Southwest

2003

ExxonMobil Travel Publications

ACKNOWLEDGMENTS

We gratefully acknowledge the help of our representatives for their efficient and perceptive inspection of the lodging and dining establishments listed; the establishments' proprietors for their cooperation in showing their facilities and providing information about them; the many users of previous editions of the Mobil Travel Guides who have taken the time to share their experiences; and for their time and information, the thousands of chambers of commerce, convention and visitors bureaus, city, state, and provincial tourism offices, and government agencies who assisted in our research.

Mobil, Mobil 1, Exxon, Speedpass, and Mobil Travel Guide are trademarks of Exxon Mobil Corporation or one of its subsidiaries. All rights reserved. Reproduction by any means including but not limited to photography, electrostatic copying devices, or electronic data processing is prohibited. Use of the information contained herein for solicitation of advertising or listing in any other publication is expressly prohibited without written permission from Exxon Mobil Corporation. Violations of reserved rights are subject to prosecution.

PHOTO CREDITS

Bachmann/ImageFinders: 329; **Randa Bishop Photography:** 607; **FPG/Getty Images:** Jerry Driendl: 470; David McGlynn: 553; Heath Robbins: 583; Travelpix: 139; **Robert Holmes Photography:** 295; **Bill Hudson/Flagstaff Convention and Vistors Bureau:** 15; **Dewitt Jones Photography:** 595; **Lani/Photri, Inc.:** 631; **Dianne Dietrich Leis/Dietrich Photography:** 358; **James Rowan Photography:** 146; **SuperStock:** 1, 23, 29, 36, 39, 50, 61, 76, 95, 102, 125, 164, 176, 197, 215, 238, 268, 273, 278, 287, 292, 318, 345, 353, 367, 372, 374, 404, 435, 453, 460, 465, 489, 500, 560, 588, 590, 602, 642; **Unicorn Stock Photos:** Robert E. Barber: 540; P. Harrington: 263.

Maps © MapQuest 2002, www.mapquest.com

Printed by Publications International, Ltd.
7373 North Cicero Avenue
Lincolnwood, Illinois 60712

info@mobiltravelguide.com

The information contained herein is derived from a variety of third-party sources. Although every effort has been made to verify the information obtained from such sources, the publisher assumes no responsibility for inconsistencies or inaccuracies in the data or liability for any damages of any type arising from errors or omissions.

Neither the editors nor the publisher assumes responsibility for the services provided by any business listed in this guide or for any loss, damage, or disruption in your travel for any reason.

ISBN 0-7627-2617-2

Manufactured in China.

10 9 8 7 6 5 4 3 2 1

CONTENTS

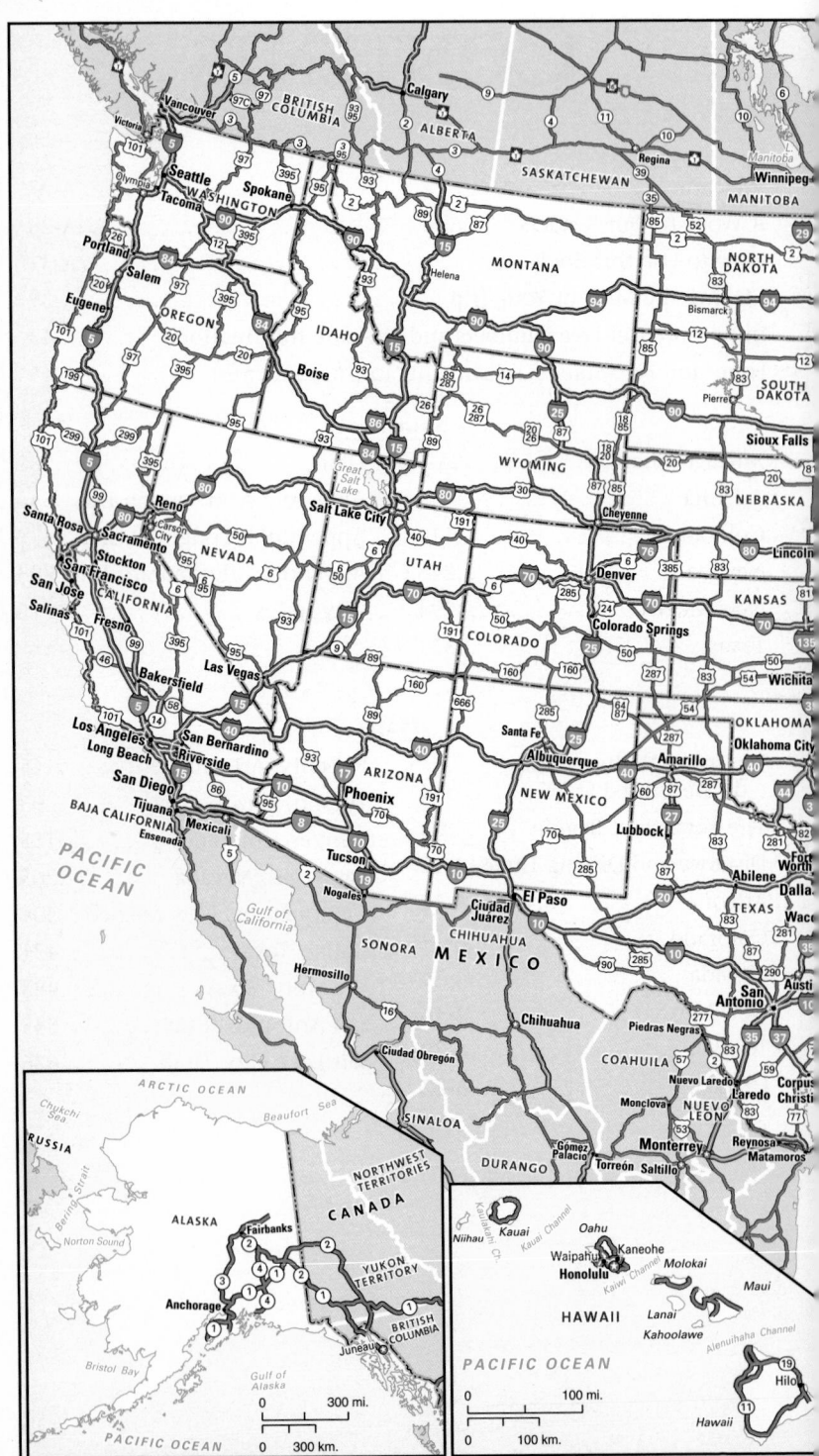

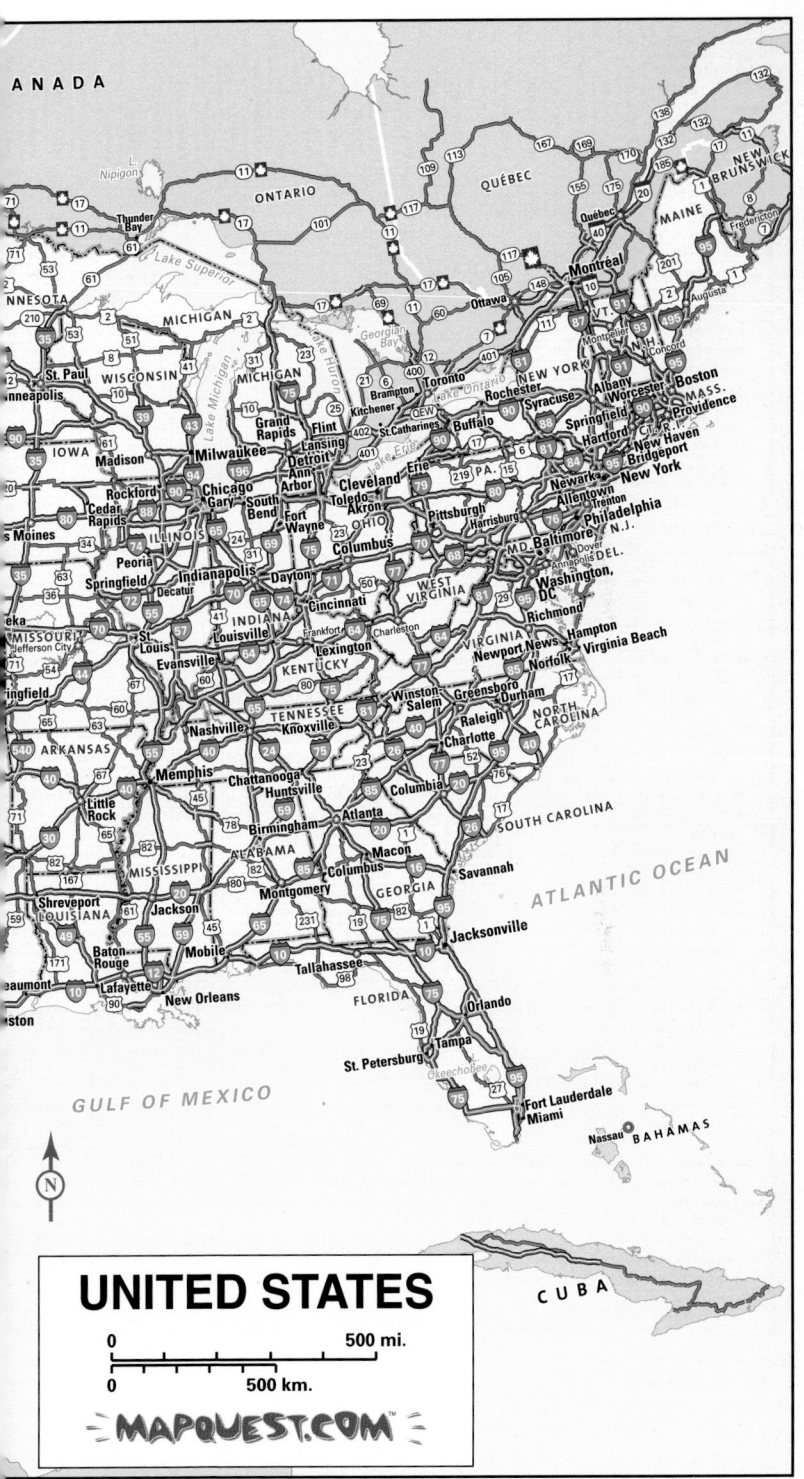

UNITED STATES

0   500 mi.

0   500 km.

MAPQUEST.COM

A-6 MILEAGE CHART

Distances in chart are in miles. To convert miles to kilometers, multiply the distance in miles by 1.609

Example:
New York, NY to Boston, MA = 215 miles or 346 kilometers (215 x 1.609)

	Albuquerque, NM	Atlanta, GA	Baltimore, MD	Billings, MT	Birmingham, AL	Bismarck, ND	Boise, ID	Boston, MA	Buffalo, NY	Burlington, VT	Charleston, SC	Charleston, WV	Charlotte, NC	Cheyenne, WY	Chicago, IL	Cincinnati, OH	Cleveland, OH	Dallas, TX	Denver, CO	Des Moines, IA	Detroit, MI	El Paso, TX	Houston, TX	Indianapolis, IN	Jackson, MS	Kansas City, MO
ALBUQUERQUE, NM		1490	1902	991	1274	1333	966	2240	1808	2178	1793	1568	1649	538	1352	1409	1619	754	438	1091	1608	263	994	1298	1157	894
ATLANTA, GA	1490		679	1889	150	1559	2218	1100	910	1158	317	503	238	1482	717	476	726	792	1403	967	735	1437	800	531	386	801
BALTIMORE, MD	1902	679		1959	795	1551	2401	422	370	481	583	352	441	1665	708	521	377	1399	1690	1031	532	2045	1470	600	1032	1087
BILLINGS, MT	991	1889	1959		1839	413	626	2254	1796	2181	2157	1755	2012	455	1246	1552	1597	1433	554	1007	1534	1255	1673	1432	1836	1081
BIRMINGHAM, AL	1274	150	795	1839		1509	2170	1215	909	1241	466	578	389	1434	667	475	725	647	1356	919	734	1292	678	481	241	753
BISMARCK, ND	1333	1559	1551	413	1509		1039	1846	1388	1773	1749	1347	1604	594	838	1144	1189	1342	693	675	1126	1597	1582	1024	1548	801
BOISE, ID	966	2218	2401	626	2170	1039		2697	2239	2624	2520	2182	2375	737	1708	1969	2040	1711	833	1369	1977	1206	1952	1852	2115	1376
BOSTON, MA	2240	1100	422	2254	1215	1846	2697		462	214	1003	741	861	1961	1003	862	654	1819	2004	1326	741	2465	1890	940	1453	1427
BUFFALO, NY	1808	910	370	1796	909	1388	2239	462		375	899	431	695	1502	545	442	197	1393	1546	868	277	2039	1513	508	1134	995
BURLINGTON, VT	2178	1158	481	2181	1241	1773	2624	214	375		1061	782	919	1887	930	817	567	1763	1931	1253	652	2409	1916	878	1479	1364
CHARLESTON, SC	1793	317	583	2157	466	1749	2520	1003	899	1061		468	204	1783	907	622	724	1109	1705	1204	879	1754	1110	721	703	1102
CHARLESTON, WV	1568	503	352	1755	578	1347	2182	741	431	782	468		265	1445	506	209	255	1072	1367	802	410	1718	1192	320	816	764
CHARLOTTE, NC	1649	238	441	2012	389	1604	2375	861	695	919	204	265		1637	761	476	501	1131	1559	1057	675	1677	1041	575	625	956
CHEYENNE, WY	538	1482	1665	455	1434	594	737	1961	1502	1887	1783	1445	1637		972	1233	1304	979	100	633	1241	801	1220	1115	1382	640
CHICAGO, IL	1352	717	708	1246	667	838	1708	1003	545	930	907	506	761	972		302	346	936	1015	337	283	1543	1108	184	750	532
CINCINNATI, OH	1409	476	521	1552	475	1144	1969	862	442	817	622	209	476	1233	302		253	958	1200	599	261	1605	1079	116	700	590
CLEVELAND, OH	1619	726	377	1597	725	1189	2040	654	197	567	724	255	501	1304	346	253		1208	1347	669	171	1854	1328	319	950	806
DALLAS, TX	754	792	1399	1433	647	1342	1711	1819	1393	1763	1109	1072	1031	979	936	958	1208		887	752	1218	647	241	913	406	554
DENVER, CO	438	1403	1690	554	1356	693	833	2004	1546	1931	1705	1367	1559	100	1015	1200	1347	887		676	1284	701	1127	1088	1290	603
DES MOINES, IA	1091	967	1031	1007	919	675	1369	1326	868	1253	1204	802	1057	633	337	599	669	752	676		606	1283	992	481	931	194
DETROIT, MI	1608	735	532	1534	734	1126	1977	741	277	652	879	410	675	1241	283	261	171	1218	1284	606		1799	1338	318	960	795
EL PASO, TX	263	1437	2045	1255	1292	1597	1206	2465	2039	2409	1754	1718	1677	801	1543	1605	1854	647	701	1283	1799		758	1489	1051	1089
HOUSTON, TX	994	800	1470	1673	678	1582	1952	1890	1513	1916	1110	1192	1041	1220	1108	1079	1328	241	1127	992	1338	758		1035	445	795
INDIANAPOLIS, IN	1298	531	600	1432	481	1024	1852	940	508	878	721	320	575	1115	184	116	319	913	1088	481	318	1489	1033		675	485
JACKSON, MS	1157	386	1032	1836	241	1548	2115	1453	1134	1479	703	816	625	1382	750	700	950	406	1290	931	960	1051	445	675		747
KANSAS CITY, MO	894	801	1087	1081	753	801	1376	1427	995	1364	1102	764	956	640	532	590	806	554	603	194	795	1089	795	485	747	
LAS VEGAS, NV	578	2067	2445	965	1852	1378	760	2757	2299	2684	2371	2122	2225	843	1768	1955	2040	1331	756	1429	2037	717	1474	1843	1735	1358
LITTLE ROCK, AR	900	528	1072	1530	381	1183	1808	1493	1066	1437	900	745	754	1076	662	632	882	327	984	567	891	974	447	587	269	382
LOS ANGELES, CA	806	2237	2705	1239	2092	1702	1033	3046	2572	2957	2554	2374	2453	1116	2042	2215	2314	1440	1091	1744	2310	801	1558	2104	1851	1632
LOUISVILLE, KY	1320	419	602	1547	369	1139	1933	964	545	915	610	251	464	1197	299	106	356	852	1118	595	366	1499	972	112	594	516
MEMPHIS, TN	1033	389	933	1625	241	1337	1954	1353	927	1297	760	606	614	1217	539	493	742	466	1116	720	752	1112	586	464	211	536
MIAMI, FL	2155	661	1109	2554	812	2224	2883	1529	1425	1587	583	994	730	2147	1382	1141	1250	1367	2069	1632	1401	1959	1201	1196	915	1466
MILWAUKEE, WI	1426	813	805	1175	763	747	1748	1100	642	1027	1003	601	857	1012	89	398	443	1010	1055	378	380	1617	1193	279	835	573
MINNEAPOLIS, MN	1339	1129	1121	839	1079	431	1465	1417	958	1343	1319	1173	881	409	714	760	999	924	246	697		1530	1240	596	1151	441
MONTRÉAL, QC	2172	1241	564	2093	1289	1685	2535	313	397	92	1145	822	1003	1799	841	815	588	1772	1843	1165	564	2363	1892	872	1514	1359
NASHVILLE, TN	1248	242	716	1648	194	1315	1916	1194	815	1160	543	395	397	1240	474	281	531	681	1162	725	541	1328	801	287	423	559
NEW ORLEANS, LA	1276	473	1142	1955	351	1734	2234	1563	1254	1588	783	926	713	1502	935	820	1070	525	1409	1117	1079	1143	360	826	185	932
NEW YORK, NY	2015	869	192	2049	985	1641	2491	215	400	299	773	515	631	1755	797	636	466	1589	1799	1121	622	2235	1660	715	1223	1202
OKLAHOMA CITY, OK	546	944	1354	1227	779	1166	1632	1366	1102	764	916	1022	1102	773	807	863	1073	209	681	546	1062	737	449	752	612	348
OMAHA, NE	973	989	1168	904	941	616	1234	1463	1005	1390	1290	952	1144	497	474	736	606	541	136	742	1236	910	618	935	388	
ORLANDO, FL	1934	440	904	2333	591	2003	2662	1324	1221	1383	379	790	525	1926	1161	920	1045	1146	1847	1411	1180	1738	980	975	694	1249
PHILADELPHIA, PA	1954	782	104	2019	897	1611	2462	321	414	381	685	454	543	1725	768	591	437	1501	1744	1091	592	2147	1572	655	1115	1141
PHOENIX, AZ	466	1868	2366	1199	1723	993		2706	2274	2644	2184	2035	2107	1004	1819	1876	2085	1077	904	1558	2074	432	1188	1764	1482	1360
PITTSBURGH, PA	1670	676	246	1719	763	1311	2161	592	217	587	642	217	438	1425	467	292	136	1246	1460	791	292	1893	1366	370	988	857
PORTLAND, ME	2338	1197	520	2352	1313	1944	2795	107	560	233	1101	839	959	2059	1101	960	751	1917	2102	1424	838	2563	1988	1038	1550	1525
PORTLAND, OR	1395	2647	2830	889	2599	1301	432	3126	2667	3052	2948	2610	2802	1166	2137	2398	2469	2140	1261	1798	2405	1767	2381	2280	2544	1805
RAPID CITY, SD	841	1511	1626	379	1463	320	930	1921	1463	1848	1824	1422	1678	305	913	1219	1264	1077	404	629	1201	1105	1318	1101	1458	710
RENO, NV	1020	2440	2623	960	2392	1372	430	2919	2460	2845	2741	2403	2595	959	1930	2191	2262	1933	1054	1591	2198	1315	2072	2073	2337	1598
RICHMOND, VA	1876	527	150	2053	678	1645	2404	550	428	322	289	760	347	1309	1688	1126	627	1993	1230	641	914					
ST. LOUIS, MO	1051	549	841	1341	501	1053	1628	1181	749	1119	850	512	704	892	294	350	560	635	855	436	549	1242	863	239	505	252
SALT LAKE CITY, UT	624	1916	2100	548	1868	960	342	2395	1936	2322	2218	1880	2072	436	1406	1667	1738	1410	531	1067	1675	864	1650	1549	1813	1074
SAN ANTONIO, TX	818	1000	1671	1500	878	1599	1761	2092	1665	2036	1310	1344	1241	1481	271	1446	1500	556	200	1186	644	812				
SAN DIEGO, CA	825	2166	2724	1302	2021	1765	1096	3065	2632	3020	2483	2393	2405	1179	2105	2234	2437	1375	1092	1766	2373	730	1487	2122	1780	1695
SAN FRANCISCO, CA	1111	2618	2840	1176	2472	1749	646	3135	2677	3062	2934	2620	2759	1176	2146	2407	2478	1827	1271	1807	2415	1181	1938	2290	2232	1814
SEATTLE, WA	1463	2705	2775	816	2657	1229	500	3070	2612	2997	2973	2571	2827	1234	2062	2368	2413	2208	1329	1822	2350	1944	2449	2249	2612	1872
TAMPA, FL	1949	455	960	2348	606	2018	2617	1380	1276	1438	434	845	581	1941	1176	935	1101	1161	1862	1426	1194	1753	995	990	709	1259
TORONTO, ON	1841	958	565	1762	958	1354	2204	570	106	419	1006	537	802	1468	510	484	303	1441	1512	834	233	2032	1561	541	1183	1028
VANCOUVER, BC	1597	2838	2908	969	2791	1362	633	3204	2745	3130	3106	2705	2960	1368	2196	2501	2547	2342	1463	1956	2483	2087	2583	2383	2746	2007
WASHINGTON, DC	1896	636	38	1953	758	1545	2395	458	384	517	539	346	397	1659	701	517	370	1362	1686	1025	526	2008	1431	596	996	1083
WICHITA, KS	707	989	1276	1067	838	934	1346	1616	1184	1554	1291	953	1145	613	728	785	995	367	521	390	984	898	608	674	771	192

LOS ANGELES, CA	LOUISVILLE, KY	MEMPHIS, TN	MIAMI, FL	MILWAUKEE, WI	MINNEAPOLIS, MN	MONTRÉAL, QC	NASHVILLE, TN	NEW ORLEANS, LA	NEW YORK, NY	OKLAHOMA CITY, OK	OMAHA, NE	ORLANDO, FL	PHILADELPHIA, PA	PHOENIX, AZ	PITTSBURGH, PA	PORTLAND, ME	PORTLAND, OR	RAPID CITY, SD	RENO, NV	RICHMOND, VA	ST. LOUIS, MO	SALT LAKE CITY, UT	SAN ANTONIO, TX	SAN DIEGO, CA	SAN FRANCISCO, CA	SEATTLE, WA	TAMPA, FL	TORONTO, ON	VANCOUVER, BC	WASHINGTON,DC	WICHITA, KS
806	1320	1033	2155	1426	1339	2172	1248	1276	2015	546	973	1934	1954	466	1670	2338	1395	841	1020	1876	1051	624	818	825	1111	1463	1949	1841	1597	1896	707
2237	419	389	661	813	1129	1241	242	473	869	944	989	440	782	1868	676	1197	2647	1511	2440	527	549	1916	1000	2166	2618	2705	455	958	2838	636	989
2705	602	933	1109	805	1121	564	716	1142	192	1354	1168	904	104	2366	246	520	2830	1626	2623	152	841	2100	1671	2724	2842	2775	960	565	2908	38	1276
1239	1547	1625	2554	1175	839	2093	1648	1955	2049	1227	904	2333	2019	1199	1719	2352	889	379	960	2053	1341	548	1500	1302	1076	816	2348	1762	949	1953	1067
2092	369	241	812	763	1079	1289	194	351	985	729	941	591	897	1723	763	1313	2599	1463	2392	678	501	1868	878	2021	2472	2657	606	958	2791	758	838
1702	1139	1337	2224	767	431	1685	1315	1734	1641	1136	616	2003	1611	1662	1311	1944	1301	320	1372	1645	1053	960	1599	1765	1749	1229	2018	1354	1362	1545	934
1033	1933	1954	2883	1748	1465	2535	1976	2234	2491	1506	1234	2662	2462	993	2161	2795	432	930	430	2496	1628	342	1761	1096	646	500	2677	2204	633	2395	1346
3046	964	1353	1529	1100	1417	313	1136	1563	215	1694	1463	1324	321	2706	592	107	3126	1921	2919	572	1181	2395	2092	3065	3135	3070	1380	570	3204	458	1616
2572	545	927	1425	642	958	397	716	1254	400	1262	1005	1221	414	2274	217	560	2667	1433	2440	485	749	1936	1665	2632	2612	2612	1276	106	2745	384	1184
2957	915	1297	1587	1027	1343	92	1086	1588	299	1632	1390	1383	371	2644	587	233	3052	1848	2845	630	1179	2322	2036	3020	3062	2997	1438	419	3130	517	1554
2554	610	760	583	1003	1319	1145	543	783	773	1248	1290	379	685	2184	642	1101	2948	1824	2741	428	850	2218	1310	2483	2934	2973	434	1006	3106	539	1291
2374	251	606	994	601	918	822	395	926	515	1022	952	790	454	2035	217	839	2610	1422	2403	322	512	1880	1344	2392	2560	2527	775	845	2705	346	953
2453	464	614	730	857	1173	1003	371	813	1102	1144	525	543	2107	1409	959	2802	1678	2595	289	704	2072	1241	2405	2759	2827	581	802	2960	397	1145	
1116	1197	1217	2147	1012	881	1799	1240	1502	1755	773	497	1926	1755	773	305	959	1760	892	436	1046	1179	1176	1341	1941	1468	1368	1659	613			
2042	299	539	1382	89	409	841	474	935	797	807	474	1161	768	1819	467	1101	2137	913	1930	802	294	1406	1210	2105	2146	2062	1176	510	2196	701	728
2374	356	742	1250	443	760	588	531	1070	466	1073	806	1045	437	2085	136	751	2469	1264	2262	471	560	1667	1231	2234	2407	2368	935	484	2501	517	785
1446	852	466	1367	1010	999	1772	681	525	1589	209	669	1146	1501	1077	1246	1917	2140	1077	1933	1309	635	1410	271	1375	1827	2208	1161	1441	2342	1362	367
1703	595	720	1632	378	246	1165	725	1117	1121	546	136	1411	1091	1558	791	1424	1798	629	1591	1126	436	1067	1009	1766	1807	1822	1426	834	1956	1025	390
2310	366	752	1401	380	697	564	541	1079	622	1062	743	1180	592	2074	292	838	2405	1201	2198	627	549	1675	1490	2373	2415	2350	1194	233	2483	526	984
1558	972	586	1201	1193	1240	1892	801	360	1660	449	910	980	1572	1188	1366	1988	2381	1318	2072	1330	863	1650	200	1487	1938	2449	995	1561	2583	1433	608
2104	112	464	1196	279	596	872	287	826	715	752	618	975	655	1764	370	1038	2280	1101	2073	641	239	1549	1186	2122	2290	2249	990	541	2383	596	674
1851	594	211	915	835	1151	1514	423	185	1223	612	935	694	1135	1482	988	1550	2544	1458	2337	910	598	1813	644	1780	2232	2612	709	1183	2746	996	771
274	1874	1611	2733	1808	1677	2596	1826	1854	2552	1124	1294	2512	2500	285	2215	2855	1188	1035	442	2444	1610	417	1722	337	575	1256	2526	2265	1390	2441	1276
1706	526	140	1190	747	814	1446	345	455	1262	355	570	969	1175	1367	920	1590	2237	1093	2030	983	416	1507	600	1703	2012	2305	984	1115	2439	1036	464
2126		386	1084	394	711	920	175	714	739	774	704	863	678	1786	394	1062	2362	1215	2155	722	264	1631	125	2144	2372	2364	878	589	2497	596	705
1839	386		1051	624	940	1306	215	396	1123	487	724	830	1035	1500	780	1451	2382	1247	2175	843	294	1652	739	1841	2144	2440	845	975	2574	896	597
2759	1084	1051		1478	1794	1296	1609	1654	232	1211	2390	1167	1627	3105	954	1214	2581	1401	2688	1340	3370	246	3267	3164	101	317	2899	2426	998	660	3003
2082	394	624	1478		337	939	569	1020	894	880	514	1257	865	1892	564	1889	2063	842	1970	899	367	1446	1343	2145	2186	1991	1272	607	2104	769	769
1951	711	940	1794	337		1255	886	1337	1211	793	383	1573	1181	1805	881	1515	1727	606	1839	1216	621	1315	1257	2014	2055	1654	1588	924	1788	1115	637
2054	925	1376	1675	569	886	1094		539	906	703	747	686	818	1715	569	1234	2405	1269	2198	626	307	1675	954	2056	2360	2479	1522	330	941	600	748
1917	714	396	874	1020	1337	1632	539		1332	731	1121	653	1245	1548	1108	1660	2663	1643	2431	1002	690	1932	560	1846	2298	2731	668	1302	2865	1106	890
2820	739	1123	1299	894	1211	383	906	1332		1469	1258	1094	91	2481	367	313	2920	1716	2713	342	956	2189	1861	2839	2929	2864	1150	372	2998	228	1391
1352	714	842	1792	383	906	1737	1469		463	1388	1408	1012	1732	1934	871	1727	1331	505	1204	466	1370	1657	2002	1403	1295	2136	1350	161			

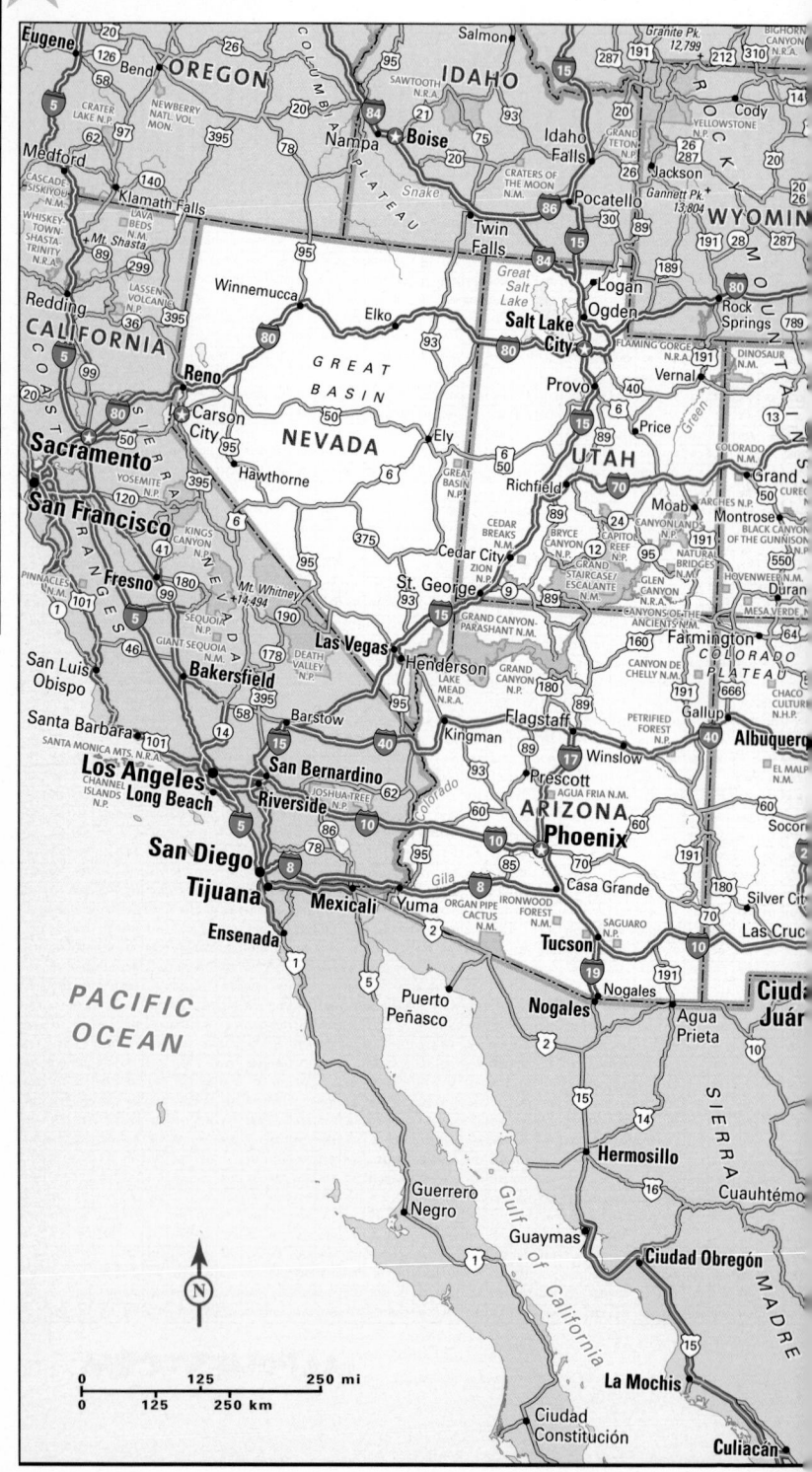

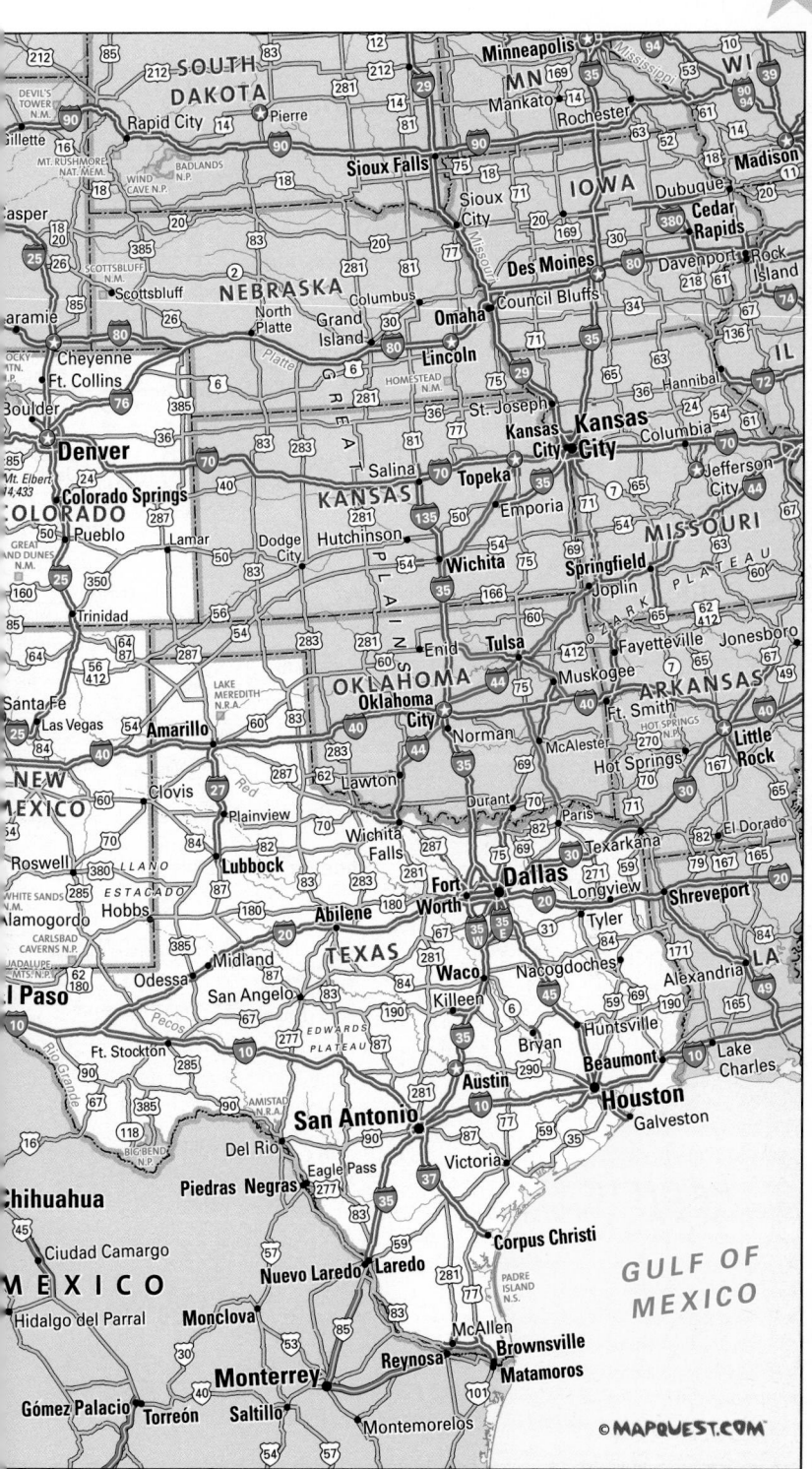

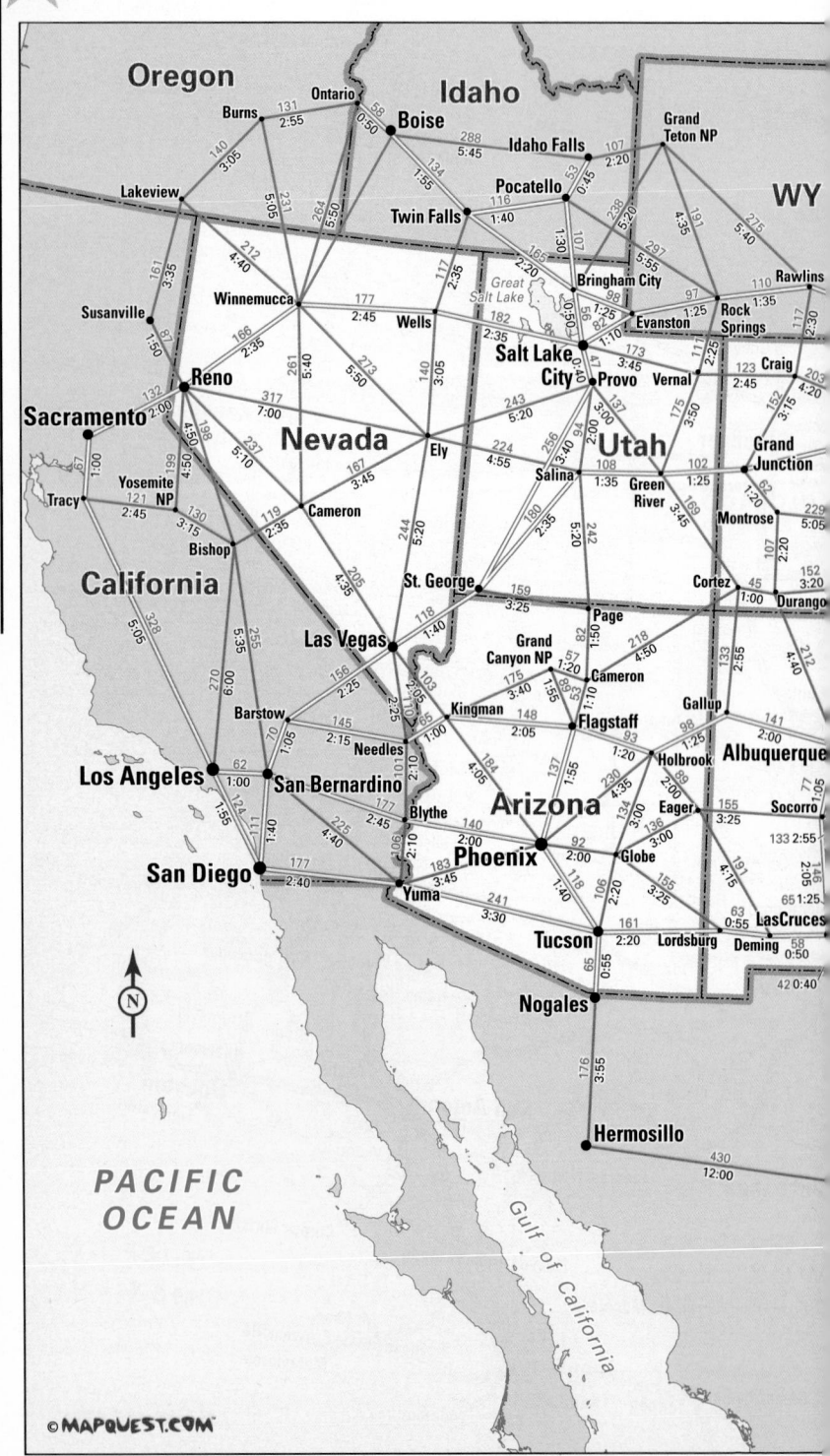

© MAPQUEST.COM

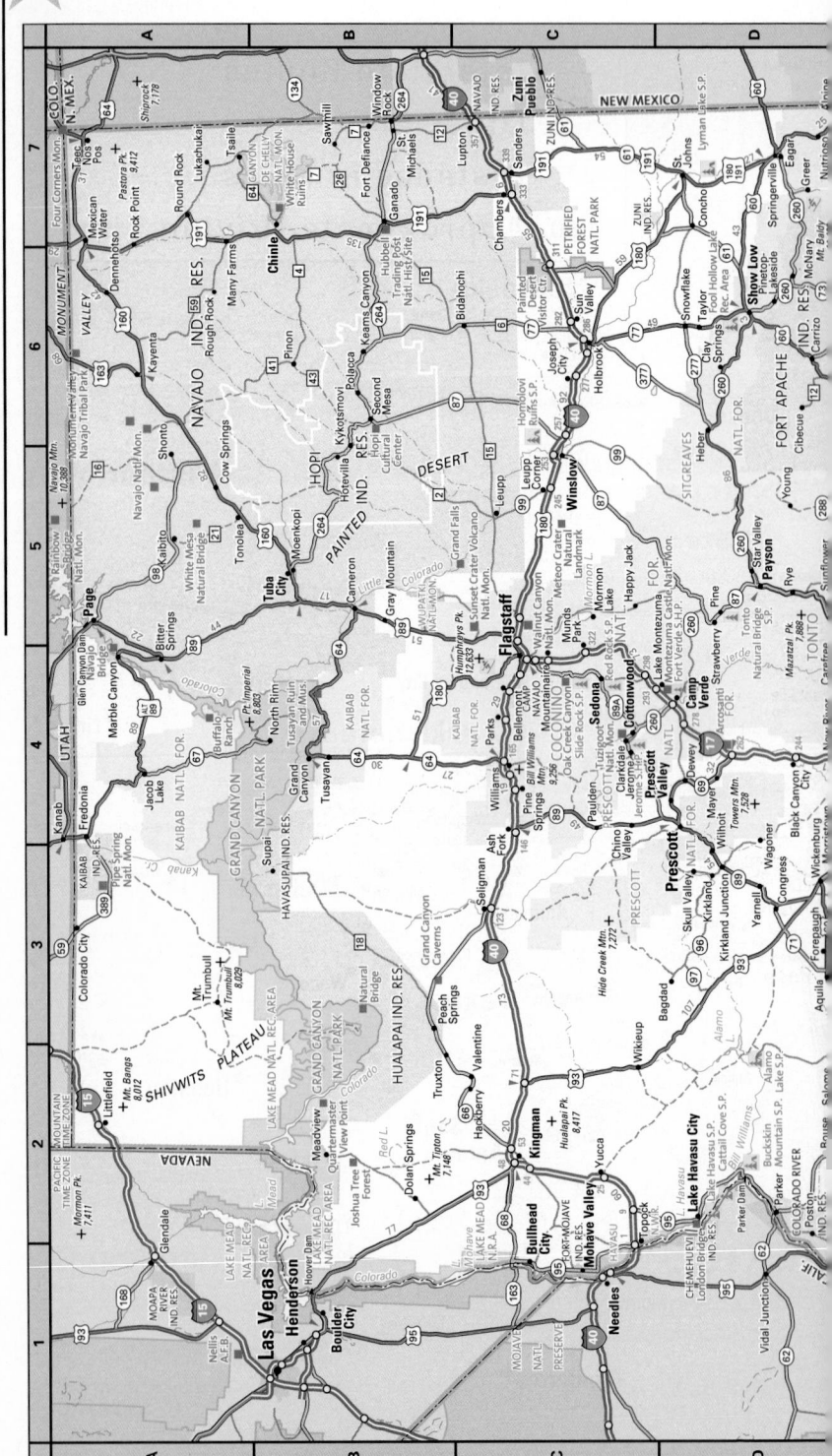

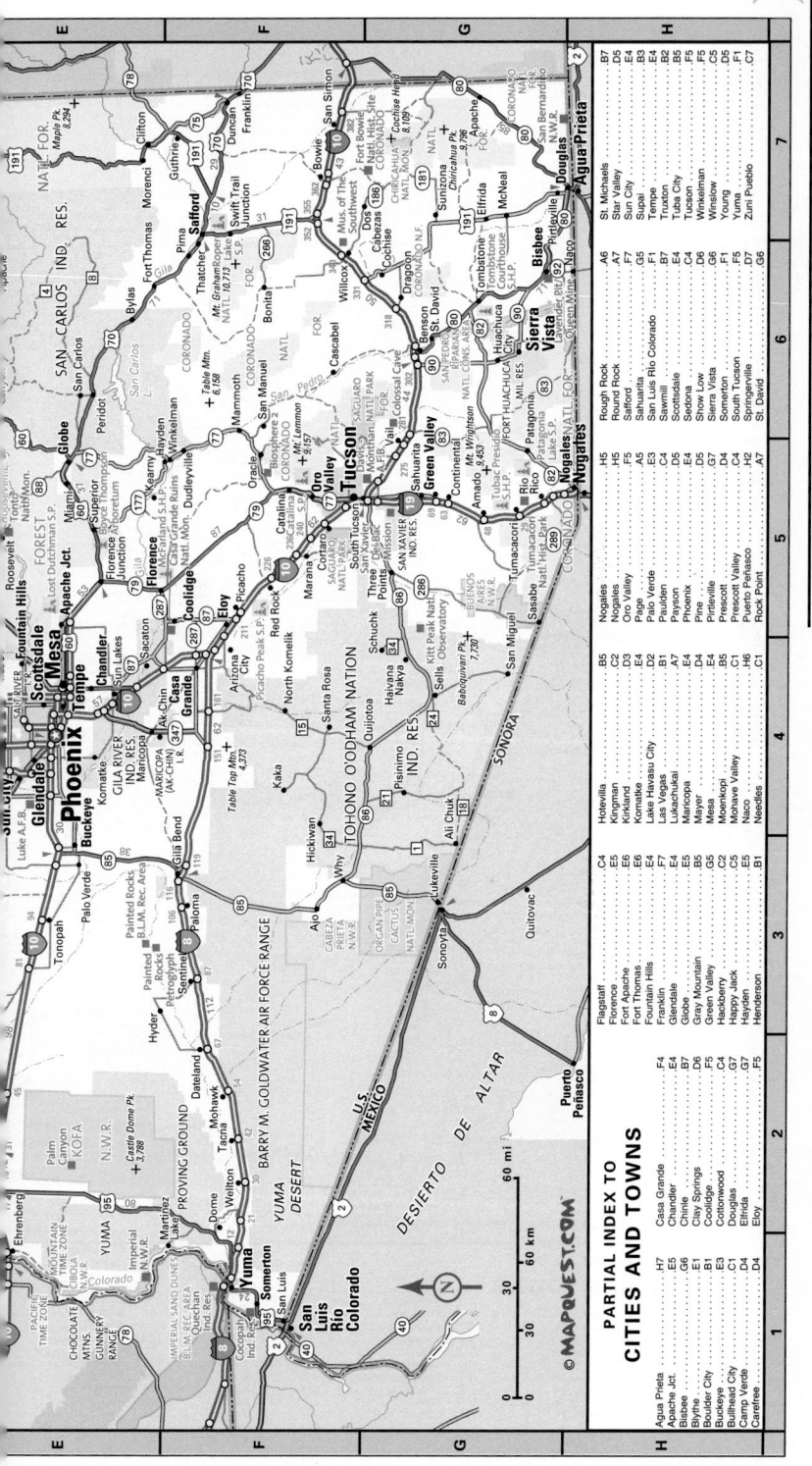

© MAPQUEST.COM

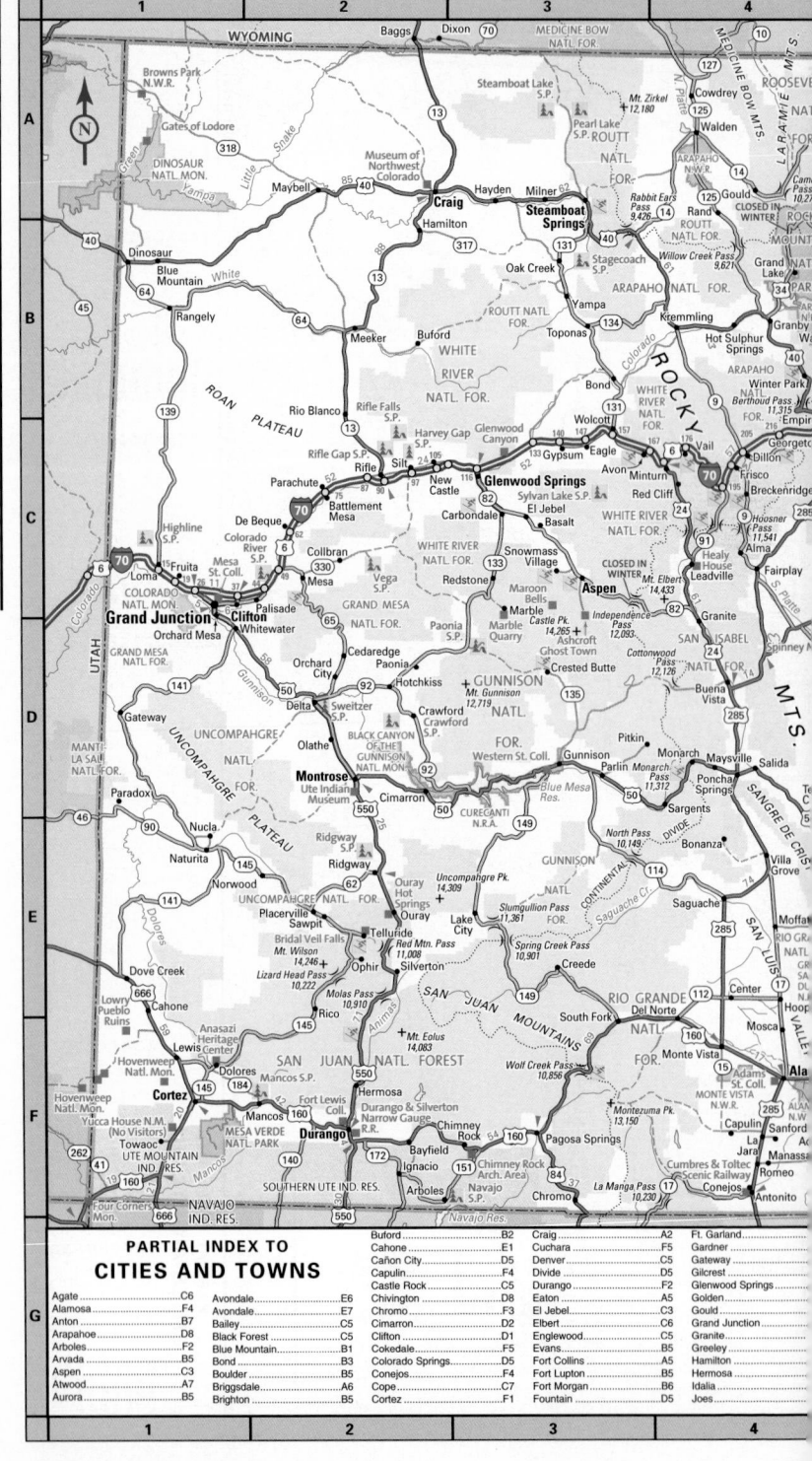

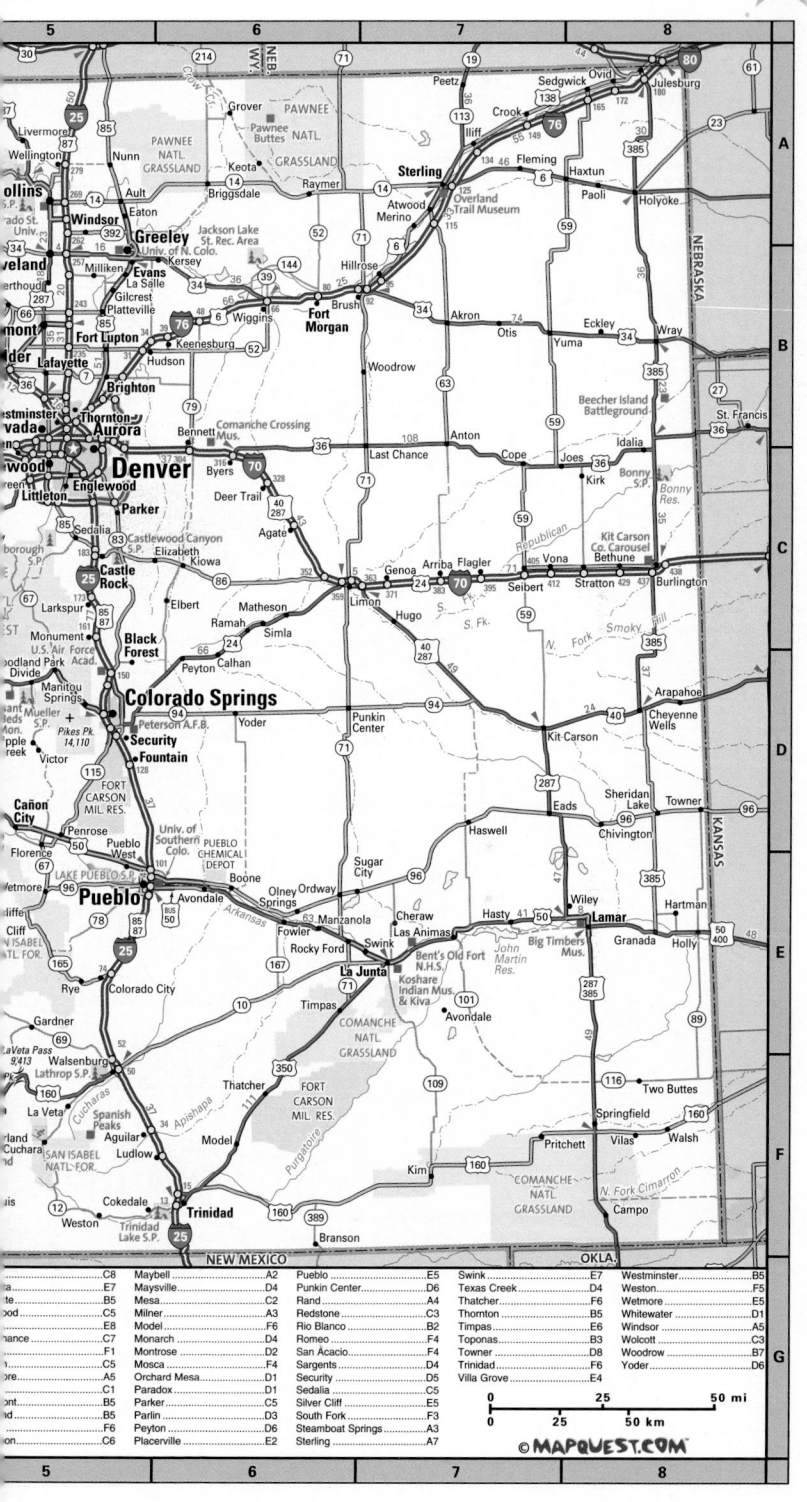

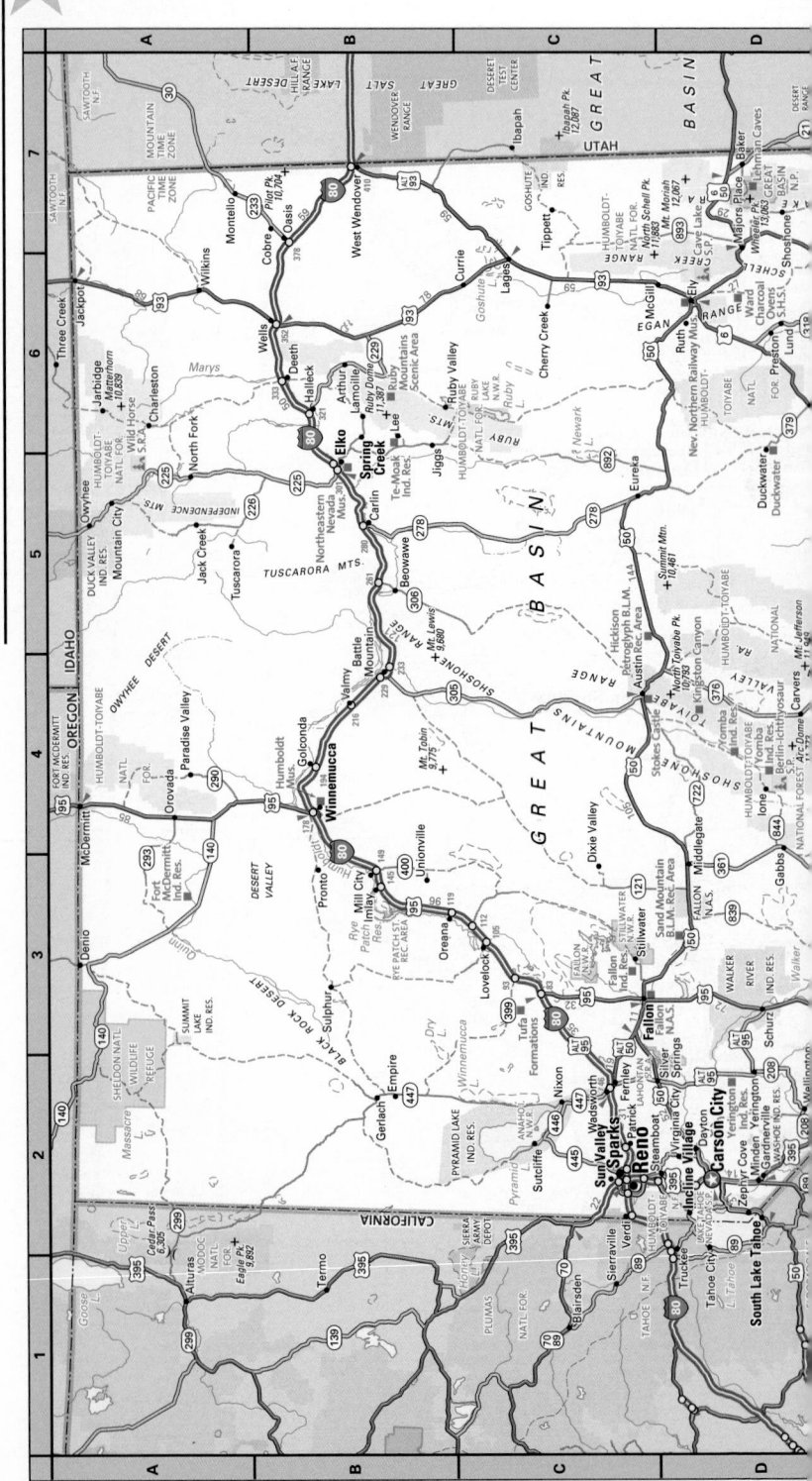

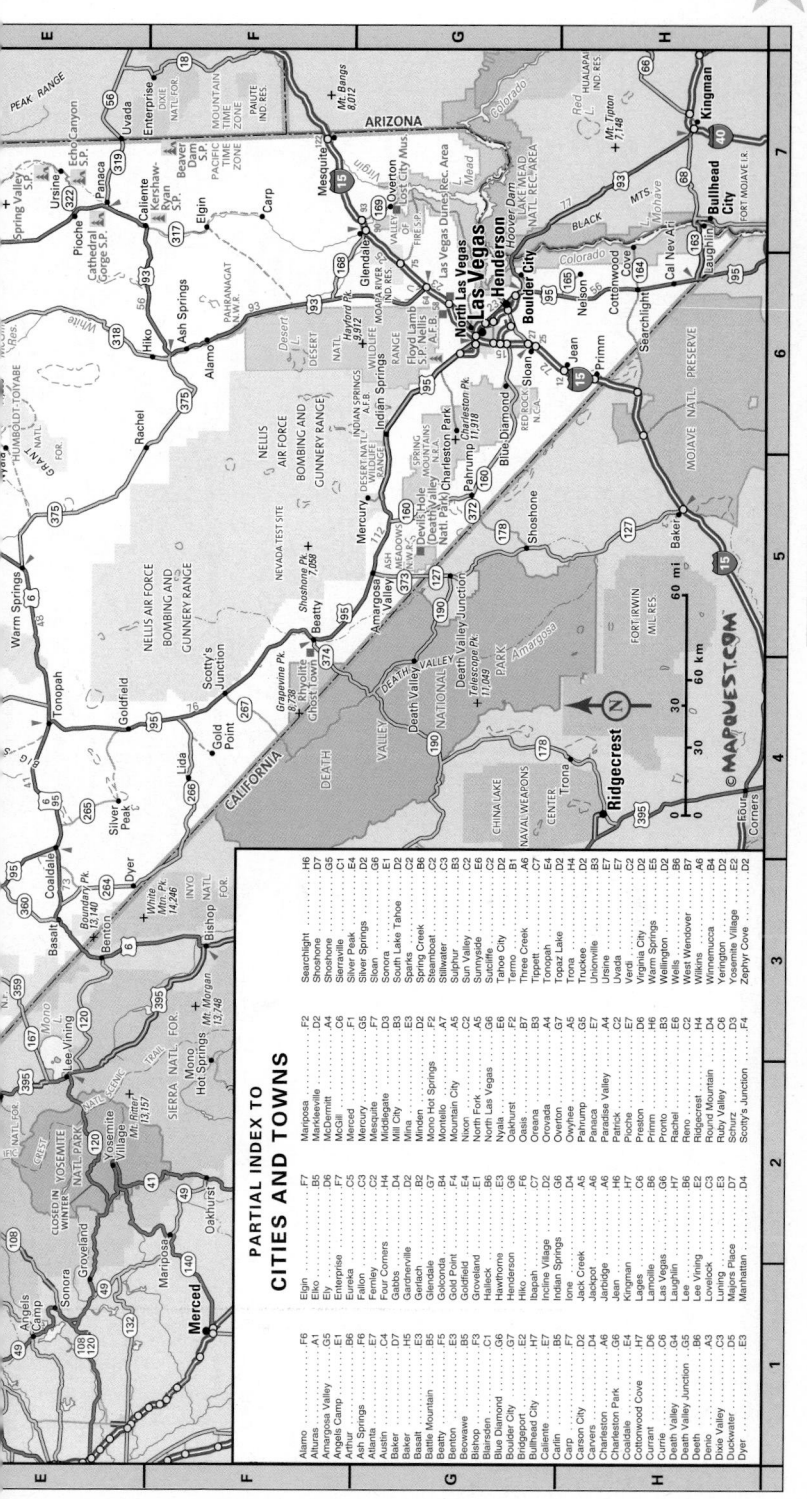

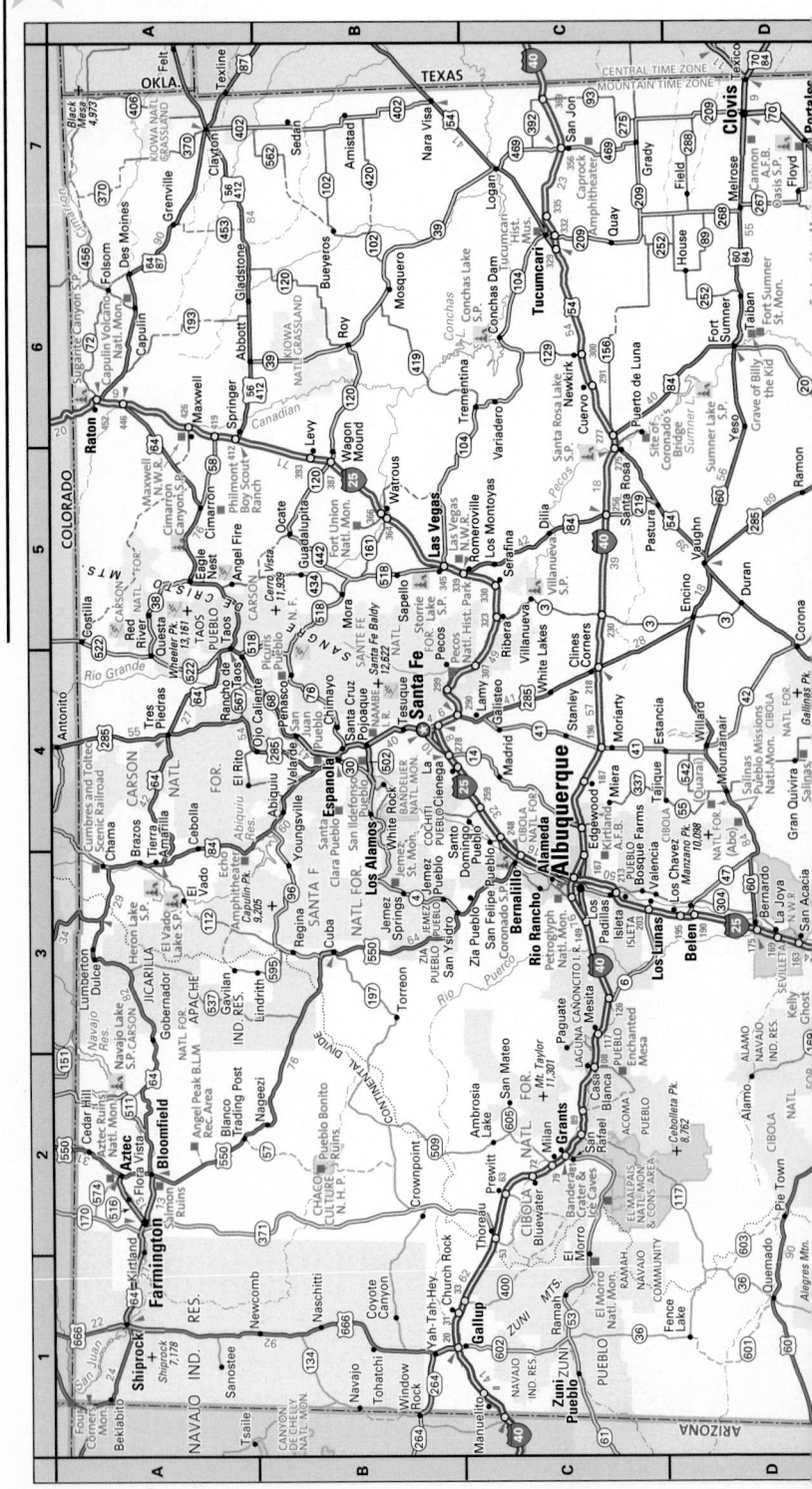

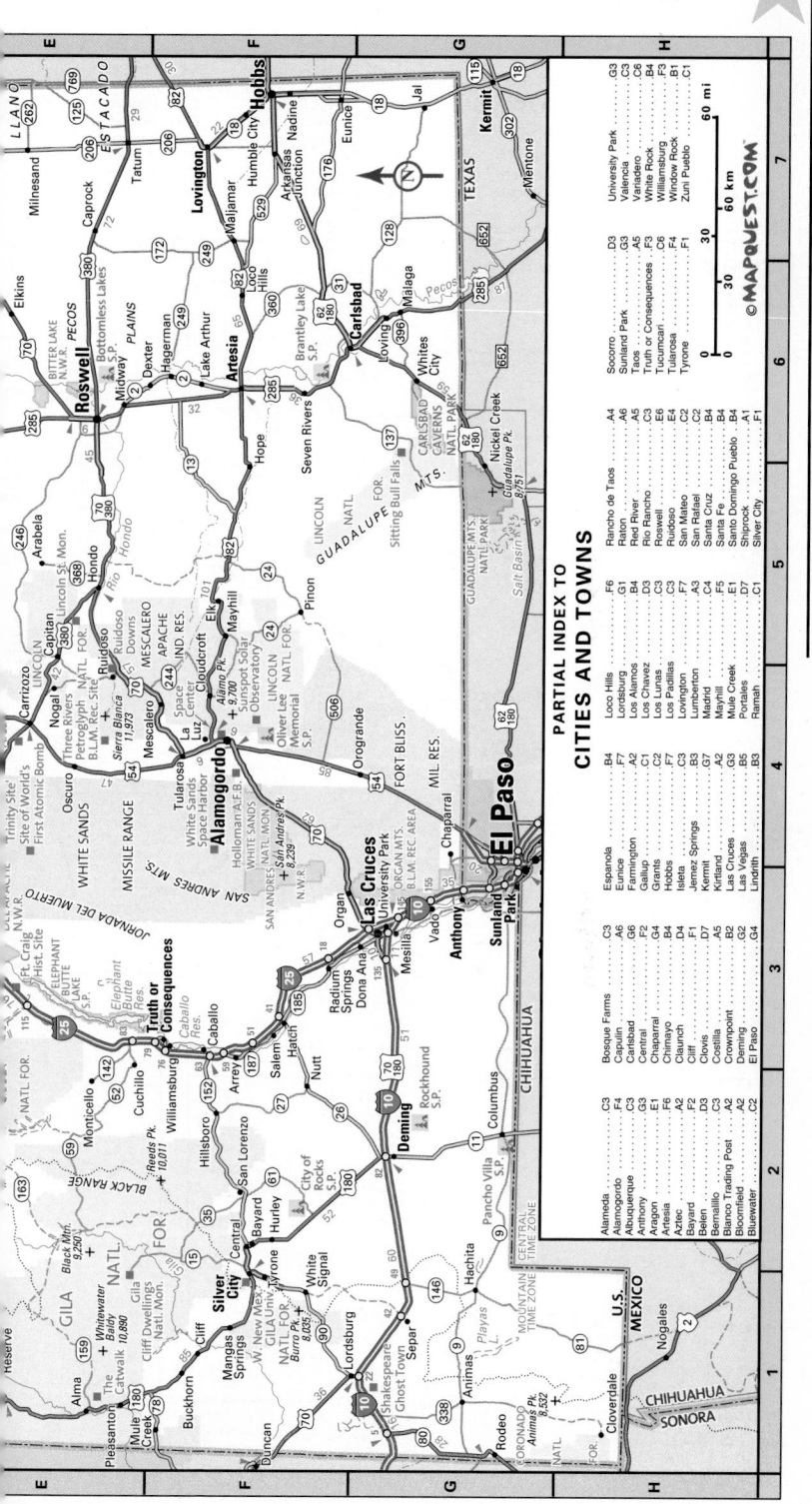

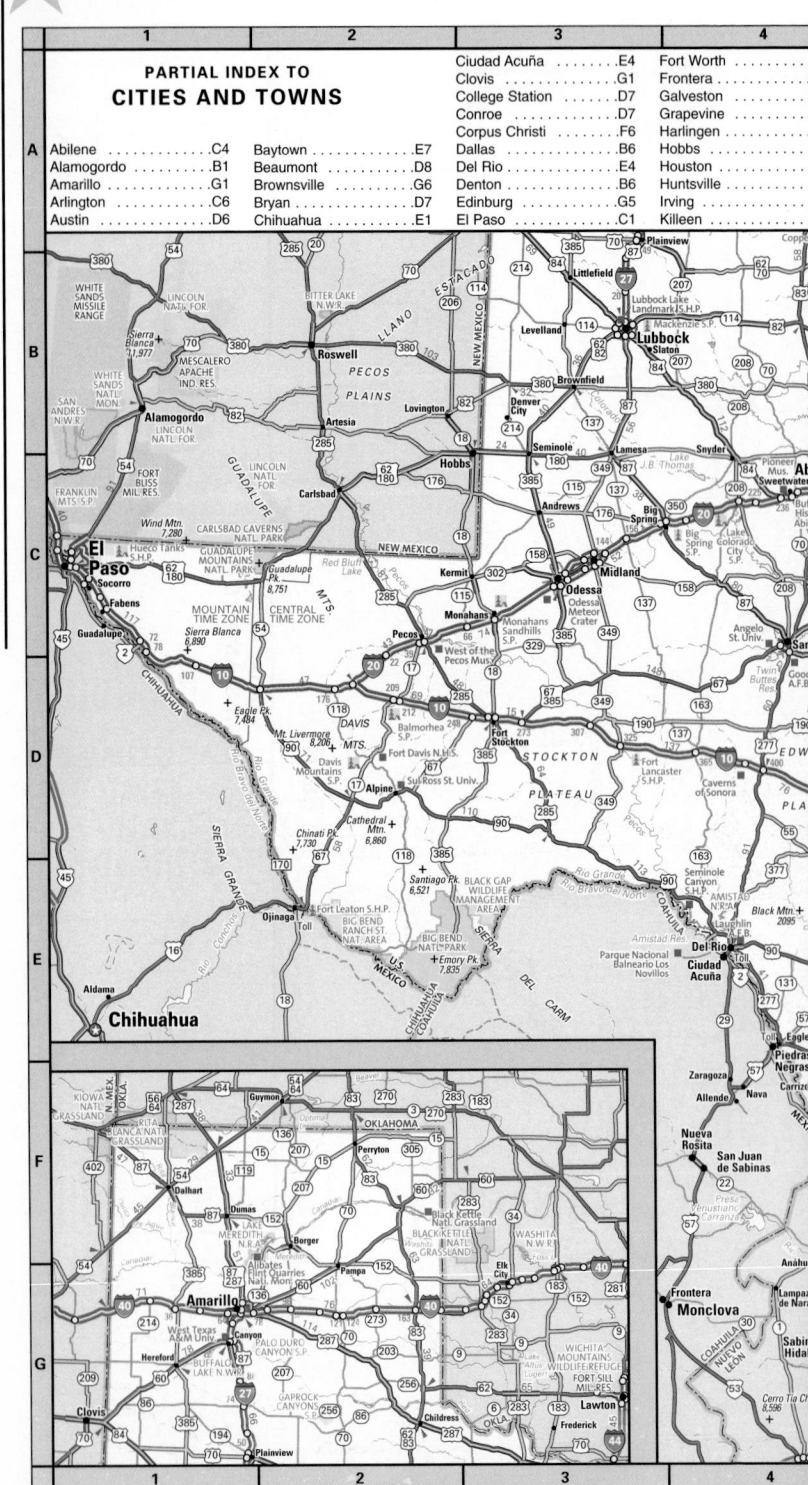

GULF OF MEXICO

0 40 80 mi
0 40 80 km

© MAPQUEST.COM

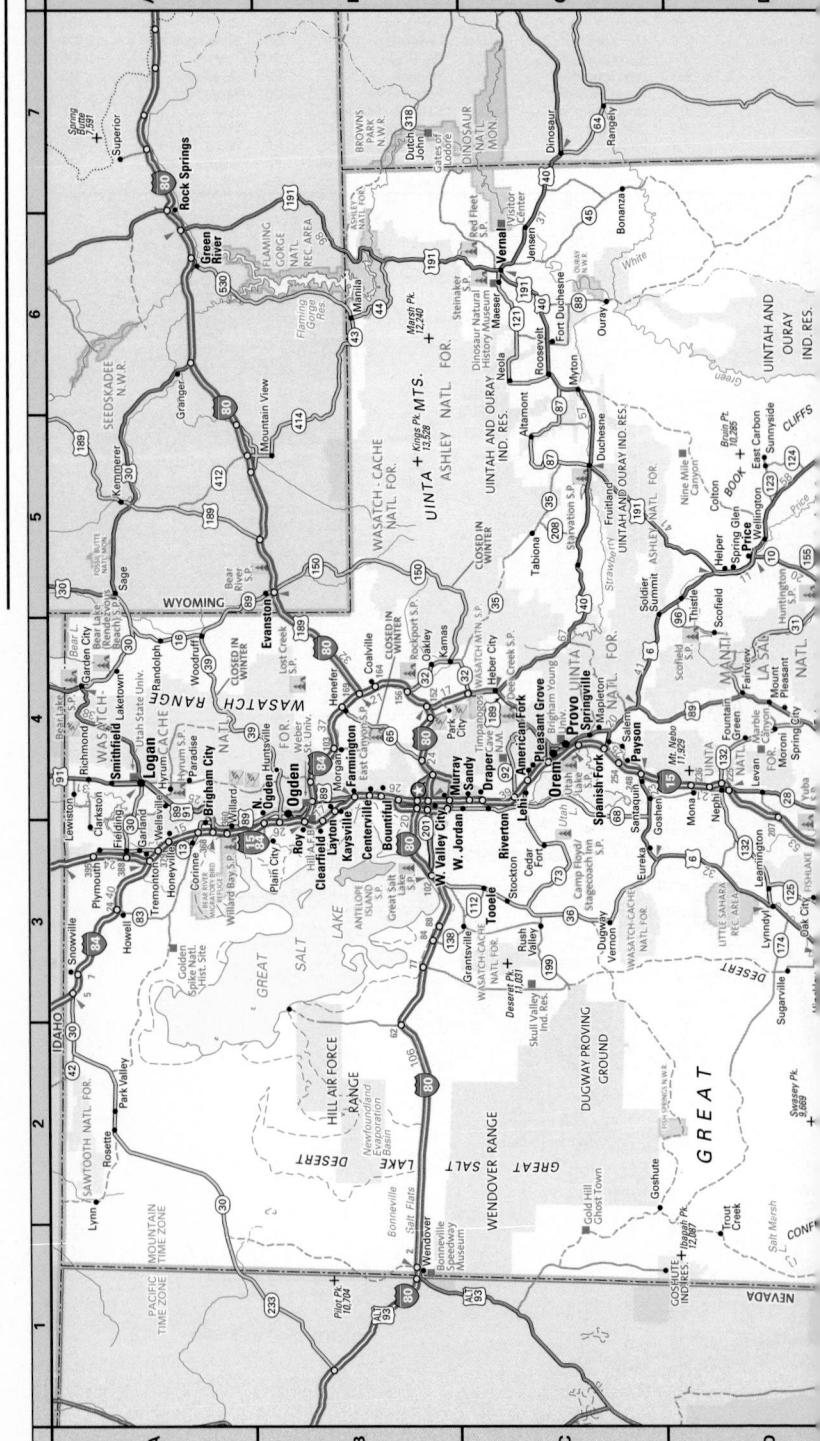

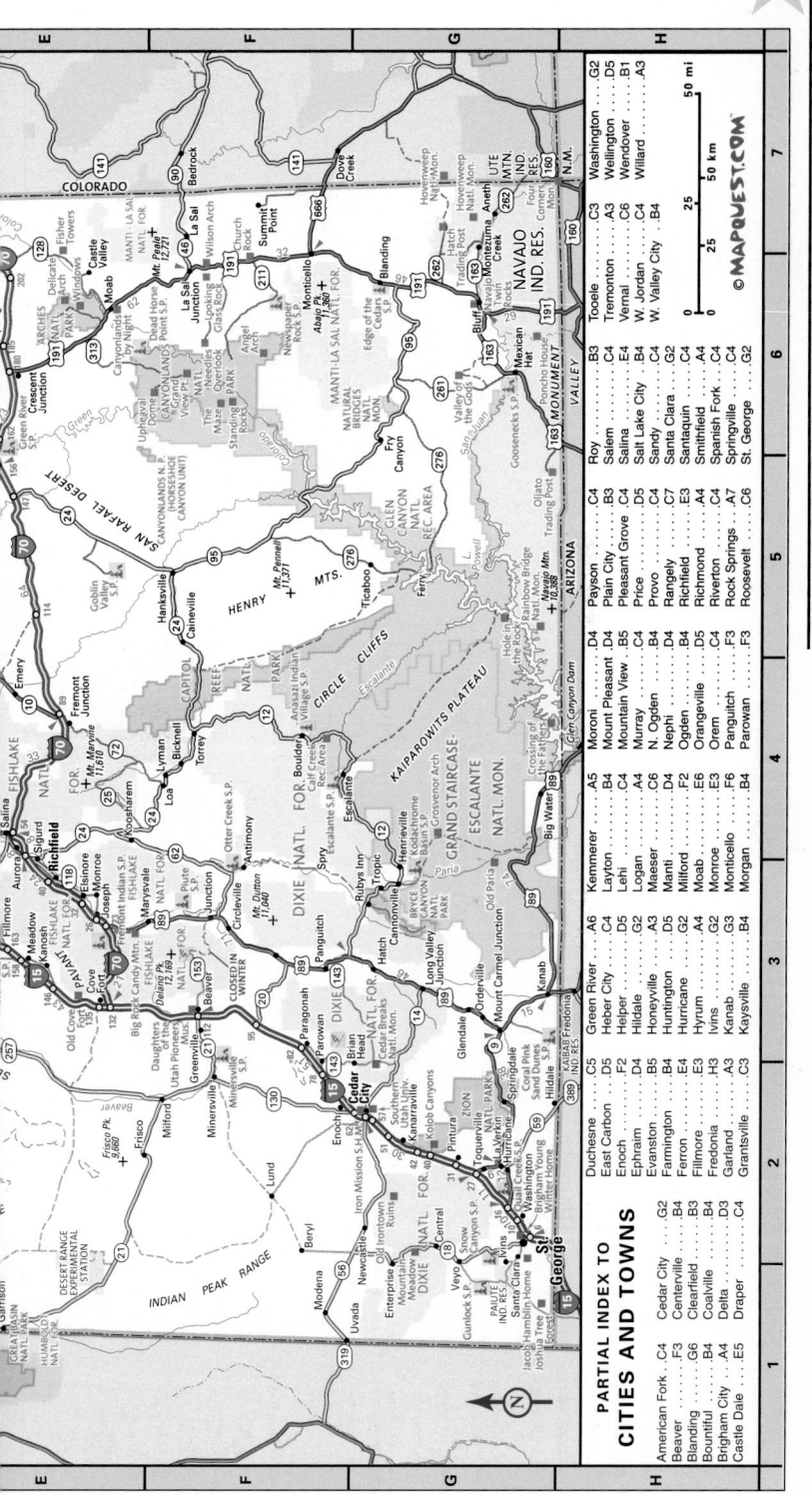

© MAPQUEST.COM

MAP LEGEND

TRANSPORTATION

CONTROLLED-ACCESS HIGHWAYS

Free

Toll; Toll Booth

Under Construction

Interchange and Exit Number

Ramp
Downtown maps only

OTHER HIGHWAYS

Primary Highway

Secondary Highway

Multilane Divided Highway
Primary and secondary highways only

Other Paved Road

Unpaved Road
Check conditions locally

HIGHWAY MARKERS

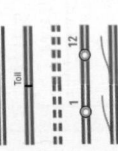

Interstate Route

US Route

State or Provincial Route

County or Other Route

Business Route

Trans-Canada Highway

Canadian Provincial Autoroute

Mexican Federal Route

OTHER SYMBOLS

Distances Along Major Highways
Miles in US; kilometers in Canada and Mexico

Tunnel; Pass

One-Way Street

Airport

Railroad
Downtown maps only

Auto Ferry; Passenger Ferry

RECREATION AND FEATURES OF INTEREST

National Park

National Forest; National Grassland

Other Large Park or Recreation Area

Military Lands

Indian Reservation

Small State Park with and without Camping

Public Campsite

Trail

Point of Interest

Golf Course
Professional tournament location

Hospital
City maps only

Ski Area

CITIES AND TOWNS

National Capital; State or Provincial Capital

County Seat
State maps only

Cities, Towns, and Populated Places
Type size indicates relative importance

Urban Area
State and province maps only

Large Incorporated Cities

OTHER MAP FEATURES

JEFFERSON   County Boundary and Name

Time Zone Boundary

+ Mt. Olympus   Mountain Peak; Elevation
  7,965   Feet in US; meters in Canada and Mexico

Perennial; Intermittent River

Perennial; Intermittent or Dry Water Body

Dam

Swamp

It pays for all kinds of fuel.

Speedpass: **today's way to pay.** Don't go on the road without *Speedpass*. You can pay for gas at the pump or just about anything inside our store. It's fast, free, and links to a check card or major credit card you already have. To join the millions who use *Speedpass*, call **1-87-SPEEDPASS** or visit speedpass.com.

We're drivers too.

With the right gas, a kid could go pretty far.

Next time you stop at an Exxon or Mobil station, consider a new destination: college. ExxonMobil is working with Upromise to help you save for a child's education. How do you start saving? Just join at upromise.com and register your credit cards. It's FREE to join. Then when you buy Exxon or Mobil gas with a credit card registered with Upromise, one cent per gallon will be contributed to your Upromise account.* This account helps you pay for the college education of any child you choose. Contributions from other Upromise participants, like GM, AT&T and Toys"R"Us, are also added to this account.** One more thing: be sure to register the credit card you linked to your *Speedpass*. That way, *Speedpass* gasoline purchases can also contribute to your account. To get your FREE *Speedpass*, go to speedpass.com or call toll free 1-87-SPEEDPASS. Upromise is an easy way to help you save for a child's education. How do we know? We're drivers too.

Join Upromise for FREE at upromise.com
For your FREE *Speedpass*, call 1-87-SPEEDPASS
or visit speedpass.com.
You must have Internet access and a valid email address to join Upromise.
*No contributions are made for diesel fuel purchases.
** Specific terms and conditions apply for each company's contributions.
   Visit upromise.com for details.
Available at Exxon and Mobil stations that accept *Speedpass*.
©2002 Exxon Mobil Corporation. All rights reserved.

 **Mobil**

We're drivers too.

WELCOME

Dear Traveler,

Since its inception in 1958, Mobil Travel Guide has served as a trusted aid to auto travelers in search of value in lodging, dining, and destinations. Now in its 45th year, Mobil Travel Guide is the hallmark of our ExxonMobil family of travel publications, and we're proud to offer an array of products and services from our Mobil, Exxon, and Esso brands in North America to facilitate life on the road.

Whether business or pleasure venues, our nationwide network of independent, professional evaluators offers their expertise on thousands of travel options, allowing you to plan a quick family getaway, a full-service business meeting, or an unforgettable Five-Star celebration.

Your feedback is important to us as we strive to improve our product offerings and better meet today's travel needs. Whether you travel once a week or once a year, please take the time to complete the customer feedback form at the back of this book. Or, contact us at www.mobiltravelguide.com. We hope to hear from you soon.

Best wishes for safe and enjoyable travels.

Lee R Raymond

Lee R. Raymond
Chairman
Exxon Mobil Corporation

A WORD TO OUR READERS

In this day and age the travel industry is ever-changing, and having accurate, reliable travel information is indispensable. Travelers are back on the roads in enormous numbers. They are going on day trips, long weekends, extended family vacations, and business trips. They are traveling across the country- stopping at National Parks, major cities, small towns, monuments, and landmarks. And for 45 years, the Mobil Travel Guide has been providing this invaluable service to the traveling consumer and is committed to continuing this service well into the future.

You, the traveler, deserve the best food and accommodations available in every city, town, or village you visit. But finding suitable accommodations can be problematic. You could try to meet and ask local residents about appropriate places to stay and eat, but that time-consuming option comes with no guarantee of getting the best advice.

The Mobil Travel Guide One- to Five-Star rating system is the oldest and most respected lodging and restaurant inspection and rating program in North America. This trusted, well-established tool directs you to satisfying places to eat and stay, as well as to interesting events and attractions in thousands of locations. Mobil Corporation (now known as Exxon Mobil Corporation, following a 1999 merger) began producing the Mobil Travel Guides in 1958, following the introduction of the US Highway system in 1956. The first edition covered only 5 southwestern states. Since then, the Mobil Travel Guide has become the premier travel guide in North America, covering the 48 contiguous states and major cities in Canadian provinces. Now, ExxonMobil presents the latest edition of our annual Travel Guides series.

For the past 45 years, Mobil Travel Guide has been inspecting and rating lodging and restaurants throughout the United States and Canada. Each restaurant, motel, hotel, inn, resort, guest ranch, etc., is inspected and must meet the basic requirements of cleanliness and service to be included in the Mobil Travel Guide. Highly trained quality assurance team members travel across the country generating exhaustive inspections reports. Mobil Travel Guide management's careful scrutiny of findings detailed in the inspection reports, incognito inspections, where we dine in the restaurant and stay overnight at the lodging to gauge the level of service of the hotel and restaurant, review of our extensive files of reader comments and letters are all used in the final ratings determinations. All of this information is used to arrive at fair, accurate, and useful assessments of lodgings and restaurants. Based upon these elements, Mobil Travel Guide determines those establishments eligible for listing. Only facilities meeting Mobil Travel Guide standards of cleanliness, maintenance and stable management are listed in the Guide. Deteriorating, poorly managed establishments are deleted. A listing in the Mobil Travel Guide constitutes a positive quality recommendation; every rating is an accolade; a recognition of achievement. Once an establishment is chosen for a listing, Mobil's respected and world-famous one- to five-star rating system highlights their distinguishing characteristics.

Although the ten-book set allows us to include many more hotels, restaurants, and attractions than in past years, space limitations still make it impossible for us to include every hotel, motel, and restaurant in America. Instead, our database consists of a generous, representative sampling, with information about places that are above-average in their type. In essence, you can confidently patronize any of the restaurants, places of lodging, and attractions contained in the *Mobil Travel Guide* series.

What do we mean by "representative sampling"? You'll find that the *Mobil Travel Guide* books include information about a great variety of establishments. Perhaps you favor rustic lodgings and restaurants, or perhaps you're most comfortable with elegance and high style. Money may be no object or, like most of us, you may be on a budget. Some travelers place a high premium on 24-hour room service or special menu items. Others look for quiet seclusion. Whatever your travel needs and desires, they will be reflected in the *Mobil Travel Guide* listings.

Allow us to emphasize that we have charged no establishment for inclusion in our guides. We have no relationship with any of the businesses and attractions we list and act only as a consumer advocate. In essence, we do the investigative legwork so you won't have to.

Look over the "How to Use This Book" section that follows. You'll discover just how simple it is to quickly and easily gather all the information you need—before your trip or while on the road. For terrific tips on saving money, travel safety, and other ways to get the most out of your travels, be sure to read our special section, "Making the Most of Your Trip."

Keep in mind that the hospitality business is ever-changing. Restaurants and places of lodging—particularly small chains or stand-alone establishments—can change management or even go out of business with surprising quickness. Although we have made every effort to double-check information during our annual updates, we nevertheless recommend that you call ahead to be sure a place you have selected is open and still offers all the features you want. Phone numbers are provided, and, when available, we also list fax and Web site information.

We hope that all your travel experiences are easy and relaxing. If any aspects of your accommodations or dining motivate you to comment, please drop us a line. We depend a great deal on our readers' remarks, so you can be assured that we will read and assimilate your comments into our research. General comments about our books are also welcome. You can write us at Mobil Travel Guides,

1460 Renaissance Drive, Suite 401, Park Ridge, IL 60068, or send email to info@mobiltravelguide.com.

Take your *Mobil Travel Guide* books along on every trip. You'll be pleased by their convenience, ease of use, and breadth of dependable coverage.

Happy travels in the new millennium!

EDITORIAL CONTRIBUTORS AND CONSULTANTS FOR DRIVING TOURS, WALKING TOURS, ATTRACTIONS, EVENTS, AND PHOTOGRAPHY:

June Naylor has written about travel in Texas, the Southwest, and the US for newspapers, books, and magazines since 1985. She is the award-winning author of several Texas travel guides including *Texas Off the Beaten Path* and *Quick Escapes from Dallas-Fort Worth*. A longtime Texas resident, she is also a dining critic and contributing travel writer for the *Fort Worth Star-Telegram* and co-host of a weekly food and road trip radio show in the Dallas-Fort Worth area.

Don Laine and his wife **Barb**, residents of northern New Mexico since 1970, have co-authored and contributed to over two dozen travel books, including *Little-Known Southwest—Outdoor Destinations Beyond the Parks,* and *New Mexico & Arizona State Parks*.

Eric Peterson is a Denver-based freelance writer and Colorado native who has contributed to numerous guidebooks about the Western US. His recent writing credits include *Frommer's Colorado, Frommer's Texas,* and *Frommer's Yellowstone and Grand Teton National Parks*. When not on the road in his Jeep (220,000 miles and still kicking), Peterson writes about the Mile High City's high-tech economy and punk-rock underworld.

HOW TO USE THIS BOOK

The *Mobil Travel Guides* are designed for ease of use. Each state has its own chapter. The chapter begins with a general introduction, which provides both a general geographical and historical orientation to the state; it also covers basic statewide tourist information, from state recreation areas to seatbelt laws. The remainder of each chapter is devoted to the travel destinations within the state—cities and towns, state and national parks, and tourist areas—which, like the states, are arranged alphabetically.

The following is an explanation of the wealth of information you'll find regarding those travel destinations—information on the area, on things to see and do there, and on where to stay and eat.

Maps and Map Coordinates

Next to most destinations are a set of map coordinates. These are referenced to the appropriate state map in the front of this book. In addition, we have provided maps of selected larger cities.

Destination Information

Because many travel destinations are close to other cities and towns where visitors might find additional attractions, accommodations, and restaurants, cross-references to those places are included whenever possible. Also listed are addresses and phone numbers for travel information resources—usually the local chamber of commerce or office of tourism—as well as pertinent vital statistics and a brief introduction to the area.

What to See and Do

Almost 20,000 museums, art galleries, amusement parks, universities, historic sites and houses, plantations, churches, state parks, ski areas, and other attractions are described in the *Mobil Travel Guides*. A white star on a red background ✪ signals that the attraction is one of the best in the state. Because municipal parks, public tennis courts, swimming pools, and small educational institutions are common to most towns, they are generally not represented in the city.

Following the attraction's description, you'll find the months and days it's open, address/location and phone number, and admission costs (see the inside front cover for an explanation of the cost symbols). Note that directions are given from the center of the town under which the attraction is listed, which may not necessarily be the town in which the attraction is located. Zip codes are listed only if they differ from those given for the town.

Driving and Walking Tours

The driving tours are usually day trips—though they can be longer—that make for interesting side trips. This is a way to get off the beaten track and visit an area often overlooked. These trips frequently cover areas of natural beauty or historical significance. The walking tours focus on a particularly interesting area of a city or town. Again, these can be a break from more everyday tourist attractions. The tours often include places to stop for a meal or snack.

Special Events

Special events can either be annual events that last only a short time, such as festivals and fairs, or longer, seasonal events such as horse racing, summer theater and concerts, and professional sports. Special event listings might also include an infrequently occurring occasion that marks a certain date or event, such as a centennial or other commemorative celebration.

Major Cities

Additional information on airports and ground transportation, and suburbs, may be included for large cities.

Lodging and Restaurant Listings

ORGANIZATION

For both lodgings and restaurants, when a property is in a town that does not have its own heading, the listing appears under the town nearest its location with the address and town immediately after the establishment name. In large cities, lodgings located within five miles of major commercial airports are listed under a separate "Airport" heading, following the city listings.

LODGING CLASSIFICATIONS

Each property is classified by type according to the characteristics below. Because the following features and services are found at most motels and hotels, they are not shown in those listings:

- Year-round operation with a single rate structure unless otherwise quoted
- European plan (meals not included in room rate)
- Bathroom with tub and/or shower in each room
- Air-conditioned/heated, often with individual room control
- Cots
- Daily maid service
- In-room phones
- Elevators

Motels/Motor Lodges. Accommodations are in low-rise structures with rooms easily accessible to parking (which is usually free). Properties have outdoor room entry and small, functional lobbies. Service is often limited, and dining may not be offered in lower-rated motels and lodges. Shops and businesses are found only in higher-rated properties, as are bellhops, room service, and restaurants serving three meals daily.

Hotels. To be categorized as a hotel, an establishment must have most of the following facilities and services: multiple floors, a restaurant and/or coffee shop, elevators, room service, bellhops, a spacious lobby, and recreational facilities. In addition, the following features and services not shown in listings are also found:

- Valet service (one-day laundry/cleaning service)
- Room service during hours restaurant is open
- Bellhops
- Some oversize beds

Resorts. These specialize in stays of three days or more and usually offer American plan and/or housekeeping accommodations. Their emphasis is on recreational facilities, and a social director is often available. Food services are of primary importance, and guests must be able to eat three meals a day on the premises, either in restaurants or by having access to an on-site grocery store and preparing their own meals.

All Suites. All Suites' guest rooms consist of two rooms, one bedroom and one living room. Higher rated properties offer facilities and services comparable to regular hotels.

B&Bs/Small Inns. Frequently thought of as a small hotel, a bed-and-breakfast or an inn is a place of homelike comfort and warm hospitality. It is often a structure of historic significance, with an equally interesting setting. Meals are a special occasion, and refreshments are frequently served in late afternoon. Rooms are usually individually decorated, often with antiques or furnishings representative of the locale. Phones, bathrooms, or TVs may not be available in every room.

Guest Ranches. Like resorts, guest ranches specialize in stays of three days or more. Guest ranches also offer meal plans and extensive outdoor activities. Horseback riding is usually a feature; there are stables and trails on the ranch property, and trail rides and daily instruction are part of the program. Many guest ranches are working ranches, ranging from casual to rustic, and guests are encouraged to participate in ranch life. Eating is often family style and may also include cookouts. Western saddles are assumed; phone ahead to inquire about English saddle availability.

Extended Stay. These hotels specialize in stays of three days or more and usually offer weekly room rates. Service is often limited and dining might not be offered at lower-rated extended-stay hotels.

Villas/Condos. Similar to Cottage Colonies, these establishments are usually found in recreational areas. They are often separate houses, often luxuriously furnished, and rarely offer restaurants and only a small variety of services on the premises.

Conference Centers. Conference Centers are hotels with extended meeting space facilities designed to house multiday conferences and seminars. Amenities are often geared toward groups staying for longer than one night and often include restaurants and fitness facilities. Larger Conference Center Hotels are often referred to as Convention Center Hotels.

Casinos. Casino Hotels incorporate areas that offer games of chance like Blackjack, Poker, Slot machines, etc. and are only found in states that legalize gambling. Casino Hotels offer a wide range of services and amenities, comparable to regular hotels.

Cottage Colonies. These are housekeeping cottages and cabins that are usually found in recreational areas. Any dining or recreational facilities are noted in our listing.

DINING CLASSIFICATIONS

Restaurants. Most dining establishments fall into this category. All have a full kitchen and offer table service and a complete menu. Parking on or near the premises, in a lot or garage, is assumed. When a property offers valet or other special parking features, or when only street parking is available, it is noted in the listing.

Unrated Dining Spots. These places, listed after Restaurants in many cities, are chosen for their unique atmosphere, specialized menu, or local flavor. They include delis, ice-cream parlors, cafeterias, tearooms, and pizzerias. Because they may not have a full kitchen or table service, they are not given a *Mobil Travel Guides* rating. Often they offer extraordinary value and quick service.

QUALITY RATINGS

The *Mobil Travel Guides* have been rating lodgings and restaurants on a national basis since the first edition was published in 1958. For years the guide was the only source of such ratings, and it remains among the few guidebooks to rate restaurants across the country.

All listed establishments were inspected by experienced field representatives or evaluated by a senior staff member. Ratings are based upon their detailed inspection reports of the individual properties, on written evaluations of staff members who stay and dine anonymously, and on an extensive review of comments from our readers.

You'll find a key to the rating categories, ★ through ★★★★★, on the inside front cover. All establishments in the book are recommended. Even a ★ place is clean, convenient, limited service, usually providing a basic, informal experience. Rating categories reflect both the features the property offers and its quality in relation to similar establishments.

For example, lodging ratings take into account the number and quality of facilities and services, the luxury of appointments, and the attitude and professionalism of staff and management. A ★ establishment provides a comfortable night's lodging. A ★★ property offers more than a facility that rates one star, and the decor is well planned and integrated. Establishments that rate ★★★ are well-appointed, with full services and amenities; the lodging experience is truly excellent, and the range of facilities is extensive. Properties that have been given ★★★★ not only offer many services but also have their own style and personality; they are luxurious, creatively decorated, and superbly maintained. The ★★★★★ properties are among the best in North America, superb in every respect and entirely memorable, year in and year out.

Restaurant evaluations reflect the quality of the food and the ingredients, preparation, presentation, service levels, as well as the property's decor and ambience. A restaurant that has fairly simple goals for menu and decor but that achieves those goals superbly might receive the same number of stars as a restaurant with somewhat loftier ambitions, but the execution of which falls short of the mark. In general, ★ indicates a restaurant that's a good choice in its area, usually fairly simple and perhaps catering to a clientele of locals and families; ★★ denotes restaurants that are more highly recommended in their area; ★★★ restaurants are of national caliber, with professional and attentive service and a skilled chef in the kitchen; ★★★★ reflect superb dining choices, where remarkable food is served in equally remarkable surroundings; and ★★★★★ represent that rare group of the best restaurants in the country, where in addition to near perfection in every detail, there's that special something extra that makes for an unforgettable dining experience.

A list of the four-star and five-star establishments in each region is located just before the state listings.

Each rating is reviewed annually and each establishment must work to maintain its rating (or improve it). Every effort is made to assure that ratings are fair and accurate; the designated ratings are published purely as an aid to travelers. In general, properties that are very new or have recently undergone major management changes are considered difficult to assess fairly and are often listed without ratings.

LODGINGS

Each listing gives the name, address, directions (when there is no street address), neighborhood and/or directions from downtown (in major cities), phone number (local and 800), fax number, number and type of rooms available, room rates, and seasons open (if not year-round). Also included are details on recreational and dining facilities on the property or nearby, the presence of a luxury level, and credit card information. A key to the symbols at the end of each listing is on the inside front cover. (Note that Exxon or Mobil Corporation credit cards cannot be used for payment of meals and room charges.)

All prices quoted in the *Mobil Travel Guide* publications are expected to be in effect at the time of publication and during the entire year; however, prices cannot be guaranteed. In some localities there may be short-term price variations because of special events or holidays. Whenever possible, these price charges are noted. Certain resorts have complicated rate structures that vary with the time of year; always confirm listed rates when you make your plans.

RESTAURANTS

Each listing gives the name, address, directions (when there is no street address), neighborhood and/or directions from downtown (in major cities), phone number, hours and days of operation (if not open daily year-round), reservation policy, cuisine (if other than American), price range for each meal served, children's menu (if offered), specialties, and credit card information. In addition, special features such as chef ownership, ambience, and entertainment are noted. By carefully reading the detailed restaurant information and comparing prices, you can easily determine whether the restaurant is formal and elegant or informal and comfortable for families.

TERMS AND ABBREVIATIONS IN LISTINGS

The following terms and abbreviations are used throughout the listings:

A la carte entrees With a price, refers to the cost of entrees/main dishes that are not accompanied by side dishes.

AP American plan (lodging plus all meals).

Bar Liquor, wine, and beer are served in a bar or cocktail lounge and usually with meals unless otherwise indicated (e.g., "wine, beer").

Business center The property has a designated area accessible to all guests with business services.

Business servs avail The property can perform/arrange at least two of the following services for a guest: audiovisual equipment rental, binding, computer rental, faxing, messenger services, modem availability, notary service, obtaining office supplies, photocopying, shipping, and typing.

Cable Standard cable service; "premium" indicates that HBO, Disney, Showtime, or similar cable services are available.

Ck-in, ck-out Check-in time, check-out time.

Coin lndry Self-service laundry.

Complete meal Soup and/or salad, entree, and dessert, plus nonalcoholic beverage.

Continental bkfst Usually coffee and a roll or doughnut.

Cr cds: A, American Express; C, Carte Blanche; D, Diners Club; DS, Discover; ER, enRoute; JCB, Japanese Credit Bureau; MC, MasterCard; V, Visa.

D Followed by a price, indicates room rate for a "double"—two people in one room in one or two beds (the charge may be higher for two double beds).

Downhill/X-country ski Downhill and/or cross-country skiing within 20 miles of property.

Each addl Extra charge for each additional person beyond the stated number of persons at a reduced price.

Early-bird dinner A meal served at specified hours, typically around 4:30-6:30 pm.

Exc Except.

Exercise equipt Two or more pieces of exercise equipment on the premises.

Exercise rm Both exercise equipment and room, with an instructor on the premises.

Fax Facsimile machines available to all guests.

Golf privileges Privileges at a course within ten miles.

Hols Holidays.

In-rm modem link Every guest room has a connection for a modem that's separate from the phone line.

Kit. or **Kits.** A kitchen or kitchenette that contains stove or microwave, sink, and refrigerator and that is either part of the room or a separate room. If the kitchen is not fully equipped, the listing will indicate "no equipt" or "some equipt."

Luxury level A special section of a lodging, covering at least an entire floor, that offers increased luxury accommodations. Management must provide no less than three of these four services: separate check-in and check-out, concierge, private lounge, and private elevator service (key access). Complimentary breakfast and snacks are commonly offered.

MAP Modified American plan (lodging plus two meals).

Movies Prerecorded videos are available for rental.

No cr cds accepted No credit cards are accepted.

No elvtr In hotels with more than two stories, it's assumed there are elevators; only their absence is noted.

No phones Phones, too, are assumed; only their absence is noted.

Parking There is a parking lot on the premises.

Private club A cocktail lounge or bar available to members and their guests. In motels and hotels where these clubs exist, registered guests can usually use the club as guests of the management; the same is frequently true of restaurants.

Prix fixe A full meal for a stated price; usually one price is quoted.

Res Reservations.

S Followed by a price, indicates room rate for a "single," i.e., one person.

Serv bar A service bar, where drinks are prepared for dining patrons only.

Serv charge Service charge is the amount added to the restaurant check in lieu of a tip.

Table d'hôte A full meal for a stated price, dependent upon entree selection; no a la carte options are available.

Tennis privileges Privileges at tennis courts within five miles.

TV Indicates color television.

Under certain age free Children under that age are not charged if staying in room with a parent.

Valet parking An attendant is available to park and retrieve a car.

VCR VCRs in all guest rooms.

VCR avail VCRs are available for hookup in guest rooms.

Special Information for Travelers with Disabilities

The *Mobil Travel Guides* Ⓓ symbol shown in accommodation and restaurant listings indicates establishments that are at least partially accessible to people with mobility problems.

The *Mobil Travel Guides* criteria for accessibility are unique to our publication. Please do not confuse them with the universal symbol for wheelchair accessibility. When the Ⓓ symbol appears following a listing, the establishment is equipped with facilities to accommodate people using wheelchairs or crutches or otherwise needing easy access to doorways and rest rooms. Travelers with severe mobility problems or with hearing or visual impairments may or may not find facilities they need. Always phone ahead to make sure that an establishment can meet your needs.

All lodgings bearing our Ⓓ symbol have the following facilities:
- ISA-designated parking near access ramps
- Level or ramped entryways to building
- Swinging building entryway doors minimum 39"
- Public rest rooms on main level with space to operate a wheelchair; handrails at commode areas
- Elevators equipped with grab bars and lowered control buttons
- Restaurants with accessible doorways; rest rooms with space to operate wheelchair; handrails at commode areas
- Minimum 39" width entryway to guest rooms
- Low-pile carpet in rooms
- Telephone at bedside and in bathroom
- Bed placed at wheelchair height
- Minimum 39" width doorway to bathroom
- Bath with open sink—no cabinet; room to operate wheelchair
- Handrails at commode areas; tub handrails

- Wheelchair-accessible peephole in room entry door
- Wheelchair-accessible closet rods and shelves

All restaurants bearing our [D] symbol offer the following facilities:

- ISA-designated parking beside access ramps
- Level or ramped front entryways to building
- Tables to accommodate wheelchairs
- Main-floor rest rooms; minimum 39" width entryway
- Rest rooms with space to operate wheelchair; handrails at commode areas

In general, the newest properties are apt to impose the fewest barriers.

To get the kind of service you need and have a right to expect, do not hesitate when making a reservation to question the management in detail about the availability of accessible rooms, parking, entrances, restaurants, lounges, or any other facilities that are important to you, and confirm what is meant by "accessible." Some guests with mobility impairments report that lodging establishments' housekeeping and maintenance departments are most helpful in describing barriers. Also inquire about any special equipment, transportation, or services you may need.

MAKING THE MOST OF YOUR TRIP

A few hardy souls might look with fondness upon the trip where the car broke down and they were stranded for a week. Or maybe even the vacation that cost twice what it was supposed to. For most travelers, though, the best trips are those that are safe, smooth, and within their budget. To help you make your trip the best it can be, we've assembled a few tips and resources.

Saving Money

ON LODGING

After you've seen the published rates, it's time to look for discounts. Many hotels and motels offer them—for senior citizens, business travelers, families, you name it. It never hurts to ask—politely, that is. Sometimes, especially in late afternoon, desk clerks are instructed to fill beds, and you might be offered a lower rate, or a nicer room, to entice you to stay. Look for bargains on stays over multiple nights, in the off-season, and on weekdays or weekends (depending on location). Many hotels in major metropolitan areas, for example, have special weekend package plans that offer considerable savings on rooms; they may include breakfast, cocktails, and meal discounts. Prices can change frequently throughout the year, so phone ahead.

Another way to save money is to choose accommodations that give you more than just a standard room. Rooms with kitchen facilities enable you to cook some meals for yourself, reducing restaurant costs. A suite might save money for two couples traveling together. Even hotel luxury levels can provide good value, as many include breakfast or cocktails in the price of the room.

State and city sales taxes, as well as special room taxes, can increase your room rates as much as 25 percent per day. We are unable to include this specific information in the listings, but we strongly urge that you ask about these taxes when placing reservations to understand the total cost of your lodgings.

Watch out for telephone-usage charges that hotels frequently impose on long-distance calls, credit-card calls, and other phone calls—even those that go unanswered. Before phoning from your room, read the information given to you at check-in, and then be sure to read your bill carefully before checking out. You won't be expected to pay for charges that they did not spell out. (On the other hand, it's not unusual for a hotel to bill you for your calls after you return home.) Consider using your cell phone; or, if public telephones are available in the hotel lobby, your cost savings may outweigh the inconvenience.

ON DINING

There are several ways to get a less expensive meal at a more expensive restaurant. Early-bird dinners are popular in many parts of the country and offer considerable savings. If you're interested in sampling a 4- or 5-star establishment, consider going at lunchtime. While the prices then are probably relatively high, they may be half of those at dinner and come with the same ambience, service, and cuisine.

ON PARK PASSES

Although many national parks, monuments, seashores, historic sites, and recreation areas may be used free of charge, others charge an entrance fee (ranging from $1 to $6 per person to $5 to $15 per carload) and/or a "use fee" for special services and facilities. If you plan to make several visits to federal recreation areas, consider one of the following National Park Service money-saving programs:

Park Pass. This is an annual entrance permit to a specific unit in the National Park Service system that normally charges an entrance fee. The pass admits the permit holder and any accompanying passengers in a private noncommercial vehicle or, in the case of walk-in facilities, the holder's spouse, children, and parents. It is valid for entrance fees only. A Park Pass may be purchased in person or by mail from the National Park Service unit at which the pass will be honored. The cost is $15 to $20, depending upon the area.

Golden Eagle Passport. This pass, available to people who are between 17 and 61, entitles the purchaser and accompanying passengers in a private noncommercial vehicle to enter any outdoor National Park Service unit that charges an entrance fee and admits the purchaser and family to most walk-in fee-charging areas. Like the Park Pass, it is good for one year and does not cover use fees. It may be purchased from the National Park Service, Office of Public Inquiries, Room 1013, US Department of the Interior, 18th and C sts NW, Washington, D.C. 20240, phone 202/208-4747; at any of the ten regional offices throughout the country; and at any National Park Service area that charges a fee. The cost is $50.

Golden Age Passport. Available to citizens and permanent residents of the United States 62 years or older, this is a lifetime entrance permit to fee-charging recreation areas. The fee exemption extends to those accompanying the permit holder in a private noncommercial vehicle or, in the case of walk-in facilities, to the holder's spouse and children. The passport also entitles the holder to a 50 percent discount on use fees charged in park areas but not to fees charged by concessionaires. Golden Age Passports must be obtained in person. The applicant must show proof of age, i.e., a driver's license, birth certificate, or signed affidavit attesting to age (Medicare cards are not acceptable proof). These passports are available at most park service units where they're used, at National Park Service headquarters (see above), at park system regional offices, at National Forest Supervisors' offices, and at most Ranger Station offices. The cost is $10.

Golden Access Passport. Issued to citizens and permanent residents of the United States who are physically disabled or visually impaired, this passport is a free lifetime entrance permit to fee-charging recreation areas. The fee exemption extends to those accompanying the permit holder in a private noncommercial vehicle or, in the case of walk-in facilities, to the holder's spouse and children. The passport also entitles the holder to a 50 percent discount on use fees charged in park areas but not to fees charged by concessionaires. Golden Access Passports must be obtained in person. Proof of eligibility to receive federal benefits is required (under programs such as Disability Retirement, Compensation for Military Service-Connected Disability, Coal Mine

Safety and Health Act, etc.), or an affidavit must be signed attesting to eligibility. These passports are available at the same outlets as Golden Age Passports.

FOR SENIOR CITIZENS

Look for the senior-citizen discount symbol in the lodging and restaurant listings. Always call ahead to confirm that the discount is being offered, and be sure to carry proof of age. At places not listed in the book, it never hurts to ask if a senior-citizen discount is offered. Additional information for mature travelers is available from the American Association of Retired Persons (AARP), 601 E St NW, Washington, D.C. 20049, phone 202/434-2277.

Tipping

Tipping is an expression of appreciation for good service, and often service workers rely on tips as a significant part of their income. However, you never need to tip if service is poor.

IN HOTELS

Door attendants in major city hotels are usually given $1 for getting you a cab. Bellhops expect $1 per bag, usually $2 if you have only one bag. Concierges are tipped according to the service they perform. It's not mandatory to tip when you've asked for suggestions on sightseeing or restaurants or help in making reservations for dining. However, when a concierge books you a table at a restaurant known to be difficult to get into, a gratuity of $5 is appropriate. For obtaining theater or sporting event tickets, $5-$10 is expected. Maids, often overlooked by guests, may be tipped $1-$2 per days of stay.

AT RESTAURANTS

Coffee shop and counter service waitstaff are usually given 8 percent–10 percent of the bill. In full-service restaurants, tip 15 percent of the bill, before sales tax. In fine restaurants, where the staff is large and shares the gratuity, 18 percent–20 percent for the waiter is appropriate. In most cases, tip the maitre d' only if service has been extraordinary and only on the way out; $20 is the minimum in upscale properties in major metropolitan areas. If there is a wine steward, tip him or her at least $6 a bottle, more if the wine was decanted or if the bottle was very expensive. If your bus person has been unusually attentive, $2 pressed into his hand on departure is a nice gesture. An increasing number of restaurants automatically add a service charge to the bill instead of a gratuity. Before tipping, carefully review your check. If you are in doubt, ask your server.

AT AIRPORTS

Curbside luggage handlers expect $1 per bag. Car-rental shuttle drivers who help with your luggage appreciate a $1 or $2 tip.

Staying Safe

The best way to deal with emergencies is to be prepared enough to avoid them. However, unforeseen situations do happen, and you can prepare for them.

IN YOUR CAR

Before your trip, make sure your car has been serviced and is in good working order. Change the oil, check the battery and belts, and make sure tires are inflated properly (this can also improve gas mileage). Other inspections recommended by the car's manufacturer should be made, too.

Next, be sure you have the tools and equipment to deal with a routine breakdown: jack, spare tire, lug wrench, repair kit, emergency tools, jumper cables, spare fan belt, auto fuses, flares and/or reflectors, flashlights, first-aid kit, and, in winter, windshield wiper fluid, a windshield scraper, and snow shovel.

Bring all appropriate and up-to-date documentation—licenses, registration, and insurance cards—and know what's covered by your insurance. Also bring an extra set of keys, just in case.

En route, always buckle up! In most states it is required by law.

If your car does break down, get out of traffic as soon as possible—pull well off the road. Raise the hood and turn on your emergency flashers or tie a white cloth to the roadside door handle or antenna. Stay near your car. Use flares or reflectors to keep your car from being hit.

IN YOUR LODGING

Chances are slim that you will encounter a hotel or motel fire. The ▣ in a listing indicates that there were smoke detectors and/or sprinkler systems in the rooms we inspected. Once you've checked in, make sure that any smoke detector in your room is working properly. Ascertain the locations of fire extinguishers and at least two fire exits. Never use an elevator in a fire.

For personal security, use the peephole in your room's door.

PROTECTING AGAINST THEFT

To guard against theft wherever you go, don't bring anything of more value than you need. If you do bring valuables, leave them at your hotel rather than in your car, and if you have something very expensive, lock it in a safe. Many hotels have one in each room; others will store your valuables in the hotel's safe. And of course, don't carry more money than you need; use traveler's checks and credit cards, or visit cash machines.

For Travelers with Disabilities

A number of publications can provide assistance. The most complete listing of published material for travelers with disabilities is available from The Disability Bookshop, Twin Peaks Press, Box 129, Vancouver, WA 98666, phone 360/694-2462.

The Reference Section of the National Library Service for the Blind and Physically Handicapped (Library of Congress, Washington, D.C. 20542, phone 202/707-9276 or 202/707-5100) provides information and resources for persons with mobility problems and hearing and vision impairments, as well as information about the NILS talking program (or visit your local library).

IMPORTANT TOLL-FREE NUMBERS AND ONLINE INFORMATION

Hotels and Motels

Adams Mark   800 444-2326
   www.adamsmark.com
Amerisuites   800 833-1516
   www.amerisuites.com
AMFA Parks & Resorts   800 236-7916
   www.amfac.com
Baymont Inns   800 229-6668
   www.baymontinns.com
Best Western   800 780-7234
   www.bestwestern.com
Budget Host Inn   800 283-4678
   www.budgethost.com
Candlewood Suites   888 226-3539
   www.candlewoodsuites.com
Clarion Hotels   800 252-7466
   www.choicehotels.com
Clubhouse Inns   800 258-2466
   www.clubhouseinn.com
Coast Hotels & Resorts   800 663-1144
   www.coasthotels.com
Comfort Inns   800 252-7466
   www.choicehotels.com
Concorde Hotels   800 888-4747
   www.concorde-hotel.com
Country Hearth Inns   800 848-5767
   www.countryhearth.com
Country Inns   800 456-4000
   www.countryinns.com
Courtyard by Marriott   888 236-2437
   www.courtyard.com
Crown Plaza Hotels   800 227-6963
   www.crowneplaza.com
Days Inn   800 544-8313
   www.daysinn.com
Delta Hotels   800 268-1133
   www.deltahotels.com
Destination Hotels & Resorts
   800 434-7347
   www.destinationhotels.com
Doubletree   800 222-8733
   www.doubletree.com
Drury Inns   800 378-7946
   www.druryinn.com
Econolodge   800 553-2666
   www.econolodge.com
Embassy Suites   800 362-2779
   www.embassysuites.com
Fairfield Inns   800 228-2800
   www.fairfieldinn.com

Fairmont Hotels   800 441-1414
   www.fairmont.com
Family Inns of America 800 251-9752
   www.familyinnsofamerica.com
Forte Hotels   800 300-9147
   www.fortehotels.com
Four Points by Sheraton
   888 625-5144   www.starwood.com
Four Seasons   800 545-4000
   www.fourseasons.com
Hampton Inns   800 426-7866
   www.hamptoninn.com
Hilton   800 774-1500
   www.hilton.com
Holiday Inn   800 465-4329
   www.holiday-inn.com
Homestead
   Studio Suites   888 782-9473
   www.stayhsd.com
Homewood Suites   800 225-5466
   www.homewoodsuites.com
Howard Johnson   800 406-1411
   www.hojo.com
Hyatt   800 633-7313
   www.hyatt.com
Inn Suites Hotels & Suites
   800 842-4242   www.innsuites.com
Inter-Continental   888 567-8725
   www.interconti.com
Jameson Inns   800 526-3766
   www.jamesoninns.com
Kempinski Hotels   800-426-3135
   www.kempinski.com
Kimpton Hotels   888-546-7866
   www.kimptongroup.com
La Quinta   800-531-5900
   www.laquinta.com
Leading Hotels of the World
   800-223-6800   www.lhw.com
Loews Hotels   800-235-6397
   www.loewshotels.com
Mainstay Suites   800-660-6246
   www.choicehotels.com
Mandarin Oriental   800-526-6566
   www.mandarin-oriental.com
Marriott   888-236-2427
   www.marriott.com
Nikko Hotels   800-645-5687
   www.nikkohotels.com
Omni Hotels   800-843-6664
   www.omnihotels.com
Preferred Hotels & Resorts Worldwide
   www.preferredhotels.com
   800-323-7500

Quality Inn   800-228-5151
    www.qualityinn.com
Radisson Hotels   800-333-3333
    www.radisson.com
Ramada   888-298-2054
    www.ramada.com
Red Lion Inns   800-733-5466
    www.redlion.com
Red Roof Inns   800-733-7663
    www.redroof.com
Regal Hotels   800-222-8888
    www.regal-hotels.com
Regent International   800-545-4000
    www.regenthotels.com
Renaissance Hotels   888-236-2427
    www.renaissancehotels.com
Residence Inns   888-236-2427
    www.residenceinn.com
Ritz Carlton   800-241-3333
    www.ritzcarlton.com
Rodeway Inns   800-228-2000
    www.rodeway.com
Rosewood Hotels & Resorts
    888-767-3966
    www.rosewood-hotels.com
Sheraton   888-625-5144
    www.sheraton.com
Shilo Inns   800-222-2244
    www.shiloinns.com
Shoney's Inns   800-552-4667
    www.shoneysinn.com
Sleep Inns   800-453-3746
    www.sleepinn.com
Small Luxury Hotels   800-525-4800
    www.slh.com
Sofitel   800-763-4835
    www.sofitel.com
Sonesta Hotels & Resorts
    800-766-3782   www.sonesta.com
SRS Worldhotels   800-223-5652
    www.srs-worldhotels.com
Summerfield Suites   800-833-4353
    www.summerfieldsuites.com
Summit International   800-457-4000
    www.summithotels.com
Swissotel   800-637-9477
    www.swissotel.com
The Peninsula Group
    www.peninsula.com
Travelodge   800-578-7878
    www.travelodge.com
Westin Hotels & Resorts
    800-937-8461   www.westin.com
Wingate Inns   800-228-1000
    www.wingateinns.com
Woodfin Suite Hotels
    www.woodfinsuitehotels.com
    800-966-3346
Wyndham Hotels & Resorts
    800-996-3426   www.wyndham

Airlines

Air Canada   888-247-2262
    www.aircanada.ca
Alaska   800-252-7522
    www.alaska-air.com
American   800-433-7300
    www.aa.com
America West   800-235-9292
    www.americawest.com
British Airways   800-247-9297
    www.british-airways.com
Continental   800-523-3273
    www.flycontinental.com
Delta   800-221-1212
    www.delta-air.com
Island Air   800-323-3345
    www.islandair.com
Mesa   800-637-2247
    www.mesa-air.com
Northwest   800-225-2525
    www.nwa.com
Southwest   800-435-9792
    www.southwest.com
United   800-241-6522
    www.ual.com
US Air   800-428-4322
    www.usair.com

Car Rentals

Advantage   800-777-5500
    www.arac.com
Alamo   800-327-9633
    www.goalamo.com
Allstate   800-634-6186
    www.bnm.com/as.htm
Avis   800-831-2847
    www.avis.com
Budget   800-527-0700
    www.budgetrentacar.com
Dollar   800-800-4000
    www.dollarcar.com
Enterprise   800-325-8007
    www.pickenterprise.com
Hertz   800-654-3131
    www.hertz.com
National   800-227-7368
    www.nationalcar.com
Payless   800-729-5377
    www.800-payless.com
Rent-A-Wreck.com   800-535-1391
    www.rent-a-wreck.com
Sears   800-527-0770
    www.budget.com
Thrifty   800-847-4389
    www.thrifty.com

FOUR-STAR AND FIVE-STAR ESTABLISHMENTS IN THE SOUTHWEST

Arizona

★★★★★ Restaurant
Mary Elaine's, *Scottsdale*

★★★★ Lodgings
Arizona Biltmore Resort and Spa, *Phoenix*
The Boulders, *Carefree*
Canyon Villa Inn, *Sedona*
Enchantment Resort, *Sedona*
The Fairmont Scottsdale Princess, *Scottsdale*
Four Seasons Resort Scottsdale at Troon North, *Scottsdale*
Hyatt Regency Scottsdale Resort at Gainey Ranch, *Scottsdale*
The Lodge at Ventana Canyon, *Tucson*
Loews Ventana Canyon Resort, *Tucson*
Marriott's Camelback Inn, *Scottsdale*
Omni Tucson National Golf Resort & Spa, *Tucson*
The Phoenician, *Scottsdale*
The Ritz-Carlton, Phoenix, *Phoenix*
Royal Palms Hotel and Casita, *Phoenix*
The Wigwam, *Litchfield Park*

★★★★ Restaurants
Acacia, *Scottsdale*
Arizona Kitchen, *Litchfield Park*
Golden Swan, *Scottsdale*
The Gold Room, *Tucson*
La Hacienda, *Scottsdale*
Latilla Room, *Carefree*
Marquesa, *Scottsdale*
The Tack Room, *Tucson*
T Cook's, *Phoenix*
The Terrace Dining Room, *Scottsdale*
The Ventana Room, *Tucson*

Colorado

★★★★★ Lodgings
The Broadmoor Resort, *Colorado Springs*
The Little Nell, *Aspen*
Tall Timber, *Durango*

★★★★ Lodgings
Brown Palace Hotel, *Denver*
C Lazy U Ranch, *Granby*
The Home Ranch, *Steamboat Springs*
Hotel Jerome, *Aspen*
The Lodge & Spa at Cordillera, *Vail*
The Lodge at Vail, *Vail*
Omni Interlocken Resort, *Denver*
Park Hyatt Beaver Creek Resort, *Vail*
The St. Regis Aspen, *Aspen*
Vista Verde Ranch, *Steamboat Springs*

★★★★ Restaurants
Flagstaff House Restaurant, *Boulder*
Kevin Taylor Restaurant, *Denver*
Mirabelle at Beaver Creek, *Vail*
Montagna, *Aspen*
Palace Arms, *Denver*
Penrose Room, *Colorado Springs*
Piñon's, *Aspen*
Q's, *Boulder*
Renaissance, *Aspen*
Restaurant Conundrum, *Aspen*
Splendido at the Chateau, *Vail*
Tante Louise, *Denver*
The Wildflower, *Vail*

Nevada

★★★★ Lodgings

Bellagio Las Vegas, *Las Vegas*

Four Seasons Hotel Las Vegas, *Las Vegas*

Hyatt Regency Las Vegas Resort, *Las Vegas*

Venetian Resort Hotel & Casino, *Las Vegas*

★★★★ Restaurants

Aqua, *Las Vegas*

Le Cirque, *Las Vegas*

Lutece, *Las Vegas*

Nobu, *Las Vegas*

Picasso, *Las Vegas*

Renoir, *Las Vegas*

New Mexico

★★★★ Lodging

Inn Of The Anasazi, *Santa Fe*

★★★★ Restaurant

Geronimo, *Santa Fe*

Texas

★★★★★ Lodging

The Mansion On Turtle Creek, *Dallas*

★★★★ Lodgings

Barton Creek Resort, *Austin*

Four Seasons Hotel Houston, *Houston*

Four Seasons Resort and Club Dallas at Las Colinas, *Dallas/Fort Worth Airport Area*

Four Seasons Hotel Austin, *Austin*

Hotel Crescent Court, *Dallas*

The Houstonian Hotel, Club & Spa, *Houston*

Omni Houston Hotel, *Houston*

The St. Regis, Houston, *Houston*

The Westin La Cantera Resort, *San Antonio*

★★★★ Restaurants

Abacus, *Dallas*

Brennan's, *Houston*

Cafe Annie, *Houston*

Cafe at the Four Seasons, *Austin*

The French Room, *Dallas*

La Reserve, *Houston*

Le Reve, *San Antonio*

Nana, *Dallas*

Quattro, *Houston*

Restaurant at the Mansion on Turtle Creek, *Dallas*

The Riviera, *Dallas*

Scott Cellar, *Houston*

Tony's, *Houston*

Utah

★★★★ Lodgings

The Blue Boar Inn, *Heber City*

The Grand America, *Salt Lake City*

Stein Eriksen Lodge, *Park City*

★★★★ Restaurants

The Blue Boar Inn Restaurant, *Heber City*

The Glitretind, *Park City*

Riverhorse Cafe, *Park City*

The Tree Room, *Provo*

ARIZONA

This rapidly growing state has more than tripled its population since 1940. Its irrigated farms grow citrus fruits, cotton, vegetables, and grain on lush green lands that contrast sharply with the surrounding desert. It also produces 60 percent of the nation's copper.

As a vacation state, its progress has been spectacular. In winter, the areas around Phoenix, Tucson, and Yuma offer sunshine, relaxation, and informal Western living. Air conditioning and swimming pools make year-round living pleasant. In summer, the northern mountains, cool forests, spectacular canyons, trout streams, and lakes offer a variety of vacation activities, including hunting and fishing camps, ghost and mining towns, meadows filled with wildflowers, intriguing ancient Native American villages, cliff dwellings, and dude ranches.

Francisco Vasquez de Coronado crossed the area in 1540 on his ill-fated search for the nonexistent gold of Cibola. Grizzled prospectors panned for gold in mountain streams and hit pay dirt. The missions built by Father Kino and his successors date back as far as 1692. Irrigation ditches, built by the Hohokam people hundreds of years earlier, have been incorporated into modern systems.

Population: 5,130,632
Area: 113,642square miles
Elevation: 70-12,633 feet
Peak: Humphreys Peak
(Coconino County)
Entered Union: February 14, 1912 (48th state)
Capital: Phoenix
Motto: God enriches
Nickname: Grand Canyon State
Flower: Saguaro (sah-WAH-ro) Cactus Blossom
Bird: Cactus Wren
Tree: Palo Verde
Fair: October, 2003 in Phoenix
Time Zone: Mountain
Website:
www.arizonaguide.com

Grand Canyon

The state has 23 reservations and one of the largest Native American populations in the United States. More than half of the Native American population is Navajo. Craft specialties include basketry, pottery, weaving, jewelry, and kachina dolls.

Arizona is a state of contrasts. It has modern and prehistoric civilizations, mountains, deserts, and modern agriculture. Arizona offers fascinating adventures for everyone.

When to Go/Climate

We recommend visiting Arizona in the spring or fall, when temperatures are milder and the heavy tourist traffic is over.

AVERAGE HIGH/LOW TEMPERATURES (°F)

PHOENIX

Jan 66/49	**May** 94/64	**Sept** 98/73
Feb 71/45	**June** 104/73	**Oct** 88/61
Mar 76/49	**July** 106/81	**Nov** 75/49
Apr 85/55	**Aug** 104/79	**Dec** 66/42

FLAGSTAFF

Jan 42/15	**May** 67/33	**Sept** 74/41
Feb 45/18	**June** 78/41	**Oct** 63/31
Mar 49/21	**July** 82/51	**Nov** 51/22
Apr 58/27	**Aug** 79/49	**Dec** 43/16

Parks and Recreation Finder

Directions to and information about the parks and recreation areas below are given under their respective town/city sections. Please refer to those sections for details.

NATIONAL PARK AND RECREATION AREAS

Key to abbreviations. I.H.S. = International Historic Site; I.P.M. = International Peace Memorial; N.B. = National Battlefield; N.B.P. = National Battlefield Park; N.B.C. = National Battlefield and Cemetery; N.C.A. = National Conservation Area; N.E.M. = National Expansion Memorial; N.F. = National Forest; N.G. = National Grassland; N.H.P. = National Historical Park; N.H.C. = National Heritage Corridor; N.H.S. = National Historic Site; N.L. = National Lakeshore; N.M. = National Monument; N.M.P. = National Military Park; N.Mem. = National Memorial; N.P. = National Park; N.Pres. = National Preserve; N.R.A. = National Recreational Area; N.R.R. = National Recreational River; N.Riv. = National River; N.S. = National Seashore; N.S.R. = National Scenic Riverway; N.S.T. = National Scenic Trail; N.Sc. = National Scientific Reserve; N.V.M. = National Volcanic Monument.

Place Name	Listed Under
Apache-Sitgreaves N.F.	SPRINGERVILLE
Canyon de Chelly N.M.	same
Casa Grande Ruins N.M.	same
Chiricahua N.M.	same
Coconino N.F.	FLAGSTAFF
Grand Canyon N.P.	same
Glen Canyon N.R.A.	PAGE
Hubbell Trading Post N.H.S.	GANADO
Kaibab N.F.	WILLIAMS
Montezuma Castle N.M.	same
Navajo N.M.	same

CALENDAR HIGHLIGHTS

JANUARY

Fiesta Bowl (Tempe). ASU Sun Devil Stadium. College football. Phone 480/350-0900.

Native American Festival (Litchfield Park). Approx 100 Native American craft vendors. Native American dancing and other authentic entertainment. Phone West Valley Fine Arts Council 623/935-6384.

Touchstone Energy Tucson Open (Tucson). Omni Tucson National Golf Resort & Spa and The Gallery Golf Club. $3-million tournament featuring top pros. Phone 800/882-7660.

FEBRUARY

Winter Fest (Flagstaff). Features art contest and exhibit, theater performances, workshops, sled dog and other races, and games; Winterfaire with arts and crafts; entertainment. Phone 800/842-7293.

Arabian Horse Show (Scottsdale). WestWorld. The largest Arabian horse show in the world. More than 2,000 champion horses. Barn parties and more than 300 commercial vendors. Phone 480/515-1500.

Arizona Renaissance Festival (Apache Junction). Hundreds of participants enjoy music, theater, crafts exhibits, and games. Concessions. Jousting tournament at King's Jousting Arena. Phone 520/463-2700.

MARCH

Spring Festival of the Arts (Tempe). Downtown. Artists' exhibits, food, entertainment, family activities. Phone Mill Avenue Merchants Association 480/967-4877.

SEPTEMBER

Southwestern Navajo Nation Fair (Dilkon). Navajo Nation Fairgrounds. Navajo traditional song and dance; Inter-tribal powwow; All-Indian Rodeo; parade, concerts, exhibits. Phone 520/657-3376.

Sedona Jazz on the Rocks (Sedona). More than 5,000 people attend this outdoor jazz festival, featuring internationally renowned artists. Phone 520/282-1985.

OCTOBER

Arizona State Fair (Phoenix). State Fairgrounds. Phone 602/252-6771.

DECEMBER

Tostitos Fiesta Bowl Block Party (Tempe). Includes games, rides, entertainment, pep rally, fireworks, food. Phone 480/784-4444.

Organ Pipe Cactus N.M.	same
Petrified Forest N.P.	same
Pipe Spring N.M.	same
Prescott N.F.	PRESCOTT
Saguaro N.P.	same
Sunset Crater Volcano N.M.	same
Tonto N.F.	PAYSON
Tumacacori N.H.	same
Tuzigoot N.M.	COTTONWOOD
Walnut Canyon N.M.	FLAGSTAFF
Wupatki N.M.	same

STATE PARK AND RECREATION AREAS

Key to abbreviations. I.P. = Interstate Park; S.A.P. = State Archaeological Park; S.B. = State Beach; S.C.A. = State Conservation Area; S.C.P. = State Conservation Park; S.Cp. = State Campground; S.F. = State Forest; S.G. = State Garden; S.H.A. = State Historic Area; S.H.P. = State Historic Park; S.H.S. = State Historic Site; S.M.P. = State Marine Park; S.N.A. = State Natural Area; S.P. = State Park; S.P.C. = State Public Campground; S.R. = State Reserve; S.R.A. = State Recreation Area; S.Res. = State Reservoir; S.Res.P. = State Resort Park; S.R.P. = State Rustic Park.

Place Name	Listed Under
Buckskin Mountain S.P.	PARKER
Dead Horse Ranch S.P.	COTTONWOOD
Fort Verde S.H.P.	COTTONWOOD
Homolovi Ruins S.P.	WINSLOW
Jerome S.H.P.	COTTONWOOD
Lake Havasu S.P. (Cattail Cove and Windsor Beach units)	LAKE HAVASU CITY
Lost Dutchman S.P.	MESA
Lyman Lake S.P.	SPRINGERVILLE
McFarland S.H.P.	FLORENCE
Patagonia Lake S.P.	PATAGONIA
Picacho Peak S.P.	CASA GRANDE
Red Rock S.P.	SEDONA
Riordan S.H.P.	FLAGSTAFF
Roper Lake S.P.	SAFFORD
Slide Rock S.P.	SEDONA
Tubac Presidio S.H.P.	NOGALES
Yuma Territorial Prison S.H.P.	YUMA

Water-related activities, hiking, riding, various other sports, picnicking, camping, and visitor centers are available at all parks. There is a $5/car day-use fee at state parks; $45 and $75 annual day-use permits are available. Camping $10-$16/day. Arizona also has nine state historic parks ($3-$6; guided tours additional fee). For further information contact Arizona State Parks, Public Information Officer, 1300 W Washington, Phoenix 85007, phone 602/542-1996.

SKI AREAS

Place Name	Listed Under
Arizona Snowbowl	FLAGSTAFF
Mormon Lake Ski Center	FLAGSTAFF
Sunrise Park Resort	McNARY
Williams Ski Area	WILLIAMS

FISHING AND HUNTING

Both are excellent in a number of sections of the state. Nonresident fishing licenses: one-day (except Colorado River), $12.50; five-day, $26; four-month, $37.50; general, $51.50; Colorado River, all species, $42.50; trout stamp, $49.50. Urban fishing (for 14 lakes in six cities), $12.00. Inquire for fees to fish on Native American reservations. Nonresident hunting licenses: three-day small game, $38; general, $85.50. Tags cost from $50.50 for turkey to $3,755 for buffalo. Permits for most big-game species available by drawing only. Combination nonresident licenses (fishing and hunting), $177.50 (including trout stamp). Fees subject to change. For updated information contact the Arizona Game & Fish Department, 2222 W Greenway Rd, Phoenix 85023, phone 602/942-3000.

Driving Information

Safety belts are mandatory for all persons in front seat of vehicle. Children under four years or under 40 pounds in weight must be in an approved safety seat anywhere in vehicle. For further information phone 602/223-2000.

INTERSTATE HIGHWAY SYSTEM

Use the following list as a guide to access Interstate highways in Arizona. You should always consult a map to confirm driving routes.

Highway Number	Cities/Towns within ten miles
Interstate 8	Casa Grande, Gila Bend, Yuma.
Interstate 10	Casa Grande, Chandler, Glendale, Litchfield Park, Mesa, Phoenix, Scottsdale, Tempe, Tucson, Willcox.
Interstate 17	Cottonwood, Flagstaff, Glendale, Phoenix, Scottsdale, Sedona, Tempe.
Interstate 19	Nogales, Tucson.
Interstate 40	Flagstaff, Holbrook, Kingman, Seligman, Williams, Winslow.

Additional Visitor Information

Arizona Highways is an excellent monthly magazine; contact 2039 W Lewis Ave, Phoenix 85009. Several informative booklets may be obtained from the Arizona Office of Tourism, 2702 N 3rd St, Suite 4015, Phoenix 85004, phone 602/230-7733 or 888/520-3434.

YOU'VE SEEN THE GRAND CANYON—NOW WHAT?

This loop drive, a side trip for visitors to the South Rim of Grand Canyon National Park, combines scenic beauty with archeological, historical, geologic, and scientific sites. It can be done in one full day or divided into a day and a half with an overnight stop in Flagstaff.

From Grand Canyon Village head south on AZ 64/US 180, turning southeast on US 180 at Valle for a slow but beautiful drive through the San Francisco Mountains. Those interested in the history of the area, including prehistoric peoples and American Indians, will want to stop at the Museum of Northern Arizona. Then continue along US 180 to the turnoff to Lowell Observatory, which has been the site of many important astronomical discoveries since its founding in 1894. Guided tours of the facilities are offered, and there's a public observatory. Kids especially like the interactive displays in the exhibit hall and the Pluto Walk, a trip through the Solar System.

You are now on the north edge of Flagstaff, and the city is a good spot to spend the night. Flagstaff's top attractions include Riordan Mansion State Historic Park, where you'll step back into the early 20th century to the rustic elegance of the home of two wealthy brothers, Tim and Mike Riordan, who were very successful in the timber industry. Actually two homes in one large log building, the mansion is somewhat unique among historic homes in that it contains practically all of its original furnishings—the exact pieces bought by the Riordan brothers and their wives (also two siblings) in 1904. The mansion was constructed and then furnished in American Arts and Crafts style, also called Craftsman, a style of furniture that was simple, well-made, and durable.

From Flagstaff go east on I-40, and take the turnoff to Walnut Canyon National Monument to see dozens of small cliff dwellings built by the Sinagua people some 800 years ago. You'll explore the monument on two trails. One is a fairly easy walk along a mesa-top; the other is a bit more strenuous, but provides a much closer look at the cliff dwellings as it drops about 400 feet into Walnut Canyon.

Leaving the monument, head back toward Flagstaff on I-40 and go north on US 89 to the Sunset Crater Volcano/Wupatki national monuments loop road, where you'll find an extinct volcano, fields of lava rock, and ruins of prehistoric stone pueblos. Wupatki National Monument's main attraction is Wupatki Pueblo, a 100-room dwelling, three stories high in places, built in the 12th century by the Sinaguans. This handsome apartment house was constructed of red sandstone slabs, blocks of pale beige limestone, and chunks of brown basalt, cemented together with clay. Nearby, Sunset Crater Volcano National Monument offers an intimate look at a dormant volcano, with its rugged landscape of jet black basalt, twisted into myriad shapes ranging from humorous to grotesque. Sunset Crater's primary eruption was in the winter of 1064-1065, and archeologists continue to speculate as to how this tremendous event affected the people who lived in this area at the time, primarily the Sinagua at nearby Wupatki and Walnut Canyon.

After rejoining US 89, continue north into the Navajo Reservation and the community of Cameron, with the historic but still operating Cameron Trading Post, which sells museum-quality items as well as more affordable rugs, baskets, jewelry, and other American Indian crafts. From Cameron, head west on AZ 64 back into the national park. **(APPROX 215 MI)**

Bisbee

(G-6) *See also Douglas, Sierra Vista, Tombstone*

Founded 1880 **Pop** 6,090 **Elev** 5,400 ft **Area code** 520 **Zip** 85603
Information Greater Bisbee Chamber of Commerce, 7 Main St, Box BA; 520/432-5421

Nestled in the foothills of the Mule Mountains of southeastern Arizona, Bisbee once was a tough mining town known as "Queen of the Copper Camps." Today, Bisbee is rich in architecture and culture with many art galleries, period hotels, and bed and breakfasts.

What to See and Do

Bisbee Mining and Historical Museum. Housed in the 1897 office building of the Copper Queen Consolidated Mining Company. Depicts early development of this urban center through displays on mining, minerals, social history, and period offices; historical photographs. Shattuck Memorial Research Library. (Daily; closed Jan 1, Thanksgiving, Dec 25) 207B Youngblood Hill. Also operates Muheim Heritage House (early 1900s). (Fri-Tues) 5 Copper Queen Plaza. Phone 520/432-7071 or 520/432-7848. ¢¢

Bisbee Restoration Association & Historical Museum. Local historical and pioneer artifacts; Native American relics. (Mon-Sat; closed hols) 37 Main St. Phone 520/432-4106 or 520/432-2386. **Donation**

Mine tours. On US 80 near Old Bisbee. Phone 520/432-2071. Tours incl

Lavender Pit. A 340-acre open-pit copper mine, now inactive. Approx one-hr van tour of surface mine and historic district (daily; closed Thanksgiving, Dec 25). Lavender Viewpoint (daily; free). Phone 520/432-2071. ¢¢¢

Queen Mine. Approx one-hr guided tour on mine train; takes visitors 1,800 ft into mine tunnel. Mine temperature 47°F-49°F; jacket recommended. (Daily; closed Thanksgiving, Dec 25). Phone 520/432-2071. ¢¢

Hotel

★★ **COPPER QUEEN HOTEL.** *11 Howell Ave (85603). 520/432-2216; fax 520/432-4298; toll-free 800/247-5829. www.copperqueen.com.* 47 rms, 4 story. S, D $70-$105; each addl $10. Crib $10. TV; cable. Heated pool. Restaurant 7 am-2:30 pm, 5:30-9 pm. Bar 11-1 am; entertainment Fri-Sat. Ck-out 11 am. Meeting rm. Business servs avail. Built in 1902. Cr cds: A, C, D, DS, MC, V.
🄳 ⛲ 🏊 🐾

B&Bs/Small Inns

★★ **CALUMET AND ARIZONA GUEST HOUSE.** *608 Powell St (85603). 520/432-4815.* 6 air-cooled rms, 4 share bath, 2 story. No rm phones. S $45-$55; D $60-$70; each addl $15. TV in sitting rm; cable, VCR (movies). Complimentary full bkfst. Restaurant nearby. Ck-out 11 am. Concierge serv. Totally nonsmoking. Patios. Cr cds: MC, V.
🏊 🐾

★ **HOTEL LA MORE/THE BISBEE INN.** *45 Ok St (85603). 520/432-5131; fax 520/432-5343. www.bisbeeinn.com.* 19 rms, 6 share bath, 2 story. S $45-$60; D $50-$75; each addl $15; wkly rates. Crib free. TV in sitting rm; cable. Complimentary full bkfst. Ck-out 11 am, ck-in after 3 pm. Restored 1917 hotel. Totally nonsmoking. Cr cds: A, C, D, DS, ER, JCB, MC, V.
🏊 🐾

★ **SCHOOL HOUSE INN.** *818 Tombstone Canyon (85603). 520/432-2996.* 9 rms, 2 story, 3 suites. No A/C. No rm phones. S $50-$60; D $55-$65; each addl $10; suites $70-$75. Children over 13 yrs only. TV in den; cable. Complimentary full bkfst. Restaurant nearby. Ck-out 11 am, ck-in 3-5 pm. Concierge serv. Balconies. Totally nonsmoking. Cr cds: A, C, D, DS, JCB, MC, V.
🄳 🏊 🐾

Bullhead City

(C-1) *See also Kingman; also see Laughlin, NV*

Founded 1946 **Pop** 21,951 **Elev** 540 ft
Area code 928
Information Chamber of Commerce, 1251 US 95, 86429; 928/754-4121

What to See and Do

Davis Dam and Power Plant. Dam (200 ft high, 1,600 ft long) impounds Lake Mohave, which has a surface area of 28,500 acres and reaches 67 mi upstream to Hoover Dam. Self-guided tour through power plant (daily). 4 mi N on Colorado River. Phone 928/754-3628. **FREE**

Fishing, camping. Trout, bass, bluegill, crappie, and catfish. Campsites, picnic grounds at Katherine, 5 mi N, a part of the Lake Mead National Recreation Area (see NEVADA). Standard fees. Phone 928/754-3245.

Motels/Motor Lodges

★★ **BEST WESTERN.** *1126 Hwy 95 (86429). 928/754-3000; fax 928/754-5234; toll-free 800/780-7234. www. bestwestern.com.* 88 rms, 2 story. S, D $45-$75; under 12 free; higher rates special events. Crib free. Pet accepted; $5. TV; cable (premium). Pool; whirlpool. Complimentary continental bkfst. Restaurant nearby. Ck-out noon. Business servs avail. Refrigerators; microwaves avail. Cr cds: A, C, D, DS, MC, V.
D ⮐ ⊠ ⬚ SC ⬚

★ **LAKE MOHAVE RESORT.** *Katherines Landing (86430). 928/754-3245; fax 928/754-1125; res 800/752-9669. www.sevencrowns.com.* 49 rms, 1-2 story, 14 kits. S, D $80-$90; each addl $6; kit. units $100-$110; under 5 free. Pet accepted, some restrictions; $5. Restaurant 7 am-9 pm mid-Apr-Nov. Bar 4-10 pm. Ck-out 11 am. Business servs avail. Boat rental. Private patios, balconies. Spacious grounds. View of lake. Cr cds: DS, MC, V.
D ⮐ ⬚ ⊠ ⬚

★ **LODGE ON THE RIVER.** *1717 Hwy 95 (86503). 928/758-8080; fax 928/758-8283; toll-free 888/200-7855.*

64 rms, 2 story, 13 suites. S $30-$65; D $35-$78; each addl $6; suites $49-$95; under 12 free; wkly rates. Crib $6. TV; cable. Pool. Restaurant nearby. Ck-out 11 am. Some refrigerators; microwaves avail. On river. Cr cds: A, D, DS, MC, V.
D ⬚ ⊠ ⬚

Restaurant

★ **EL ENCANTO.** *1884 S Hwy 95 (86442). 928/754-5100.* Hrs: 11 am-11 pm. Closed some major hols. Res accepted. Mexican, Amer menu. Bar. Lunch $3-$5.25, dinner $5.60-$10. Child's menu. Outdoor dining. Mexican decor. Cr cds: A, MC, V.
D

Canyon de Chelly National Monument

See also Ganado

(In NE corner of state at Chinle)

The smooth red sandstone walls of the canyon extend straight up as much as 1,000 feet from the nearly flat sand bottom. When William of Normandy defeated the English at the Battle of Hastings in 1066, the Pueblo had already built apartment houses in these walls. Many ruins are still here.

The Navajo came long after the original tenants had abandoned these structures. In 1864, Kit Carson's men drove nearly all the Navajo out of the area, marching them on foot 300 miles to the Bosque Redondo in eastern New Mexico. Since 1868, Navajo have returned to farming, cultivating the orchards, and grazing their sheep in the canyon. In 1931, Canyon de Chelly (pronounced "de-SHAY") and its tributaries, Canyon del Muerto and Monument Canyon, were designated a national monument.

There are more than 60 major ruins, some dating from circa A.D. 300, in these canyons. White House, Antelope House, and Mummy Cave are among the most picturesque.

Most ruins are inaccessible but can be seen from either the canyon bottom or from the road along the top of the precipitous walls. Two spectacular, 16-mile rim drives can be made by car in any season. Lookout points, sometimes a short distance from the road, are clearly marked. The only self-guided trail (2½-miles round trip) leads to the canyon floor and White House ruin from White House Overlook. Other hikes can be made only with a National Park Service permit and an authorized Navajo guide (fee). Only four-wheel drive vehicles are allowed in the canyons; each vehicle must be accompanied by an authorized Navajo guide (fee) and requires a National Park Service permit obtainable from a ranger at the visitor center.

The visitor center has an archaeological museum and rest rooms. (Daily; free) Rim drive guides and White House Trail guides at visitor center bookstore. Picnic areas and campgrounds (free).

What to See and Do

⭐ **Canyon Tours.** Offered by Thunderbird Lodge (see HOTELS). Lodge personnel conduct jeep tours into the canyons; half-day (daily) and full-day (Apr-Oct, daily) trips. Phone 928/674-5841 or 800/679-2473. ¢¢¢¢

Motels/Motor Lodges

★★ **BEST WESTERN CANYON DE CHELLY.** *100 Main St (Rte 7), Chinle (86503). 928/674-5874; fax 928/674-3715; res 800/528-1234. www.bestwestern.com.* 99 rms. Early May-Oct: S $108; D $112; each addl $4; under 12 free; lower rates rest of yr. Crib free. TV; cable. Indoor pool. Complimentary coffee in rms. Restaurant 6:30 am-10 pm; Nov-Mar to 9 pm. Ck-out 11 am. Gift shop. Picnic tables. Navajo decor. Cr cds: A, C, D, DS, MC, V.
🔧 🐾 ☂ ⚒

★★ **HOLIDAY INN GARCIA TRADING POST.** *Indian Rte 7; PO Box 1889, Chinle (86503). 928/674-5000; fax 928/674-8264; toll-free 800/465-4329. www.holiday-inn.com.* 108 rms, 2 story. May-Oct: S, D $69-$109; under 18 free; lower rates rest

of yr. Crib free. TV; cable (premium). Heated pool. Restaurant 6 am-2 pm, 5-10 pm; winter hrs vary. Rm serv. Ck-out noon. Meeting rm. Business servs avail. Sundries. Gift shop. Balconies. Cr cds: A, C, D, DS, JCB, MC, V.
🔧 ☂ ⚒ 🐾 SC

Hotel

★★ **THUNDERBIRD LODGE.** *Hwy 191 and Rte 7, Chinle (86503). 928/674-5841; fax 928/674-5844; toll-free 800/679-2473. www.tbirdlodge.com.* 72 rms in motel, lodge. Mar-Oct: S $65-$97; D $70-$106; each addl $4; lower rates rest of yr. Crib $6. TV; cable. Restaurant 6:30 am-9 pm; winter hrs vary. Ck-out 11 am. Meeting rm. Business servs avail. Airport transportation. Canyon tours avail. Cr cds: A, C, D, DS, MC, V.
🔧 ⚒ 🐾

Carefree

(D-4) *See also Chandler, Mesa, Phoenix, Scottsdale, Tempe*

Pop 2,927 **Elev** 2,389 ft
Area code 480 **Zip** 85377
Information Carefree/Cave Creek Chamber of Commerce, 748 Easy St, Marywood Plaza, Box 734; 480/488-3381

The immense Tonto National Forest (see PAYSON) stretches to the north and east; the Ranger District office for the forest's Cave Creek District is located here. Located in the center of town is the largest and most accurate sundial in the Western Hemisphere.

Special Event

Fiesta Days. PRCA rodeo, parade. Usually first wkend Apr. Phone 480/488-4043.

Resort

★★★★ **THE BOULDERS.** *34631 N Tom Darlington Dr (85377). 480/488-9009; fax 480/488-4118; res 888/472-6229. www.wyndham.com/boulders.* Designed by architect Bob Bacon, this tranquil hideaway is in perfect harmony with its Sonoran desert surroundings. The traditional pueblo-style adobe buildings seem to disappear into the land and the unusual granite boulders, naturally sculpted by nature, create a surreal atmosphere. A daily schedule is delivered with nightly cookies to each casita so guests can plan their next day of activities. 205 casitas, 1-2 story; also patio homes. S, D $495-$985; each addl $25; under 18 free; MAP avail; lower rates rest of yr. Serv charge $27/day. Crib free. Pet accepted, $100. TV; cable (premium), VCR. 4 heated pools; whirlpool, poolside serv. Dining rms (public by res) 6 am-10 pm (see also LATILLA). Box lunches, snack bar. Rm serv. Bar 11-1 am. Ck-out noon, ck-in 4 pm. Grocery, package store 2 blks. Coin lndry 2 mi. Meeting rms. Business center. In-rm modem link. Gift shop. Tennis, pro. 36-hole golf, greens fee $230, pro, putting green, driving range. Entertainment. Exercise rm; sauna, steam rm. Massage. Minibars, fireplaces. Private patios. Cr cds: A, C, D, DS, ER, JCB, MC, V.

D

Restaurants

★★ **CANTINA DEL PEDREGAL.** *34505 N Scottsdale Rd, Scottsdale (85602).* 480/488-0715. Hrs: 11:30 am-10 pm. Closed Thanksgiving, Dec 25. Res accepted. Mexican menu. Bar. Lunch $6-$12.50, dinner $11.50-$19.50. Child's menu. Specialties: fajitas, chili rellenos. Patio dining. Colorful decor. Cr cds: A, D, DS, ER, JCB, MC, V.

D

★★★★ **LATILLA ROOM.** *34631 N Tom Darlington Dr (85377).* 480/488-9009. *www.wyndham.com/boulders* Housed in The Boulders, this restaurant has a sleek, modern decor juxtaposed with a rustic, circular, exposed-beam latilla ceiling. Floor-to-ceiling windows afford beautiful waterfall views. The American cuisine, including Chilean sea bass roasted in tomato concasse, is just as unique as the room. Golden Door Spa cuisine is also available for health conscious visitors. Regional American menu. Specializes in pan-roasted seabass. Own baking. Hrs: 6-10 pm; Sun brunch (Dec-May) 11:30

am-2 pm. Bar 11-1 am. A la carte entrees: dinner $24-$34. Sun brunch $9-$15. Entertainment. Outdoor dining. Jacket. Totally nonsmoking. Cr cds: A, C, D, DS, ER, JCB, MC, V.

D

Casa Grande

(F-4) *See also Florence, Gila Bend, Phoenix*

Pop 25,224 **Elev** 1,405 ft
Area code 520 **Zip** 85222
Information Chamber of Commerce, 575 N Marshall St; 520/836-2125 or 800/916-1515
Web www.casagrandechamber.org

What to See and Do

Casa Grande Ruins National Monument. (see). Approx 14 mi E on AZ 84, 287, then 9 mi N on AZ 87.

Casa Grande Valley Historical Society & Museum. Exhibits tracing Casa Grande Valley growth from prehistoric times to present with emphasis on farm, ranch, mining, and domestic life. Gift shop. (Mid-Sept-Memorial Day wkend, Tues-Sun; closed hols) 110 W Florence Blvd. Phone 520/836-2223. ¢

Factory outlet stores. Two different outlet malls: Factory Stores of America, 440 N Camino Mercado; 520/986-7616; and Tanger Factory Outlet Center, 2300 E Tanger Dr; 520/836-9663.

Picacho Peak State Park. This 3,400-acre park incl a sheer-sided peak rising 1,500 ft above the desert floor, which was a landmark for early travelers. The only Civil War battle in Arizona was fought near here. Colorful spring wildflowers; desert nature study. Hiking, picnicking (shelter). Interpretive center programs (seasonal). 24 mi SE off I-10, Picacho Peak exit. Phone 520/466-3183.

Special Event

O'Odham Tash-Casa Grande's Indian Days. Rodeo, parades, ceremonial dances, arts and crafts, chicken scratch dance and bands; Native American foods, barbecue. Res advised. Phone 520/836-4723. Mid-Feb.

Casa Grande Ruins National Monument

(F-4) *See also Casa Grande, Chandler, Florence, Phoenix*

(33 mi SE of Chandler on AZ 87, 1 mi N of Coolidge)

The Hohokam people existed in the Salt and Gila river valleys for hundreds of years before abandoning the region sometime before 1450. They built irrigation canals in order to grow beans, corn, squash, and cotton. Casa Grande (Big House) was built during the 14th century.

Casa Grande was constructed of caliche-bearing soil (a crust of calcium carbonate on stony soil) and is four stories high (although the first story was filled in with dirt). The top story probably provided an excellent view of the surrounding country and may have been used for astronomical observations.

After being occupied for some 100 years, Casa Grande was abandoned. Father Kino, the Jesuit missionary and explorer, sighted and named it Big House in 1694.

Casa Grande is the only structure of its type and size in southern Arizona. It is covered by a large protective roof. There is a museum with archaeological exhibits (daily); self-guided tours. Contact Superintendent, 1100 Ruins Dr, Coolidge 85228; phone 520/723-3172. ¢

Chandler

(E-4) *See also Mesa, Phoenix, Scottsdale, Tempe*

Pop 176,581 **Elev** 1,213 ft
Area code 480
Information Chandler Chamber of Commerce, 25 S Arizona Pl, 85225; 480/963-4571 or 800/963-4571
Web www.chandlerchamber.com

What to See and Do

Casa Grande Ruins National Monument. (see). 33 mi SE on AZ 87.

Gila River Arts & Crafts Center. Gallery featuring the works of outstanding Native American artists and artisans from more than 30 tribes. Restaurant features Native American food. Museum preserves cultural heritage of Pima and Maricopa tribes. Gila Heritage Park features five Native American villages. (Daily; closed hols) 15 mi S via AZ 93 at jct I-10 (exit 175), on Gila River Indian Reservation. Phone 480/963-3981. **FREE**

Special Events

Chandler Ostrich Festival. Features ostrich racing, food, entertainment, and arts and crafts. Early Mar. Phone 480/963-0571.

ASA Amateur Softball National Tournament. Phone 480/782-2000 or 480/782-2727. Sept.

Motels/Motor Lodges

★★ **FAIRFIELD INN.** *7425 W Chandler Blvd (85226). 480/940-0099; fax 480/940-7336; res 800/228-2800. www.fairfieldinn.com.* 66 rms, 3 story, 18 suites. Jan-Apr: S $94.95; D $104.95; suites $104.95-$114.95; higher rates for special events; lower rates rest of yr. Crib free. TV; cable (premium). Heated pool; whirlpool. Complimentary continental bkfst. Coffee in rms. Restaurant nearby. Ck-out noon. Business servs avail. In-rm modem link. Coin lndry. Some refrigerators; microwaves avail. Cr cds: A, D, DS, MC, V.
🅳 ⬚ ✈ ⬚ 🔥

★★ **HAMPTON INN.** *7333 W Detroit St (85226). 480/753-5200; fax 480/753-5100; res 800/426-7866. www.hamptoninn.com.* 101 rms, 6 story. Jan-Mar: S, D $109-$129; under 18 free; lower rates rest of yr. Crib free. TV; cable (premium). Complimentary continental bkfst. Complimentary coffee in rms. Restaurant adj open 24 hrs. Ck-out noon. Meeting rm. Business servs avail. In-rm modem link. Pool; whirlpool. Airport transportation (Mon-Fri). Some in-rm whirlpools. Cr cds: A, D, DS, JCB, MC, V.

D ⌂ ⌑ ⌦ SC

★★ **WYNDHAM GARDEN HOTEL.**
*7475 W Chandler Blvd (85226).
480/961-4444; fax 480/940-0269; res
800/889-8846. www.wyndham.com/
chandler.* 159 rms, 4 story, 19 suites.
Mid-Jan-mid-May: S $109-$159; D
$119-$169; each addl $10; suites
$129-$179; lower rates rest of yr. Crib
free. TV; cable. Heated pool; whirlpool, poolside serv. Coffee in rms.
Complimentary newspaper. Restaurant 6:30 am-2 pm, 5-10 pm. Rm
serv. Bar 4-11 pm. Ck-out noon.
Coin lndry. Meeting rms. Business
servs avail. Valet serv. Exercise
equipt. Some refrigerators. Cr cds: A,
C, D, DS, MC, V.

D ⌂ ⌇ ⌑ ⌦ SC

Resort

★★★ **SHERATON SAN MARCOS
GOLF RESORT.** *One San Marcos Pl
(85225). 480/812-0900; fax 480/963-
6777; toll-free 800/528-8071. www.
sanmarcosresort.com.* 295 rms, 4 story.
Jan-May: S, D $225, suites $295; each
addl $10; under 18 free; wkend, hol
rates; golf plans; lower rates rest of
yr. Crib free. Pet accepted; $50
deposit. TV; cable (premium). Complimentary coffee in rms. Restaurant
6:30 am-10 pm. Box lunches, snack
bar, picnics. Bar 11-1 am. Ck-out
noon, ck-in 3 pm. Pool; wading pool,
whirlpool, poolside serv. Grocery,
package store 1 blk. Coin lndry 2
blks. Convention facilities. Business
center. Bellhops. Valet serv.
Concierge. Shopping arcade. Barber,
beauty shop. Sports dir. Lighted tennis, pro. 18-hole golf, greens fee
$109 with cart, pro, putting green,
driving range. Exercise equipt. Cr
cds: A, C, D, DS, ER, JCB, MC, V.

D ⌇ ⌦ ⌂ ⌇ ⌑ ⌦ SC ⌦ ⌦

Restaurant

★★ **C-FU GOURMET.** *2051 W
Warner (85224). 480/899-3888.* Hrs:
10 am-2:30 pm, 4:30-9:30 pm. Res
accepted. Chinese menu. Bar. Lunch
$5-$9, dinner $10-$25. Specializes in
seafood, dim sum. Chinese decor.
Live seafood tanks. Cr cds: A, MC, V.

D ⌦

Chiricahua National Monument

See also Willcox

*(32 mi SE of Willcox on AZ 186, then 3
mi E on AZ 181)*

This national monument features 20
square miles of picturesque natural
rock sculptures and deep twisting
canyons.

The Chiricahua (Cheer-a-CAH-
wah) Apaches hunted in the Chiricahua Mountain range. Cochise,
Geronimo, "Big Foot" Massai, and
other well-known Apaches undoubtedly found their way into this region
during the 1870s and 1880s. A visitor
center, two miles from the entrance,
has geological, zoological, and historical displays. (Daily)

At Massai Point Overlook, geologic
exhibits explain the volcanic origin
of the monument. The road up
Bonita Canyon leads to a number of
other outlook points; there are also
20 miles of excellent day-use trails to
points of special interest.

Picnicking and camping sites are
located within the national monument. Campground/night; 26-foot
limit on trailers. Contact Superintendent, HCR #2, Box 6500, Willcox
85643; phone 520/824-3560.

Clifton

(E-7) *See also Safford*

Settled 1872 **Pop** 2,596 **Elev** 3,468 ft
Area code 520 **Zip** 85533

What to See and Do

Old Jail & Locomotive. Jail blasted
out of mountainside; first occupied
by the man who built it. S Coronado
Blvd. Phone 520/824-3560.

Cottonwood

(C-4) See also Flagstaff, Prescott, Sedona

Pop 9,179 **Elev** 3,314 ft
Area code 928 **Zip** 86326
Information Chamber of Commerce, 1010 S Main St; 928/634-7593

What to See and Do

Dead Horse Ranch State Park. This 320-acre park offers fishing; nature trails, hiking, picnicking (shelter), camping (dump station). Visitor center. Standard fees. At Verde River, N of town on 10th St. Phone 928/634-5283.

Fort Verde State Historic Park. Four original buildings of US Army fort, a major base during the campaigns of 1865-1890; museum; two furnished officers' quarters; post doctor's quarters; military artifacts. Picnicking. (Daily; closed Dec 25) 15 mi SE on AZ 279/260 in town of Camp Verde. Phone 928/567-3275. ¢¢

Jerome. Historic old copper-mining town with cobblestone streets and renovated structures now housing gift, jewelry, antique, and pottery shops; art galleries; restaurants; and hotels. Views of Verde Valley and the Mogollon Rim. 8 mi W on US 89A, 3,200-5,200 ft almost straight up. Phone 928/634-2900. Also in Jerome is

Jerome State Historic Park. Douglas Memorial Mining Museum depicts history of Jerome, mining in Arizona; housed in former house of "Rawhide" Jimmy Douglas (fee). Picnicking. No overnight facilities. (Daily; closed Dec 25) Off US 89A. Phone 928/634-5381. ¢¢

Montezuma Castle National Monument. (see). 2800 Montezuma Castle Rd, Campe Verde, AZ 86322. Phone (928)567-3322 ¢

Tuzigoot National Monument. Excavated pueblo occupied from A.D. 1000-1450. Visitor center, museum with artifacts of Sinagua culture. (Daily) 2 mi NW via N Main St, follow signs. Phone 928/634-5564. ¢¢

Verde Canyon Railroad. Scenic excursion train takes passengers through the Verde Canyon on a four-hr round trip from Clarkdale to Perkinsville. Panoramic views of rugged, high-desert area; Verde River; Native American ruins. Some open-air viewing cars. Starlight rides (summer). (Daily; schedule varies; closed Jan 1, Thanksgiving, Dec 25) 2 mi NW via US 89A. Contact 300 N Broadway, Clarkdale 86324. Phone 928/639-0010 or 800/293-7245. ¢¢¢¢

Special Events

Verde Valley Fair. Fairgrounds. First wkend May. Phone 928/634-3290.

Paseo de Casas. In Jerome. Tour of unique old homes. Third wkend May. Phone 928/634-5477.

Fort Verde Days. In Camp Verde. Parade, dancing, barbecue, reenactments. Second wkend Oct. Phone 928/567-9294.

Motels/Motor Lodges

★★ **BEST WESTERN COTTONWOOD INN.** *993 S Main St (86326). 928/634-5575; fax 928/634-5576; res 800/377-6414. www.cottonwoodinn-az.com.* 77 rms, 2 story. Mar-Oct: S, D $69-$109; each addl $6; suites $89-$109; under 12 free; lower rates rest of yr. Crib free. TV; cable. Heated pool; whirlpool. Complimentary continental bkfst. Coffee in rms. Restaurant 6 am-10 pm. Rm serv. Ck-out 11 am. Coin lndry. Meeting rm. Business servs avail. Some refrigerators. Cr cds: A, C, D, DS, V.

★★ **QUALITY INN.** *301 W Hwy 89A (86326). 928/634-4207; fax 928/634-5764; toll-free 800/228-5151. www.qualityinn-az.com.* 52 rms, 2 story. Mar-May, Sept-Oct: S $59-$99; D $65-$109; each addl $5; under 18 free; lower rates rest of yr. Crib free. TV; cable (premium). Heated pool; whirlpool. Complimentary continental bkfst. Coffee in rms. Restaurant 11 am-9 pm. Bar. Ck-out 11 am. Meeting rms. Business servs avail. Cr cds: A, C, D, DS, MC, V.

Douglas

(G-7) *See also Bisbee*

Founded 1901 **Pop** 14,312 **Elev** 3,990 ft **Area code** 520 **Zip** 85607
Information Chamber of Commerce, 1125 Pan American; 520/364-2477

What to See and Do

Agua Prieta, Sonora, Mexico. Just across the border. (For border crossing regulations, see MAKING THE MOST OF YOUR TRIP.) It is a pleasant place with shops, a historical museum of the days of Pancho Villa, restaurants, and cabarets.

Special Events

Horse races. Cochise County Fairgrounds, N on Leslie Canyon Rd. Mid-Apr-mid-Sept. Phone 520/364-3819.

Cinco de Mayo. Mexican independence festival. Early May.

Douglas Fiestas. Mid-Sept.

Cochise County Fair & College Rodeo. Cochise County Fairgrounds. Third wkend Sept. Phone 520/364-3819.

Flagstaff

(C-4) *See also Cottonwood, Sedona, Williams, Winslow*

Settled 1876 **Pop** 52,894 **Elev** 6,910 ft **Area code** 928
Information Chamber of Commerce, 101 W Rte 66, 86001; 928/774-4505
Web www.flagstaffchamber.org

In 1876, the Boston Party, a group of men who had been lured west, made camp in a mountain valley on the Fourth of July. They stripped a pine tree of its branches and hung a flag at its top. Afterward, the tree was used as a marker for travelers who referred to the place as the spring by the flag staff. In 1882, Flagstaff became a railroad town when the Atlantic and Pacific Railroad (now the Santa Fe) was built.

Flagstaff, home of Northern Arizona University (1899), is an educational and cultural center. Tourism is Flagstaff's main industry; the city is a good place to see the Navajo country, Oak Creek Canyon, the Grand Canyon (see), and Humphreys Peak (12,670 feet), the tallest mountain in Arizona. Tall pine forests of great beauty abound in the surrounding area. A Ranger District Office of the Coconino National Forest is located here.

What to See and Do

Arizona Historical Society Pioneer Museum. History of northern Arizona. (Mon-Sat; closed hols) 2½ mi NW on Fort Valley Rd (US 180). Phone 928/774-6272. **FREE**

Arizona Snowbowl Ski & Summer Resort. Resort has two triple, two double chairlifts; patrol, school, rentals; restaurants, bars, lounge; lodges. Thirty-two trails, longest run more than two mi; vertical drop 2,300 ft. (Mid-Dec-mid-Apr, daily) Skyride (Memorial Day-Labor Day; fee) takes riders to 11,500-ft elevation. 7 mi NW off US 180 at Snowbowl Rd in Coconino National Forest. Phone 928/779-1951. ¢¢¢¢

Coconino National Forest. Surrounds city of Flagstaff and the community of Sedona (see). Outstanding scenic areas incl Humphreys Peak, Arizona's highest point; parts of the Mogollon Rim and the Verde River Valley; the red rock country of Sedona and Oak Creek Canyon, where Zane Grey wrote *Call of the Canyon;* the San Francisco Peaks; seven wilderness areas; the eastern portions of Sycamore Canyon and Kendrick wilderness areas and the northern portion of Mazatzal Wilderness area; extinct volcanoes; high country lakes. Fishing; hunting on almost two million acres, winter sports, picnicking, camping (fee). Standard fees. Phone 928/527-3600.

Lowell Observatory. Established by Percival Lowell in 1894; the planet Pluto was discovered here in 1930. Guided tours; slide presentations; telescope viewing (seasonal). Museum, gift shop. Telescope domes are unheated; appropriate clothing advised. 1 mi W on Mars Hill Rd, off Santa Fe Ave. Phone 928/774-2096. ¢¢

Wupatki National Monument

Mormon Lake Ski Center. Terrain incl snowy meadows, huge stands of pine, oak, and aspen, old logging roads, and turn-of-the-century railroad grades. School. Has 21 mi of marked, groomed trails; restaurant, bar; motel, cabins. Rentals. Guided tours. 28 mi SE off Lake Mary Rd on Mormon Lake Rd. Phone 928/354-2240. ¢¢

Museum of Northern Arizona. Exhibits on the archaeology, geology, biology, paleontology, and fine arts of the Colorado Plateau; offers Hispanic, Hopi, Navajo, Zuni, and Pai exhibits and summer marketplaces, revealing the region's artistic traditions, Native cultures, and natural sciences. Museum shop, bookstore. (Daily; closed Jan 1, Thanksgiving, Dec 25) 3 mi NW on US 180 (Fort Valley Rd). Phone 928/774-5213. ¢¢

Oak Creek Canyon. This spectacular gorge may look familiar to you. It's a favorite location for western movies. The northern end of the road starts with a lookout point atop the walls and descends nearly 2,000 ft to the stream bed. The creek has excellent trout fishing. At the southern mouth of the canyon is Sedona (see), a resort town. 14 mi S on US 89A. Phone 928/282-3034.

Riordan State Historic Park. Features a mansion built in 1904 by Michael and Timothy Riordan. The brothers played a significant role in the development of Flagstaff and northern Arizona. Original artifacts, handcrafted furniture, mementos. Picnic area; no overnight facilities. Guided tours. (Daily; closed Dec 25) W on I-40, exit Flagstaff/Grand Canyon, then N on Milton Rd; turn right at sign past second light. Phone 928/779-4395. ¢¢

Special Events

Winter Festival. Features art contest and exhibit; theater performances; workshops; sled dog and other races, games; Winterfaire, with arts and crafts; entertainment. Feb.

Zuni Artists' Exhibition. The Museum of Northern Arizona. Five days beginning Sat before Memorial Day. Phone 928/774-5213.

Hopi Artists' Exhibition. The Museum of Northern Arizona. Late June-early July. Phone 928/774-5213.

Flagstaff Festival of the Arts. Northern Arizona University campus, SW edge of city. Symphonic/pops concerts, chamber music; theater; dance; art exhibits; poetry; film classics. July-early Aug. Phone 800/266-7740.

Navajo Artists' Exhibition. The Museum of Northern Arizona. Last wkend July-first wkend Aug. Phone 928/774-5213.

Coconino County Fair. Labor Day wkend. Phone 928/774-5139.

Motels/Motor Lodges

★★ **BEST WESTERN PONY SOLDIER MOTEL.** *3030 E Rte 66 (86004). 928/526-2388; fax 928/527-8329; res 800/780-7234. www.bestwestern.com.* 75 rms, 2 story. Apr-Oct: S, D $79-$109; each addl $5; suites $119; under 18 free; lower rates rest of yr. Crib $5. TV; cable (premium). Indoor pool. Barber/beauty shop. Complimentary continental bkfst. Restaurant 4:30-9:30 pm; Fri, Sat to 10 pm. Ck-out 11 am. Business servs avail. Gift shop. Downhill ski 15 mi. Refrigerators in suites. Cr cds: A, C, D, DS, MC, V.

★★ **DAYS INN.** *1000 W Rte 66 (86001). 928/774-5221; fax 928/774-4977; res 800/329-7466. www.daysinn.com.* 157 rms, 2 story. Mid-June-mid-Sept: S, D $35-$119; under 18 free; higher rates: hols, special events; lower rates rest of yr. Crib free. Pet accepted, some restrictions; $10. TV; cable (premium). Complimentary coffee in lobby. Complimentary continental bkfst. Ck-out 11 am. Meeting rms. Business servs avail. Bellhops. Valet serv. Sundries. Gift shop. Coin lndry. Pool. Cr cds: A, D, DS, MC, V.

★★ **DAYS INN EAST.** *3601 E Lockett Rd (86004). 928/527-1477; fax 928/527-0228; toll-free 800/435-4363. www.daysinnflagstaffeast.com.* 54 rms, 3 story. Mid-Mar-Oct: S, D $42-$139; under 18 free; higher rates: hols, special events; lower rates rest of yr. Crib free. TV; cable. Indoor pool; whirlpool. Complimentary continental bkfst. Restaurant adj 6 am-11 pm. Ck-out 11 am. Coin lndry. Business servs avail. Some refrigerators. Cr cds: A, D, DS, JCB, MC, V.

★★ **FAIRFIELD INN.** *2005 S Milton Rd (86001). 928/773-1300; fax 928/773-1462; res 800/228-2800. www.fairfieldinn.com/flgfi.* 134 rms, 3 story. Mid-May-Oct: S, D $65-$119; under 18 free; lower rates rest of yr. Crib free. TV; cable (premium). Pool. Complimentary continental bkfst. Ck-out noon. Meeting rm. In-rm modem link. Downhill/x-country ski 15 mi. Some refrigerators. Cr cds: A, D, DS, JCB, MC, V.

★★ **HAMPTON INN.** *3501 E Lockett Rd (86004). 928/527-1477; fax 928/527-0228; toll-free 800/453-4363. www.hamptoninnflagstaff.com.* 50 rms, 3 story. Mid-May-Sept: S, D $59-$149; under 18 free; higher rates: hols, special events; lower rates rest of yr. Crib free. TV; cable (premium). Complimentary continental bkfst. Coffee in rms. Restaurant nearby. Ck-out 11 am. Business servs avail. Downhill ski 15 mi. Indoor pool; whirlpool. Cr cds: A, C, D, DS, MC, V.

★★ **HAMPTON INN AND SUITES.** *2400 S Beulah Blvd (86001). 928/913-0900; fax 928/913-0800; toll-free 800/426-7866. www.flagstaffhampton.com.* 126 rms, 5 story, 39 kit. suites. June-Aug: S, D $69-$99; kit. suites $99-$129; under 18 free; higher rates graduation; lower rates rest of yr. Crib free. TV; cable (premium). Heated indoor pool; whirlpool. Complimentary continental bkfst. Coffee in suites. Restaurant adj 10 am-10 pm. Ck-out noon. Meeting rms. Business servs avail. In-rm modem link. Bellhops. Sundries. Coin lndry. Valet serv. Exercise equipt; sauna. Many fireplaces; some in-rm whirlpools; refrigerators, microwaves, VCRs in suites. Cr cds: A, C, D, DS, MC, V.

★★★ **HILTON GARDEN INN.** *350 W Forest Meadows St (86001). 928/226-8888; fax 928/556-9059; toll-free 800/333-0785. www.hiltongardeninn.com.* 90 rms, 3 story. Apr-Oct: S, D $69-$139; each addl $10; under 18 free; pkg plans; higher rates special events; lower rates rest of yr. Crib free. TV; cable (premium). Complimentary coffee in rms. Restaurant adj 6:30 am-10 pm. Rm serv 11 am-10 pm. Ck-out noon. Business servs avail. In-rm modem link. Valet serv. Coin lndry. Downhill/x-country ski 15 mi. Exercise equipt; sauna. Heated indoor pool; whirlpool. Refrigerators, microwaves. Cr cds: A, C, D, DS, JCB, MC, V.

★★ **HOLIDAY INN FLAGSTAFF.**
*2320 E Lucky Ln (86004). 928/714-
1000; fax 928/779-2610; toll-free
800/533-2754. www.holiday-inn.com/
flagstaffaz.* 156 rms, 5 story. Mid-
May-mid-Oct: S, D $59-$119; each
addl $10; under 18 free; lower rates
rest of yr. Crib free. Pet accepted,
$25. TV; cable. Indoor pool; whirl-
pool. Coffee in rms. Restaurant 6-9
am, 5-10 pm. Rm serv. Bar 5 -10 pm.
Free airport transportation. Ck-out
noon. Coin lndry. Meeting rms. In-
rm modem link. Exercise equipt.
Valet serv. Downhill ski 11 mi.
Refrigerators avail. Cr cds: A, C, D,
DS, MC, V.

★★ **QUALITY INN.** *2000 S Milton
Rd (86001). 928/774-8771; fax
928/773-9382; res 800/228-5151.
www.qualityinnflagstaffaz.com.* 95
rms, 2 story. May-Oct: S, D $79-$129;
each addl $5; under 18 free; lower
rates rest of yr. Crib free. Pet
accepted; $50 deposit and $10/day.
TV; cable. Heated pool. Coffee in
rms. Complimentary continental
bkfst. Restaurant adj open 24 hrs.
Ck-out 11 am. Business servs avail.
Airport transportation. Downhill ski
15 mi. Cr cds: A, D, DS, MC, V.

★★ **RAMADA LIMITED.** *2755 Woodlands Village Blvd (86001). 928/773-
1111; fax 928/774-1449; toll-free
877/703-0291. www.ramada.com.* 89
suites, 2 story. May-Sept: S, D $59-
$129; each addl $10; under 17 free;
lower rates rest of yr. Crib free. Pet
accepted, $10. TV; cable (premium).
Heated pool; whirlpool. Complimentary continental bkfst. Restaurant
nearby. Ck-out 11 am. Coin lndry.
Meeting rms. Business servs avail.
Sundries. Exercise equipt; sauna.
Refrigerators, microwaves. Cr cds: A,
C, D, DS, MC, V.

Hotels

★★★ **LITTLE AMERICA HOTEL.**
*2515 E Butler Ave (86004). 928/779-
7900; fax 928/779-7983; toll-free
800/352-4386. www.littleamerica.com.*
247 rms, 2 story. May-Oct: S, D $119-
$129; each addl $10; suites $150-
$250; under 12 free; lower rates rest

of yr. Crib free. TV; cable (premium),
VCR avail. Heated pool; whirlpool.
Playground. Restaurant 6 am-midnight. Rm serv 6 am-11 pm; Fri, Sat
to midnight. Bar 11-1 am; entertainment. Ck-out 1 pm. Coin lndry.
Meeting rms. In-rm modem link.
Valet serv. Concierge. Gift shop. Sundries. Downhill ski 15 mi. Exercise
equipt. Lawn games. Refrigerators;
some fireplaces. Cr cds: A, C, D, DS,
JCB MC, V.

★★ **RADISSON WOODLANDS
HOTEL.** *1175 W Rte 66 (86001).
928/773-8888; fax 928/773-0597; res
800/333-3333. www.radisson.com.* 183
rms, 4 story, 15 suites. Memorial
Day-Mid-Oct: S, D $109-$129; each
addl $8; suites $129-$169; under 12
free; ski plans; lower rates rest of yr.
TV; cable (premium). Heated pool;
whirlpool. Coffee in rms. Restaurant
(see also SAKURA). Rm serv. Bar. Ck-
out noon. Coin lndry. Meeting rms.
Business servs avail. In-rm modem
link. Sundries. Gift shop. Downhill/
.x-country ski 11 mi. Exercise equipt;
sauna. Microwaves avail. Refrigerator
in suites. Cr cds: A, C, D, DS, JCB,
MC, V.

B&B/Small Inn

★★★ **INN AT 410 BED & BREAK-
FAST.** *410 N Leroux St (86001).
928/774-0088; fax 928/774-6354; toll-
free 800/774-2008. www.inn410.com.*
9 rms, 1 with shower only, 2 story, 4
suites. No rm phones. Mar-Oct: S, D,
suites $135-$190; each addl $25;
wkends Apr-late-Oct (2-day min),
hols. Complimentary full bkfst; afternoon refreshments. Coffee in rms.
Restaurant nearby. Ck-out 11 am, ck-
in 4-6 pm. Luggage handling.
Concierge serv. Downhill ski 14 mi;
x-country ski 7 mi. Refrigerators. Picnic tables. Built in 1907; antiques.
Some fireplaces. Totally nonsmoking.
Cr cds: MC, V.

All Suites

★★ **AMERISUITES FLAGSTAFF.**
*2455 S Beulah Blvd (86001). 928/774-
8042; fax 928/774-5524; res 800/833-
1516. www.amerisuites.com.* 117 kit.

suites, 5 story. May-Sept: S $109-
$149; D $119-$159; each addl $10;
under 18 free; higher rates special
events; lower rates rest of yr. Crib
free. Pet accepted, some restrictions.
TV; cable, VCR. Heated indoor pool;
whirlpool. Complimentary continental bkfst, coffee in rms. Ck-out noon.
Coin lndry. Business center. In-rm
modem link. Valet serv. Free airport,
RR station, bus depot transportation.
Exercise equipt. Refrigerators. Cr cds:
A, C, D, DS, ER, JCB, MC, V.

★★ EMBASSY SUITES. *706 S Milton
Rd (86001). 928/774-4333; fax
928/774-0216; toll-free 800/774-4333.
www.embassysuitesflagstaff.com.* 119
suites, 3 story. Mid-Apr-mid-Sept:
suites $89-$179; each addl $10; ski,
hol rates; lower rates rest of yr. Crib
free. Pet accepted, some restrictions;
$50. TV; cable (premium). Heated
pool; whirlpool. Complimentary full
bkfst. Coffee in rms. Ck-out noon.
Meeting rms. Business servs avail. In-
rm modem link. Coin lndry. Valet
serv. Downhill ski 12 mi. Exercise
equipt. Refrigerators, microwaves.
Picnic tables. Cr cds: A, C, D, DS,
MC, V.

Restaurants

★★ BUSTER'S. *1800 S Milton Rd
(86001). 928/774-5155.* Hrs: 11:30
am-10 pm; early bird dinner 4:30-
6:30 pm. Closed Thanksgiving, Dec
25. Res accepted. Bar to 1 am. Lunch
$5.50-$8.95, dinner $9.95-$19.95.
Child's menu. Specializes in fresh
seafood. Oyster bar. Casual dining.
Cr cds: A, D, DS, MC, V.

★★ COTTAGE PLACE. *126 W Cottage Ave (86001). 928/774-8431. www.
cottageplace.com.* Hrs: 5-9:30 pm.
Closed Mon. Res accepted. No A/C.
Continental menu. Wine, beer. Dinner $15-$25. Child's menu. Specialties: châteaubriand, scallops en
croute, lamb chops. Own desserts.
Intimate dining in 1909 cottage. Former residence of town mayor. Cr cds:
A, MC, V.

★ KACHINA DOWNTOWN. *522 E
Rte 66 (86001). 928/779-1944.* Hrs:
11 am-9 pm; Sun to 8 pm. Closed

some major hols. Res accepted. Mexican menu. Bar. Child's menu. Lunch,
dinner $6-$18. Cantina decor. Cr cds:
A, D, DS, ER, JCB, MC, V.

★★ MAMMA LUISA. *2710 N Steves
Blvd (86004). 928/526-6809.* Hrs: 5-
10 pm. Closed Thanksgiving, Dec.
25. Res accepted. Italian, vegetarian
menu. Serv bar. Dinner $7.95-$15.95.
Child's menu. Specialties: chicken
rollantini, veal saltimbocca, fresh-
baked garlic bread. Cr cds: A, D, DS,
MC, V.

★★ SAKURA. *1175 W US 66
(86001). 928/773-9118. www.radisson.
com.* Hrs: 11:30 am-2 pm, 5-10 pm;
Sun from 5 pm. Res accepted. Japanese menu. Bar to 1 am. Lunch $4.95-
$9.95, dinner $7.95-$18.95. Child's
menu. Specialties: flaming shrimp.
Teppanyaki cooking, sushi bar. Cr
cds: A, D, DS, MC, V.

★ SALSA BRAVA. *1800 S Milton Rd
(86001). 520/774-1083.* Hrs: 11 am-9
pm; Fri to 10 pm; Sat, Sun 8 am-10
pm. Closed major hols. Mexican
menu. Bar. Bkfst $3.29-$6.95, lunch
$4.95-$6.95, dinner $5.95-$8.50.
Child's menu. Specializes in carnitas.
Outdoor dining. Casual atmosphere.
Salsa bar. Cr cds: A, MC, V.

Florence

(E-5) *See also Casa Grande*

Pop 17,054 **Elev** 1,490 ft
Area code 520 **Zip** 85232

Information Chamber of Commerce,
Box 929; 520/868-9433 or 800/437-
9433; or the Pinal County Visitor
Center, PO Box 967; 520/868-4331
Web www.florenceaz.org

What to See and Do

**Casa Grande Ruins National Monu-
ment.** (see). 10 mi W via AZ 287,
then S on AZ 87.

McFarland State Historic Park.
(1878) First of three courthouses
built here; restored adobe building
with interpretive center, displays of

early Arizona and US legal history, and the personal collections of Governor Ernest McFarland, also a US Senator and state supreme court justice. (Thurs-Mon; closed Dec 25) Ruggles Ave and Main St. Phone 520/868-5216. ¢

Pinal County Historical Society Museum. Exhibits depict early life in the area. (Tues-Sat, Sun afternoons; closed hols, also mid-July-Aug) 715 S Main St. Phone 520/868-4382. **Donation**

Special Event

Junior Parada. Three-day celebration features parade and rodeo. Sat of Thanksgiving wkend. Phone 520/868-9433.

B&B/Small Inn

★★ **RANCHO SONORA INN & RV PARK.** *9198 N Hwy 79 (85232). 520/868-8000; res 800/205-6817. www.ranchosonora.com.* 11 rms, 3 casitas. Some rm phones. S, D $74-$79; casitas $105-$150; under 5 free. Pet accepted, some restrictions. TV; cable (premium); VCR avail (free movies). Complimentary continental bkfst. Restaurant nearby. Ck-out 11 am, ck-in 2 pm. Business servs avail. Coin lndry. Pool; whirlpool. Some refrigerators, microwaves. Picnic tables, grills. Built in 1930. Original adobe, western and traditional decor. Courtyard. Cr cds: A, D, DS, MC, V.

Ganado

(B-7) *See also Canyon de Chelly National Monument, Window Rock*

Pop 1,505 **Elev** 6,386 ft
Area code 928 **Zip** 86505

What to See and Do

Hubbell Trading Post National Historic Site. The oldest continuously operating trading post (1878) on the Navajo Reservation; named for founder John Lorenzo Hubbell, who began trading with the Navajo in 1876. Construction of the present-day post began in 1883. The visitor center houses exhibits; Navajo weavers and a silversmith can be observed at work; tours of the Hubbell house, containing paintings, Navajo rugs, and Native American arts and crafts; self-guided tour of the grounds (ranger-conducted programs in summer). (Daily; closed Jan 1, Thanksgiving, Dec 25) 1 mi W on AZ 264. Phone 928/755-3475 or 928/755-3477. **FREE**

Gila Bend

(F-3) *See also Casa Grande*

Pop 1,980 **Elev** 736 ft **Area code** 520
Zip 85337

Motel/Motor Lodge

★★ **BEST WESTERN SPACE AGE LODGE.** *401 E Pima St (85337). 520/683-2273; toll-free 800/780-7234. www.bestwestern.com.* 41 rms. Jan-Apr: S $60-$70; D $65-$85; each addl $4; under 17 free; lower rates rest of yr. Crib free. Pet accepted. TV; cable (premium). Pool; whirlpool. Coffee in rms. Restaurant open 24 hrs. Ck-out noon. Some refrigerators. Cr cds: A, C, D, DS, V.

Glendale

(E-4) *See also Litchfield Park, Mesa, Phoenix, Scottsdale, Tempe*

Founded 1892 **Pop** 218,812
Elev 1,150 ft **Area code** 623
Information Chamber of Commerce, 7105 N 59th Ave, Box 249, 85311; 623/937-4754 or 800/437-8669

What to See and Do

Arizona's Antique Capital. Shopping area in downtown Glendale incl antique stores, specialty shops, and candy factory. (Most stores open Mon-Sat) 5850 W Glendale Ave. Phone 623/930-4500.

Motels/Motor Lodges

★★ **HAMPTON INN.** *8408 W Paradise Ln, Peoria (85382). 623/486-9918; fax 623/486-4842; toll-free 800/426-7866. www.hamptoninn.com.* 112 rms, 5 story. Jan-mid-Apr: S $99-$159; D $109-$159; each addl $10; under 18 free; golf plans; lower rates rest of yr. Crib free. TV; cable (premium), VCR avail. Complimentary continental bkfst. Complimentary coffee in rms. Restaurant nearby. Ck-out noon. Meeting rms. Business servs avail. In-rm modem link. Valet serv. Coin lndry. Exercise equipt. Pool; whirlpool. Refrigerators, microwaves; some in-rm whirlpools, wet bars. Cr cds: A, C, D, DS, JCB, MC, V.

[icons]

★★ **HOLIDAY INN EXPRESS.** *7885 W Arrowhead Towne Center Dr (85308). 623/412-2000; fax 623/412-5522; res 800/465-4329. www.holiday-inn.com.* 60 rms, 2 story. Mid-Jan-Mar: S, D $49-$149; each addl $10; under 18 free; lower rates rest of yr. Crib free. TV; cable (premium). Heated pool; whirlpool. Complimentary continental bkfst. Restaurant nearby. Ck-out 11 am. Business servs avail. Coin lndry. Exercise equipt. Many refrigerators; microwaves avail. Cr cds: A, MC.

[icons]

★★ **LA QUINTA INN AND SUITES.** *16321 N 83 Ave, Peoria (85382). 623/487-1900; fax 623/487-1919; toll-free 800/687-6667. www.laquinta.com.* 108 rms, 5 story. Jan-Apr: S, D $47-$129; each addl $10; suites $175-$200; under 18 free; golf plans; lower rates rest of yr. Crib free. Pet accepted, some restrictions; $25 deposit. TV; cable (premium). Complimentary continental bkfst. Complimentary coffee in rms. Restaurant nearby. Ck-out noon. Meeting rm. Business servs avail. In-rm modem link. Valet serv. Coin lndry. Exercise equipt. Pool; whirlpool. Many refrigerators, microwaves. Cr cds: A, C, D, DS, V.

[icons]

★★ **SPRINGHILL SUITES.** *7810 W Bell Rd (85308). 623/878-6666; fax 623/878-6611; res 888/287-9400. www.springhillsuites.com.* 89 suites, 4 story. Oct-Apr: suites $89-$139; under 18 free; lower rates rest of yr. Crib free. TV; cable (premium). Complimentary continental bkfst. Complimentary coffee in rms. Restaurant opp open 24 hrs. Ck-out noon. Business servs avail. In-rm modem link. Valet serv. Coin lndry. Lighted tennis privileges, pro. Pool; whirlpool. Refrigerators, microwaves, wet bars. Cr cds: A, C, D, DS, MC, V.

[icons]

★★ **WINDMILL INN AT SUN CITY WEST.** *12545 W Bell Rd, Surprise (85374). 623/583-0133; fax 623/583-8366; res 800/547-4747. www.windmillinns.com.* 127 rms, 3 story. Mid-Jan-mid-Apr: S, D $116-$145; each addl $6; under 18 free; lower rates rest of yr. Crib free. Pet accepted, some restrictions. TV; cable (premium). Heated pool; whirlpool. Complimentary continental bkfst. Restaurant adj 6 am-10 pm. Ck-out 11 am. Coin lndry. Meeting rms. Business servs avail. Golf privileges. Microwaves, refrigerators avail. Grills. Cr cds: A, D, DS, MC, V.

[icons]

Globe

(E-5) *See also San Carlos*

Settled 1876 **Pop** 7,486 **Elev** 3,509 ft **Area code** 928 **Zip** 85501

Information Greater Globe-Miami Chamber of Commerce, 1360 N Broad St, Box 2539, 85502; 928/425-4495 or 800/804-5623

What to See and Do

Besh-Ba-Gowah Indian Ruins. Ruins of a village inhabited by the Salado from 1225-1400. More than 200 rms. Visitor center, museum. 15-min video presentation.(Daily; closed Jan 1, Thanksgiving, Dec 25) From end of S Broad St turn right across bridge, continue on Jess Hayes Rd. Phone 928/425-0320. ¢¢

Boyce Thompson Southwestern Arboretum. Large collection of plants from arid parts of world added to native flora in high Sonoran Desert setting at foot of Picket Post Mtn; labeled plants in 39-acre garden. Picnicking. Book store. Visitor center features biological and historical displays. (Daily; closed Dec 25) 28 mi W on US 60; 3 mi W of Superior. Phone 928/689-2811. ¢¢¢

Gila County Historical Museum.
Exhibit of artifacts of Gila County, incl those of the Apache. (Mon-Sat; closed hols) 1 mi N on US 60. Phone 928/425-7385. **Donation**

Special Events

Gila County Fair. Four days mid-Sept.
Apache Days. Fourth wkend Oct.

Motel/Motor Lodge

★ **HOLIDAY INN EXPRESS GLOBE.**
2119 Old West Hwy 60 (85502). 928/425-7008; fax 928/425-6410; res 800/465-4329. www.holiday-inn.com. 45 rms, 2 story. S, D $56-$70; each addl $7; under 18 free. Crib free. Pet accepted. TV; cable (premium). Complimentary continental bkfst. Restaurant opp 11 am-9 pm. Ck-out noon. Meeting rms. Business servs avail. Coin lndry. Some refrigerators. Cr cds: A, C, D, DS, JCB, MC, V.
🄳 🐾 🛒 🔥

Grand Canyon National Park

(B-4) *See also Flagstaff, Williams*

Approx 50 mi N on US 180 (AZ 64) to South Rim.

Every minute of the day, the light changes the colors and form of this magnificent spectacle. Sunrises and sunsets are particularly superb.

In 1540, Spanish explorer de Cardenas became the first European to see this canyon of the Colorado River, but he and his party were unable to cross and soon left. In 1857, American Lieutenant Joseph Ives said the region was "altogether valueless.... Ours has been the first and will doubtless be the last party of whites to visit this profitless locality."

As much as 18 miles wide and about a mile deep, the canyon has wildlife that includes at least 287 different species of birds, 76 species of mammals, 35 species of reptiles, and 6 species of amphibians.

The South Rim (see), open all year, has the greatest number of services and is the most popular to visit. The North Rim (see), blocked by heavy snows in winter, is open from approximately mid-May-mid-October. One rim can be reached from the other by a 220-mile drive. The South Rim has an altitude of about 7,000 feet; the North Rim is about 8,100 feet. The river is some 4,600 feet below the South Rim. It is seven miles via the South Kaibab Trail and nine miles via the Bright Angel Trail from the South Rim to the bottom of the canyon.

The park encompasses more than one million acres. Of the Grand Canyon's 277-mile length, the first 50 or so miles along the Colorado River comprise what is known as Marble Canyon, where 3,000-foot, near-vertical walls of sandstone and limestone may be seen. US 89A crosses Navajo Bridge 467 feet above the Colorado River.

Pets must be on a leash and are excluded from trails below the rim. For further information contact Trip Planner, Grand Canyon National Park, PO Box 129, Grand Canyon 86023; 928/638-7888. Per vehicle ¢¢¢¢

North Rim (Grand Canyon National Park)

(B-4)

(220 mi NW of Flagstaff: 116 mi N via US 89, 58 mi W via US 89A, then 46 mi S via AZ 67)

What to See and Do

Camping. Campsites, trailer parking space at North Rim Campground (seven-day limit; no hookups). For camping res phone 800/365-2267. ¢¢¢¢
⭐ **Drive to Cape Royal.** About 23 mi from Bright Angel Point over paved road. Several good viewpoints along way. Many think the view from here is better than from the South Rim.

Archaeology and geology talks in summer and fall.

Hiking. Six trails (¼ mi-10 mi); some are self-guided.

Muleback trips. Into canyon (daytime only). Also horseback trips (along rim only, not into canyon).

Programs. By naturalists; occasionally other events. Consult information board at Grand Canyon Lodge for schedule. **FREE**

Motel/Motor Lodge

★ ★ **GRAND CANYON LODGE.** *General Delivery, at Canyon Rim, S on AZ 67, North Rim (86052). 520/638-2611; fax 520/638-2554. www.grand canyonnorthrim.com.* 201 units; 161 cabins, 40 motel rms. May-Oct: S, D $55-$91; each addl $5; under 16 free. Closed rest of yr. Crib $5. Restaurant 6:30-10 am, 11:30 am-2:30 pm, 5-9:30 pm. Bar 11:30 am-10:30 pm. Ck-out 11 am. Business servs avail. Bellhops. Sundries. Gift shop. Game rm. View of canyon. Cr cds: A, D, DS, JCB, MC, V.

D ⚡ 🖺 🔥

South Rim (Grand Canyon National Park)

(B-4)

(Approx 80 mi NW of Flagstaff via US 180)

What to See and Do

Camping. Sites (no hookups) at Mather Campground (fee); res can be made through BIOSPHERICS. Phone 800/365-2267. ¢¢¢¢

⭐ **Drives to viewpoints.** There are West Rim and East Rim drives out from Grand Canyon Village; each is rewarding. Grandview Point and Desert View on the East Rim Drive are especially magnificent. West Rim Drive is closed to private vehicles early Apr-early Oct. Free shuttle buses serve West Rim and Village area during this period.

Evening programs. Every night all yr by Park Service ranger-naturalist in outdoor amphitheater; inside Shrine of the Ages Building during the colder months; daytime talks given all yr at Yavapai Observation Station and at Visitor Center. **FREE**

Grand Canyon IMAX Theatre. Large screen film (35-min) highlighting features of Grand Canyon. (Daily) AZ 64/US 180, 1 mi S of park entrance. Phone 928/638-2203. ¢¢

Guided river trips. Res should be made well in advance.

Multiday trips. Within the park. Phone 928/638-7888 for a written list of commercial outfitters.

One-day trips. Avail from Page to Lees Ferry, in Glen Canyon National Recreation Area. Phone 928/645-3279.

Hiking down into canyon. Not recommended except for those in good physical condition, because heat and 4,500-ft climb back are exhausting. Consult Backcountry Office staff before attempting this. (**Caution:** always carry sufficient water and food; neither is avail along trails.) Res and fees required for camping below the rim; by mail from Backcountry Office, PO Box 129, Grand Canyon 86023, or in person at Backcountry, located adj to Maswik Lodge.

Kaibab National Forest. Adj to both North and South rims are units of this 1½ million-acre forest (see WILLIAMS). The Ranger District office for the Tusayan District is located in Tusayan, four mi south of the park. Phone 928/638-2443.

Mule trip into canyon. Easier than walking and quite safe; a number of trips are scheduled, all with guides. There are some limitations. Trips take one, two, or three days. Res should be made several months in advance (preferably one yr prior). Phone 303/297-2757.

Scenic flights over Grand Canyon. Many operators offer air tours of the Canyon. Flights out of many different airports. For a partial list of companies contact the Grand Canyon Chamber of Commerce, PO Box 3007, Grand Canyon 86023.

Tusayan Museum. Exhibits on prehistoric man in the Southwest. Excavated pueblo ruin (ca 1185) nearby. (Daily, weather permitting) East Rim

Dr, 22 mi E of Grand Canyon Village. **FREE**

Visitor Center. National Park Service. Grand Canyon Village. Has information, maps, pamphlets, and exhibits. (Daily) **FREE**

Yavapai Observation Station. Scenic views, exhibits, information. (Daily) On rim, 1 mi E of Grand Canyon Village. **FREE**

Motels/Motor Lodges

★★ **BEST WESTERN GRAND CANYON SQUIRE INN.** *Hwy 64, Grand Canyon (86023). 928/638-2681; fax 928/638-2782; res 800/780-7234. www.bestwestern.com.* 250 rms, 3 story. Apr-Oct: S, D $150-$175; each addl $10; under 12 free; lower rates rest of yr. Crib free. TV; cable (premium). Heated pool; whirlpool. Restaurant 6:30 am-10 pm. Bar 10 am-midnight. Ck-out noon. Coin lndry. Convention facilities. Business servs avail. Concierge. Sundries. Gift shop. Beauty shop. Exercise equipt; sauna. Game rm. Rec rm. Bowling alley on premises. Cowboy museum, mural of Grand Canyon. Cr cds: A, DS, MC, V.

D 🐕 🏊 🛪 ✈ 🖼 🔥

★ **BRIGHT ANGEL LODGE.** *1 Main St, Grand Canyon (86023). 928/638-2631; fax 928/638-9247. www. xanterra.com.* 89 rms: 39 in lodge, 15 with bath; 50 cabins. No A/C. S, D $58-$114; each addl $7; suite $227. Crib free. TV in some rms. Restaurant 6:30 am-10 pm. Bar 11-1 am; Sun from noon. Ck-out 11 am. Bellhops. Sundries. Gift shop. Barber, beauty shop. Fireplace in some cabins. Some canyon-side rms. Canyon tour serv. Cr cds: A, C, D, DS, JCB, MC, V.

D 🖼 🔥

Grand Canyon National Park

★ **GRAND CANYON PARK NATIONAL LODGES.** *1 Main St, Grand Canyon. 928/638-2631; fax 928/638-0950; res 888/297-2757. www.grandcanyonlodges.com.* 278 rms, 2 story. S, D $127-$287; each addl $9-$11; under 18 free. Crib free. TV; cable. Restaurant 6 am-10 pm. Bar 11-1 am. Ck-out 11 am. Business servs avail. Bellhops. Sundries. Gift shop. Some private patios, balconies. Canyon tour serv. Cr cds: A, D, DS, MC, V.

★ **KACHINA LODGE.** *1 Main St, Grand Canyon (86023). 928/638-2631; fax 928/638-9247. www.xanterra.com.* 49 air-cooled rms, 2 story. S, D $107-$117; each addl $9. Crib free. TV; cable. Restaurant adj 6:30 am-2 pm, 5-10 pm. Ck-out 11 am. Bellhops. Canyon tour serv. Cr cds: A, C, D, DS, JCB, MC, V.

★★ **QUALITY INN.** *AZ 64 Grand Canyon, Grand Canyon (86023). 928/638-2673; fax 928/638-9537; toll-free 800/221-2222. www.grandcanyon qualtiyinn.com.* 232 rms, 3 story. Apr-Oct: S, D $73-$118; each addl $10; under 18 free; lower rates rest of yr. Crib $10. TV; cable. Pool; whirlpool. Complimentary coffee in rms. Restaurant 6 am-10 pm. Ck-out 11 am. In-rm modem link. Gift shop. Some minibars. Balconies. Atrium. Cr cds: A, C, D, DS, ER, JCB, MC, V.

★ **RODEWAY INN RED FEATHER LODGE.** *Hwy 64, Grand Canyon (86023). 928/638-2414; fax 928/638-2707; res 800/228-2000. www.red featherlodge.com.* 234 rms, 2- and 3-story. May-Oct: S, D $100-$175; each addl $10; under 18 free; lower rates rest of yr. Crib free. Pet accepted; $45. TV; cable. Restaurant adj 6 am-10 pm. Ck-out 11 am. Business servs avail. Exercise equipt. Cr cds: A, D, DS, MC, V.

★ **THUNDERBIRD LODGE.** *1 Main St, Grand Canyon (86023). 928/638-2631; fax 928/638-9247; res 303/297-2757. www.xanterra.com.* 55 air-cooled rms, 2 story. S, D $102-$112; each addl $9. Crib free. TV; cable. Restaurant adj 6:30 am-10 pm. Ck-out 11 am. Meeting rms. Bell-

hops. Some canyon-side rms. Canyon tour serv. Cr cds: A, C, D, DS, JCB, MC, V.

★ **YAVAPAI LODGE.** *1 Main St, Grand Canyon (86023). 928/638-2631; fax 928/638-9247. www.xanterra.com.* 358 rms, 2 story. No A/C. S, D $83-$98; each addl $9. Crib free. TV; cable. Restaurant 6 am-9 pm. Ck-out 11 am. Bellhops. Gift shop. Sundries. Canyon tour serv. Cr cds: A, C, D, DS, JCB, MC, V.

Hotel

★★★ **EL TOVAR.** *1 Main St, Grand Canyon (86023). 928/638-2631; fax 928/638-9247. www.amfac.* 78 rms, 4 story. S, D $112-$169; each addl $11; suites $192-$277. Crib free. TV; cable. Restaurant (see also EL TOVAR DINING ROOM). Bar 11-1 am; Sun from noon. Ck-out 11 am. Concierge. Gift shop. Built 1905. Some suites with balcony overlooking canyon. Cr cds: A, C, D, DS, JCB, MC, V.

Restaurants

★★★ **EL TOVAR DINING ROOM.** *1 Main St, South Rim (86023). 928/638-2631.* Hrs: 6:30 am-2 pm, 5-10 pm. Res required. Bar. Wine cellar. Bkfst $2.50-$11.20, lunch $3.25-$17, dinner $14.75-$24.75. Child's menu. Specialties: shrimp toast with mango and prickly pear vinaigrette, smoked corn chowder, vegetable empanada with roasted pepper coulis. Stone fireplaces. Native American murals. Overlooks Grand Canyon. Totally nonsmoking. Cr cds: A, C, D, DS, ER, MC, V.

★ **STEAKHOUSE AT THE GRAND CANYON.** *AZ 64 & US 180, Grand Canyon (86023). 928/638-2780.* Hrs: 11 am-10 pm. Bar. Lunch, dinner $6.95-$22.95. Child's menu. Specialty: beef, chicken cooked on open oak wood fire. Hayrides, stagecoach rides Mar-Oct. Old West decor; brick fireplace. Covered wagon in front yard. Cr cds: MC, V.

Greer

(D-7) *See also McNary, Pinetop, Springerville*

Pop 125 **Elev** 8,380 ft **Area code** 520 **Zip** 85927

Within the Apache-Sitgreaves National Forests, this town is 18 miles southwest of Springerville (see) on AZ 273. Cross-country and downhill skiing are available nearby from December to March; fishing, hunting, backpacking, bicycling, and camping are popular at other times of year.

Motel/Motor Lodge

★ **GREER LODGE.** *44 Main St (85927). 520/735-7516; fax 520/735-7720; toll-free 888/475-6343. www. greerlodge.com.* 8 rms in main lodge, 3 story, 3 cabins. No A/C. No elvtr. No rm phones. S $90; D $150; each addl $15; kit. units $75-$110; each addl $15; package plans. Crib avail. Pet accepted in cabins; $10/day. TV in lobby and lounge. Restaurant (public by res) 7-10 am, 11:30 am-2:30 pm, 5-8:30 pm. Bar 10 am-10 pm. Ck-out 11 am. Meeting rm. X-country ski 5 mi. Ice skating; skates provided. Sleigh rides. Stocked trout pond. Picnic tables, grills. Sun deck. Fireplace, piano in living rm. On 9 acres; overlooks Little Colorado River. Cr cds: A, D, DS, MC, V.

[D] [icons]

B&B/Small Inn

★ ★ ★ **RED SETTER INN.** *8 County Rd 1120 (85927). 520/735-7441; fax 520/735-7425; res 888/994-7337. www.redsetterinn.com.* 12 rms, 3 story. S, D $125-$195; each addl $25; wkends (2-day min); hols (3-day min). Children over 16 yrs only. TV in common rm; VCR (movies). Complimentary full bkfst; afternoon refreshments. Restaurant nearby. Ck-out 10:30 am, ck-in 3-7 pm. Business servs avail. Luggage handling. Concierge serv. Downhill ski 15 mi; x-country ski 5 mi. Some in-rm whirlpools, fireplaces. Many balconies. On river. Antiques; Irish Setter theme. Totally nonsmoking. Cr cds: A, MC, V.

[icons]

Restaurant

★ **MOLLY BUTLER.** *109 Main St (85927). 520/735-7226. www.molly butlerlodge.com.* Hrs: 5-9 pm. Res accepted. No A/C. Bar 8-1 am. Dinner $6.95-$32.50. Specializes in steak, seafood. Old West atmosphere; 2 dining areas; rustic decor. Scenic view of valley meadows, mountains. Cr cds: MC, V.

[D]

Holbrook

(C-6) *See also Hopi Indian Reservation, Navajo Indian Reservation, Winslow*

Pop 4,917 **Elev** 5,083 ft **Area code** 928 **Zip** 86025

Information Chamber of Commerce, 100 E Arizona St; 928/524-6558 or 800/524-2449

What to See and Do

Apache-Sitgreaves National Forests. (see). 46 mi S on AZ 77 to Show Low (see).

Navajo County Historical Museum. Exhibits on Navajo, Apache, Hopi, and Hispanic culture; petrified forest; local history; dinosaurs. (May-Sept, Mon-Sat; rest of yr, Mon-Fri; closed hols) 100 E Arizona, in Old County Courthouse. Phone 928/524-6558. **Donation**

Petrified Forest National Park. (see). I-90 to Millersport Hwy, N to SUNY-Buffalo exit. Also at 3435 Main St, near Bailey Ave in Buffalo. Phone 928/524-6228.

Special Events

Old West Celebration. Second wk June. Phone 928/524-6558.

Navajo County Fair. Mid-Sept. Phone 928/524-6407.

Motels/Motor Lodges

★★ **BEST WESTERN ARIZONIAN INN.** *2508 Navajo Blvd (86025). 928/524-2611; fax 928/524-2253; res 800/780-7234. www.bestwestern.com.* 70 rms, 2 story. June-Aug: S $46-$63; D $50-$69; each addl $4; under 17 free; lower rates rest of yr. Crib $5. Pet accepted, some restrictions. TV; cable (premium). Heated pool. Complimentary coffee in lobby. Restaurant open 24 hrs. Ck-out 11 am. Some refrigerators, microwaves. Cr cds: A, C, D, DS, MC, V.

★★ **COMFORT INN.** *2602 E Navajo Blvd (86025). 928/524-6131; fax 928/524-2281; toll-free 800/228-5150. www.comfortinn.com.* 60 rms, 2 story. May-Sept: S $60; D $65; each addl $5; under 18 free; wkly, wkend rates; lower rates rest of yr. Crib free. Pet accepted, some restrictions. TV; cable (premium). Pool. Complimentary coffee in lobby. Restaurant adj open 24 hrs. Ck-out 11 am. Coin lndry. Some refrigerators, microwaves. Cr cds: A, C, D, DS, MC, V.

★ **ECONO LODGE INN.** *2596 Navajo Blvd (86001). 928/524-1448; fax 928/524-1493; res 800/446-6900. www.econolodge. com.* 63 rms, 2 story. June-Aug: S $44; D $50; each addl $5; under 18 free; lower rates rest of yr. Crib free. Pet accepted. TV; cable (premium). Heated pool. Complimentary bkfst. Restaurant adj. Ck-out 11 am. Coin lndry. Some refrigerators. Picnic table. Cr cds: A, C, D, DS, ER, JCB, MC, V.

★★ **HOLIDAY INN EXPRESS.** *1308 Navajo Blvd (86025). 928/524-1466; fax 928/524-1788; res 800/465-4329. www.holiday-inn.com.* 59 rms, 2 story. Late May-late Aug: S $59; D $63; each addl $4; suites $69-$83; under 17 free; lower rates rest of yr. Crib $4. Pet accepted. TV; cable. Indoor pool; whirlpool. Complimentary continental bkfst. Restaurant nearby. Ck-out 11 am. Coin lndry. Meeting rm. Refrigerator, microwave in suites. Cr cds: A, C, D, DS, MC, V.

Restaurant

★★ **MESA ITALIANA.** *2318 N Navajo Blvd (86025). 928/524-6696.* Hrs: 11 am-9 pm. Closed Mon. Italian menu. Bar to 1 am. Lunch $3.50-$8.95, dinner $6.95-$14.95. Child's menu. Specialties: pasta primavera, chicken Jerusalem, pasta pescatore. Casual dining. Cr cds: A, DS, MC, V.

Hopi Indian Reservation

See also Canyon de Chelly National Monument, Holbrook, Kayenta, Page

Completely surrounded by the Navajo Indian Reservation (see) is the 1½ million-acre Hopi Indian Reservation. The Hopi are pueblo people of Shoshonean ancestry who have lived here for more than 1,000 years. The Hopi have a complex religious system. Excellent farmers, they also herd sheep, as well as craft pottery, silver jewelry, kachina dolls, and baskets. They live in some of the most intriguing towns on the North American continent.

Both the Navajo and Hopi are singers and dancers—each in their own style. The Hopi are most famous for their Snake Dance, which may not be viewed by visitors, but there are dozens of other beautiful ceremonies that visitors are allowed to watch. However, the photographing, recording, or sketching of any events on the reservation is prohibited.

All major roads leading into and across the Navajo and Hopi Reservations are paved. Do not venture off the main highways.

The Hopi towns are located, for the most part, on three mesas. On the first mesa is Walpi, founded around 1680, one of the most beautiful Hopi pueblos. It is built on the tip of a narrow, steep-walled mesa, along with its companion villages, Sichomovi and Hano, which are inhabited by the Tewa and the Hano. Hanoans speak a Tewa language as well as Hopi. You can drive to Sichomovi and walk along a narrow connecting mesa to Walpi. Only passenger cars are allowed on the mesa; no RVs or trailers. Individuals of Walpi and First Mesa Villages offer Hopi pottery and kachina dolls for sale; inquire locally.

The second mesa has three towns: Mishongnovi, Shipaulovi, and Shongopovi, each fascinating in its own way. The Hopi Cultural Center, located on the second mesa, includes a museum and craft shops (daily), a restaurant serving both Hopi and American food, and a motel; reservations (phone 520/734-2421) for May-August should be made at least three months in advance. Near the Cultural Center is a primitive campground (free). The third mesa has Oraibi, the oldest Hopi town, and its three offshoots, Bacabi, Kyakotsmovi, and Hotevilla, a town of considerable interest. A restaurant, a small motel, and tent and trailer sites can be found at Keams Canyon. There are not many places to stay, so plan your trip carefully.

Kayenta

(A-6) *See also Hopi Indian Reservation, Navajo Indian Reservation*

Pop 4,922 **Elev** 5,641 ft
Area code 928 **Zip** 86033

What to See and Do

Crawley's Monument Valley Tours, Inc. Guided tours in back-country vehicles to Monument Valley, Mystery Valley, and Hunt's Mesa. Half- and full-day rates. (Daily) Phone 928/697-3734 or 928/697-3463. ¢¢¢¢

Guided tours. Avail through **Bennett Tours**, phone 800/862-8270; **Daniel's Guided Tours**, phone 800/596-8427; **Totem Pole Tours**, phone 800/345-8687; **Goulding's Monument Valley Lodge**, phone 801/727-3231. Fees and schedules vary.

Monument Valley Navajo Tribal Park. Self-guided tours of the valley (road conditions vary, inquire locally). Camping (at Park Headquarters only; fee). (Daily; closed Jan 1, Dec 25) 25

mi NE off US 163. Phone 801/727-3287. Park ¢¢

Motel/Motor Lodge

★★ **HOLIDAY INN.** *Jct US 160 and 163 (86033).* 928/697-3221; *fax 928/697-3349; toll-free 800/465-4329. www.holiday-inn.com.* 162 rms, 2 story. Apr-Nov: S, D $89-$150; each addl $10; suites $120-$160; under 19 free; lower rates rest of yr. Crib free. TV; cable. Pool; wading pool. Restaurant 6 am-10 pm. Rm serv. Ck-out noon. Business servs avail. Coin lndry. Sundries. Gift shop. Cr cds: A, C, D, DS, JCB, MC, V.

Kingman

(C-2) *See also Bullhead City, Lake Havasu City*

Pop 20,069 **Elev** 3,341 ft
Area code 928 **Zip** 86401
Information Chamber of Commerce, 333 W Andy Devine, Box 1150, 86402; 928/753-6106
Web www.kingmanchamber.org

Kingman is the seat of Mohave County. It lies at the junction of two transcontinental highways, I-40 reaching from the East to the West coast, and US 93 from Fairbanks, Alaska, to Guatemala, Mexico. It is a convenient stop on the way to the Grand Canyon, Las Vegas, or Los Angeles. Nearby are Lakes Mead, Mohave, and Havasu, with year-round swimming, waterskiing, fishing, and boating. To the south are the beautiful Hualapai Mountains. This city lies at the heart of historic Route 66 and once was a rich silver and gold mining area; several ghost towns are nearby.

What to See and Do

Bonelli House. (1894) One of the earliest permanent structures in the city. Restored and furnished with many original pieces. (Mon, Thurs-Sun afternoons; closed hols) 430 E Spring

St. Phone 928/753-1413 or 928/753-3195. **FREE**

Mohave Museum of History & Art. Exhibits trace local and state history; portrait collection of US presidents and first ladies; Andy Devine display; turquoise display; rebuilt 1926 pipe organ; Native American displays. Local artists' gallery. (Daily; closed hols) 400 W Beale St, ¼ mi E of I-40, Beale St/Las Vegas exit. Phone 928/753-3195. ¢¢

Oatman. In the 1930s, this was the last stop in Arizona before entering the Mojave Desert in California. Created in 1906 as a tent camp, it flourished as a gold mining center until 1942, when Congress declared that gold mining was no longer essential to the war effort. The ghost town has been kept as authentic as possible; several motion pictures have been filmed here. Wild burros abound, many roaming streets that are lined with historic buildings, former mine sites, old town jail, old and modern hotels, museum, turquoise and antique shops. Gunfights staged (daily). Contact the Oatman Chamber of Commerce. 28 mi SW, located on old US 66. Phone 928/768-6222. **FREE**

Powerhouse Visitor Center. Renovated power generating station (1907). Houses Historic Route 66 Association of Arizona, Tourist Information Center, Carlos Elmer Memorial Photo Gallery, model railroad shop, gift shop, deli. (Daily; closed holidays) 120 W Andy Devine Ave. Phone 928/753-6106. **FREE**

Special Events

Mohave County Fair. First wkend after Labor Day. Phone 928/753-2636.

Andy Devine Days & PRCA Rodeo. Sports tournaments, parade, other events. Two days late Sept. Phone 928/753-6106.

Motels/Motor Lodges

★★ **BEST WESTERN WAYFARERS INN.** *2815 E Andy Devine Ave (86041). 928/753-6271; fax 928/753-9608; toll-free 800/548-5695. www.bestwestern.com.* 101 rms, 2 story. Mid-May-Sept: S $60-$65; D $67-$70; suites $90; under 12 free; lower rates rest of yr. Crib $5. Pet accepted.

TV; cable (premium). Complimentary full breakfast. Heated pool. Ck-out noon. Coin lndry. Refrigerators, microwaves. Cr cds: A, C, D, DS, MC, V.

★ **DAYS INN.** *3023 E Andy Devine Ave (86401). 928/753-7500; fax 928/753-4686; toll-free 800/329-7466. www.daysinn.com.* 60 rms, 2 story, 40 kit. units. May-Sept: S, D $55-$75; kit. units $60; higher rates hols; lower rates rest of yr. Crib free. Pet accepted; $3. TV; cable (premium). Heated pool; whirlpool. Coffee in lobby. Restaurant opp 6 am-11 pm. Coin lndry. Business servs avail. In-rm modem link. Microwaves avail. Cr cds: A, C, D, DS, JCB, MC, V.

★★ **QUALITY INN.** *1400 E Andy Devine Ave (86401). 928/753-4747; fax 928/753-5175; res 800/228-5151. www.qualityinn.com.* 98 rms, 1-2 story. June-Aug: S, D, kit. units $54-$69; each addl $10; under 18 free; lower rates rest of yr. Crib free. Pet accepted. TV; cable (premium). Pool; whirlpool. Complimentary continental bkfst. Complimentary coffee in rms. Restaurant adj 7 am-10 pm. Ck-out noon. Meeting rm. Business servs avail. Free airport transportation. Exercise equipt; sauna. Cr cds: A, D, MC, V.

Lake Havasu City

(D-2) *See also Kingman, Parker*

Founded 1964 **Pop** 41,938 **Elev** 600 ft **Area code** 928 **Zip** 86403

Information Lake Havasu Tourism Bureau, 314 London Bridge Rd; 928/855-4115 or 800/242-8278

Web www.havasuchamber.com

What to See and Do

Lake Havasu State Park. There are 13,000 acres along 23 mi of shoreline. **Windsor Beach Unit,** 2 mi N on old US 95 (London Bridge Rd),

London Bridge

has swimming, fishing, boating (ramps); hiking, ramadas, camping (dump station). Phone 928/855-2784. **Cattail Cove Unit,** 15 mi S, ½ mi W of US 95, has swimming, fishing, boating (ramps); camping (incl some water-access sites; fee). Standard fees. Phone 928/855-1223. 699 London Bridge Rd.

London Bridge Resort & English Village. English-style village on 21 acres; home of the world-famous London Bridge. Specialty shops, restaurants, boat rides, nine-hole golf course, accommodations. Village (daily). 1477 Queens Bay. Phone 928/855-0888 or 928/855-0880. ¢

Sightseeing. Outback Off-Road Adventures, phone 928/680-6151; Lake Havasu Boat Tours, phone 928/855-7979; Bluewater Jet Boat Tours, phone 928/855-7171; Dixie Bell Boat Tours, phone 928/453-6776; London Jet Boat Tours, phone 888/505-3545. ¢¢¢¢¢

Topock Gorge. Scenic steep volcanic banks along Colorado River. Migratory birds winter here; herons, cormorants, and egrets nest (Apr-May). Fishing; picnicking. 10 mi N on lake (accessible only by boat), S boundary of Havasu National Wildlife Refuge. **FREE**

Motel/Motor Lodge

★ ★ **HOLIDAY INN.** *245 London Bridge Rd, Lake Havasu (85204). 928/855-4071; fax 928/855-2379; toll-free 888/428-2465. www.holiday-inn. com.* 162 rms, 4 story. Feb-Nov: S $49-$78; D $57-$84; each addl $8; suites $97-$135; under 18 free; wkly rates; golf plan; higher rates: hols, special events; lower rates rest of yr. Crib free. Pet accepted, some restrictions. TV; cable (premium). Heated pool. Restaurant 6 am-10 pm. Rm serv. Bar 11-1 am; Sun from noon. Ck-out noon. Coin lndry. Meeting rms. Business servs avail. In-rm modem link. Free airport transportation. Game rm. Refrigerators. Balconies. On lake; state park adj. Cr cds: A, C, D, DS, JCB, MC, V.

Restaurant

★ ★ **SHUGRUE'S.** *1425 McCulloch Blvd (86403). 928/453-1400.* Hrs: 11

am-10 pm. Closed Dec 25. Res accepted. Bar to 1 am. Lunch $5.25-$7.95, dinner $9.95-$32.95. Child's menu. Specializes in fresh seafood, steak, chicken. Multilevel dining. Nautical decor. Overlooks London Bridge. Cr cds: A, MC, V.

Lake Mead National Recreation Area

(see Nevada)

Litchfield Park

See also Glendale, Mesa, Phoenix, Scottsdale, Tempe

Pop 3,810 **Elev** 1,027 ft
Area code 623 **Zip** 85340
Information Southwest Valley Chamber of Commerce, 289 N Litchfield Rd, Goodyear 85338; 623/932-2260.
Web www.southwestvalleychamber.org

What to See and Do

Duncan Family Farms. Two-thousand-acre working fruit and vegetable farm allows guests to pick their own organic produce. Petting zoo; farm play yard with "kittie kattle train," swings, giant maze. Country market and bakery. Seasonal festivals. (Fri-Sun; closed hols) 5 mi S in Goodyear; off of Cotton Ln at 17203 W Indian School Rd. Phone 623/853-9880. **FREE**

Wildlife World Zoo. Houses a family of dromedaries (single-humped camels); exotic bird aviary; three species of rare antelope; monkeys, kangaroos, wallabies, leopards, tigers; all five species of the world's flightless birds. Petting zoo; concession. (Daily) 3 mi W on Northern Ave. Phone 623/935-WILD. ¢¢¢

Special Events

Native American Festival. 387 E Indian School Rd. Approx 100 Native American craft vendors. Native American dancing and other authentic entertainment both days. Third wkend Jan.

Goodyear Rodeo Days. In Goodyear. Incl entertainment, family games, dance. Late Feb. Phone 623/932-2260.

Billy Moore Days. Held in Avondale and Goodyear. Carnival, entertainment, parade, other events. Mid-Oct. Phone 623/932-2260.

Motel/Motor Lodge

★★ **HOLIDAY INN EXPRESS.** *1313 N Litchfield Rd, Goodyear (85338). 623/535-1313; fax 623/535-0950; res 800/465-4329. www.holiday-inn.com.* 90 rms, 3 story. Jan-May: S, D $129-$149; each addl $10; family rates; higher rates special events; lower rates rest of yr. Crib free. Pet accepted. TV; cable (premium). Complimentary continental bkfst. Restaurant adj 6:30 am-10 pm. Ck-out noon. Meeting rms. Business servs avail. In-rm modem link. Valet serv. Coin lndry. Exercise equipt. Pool; whirlpool. Game rm. Many in-rm whirlpools, refrigerators, microwaves, wet bars. Cr cds: A, C, D, DS, MC, V.

Resort

★★★★ **THE WIGWAM.** *300 Wigwam E Blvd (85340). 623/935-3811; fax 623/856-1081; toll-free 800/935-3737. www.wigwamresort.com.* Originally built in 1918 by Goodyear as a private company lodge for visiting executives, this golf resort now offers 331 adobe-style casitas just 20 minutes from downtown Phoenix. On the 463-acre property there are three 18-hole championship golf courses, two of which were designed by Robert Trent Jones, Sr. 331 units, 1-2 story casitas. Jan-May: S, D $369-$429; each addl $25; suites $429-$539; under 18 free; golf plan; AP and MAP avail; family rates avail hol seasons; lower rates rest of yr. Crib avail. Pet accepted; some restrictions. TV; cable (premium). 2 pools; whirlpool, poolside serv. Playground. Supervised child's activities (June-

Sept and hols); ages 5-12. Dining rms (public by res) 6:30-10:30 am, 11:30 am-2:30 pm, 5-10 pm (see also ARIZONA KITCHEN). Rm serv 24 hrs. Box lunches, bkfst rides, steak frys. Bar 11-1 am. Ck-out noon, ck-in 4 pm. Meeting rms. Business center. Concierge. Valet serv. Gift shop. Barber, beauty shop. Airport transportation. Lighted tennis, pro. 54-hole golf, greens fee $120 (incl cart), pro, putting greens. Stagecoach, hayrides. Bicycles. Skeet, trapshooting. Indoor, outdoor games. Soc dir; entertainment, dancing. Exercise equipt; sauna, steam rm. Some refrigerators, minibars, wet bars, fireplaces. Library. Private patios. Cr cds: A, D, DS, MC, V.

Restaurant

★ ★ ★ ★ **ARIZONA KITCHEN.** *300 Wigwam Blvd (85340). 623/935-3811. www.wigwamresort.com.* Located in The Wigwam, 20 minutes outside of Phoenix, this restaurant is a top destination for anyone seeking authentic Arizona cuisine inspired by the flavors and cooking techniques of the Southwest. The red brick dining room with its adobe accents and the show kitchen create an exciting atmosphere where flavors from the mesquite grill weave their way through the menu. Southwestern menu. Specialties: smoked corn chowder, grilled sirloin of buffalo, mesquite-dusted Chilean sea bass. Hrs: 6-10 pm. Bar 4 pm-midnight. Wine list. Res required. A la carte entrees: dinner $19-$33. Prix fixe: $24-$35. Cr cds: A, D, DS, MC, V.

Marble Canyon

(A-4) *See also Page*

Pop 150 **Elev** 3,580 ft **Area code** 928 **Zip** 86036

What to See and Do

Marble Canyon. Part of Grand Canyon National Park (see). Phone 800/433-2543.

River-running trips. Multiday trips on the Colorado River. For a list of commercial operators contact Grand Canyon National Park, PO Box 129, Grand Canyon 86023. Phone 928/638-7888.

Motels/Motor Lodges

★ **CLIFF DWELLERS LODGE.** *Hwy 89A (85321). 928/355-2228; fax 928/355-2271; toll-free 800/433-2543. www.leesferry.com.* 20 rms. S, D $60-$82. Restaurant 5 am-10 pm (winter hrs may vary). Ck-out 11 am. Business servs avail. Gift shop. Hiking, fishing; river raft trips. Cr cds: A, DS, MC, V.

★ **MARBLE CANYON LODGE.** *Hwy 89A (86036). 928/355-2225; fax 928/355-2227; toll-free 800/726-1789.* 58 rms, some kits. May-Aug: S $45; D $55-$60; suites $125; kit. units $55; under 12 free; some lower rates rest of yr. Crib free. Pet accepted. Complimentary coffee in rms. Restaurant 6 am-9 pm; Dec-Mar from 6:30 am. Bar 6 am-9 pm. Ck-out 11 am. Coin lndry. Meeting rms. Business servs avail. Sundries. Hiking. 3,500-ft paved landing strip. Shuttle serv for river rafting. Cr cds: A, DS, MC, V.

McNary

(D-6) *See also Greer, Pinetop, Show Low, Springerville*

Pop 349 **Elev** 7,316 ft **Area code** 928 **Zip** 85930

McNary is in the northeastern section of the Fort Apache Indian Reservation. "Hon-dah" is Apache for "be my guest," and visitors find a warm welcome here. The White Mountain Apaches have a number of recreation areas on their reservation. Trout fishing, exploring, and camping are available. For further information contact White Mountain Recreation

Enterprise, Game & Fish Dept, Box 220, Whiteriver 85941; 928/338-4385.

What to See and Do

Hawley Lake. Summer activities incl fishing; camping, hiking, and cabin rental. (May-Oct) 12 mi E on AZ 260, then S 11 mi on AZ 473. Phone 928/335-7511 or 928/338-4417.

Sunrise Park Resort. Resort has two quad, four triple, double chairlift, three rope tows; patrol, school, rentals; cafeteria, restaurants, bars. Sixty-five runs. Also snowboarding. (Nov-mid-Apr, daily) Summer activities incl swimming, fishing, canoeing; hiking, horseback riding, tennis. Camping. 20 mi E on AZ 260, then S on AZ 273, on Fort Apache Indian Reservation. Phone 928/735-7669 or 800/772-7669. ¢¢¢¢

Mesa

(E-4) *See also Casa Grande, Chandler, Phoenix, Scottsdale, Tempe*

Founded 1878 **Pop** 396,375
Elev 1,241 ft
Information Convention & Visitors Bureau, 120 N Center, 85201; 480/827-4700 or 800/283-6372
Web www.mesachamber.org

Mesa, Spanish for "table," sits atop a plateau overlooking the Valley of the Sun and is one of the state's largest and fastest-growing cities. Mesa offers year-round golf, tennis, hiking, and water sports. It also provides easy access to other Arizona and Southwest attractions.

What to See and Do

Arizona Museum for Youth. Fine arts museum with changing hands-on exhibits for children. (Tues-Sun; closed hols) 35 N Robson. Phone 480/644-2467. ¢¢

Arizona Temple Visitor Center. Murals; ten-ft replica of Thorvaldsen's *Christus* statue; history of prehistoric irrigation; films; dioramas; information. Temple gardens (site of concert series) have large variety of trees, cacti, and shrubs collected from all over the world; extensive light display during Christmas season. The Church of Jesus Christ of Latter-day Saints (Mormon) Arizona Temple is located just south of visitor center (not open to the public). Tours of the visitor center (daily). 525 E Main St. Phone 480/964-7164. **FREE**

Boyce Thompson Southwestern Arboretum. Three hundred acres of gardens and natural areas incl cacti, streamside forest, desert lake, hidden canyon, herb garden. Bookstore. Mi of nature trails. (Daily; closed Dec 25) E via US 60 to Superior. Phone 520/689-2811. ¢¢¢

Champlin Fighter Museum. Large vintage fighter aircraft collection of WWI, WWII, Korean, and Vietnam War planes; also art gallery with paintings of aircraft in combat; extensive collection of photos of fighter aces from WWI to Vietnam. (Daily) Falcon Field, 4636 Fighter Aces Dr. Phone 480/830-4540. ¢¢¢

Dolly Steamboat Cruises. Narrated tours and twilight dinner cruises of Canyon Lake, following the original path of the Salt River. Phone 480/827-9144. ¢¢¢¢

Lost Dutchman State Park. A 300-acre park in the Superstition Mtns area. Hiking, picnicking (shelter), improved camping (dump station). Interpretive trails and access to nearby forest service wilderness area. (Daily; closed Dec 25) Standard fees. 14 mi E via US 60/89 to Apache Junction, then 5 mi NE via AZ 88 (Apache Tr Hwy). Phone 480/982-4485.

Mesa Southwest Museum. Displays trace Mesa history from dinosaurs to Space Age and emphasize Arizona history and archaeology. Participatory exhibits incl panning for gold, "legendarium," and 1890s territorial jail cells. Changing exhibits; animated dinosaurs; Native American and pioneer celebrations. (Tues-Sun; closed hols) 53 N MacDonald. Phone 480/644-2230. ¢¢¢

River tubing. Salt River Recreation Inc. Fee incl tube rental and shuttle bus service to various points on the Salt River. (Mid-Apr-Sept) 15 mi NE in Tonto National Forest (see PAYSON): E on US 60 to Power Rd, then N to jct Usery Pass Hwy. Phone 480/984-3305. ¢¢¢

Special Events

Arizona Renaissance Festival. Phone 520/463-2700. Wkends Feb-mid-Mar.

Mesa Territorial Day Festival. Sirrine House, 160 N Center. Arizona's birthday party celebrated in Old West style. Western arts and crafts, music, food. Phone 480/644-2760. Second Sat in Feb.

Baseball Spring Training. Ho Ho Kam Park. Chicago Cubs. Late Feb-late Mar. Phone 480/964-4467.

Motels/Motor Lodges

★★ **BEST WESTERN DOBSON RANCH INN AND RESORT.** *1666 S Dobson Rd (85202). 480/831-7000; res 800/780-7234. www.bestwestern.com.* 213 rms, 2 story. Jan-Apr: S $120-$145; D $130-$165; each addl $15; suites $180-$200; under 12 free; wkend rates; lower rates rest of yr. Crib $3. TV; cable (premium). Heated pool; whirlpool. Complimentary full bkfst, newspaper. Coffee in rms. Restaurant 6:30 am-10 pm. Rm serv. Bar 10-1 am. Ck-out noon. Meeting rms. In-rm modem link. Valet serv. Sundries. Exercise equipt. Refrigerators avail. Cr cds: A, C, D, DS, MC, V.
🄳 ⛱ 🛅 🐕 🔥 SC

★★ **BEST WESTERN SUPERSTITION SPRINGS INN.** *1342 S Power Rd (85206). 480/641-1164; fax 480/641-7253; toll-free 800/780-7234. www.bestwestern.com.* 59 rms, 2 story. Jan-mid-Apr: S, D $120-$139; each addl $10; under 15 free; lower rates rest of yr. Crib free. Pet accepted, some restrictions; $10. TV; cable (premium). Complimentary continental bkfst. Restaurant adj open 24 hrs. Ck-out 11 am. Meeting rms. Business servs avail. In-rm modem link. Coin lndry. 18-hole golf privileges, pro, putting green, driving range. Exercise equipt. Pool; whirlpool. Many refrigerators, microwaves. Cr cds: A, C, D, DS, JCB, MC, V.
🐕 🔥 🛅 🛅 ⛱ 🄳 ⊠

★★ **COURTYARD BY MARRIOTT.** *1221 S Westwood Ave (85210). 480/461-3000; fax 480/461-0179; toll-free 800/321-2211. www.courtyard.com.* 149 units, 3 story. Jan-Apr: S, D $109-$169; suites $159-$169; wkend rates (off-season); lower rates rest of yr. Crib free. TV; cable (premium). Heated pool; whirlpool. Complimentary coffee in rms. Restaurant 6-10 am; Fri to 10 pm; Sat, Sun 7 am-noon. Bar 5-10 pm. Ck-out noon. Coin lndry. Meeting rms. Business servs avail. In-rm modem link. Valet serv. Sundries. Exercise equipt. Refrigerator, microwave in suites. Many balconies. Cr cds: A, C, D, DS, MC, V.
🄳 ⛱ 🛅 🐕 🔥

★ **DAYS INN.** *5531 E Main St (85205). 480/981-8111; fax 480/396-8027; res 800/329-7466. www.daysinn.com.* 61 rms, 2 story. Jan-mid-Apr: S, D $80-$95; under 12 free; lower rates rest of yr. Crib free. Pet accepted. TV; cable. Heated pool; whirlpool. Complimentary continental bkfst. Restaurant nearby. Ck-out 11 am. Business servs avail. Some refrigerators, microwaves. Cr cds: A, C, D, DS, JCB, MC, V.
🄳 ⛱ 🐕 🔥 SC 🐾

★★ **DAYS INN.** *333 W Juanita Ave (85210). 480/844-8900; fax 480/844-0973; res 800/329-7466. www.daysinn.com.* 124 units, 3 story. Mid-Jan-mid-Apr: S, D $89-$109; each addl $6; under 18 free; lower rates rest of yr. Crib free. TV; cable (premium), VCR avail (movies). Heated pool; whirlpool. Complimentary continental bkfst. Ck-out 11 am. Coin lndry. Meeting rms. Business servs avail. Exercise equipt; sauna. Refrigerators. Cr cds: A, D, DS, MC, V.
🄳 ⛱ 🐕 🔥 🛅

★★ **FAIRFIELD INN.** *1405 S Westwood (85210). 480/668-8000; fax 480/668-7313; res 800/228-2800. www.fairfieldinn.com.* 66 rms, 3 story. Jan-Apr: S, D $79-$109; under 18 free; lower rates rest of yr. Crib free. TV; cable (premium). Complimentary continental bkfst. Restaurant nearby. Ck-out noon. Business servs avail. In-rm modem link. Pool; whirlpool. Some refrigerators, microwaves. Cr cds: A, D, DS, MC, V.
🄳 ⛱ 🐕 🔥 SC

★★ **HAMPTON INN PHOENIX/MESA.** *1563 S Gilbert Rd (85204). 480/926-3600; fax 480/926-4892; toll-free 800/426-7866. www.hamptoninn.com.* 118 rms, 4 story.

Jan-mid-Apr: S $119-$129; D $129-$139; under 18 free; lower rates rest of yr. Crib free. Pet accepted. TV; cable (premium). Heated pool; whirlpool. Complimentary continental bkfst. Coffee in rms. Ck-out noon. Coin lndry. Meeting rms. Business servs avail. In-rm modem link. Health club privileges. Refrigerators. Cr cds: A, C, D, DS, MC, V.

D ⊠ ⊠ ⊠ SC ➤

★★ **LA QUINTA INN AND SUITES.** *6530 E Superstition Springs Blvd (85206). 480/654-1970; fax 480/654-1973; res 800/687-6667. www. laquinta.com.* 107 rms, 6 story. Mid-Oct-mid-Apr: S, D $119-$129; suites $175; under 18 free; higher rates special events; lower rates rest of yr. Crib free. Pet accepted, some restrictions. TV; cable (premium). Complimentary continental bkfst. Complimentary coffee in rms. Restaurant nearby. Ck-out noon. Meeting rms. Business servs avail. In-rm modem link. Valet serv. Coin lndry. Exercise equipt. Pool; whirlpool. Some refrigerators, microwaves. Cr cds: A, C, D, DS, V.

D ➤ ⊠ ⊠ ⊠ 木

★ **QUALITY INN ROYAL.** *951 W Main St (85201). 480/833-1231; toll-free 800/333-5501. www.qualityinn. com.* 96 rms, 2 story. Mid-Jan-mid-Apr: S, D $99-$165; each addl $10; under 18 free; golf plans; higher rates Fiesta Bowl; lower rates rest of yr. Crib avail. Pet accepted; $25. TV; cable (premium). Heated pool; whirlpool. Restaurant. Complimentary continental bkfst. Coffee in rms. In-rm modem link. Ck-out 11:30 am. Guest lndry. Meeting rm. Business servs avail. Valet serv. Exercise equipt; sauna. Some refrigerators, bathrm phones; microwaves avail. Private patios, balconies. Cr cds: A, C, D, DS, JCB, MC, V.

➤ D ⊠ 木 ⊠ ⊠

Hotels

★★★ **HILTON PHOENIX EAST/MESA.** *1011 W Holmes Ave (85210). 480/833-5555; fax 480/649-1886; res 800/445-8667. www.mesa pavilion.hilton.com.* 263 rms, 8 story, 47 suites. Jan-May: S $160-$200; D $175-$215; each addl $15; under 18 free; some wkend rates; lower rates rest of yr. Crib free. TV; cable (premium), VCR avail. Heated pool;

poolside serv (in season). Coffee in rms. Restaurant 6:30 am-10 pm. Bar 11-1 am; seasonal entertainment. Ck-out noon. Convention facilities. Business center. In-rm modem link. Gift shop. Tennis privileges. Golf privileges. Exercise equipt. Refrigerators, wet bar in suites; some bathrm phones; microwaves avail. Luxury level. Cr cds: A, C, D, DS, MC, V.

D 木 木 ⊠ 木 ⊠ ⊠ 木

★★★ **SHERATON PHOENIX EAST HOTEL & CONVENTION CENTER.** *200 N Centennial Way (85201). 480/898-8300; fax 480/964-9279; res 800/325-3535. www.sheratonmesa. com.* 273 rms, 12 story. Mid-Jan-Mar: S, D $89-$179; each addl $10; suites $225-$300; under 18 free; lower rates rest of yr. Crib free. Pet accepted; $25 deposit and $50/day. TV; cable (premium), VCR avail. Heated pool; whirlpool. Coffee in rms. Restaurant 6 am-10 pm. Bar 4 pm-1 am. Ck-out noon. Convention facilities. Business servs avail. Exercise equipt. Refrigerators avail. Some balconies. Elaborate landscaping with palm trees, fountain. Luxury level. Cr cds: A, D, DS, JCB, MC, V.

D ➤ ⊠ 木 ⊠ ⊠

Resorts

★★★ **ARIZONA GOLF RESORT AND CONFERENCE CENTER.** *425 S Power Rd (85206). 480/832-3202; fax 480/981-0151; toll-free 800/528-8282. www.azgolfresort.com.* 187 kit. units, 1-2 story. Jan-Apr: S, D $89-$169; each addl $15-$25; suites $215-$440; under 16 free; golf plans; lower rates rest of yr. Crib free. Pet accepted. TV; cable (premium), VCR avail. Heated pool. Coffee in rms. Dining rm 6 am-9 pm. Bar 10 am-midnight. Ck-out noon, ck-in 3 pm. Coin lndry. Gift shop. Meeting rms. Business servs avail. Valet serv. Lighted tennis. 18-hole golf, pro, putting green, driving range. Exercise equipt. Refrigerators, microwaves. Private patios, balconies. Picnic tables, grill. Cr cds: A, C, D, DS, ER, JCB, MC, V.

D ➤ 木 木 ⊠ 木 ⊠ ⊠

★★★ **GOLD CANYON GOLF RESORT.** *6100 S Kings Ranch Rd, Gold Canyon (85218). 480/982-9090; fax 480/983-9554; toll-free 800/624-6445. www.gcgr.com* 101 units. Jan-mid-

May: S, D $160-$270; each addl $10; under 18 free; lower rates rest of yr. Crib free. Pet accepted; $50. TV; cable, VCR avail. Heated pool; whirlpool, poolside serv. Dining rm 6:30 am-10 pm. Rm serv. Box lunches, cookouts, bkfst trail rides. Bar 10:30-1 am. Ck-out 11 am, ck-in 4 pm. Meeting rms. Business servs avail. In-rm modem link. Concierge. Valet serv. Lighted tennis. 36-hole golf, greens fee $80-$135 (incl cart), pro, driving range, putting green. Bicycle rentals. Refrigerators, fireplaces; many whirlpools. Private patios. In foothills of Superstition Mountains on 3,300 acres. Cr cds: A, D, DS, JCB, MC, V.

D 🦅 🏋 🎿 ➰ 🏊 🔥

Restaurants

★★ **LANDMARK.** *809 W Main St (85201). 480/962-4652. www.lmrk. com.* Hrs: 11 am-9 pm, Sun to 7 pm. Closed July 4, Thanksgiving, Dec 25. Serv bar. Lunch $5.95-$8.95, dinner $9.95-$24.95. Child's menu. Specializes in seafood, beef, chicken. Salad bar. Parking. Former Mormon church (ca 1905). Antiques, original artwork. Totally nonsmoking. Cr cds: A, DS, MC, V.

D

★ **MATTA'S.** *932 E Main St (85203). 480/964-7881. www.mattas.com.* Hrs: 11 am-9 pm; Fri, Sat to 10 pm. Closed major hols. Res accepted. Mexican, Amer menu. Bar. Lunch $2.50-$6.95, dinner $6.50-$13.95. Child's menu. Specializes in tacos, chimichangas, chile rellenos. Mariachi band Fri, Sat. Family-owned. Cr cds: A, D, DS, MC, V.

D

★★ **MICHAEL MONTI'S MESA GRILL.** *1233 S Alma School Rd (85210). 480/844-1918. www.montis. com.* Hrs: 11 am-4 pm, 5-10 pm; Sat from noon; Sun 5-9 pm. Closed Dec 25. Res accepted. Bar. Lunch $6.25-$9.95, dinner $9.95-$25.39. Child's menu. Specializes in filet mignon. Pianist Tues-Sat. Garage parking. Totally nonsmoking. Cr cds: A, D, DS, JCB, MC, V.

D

Montezuma Castle National Monument

See also Cottonwood, Flagstaff

(20 mi SE of Cottonwood on AZ 260, then N and E off I-17)

This five-story, 20-room structure was built by Native Americans more than 800 years ago and is one of the most remarkable cliff dwellings in the United States. Perched under a protective cliff, which rises 150 feet, the dwelling is 70 feet straight up from the talus.

Visitors are not permitted to enter the castle, but there is a self-guided trail offering a good view of the structure and of other ruins in the immediate area. Castle "A," a second ruin, is nearby. Montezuma Well, about 11 miles northeast, is a 470-foot-wide limestone sinkhole, with a lake 55 feet deep. Around the rim are well-preserved cliff dwellings. An irrigation system built by the inhabitants about 800 years ago leads from the spring. Limited picnicking; no camping. The Castle Visitor Center and a self-guided trail are both accessible to wheelchairs. (Daily) Contact the Chief Ranger, Box 219, Camp Verde 86322; phone 520/567-3322.

Navajo Indian Reservation

See also Holbrook, Kayenta, Page, Winslow

The Navajo Nation is the largest Native American tribe and reservation in the United States. The reservation covers more than 25,000 square miles within three states: the larger portion in northeast Arizona and the rest in New Mexico and Utah.

More than 400 years ago, the Navajo people (the Dineh) moved into the arid southwestern region of the United States and carved out a way of life that was in harmony with the natural beauty of present-day Arizona, New Mexico, and Utah. In the 1800s, this harmonious life was interrupted by westward-moving settlers and the marauding cavalry. For the Navajo, this conflict resulted in their forced removal from their ancestral land and the "Long Walk" to Fort Sumner, New Mexico. This forced removal of the Navajo was judged a failure; in 1868, they were allowed to return to their homeland.

Coal, oil, and uranium have been discovered on the reservation. The income from these, which is handled democratically by the tribe, has helped improve its economic and educational situation.

The Navajo continue to practice many of their ancient ceremonies, including the Navajo Fire Dance and the Yei-bi-chei (winter) and Enemy Way Dances (summer). Many ceremonies are associated with curing the sick and are primarily religious in nature. Visitors must obtain permission to view these events; photography, recording, and sketching are prohibited.

Most of the traders on the reservation are friendly and helpful. Do not hesitate to ask them when and where the dances take place. Navajo Tribal rangers, who patrol tribal parks, also are extremely helpful and can answer almost any question that may arise.

There are a number of paved roads across the Navajo and Hopi Reservations (see)—as well as some unpaved gravel and dirt roads. During the rainy season (mostly August to September), the unpaved roads are difficult or impassable; it is best to stay off them.

Some of the most spectacular areas in Navajoland are Canyon de Chelly National Monument (see); Navajo National Monument (see); Monument Valley Navajo Tribal Park, north of Kayenta (see); Four Corners Monument; and Rainbow Bridge National Monument (see Utah). Hubbell Trading Post National Historic Site is in Ganado (see).

Accommodations on the reservation are limited; reservations are needed months in advance. For information contact the Navajoland Tourism Dept, Box 663, Window Rock 86515; phone 520/871-6436 or 520/871-7371.

Montezuma Castle National Monument

Navajo National Monument

See also Kayenta

(19 mi SW of Kayenta on US 160, then 9 mi N on paved road AZ 564 to Visitor Center)

This monument comprises three scattered areas totaling 600 acres and is surrounded by the Navajo Nation. Each area is the location of a large and remarkable prehistoric cliff dwelling. Two of the ruins are accessible by guided tour.

Headquarters for the monument and the visitor center are near Betatakin, the most accessible of the three cliff dwellings. Guided tours, limited to 25 people (Betatakin tour), are arranged on a first-come, first-served basis (May-September; tours sometimes possible earlier in spring and late in fall; phone for schedule). Hiking distance is four miles round-trip including a steep 700-foot trail and takes five to six hours. Because of hot temperatures, high elevations, and rugged terrain, this tour is recommended only for those in good physical condition. Betatakin may also be viewed from the Sandal Trail overlook—a ½-mile, one-way, self-guided trail. (Daily)

The largest and best preserved ruin, Keet Seel (Memorial Day-Labor Day, phone for schedule), is 8½ miles one-way by foot or horseback from headquarters. A permit is required either way, and reservations can be made up to two months in advance. Primitive campground available for overnight hikers. The horseback trip takes all day; horses should be reserved when making reservations (fee for horses and for guide; no children under 12 unless previous riding experience).

The visitor center has a museum and film program. There are picnic tables, a campground, and a craft shop at the headquarters area. (Daily; closed Jan 1, Thanksgiving, Dec 25) Contact the Superintendent, HC-71, Box 3, Tonalea 86044-9704; phone 928/672-2367. **FREE**

Nogales

(H-5) *See also Patagonia, Tucson*

Founded 1880 **Pop** 20,878 **Elev** 3,869 ft **Area code** 520 **Zip** 85621
Information Nogales-Santa Cruz County Chamber of Commerce, 123 W Kino Park Pl; 520/287-3685
Web www.nogaleschamber.com

What to See and Do

Pimeria Alta Historical Society Museum. History of southern Arizona and northern Sonora, from A.D. 1000-present. Photo collection; library; archives; self-guided walking tours. (Tues-Sat; closed hols) 136 N Grand Ave, in former City Hall. Phone 520/287-4621. **FREE**

Tubac Presidio State Historic Park. Arizona's first European settlement, where a presidio (military post) was built in 1752. Spanish colonial and territorial ruins. Picnicking. Museum with exhibits and underground view of the remains of the presidio's main building. (Daily; closed Dec 25) 20 mi N off I-19. Phone 520/398-2252. ¢¢

Tumacacori National Historical Park. (see). 1891 E Frontage Rd. Phone 520/398-2341. ¢¢

Motel/Motor Lodge

★ **SUPER 8 MOTEL.** *547 W Mariposa Rd (85621). 520/281-2242; fax 520/281-0125; res 800/800-8000. www.super8.com.* 117 rms, 3 story. No elvtr. S $45-$55; D $56-$65; under 12 free. Crib $10. Pet accepted; $5/day. TV; cable. Pool; whirlpool. Restaurant 6 am-9 pm. Bar 3-11 pm. Ck-out noon. Coin lndry. Business servs avail. Meeting rms. Valet serv. Refrigerators, microwaves. Cr cds: A, D, DS, MC, V.
🄳 🐾 ⚦ 🚱 🔥 🆂🅲

Resort

★ ★ ★ **RIO RICO RESORT AND COUNTRY CLUB.** *1069 Camino Car-*

alampi, Rio Rico (85648). *520/281-1901; fax 520/281-7132; toll-free 800/288-4746. www.rioricoresort.com.* 180 units, 2-3 story. No elvtr. Jan-Apr: S, D $180; each addl $15; suites $250-$1,000; under 18 free; golf, tennis, horseback riding plans; lower rates mid-Apr-Sept. Crib free. Pet accepted; $50 refundable. TV; cable (premium). Heated pool; whirlpool, poolside serv. Coffee in rms. Dining rm 6 am-2 pm, 5-9 pm. Box lunches, picnics. Rm serv. Bar 11-1 am; entertainment wkends. Ck-out noon, ck-in 4 pm. Grocery ½ mi. Meeting rms. Business center. Valet serv. Gift shop. Airport transportation. Lighted tennis. 18-hole golf, $85 with cart, pro, putting green, driving range. Stables. Exercise equipt; sauna. Lawn games. Some microwvaes, refrigerators. Private patios, balconies. Western cook-outs. On mesa top with scenic view. Cr cds: A, C, D, DS, ER, JCB, MC, V.

Restaurant

★ **MR C'S.** *282 W View Point Dr (85621). 520/281-9000.* Hrs: 11:30-1 am. Closed Jan 1, Dec 25; also Sun. Res accepted. Bar. Lunch $6-$15, dinner $9.95-$30. Child's menu. Specialties: guaymas shrimp, fresh fish and steak. Salad bar. Entertainment. Hilltop location; supper club atmosphere. Cr cds: A, C, D, DS, MC, V.

Oak Creek Canyon

(see Flagstaff)

Organ Pipe Cactus National Monument

(Park entrance 15 mi S of Ajo on AZ 85; Visitor Center 35 mi S of Ajo on AZ 85)

This 516-square-mile Sonoran desert area on the Mexican border is Arizona's largest national monument. The organ pipe cactus grows as high as 20 feet and has 30 or more arms, which resemble organ pipes. The plant blooms in May and June. Blossoms, usually at branch tips, are white with pink or lavender touches. Depending on the rainfall, during February and March, parts of the area may be covered with Mexican goldpoppy, magenta owl clover, blue lupine, and bright orange mallow. Mesquite, saguaro, several species of cholla, barrel cacti, paloverde trees, creosote bush, ocotillo, and other desert plants thrive here.

There are two graded scenic drives, which are self-guided: the 53-mile Puerto Blanco and the 21-mile Ajo Mountain drives. There is a 208-site campground near headquarters (May-mid-January, 30-day limit; mid-January-April, 14-day limit; 35-foot RV limit; fee), no reservations; groceries (five miles). Information service and exhibits are at the visitor center (daily). Standard fees. Contact the Superintendent, Rte 1, Box 100, Ajo 85321; phone 520/387-6849.

B&B/Small Inn

★★ **GUEST HOUSE INN.** *700 Guest House Rd, Ajo (85321). 520/387-6133; fax 520/387-3995. www.wgn.net/ ~morris/ajo.* 4 rms. No rm phones. Sept-May: S $59-$69; D $69-$79; each addl $10; lower rates rest of yr. TV in sitting rm; cable, VCR avail. Complimentary full bkfst. Restaurant nearby. Ck-out 11 am, ck-in 2 pm. Former executive guest house built in 1925; stately dining rm. Bird watching. Totally nonsmoking. Cr cds: D, MC, V.

Page

(A-5) *See also Marble Canyon, Navajo Indian Reservation*

Pop 6,809 **Elev** 4,000 ft
Area code 928 **Zip** 86040

weap Lodge & Marina. Phone 800/528-6154.

Glen Canyon National Recreation Area. More than one million acres incl Lake Powell. Campfire program (Memorial Day-Labor Day). Swimming, waterskiing, fishing, boating (ramps, marina); hiking, picnicking, restaurants, lodge, camping. Developed areas in Utah incl Bullfrog, Hite, Halls Crossing, Dangling Rope (accessible by boat only); many of these have ranger stations, marinas, boat rentals and trips, supplies, camping, and lodging. Lees Ferry on Colorado River (approx 15 mi downstream from dam, but a 45-mi drive SW from Page) has a launch ramp and camping. Visitor center on canyon rim, adj to Glen Canyon Bridge on US 89, has historical exhibits. Ranger station, 7 mi N of dam at Wahweap. (Daily; closed Jan 1, Dec 25) Guided tours (summer). Phone 928/608-6404. ¢¢¢

John Wesley Powell Memorial Museum. Fluorescent rock collection, Native American artifacts; books, videos; replica of Powell's boat. (Mid-Mar-mid-Dec, schedule varies) 6 N Lake Powell Blvd. Phone 928/645-9496. ¢

Rainbow Bridge National Monument. (see UTAH) Approx 60 mi NE in Utah, NW of Navajo Mtn. Phone 928/608-6404.

Scenic flights over area. Trips vary from 30 min to more than two hrs. (Daily; closed Jan 1, Thanksgiving, Dec 25) Page Airport in Classic Helicopter Bldg, ½ mi NE on US 89. For fee information contact Scenic Air, Box 1385. Phone 928/645-2494.

Wilderness River Adventures. Half-day smoothwater trip on the Colorado River in Glen Canyon in raftlike neoprene boats. (Mar-Oct) Phone 800/528-6154. ¢¢¢¢

Organ Pipe Cactus National Monument

Information Page/Lake Powell Chamber of Commerce, 644 N Navajo, Tower Plaza, Box 727; 928/645-2741 or 888/261-7243.
Web www.powellguide.com

Page is at the east end of the Glen Canyon Dam, on the Colorado River. The dam, 710 feet high, forms Lake Powell, a part of the Glen Canyon National Recreation Area. The lake, 186 miles long with 1,900 miles of shoreline, is the second-largest man-made lake in the United States.

The dam was built for the Bureau of Reclamation for water storage and the generation of electric power. The lake is named for John Wesley Powell, the intrepid and brilliant geologist who lost an arm at the Battle of Shiloh, led an expedition down the Colorado in 1869, and was later director of the US Geological Survey.

What to See and Do

Boat trips on Lake Powell. One-hr to one-day trips, some incl Rainbow Bridge National Monument. Houseboat and powerboat rentals. Res advised. 6 mi N on US 89 at Wah-

Motels/Motor Lodges

★★ **BEST WESTERN ARIZONA INN.** *716 Rim View Dr (86040). 928/645-2466; fax 928/645-2053; toll-free 800/826-2718.* 103 units, 3 story. Apr-Oct: S $62-$92; D $79-$92; each addl $5; suites $125; under 18 free; lower rates rest of yr. Crib free. Pet accepted. TV; cable, VCR (movies). Pool; whirlpool. Restaurant 6 am-10 pm. Bar. Ck-out noon. Meeting rm. Business servs avail. Airport transportation. Overlooking Glen Canyon Dam and Lake Powell. Cr cds: A, D, DS, MC, V.

★★ **BEST WESTERN PAGE INN.** *207 N Lake Powell Blvd (86040). 928/645-2451; fax 928/645-9552; res 800/780-7234. www.bwwestoninn.domainvalet.com.* 90 rms, 3 story. S $58-$62; D $63-$150; each addl $5; under 17 free. Crib $3. Pet accepted, some restrictions; $10. TV; cable (premium), VCR avail (movies). Heated pool; whirlpool. Complimentary continental bkfst. Restaurant adj 5:30 am-10 pm. Ck-out 11 am. Business servs avail. In-rm modem link. Free airport transportation. Some rms with balconies and views of Lake Powell. Cr cds: A, C, D, DS, MC, V.

★ **EMPIRE MOTEL.** *107 S Lake Powell Blvd (86040). 928/645-2406; fax 928/645-2647; res 800/551-9005. www.empiremotel.com.* 69 rms, 2 story. Apr-Oct: S $58; D $63; each addl $5; under 12 free with 2 adults; some lower rates rest of yr. Crib $5. Pet accepted. TV; cable. Pool. Restaurant 7:30 am-8:30 pm. Ck-out 11 am. Gift shop. Free airport transportation. Balconies. Cr cds: A, DS, MC, V.

★★★ **WAHWEAP LODGE AND MARINA.** *100 Lakeshore Dr (86040). 928/645-2433; fax 928/645-1031; res 800/528-6134. www.visitlakepowell.com.* 350 rms in 8 bldgs, 2 story. May-Oct: S, D $125-$149; each addl $10; suites $227; under 18 free; lower rates rest of yr. Crib free. Pet accepted. TV; cable. 2 pools; whirlpool, poolside serv. Restaurants 6 am-10 pm. Bar 11-1 am; Sun from noon. Ck-out 11 am. Coin lndry. Meeting rms. Business servs avail. Bellhops. Concierge. Sundries. Gift shop. Free airport transportation. Golf privileges. Exercise equipt. Private patios, balconies. On lake. Boats, motorboats, scenic boat trips. Host for national bass fishing tournaments. Cr cds: A, C, D, DS, MC, V.

Restaurants

★★ **BELLA NAPOLI.** *810 N Navajo Dr (86040). 928/645-2706.* Hrs: 5-10 pm. Closed mid-Nov-Feb. Italian menu. Wine list. Dinner $7-$17. Specialties: scampi, chicken tetrazzini. Cr cds: A, DS, MC, V.

★ **KEN'S OLD WEST.** *718 Vista (86040). 928/645-5160.* Hrs: 4-11 pm. Closed Jan 1, Thanksgiving, Dec 25. Bar to 1 am. Dinner $5.95-$18.95. Child's menu. Specializes in steak, barbecued ribs. Salad bar. Country band. Patio dining. Cr cds: A, D, DS, MC, V.

Parker

(D-2) *See also Lake Havasu City*

Founded 1908 **Pop** 3,140 **Elev** 413 ft
Area code 928 **Zip** 85344
Information Chamber of Commerce, 1217 California Ave; 928/669-2174
Web www.coloradoriverinfo.com/parker

What to See and Do

Buckskin Mountain State Park. On 1,676 acres. Scenic bluffs overlooking the Colorado River. Swimming, fishing, boating (ramp, marina); nature trails, hiking, picnicking (shelter), concession, camping (electric hookups, dump station), riverside cabanas (fee). 11 mi NE on AZ 95. Phone 520/667-3231. **River Island Unit** has boating (ramp); picnicking (shelter), camping (water hook-ups). (Daily) Standard fees. ½ mi N of main unit. Phone 928/667-3386 or 928/667-3231. 11 mi NE on AZ 95.

★ **Colorado River Indian Tribes Museum, Library and Gaming Casino.** Museum contains exhibits that interpret the history of the four Colorado

River Tribes: Mohave, Chemehuevi, Navajo, and Hopi. Authentic Native American arts and crafts for sale. Bluewater Casino is open 24 hrs; slots, poker, bingo. Operated by the Colorado River Indian Tribes. (Mon-Sat; closed hols) 2nd Ave at Mohave Rd. Phone 928/669-9211. **FREE** The museum is part of the

Colorado River Indian Tribes Reservation. More than 278,000 acres in Arizona and California. Fishing, boating, waterskiing; hunting (tribal permit required), camping (fee). Phone 928/669-9211.

La Paz County Park. A 540-acre park with 4,000 ft of Colorado River beach frontage. Swimming, waterskiing, fishing, boating (ramps); tennis court, golf course, driving range, picnicking (shelter), playground, camping (electric hookups, dump station). Fee for some activities. 8½ mi N on AZ 95. Phone 928/667-2069.

Parker Dam & Power Plant. One of the deepest dams in the world, 65 percent of its structural height of 320 ft is below the riverbed. Only 85 ft of the dam is visible while another 62 ft of its superstructure rises above the roadway, across the top of the dam. (Daily) 17 mi N via AZ 95, Riverside Dr exit. Phone 760/663-3712. **FREE**

Special Events

Parker 400 Off Road Race. Three Arizona loops. Four hundred mi of desert racing. Phone 928/669-2174. Late Jan.

La Paz County Fair. Carnival, livestock auction, farm olympics, entertainment. Mid-Mar. Phone 928/669-8100.

Parker Enduro-Aquasports Weekend. Longest and oldest boat racing event in country. Phone 928/669-2174 or 928/855-2208. May.

Holiday Lighted Boat Parade. Decorated boats parade on the 11-mi strip to selected site for trophy presentation; viewing from both sides of the river. Late Nov.

Motel/Motor Lodge

★ **KOFA INN.** *1700 S California Ave (85344). 928/669-2101; fax 928/669-6902; res 800/742-6072.* 41 rms, 1-2 story. S $41; D $45; each addl $4. TV;

cable. Pool. Restaurant adj open 24 hrs. Ck-out noon. Sundries. Cr cds: A, C, D, MC, V.

🄳 🖭 🐾 🌊

Patagonia

(G-5) *See also Nogales, Sierra Vista*

Pop 881 **Elev** 4,057 ft **Area code** 520 **Zip** 85624
Information Information/Visitors Center, Horse of a Different Color Emporium, Box 241; 520/394-0060 or 888/794-0060

What to See and Do

Patagonia Lake State Park. A 265-acre park with a lake. Swimming beach, fishing, boating (ramp, rentals, marina); hiking, picnicking, concession, ramadas, camping (dump station). Standard fees. 8 mi S on AZ 82, then 4 mi N on Patagonia Lake Rd. Phone 520/287-6965.

Patagonia-Sonoita Creek Preserve. The 312 acres extend downstream along Sonoita Creek for more than one mi. Bordered by willows, cottonwoods, and ash, it provides a perfect sanctuary for more than 250 species of birds. Along AZ 82; watch for directional signs to the entrance. Phone 520/394-2400.

Payson

(D-5) *See also Phoenix*

Founded 1882 **Pop** 13,620 **Elev** 5,330 ft **Area code** 928 **Zip** 85541
Information Chamber of Commerce, Box 1380, 85547; 928/474-4515 or 800/6-PAYSON
Web www.rimcountry.com

What to See and Do

Tonto National Forest. This area incl almost three million acres of desert and mountain landscape. Six lakes along the Salt and Verde rivers provide opportunities for fishing, boating, hiking, and camping. Seven wilderness areas are located within the forest's boundaries, providing hiking and bridle trails. The forest also features Tonto Natural Bridge, the largest natural travertine bridge in the world. Scenic attractions incl the Apache Trail, Four Peaks, the Mogollon Rim, and Sonoran Desert country. Phone 602/225-5200.

Special Events

World's Oldest Continuous PRCA Rodeo. Third wkend Aug. Phone 928/474-4515.

Old-Time Fiddler's Contest & Festival. Late Sept. Phone 928/474-3398.

Motel/Motor Lodge

★★ **HOLIDAY INN EXPRESS.** *206 S Beeline Hwy (85541). 928/472-7484; fax 928/472-6283; res 800/465-4329. www.holiday-inn.com.* 44 rms, 3 story. June-Aug: S $89-$109; D $99-$119; each addl $10; suites $119-$169; under 19 free; higher rates special events; lower rates rest of yr. Crib free. TV. Indoor pool; whirlpool. Complimentary continental bkfst, afternoon refreshments. Restaurant nearby. Ck-out 11 am. Coin lndry. Meeting rms. Business servs avail. Sundries. Refrigerator in suites; microwave avail. Cr cds: A, D, DS, MC, V.

D 🐾 ⚓ ⚒ ☀ 🔥

Hotels

★★ **INN OF PAYSON.** *801 N Beeline Hwy (85541). 928/474-3241; fax 928/472-6564; toll-free 800/247-9477. www.innofpayson.com.* 99 rms, 2-story. May-Sept: S, D $59-$89; each addl $10; apt (2 bdrm) $149; under 16 free; lower rates rest of yr. Crib $10. Pet accepted; $10/day. TV; cable (premium). Heated pool; whirlpool. Complimentary continental bkfst. Complimentary coffee in rms. Restaurant 11 am-2 pm, 5-9 pm, Fri-Sat to 10 pm. Bar from 4 pm. Ck-out 11 am. Meeting rm. Business servs avail. Refrigerators; some in-rm fireplaces. Private patios. Cr cds: A, D, DS, JCB, MC, V.

D 🐾 ⚓ ⚒ ☀ 🔥

★★ **MAJESTIC MOUNTAIN INN.** *602 E Hwy 260 (85541). 928/474-0185; fax 928/472-6097; toll-free 800/408-2442. www.majesticmountain inn.com.* 50 rms, 1 story. Feb-Nov: S $55-$99; D $64-$99; each addl $6;

lower rates rest of yr. Crib free. TV; cable (premium), VCR avail (movies). Pool. Complimentary coffee in rms. Restaurant adj 10:30 am-9 pm. Ck-out 11 am. Meeting rms. Health club privileges. Some fireplaces, in-rm whirlpools. Refrigerators. Picnic tables. Grills. Cr cds: A, C, D, DS, MC, V.

D ⚓ ✈ ⚒ 🔥

Restaurants

★ **LA CASA PEQUENA.** *911 S Beeline Hwy (85541). 928/474-6329.* Hrs: 11 am-10 pm. Closed Thanksgiving, Dec 25. Mexican, Amer menu. Bar to 1 am. Lunch $4.25-$7.95, dinner $5.50-$13.95. Specialties: La Casa chimichanga, chicken Acapulco, chicken fajitas. Entertainment Fri, Sat. Mexican decor; large collection of wheeled decanters. Surrounded by gardens. Cr cds: MC, V.

D ⚒

★ **MARIO'S.** *600 E AZ 260 (85541). 928/474-5429.* Hrs: 10:30 am-9 pm; Fri, Sat to 10 pm. Closed Memorial Day, Dec 25. Italian, Amer menu. Bar. Lunch $3.25-$7, dinner $5.25-$13.25. Child's menu. Specializes in pasta, pizza. Own bread. Entertainment wkends. Cr cds: A, D, DS, MC, V.

D ⚒

Petrified Forest National Park

See also Holbrook

(North entrance: 25 mi E of Holbrook on I-40. South entrance: 19 mi E of Holbrook on US 180)

These 93,532 acres include one of the most spectacular displays of petrified wood in the world. The trees of the original forest may have grown in upland areas and then washed down onto a floodplain by rivers. Subsequently, the trees were buried under sediment and volcanic ash, causing the organic wood to be filled gradually with mineral compounds, especially quartz. The grain, now multicolored by the compounds, is still visible in some specimens.

The visitor center is located at the entrance off I-40. The Rainbow Forest Museum (off US 180) depicts the paleontology and geology of the Triassic Era. (Daily; closed December 25) Service stations and cafeteria at the north entrance; snacks only at south entrance. Prehistoric Pueblo inhabitants left countless petroglyphs of animals, figures, and symbols carved on sandstone throughout the park.

The park contains a portion of the Painted Desert, a colorful area extending 200 miles along the north bank of the Little Colorado River. This highly eroded area of mesas, pinnacles, washes, and canyons is part of the Chinle formation, a soft shale, clay, and sandstone stratum of Triassic age. The sunlight and clouds passing over this spectacular scenery create an effect of constant, kaleidoscopic change. There are very good viewpoints along the park road.

Picnicking facilities at Rainbow Forest and at Chinle Point on the rim of the Painted Desert; no campgrounds. **Important:** It is forbidden to take even the smallest piece of petrified wood or any other object from the park. Nearby curio shops sell wood taken from areas outside the park. (Daily; closed December 25) Standard fees. Contact the Superintendent, Box 2217, Petrified Forest National Park 86028; phone 520/524-6228.

Phoenix (E-4)

Settled 1864 **Pop** 1,321,045
Elev 1,090 ft **Area code** 602
Information Phoenix & Valley of the Sun Convention & Visitors Bureau, One Arizona Center, 400 E Van Buren St, Suite 600, 85004; 602/254-6500
Web www.phoenixchamber.com

Suburbs Glendale, Mesa, Scottsdale, Tempe.

The capital of Arizona lies on flat desert, surrounded by mountains and green irrigated fields of cotton, lettuce, melons, alfalfa and groves of oranges, grapefruit, lemons, and olives. It is a resort area as well as an industrial area. It is also the home of Grand Canyon University (1949). The sun shines practically every day. Most rain falls in December, with some precipitation in summer. There is swimming, fishing, boating, horseback riding, golf, and tennis. Phoenix, like Tucson, is a health center, known for its warm temperatures and low humidity. As a vacation spot, it is both sophisticated and informal.

Additional Visitor Information

Phoenix Metro Magazine, available at newsstands, has up-to-date information on cultural events and articles of interest to visitors.

The Phoenix & Valley of the Sun Convention & Visitors Bureau has helpful information for visitors; contact them at One Arizona Center, 400 E Van Buren St, Suite 600, 85004; phone 602/254-6500; visitor information, phone 602/252-5588.

Transportation

Car Rental Agencies. See IMPORTANT TOLL-FREE NUMBERS.
Public Transportation. Buses (Valley Metro Transit System), phone 602/253-5000.
Rail Passenger Service. Amtrak, phone 800/872-7245.

Airport Information

Phoenix Sky Harbor Intl Airport. Information 602/273-3300; lost and found 602/273-3307; weather 602/265-5550; cash machines, Terminals 2-4.

What to See and Do

Arizona Mining & Mineral Museum. Collections of minerals, ores, gems; petrified wood; mining exhibits. Maintained by the Arizona Department of Mines and Mineral Resources. (Mon-Sat; closed hols) 1502 W Washington. Phone 602/255-3791. **FREE**

Arizona Science Center. Features energy, technology, and life sciences exhibits. Visitor participation encouraged. (Daily; closed Thanksgiving, Dec 25) 600 E Washington St. Phone 602/716-2000. ¢¢¢

Arizona State Capitol Museum. Built of native stone with a landscaped area incl a large variety of native trees, shrubs, and cacti. Four-story restored Capitol Museum exhibits incl re-creation of the original 1912 governor's office and the early House and Senate chambers and galleries. (Mon-Fri; closed hols) 1700 W Washington St. Phone 602/542-4581 or 602/542-4675. **FREE**

Desert Botanical Garden. Incl 150 acres of plants from the world's deserts; self-guided nature walk; public lectures; Cactus Show (Apr). (Daily; closed July 4, Dec 25) 1201 N Galvin Pkwy, in Papago Park. Phone 480/941-1217. ¢¢

Dog racing. Phoenix Greyhound Park, 40th and E Washington Sts. (Daily) Phone 602/273-7181.

★ **The Heard Museum.** The arts and lifestyles of Southwest Native American culture, prehistoric to contemporary representation. Changing exhibits incl art from throughout the world and Native American art. Also features Goldwater katsina doll collection; artist demonstrations. (Daily; closed hols) 2301 N Central Ave. Phone 602/252-8848 or 602/252-8840. ¢¢¢

Heritage Square. Historical city park has eight turn-of-the-century houses, incl restored 1895 Victorian Rosson House (Wed-Sun; fee) and Arizona Doll & Toy Museum. Also open-air Lath House Pavilion. (Daily) 7th St and Monroe. Phone 602/262-5071 or 602/262-5029. **FREE**

★ **Mystery Castle.** Unique stone and sand castle built by one man, over a period of 18 yrs, for his daughter. The castle features 18 furnished rms, 13 fireplaces, a cantilevered stairway, and a chapel. Tours. (Oct-early July, Thurs-Sun) 800 E Mineral Rd. 7 mi S via Central Ave, E on Baseline Rd, S on 7th St, then E on Mineral Rd. Phone 602/268-1581. ¢¢

Phoenix Art Museum. Permanent and traveling exhibits; Western, contemporary, decorative arts, European galleries; Thorne miniature rms; Arizona Costume Institute; Asian art; sculpture court. Tours avail. Special exhibits (fee). Store; cafe. (Tues-Sun; closed hols) 1625 N Central Ave. Phone 602/257-1880. ¢¢

Phoenix Mountains Preserve. Located in both the northern and southern parts of the city, the parks offer more than 23,500 acres of unique desert mountain recreational activities. Hiking, riding, and picnicking daily. Phone 602/262-6861. **FREE**

Echo Canyon. (Camelback Mtn) Hiking trails, incl trail to top of Camelback Mtn. E McDonald and Tatum Blvd. Phone 602/256-3220.

North Mountain Recreation Area. Hiking on mountain trails. Picnicking (shelter). 10600 N 7th St. Phone 602/262-7901.

South Mountain. Offers 16,000 acres in a rugged mountain range. Hiking trails, park drives to scenic overlooks, picnicking (shelter). 10919 S Central. Phone 602/262-6111.

Squaw Peak Park. Hiking trail (1¼ mi) offers panoramic view of city; park also offers access to other mountain trails. Picnicking (shelter). 2701 E Squaw Peak Dr (22nd St and Lincoln Dr). Phone 602/262-7901.

Phoenix Museum of History. More than 2,000 yrs of Arizona history; changing exhibits. (Daily; closed hols) 105 N 5th St. Phone 602/253-2734. ¢¢

Phoenix Zoo. A 125-acre zoo; home to more than 1,300 mammals, birds, and reptiles, most in naturalistic exhibits. Features rare Sumatran tigers; Tropical Flights aviary; African savannah; Arizona Trail exhibit, with native animals; children's zoo; safari train tours; refreshment centers. (Daily; closed Dec 25) 455 N Galvin Pkwy, in Papago Park. Phone 602/273-1341. ¢¢¢ Opp zoo is

Hall of Flame Firefighting Museum. The nation's largest collection of antique fire equipment, hand- and horse-drawn (from 1725) and motorized (1906-1961); fire communications, firemarks, artwork, models, and memorabilia. (Daily; closed Jan 1, Thanksgiving, Dec 25) 6101 E Van Buren St. Phone 602/275-3473. ¢¢¢

Professional sports.

Arizona Diamondbacks (MLB). Bank One Ballpark, 401 E Jefferson. Phone 602/514-8400.

Phoenix Coyotes (NHL). America West Arena, ALLTEL Ice Den, 9375

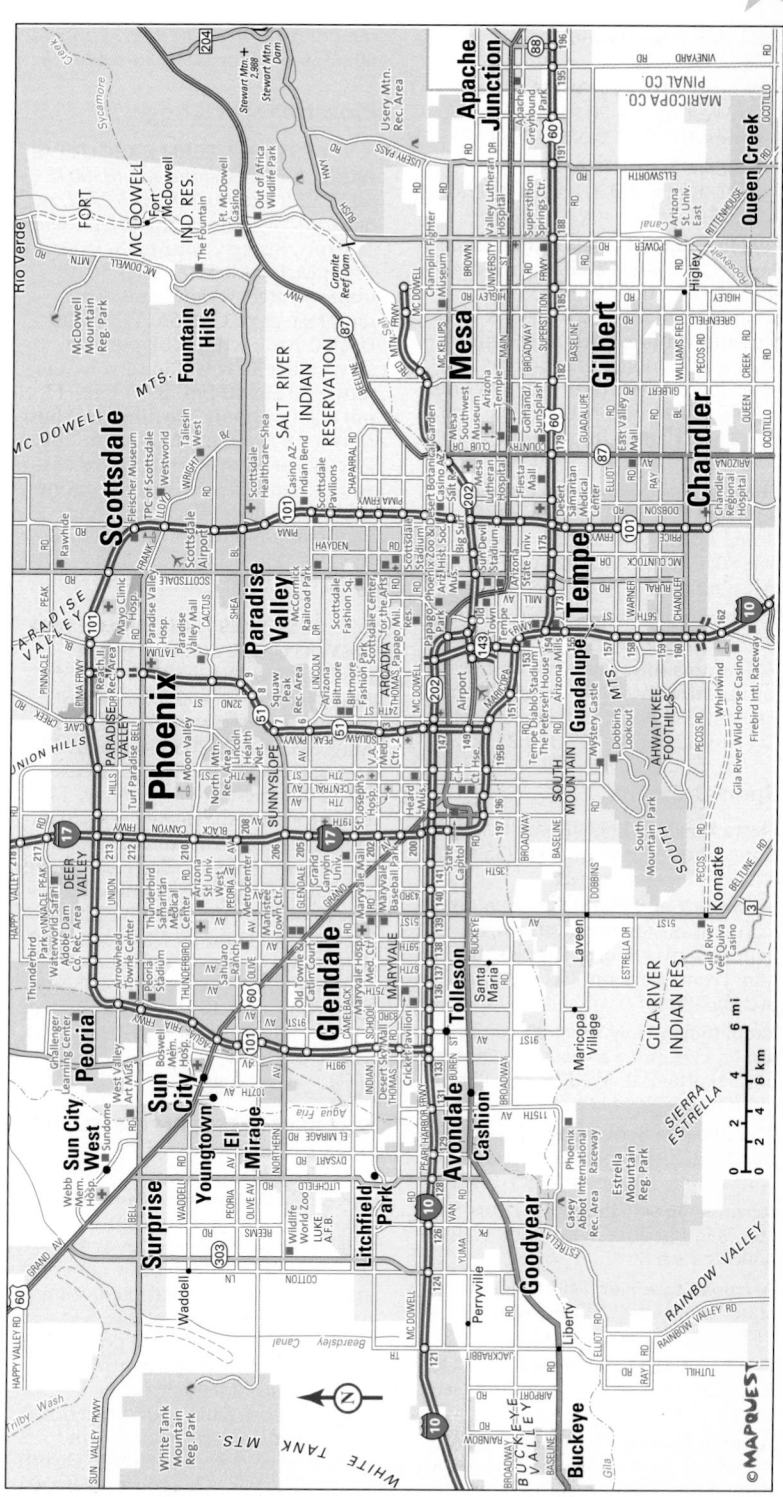

E Bell Rd, Scottsdale. Phone 480/784-4444.

Phoenix Mercury (WNBA). America West Arena, 201 E Jefferson St. Phone 602/252-WNBA.

Phoenix Suns (NBA). America West Arena, 201 E Jefferson. Phone 602/379-7867.

Pueblo Grande Museum and Cultural Park. A Hohokam archaeological site and ruin, thought to have been occupied between A.D. 300-1450. Museum features permanent and changing exhibits. Interpretive trail. Tours (Sept-May). (Daily; closed hols) 4619 E Washington St, approx 1 mi NE of Sky Harbor International Airport. Phone 602/495-0901. ¢

Thoroughbred Horse Racing. (Late Sept-early May, Mon, Tues, Fri-Sun; closed hols) Turf Paradise, 1501 W Bell Rd, 10 mi N on I-17 to Bell Rd exit. Phone 602/942-1101.

Tonto National Forest. (see). 20 mi NE on AZ 87.

Wilderness Alive. 1-5 day whitewater rafting trips through the Salt River Canyon. PO Box 1550, Buena Vista, CO 81211. Phone 719-395-2112.

Special Events

Fiesta Bowl. College football classic game. Early Jan. Phone 480/350-0900.

Indian Fair and Market. Native American artisans, demonstrations, dances, native foods. First wkend Mar. Heard Museum (see). Phone 602/252-8840.

Yaqui Indian Holy Week Ceremonials. Fri eves prior to Easter, beginning first Fri after Ash Wednesday. Phone 602/883-2838.

The Phoenix Symphony. May. Symphony Hall, 455 N 3rd St, at 2nd St and Adams. Phone 602/495-1999.

Arizona Opera Company. Thurs-Sun, Oct-Mar. Phoenix Symphony Hall, 4600 N 12th St.

Arizona State Fair. Mid to late Oct. State Fairgrounds. Phone 602/252-6771.

Cowboy Artists of America. Late Oct-mid-Nov. Phoenix Art Museum (see). Phone 602/257-1880.

Arizona Theatre Company. 502 W Roosevelt. Professional regional company performs both classic and con-

temporary works. Oct-May. Phone 602/256-6899 or 602/256-6995.

Motels/Motor Lodges

★★ **BEST WESTERN EXECUTIVE PARK.** *1100 N Central Ave (85004). 602/252-2100; fax 602/252-2731; res 800/780-7234. www.bestwestern.com.* 107 rms, 8 story. Jan-Apr: S, D $109-$129; each addl $10; suites $210; under 18 free; wkend rates; lower rates rest of yr. Crib $5. TV; cable. Heated pool; whirlpool, poolside serv. Coffee in rms. Rm serv. Restaurant 6:30 am-10 pm. Bar 11 am-11 pm. Ck-out noon. Meeting rms. Business servs avail. In-rm modem link. Free airport transportation. Exercise equipt; sauna. Some bathrm phones, refrigerators, wet bars. Balconies. Panoramic mountain views. Cr cds: A, C, D, DS, MC, V.

[D] [⇌] [🏃] [⊠] [🔥] [⬛]

★★ **BEST WESTERN GRACE INN AHWATUKEE.** *10831 S 51st St (85044). 480/893-3000; fax 480/496-8303; res 800/843-6010. www.bestwestern.com.* 160 rms, 6 story. Jan-May: S $165; D $205; each addl $10; suites $120-$175; under 17 free; lower rates rest of yr. Crib free. TV; cable (premium). Heated pool; poolside serv. Coffee in rms. Restaurant 6 am-10 pm. Rm serv. Bar 11:30-1 am; Sun from noon; entertainment. Ck-out noon. Meeting rms. Business servs avail. Bellhops. Valet serv. Sundries. Free airport transportation. Lighted tennis. Lawn games. Refrigerators; microwaves avail. Many balconies. Luxury level. Cr cds: A, C, D, DS, JCB, MC, V.

[D] [⇌] [✈] [⊠] [🔥] [SC] [🐾]

★★ **BEST WESTERN INN SUITES.** *1615 E Northern Ave (85020). 602/997-6285; fax 602/943-1407; res 800/752-2204. www.bestwestern.com.* 105 rms, 2 story, 4 kits. Jan-mid-Apr: S, D $119-$129; kit. suites $149-$169; under 19 free; lower rates rest of yr. Crib free. Pet accepted; some restrictions; $25 refundable. TV; cable (premium). Heated pool; whirlpool. Complimentary continental bkfst. Complimentary coffee in rms. Ck-out noon. Coin lndry. Meeting rms. Business servs avail. In-rm modem link. Exercise equipt. Health club privileges. Playground. Refrigerators, microwaves. Picnic tables, grills. Cr cds: A, C, D, DS, MC, V.

🅳 🛇 ➳ 🛉 🏕 🔥 SC

★★ **COURTYARD BY MARRIOTT.**
2621 S 47th St (85034). 480/966-4300; fax 480/966-0198; res 800/321-3211. www.courtyard.com. 145 units, 4 story. Jan-early May: S, D $159-$169; each addl $10; suites $179-$189; wkend, wkly rates; lower rates rest of yr. Crib free. TV; cable (premium). Heated pool; whirlpool. Complimentary coffee in rms. Restaurant 6 am-2 pm, 5-10 pm; wkends 7 am-noon, 5-10 pm. Bar 4-11 pm. Ck-out noon. Coin lndry. Meeting rms. Business servs avail. In-rm modem link. Valet serv. Free airport transportation. Exercise equipt. Health club privileges. Refrigerator in suites. Many balconies. Cr cds: A, D, DS, MC, V.

🅳 ➳ 🛉 ✈ 🏕 🔥

★★ **COURTYARD BY MARRIOTT CAMELBACK.** *2101 E Camelback Rd (85016). 602/955-5200; fax 602/955-1101; res 800/321-2211. www.courtyard.com.* 155 rms, 4 story. Jan-May: S, D $99-$179; suites $185-$195; under 13 free; wkend, wkly, hol rates; lower rates rest of yr. Crib free. TV; cable (premium). Heated pool; whirlpool. Complimentary coffee in rms. Restaurant 6:30-10:30 am; Sat, Sun 7 am-noon. Rm serv. Bar 4-11 pm. Ck-out noon. Coin lndry. Meeting rms. Business servs avail. In-rm modem link. Valet serv. Exercise equipt. Refrigerator, microwave in suites. Balconies. Cr cds: A, D, DS, MC, V.

🅳 ➳ 🛉 🏕 🔥 SC

★★ **COURTYARD BY MARRIOTT - PHOENIX NORTH.** *9631 N Black Canyon Hwy (85021). 602/944-7373; fax 602/944-0079; res 800/321-2211. www.courtyard.com/phxmc.* 146 rms, 3 story. Jan-mid-Apr: S, D $149-$159, suites $169-$179; under 18 free; wkend rates; lower rates rest of yr. Crib free. TV; cable (premium). Heated pool; whirlpool. Complimentary coffee in rms. Restaurant 5-10 pm. Ck-out noon. Coin lndry. Business servs avail. In-rm modem link. Valet serv. Exercise equipt. Some refrigerators; microwaves

avail. Balconies. Cr cds: A, C, D, DS, JCB, MC, V.

🅳 ➳ 🛉 🏕 🔥

★★ **FAIRFIELD INN PHOENIX/AIRPORT.** *4702 E University Dr (85034). 480/829-0700; fax 480/829-8068; res 800/228-2800. www.fairfieldinn.com.* 90 rms, 3 story, 18 suites. Jan-Apr: S, D $119-$139; suites $129-$149; under 18 free; higher rates special events; lower rates rest of yr. Crib free. TV; cable (premium), VCR avail. Complimentary continental bkfst. Restaurant adj from 6:30 am. Ck-out noon. Business servs avail. In-rm modem link. Valet serv. Coin lndry. Pool; whirlpool. Refrigerator, microwave in suites; microwaves & refrigerators avail. Cr cds: A, C, D, DS, MC, V.

🅳 ➳ ✈ 🏕 🔥 SC

★★ **HAMPTON INN I-17 PHOENIX/METROCENTER.** *8101 N Black Canyon Hwy (85021). 602/864-6233; fax 602/995-7503; res 800/426-7866. www.hamptoninn.com.* 147 rms, 3 story. Jan-mid-Apr: S, D $79-$99; under 18 free; higher rates special events; lower rates rest of yr. Crib free. Pet accepted, some restrictions; $25. TV; cable (premium). Heated pool; whirlpool. Complimentary continental bkfst. Ck-out noon. Meeting rm. Business servs avail. In-rm modem link. Grill. Cr cds: A, C, D, DS, ER, JCB, MC, V.

🅳 🐾 ➳ 🏕 🔥 SC

★★ **HOLIDAY INN PHOENIX WEST.** *1500 N 51st Ave (85043). 602/484-9009; fax 602/484-0108; toll-free 800/465-4329. www.holiday-inn.com.* 144 rms, 4 story. Jan-Apr: S, D $75-$139; each addl $10; suites $259; under 18 free; higher rates special events; lower rates rest of yr. Crib free. Pet accepted; $25. TV; cable (premium), VCR avail. Pool; whirlpool, poolside serv. Coffee in rms. Restaurant 6 am-10 pm; wkend hrs vary. Bar 11 pm-1 am. Ck-out noon. Meeting rms. Business servs avail. Gift shop. Golf privileges, pro, putting green, driving range. Exercise equipt; sauna. Some refrigerators. Balconies. Cr cds: A, C, D, DS, MC, V.

🅳 🏌 ➳ 🛉 🏕 🔥 SC

★★ **HOLIDAY INN SELECT - PHOENIX AIRPORT.** *4300 E Wash-*

ington St (85034). 602/273-7778; fax 602/275-5616; toll-free 800/465-4329. www.holiday-inn.com/phx-airport. 301 rms, 10 story. Jan-mid-Apr: S $169; D $179; each addl $10; under 18 free; higher rates: special events; lower rates rest of yr. Crib free. Pet accepted, $50 deposit. TV; cable (premium). Heated pool; whirlpool, poolside serv. Coffee in rms. Restaurant 6 am-10 pm. Bar 11-1 am; entertainment Fri, Sat. Ck-out noon. Coin lndry. Convention facilities. Business servs avail. In-rm modem link. Valet serv. Gift shop. Garage parking. Free airport transportation. Exercise equipt. Game rm. Some refrigerators; microwaves avail. Cr cds: A, C, D, DS, JCB, MC, V.

★★ **HOMEWOOD SUITES BY HILTON.** *2001 E Highland Ave (85016). 602/508-0937; fax 602/508-0854; res 800/225-4663. www. homewoodsuites.com.* 124 kit. suites, 4 story. Jan-Apr: Suites $179-$274; each addl $10; under 18 free; wkly, wkend, hol rates; lower rates rest of yr. Crib free. Pet accepted, some restrictions; $100. TV; cable (premium), VCR. Complimentary continental bkfst. Complimentary coffee in rms. Restaurant adj 11 am-11 pm. Ck-out noon. Meeting rm. Business center. In-rm modem link. Valet serv. Sundries. Coin lndry. Exercise equipt. Health club privileges. Pool. Refrigerators, microwaves; some fireplaces. Grills. Cr cds: A, C, D, DS, MC, V.

★★ **LA QUINTA INN.** *2725 N Black Canyon Hwy (85009). 602/258-6271; fax 602/340-9255; toll-free 800/531-5900. www.laquinta.com.* 140 rms, 2 story. Jan-Apr: S, D $95-$110; each addl $10; under 18 free; lower rates rest of yr. Crib free. Pet accepted, some restrictions. TV; cable (premium). Heated pool. Complimentary continental bkfst. Coffee in rms. Restaurant adj open 24 hrs. Ck-out noon. Coin lndry. Business servs avail. Valet serv. Some refrigerators. Cr cds: A, D, DS, MC, V.

★★ **PHOENIX INN.** *2310 E Highland Ave (85016). 602/956-5221; fax 602/468-7220; toll-free 800/956-5221. www.phoenixinn.com.* 120 rms, 4 story. Jan-May: S, D $119-$165; each

addl $10; suites $209-$239; under 18 free; lower rates rest of yr. Crib free. TV; cable (premium), VCR avail. Heated pool; whirlpool. Complimentary continental bkfst. Complimentary coffee in rms. Restaurant nearby. Ck-out noon. Meeting rm. Business servs avail. In-rm modem link. Bellhops. Coin lndry. Free airport transportation. Exercise equipt. Health club privileges. Refrigerators, microwaves. Cr cds: A, D, DS, MC, V.

★★ **QUALITY INN SOUTH MOUNTAIN.** *5121 E La Puente Ave (85044). 480/893-3900; res 800/228-5151. www.qualityinn.com.* 193 rms, 4 story. Jan-Apr: S, D $99-$129; under 17 free; lower rates rest of yr. Crib $10. Pet accepted; $25. TV; cable. Heated pool; whirlpool. Complimentary continental bkfst. Coffee in rms. Restaurant 6:30-10 am, 5-10 pm. Ck-out 11 am. Coin lndry. Meeting rms. Business servs avail. In-rm modem link. Some refrigerators; microwaves avail. Cr cds: A, C, D, DS, MC, V.

★★ **RED LION.** *12027 N 28th Dr (85029). 602/866-7000; fax 602/942-7512; res 800/RED-LION. www. redlion.com.* 171 rms, 4 story. Mid-Jan-mid-Apr: S, D $69-$109; each addl $10; suites $159-$179; under 18 free; lower rates rest of yr; rates vary special events. Crib free. Pet accepted, some restrictions; $75 refundable. TV; cable (premium). Heated pool; whirlpool, poolside serv. Complimentary coffee in rms. Restaurant 6 am-10 pm. Rm serv. Bar 4-11 pm. Ck-out noon. In-rm modem link. Meeting rms. Exercise equipt. Business servs avail. Some refrigerators, microwaves. Cr cds: A, C, D, DS, MC, V.

★★ **WYNDHAM GARDEN HOTEL NORTH.** *2641 W Union Hills Dr (85027). 602/978-2222; fax 602/978-9139; res 800/996-3426. www. wyndham.com.* 166 rms, 2 story. Jan-Apr: S $149; D $159; each addl $10; under 18 free; lower rates rest of yr. TV; cable (premium). Heated pool; whirlpool, poolside serv. Coffee in rms. Restaurant 6:30 am-10 pm. Rm serv 5-10 pm. Bar 4:30-11 pm. Ck-out noon. Meeting rms. Business servs avail. In-rm modem link. Valet serv. Sundries. Exercise equipt. Some refrigerators. Some private patios. Cr cds: A, C, D, DS, MC, V.

Hotels

★★★ **HILTON PHOENIX AIRPORT HOTEL.** *2435 S 47th St (85034). 480/894-1600; fax 480/921-7844; toll-free 800/728-6357. www.hilton.com.* 255 units, 4 story. Jan-mid-Mar: S $149-$299; D $164-$314; each addl $15; suites $299-$429; under 18 free; lower rates rest of yr. Crib free. TV; cable (premium), VCR avail. Pool; whirlpool, poolside serv. Coffee in rms. Restaurant 6 am-2 pm, 5-10 pm; Sun 5-9 pm. Rm serv to midnight. Bar 11 am-midnight. Ck-out noon. Convention facilities. Business center. In-rm modem link. Bellhops. Valet serv. Concierge. Sundries. Gift shop. Free airport transportation. Exercise equipt. Minibars. Many balconies. Luxury level. Cr cds: A, C, D, DS, MC, V.

★★★ **HYATT REGENCY.** *122 N 2nd St (85004). 602/252-1234; fax 602/254-9472; toll-free 800/233-1234. www.hyatt.com.* 712 rms, 24 story. Oct-Apr: S, D $215-$299; suites $550-$1550; under 18 free; wkend rates; lower rates rest of yr. Crib free. Garage $14/day, valet $18. TV; cable (premium), VCR avail. Heated pool; whirlpool, poolside serv. Restaurant 5:30 am-midnight (see also COMPASS). Bar 11-1 am. Ck-out noon. Meeting rms. Business center. Concierge. Shopping arcade. Barber, beauty shop. Exercise equipt. Health club privileges. Wet bar in some suites. Refrigerators avail. Some balconies. Cr cds: A, C, D, DS, ER, JCB, MC, V.

★★★ **MARRIOTT PHOENIX AIRPORT.** *1101 N 44th St (85008). 602/273-7373; res 800/228-9290. www.marriott.com.* 345 rms, 12 story, 2 suites. S, D $199-$225; suites $275; under 18 free. Crib avail. TV; cable (premium). Pool; whirlpool. Restaurant 6:30 am-10 pm. Bar to 11 pm. Rm serv 24 hrs. Ck-out noon. Meeting rms. Business center. In-rm modem link. Concierge. Exercise equipt. Many refrigerators in suites. Cr cds: A, C, D, DS, JCB, MC, V.

★★ **RADISSON PHOENIX AIRPORT HOTEL.** *3333 E University Dr (85034). 602/437-8400; fax 602/470-0998; toll-free 800/333-3333. www.radisson.com.* 163 rms, 6 story. Jan-Mar: S, D $107-$199; each addl $10; under 18 free; hol rates; lower rates rest of yr. Crib $10. TV; cable (premium). Heated pool; whirlpool, poolside serv. Complimentary coffee in rms. Restaurant 6 am-10 pm. Rm serv. Bar 11-1 am. Ck-out noon, ck-in 3 pm. Meeting rms. Business servs avail. Bellhops. Valet serv. Sundries. Gift shop. Coin lndry. Free airport transportation. Exercise equipt; sauna. Some refrigerators; microwaves avail. Some balconies. Cr cds: A, C, D, DS, MC, V.

★★★★ **THE RITZ-CARLTON, PHOENIX.** *2401 E Camelback (85016). 602/468-0700; fax 602/468-0713; res 800/241-3333. www.ritzcarlton.com.* This urban oasis is located in the financial district near exclusive residences, restaurants, and shops. Many rooms have spectacular views of the Phoenix Mountain Preserve or skyline. If classic Ritz service is not enough, request the 11th-floor Club Level for a lounge with a view, private concierge, and complimentary meals. Bistro 24 offers European Bistro cuisine Americana style. 281 rms, 11 story. Jan-May: S, D $199-$355; suites $265-$500; under 12 free; lower rates rest of yr. Crib avail. TV; cable (premium), VCR avail. Pool; poolside serv. Restaurant (see BISTRO 24). Rm serv 24 hrs. Bar 5 pm-1 am; Sat, Sun from 11 am. Ck-out noon, ck-in 3 pm. Convention facilities. Business center. Concierge. Gift shop. Covered parking. Airport, railroad station, bus depot transportation. Exercise rm; sauna. Massage. Spa. Bicycle rentals. Bathrm phones, minibars; microwaves avail. Luxury level. Cr cds: A, C, D, DS, JCB, MC, V.

★★★ **SHERATON CRESCENT HOTEL.** *2620 W Dunlap Ave (85021). 602/943-8200; fax 602/371-2857; res*

800/325-3535. www.sheraton.com. 342 rms, 8 story. Early Jan-mid-May: S, D $165-$269; suites $550-$650; some wkend rates; lower rates rest of yr. Crib free. Pet accepted, some restrictions; $100 refundable. TV; cable (premium), VCR avail. Heated pool; whirlpool, poolside serv. Complimentary coffee in rms. Restaurant 6 am-10 pm. Bar 11-1 am. Ck-out noon. Convention facilities. Business center. Gift shop. Free covered parking. Lighted tennis. Exercise rm; sauna, steam rm. Lawn games. Refrigerators avail. Balconies. Some fireplaces. Luxury level. Cr cds: A, C, D, ER, DS, MC, V.

★★ **WYNDHAM PHOENIX AIRPORT.** *427 N 44th St (85008). 602/220-4400; fax 602/231-8703; res 800/996-3426. www.wyndham.com.* 210 rms, 7 story, 24 suites. Jan-May: S, D $159-$229; each addl $10; under 18 free; lower rates rest of yr. Pet accepted. Crib free. TV; cable. Heated pool; whirlpool, poolside serv. Coffee in rms. Restaurant 6:30 am-2 pm, 5-10 pm; Sat, Sun from 7 am. Rm serv 6:30 am-10 pm. Bar 4 pm-midnight. Ck-out noon. Meeting rms. Business center. Valet serv. Sundries. Free airport transportation. Exercise equipt. Some bathrm phones. Refrigerators. Cr cds: A, C, D, JCB, MC, V.

Resorts

★★★★ **ARIZONA BILTMORE RESORT AND SPA.** *2400 E Missouri Rd (85016). 602/955-6600; fax 602/954-2571; res 800/950-0086. www.arizonabiltmore.com.* The influence of Frank Lloyd Wright is evident in the design of this 1929 landmark from the mission-style furniture in the 736 guestrooms to the concrete-block sculptures that grace the immaculate landscape. But along with this homage to the past have come modern additions including a 20,000-square-foot spa, two adjacent championship golf courses, and the Paradise Pool complex with its water slide and cabanas. 736 rms, 2-4 story. Jan-May: S, D $395-$495; each addl $30; suites $620-$1,745; golf plan; lower rates rest of yr. Crib avail. TV; cable (premium). 8 heated pools; wading pool, whirlpool, poolside serv. Supervised child's cabana club. Restaurants 5:30 am-midnight. Bar 10-1 am. Ck-out noon, ck-in 4 pm. Concierge. Shopping arcade. Barber, beauty shop. Lighted tennis. 36-hole golf, greens fee $165 (incl cart), putting greens, driving range. Bicycle rentals. Lawn chess, jeep tours and hot-air ballooning. Rec rm. Spa. Salon. Fitness center; sauna. Refrigerators. Sun decks. Most with private patios and mountain views,

Encanto Park

balconies. Cr cds: A, C, D, DS, JCB, MC, V.

D ⚡ 📠 ≈ 🎾 🏊 🔥

★ ★ ★ **HILTON POINTE SQUAW PEAK.** *7677 N 16th St (85020). 602/997-2626; fax 602/997-2391; res 800/445-8667. www.pointehilton.com.* 563 suites, 4 story. Jan-Apr: S, D $159; suites $199-$319; under 18 free; golf plans; hols (4-day min); lower rates rest of yr. Crib free. Pet accepted; $150 deposit. TV; cable (premium), VCR avail. Complimentary coffee in rms. Restaurant 6 am-11 pm. Snack bar. Rm serv 6 am-midnight. Bar 11-2 am. Ck-out noon, ck-in 4 pm. Coin lndry. Convention facilities. Business center. Bellhops. Valet serv. Concierge. Shopping arcade. Barber, beauty shop. Airport transportation. Lighted tennis. 18-hole golf privileges, greens fee $119, pro, putting green, driving range. Bicycle rentals. Exercise rm; sauna, steam rm. Massage. Spa. Heated pool; wading pool, whirlpool, poolside serv. Playground. Supervised children's activities; ages 4-12. Many refrigerators, microwaves; minibar, wet bar in suites. Balconies. Cr cds: A, C, D, DS, ER, JCB, MC, V.

D ⚡ 📠 ≈ 🎾 🏊 🔥 🎾 🔥 ➳

★ ★ ★ **HILTON POINTE TAPATIO CLIFFS.** *11111 N 7th St (85020). 602/866-7500; fax 602/866-6347; res 602/997-6000. www.hilton.com.* 585 suites, 6 story. Mid-Jan-May: S, D $219-$399; each addl $15-$25; under 18 free; wkend, hol rates; golf plan; lower rates rest of yr. Crib free. Pet accepted, some restrictions; $100 deposit. TV; cable (premium), VCR avail. Supervised children's activities May-Sept; ages 3-12. Complimentary coffee in rms. Restaurant (see also DIFFERENT POINTE OF VIEW). Box lunches, snack bar, picnics. Bar 10-1 am; entertainment. Ck-out noon, ck-in 4 pm. Grocery, pkg store 1 mi. Coin lndry. Convention facilities. Business center. In-rm modem link. Bellhops. Valet serv. Concierge. Shopping arcade. Barber, beauty shop. Sports dir. Lighted tennis, pro. 18-hole golf, greens fee $130-$140, pro, putting green, driving range. Horse stables. Bicycle rentals. Game rm. Exercise rm; sauna, steam rm. Spa. Health club privileges. Pool; whirlpool, poolside serv. Refrigera-

tors, minibars, wet bars; some bathrm phones, fireplaces. Balconies. Picnic tables. Luxury level. Cr cds: A, C, D, DS, JCB, MC, V.

D ⚡ 🎾 📠 ≈ 🎾 🏊 🔥 🎾 ➳

★ ★ **THE LEGACY GOLF RESORT.** *6808 S 32nd St (85042). 602/305-5500; fax 602/305-5501; toll-free 888/828-3673. www.legacygolfresort. com.* 328 rms, 2 story. S, D $199-$249; under 18 free. Crib avail. TV; cable (premium). Pool; whirlpool. Restaurant 6:30 am-10 pm. Bar to 10 pm. Ck-out 11 am. Concierge. Exercise rm. Golf, 18 holes. Lighted tennis. Refrigerators, microwaves. Balconies. Cr cds: A, C, D, DS, MC, V.

D 🎾 📠 ≈ 🎾 🏊 🔥

★ ★ ★ **POINTE SOUTH MOUNTAIN RESORT.** *7777 S Pointe Pkwy (85044). 602/438-9000; fax 602/431-6535; toll-free 877/800-4888. www. pointesouthmtn.com.* 640 suites, 2-5 story. Jan-May: S, D $155-$325; each addl $15; under 18 free; higher rates rest of yr. TV; cable (premium). 6 heated pools; wading pool, whirlpool, poolside serv. Supervised child's activities; ages 5-12. Complimentary coffee in rms. Dining rm (see also RUSTLER'S ROOSTE). Rm serv. Bar 11-1 am. Ck-out noon, ck-in 4 pm. Coin lndry. Convention facilities. Business center. Beauty shop. Sports dir. Lighted tennis, pro. 18-hole golf, greens fee $135 (incl cart), pro, putting green. Bicycles. Exercise rm, sauna. Massage. Rec rm. Minibars. Private patios, balconies. Cr cds: A, C, D, DS, JCB, MC, V.

🎾 🎾 📠 🔥 ≈ 🎾 🎾

★ ★ ★ ★ **ROYAL PALMS HOTEL AND CASITA.** *5200 E Camelback Rd (85018). 602/840-3610; fax 602/840-6927; toll-free 800/672-6011. www. royalpalmshotel.com.* Originally built in 1929 as a luxurious private residence, this Spanish colonial mansion's restoration has maintained the character of the original structure. Located between Biltmore and downtown, the hotel's huge mahogany doors lead to a warm lobby alive with the feel of a private home. All 116 casitas and guestrooms are designed for privacy in this tranquil Valley of the Sun setting. 116 rms, 1-2 story. Jan-May: S, D $365; each addl $25; suites $405-$3,500; under

18 free; lower rates rest of yr. Serv charge $18/day. Crib free. TV; cable (premium). Pool; poolside serv. Restaurant. Rm serv 24 hrs. Bar 11 am-midnight; Fri, Sat to 1 am. Ck-out noon. Meeting rms. Business center. Valet serv. Tennis, pro. Exercise equipt. Minibars. Some balconies. Spanish architecture; antiques. Totally nonsmoking. Cr cds: A, C, D, DS, MC, V.

B&B/Small Inn

★★★ **MARICOPA MANOR B&B INN.** *15 W Pasadena Ave (85013). 602/274-6302; fax 602/266-3904; toll-free 800/292-6403. www.maricopa manor.com.* 6 rms, 1 kit. Sept-May: S, D, kit. unit $129-$189; each addl $25; lower rates rest of yr. TV; cable (premium). Pool; whirlpool. Complimentary continental bkfst in rms. Restaurant nearby. Ck-out 11 am, ck-in 4-6 pm. Business servs avail. Health club privileges. Many microwaves. Picnic tables. Restored Spanish mission-style mansion (1928); antiques, library/sitting rm. Refrigerators. Balconies. Gardens, fountains. Totally nonsmoking. Cr cds: A, C, D, DS, MC, V.

All Suites

★★★ **DOUBLETREE GUEST SUITES-GATEWAY CENTER.** *320 N 44th St (85008). 602/225-0500; fax 602/231-0561; res 800/222-8733. www.doubletree.com.* 242 suites, 6 story. Jan-Apr: S, D $109-$219; each addl $10; wkend rates; lower rates rest of yr. Crib free. TV; cable (premium), VCR avail. Heated pool; whirlpool, poolside serv. Complimentary coffee in rms. Restaurant 6 am-10 pm; Sat, Sun from 7 am. Bar 11 am-midnight. Ck-out noon. Meeting rms. Business center. Gift shop. Free airport transportation. Exercise equipt. Refrigerators, microwaves. Atrium. Cr cds: A, C, D, DS, MC, V.

★★★ **EMBASSY SUITES.** *2630 E Camelback Rd (85016). 602/955-3992; fax 602/955-6479; toll-free 800/362-2779. www.embassy-suites.com.* 232 kit. suites, 5 story. Jan-May: S, D $139-$289; each addl $15; under 13

free; lower rates rest of yr. Crib free. TV; cable (premium). Heated pool; whirlpool, poolside serv. Complimentary full bkfst; afternoon refreshments. Complimentary coffee in rms. Restaurant 11 am-10 pm. Bar to midnight. Ck-out 1 pm. Meeting rms. Business servs avail. In-rm modem link. Coin lndry. Gift shop. Tennis privileges. Golf privileges. Exercise equipt. Health club privileges. Refrigerators, microwaves. Private patios, balconies. Atrium with lush garden and fish pond. Cr cds: A, C, D, DS, JCB, MC, V.

★★ **EMBASSY SUITES PHOENIX AIRPORT.** *1515 N 44th St (85008). 602/244-8800; fax 602/244-8114; res 800/447-8483. www.embassysuites. com.* 229 suites, 4 story. Jan-Apr: S, D $169-$219; each addl $10; under 18 free; lower rates rest of yr. Pet accepted, $50. Crib free. TV; cable (premium). Heated pool; whirlpool, poolside serv. Complimentary full bkfst. Complimentary coffee in rms. Restaurant 11 am-10 pm. Bar. Ck-out noon. Coin lndry. Meeting rms. Business servs avail. Gift shop. Free airport transportation. Refrigerators, microwaves. Balconies. Grills. Glass-enclosed elvtr overlooks courtyard. Cr cds: A, C, D, DS, ER, JCB, MC, V.

★★★ **EMBASSY SUITES PHOENIX-NORTH.** *2577 W Greenway Rd (85023). 602/375-1777; fax 602/993-5963; toll-free 800/527-7715. www.embassy-suites.com.* 314 suites, 3 story. Jan-mid-May: S, D $119-$169; under 18 free; lower rates rest of yr. TV; cable (premium). Heated pool; wading pool, whirlpool. Complimentary full bkfst. Coffee in rms. Restaurant 6 am-10 pm. Rm serv. Bar 11-1 am. Ck-out noon. Coin lndry. Meeting rms. Business servs avail. In-rm modem link. Bellhops. Valet serv. Lighted tennis. Exercise equipt. Lawn games. Refrigerators. Cr cds: A, C, D, DS, MC, V.

★★★ **HILTON SUITES.** *10 E Thomas Rd (85012). 602/222-1111; fax 602/265-4841; res 800/445-8667. www.phoenixsuites.hilton.com.* 226 suites, 11 story. Jan-May: S, D $89-$279; each addl $15; under 18 free; wkend, hol rates; lower rates rest of yr. Crib free. Pet accepted; $300 deposit. TV; cable (premium), VCR avail. Indoor pool; whirlpool. Complimentary full bkfst. Coffee in rms. Restaurant 11 am-2 pm, 5:30-10 pm; Sat, Sun from 5:30 pm. Bar 4 pm-midnight. Ck-out noon. Meeting rms. Business center. In-rm modem link. Concierge. Gift shop. Exercise equipt; sauna. Refrigerators, microwaves. Some balconies. Cr cds: A, C, D, DS, JCB, MC, V.

Restaurants

★ ★ ★ **AVANTI OF PHOENIX.** *2728 E Thomas Rd (85016). 602/956-0900. www.avanti-az.com.* Hrs: 11 am-2 pm, 5-10 pm; Sat, Sun from 5:30 pm. Closed July 4, Dec 25. Res accepted. Continental, Italian menu. Bar. Wine list. Lunch $8.95-$15.95, dinner $17.95-$35.95. Specializes in osso buco. Own desserts. Entertainment Thurs-Sat. Valet parking. Patio dining in season. Cr cds: A, D, DS, MC, V.

★ **BABY KAY'S CAJUN KITCHEN.** *2119 E Camelback Rd (85016). 602/955-0011. www.baby kays.com.* Hrs: 11 am-3 pm, 5-10 pm; Fri, Sat to 11 pm; Sun 11 am-9 pm. Closed Thanksgiving, Dec 25. Cajun menu. Bar. Lunch $7.95-$13.95, dinner $8.50-$18.95. Specialties: crawfish etouffée. Blues/jazz Tues-Sat. Outdoor dining. Casual dining. Cr cds: A, D, DS, MC, V.

★ ★ ★ **BISTRO 24.** *2401 E Camelback Rd (85016). 602/952-2424. www. ritzcarlton.com.* Hrs: 6 am-11 pm; Fri, Sat to midnight; Sun brunch 11 am-2:30 pm. Res accepted. Bar. Wine cellar. Bkfst $6.25-$11, lunch $9-$15, dinner $19-$30. Sun brunch $17-$30. Child's menu. Specialties: duck confit, marinated filet mignon, filet of sole meuniere. Own baking. Valet parking. Outdoor dining on streetside patio. European bistro, Americana style. Cr cds: A, D, DS, JCB, MC, V.

★ ★ ★ **CHRISTOPHER'S FERMIER BRASSERIE.** *2584 E Camelback Rd (85016). 602/522-2344. www.fermier. com.* French menu. Menu changes

daily. Hrs: 11 am-3 pm, 5-10 pm. Sat, Sun from noon. Closed hols. Res accepted. Specialty: truffle-infused sirloin. Lunch $9.95-$14; dinner $16.95-$26.95. Cr cds: A, D, DS, JCB, MC, V.

★ ★ **COMPASS.** *122 N 2nd St (85004). 602/440-3166. www.hyatt. com.* Hrs: 11:30 am-2 pm, 5:30-10 pm; Sun brunch 10 am-2 pm. Res accepted. Bar to midnight. Lunch $7.50-$12, dinner $24-$34. Sun brunch $27. Child's menu. Specializes in Dungeness crab cakes. Own baking. Valet parking. Revolving dining area on 24th flr; panoramic view of city. Totally nonsmoking. Cr cds: A, D, DS, MC, V.

★ ★ ★ **DIFFERENT POINTE OF VIEW.** *11111 N 7th St (85020). 602/863-0912. www.hilton.com.* Hrs: 5:30-10 pm. Closed Sun, Mon (mid-June-Oct). Res accepted. Regional Amer menu. Bar 5 pm-1 am. Wine cellar. A la carte entrees: dinner $23-$36. Prix fixe: dinner (mid-June-mid-Sept) $29.95. Sun brunch (Oct-Father's Day) $34.95. Child's menu. Specializes in steak, seafood, regional dishes. Own baking. Entertainment Wed-Sat. Valet parking. Outdoor dining. On mountaintop, view of surrounding mountain ranges. Totally nonsmoking. Cr cds: A, D, DS, MC, V.

★ ★ **FISH MARKET.** *1720 E Camelback Rd (85016). 602/277-3474.* Hrs: 11 am-9:30 pm; Fri, Sat to 10 pm; Sun noon-9:30 pm. Closed Thanksgiving, Dec 25. Res accepted. Bar. Lunch $8-$20, dinner $10-$49.50. Child's menu. Specializes in fresh fish, live shellfish, smoked fish. Oyster bar. Outdoor dining. Nautical decor. Retail fish market. Sushi bars. Cr cds: A, D, DS, MC, V.

★ ★ ★ **GREEKFEST.** *1940 E Camelback Rd (85016). 602/265-2990. www. thegreekfest.com.* Hrs: 11 am-2:30 pm, 5-10 pm; Fri, Sat to 11 pm; Sun 5-9 pm. Closed Jan 1, Dec 25. Res accepted. Greek menu. Bar. Lunch $4.95-$12, dinner $8.50-$30. Child's menu. Specialties: solomos chios.

Parking. Outdoor dining. Greek decor; festive atmosphere. Cr cds: A, D, DS, MC, V.
[D] [⌐]

★★★ **HARRIS'.** *3101 E Camelback Rd (85016). 602/508-8888. www. harrisrestaurantphx.com.* Hrs: 11:30 am-2 pm, 5:30-10 pm. Closed Dec 25, also Sun (summer). Res accepted. Bar 11 am-10 pm; Sat, Sun 5-10 pm. Wine cellar. Lunch $8.95-$10.95, dinner $14-$34. Specializes in dry-aged Angus beef. Pianist Thurs-Sat. Valet parking. Outdoor dining. Southwestern decor. Cr cds: A, D, DS, MC, V.
[D]

★★ **HAVANA CAFE.** *4225 E Camelback Rd (85018). 602/952-1991.* Hrs: 11:30 am-10 pm; Sun 4-9 pm. Closed some major hols. Cuban, Spanish menu. Bar. A la carte entrees: lunch $4.95-$11.95, dinner $8.95-$25. Specialties: pollo Cubano, masas de puerco fritas, paella. Patio dining. Totally nonsmoking. Cr cds: A, D, DS, MC, V.

★★ **HOUSTON'S.** *2425 E Camelback Rd, Ste 110 (85016). 602/957-9700. www.houstons.com.* Hrs: 11 am-11 pm; Fri, Sat to midnight. Closed Thanksgiving, Dec 25. Bar. Lunch, dinner $7-$19 Specializes in ribs, fresh grilled fish. Outdoor dining. Cr cds: A, MC, V.
[D]

★★★ **LA FONTANELLA.** *4231 E Indian School Rd (85018). 602/955-1213. www.lafontanella.com.* Hrs: 11 am-2 pm, 4:30-9:30 pm; Sat, Sun from 4:30 pm. Closed Dec 25. Res accepted. Italian menu. Bar. Lunch $6-$9.50, dinner $11.75-$23.75. Specialties: rack of lamb, osso buco, pasta with seafood. Own desserts. Cr cds: A, D, DS, MC, V.
[D]

★★ **LE RHONE.** *9401 W Thunderbird Rd, Peoria (85381). 623/933-0151. www.lerhone.com.* Hrs: 5:30-8:30 pm. Closed Mon; Jan 1. Res accepted. Swiss, Continental menu. Bar. Complete meals: dinner $19.90-$34.75. Specialties: châteaubriand, jumbo gulf shrimp Provençale, rack of lamb. Pianist. Cr cds: A, D, DS, MC, V.
[D]

★★ **LOMBARDI'S.** *455 N 3rd St (85004). 602/257-8323. www. lombardisrestaurant.com.* Hrs: 11 am-11 pm; Sun to 10 pm. Closed some hols. Res accepted. Italian menu. Bar. A la carte entrees: lunch $8-$14.95, dinner $10-$18. Child's menu. Specialty: frutti de mare. Patio dining. Open kitchen. Cr cds: A, D, MC, V.
[D] [⌐]

★ **MARILYN'S.** *12631 N Tatum Blvd (85032). 602/953-2121.* Hrs: 11 am-10 pm; Sun, Mon to 9 pm; Fri, Sat to 10:30 pm. Closed Thanksgiving, Dec 25. Mexican menu. Bar. Lunch $4.95-$7.50, dinner $7-$14.95. Child's menu. Specialties: fajitas, spinach enchilada, pollo fundido. Southwestern decor; fiesta atmosphere. Cr cds: A, D, DS, MC, V.
[D] [⌐]

★★ **MONTI'S.** *12025 N 19th Ave (85029). 602/997-5844.* Hrs: 11 am-10 pm; Fri, Sat to 11 pm; early-bird dinner 3-6:30 pm. Closed Dec 25. Res accepted. Bar. Lunch $4.10-$8.80, dinner $5.30-$34.15. Child's menu. Specializes in sirloin, small filet. Parking. Outdoor dining. Western motif. Family-owned. Cr cds: A, D, DS, MC, V.
[D] [⌐]

★★ **PIZZERIA BIANCO.** *623 E Adams St (85004). 602/258-8300.* Hrs: 11:30 am-2 pm, 5:30-10 pm; Sat, Sun from 5:30 pm; Sun to 9 pm. Closed Mon; hols. Italian menu. Bar. A la carte entrees: lunch $4.50-$10.50, dinner $8.50-$12. Specializes in wood-fired pizzas, organic salads. Own dough, mozzarella. Totally nonsmoking. Cr cds: MC, V.
[D]

★ **PRONTO RISTORANTE.** *3950 E Campbell (85018). 602/956-4049. www.prontoristorante.com.* Hrs: 11:30 am-2:30 pm, 5:30-10 pm; Fri, Sat to 10:30 pm. Closed Sun; Thanksgiving, Dec 25. Res accepted. Regional Italian menu. Bar. Lunch $5.95-$9.95, dinner $10.95-$17.95. Specialties: capellini alla pescarese, veal Marsala, gnocchi di patate. 3 dining areas. Dinner theater Fri, Sat. Stained-glass; antique instruments. Cr cds: A, D, DS, MC, V.
[D] [⌐]

★ ★ ★ **ROXSAND.** *2594 E Camelback Rd (85016). 602/381-0444. www. roxsand.net.* Hrs: 11 am-10 pm; Fri, Sat to 10:30 pm; Sun noon-9:30 pm. Closed most major hols. Res accepted. Bar. Wine list. Child's menu. Specialty: Chilean sea bass with horseradish crust. Lunch $8.25-$11.95, dinner $17.95-$33. Menu changes seasonally. Valet parking. Outdoor dining. Cr cds: A, MC, V.
D

★ ★ **RUSTLER'S ROOSTE.** *7777 S Pointe Pkwy (85044). 602/431-6474. www.rustlersrooste.com.* Hrs: 5-10 pm; Fri, Sat to 11 pm. Bar 4 pm-1 am. Dinner $12.95-$28.95. Child's menu. Specializes in steak, enchiladas, rattlesnake appetizer. Entertainment. Valet parking. Outdoor dining. Rustic decor. Cr cds: A, D, DS, MC, V.
D

★ ★ **RUTH'S CHRIS STEAK HOUSE.** *2201 E Camelback Rd (85016). 602/957-9600. www. ruthschris.com.* Hrs: 5-10 pm; Fri, Sat to 10:30 pm. Closed Thanksgiving, Dec 25. Res accepted. Bar. Dinner $23.95-$31.95. Specializes in steaks. Valet parking. Outdoor dining. Cr cds: A, D, DS, JCB, MC, V.
D

★ ★ **STEAMERS SEAFOOD AND RAW BAR.** *2576 E Camelback Rd (85016). 602/956-3631. www.steamers genuineseafood.com.* Hrs: 11:30 am-10 pm; Fri, Sat to 11 pm. Closed Thanksgiving, Dec 25. Res accepted. Bar to 11 pm. Lunch $7.95-$17.95, dinner $19.95-$41.95. Child's menu. Specializes in pan-seared halibut. Raw bar. Valet parking. Outdoor dining. Bright and colorful, spacious dining area. Cr cds: A, D, DS, MC, V.
D

★ ★ ★ **TARBELL'S.** *3213 E Camelback Rd (85018). 602/955-8100. www.tarbells.com.* Hrs: 5-11 pm; Sun to 10 pm. Closed most major hols. Res accepted. Bar. Wine cellar. Dinner $17-$33. Specialties: grilled salmon on a crispy potato cake. Own baking. Open kitchen with wood-burning oven. Cr cds: A, D, DS, JCB, MC, V.
D

★ ★ ★ ★ **T. COOK'S.** *5200 E Camelback Rd (85018). 602/808-0766. www. royalpalmshotel.com.* The French and Spanish inspired Mediterranean cuisine of chef Derek Morgan has found a perfect home in this rustic yet elegant dining room located in the Royal Palms Hotel. The stunning Spanish/Mediterranean architecture and decor provide the perfect setting for a special romantic evening. Only the freshest ingredients are used in preparing dishes such as lobster and parsnip bisque with creme fraiche and osetra caviar and delicate Petrale sole with preserved lemon, Swiss chard and glazed radishes. Impeccable service makes dining carefree. Outdoor seating is available. Hrs: 6 am-2 pm, 6-10 pm; Sun brunch 10 am-2 pm. Res accepted. Mediterranean menu. Bar 10 am-midnight; Fri, Sat to 1 am. Wine list. Bkfst $6-$14, lunch $9-$15, dinner $18-$30. Sun brunch $12-$28. Specialties: T Cook's Mediterranean paella, lobster tortellini, Mediterranean antipasto platter Pianist. Valet parking. Outdoor dining. Mediterranean decor; hand-painted walls. Cr cds: A, D, DS, MC, V.
D

★ ★ **TOMASO'S.** *3225 E Camelback Rd (85016). 602/956-0836.* Hrs: 11:30 am-2:30 pm, 5-10:30 pm; Sat, Sun from 5 pm. Closed Super Bowl Sun, Thanksgiving. Res accepted. Italian menu. Bar. A la carte entrees: lunch $8-$14, dinner $12-$26.95. Child's menu. Specializes in costata alla valdostana. Cr cds: A, D, DS, MC, V.
D

★ ★ **TOP OF THE MARKET.** *1720 E Camelback Rd (85016). 602/277-3474. www.thefishmarket.com.* Hrs: 5-9:30 pm; Fri, Sat to 10 pm. Closed Thanksgiving, Dec 25. Res accepted. Bar. A la carte entrees: dinner $16.25-$47.50. Child's menu. Specializes in seafood, pasta, pizza. Parking. Nautical decor. Wood-burning pizza oven. View of Squaw Peak Mtn. Cr cds: A, C, D, DS, MC, V.
D

★ **TUCCHETTI.** *2135 E Camelback Rd (85016). 602/957-0222. www. tucchetti.com.* Hrs: 11:15 am-9:30 pm; Fri to 10:30 pm; Sat noon-10:30 pm; Sun 4:30-9 pm. Closed Thanksgiving,

Dec 25. Res accepted. Italian menu. Bar. A la carte entrees: lunch, dinner $6.95-$18.95. Child's menu. Specializes in baked spaghetti. Outdoor dining. Italian atmosphere. Cr cds: A, D, DS, JCB, MC, V.

D

★ ★ ★ **VINCENT GUERITHAULT ON CAMELBACK.** *3930 E Camelback Rd (85018).* 602/224-0225. Southwestern, Amer menu. Specializes in grilled rack of lamb. Own baking, ice cream. Hrs: 11:30 am-2:30 pm, 6-10:30 pm; Sat from 5:30 pm. Closed major hols; also Sun June-Sept. Res accepted. Bar. Wine list. A la carte entrees: lunch $7.50-$11.50, dinner $23-$26. Valet parking. Open-air market on Sat, mid-Oct-mid-Apr. Cr cds: A, D, MC, V.

D

★ ★ ★ **WRIGHT'S.** *2400 Missouri Rd (85016).* 602/954-6600. *www.arizona biltmore.com.* Contemporary Amer cuisine. Hrs: 11 am-2 pm; 6-10 pm; Sun brunch 10 am-2 pm. A la carte entrees: lunch $12-$17; dinner $28-$36. Chef's tasting menu $75. Champagne brunch $48. Res required. Valet. Pianist and trio. Cr cds: A, D, DS, MC, V.

D

★ ★ **ZEN 32.** *3160 E Camelback (85016).* 602/954-8700. *www.zen32. com.* Specializes in sushi, lobster ravioli, grilled asian salmon. Hrs: 11 am-midnight. Res accepted. Wine, beer. Lunch $7-$10; dinner $12-$20. Entertainment: Japanese animation. Cr cds: A, C, D, MC, V.

D ⊠

Unrated Dining Spots

CHOMPIE'S. *3202 E Greenway Rd (85032).* 602/971-8010. *www. chompies.com.* Hrs: 6 am-9 pm; Mon to 8 pm; Fri to 9:30 pm; Sun 6:30 am-8 pm. Kosher deli menu. Wine, beer. Bkfst $2.50-$6, lunch $3.50-$7, dinner $5.95-$10.95. Child's menu. Specializes in beef, chicken, fish. Own baking. Family-owned New York-style kosher deli, bakery and bagel factory. Cr cds: A, MC, V.

D ⊠

DUCK AND DECANTER. *1651 E Camelback Rd (85016).* 602/274-5429. *www.duckanddecanter.com.* Hrs: 9 am-

7 pm; Thurs, Fri to 9 pm; Sun from 10 am. Closed some major hols. Bar. A la carte entrees: lunch, dinner $2.75-$5.95. Child's menu. Specialty: albacore tuna sandwich. Guitarist Fri-Sun evenings. Outdoor dining. Gourmet, wine shop. Totally non-smoking. Cr cds: A, D, DS, MC, V.

D

ED DEBEVIC'S. *2102 E Highland Ave (85016).* 602/956-2760. *www.ed debevics.com.* Hrs: 11 am-9 pm; Fri, Sat 10 pm. Closed Thanksgiving, Dec 25. Bar. A la carte entrees: lunch, dinner $2.75-$6.95. Child's menu. Specializes in hamburgers, malts, french fries. Nostalgic 50s-style diner; tabletop jukeboxes. Costumed servers improvise routine of songs, dances, skits, irreverent humor. Cr cds: A, D, MC, V.

D

HARD ROCK CAFE. *3 S 2nd St, Ste 117 (85004).* 602/261-7625. *www. hardrock.com.* Hrs: 11 am-11 pm; Fri, Sat to midnight. Closed Dec 25. Bar to 1 am. Lunch, dinner $5.99-$14.99. Child's menu. Specializes in burgers, chicken. Outdoor dining. Rock-and-roll memorabilia. Cr cds: A, D, DS, MC, V.

D

Pinetop

(D-6) *See also McNary, Show Low*

Pop 3,582 **Elev** 6,959 ft
Area code 520 **Zip** 85935
Information Pinetop-Lakeside Chamber of Commerce, 102-C W White Mtn Blvd, PO Box 4220; 520/367-4290
Web www.pinetoplakeshidechamber.com

Trout fishing, horseback riding, hiking, biking, and golfing are popular summer activities here; skiing and snowmobiling draw many winter visitors.

Motels/Motor Lodges

★ ★ **BEST WESTERN HOTEL.** *404 S White Mtn Blvd (85935).* 520/367-6667; fax 520/367-6672; toll-free 800/780-7234. *www.innofpinetop.com.* 41 rms, 2 story. June-mid-Sept, mid-

Dec-Mar: S, D $69-$99; suite $199; each addl $5; under 12 free; higher rates: hols, special events; lower rates rest of yr. Crib free. TV; cable (premium). Complimentary continental bkfst. Ck-out 11 am. Business servs avail. Whirlpool. Some refrigerators, microwaves. Cr cds: A, C, D, DS, ER, JCB, MC, V.

⊡ ⛄ ⌁ ⊠ 🔥 SC

★★ **PINETOP COMFORT INN.**
1637 E White Mountain Blvd (85044).
520/368-6600; res 800/228-5150.
www.comfortinn.com. 55 rms, 2 story.
May-Oct, Dec-Mar: S, D $55-$69; each addl $8; under 18 free; higher rates hol wkends (2-day min); lower rates rest of yr. TV; cable, VCR avail. Complimentary continental bkfst. Ck-out 11 am. Meeting rm. Business servs avail. In-rm modem link. Whirlpool. Refrigerators; some fireplaces. Cr cds: A, D, DS, JCB, MC, V.

⊡ ⛄ ⌁ ⊠ 🔥 SC

Restaurant

★★ **CHARLIE CLARK'S STEAK HOUSE.** *1701 E White Mtn Blvd (AZ 260) (85935).* 520/367-4900. Hrs: 5-10 pm. Bar 11-1 am. Dinner $8.95-$19.95. Child's menu. Specializes in beef, seafood, steak. Cr cds: A, C, D, MC, V.

⊡ ⊣

Pipe Spring National Monument

Also see Kanab, UT

(14 mi W of Fredonia on spur off AZ 389)

Located on the Kaibab-Paiute Indian Reservation, the focal point of this monument is a beautifully built sandstone Mormon fort, dating back to 1870. Several years earlier, Brigham Young had ordered the exploration of this region north of the Grand Canyon. According to legend, rifleman William "Gunlock Bill" Hamblin gave the place its name by shooting the bottom out of a smoking pipe at 50 paces.

The fort, actually a fortified ranchhouse, was built under the direction of Bishop Anson P. Winsor to protect the families caring for the church's cattle. Cattle drives, headed for the railroad in Cedar City, Utah, began here.

Guide service (daily); living history demonstrations (June-Sept). Kaibab Paiute Campground (fee), ½ mile N of access road to visitor center. Area closed Jan 1, Thanksgiving, Dec 25. Contact the Superintendent, HC 65, Box 5, Fredonia 86022; phone 928/643-7105. ¢¢

Prescott

(D-4) *See also Cottonwood*

Founded 1864 **Pop** 33,938 **Elev** 5,368 ft **Area code** 928

Information Chamber of Commerce, 117 W Goodwin St, PO Box 1147, 86302; 928/445-2000 or 800/266-7534

Web www.prescott.org

When President Lincoln established the territory of Arizona, Prescott became the capital. In 1867, the capital was moved to Tucson and then back to Prescott in 1877. After much wrangling, it was finally moved to Phoenix in 1889.

Tourism and manufacturing are now Prescott's principal occupations. The climate is mild during summer and winter. The Prescott National Forest surrounds the city; its headquarters are located here.

What to See and Do

Arcosanti. Architectural project by Paolo Soleri and the Cosanti Foundation. This prototype town is being constructed as a functioning example of "arcology," a fusion of architecture and ecology. Guided tours. (Daily; closed hols) 36 mi SE on AZ 69 to Cordes Jct, then 2 mi E on unnumbered road (follow signs or inquire locally for directions). Phone 928/632-7135. **Donation**

Prescott National Forest. Minerals and varied vegetation abound in this forest (more than one million acres). Within the forest are Juniper Mesa, Apache Creek, Granite Mtn, Castle Creek, Woodchute, and Cedar Bench wilderness areas, and parts of Sycamore Canyon and Pine Mtn wilderness areas. Fishing (Granite Basin, Lynx lakes); hunting, picnicking, camping. 20 mi NE on US 89A or 1 mi SW on US 89. Phone 928/445-1762.

Sharlot Hall Museum. Period houses incl the Territorial Governor's Mansion (1864), restored in 1929 by poet-historian Sharlot Hall; Fort Misery (1864); William Bashford house (1877); and John C. Frémont house (1875). Period furnishings. Museum, library, and archives. Also on grounds are grave of Pauline Weaver; rose and herb garden; pioneer schoolhouse. All buildings (daily; closed Jan 1, Thanksgiving, Dec 25). 415 W Gurley St. Phone 928/445-3122. ¢

Smoki Museum. Native American artifacts, ancient and modern. (May-Sept, daily; rest of yr, Mon, Tues, Thurs; also Sun afternoons) 147 N Arizona St. Phone 928/445-1230. ¢¢

Special Events

Phippen Museum Fine Art Show & Sale. Over 50 artists. Memorial Day wkend. Phone 928/778-1385.

Territorial Prescott Days. Art show, craft demonstrations, old-fashioned contests, home tours. Early June. Courthouse Plaza, and throughout city. Phone 928/445-0204.

Bluegrass Festival. Mid-June. Courthouse Plaza. Phone 928/445-0204.

Prescott Frontier Days Rodeo. Also parade and laser show. Late-June-July 4. Fairgrounds on Miller Valley Rd. Phone 928/445-3103.

Motels/Motor Lodges

★★ **BEST WESTERN PRESCOT-TONIAN.** 1317 E Gurley St (86301). 928/445-3096; fax 928/778-2976; res 800/780-7234. www.bestwestern.com. 121 rms, 2-3 story. No elvtr. Apr-Oct: S $59-$89; D $69-$89; each addl $10; suites $125-$200; higher rates special

events; lower rates rest of yr. Crib free. Pet accepted. TV; cable. Pool; whirlpool. Coffee in rms. Restaurant 6 am-10 pm. Bar 11 am-10 pm. Ck-out noon. Coin lndry. Business servs avail. Meeting rms. In-rm modem link. Refrigerators. Some private patios, balconies. Cr cds: A, C, D, DS, MC, V.

⊡ 🐾 ➳ ⊠ 🔥 SC

★ **COMFORT INN.** 1290 White Spar Rd (86303). 928/778-5770; fax 928/771-9373; res 800/228-5150. www.prescottcomfortinn.com. 61 rms, 2 story, 11 kit. units. Apr-Oct: S, D $89-$99; each addl $10; kit. units $100; under 18 free; higher rates: wkends, some hols; lower rates rest of yr. Crib free. TV; cable. Complimentary continental bkfst. Complimentary coffee in rms. Restaurant nearby. Ck-out 11 am. Whirlpool. Some refrigerators. Cr cds: A, C, D, DS, MC, V.

⊡ 🌠 ⊠ 🦺

★ **DAYS INN OF PRESCOTT VAL-LEY.** 7875 E Hwy 69, Prescott Valley (86314). 928/772-8600; fax 928/772-0942; res 800/329-7466. www.daysinn.com. 59 rms, 2 story. S $59-$69; D $69-$79; each addl $10; suites $99-$109; under 12 free; hols (2-day min); higher rates special events. Crib free. Pet accepted; $50. TV; cable (premium). Complimentary continental bkfst. Restaurant adj open 24 hrs. Ck-out 11 am. Meeting rm. Business servs avail. Pool; whirlpool. Some refrigerators; microwave, wet bar in suites. Cr cds: A, C, D, DS, JCB, MC, V.

⊡ 🐾 ➳ ⊠ 🔥 SC

★★ **HOLIDAY INN EXPRESS - PRESCOTT.** 3454 Ranch Dr (86303). 928/445-8900; fax 928/778-2629; res 800/465-4329. www.hiexpress.com/prescottaz. 76 rms, 3 story. Mid-Apr-mid-Oct: S, D $79-$109; each addl $10; suites $109-$159; under 17 free; hols (2-day min); higher rates special events; lower rates rest of yr. Crib free. TV; cable (premium). Complimentary continental bkfst. Restaurant nearby. Ck-out 11 am. Meeting rm. In-rm modem link. Valet serv. Coin lndry. Exercise equipt. Indoor pool; whirlpool. Some refrigerators, microwaves;

minibar, wet bar in suites. Cr cds: A, C, D, DS, JCB, MC, V.

Casino. On hill overlooking city. Cr cds: A, C, D, DS, JCB, MC, V.

Hotels

★★★ **FOREST VILLAS HOTEL.**
3645 Lee Circle (86301). 928/717-1200; fax 928/717-1400; toll-free 800/223-3449. www.forestvillas.com. 62 rms, 2 story, 15 suites. Mid-Apr-Oct: S $69-$85; D $79-$95; each addl $10; suites $125-$208; under 13 free; wkly rates; lower rates rest of yr. Crib free. TV; cable (premium). Heated pool; whirlpool. Complimentary continental bkfst. Complimentary coffee in rms. Ck-out 11 am. Meeting rms. Business servs avail. Free garage parking. Refrigerators. Balconies. European decor with grand staircase. Cr cds: A, C, D, DS, MC, V.

★★ **HASSAYAMPA INN.** *122 E Gurley St (86301). 928/778-9434; fax 928/445-8590; toll-free 800/322-1927. www.hassayampainn.com.* 68 rms, 4 story. Apr-Oct: S, D $109-$179; each addl $15; suites $159-$209; under 6 free; lower rates rest of yr. Crib free. TV; cable, VCR avail. Complimentary full bkfst. Restaurant 6:30 am-2 pm, 5-9 pm; Fri, Sat to 9:30 pm. Bar 11 am-11 pm. Ck-out noon. Convention facilities. Business servs avail. Maintained vintage hotel (1927); original wall stenciling, decorative tiles. On National Register of Historic Places. Cr cds: A, D, DS, MC, V.

Resort

★★ **PRESCOTT RESORT CONFERENCE CENTER & CASINO.** *1500 Hwy 69 (86301). 928/776-1666; fax 928/776-8544; toll-free 800/967-4637. www.prescottresort.com.* 160 rms, 5 story, 80 suites. Apr-Oct: S, D $125; suites $145; under 18 free; golf plans; lower rates rest of yr. Crib free. TV; cable (premium). Indoor/outdoor pool; whirlpool, poolside serv. Restaurant 6:30 am-9:30 pm. Bar 11-12:30 am; entertainment Fri-Sat. Ck-out noon. Meeting rms. Business servs avail. Gift shop. Barber, beauty shop. Lighted tennis. Racquetball court. Exercise equipt; sauna. Bathrm phones, refrigerators. Balconies.

B&Bs/Small Inns

★★ **HOTEL VENDOME.** *230 S Cortez St (86303). 928/776-0900; fax 928/771-0395; toll-free 888/468-3583. www.vendomehotel.com.* 21 rms, 2 story, 4 suites. May-Nov: S, D $79-$99; suites $119-$159; under 18 free; higher rates: major hols, special events; lower rates rest of yr. Crib free. TV; cable. Complimentary continental bkfst. Restaurant nearby. Bar 10-1 am. Ck-out 11 am. Business servs avail. Vintage (1917) lodging house. Cr cds: A, DS, MC, V.

★★ **PLEASANT STREET INN.** *142 S Pleasant St (86303). 928/445-4774; fax 928/777-8696. www.cwdesigners. com/pleasantstreet.* 4 rms, 2 with shower only, 2 suites. S, D $95; suites $130; hols (2-day min). Complimentary full bkfst. Restaurant nearby. Ck-out 11 am, ck-in 2 pm. Street parking. Built in 1906; Victorian decor. Totally nonsmoking. Cr cds: A, DS, MC, V.

Restaurants

★★ **GURLEY STREET GRILL.** *230 Gurley St (86301). 928/445-3388.* Hrs: 11-1 am. Closed Dec 25. Bar. Lunch $4.95-$8.50, dinner $5.95-$13.99. Child's menu. Specializes in fresh pasta, pizza, chicken. Patio dining. Pub-style atmosphere. Open kitchen. In Arizona's 1st territorial capital bldg (ca 1890). Cr cds: A, DS, MC, V.

★★ **MURPHY'S.** *201 N Cortez (86301). 928/445-4044.* Hrs: 11 am-11 pm; winter hrs vary; early-bird dinner Sun-Thurs 4:30-6 pm; Sun brunch to 3 pm. Closed day after Labor Day, Dec 25. Bar to 1 am. Lunch $5.25-$9.95, dinner $10.95-$20.95. Sun brunch $9-$15. Child's menu. Specialties: mesquite-broiled fresh fish, 21-day aged beef hand-cut steak, prime rib. Own bread. Memorabilia from turn-of-the-century on display. Restored (ca 1890) mercantile building. Cr cds: A, DS, MC, V.

★ **PINE CONE INN.** *1245 White Spar Rd (86303). 928/445-2970.* Hrs: 11 am-10:30 pm; Sun from 8 am; early-bird dinner 4-6 pm. Closed Dec 24-26. Res accepted. Bar to midnight. Bkfst $2.50-$5.25, lunch $4-$8.25, dinner $7-$18. Specializes in steak, seafood. Entertainment Tues-Sun. Family-owned. Cr cds: A, DS, MC, V.

Safford

(F-7) *See also Willcox*

Founded 1874 **Pop** 9,232 **Elev** 2,920 ft **Area code** 928 **Zip** 85546

Information Graham County Chamber of Commerce, 1111 Thatcher Blvd; 928/428-2511

Web www.graham-chamber.com

What to See and Do

Roper Lake State Park. This 320-acre park incl a small artificial lake, a swimming beach, and natural hot springs with tubs for public use; fishing (dock), boat launch (no gas-powered motors); nature trails, hiking, picnicking (shelter), camping, tent and trailer sites (hook-ups, dump station). Fishing dock accessible to the disabled. **Dankworth Unit,** 6 mi S, is a day-use area with fishing and picnicking. Standard fees. 6 mi S, ½ mi E of US 666. Phone 928/428-6760.

The Swift Trail. AZ 366 snakes its way 36 mi SW from Safford to the high elevations of the Pinaleño Mtns in Coronado National Forest; splendid view from the top, where Mt Graham towers 10,713 ft. There are five developed campgrounds (mid-Apr-mid-Nov, weather permitting); trout fishing at Riggs Flat Lake and in the streams. The upper elevations of AZ 366 are closed from mid-Nov-mid-Apr. Phone 928/428-4150. ¢¢¢

Special Events

Fiesta de Mayo. Mexican-American commemoration of *Cinco de Mayo* (May 5th), date of Mexican independence from Europe. First wkend May. Phone 928/428-4920.

Pioneer Days. Commemorates Mormon settlement. Late July.

Graham County Fair. Mid-Oct. Phone 928/428-6240.

Motels/Motor Lodges

★★ **BEST WESTERN DESERT INN.** *1391 Thatcher Blvd (85546). 928/428-0521; fax 928/428-7653; res 800/780-7234. www.bestwestern.com.* 70 rms, 2 story. S $59-$80; D $65; each addl $6; under 17 free. TV; cable. Pet accepted. Heated pool. Coffee in rms. Restaurant adj 6 am-10:30 pm. Bar 11 am-11 pm; Sun from noon. Ck-out 11 am. Coin lndry. Business servs avail. Free airport, bus depot transportation. Refrigerators. Cr cds: A, D, DS, MC, V.

★ **COMFORT INN.** *1578 W Thatcher Blvd (85546). 928/428-5851; fax 928/428-4968; res 800/228-5150. www.comfortinn.com.* 45 rms, 2 story. S $58; D $68; each addl $5; under 18 free; golf plans. Crib $3. Pet accepted, some restrictions. TV; cable (premium). Heated pool. Complimentary continental bkfst. Coffee in rms. Ck-out 11 am. Business servs avail. In-rm modem link. Some refrigerators, microwaves. Cr cds: A, C, D, DS, MC, V.

Restaurant

★ **CASA MANANA.** *502 1st Ave (85546). 928/428-3170.* Hrs: 11 am-9 pm; Fri, Sat to 10 pm. Closed Sun; Jan 1, Thanksgiving, Dec 25. Res accepted. Mexican, Amer menu. Beer, wine. A la carte entrees: lunch, dinner $3.50-$14. Specialties: green chili chimichangas, fajitas, fried ice cream. Spanish decor. Cr cds: DS, MC, V.

Saguaro National Park

See also Tucson

(Rincon Mtn District: 17 mi E of Tucson via Broadway and Old Spanish Tr. Tucson Mtn District: 16 mi W of Tucson via Speedway and Gates Pass Rd)

Saguaro National Park

The saguaro (sah-WAH-ro) cactus may grow as high as 50 feet and may live to be 200 years old. The fluted columns, spined with sharp, tough needles, may branch into fantastic shapes. During the rainy season, large saguaros can absorb enough water to sustain themselves during the dry season.

The saguaro's waxy, white blossoms (Arizona's state flower), which open at night and close the following afternoon, bloom in May and June; the red fruit ripens in July. The Tohono O'Odham eat this fruit fresh and dried; they also use it to make jellies, jams, and wines.

Wildlife is abundant. Gila woodpeckers and gilded flickers drill nest holes in the saguaro trunks. Once vacated, these holes become home to many other species of birds, including the tiny elf owl. Peccaries (piglike mammals), coyotes, mule deer, and other animals are often seen. Yuccas, agaves, prickly pears, mesquite, paloverde trees, and many other desert plants grow here.

The Rincon Mountain District offers nature trails, guided nature walks (winter), eight-mile self-guided drive (fee), mountain hiking, bridle trails, picnicking (no water), back-country camping. Visitor center with museum and orientation film.

The Tucson Mountain District offers nature trails, a six-mile self-guided drive, and hiking and bridle trails. Five picnic areas (no water). Visitor center; exhibits, slide program (daily). Contact the Superintendent, 3693 S Old Spanish Tr, Tucson 85730; phone 520/733-5100 or 520/733-5153. **FREE**

San Carlos

(E-6) *See also Globe*

Pop 2,918 **Elev** 2,635 ft
Area code 520 **Zip** 85550
Information San Carlos Recreation & Wildlife Department, PO Box 97; 520/475-2343

The San Carlos Apache Indian Reservation covers almost two million acres ranging from desert to pine forests. Many lakes, rivers, and ponds offer fishing (fee) year-round for trout, bass, and catfish. Hunting for small game, large game, and waterfowl is also year-round. Camping (fee). Apache guides may be hired to lead visitors into the wilderness portions of the reservation. Sunrise ceremonial dances are held from time to time.

Scottsdale

(E-4) *See also Chandler, Glendale, Mesa, Phoenix, Tempe*

Pop 202,705 **Elev** 1,250 ft
Area code 602/480
Information Chamber of Commerce, 7343 Scottsdale Mall, 85251; 480/945-8481 or 800/877-1117
Web www.scottsdalechamber.com

Scottsdale is a popular resort destination located on the eastern border of Phoenix. It is renowned for outstanding art galleries, excellent shopping and dining, lush golf courses, abundant recreational activities, and Western and Native American heritage.

What to See and Do

Cosanti Foundation. Earth-formed concrete structures and studios by Italian architect Paolo Soleri; constructed by Soleri's students. Soleri windbells made in crafts areas. (Daily; closed hols) 6433 Doubletree Ranch Rd. Phone 480/948-6145 or 800/752-3187. **FREE**

Gray Line sightseeing tours. Contact PO Box 21126, Phoenix 85036. Phone 602/495-9100 or 800/732-0327.

Hot Air Expeditions. Hot-air balloon flights offer spectacular views of Sonoran Desert. Contact 2243 E Rose/Garden/Loop, Phoenix 85024. Phone 480/502-6999 or 800/831-7610.

McCormick Steelman Railroad Park. This 30-acre city park was created by civic support and volunteer labor. Displays incl a full-size Baldwin steam engine, baggage car, and the Roald Amundsen Pullman car; exhibits by model railroad clubs; railroad hobby and artifact shops. Train rides aboard the steam-powered, nearly half-size *Paradise and Pacific* on one mi of 15-inch gauge track (fee). Museum, playground with 1929 carousel, picnic areas, desert arboretum; park office. (Daily; closed Thanksgiving, Dec 25) 7301 E Indian Bend Rd. Phone 480/312-2312. Train rides ¢

Rawhide 1880s Western Town. Town re-created in the image of the Old West; steakhouse and saloon; 20 shops; Native American village; displays; rodeos; cowboy gunfights; stagecoach ride; petting ranch. (Daily; closed Dec 25) Fee for some attractions. 23023 N Scottsdale Rd. Phone 480/502-5600.

Scottsdale Center for the Arts. Offers theater, dance; classical, jazz and popular music; lectures; outdoor festivals and concerts. Sculpture garden; art exhibits (daily; closed hols). 7380 E 2nd St. Phone 480/994-2787. ¢¢

⭐ **Taliesin West.** Winter house of Frank Lloyd Wright; now campus of the Taliesin Foundation; historic landmark of notable design. Tours; bookstore. (Daily; closed hols) At Cactus Rd and Frank Lloyd Wright Blvd. Phone 480/860-2700. ¢¢¢¢

WestWorld of Scottsdale. A 360-acre recreation park and event facility at base of McDowell Mtns. Hosts concerts, sports competitions, special events. (Daily) 16601 N Pima Rd. Phone 480/312-6802.

Wild West Jeep Tours. Four-hr guided desert tour. Explore an ancient ruin. (Daily) Phone 480/922-0144. ¢¢¢¢

Special Events

Parada del Sol & Rodeo. Phone 480/990-3179 (parade) or 480/502-5600 (rodeo). Mid-Feb.

Arabian Horse Show. WestWorld, 16601 N Pima Rd. Phone 480/515-1500. Two wks mid-Feb.

Baseball Spring Training. Scottsdale Stadium. San Francisco Giants. Phone 480/312-2580. Mar. Phone 480/312-2586.

The Tradition at Superstition Mountain. Superstition Mountain Golf & Country Club, 8000 E Club Village Dr. Senior PGA Tour golf tournament. Phone 800/508-9999. Early Apr.

Motels/Motor Lodges

★ ★ **BEST WESTERN.** *7515 E Butherus Dr (85260). 480/951-4000; fax 480/483-9046; toll-free 800/334-1977. www.bestwestern.com.* 120 suites, 4 story. Mid-Jan-mid-Apr: S, D $115-$159; under 12 free; golf plans; lower rates rest of yr. Crib free. Pet accepted, some restrictions; $50 deposit. TV; cable. Heated pool; whirlpool, poolside serv. Complimentary full bkfst. Restaurant 6 am-10 pm. Rm serv. Bar 3-10 pm. Ck-out noon. Coin lndry. Meeting rms. Business servs avail. In-rm modem link. Valet serv. Exercise equipt. Refrigerators, microwaves. Some balconies. Cr cds: A, D, DS, MC, V.

★★ **BEST WESTERN PAPAGO INN AND RESORT HOTEL.** *7017 E McDowell Rd (85257). 480/947-7335; fax 480/994-0692; res 800/780-7234. www.papagoinn.com.* 56 rms, 2 story. Jan-Apr: S, D $109-$179; each addl $5; under 17 free; lower rates rest of yr. Crib free. TV; cable (premium). Heated pool; poolside serv. Coffee in rms. Restaurant. Rm serv. Bar 10-1 am. Ck-out noon. Coin lndry. Business servs avail. Valet serv. Free airport transportation. Exercise equipt; sauna. Bathrm phones, refrigerators; some microwaves. Shopping mall adj. Aviary in courtyard. Cr cds: A, D, DS, JCB, MC, V.

★★ **COMFORT INN.** *7350 E Gold Dust Ave (85258). 480/596-6559; fax 480/596-0554; toll-free 888/296-9776. www.zmchotels.com.* 123 rms, 3 story. Jan-Apr: S, D $89-$134; each addl $10; suite $185; under 18 free; golf plans; lower rates rest of yr. Crib free. TV; cable (premium). Complimentary continental bkfst. Complimentary coffee in rms. Restaurant nearby. Rm serv 11 am-9 pm. Ck-out noon. In-rm modem link. Meeting rms. Business servs avail. Valet serv. Coin lndry. Health club privileges. Pool; whirlpool. Refrigerators; some in-rm whirlpools; microwaves avail. Cr cds: A, C, D, DS, MC, V.

★★ **COUNTRY INN AND SUITES.** *10801 N 89th Pl (85260). 480/314-1200; fax 480/314-7367; toll-free 800/456-4000. www.countryinns.com/scottsdaleaz_central.* 163 rms, 3 story, 92 suites. Jan-May: S, D $49-$139; each addl $10; suites $159-$189; under 18 free; lower rates rest of yr. Pet accepted; $50. Crib free. TV; cable (premium). Complimentary continental bkfst. Complimentary coffee in rms. Restaurant adj 7 am-11 pm. Ck-out noon. Meeting rms. Business servs avail. In-rm modem link. Bellhops. Coin lndry. Exercise equipt. Heated pool; wading pool, whirlpool. Refrigerator, microwave, wet bar in suites. Grill. Cr cds: A, D, DS, MC, V.

★★ **FAIRFIELD INN SCOTTSDALE NORTH.** *13440 N Scottsdale Rd (85254). 480/483-0042; fax 480/483-3715; res 800/228-2800. www.fairfieldinn.com.* 132 rms, 3 story. Jan-Apr: S, D $99-$135; under 18 free; lower rates rest of yr. TV; cable (premium). Pool; whirlpool. Complimentary continental bkfst. Restaurant nearby. Ck-out noon. Coin lndry. Business servs avail. In-rm modem link. Valet serv. Refrigerators avail. Picnic table. Cr cds: A, D, DS, MC, V.

★★ **HAMPTON INN.** *4415 N Civic Center Plaza (85251). 480/941-9400; fax 480/675-5240; res 800/426-7866. www.hamptoninnoldtown.com.* 126 rms, 5 story. Jan-Apr: S, D $120-$160; under 18 free; higher rates special events; lower rates rest of yr. Crib free. Pet accepted; $50 fee. TV; cable (premium). Complimentary continental bkfst. Coffee in rms. Restaurant adj 6 am-11 pm. Bar. Ck-out noon. Meeting rms. Business servs avail. Valet serv. Coin lndry. Tennis privileges. Pool. Cr cds: A, D, DS, MC, V.

★★ **HILTON GARDEN INN.** *7324 E Indian School Rd (85251). 480/481-0400; fax 480/481-0800; res 800/445-8667. www.scottsdale.gardeninn.com.* 200 rms, 7 story, 48 suites. Jan-Apr: S, D $199; suites $269; under 18 free; lower rates rest of yr. Crib avail. Parking garage. Pool, whirlpool. TV; cable (premium). Complimentary coffee in rms, newspaper, toll-free calls. Restaurant 6:30 am-10 pm. Bar. Ck-out noon, ck-in 3 pm. Meeting rms. Business center. Coin lndry. Gift shop. Exercise equipt. Refrigerators. Cr cds: A, C, D, DS, JCB, MC, V.

★★ **HOLIDAY INN SUNSPREE.** *7601 E Indian Bend Rd (85250). 480/991-2400; fax 480/998-2261; res 800/852-5205. www.holiday-inn.com.*

200 rms, 3 story. Jan-Apr: S, D $145-$169; each addl $10; under 18 free; package plans; lower rates rest of yr. TV; cable (premium). Heated pool; poolside serv. Supervised children's activities (May-Aug). Coffee in rms. Dining rm 6:30 am-10 pm. Box lunches. Rm serv. Bar 11-1 am. Ck-out noon. Convention facilities. Business servs avail. Valet serv. Gift shop. Coin lndry. Lighted tennis, pro. Golf. Bicycles (rentals). Lawn games. Exercise equipt. Refrigerators. Some private patios. Cr cds: A, D, DS, ER, JCB, MC, V.

⬛ 🏌 🏊 ⛴ 🛶 🔥 ⛷

★★ **HOMEWOOD SUITES.** *9880 N Scottsdale Rd (85253). 480/368-8705; fax 480/368-8725. www.homewood suites.com.* 114 suites, 3 story. Dec-Apr: S, D $159-$259; under 18 free; lower rates rest of yr. Crib free. TV; cable (premium), VCR. Complimentary continental bkfst. Complimentary coffee in rms. Restaurant nearby. Ck-out noon. Meeting rms. Business servs avail. In-rm modem link. Bellhops. Valet serv. Coin lndry. Sundries. Grocery store. Exercise equipt. Pool. Refrigerators, microwaves. Grills. Cr cds: A, D, DS, MC, V.

⬛ 🐾 🏊 ⛴ 🛶 🔥

★★ **HOSPITALITY SUITE RESORT.** *409 N Scottsdale Rd (85257). 480/949-5115; fax 480/941-8014; res 800/445-5115. www.hospitalitysuites.com.* 210 kit. suites (1-2 rm), 2-3 story. Mid-Jan-mid-Apr: S, D $69-$179; under 18 free; lower rates rest of yr. Crib $10. Pet accepted, some restrictions; $100 refundable. TV; cable (premium). 3 heated pools; whirlpool, poolside serv. Complimentary full bkfst. Coffee in rms. Restaurant 6:30 am-10 pm. Rm serv. Bar 11-1 am. Ck-out 11 am. Coin lndry. Meeting rms. Business servs avail. Bellhops. Valet serv. Free airport transportation. Lighted tennis. Lawn games. Health club privileges. Refrigerators, microwaves. Picnic tables; grills. Cr cds: A, C, D, DS, MC, V.

⬛ 🐾 🏌 🏊 🛶 🔥

★★ **HOTEL WATERFRONT IVY.** *7445 E Chapparral Rd (85250). 480/994-5282; fax 480/994-5625; res 877/770-7772. www.hotelwaterfront ivy.com.* 111 rms, 2 story, 69 kit. units. Early Jan-Apr: S, D $149-$299; package plans; lower rates rest of yr.

Crib free. TV; cable (premium), VCR avail (movies). Complimentary bkfst buffet, evening refreshments. Coffee in rms. Restaurant nearby. Ck-out noon. Meeting rms. Business servs avail. Valet serv. Coin lndry. Exercise equipt. Tennis. 5 pools; whirlpools. Playground. Refrigerators, microwaves. Cr cds: A, D, DS, MC, V.

⬛ 🏌 🏊 ⛴ 🛶 🔥

★★ **LA QUINTA INN AND SUITES.** *8888 E Shea Blvd. (85260). 480/614-5300; fax 480/614-5333; res 800/531-5900. www.laquinta.com.* 140 rms, 3 story. Jan-Apr: S $69-$119; D $79-$129; each addl $10; under 18 free; lower rates rest of yr. Crib free. Pet accepted, some restrictions. TV; cable (premium). Complimentary continental bkfst. Complimentary coffee in rms. Restaurant adj 7 am-11 pm. Ck-out noon. Meeting rms. Business servs avail. Coin lndry. Exercise equipt. Pool; whirlpool. Some refrigerators, microwaves. Cr cds: A, C, D, DS, V.

⬛ 🐾 🏊 ⛴ 🛶 🔥

★★ **SPRINGHILL SUITES.** *17020 N Scottsdale Rd (85255). 480/922-8700; fax 480/948-2276; res 888/287-9400. www.marriott.com.* 123 rms, 4 story. Jan-Apr: S, D $129-$149; under 18 free; lower rates rest of yr. Crib free. TV; cable (premium), VCR avail. Complimentary continental bkfst. Complimentary coffee in rms, newspaper, toll-free calls. Restaurant opp 7 am-midnight. Rm serv 5-10 pm. Ck-out noon. Meeting rm. Business servs avail. In-rm modem link. Bellhops. Valet serv. Coin lndry. Pool; whirlpool. Refrigerators, microwaves, wet bars. Picnic tables. Cr cds: A, D, DS, MC, V.

⬛ 🏊 🛶 🔥 SC

Hotels

★★ **COURTYARD BY MARRIOTT MAYO CLINIC.** *13444 E Shea Blvd (85259). 480/860-4000; fax 480/860-4308; res 800/321-2211. www.courtyard.com.* 124 rms, 2 story, 8 suites. Jan-mid-May: S, D $89-$159; suites $109-$179; lower rates rest of yr. Crib free. TV; cable (premium). Heated pool; whirlpool. Complimentary coffee in rms. Restaurant 6:30 am-9 pm; Sat, Sun 7 am-2 pm, 5-9 pm. Rm serv. Bar 4-11 pm. Ck-out noon. Coin lndry. Meeting rms. Business servs avail. Valet serv. Exercise equipt. Refrigerators, microwaves avail. Many balconies. Cr cds: A, C, D, DS, MC, V.

⬛ ▨ ▧ ▨ ▨

★ ★ **COURTYARD BY MARRIOTT NORTH SCOTTSDALE.** *17010 N Scottsdale Rd (85255). 480/922-8400; fax 480/948-3481; toll-free 800/321-2211. www.courtyard.com.* 153 rms, 3 story. Jan-Apr: S, D $149-$169; suites $179-$199; under 18 free; golf plans; lower rates rest of yr. Crib free. TV; cable (premium), VCR avail. Complimentary coffee in rms. Restaurant 6 am-11 pm. Rm serv 6-11 am, 5-10 pm. Bar 5-11 pm. Ck-out noon. Meeting rms. Business servs avail. In-rm modem link. Bellhops. Valet serv. Coin lndry. Exercise equipt. Pool; whirlpool. Some in-rm whirlpools; refrigerator, microwave, wet bar in suites. Some balconies. Cr cds: A, C, D, DS, MC, V.

⬛ ▨ ▧ ▨ ▨ SC

★ ★ ★ **HILTON SCOTTSDALE RESORT & VILLAS.** *6333 N Scottsdale Rd (85250). 480/948-7750; fax 480/315-2097; toll-free 800/528-3119. www.scottsdaleresort.hilton.com.* 185 rms, 3 story, 10 suites. S, D $185-$275; suites $300-$475; under 18 free. Crib free. TV; cable (premium), VCR avail. 2 pools; wading pool. Restaurant 7 am-10 pm. Bar to midnight. Ck-out noon. Meeting rms. Business center. In-rm modem link. Concierge. Exercise equipt. Spa. Minibar; refrigerators. Cr cds: A, C, D, DS, ER, JCB, MC, V.

⬛ ▨ ▧ ▨ ▨ ▧

Resorts

★ ★ **DOUBLETREE LA POSADA RESORT.** *4949 E Lincoln Dr (85253). 602/952-0420; fax 602/840-8576; toll-free 800/222-8733. www.doubletree. com.* 253 rms, 9 suites. Jan-May: S, D $264-$290; each addl $20; suites $375-$750; under 18 free; package plan; lower rates rest of yr. Crib free. Pet accepted, some restrictions. TV; cable (premium). 2 heated pools; whirlpool, poolside serv. Complimentary coffee in rms. Restaurant 6 am-10 pm; Fri, Sat to 11 pm. Rm serv. Bar noon-1 am. Ck-out noon. Convention facilities. Business servs avail. Bellhops. Valet serv. Sundries.

Gift shop. Barber, beauty shop. Lighted tennis, pro. Golf privileges, 2 putting greens. Racquetball. Exercise equipt; sauna. Lawn games. Bicycle rentals. Minibars; some refrigerators. Private patios. Multiple cascading waterfalls; lagoon-like pool. At foot of Camelback Mtn. Cr cds: A, C, D, DS, MC, V.

◀ ▧ ▨ ▨ ▧

★ ★ ★ **DOUBLETREE PARADISE VALLEY RESORT.** *5401 N Scottsdale Rd (85250). 480/947-5400; fax 480/946-1524; res 800/222-8733. www.doubletree.com.* 375 rms, 2 story, 12 suites. Jan-mid-May: S, D $205-$300; each addl $10; suites $350-$2,000; under 18 free; wkend rates; golf plans; lower rates rest of yr. Crib free. TV; cable (premium). 2 heated pools; whirlpool, poolside serv. Coffee in rms. Restaurants 6:30 am-11 pm. Rm serv. Bar 11-1 am. Ck-out noon. Convention facilities. Business servs avail. Concierge. Gift shop. Barber, beauty shop. 2 lighted tennis courts. Golf privileges. Exercise rm; sauna, steam rm. Massage. Bathrm phones, minibars. Refrigerators avail. Private patios, balconies. Grill. Extensive grounds elaborately landscaped; patio area overlooks courtyard. Cr cds: A, D, DS, ER, JCB, MC, V.

▧ ⬛ ▨ ▧ ▨ ▧ ▨ ▨

★ ★ ★ ★ **THE FAIRMONT SCOTTSDALE PRINCESS.** *7575 E Princess Dr (85255). 480/585-4848; fax 480/585-0086; res 800/441-1414. www. fairmont.com.* As if the McDowell Mountain backdrop wasn't enough, this resort's Spanish colonial architecture and pink facade are breathtaking as well. The 450-acre property is a Sonoran Desert oasis with two 18-hole golf courses, Sonoran Splash water slide facility, three pools, seven tennis courts, a spa and fitness center, and 61,000 square feet of meeting space. Several nationally recognized restaurants are here, including the Catalan restaurant Marquesa. 650 rms, 3-4 story, 75 suites, 119 casitas. Jan-Mar: S, D $479-$539; each addl $30; suites $689-$3,800; casitas $639-$739; under 16 free; golf, tennis, spa, hol plans; lower rates rest of yr. TV; cable, VCR avail. 3 pools; whirlpool, poolside serv. Supervised child's activities (Memorial Day-Labor Day and hols); ages 5-12. Dining rms 6:30 am-11 pm (see also LA HACIENDA and MARQUESA). Rm serv 24 hrs. Bars 11-1 am. Ck-out noon, ck-in 4 pm. Convention facilities. Business center. Concierge. Shopping arcade. Barber, beauty shop. Valet parking. Lighted tennis, pro. 36-hole golf, greens fee $91-$214, pro, putting green, driving range. Lawn games. Exercise rm; sauna, steam rm. Massage. Stocked lagoons; equipt avail for guests. Bathrm phones, refrigerators, minibars; some fireplaces. Private patios, balconies. Cr cds: A, C, D, DS, JCB, MC, V.

★★★★ **FOUR SEASONS RESORT SCOTTSDALE AT TROON NORTH.** *10600 E Crescent Moon Dr (85255). 480/515-5700; fax 480/515-5599. www.fourseasons.com.* Luxurious resort in the foothills of Pinnacle Peak in northern Scottsdale. Spacious beautifully appointed guestrooms with fireplaces and large bathrooms, fine dining in Acacia, golf at Troon North and a host of leisure activities combine with a pampering staff to make this a memorable destination. 210 rms, 2 story. Jan-June: S, D $425-$650; suites $795-$1,150; under 17 free; golf plan. Crib free. Pet accepted, some restrictions. TV; cable (premium), VCR avail. Pool; wading pool, whirlpool, poolside serv. Complimentary coffee in rms. Restaurant 7 am-10 pm (see also ACACIA). Rm serv 24 hrs. Bar to midnight. Ck-out noon, ck-in 4 pm. Meeting rms. Business center. In-rm modem link. Bellhops. Valet serv. Concierge. 4 lighted tennis courts, pro. 36-hole golf, greens fee $248. Putting green, driving range. Exercise rm; sauna, steam rm. Massage. Bathrm phones, minibars. Balconies, patios. Cr cds: A, C, D, DS, ER, JCB, MC, V.

★★★★ **HYATT REGENCY SCOTTSDALE RESORT AT GAINEY RANCH.** *7500 E Doubletree Ranch Rd (85258). 480/991-3388; fax 480/483-5550; toll-free 800/233-1234. www.hyatt.com.* The strikingly expansive 560-acre Gainey Ranch boasts 43,000 square feet of meeting space and a 2 ½ acre "water playground" with pools, water slides, sand, whirlpools, and bars. Rest in one of 493 rooms and suites surrounded by warm tones

with subtle southwestern accents, or sample the various dining options, including the gourmet southwestern eatery Golden Swan, which has spectacular lagoon and garden views. 486 units in main bldg, 4 story, 7 casitas (1-4 bedrm) on lake. Jan-mid-June: S, D $350-$525; suites $600-$3,000; under 18 free; golf plans; lower rates rest of yr. Crib free. TV; cable (premium), VCR avail. 10 pools; wading pool, poolside serv; clock tower with waterslide, sand beach. Playground. Supervised child's activities; ages 3-5, 6-12. Restaurants (public by res) 6:30 am-10:30 pm (see also GOLDEN SWAN). Rm serv 24 hrs. Bar noon-1 am. Ck-out noon, ck-in 4 pm. Meeting rms. Business center. In-rm modem link. Concierge. Gift shop. Free valet parking. Rec dir. 8 tennis courts, 4 lighted, pro. 27-hole golf, greens fee $160, pro, putting green, driving range. Bicycles. Exercise rm, sauna, steam rm. Massage. Body treatments. Beauty salon. Minibars; microwaves avail. Fireplace, wet bar in casitas. Balconies. Luxury level. Cr cds: A, C, D, DS, JCB, MC, V.

★★★★ **MARRIOTT'S CAMEL-BACK INN.** *5402 E Lincoln Dr (85253). 480/948-1700; fax 480/951-8469; toll-free 800/242-2635. camelbackinn.com.* This resort, golf club, and spa is situated on 125 Sonoran Desert acres at the base of Mummy Mountain. In the evening, the garden lights look like flickering candles illuminating the cactus-lined entranceway. Since 1936, the recreation options have grown to include 36 holes of championship golf, six tennis courts, a 27,000-square-foot spa, and 40,000 square feet of conference space. 453 rms, 1-2-story casitas. Jan-May: S, D $399-$450; suites $600-$2,000; under 18 free; wkend rates; golf, tennis, spa, package plans; lower rates rest of yr. Crib free. Pet accepted. TV; cable (premium), VCR avail. 3 pools; whirlpool, poolside serv, lifeguards. Supervised child's activities hols only; ages 5-12. Dining rms 6:30 am-10 pm (see CHAPARRAL DINING ROOM). Rm serv to midnight. Box lunches. Bars 11-1 am. Ck-out noon, ck-in 4 pm. Business center. In-rm modem link. Valet serv. Concierge. Barber, beauty shop. Gift and sport shops. Lighted tennis, pro. 36-hole golf, greens fee $90-$155 (incl cart), pros, putting greens, driving range, golf school. Bicycle rental. Lawn games. Soc dir; entertainment; movies winter and spring hols. Extensive exercise rm; sauna, steam rm. Spa. Refrigerators, minibars. Wet bar, microwave; fireplace, private pool in some suites. Private patios; many balconies. Cr cds: A, C, D, DS, ER, JCB, MC, V.

★★★ **MARRIOTT'S MOUNTAIN SHADOWS RESORT & GOLF CLUB.** 5641 E Lincoln Dr (85253). 480/948-7111; fax 480/951-5430; res 800/228-9290. www.marriott.com. 318 rms, 19 suites, 1-2 story. Jan-mid-May: S, D $99-$239; suites $300-$750; under 18 free; lower rates rest of yr. Crib free. TV; cable (premium). 3 heated pools; whirlpool. Dining rms 6:30 am-midnight. Rm serv. Box lunches. Snack bar. Bars 11-1 am. Ck-out noon, ck-in 4 pm. Convention facilities. Business center. Valet serv. Gift shop. Lighted tennis, pro. 54-hole golf, greens fee $60-$105 (incl cart), pro, putting greens, driving range. Lawn games. Playground. Exercise rm; sauna. Minibars; many bathrm phones; wet bar in suites; microwave avail. Private patios, balconies. On 70 acres; 3 acres of gardens. Cr cds: A, D, DS, MC, V.

★★★ **MILLENNIUM RESORT SCOTTSDALE MCCORMICK RANCH.** 7401 N Scottsdale Rd (85253). 480/948-5050; fax 480/948-9113; toll-free 800/243-1332. www.millennium-hotels.com/scottsdale. 125 rms, 3 story, 51 kit. villas (2-3 bedrm). Jan-Apr: S, D $195-$325; each addl $10; villas $350-$510; under 18 free; golf, tennis plans; lower rates rest of yr. Crib free. TV; cable (premium). Heated pool; whirlpool, poolside serv. Coffee in rms. Dining rm 6:30 am-10 pm. Rm serv. Bar 11-1 am. Ck-out noon, ck-in 3 pm. Convention facilities. Business center. Valet serv. Valet parking. Concierge. Gift shop. Lighted tennis. Dock; sailboats, paddleboats. Exercise equipt. Health club privileges. Sightseeing, desert trips. Lawn games. Soc dir. Minibars. Wet bar, fireplace in villas. Private patios, balconies. 10 acres on Camelback Lake; view of

McDowell Mtns. Cr cds: A, D, DS, MC, V.

★★★ **ORANGE TREE GOLF RESORT.** 10601 N 56th St (85254). 480/948-6100; fax 480/483-6074; toll-free 800/228-0386. www.orangetree.com. 160 suites, 2 story. Jan-May: S, D $150-$275; under 18 free; golf plan; lower rates rest of yr. Crib free. TV; cable (premium), VCR (movies). Heated pool; wading pool, whirlpool, poolside serv. Supervised children's activities. Coffee in rms. Dining rm 6 am-10 pm. Box lunches. Snack bar. Picnics. Rm serv. Bar 11-1 am; entertainment Wed-Sat. Ck-out 11 am, ck-in 4 pm. Grocery, pkg store 1 mi. Coin lndry. Meeting rms. Business servs avail. Bellhops. Valet serv. Concierge. Gift shop. Sports dir. 18-hole golf, greens fee $100 (incl cart), pro. Exercise equipt. Massage. Bathrm phones, refrigerators, microwaves. Private patios, balconies. Golf resort with country club atmosphere. Cr cds: A, D, DS, MC, V.

★★★★ **THE PHOENICIAN.** 6000 E Camelback Rd (85251). 480/941-8200; fax 480/947-4311. www.thephoenician.com. At the base of Camelback Mountain, this prestigious, 250-acre Sonoran Desert oasis provides extravagance and luxury from the $8 million art collection to the Valley of the Sun view from the stunningly appointed lobby. It's truly a world in and of itself with a spa, a 27-hole championship golf course, 12 tennis courts, 9 pools, and several world-class restaurants. 654 rms: 468 rms in main bldg, 4-6 story, 119 casitas. Jan-May: S, D, casitas $525-$695; each addl $50; suites $1,225-$5,500; villas $3,100-$3,500; under 17 free; golf plans; lower rates rest of yr. Crib free. TV; cable (premium), VCR avail (movies). 7 pools; 2 wading pools, whirlpool, poolside serv. Supervised child's activities; ages 5-12. Dining rms (public by res) 6 am-10 pm (see also MARY ELAINE'S, THE TERRACE DINING ROOM, and WINDOWS ON THE GREEN). Rm serv 24 hrs. Bar 11-1 am; entertainment. Ck-out noon, ck-in 4 pm. Convention facilities. Business center. In-rm modem link. Bellhops. Valet serv. Concierge. Shopping arcade. Barber, beauty shop. Airport transportation. Sports dir. 12 lighted tennis courts, pro. 27-hole golf, greens fee $90-$175, pro, putting green, driving range. Hiking. Bicycle rentals. Lawn games. Exercise rm; sauna, steam rm. Spa. Bathrm phones, minibars; some refrigerators, wet bars; microwaves avail. Balconies. Picnic tables. Cr cds: A, D, DS, MC, V.

[icons]

★ ★ ★ **RADISSON RESORT & SPA.**
7171 N Scottsdale Rd (85253). 480/991-3800; fax 480/948-1381; res 800/333-3333. www.radisson.com. 318 rms, 2 story, 34 suites. Jan-May: S, D $189-$259; each addl $20; suites $249-$289; under 18 free; lower rates rest of yr. Crib free. TV; cable (premium). 4 heated pools; whirlpool, poolside serv. Supervised children's activities (Late June-mid-Sept); ages 4-12. Dining rms 6:30 am-10 pm. Rm serv. Snack bar. Bar 11-1 am. Ck-out noon, ck-in 4 pm. Coin lndry. Convention facilities. Business center. Valet serv. Concierge. Gift shop. Barber, beauty shop. Lighted tennis, pro. Exercise equipt; sauna. Many refrigerators, mini-bars; some wet bars. Private patios, balconies. On 76 acres. Cr cds: A, D, DS, JCB, MC, V.

[icons]

★ ★ ★ **RENAISSANCE SCOTTS-DALE RESORT.** 6160 N Scottsdale Rd (85253). 480/991-1414; fax 480/951-3350; res 800/468-3571. www.renaissancehotels.com. 107 suites, 64 rms. Jan-May: S, D $89-$219; each addl $10; suites $285-$330; kit. units $345-$360; under 18 free; package plans; lower rates rest of yr. Crib free. Pet accepted, some restrictions. TV; cable (premium), VCR avail (movies). 3 heated pools; whirlpools, poolside serv. Complimentary continental bkfst. Restaurant 7 am-10:30 pm. Rm serv 24 hrs. Bar noon-11 pm. Ck-out noon. Meeting rms. Business servs avail. Bellhops. Concierge. Valet serv. Lighted tennis, pro. Golf privileges, putting green. Health club privileges. Lawn games. Bicycle rentals. Refrigerators, minibars; some bathrm phones, fireplaces; microwaves avail. Whirlpool on patios. Adj to Borgata shopping complex. Cr cds: A, C, D, DS, JCB, MC, V.

[icons] SC

★ ★ ★ **SANCTUARY AT CAMEL-BACK MOUNTAIN.** 5700 E McDonald Dr, Paradise Valley (85253). 480/948-2100. www.gardinersresort.com. 82 rms, 1 story. S, D $205-$450. Crib avail. TV; cable (premium). Pool; whirlpool. Restaurant 6:30 am-10 pm. Bar to midnight. Ck-out noon, ck-in 3 pm. Meeting rms. Business center. In-rm modem link. Concierge. Exercise rm. Spa. Minibars; many refrigerators in suites. Cr cds: A, C, D, DS, MC, V.

[icons]

★ ★ ★ **SCOTTSDALE PLAZA.** 7200 N Scottsdale Rd (85253). 480/948-5000; fax 480/998-5971; res 800/832-2025. www.scottsdaleplaza.com. 404 rms, 2 story, 180 suites. Jan-May: S, D $295-$325; each addl $10; suites $325-$3,500; golf, pkg plans; under 17 free; wkend rates; lower rates rest of yr. Crib $10. TV; cable, VCR avail. 5 heated pools; poolside serv. Dining rms 6 am-11 pm (see also REMING-TON). Rm serv. Bar 11-1 am; entertainment. Ck-out noon, ck-in 3 pm. Valet serv. Convention facilities. Business center. Concierge. Sundries. Gift shop. Beauty shop. Lighted tennis, pro. Racquetball. Putting green. Bike rentals. Lawn games. Exercise equipt, sauna. Refrigerators, minibars; many wet bars; microwaves avail. Fireplaces in suites. Spanish Colonial-style buildings on 40 acres; waterfall. Cr cds: A, D, DS, MC, V.

[icons]

★ ★ ★ **SUNBURST RESORT.** 4925 N Scottsdale Rd (85251). 480/945-7666; fax 480/946-4056; toll-free 800/528-7867. www.sunburstresort.com. 210 units, 7 with shower only. 2 story. Jan-Apr: S, D $259-$289; each addl $10; suites $395-$495; under 18 free; family, wkend, hol rates; golf plans; lower rates rest of yr. Crib free. TV; cable (premium). 2 heated pools; whirlpool, poolside serv. Complimentary coffee in rms. Restaurant 6 am-10 pm. Rm serv. Box lunches, snacks. Bar 10-1 am. Ck-out noon, ck-in 3 pm. Gift shop. Grocery, coin lndry 1 mi. Bellhops. Concierge. Valet serv. Meeting rms. Business servs avail. In-rm modem link. Exercise equipt. Refrigerators, minibars. Balconies. Cr cds: A, C, D, DS, MC, V.

[icons] SC

B&Bs/Small Inns

★ ★ ★ **HERMOSA INN.** *5532 N Palo Cristi Rd, Paradise Valley (85253). 602/955-8614; fax 602/955-8299; toll-free 800/241-1210. www.hermosainn. com.* 35 units, 5 suites, 4 houses, 13 kit. units. Jan-mid-Apr: S, D $95-$265; each addl $25; suites/houses $415-$595; under 6 free; lower rates rest of yr. Crib $25. TV; cable. Heated pool; whirlpool. Complimentary continental bkfst. Restaurant (see also LON'S). Rm serv. Ck-out noon, ck-in 3 pm. Concierge serv. Luggage handling. Tennis, pro. Many fireplaces, wet bars. Cr cds: A, C, D, DS, MC, V.

⬚⬚⬚⬚⬚ SC

★ ★ ★ **INN AT CITADEL.** *8700 E Pinnacle Peak Rd (85255). 480/585-6133; fax 480/585-3436; toll-free 800/927-8367. www.citadelinn.com.* 11 suites. Jan-Mid-May: S, D $79-$249; lower rates rest of yr. Crib free. Pet accepted. TV; cable (premium). Complimentary continental bkfst. Coffee in rms. Restaurant adj 6 am-11 pm. Rm serv. Ck-out noon, ck-in 3 pm. Business servs avail. Some balconies, minibars. Each rm individually decorated with antiques, artwork. View of Sonoran Desert, city. Cr cds: A, D, DS, MC, V.

D ⬚⬚⬚

★ ★ ★ **SOUTHWEST INN AT EAGLE MOUNTAIN.** *9800 N Summer Hill Blvd, Fountain Hill (85268). 480/816-3000; fax 480/816-3090; toll-free 800/992-8083. www.southwestinn. com.* 42 rms, 2 story, 11 suites. Jan-May: S, D $109-$199; each addl $10; suites $149-$259; under 13 free; package plans; lower rates rest of yr. Crib free. TV; cable (premium), VCR. Complimentary continental bkfst. Complimentary coffee in rms. Ck-out 11 am, ck-in 3 pm. Meeting rms. Business servs avail. In-rm modem link. Bellhops. Concierge serv. Gift shop. Lighted tennis privileges, pro. 18-hole golf privileges, pro, putting green, driving range. Heated pool; whirlpool. Bathrm phones, in-rm whirlpools, refrigerators, fireplaces. Balconies. Totally nonsmoking. Cr cds: A, D, DS, MC, V.

D ⬚⬚⬚⬚⬚ SC

All Suites

★ ★ **AMERISUITES.** *7300 E 3rd Ave (85251). 480/423-9944; fax 480/423-2991; toll-free 800/833-1516. www. amerisuites.com.* 128 rms, 6 story. Jan-Apr: suites $149-$189; each addl $10; under 18 free; lower rates rest of yr. Crib avail. Pet accepted, fee, some restrictions. Parking lot. Pool. TV; cable (premium), VCR avail. Complimentary continental bkfst, coffee in rms, newspaper, toll-free calls. Restaurant nearby. Ck-out noon, ck-in 3 pm. Meeting rms. Business center. Coin lndry. Valet serv. Exercise equipt. Refrigerators, microwaves. Cr cds: A, C, D, DS, ER, JCB, MC, V.

D ⬚⬚⬚⬚⬚⬚

★ ★ **CHAPARRAL SUITES.** *5001 N Scottsdale Rd (85250). 480/949-1414; fax 480/947-2675; toll-free 800/528-1456. www.chaparralsuites.com.* 311 suites, 4 story. Jan-Apr: S $189; D $199; each addl $10; under 18 free; lower rates rest of yr. Crib free. Pet accepted, some restrictions. TV; cable (premium), VCR avail (movies). 2 heated pools; poolside serv. Complimentary full bkfst, newspaper, evening refreshments. Coffee in rms. Restaurants 11 am-2:30 pm, 5-10 pm; Fri, Sat to 11 pm. Bars to 1 am. Ck-out noon. Coin lndry. Meeting rms. Business servs avail. Concierge. Gift shop. Free airport transportation. Lighted tennis. Exercise equipt. Rec rm. Game rm. Refrigerators; some bathrm phones; microwaves avail. Cr cds: A, C, D, DS, MC.

⬚⬚⬚⬚⬚⬚⬚ D

★ ★ **GAINEY SUITES HOTEL.** *7300 E Gainey Suites Dr (85258). 480/922-6969; fax 480/922-1689; toll-free 800/970-4666. www.gaineysuiteshotel. com.* 164 rms, 3 story. Jan-Apr: S $179; D $ 269; suites $145; lower rates rest of yr. Crib avail. Pool, whirlpool. TV; cable. Complimentary continental bkfst, coffee in rms, newspaper, toll-free calls. Evening reception. Restaurant nearby. Ck-out noon, ck-in 3 pm. Meeting rms. Business center. Bellhops. Concierge serv. Dry cleaning, coin lndry. Gift shop. Salon/ barber avail. Exercise equipt. Hiking trail. Picnic facilities. Cr cds: A, C, D, DS, MC, V.

D ⬚⬚⬚⬚⬚⬚ SC ⬚

★ ★ ★ **MARRIOTT AT MCDOWELL MOUNTAINS SCOTTSDALE.** *16770 N Perimeter Dr (85260). 480/502-3836; fax 480/502-0653; toll-free 800/288-6127. www.marriottscottsdale. com.* 270 rms, 3 story. Nov-Apr: S, D $269; lower rates rest of yr. Crib avail. Valet parking avail. Pool, whirlpool. TV; cable (premium), VCR avail. Complimentary coffee in rms, newspaper, toll-free calls. Restaurant 6:30 am-10 pm. Bar. Ck-out noon, ck-in 4 pm. Conference center, meeting rms. Business center. Bellhops. Concierge serv. Dry cleaning, coin lndry. Gift shop. Exercise equipt, steam rm. Golf. Hiking trail. Video games. Cr cds: A, D, DS, JCB, MC, V.

★ ★ ★ **MARRIOTT SUITES SCOTTSDALE.** *7325 E 3rd Ave (85251). 480/945-1550; fax 480/945-2005; toll-free 800/228-9290. www. marriott.com.* 251 suites, 8 story. Jan-May: S, D $199-$249; lower rates rest of yr. Crib $10. TV; cable (premium). Heated pool; whirlpool, poolside serv. Complimentary coffee in rms. Restaurant 6:30 am-10 pm; Sat, Sun 7 am-11 pm. Bar 5-11 pm. Ck-out noon. Coin lndry. Gift shop. Convention facilities. Business center. Valet; covered parking. Exercise equipt; sauna. Refrigerators; microwaves avail. Many private patios, balconies. Cr cds: A, C, D, DS, MC, V.

★ ★ **SUMMERFIELD SUITES.** *4245 N Drinkwater Blvd (85251). 480/946-7700; fax 480/946-7711; toll-free 800/833-4353. www.wyndham.com.* 163 suites. Feb-Apr: suites $199; lower rates rest of yr. Crib free. Pet accepted, some restrictions, fee. Pool, whirlpool. Sundries. TV; cable (premium), VCR avail. Complimentary full bkfst, coffee in rms, newspaper, toll-free calls. Restaurant nearby. Ck-out noon, ck-in 4 pm. Meeting rms. Business servs avail. Bellhops. Concierge serv. Coin lndry. Salon/barber avail. Exercise equipt. Golf. Bike rentals. Cr cds: A, C, D, DS, JCB, MC, V.

Extended Stay

★ ★ **RESIDENCE INN BY MARRIOTT.** *6040 N Scottsdale Rd (85253).* *480/948-8666; fax 480/443-4869; toll-free 800/331-3131. www.residence inn.com.* 122 kit. suites, 2 story. Jan-Apr: studio $186-$206; 2-bedrm $269-$289; wkly, monthly rates; lower rates rest of yr. Crib free. Pet accepted, $50 deposit and $6/day. TV; cable (premium), VCR avail. Heated pool; whirlpool; poolside serv. Complimentary continental bkfst. Complimentary coffee in rms. Restaurant opp 6 am-10 pm. Ck-out noon. Coin lndry. Business servs avail. Valet serv. Lighted tennis privileges. 36-hole golf privileges, pro, putting green, driving range. Exercise equipt. Refrigerators, microwaves. Grills. Cr cds: A, C, D, DS, JCB, MC, V.

Restaurants

★ ★ ★ ★ **ACACIA.** *10600 E Crescent Moon Dr (85255). 480/515-5700. www.fourseasons.com.* Casual sophistication combined with spectacular views of Pinnacle Peak and the city below create an ideal setting for the fresh seafood and finest USDA and certified prime beef of this Four Seasons restaurant. The knowledgeable, attentive staff is everything one would expect. The steak house menu includes bone-in ribeye, filet mignon, and a 24-oz porterhouse steak. Specializes in grilled double cut lamb chops, five spiced ahi tuna, live Maine lobster. Hrs: 6-10 pm, Fri, Sat to 10:30 pm. Res accepted. Dinner $22-$34. Wine list. Cr cds: A, C, D, DS, ER, JCB, MC, V.

★ ★ **BANDERA.** *3821 N Scottsdale Rd (85251). 480/922-7775. www. houstons.com.* Hrs: 5-10 pm; Fri to 11 pm; Sat 4:30-11 pm; Sun from 4:30 pm. Closed Thanksgiving, Dec 25. Bar. Dinner $10.95-$19.95. Child's menu. Specialties: wood-fired, spit-roasted chicken; black bean chicken chili; millionaire's club filet. Parking. Totally nonsmoking. Cr cds: A, D, MC, V.

★ ★ **BUSTER'S.** *8320 N Hayden (85258). 480/951-5850. www.busters restaurant.com.* Hrs: 11:30 am-10 pm; June-Aug to 9 pm; early-bird dinner 4-6 pm. Closed Dec 25. Res accepted. Bar. Amer menu. Lunch $6.45-

$10.95, dinner $16-$21. Child's menu. Specialties: chicken Sonoma with artichoke hearts and mushrooms. Parking. Outdoor dining. Overlooks Lake Marguerite. Cr cds: A, D, DS, MC, V.
D

★★★ **CHAPARRAL DINING ROOM.** *5402 E Lincoln Dr (85253). 480/948-1700. www.camelbackinn. com.* Hrs: 5:30-10 pm; Fri, Sat from noon. Res accepted. Bar to midnight. Wine cellar. A la carte entrees: lunch, dinner $19-$35. Specialties: lobster bisque, Dover sole, rack of lamb, souflees. Own baking. Valet parking. Jacket (in season). Cr cds: A, D, DS, ER, JCB, MC, V.
D

★★ **CHART HOUSE.** *7255 McCormick Pkwy (85258). 480/951-2250. www.chart-house.com.* Hrs: 5-10 pm; Sun 4:30-9 pm. Res accepted. Bar. Dinner $15-$40. Child's menu. Specialty: macadamia-crusted halibut. Salad bar. Parking. Outdoor dining. All dining areas have view of McCormick Lake. Cr cds: A, D, DS, MC, V.
D

★ **CHOMPIE'S.** *9301 E Shea Blvd (85260). 480/860-0475. www. chompies.com.* Hrs: 6 am-9 pm; Sun, Mon to 8 pm. Kosher deli menu. Wine, beer. Bkfst $1.75-$8.50, lunch $4.50-$10.95, dinner $7.95-$13.95. Specialties: Nova Scotia lox, matzo brie, mile-high sandwiches. New York-style decor. Cr cds: A, MC, V.
D

★★ **CREW.** *34505 N Scottsdale Rd, Ste 32 (85262). 480/488-8840. www. creweats.com.* Hrs: 11:30 am-9:30 pm. Closed Thanksgiving, Dec 25. Res accepted. Wine list. Specializes in pan-seared trout. Lunch $5-$9.50; dinner $14.50-$23. Child's menu. Entertainment. Cr cds: A, D, DS, MC, V.
D

★★ **DON AND CHARLIE'S AMERICAN RIB AND CHOP HOUSE.** *7501 E Camelback Rd (85251). 480/990-0900. www.donandcharlies.com.* Hrs: 5-10 pm; Fri, Sat to 10:30 pm; Sun 4:30-9 pm. Closed Thanksgiving. Res accepted. Bar. Dinner $11.95-$29.95.

Child's menu. Specialties: barbecued ribs, prime center cut steak. Own pies, cakes. Parking. Photos of celebrities, sports memorabilia on walls. Totally nonsmoking. Cr cds: A, D, DS, MC, V.
D

★★ **EL CHORRO LODGE.** *5550 E Lincoln Dr (85253). 480/948-5170. www.elchorro.com.* Hrs: 11 am-4 pm, 6-10 pm; Sat, Sun from 6 pm. Res accepted. Bar. Lunch $8-$16.25, dinner $13-$62. Specialties: châteaubriand, rack of lamb, prime beef. Piano, guitar Thurs-Sat. Valet parking. Outdoor dining. Western decor, paintings. Fireplaces. Family-owned. Cr cds: A, D, DS, MC, V.
D

★★★★ **GOLDEN SWAN.** *7500 E Doubletree Rd (85258). 480/483-5572. www.scottsdale.hyatt.com.* Housed in the Hyatt Regency Scottsdale Resort at Gainey Ranch, this restaurant serves regional American cuisine with the expected nod to southwestern flavors. It is a popular destination for the Sunday Chef's Brunch, where visitors are invited into the kitchen to observe and interact with the chefs. Dine indoors or out for a view of the lagoon, lily pond, and mountains. Southwestern gourmet cuisine. Specialties: free range hen baked in red rock clay; grilled Pacific salmon filet with mesquite honey barbecue sauce; sauteed veal chop. Own pastries. Hrs: 6-10 pm; Sun brunch 9:30 am-2:30 pm. Closed Sun, Mon (July 4-Labor Day). Bar. Res accepted. A la carte entrées: dinner $28-$31. Sun brunch $42, $28 for children. Valet parking. Braille menu. Totally nonsmoking. Cr cds: A, D, DS, JCB, MC, V.
D

★★★ **HAPA.** *6204 N Scottsdale Rd (85253). 480/998-8220. www. restauranthapa.com.* Hrs: 11:30 am-2:30 pm, 5:30-10 pm. Closed Sun; most major hols; 2 wks in summer. Res accepted. Asian Amer menu. Bar to midnight. Wine list. Lunch $5-$12, dinner $14-$23. Specialties: fiery squid salad, caramelized Chinese mustard beef tenderloin, miso-marinated sea bass. Parking. Outdoor dining. Asian Amer decor. Cr cds: A, MC, V.

D

★★ **HOUSTON'S.** *6113 N Scottsdale Rd (85250). 480/922-7775. www. houstons.com.* Hrs: 11 am-10 pm; Fri to 11 pm; Sat 11 am-11 pm. Closed Dec 25. Bar. Lunch, dinner $8-$25. Child's menu. Specializes in barbecued baby ribs. Outdoor dining. Upscale casual dining. Cr cds: A, MC, V.

D

★★★★ **LA HACIENDA.** *7575 E Princess Dr (85255). 480/585-4848. www.fairmont.com.* This turn-of-the-century Mexican ranch house is located at The Fairmont Scottsdale Princess Hotel and is one of the country's highest regarded destinations for Mexican cuisine. Specialties from Old Colonial Mexico include the dramatic signature Cochinillo Asado, a spit-roasted suckling pig marinated in bitter orange, pepper, and tamarind and carved tableside. Strolling mariachis and a courtyard view create an impressive dining space. Mexican menu. Specialties: filete al chipotle (charbroiled beef tenderloin), charbroiled lambchops crusted with pumpkin seed, suckling pig. Own baking. Hrs: 6-10 pm. Closed Wed. Bar from 5 pm. Wine list. Res accepted. A la carte entrees: dinner $22-$31. Child's menu. Strolling mariachis. Valet parking. Outdoor dining. Cr cds: A, D, DS, MC, V.

D

★★ **LANDRY'S PACIFIC FISH COMPANY.** *4321 N Scottsdale Rd (85251). 480/941-0602.* Hrs: 11 am-10 pm; Fri, Sat to 11 pm; Sun noon-10 pm; June-July hrs vary. Closed Thanksgiving, Dec 25. Res accepted. Bar. Lunch $7.95-$13.99, dinner $15-$25. Child's menu. Entertainment wkends. Free valet parking. Outdoor dining. 2 floors of dining; nautical decor, memorabilia; open kitchen. Cr cds: A, D, DS, MC, V.

D ⊒

★★★ **L'ECOLE.** *8100 E Camelback Rd (85251). 480/990-7639. www. scichefs.com.* Hrs: 11:30 am-1:30 pm, 6:30-8:30 pm. Closed Sat, Sun; major hols. Res required. Contemporary Amer menu. Serv bar. Wine list.

Complete meals: lunch $7-$12, dinner $24.95-$29.95. Specializes in fish, poultry, beef. Own baking. Tableside cooking. Menu changes wkly. Parking. Primarily staffed by students of the Scottsdale Culinary Institute. Cr cds: A, DS, MC, V.

D

★★★ **LON'S.** *5532 N Palo Cristi Rd, Paradise Valley (85253). 602/955-7878. www.lons.com.* Hrs: 11:30 am-2 pm, 6-10 pm; Sun brunch 10 am-2 pm. Closed Jan 1, Memorial Day, July 4, Labor Day. Res accepted. Contemporary Amer menu. Bar. Wine list. Lunch $8.95-$14.95, dinner $16.95-$24.95. Sun brunch $7.95-$12. Specialties: seared breast of duck, wood-grilled veal t-bone, seared Ahi tuna. Parking. Outdoor dining. Old Arizona adobe. Totally nonsmoking. Cr cds: A, MC, V.

D

★★★ **MANCUSO'S.** *6166 N Scottsdale Rd (85253). 480/948-9988. www. mancusosrestaurant.com.* Hrs: 5-10:30 pm. Closed Dec 25. Res accepted. Northern Italian, Continental menu. Bar. Complete meals: dinner $16.95-$28.95. Specializes in osso buco. Piano lounge. Valet parking. Ambiance of castle interior. Cr cds: A, C, D, DS, MC, V.

D ⊒

★★ **MARCO POLO SUPPER CLUB.** *8608 E Shea Blvd (85260). 480/483-1900. www.marcopolosupperclub.com.* Hrs: 5-10 pm; Fri, Sat to 11 pm. Res accepted. Continental menu. Bar to 1 am. A la carte entrees: dinner $11.95-$30. Specialties: lobster spedini with penne alfredo and spinach. Musicians. Valet parking. Outdoor dining. Family photographs adorn walls. Cr cds: A, DS, MC, V.

D ⊒

★★★ **MARIA'S WHEN IN NAPLES.** *7000 E Shea Blvd (85254). 480/991-6887. www.mariaswheninnaples.com.* Hrs: 11:30 am-2:30 pm, 5-10 pm; Sat, Sun from 5 pm. Closed most major hols. Res accepted. Italian menu. Bar. Lunch $6.95-$10.95, dinner $12.95-$22.95. Specializes in pasta, veal. Own desserts. Parking. Outdoor dining. Open kitchen. Multi-tiered dining. Cr cds: A, D, DS, MC, V.

D

★★★★ **MARQUESA.** *7575 E Princess Dr (85255). 480/585-4848. www.fairmont.com.* Under Fairmont management, this long-respected Scottsdale Princess restaurant has broadened its menu to the foods of the Mediterranean Riviera. Luckily, the dining room remains unchanged: luxuriously upholstered chairs, a stone fireplace, Spanish colonial antiques, and a view of the McDowell Mountains. Starters like delicate shrimp "raviolis" with lamb gravy are excellent, as are the fine selection of wines, sherries, and cordials. Mediterranean Riviera cuisine. Hrs: 6-10 pm; Sun brunch 10:30 am-2:30 pm. Closed Sun, Mon. Bar. Wine cellar. Res accepted. A la carte entrees: dinner $27-$42. Sun brunch $49 (late fall-Father's Day). Child's menu. Entertainment. Flamenco guitarist Sun brunch. Valet parking. Outdoor dining. Cr cds: A, D, DS, MC, V.
D

★★★★★ **MARY ELAINE'S.** *6000 E Camelback Rd (85251). 480/423-2444. www.thephoenician.com.* Never mind the extraordinary prices: this bastion of luxury is worth the price tag. The impeccable service staff will anticipate your every need, whether it's a stool on which to rest your handbag or guidance navigating the impressive wine list. Seafood is the specialty, with heavenly choices including pan-seared New Zealand John Dory, Sea of Cortez scallops, and roasted American red snapper. French menu. Specializes in fresh seafood from around the world, rack of lamb, veal, Artisan game. Hrs: 6-10 pm; Fri, Sat to 11 pm. Closed Sun & Mon. Bar. Wine cellar. Res accepted. A la carte entrees: dinner $40-$45. Complete meals: dinner $70-$100. Child's menu. Entertainment. Valet parking. Jacket. Cr cds: A, D, DS, JCB, MC, V.
D

★★★ **MICHAEL'S.** *8700 E Pinnacle Peak Rd (85255). 480/515-2575. www.michaelsrestaurant.com.* Hrs: 6-10 pm. Closed some hols. Res accepted. Contemporary Amer menu. Bar 5 pm-midnight. Wine cellar. A la carte entrees: dinner $17.95-$27.95. Specialties: seared Chilean sea bass. Jazz Fri, Sat. Outdoor dining. Unique decor with waterfall. Cr cds: A, D, MC, V.
D

★★ **OCEANA.** *8900 E Pinnacle Peak Rd (85255). 480/515-2277. www.restaurantoceana.com.* Hrs: 5:30-10 pm. Closed most major hols; Sun (May-Aug); 1st 2 wks of Aug. Res accepted. Seafood menu. Bar. Dinner $23-$43. Specialties: seared ahi tuna with foie gras. Parking. Outdoor dining. Intimate atmosphere. Cr cds: A, D, DS, MC, V.
D

★★★ **PALM COURT.** *7700 E McCormick Pkwy (85258). 480/596-7700.* Hrs: 7-11 am, 11:30 am-2 pm, 5-10 pm; Sun brunch 10:30 am-2 pm, dinner 5-10 pm. Res accepted. Bar 10:30-1 am. Wine cellar. Bkfst $5.50-$10, lunch $7.50-$20, dinner $21-$31. Prix fixe: dinner $52. Sun brunch $26. Serv charge 18%. Child's menu. Specialties: Dover sole with almondine butter sauce. Pianist brunch, evenings. Valet parking. Intimate dining; tableside cooking and preparation. Jacket (dinner). Totally nonsmoking. Cr cds: A, D, DS, MC, V.

★ **PISCHKE'S PARADISE.** *7217 E 1st St (85251). 480/481-0067. www.pischkesparadise.com.* Hrs: 7 am-11 pm; Sun 8 am-10 pm. Closed most major hols. Bar. Bkfst $3-$9, lunch $5-$10, dinner $6-$18. Specialties: Cajun Caesar salad, six-egg omelettes. Outdoor dining. Colorful prints, photos above bar. Cr cds: A, DS, MC, V.
D

★ **QUILTED BEAR.** *6316 N Scottsdale Rd (85253). 480/948-7760.* Hrs: 7 am-10 pm; Sun from 8 am. Res accepted. Bkfst $1.99-$7.95, lunch $4.95-$10, dinner $6.95-$21.95. Child's menu. Specializes in prime rib, seafood. Salad bar. Own soups. Outdoor dining. Colorful decor; stained-glass windows. Cr cds: A, D, DS, MC, V.
D

★★★ **RAZZ'S.** *10315 N Scottsdale Rd (85253). 480/905-1308. www.razzsrestaurant.com.* Hrs: 5-10 pm. Closed Sun, Mon; most major hols; also July-Aug. Res accepted, required Fri, Sat. Contemporary international menu. Bar. Dinner $15.95-$22.95. Child's menu. Specialties: duck cakes with nopalito cactus sauce, rack of lamb with tamarind, cashew and rosemary-encrusted salmon filet. Own baking. Parking. Chef-owned. Cr cds: A, D, DS, MC, V.

D ✂

★★★ **REMINGTON.** 7200 N Scottsdale Rd (85253). 480/951-5101. Hrs: 11 am-2:30 pm, 5-10 pm; Sat, Sun from 5 pm. Res accepted. Bar 4:30 pm-midnight. Wine cellar. A la carte entrees: lunch $8.75-$16, dinner $18.50-$39.50. Specializes in crab cakes. Jazz. Outdoor dining. Elegant Southwestern decor; columns, vaulted dome ceiling with sky mural. Cr cds: A, D, DS, MC, V.

D ✂

★★★ **ROARING FORK.** 7243 E Camelback Rd (85251). 480/947-0795. www.roaringfork.com. Hrs: 11 am-3 pm, 6-10 pm; Fri to 11 pm; Sat 6-11 pm. Closed Sun; most major hols; hrs vary June-Aug. Res accepted. Bar. Wine cellar. Lunch $7-$12, dinner $13-$25. Child's menu. Specialties: sugar and chile-cured duckling, campfire-style salmon, grilled beef tenderloin with horseradish shellac. Valet parking wkends. Outdoor dining. Western artwork. Cr cds: A, D, DS, MC, V.

D

★★★ **RUTH'S CHRIS STEAK HOUSE.** 7001 N Scottsdale Rd (85253). 480/991-5988. www.ruths chrissteakhouse.com. Hrs: 5-10 pm; Fri, Sat to 10:30 pm. Closed Thanksgiving, Dec 25. Res accepted. Bar. A la carte entrees: dinner $17.95-$43.50. Specializes in USDA prime-aged, corn-fed Midwestern beef; fresh seafood, live Maine lobster. Outdoor dining. Traditional steakhouse. Cr cds: A, D, DS, MC, V.

D

★★ **SALT CELLAR.** 550 N Hayden Rd (85257). 480/947-1963. www.salt cellarrestaurant.com. Hrs: 5-11 pm; Fri, Sat to midnight. Closed Dec 25. Res accepted. Bar 4 pm-1 am. Dinner $22-$27. Child's menu. Specializes in seafood, prime steaks. Parking. Restaurant located underground, in former salt cellar. Rustic, nautical decor. Cr cds: A, MC, V.

✂

★★ **SUSHI ON SHEA.** 7000 E Shea Blvd (85254). 480/483-7799. www. sushionshea.com. Hrs: 11:30 am-2:30 pm, 5:30-10 pm; Fri, Sat to 11 pm; Sun from 5:30 pm. Closed most major hols. Japanese menu. Bar. Lunch $4.50-$10, dinner $8.25-$15. Child's menu. Specializes in chicken, sushi, tempura. Aquarium; sushi bar. Totally nonsmoking. Cr cds: A, D, DS, MC, V.

D

★★★★ **THE TERRACE DINING ROOM.** 6000 E Camelback Rd (85251). 480/423-2530. www.the phoenician.com. Housed at the luxurious Phoenician resort, this dining room and its covered patio overlook a pristine croquet lawn and flower garden. The menu offers New American cuisine such as pecan-crusted colorado rack of lamb, pancetta-wrapped Atlantic salmon provencal. Diners always have the "Choices Cuisine" option, a special section of the menu devoted to more health-conscious selections. Continental/American menu. Hrs: 6 am-10 pm; Sun brunch 10 am-2 pm. A la carte entrees: bkfst $8-$11, lunch $9-$14, dinner $19-$35. Prix fixe: dinner $30-$50. Sun brunch $52. Child's menu. Entertainment. Valet parking. Cr cds: A, D, DS, MC, V.

D

★★ **VIC'S AT PINNACLE PEAK.** 8711 E Pinnacle Peak Rd (85255). 480/998-2222. Hrs: 11:30 am-9 pm; Fri, Sat to 10 pm; early-bird dinner 4-6 pm. Res accepted. Bar to midnight. Lunch $5.99-$9.99, dinner $19-$29. Child's menu. Specializes in walleyed pike. Parking. Outdoor dining. Mission courtyard architecture with bell tower; antiques, art work. View of desert gardens. Cr cds: A, MC, V.

D

★★★ **WINDOWS ON THE GREEN.** 6000 E Camelback Rd (85251). 480/423-2530. www.the phoenician.com. Hrs: 5-10 pm. Closed Tues & Wed. Res accepted. Southwestern menu. Bar 4-11 pm. Wine cellar. Dinner $19-$25. Child's menu. Valet parking. Outdoor dining. View overlooking golf course. Cr cds: A, D, DS, MC, V.

D

Sedona

(C-4) *See also Cottonwood, Flagstaff*

Founded 1902 **Pop** 10,192 **Elev** 4,400 ft **Area code** 928
Information Sedona-Oak Creek Canyon Chamber of Commerce, PO Box 478, 86339; 928/282-7722 or 800/288-7336
Web www.sedonachamber.com

Known worldwide for the beauty of the red rocks surrounding the town, Sedona has grown from a pioneer settlement into a favorite film location. This is a resort area with numerous outdoor activities, including hiking, fishing, and biking, that can be enjoyed all year. Also an art and shopping destination, Sedona boasts Tlaquepaque (T-lock-ay-POCK-ay), a 4½-acre area of gardens, courtyards, fountains, galleries, shops, and restaurants. A Ranger District office of the Coconino National Forest is here.

What to See and Do

Chapel of the Holy Cross. Chapel perched between two pinnacles of uniquely colored red sandstone. Open to all for prayer and meditation. (Daily) 2½ mi S on AZ 179. Phone 928/282-4069. **FREE**

Jeep tours. Two-hr back country trips. (Daily) Other tours also avail. Contact Sedona Red Rock Jeep Tours, phone 800/8-SEDONA; on Red Rock Jeep Tours, phone 928/282-6826. ¢¢¢¢

Oak Creek Canyon. A beautiful drive along a spectacular fishing stream, north toward Flagstaff (see). Phone 928/282-2085. In the canyon is

Slide Rock State Park. A 43-acre day-use park on Oak Creek. Swimming, natural sandstone waterslide, fishing; hiking, picnicking. Concessions. Standard fees. 7 mi N on US 89A. Phone 928/282-3034. ¢

Sedona Cultural Park. A five-acre park that is home to the Georgia Frontiere Performing Arts Pavilion (seating 1,200-5,500), plus nature trails, picnic areas, and splendid views of of the surrounding red rock country. Performing arts season (May-Oct) features classical, jazz, country, and popular music, plus live theater and outdoor cinema. (Daily) Cultural Park Pl, off US 89A. Phone 928/282-0747. ¢¢¢¢

Tlaquepaque. Consists of 40 art galleries and stores set in a Spanish-style courtyard; cafes. (Daily exc hols) On AZ 179. Phone 928/282-4838. **FREE**

Verde Canyon Railroad. 20 mi SW via US 89A, in Clarkdale. (See COTTONWOOD) Phone 800/293-7245.

Special Events

Sedona Film Festival. First full wkend Mar. Phone 928/282-0747.

Sedona Jazz on the Rocks. Late Sept. Phone 928/282-1985.

Red Rock Fantasy of Lights. Late Nov-mid-Jan. Phone 928/282-1777.

Motels/Motor Lodges

★★ **BEST WESTERN ARROYO ROBLE.** *400 N Hwy 89A (86336). 928/282-4001; res 800/780-7234. www.bestwesternsedona.com.* 66 rms, 5 story, 8 villas. Mid-Feb-Nov: S, D $100-$149; each addl $10; suite $159-$179; cottage $179; villas $299; under 12 free; lower rates rest of yr. Crib free. TV; cable (premium). Heated indoor/outdoor pools; whirlpools. Complimentary continental bkfst, coffee in rms. Ck-out 11 am. Coin lndry. Business servs avail. In-rm modem link. Lighted tennis $5/person. Racquetball. Exercise equipt; sauna; steam rm. Microwave avail. Some private patios, balconies, fireplaces, whirlpools. Grills. Views of red sandstone buttes. Cr cds: A, C, D, DS, MC, V.
⊡ ⬧ ⬧ ⬧ ⬧ ⬧ ⬧ ⬧ SC

★★ **BEST WESTERN INN OF SEDONA.** *1200 W Hwy 89A (86336). 928/282-3072; fax 928/282-7218; res 800/780-7234. www.innofsedona.com.* 110 rms, 3 story. Mar-May, Sept-Oct: S, D $79-$179; suite $189; each addl $10; under 12 free; hols (2-day min); lower rates rest of yr. Crib free. Pet accepted; $10/day. TV; cable (premium). Complimentary continental bkfst, coffee in rms. Restaurant adj

11 am-9 pm. Ck-out 11 am. Meeting rms. Business servs avail. In-rm modem link. Concierge. Valet serv. Airport transportation. Exercise equipt. Heated pool; whirlpool. Many refrigerators; some fireplaces, balconies. Cr cds: A, C, D, DS, MC, V.

Courthouse Rock, Sedona

★★ **DESERT QUAIL INN.** *6626 State Rte 179 (86351). 928/284-1433; fax 928/284-0487; toll-free 800/385-0927. www.desertquailinn.com.* 41 rms, 1 suite, 2 story. S, D $69-$149; suite $139-$169; each addl $10; under 13 free; golf plan; higher rates: hols (2-day min), special events. Crib free. Pet accepted, some restrictions; $10/day/pet. TV; cable. Pool. Complimentary coffee in rms. Restaurant nearby. Ck-out 11 am. Coin lndry. In-rm modem link. Golf privileges. Some fireplaces. Refrigerators; microwaves avail. Cr cds: A, C, D, DS, MC, V.

★★ **HAMPTON INN.** *1800 W Hwy 89A (86336). 928/282-4700; fax 928/282-0004; res 800/426-7866. www.sedonahamptoninn.com.* 56 rms, 2 story. Sept-Oct: S, D $89-$129; suites $129-$159; under 18 free; lower rates rest of yr. Crib free. TV; cable (premium). Complimentary continental bkfst, coffee in rms. Restaurant nearby. Ck-out noon. Meeting rm. In-rm modem link. Valet serv. Heated pool; whirlpool. Refrigerators, microwaves; in-rm whirlpool. Cr cds: A, C, D, DS, JCB, MC, V.

★★ **LOS ABRIGADOS LODGE.** *270 N Hwy 89A (86336). 928/282-7125; fax 928/282-1825. www.ilxresorts.com.* 32 rms, 7 suites, 2 story. Mar-Dec: S, D $119-$139; suites $169. Crib free. TV; cable (premium), VCR (movies). Heated pool; whirlpool; poolside serv. Ck-out 11 am. Coffee in rms. Meeting rm. In-rm modem link. Coin lndry. Concierge. Valet serv. Exercise equipt. Gift shop. Refrigerators, microwaves, fireplaces, balconies. Cr cds: A, D, DS, MC, V.

★★ **SKY RANCH LODGE.** *1105 Airport Rd (86339). 928/282-6400; fax 928/282-7682; toll-free 888/708-6400. www.skyranchlodge.com.* 94 rms, 1-2 story, 20 kit. units, 2 cottages. S, D $80-$149; each addl $8; cottages $179; under 12 free. Crib free. Pet accepted, some restrictions; $10/day/pet. TV; cable. Pool; whirlpool. Complimentary coffee in rms. Restaurant nearby. Ck-out 11 am. Coin lndry. Business servs avail. Gift shop. Balconies. Some refrigerators, fireplaces. Cr cds: A, MC, V.

Hotel

★ ★ **KOKOPELLI SUITES.** *3119 W AZ 89 (86336). 928/204-1146; fax 928/204-5851; toll-free 800/789-7393. www.kokopellisuites.com.* 46 suites, 2 story. Mar-May, Sept-Nov: suites $69-$239; under 12 free; special events (2-day min); lower rates rest of yr. Crib $10. TV; cable. Heated pool; whirlpool. Complimentary continental bkfst. Coffee in rms. Restaurant nearby. Ck-out 11 am. Coin lndry. In-rm modem link. Refrigerators, microwaves; some in-rm whirlpools, fireplaces. Cr cds: A, C, D, DS, MC, V.

D ⛱ 🏊 🐾 SC

Resorts

★ ★ ★ ★ **ENCHANTMENT RESORT.** *525 Boynton Canyon Rd (86336). 928/282-2900; fax 928/282-9249; toll-free 800/826-4180. www.enchantment resort.com.* The geometrically designed buildings of this resort sit five miles from Sedona in Boynton Canyon, surrounded by the red rock and cedar forests of Coconino National Forest. Guests can choose an adobe casita, hacienda, or standard guestroom, all with private decks and beautiful canyon views. The property's Mii Amo Spa offers treatments using natural ingredients and traditional Native American practices. 220 units, 2 stories, 56 kit. casitas (2-bedrm). S, D $175-$375; suites $375-$805; kit. casitas $535-$1,045; special events (2-day min); lower rates rest of yr. Valet parking avail. Crib free. TV; cable (premium), VCR avail (movies). 6 heated pools, whirlpool, poolside serv. Supervised children's activities; ages 4-12. Complimentary coffee in rms. Restaurant (see YAVAPAI). Rm serv. Box lunches, snacks, picnics. Bar 11-1 am; entertainment Fri, Sat. Ck-out noon, ck-in 4 pm. Bellhops. Concierge. Valet serv. Coin lndry. Gift shop. Shopping arcade. Meeting rms. Business center. In-rm modem link. Golf; pro shop; putting green. Lighted tennis (fee), pro. Hiking. Bicycle rentals. Lawn games. Exercise rm $18; steam rm, sauna. Spa. Massage. Patios; some balconies, fireplaces, refrigerators. Picnic tables. Cr cds: A, C, D, DS, MC, V.

D ⛷ 🏌 ⛱ 🎾 🏊 🐾 🏃

★ ★ ★ **L'AUBERGE DE SEDONA.** *301 L'Auberge Ln (86336). 928/282-1661; fax 928/282-2885; toll-free 800/272-6777. www.lauberge.com.* 26 rooms, 2 story, 34 cottages. S, D $230-$275; cottage $280-$450; each addl $20; under 12 free. Crib free. TV; cable. Heated pool; whirlpool; poolside serv. Complimentary coffee in rms, library. Dining rm (see also L'AUBERGE). Rm serv. Bar 11 am-10 pm. Coffee in rms. Ck-out 11 am. Concierge. Bellhops. Gift shop. Business servs avail. In-rm modem link. Valet serv. Free airport transportation. Lawn games. Refrigerators, minibars, fireplaces. Some balconies. Romantic atmosphere; on Oak Creek. Cr cds: A, D, DS, MC, V.

D 🐾 🏌 ⛱ 🏊 🐾

★ ★ **LOS ABRIGADOS RESORT & SPA.** *160 Portal Ln (85901). 928/282-1777; fax 928/282-0199; toll-free 800/521-3131. www.ilxresorts.com.* 172 suites (1 and 2 bdrms), 1 cottage, 1-2 story. S, D $225-$395; each addl $20; cottage $1,500; under 16 free. Crib free. TV; cable (premium), VCR. 2 pools; whirlpool, poolside serv. Playground. Dining rm (see also JOEY BISTRO). Box lunches; steak fry area on Oak Creek. Rm serv. Bar 11-1 am. Ck-out noon, ck-in 4 pm. Coin lndry. Business servs avail. Valet serv. Concierge. Gift shop. Beauty shop. Sports dir. Tennis. Lawn games. Exercise rm; sauna, steam rm. Fishing in Oak Creek. Refrigerators, microwaves; some fireplaces. Private patios, balconies. Grills. Spanish-style stucco and tile-roofed buildings set among buttes of Oak Creek Canyon. Former ranch site and early movie location. Cr cds: A, C, D, DS, MC, V.

D 🐾 🏌 ⛱ 🎾 🏊 🐾 SC

★ **QUAIL RIDGE RESORT.** *120 Canyon Circle Dr (86351). 928/284-9327; fax 928/284-0832. www.quail ridgeresort.com.* 14 kit. units, shower only, 2 story, 5 suites, 9 chalets. Suites $96-$112; chalets $130-$194; wkly, wkend rates (2-day min); hols (3-day min); lower rates rest of yr. Crib $10. Pet accepted. TV; cable (premium). Heated pool; whirlpool. Restaurant nearby. Coffee in rms. Ck-out 11 am. Business servs avail. In-rm modem link. Coin lndry. Tennis. Refrigerators. Microwaves avail. Picnic table, grills. Totally nonsmoking. Cr cds: A, C, D, DS, MC, V.

★★ **RADISSON POCO DIABLO.** *1752 S Hwy 179 (86336). 928/282-7333; fax 928/282-9712; toll-free 800/333-3333. www.radisson.com.* 137 rms, 2 story. S, D $109-$209; each addl $20; under 18 free. Crib free. TV; cable (premium). Heated pool; whirlpool, poolside serv. Coffee in rms. Dining rm (public by res) 7 am-9 pm; Fri, Sat to 11 pm. Rm serv. Bar 11-1 am. Ck-out 11 am. Meeting rms. Business servs avail. In-rm modem link. Valet serv. Concierge. Lighted tennis, pro. 9-hole, par-3 golf, greens fee $10. Playground. Hiking. Basketball. Racquetball. Game rm. Massage. Coin lndry. Exercise equipt. Refrigerators; some in-rm spas, fireplaces, balconies. Views of Red Rock mtns. Cr cds: A, C, D, DS, ER, JCB, MC, V.

B&Bs/Small Inns

★★★ **ADOBE VILLAGE GRAHAM INN.** *150 Canyon Circle Dr (86351). 928/284-1425; fax 928/284-0767; toll-free 800/228-1425. www.sedonasfinest. com.* 7 rms in inn, 2 story; 4 kit. casitas. Inn: S $184-$454, D $199-$469; suite S $354-$554, D $369-$569; casitas: S $414-$424, D $429-$439; each addl $20; wkends 2-day min, hols 3-day min. Crib free. TV; cable, VCR (movies). CD player. Heated pool; whirlpool. Complimentary drinks in casitas and sitting rm. Complimentary full bkfst; afternoon refreshments. Dining rm opp 8-9:30 am. Ck-out 11 am, ck-in 3-6 pm. Business servs avail. In-rm modem link. Coin lndry. Luggage handling. Concierge serv. Gift shop. Valet serv. Bicycles avail. Fireplaces, in-rm whirlpools. Bathrm phone, refrigerator, microwave, wet bar, fireplace in casitas. Balconies. Guest library. Totally nonsmoking. Cr cds: A, DS, MC, V.

★★★ **APPLE ORCHARD INN.** *656 Jordan Rd (86336). 928/282-5328; fax 928/204-0044; toll-free 800/663-6968. www.appleorchardbb.com.* 6 rms, 2 story. S, D $135-$230; each addl $20; hols, wkends 2-day min. Children over 12 yrs only. TV; cable, VCR

(movies). Heated pool; whirlpool. Complimentary full bkfst. Restaurant nearby. Ck-out 11 am, ck-in 3-6 pm. Business servs avail. Coin lndry. Luggage handling. Valet serv. Refrigerators; many in-rm whirlpools. Some fireplaces, balconies. Totally nonsmoking. Cr cds: A, MC, V.

★★ **A TOUCH OF SEDONA BED AND BREAKFAST.** *595 Jordan Rd (86336). 928/282-6462; fax 928/282-1534; toll-free 800/600-6462. www. touchsedona.com.* 5 rms, 3 with shower only. No rm phones. Apr-June, Aug-Nov: S, D $119-$169; each addl $15; wkends, hols (2-, 3-day min); lower rates rest of yr. Crib free. TV; cable (premium), VCR avail. Complimentary full bkfst; afternoon refreshments. Restaurant nearby. Ck-out 11 am, ck-in 4-6 pm. Luggage handling. Concierge serv. Valet serv. Refrigerators. Balconies. Picnic tables. Totally nonsmoking. Cr cds: A, DS, MC, V.

★★★ **B & B AT SADDLEROCK RANCH.** *255 Rockridge Dr (86336). 928/282-7640; fax 928/282-6829. www.saddlerockranch.com.* 3 rms. Mid-Mar-mid-June, mid-Sept-mid Nov (min stay required): S $154-$1749; D $169-$189; each addl $20. Children over 14 yrs only. TV; cable, VCR. Pool; whirlpool. Complimentary full bkfst; afternoon refreshments. Ck-out 11 am, ck-in 4-6 pm. Luggage handling. Concierge serv. Business servs avail. Original house (1926) was part of 6,000-acre ranch. Many antiques, Native American artifacts. Many Western movies filmed here. Cr cds: MC, V.

★★★★ **CANYON VILLA INN.** *125 Canyon Circle Dr (86351). 928/284-1226; fax 928/284-2114; toll-free 800/453-1166. www.canyonvilla.com.* With the red-rock landscape as a backdrop, this cozy inn blends Mediterranean elegance with rustic Southwestern accents. All 11 guest-rooms include breakfast and after-noon hors d'oeuvres and have French doors opening to private balconies or patios (most with direct views of Courthouse Butte and Bell Rock). Simply enjoy the setting or explore nearby recreations including golf, hiking, and horseback riding. 11 rms, 2

story. S $179-$269; D $189-$279; wkends (2-day min); hols (3-day min); each addl $25. Children over 11 yrs only. TV; cable (premium). Heated pool. Complimentary full bkfst; afternoon refreshments. Restaurant nearby. Ck-out 11 am, ck-in 3-6 pm. Business servs avail. In-rm modem link. Luggage handling. Patios, balconies. Some fireplaces. Totally nonsmoking. Cr cds: A, DS, MC, V.
🄳 ⊠ ⊠ 🔥

★★★ **CASA SEDONA BED AND BREAKFAST.** *55 Hozoni Dr (86336). 928/282-2938; fax 928/282-2259; toll-free 800/525-3756. www.casasedona. com.* 16 rms, 2 story. S $170-$250; D $180-$260; each addl $30; wkend, hols (2-day min). Children over 12 only. TV; cable (premium), VCR (movies). Whirlpool. Complimentary full bkfst. Ck-out 11 am, ck-in 3-6 pm. Meeting rm. Business servs avail. In-rm modem link. Bellhops. Concierge serv. Valet serv. Refrigerators, fireplaces. Balconies. Picnic tables. Each rm with view of Red Rocks. Totally nonsmoking. Cr cds: MC, V.
🄳 ⊠ 🔥

★★★ **THE INN ON OAK CREEK.** *556 Hwy 179 (86336). 928/282-7896; fax 928/282-0696; toll-free 800/499-7896. www.sedona-inn.com.* 9 rms, 2 story, 2 suites. S $165-$260; D $180-$275; each addl $20; suites $210-$305; wkends, hols (2-day min). Children over 10 yrs only. TV; cable (premium), VCR (movies). Complimentary full bkfst; afternoon refreshments. Restaurant nearby. Ck-out 11 am, ck-in 3-6 pm. Business servs avail. In-rm modem link. Luggage handling. Valet serv. Concierge serv. In-rm whirlpools, fireplaces. Many balconies. On river. Views of Oak Creek and Red Rocks. Totally nonsmoking. Cr cds: A, DS, MC, V.
🄳 ⚓ 🛶 ⊠ 🔥

★★★ **THE LODGE AT SEDONA.** *125 Kallof Pl (86336). 928/204-1942; fax 928/204-2128; toll-free 800/619-4467. www.lodgeatsedona.com.* 14 rms, 2 story. D $140-$275; wkends (2-day min); each addl $30. TV; cable (premium) in sitting rm. Complimentary full bkfst; afternoon refreshments. Ck-out 11 am, ck-in 4-8 pm. Concierge serv. Gift shop. Meeting

rm. Business servs avail. Lawn games. Health club privileges. Some in-rm whirlpools, fireplaces. Picnic tables. Antiques. Library. Located on 2½ acres. Gardens, labyrinth. Totally nonsmoking. Cr cds: DS, MC, V.
🄳 ⊠ 🔥

★★★ **SOUTHWEST INN AT SEDONA.** *3250 W Hwy 89A (86336). 928/282-3344; fax 928/282-0267. www.swinn.com.* 28 rms, 2 story. Mid-Mar-May, Sept-Oct: S, D $139-$199; each addl $10; suites $189-$239; under 13 free; wkends, hols, special events (2-day min); lower rates rest of yr. Crib free. TV; cable (premium), VCR (movies). Heated pool; whirlpool. Complimentary continental bkfst, coffee in rms. Restaurant opp 11:30 am-9 pm. Ck-out 11 am. Bellhops. Concierge. Meeting rm. Business servs avail. In-rm modem link. Exercise equipt. Refrigerators, fireplaces; microwaves avail. Balconies. Golf nearby. Totally nonsmoking. Cr cds: A, C, D, DS, MC, V.
🄳 🏋 🛶 ⊠ 🔥 🏃

★★★ **TERRITORIAL HOUSE BED AND BREAKFAST.** *65 Piki Dr (86336). 928/204-2737; fax 928/204-2230; toll-free 800/801-2737. www. territorialhousebb.com.* 4 rms, 2 with shower only, 2 story, 1 suite. No A/C. 3 rm phones. S $105-$170; D $115-$185; each addl $20; suite $175-$250; min stay wkends, hols. TV; cable (premium), VCR (movies). Complimentary full bkfst; afternoon refreshments. Ck-out 11 am, ck-in 4-6 pm. Business servs avail. Whirlpool. Coin lndry. Refrigerators, microwaves avail. Some balconies. Converted Western ranch house; stone fireplace. Totally nonsmoking. Cr cds: A, DS, MC, V.
⊠ 🔥

Cottage Colony

★★ **BRIAR PATCH INN.** *3190 N Hwy 89A (86336). 928/282-2342; fax 928/282-2399; toll-free 888/809-3030. www.briarpatchinn.com.* 17 cottages, 13 with shower only. No rm phones. S, D $169-$325; each addl $25. Crib free. TV; cable (premium); CD players. Complimentary full bkfst, coffee in rms. Ck-out noon, ck-in 2 pm. Meeting house. Business servs avail.

Gift shop. Massage. Refrigerators. Some fireplaces. Picnic tables. Some antiques. Library. Swimming hole on Oak Creek. Located on 9 acres. Cr cds: A, MC, V.

D ⬚ ⬚ ⬚ ⬚

All Suites

★ ★ ★ **HILTON SEDONA RESORT & SPA.** *90 Ridge Trail Dr (86351). 928/284-4040; fax 928/284-6940. www.hiltonsedona.com.* 219 rms, 3 story. S, D $109-$249; special events (2-day min); under 18 free. Crib avail. Pet accepted; $50. TV; cable (premium). Heated pool; wading pool; whirlpool; poolside servs avail. Supervised children's activities. Restaurant 6:30 am-10 pm. Rm serv. Bar 11 am-11 pm; Fri, Sat to midnight. Coffee in rms. Ck-out noon. Meeting rms. Business servs avail. In-rm modem link. Bellhops. Valet serv. Concierge. Gift shop. Coin lndry. Exercise rm. 18-hole golf; greens fee $59-$109, pro, pro shop, cart avail. Lighted tennis. Spa. Massage. Fireplaces. Minibars. Balconies. Cr cds: A, C, D, DS, MC, V.

D ⬚ ⬚ ⬚ ⬚ ⬚ ⬚ ⬚

★ ★ ★ **SEDONA REAL INN.** *95 Arroyo Pinon Dr (86336). 928/282-1414; fax 928/282-0900; toll-free 800/353-1239. www.sedonareal.com.* 47 suites, 2 story. Mar-Nov, Dec-Jan: S, D $120-$250; each addl $10; under 12 free; golf plans; lower rates rest of yr. Crib free. TV; cable (premium), VCR (movies). Complimentary continental bkfst. Coffee in rms. Restaurant nearby. Ck-out 11 am. Meeting rm. Coin lndry. In-rm modem link. Concierge. Bellhops. Valet serv. Exercise equipt. Heated pool; whirlpool. Refrigerators, microwaves, fireplaces. Some balconies. Cr cds: A, DS, MC, V.

D ⬚ ⬚ ⬚ SC ⬚

Restaurants

★ ★ **COWBOY CLUB.** *241 N AZ 89A (86336). 928/282-4200. www.cowboyclub.com.* Hrs: 11 am-4 pm, 5-10 pm. Closed Thanksgiving, Dec 25. Res accepted. High desert menu. Bar. Lunch $5.95-$11.95, dinner $9.95-$32.95. Child's menu. Specializes in rattlesnake, buffalo, burgers. Parking. Cr cds: A, DS, MC, V.

D

★ **EL RINCON RESTAURANTE MEXICANO.** *336 AZ 179 #A112 (86336). 520/282-4648. www.rincon rerstaurants.com.* Hrs: 11 am-9 pm; Sun noon-5 pm; winter hrs vary. Closed Mon; Jan 1, Thanksgiving, Dec 25. Res accepted. Mexican menu. Bar. A la carte entrees: lunch, dinner $8.75-$14. Child's menu. Specializes in chimichangas, tamales, Navajo pizzas. Outdoor dining. Totally nonsmoking. Cr cds: MC, V.

D

★ ★ ★ **HEARTLINE CAFE.** *1610 W AZ 89A (86336). 928/282-0785. www.heartlinecafe.com.* Hrs: 11:30 am-3 pm, 5-9:15 pm; Tues, Wed from 5 pm. Res accepted. Eclectic menu. Bar. Wine cellar. Lunch $6.95-$13.50, dinner $15-$27. Child's menu. Specialties: mesquite-crusted rack of lamb, pecan-crusted local trout, crab cakes. Patio dining. Cottage surrounded by English garden. Smoking on patio only. Cr cds: A, D, DS, MC, V.

D ⬚

★ **HIDEAWAY.** *179 Country Sq (86336). 928/282-4204. www.sedona.net/hideaway.* Hrs: 11 am-9 pm. Closed Thanksgiving, Dec 24, 25. Italian menu. Bar. Lunch $7.50-$9, dinner $9-$11.50. Specializes in pizza, antipasto salad, fettucine. Parking. Outdoor dining overlooking Oak Creek and Red Rock Mountains. Dining rm features stained-glass windows. Cr cds: A, C, D, DS, MC, V.

⬚

★ ★ ★ **JOEY BISTRO.** *160 Portal Ln (86336). 928/204-5639. www.ilx resorts.com.* Hrs: 5-10 pm; Sun brunch 10 am-2 pm. Res accepted. Southern Italian menu. Bar. Wine cellar. Dinner $12.95-$25.95. Sun brunch $15.95. Specialties: vitello Mamma, tortellini and scampi, lobster ravioli. Décor features famous and infamous "Joes". Totally nonsmoking. Cr cds: A, C, D, DS, MC, V.

D

★ ★ ★ **L'AUBERGE.** *301 L'Auberge Ln (86339). 928/282-1667. www.lauberge.com.* Hrs: 7:30-10:30 am, 11:30 am-2:30 pm, 5:30-10 pm; Sun 7:30-10

am, 11 am-3 pm (brunch), 6-10 pm. Res accepted; required dinner. French menu. Bar. Wine cellar. A la carte entrees: bkfst $8-$14, lunch $11-$18, dinner $28-$38.50. Complete meal: dinner $60-$80. Sun brunch $30. Child's menu. Specialties: rack of lamb. Parking. Outdoor dining. Elegant dining in French country atmosphere; many antiques. View of creek. Jacket (dinner). Totally nonsmoking. Cr cds: A, D, DS, MC, V.
D

★★★ **PIETRO'S.** *2445 W AZ 89A # 3 (86336). 928/282-2525. www.pietrossedona.com.* Hrs: 5:30-9:30 pm; Fri, Sat to 10 pm; Nov-Feb from 5 pm; early-bird dinner until 6:30 pm. Closed Thanksgiving, Dec 25. Res accepted. Northern Italian menu. Bar. Wine cellar. Dinner $16-$26. Specialties: veal Marsala, polenta with sausage. Totally nonsmoking. Cr cds: A, C, DS, MC, V.
D

★★★ **RENE AT TLAQUEPAQUE.** *AZ 179 (86336). 928/282-9225. www. rene-sedona.com.* Hrs: 11:30 am-2:30 pm, 5:30-8:30 pm, Fri, Sat to 9 pm. Closed Dec 25. Res accepted. Continental menu. Specializes in Colorado rack of lamb. Bar. Lunch $7.95-$11.95, dinner $18.95-$27.95. Outdoor dining. Casual, elegant dining. Totally nonsmoking. Cr cds: MC, V.
D

★ **ROSEBUDS.** *320 N AZ 89A (86336). 928/282-3022.* Hrs: 11 am-9:30 pm. Closed Dec 25. Res accepted. Bar to 10 pm. Lunch $6.95-$10.95, dinner $15.95-$24.95. Specializes in seafood, steak. Own desserts. Parking. Panoramic view of Red Rocks. Cr cds: A, C, DS, MC, V.
D

★★★ **SHUGRUE'S HILLSIDE GRILL.** *671 AZ 179 (86336). 928/282-5300. www.shugrues.com.* Hrs: 11:30 am-3 pm, 5-9:30 pm. Closed Dec 25. Res accepted. Continental menu. Bar. Lunch $7-$13, dinner $16-$28. Child's menu. Specializes in steak, seafood, lamb, seared ahi tuna. Jazz Fri-Sat. Parking. Outdoor dining. Located high upon a hill; commanding view of rock formations. Cr cds: A, D, MC, V.
D

★ **WILD TOUCAN.** *6376 AZ 179 (86351). 928/284-1604. www.wild toucan.com.* Hrs: 11 am-9 pm; wkends to 10 pm. Closed Thanksgiving, Dec 25. Res accepted. Mexican, Amer menu. Bar. Lunch $4.95-$14.95, dinner $5.95-$18.95. Child's menu. Specializes in hand-cut steaks, authentic Mexican dishes. Parking. Outdoor dining. Casual, colorful atmosphere with good view of Red Rocks. Cr cds: A, D, DS, MC, V.
D

★★★ **YAVAPAI.** *525 Boynton Canyon Rd (86336). 928/204-6000. www.enchantmentresort.com.* Southwestern menu. Specialties: rack of Colorado lamb, pan-roasted Maine lobster. Hrs: 6:30 am-2:30 pm, 5:30-9:30 pm; Sun brunch 10:30 am-2:30 pm. Res required. Bar. Wine cellar. A la carte entrees: bkfst $7.50-$12.50, lunch $7.50-$14.50, dinner $22-$40. Sun brunch $28.50. Child's menu. Entertainment Fri-Sun. Parking. Outdoor dining. Cr cds: A, C, D, DS, MC, V.
D

Seligman

(C-3) *See also Flagstaff, Williams*

Pop 456 **Elev** 5,242 ft **Area code** 928 **Zip** 86337

Information Chamber of Commerce, Box 65, 86337; 928/422-3939

What to See and Do

Grand Canyon Caverns. Incl the 18,000-sq-ft "Chapel of Ages" and other rms and tunnels; ¾-mi trail; temperature 56°F. Elevator takes visitors 210 ft underground; 50-min guided tours. Motel, restaurant; western-style cookouts (May-Sept). (Daily; closed Dec 25) Golden Age Passport accepted. 25 mi NW on AZ 66. Phone 928/422-3223. ¢¢¢¢

Sells

(G-4) *See also Tucson*

Pop 2,799 **Elev** 2,360 ft
Area code 520 **Zip** 85634
Information Tohono O'Odham
Nation Executive Office, Box 837;
520/383-2028

This is the headquarters of the
Tohono O'Odham Indian Reservation (almost three million acres). The
Papagos farm, raise cattle, and craft
pottery and baskets. The main road
(AZ 86) passes through the reservation, and side roads lead to other villages. The older houses are made of
saguaro ribs plastered with mud.
More recently, burnt adobe (mud
brick) construction and conventional
housing have been adopted.

What to See and Do

Kitt Peak National Observatory.
(National Optical Astronomy Obser-
vatories) Site of world's largest collection of ground-based optical
telescopes; 36-, 50-, 84-, and 158-
inch stellar telescopes; world's largest
solar telescope (60 inches). Visitor
center with exhibits. Tours. Observatory (daily; closed hols). Approx 36
mi NE on AZ 86, then 12 mi S on AZ
386, in the Quinlan Mtns of the
Sonoran Desert (elev 6,882 ft). Phone
520/318-8600. **Donation**

Show Low

(D-6) *See also McNary, Pinetop*

Pop 7,695 **Elev** 6,347 ft
Area code 928 **Zip** 85901
Information Show Low Regional
Chamber of Commerce, 951 W
Deuce of Clubs, PO Box 1083, 85902;
928/537-2326 or 888-SHOW-LOW
Web www.showlowchamberof
commerce.com

This town, astride the Mogollon Rim
on US 60, is a good stop for the golf
enthusiast, angler, photographer, or
nature lover.

What to See and Do

Apache-Sitgreaves National Forests.
Combined into one administrative
unit, these two forests (see
SPRINGERVILLE) encompass more
than two million acres of diverse terrain. The Sitgreaves Forest (AZ 260) is
named for Captain Lorenzo Sitgreaves, conductor of the first scientific expedition across the state in
the 1850s; part of the General
George Cook military trail is here.
Fishing; hunting, self-guided nature
hikes, picnicking, camping (dump
station; fee). Sat eve programs in
summer. Phone 928/333-4301.

Fishing. Rainbow Lake. 8 mi SE on AZ
260. **Show Low Lake.** 4 mi SE off AZ
260. **Fool Hollow Lake.** 3 mi NW.
Many others in area. Boat rentals at
some lakes. Phone 928/537-2326.

Hunting. Elk, deer, turkey, bear,
mountain lion, bighorn sheep, and
antelope. Phone 928/537-2326.

Motels/Motor Lodges

★ ★ **BEST WESTERN PAINT PONY
LODGE.** *581 W Deuce of Clubs Ave
(85901). 928/537-5773; fax 928/537-
5766; res 800/780-7234. www.best
western.com.* 50 rms, 2 story. Mid-
May-mid-Sept: S $69-$79; D $74-
$84; each addl $5; suites $129-$139;
higher rates hols; lower rates rest of
yr. Crib $5. Pet accepted. TV; cable
(premium). Complimentary continental bkfst. Restaurant 11 am-2
pm, 5-9 pm; wkend hrs vary. Rm
serv. Bar. Ck-out 11 am. Meeting
rms. Business servs avail. In-rm
modem link. Sundries. Free airport
transportation. X-country ski 17 mi.
Refrigerators; some fireplaces; microwaves avail. Cr cds: A, C, D, DS,
MC, V.

★ **DAYS INN.** *480 W Deuce of Clubs
Ave Hwy 60 (85901). 928/537-4356;
fax 928/537-8692. www.daysinn.com.*
122 rms, 2 story. S $54-$65; D $69-
$74; each addl $10; higher rates special events. Crib free. Pet accepted,
some restrictions. TV; cable (premium). Heated pool. Complimentary
full bkfst. Restaurant 6 am-10 pm.
Ck-out noon. Coin lndry. Meeting
rms. Business servs avail. Beauty
shop. Free airport transportation.

Refrigerators, microwaves. Cr cds: A, C, D, DS, JCB, MC, V.

Restaurant

★ **BRANDING IRON STEAK HOUSE.** *1261 E Deuce of Clubs Ave (85901).* 928/537-5151. Hrs: 11 am-2 pm, 5-10 pm; early-bird dinner Sun-Fri 5-7 pm. Closed Dec 25. Res accepted. Bar. Lunch $4.50-$9, dinner $10-$28. Child's menu. Specializes in steak, beef, seafood. Salad bar. Western saloon. Cr cds: C, D, DS, ER, MC, V.

Sierra Vista

(G-6) *See also Patagonia*

Pop 37,775 **Elev** 4,623 ft
Area code 520 **Zip** 85635
Information Chamber of Commerce, 21 E Wilcox; 520/458-6940

What to See and Do

Coronado National Forest. (see TUCSON) One of the larger sections of the forest lies to the south and west of Fort Huachuca Military Reservation. Picnicking, camping (fee). Parker Canyon Lake offers boating, fishing; camping (fee). A Ranger District office is located in Sierra Vista. Phone 520/670-4552.

Coronado National Memorial. Commanding view of part of Coronado's route through the Southwest in 1540-1542. Hiking trails, picnic grounds. Visitor center (daily; closed Jan 1, Dec 25). 16 mi S via AZ 92 to Coronado Memorial Rd then W on Montezuma Canyon Rd. Phone 520/366-5515. **FREE**

Fort Huachuca. Founded by the US Army in 1877 to protect settlers and travelers from hostile Apache raids, the fort is now the home of the US Army Intelligence Center, the Information Systems Command, and the Electronic Proving Ground. A historical museum is on the "Old Post," Boyd and Grierson Aves (daily; closed hols). The historic Old Post area (1885-1895) is typical of frontier post construction and is home to the post's ceremonial cavalry unit; open to public. Directions and visitor's pass at main gate, just west of Sierra Vista. Bronze statue of buffalo soldier. Phone 520/538-7111. **FREE**

Motel/Motor Lodge

★ **SUPER 8 MOTEL.** *100 Fab Ave (85635).* 520/459-5380; fax 520/459-6052; res 800/800-8000. www.inn works.com. 52 rms, 2 story. S $38-$48; D $42-$52; each addl $5; under 12 free; golf plans. Crib $4. Pet accepted; $10. TV; cable. Pool. Complimentary continental bkfst. Restaurant nearby. Ck-out 11 am. Business servs avail. Coin lndry. Refrigerators. Cr cds: A, D, DS, MC, V.

B&B/Small Inn

★★ **RAMSEY CANYON INN.** *29 E Ramsey Canyon Rd, Hereford (85638).* 520/378-3010; fax 520/378-1480. www.nature.org/arizona.com. 8 units: 6 rms in house, 2 cottages. No A/C. No rm phones. S, D $110. Children under 16 yrs cottages only. Complimentary full bkfst (exc cottages); afternoon refreshments. Ck-out 11 am, ck-in after 3 pm. Charming country inn with antiques throughout; bounded on 2 sides by Coronado National Forest. Situated on a winding mountain stream, in a wooded canyon, this is a hummingbird haven; peak season is Mar-Oct (2-day min). More than 10 species visit the inn's feeders during the year. Totally nonsmoking. Cr cds: MC, V.

Conference Center

★ **WINDEMERE HOTEL & CONFERENCE CENTER.** *2047 S Hwy 92 (85635).* 520/459-5900; fax 520/458-1347; toll-free 800/825-4656. www. windemere-hotel.com. 149 rms, 3 story. S $78; D $86; each addl $8; suites $150-$200; under 18 free; golf plans. Crib free. Pet accepted, some restrictions; $50 refundable. TV; cable. Heated pool; whirlpool. Coffee in rms. Complimentary bkfst buffet. Restaurant 6 am-2 pm, 4:30-9 pm. Rm serv. Bar 4-9 pm; entertainment.

Ck-out 11 am. Coin lndry. Meeting rms. Business servs avail. Valet serv. Health club privileges. Some refrigerators, microwaves. Cr cds: A, C, D, DS, ER, JCB, MC, V.

[D] [🐾] [≈] [⊠] [🔥] [SC]

Restaurant

★ ★ **MESQUITE TREE.** *AZ 92S and Carr Canyon Rd (85635).* 520/378-2758. Hrs: 5-9 pm; Sun, Mon to 8 pm. Closed Thanksgiving, Dec 25. Res accepted. No A/C. Bar. Dinner $7.25-$17.95. Child's menu. Specialties: prime rib, steak, Gulf shrimp scampi. Parking. Outdoor dining. Eclectic decor. Cr cds: A, C, D, DS, ER, MC, V.

[D] [SC] [⊣]

Springerville

(D-7) *See also Greer, McNary*

Pop 1,972 **Elev** 6,968 ft
Area code 928 **Zip** 85938
Information Round Valley Chamber of Commerce, 318 E Main St, PO Box 31; 928/333-2123

The headquarters for the Apache-Sitgreaves National Forests is located here.

What to See and Do

Apache-Sitgreaves National Forests. Combined into one administrative unit, these two forests (see SHOW LOW) encompass more than two million acres of diverse terrain. The Apache Forest (on US 180/666) features the Mt Baldy, Escudilla, and Bear Wallow wilderness areas and Blue Range Primitive Area, which are accessible only by foot or horseback, and the Coronado Trail (US 666), the route followed by the explorer in 1540. Lake and stream fishing; big-game hunting, picnicking, camping (fee charged in some campgrounds). Phone 928/333-4301.

Lyman Lake State Park. There are 1,180 acres bordering on a 1,500-acre reservoir near headwaters of the Little Colorado River; high desert, juniper country. Swimming, water-skiing, fishing (walleye, trout, channel and blue catfish), boating (ramps); hiking, picnicking (shelter), tent and trailer sites (dump station). Standard fees. 18 mi N on US 180/666. Phone 928/337-4441.

Madonna of the Trail. Erected in 1927, the statue is one of 12 identical monuments placed in states along the National Old Trails Highway to commemorate pioneer women who trekked west. Main St. Phone 928/333-2123.

Sunset Crater Volcano National Monument

See also Flagstaff

(15 mi N of Flagstaff on US 89, then 2 mi E on Sunset Crater/Wupatki Loop Road)

Between the growing seasons of 1064 and 1065, violent volcanic eruptions built a large cone-shaped mountain of cinders and ash called a cinder cone volcano. Around the base of the cinder cone, lava flowed from cracks, creating the Bonito Lava Flow on the west side of the cone and the Kana'a Lava Flow on the east side. The approximate date of the initial eruption was determined by examining tree rings of timber found in the remains of Native American pueblos at Wupatki National Monument (see).

This cinder cone, now called Sunset Crater, stands about 1,000 feet above the surrounding terrain. Mineral deposits around the rim stained the cinders, giving the summit a perpetual sunset hue, thus the name Sunset Crater. Along the Lava Flow Trail at the base of the cone, visitors will find "squeeze-ups" and other geologic features related to lava flows.

Park rangers are on duty all year. Do not attempt to drive off the roads; the cinders are soft, and the surrounding landscape is very fragile. The US Forest Service maintains a

campground (May-mid-September; fee) opposite the visitor center. Guided tours and naturalist activities are offered during the summer. Visitor center (daily; closed December 25). A 20-mile paved road leads to Wupatki National Monument (see). Phone 520/556-7042.

Tempe

(E-4) *See also Chandler, Glendale, Mesa, Phoenix, Scottsdale*

Founded 1871 **Pop** 158,625
Elev 1,160 ft **Area code** 480
Information Chamber of Commerce, 909 E Apache Blvd, PO Box 28500, 85285; 480/967-7891
Web www.tempechamber.org

Founded as a trading post by the father of former Senator Carl Hayden, this city is now the site of Arizona State University, the state's oldest institution of higher learning.

What to See and Do

Arizona State University. (1885) 52,000 students. Divided into 13 colleges. Incl on the 700-acre main campus are several museums and collections featuring meteorites; anthropology and geology exhibits; the Charles Trumbull Hayden Library, the Walter Cronkite School of Journalism, and the Daniel Noble Science and Engineering Library. In town center on US 60/80/89. Also on campus are

Grady Gammage Memorial Auditorium. (1964) Last major work designed by Frank Lloyd Wright. Guided tours (Mon-Fri). **FREE**

Nelson Fine Arts Center and Ceramics Reserach Center. Exhibits of American paintings and sculpture; Latin American art; comprehensive print collection; American crockery and ceramics. Tours avail. Phone 480/965-ARTS.

Niels Petersen House Museum. Built in 1892 and remodeled in the 1930s. Restoration retains characteristics of both the Victorian era and the 1930s.

Half-hr, docent-guided tours avail. (Tues-Thurs, Sat) 1414 W Southern Ave. Phone 480/350-5151. **FREE**

Professional sports.

Arizona Cardinals (NFL). Sun Devil Stadium, Mill at University Dr, ASU campus. Phone 800/999-1402.

Tempe Historical Museum. Exhibits relating the history of Tempe from the prehistoric Hohokam to the present; artifacts, videos, interactive exhibits. Research library. Gift shop. (Mon-Thurs; Sat-Sun; closed hols) 809 E Southern. Phone 480/350-5100. **FREE**

Special Events

Tostitos Fiesta Bowl. ASU Sun Devil Stadium. College football. Early Jan. ASU Sun Devil Stadium. Phone 480/350-0900.

Baseball Spring Training. Anaheim Angels. Phone 888/99-HALOS. Late Feb-late Mar. Tempe Diablo Stadium.

Spring Festival of the Arts. Last wkend Mar. Phone 480/965-2278.

Fall Festival of the Arts. First wkend Dec. Phone 480/965-2278.

Tostitos Fiesta Bowl Block Party. Incl games, rides, entertainment, pep rally, fireworks, food. Dec 31. Phone 480/350-0900.

Motels/Motor Lodges

★★ **COUNTRY INN & SUITES.** *1660 W Elliot (85284). 480/345-8585; fax 480/345-7461; res 800/456-4000. www.countryinns.com.* 139 kit. suites, 3 story. Jan-mid-May: kit. suites $79-$129, each addl $10; under 18 free; lower rates rest of yr. Crib free. Pet accepted, some restrictions. $50 deposit. TV; cable (premium). Pool; wading pool, whirlpool. Complimentary continental bkfst. Complimentary coffee in rms. Restaurant nearby. Ck-out noon. Coin lndry. Meeting rms. Business servs avail. Valet serv. Free airport transportation. Health club privileges. Refrigerators, microwaves. Cr cds: A, D, DS, MC, V.

★★ **COURTYARD BY MARRIOTT.** *601 S Ash Ave (85281). 480/966-2800; fax 480/829-8446; res 480/951-5400. www.courtyard.com.* 160 rms, 3 story.

Jan-mid-May: S, D $89-$169; suites $169-$179; under 18 free; lower rates rest of yr. Crib free. TV; cable (premium). Complimentary coffee in rms. Restaurant 6-10 am; Sat, Sun 7-11 am. Bar 4-11 pm. Ck-out noon. Meeting rms. Business servs avail. In-rm modem link. Valet serv. Coin lndry. Exercise equipt. Heated pool; whirlpool. Airport transportation. Some in-rm whirlpools; refrigerator, wet bar in suites. Some balconies. Cr cds: A, C, D, DS, MC, V.

D ⚹ ⊠ ⌧ 🔥 ⊠

★★ **HOLIDAY INN EXPRESS.** 5300 S Priest Dr (85283). 480/820-7500; fax 480/730-6626; toll-free 800/465-4329. www.holiday-inn.com. 160 rms, 4 story. Jan-Apr: S $80-$130; D $90-$140; each addl $5; under 18 free; lower rates rest of yr. Crib free. Pet accepted; $5/day. TV; cable (premium). Pool; whirlpool. Complimentary continental bkfst. Ck-out noon. Meeting rm. Business servs avail. Exercise equipt. Free airport transportation. Refrigerators. Cr cds: A, C, D, DS, MC, V.

D ⚹ ⊠ ⌧ 🔥 SC ⚹

★★ **HOLIDAY INN PHOENIX-TEMPE/ASU.** 915 E Apache Blvd (85281). 480/968-3451; fax 480/968-6262; res 800/465-4329. www.holiday-inn.com/phx-tempeasu. 190 rms, 4 story. Jan-Apr: S, D $64-$139; suites, studio rms $159-$189; under 19 free; lower rates rest of yr. Crib free. Pet accepted. TV; cable (premium). Heated pool; whirlpool, poolside serv. Complimentary coffee in rms. Restaurant 6 am-10 pm. Rm serv. Bar 11-1 am. Ck-out 1 pm. Free lndry facilities. Meeting rms. Business servs avail. Bellhops. Valet serv. Gift shop. Free airport transportation. Exercise equipt. Health club privileges. Refrigerators; microwaves avail. Some private patios, balconies. Cr cds: A, C, D, DS, JCB, MC, V.

D ⚹ ⊠ ⚹ ⌧ ⊠ 🔥

★★ **LA QUINTA INN.** 911 S 48th St (85281). 480/967-4465; fax 480/921-9172; toll-free 800/531-5900. www.laquinta.com. 128 rms, 3 story. Jan-Apr: S, D $99-$119; each addl $6; suites $129-$139; under 18 free; lower rates rest of yr. Crib free. Pet accepted, some restrictions. TV; cable (premium). Heated pool. Complimentary continental bkfst. Restau-

rant adj open 24 hrs. Ck-out noon, ck-in 1 pm. Coin lndry. Exercise rm. Business servs avail. Free airport transportation. Putting green. Some refrigerators. Cr cds: A, C, D, DS, MC, V.

D ⚹ ⊠ ⌧ 🔥 SC ⚹ ✈

★ **RODEWAY INN.** 1550 S 52nd St (85281). 480/967-3000; fax 480/966-9568; res 800/228-2000. www.rodewayinn.com. 100 rms, 2 story. Jan-Apr: S, D $79-$99; suite $119-$129; under 18 free; lower rates rest of yr. Crib free. Pet accepted, some restrictions; $10. TV; cable (premium). Heated pool; whirlpool. Complimentary continental bkfst. Complimentary coffee in rms. Restaurant adj 6 am-10 pm. Ck-out noon. Coin lndry. Free airport transportation. Refrigerators, microwaves avail. Cr cds: A, C, D, DS, MC, V.

⚹ ⊠ ⌧ 🔥 ⚹ D ✈

Hotels

★★★ **SHERATON PHOENIX AIRPORT HOTEL.** 1600 S 52nd St (85281). 480/967-6600; fax 480/966-2392; res 800/325-3535. www.sheraton.com/phoenixairport. 210 rms, 4 story. Jan-Apr: S $69-$245; D $79-$225; each addl $10; under 18 free; lower rates rest of yr. Crib free. TV; cable (premium). Pool; whirlpool, poolside serv. Coffee in rms. Restaurant 6 am-10 pm. Rm serv. Bar 11 am-midnight. Ck-out noon. Meeting rms. Business servs avail. Bellhops. Valet serv. Sundries. Exercise rm. Free airport transportation. Bathrm phones. Private patios, balconies. Cr cds: A, C, D, DS, MC, V.

D ⊠ ⚹ ✈ ⌧ 🔥 SC

★★ **TWIN PALMS.** 225 E Apache Blvd (85281). 480/967-9431; fax 480/968-1877; toll-free 800/367-0835. www.twinpalmshotel.com. 140 rms, 7 story. Jan-Apr: S $99-$129; D $109-$159; each addl $10; under 18 free; lower rates rest of yr. Crib free. TV; cable (premium). Complimentary coffee in rms. Restaurant adj open 24 hrs. Bar 4 pm-1 am. Ck-out noon. Meeting rms. Business servs avail. Coin lndry. Free airport transportation. Health club privileges. Pool. Microwaves, refrigerators avail. Many balconies. Cr cds: A, C, D, DS, JCB, MC, V.

⬛ ⬛ **D** ⬛ ⬛

★★ **WYNDHAM BUTTES RESORT.** *2000 Westcourt Way (85282). 602/225-9000; fax 602/438-8622; toll-free 800/843-1986. www.wyndham. com.* 353 rms, 4-5 story. Jan-May: S, D $175-$325; each addl $10; suites $425-$700; under 18 free; golf, wkend plans; lower rates rest of yr. Crib $10. TV; cable (premium). 2 pools; poolside serv. Complimentary coffee in rms. Restaurants 6 am-10 pm; Fri, Sat to 11 pm (see also TOP OF THE ROCK). Rm serv 5:30 am-midnight. Bar 5 pm-1 am. Ck-out noon. Meeting rms. Business center. Concierge. Gift shop. Lighted tennis. Exercise equipt; sauna. Massage. Minibars. Some private patios. Large resort built into mountainside. Heliport. Luxury level. Cr cds: A, C, D, DS, ER, JCB, MC, V.

D ⬛ ⬛ ⬛ ⬛ ⬛ ⬛

Resorts

★★★ **FIESTA INN RESORT.** *2100 S Priest Dr (85282). 480/967-1441; fax 480/967-0224; toll-free 800/501-7590. www.fiestainnresort.com.* 270 rms, 3 story. Jan-May: S, D $65-$179; each addl $10; suites $225-$275; under 18 free; lower rates rest of yr. Crib free. TV; cable (premium), VCR avail (free movies). Heated pool; whirlpool, poolside serv. Coffee in rms. Restaurant 6:30 am-10 pm. Rm serv. Bar 11-1 am. Ck-out 11 am. Meeting rms. Business center. Bellhops. Valet serv. Concierge. Sundries. Free airport transportation. Lighted tennis, pro. 18-hole golf privileges, putting green, driving range, pro. Exercise equipt; sauna. Refrigerators. Mexican antiques. Cr cds: A, D, DS, MC, V.

⬛ ⬛ ⬛ ⬛ ⬛ ⬛ **D**

★★★ **TEMPE MISSION PALMS.** *60 E 5th St (85281). 480/894-1400; fax 480/968-7677; toll-free 800/547-8705. www.destinationhotels.com.* 303 rms, 4 story. Jan-May: S, D $159-$279; each addl $10; suites $395-$495; under 18 free; golf packages; higher rates: Fiesta Bowl, art festival; lower rates rest of yr. Crib free. TV; cable (premium). Heated pool; whirlpool, poolside serv. Complimentary coffee

in rms. Restaurant 6:30 am-9:30 pm. Bar 11-1 am. Ck-out noon. Convention facilities. Business center. In-rm modem link. Shopping arcade. Free airport transportation. Lighted tennis. Exercise equipt. Health club privileges. Refrigerator in suites. Cr cds: A, C, D, DS, JCB, MC, V.

D ⬛ ⬛ ⬛ ⬛ ⬛ ⬛ ⬛

All Suites

★★★ **EMBASSY SUITES PHOENIX/TEMPE.** *4400 S Rural Rd (85282). 480/897-7444; fax 480/897-6830; res 800/362-2779. www.embassy suitestempe.com.* 224 suites, 1-3 story. Jan-Apr: S, D $119-$199; each addl $10; under 18 free; wkend rates; higher rates for special events; lower rates rest of yr. Crib free. TV; cable (premium). Heated pool; whirlpool, poolside serv. Complimentary full bkfst. Coffee in rms. Restaurant 11 am-10 pm; Fri, Sat to 11 pm. Bar 11-1 am. Ck-out 1 pm. Meeting rms. Business servs avail. Free airport transportation. Exercise equipt; sauna. Game rm. Coin lndry. Refrigerators, microwaves. Private patios, balconies. Cr cds: A, C, D, DS, MC, V.

D ⬛ ⬛ ⬛ ⬛ ⬛ **SC**

★★ **INN SUITES HOTELS TEMPE/PHOENIX AIRPORT.** *1651 W Baseline Rd (85283). 480/897-7900; fax 480/491-1008; res 800/841-4242. www.innsuites.com.* 170 rms, 2-3 story, 79 kits. Jan-Apr: S, D $79-$129; suites, kit. units $99-$139; under 18 free; lower rates rest of yr. Crib free. Pet accepted; $25. TV; cable (premium). Heated pool; whirlpool. Playground. Complimentary continental bkfst. Complimentary coffee in rms. Restaurant 6 am-2 pm, 4-10 pm; Oct-Apr 6 am-10 pm. Ck-out noon. Coin lndry. Meeting rms. Business center. In-rm modem link. Valet serv. Free airport transportation. Lighted tennis. Exercise equipt. Refrigerators, microwaves. Some private patios, balconies. Grills. Cr cds: A, C, D, DS, MC, V.

D ⬛ ⬛ ⬛ ⬛ ⬛ ⬛ **SC** ⬛

Restaurants

★★ **BYBLOS.** *3332 S Mill Ave (85282). 480/894-1945.* Hrs: 11 am-3 pm, 5-10 pm; Fri, Sat to 10:30 pm;

Sun 4-9:30 pm. Closed Mon; Jan 1, Dec 25; 1st 2 wks July. Res accepted. Mediterranean menu. Bar. Lunch $4.75-$6.95, dinner $7.95-$16.95. Child's menu. Specializes in lamb, seafood, vegetarian dishes. Own baking. Belly dancing last Sun of month. Family-owned. Cr cds: A, D, DS, MC, V.

D ⊒

★★ **HOUSE OF TRICKS.** *114 E 7th St (85281). 480/968-1114. www.house oftricks.com.* Hrs: 11 am-10 pm. Closed Sun; most major hols; also first 2 wks Aug. Res accepted. Contemporary Amer menu. Patio bar. A la carte entrees: lunch $5.95-$8.50, dinner $12.75-$20. Specialty: ahi tuna with lavender and herb crust. Parking. Outdoor dining. Restored cottage (1918); hardwood and tile floors, stone fireplace. Cr cds: A, D, DS, MC, V.

D

★★ **LO CASCIO.** *2210 N Scottsdale Rd (85281). 602/949-0334.* Hrs: 11 am-2 pm, 5-10 pm; Fri, Sat 5-11 pm; early bird 5-6 pm. Closed hols; also Mon during summer. Res accepted. Southern Italian menu. Serv bar. Lunch $5.50-$7.95, dinner $7.95-$16.95. Child's menu. Specialties: penne alforno, mozzarella marinara. Cr cds: A, DS, MC, V.

D SC ⊒

★ **MACAYO.** *300 S Ash Ave (85281). 480/966-6677. www.macayo.com.* Hrs: 11 am-11 pm; Fri, Sat to midnight. Mexican menu. Bar. Lunch $4.50-$7.75, dinner $7.25-$11.50. Child's menu. Specialty: Baja chimichanga. Parking. Outdoor dining. Old Mexican-style cantina, located in a converted train station. Cr cds: A, D, DS, MC, V.

D SC ⊒

★★ **MARCELLO'S PASTA GRILL.** *1701 E Warner Rd (85284). 480/831-0800. www.marcellospastagrill.com.* Hrs: 11 am-10 pm; Fri to 11 pm; Sat 4-11 pm; Sun 4-9 pm. Closed some major hols. Res accepted. Italian menu. Bar. Lunch $4.95-$7.50, dinner $8.95-$16.95. Child's menu. Specializes in veal, seafood, pasta. Outdoor dining. Italian decor. Cr cds: A, D, MC, V.

D ⊒

★ **SIAMESE CAT.** *5034 S Price Rd (85282). 480/820-0406. www.the siamesecat.com.* Hrs: 11 am-2 pm, 5-9 pm; Fri, Sat to 10 pm. Closed some major hols. Res accepted. Thai menu. Wine, beer. Lunch $3.95-$9.95, dinner $4.95-$9.95. Specialties: pad ta lae, pad pak gratiem, prik Thai. Cr cds: A, MC, V.

★★ **TOP OF THE ROCK.** *2000 Westcourt Way (85282). 602/431-2370. www.wyndham.com.* Hrs: 5-10 pm; Fri, Sat to 11 pm; Sun brunch 10 am-2 pm. Res accepted. Bar to 1 am. Dinner $23-$31. Child's menu. Specialties: lobster Napoleon. Entertainment Fri, Sat. Valet parking. Outdoor dining. Comfortable dining with view of mountains and city. Cr cds: A, C, D, DS, ER, MC, V.

D

Tombstone

(G-6) *See also Bisbee*

Founded 1879 **Pop** 1,504 **Elev** 4,540 ft **Area code** 520 **Zip** 85638
Information Tombstone Chamber of Commerce, PO Box 995; 888/457-3929.
Web www.tombstone.org

Shortly after Ed Schieffelin discovered silver, Tombstone became a rough-and-tumble town with saloons, bawdyhouses, and lots of gunfighting. Tombstone's most famous battle was that of the O.K. Corral, between the Earps and the Clantons in 1881. Later, water rose in the mines and could not be pumped out; fires and other catastrophes occurred, but Tombstone was "the town too tough to die." Now a health and winter resort, it is also a museum of Arizona frontier life. In 1962, the town was designated a National Historic Landmark by the US Department of the Interior.

What to See and Do

Bird Cage Theatre. Formerly a frontier cabaret (1880s), this famous landmark has seen many of the West's most famous characters. In its heyday it was known as "the wildest and wickedest nightspot between

Basin Street and the Barbary Coast." The upstairs "cages," where feathered girls plied their trade, inspired the refrain, "only a bird in a gilded cage." Original fixtures, furnishings. (Daily) Allen and 6th Sts. Phone 520/457-3421. ¢¢

Boothill Graveyard. About 250 marked graves, some with unusual epitaphs, many of famous characters. NW on US 80 W. Phone 520/457-9344.

Crystal Palace Saloon. Restored. Dancing Fri-Sun eves. (Daily) 5th and Allen Sts. Phone 520/457-3611.

Office of the Tombstone Epitaph. The oldest continuously published newspaper in Arizona, founded in 1880; it is now a monthly journal of Western history. Office houses collection of early printing equipt. (Daily) 5th St, near Allen St. Phone 520/457-2211. **FREE**

O.K. Corral. Restored stagecoach office and buildings surrounding gunfight site; life-size figures; Fly's Photography Gallery (adj) has early photos. (Daily; closed Dec 25) Allen St, between 3rd and 4th Sts. Phone 520/457-3456. ¢¢¢

Rose Tree Inn Museum. Largest rose bush in the world, spreading over 9,000 sq ft; blooms in Apr. Museum in 1880 boarding house (oldest house in town); original furniture, documents. (Daily; closed Dec 25) Toughnut and 4th Sts. Phone 520/457-3326. ¢¢

St. Paul's Episcopal Church. (1882) Oldest Protestant church still in use in state; original fixtures. N 3rd and Safford Sts.

Tombstone Courthouse State Historic Park. (1882) Victorian building (1882) houses exhibits recalling Tombstone in the turbulent 1880s.

GUNFIGHTS AND SALOONS

Begin exploring "The Town too Tough to Die" on Toughnut Street. At the corner of Third and Toughnut, explore the gorgeous Cochise County Courthouse, now a museum and state historic park. Built in 1882, it's a beautiful testament to Victorian Neoclassical architecture; check out the town gallows in the courtyard, and browse the book shop. To the west a few steps, Victoria's B&B Wedding Chapel (on Toughnut between Second and Third) is located in an 1880s home. To the east one block, the Rose Tree Museum at Fourth and Toughnut occupies another 1880s home; inside its courtyard is a century-old rose tree that blooms every April and covers an 8,000-square-foot space. At Fifth and Toughnut streets, Nellie Cashman's is the oldest restaurant in town, specializing in homemade pies.

Now follow Third Street north one block to Allen Street, essentially the main drag of historic Tombstone. Stop in between Third and Fourth streets on Allen, where the Historama offers a 30-minute presentation (narrated by Vincent Price) that tells the town story in film and animated figures. Next door, see life-size figures in the OK Corral, the alleged site of the legendary gunfight between the Earp and Clanton brothers and Doc Holliday. (Actually, it took place on nearby Fremont Street.) Across the street, Tombstone Art Gallery offers works by local artisans and crafters.

On the corner of Allen and Fifth streets, the Crystal Palace Saloon has been restored to its 1879 glory, looking every bit the lusty watering hole and gambling den of legend. In the block of Allen between Fifth and Sixth streets, the Prickly Pear Museum is chock-full of military history; on Allen at Sixth, find the famous old Bird Cage Theater Museum. The Pioneer Home Museum, between Eighth and Ninth streets, continues telling the rowdy-days story.

From Fifth and Allen, walk north a half-block to the Tombstone Epitaph Museum to see an 1880s printing press and newsroom equipment and buy a copy of the 1881 Epitaph report of the OK Corral shoot-out. Continue walking north on Fifth, crossing Fremont Street and turning left onto Safford Street. Walk west on Safford three blocks to Second and Safford, where the two-story adobe called Buford House B&B occupies an 1880s home bearing a National Historic Landmark plaque.

Tombstone and Cochise County history. (Daily; closed Dec 25) Toughnut and 3rd Sts, off US 80. Phone 520/457-3311. ¢¢

Tombstone Historama. Electronic diorama and film narrated by Vincent Price tell story of Tombstone. (Daily; hrly showings; closed Dec 25) Adj to O.K. Corral. Phone 520/457-3456. ¢¢

Special Events

Territorial Days. Commemorates formal founding of the town. Fire-hose cart races and other events typical of a celebration in Arizona's early days. Second wkend Mar. Phone 520/457-9317.

Wyatt Earp Days. Also fiddlers' contests. Memorial Day wkend. Phone 520/457-3434.

Wild West Days and Rendezvous of Gunfighters. Labor Day wkend. Phone 520/457-9465.

Helldorado. Three days of reenactments of Tombstone events of the 1880s. Third wkend Oct.

Motel/Motor Lodge

★ ★ **BEST WESTERN LOOKOUT LODGE.** *US Hwy 80 (85638). 520/457-2223; fax 520/457-3870; res 800/780-7234. www.bestwestern.com.* 40 rms, 2 story. S $58-$65; D $62-$69; each addl $5; under 12 free; higher rates special events. Crib free. Pet accepted, some restrictions; $50 and $5/day. TV; cable. Heated pool. Complimentary continental bkfst. Restaurant nearby. Ck-out 11 am. Business servs avail. Cr cds: A, C, D, DS, MC, V.

Restaurants

★ **BIG NOSE KATE'S SALOON.** *417 E Allen St (85638). 520/457-3107. www.bignosekates.com.* Hrs: 11 am-8 pm. Closed Thanksgiving, Dec 25. Mexican menu. No A/C. Bar 10 am-10 pm; Thurs-Sat to midnight. Lunch, dinner $2.50-$16.95. Child's menu. Specializes in authentic Mexican entrees, burgers, pizza. Entertainment. Street parking. Outdoor dining. Original 1880 bldg; mine shaft at basement level; retail Western wear. Cr cds: MC, V.

★ **LONGHORN.** *501 E Allen (85638). 520/457-3405. www.bignose kates.com.* Hrs: 7 am-8 pm. Closed Thanksgiving, Dec 25. Res accepted. Wine, beer. Bkfst $2.50-$10, lunch, dinner $5.95-$29.95. Specialties: hamburgers, mesquite-smoked ribs, T-bone steak. Street parking. Western decor. Family-owned. Cr cds: MC, V.

★ **NELLIE CASHMAN'S.** *117 S 5th (85638). 520/457-2212.* Hrs: 7 am-9 pm. No A/C. Bkfst $3-$8, lunch $3.50-$7, dinner $9-$22. Specializes in chicken, pork, steak. Outdoor dining. In historic adobe building (1879); established in 1882 by Nellie Cashman, "the angel of Tombstone," at height of silver boom. Antique decor. Cr cds: A, DS, MC, V.

Tucson

(F-5) *See also Nogales*

Founded 1775 **Pop** 486,669
Elev 2,386 ft **Area code** 520
Information Metropolitan Tucson Convention & Visitors Bureau, 110 S Church Ave, #7199, 85701; 520/624-1817
Web www.visittucson.org

Tucson (TOO-sahn) offers a rare combination of delightful Western living, colorful desert and mountain scenery, and cosmopolitan culture.

It is one of several US cities that developed under four flags. The Spanish standard flew first over the Presidio of Tucson, built to withstand Apache attacks in 1776. Later, Tucson flew under the flags of Mexico, the Confederate States and, finally, the United States.

Today, Tucson is a resort area, an educational and copper center, a cotton and cattle market, headquarters for the Coronado National Forest, and a place of business for several large industries. Health-seekers, under proper medical advice, nearly always find relief. The city's shops, restaurants, resorts, and points of interest are varied and numerous.

What to See and Do

Arizona Historical Society Fort Lowell Museum. Reconstruction of commanding officer's quarters. Exhibits, period furniture. (Wed-Sat; closed hols) 2900 N Craycroft Rd; in Fort Lowell County Park, N end of Craycroft Rd. Phone 520/885-3832. **FREE**

Arizona Historical Society Frémont House Museum. (ca 1880) Adobe house restored and furnished in period style. Once occupied by John C. Frémont's daughter, Elizabeth, when he was territorial governor (1878-1881). Special programs all yr, incl slide shows on Arizona history (Sat; free) and walking tours of historic sites (Nov-Mar, Sat; fee; registration in advance). Museum (Wed-Sat). 151 S Granada Ave, in the Tucson Community Center Complex, Downtown. Phone 520/622-0956.

Arizona Historical Society Museum, Library, and Archives. Exhibits depicting state history from the Spanish colonial period to present; Arizona mining hall; photography gallery. Research library (Mon-Sat) contains collections on Western history; manuscripts. (Mon-Sat, also Sun afternoons; closed hols) 949 E 2nd St at Park Ave. Phone 520/628-5774. **Donation**

Catalina State Park. A 5,500-acre desert park with vast array of plants and wildlife; bird area (nearly 170 species). Nature and horseback riding trails, hiking, trail access to adj Coronado National Forest; picnicking, camping (dump station). Standard fees. 9 mi N on US 77. Phone 520/628-5798. ¢¢

Colossal Cave. Fossilized marine life provides evidence of ocean that once covered Arizona desert. 70°F yr-round. Forty-five-min to one-hr guided tours. (Daily) 19 mi SE on I-10 to Vail, exit 279, then 7 mi N on Colossal Cave Rd. Phone 520/647-7275. ¢¢

Columbia University's Biosphere 2 Center. An ambitious attempt to learn more about our planet's ecosystems began in Sept 1991 with the first of a series of missions in this 3½-acre, glass-enclosed, self-sustaining model of Earth. Isolated from the outside, a rotating crew of researchers rely entirely on the air, water, and food generated and recycled within the structure. It contains over 3,500 species of plants and animals in multiple ecosystems, incl a tropical rain forest with an 85-ft-high mountain. Visitors are permitted within the biospherian living areas of the enclosure. They may also view the interior from outside as well as enjoy many other exhibits located throughout the campus. Because of variance in research schedule, the biospherian crew may not always be present. Walking tours (wear comfortable shoes) incl multimedia introduction to Biosphere 2. Visitor center, gift shop, restaurant. (Daily; closed Dec 25) 35 mi N on US 89 to AZ 77 milepost 96.5, then ½ mi N to Biosphere 2 Rd. Phone 520/896-6200. ¢¢¢¢

Coronado National Forest. Mt Lemmon Recreation Area, part of this forest (almost two million acres), offers fishing; bird-watching, hiking, horseback riding, picnicking, skiing, camping (fee). Madera Canyon offers recreation facilities, lodge. Peña Blanca Lake and Recreation Area (see NOGALES) and the Chiricahua Wilderness area in the southeast corner of the state are part of the 12 areas that make up the forest. The Santa Catalina Ranger District, located in Tucson (phone 520/749-8700), has its headquarters at Sabino Canyon, 12 mi NE on Sabino Canyon Rd; a ¼-mi nature trail begins at the headquarters, as does a shuttle ride almost 4 mi into Sabino Canyon (fee). Northeast, east and south of city. Phone 520/670-4552.

Gray Line bus tours. Contact PO Box 1991, 85702. Phone 520/622-8811.

Greyhound racing. Pari-mutuel wagering. Tucson Greyhound Park, S 4th Ave at 36th St. Phone 520/884-7576.

International Wildlife Museum. Incl hundreds of wildlife exhibits from around the world; hands-on, interactive computer displays; videos; cafe. (Daily; closed Thanksgiving, Dec 25) 4800 W Gates Pass Rd, on Speedway 5 mi W of I-10. Phone 520/617-1439. ¢¢¢

Kitt Peak National Observatory. (see). 44 mi SW on AZ 86, then 12 mi S on AZ 386.

Old Town Artisans. Restored adobe buildings (ca 1850s) in the historic El Presidio neighborhood are a marketplace for handcrafted Southwestern and Latin American art. Courtyard cafe. (Daily; closed hols) 186 N Meyer Ave. Phone 520/623-6024.

Picacho Peak State Park. (see). 40 mi NW on I-10, Picacho Peak exit.

Pima Air & Space Museum. Aviation history exhibits with an outstanding collection of more than 250 aircraft, both military and civilian. (Daily; closed Thanksgiving, Dec 25) 6000 E Valencia Rd; I-10 to exit 267 (Valencia Rd), then E. Phone 520/574-0462. ¢¢

Reid Park. Picnicking; zoo; rose garden; outdoor performance center. (Daily exc Dec 25) 22nd and Country Club Rd. Phone 520/791-4873. ¢¢

Skiing. Mount Lemmon Ski Valley. Double chairlift, two tows; patrol, school, rentals; snack bar, restaurant. Fifteen runs, longest run one mi; vertical drop 900 ft. (Late Dec-mid-Apr, daily) Chairlift operates rest of yr (daily; fee). Nature trails. 35 mi NE via Mt Lemmon Hwy. Phone 520/576-1400.

Titan Missile Museum. Deactivated Titan II missile on display; memorabilia, models, rocket engine that powered the missile, support vehicles, UH1F helicopter, various exhibits. A one-hr guided tour begins with a briefing and incl visit down into the missile silo (may be strenuous; comfortable walking shoes required in the missile silo). The silo may also be viewed from a glass observation area located at the museum level. (Nov-Apr, daily; rest of yr, Wed-Sun). Located in Green Valley, approx 20 mi S via I-19, exit 69 (Duval Mine Rd), then W, past La Canada, turn right and follow signs. Phone 520/625-7736. ¢¢¢

Tohono Chul Park. A 37-acre preserve with more than 400 species of arid climate plants; nature trails; demonstration garden; geology wall; recirculating stream; ethnobotanical garden. Many varieties of wild birds visit the park. Exhibits, galleries, tea rm, and gift shops in restored adobe house (daily; closed July 4). (Daily) Ina and Oracle Rds, entrance at 7366 N Paseo del Norte. Phone 520/575-8468. **Donation**

Tucson Botanical Gardens. Gardens incl Mediterranean and landscaping plants; native wildflowers; tropical greenhouse; xeriscape/solar demonstration garden. Tours, botanical classes; special events. Picnic area (free). (Daily; closed hols) 2150 N Alvernon Way. Phone 520/326-9255. ¢¢

Tucson Mountain Park. More than 18,000 acres of saguaro cactus and mountain scenery. Picnic facilities. Gilbert Ray Campground (electric hookups, dump station; fee). 12 mi W, via AZ 86 (Ajo Way) about 6 mi to Kinney Rd, turn right. Phone 520/883-4200 or 520/740-2690. Also here is

Arizona-Sonora Desert Museum. Live desert creatures: mountain lions, beavers, bighorn sheep, birds, tarantulas, prairie dogs, snakes, otters, and many others. Nature trails through labeled desert botanical gardens. Underground earth sciences center with limestone caves; geological, mineral, and mining exhibits. Orientation rm provides information on natural history of deserts. (Daily) Phone 520/883-2702. ¢¢¢

★ **Tucson Museum of Art.** Housed in six renovated buildings within the boundaries of El Presidio Historic District (ca 1800). Pre-Columbian, Spanish colonial, and Western artifacts; decorative arts and paintings; art of the Americas; contemporary art and crafts; changing exhibits. Mexican heritage museum; historic presidio rm; 6,000-volume art resource library; art school. (Labor Day-Memorial Day, Mon-Sat, also Sun afternoons; rest of yr, Tues-Sun; closed hols) Free admission Sun. 140 N Main Ave. Phone 520/624-2333. ¢¢

University of Arizona. (1885) 35,000 students. The 343-acre campus is beautifully landscaped, with handsome buildings. Visitor center, located at University Blvd and Cherry Ave, has campus maps and information on attractions and activities. Tours (Mon-Sat). N Park Ave and E University Blvd. Phone 520/621-5130. On campus are

Arizona State Museum. Exhibits on the Native American cultures of Arizona and the Southwest from 10,000 yrs ago to the present. (Daily; closed hols) N Park Ave and

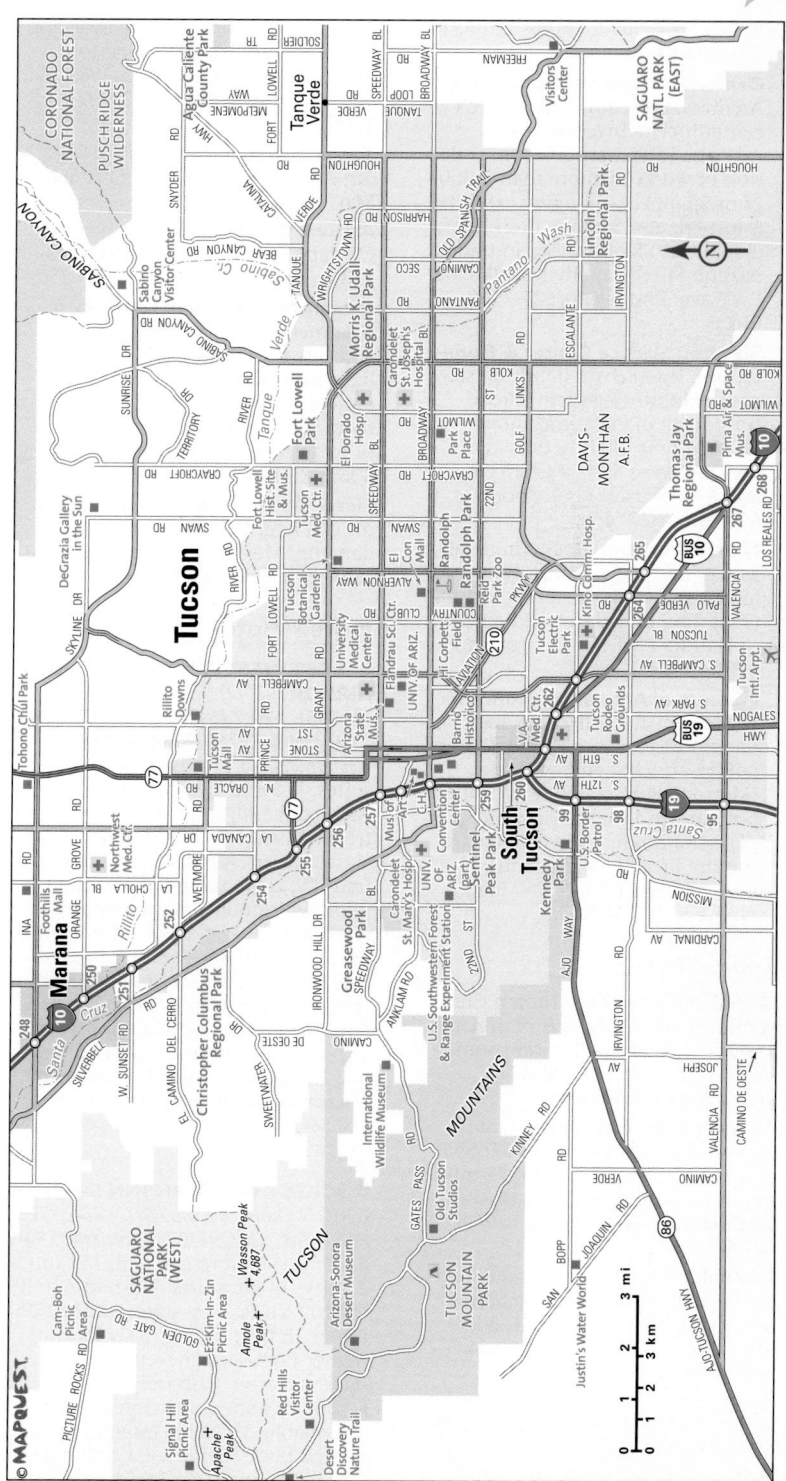

© MAPQUEST

E University Blvd. Phone 520/621-6281. **FREE**

Center for Creative Photography.
Archives, museum, and research
center incl archives of Ansel
Adams and Richard Avedon, collection of works by more than 2,000
photographers; changing exhibits.
(Mon-Fri, also Sat-Sun afternoons;
closed hols) S of pedestrian underpass on Speedway Blvd, 1 blk E of
Park Ave. Phone 520/621-7968.
FREE

Flandrau Science Center & Planetarium. Interactive, hands-on science exhibits (Tues-Sun; closed
hols; free); planetarium shows
(limited hrs). Nightly telescope
viewing (Wed-Sat). N Cherry Ave
and E University Blvd. Phone
520/621-7827. ¢¢

Mineral Museum. Rocks, minerals,
gemstones, and cuttings; paleontological materials. Meteorite exhibit.
(Tues-Sun; closed hols) Basement
of Flandrau Science Center. Phone
520/621-4227. ¢¢

Museum of Art. Art museum (free)
with extensive collection, incl
Renaissance, baroque, and contemporary art; changing exhibits.
(Mon-Fri, Sun; closed hols) Music
building and theater, in which
plays are produced by students.
Inquire locally for programs. N
Park Ave and E Speedway Blvd.
Phone 520/621-7567.

Special Events

Gem & Mineral Show. Tucson Convention Center. Displays of minerals;
jewelry; lapidary skills; Smithsonian
Institution collection. Mid-Feb.
Phone 520/322-5773.

Chrysler Classic of Tucson. Omni
Tucson National Golf Resort & Spa
and The Gallery Golf Club. $3-million tournament featuring top pros.
Late-Feb-early-Mar. Phone 520/297-2271.

Baseball. Colorado Rockies, Chicago
White Sox, and Arizona Diamondbacks spring training; late Feb-late
Mar. AAA Arizona Diamondbacks'
minor league team, Tucson
Sidewinders; Apr-Sept. Phone
520/434-1111. Hi Corbett Field, Tucson Electric Park.

Arizona Theatre Company. The Temple of Music & Art. The State Theatre
of Arizona performs both classic and
contemporary works. Eve performances Tues-Sun; matinees Wed, Sat,
and Sun. Phone 520/622-2823. Sept-May.

Tucson Symphony Orchestra. 2175 N
6th Ave. Phone 520/882-8585. Sept-May.

Arizona Opera. Tucson Convention
Center Music Hall. Phone 520/293-4336. Fri-Sun, Oct-Mar.

Tucson: Meet Yourself. Downtown.
Commemorates Tucson's cultural
and historic heritage with a torchlight pageant, Native American
dances, children's parade, Mexican
fiesta, frontier encampment, and
other events. Oct. Phone 520/882-3060. Also incl is

Fiesta del Presidio. Tucson Museum
of Art Plaza. Low-rider car show,
dancing, Mexican fiesta events, costumes, food. Phone 520/624-2333.

Motels/Motor Lodges

★ **BEST WESTERN INN AT THE
AIRPORT.** *7060 S Tucson Blvd
(85706). 520/746-0271; fax 520/889-7391; res 800/780-7234. www.best
western.com.* 149 rms, 3 story, 3
suites. Jan-mid-Apr: S, D $89-$119;
each addl $10; suites $150; under 18
free; wkend rates; higher rates gem
show; lower rates rest of yr. Crib
free. TV; cable (premium). Heated
pool; whirlpool. Complimentary
continental bkfst. Restaurant 5 am-2
pm, 5-10 pm. Bar 4 pm-midnight;
Sun to 10 pm. Ck-out noon. Meeting
rms. Business servs avail. Bellhops.
Sundries. Valet serv. Coin lndry. Free
airport transportation. Lighted tennis. Refrigerators; some balconies;
microwaves avail. Cr cds: A, C, D,
DS, MC, V.

[D] [icons]

★★ **BEST WESTERN INN SUITES.**
6201 N Oracle Rd (85704). 520/297-8111; fax 520/297-2935; res 800/554-4535. www.bestwestern.com. 159 rms,
2 story, 74 kit. suites. Jan-mid-Apr: S,
D $109-$129; 2-rm suites $129-$179;
under 18 free; wkend, wkly rates;
higher rates special events; lower
rates rest of yr. Crib free. Pet
accepted, some restrictions; $25
refundable. TV; cable (premium).
Heated pool; whirlpool. Complimentary bkfst buffet. Coffee in rms.
Restaurant adj 6 am-midnight. Rm

serv. Ck-out noon. Coin lndry. Meeting rms. Business servs avail. Valet serv. Lighted tennis. Exercise equipt. Refrigerators; some in-rm whirlpools. Some private patios, balconies. Grills. Microwaves avail. Cr cds: A, C, D, DS, MC, V.

"Gunfight" in Old Tucson

★★ **BEST WESTERN ROYAL SUN INN.** *1015 N Stone Ave (85705). 520/622-8871; fax 520/623-2267; res 800/545-8858. www.bestwestern.com.* 59 rms, 2 story, 20 suites. Jan-Apr: S, D $89-$129; each addl $10; suites $99-$159; higher rates gem show; lower rates rest of yr. Crib free. TV; cable (premium), VCR (movies). Heated pool; whirlpool, poolside serv. Coffee in rms. Restaurant 6 am-9 pm. Rm serv. Bar 4 pm-1 am. Meeting rm. Business servs avail. Valet serv. Bathrm phones, refrigerators; some wet bars. Balconies. Cr cds: A, C, D, DS, MC, V.

★★ **CLARION HOTEL RANDOLPH PARK.** *102 N Alvernon Way (85711). 520/795-0330; fax 520/326-2111; toll-free 800/227-6086. www.clarionhotel. com.* 157 rms, 3 story. Jan-Mar: S, D $109-$139; each addl $10; suites $99-$149; under 18 free; lower rates rest of yr. Crib free. Pet accepted, $50. TV; cable (premium). Heated pool; wading pool. Complimentary bkfst. Coffee in rms. Ck-out noon. Meeting rms. Business center. In-rm modem link. Exercise equipt. Refrigerators, microwaves. Some balconies. Cr cds: A, C, D, DS, ER, MC, V.

★★ **CLARION HOTEL TUCSON AIRPORT.** *6801 S Tucson Blvd (85706). 520/746-3932; fax 520/889-9934; toll-free 800/526-0550. www. clarionhoteltucson.com.* 189 rms, 2 story. Jan-Mar: S, D $99-$139; under 18 free; wkend rates; lower rates rest of yr. Crib free. TV; cable (premium). Heated pool; whirlpool, poolside serv. Complimentary bkfst buffet. Restaurant 6 am-11 pm. Rm serv. Bar. Ck-out noon. Coin lndry. In-rm modem link. Meeting rms. Business center. Bellhops. Valet serv. Sundries.

Free airport transportation. Exercise equipt. Refrigerators. Picnic tables, grills. Cr cds: A, C, D, DS, ER, JCB, MC, V.

★★ **CLARION SANTA RITA HOTEL & SUITES.** *88 E Broadway (85701). 520/622-4000; fax 520/620-0376; res 800/252-7466. www.clarion hotel.com.* 161 rms, 8 story, 31 suites. Mid-Jan-Easter: S, D $59-$129; each addl $10; suites $109-$289; under 18 free; higher rates special events; lower rates rest of yr. Crib free. Pet accepted, some restrictions; $25. TV; cable (premium). Complimentary bkfst. Complimentary coffee in rms. Restaurant (see also CAFE POCA COSA). No rm serv. Ck-out noon. Meeting rms. Business center. In-rm modem link. Coin lndry. Exercise equipt. Pool; whirlpool. Refrigerators, microwaves. Some balconies. Cr cds: A, C, D, DS, MC, V.

★★ **COURTYARD BY MARRIOTT.** *201 S Williams Blvd (85711). 520/745-6000; fax 520/745-2393; toll-free 800/228-9290. www.courtyard. com.* 153 rms, 3 story. Mid-Jan-Mar: S, D $159-$184; higher rates special events (2-3-day min); lower rates rest of yr. Crib free. TV; cable (premium). Complimentary coffee in rms. Restaurant 6-10 am, 5-10 pm. Rm serv from 5 pm. Bar 4-11 pm. Ck-out noon. In-rm modem link. Meeting rms. Valet serv. Sundries. Exercise equipt. Pool; whirlpool, poolside serv. Some balconies. Cr cds: A, D, DS, MC, V.

[D] [≈] [🛇] [🛇] [🔥] [SC]

★★ **COURTYARD BY MARRIOTT AIRPORT.** 2505 E Executive Dr (85706). 520/573-0000; fax 520/573-0470; toll-free 800/321-2211. www.courtyard.com. 149 rms, 3 story. Jan-mid-May: S, D $129-$159; under 12 free; lower rates rest of yr. Crib free. TV; cable (premium). Heated pool; whirlpool. Complimentary coffee in rms. Restaurant 6-10 am, 5-10 pm; Sat, Sun 7-11 am. Bar 4-11 pm. Ck-out noon. Coin lndry. Meeting rms. Business servs avail. In-rm modem link. Valet serv. Free airport transportation. Exercise equipt. Some microwaves; refrigerator avail. Balconies, patios. Cr cds: A, D, DS, MC, V.

[D] [≈] [🛇]

★★ **HAMPTON INN TUCSON AIRPORT.** 6971 S Tucson Blvd (85706). 520/889-5789; fax 520/889-4002; res 800/426-7866. www.hamptoninn.com. 126 units, 4 story. Jan-Apr: S $59-$99; D $69-$109; suites $119-$129; under 18 free; higher rates special events; lower rates rest of yr. Crib free. TV; cable (premium). Heated pool; whirlpool. Complimentary continental bkfst. Coffee in rms. Restaurant nearby. Ck-out noon. Coin lndry. Business servs avail. Free airport transportation. Some refrigerators. Some private patios, balconies. Cr cds: A, C, D, DS, MC, V.

[D] [≈] [🛇] [🔥]

★★ **HOLIDAY INN PALO VERDE.** 4550 S Palo Verde Rd (85714). 520/746-1161; fax 520/741-1170; res 800/465-4329. www.holiday-inn.com. 299 rms, 6 story, 53 suites. Jan-mid-May: S, D $98-$175; each addl $10; suites $115-$185; under 18 free; lower rates rest of yr. Crib free. TV; cable (premium), VCR avail. Heated pool; whirlpool, poolside serv. Restaurant 6 am-2:30 pm; dining rm 5-10 pm. Rm serv. Bar 11 am-11 pm, Sun noon-10 pm. Ck-out noon. Coin lndry. Convention facilities. Business servs avail. Bellhops. Valet serv. Gift shop. Free airport transportation. Lighted tennis. Exercise equipt. Some refrigerators; microwaves avail. On 15 acres. Cr cds: A, C, D, DS, ER, JCB, MC, V.

[D] [🚴] [≈] [🛇] [🔥]

★ **RAMADA FOOTHILLS RESORT.** 6944 E Tanque Verde Rd (85715). 520/886-9595; fax 520/721-8466; res 800/272-6232. www.ramadafoothills tucson.com. 113 units, 2 story, 61 suites. Jan-Apr: S, D $80-$140; each addl $10; suites $100-$160; under 18 free; lower rates rest of yr. Crib free. Pet accepted, some restrictions; $25. TV; cable (premium). Heated pool; whirlpool. Continental bkfst. Restaurant adj 24 hrs. Ck-out noon. Coin lndry. Meeting rm. Business servs avail. In-rm modem link. Sauna. Refrigerators, microwaves. Cr cds: A, C, D, DS, ER, JCB, MC, V.

[D] [🐾] [≈] [🛇] [🔥] [SC]

★★ **SMUGGLERS INN.** 6350 E Speedway Blvd (85710). 520/296-3292; fax 520/722-3713; toll-free 866/517-6870. www.smugglersinn.com. 149 rms, 2 story, 28 kits. Jan-mid-May S $89-$119; D $99-$129; each addl $10; suites, kit. units $129-$139; under 15 free. Crib free. TV; cable (premium), VCR avail. Heated pool; whirlpool. Complimentary coffee in rms. Restaurant 6:30 am-9:30 pm. Rm serv. Bar 11:30-1 am; Sun from noon. Ck-out noon. Coin lndry. Meeting rms. Business servs avail. Valet serv. Bathrm phones. Private patios, balconies. Some refrigerators; microwaves avail. Cr cds: A, D, DS, MC, V.

[D] [≈] [🛇] [🔥]

Hotels

★★ **COUNTRY INN AND SUITES - TUCSON.** 7411 N Oracle Rd (85704). 520/575-9255; fax 520/575-8671; toll-free 800/456-4000. www.country inns.com. 156 kit. suites, 3 story. Jan-Apr: S, D $99-$134; under 18 free; lower rates rest of yr. Crib free. TV; cable (premium). Heated pool; whirlpool. Complimentary continental bkfst. Coffee in rms. Restaurant opp 6 am-10 pm. Ck-out noon. Coin lndry. Meeting rm. Business servs avail. In-rm modem link. Valet serv. Free airport, RR station, bus depot transportation. Putting green. Health club privileges. Refrigerators, microwaves. Gazebo. Cr cds: A, D, DS, MC, V.

[D] [≈] [🛇] [🔥] [SC]

★★★ **DOUBLETREE HOTEL REID PARK.** 445 S Alvernon Way (85711).

520/881-4200; fax 520/323-5225; res 800/222-8733. www.doubletreehotels. com. 295 rms, 2-9 story. Mid-Jan-mid-Apr: S, D $149-$179; each addl $20; suites $225-$375; under 18 free; lower rates rest of yr. Crib free. Pet accepted, some restrictions; $50 refundable. TV; cable (premium), VCR avail. Heated pool; whirlpool, poolside serv. Restaurant 6 am-11 pm. Rm serv. Bars 11-1 am, Sun from noon. Ck-out noon. Meeting rms. Business center. Bellhops. Valet serv. Gift shop. Beauty shop. Lighted tennis. Exercise equipt. Some private patios. Cr cds: A, C, D, DS, MC, V.

★★ **FOUR POINTS BY SHERA-TON.** 1900 E Speedway Blvd (85719). 520/327-7341; fax 520/327-0276; toll-free 800/325-3535. www.fourpoints. com. 150 rms, 7 story. Jan-Apr: S, D $85-$179; each addl $10; under 16 free; lower rates rest of yr. Crib free. TV; cable (premium). Heated pool; whirlpool. Restaurant 6:30 am-10 pm. Rm serv. Bar 11-1 am; Sun to 8 pm. Ck-out noon. Meeting rms. Some refrigerators. Cr cds: A, C, DS, JCB, MC, V.

★★★ **HILTON TUCSON EAST.** 7600 E Broadway, Tucson (85710). 520/721-5600; fax 520/721-5696; toll-free 800/445-8667. www.tucsoneast. hilton.com. 233 rms, 7 story. Jan-Mar: S $180-$214; D $190-$224; each addl $14; suites $250-$425; under 18 free; some wkend rates; lower rates rest of yr. Crib free. TV; cable (premium). Heated pool; whirlpool, poolside serv. Complimentary coffee in rms. Restaurant 6 am-10 pm; Sat, Sun from 6:30 am. Bar 11-1 am. Rm serv 6 am-11 pm. Ck-out noon. Convention facilities. Exercise rm. Business center. Concierge. Gift shop. Luxury level. Cr cds: A, D, DS, JCB, MC, V.

★★★ **MARRIOTT UNIVERSITY PARK.** 880 E 2nd St (85719). 520/792-4100; fax 520/882-4100; res 800/228-9290. www.marriott.com. 250 rms, 9 story. Mid-Jan-Apr: S, D $129-$164; each addl $15; suites $154-$194; under 18 free; wkend rates; golf plans; higher rates special events; lower rates rest of yr. Crib free. TV; cable (premium). Complimentary

coffee in rms. Restaurant 6 am-10 pm. Bar 10-1 am. Ck-out noon. Convention facilities. Business center. In-rm modem link. Concierge. Gift shop. Exercise equipt; sauna. Pool; whirlpool, poolside serv. Many balconies. Refrigerator, microwave, wet bar in suites. Luxury level. Cr cds: A, C, D, DS, ER, JCB, MC, V.

★★ **RADISSON HOTEL CITY CEN-TER.** 181 W Broadway Blvd (85701). 520/624-8711; fax 520/624-9963; toll-free 800/333-3333. www.radisson.com. 307 rms, 14 story. Oct-Apr: S, D $109-$139; each addl $10; suites $149-$220; under 18 free; lower rates rest of yr. Crib free. Pet accepted, some restrictions; $25 refundable. TV; cable (premium). Heated pool; poolside serv. Complimentary coffee in rms. Restaurant 6 am-2 pm, 5-10 pm. Bar 5 pm-midnight; wkends to 1 am. Ck-out noon. Convention facilities. Concierge. Gift shop. Free garage parking. Exercise equipt. Microwaves avail. Adj to Tucson Convention Center, music hall, theater, government offices. Cr cds: A, C, D, DS, JCB, MC, V.

★★ **SHERATON TUCSON HOTEL & SUITES.** 5151 E Grant Rd (85712). 520/323-6262; fax 520/325-2989; res 800/325-3535. www.sheraton.com. 216 rms, 4 story. Mid-Jan-May: S, D $139-$249; under 18 free; wkend rates; lower rates rest of yr. Crib free. TV; cable (premium). Heated pool; poolside serv. Coffee in rms. Complimentary continental bkfst. Restaurant 11:30 am-11 pm. Bar 11-1 am. Ck-out noon. Coin lndry. Meeting rms. Gift shop. Exercise equipt; sauna. Refrigerators; microwaves avail. Glass-enclosed elevators. Cr cds: A, C, D, DS, ER, JCB, MC, V.

Resorts

★★★ **ARIZONA INN.** 2200 E Elm St (85719). 520/325-1541; fax 520/881-5830; toll-free 800/933-1093. www.arizonainn.com. 71 rms, 2 story, 15 suites, 5 houses. Mid-Jan-mid-Apr: S, D $195-$239; suites $299-$369; houses $595-$2,500; each addl $15;

under 2 free (summer); lower rates rest of yr. Crib free. TV; cable, VCR avail. Heated pool. Dining rm 6-10 am, 11 am-2 pm, 6-10 pm. Rm serv. Pianist 6-10 pm. Ck-out noon, ck-in 3 pm. Luggage handling. Concierge serv. Business servs avail. In-rm modem link. Exercise equipt. Lighted tennis. Refrigerators, microwaves avail. Some patios, balconies. Adobe-style bldgs (1930) on 15 acres of landscaped lawns and gardens. Individually decorated rms with antiques. Cr cds: A, D, MC, V.

★★★ **THE GOLF VILLAS AT ORO VALLEY.** *10950 N La Canada (85737). 520/498-0098; fax 520/498-5150; toll-free 888/388-0098. www.the golfvillas.com.* 79 rms, 2 story. Jan-Apr: suites $289-$499; lower rates rest of yr. Crib avail. Pet accepted. Valet parking avail. Pool. TV; cable (premium), VCR avail. Complimentary coffee in rms, newspaper. Restaurant nearby. Ck-out noon, ck-in 3 pm. Business center. Bellhops. Concierge serv. Gift shop. Exercise equipt, sauna. Hiking trail. Picnic facilities. Cr cds: A, DS, JCB, MC, V.

★★★★ **THE LODGE AT VENTANA CANYON.** *6200 N Clubhouse Ln (85750). 520/577-1400; fax 520/577-4065; res 888/472-6229. www.wyndham.com.* This Wyndham Resort in the Santa Catalina foothills offers 50 intimate suites surrounded by 600 acres of Sonoran Desert terrain. The strikingly beautiful landscape is the backdrop for two 18-hole Tom Fazio-designed championship golf courses. Suites offer views of the golf courses, city lights, and mountains. Due to the resort's size, groups can reserve suites for exclusive use. 50 kit. units, 2 story. Jan-Apr: 1-bedrm $345-$495; 2-bedrm $495-$695; each addl $25; under 18 free; family, wkly, wkend, hol, golf plans; lower rates rest of yr. Serv charge $20/day. Crib $10. TV; cable, VCR avail. Heated pool; wading pool, whirlpool, poolside serv. Complimentary coffee in rms. Restaurant 7 am-10 pm. Rm serv. Box lunches, snacks, picnics. Bar 3 pm-midnight. Ck-out noon, ck-in 4 pm. Gift shop. Guest lndry. Bellhops. Concierge. Valet serv. Meeting rms. Business servs avail. Lighted tennis, pro. 36-hole golf, greens fee $56-

$199, pro, putting green, driving range. Bicycle rental. Jogging track. Exercise rm; sauna, steam rm. Lawn games. Massage. Minibars; microwaves avail. Balconies. Cr cds: A, C, D, DS, JCB, MC, V.

★★★★ **LOEWS VENTANA CANYON RESORT.** *7000 N Resort Dr (85750). 520/299-2020; fax 520/299-6832; res 800/235-6397. www.loews hotels.com.* This luxurious Sonoran Desert retreat has everything you'll need for entertainment or relaxation, including two PGA golf courses, a full-service spa, and eight tennis courts. Each room has a furnished patio and most have spectacular, desert-sunset views. Add to this 37,000 square feet of function space and a plethora of dining options and you might never need to leave. 398 rms, 4 story. Jan-May: S, D $249-$409; each addl $25; suites $750-$2,450; under 18 free; lower rates rest of yr. Crib free. TV; cable, VCR avail. Heated pool; whirlpool, poolside serv. Playground. Supervised children's activities; ages 4-12. Dining rms. Afternoon tea. Rm serv 24 hrs. Bar 11-1 am. Ck-out noon, ck-in 3 pm. Meeting rms. Business center. In-rm modem link. Concierge. Shopping arcade. Beauty shop. Lighted tennis. Two 18-hole golf, greens fee $80-$169, putting green, driving range, pro shop. Bicycle rentals. Lawn games. Extensive exercise rm; sauna, steam rm. Spa. Bathrm phones, minibars; some refrigerators; microwaves avail. Private patios, balconies. Picnic tables. Cr cds: A, D, DS, JCB, MC, V.

★★★★ **OMNI TUCSON NATIONAL GOLF RESORT & SPA.** *2727 W Club Dr (85742). 520/297-2271; fax 520/297-7544; toll-free 800/528-4856. www.omnihotels.com.* The main attractions at this resort are the three nine-hole golf courses and the long, picturesque fairways, which afford beautiful Sonoran Desert views. Rooms are a mixture of casita suites, haciendas, and traditional guestrooms nestled in the foothills of the Santa Catalina Mountains. Resident PGA professionals offer golf lessons, while more extensive clinics are conducted by John Jacob's School of Golf. 167 units, 2 story. Jan-Apr: S, D $229-$274; each addl $10; suites $254-$390; under 18 free; golf plans; lower rates rest of yr. Pet accepted, some restrictions; $50 deposit. TV; cable (premium), VCR avail. 2 pools; whirlpool, poolside serv. Restaurant 6:30 am-11 pm. Box lunches, snack bar. Bars 10-1 am; Sun from noon. Ck-out noon, ck-in 4 pm. Convention facilities. Business servs avail. Concierge. Gift shop. Barber, beauty shop. Sports dir. Lighted tennis, pro. 27-hole championship golf, greens fee $85-$179, pro, putting green, driving ranges. Soc dir. Entertainment. Exercise rm; sauna, steam rm. Massage. Lawn games. Wet bars, minibars; many fireplaces. Private patios, balconies. Cr cds: A, C, D, DS, JCB, MC, V.

🅳 ⬛ ⬛ ⬛ ⬛ ⬛ ⬛ ⬛

★ ★ ★ **SHERATON EL CONQUISTADOR.** *10000 N Oracle Rd (85737). 520/544-5000; fax 520/544-1222; res 800/325-3535. www.sheratonel conquistador.com.* 428 rooms, five restaurants, and 45,000 square feet of meeting space. 428 rms. Jan-May: S, D $230-$300; suites, studio rms $275-$610; under 17 free; golf, tennis plans; lower rates rest of yr. Crib free. Pet accepted, some restrictions. TV; cable (premium), VCR avail. Pools; whirlpools, poolside serv. Supervised child's activities; ages 5-12. Coffee in rms. Dining rms 6 am-11 pm (see also LAST TERRITORY). Rm serv to 2 am. Bar to 1 am; Sun from 10:30 am; entertainment. Ck-out noon, ck-in 4 pm. Convention facilities. Business center. Bellhops. Valet serv. Concierge. Shopping arcade. Beauty shop. Pro shop. Sports dir. Lighted tennis, pro. 45-hole golf, greens fee (incl cart) $95-$135 ($48-$60 in summer), pro, putting green, driving range. Bicycles. Bkfst and evening horseback rides; hayrides. Exercise rm; sauna. Massage. Lawn games. Basketball. Hiking and nature trails. Minibars; some bathrm phones, wet bars, fireplaces; microwaves avail. Private patios, balconies. Cr cds: A, C, D, DS, ER, JCB, MC, V.

🅳 ⬛ ⬛ ⬛ ⬛ ⬛ ⬛ ⬛ ⬛

★ ★ ★ **THE WESTIN LA PALOMA.** *3800 E Sunrise Dr (85718). 520/742-6000; fax 520/577-5878; res 800/937-8461. www.westinlapalomaresort.com.* 487 units, 3 story. Jan-May: S, D $319-$480; each addl $30; suites $445-$1,995; under 18 free; golf, tennis plans; lower rates rest of yr. Serv charge $10/day. Crib free. TV; cable (premium). 2 pools; whirlpool, poolside serv, water slide. Supervised children's activities; ages 3-12 yrs. Coffee in rms. Dining rm 6:30 am-10 pm (see also JANOS). Box lunches, snack bar, picnics. Rm serv 24 hrs. Bar 11-1 am. Ck-out noon, ck-in 4 pm. Package store 2 mi. Convention facilities. Business center. Bellhops. Valet serv. Concierge. Shopping arcade. Valet parking. 10 lighted tennis courts (4 clay), pro. 27-hole golf (Jack Nicklaus Signature Design), greens fee $185-$205, pro, putting green, driving range. Lawn games. Horseback privileges 15 mi. Rec rm. Exercise rm; steam rm. Massage. Some fireplaces; microwaves avail; whirlpool, sauna in suites. Cr cds: A, C, D, DS, JCB, MC, V.

🅳 ⬛ ⬛ ⬛ ⬛ ⬛ ⬛ ⬛

★ ★ ★ **WESTWARD LOOK RESORT.** *245 E Ina Rd (85704). 520/297-1151; fax 520/297-9023; toll-free 800/722-2500. www.westward look.com.* 243 rms, 2 story. Mid-Jan-Apr: S, D $169-$369; each addl $10; under 16 free; golf plans; hol rates; higher rates special events; lower rates rest of yr. Crib free. Pet accepted, some restrictions; $75. TV; cable (premium). 3 heated pools; whirlpools. Complimentary coffee in rms. Restaurants 6 am-10 pm (see also GOLD ROOM). Rm serv. Box lunches, snacks, picnics. Bar 4 pm-1 am; entertainment Thurs-Sat. Ck-out noon, ck-in 4 pm. Coin lndry 6 mi. Spa. Gift shop. Grocery ¼ mi. Bellhops. Valet serv. Concierge. Meeting rms. Business center. Sports dir. Lighted tennis, pro. Lawn games. Exercise rm. Some refrigerators, minibars. Balconies/patios. Bicycles. Cr cds: A, C, D, DS, JCB, MC, V.

🅳 ⬛ ⬛ ⬛ ⬛ ⬛ ⬛ ⬛

B&Bs/Small Inns

★ ★ **ADOBE ROSE INN BED AND BREAKFAST.** *940 N Olsen Ave (85719). 520/318-4644; fax 520/325-0055; toll-free 800/328-4122. www. aroseinn.com.* 7 rms, 4 with shower only, 2 suites. 4 rm phones; phones in suites. Jan-mid-May: S $95-$115;

D $95-$135; each addl $15; suites $150; wkly rates; higher rates special events; lower rates rest of yr. Children over 10 yrs only. Pool; whirlpool. TV; cable, some VCRs. Complimentary full bkfst. Restaurant nearby. Ck-out 11 am, ck-in 3-6 pm. Luggage handling. Concierge serv. Refrigerators; microwaves avail. Picnic tables. Totally nonsmoking. Cr cds: A, MC, V.

★★ **CAR-MAR'S SOUTHWEST BED AND BREAKFAST.** 6766 W Oklahoma St (85735). 520/578-1730; fax 520/578-7272; toll-free 888/578-1730. www.members.aol.com/carmarbb. 4 rms, 2 share bath. Jan-Apr: S, D $75-$145; under 5 free; wkly rates; lower rates rest of yr. TV in some rms; cable (premium), VCR avail (movies). Complimentary full bkfst. Complimentary coffee in rms. Restaurant nearby. Ck-out 11 am, ck-in 4-6 pm. Business servs avail. Luggage handling. Concierge serv. Pool; whirlpool. Some refrigerators, microwaves. Picnic tables, grills. Antiques, hand-made furniture. Totally nonsmoking. Cr cds: MC, V.

★★ **CASA ALEGRE BED AND BREAKFAST INN.** 316 E Speedway Blvd (85705). 520/628-1800; fax 520/792-1880; toll-free 800/628-5654. www.casaalegreinn.com. 4 rms, 2 with shower only. No rm phones. Jan-May: S, D $80-$135; under 12 free; wkly, monthly rates; lower rates rest of yr. TV, VCR (free movies). Pool; whirlpool. Complimentary full bkfst. Restaurant nearby. Ck-out 11 am, ck-in 4-6 pm. Covered parking. Bungalow (1915); period furnishings. Totally nonsmoking. Cr cds: DS, MC, V.

★★ **CATALINA PARK INN.** 309 E 1st St (85705). 520/792-4541; toll-free 800/792-4885. www.catalinaparkinn. com. 6 rms, 2 story. Dec-Apr: S, D $114-$144; wkly, monthly rates; special events (2-day min); lower rates rest of yr. Closed mid June-Aug. Children over 10 yrs only. TV; cable, VCR avail. Complimentary full bkfst; afternoon refreshments. Ck-out 11 am, ck-in 4-6 pm. Luggage handling. Concierge serv. House built in 1927 detailed with Mexican mahogany;

unique antiques. Totally nonsmoking. Cr cds: A, DS, MC, V.

★ **PEPPERTREE'S BED AND BREAKFAST INN.** 724 E University Blvd (85719). 520/622-7167; toll-free 800/348-5763. www.peppertreesinn. com. 6 units, 1-2 story, 4 kit. units, 3 rms with showers only. Mid-Dec-Apr: S $98; D $108; suites $125-$185; higher rates special events; hols (2-day min); lower rates rest of yr. Crib free. TV in sitting rm; VCR. Complimentary full bkfst. Restaurant nearby open 24 hrs. Ck-out 11 am, ck-in 3-6 pm. Concierge serv. Refrigerators. Picnic tables. Totally nonsmoking. Cr cds: DS, MC, V.

★★★ **SUNCATCHER BED AND BREAKFAST TUCSON DESERT RETREAT.** 105 N Avenida Javalina (85748). 520/885-0883; fax 520/885-0883; toll-free 877/775-8355. www. thesuncatcher.com. 4 rms, 1 with shower only. Sept-May (2-day min): S, D $90-$135; lower rates rest of yr. TV; VCR (movies). Heated pool; whirlpool. Complimentary full bkfst; evening refreshments. Ck-out noon, ck-in 3 pm. Business servs avail. Luggage handling. Concierge serv. Picnic table. Totally nonsmoking. Cr cds: A, DS, MC, V.

Guest Ranches

★★★ **TANQUE VERDE GUEST RANCH.** 14301 E Speedway Blvd (85748). 520/296-6275; fax 520/721-9426; toll-free 800/234-3833. www. tanqueverderanch.com. 75 rms in casitas. AP, mid-Dec-Apr: S $300-$390; D $350-$470; each addl $90-$100; lower rates rest of yr. Serv charge 15%. Crib $15. TV avail; VCR avail. 2 heated pools, 1 indoor; wading pool. Supervised children's activities; ages 4-11. Dining rm (public by res) 8-9 am, noon-1:30 pm, 6-8 pm. Box lunches, picnics, cookouts. Ck-out noon, ck-in 2 pm. Coin lndry. Pkg store. Meeting rms. Business servs avail. Gift shop. Free airport, RR station, bus depot transportation (4-night min). Sports dir. Tennis, pro. 18-hole golf privileges. Indoor, outdoor games. Soc dir; entertainment, dancing. Rec rm. Exercise equipt. Sightseeing trips; overnight trail rides avail; rodeos. Full-time naturalist (2 walks/day). Refrigerators; many fireplaces. Private patios. Cr cds: A, DS, MC, V.

★ ★ ★ **WHITE STALLION RANCH.** 9251 W Twin Peaks Rd (85743). 520/297-0252; fax 520/744-2786; toll-free 888/977-2624. www.wsranch. 41 rms in cottages. AP, mid-Dec-May: S $156-$165; D $240-$310; suites $312-$368; each addl $89; wkly rates; lower rates Sept-mid-Dec. Closed June-Aug. Crib free. Heated pool. Family-style meals. Box lunches, cookouts. Bar. Ck-out 11 am, ck-in 2 pm. Coin lndry. Meeting rms. Business servs avail. Gift shop. Free airport, RR station, bus depot transportation (4-night min). Tennis. Lawn games. Bkfst rides, hayrides, rodeos, bonfires with entertainment. Rec rm. Refrigerators, fireplaces. Library. Informal ranch on 3,000 acres. Petting zoo. Team penning (working cattle in the arena).

All Suites

★ ★ ★ **DOUBLETREE GUEST SUITES.** 6555 E Speedway Blvd (85710). 520/721-7000; fax 520/721-1991; res 800/222-8733. www.double treetucson.com. 304 suites, 5 story. S $75-$144; D $85-$154; Jan-mid-Apr: suites $125-$250; under 18 free; pkg plans; lower rates rest of yr. Crib free. Pet accepted, some restrictions; $25. TV; cable (premium). Heated pool; whirlpool, poolside serv. Restaurant 6 am-11 pm. Bar. Ck-out noon. Coin lndry. Convention facilities. Business center. Gift shop. Exercise equipt. Refrigerators; microwaves. Balconies. Cr cds: A, C, D, DS, ER, JCB, MC, V.

★ ★ **EMBASSY SUITES.** 7051 S Tucson Blvd (85706). 520/573-0700; fax 520/741-9645; res 800/362-2779. www.embassysuites.com. 204 suites, 3 story. Jan-June: S, D $149-$189; each addl $10; under 12 free; wkend rates; lower rates rest of yr. Crib free. Pet accepted, $15 refundable. TV; cable (premium). Heated pool; whirlpool, poolside serv. Complimentary full bkfst. Coffee in rms. Restaurant 11 am-10 pm; Fri, Sat to 11 pm. Bar to

midnight. Ck-out 1 pm. Coin lndry. Meeting rms. Business servs avail. Gift shop. Free airport transportation. Exercise equipt. Wet bars, refrigerators, microwaves. Cr cds: A, C, D, DS, MC, V.

★ ★ **EMBASSY SUITES HOTEL TUCSON-BROADWAY.** 5335 E Broadway (85711). 520/745-2700; fax 520/790-9232; res 800/362-2779. www.embassysuites.com. 142 suites, 3 story. No elvtr. Jan-Apr: S, D $139-$199; each addl $10; under 18 free; lower rates rest of yr. Crib free. Pet accepted, some restrictions. TV; cable (premium). Heated pool; whirlpool. Complimentary full bkfst; evening refreshments. Coffee in rms. Restaurant opp 8 am-10 pm. Rm serv. Ck-out noon. Coin lndry. Meeting rms. Business servs avail. Bellhops. Gift shop. Valet serv. Sundries. Refrigerators, microwaves. Grills. Cr cds: A, C, D, DS, JCB, MC, V.

★ ★ **WINDMILL INN AT ST. PHILIP'S PLAZA.** 4250 N Campbell Ave (85718). 520/577-0007; fax 520/577-0045; toll-free 800/547-4747. www.windmillinns.com. 122 suites, 3 story. Jan-Apr: suites $135-$395; each addl $10; under 18 free; lower rates rest of yr. Pet accepted, some restrictions. TV; cable (premium). Heated pool; whirlpool. Complimentary continental bkfst. Restaurant adj 11 am-11 pm. Ck-out 11 am. Coin lndry. Meeting rms. Business servs avail. Bathrm phones, refrigerators, microwaves, wet bars. Bicycles. Library. Cr cds: A, D, DS, MC, V.

Restaurants

★ ★ **CAFE POCA COSA.** 88 E Broadway (85701). 520/622-6400. Hrs: 11 am-9 pm; Fri, Sat to 10 pm. Closed Sun; most major hols; mid-July-early-Aug. Res accepted. Mexican menu. Bar. Lunch $6.50-$9, dinner $11-$16. Specialties: mole negro, pastel de elote tropical. Menu changes daily. Outdoor dining. 3-tiered circular fountain. Totally non-smoking. Cr cds: MC, V.

★★ **CAPRICCIO.** *4825 N 1st Ave (85718).* 520/887-2333. Hrs: 5:30-9:30 pm. Closed Sun; Jan 1, Thanksgiving, Dec 25; also Mon mid-May-Aug. Res accepted. Continental menu. Serv bar. Dinner $15-$24.50. Specialties: roast duckling with green peppercorn sauce, smoked chicken pâte, ravioli con vitello. Own pastries. Parking. Tableside appetizers and flambé. Cr cds: A, DS, MC, V.
[D]

★★★ **CATALINA GRILLE.** *2727 W Club Dr (85742).* 520/877-2377. *www.omnihotels.com.* Hrs: 5:30-9:30 pm. Closed Sun. Res accepted. Bar. Wine list. A la carte entrees: dinner $16.95-$31.95. Specialties: polenta and prawns, certified black angus beef, seafood. Outdoor dining; view of mountains and golf course. Large murals; fireplace. Regional menu with daily specials. Cr cds: A, DS, MC, V.
[D]

★★ **CHAD'S STEAKHOUSE.** *3001 N Swan (85712).* 520/881-1802. Hrs: 4-10 pm; Sun to 9 pm. Closed Thanksgiving, Dec 25. Res accepted. Bar. Dinner $8.95-$17.95. Child's menu. Specializes in steak, seafood. Parking. Family-owned. Cr cds: A, C, D, DS, ER, MC, V.
[D]

★★ **CITY GRILL.** *6464 E Tanque Verde (85715).* 520/733-1111. *www. metrorestaurants.com.* Hrs: 11 am-10 pm; Fri, Sat to 11 pm; Sun to 9 pm. Closed most major hols. Res accepted. Bar to midnight; wkends to 1 am. Lunch, dinner $5.95-$15.95. Child's menu. Specialties: wood-fired pizza, Angus prime rib, spit-fired rotisserie. Outdoor dining. Cr cds: A, C, D, DS, ER, MC, V.
[D] [⊐]

★ **DELECTABLES.** *533 N 4th Ave (85705).* 520/884-9289. *www. delectables.com.* Hrs: 11 am-9 pm. Closed major hols. Res accepted. Bar. Lunch, dinner $4.50-$13.95. Specializes in crepes, quiche, chicken Picatta. Child's menu. Own desserts. Outdoor dining. Cr cds: A, C, D, DS, ER, MC, V.
[D] [SC]

★★★ **EVANGELOS SCORDATO'S.** *4405 W Speedway Blvd (85745).* 520/792-3055. Hrs: 5-10 pm; Sun 4-9 pm. Closed Sun, Mon (June-Aug); July 4, Thanksgiving, Dec 25. Res accepted. Italian, Continental menu. Bar. Wine cellar. A la carte entrees: dinner $15.95-$21.95. Child's menu. Specializes in veal, fresh seafood, steak. Own pastries. Outdoor dining. Desert, mountain view. Cr cds: A, C, D, DS, ER, MC, V.
[D]

★★★ **FUEGO.** *6958 E Tanque Verde Rd (85715).* 520/886-1745. *www. snnewpages.com/fuego.* Hrs: 5-10 pm; Fri, Sat to 11 pm; hrs vary June-Sept. Closed some major hols. Res accepted. Southwestern menu. Bar. Wine cellar. Dinner $6.95-$27.95. Child's menu. Specializes in fresh seafood, ostrich, Southwestern dishes. Outdoor dining. Southwestern decor. Cr cds: A, MC, V.
[D] [SC]

Pima County Courthouse

★★★★ **THE GOLD ROOM.** *245 E Ina Rd (85704). 520/297-1151. www. westwardlook.com.* This bright dining room is aptly named and resides in the Westward Look Resort, an 80-acre Sonoran Desert property. The window-wrapped dining room affords beautiful views of the city and the Southwestern cuisine takes advantage of local ingredients and fresh herbs grown in the resort's own garden. One menu highlight is a mesquite-grilled buffalo sirloin with cabernet-chipotle-maple glace. Contemporary American menu. Hrs: 6 am-4 pm, 5:30-10 pm. Res accepted. Bkfst $5-$12, lunch $9.50-$16.50, dinner $19.75-$38. Sun brunch $26.50. Child's menu. Specialties: medallions of buffalo. Valet parking. Outdoor dining. Totally nonsmoking. Cr cds: A, C, D, DS, ER, JCB, MC, V.
D

★★★ **THE GRILL AT HACIENDA DEL SOL.** *5601 N Hacienda del Sol Rd (85718). 520/529-3500. www.hacienda delsol.com.* Contemporary American menu. Hrs: 6-10 pm; Sun brunch 10 am-2 pm; hrs vary off-season. Res accepted. Wine list. Dinner $18-$32. Child's menu. Menu changes seasonally. Cr cds: A, C, D, DS, MC, V.
D

★★★ **JANOS RESTAURANT.** *3770 E Sunrise Dr (85718). 520/615-6100. www.janos.com.* French-inspired Southwestern regional cuisine. Specialties: pepito-roasted venison, mushroom and brie relleno, lobster bisque. Own baking, pastas, brioche. Hrs: from 5:30 pm. Closed Sun; Jan 1, Dec 25; also Mon mid-May-Nov. Bar. Wine cellar. Res accepted. Dinner $22-$35. Outdoor dining. Chef-owned. Cr cds: A, D, MC, V.
D

★★★ **KINGFISHER.** *2564 E Grant (85716). 520/323-7739. www. kingfisherbarandgrill.com.* Hrs: 11 am-midnight; wkends from 5 pm. Closed some major hols. Res accepted. Bar. Wine cellar. Lunch $5-$9.75, dinner $7-$18.75. Child's menu. Specialties: grilled baby back ribs, mixed grill pasta, mesquite-grilled salmon. Blues/jazz band Mon. Parking. Mod-

ern decor and artwork. Cr cds: A, C, D, DS, ER, MC, V.
D ⅃

★★ **LA FUENTE.** *1749 N Oracle Rd (85705). 520/623-8659.* Hrs: 11 am-10 pm; Fri-Sun to 11 pm; Sat from noon; Sun brunch 11:30 am-2 pm. Closed most major hols. Res accepted. Mexican menu. Lunch $4.50-$17.95, dinner $6.75-$17.95. Sun brunch $9.95. Child's menu. Specialties: chicken mole poblano, pastel azteca, nopalitas. Entertainment. Family-owned. Cr cds: A, D, MC, V.
D

★★ **LA PLACITA CAFE.** *2950 N Swan Rd (85712). 520/881-1150.* Hrs: 11:30 am-2:30 pm, 5-9:30 pm; Sun from 5 pm. Closed Jan 1, Thanksgiving, Dec 25. Res accepted. Mexican menu. Serv bar. Lunch $5.95-$7.25, dinner $5.95-$15.95. Specialties: bistec Mexicana al minuto, pescado cabrilla (estilo hermosillo), chiles rellenos. Own tortillas. Outdoor dining. Sonoran decor; turn-of-the-century Tucson prints, raised-hearth tile fireplace, serape drapes. Cr cds: A, C, D, DS, ER, MC, V.
D

★★ **LAST TERRITORY.** *10000 N Oracle Rd (85737). 520/544-5000. www.sheratonelconquistador.com.* Hrs: 5-10 pm; early-bird dinner to 7 pm. Closed Mon. Res accepted. Bar. Dinner $14.95-$22. Child's menu. Western musicians. Specialties: cowboy porterhouse steak, T-bone chili, wild game. Outdoor dining. Cowboy motif. Cr cds: A, C, D, DS, ER, JCB, MC, V.
D ⅃

★★ **LE BISTRO.** *2574 N Campbell Ave (85719). 520/327-3086. www. lebistrotucson.com.* Hrs: 11 am-2:30 pm; 5-9:30 pm; Fri to 11 pm; Sat 5-11 pm; Sun from 5 pm. Closed Thanksgiving, Dec 25. Res accepted. Serv bar. A la carte entrees: lunch $5.95-$11.95, dinner $8.25-$18.95. Specialties: blackened scallops, crispy duck with raspberry vinegar sauce, salmon with ginger crust. Own desserts. Cr cds: A, C, DS, ER, MC, V.
D

★★ **METROPOLITAN GRILL.** *7892 N Oracle Rd (85704). 520/531-1212.*

www.metrorestaurants.com. Hrs: 11 am-10 pm; Fri, Sat to 10:30 pm. Closed Dec 25. Res accepted. Bar to 1 am. Lunch $5.95-$9.95, dinner $8.95-$15.95. Child's menu. Specializes in beef, fresh fish, pork chops. Outdoor dining. Exhibition kitchen with wood-fired pizza oven. Cr cds: A, C, D, DS, ER, MC, V.
D ⊟

★★★ **OLIVE TREE.** 7000 E Tanque Verde Rd (85715). 520/298-1845. Hrs: 5-10 pm. Closed Mon (June-Sept); also some major hols. Res accepted. Mediterranean, Greek menu. Bar. Wine list. Dinner $13.95-$26.95. Child's menu. Specializes in lamb, pasta, seafood. Courtyard dining. 2 intimate dining rms. Cr cds: A, MC, V.
D ⊟

★ **PINNACLE PEAK.** 6541 E Tanque Verde Rd (85715). 520/296-0911. Hrs: 5-10 pm. Closed Thanksgiving, Dec 25. Bar. Dinner $4.95-$13.95. Child's menu. Specializes in steak, ribs. Open mesquite grills. Old West atmosphere with gunfights Thurs-Sun. Family-owned. Cr cds: A, DS, MC, V.
D

★★ **PRESIDIO GRILL.** 3352 E Speedway (85716). 520/327-4667. www.dotucson.com. Hrs: 11 am-10 pm; Fri, Sat to midnight; Sun from 10 am. Closed most major hols. Res accepted. Bar. Wine list. Bkfst $3.75-$7.95, lunch $5.95-$10.95, dinner $5.95-$19.95. Child's menu. Specialties: blackened prime rib, chicken pasta, roasted whole garlic with brie. Bistro atmosphere. Cr cds: A, C, D, DS, ER, MC, V.
D

★ **SERI MELAKA.** 6133 E Broadway (85711). 520/747-7811. www.seri melaka.com. Hrs: 11 am-9:30 pm; wkends to 10 pm; early-bird dinner Mon-Fri 4:30-6 pm. Res accepted. Malaysian, Chinese menu. Serv bar. Lunch $4.65-$6.95, dinner $6.95-$34.95. Buffet lunch $5.95. Specialties: sambal, satay, rendang. Malaysian and Chinese decor. Cr cds: A, DS, MC, V.
D

★★★ **SOLEIL.** 3001 E Skyline Dr (85718). 520/299-3345. Mediterranean menu. Menu changes seasonally. Hrs: 11 am-10 pm; hrs vary in summer.

Closed Mon. Res accepted. Wine list. Lunch $5.50-$13; dinner $16-$29. Cr cds: A, C, D, DS, JCB, MC, V.
D

★★★★ **THE TACK ROOM.** 7300 E Vactor Ranch Tr (85715). 520/722-2800. www.emol.org/emol/thetackroom. This four-acre property began as a private hacienda in 1940, was then a guest ranch, and now continues a 35-year-old, fine-dining tradition. The adobe destination with old-western character attracts loyal locals and visitors from around the world for its Southwest-inspired Continental cuisine. A visit might include Arizona four-pepper steak with poblano potato cake likely accompanied by a wine from the extensive cellar. Southwestern, American cuisine. Specialties: rack of lamb with mesquite honey and lime, roast duckling with pistachio crust and glaze of jalapeno and lime, Arizona four-pepper steak. Own baking. Hrs: from 6 pm. Closed Mon off-season; also first 2 wks of July. Bar from 5:30 pm. Wine cellar. Res accepted. A la carte entrees: dinner $28.50-$38.50. Child's menu. Valet parking. Family-owned. Cr cds: A, D, DS, MC, V.
D

★★★★ **THE VENTANA ROOM.** 7000 N Resort Dr (85750). 520/299-2020. www.ventanaroom.com. Take in views of the city lights and the Catalina Mountains at this restaurant located in Loews Ventana Canyon Resort. The contemporary American menu offers specialties such as grilled dry-aged sirloin with roquefort, chanterelle mushroom bread pudding, and port wine sauce. Guests can also choose one of chef Jeffrey Russell's tasting menus to enjoy in the opulent, romantic dining room. Contemporary American menu. Specialties: grilled filet of Dover sole, mixed grill of game, trio of foie gras. Own pastries. Hrs: 6-9 pm; Fri, Sat to 10 pm. Bar. Wine cellar. Res accepted. A la carte entrees: dinner $32-$45. Valet parking. Totally nonsmoking. Cr cds: A, D, DS, JCB, MC, V.
D

Unrated Dining Spots

BLUE WILLOW. 2616 N Campbell Ave (85719). 520/327-7577. Hrs: 8 am-10 pm; Thur, Fri, Sat to midnight;

Sun to 9 pm. Closed Thanksgiving, Dec 25. Wine, beer. Bkfst $2.25-$6.75, lunch $3.50-$7.95, dinner $3.50-$10.50. Specializes in omelettes, desserts. Outdoor dining. Totally nonsmoking. Cr cds: A, DS, MC, V.
D

MILLIE'S WEST PANCAKE HAUS. *6530 E Tanque Verde Rd (85715). 520/298-4250.* Hrs: 6:30 am-3 pm. Closed Mon; Jan 1, Thanksgiving, Dec 25. Res accepted. Bkfst $3.50-$5.50, lunch $4-$8. Child's menu. Specializes in pancakes. Country inn atmosphere; 2 dining rms. Fireplace; collection of plates and prints displayed. Cr cds: MC, V.
D

TOHONO CHUL TEA ROOM. *7366 N Paseo del Norte (85704). 520/797-1222. www.tohonochulpark.org.* Hrs: 8 am-5 pm. Closed most major hols. Bkfst $2.50-$8.95, lunch $6.95-$9.95. Child's menu. Specializes in scones, salads, homemade soups. Own desserts. Outdoor dining. Adobe house in park dedicated to arid flora and landscape. Gift shop. Cr cds: A, MC, V.
D

Tumacacori National Historical Park

(G-5) *See also Nogales, Patagonia, Tucson*

(Exit 29 on I-19, 48 mi S of Tucson, 18 mi N of Nogales)

Father Kino, a Jesuit missionary, visited the Pima village of Tumacacori in 1691. Work began on the present historic mission church in 1800. It was completed in 1822, but was abandoned in 1848.

There is a beautiful patio garden and a museum with fine dioramas (daily; closed Thanksgiving, December 25). Self-guided trail; guided tours (December-April, daily; advance notice needed rest of year). There is a fiesta held on the first weekend in December with entertainment, music, and food. Contact the Superintendent, PO Box 67, Tumacacori 85640; phone 520/398-2341.

Resort

★ ★ **TUBAC GOLF RESORT.** *1 Otero Rd, Tubac (85646). 520/398-2211; fax 520/398-9261; toll-free 800/848-7893. www.tubacgolfresort.com.* 46 rms, 10 kits. Mid-Jan-mid-Apr: S, D $140-$150; each addl $15; suites $170-$235; lower rates rest of yr. Crib free. TV. Heated pool. Complimentary coffee in rms. Restaurant 7 am-9 pm. Bar to 10 pm. Ck-out noon. Coin lndry. Meeting rm. Tennis. 18-hole golf, greens fee $63 (incl cart), pro, putting green, pro shop. Refrigerators. Many fireplaces. Many private patios. Contemporary Southwest decor. Pool area has mountain view. Cr cds: A, DS, MC, V.

Walnut Canyon National Monument

(see Flagstaff)

Wickenburg

(D-3) *See also Phoenix*

Founded 1863 **Pop** 5,082 **Elev** 2,070 ft **Area code** 928

Information Chamber of Commerce, Santa Fe Depot, 216 N Frontier St, 85390; 928/684-5479 or 928/684-0977

Web www.wickenburgchamber.com

Wickenburg was first settled by early Hispanic families who established ranches in the area and traded with the local Native Americans. The town was relatively unpopulated until a Prussian named Henry Wickenburg picked up a rock to throw at a stubborn burro and stumbled onto the richest gold find in Arizona, the

Vulture Mine. His find began a $30-million boom and the birth of a town. Today Wickenburg is the oldest town north of Tucson and is well-known for its area dude ranches.

What to See and Do

Desert Caballeros Western Museum.
Western art gallery; diorama rm; street scene (ca 1915); period rms; mineral display; Native American exhibit. (Daily; closed hols) 21 N Frontier St. Phone 928/684-2272. ¢¢

Frontier Street. Preserved in early 1900s style. Train depot (houses Chamber of Commerce), brick Hassayampa building (former hotel) and many other historic buildings. Phone 928/684-5479.

The Jail Tree. This tree was used from 1863-1890 (until the first jail was built) to chain rowdy prisoners. Friends and relatives visited the prisoners and brought picnic lunches. Escapes were unknown. Tegner and Wickenburg Way. Phone 928/684-5479.

Little Red Schoolhouse. Pioneer schoolhouse. Four blks N of Wickenburg Way on Tegner. Phone 928/684-5479.

Old 761 Santa Fe Steam Locomotive. This engine and tender ran the track between Chicago and the West. At Apache and Tegner, behind Town Hall. Phone 928/684-5479.

Special Events

Gold Rush Days. Bonanza days revived, with chance to pan for gold and keep all you find. Rodeo; parade. Second full wkend Feb. Phone 928/684-5479.

Septiembre Fiesta. Celebration of Hispanic heritage. First Sat Sept. Phone 928/684-5479.

Bluegrass Music Festival. Four-Corner States Championship. Second full wkend Nov. Phone 928/684-5479.

Motels/Motor Lodges

★★ **AMERICINN MOTEL.** *850 E Wickenburg Way (85358). 928/684-5461; toll-free 800/634-3444. www.americinn.com.* 29 rms, 2 story. Nov-May: S $53-$62; D $59-$68; each addl $6; under 16 free; lower rates rest of yr. Crib free. TV; cable (premium). Heated pool; whirlpool.

Restaurant 7 am-1:30 pm, 5-8:30 pm; closed Mon. Rm serv. Bar (exc Mon). Ck-out 11 am. Business servs avail. Some microwaves. Private patios, some balconies. Cr cds: A, C, D, DS, MC, V.
🅳 ⛵ 🏂 🔥

★ **BEST WESTERN RANCHO GRANDE MOTEL.** *293 E Wickenburg Way (85390). 928/684-5445; fax 928/684-7380; res 800/854-7235. www.bwranchogrande.com.* 80 rms, 1-2 story, 24 kits. Nov-Apr: S $63-$94; D $66-$104; each addl $3; suites $94-$115; higher rates special events; lower rates rest of yr. Crib $3. Pet accepted. TV; cable, VCR avail (movies). Heated pool; whirlpool. Playground. Complimentary coffee in rms. Restaurant nearby. Ck-out noon. Business servs avail. Bellhops. Valet serv. Free airport transportation. Tennis. Refrigerators; some bathrm phones, microwaves. Some private patios, balconies. Cr cds: A, C, D, DS, ER, JCB, MC, V.
🅳 🏇 🎿 ⛵ 🏂 🔥

Guest Ranches

★★ **FLYING E RANCH.** *2801 W Wickenburg Way (85390). 928/684-2690; fax 928/684-5304; toll-free 888/684-2650. www.flyingeranch.com.* 17 units. AP (3-day min), Nov-Apr: S $145-$185; D $230-$295; each addl $40-$100; family rates. Closed rest of yr. TV; VCR avail. Heated pool. Family-style meals. Bkfst cookouts, chuckwagon dinners. Setups. Ck-out 11 am, ck-in varies. Business servs avail. Trail rides (fee); hay rides. Lighted tennis. Shuffleboard. Exercise equipt; sauna. Occasional entertainment; square, line dancing. Refrigerators. On 20,000-acre cattle ranch in shadow of Vulture Peak. No credit cards accepted.
🎿 🎿 ⛵ 🚶 🔥

★★★ **RANCHO DE LOS CABALLEROS.** *1551 S Vulture Mine Rd (85390). 928/684-5484; fax 928/684-2267; toll-free 800/684-5030. www.sunc.com.* 79 rms, 33 kit. units. AP, Feb-mid-May: S $239-$299; D $379-$439; under 5 free; golf plans; hol rates; lower rates Oct-Jan. Closed rest of yr. Crib free. TV. Pool; poolside serv. Playground. Free supervised children's activities; ages 5-12. Complimentary coffee in rms. Restaurant

7-9 am, 12:30 am-1:30 pm, 6:30-8:30 pm. Box lunches, snacks. Bar 10:30 am-midnight; entertainment Wed, Fri, Sat. Ck-out 1 pm, ck-in 4 pm. Grocery 2 mi. Coin lndry. Bellhops. Meeting rms. Business servs avail. Airport transportation. Tennis, pro. 18-hole golf, greens fee $75, pro, putting green, driving range, pro shop. Horse stables. Hiking. Bicycles. Hot air ballooning. Trap and skeet shooting. Soc dir. Massage. Some refrigerators, microwaves.

Willcox

(F-6) *See also Safford*

Pop 3,733 **Elev** 4,200 ft
Area code 520 **Zip** 85643
Information Chamber of Commerce, Cochise Information Center, 1500 N Circle I Rd; 520/384-2272 or 800/200-2272

What to See and Do

Amerind Foundation. Amerind (short for American Indian) Museum contains one of the finest collections of archaeological and ethnological artifacts in the country. Displayed in art gallery are paintings by Anglo and Native American artists. Picnic area, museum shop. (Sept-May, daily; rest of yr, Wed-Sun; closed hols) Approx 1 mi SW via I-10, exit 318 on Dragoon Rd in Dragoon. Phone 520/586-3666. ¢¢

Cochise Information Center . (Daily; closed Jan 1, Thanksgiving, Dec 25) 1 mi N via Circle I Rd just off Fort Grant Rd, exit from I-10. Phone 520/384-2272 or 800/200-2272.
FREE

Cochise Stronghold. Rugged canyon once sheltered Chiricahua Apache; unique rock formations provide protection and vantage points. Camping, picnicking; nature, hiking, horseback, and history trails. (Daily) SW via I-10 to US 191 S, then W on Ironwood Rd. Phone 520/364-3468.

Fort Bowie National Historic Site. Visitors pass ruins of Butterfield Stage Station, post cemetery, Apache Spring, and the first Fort Bowie on the way to ruins of the second Fort Bowie. Visitor center. Carry water in summer, beware of flash floods and rattlesnakes. Do not climb on ruins or disturb any of the site's features. 22 mi SE on AZ 186, then 6 mi NE on graded road leading east into Apache Pass and two mi to trailhead, then walk 1½ mi on foot trail to the fort ruins. Phone 520/847-2500.
FREE

The Rex Allen Arizona Cowboy Museum & Cowboy Hall of Fame. Museum dedicated to Willcox-native Rex Allen, the "last of the Silver Screen Cowboys." Details his life from ranch life in Willcox to radio, TV, and movie days. Also special exhibits on pioneer settlers and ranchers. Cowboy Hall of Fame pays tribute to real cattle industry heroes. Gift shop. (Daily; closed Jan 1, Thanksgiving, Dec 25) 150 N Railroad Ave. Phone 520/384-4583. ¢

Special Events

Wings Over Willcox/Sandhill Crane Celebration. Tours of bird-watching areas, trade shows, seminars, workshops. Third wkend Jan. Phone 520/384-2272.

Rex Allen Days. PRCA Rodeo, concert by Rex Allen, Jr., parade, country fair, Western dances, softball tournament. First wkend Oct. Phone 520/384-2272.

Motels/Motor Lodges

★★ **BEST WESTERN PLAZA INN.** *1100 W Rex Allen Dr (85643). 520/384-3556; fax 520/384-2679; res 800/262-2645. www.bestwestern.com.* 91 rms, 2 story. S, D $59-$109; each addl $10; under 12 free. Crib free. Pet accepted, some restrictions; $8. TV; cable. Heated pool. Complimentary full bkfst. Coffee in rms. Restaurant 6 am-9 pm; Fri, Sat to 10 pm. Rm serv. Bar 4 pm-1 am. Ck-out noon. Coin lndry. Meeting rms. Business servs avail. Many refrigerators. Cr cds: A, C, D, DS, MC, V.

★★ **DAYS INN.** *724 N Bisbee Ave (85643). 520/384-4222; fax 520/384-3785; toll-free 800/329-7466. www.*

daysinn.com. 73 rms, 2 story. June-Aug and Nov-Feb: S $40-$42; D $45-$52; each addl $5; under 13 free; lower rates rest of yr. Crib $5. Pet accepted, some restrictions; $5. TV; cable (premium). Heated pool. Complimentary continental bkfst. Restaurant opp open 24 hrs. Ck-out 11 am. Coin lndry. Business servs avail. Cr cds: A, C, D, DS, MC, V.

B&B/Small Inn

★ ★ **CHIRICAHUA FOOTHILLS.** *6310 Pinery Canyon Rd (85643). 520/824-3632.* 5 air-cooled rms. No rm phones. S $65; D $70; under 12 free. 2 TV rms; VCR avail (movies). Complimentary full bkfst. Ck-out 11 am, ck-in 3 pm. Picnic tables. Working cattle ranch. Totally nonsmoking. No credit cards accepted.

Williams

(C-4) *See also Flagstaff, Seligman*

Settled 1880 **Pop** 2,842 **Elev** 6,750 ft
Area code 928 **Zip** 86046
Information Williams-Grand Canyon Chamber of Commerce, 200 W Railroad Ave; 928/635-4061

What to See and Do

Grand Canyon National Park. (see). Hwy 180. Phone 928/638-7888. ¢¢¢

⭐ **Grand Canyon Railway.** First operated by Santa Fe Railroad in 1901 as an alternative to the stagecoach, this restored line carries passengers northward aboard authentically refurbished steam locomotives and coaches. Full-day round trips incl 3½-hr layover at canyon. At Williams depot, there is a museum of railroad history. Railway (close Jan 1, Dec 25). Phone 800/843-8724. ¢¢¢¢

Kaibab National Forest. More than 1 ½ million acres; one area surrounds Williams and incl Sycamore Canyon and Kendrick Mtn wilderness areas and part of National Historic Rte 66; a second area is 42 mi N on US 180 (AZ 64) near South Rim of Grand Canyon; a third area lies north of Grand Canyon (outstanding views of the canyon from seldom-visited vista points in this area) and incl Kanab Creek and Saddle Mtn wilderness areas, the Kaibab Plateau, and the North Rim Parkway National Scenic Byway. The forest is home for a variety of wildlife unique to this area, incl mule deer and the Kaibab squirrel. Fishing (trout); hunting, picnicking, camping (fee). Phone 928/635-2681. Also in forest is

Williams Ski Area. Pomalift, rope tow; patrol, school, rentals; snack bar. Vertical drop 600 ft. (Mid-Dec-Easter, Mon, Thurs-Sun) Sledding slopes and x-country trails nearby. 4 mi S of town, on the N slopes of Bill Williams Mtn. Phone 928/635-9330. ¢¢¢¢

Special Events

Bill Williams Rendezvous Days. Black powder shoot, carnival, street dances, pioneer arts and crafts. Memorial Day wkend.

Labor Day Rodeo. Professional rodeo and Western celebration. Labor Day wkend. Phone 928/635-4061.

Motels/Motor Lodges

★ **BEST VALUE INN - NORRIS MOTEL.** *1001 W Rte 66 (86046). 928/635-2202; fax 928/635-9202; res 888/351-2378. www.bestvalueinn.com.* 33 rms. May-Sept: S $26-$59; D $30-$77; each addl $5; under 12 free; ski plans; lower rates rest of yr. Crib $7. TV; cable (premium). Pool. Complimentary coffee in lobby. Restaurant nearby. Ck-out 11 am. Business servs avail. In-rm modem link. Free RR station transportation. Golf privileges. Downhill ski 4 mi. Whirlpool. Refrigerators; microwaves avail. Grills. Cr cds: A, DS, MC, V.

★ ★ **BEST WESTERN WILLIAMS.** *2600 W Rte 66 (86046). 928/635-4400; fax 928/635-5488; res 800/780-7234. www.bestwestern.com.* 79 rms, 2 story, 10 suites. Mid-May-Aug: S $79-$135; D $89-$135; each addl $10; suites $125-$181; under 12 free; ski plan; lower rates rest of yr. Crib free. TV; cable (premium). Complimentary full bkfst. Complimentary coffee in rms. Restaurant adj open 24 hrs. Bar 5-10 pm. Ck-out noon. Meeting rms.

Business servs avail. In-rm modem link. Bellhops. Gift shop. Coin lndry. Downhill ski 5 mi. Pool; whirlpool. Bathrm phones. 1 mi to lake. Cr cds: A, C, D, DS, MC, V.

★ **EL RANCHO MOTEL.** *617 E Rte 66 (86046). 928/635-2552; fax 928/635-4173; toll-free 800/228-2370. www.thegrandcanyon.com\elrancho.* 25 rms, 2 story, 2 suites. Mid-May-Sept: S, D $52-$73; each addl $5; suites $95-$105; lower rates rest of yr. Crib $3. TV; cable (premium), VCR avail. Heated pool. Complimentary coffee in rms. Restaurant opp 6 am-2 pm; 5-10 pm. Ck-out 11 am. Downhill ski 4 mi. Refrigerators, microwaves. Cr cds: A, DS, MC, V.

★★ **FRAY MARCOS HOTEL.** *235 N Grand Canyon Blvd (86046). 928/635-4010; fax 928/635-2180; toll-free 800/843-8724. www.thetrain.com.* 196 rms, 2 story. Apr-mid-Sept: S, D $79-$119; each addl $10; under 16 free; lower rates rest of yr. Crib free. TV; cable (premium). Complimentary coffee in lobby. Restaurant 4-10 pm. Bar. Ck-out 11 am. Business servs avail. Bellhops. Sundries. Gift shop. Cr cds: A, DS, MC, V.

★★ **HOLIDAY INN WILLIAMS.** *950 N Grand Canyon Blvd (86046). 928/635-4114; fax 928/635-2700; res 800/465-4329. www.holiday-inn.com.* 120 rms, 2 story, 12 suites. S, D $79-$99; each addl $10; suites $99-$119; under 19 free; higher rates hols; lower rates rest of yr. Crib free. Pet accepted. TV; cable. Complimentary coffee in lobby. Restaurant 6-10 am, 5-10 pm; summer hrs 6 am-10 pm. Rm serv. Bar from 5 pm. Ck-out 11 am. Meeting rm. Business servs avail. Bellhops. Gift shop. Coin lndry. Downhill ski 5 mi. Indoor pool; whirlpool. Some refrigerators. Wet bars in suites. Cr cds: A, C, D, DS, MC, V.

★ **MOTEL 6.** *831 W Bill Williams Ave (86046). 928/635-9000; fax 928/635-2300; res 800/466-8356. www.motel6. com.* 52 rms, 2 story. June-Sept: S, D $45-$69; each addl $6; under 18 free; higher rates hols; lower rates rest of

yr. Crib free. Pet accepted. TV, cable. Indoor pool; whirlpool. In-rm modem link. Restaurant opp 11 am-9 pm. Ck-out 11 am. Coin lndry. Business servs avail. Cr cds: A, D, DS, MC, V.

★ **MOUNTAINSIDE INN.** *642 E Rte 66 (86046). 928/635-4431; fax 928/635-2292; res 866/635-2986. www.mtnsideinn.com.* 96 rms, 2 story. Apr-Oct: S, D $95-$125; each addl $10; under 18 free; 2-day min stay hols; lower rates rest of yr. Crib free. Pet accepted. TV, cable. Heated pool; whirlpool. Restaurant 6 am-2 pm, 4-10 pm. Rm serv (evening only). Bar. Ck-out noon. Gift shop. Downhill ski 4 mi. Microwaves avail. Picnic tables. Cr cds: A, D, DS, MC, V.

B&B/Small Inn

★★ **TERRY RANCH BED AND BREAKFAST.** *701 Quarterhorse Rd (86046). 928/635-4171; fax 928/635-2488; toll-free 800/210-5908. www. terryranchbnb.com.* 4 rms. No A/C. No rm phones. May-Sept: S, D $90-$120; each addl $15; lower rates rest of yr. TV in common rm; cable (premium), VCR avail (movies). Complimentary full bkfst; afternoon refreshments. Restaurant nearby. Ck-out 10 am, ck-in 4-6 pm. Luggage handling. Concierge serv. Some in-rm fireplaces, whirlpools. Picnic tables, grills. Antiques. Country Victorian log house. Totally nonsmoking. Cr cds: A, DS, MC, V.

Restaurant

★ **ROD'S STEAK HOUSE.** *301 E Bill Williams Ave (86046). 928/635-2671. www.rods-steakhouse.com.* Hrs: 11:30 am-9:30 pm. Closed Thanksgiving, Dec 24, 25. Res accepted. Bar. Lunch $3.50-$7.50, dinner $7-$23. Child's menu. Specialties: mesquite-broiled steak, prime rib. Paintings of the Old West, stained-glass windows. Cr cds: MC, V.

Window Rock (B-7)

Pop 3,059 **Elev** 6,880 ft
Area code 928
Information Navajoland Tourism
Department, PO Box 663; 928/871-
6436 or 928/871-7371

What to See and Do

Canyon de Chelly National Monument. (see). Phone 928/674-5500.

Guided tours of Navajoland. Various
organizations and individuals offer
walking and driving tours of the
area. Fees and tours vary; phone for
information. Phone 928/871-6436.

> **Hozhoni Tours.** Contact PO Box
> 1995, Kayenta 86033. Phone
> 520/697-8198.

> **Roland's Navajo Land Tours.** Contact PO Box 1995, Kayenta 86033.
> Phone 520/697-8198.

> **Stanley Perry, Step-On Tours.** Contact PO Box 2381.

Navajo Nation Museum. Established
in 1961 to preserve Navajo history,
art, culture, and natural history; permanent and temporary exhibits. Literature and Navajo information
avail. (Mon-Fri; closed tribal and
other hols) E of jct AZ 264 and
Indian Rte 12, on AZ 264 in Navajo
Arts & Crafts Enterprise Center.
Phone 520/871-6673. **Donation**

Navajo Nation Zoological and Botanical Park. Features a representative
collection of animals and plants of
historical or cultural importance to
the Navajo people. (Daily; closed Jan
1, Dec 25) E of jct AZ 264 and Indian
Rte 12, on AZ 264. Phone 928/871-
6573. **FREE**

St. Michaels. Catholic mission, established in 1898, which has done
much for the education and health
of the tribe. Original mission building now serves as a museum depicting history of the area. Gift shop.
(Memorial Day-Labor Day, daily) 3
mi W. Phone 928/871-4172. **FREE**

Special Events

Powwow and PRCA Rodeo. July 4.
Phone 928/871-6478.

Navajo Nation Fair. Navajo Nation
Fairgrounds. Navajo traditional song
and dance; Intertribal powwow; All-
Indian Rodeo; parade; concerts;
exhibits. Early Sept. Contact PO
Drawer U. Phone 928/871-6478.

Winslow

(C-5) *See also Holbrook, Hopi Indian
Reservation, Navajo Indian Reservation*

Founded 1880 **Pop** 9,520 **Elev** 4,880
ft **Area code** 928 **Zip** 86047
Information Chamber of Commerce,
300 W North Rd, PO Box 460; /289-
2434 or 928/289-2435

What to See and Do

Homolovi Ruins State Park. This
park contains six major Anasazi ruins
dating from A.D. 1250-1450. Arizona
State Museum conducts occasional
excavations (June, July). Trails. Visitor center; interpretive programs.
Standard fees. (Daily; closed Dec 25)
3 mi E on I-40, then 1 mi N on AZ
87. Phone 928/289-4106.

Meteor Crater. Crater is one mi from
rim to rim and 560 ft deep. The
world's best preserved meteorite
crater was used as training site for
astronauts. Museum; lecture; Astronaut Wall of Fame; telescope on
highest point of the crater's rim
offers excellent view of surrounding
area. (Daily) 20 mi W on I-40, then 5
mi S on Meteor Crater Rd. Phone
928/289-2362. ¢¢

Old Trails Museum. Operated by the
Navajo County Historical Society;
exhibits and displays of local history,
Native American artifacts, and early
Americana. (Apr-Oct, Tues-Sat; rest of
yr, Tues, Thurs, and Sat; closed hols)
212 N Kinsley Ave. Phone 928/289-
5861. **FREE**

Motels/Motor Lodges

★★ **BEST WESTERN ADOBE INN.**
*1701 N Park Dr (86047). 928/289-
4638; fax 928/289-5514; res 800/780-
7234. www.bestwestern.com.* 72 rms, 2
story. June-Aug: S $50-$56; D $54-
$58; suites $68; under 18 free; lower
rates rest of yr. Crib $4. Pet accepted,
some restrictions. TV; cable (premium), VCR avail. Indoor pool;
whirlpool. Restaurant 6 am-2 pm, 4-
10 pm; Sun to 9 pm. Rm serv. Bar 4-
11 pm, Sun to 10 pm. Ck-out 11 am.

Coin lndry. Meeting rms. Business servs avail. Free airport, RR station, bus depot transportation. Cr cds: A, C, D, DS, MC, V.

★ **ECONO LODGE.** *1706 N Park Dr (86047). 928/289-4687; fax 928/289-9377; toll-free 800/228-5050. www. econolodge.com.* 73 rms, 2 story. Late May-Sept: S, D $45-$59; under 18 free; lower rates rest of yr. Pet accepted; $5/day. TV; cable (premium), VCR avail. Pool. Complimentary coffee in rms. Ck-out 11 am. Coin lndry. Business servs avail. Some refrigerators, microwaves. Cr cds: A, C, D, DS, JCB, MC, V.

Wupatki National Monument

See also Flagstaff

(35 mi N of Flagstaff on US 89)

The nearly 2,600 archeological sites of the Sinagua and Anasazi cultures were occupied between 1100 and 1250. The largest of them, Wupatki Pueblo, was three stories high, with about 100 rooms. The eruption of nearby Sunset Crater (see) spread volcanic ash over an 800-square-mile area and for a time made this an active farming center.

The half-mile ruins trail is self-guided; books are available at its starting point. The visitor center and main ruin are open daily (closed December 25). Rangers on duty. Wupatki National Monument and Sunset Crater Volcano National Monument (see) are located on a 35-mile paved loop off of US 89. Nearest camping at Bonito Campground (May-October; phone 520/526-0866). Contact the Superintendent, 6400 US 89A, Flagstaff 86004; phone 520/526-1157.

Yuma (F-I)

Founded 1849 **Pop** 77,515 **Elev** 138 ft
Area code 928
Information Convention & Visitors Bureau, 377 Main St, PO Box 11059, 85366; 928/783-0071
Web www.visityuma.com

What to See and Do

Arizona Historical Society Sanguinetti House. Former home of E. F. Sanguinetti, pioneer merchant; now a division of the Arizona Historical Society. Artifacts from Arizona Territory, incl documents, photographs, furniture, and clothing. Gardens and exotic birds surround museum. Historical library open by appt. (Tues-Sat; closed hols) 240 Madison Ave. Phone 928/782-1841. **FREE**

Fort Yuma-Quechan Museum. Part of one of the oldest military posts (1855) associated with the Arizona Territory; offered protection to settlers and secured the Yuma Crossing. Fort Yuma is headquarters for the Quechan Tribe. Museum houses tribal relics of southwestern Colorado River Yuman groups. (Daily; closed hols) Fort Yuma. Phone 619/572-0661. ¢

Imperial National Wildlife Refuge. Bird-watching; photography. Fishing; hunting, hiking. Interpretive center/office (Mon-Fri). 40 mi N via US 95. Phone 928/783-3371. **FREE**

Yuma River Tours. Narrated historical tours on the Colorado River; half- and full-day trips. Sunset dinner cruise. Also jeep tours to sand dunes. (Mon-Fri; fees vary) 1920 Arizona Ave. Phone 928/783-4400.

Yuma Territorial Prison State Historic Park. Remains of 1876 prison; museum, original cell blocks. Southwest artifacts and prison relics. (Daily; closed Dec 25) Off I-8, Giss Pkwy exit. Phone 928/783-4771. ¢¢ Nearby is

Yuma Valley Railway. Tracks run 12 mi through fields along the Colorado River levee and Morelos Dam. Two-hr trips; dinner trips. (Nov-Mar, Sat and Sun; Apr-May, Oct, Sat only; June by appt only; closed July-Sept)

Levee at 8th St. Phone 928/783-3456.
¢¢¢

Special Events

Midnight at the Oasis Festival. First
full wkend Mar. Phone 928/343-
1715.

Yuma County Fair. Five days early
Apr. Phone 928/726-4420.

Motels/Motor Lodges

★★ **AIRPORT TRAVELODGE.** *711 E
32nd St (85365). 928/726-4721; fax
928/344-0452; res 800/578-7878.
www.travelodge.com.* 80 rms, 2 story. S
$54; D $62; each addl $5; suites $78;
under 14 free; higher rates special
events (2-day min); lower rates rest
of yr. Crib free. Pet accepted, some
restrictions; $25 deposit. TV; cable
(premium), VCR avail (movies).
Complimentary continental bkfst.
Complimentary coffee in rms.
Restaurant 11 am-10 pm. Bar. Ck-out
noon. Business servs avail. Coin
lndry. Health club privileges. Pool;
whirlpool. Refrigerators; microwaves
avail. Wet bar in suites. Picnic tables,
grills. Cr cds: A, DS, MC, V.
[D] [⮌] [≈] [✈] [⊿] [♨]

★ **INTERSTATE 8 INN.** *2730 S 4th
Ave (85364). 928/726-6110; fax
928/726-7711; toll-free 800/821-7465.*
120 rms, 2 story. Jan-Mar: S $26-$39;
D $34-$56; each addl $6; under 13
free; higher rates special events;
lower rates rest of yr. Crib free. Pet
accepted, some restrictions. TV; cable
(premium), VCR avail (movies).
Complimentary coffee in lobby.
Restaurant adj 6 am-11 pm. Ck-out
11 am. Business servs avail. Coin
lndry. Pool; whirlpool. Refrigerators;
microwaves avail. Picnic tables, grills.
Cr cds: A, C, D, DS, JCB, MC, V.
[⊿] [♨] [≈]

★★ **LA FUENTE INN.** *1513 E 16th
St (85365). 928/329-1814; fax
928/343-2671; res 877/202-3353.
www.lafuenteinn.com.* 50 rms, 2 story,
46 suites. Jan-May: S $68-$80; D $78-
$90; suites $95; under 12 free; higher
rates special events; lower rates rest
of yr. Crib free. TV; cable (premium),
VCR avail (movies). Heated pool;
whirlpool. Complimentary continental bkfst, afternoon refreshments.
Coffee in rms. Restaurant adj open
24 hrs. Ck-out noon. Coin lndry.

Business servs avail. Meeting rm.
Exercise equipt. Health club privi-
leges. Airport transportation. Refrig-
erators; many wet bars, microwaves.
Near Yuma Airport. Cr cds: A, D, DS,
MC, V.
[D] [≈] [⫯] [✈] [⊿] [♨] [SC]

★★ **SHILO INN.** *1550 S Castle Dome
Ave (85365). 928/782-9511; fax
928/783-1538; toll-free 800/222-2244.
www.shiloinns.com.* 134 rms, 4 story,
16 kits. S, D $89-$159; each addl
$12; kit. units $109-$260; under 12
free. Crib free. Pet accepted, some
restrictions; $10/day. TV; cable (pre-
mium), VCR. Heated pool; whirlpool,
poolside serv. Complimentary full
bkfst. Restaurant 6 am-10 pm. Bar to
midnight. Ck-out noon. Coin lndry.
Meeting rms. Business servs avail. In-
rm modem link. Exercise equipt;
sauna, steam rm. Airport transportation. Refrigerators, microwaves avail.
Private patios, balconies. Cr cds: A,
D, DS, MC, V.
[D] [⮌] [⫯] [⌇] [≈] [⫯] [✈] [⊿] [♨] [SC]

All Suites

★★ **BEST WESTERN INN SUITES.**
*1450 S Castle Dome Ave (85365).
928/783-8341; fax 928/783-1349; toll-
free 800/922-2034. www.bestwestern.
com.* 166 rms. Jan-Apr: S, D $99; 2-
rm suites $94-$139; under 20 free;
higher rates opening wk dove season;
lower rates rest of yr. Crib free. Pet
accepted. TV; cable (premium), VCR
avail. Heated pool; whirlpool. Complimentary continental bkfst. Coffee
in rms. Ck-out noon. Coin lndry.
Business center. In-rm modem link.
Valet serv. Lighted tennis. Exercise
equipt. Refrigerators, microwaves.
Library. Cr cds: A, C, D, DS, MC, V.
[D] [⮌] [⌇] [≈] [⫯] [⊿] [♨] [SC] [⫯]

★★ **RADISSON SUITES INN.** *2600
S 4th Ave (85364). 928/726-4830; fax
928/341-1152; res 800/333-3333.
www.radisson.com.* 164 suites, 3 story.
Oct-Apr: S $106; D $116; each addl
$10; under 16 free; lower rates rest of
yr. Crib free. Pet accepted. TV; cable
(premium). Heated pool; whirlpool.
Complimentary continental bkfst.
Complimentary coffee in rms.
Restaurant adj open 24 hrs. Ck-out
noon. Meeting rms. Business servs
avail. Bellhops. Valet serv. Free airport, RR station, bus depot transportation. Health club privileges.

Refrigerators, microwaves, wet bars.
Cr cds: A, C, D, DS, ER, JCB, MC, V.

Restaurants

★ **THE CROSSING.** *2690 S 4th Ave
(85364). 928/726-5551.* Hrs: 11 am-
9:30 pm; Sun to 8:30 pm. Res
accepted. Italian, Amer menu. Wine,
beer. Lunch, dinner $3.95-$14.95.
Child's menu. Specialties: prime rib,
catfish, buffalo wings. Casual dining.
Cr cds: A, C, MC, V.

★ ★ **HUNTER STEAKHOUSE.** *2355
S 4th Ave (85364). 928/782-3637.*
Hrs: 11:30 am-2 pm, 5-9 pm; Sat,
Sun from 4 pm; early-bird dinner
Mon-Sat 5-6 pm, Sun 4-6 pm. Closed
Dec 25. Res accepted. Bar to 11 pm.
Lunch $5-$8, dinner $10-$30.
Child's menu. Specializes in beef,
steak, fresh seafood. Cr cds: A, C, D,
DS, ER, MC, V.

★ ★ **MANDARIN PALACE.** *350 E
32nd St (85364). 928/344-2805.* Hrs:
11 am-10 pm; Fri, Sat to 11 pm. Res
accepted. Chinese, Amer menu. Bar.
A la carte entrees: lunch $5.50-$6.95,
dinner $7.25-$24.95. Specialties:
crispy beef a la Szechwan, rainbow
shrimp, crispy Mandarin duck. Elegant Oriental decor. Cr cds: A, C, D,
DS, ER, MC, V.

COLORADO

From the eastern plains westward through the highest Rockies, Colorado's terrain is diverse, fascinating, and spectacularly beautiful. The highest state in the Union, with an average elevation of 6,800 feet and with 53 peaks above 14,000 feet, Colorado has attracted sports enthusiasts and vacationers as well as high-technology research and business.

When gold was discovered near present-day Denver in 1858, an avalanche of settlers poured into the state; when silver was discovered soon afterward, a new flood came. Mining camps, usually crude tent cities clinging to the rugged slopes of the Rockies, contributed to Colorado's colorful, robust history. Some of these mines still operate, but most of the early mining camps are ghost towns today. Thousands of newcomers arrive yearly, drawn to Colorado's Rockies by the skiing, hunting, fishing, and magnificent scenery.

Throughout the state there are deep gorges, rainbow-colored canyons, mysterious mesas, and other strange and beautiful land-mass variations carved by ancient glaciers and eons of erosion by wind, rain, and water. Great mountains of shifting sand lie trapped by the Sangre de Cristo Mountains in Great Sand Dunes National Monument (see); fossils 140 million years old lie in the quarries of Dinosaur National Monument (see).

Spaniards penetrated the area by the mid-1500s. American exploration of the area first took place in 1806, three years after a good portion of the region became American prop-erty through the Louisiana Purchase. Leader of the party was Lieutenant Zebulon M. Pike, for whom Pikes Peak is named. Pike pro-nounced the 14,110-foot mountain unclimbable. Today, one may drive to the top on a good gravel highway (first five miles paved). Colorado became a territory in 1861 and earned its "Centen-nial State" nickname by becoming a state in 1876, 100 years after the signing of the Declaration of Independence.

Population: 4,301,261
Area: 104,100square miles
Elevation: 3,350-14,433 feet
Peak: Mount Elbert (Lake County)
Entered Union: August 1, 1876 (38th state)
Capital: Denver
Motto: Nothing Without Providence
Nickname: Centennial State, Silver State
Flower: Rocky Mountain Columbine
Bird: Lark Bunting
Tree: Colorado Blue Spruce
Fair: August, 2003, in Pueblo
Time Zone: Mountain
Website: www.colorado.com

Colorado produces more tin, molybdenum, uranium, granite, sandstone, and basalt than any other state. The mountain area also ranks high in production of coal, gold, and silver; the state as a whole has vast deposits of brick clay and oil. Its extensively irrigated plateaus and plains are good grazing lands for live-stock and rich producers of potatoes, wheat, corn, sugar beets, cauliflower, fruit, and flowers.

When to Go/Climate

Most of Colorado falls in a semiarid climate zone. Springs are short; summers dry. Winters are surprisingly mild along the Front Range, but annual snowfall in the mountains often exceeds 20 ft.

AVERAGE HIGH/LOW TEMPERATURES (°F)
DENVER

Jan 43/16	**May** 71/44	**Sept** 77/48
Feb 47/20	**June** 81/52	**Oct** 66/36
Mar 52/26	**July** 88/59	**Nov** 53/25
Apr 62/35	**Aug** 86/57	**Dec** 45/17

COLORADO SPRINGS

Jan 41/16	**May** 69/42	**Sept** 74/47
Feb 45/19	**June** 79/51	**Oct** 64/36
Mar 50/25	**July** 84/57	**Nov** 51/25
Apr 60/33	**Aug** 81/55	**Dec** 42/17

Parks and Recreation Finder

Directions to and information about the parks and recreation areas below are given under their respective town/city sections. Please refer to those sections for details.

NATIONAL PARK AND RECREATION AREAS

Key to abbreviations. I.H.S. = International Historic Site; I.P.M. = International Peace Memorial; N.B. = National Battlefield; N.B.P. = National Battlefield Park; N.B.C. = National Battlefield and Cemetery; N.C.A. = National Conservation Area; N.E.M. = National Expansion Memorial; N.F. = National Forest; N.G. = National Grassland; N.H.P. = National Historical Park; N.H.C. = National Heritage Corridor; N.H.S. = National Historic Site; N.L. = National Lakeshore; N.M. = National Monument; N.M.P. = National Military Park; N.Mem. = National Memorial; N.P. = National Park; N.Pres. = National Preserve; N.R.A. = National Recreational Area; N.R.R. = National Recreational River; N.Riv. = National River; N.S. = National Seashore; N.S.R. = National Scenic Riverway; N.S.T. = National Scenic Trail; N.Sc. = National Scientific Reserve; N.V.M. = National Volcanic Monument.

Place Name	Listed Under
Arapaho N.F.	DILLON
Black Canyon of the Gunnison N.M.	same
Colorado N.M.	same
Dinosaur N.M.	same
Florissant Fossil Beds N.M.	same
Grand Mesa N.F.	GRAND JUNCTION
Great Sand Dunes N.M.	same
Hovenweep N.M.	CORTEZ
Mesa Verde N.P.	same
Rocky Mountain N.P.	same
Pike N.F.	COLORADO SPRINGS
Routt N.F.	STEAMBOAT SPRINGS
San Isabel N.F.	PUEBLO

STATE PARK AND RECREATION AREAS

Key to abbreviations. I.P. = Interstate Park; S.A.P. = State Archaeological Park; S.B. = State Beach; S.C.A. = State Conservation Area; S.C.P. = State Conservation Park; S.Cp. = State Campground; S.F. = State Forest; S.G. = State Garden; S.H.A. = State Historic Area; S.H.P. = State Historic Park; S.H.S. = State Historic Site; S.M.P. = State Marine Park; S.N.A. = State Natural Area; S.P. = State Park; S.P.C. = State Public Campground; S.R. = State Reserve; S.R.A. = State Recreation

Area; S.Res. = State Reservoir; S.Res.P. = State Resort Park; S.R.P. = State Rustic Park.

Place Name	Listed Under
Bonny Lake S.P.	BURLINGTON
Boyd Lake S.P.	LOVELAND
Chatfield S.P.	DENVER
Cherry Creek S.P.	DENVER
Crawford S.P.	DELTA
Lake Pueblo S.P.	PUEBLO
Steamboat Lake S.P.	STEAMBOAT SPRINGS
Sweitzer S.P.	DELTA

CALENDAR HIGHLIGHTS

JANUARY

National Western Livestock Show, Horse Show & Rodeo (Denver). National Western Complex and Coliseum. Phone 303/297-1166.

Winterskol Carnival (Aspen). Parade, fireworks, skiing, and ice-skating. Phone 970/925-1940.

MAY

Bolder Boulder (Boulder). 10K race includes citizens race and world-class heats. Phone 303/444-7223.

JUNE

FIBArk River International Whitewater Boat Race (Salida). Twenty-six-mile kayak race. Other events include slalom, raft, foot, and bicycle races. Phone 719/539-2068.

Colorado Stampede (Grand Junction). Rodeo. Phone 970/245-7723.

AUGUST

Pikes Peak Marathon (Colorado Springs). Footrace on Barr's Trail from cog depot to top of Pikes Peak and back. Phone 719/473-2625.

Jazz (Telluride). Town Park and local nightclubs. Mainstream jazz with international flavors, performed in various locales throughout the city. Phone 800/525-3455.

Boulder County Fair & Rodeo (Longmont). Fairgrounds. Phone 303/441-3927.

Colorado State Fair (Pueblo). Fairgrounds, Prairie Ave. PRCA rodeo, grandstand and amphitheater entertainment, livestock and agricultural displays, industrial and high technology displays, arts and crafts, carnival. Phone 800/876-4567.

SEPTEMBER

Vintage Auto Race & Concours d'Elegance (Steamboat Springs). Mount Werner Circle and downtown. Vintage auto racing, exhibition of restored vintage automobiles, art show of works by automotive artists. Phone 970/879-3120.

Telluride Airmen's Rendezvous & Hang Gliding Festival (Telluride). Pilots converge on Telluride for a week of hang gliding and paragliding. Climax is the World Aerobatic Hang Gliding Championship in Town Park. Pilots phone 970/728-5793.

Water-related activities, hiking, riding, various other sports, picnicking, and visitor centers, as well as camping, are available in many of these areas. Interpretive and watchable wildlife programs are available as well. A parks pass is required, good for driver and passengers; annual pass, $50; one-day pass, $3-$6/car. Passes are available at self-service dispensers at all state parks and park offices. Camping is available in most parks. Reservations can be made by phoning 303/470-1144 or 800/678-2267 from 8 am to 4:30 pm, Monday through Friday. Reservations cost $7 and a campground fee of $6-$16 is charged, depending on service offered. Electrical hookups are $5-$8 per night.

Fishing, camping, and picnicking are possible in most parks. For further information, or a free Colorado State Parks Guide, contact Colorado State Parks, 1313 Sherman #618, Denver 80203, phone 303/866-3437.

SKI AREAS

Place Name	Listed Under
Arrowhead at Vail Ski Area	VAIL
Aspen Highlands Ski Area	ASPEN
Aspen Mountain Ski Area	ASPEN
Beaver Creek Ski Area	VAIL
Breckenridge Ski Area	BRECKENRIDGE
Buttermilk Ski Area	ASPEN
Copper Mountain Resort Ski Area	DILLON
Crested Butte Mountain Resort Ski Area	CRESTED BUTTE
Eldora Mountain Resort	BOULDER
Howelsen Ski Complex	STEAMBOAT SPRINGS
Keystone Resort Ski Area	DILLON
Purgatory-Durango Ski Resort	DURANGO
Ski Cooper Ski Area	LEADVILLE
Snowmass Ski Area	SNOWMASS VILLAGE
Steamboat Ski Area	STEAMBOAT SPRINGS
Telluride Ski Resort	TELLURIDE
Vail Ski Area	VAIL
Winter Park Resort	WINTER PARK

For skiing information contact Colorado Ski Country USA, 1560 Broadway, Suite 2000, Denver 80202, phone 303/837-0793.

FISHING AND HUNTING

Nonresident fishing licenses: annual $40.25; five-day, $18.25; one-day, $5.25; additional one-day stamp, $5; second-rod stamp, $4. Many varieties of trout can be found in Colorado: rainbow and brown in most streams, lakes, and in western Colorado River, brook in all mountain streams, and cutthroat in most mountain lakes. Mackinaw can be found in many lakes and reservoirs. Kokanee salmon are also found in many reservoirs.

Nonresident hunting licenses: elk, $250.25; deer, $150.25; small game, $40.25. For information on regulations write the Division of Wildlife, 6060 Broadway, Denver 80216, phone 303/297-1192.

Driving Information

Safety belts are mandatory for all persons in front seat of vehicle. Children under four years and under 40 pounds in weight must be in an approved safety seat anywhere in vehicle. For further information phone 303/239-4500.

INTERSTATE HIGHWAY SYSTEM

The following alphabetical listing of Colorado towns in *Mobil Travel Guide* shows that these cities are within ten miles of the indicated Interstate highways. A highway map should, however, be checked for the nearest exit.

Highway Number	Cities/Towns within ten miles
Interstate 25	Colorado Springs, Denver, Englewood, Fort Collins, Lakewood, Longmont, Loveland, Manitou Springs, Pueblo, Trinidad, Walsenburg.
Interstate 70	Breckenridge, Burlington, Central City, Denver, Dillon, Evergreen, Georgetown, Glenwood Springs, Golden, Grand Junction, Idaho Springs, Lakewood, Limon, Vail.
Interstate 76	Denver, Fort Morgan, Sterling.

Additional Visitor Information

Colorado Outdoors magazine is published six times annually by State Department of Wildlife, 6060 Broadway, Denver 80216, phone 303/297-1192. *Colorado, Official State Vacation Guide* is available from The Colorado Travel & Tourism Authority, PO Box 3524, Englewood 80155, phone 800/COLORADO. A pamphlet on guest ranches is available from the Colorado Dude & Guest Ranch Association, PO Box 2120, Granby 80446, phone 970/724-3653.

There are seven welcome centers in Colorado providing brochures and travel information. Their locations are as follows: I-70 westbound in Burlington; I-70 eastbound in Fruita; US 40 eastbound in Dinosaur; I-25 northbound in Trinidad; US 160/666 northbound in Cortez; US 50 westbound in Lamar; I-76 westbound in Julesburg.

Gold mining towns abound in Colorado, as they do in many western states. Though not all towns can be reached by passenger cars, Colorado has developed the jeep tour to great advantage. Some information on ghost towns and jeep trips is listed under Breckenridge, Gunnison, Ouray, Salida, and Silverton.

COLORADO'S GOLD MINES

The San Juan Skyway is a spectacular scenic 236-mile loop out of Durango that ranges over five mountain passes as it wanders through the San Juan Mountains. From Durango, head west on US 160 to Hesperus, where you can take a side trip into La Plata Canyon to see mining ruins and a few ghost towns. Continuing west, you'll pass Mesa Verde National Park and come to CO 145 shortly before Cortez. Head north to the town of Dolores and the Anasazi Heritage Center, which features a large display of artifacts, most more than 1,000 years old. The road now follows the Dolores River, a favorite of trout anglers, and climbs the 10,222-foot Lizard Head Pass, named for the imposing rock spire looming overhead. Descending from the pass, take a short side trip into Telluride, a historic mining town and ski resort nestled in a beautiful box canyon. Follow the San Miguel River valley to CO 62, and turn north to cross the 8,970-foot Dallas Divide. After the historic railroad town of Ridgway and Ridgway State Park, where you might stop for a swim or picnic, turn south on US 550 and drive to Ouray, a picturesque old mining town. Continue over the 11,008-foot Red Mountain Pass; there is a monument here dedicated to snowplow operators who died while trying to keep the road open during winter storms. Next stop is Silverton, a small mining town and the northern terminus of the Durango and Silverton Narrow Gauge Railroad. South of Silverton is the 10,910-foot Molas Divide, after which the road almost parallels the rails as they follow the Animas River back to Durango. This tour can be done in one long day by those who want to see only the mountain scenery, but is better over two or three days, with stops at Mesa Verde National Park and the historic towns along the way. **(APPROX 236 MI)**

Alamosa

(F-4) *See also Monte Vista*

Founded 1878 **Pop** 7,960 **Elev** 7,544 ft **Area code** 719 **Zip** 81101
Information Alamosa County Chamber of Commerce, Cole Park; 719/589-3681 or 800/BLU-SKYS
Web www.alamosachamber.com

What to See and Do

Cole Park. Old Denver and Rio Grande Western narrow-gauge train on display. Chamber of Commerce located in old train station. Tennis, bicycle trails, picnicking, playgrounds. 425 4th St, on Rio Grande River. **FREE**

Cumbres & Toltec Scenic Railroad, Colorado Limited. Round-trip excursion to Osier on 1880s narrow-gauge steam railroad. Route passes through backwoods country and mountain scenery, incl the Phantom Canyon and the Toltec Gorge. Warm clothing advised due to sudden weather changes. (Memorial Day-mid-Oct, daily) Also trips to Chama, NM, via the **New Mexico Express** with van return. Res advised. 28 mi S in Antonito. Contact Box 789, Chama, NM 87520. Phone 505/756-2151. ¢¢¢¢

Fort Garland Museum. Army post (1858-1883) where Kit Carson held his last command. Restored officers' quarters; collection of Hispanic folk art. (Apr-Oct, daily; rest of yr, Mon, Thurs-Sun) 25 mi E on US 159 at Fort Garland. Phone 719/379-3512. ¢¢

Great Sand Dunes National Monument. (see). 9 mi on Rte 145 just outside East Durham. Phone 505/479-6124. ¢¢

Special Events

Sunshine Festival. Cole Park. Arts, crafts, food booths, bands, horse rides, parade, pancake bkfst, contests. First full wknd June. Phone 719/589-6077.

Early Iron Festival. Auto show. Labor Day wknd. Phone 719/589-6077.

Motels/Motor Lodges

★★ **BEST WESTERN INN.** *1919 Main St (81101). 719/589-2567; fax 719/589-0767; toll-free 800/459-5123. www.bestwestern.com/alamosainn.* 53 rms, 2 story. Mid-May-mid-Sept: S $52-$82; D $66-$96; each addl $8; suites $96-$135; under 12 free; lower rates rest of yr. Crib $8. Pet accepted, some restrictions. TV; cable (premium). Indoor pool; whirlpool. Complimentary continental bkfst. Coffee in rms. Restaurant 6 am-10 pm. Bar 4 pm-midnight. Ck-out 11 am. Meeting rms. Business servs avail. Free airport, bus depot transportation. Cr cds: A, C, D, DS, MC, V.
D ⊠ ⚡ ≋ ✈ ⊠ ⚒

★★ **HOLIDAY INN.** *333 Santa Fe Ave (81101). 719/589-5833; fax 719/589-4412; res 800/465-4329. www.holiday-inn.com.* 127 rms, 2 story. June-Aug: S $79; D $94; each addl $10; suites $110; under 18 free; lower rates rest of yr. Crib free. Pet accepted. TV; cable, VCR avail (movies $6). Indoor pool; whirlpool. Sauna. Complimentary coffee in lobby. Restaurant 6 am-9 pm. Rm serv. Bar 5 pm-2 am, Sun to midnight. Ck-out noon. Coin lndry. Meeting rms. Business center. In-rm modem link. Gift shop. Free airport, bus depot transportation. Game rm. Rec rm. Cr cds: A, D, DS, MC, V.
D ⊠ ≋ ⊠ ⚒ ⚹

B&Bs/Small Inns

★★★ **COTTONWOOD INN.** *123 San Juan Ave (81101). 719/589-3882; fax 719/589-6437; toll-free 800/955-2623. www.cottonwoodinn.com.* 9 air-cooled rms in 2 buildings, 2 share bath, 2 story, 4 kit. suites. S $44-$89; D $48-$93; each addl $10-$15; kit. units $93. Crib free. TV in sitting rm. Complimentary full bkfst. Restaurant nearby. Ck-out 11 am, ck-in 4-7 pm. Business servs avail. Each rm individually decorated; artwork by area artists. Some antiques. Totally nonsmoking. Cr cds: A, DS, MC, V.
⊠ ⚒ ⚹

★★ **ZAPATA RANCH.** *5303 State Hwy 150, Mosca (81146). 719/378-2356; fax 719/378-2428.* 15 rms, 1 suite. No rm phones. July-mid-Sept:

S, D $150-$180; suite $230; golf plan; lower rates mid-Sept-Dec. Closed Jan-mid-Mar. Crib free. Heated pool; whirlpool. Complimentary full bkfst. Coffee in rms. Dining rm 7:30-10 am, 11 am-3 pm, 6-9 pm. Ck-out 11 am, ck-in 3 pm. 18-hole golf privileges, greens fee $35, pro, putting green, driving range. Exercise equipt; sauna. Massage. Picnic tables. Ranch house built 1889; rustic decor, hand-made furniture. Bison on grounds. Totally nonsmoking. Cr cds: A, DS, MC, V.

Restaurant

★ **TRUE GRITS STEAKHOUSE.** *100 Santa Fe Ave (81101). 719/589-9954.* Hrs: 11 am-10 pm. Closed Thanksgiving, Dec 25. Res accepted. Bar. Lunch $3.95-$6.95, dinner $6.95-$18.99. Child's menu. Specializes in steak. John Wayne memorabilia. Casual dining. Cr cds: DS, MC, V.

Aspen

(C-3) *See also Snowmass Village*

Settled 1879 **Pop** 5,914 **Elev** 7,908 ft
Area code 970 **Zip** 81611
Information Aspen Chamber Resort Association, 425 Rio Grande Place; 970/925-1940 or 800/26-ASPEN
Web www.aspen.com

What to See and Do

Ashcroft Ghost Town. Partially restored ghost town and mining camp features 1880s buildings, hotel. Guided tours (June-Aug 11 am and 2 pm, daily) Self-guided tours avail daily. 10 mi S. Phone 970/925-3721. ¢¢

HeritageAspen: Aspen's Historical Society. Exhibits depict Aspen area history. (Early June-Sept and mid-Dec-mid-Apr, Tues-Fri; rest of yr by appt; closed Dec 25) 620 W Bleeker St. Phone 970/925-3721. ¢¢¢¢

Recreation. Swimming, fishing, river rafting; hunting (deer, elk), hiking, climbing, horseback riding, golf, tennis, ice-skating, camping, pack trips, kayaking, hang gliding, paragliding, sailplaning, ballooning. There are 1,000 mi of trout streams and 25 lakes within a 20-mi radius of Aspen, plus many more in the surrounding mountains. More than ten public campgrounds. Contact the Aspen Chamber Resort Association for details.

River rafting.

Blazing Adventures. Half-day, full-day, and overnight trips on the Arkansas, Roaring Fork, Colorado, and Gunnison rivers. Trips range from scenic floats for beginners to exciting runs for experienced rafters. (May-Oct; res required) Transportation to site. Phone 800/282-7238. ¢¢¢¢

Scenic drive to Independence Pass. A 12,095-ft pass in magnificent mountain scenery. (June-Oct; road closed rest of yr) SE on CO 82.

Skiing.

Aspen Highlands. Three quad, triple chairlift; patrol, school, rentals, snowmaking; three restaurants, bar. One hundred twelve runs; longest run 3½ mi; vertical drop 3,635 ft. (Dec-mid-Apr, daily) Snowboarding. Shuttle bus service to and from Aspen. Half-day rates. 1½ mi SW on Maroon Creek Rd in White River National Forest (see GLENWOOD SPRINGS). Phone 970/925-1220 or 800/525-6200. ¢¢¢¢

Aspen Mountain. Three quad, four double chairlifts; gondola; patrol, school, snowmaking; restaurants, bars. Seventy-six runs; longest run three mi; vertical drop 3,267 ft. (Dec-mid-Apr, daily) Shuttle bus service to Buttermilk, Aspen Highlands, and Snowmass. ¢¢¢¢

Buttermilk. Quad, five double chairlifts, surface lift; patrol, school, rentals, snowmaking; cafeteria, restaurants, bar, nursery. Forty-three runs; longest run three mi; vertical drop 2,030 ft. Snowboarding. (Dec-mid-Apr, daily) Shuttle bus service from Ajax and Snowmass. 2 mi W on CO 82. Phone 970/925-1221. ¢¢¢¢

Snowmass. 12 mi NW (see SNOWMASS VILLAGE).

Special Events

Winterskol Carnival. Mid-Jan. Phone 970/925-1940.

Aspen Music Festival. Aspen Music Tent, Wheeler Opera House, and Harris Concert Hall. Symphonies, chamber music concerts, opera, jazz. Phone 970/925-3254. June-Aug.

Aspen Theater in the Park. Performances nightly and afternoons. Phone 970/925-3254. June-Aug.

Motels/Motor Lodges

★★★★ **HOTEL JEROME.** *330 E Main St (81611). 970/920-1000; fax 970/925-2784; toll-free 800/331-7213. www.hoteljerome.com.* This 1889 Victorian building is on the National Register of Historic Places and houses 93 rooms uniquely decorated with country fabrics, down comforters, and carved armoires. In operation since 1890, the hotel's J-Bar is a popular casual dining destination featuring seasonal, live entertainment. 93 rms, 3-4 story. Mid-Nov-mid-Mar: S $215-$525, D $325-$655; suites $355-$1,650; lower rates rest of yr. Pet accepted. Garage $10. TV; cable (premium), VCR (movies $7). Heated pool; whirlpools, poolside serv. Restaurant 7 am-10 pm (see also CENTURY ROOM). Rm serv 24 hrs. Bar noon-2 am. Ck-out 11 am. Meeting rms. Business servs avail. In-rm modem link. Concierge. Gift shop. Free airport transportation. Downhill ski 4 blks; x-country ski 1 mi. Exercise equipt. Massage. Bathrm phones, refrigerators; some in-rm whirlpools. Cr cds: A, D, MC, V.

⊡ ➤ ⚓ ♨ ⚒ ≋ ⚘ ✈ ⌦ ♿

★★ **INNSBRUCK INN.** *233 W Main St (81611). 970/925-2980; fax 970/925-6960. www.preferredlodging. com.* 30 rms, some A/C, 2 kit. units, 2 story. Mid-Nov-mid-Apr: S, D $139-$195-$250; each addl $20; suites (to 4 persons) $399; under 16, $10; higher rates Christmas hols; lower rates rest of yr. Crib free. Pet accepted. TV; cable (premium), VCR avail. Heated pool; whirlpool. Complimentary continental bkfst. Restaurant nearby. Ck-out 11 am. In-rm modem link. Downhill/x-country ski ½ mi. Some refrigerators; microwaves avail. Cr cds: A, D, MC, V.

⊡ ➤ ♨ ≋ ⌦ ♨

Hotels

★★ **ASPEN SQUARE CONDOMINIUM HOTEL.** *617 E Cooper Ave (81611). 970/925-1000; fax 970/925-1017; toll-free 800/862-7736. www. aspensquarehotel.com.* 104 air-cooled condo apts with kit., 3-4 story. Late-Nov-Apr: $165-$295; each addl (after 4th person) $15; higher rates Christmas; under 12 free. lower rates rest of yr. Crib free. TV; cable (premium), VCR. Heated pool; whirlpool. Restaurant adj 7:30 am-3:30 pm. Coffee in rms. Ck-out 10 am. Coin lndry. Meeting rms. Business servs avail. In-rm modem link. Gift shop. Bellhops. Concierge. Coin lndry. Free garage parking. Downhill ski adj; x-country ski 1 mi. Valet serv. Exercise equipt. Health club privileges. Refrigerators. Fireplaces. Balconies. Cr cds: A, MC, V.

⚓ ⚒ ♨ ≋ ⚘ ⌦ ♿

★★ **HOTEL ASPEN.** *110 W Main St (81611). 970/925-3441; fax 970/920-1379; toll-free 800/527-7369. www. aspen.com/ha.* 45 rms, 2-3 story. No elvtr. Mid-Feb-late-Mar: S, D $149-$399; each addl $20; under 13 free; higher rates hols; lower rates rest of yr. Crib free. Pet accepted. TV; cable (premium), VCR. Heated pool; whirlpool. Complimentary continental bkfst, coffee in rms. Ck-out 11 am. Business servs avail. In-rm modem link. Parking $1/day. Valet serv. Free ski shuttle. Downhill ski 8 blks. Health club privileges. Refrigerators, wet bars, fireplaces, microwaves. Patios, balconies. Totally nonsmoking. Cr cds: A, D, DS, MC, V.

♨ ♨ ≋ ⌦ ♨

★★ **MOLLY GIBSON LODGE.** *101 W Main St (81611). 970/925-3434; fax 970/925-2582; toll-free 800/356-6559. www.mollygibson.com.* 52 rms, 2 story, 6 kits. Feb-Mar: S, D $195-$395; each addl $10; suites $295-$425; lower rates rest of yr. Crib free. TV; cable (premium), VCR (movies). Heated pools; 2 whirlpools. Complimentary continental bkfst. Restaurant nearby. Bar 4-9 pm in winter. Ck-out 10 am. Meeting rm. Business center. In-rm modem link. Bellhops. Valet serv. Exercise equipt. Free airport transportation. Downhill/x-country ski 6 blks. Free bicycle rentals. Refrigerators; some in-rm whirlpools, fireplaces, balconies. Cr cds: A, D, DS, MC, V.

Resorts

★★ **LIMELITE LODGE.** *228 E Cooper St (81611). 970/925-3025; fax 970/925-5120; toll-free 800/433-0832. www.aspen.com/limelite.* 63 rms, 34 A/C, 29 air-cooled, 1-3 story. No elvtr. Mid-Dec-Mar: S, D $77-$275; each addl $15 kit. units $118-$350; under 12 free; ski plans; higher rates hols; varied lower rates rest of yr. Pet accepted. TV; cable (premium), VCR avail. 2 heated pools; whirlpools, sauna. Playground opp. Complimentary continental bkfst.Coffee in rms. Restaurant nearby. Ck-out 11 am. Coin lndry. Business servs avail. In-rm modem link. Downhill ski 3 blks. Refrigerators. Cr cds: A, C, D, DS, MC, V.

★★★★★ **THE LITTLE NELL.** *675 E Durant Ave (81611). 970/920-4600; fax 970/920-6345; toll-free 800/525-6200. www.thelittlenell.com.* Enjoy splendid downtown or mountain views from one of 92 rooms at this western American alpine retreat. In the winter, ski in from the lifts, conveniently located behind the main building, and take the chill off by the roaring lobby fire or the guest room gas fireplaces. In the summer, there's swimming, hiking, and mountain biking. 92 rms, 4 story, 14 suites. Dec-Mar: S, D $285-$650; suites $900-$3,900; lower rates rest of year. Crib free. Pet accepted. Garage; valet parking $15. TV; cable (premium), VCR (movies). Heated pool; whirlpool, poolside serv. Restaurant (see also MONTAGNA). Bar 3 pm-midnight; entertainment Thurs-Sat. Ck-out noon. Meeting rms. Business center. In-rm modem link. Concierge. Shopping arcade. Free airport transportation. Downhill ski on site. Exercise rm; steam rm. Massage. Bathrm phones, refrigerators, minibars, gas fireplaces; microwaves avail. Cr cds: A, D, DS, ER, MC, V.

★★★★ **THE ST. REGIS ASPEN.** *315 E Dean St (81611). 970/920-3300; fax 970/925-8998; res 800/325-3589. www.stregisaspen.com.* Experience this hotel's well-known luxury in a cozy mountain atmosphere accented with leather, stone, and crackling fireplaces. At the base of Aspen Mountain between the gondola and Lift 1A, the 257 rooms and suites are decorated with leather chairs, khaki walls, and plaid-accented furnishings. Boston chef Todd English's famous Olives restaurant has an outpost here showcasing refined, Mediterranean cuisine. 257 rms, 6 story. Early Jan-late Mar and early June-early Oct: S, D $219-$595; each addl $25; suites $595-$4,000; under 18 free; ski plans; lower rates rest of yr. Crib free. Pet accepted. Valet parking $19. TV; cable (premium), VCR avail (movies). Heated pool; whirlpools, poolside serv (summer). Supervised children's activities (Nov-mid-Apr); ages 3-16. Restaurant. Rm serv 24 hrs. Bar 11-1 am; entertainment. Ck-out noon. Convention facilities. Business center. In-rm modem link. Concierge. Gift shop. Beauty shop. Golf privileges. Downhill ski 1 blk; x-country ski 1 ½ mi; rental equipt. Hiking. Bicycle rentals. Exercise rm; saunas, steam rms. Massage. Bathrm phones, minibars; microwaves avail. Some balconies. Luxury level. Cr cds: A, C, D, DS, JCB, MC, V.

B&Bs/Small Inns

★ **ASPEN MOUNTAIN LODGE.** *311 W Main St (81611). 970/925-7650; fax 970/925-5744; res 800/362-7736. www.aspenmountainlodge.com.* 38 rms, 4 story. No elvtr. Mid-Feb-late Mar: S, D $89-$189; under 12 free; ski plan; lower rates rest of yr. Closed mid-Apr-late May. TV; cable. Heated pool; whirlpool. Complimentary buffet bkfst. Restaurant nearby. Ck-out 11 am. In-rm modem link. Downhill/x-country ski 6 blks. Refrigerators, wet bars. 4-story river rock fireplace. Some balconies. Cr cds: A, DS, MC, V.

★★ **BOOMERANG LODGE.** *500 W Hopkins Ave (81611). 970/925-3416; fax 970/925-3314; toll-free 800/992-8852. www.boomeranglodge.com.* 34 air-cooled units, 2-3 story, 11 kits. Jan-late Mar: S, D $141-$391; each addl $10; studio rms $207-$281; 2-3-bedrm apts $408-$587; under 12 free (summer); higher rates Dec 25; lower rates rest of yr. Crib $4. TV; cable, VCR avail. Heated pool; whirlpool, sauna. Complimentary continental bkfst. Restaurant nearby. Ck-out 11 am. Guest lndry. Business servs avail. In-rm modem link. Downhill/x-country ski 5 blks. Some refrigerators, fireplaces; microwaves avail. Private patios, balconies. Garden picnic area, mountain views. Cr cds: A, D, DS, MC, V.

★ ★ ★ **HOTEL LENADO.** *200 S Aspen St (81611). 970/925-6246; fax 970/925-3840. www.hotellenado.com.* 19 rms, 3 story. Mid-Dec-Apr: S, D $425-$485; lower rates rest of yr. Whirlpool. Pet accepted; $500 deposit. TV; cable (premium), VCR avail. Complimentary full bkfst (in season), continental bkfst (off season); afternoon refreshments. Bar 4 pm-midnight. Coffee in rms. Ck-out noon, ck-in 4 pm. Meeting rms. In-rm modem link. Luggage handling. Valet serv. Downhill/x-country ski 6 blks. Some refrigerators, in-rm whirlpools, wet bars. Balconies. Library. Cr cds: A, D, MC, V.

★ ★ ★ **SARDY HOUSE HOTEL.** *128 E Main St (81611). 970/920-2525; fax 970/920-4478; toll-free 800/321-3457. www.sardyhouse.com.* 20 units, 3 story. Late-Nov-mid-Apr: S, D $195-$275; suites $300-$500; higher rates winter hols. Crib avail. Pet accepted. TV; cable (premium), VCR (free movies) in suites. Heated pool; whirlpool. Sauna. Complimentary full bkfst. Dining rm 7:30-10:30 am, 6-9:30 pm. Rm serv. Bar 4:30 pm-midnight. Ck-out noon, ck-in 4 pm. Meeting rm. Business servs avail. In-rm modem link. Luggage handling. Valet serv. Downhill/x-country ski 5 blks. Health club privileges. Some refrigerators, bathrm phones, in-rm steam baths, coffeemakers, fireplaces, balconies. 1892 house with winding staircase and oak balustrade; panoramic mountain views. Cr cds: A, D, MC, V.

★ ★ **SHENANDOAH INN.** *0600 Frying Pan Rd, Basalt (81621). 970/927-4991; fax 970/927-4990; toll-free 800/804-5520. www.shenandoahinn.*

com. 4 rms, 1 cabin, private baths, 2 story. No A/C. D $100-$130; cabin $175; each addl $25; wkly rates; wkends (2-day min). Children over 12 yrs only. TV in common rm; VCR avail (movies). Whirlpool. Complimentary full bkfst. Restaurant nearby. Ck-out 11 am, ck-in 4-7 pm. Business servs avail. In-rm modem link. Luggage handling. Refrigerators. Downhill ski 17 mi; x-country ski 3 mi. On river. Cabin built in 1896. Totally nonsmoking. Cr cds: A, MC, V.

Conference Center

★ ★ ★ **ASPEN MEADOWS.** *845 Meadows Rd (81611). 970/925-4240; fax 970/925-7790; toll-free 800/452-4240. www.aspenmeadows.com.* 98 suites in 6 bldgs, 58 with shower only. No A/C. June-Sept: S, D $195-$260; each addl $20; under 12 free; lower rates rest of yr. Crib $10. Garage parking $5. TV; cable (premium), VCR (movies $5.95). Heated pool; whirlpool. Complimentary coffee in rms. Restaurant 7-9:30 am, noon-2 pm, 6-9 pm. Rm serv. Bar 4-10 pm. Ck-out 11 am. Conference facilities. Business center. In-rm modem link. Bellhops. Sundries. Coin lndry. Valet serv. Free airport transportation. Tennis. 18-hole golf privileges. Downhill/x-country ski 1 mi. Exercise rm; steam rm. Massage. Mountain bike rentals. Wet bars; microwaves avail. Balconies. Picnic tables. On 40-acres; Bauhaus-style architecture. Cr cds: A, C, D, DS, MC, V.

Restaurants

★ ★ ★ **AJAX TAVERN.** *685 E Durant (81611). 970/920-9333. www.ajax tavern.com.* Hrs: 11:30 am-10 pm. Closed mid-Apr-mid-May. Res accepted. Bar. A la carte entrees: lunch $8-$17.50, dinner $10.50-$32. Child's menu. Specialties: lamb sirloin, seafood pastina risotto. Valet parking. Outdoor dining. English tavern decor. Cr cds: A, C, D, DS, MC, V.

★★★ **CACHE CACHE.** *205 S Mill St (81611).* 970/925-3835. *www.cache cache.com.* Hrs: 5:30-10:30 pm. Closed mid-Apr-May, Nov. Res accepted. French menu. Bar. Dinner $14-$27. Specialties: osso buco, Chilean sea bass, Long Island duck with blood orange sauce. Patio dining. Casual dining. Cr cds: A, MC, V.

★★ **CANTINA.** *411 E Main St (81611).* 970/925-3663. Hrs: 11 am-10:30 pm. Mexican, Amer menu. Bar to 1 am. Lunch $5.95-$8.95, dinner $7.95-$18.95. Child's menu. Specialties: wild game fajitas, cantina camarones, chimichanga. Outdoor dining. Mexican decor. Cr cds: A, D, DS, MC, V.
D ⊒

★★★ **CENTURY ROOM.** *330 E Main St (81611).* 970/920-1000. *www. hoteljerome.com.* Hrs: 6-10 pm. Res accepted. Bar 11:30-2 am. Wine list. Dinner $24-$34. Specializes in Colorado trout, game, rack of lamb. Entertainment. Valet parking. Outdoor dining. Antiques. Cr cds: A, D, DS, MC, V.
D SC

★★ **THE CHART HOUSE.** *219 E Durant Ave (81611).* 970/925-3525. Hrs: 5:30-10 pm. Res accepted. Bar. Dinner $14.95-$30. Child's menu. Specializes in prime rib, seafood, steak. Salad bar. Cr cds: A, D, DS, MC, V.

★★ **GUIDO'S SWISS INN.** *403 S Galena St (81611).* 970/925-7222. Hrs: 5:30-10 pm. Closed mid-Apr-mid-June & mid Oct-Thanksgiving. Res accepted. Swiss, French menu. Bar. Dinner $16-$26. Child's menu. Specialties: Wiener schnitzel, rack of lamb. Outdoor dining. European chalet decor; scenic view of mountains. Family-owned. Cr cds: A, DS, MC, V.
D SC

★★★ **JIMMY'S AN AMERICAN RESTAURANT.** *205 S Mill St (81611).* 970/925-6020. Hrs: 5-11 pm. Closed Thanksgiving, Dec 25. Res accepted. Contemporary Amer menu. Bar. A la carte entrees: dinner $10-$34. Specializes in steaks, chops, seafood. Street parking. Outdoor dining. Totally nonsmoking. Cr cds: A, MC, V.

★★ **LA COCINA.** *308 E Hopkins (81611).* 970/925-9714. Hrs: 5-10 pm. Closed Dec 25; also mid-Apr-May, Nov. Mexican menu. Bar. Dinner $6.50-$10.75. Child's menu. Specializes in posole, blue corn tortillas, guacamole. Outdoor dining. Cr cds: MC, V.

★★ **L'HOSTARIA.** *620 E Hyman Ave (81611).* 970/925-9022. *www. lhostaria.com.* Hrs: 5:30-10:30 pm; summer hrs vary. Closed mid-Apr-mid May. Res accepted. Italian menu. Bar. A la carte entrees: dinner $9.50-$26. Specialties: grilled ahi, breaded veal cutlet, homemade tortelloni. Outdoor dining. Italian contemporary decor. Cr cds: A, D, MC, V.
D

★ **MAIN STREET BAKERY & CAFE.** *201 E Main St (81611).* 970/925-6446. Hrs: 7 am-9:30 pm; Sun, Mon to 5 pm. Closed Thanksgiving, Dec 25. No A/C. Wine, beer. Bkfst $4.95-$10.95, lunch $4.95-$9.95, dinner $12-$25. Child's menu. Specialties: cinnamon raisin french toast, pumpkin seed crusted rainbow trout. Own baking. Parking. Outdoor dining in shaded courtyard. Totally nonsmoking. Cr cds: A, MC, V.
D

★★★ **MATSUHISA.** *303 E Main St (81611).* 970/544-6628. Specializes in black cod with miso, new style sushi. Hrs: 6-10 pm. Res accepted. Wine list. Dinner $15-$35. Street parking. New Japanese style decor. Cr cds: A, D, DS, MC, V.
D

★★ **MEZZALUNA.** *624 E Cooper Ave (81611).* 970/925-5882. Specializes in wood-oven pizza, seared tuna. Hrs: 11:30 am-10:30 pm. Res accepted. Wine, beer. Lunch $5.95-$15; dinner $11.50-$25. Entertainment. Cr cds: A, D, DS, MC, V.
D

★★★★ **MONTAGNA.** *675 E Durant Ave (81611).* 970/920-6313. *www.the littlenell.com.* This elegant dining room at the base of Aspen Mountain features sparkling crystal, crisp white linens, an award-winning wine list, and a team of professional servers who dote on every guest. Chef Paul

Skiing in Aspen

Wade's American alpine cuisine constantly impresses diners with its intriguing combination of flavors, textures, and colors. Contemporary French cuisine. Specialties: Colorado rack of lamb with spaghetti squash, stuffed zuchini tart, butternut squash ruby trout with white truffle gnocchi, spinach and pine nut froth. Hrs: 7-10:30 am, 11:30 am-2:30 pm, 6-10 pm; Sun brunch noon-2:30 pm. Res accepted. Bar 3 pm-2 am. Wine cellar. A la carte entrees: bkfst $7-$15.50, lunch $10-$16, dinner $27-$40. 5-course degustation menu: dinner $75. Sun brunch $10.50-$16.50. Valet parking. Outdoor dining (seasonal). Cr cds: A, D, DS, MC, V.
🄳

★★ **MOTHERLODE.** *314 E Hyman Ave (81611). 970/925-7700. www. motherloderestaurant.com.* Hrs: 11:30 am-2:30 pm, 5:30-10:30 pm, winter from 5:30 pm. Closed Thanksgiving; also mid-Apr-May. Italian menu. Bar to 1:30 am. Lunch $5.95-$8.95, dinner $13-$23. Specializes in pasta, seafood. Outdoor dining. Casual dining. Family-owned. Cr cds: A, C, D, DS, MC, V.
🄳

★★★ **OLIVES.** *315 E Dean St (81611). 970/920-7356. www.stregis aspen.com.* Specializes in ribeye, grilled roasted chicken, tuna tartare.

Hrs: 7 am-2 pm. Res accepted. Wine, beer. Lunch $9.75-$14; dinner $30-$40. Child's menu. Open viewing kitchen. Cr cds: A, C, D, DS, MC, V.
🄳

★★ **PACIFICA.** *307 S Mill St (81611). 970/920-9775.* Hrs: 11:30 am-midnight. Bar. Lunch $7-$14, dinner $19-$28. Specialties: spicy catfish, paella risotto, tuna quesadillas. Child's menu. Outdoor dining. On mall; overlooks Wagner Park. Cr cds: A, D, DS, MC, V.
🄳

★★ **PINE CREEK COOKHOUSE.** *12500 Castle Creek Rd (81611). 970/925-1044. www.pinecreekcook house.com.* Sittings: noon & 1:30 pm, 6 & 8:30 pm. Winter hrs vary. Closed May & Oct-mid-Nov. Res accepted. No A/C. Continental menu. Bar. Lunch $8.95-$14.95, dinner $19-$33. Specialties: rainbow trout, spinach crepe, rack of lamb. Salad bar (lunch). Parking. Outdoor dining. Unique dining in cabin located in a scenic valley in the Elk Mtns (elev 9,800 ft); overlooks Castle Creek. Arrive via x-country ski trail or horse-drawn sleigh in winter ($20 per person). Totally nonsmoking. Cr cds: A, MC, V.

★★★★ **PIÑON'S.** *105 S Mill St (81611). 970/920-2021.* This comfortable earth-toned restaurant is typical for ski-town dining - impeccable food paired with a rustic, laid-back setting. The creative Colorado-American menu includes dishes such as coriander-grilled caribou with whipped yams and potatoes and sun-dried currant sauce. Chef Rob Mobillian's creative culinary interpretations served in this dimly lit, romantic atmosphere have even been known to attract a few celebrities. Contemporary American menu. Specialties: caribou, pheasant, ahi tuna. Hrs: 6-10 pm. Closed mid-Apr-early-June, Oct-Dec. Res accepted. Bar. Wine cellar. Dinner $22-$40. Western decor. View of mountains. Totally nonsmoking. Cr cds: A, MC, V.

D

★★ **POPPIES BISTRO CAFE.** 834 W Hallam (81611). 970/925-2333. www.poppiesbistrocafe.com. Hrs: 6-10:30 pm. Closed mid-Apr-mid-June and late Oct-mid-Nov. Res accepted. No A/C. Continental menu. Bar. Dinner $19-$34. Specialties: lobster relleno, steak au poivre, sauteed pheasant breast. Own baking, pasta. Parking. Intimate dining in Victorian house (1889). Period furnishings; antiques. Cr cds: A, MC, V.

D

★★★★ **RENAISSANCE.** 304 E Hopkins (81611). 970/925-2402. www.renaissancerestaurant.com. This modern fine-dining restaurant offers creative, worldly cuisine with a rustic feel. Nationally recognized chef Charles Dale turns out specialties that include foie gras with Coca Cola sauce, and chocolate souffle. Modern French menu. Specialties: spinach with crab tart, sea bass with artichokes and shiitake mushrooms, fresh sautéed foie gras. Menu changes nightly. Own baking. Hrs: 6-10:30 pm. Res accepted. Bar. Extensive wine list. A la carte entrees: dinner $24-$32. Child's menu. Street parking. Outdoor dining. Cr cds: A, D, MC, V.

D

★★★★ **RESTAURANT CONUN-DRUM.** 325 E Main St (81611). 970/925-9969. This elegant restaurant serves up an American menu with international influences. Favorites include roasted Chilean sea bass in pancetta with a port and black truffle vinaigrette. Dishes incorporate very fresh ingredients, and the wine list is extensive. American cuisine with European influences. Hrs: 6-10 pm. Res accepted. Wine list. Dinner $22-$32. Cr cds: A, MC, V.

D ⊠

★★★ **SYZYGY.** 520 E Hyman Ave (81611). 970/925-3700. Hrs: 6 pm-midnight. Closed mid-Apr-May. Res accepted. Bar. A la carte entrees: dinner $17-$33. Specialties: elk tenderloin, halibut with morels, soft shell crab. Own pastries. Jazz band Wed-Sun. Art deco decor; water wall fountains. Cr cds: A, D, DS, MC, V.

D ⊠

★★ **TAKAH SUSHI.** 420 E Hyman Ave (81611). 970/925-8588. www.takahsushi.com. Hrs: 5:30-11 pm; summer from 6 pm. Closed Thanksgiving; mid Apr-May. Res accepted. Japanese menu. Bar. Dinner $15-$25. Specialties: sushi, sashimi, crispy duck. Contemporary Oriental decor. Totally nonsmoking. Cr cds: A, D, DS, MC, V.

★★ **UTE CITY.** 501 E Hyman Ave (81611). 970/920-4699. Hrs: 11:30 am-11 pm. Res accepted. Bar 11:30-2 am. Lunch $8.25-$12.25, dinner $15-$42. Specialties: crab cakes, wild game, home-smoked salmon. Entertainment wkends. Originally a bank (1890). Murals. Cr cds: A, DS, MC, V.

D

★★ **WIENERSTUBE.** 633 E Hyman Ave (81611). 970/925-3357. Hrs: 7 am-2:30 pm. Closed Mon. Continental menu. Bar. Bkfst $1.75-$9.95, lunch $4.50-$16.25. Specializes in wienerschnitzel, Austrian sausages. Outdoor dining. Cr cds: A, C, D, DS, MC, V.

D

Unrated Dining Spots

BOOGIE'S DINER. 534 E Cooper Ave (81611). 970/925-6610. www.boogies.com. Hrs: 8 am-10 pm. Closed mid-Apr-mid-June. Res accepted. Bar 11 am-closing. Bkfst $3.75-$5.95, lunch, dinner $1.95-$7.95. Child's menu. Specialty: meat loaf. Diner. Cr cds: A, MC, V.

D SC

CRYSTAL PALACE DINNER THE-ATER. *300 E Hyman (81612). 970/925-1455. www.cpalace.net.* Hrs: 5:30 pm-12:30 am (winter); 7:30-11:30 pm (summer); wkends 5:30 pm-12:30 am. Closed Sun & Mon (summer); also mid-Apr-mid-June & Sept-Nov. Res required. Continental menu. Bar. Complete meals: dinner $60. Serv charge 18%. Child's menu. Specialties: prime rib, salmon Bearnaise, rack of lamb. Dinner theater. Victorian decor. Cr cds: A, C, D, DS, MC, V.

Aurora (B-5)

(see Denver International Airport Area)

Beaver Creek

(see Vail)

Black Canyon of the Gunnison National Monument

(D-2) *See also Montrose*

(15 mi NE of Montrose via US 50, CO 347)

Within this monument, 12 of the most spectacular miles of the rugged gorge of the Gunnison River slice down to a maximum depth of 2,660 feet. At one point the river channel is only 40 feet wide. Narrowest width between north and south rims at the top is 1,100 feet. The combination of dark, weathered rock and lack of sunlight due to the narrowness of the canyon give the monument its name.

Piñon trees, some more than 800 years old, add to the spectacular scenery, along with numerous mule deer. There are scenic drives along

South Rim (road plowed to Gunnison Point in winter) and North Rim (approximately May to October). There are also hiking areas and concessions (June-Labor Day). The visitor center is located at Gunnison Point on the South Rim. A descent into the canyon requires a free hiking permit from the visitor center. Cross-country skiing is open in winter from Gunnison Point to High Point. Interpretive programs are offered (summer only). Contact Superintendent, 102 Elk Creek, Gunnison 81230; phone 970/641-2337. Per vehicle ¢¢

Boulder

(B-5) *See also Denver, Longmont, Lyons*

Settled 1858 **Pop** 94,673 **Elev** 5,344 ft **Area code** 303

Information Convention & Visitors Bureau, 2440 Pearl St, 80302; 303/442-2911 or 800/444-0447

Web www.ci.boulder.co.us

What to See and Do

Boulder Creek Path. A nature and exercise trail that runs some 16 mi through the city and into the adj mountains, with no street crossings, leading past a sculpture garden, restored steam locomotive, and several city parks. (Daily) From 55th St and Pearl Pkwy to Boulder Canyon. Phone 303/413-7200. **FREE**

Boulder History Museum. Collections of Boulder history from 1858-present including 20,000 artifacts, 111,000 photgraphs, and 486,000 documents; permanent and rotating interpretive exhibits; educational programs. (Tues-Fri 10 am-4 pm, Sat, Sun noon-4 pm) Harbeck House (1899), 1206 Euclid Ave. Phone 303/449-3464. ¢¢

Boulder Museum of Contemporary Art. Exhibits of contemporary and regional painting, sculpture, other media; experimental performance series (Thurs, fee); changing exhibits with local, domestic, and international artists. Lectures, workshops, and special events. (Tues-Sun; closed hols) 1750 13th St. Phone 303/443-2122. ¢¢

Boulder Reservoir. Swimming (Memorial Day-Labor Day, daily), waterskiing, fishing, boating (daily; get permit for power boat at main gate), rentals; picnicking. (Daily) 2 mi N on CO 119. Phone 303/441-3461. ¢¢

Downtown Mall. Pedestrian shopping mall offers fine shops and restaurants, acrobatic shows, mime performances, strolling musicians; periodic art and cultural festivals. Pearl St between 9th and 15th Sts.

Industrial Tour. Celestial Seasonings. This maker of herbal and black teas gives tours covering the history of the company, its product line, and a walk-through of the manufacturing plant. 4600 Sleepytime Dr. Phone 303/530-5300.

Leanin' Tree Museum of Western Art. Museum displaying the original works of art used in many of the greeting cards produced by Leanin' Tree, a major greeting card publisher. (Daily) 6055 Longbow Dr. Phone 303/530-1442. **FREE**

National Center for Atmospheric Research. Designed by I. M. Pei. Exhibits on global warming, weather, the sun, aviation hazards, and supercomputing. Also 400-acre nature preserve on site. Guided tours (summer, Mon-Sat afternoons; rest of yr, Wed). (Daily) 1850 Table Mesa Dr. **FREE**

Skiing. Eldora Mountain Resort. Two quad, two triple, four double chairlifts; four surface lifts; patrol, school, rentals, snowmaking; cafeteria, bar, nursery. Fifty-three runs; longest run three mi; vertical drop 1,400 ft. (Mid-Nov-early Apr) X-country skiing (27 mi). 21 mi W on CO 119 near Nederland. Phone 303/440-8700. ¢¢¢¢

University of Colorado. (1876) 25,000 students. Tours of campus. Phone 303/492-1411. On the 786-acre campus, the distinctive native sandstone and red-tile buildings incl Old Main, Norlin Library, and

> **Fiske Planetarium and Science Center.** Programs using a new computerized control system giving a three-dimensional effect; science classes for all ages, special events (fees). Lobby exhibits. Phone 303/492-5001. ¢¢

Macky Auditorium Concert Hall. Artist Series, guest artists, Boulder Philharmonic Orchestra. Concerts during academic yr. 17th St and University Ave. Phone 303/492-6309.

Sommers-Bausch Observatory. Stargazing. (Weather permitting, school yr; closed school hols) Res required Fri. Phone 303/492-6732. **FREE**

University of Colorado Museum. Displays relics and artifacts of early human life in the area, plus regional geological, zoological, and botanical collections. Changing exhibits. (Daily; closed school hols) Broadway and 15th St, in Henderson Building. Phone 303/492-6892. **FREE**

Special Events

Boulder Bach Festival. Concerts of the music of Johann Sebastian Bach. Phone 303/494-3159. Late Jan.

Kinetic Conveyance Sculpture Challenge. People-powered sculpture race across land and water. Early May. Phone 303/444-5600.

Bolder Boulder. Ten-km race. Incl citizens race and world-class heats. Phone 303/444-7223. Memorial Day.

Colorado Music Festival. Chautauqua Park, 900 Baseline Rd. Entertainment, lectures. Phone 303/449-1397. Eight wks June-Aug.

Colorado Shakespeare Festival. Mary Rippon Outdoor Theater, University of Colorado. Three Shakespeare plays in repertory. Phone 303/492-1397 or 303/492-7355. June-Aug.

Motels/Motor Lodges

★★ **COURTYARD BY MARRIOTT BOULDER.** *4710 Pearl E Cir (80301). 303/440-4700; fax 303/440-8975; toll-free 888/236-2427. www.courtyard. com.* 149 rms, 3 story. May-Oct: S, D $139-$159; suites $155-$179; under 12 free; wkly rates; lower rates rest of yr. Crib free. TV; cable (premium). Heated indoor pool; whirlpool. Complimentary coffee in rms. Restaurant 6:30-10 am, 6-10 pm; Fri to 10 am, Sat to 11 am; Sun 7 am-noon, 6-10 pm. Bar 5-10:30 pm. Ck-out noon. Coin lndry. Meeting rms. Business servs avail. In-rm modem link. Valet serv. Airport transportation. Exercise equipt. Refrigerator in suites. Balconies. Cr cds: A, D, DS, JCB, MC, V.

★★ HAMPTON INN. *912 W Dillon Rd, Louisville (80027). 303/666-7700; fax 303/666-7374; res 800/426-7866. www.stonebridgecompanies.com.* 80 rms, 3 story. Late May-Sept: S, D $89-$109; each addl $10; under 18 free; higher rates special events; lower rates rest of yr. Crib free. TV; cable (premium). Complimentary continental bkfst. Complimentary coffee in rms. Restaurant nearby. Ck-out 11 am. Meeting rms. Business center. In-rm modem link. Valet serv. Coin lndry. Airport transportation. Exercise equipt. Indoor pool; whirlpool. Bathrm phones, refrigerators, microwaves. Cr cds: A, C, D, DS, JCB, MC, V.

Hotels

★★ THE BOULDER BROKER INN. *555 30th St (80303). 303/444-3330; fax 303/444-6444. www.boulderbrokerinn.com.* 118 rms, 4 story. May-Sept: S, D $75-$159; each addl $6; suites $199-$299; under 18 free; wkend rates; lower rates rest of yr. Crib free. Pet accepted. TV; cable (premium). Heated pool; whirlpool, poolside serv. Complimentary bkfst Mon-Fri. Restaurant 6:30-10:30 am, 11 am-2 pm, 5-10 pm; Sat-Sun from 7:30 am. Rm serv. Bar 11-2 am, Sun to midnight; entertainment. Coffee in rms. Ck-out noon. Meeting rms. Business center. In-rm modem link. Bellhops. Concierge. Valet serv. Health club privileges. Airport transportation. Bathrm phone in suites. Refrigerators avail. Cr cds: A, C, D, DS, MC, V.

★★★ HOTEL BOULDERADO. *2115 13th St (80302). 303/442-4344; fax 303/442-4378; toll-free 800/433-4344. www.boulderado.com.* 160 rms, 5 story. S $135-$185; D $235-$325; each addl $12; suites $275; under 12 free. Crib free. TV; cable (premium), VCR avail. Restaurant (see Q's). Rm serv. Bars 10:30-1 am; entertainment. Coffee in rms. Ck-out 11 am. Meeting rms. Business center. In-rm

modem link. Health club privileges. Gift shop. Bellhops. Coin lndry. Valet serv. Many refrigerators. Some balconies. Restored historic hotel (1909); authentic Victorian furnishings. Cr cds: A, C, D, DS, ER, MC, V.

★★★ MARRIOTT BOULDER. *2660 Canyon Blvd (80302). 303/440-8877; toll-free 888/236-2427. www.marriott.com.* 155 rms, 5 story. S, D $179-$259; under 18 free. Valet parking. Crib avail. TV; cable (premium). Heated indoor pool; whirlpool. Restaurant 6:30 am-10 pm. Rm serv. Bar to midnight. Coffee in rms. Ck-out noon. Meeting rms. Business center. In-rm modem link. Coin laundry. Concierge. Bellhops. Valet serv. Exercise equipt. Minibars; many refrigerators in suites. Cr cds: A, C, D, DS, MC, V.

★★★ MILLENIUM HARVEST HOUSE. *1345 28th St (80302). 303/443-3850; fax 303/443-1480; res 800/222-8888.* 269 rms, 4-5 story. S, D $130-$230; suites $220-$550; family rates. Crib free. TV; cable (premium), VCR avail. 2 heated pools, 1 indoor; wading pool, whirlpool, poolside serv. Coffee in lobby. Restaurant 6:30 am-10 pm. Bar 5-11 pm. Ck-out noon. Coin lndry. Meeting rms. Business center. In-rm modem link. Gift shop. Tennis, pro. Valet serv. Exercise equipt. Lawn games. Some refrigerators, microwaves avail. Some private patios, balconies. Cr cds: A, D, DS, MC, V.

B&Bs/Small Inns

★★★ ALPS BORDER CANYON INN. *38619 Boulder Canyon Dr (80302). 303/444-5445; fax 303/444-5522; toll-free 800/414-2577. www.alpsinn.com.* 12 rms, 2 story. No A/C. S, D $119-$225; each addl $35; lower rates Jan-May. Children over 12 yrs only. TV in sitting rm; cable (premium), VCR (movies). Complimentary full bkfst; refreshments in sitting rm. Restaurant nearby. Ck-out 11 am, ck-in 4-9 pm. Business servs avail. In-rm modem link. Downhill/x-country ski 18 mi. Game rm. Some in-rm whirlpools, balconies. Rms individually furnished. Fireplaces, many antiques. Hiking trails. Entrance to inn is original log cabin (1870s) which served as both stage-coach stop and bordello. Totally nonsmoking. Cr cds: A, C, D, DS, MC, V.

★★ **BRIAR ROSE BED & BREAK-FAST.** *2151 Arapahoe Ave (80302). 303/442-3007; fax 303/786-8440. www.briarrosebb.com.* 9 rms, 8 A/C, 2 story. May-Dec: S $90-$165; D $165-$199; each addl $15; lower rates rest of yr. Children over 6 yrs only; $15. Crib avail. TV in living rm. Complimentary continental bkfst; afternoon refreshments. Ck-out noon, ck-in 3-9 pm. Business servs avail. In-rm modem link. Some fireplaces, balconies. English country-style home (1897); antiques. Totally nonsmoking. Cr cds: A, C, D, MC, V.

★ **SANDY POINT INN.** *6485 Twin Lakes Rd (80301). 303/530-2939; fax 303/530-9101; toll-free 800/322-2939. www.sandypointinn.com.* 33 kit. units, 2 story. June-Aug: S $59-$99; D $69-$104; each addl $10; under 12 free; wkly rates; higher rates special events; lower rates rest of yr. Crib free. TV; cable (premium), VCR avail. Complimentary continental bkfst, coffee in rms. Restaurant nearby. Ck-out 11 am, ck-in 3 pm. In-rm modem link. Coin lndry. Health club privileges. Playground. Refrigerators, microwaves. Picnic tables, grills. Totally nonsmoking. Cr cds: A, D, DS, Enroute, MC, V.

Extended Stay

★★ **RESIDENCE INN BY MAR-RIOTT.** *3030 Center Green Dr (80301). 303/449-5545; fax 303/449-2452; toll-free 800/331-3131. www.residenceinn. com.* 128 kit. suites, 2 story. S, D $89-$220. Crib free. Pet accepted; $50 (nonrefundable). TV; cable (premium). Heated pool; whirlpool. Complimentary continental bkfst, coffee in rms. Ck-out noon. Coin lndry. Meeting rms. Business servs avail. In-rm modem link. Valet serv. Health club privileges. Microwaves. Some fireplaces. Lighted tennis. Pic-

nic tables, grills. Playground. Cr cds: A, DS, JCB, MC, V.

Restaurants

★ **ANTICA ROMA CAFFE.** *1308 Pearl St (80302). 303/442-0378. www. anticaroma.com.* Hrs: 11:30 am-3:30 pm, 5-10 pm. Closed Dec 25. Italian menu. Bar. A la carte entrees: lunch $4-$8, dinner $10-$18. Child's menu. Specialties: il cioppino, saltimbocca alla romana, frutti di mare. Entertainment Tues. Outdoor dining. Totally nonsmoking. Cr cds: A, D, DS, MC, V.

★★ **DANDELION.** *1011 Walnut St (80302). 303/443-6700. www. citysearch.com.* Hrs: 11 am-10 pm; Fri to 11 pm; Sat 5-11 pm; Sun 5-9 pm. Closed Memorial Day. Res accepted. Contemporary Amer, Mediterranean menu. Bar. A la carte entrees: lunch $6-$10, dinner $13-$20. Specialties: grilled venison over potato leeks, pan roasted salmon. Outdoor dining. Contemporary atmosphere. Totally nonsmoking. Cr cds: A, D, MC, V.

★ **EUROPEAN CAFE.** *2460 Arapahoe (80302). 303/938-8250.* Hrs: 11 am-2 pm; 5:30-10 pm; Sat from 5:30 pm. Closed Sun; Memorial Day, July 4, Labor Day. Res accepted. French, Californian menu. A la carte entrees: lunch $7-$10, dinner $14-$26. Specialties: blackened tuna with ginger, filet mignon, rack of lamb. Parking. Contemporary decor. Cr cds: A, MC, V.

★★★★ **FLAGSTAFF HOUSE RESTAURANT.** *1138 Flagstaff Rd (80302). 303/442-4640. www.flagstaff house.com.* It's no wonder this restaurant has become a special destination with its setting 6,000 feet up Flagstaff Mountain. The creative tiered seating and floor-to-ceiling windows afford everyone a fantastic view of the eastern plains while they dine on Chef Mark Monette's unique, Asian-accented French cuisine. This landmark has been owned and operated by the Monette family since 1971. Amer menu. Specializes in Colorado beef, fresh seafood, game. Own baking. Hrs: 5-10 pm. Closed hols. Res accepted. Bar 5 pm-midnight. Wine cellar. A la carte entrees: dinner $24-$52. Prix fixe: dinner $65. Valet parking. Tableside serv. Chef-owned. Cr cds: A, D, DS, MC, V.

D

★★ **FULL MOON GRILL.** 2525 Arapahoe Ave (80302). 303/938-8800. www.fullmoongrill.com. Hrs: 11:30 am-2 pm, 5-9:30 pm; Fri to 10 pm; Sat 5-10 pm; Sun 5-9:30 pm. Closed most major hols. Res accepted. Northern Italian menu. Bar. Lunch $7.95-$10.95, dinner $9.95-$19.95. Specializes in fresh seafood, pasta. Outdoor dining. Contemporary atmosphere. Totally nonsmoking. Cr cds: A, DS, MC, V.

D

★★★ **THE GREENBRIAR INN.** 8735 N Foothills Hwy (US 36) (80302). 303/440-7979. www.greenbriarinn.com. Hrs: 5-10 pm; Sun brunch 11 am-2:30 pm. Closed Mon; Jan 1. Res accepted. Bar to 2 am. Wine list. A la carte entrees: dinner $18-$32. Sun brunch $20. Specialties: rack of Colorado lamb, fresh seafood, venison. Parking. Patio dining. Gardens. Cr cds: A, C, D, MC, V.

D

★★★ **JOHN'S RESTAURANT.** 2328 Pearl St (80302). 303/444-5232. www.johnsrestaurantboulder.com. Hrs: 5:30-10 pm. Closed Sun, Mon; July 4, Dec 25. Res accepted. Continental menu. Serv bar. Dinner $15.50-$24. Specialties: filet mignon with stilton-ale sauce, salmon Brettonne, breast of duck. Own sauces, ice cream. Located in cottage. Totally nonsmoking. Cr cds: A, DS, MC, V.

D

★★ **LAUDISIO.** 2785 Iris (80304). 303/442-1300. www.laudisio.com. Hrs: 11:30 am-2 pm; 5:30-9:30 pm; Fri to 10 pm; Sat 5:30-10 pm; Sun 5:30-9:30 pm. Closed major hols. Res accepted. Italian menu. Bar. A la carte entrees: lunch $6-$9.50, dinner $10-$24. Child's menu. Specialties: polenta Boulder, chicken scarpariello, zuppa di pesce. Outdoor dining. Italian decor. Cr cds: A, C, D, DS, ER, MC, V.

D SC ⌐

★★ **THE MEDITERRANEAN.** 1002 Walnut St (80302). 303/444-5335. www.themedboulder.com. Hrs: 11:30 am-10 pm; Fri, Sat to 11 pm; Sun from 5 pm. Closed most major hols. Mediterranean menu. Bar. Lunch $4.95-$5.95, dinner $7-$17. Child's menu. Specializes in paella, tapas. Outdoor dining. Mediterranean decor, artwork. Cr cds: A, D, MC, V.

D

★★★★ **Q'S.** 2115 13th St (80302). 303/442-4880. Visit this restaurant in the historic Hotel Boulderado for a taste of chef John Platt's contemporary American cuisine highlighting the freshest seafood, meat, game, and produce of the season. The food is intricate and artistic, including a pan-roasted Colorado lamb loin with sage, juniper, white onion tart, and chanterelle mushrooms. There's even live music during weekend brunch service. Contemporary American menu. Specializes in fresh seafood, lamb, beef, desserts. Hrs: 6:30 am-2 pm, 5-10 pm; Sat, Sun brunch 7 am-2 pm. Res accepted. Bar. Wine list. A la carte entrees: bkfst $5-$10, lunch $6-$12, dinner $17-$27. Child's menu. Parking. Contemporary art on display. Totally nonsmoking. Cr cds: A, C, D, DS, MC, V.

★★ **RHUMBA.** 950 Pearl St (80302). 303/442-7771. www.rhumbarestaurant.com. Specializes in jerk chicken, garam masala crusted halibut. Hrs: 11:30 am-10 pm; Fri, Sat to 11 pm. Res accepted. Wine list. Lunch $5.95-$9.95; dinner $6.95-$20.95. Child's menu. Entertainment: Caribbean Sat, Sun. Cr cds: A, D, MC, V.

D

★ **ROYAL PEACOCK.** 5290 Arapahoe Ave (80303). 303/447-1409. Hrs: 11:30 am-2:30 pm, 5:30-10:30 pm; Sat from 5:30 pm; Sun 5-10 pm. Res accepted. East Indian menu. Bar. Lunch $6.25-$11, dinner $7-$22. Lunch buffet $6.95. Specializes in curry, tandoori, wild game. Parking. Outdoor dining. East Indian decor. Cr cds: A, C, D, DS, ER, MC, V.

D

★★★ **TRIO'S.** 1155 Canyon Blvd (80302). 303/442-8400. www.triosgrille.com. Hrs: 11 am-midnight; Fri, Sat to 2 am; Sun brunch 10 am-3 pm. Closed most major hols. Res accepted. Bar. Lunch $6-$11, dinner $18-$25. Sun brunch $5-$11. Specialties: crayfish hash, wood oven pizza, smoked salmon. Jazz Mon-Sat. Parking. Contemporary decor. Gallery adj. Cr cds: A, C, D, DS, MC, V.

D

Breckenridge

(C-4) *See also Dillon, Fairplay*

Settled 1859 **Pop** 2,408 **Elev** 9,602 ft
Area code 970 **Zip** 80424
Information Breckenridge Resort Chamber, 311 S Ridge St, PO Box 1909, phone 970/453-2913; or Guest Services and Activities Center, 137 S Main St, 970/453-5579
Web www.gobreck.com

What to See and Do

Ghost towns. Lincoln City, Swandyke, Dyersville, others. Some can be reached only by jeep or on horseback; inquire locally.

Skiing. Breckenridge Ski Area. Six high-speed quad, triple, seven double chairlifts; five surface lifts, six carpet lifts; school, rentals, snowmaking; four cafeterias, five restaurants on mountain, picnic area; four nurseries (from two months old). One hundred twelve runs on three interconnected mountains; longest run three mi; vertical drop 3,398 ft. (Mid-Nov-early May, daily) X-country skiing (23 km), heliskiing, ice-skating, snowboarding, sleigh rides. Shuttle bus service. Multiday, ½-day, and off-season rates. Chairlift and alpine slide operate in summer (mid-June-mid-Sept). Ski Hill Rd, 1 mi W off CO 9. Phone 970/453-5000. ¢¢¢¢

Walking tours. Through historic district; also tours to abandoned mines, gold panning, and assay demonstrations. Led by Summit Historical Society. (Mon-Sat) Phone 970/453-9022. ¢¢

Special Events

International Snow Sculpture Championships. Teams from around the world create works of art from 12-ft-tall, 20-ton blocks of artificial snow. Jan.

Ullr Fest & World Cup Freestyle. Honoring Norse god of snow. Parades, fireworks, Nordic night, and ski competition. Seven days mid-Jan.

Breckenridge Music Festival. Classical music performances, elderhostels, music camps, children's programs, and workshops. Phone 970/453-2120. June-Aug.

Backstage Theatre. Downtown. Melodramas, musicals, comedies. Contact PO Box 297. Phone 970/453-0199. July-Labor Day, mid-Dec-Mar.

No Man's Land Day Celebration. Celebrates time when Colorado became a state of the Union, while the Breckenridge area was mistakenly forgotten in historic treaties. This area became part of Colorado and the US at a later date. Celebration features emphasis on Breckenridge life in the 1880s; parade, dance, games. Second wkend Aug.

Resorts

★★★ **BEAVER RUN RESORT.** *620 Village Rd (80424). 970/453-6000; fax 970/453-4284; res 800/525-2253. www.beaverrun.com.* 567 kit. suites, 8 story. Mid-Nov-mid-Apr: kit. suites $210-$710; lower rates rest of yr. Crib free. TV; cable (premium). 2 heated pools, 1 indoor/outdoor; whirlpool, poolside serv in winter. Complimentary coffee in rms. Restaurant 7 am-10 pm. No rm serv. Bar 11-2 am; seasonal entertainment. Ck-out 11 am. Coin lndry. Convention facilities. Business center. Concierge. Shopping arcade. Tennis. Downhill ski on site; x-country ski 1 mi. Exercise equipt; sauna. Rec rm. Miniature golf. Fireplaces. Some in-rm whirlpools. Balconies. Cr cds: A, D, MC, V.

D ⚡ ⌿ ⅀ ≈ ⫟ ⊠ 🔥 🏃

★★★ **GREAT DIVIDE LODGE BRECKENRIDGE.** *550 Village Rd (80424). 970/453-4500; fax 970/453-1983; res 800/321-8444. www.greatdividelodge.com.* 208 rms, 10 story. Mid-Dec-mid-Apr: S, D $155-$299; suites $300-$500; children free; ski plans; higher rates special events; lower rates rest of yr. TV; cable (premium). Indoor pool; whirlpool. Coffee in rms. Restaurant 7 am-10 pm. Bar 11 am-11 pm. Ck-out 10 am.

Meeting rms. Business servs avail. Concierge. Sports shop. Garage. Airport, bus depot transportation. Downhill/x-country ski ½ blk. Exercise equipt; sauna. Massage. Refrigerators, wet bars. Some balconies. Cr cds: A, C, D, DS, JCB, MC, V.

⬛🏊🍴🔁🔥 SC

★★★ **LODGE & SPA AT BRECKENRIDGE.** *112 Overlook Dr (80424). 970/453-9300; fax 970/453-0625; res 800/736-1607. www.thelodgeatbreck. com.* 45 air-cooled rms, 4 story. Feb-Apr: S, D $135-$275; each addl $25; under 16 free; package plans; hols 5-day min; higher rates Christmas; lower rates rest of yr. Crib free. Pet accepted, some restrictions; $25. Free valet parking. TV; cable (premium), VCR avail. Complimentary coffee in rms. Restaurant (see TOP OF THE WORLD). Rm serv. Bar 5 pm-midnight. Ck-out 11 am. Meeting rms. Business center. In-rm modem link. Bellhops. Valet serv. Concierge. Sundries. Gift shop. 18-hole golf privileges, greens fee $90 (with cart), pro, putting green, driving range. Downhill/x-country 2 mi. Exercise rm; sauna, steam rm. Massage. Indoor pool; whirlpool, poolside serv. Minibars; some refrigerators, microwaves, wet bars, fireplaces. Some balconies. Picnic tables. Cr cds: A, D, DS, MC, V.

⬛🔁🔥

★★ **RIVER MOUNTAIN LODGE.** *100 S Park Ave (80424). 970/453-4711; fax 970/453-1763; toll-free 800/627-3766.* 150 kit. condo units, 3-4 story. S, D $89-$599. TV; cable, VCR avail (movies $6). Pool; whirlpool. Ck-out 10 am. Coffee in lobby. Restaurant. Guest lndry in condos. Meeting rms. Business servs avail. Concierge. Covered parking. Airport, bus depot transportation. Downhill/x-country ski 1 mi. Exercise equipt; sauna. Refrigerators, microwaves; some fireplaces. Cr cds: A, DS, MC, V.

⬛🔁🔥

B&Bs/Small Inns

★★★ **ALLAIRE TIMBERS INN.** *9511 Hwy 9 (80424). 970/453-7530; fax 970/453-8699; toll-free 800/624-4904. www.allairetimbers.com.* 10 rms,

2 story, 2 suites. Mid-Feb-Mar: S, D $145-$160; suites $220-$250; ski, golf plans; lower rates rest of yr. Children over 13 yrs only. TV; cable. Complimentary full bkfst. Restaurant nearby. Ck-out 11 am, ck-in 3-7 pm. Business servs avail. Concierge. Downhill/x-country ski 2 mi. Balconies. Rms named for historic Mt passes. Totally nonsmoking. Cr cds: A, MC, V.

🔁🔥

★★★ **BED & BREAKFAST ON NORTH MAIN ST.** *303 N Main St (80424). 970/453-2975; fax 970/453-5258; toll-free 800/795-2975. www. breckenridge-inn.com.* 10 rms, 1 cottage. No A/C. Some rm phones. Feb-Mar: S, D $130-$185; cottage $205; higher rates Dec 25-Jan 1; lower rates rest of yr. Closed 3 wks May, last wk Oct, 1st 2 wks Nov. Adults only. TV in some rms; cable. Complimentary full bkfst; afternoon refreshments. Ck-out 11 am, ck-in by appt. Concierge serv. Downhill/x-country ski 1 mi. Health club privileges. Whirlpool, refrigerator in cottage. Picnic tables. Antiques, fireplaces. Totally nonsmoking. Cr cds: A, DS, MC, V.

🔁🔥

★★ **EVANS HOUSE BED & BREAKFAST.** *102 S French St (80424). 970/453-5509. www.coloradoevans house.com.* 6 rms, 2 story, 2 suites. No A/C. Dec-Mar: S, D $100-$140; each addl $30; lower rates rest of yr. Crib $30. TV; cable. Complimentary full bkfst. Restaurant nearby. Ck-out 10 am, ck-in 4-6 pm. Business servs avail. Luggage handling. Downhill/x-country ski 1 mi. Exercise equipt. Whirlpool. Health club privileges. Picnic table. House built 1886. Totally nonsmoking. Cr cds: A, D, DS, MC, V.

⬛🔁🔥

★★★ **HUNT PLACER INN.** *275 Ski Hill Rd (80424). 970/453-7573; fax 970/453-2335; toll-free 800/472-1430. www.huntplacerinn.com.* 8 rms, 3 story, 3 suites. No rm phones. Mid-Feb-Mar (4-day min): S, D $119-$164; suites $179-$189; 5-day min late Dec-early Jan; lower rates rest of yr. Children over 12 yrs only. TV; cable, VCR avail. Complimentary full bkfst. Ck-out 11 am. Meeting rm.

Downhill ski 1 mi; x-country ski on site. Game rm. Fireplaces. Balconies. Chalet-style inn. Totally nonsmoking. Cr cds: A, C, D, DS, MC, V.

★★ **RIDGE STREET INN.** *212 N Ridge St (80424). 970/453-4680; fax 970/547-1477; toll-free 800/452-4680. www.colorado.net/ridge.* 6 rms, 2 share bath, 2 story. No A/C. No rm phones. Nov-Mar: S, D $98-$150; lower rates rest of yr. Children over 6 yrs only. Complimentary full bkfst. Downhill/x-country ski 3 mi. Health club privileges. Victorian house; view of mountains. Totally nonsmoking. Cr cds: MC, V.

★★ **SWAN MOUNTAIN INN.** *16172 CO 9 (84035). 970/453-7903; res 800/578-3687. www.swanmountain inn.com.* 4 rms, 1 share bath, 2 story. Late Dec-early Jan, Mar (3-day min): S, D $70-$145; under 3 free; MAP avail; wkend, hol rates; lower rates rest of yr. Crib free. TV; cable, VCR (movies). Whirlpool. Complimentary full bkfst. Restaurant (see SWAN MOUNTAIN INN). Bar. Ck-out 11 am, ck-in 4 pm. Meeting rms. Downhill ski 5 mi; x-country ski 1 mi. Picnic tables. Rustic log cabin with front porch. Totally nonsmoking. Cr cds: DS, MC, V.

Restaurants

★ **BRECKENRIDGE BREWERY.** *600 S Main St (80424). 970/453-1550. www.breckenridgebrewery.com.* Hrs: 11 am-midnight. Closed Dec 25. Bar to 2 am. Lunch $5.95-$8, dinner $7.95-$18. Child's menu. Specializes in baby-back ribs, fish 'n chips, fajitas. Parking. Outdoor dining. Microbrewery; tours wkends. Second-story dining arranged around brew kettles. Cr cds: A, D, DS, MC, V.

★ **BRIAR ROSE.** *109 E Lincoln St (80424). 970/453-9948.* Hrs: 5-10 pm; summer from 6 pm. Res accepted. Continental menu. Bar 4:30 pm-2 am. Dinner $15-$50. Child's menu. Specializes in prime rib, game, steak. Entertainment (ski season). 1890s Victorian decor; on site of old min-

ing boarding house. Cr cds: A, DS, MC, V.

★★ **CAFE ALPINE.** *106 E Adams (80424). 970/453-8218. www.cafe alpine.com.* Hrs: 11 am-10 pm. Res accepted. Continental menu. Bar. Lunch $5-$9, dinner $12-$24. Child's menu. Specializes in regional cuisine, tapas. Outdoor dining. Cozy, informal dining in 3 rms. Totally nonsmoking. Cr cds: A, DS, MC, V.

★★ **HEARTHSTONE.** *130 S Ridge St (80424). 970/453-1148. www.storm restaurants.com.* Hrs: 11:30 am-10 pm; winter from 3 pm. Res accepted. No A/C. Bar. Lunch $4.95-$7.95 (summer only), dinner $12.50-$21.95. Child's menu. Specializes in prime rib, fresh seafood. Parking. Outdoor dining. In Victorian house (1886). View of mountains and ski area. Cr cds: A, MC, V.

★★ **HORSESHOE 2.** *115 S Main (80424). 970/453-7463.* Hrs: 11 am-10 pm; Fri-Sun from 8 am. No A/C. Bar to 2 am. Bkfst $2.25-$6.95, lunch $4-$9.95, dinner $4.25-$17. Child's menu. Outdoor dining. Former miners' supply store (1880). Totally nonsmoking. Cr cds: A, MC, V.

★★ **MI CASA MEXICAN CANTINA.** *600 S Park St (80424). 970/453-2071. www.stormrestaurants. com.* Hrs: 11:30 am-9 pm. No A/C. Mexican, Amer menu. Bar. Lunch, dinner $5.95-$14.95. Child's menu. Specialties: chimichanga, fajitas, fresh seafood, deep-fried ice cream. Parking. Mexican decor. Outdoor dining. Cr cds: A, MC, V.

★★★ **PIERRE'S RIVERWALK CAFE.** *137 S Main (80424). 970/453-0989.* Hrs: 11:30 am-2:30 pm, 5:30-10 pm; winter hrs vary. Closed Dec 25; also May and 1st 2 wks Nov. Res accepted. French, Amer menu. Bar. Lunch $6.25-$9, dinner $15-$26. Specialties: Rocky Mountain trout, rack of lamb. Parking. Outdoor dining. Chef-owned. Cr cds: MC, V.

★ **POIRRIER.** *224 S Main (80424). 970/453-1877. www.poirrierscajuncafe.*

com. Hrs: 11:30 am-2:30 pm, 5:30-9:30 pm. No A/C. Bar. Lunch $4.95-$9, dinner $8.95-$19.95. Child's menu. Specializes in seafood platter, crawfish, gumbos. Outdoor dining. Family-owned. Cajun/Louisiana decor. Totally nonsmoking. Cr cds: A, D, DS, MC, V.
D

★★ **ST. BERNARD INN.** *103 S Main St (80424).* 970/453-2572. Hrs: 5:30-10 pm. Closed May. Res accepted. No A/C. Continental menu. Bar. Dinner $13.50-$25. Child's menu. Specialties: beef tenderloin, cannelloni di mare, seafood. Parking. In historic mercantile building. Old mining memorabilia. Cr cds: A, D, DS, MC, V.
D ⟂

★★ **SALT CREEK.** *110 E Lincoln Ave (80424).* 970/453-4949. Hrs: 11:30 am-2 pm, 5-10 pm; hrs extended ski season. Barbecue menu. Bar. Lunch $4.95-$7.95, dinner $8.95-$23.95. Child's menu. Specializes in Angus beef steaks. Outdoor dining. Casual Western atmosphere. Cr cds: DS, MC, V.
D

★★ **SWAN MOUNTAIN INN.** *16172 CO 9 (80424).* 970/453-7903. *www.swanmountaininn.com.* Hrs: 7:30-10 am, 11:30 am-2 pm, 5:30-9 pm; Sat, Sun 7:30 am-2 pm, 5:30-9 pm; winter hrs vary. Res accepted. No A/C. Continental menu. Bar. Bkfst $6.50-$9.50, lunch $6.95-$7.95, dinner $9.95-$20.95. Child's menu. Specialties: marinated pork tenderloin, black raspberry roast duckling, filet mignon with snow crab and bearnaise. Parking. Outdoor dining. Log structure; view of mountains. Cr cds: A, MC, V.
SC

★★ **TOP OF THE WORLD.** *112 Overlook Dr (80424).* 970/453-9300. *www.colorado.net/thelodge.* Hrs: 7-10 am, 5-10 pm. Res accepted. Continental menu. Bar 5 pm-midnight. Bkfst $9-$15, dinner $18-$40. Child's menu. Specialties: sauteed medallion of Sonoma foie gras, ahi tuna sushimi, herb-crusted rack of lamb. Parking. Mountain views. Totally nonsmoking. Cr cds: A, D, MC, V.
D

Buena Vista

(D-4) *See also Leadville, Salida*

Founded 1879 **Pop** 2,195 **Elev** 7,955 ft **Area code** 719 **Zip** 81211

Information Chamber of Commerce, 343 S US 24, Box 2021; 719/395-6612

Web www.fourteenernet.com/buenavista

What to See and Do

Hiking, camping, mountain biking, snowmobiling, and cross-country skiing. Equipt rentals, supplies, maps, and information on trails and routes may be obtained from Trailhead Ventures. Phone 719/395-8001.

River rafting.

Arkansas River Tours. Quarter-day to three-day, mild to wild whitewater rafting and fishing trips on the Arkansas River. (May-Aug) Contact PO Box 337, Cotopaxi, 81223. Phone 800/321-4352. ¢¢¢¢

Bill Dvorak's Kayak & Rafting Expeditions. Half-day to 12-day trips on the Arkansas, Colorado, Dolores, Green, Gunnison, North Platte, Rio Chama, Rio Grande, and San Miguel rivers. Guided fishing trips; kayak instruction. (Mid-Apr-early Oct) Phone 719/539-6851 or 800/824-3795. ¢¢¢¢

Noah's Ark Whitewater Rafting Company. Half-day to three-day trips on the Arkansas River. (Mid-May-late Aug) Phone 719/395-2158. ¢¢¢¢

Wilderness Aware. Half-day to ten-day river rafting trips on the Arkansas, Colorado, Dolores, North Platte, and Gunnison rivers. (May-Sept) Phone 719/395-2112 or 800/462-7238. ¢¢¢¢

Motels/Motor Lodges

★★ **BEST WESTERN VISTA INN.** *733 US 24 N (81211).* 719/395-8009; fax 719/395-6025; toll-free 800/809-3495. www.bestwestern.com. 41 rms, 2 story. Late-May-Sept: S, D $99-$120; each addl $5; under 12 free; package plans; lower rates rest of yr. Crib free. TV; cable (premium). 3 hot springs whirlpools. Complimentary continental bkfst, coffee in rms. Restaurant opp 5-10 pm. Ck-out 11 am. Meeting rms. Business servs avail. In-rm modem link. Coin lndry. Valet serv. X-country ski 1 mi. Golf privileges. Fishing. Bike rentals. Hiking. Exercise equipt. Refrigerators, microwaves. Cr cds: A, C, D, DS, MC, V.

★ **GREAT WESTERN SUMAC LODGE.** *428 US 24 S (81212). 719/395-8111; fax 719/395-2560; toll-free 888/786-2290.* 30 rms, 2 story. Late-May-Sept: S, D $56-$73; each addl $5; lower rates rest of yr. Pet accepted; $5. TV; cable (premium). Complimentary coffee in lobby. Restaurant nearby. Ck-out 11 am. In-rm modem link. Mountain view. Cr cds: A, C, DS, MC, V.

Restaurants

★ ★ **BUFFALO BAR & GRILL.** *710 US 24 N (81211). 719/395-6472.* Hrs: 5-10 pm. Res accepted. Bar. Dinner $6.50-$18.95. Child's menu. Specializes in steak, seafood. Parking. Cr cds: A, DS, MC, V.

★ **CASA DEL SOL.** *333 US 24 N (81211). 719/395-8810.* Hrs: 11:30 am-3 pm, 4:30-9 pm; winter hrs vary. Closed late May-Labor Day. Mexican menu. Lunch $4.50-$8.95, dinner $10-$15. Child's menu. Specialty: pechuga Suiza. Own desserts. Parking. Outdoor dining. In 1880 miner's cabin. Totally nonsmoking. Cr cds: DS, MC, V.

Burlington (C-8)

Pop 3,678 **Elev** 4,160 ft
Area code 719 **Zip** 80807
Information Chamber of Commerce, 415 15th St, PO Box 62; 719/346-8070

What to See and Do

Bonny Lake State Park. A 2,000-acre lake has swimming, waterskiing, fishing, boating (ramps); picnicking, concession, camping. Standard fees.

(Daily) 23 mi N on US 385, near Idalia. Phone 303/354-7306. Per vehicle ¢¢

Kit Carson County Carousel. Built in 1905, this restored carousel houses a 1912 Wurlitzer Monster Military Band organ. (Memorial Day-Labor Day, daily, afternoon-mid-eve) Fairgrounds, Colorado Ave and 15th St. Fee for 20-min tour and 4-min ride ¢

Old Town. Historical village with 20 buildings reflects Colorado prairie heritage. Also cancan shows, gunfights, and melodramas (summer); two-day hoedown (Labor Day wkend). (Daily; closed hols) 420 S 14th St. Phone 719/346-7382 or 800/288-1334. ¢¢

Special Events

Little Britches Rodeo. Fairgrounds. Late May. Phone 719/389-0333.
Kit Carson County Fair & Rodeo. Fairgrounds. Phone 719/346-8133. Early Aug.

Motels/Motor Lodges

★ **CHAPARRAL MOTOR INN.** *405 S Lincoln (80807). 719/346-5361; fax 719/346-8502; res 800/283-4678.* 39 rms. June-Sept: S $33-$43; D $34-$44; each addl $4; under 12 free; lower rates rest of yr. Crib $5. Pet accepted, some restrictions. TV; cable (premium). Heated pool; whirlpool. Playground. Restaurant adj 6 am-11 pm. Ck-out 11 am. Cr cds: A, C, D, DS, MC, V.

★ **SLOANS MOTEL.** *1901 Rose Ave (80807). 719/346-5333; fax 719/346-9536; res 888/315-2378.* 29 rms, 1-2 story. S $31-$36; D $35-$45; each addl $3. Crib free. TV; cable (premium). Pool. Restaurant nearby. Ck-out 10:30 am. Bus depot transportation. Refrigerators, microwaves avail. Cr cds: A, C, D, DS, MC, V.

Cañon City

(D-5) *See also Colorado Springs, Cripple Creek, Pueblo*

Founded 1859 **Pop** 15,431 **Elev** 5,332 ft **Area code** 719 **Zip** 81212

Information Chamber of Commerce, 403 Royal Gorge Blvd, PO Bin 749; 719/275-2331 or 800/876-7922
Web www.canoncitychamber.com.

What to See and Do

Cañon City Municipal Museum. Complex incl outdoor buildings; Rudd Cabin, a pioneer log cabin constructed in 1860, and Stone House, built in 1881. Second-floor Municipal Building galleries display minerals and rocks, artifacts from settlement of the Fremont County region, and guns. (Early May-Labor Day, Tues-Sun; rest of yr, Tues-Sat; closed hols) 612 Royal Gorge Blvd (US 50). Phone 719/276-5279. ¢

Colorado Territorial Prison Museum and Park. Housed in the women's prison facility (1935), this museum and resource center displays exhibits and memorabilia of the Colorado prison system. Picnicking is permitted on the grounds. Adj is an active medium-security prison. (Summer, daily; winter, Thurs-Sun; closed hols) 1st and Macon Aves. Phone 719/269-3015. ¢¢

Fremont Center for the Arts. Community art center; features visual art exhibits, cultural programs. (Tues-Sat; closed hols) 505 Macon Ave. Phone 719/275-2790. ¢

Rafting. There are many rafting companies in the area. For information contact the Cañon City Chamber of Commerce. Phone 800/876-7922.

⭐ **Royal Gorge.** Magnificent canyon with cliffs rising more than 1,000 ft above Arkansas River. Royal Gorge Suspension Bridge, 1,053 ft above river, is highest in the world (recreational vehicles larger than small van or small camper not permitted on bridge). Royal Gorge Incline Railway, the world's steepest, takes passengers 1,550 ft to bottom of canyon. A 2,200-ft aerial tramway glides across the spectacular canyon. Theater; entertainment gazebo; petting zoo; restaurants; gift shops. (Daily) 8 mi W on US 50, then 4 mi SW. Phone 719/275-7507.

Royal Gorge Frontier Town and Railway. Old West theme park incl old Western town with 30 authentic buildings; restaurant and saloon. Other activities here are daily gun-fights, horse-drawn trolley ride, magic shows, and entertainment. Also three-mi, 30-min train ride to rim of Royal Gorge. Railway (Mar-Dec, daily). Park (May-Sept, daily). 8 mi W via US 50, 1 mi S to Royal Gorge. Phone 719/275-5149 or 719/275-5485. ¢¢¢¢

Royal Gorge Route. Travel by train through the Royal Gorge on two-hr round-trip departing from Cañon City. (Summer; daily)

Special Events

Blossom & Music Festival. First wkend May. Phone 719/569-2403.
Royal Gorge Rodeo. First wkend May.

Motels/Motor Lodges

★★ **BEST WESTERN ROYAL GORGE.** *1925 Fremont Dr (81212). 719/275-3377; fax 719/275-3931; res 800/780-7234. www.bestwestern.com.* 67 rms, 2 story. May-Sept: S $44-$69; D $49-$89; each addl $5; under 12 free; lower rates rest rest of yr. Crib free. Pet accepted, some restrictions; $15 (nonrefundable). TV; cable (premium). Heated pool; whirlpool, poolside serv. Playground. Coffee in rms. Restaurant 6 am-9 pm. Bar noon-10 pm. Ck-out 11 am. Coin lndry. In-rm modem link. Some refrigerators; microwaves avail. Picnic tables. Cr cds: A, C, D, DS, MC, V.
D 🐾 🏊 ⊠ 🔥

★★★ **CANON INN.** *3075 E US 50 (81212). 719/275-8676; fax 719/275-8675; toll-free 800/525-7727. www.canoninn.com.* 152 rms, 2 story. May-Sept: S $65-$90; D $80-$100; each addl $7; under 16 free; lower rates rest of yr. Crib free. Pet accepted; $50. TV; cable (premium). Heated pool; whirlpools. Restaurant 5:30 am-10 pm. Rm serv. Bar 4 pm-2 am. Ck-out 11 am. Coin lndry. Meeting rms. Business servs avail. Valet serv. Free airport, bus depot transportation. Some bathrm phones, refrigerators; microwaves avail. Cr cds: A, C, D, DS, MC, V.
D 🐾 🏊 ⊠ 🔥

Restaurant

★★ **MERLINO'S BELVEDERE.** *1330 Elm Ave (81212). 719/275-5558; toll-*

free 800/625-2526 www.belvedere restaurant.com. Hrs: 5-10 pm; Fri, Sat 4:30-10 pm; Sun noon-9 pm; winter hrs vary. Closed Thanksgiving, Dec 25. Italian, Amer menu. Bars. Dinner $8.25-$18.50. Child's menu. Specializes in homemade pasta, steak. Own soups. Parking. Mediterranean decor. Bakery on premises. Family-owned. Cr cds: A, D, DS, MC, V.

D ⊒

Central City

(C-5) *See also Denver, Georgetown, Golden, Idaho Springs*

Settled 1859 **Pop** 515 **Elev** 8,496 ft **Area code** 303 **Zip** 80427
Information Gilpin County Chamber of Commerce, PO Box 343, Blackhawk, 80422; 303/582-5077 or 800/331-5825

What to See and Do

Gilpin County Historical Society Museum. Exhibits, housed in an early schoolhouse (1870) under continuing restoration, re-create early gold-mining life in Gilpin County; replicas of a Victorian house and period shops with authentic furnishings; collection of antique dolls; personal effects of sheriff gunned down in 1896. (Memorial Day wkend-Labor Day, daily; or by appt) 228 E High St. Phone 303/582-5283. ¢¢ Also maintained by the Historical Society is

The Thomas House Museum. (1874) On display are the belongings of one family who lived in this house. (Memorial Day wkend-Labor Day, Thurs-Sun; rest of yr, by appt) 209 Eureka St. Phone 303/582-5283. ¢¢

Site of First Gold Lode Discovery in Colorado. Granite monument marks spot where John H. Gregory first found gold May 6, 1859. Boundary of Central City and Black Hawk.

Special Event

Central City Music Festival. Three days of great sounds. Late Aug.

Restaurant

★★ **BLACK FOREST RESTAURANT.** *24 Big Springs Dr, Nederland (80466). 303/279-2333.* Hrs: 8 am-10 pm; Sun to 9 pm. Res accepted. German, Amer menu. Bar to 1 am. Lunch $4-$8.75, dinner $10.95-$22.95. Specializes in wild game. Own ice cream. Entertainment Fri-Sun. Bavarian decor. Cr cds: C.

D

Colorado National Monument

(C-1) *See also Grand Junction*

(5 mi W of Grand Junction, off CO 340)

Wind, water, a ten-mile fault, and untold eons have combined to produce spectacular erosional forms. In the 32-square-mile monument, deep canyons with sheer walls form amphitheaters for towering monoliths, rounded domes, and other geological features. Wildlife includes deer, foxes, coyotes, porcupines, and a growing herd of desert bighorn sheep. Rim Rock Drive, accessible from either Fruita or Grand Junction, is a spectacular 23-mile road along the canyon rims. There are picnicking and camping facilities within the monument (all year; fee for camping). The Saddlehorn Visitor Center has geology and natural history exhibits (daily). Interpretive programs are offered in summer. Hiking and cross-country skiing trails are open in season. For detailed information contact Superintendent, Fruita, CO 81521; phone 970/858-3617. Per vehicle ¢¢

Colorado Springs

(D-5) *See also Cañon City, Cripple Creek, Manitou Springs*

Founded 1871 **Pop** 360,890 **Elev** 6,035 ft **Area code** 719

Information Convention & Visitor Bureau, 515 S Cascade, Suite 104, 80903; 719/635-7506 or 800/368-4748

Web www.coloradosprings-travel.com

What to See and Do

Broadmoor-Cheyenne Mountain Area. 4 mi S on Nevada Ave, then W on Lake Ave to Broadmoor Hotel. Opp hotel is

Broadmoor-Cheyenne Mountain Highway. Zig-zags up east face of Cheyenne Mtn; view of plains to the east. Round-trip to Shrine of the Sun (see) is six mi. (Daily; weather permitting) Toll (incl zoo, Shrine of the Sun) ¢¢¢

Cheyenne Mountain Zoological Park. Approx 650 animals incl primate, penguin, giraffe, feline, and birds of prey collections. (Daily). ¢¢¢

El Pomar Carriage Museum. Collection of fine carriages, vehicles, Western articles of 1890s. (Daily; closed hols) Lake Ave and Lake Circle. Phone 719/577-5710. **FREE** Around hotel grounds and golf course is start of

Shrine of the Sun. Memorial to Will Rogers. Built of Colorado pink granite and steel. Contains Rogers memorabilia. (Daily)

Colorado Springs Fine Arts Center. Permanent collections incl Native American and Hispanic art, Guatemalan textiles, 19th- and 20th-century American Western paintings, graphics, and sculpture by Charles M. Russell and other American artists. Changing exhibits; painting and sculpture classes; repertory theater performances; films. (Tues-Sun; closed hols) 30 W Dale St. Phone 719/634-5581. ¢¢

Colorado Springs Pioneer Museum. Exhibits portray

the history of Pikes Peak region. (Tues-Sat, also Sun afternoons in the summers; closed hols) 215 S Tejon St. Phone 719/385-5990. **FREE**

Flying W Ranch. A working cattle and horse ranch with chuckwagon suppers and Western stage show. More than 12 restored buildings with period furniture. (Mid-May-Sept, daily; rest of yr, Fri and Sat; closed Dec 25-Feb) Res required. 3330 Chuckwagon Rd, 8 mi NW on 30th St, 2 mi W of I-25 on Garden of the Gods Rd. Phone 719/598-4000 or 800/232-FLYW. ¢¢¢¢

Focus on the Family. Welcome center with interactive displays, a 20-min video, and a children's play area, at the headquarters of this popular Christian ministry. (Mon-Sat; closed hols) 8685 Explorer Dr (I-25 exit 151). Phone 719/531-3328. **FREE**

⭐ **Garden of the Gods.** Outstanding geological formations, incl famous Balanced Rock and Kissing Camels. Hands-on exhibits; cafe; gift shop. Dramatic views at sunrise and sunset. Visitor center at 1805 N 30th in town (daily). Guided nature walks. Park (all yr). I-25 exit 146, W on Garden of the Gods Rd to mountains, left on 30th St for ½ mi. Phone 719/634-6666. **FREE** In the park is

Garden of the Gods Trading Post. Established in 1900. Southwestern art gallery displays contemporary Native American jewelry, Santa Clara pottery, Hopi kachinas. Gift shop. (Daily) Near Balanced Rock, at south end of park. Phone

Garden of the Gods

719/685-9045 or 800/874-4515. **FREE**

Gray Line bus tours. Contact 3704 W Colorado Ave, 80904. Phone 719/633-1747 or 800/345-8197.

Industrial Tour. Van Briggle Art Pottery Company. Exhibitions of "throwing potter's wheel"; self-guided tours. (Mon-Sat; closed Jan 1, Thanksgiving, Dec 25) 600 S 21st St at W US 24. Phone 719/633-7729 or 800/847-6341. **FREE**

Magic Town. Theatrical sculpture, created by sculptor Michael Garman, is a combination of miniature cityscapes and characters together with theatre techniques. Gift shop. (Daily) 2418 W Colorado Ave. Phone 719/471-9391. ¢¢

May Natural History Museum. Collection of more than 7,000 invertebrates from the tropics. Also here is **Museum of Space Exploration** with hundreds of models and NASA space photos and movies. (May-Sept, daily) Campground (fee). 9 mi SW on CO 115. Phone 719/576-0450 or 800/666-3841. Both museums ¢¢

McAllister House Museum. (1873) Six-rm, Gothic-style cottage; Victorian furnishings. Carriage house. Guided tours. (May-Aug, Wed-Sun; rest of yr, Thurs-Sat; closed Jan) 423 N Cascade Ave. Phone 719/635-7925. ¢¢

Museum of the American Numismatic Association. Displays and research collections of coins, tokens, medals, paper money; changing exhibits; library. (Mon-Sat; closed hols) 818 N Cascade Ave. Phone 719/632-2646 or 800/367-9723. **FREE**

Old Colorado City. Renovated historic district features more than 100 quaint shops, art galleries, and restaurants. (Daily) 3 mi W on US 24. Phone 719/577-4112. **FREE**

Palmer Park. Magnificent views from scenic roads and trails among its 710 acres on Austin Bluffs. Picnic areas. On Maizeland Rd off N Academy Blvd. **FREE**

Peterson Air & Space Museum. Display of 17 historic aircraft from WWII-present, plus exhibits on the history of the Air Force base. (open on restricted basis, call for times) Main gate, off US 24. Phone 719/556-4915. **FREE**

Pike National Forest. The more than 1,100,000 acres north and west of town via US 24 incl world-famous Pikes Peak; picnic grounds, camp-grounds (fee); Wilkerson Pass (9,507 ft), 45 mi W on US 24, with visitor information center (Memorial Day-Labor Day); Lost Creek Wilderness, NW of Lake George; Mt Evans Wilderness, NW of Bailey. Contact the Supervisor, 1920 Valley Dr, Pueblo 81008. There is also a Ranger District office in Colorado Springs at 601 S Weber; phone 719/636-1602. Phone 719/545-8737. **FREE**

★ **Pikes Peak.** (14,110 ft) Toll road climbs 7,309 ft. (Daily; weather permitting) Closed during annual Hill Climb in July (see SPECIAL EVENTS). 10 mi W on US 24 to Cascade, then 19 mi on toll road to summit. Phone 719/684-9383. ¢¢¢

   Cog railway. Up to eight trips daily (May-Oct, inquire for schedule). Res required. 515 Ruxton Ave in Manitou Springs, 5 mi W on US 24. Phone 719/685-5401. Round trip ¢¢¢¢

Pikes Peak Auto Hill Climb Educational Museum. More than two dozen race cars plus numerous exhibits on the Pikes Peak race, considered America's second-oldest auto race. (Daily, shorter hrs in winter; closed hols) 135 Manitou Ave. Phone 719/685-4400. ¢¢

Pikes Peak Ghost Town. Authentic Old West town under one roof in an 1899 railroad building. Incl antique-furnished buildings such as general store, livery, jail, saloon, and re-created Victorian home. Also horse-less carriages and buggies and a 1903 Cadillac. Old-time nickelodeons, player pianos, arcade "movies", and shooting gallery. (Daily) US 24 W at 400 S 21st St. Phone 719/634-0696. ¢¢¢

Pro Rodeo Hall of Fame and American Cowboy Museum. Traces the rodeo lifestyle and its development over more than 100 yrs. Multimedia presentation documents rodeo's evolution from its origins in 19th-century ranch work to its present status as a major spectator sport. More than 90 exhibits of historic and modern cowboy and rodeo gear; changing Western art exhibits. The outdoor exhibits incl live rodeo animals and a replica rodeo arena.

(Daily; closed hols) 101 Pro Rodeo Dr (I-25 exit 147 Rockrimmon Blvd). Phone 719/528-4764. ¢¢¢

Rock Ledge Ranch Historic Site. A living history program demonstrating everyday life in the region; 1868 homestead, 1895 working ranch, 1907 Orchard House. Braille nature trail. (June-Labor Day, Wed-Sun; after Labor Day-Dec 25, wkends) 3202 Chambers Way, 4 mi W via I-25, Garden of Gods exit to 30th St, S to Gateway Rd at E entrance of Garden of the Gods. Phone 719/578-6777. ¢¢

Seven Falls. Only completely lighted canyon and waterfall in the world. Best seen from Eagle's Nest, reached by mountain elevator. Native American dance interpretations (summer, daily). Night lighting (summer). 7 mi SW on Cheyenne Blvd in south Cheyenne Canyon. Phone 719/632-0765. ¢¢¢

US Air Force Academy. (1955) 4,200 cadets. On 18,500 acres at foot of Rampart Range of Rocky Mtns where cadets undergo four-yr academic, military, and physical training. Striking, modern cadet chapel (daily; closed for private services; Sun service open to public.) Cadet Wing marches to lunch may be watched from wall near Chapel (academic yr). Planetarium programs for public (free). Visitor center has self-guided tour brochures, theater, and exhibits on cadet life and academy history (daily; closed Jan 1, Thanksgiving, Dec 25). N on I-25 exit 150B (South Gate) or 156B (North Gate). Phone 719/333-7742 or 800/955-4438. **FREE**

US Olympic Complex and Visitor Center. National headquarters of the US Olympic Committee, 15 national sports governing bodies, and Olympic Training Center, where more than 15,000 athletes train each yr. Guided tours incl film and walking tour of training center. (Daily) One Olympic Plaza, 2 blks N of Platte Ave (US 24 E), at Union Blvd. Phone 719/866-4618. **FREE**

World Figure Skating Hall of Fame and Museum. Exhibits on history of figure skating; art, memorabilia, library, skate gallery, video collection. (May-Sept, Mon-Sat; rest of yr, Mon-Fri; closed hols) 20 First St, off Lake Ave. Phone 719/635-5200. ¢¢

Special Events

Greyhound racing. Post Time Greyhound Park. E of I-25 between Garden of the Gods and Fillmore. Phone 719/632-1391. Apr-late Sept.

Motor sports. Pikes Peak International Raceway. S on I-25 in Fountain. Phone 719/382-RACE, 888/306-RACE, or 800/511-PPIR. May-Sept. Phone 719/382-7223.

Pikes Peak Auto Hill Climb. Pikes Peak Toll Rd. July 4. Phone 719/685-4400.

Pikes Peak Marathon. Footrace from cog depot to summit and back. Aug. Phone 719/473-2625.

Pikes Peak or Bust Rodeo. Spencer Penrose Stadium. Phone 719/635-3547. First full wk Aug.

Colorado Springs Balloon Classic. Memorial Park. Labor Day wkend.

Motels/Motor Lodges

★ **CASCADE HILLS MOTEL.** *7885 W US 24, Cascade (80424). 719/684-9977; fax 719/684-0966; toll-free 877/687-6648.* 14 rms, 8 air-cooled, 6 units A/C, shower only, 2 story, 2 kit. units, 2 cottages. Memorial Day-Sept: S $40-$75; D $45-$85; each addl $4; kit. units $85-$125; cottages $150-$200; wkly rates; lower rates rest of yr. TV; cable (premium). Whirlpool. Complimentary continental bkfst. Ck-out 10 am. Some refrigerators. Picnic tables. Cr cds: MC, V.

⊡ ⬤ ⚡ ➤ ➤ ♨

★★ **COMFORT INN.** *2115 Aerotech Dr (80916). 719/380-9000; fax 719/596-4738; res 800/228-5150. www.comfortinn.com.* 42 rms, 2 story. S $50-$119; D $60-$129; under 18 free. Crib free. TV; cable (premium), VCR avail. Complimentary continental bkfst. Coffee in rms. Restaurant nearby. Ck-out noon. Meeting rms. Business servs avail. In-rm modem link. Coin lndry. Free airport transportation. Exercise equipt. Indoor pool; whirlpool. Cr cds: A, D, DS, MC, V.

⊡ ⚡ ➤ ➤ ♨ ⚐

★★ **COMFORT INN NORTH.** *6450 Corporate Center Dr (80210). 719/262-9000; fax 719/262-9900; res 800/228-5150. www.comfortinn.com.* 70 rms, 4 story. S $59-$95; D $69-$105; each

EXPLORING "THE SARATOGA OF THE WEST"

Nestled at the foot of Pikes Peak a mere seven miles west of downtown Colorado Springs, Manitou Springs is one of the state's definitive—and most accessible—mountain communities. A walking tour of Manitou Avenue, a bustling boulevard rife with artists' studios, restaurants, and boutiques that is one of the country's largest historic districts, is a good place to begin. Start at Memorial Park on the town's east side (Manitou and Deer Path avenues), which is surrounded by ample parking and centered around Seven Minute Spring, one of ten named mineral springs in the area that are renowned for their cool, drinkable water. (As a result, Manitou has been called "The Saratoga of the West.") From the park, walk west two blocks on Manitou Avenue to the Canon Avenue intersection. This is the central business district, and most of the restaurants and galleries are within a three-block radius. One can't-miss establishment is Arcade Amusements (930 Manitou Avenue), one of the West's oldest amusement arcades, featuring an array of antique coin-operated games. The downtown area is also ground zero for the Manitou Art Project, an annually rotating installation of 20 outdoor sculptures. Just west of the Canon-Manitou intersection is the Jerome Wheeler Town Clock, a landmark named for its eponymous donor, the onetime president of Macy's Department Stores who brought his ailing wife to the area in the 19th century. Continuing west on Manitou Avenue, it's a short walk to Ruxton Avenue, which will be on the left. Head southwest on Ruxton to the Miramont Castle (9 Capitol Hill Avenue, immediately adjacent to Ruxton), one of the architectural gems of Manitou Springs. Built as a home for a Catholic priest in 1895, the castle features English Tudor and Byzantine motifs in its eclectic design. After touring Miramont Castle, you might want to continue up Ruxton Avenue on a steep, 3/4-mile hike to the Manitou & Pikes Peak Railway Depot (515 Ruxton Avenue), the departure point for a rail trip to the pinnacle of Pikes Peak (open daily in the summertime). However, Miramont is also a good place to backtrack to your car for a drive to Manitou Springs attractions that are less accessible by foot, such as the railway, the Cliff Dwellings Museum, and the Cave of the Winds.

addl $10; under 18 free. TV; cable (premium). Complimentary continental bkfst, coffee in rms. Restaurant nearby. Ck-out 11 am. Meeting rms. In-rm modem link. Coin lndry. Exercise equipt. Indoor pool; whirlpool. Bathrm phones, refrigerators, microwaves. Cr cds: A, D, DS, JCB, MC, V.

⊡ ⚊ 🏃 🛇 🔥 SC

★★ **DRURY INN.** 8155 N Academy Blvd (I-25 & N Academy Blvd) (80920). 719/598-2500; toll-free 800/325-8300. www.drury-inn.com. 118 rms, 4 story. May-early Sept: S, D $74-$109; each addl $10; under 18 free; lower rates rest of yr. Crib free. Pet accepted, some restrictions. TV; cable. Heated indoor/outdoor pool; whirlpool. Complimentary continental bkfst. Coffee in rms. Restaurant adj open 24 hrs. Ck-out noon. Coin lndry. Meeting rms. Business servs avail. In-rm modem link. Valet serv. Exercise equipt. Some refrigera-

tors; microwaves avail. Cr cds: A, C, D, DS, MC, V.

⊡ 🐾 ⚊ 🏃 🛇 🔥 SC

★★ **FAIRFIELD INN NORTH.** 7085 Commerce Center Dr (80919). 719/533-1903; fax 719/533-1903; toll-free 800/228-2800. www.fairfieldinn. com. 67 rms, 4 story. May-early Oct: S $84; D $91; each addl $8; under 18 free; lower rates rest of yr. Crib free. TV; cable (premium). Complimentary continental bkfst, coffee in rms. Restaurant nearby. Ck-out 11 am. Meeting rm. Business servs avail. Indoor pool; whirlpool. Game rm. Some refrigerators, microwaves. Cr cds: A, C, D, DS, MC, V.

⊡ ⚊ 🛇 🔥 SC

★ **FAIRFIELD INN SOUTH.** 2725 Geyser Dr (80906). 719/576-1717; res 800/228-2800. www.fairfieldinn.com. 85 rms, 3 story. Mid-May-mid-Oct: S, D $69-$89; under 18 free; lower rates rest of yr. Crib free. TV; cable (premium). Complimentary continental bkfst, coffee in rms. Restaurant nearby. Ck-out noon. Meeting rm. Business servs avail. In-rm modem link. Exercise equipt. Indoor pool; whirlpool. Some refrigerators, microwaves. Cr cds: A, C, D, DS, JCB, MC, V.

★ **GARDEN OF THE GODS MOTEL.** *2922 W Colorado Ave (80904). 719/636-5271; fax 719/477-1422; res 800/637-0703. www.pikespeak.com/gardenofgods.htm.* 32 rms, 1-2 story, 2 cottages. Mid-May-mid-Sept: S, D $49-$89; each addl $5; cottages $89.50-$120; lower rates rest of yr. Closed mid-Dec-mid-Feb. Crib $3. TV; cable. Indoor pool. Sauna. Coffee in lobby. Restaurant nearby. Ck-out 10:30 am. Microwaves avail. Cr cds: A, C, D, DS, MC, V.

★★ **HOLIDAY INN EXPRESS.** *1815 Aeroplaza Dr (80916). 719/591-6000; fax 719/591-6100; toll-free 800/465-4329. www.holiday-inn.com.* 94 rms, 4 story, 15 suites. S $59-$95; D $69-$105; suites $119-$129; under 19 free; wkend, hol rates. Crib free. TV; cable (premium). Complimentary continental bkfst. Complimentary coffee in rms. Restaurant nearby. Ck-out noon. Meeting rms. Business center. In-rm modem link. Sundries. Coin lndry. Free airport transportation. Exercise equipt. Bathrm phones. Refrigerator, microwave, wet bar in suites. Some balconies. Cr cds: A, C, D, DS, JCB, MC, V.

★ **MEL-HAVEN LODGE.** *3715 W Colorado Ave (80904). 719/633-9435; toll-free 800/762-5832.* 21 rms, 2 story, 14 kits. Mid-May-mid-Sept: S $55-$70; D $70-$105; each addl $5; suites $110-$150; kit. units $5 addl; lower rates rest of yr. TV; cable (premium). Heated pool; whirlpool. Playground. Complimentary coffee in lobby. Restaurant nearby. Ck-out 11 am. Coin lndry. Many refrigerators; microwaves avail. Picnic tables, grill. Cr cds: A, DS, MC, V.

★ **MICROTEL INN & SUITES.** *7265 Commerce Center Dr (80919). 719/598-7500; fax 719/598-4975; res 888/771-7171. www.microtelinnco.com.* 105 rms, 4 story, 69 suites. Mid-May-

mid-Sept: S $49-$79; D $89-$120; each addl $10; suites $89; under 16 free; lower rates rest of yr. Crib free. TV; cable (premium). Complimentary continental bkfst. Complimentary coffee in rms. Restaurant nearby. Ck-out 11 am. In-rm modem link. Coin lndry. Exercise equipt. Indoor pool; whirlpool. Refrigerator, microwave in suites. Cr cds: A, C, D, DS, MC, V.

★★ **RAMADA INN.** *3125 N Sinton Rd (80907). 719/633-5541; fax 719/633-3870; toll-free 888/298-2054. www.ramada.com.* 215 rms, 2 story. May-Aug: S $89; D $99; suites $175-$225; under 18 free; lower rates rest of yr. Crib free. TV; cable (premium). Complimentary coffee in lobby, rms. Restaurant 6 am-1:30 pm, 5:30-10 pm. Rm serv. Bar 5-10 pm. Ck-out noon. Meeting rms. Business servs avail. In-rm modem link. Valet serv. Coin lndry. Free airport transportation. Indoor pool. Game rm. Health club privileges. Cr cds: A, C, D, DS, ER, JCB, MC, V.

★ **RODEWAY INN.** *2409 E Pikes Peak Ave (80909). 719/471-0990; fax 719/633-3343; res 800/228-2000. www.rodewayinn.com.* 113 rms, 2 story. May-early Sept: S $75; D $85; each addl $6; kit. units $135; under 18 free; lower rates rest of yr. Crib free. TV; cable (premium). Heated pool. Complimentary continental bkfst. Coffee in rms. Restaurant adj 6 am-10 pm. Bar to midnight. Ck-out noon. Meeting rms. Business servs avail. In-rm modem link. Coin lndry. Exercise equipt. Airport transportation. Some refrigerators, microwaves, fireplaces. Cr cds: A, C, D, DS, ER, JCB, MC, V.

★★ **VILLAGER PREMIER.** *725 W Cimarron St (80905). 719/473-5530; fax 719/473-8763.* 207 rms, 2 story. Mid-May-mid-Sept: S, D $89-$105; each addl $10; suites $225; under 19 free; family, wkly rates; lower rates rest of yr. Crib free. Pet accepted; $25. Heated pool. TV; cable (premium). Complimentary continental bkfst. Restaurant opp 11 am-10 pm. Ck-out noon. Meeting rms. Business servs avail. In-rm modem link. Cr cds: A, C, D, DS, MC, V.

Hotels

★★★ **THE ANTLERS ADAM'S MARK HOTEL.** *4 S Cascade (80903). 719/473-5600; fax 719/389-0259. www.adamsmark.com.* 290 rms, some with shower only, 13 story. S $79-$176; D $89-$176; each addl $15; suites $200-$825; under 18 free; wkend rates. Crib free. Pet accepted, some restrictions. Garage $6. TV; cable (premium), VCR avail. Indoor pool; whirlpool, poolside serv. Complimentary coffee in rms. Restaurants 6:30 am-midnight; Fri, Sat to 1 am. Bars 11-1 am, Sun to midnight. Ck-out noon. Convention facilities. Business servs avail. Concierge. Gift shop. Valet parking. Exercise equipt. Microwaves avail. Cr cds: A, C, D, DS, MC, V.

★★★ **DOUBLETREE HOTEL.** *1775 E Cheyenne Mtn Blvd (80906). 719/576-8900; fax 719/576-4450; res 800/222-8733. www.doubletree.com.* 299 rms, 5 story. S, D $159-$178; each addl $15; suites $375-$475; under 18 free; wkend rates. Crib free. Pet accepted; $10. TV; cable (premium). Indoor pool; whirlpool. Coffee in rms. Restaurant 6 am-10 pm. Rm serv. Bar 11-2 am; entertainment Tues-Sat. Ck-out noon. Convention facilities. Business servs avail. In-rm modem link. Bellhops. Valet serv. Gift shop. Free airport transportation. Exercise equipt; sauna. Some bathrm phones. Private patios, balconies. Cr cds: A, C, D, DS, ER, JCB, MC, V.

★★★ **RADISSON INN & SUITES.** *1645 Newport Rd (80916). 719/597-7000; fax 719/597-4308; res 800/333-3333. www.radisson.com.* 200 rms, 2 story. May-Sept: S, D $109-$129; each addl $15; suites $160; under 18 free; wkly rates; lower rates rest of yr. Crib free. Pet accepted, some restrictions; $50. TV; cable (premium). Indoor pool; whirlpool, poolside serv. Complimentary full bkfst. Complimentary coffee in rms. Restaurant 6 am-10 pm. Rm serv 24 hrs. Bar. Ck-out noon. Coin lndry. Meeting rms. Business center. In-rm modem link.

Bellhops. Concierge. Gift shop. Free airport transportation. Exercise equipt. Game rm. Refrigerator, microwave in suites. Cr cds: A, C, D, DS, ER, JCB, MC, V.

★★★ **RADISSON INN NORTH.** *8110 N Academy Blvd (80920). 719/598-5770; fax 719/598-3434; res 800/333-3333. www.radisson.com.* 200 rms, 2-4 story. May-Sept: S $119-$149; D $129-$159; each addl $10; suites $159-$259; under 18 free; wkend rates; lower rates rest of yr. Crib free. Pet accepted, some restrictions. TV; cable (premium). Indoor pool; whirlpool. Coffee in rms. Restaurants 6:30 am-10 pm. Rm serv. Bar from 11 am. Ck-out noon. Meeting rms. Business servs avail. In-rm modem link. Coin lndry. Free airport transportation. Exercise equipt; sauna. Microwaves avail. Near USAF Academy. Cr cds: A, C, D, DS, ER, JCB, MC, V.

★★★ **SHERATON HOTEL.** *2886 S Cir Dr (80905). 719/576-5900; fax 719/576-7695; toll-free 800/981-4012. www.sheraton.com.* 500 rms, 2-4 story. Mid-May-mid-Sept: S, D $105-$155; suites $250; under 18 free; wkend rates; lower rates rest of yr. Crib $5. Pet accepted. TV; cable (premium), VCR avail. 2 pools, 1 indoor; wading pool, whirlpool. Playground. Coffee in rms. Restaurant 6 am-10 pm. Rm serv 24 hrs. Bars 11-2 am; entertainment Fri, Sat. Ck-out 11 am. Convention facilities. Business center. In-rm modem link. Bellhops. Valet. Concierge. Gift shop. Airport transportation. Lighted tennis. Putting green. Exercise equipt; steam rm, sauna. Game rm. Some refrigerators; microwaves avail. Private patios, balconies. Cr cds: A, C, D, DS, JCB, MC, V.

★★ **WYNDHAM COLORADO SPRINGS.** *5580 Tech Center Dr (80919). 719/260-1800; fax 719/260-1492; res 800/996-3426. www.wyndham.com.* 311 rms, 9 story. S $129-$159; D $149-$179; suites $275-$350; under 18 free. Crib free. TV; cable (premium), VCR avail. 2 pools, 1 indoor; poolside serv. Restaurant 6:30 am-2 pm, 5-11 pm. Bar 11 am-midnight. Ck-out noon.

Lndry facilities. Convention facilities. Business servs avail. In-rm modem link. Gift shop. Exercise equipt; sauna. Cr cds: A, C, D, DS, ER, JCB, MC, V.

Resort

★★★★★ THE BROADMOOR RESORT. *One Lake Ave (80906). 719/634-7711; fax 719/577-5700; res 800/634-7711. www.broadmoor.com.* This 3,000-acre resort began as a gambling casino in 1891 and sits at the foot of the Rockies near Cheyenne Lake. Host to many dignitaries and celebrities over the years, the beautifully manicured grounds offer three 18-hole golf courses, 12 tennis courts, a spa (utilizing treatment ingredients from the surrounding mountains), indoor and outdoor pools, and over ten restaurants and lounges. 700 rms. Mid-May-mid-Oct: S, D $190-$425; suites $450-$2,000; package plans; lower rates rest of yr. Crib free. TV; cable (premium), VCR avail. 4 heated pools, 1 indoor; whirlpool, wading pool, poolside serv, lifeguard. Supervised child's activities (June-Labor Day and Dec 25 hols); ages 3-12. Dining rm (see PENROSE ROOM and CHARLES COURT). Rm serv 24 hrs. Box lunches, snack bar. Bars noon-1 am; Sun to midnight. Ck-out noon, ck-in 4 pm. Convention facilities. Business center. In-rm modem link. Concierge. Airport, railroad station, bus depot transportation. Tennis (indoor in winter), pro. Three 18-hole golf courses, greens fee, pro, putting green, driving range. Boats. Bicycles. Horseback riding. Hot-air ballooning. Entertainment, dancing, movie theater. Exercise rm; sauna. Health spa, Massage. Fishing/hunting guide service. Minibars; some refrigerators. Balconies. Cr cds: A, C, D, DS, JCB, MC, V.

B&Bs/Small Inns

★★★ CHEYENNE CANON INN. *2030 W Cheyenne Blvd (80906). 719/633-0625; fax 719/633-8826. www.cheyennecanoninn.com.* 10 rms, 2 story. S, D $95-$200. TV; cable (premium). In-rm modem link.

Complimentary full bkfst. Whirlpool. Cr cds: A, DS, MC, V.

★★★ HEARTHSTONE INN. *506 N Cascade Ave (80903). 719/473-4413; fax 719/473-1322; toll-free 800/521-1885. www.hearthstoneinn.com.* 25 rms, 2 share bath, 3 story. No rm phones. S $80-$160; D $90-$170; each addl $15; under 4 free. Crib free. Complimentary full bkfst. Ck-out 11 am, ck-in 2-10 pm. Meeting rm. Gift shop. Some private patios, fireplaces. Restored Victorian mansion (1885); brass fixtures, carved beds, many antique furnishings. Some rms with view of Pikes Peak. Totally nonsmoking. Cr cds: A, MC, V.

★★★ HOLDEN HOUSE 1902 BED & BREAKFAST. *1102 W Pikes Peak Ave (80904). 719/471-3980; fax 719/471-4740; toll-free 888/565-3980. www.holdenhouse.com.* 5 suites, 2 story. S, D $135. Adults only. TV in sitting rm. Complimentary full bkfst; afternoon refreshments. Restaurant nearby. Ck-out 11 am, ck-in 4-6 pm. Fireplaces, antique furnishings. Victorian house (1902). Totally nonsmoking. Cr cds: A, C, D, DS, MC, V.

★★★ OLD TOWN GUEST HOUSE. *115 S 26th St (80904). 719/632-9194; fax 719/632-9026; toll-free 888/375-4210. www.oldtown-guesthouse.com.* 8 rms, 3 story. S, D $95-$175. TV; cable (premium), VCR (movies). Complimentary full bkfst. Complimentary coffee in rms. Restaurant adj 6 am-9 pm. Ck-out 11 am, ck-in 4-6 pm. In-rm modem link. Luggage handling. Valet serv. Exercise equipt. Game rm. Refrigerators; many fireplaces. Many balconies. Totally nonsmoking. Cr cds: A, DS, MC, V.

★★★ ROOM AT THE INN. *618 N Nevada Ave (80903). 719/442-1896; fax 719/442-6802; res 800/442-1896. www.roomattheinn.com.* 7 rms, 1 with shower only, 3 story. S, D $89-$135; each addl $15. Children over 12 yrs only. Whirlpool. Complimentary full bkfst; afternoon refreshments. Restaurant nearby. Ck-out 11 am, ck-in 4-6 pm. Luggage handling. Concierge serv. Queen Anne Victo-

rian home built in 1896; 3-story turret, wraparound porch. Totally non-smoking. Cr cds: A, DS, V.

Guest Ranch

★★★ **LOST VALLEY RANCH.** *29555 Goose Creek Rd, Sedalia (80135). 303/647-2311; fax 303/647-2315. www.lostvalleyranch.com.* 24 cabins (1-3 bedrm). No A/C. No rm phones. Mid-June-Labor Day, AP, wkly: $1,690 each; family rates; lower daily rates rest of yr. Pool; whirlpools. Playground. Free supervised child's activities (Memorial Day-Labor Day); ages 3-18. Coffee in cabins. Box lunches, picnics, cookouts. Ck-out Sun 10 am, ck-in Sun 2 pm. Coin lndry. Meeting rms. Business servs avail. Tennis. Trap shooting. Hayrides, wagon rides. Spring and fall cattle round-ups. Lawn games. Soc dir, entertainment, square dancing. Rec rm. Fishing school; fish cleaning, storage, cooking. Refrigerators, fireplaces. Private porches, balconies. Beautiful view of mountains. Authentic working ranch. Homesteaded in 1883.

All Suites

★★ **AMERISUITES.** *503 W Garden of The Gods Rd. (20907). 719/265-9385; fax 719/532-9514; toll-free 800/747-8483. www.amerisuites.com.* 126 suites, 4 story. Apr-Sept: S $99-$139; D $109-$149; suites $149; each addl $10; under 18 free; wkend rates; lower rates rest of yr. Crib free. TV; cable (premium). Complimentary continental bkfst. Restaurant adj 11 am-11 pm. Ck-out noon. Meeting rms. Business servs avail. In-rm modem link. Bellhops. Coin lndry. Exercise equipt. Pool. Refrigerators, microwaves. Cr cds: A, D, DS, MC, V.

★★★ **EMBASSY SUITES.** *7290 Commerce Center Dr (80919). 719/599-9100; fax 719/599-4644. www.embassysuites.com.* 207 suites, 4 story. Mid-Apr-Sept: S $125-$135; D $130-$149; each addl $10; under 12 free; lower rates rest of yr. TV; cable (premium). Indoor pool; whirlpool. Complimentary full bkfst. Coffee in rms. Restaurant 11:30 am-2:30 pm, 6-10 pm. Rm serv. Bar to midnight. Ck-out noon. Coin lndry. Meeting rms. Business servs avail. In-rm modem link. Bellhops. Gift shop. Golf privileges. Tennis privileges. Exercise equipt; sauna. Game rm. Refrigerators, microwaves. Balconies. Atrium; glass elevators. Cr cds: A, D, DS, MC, V.

Extended Stays

★★ **RESIDENCE INN BY MARRIOTT.** *3880 N Academy Blvd (80917). 719/574-0370; fax 719/574-7821; res 800/331-3131. www.residenceinn.com.* 96 kit. suites, 2

Pikes Peak

story. S $89-$138; D $129-$185; each addl $10; under 18 free. Pet accepted; $15/day. TV; cable (premium), VCR avail. Heated pool; whirlpool. Complimentary continental bkfst. Ck-out noon. Meeting rms. Business servs avail. In-rm modem link. Coin lndry. Valet serv. Free airport transportation. Health club privileges. Refrigerators, microwaves; some fireplaces. Some balconies. Grills. Cr cds: A, D, DS, MC, V.

★★ **RESIDENCE INN BY MARRIOTT SOUTH.** *2765 Geyser Dr (80906).* 719/576-0101; fax 719/576-4848; res 800/331-3131. www. residenceinn.com. 72 units, 3 story. May-Oct: S $99-$129; D $139-$169; lower rates rest of yr. Crib free. Pet accepted, some restrictions; $50. TV; cable (premium). Complimentary continental bkfst. Complimentary coffee in rms. Restaurant adj 4-11 pm. Ck-out noon. Meeting rms. Business servs avail. In-rm modem link. Valet serv. Coin lndry. Lighted tennis. Exercise equipt. Indoor pool; whirlpool. Refrigerators, microwaves; some fireplaces. Grills. Cr cds: A, C, D, DS, JCB, MC, V.

Restaurants

★★★ **CHARLES COURT.** *1 Lake Ave (80901).* 719/577-5774. Hrs: 7-11 am, 6-9:30 pm. Res accepted. Continental Amer cuisine. Bar. Wine cellar. A la carte entrees: bkfst $9-$13 dinner $28-$45. Specializes in fresh cuts of beef, Colorado wild game. Valet parking. Jacket. Cr cds: A, C, D, DS, ER, JCB, MC, V.

★★ **EDELWEISS.** *34 E Ramona Ave (80906).* 719/633-2220. www. restauranteur.com/edelweiss. Hrs: 11:30 am-2 pm, 5-9 pm; Fri, Sat to 9:30 pm; Sun 5-9 pm. German, Amer menu. Bar. Lunch $4.50-$7.25, dinner $8.25-$17.25. Specialties: Wiener schnitzel, sauerbraten. Own soups. German music and entertainment Fri, Sat. Parking. Outdoor dining. Former schoolhouse (1890). Family-owned. Cr cds: A, D, DS, MC, V.

★ **GIUSEPPE'S OLD DEPOT.** *10 S Sierra Madre (80903).* 719/635-3111. Hrs: 11 am-9:30 pm; Fri, Sat to 11 pm. Closed Thanksgiving, Dec 25. Res accepted. Italian, Amer menu. Bar. Lunch, dinner $5.95-$16.50. Child's menu. Specializes in lasagne, pizza, prime rib. Salad bar. Patio dining. Large main dining rm with several different size dining areas. In historic railroad depot (1887); railroad memorabilia on display. Cr cds: A, C, D, DS, ER, MC, V.

★★ **HATCH COVER.** *252 E Cheyenne Mtn Blvd (80906).* 719/576-5223. Hrs: 11 am-2 pm, 5-10 pm; Sat, Sun from 5 pm. Res accepted. Bar to 2 am. Lunch $3.95-$11.95, dinner $10-$35. Specializes in fresh seafood, prime rib, pasta. Parking. Aquariums. Cr cds: D, DS, MC, V.

★★ **LA PETITE MAISON.** *1015 W Colorado Ave (80904).* 719/632-4887. www.restauranteur.com. Hrs: 5-10 pm; early-bird dinner to 6:30 pm. Res accepted. Closed Sun, Mon; Jan 1, July 4, Dec 24-25. Serv bar. Dinner $11.50-$26. Specializes in duck, lamb, seasonal fresh fish. Own baking. Parking. In renovated house (1894). Totally nonsmoking. Cr cds: A, D, DS, MC, V.

★★ **MACKENZIE'S CHOP HOUSE.** *128 S Tejon (80903).* 719/635-3536. Hrs: 11 am-2 pm, 5-10 pm; Fri to 11 pm; Sat 5-11 pm; Sun (brunch) 10 am-2 pm, 4-10 pm. Closed Dec 25. Res accepted. Steak menu. Bar. Lunch $5.95-$12.95, dinner $10.95-$34.95. Sun brunch $19.95. Specializes in steaks, chops, seafood. Street parking. Outdoor dining. Built 1890. Totally nonsmoking. Cr cds: A, MC, V.

★ **MAGGIE MAE'S.** *2405 E Pikes Peak Ave (80909).* 719/475-1623. Hrs: 6 am-10 pm; Sat, Sun to 9 pm. Closed Dec 25. Mexican, Amer menu. Bar to 2 am. Bkfst $3-$6.75, lunch $4.25-$6.75, dinner $4-$8. Child's menu. Specializes in green and red chili burritos, pancakes, crepes. Parking. Cr cds: A, C, D, DS, ER, MC, V.

★ ★ ★ ★ **PENROSE ROOM.** *1 Lake Ave (80906). 719/634-7711. www. broadmoor.com.* Dress up for this lofty escape in the South Tower penthouse of The Broadmoor, a luxury resort at the foot of the Rockies. The room is named after Spencer Penrose, the owner under whom this resort gained such a fine reputation, and offers breathtaking views of the city and Cheyenne Mountain. Enjoy classic continental specialties and the signature dessert souffles. Continental menu. Specialties: châteaubriand, medallion of veal, roasted rack of Colorado lamb. Own baking. Bar. Hrs: 6-10 pm. Res accepted. Dinner $23-$35. Band trio. Jacket. Cr cds: A, D, MC, V.
D

Unrated Dining Spots

LA CREPERIE. *204 N Tejon (80903). 719/632-0984. www.restauranteur.com/ lacreperie.* Hrs: 10 am-9 pm; Sun, Mon to 3 pm. Closed most major hols. Res accepted. Continental menu. Wine, beer.Lunch $5-$8, dinner $7.50-$18. Specializes in country French cuisine. Former streetcar horse stable (1892). Country French decor. Cr cds: A, D, MC, V.
D

OLD CHICAGO. *7115 Commerce Center Dr (80919). 719/593-7678. www.oldchicago.com.* Hrs: 11-2 am; Sun to midnight. Closed Thanksgiving, Dec 25. Bar. Italian, Amer menu. Lunch $4.95-$7.95, dinner $5.95-$15.95. Child's menu. Specializes in deep-dish pizza, pasta. Parking. Sports bar atmosphere. Cr cds: A, D, MC, V.
D SC ⊸

OLD CHICAGO PASTA & PIZZA. *118 N Tejon (80903). 719/634-8812. www.rockbottom.com.* Hrs: 11 am-1 am; Sun from noon. Closed Thanksgiving, Dec 25. Res accepted. Italian menu. Bar to 2 am, Sun to midnight. Lunch $3.95-$6.50, dinner $5.95-$10.95. Child's menu. Specializes in pizza, pasta bar. Own pasta. Outdoor dining. Cr cds: A, C, D, ER, MC, V.
D ⊸

Copper Mountain (C-4)

(see Dillon)

Cortez (E-1)

Settled 1890 **Pop** 7,977

Information Cortez/Mesa Verde Visitor Info Bureau, PO Box HH; 970/565-8227 or 800/253-1616

What to See and Do

Anasazi Heritage Center and Escalante. Museum of exhibits, artifacts, and documents from excavations on public lands in southwest Colorado, incl the Dolores Archaeological Program. Represents the Northern San Juan Anasazi Tradition (A.D. 1 to 1300). Within ½-mi of the center are the Dominguez and Escalante sites—the latter discovered by a Franciscan friar in 1776. Excavations revealed kivas and other structures, pottery, and ceremonial artifacts. (Daily; closed Jan 1, Thanksgiving, Dec 25) 8 mi N on CO 145, then 2 mi NW on CO 184. Phone 970/882-4811. ¢¢

Hovenweep National Monument. Monument consists of six units of prehistoric ruins; the best preserved is at Square Tower, which incl the remains of pueblos and towers. Self-guided trail, park ranger on duty; visitor area (daily). 20 mi NW on US 666 to Pleasant View and follow signs 5 mi W on County BB, then 20 mi S on County 10. Phone 970/562-4282. ¢¢¢

Lowry Pueblo. Constructed by the Anasazi (ca 1075). Forty excavated rms incl one great and seven smaller kivas. Picnic facilities. No camping. (Daily, weather and road conditions permitting) 21 mi NW on US 666 to Pleasant View, then 9 mi W on County Rd CC. Phone 970/247-4874. **FREE**

Mesa Verde National Park. (see). 10 mi E on US 160.

Ute Mountain Tribal Park. The Ute Mountain Tribe developed this 125,000-acre park on their tribal lands, opening hundreds of largely unexplored 800-yr-old Anasazi ruins to the public. Tours begin at the Ute Mountain Visitor Center/Museum, 19 mi S via US 666 (daily); res required. Backpacking trips in summer. Primitive camping avail. Phone 970/565-9653 or 800/847-5485. Tours ¢¢¢¢

Special Events

Ute Mountain Rodeo. Phone 970/565-4485. Early-mid June.

Montezuma County Fair. Phone 970/565-1000. First wk Aug.

Motels/Motor Lodges

★★ **ANASAZI MOTOR INN.** *640 S Broadway (81321). 970/565-3773; fax 970/565-1027; res 800/972-6232. www.anasazimotorinn.com.* 87 rms, 1-2 story. June-Sept: S, D $71; each addl $6; under 18 free; lower rates rest of yr. Crib free. Pet accepted. TV; cable (premium), VCR avail. Heated pool; whirlpool. Restaurant 6 am-9 pm. Bar; entertainment Fri, Sat. Ck-out noon. Meeting rms. Business servs avail. Free airport transportation. Refrigerators avail. Cr cds: A, C, D, DS, MC, V.

★★ **BEST WESTERN TURQUOISE INN AND SUITES.** *535 E Main St (81321). 970/565-3778; fax 970/565-3439; res 800/780-7234. www.cortez bestwestern.com.* 77 rms, 2 story, 33 suites. June-Sept: S, D $89-$129; under 12 free; lower rates rest of yr. Crib free. Pet accepted; $15. TV; cable (premium). Heated pools; whirlpool. Complimentary continental bkfst. Coffee in rms. Ck-out 11 am. Coin lndry. In-rm modem link. Business servs avail. Valet serv. Gift shop. Free airport transportation. Refrigerator, microwave, kitchenette in suites. Some balconies, fireplaces, in-rm whirlpools. Cr cds: A, C, D, DS, MC, V.

★★ **COMFORT INN.** *2321 E Main St (81321). 970/565-3400; fax 970/564-9768; res 800/228-5150. www.comfort inn.com.* 150 rms, 3 story. Mid-May-mid-Oct: S, D $59-$89; each addl $6; under 18 free; ski plans; lower rates rest of yr. Crib $6. Pet accepted. TV;

cable (premium). Complimentary continental bkfst, coffee in rms. Restaurant nearby. Ck-out noon. Meeting rms. Business servs avail. In-rm modem link. Coin lndry. Heated indoor pool; whirlpool. Some in-rm whirlpools. Cr cds: A, D, MC, V.

★★ **HOLIDAY INN EXPRESS.** *2121 E Main St (81321). 970/565-6000; fax 970/565-3438; res 800/626-5652. www.coloradoholiday.com.* 100 rms, 3 story. Mid-May-Sept: S, D $69-$149; each addl $6; under 18 free. Crib free. Pet accepted, some restrictions. TV; cable (premium), VCR avail. Heated indoor pool; whirlpool. Complimentary continental bkfst. Restaurant nearby. Ck-out 11 am. Meeting rms. Business servs avail. In-rm modem link. Coin lndry. Valet serv. Business servs avail. Free airport transportation. Exercise equipt; sauna. Refrigerators in suites. Some in-rm whirlpools. Cr cds: A, D, DS, MC, V.

Restaurant

★★ **HOMESTEADERS.** *45 E Main St (81321). 970/565-6253.* Hrs: 7 am-3 pm, 5-9 pm. Closed major hols; also Sun Nov-Apr. Res accepted. Serv bar. Southwestern menu. Bkfst $2.65-$5.79, lunch $2.49-$5.75, dinner $7.50-$16. Child's menu. Specializes in homemade soups, breads, pies. Rustic Western decor. Cr cds: MC, V.

Craig

(A-2) *See also Steamboat Springs*

Pop 9,189 **Elev** 6,186 ft
Area code 970 **Zip** 81625
Information Greater Craig Area Chamber of Commerce, 360 E Victory Way; 970/824-5689 or 800/864-4405
Web www.craig-chamber.com

What to See and Do

Dinosaur National Monument. (see). Exit 21 off NY State Thruway, W on

NY 23 to NY 145W, 1 mi off NY 145 on Shady Glen Rd in East Durham. Phone 518/239-4559. ¢¢¢¢

Marcia. Private, luxury Pullman railroad car of David Moffat. Tours avail through Moffat County Visitors Center. City Park, US 40. Phone 970/824-5689. **FREE**

Museum of Northwest Colorado. Local history, Native American artifacts; wildlife photography. Cowboy and gunfighter collection. Also the Edwin C. Johnson Collection (Johnson was governor of Colorado and a US senator). (Mon-Sat). 590 Yampa Ave, Old State Armory, center of town. Phone 970/824-6360. **Donation**

Save Our Sandrocks Nature Trail. This sloped, ¾-mi trail provides a view of Native American petroglyphs on the sandrocks. Trail guide avail at the Cooperative Extension Office, 200 W Victory Way. (May-Nov) On the 900 blk of Alta Vista Dr. Phone 970/824-6673. **FREE**

Motel/Motor Lodge

★★ **HOLIDAY INN.** *300 S Hwy 13 (81625). 970/824-4000; fax 970/824-3950; toll-free 800/465-4329. www. holiday-inn.com.* 152 rms, 2 story. S $59-$79; D $69-$89; each addl $10; suites $84-$109; under 19 free. Crib free. Pet accepted. TV; cable (premium), VCR avail. Indoor pool; whirlpool, poolside serv. Coffee in rms. Restaurant 6 am-2 pm, 5-10 pm. Rm serv. Bar 4 pm-midnight. Ck-out 11 am. Coin lndry. Meeting rms. Business servs avail. Valet serv. Holidome. Exercise equipt. Game rm. Refrigerators. Microwaves avail. Cr cds: A, D, DS, MC, V.

🄳 🐾 ⛖ 🏊 🔥 🏃

Crested Butte

(D-3) *See also Gunnison*

Founded 1880 **Pop** 1,529 **Elev** 8,908 ft **Area code** 970 **Zip** 81224

Information Crested Butte Vacations, 500 Gothic Rd, PO Box A, Mount Crested Butte 81225; 800/544-8448

Web www.crestedbutteresort.com

What to See and Do

Skiing. Crested Butte Mountain Resort Ski Area. Three high-speed quad, three triple, three double chairlifts, four surface lifts, two magic carpets; patrol, school, rentals, snowmaking; cafeteria, restaurant, bar, nursery. Eighty-five runs; longest run 2½ mi; vertical drop 3,062 ft. (Late Nov-mid-Apr, daily) Multiday, half-day rates. Nineteen mi of groomed x-country trails, 100 mi of wilderness trails; snowmobiling, sleigh rides. 3 mi N on county road in Gunnison National Forest (see GUNNISON). Phone 800/810-SNOW. ¢¢¢¢

B&Bs/Small Inns

★★ **CRESTED BUTTE ATHLETIC CLUB.** *512 2nd Ave (81224). 970/349-6655; fax 970/349-7580.* 8 air-cooled rms, 2 story. Mid-Nov-mid-Apr (2-day min): S, D $125-$250; each addl $30; ski, golf plans; lower rates rest of yr. Crib free. TV; cable (premium). Heated indoor pool; whirlpool. Complimentary bkfst buffet. Coffee in rms. Restaurant opp 5-10 pm. Bar 7 am-10 pm. Ck-out 11 am, ck-in 3 pm. Concierge serv. Luggage handling. Business servs avail. Golf privileges, putting green, driving range. Downhill ski 2 mi; x-country 1 blk. Exercise equipt; steam rm. Massage. Built in 1886; many family heirlooms, fireplaces. Totally nonsmoking. Cr cds: DS, MC, V.

🛒 🏋 🌊 ⛷ 🏃 🟰 🔥

★★ **THE NORDIC INN.** *14 Treasury Rd, Mt Crested Butte (80216). 970/349-5542; fax 970/349-6487; toll-free 800/542-7669. www.nordicinncb. com.* 27 rms, 2 story, 3 kits, 2 chalets. No A/C. Thanksgiving-Apr: S, D $88-$152; each addl $10; kit. units $125-$175; chalets $230-$315; under 12 free (summer); family, wkly rates (summer); ski plans; lower rates rest of yr. Closed early-Apr-May. Crib $5. TV; cable (premium), VCR avail. Whirlpool. Complimentary continental bkfst. Restaurant nearby. Ck-out 11 am. Meeting rm. Business servs avail. In-rm modem link. Downhill ski 1 blk. Fireplace in lobby. Balconies. Cr cds: A, MC, V.

🄳 🐾 ⛖ 🟰 🔥

Restaurants

★ **DONITA'S CANTINA.** *330 Elk Ave (81224).* 970/349-6674. Hrs: 5:30-9:30 pm. Closed Thanksgiving, Dec 25, last 2 wks Apr. No A/C. Mexican menu. Dinner $8.50-$21.95. Child's menu. Specializes in Tex-Mex, vegetarian cuisine. Own desserts. Mexican decor. Former hotel (1881) with original pressed tin ceiling. Totally nonsmoking. Cr cds: A, D, DS, MC, V.
D

★ ★ **LE BOSQUET.** *6th and Belleview (81224).* 970/349-5808. Hrs: 6-10 pm; winter from 5:30 pm. Closed mid-Apr-mid-May. Res accepted. No A/C. French menu. Bar. Dinner $12.95-$36.95. Specializes in lamb, fresh seafood, chicken. Own desserts. Outdoor dining. French decor. Totally nonsmoking. Cr cds: A, DS, MC, V.
D

Cripple Creek

(D-5) *See also Cañon City, Colorado Springs, Manitou Springs*

Settled 1891 **Pop** 1,115 **Elev** 9,494 ft
Area code 719 **Zip** 80813
Information Chamber of Commerce, PO Box 650; 719/689-2169 or 800/526-8777
Web www.cripple-creek.co.us

What to See and Do

Cripple Creek District Museum. Artifacts of Cripple Creek's glory; pioneer relics, mining and railroad displays; Victorian furnishings. Heritage Art Gallery and Assay Office. Extensive activities for research. (Memorial Day-mid-Oct, daily; winter and early spring, wkends only) On CO 67. Phone 719/689-2634. ¢¢

Cripple Creek-Victor Narrow Gauge Railroad. An authentic locomotive and coaches depart from Cripple Creek District Museum. Four-mi round-trip past many historic mines. (Late May-early Oct, daily, departs every 45 min) On CO 67. Phone 719/689-2640. ¢¢¢

Imperial Casino Hotel. (1896) (see HOTELS) This hotel was constructed shortly after the town's great fire. Phone 719/689-7777 or 800/235-2922. ¢¢¢

Mollie Kathleen Gold Mine. Descend 1,000 ft on a 40-min guided tour through a gold mine. (May-Oct, daily) 1 mi N on CO 67. Phone 719/689-2465. ¢¢¢

Victor. Victor, the "city of mines," actually does have streets paved with gold (low-grade ore was used to surface streets in the early days). 5 mi S on CO 67.

Special Events

Donkey Derby Days. Last full wkend June. Phone 719/689-3315.

Veteran's Memorial Rally. Mid-Aug. Phone 719/487-8005.

Motel/Motor Lodge

★ ★ **HOLIDAY INN EXPRESS CRIPPLER.** *601 E Galena Ave (80813).* 719/689-2600; fax 719/689-3426; res 800/465-4329. www.holidayinncc.com. 67 rms, 3 story. S, D $68-$99; each addl $5; under 18 free. Crib free. TV; cable (premium). Complimentary continental bkfst. Restaurant nearby. Ck-out 11 am. Meeting rms. Concierge. Coin lndry. Picnic tables. Cr cds: A, C, D, DS, JCB, MC, V.
D 🐾 ⚙ 🏊 🔥

Hotels

★ ★ **DOUBLE HOTEL & CASINO.** *442 E Bennett Ave (80813).* 719/689-5000; fax 719/689-5050. www.decasino.com. 157 air-cooled rms, 5 story. S, D $59-$99; each addl $15; suites $129-$500. Crib free. TV; cable. Complimentary full bkfst. Restaurant 6 am-10 pm. Ck-out 11 am. Meeting rms. Business servs avail. Gift shop. Cr cds: A, D, DS, MC, V.
D 🏊 🔥

★ **IMPERIAL CASINO HOTEL.** *123 N 3rd St (80813).* 719/689-7777; fax 719/689-1008; toll-free 800/235-2922. www.imperialcasinohotel.com. 29 rms, 3 story, 18 share baths. No A/C. S, D $65-$80; each addl $10. Restaurant (see STRATTON DINING ROOM). Bars 10-2 am. Ck-out 11 am. Meeting rms. Built 1896. Victorian decor;

antiques. Gold Bar Room Theatre. Cr cds: A, DS, MC, V.

D ♿ ⚡ ⛵ 🔥 🐾

B&B/Small Inn

★★ **VICTOR HOTEL.** *4th St and Victor Ave, Victor (80860). 719/689-3553; fax 719/689-3979; toll-free 800/748-0870. www.victorhotel.com.* 30 air-cooled rms, 4 story. Mid-May-mid-Oct: S $89; D $99; under 12 free; lower rates rest of yr. Pet accepted. TV; cable (premium). Complimentary continental bkfst. Restaurant May-Sept 11 am-2 pm; Fri-Sat to 9 pm. Rm serv. Ck-out 11 am. Business servs avail. Former bank; bird-cage elevator. Cr cds: DS, MC, V.

D 🔄 ♿ ⚡ ⛵ 🔥

Restaurant

★★ **STRATTON DINING ROOM.** *123 N 3rd St (80813). 719/689-7777.* Hrs: 7-10 am, 11 am-2 pm, 5-9 pm; Sun brunch 11 am-2 pm. Bars 8-2 am. A la carte entrees: bkfst $1.25-$4.95, lunch $5.95, dinner $8.75-$14.95. Valet parking. Authentic Old West Victorian decor. Cr cds: A, DS, MC, V.

D ⛵

Delta

(D-2) *See also Montrose*

Settled 1880 **Pop** 6,400 **Elev** 4,953 ft
Area code 970 **Zip** 81416
Information Chamber of Commerce, 301 Main St; 970/874-8616

What to See and Do

Black Canyon of the Gunnison National Monument. (see).

Crawford State Park. Swimming, waterskiing, fishing, boating (ramps); winter sports, picnicking, camping. Standard fees. (Daily) 20 mi E to Hotchkiss, then 11 mi S on CO 92. Phone 970/921-5721. Per vehicle ¢¢

Sweitzer State Park. Swimming, waterskiing, fishing, boating (ramps); picnicking, bird-watching. Standard fees. (Daily) 3 mi SE off US 50. Phone 970/874-4258. ¢¢

Special Event

Deltarado Days. Delta Round-Up Club, 4 mi E. Parade, barbecue, craft booths, games, square dancing, PRCA Rodeo. Last wkend July. Phone 970/874-8616.

Motels/Motor Lodges

★★ **BEST WESTERN SUNDANCE.** *903 Main St (81416). 970/874-9781; fax 970/874-5440; res 800/780-7234. www.bestwesternsundance.com.* 41 rms, 2 story. May-Sept: S, D $50-$80; each addl $10; under 12 free; lower rates rest of yr. Pet accepted, some restrictions; $5. TV; cable (premium). Heated pool; whirlpool. Complimentary full bkfst. Complimentary coffee. Restaurant 6; Sun 6 am-2 pm. Rm serv. Bar 11-2 am. Ck-out 11 am. Coin lndry. Business servs avail. In-rm modem link. Exercise equipt. Balconies. Refrigerators, microwaves avail. Cr cds: A, C, D, DS, MC, V.

🏃 D 🐾 ⛵ 🔥 SC

★★ **COMFORT INN.** *180 Gunnison River Dr (81416). 970/874-1000; fax 970/874-4154; toll-free 800/228-5150. www.comfortinn.com.* 47 rms, 2 story, 4 suites. June-Sept: S, D $74-$89; each addl $5; suites $89-$99; under 18 free; higher rates special events; lower rates rest of yr. Crib free. Pet accepted; $5. TV; cable (premium), VCR avail (movies). Pool privileges; whirlpool. Complimentary continental bkfst, coffee in rms. Restaurant opp 6 am-10 pm. Ck-out 11 am. Business servs avail. Coin lndry. Game rm. Health club privileges; sauna. Some refrigerators, microwaves. Tennis, skiing nearby. Cr cds: A, D, DS, MC, V.

D 🏃 ⚡ 🐾 ⛵ 🔥 SC

Denver (C-5)

Settled 1858 **Pop** 544,636 **Elev** 5,280 ft **Area code** 303
Information Denver Metro Convention & Visitors Bureau, 1555 California St, Suite 300, 80202; 303/892-1112 or 800/233-6837
Web www.denver.org

Suburbs Boulder, Central City, Englewood, Evergreen, Golden, Idaho

Springs, Lakewood. (See individual alphabetical listings.)

Transportation

Airport. See DENVER INTERNATIONAL AIRPORT AREA.

Car Rental Agencies. See IMPORTANT TOLL-FREE NUMBERS.

Public Transportation. Buses (Regional Transportation District), phone 303/299-6000.

Rail Passenger Service. Amtrak 800/872-7245.

Airport Information

Denver International Airport Area. For additional accommodations, see DENVER INTERNATIONAL AIRPORT AREA, which follows DENVER.

What to See and Do

16th Street Mall. This tree-lined pedestrian promenade of red and gray granite runs through the center of Denver's downtown shopping district; outdoor cafes, shops, restaurants, hotels, fountains, and plazas line its mi-long walk. European-built shuttle buses offer transportation from either end of the promenade. 16th St, between Market St and Broadway. Along the mall are

> **Tabor Center.** A multilevel, glass-encased, state-of-the-art retail shopping and entertainment center featuring ESPN Zone, The Palm, The Cheesecake Factory and Big Bowl restaurants, a food court and a variety of specialty stores. Named after famed developer Horace A. W. Tabor, who made his millions in silver mining and built Denver's first skyscraper on this block. (Daily) On 16th St Mall, between Larimer and Arapahoe Sts. Phone 303/572-6868.

> **Larimer Square.** Restoration of the first street in Denver, this collection of shops, galleries, nightclubs, and restaurants is set among Victorian courtyards, gaslights, arcades, and buildings; carriage rides around square. (Daily) Larimer St between 14th and 15th Sts. Phone 303/534-2367.

Arvada Center for the Arts & Humanities. Performing arts center with concerts, plays, classes, demonstrations, art galleries, banquet hall. Amphitheater seats 1,200 (June-early Sept). Historical museum with old cabin and pioneer artifacts. (Daily) Museum and gallery. 6901 Wadsworth Blvd, NW in Arvada. Phone 303/431-3080. **FREE**

Byers-Evans House Museum. Restored Victorian house featuring the history of two noted Colorado pioneer families. Guided tours avail. (Tues-Sun; closed hols) 1310 Bannock St. Phone 303/620-4933. ¢¢

Chatfield State Park. Swimming beach, bathhouse, waterskiing, fishing, boating (rentals, dock), marina; hiking, biking, bridle trails; picnicking, snack bar, camping (electrical hookups, dump station). Nature center; interpretive programs. Standard fees. (Daily) 1 mi S of C-470 on Wadsworth St, near Littleton. Phone 303/791-7275. ¢¢

Cherry Creek State Park. Swimming, bathhouse, waterskiing, fishing, boating (ramps, rentals); horseback riding, picnicking (shelters), concession, camping. Model airplane field, shooting range. Standard fees. (Daily) 1 mi S of I-225 on Parker Rd (CO 83), near south Denver. Phone 303/699-3860. Per vehicle ¢¢

The Children's Museum of Denver. Hands-on, 24,000-sq ft, 2-story environment allows children to learn and explore the world around them. Exhibits include a rm with thousands of plastic balls; Kidslope, a yr-round ski slope; science center; educational programs grocery store. (June-Aug, daily; rest of yr, Tues-Sun; closed hols) Children's Museum Theater (wkends) and special events. First Fri of every month is free for seniors (60+). 2121 Children's Museum Dr, off I-25 exit 211. Phone 303/433-7433. ¢¢¢

Civic Center. West of Capitol Complex. Incl

> **Denver Art Museum.** Houses collection of art objects representing almost every culture and period, incl a fine collection of Native American arts; changing exhibits. (Tues-Sun; closed hols) Free admission Sat for Colorado residents. 100 W 14th Ave Pkwy, south side

of Civic Center. Phone 720/865-5000. ¢¢¢

Denver City and County Buildings. Courts, municipal council, and administrative offices. West side of Center. Phone 303/866-2604.

Denver Public Library. First phase of new library opened in 1995; it encompasses the old library. Largest public library in Rocky Mtn region with nearly four million items; outstanding Western History collection, Patent Depository Library, genealogy collections, and branch library system. Programs, exhibits. (Daily; closed hols) 10 W 14th Ave Pkwy. Phone 720/865-1351. **FREE**

Greek Theater. Outdoor amphitheater, summer folk dancing. South side of Center.

Comanche Crossing Museum. Memorabilia of the completion of the transcontinental railway, artifacts pertaining to area history; two buildings with period rms; restored schoolhouse (1891); Strasburg Union Pacific Depot; caboose, wood-vaned windmill (1880), and homestead on landscaped grounds. (June-Aug, afternoons daily) 30 mi E in Strasburg. Phone 303/622-4322. **Donation**

Denver Botanic Gardens. Outdoor areas with herb, rose, and Japanese gardens; rock alpine garden and alpine house; landscape demonstration gardens; Boettcher Memorial Conservatory, which houses more than 850 tropical and subtropical plants; orchid and bromeliad pavilion; education building with library. (Daily; closed Jan 1, Dec 25) 1005 York St. Phone 303/331-4000. ¢¢

Denver Firefighters Museum. Housed in Fire House No. 1; maintains atmosphere of working firehouse; firefighting equipt from mid-1800s. (Mon-Sat) 1326 Tremont Pl. Phone 303/892-1436. ¢¢

Denver Museum of Nature and Science. Ninety habitat exhibits from four continents displayed against natural backgrounds; Prehistoric Journey exhibit displays dinosaurs in re-created environments; earth sciences lab; gems and minerals; Native American collection. (Daily; closed Dec 25) 2001 Colorado Blvd, in City Park. Phone 303/322-7009. ¢¢¢ Combination tickets avail for

Charles C. Gates Planetarium. Contains a Minolta Series IV star projector; presents a variety of star and laser light shows daily. The **Phipps IMAX Theater** has an immense motion picture system projecting images on screen 4½ stories tall and 6½ stories wide. Daily showings. Phone 303/370-6300. ¢¢¢

Hall of Life. Health education center has permanent exhibits on genetics, fitness, nutrition, and the five senses. Classes and workshops (fee). (Daily) Phone 303/322-7009.

Denver Performing Arts Complex. One of the most innovative and comprehensive performing arts centers in the country. With the addition of the Temple Hoyne Buell Theatre, the complex is the second largest in the nation. The complex also contains shops and restaurants. 14th and Curtis. Phone 303/893-4100.

Auditorium Theatre. (1908) Past host to grand opera, political conventions, minstrel shows, revivalist meetings, and military maneuvers; now hosts touring Broadway productions and the Colorado Ballet. Home of Colorado Contemporary Dance. Phone 303/640-2862.

Boettcher Concert Hall. The first fully "surround" symphonic hall in the US; all of its 2,630 seats are within 75 ft of the stage. Home of the Colorado Symphony Orchestra (Sept-early June) and Opera Colorado with performances "in the round" (May). Phone 303/640-2862.

The Galleria. A walkway covered by an 80-ft-high arched glass canopy. It connects all of the theaters in the complex.

The Helen Bonfils Theatre Complex. Home of the Denver Center Theatre Company. Contains three theaters: the Stage, seating 547 in a circle around a thrust platform; the Space, a theater-in-the-round seating 450; and the Source, a small theater presenting plays by American playwrights. Also contains the **Frank Ricketson Theatre**, a 195-seat theater avail for rental for community activities, classes, and festivals.

Temple Hoyne Buell Theatre. The most recent addition to the com-

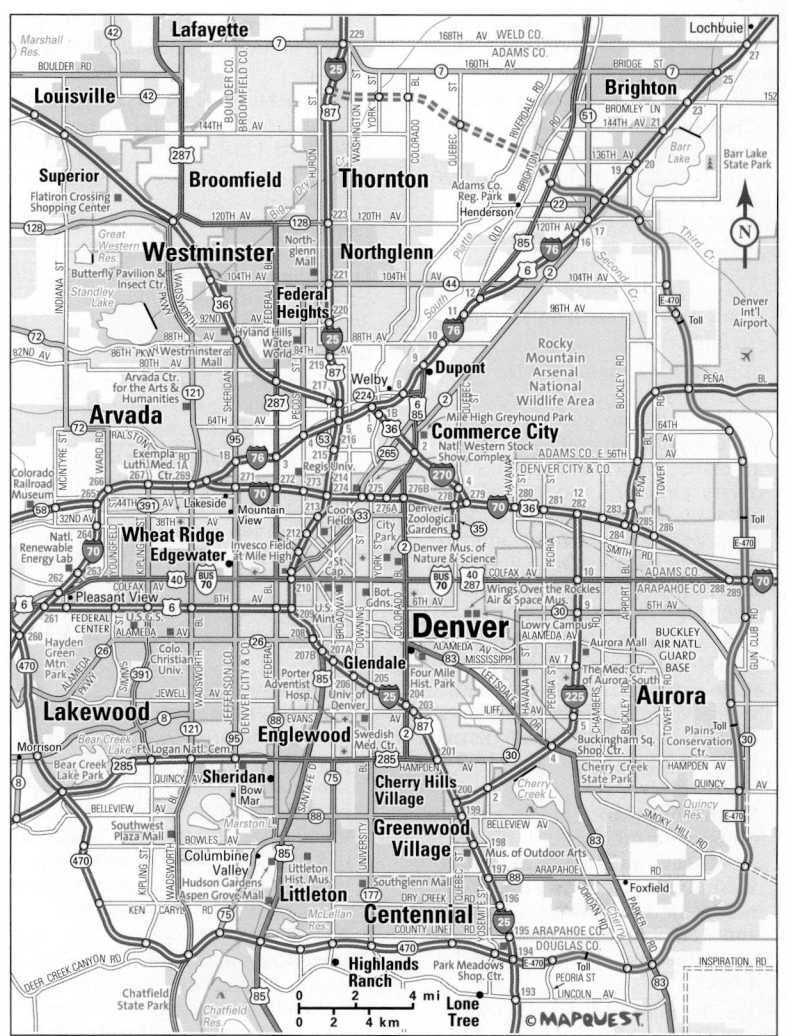

plex. The 2,800-seat theater has a glass facade and Colorado sandstone walls. It is host to Opera Colorado and Broadway plays and home of the Colorado Ballet. Phone 303/640-2862.

Elitch Gardens. Relocated into downtown area in 1995. Amusement park with over 48 major rides. Observation tower, 100-ft-high Ferris wheel, outdoor waterpark. Flower gardens, lakes, and waterfalls. (Memorial Day-Labor Day, daily) Platte River Valley. Phone 303/595-4386. ¢¢¢¢

Forney Transportation Museum. Collection of more than 300 antique cars, carriages, cycles, sleighs, steam locomotives and coaches; Costumed figures. (Mon-Sat) 4303 Brighton Blvd. Phone 303/297-1113. ¢¢¢

Molly Brown House Museum. (ca 1889) House of "the unsinkable" Molly Brown, famous socialite and heroine of the *Titanic* disaster (1912); period furnishings. Guided tours by costumed docents. (Memorial Day-Labor Day, daily; rest of yr, Tues-Sun; closed hols) 1340 Pennsylvania St. Phone 303/832-4092. ¢¢¢

Park system. More than 200 parks within city provide approx 4,400 acres of facilities for boating, fishing, and other sports. The system incl six golf courses. There are also 27 mountain parks within 72 mi of the city covering 13,448 acres of land in the Rocky Mt foothills. Phone 303/964-2500. Parks of special interest are

Cheesman Park. Park has excellent views of nearby mountain peaks with aid of dial and pointers. Congress Park swimming pool (fee) is adj. Located between Cheesman and Congress parks is the Denver Botanic Gardens (fee), with the Boettcher Memorial Conservatory. E 8th Ave and Franklin St. Phone 303/322-0066.

City Park. Contains the Denver Museum of Natural History, an 18-hole golf course, and the **Denver Zoo.** Animals in natural habitats; primates, felines, and giraffes; aviary, children's zoo, miniature railroad. (Daily) Children under 16 must be accompanied by adult at zoo. Runs between 17th and 26th Aves, York St and Colorado Blvd. Phone 303/331-4113. ¢¢¢

⭐ **Red Rocks Park.** Amphitheater (9,500-seat) in natural setting of huge red rocks. Site of Easter sunrise service and summer concerts (fee). 12 mi SW, off CO 26 between I-70 and US 285. Phone 303/697-8801.

Washington Park. Large recreation center with indoor pool (fee). Floral displays incl replica of George Washington's gardens at Mt Vernon. Park runs between S Downing and S Franklin Sts, E Louisiana and E Virginia Aves. Phone 303/698-4930.

Pearce-McAllister Cottage. (1899) Dutch Colonial Revival house contains original furnishings. Guided tours give insight into upper middle-class lifestyle of the 1920s. Second floor houses Denver Museum of Dolls, Toys, and Miniatures. (Tues-Sat, also Sun afternoons) 1880 N Gaylord St. Phone 303/322-3704. ¢¢

Professional sports.

Colorado Avalanche (NHL). Pepsi Center, 1000 Chopper Pl. Phone 303/405-1100.

Colorado Rapids (MLS). Mile High Stadium, 2755 W 17th Ave. Phone 800/844-7777.

Colorado Rockies (MLB). Coors Field, 2001 Blake St. Phone 303/292-0200.

Denver Broncos (NFL). INVESCO Field at Mile High. Phone 303/433-7466.

Denver Nuggets (NBA). Pepsi Center, 1000 Chopper Pl. Phone 303/405-1212.

Sakura Square. Denver's Japanese Cultural and Trade Center features Asian restaurants, shops, businesses; authentic Japanese gardens. Site of famed Buddhist Temple. Lawrence to Larimer Sts on 19th St. Phone 303/295-0305.

Sightseeing tours.

Colorado Bug Tours. Auto tours in classic Volkswagen convertible. Phone 888/528-5285.

Colorado History Tours. Two-hr guided walking tours; three-hr guided step-on bus tours. Res required; ten people minimum. Prices and schedules vary. Phone 303/866-4686.

Gray Line bus tours. Contact PO Box 17646, 80217. Phone 303/289-2841.

State Capitol Complex.

Colorado History Museum. Permanent and rotating exhibits on people and history of Colorado. Dioramas, full-scale mining equipt, Native American artifacts, photographs; sodhouse. Headquarters of Colorado Historical Society. (Daily; closed Jan 1, Thanksgiving, Dec 25) 1300 Broadway. Phone 303/866-3682. ¢¢

State Capitol. Colorado granite; dome (covered with gold leaf from Colorado mines) offers panoramic view. (Mon-Fri) E Colfax Ave and Sherman St. Phone 303/866-2604. **FREE**

United States Mint. Established in 1862. Tours (Mon-Fri; closed hols). Children under 14 yrs only with adult. No photography permitted in building. 320 W Colfax Ave, W of Civic Center; use Cherokee St entrance. Phone 303/405-4755. **FREE**

University of Denver. (1864) 8,500 students. Handsome 125-acre main campus with Penrose Library, Harper Humanities Gardens, Shwayder Art Building, Seely G. Mudd Building (science), William T. Driscoll University Center, and historic buildings dating from the 1800s. The 33-acre Park Hill campus at Montview Blvd and Quebec St is the site of the University of Denver Law School (Lowell Thomas Law Building) and the Lamont School of Music (Houston Fine Arts Center; for schedule phone 303/871-6400). Campus tours. S University Blvd and E Evans Ave. Phone 303/871-2711. The university maintains

> **Chamberlin Observatory.** Houses large telescope in use since 1894; lectures. Tours (Tues and Thurs; closed hols, Christmas wk; res required). Observatory Park, 2930 E Warren Ave. Phone 303/871-5172. ¢

Special Events

National Western Livestock Show, Horse Show, and Rodeo. National Western Complex and Coliseum. Phone 303/297-1166. Two wks Jan.

Greyhound racing. Mile High Greyhound Park. 7 mi NE at jct I-270 and Vasquez Blvd; 6200 Dahlia St, Commerce City. Pari-mutuels. Mid-June-mid-Feb, nightly Tues-Sat; matinee racing Mon, Fri-Sat. Satellite "off-track" betting all yr. Phone 303/288-1591.

Cherry Creek Arts Festival. Features works by 200 national artists. July 4 wkend.

Motels/Motor Lodges

★★ **BEST WESTERN DENVER STAPLETON.** 3535 Quebec St (80207). 303/333-7711; fax 303/322-2262; res 800/780-7234. www.bestwestern.com. 189 rms, 8 story. S $65-$99; D $99-$129; each addl $10; under 18 free; wkend plans. Crib free. Pet accepted, some restrictions; $50 deposit. TV; cable (premium), VCR avail. Heated indoor pool. Restaurant 11 am-2 pm, 4-10 pm. Bar 4 pm-midnight. Coffee in rms. Complimentary full bkfst. Ck-out noon. Coin lndry. Meeting rms. Business center. In-rm modem link. Valet serv. Gift shop. Airport transportation. Exercise equipt. Microwaves, refrigerators. avail. Some private patios, balconies. Cr cds: A, C, D, DS, MC, V.
🅳 ⊀ ⌁ 🛪 ⇲ 🔥 SC 🛪

★★ **COMFORT INN.** 401 17th St (80202). 303/296-0400; fax 303/312-5941; toll-free 800-252-7466. www.comfortinn.com. 231 rms, 22

suites, 22 story. S, D $79-$139; each addl $10; suites $179-$300; under 18 free; wkend rates. Covered valet parking $16. Crib free. TV; cable (premium), VCR avail. Complimentary continental bkfst, coffee in rms. Restaurant adj 6:30 am-11 pm. Rm serv 24 hrs. Bar 11 am-11 pm. Ck-out noon. Meeting rms. Business servs avail. In-rm modem link. Valet serv. Exercise equipt; $5. Barber, beauty shop. Refrigerators avail. Golf nearby. Cr cds: A, C, D, DS, MC, V.
🅳 ⊀ 🛪 ⇲ 🔥 SC

★★ **COURTYARD BY MARRIOTT DENVER STAPLETON.** 7415 E 41st Ave (80216). 303/333-3303; fax 303/399-7356; toll-free 888/236-2437. www.courtyard.com. 146 rms, 12 suites, 3 story. S, D $49-$69; each addl $10; suites $95-$105; under 18 free; wkend rates. Crib free. TV; cable (premium). Indoor pool; whirlpool. Complimentary coffee in rms. Restaurant 6-10 am, 5-10 pm; Sat, Sun 7-11 am. Bar 4-10 pm. Ck-out noon. Coin lndry. Meeting rms. Business servs avail. In-rm modem link. Valet serv. Exercise equipt. Microwaves avail; refrigerator in suites. Balconies. Cr cds: A, C, D, DS, ER, JCB, MC, V.
🅳 ⇲ 🛪 ⇲ 🔥

★★ **HOLIDAY INN NORTH GLENN.** 10 E 120th Ave, Northglenn (80233). 303/452-4100; fax 303/457-1741; toll-free 800/465-4329. www.holiday-inn.com. 235 rms, 12 suites, 6 story. Apr-Sept: S, D $89-$125; each addl $10; suites $150-$175; under 17 free; wkend rates; lower rates rest of yr. Crib avail. Pet accepted, some restrictions. TV; cable. Indoor pool; whirlpool. Restaurants 6 am-11 pm. Bar 11 am-11 pm. Coffee in rms. Ck-out noon. Convention facilities. Business servs avail. In-rm modem link. Coin lndry. Gift shop. Valet serv. Exercise equipt. Health club privileges. Golf, tennis nearby. Cr cds: A, C, D, DS, JCB, MC, V.
🅳 ⊀ ⌁ ⇲ 🛪 ⇲ 🔥 🛪

★★ **LA QUINTA INN.** 3975 Peoria Way (80239). 303/371-5640; fax 303/371-7015; toll-free 800/687-6667. www.laquinta.com. 112 rms, 2 story. S, D $69-$89; under 18 free. Crib free. Pet accepted, some restrictions.

TV; cable (premium). Heated pool. Complimentary continental bkfst. Restaurant adj open 24 hrs. Ck-out noon. Coin lndry. Business servs avail. In-rm modem link. Valet serv. Free airport transportation. Refrigerators, microwaves avail. Cr cds: A, C, D, DS, MC, V.

🅓 🐾 🐕 🔥 SC ⇆

★ ★ **LA QUINTA INN.** *3500 Park Ave W (80216).* 303/458-1222; fax 303/433-2246; res 800/531-5900. www.laquinta.com. 106 rms, 3 story. S, D $65-$95; each addl $10; under 18 free. Crib free. Pet accepted. TV; cable (premium). Pool. Complimentary continental bkfst. Restaurant adj open 24 hrs. Coin lndry. Ck-out noon. Business servs avail. In-rm modem link. Valet serv. Cr cds: A, C, D, DS, MC, V.

🅓 🐾 ⇆ 🐕 🔥

★ ★ **QUALITY INN.** *6300 E Hampden Ave (80222).* 303/758-2211; fax 303/753-0156; res 800/228-5151. www.qualityinndtc.com. 182 rms, 1-2 story. S $74-$79; D $79-$89; each addl $10; under 18 free. Crib free. Pet accepted; $6/day. TV; cable (premium). Pool; whirlpool, poolside serv. Sauna. Complimentary continental bkfst, coffee in rms. Restaurant 6 am-11 pm. Rm serv. Bar from 4 pm. Ck-out 11 am. Coin lndry. Meeting rms. Business servs avail. In-rm modem link. Health club privileges. Lawn games. Some refrigerators. Private patios, balconies. Picnic tables. Cr cds: A, C, D, DS, ER, JCB, MC, V.

🅓 🐾 ⇆ 🐕 🔥 SC

★ ★ **QUALITY INN.** *12100 W 44th Ave, Wheat Ridge (80033).* 303/467-2400; fax 303/467-0198; toll-free 800/449-0003. www.qualityinn.com. 108 rms, 5 story. May-Aug: S $54; D $69; under 18 free; lower rates rest of yr. Crib free. Pet accepted, some restrictions; $50 deposit. TV; cable (premium). Complimentary coffee in lobby. Restaurant 7 am-10 pm. Rm serv. Bar 11 am-2 am. Ck-out 11 am. Meeting rm. Business servs avail. Exercise equipt. Whirlpool. Refrigerators. On lake. Cr cds: A, D, DS, MC, V.

🅓 🐾 🐕 🔥 SC 🏃

★ ★ **QUALITY INN AND SUITES.** *4590 Quebec St (80216).* 303/320-0260; fax 303/320-7595; res 800/228-5151. www.qualityinn.com. 200 rms, 5 story. May-Sept: S $75-$80; D $80-$85; each addl $7; suites $115-$135; under 18 free; lower rates rest of yr. Crib free. TV; cable (premium). Pool; whirlpool. Complimentary continental bkfst, coffee in rms. Restaurant 6-10 am, 5:30-10 pm; Sat, Sun from 6:30 am. Rm serv. Bar 4 pm-midnight; Sat, Sun from 5 pm. Ck-out noon. Coin lndry. Meeting rms. Business servs avail. In-rm modem link. Valet serv. Gift shop. Free airport transportation. Exercise equipt. Refrigerators, microwaves. Golf nearby. Cr cds: A, C, D, DS, JCB, MC, V.

🅓 🐕 🏃 🕍 ⇆ 🐕 👋 🏃

Hotels

★ ★ **ADAM'S MARK.** *1550 Court Pl (80202).* 303/893-3333; fax 303/626-2542; res 800/444-2326. www.adamsmark.com. 1,225 rms, 2 bldgs, 8 & 22 story. S, D $175-$185; each addl $15; suites $375-$1,200; under 18 free; wkend rates. Crib free. Pet accepted, some restrictions; $100 deposit. Garage $15; in/out privileges. TV; cable (premium). Pool; poolside serv. Restaurants 6:30 am-11 pm. Rm serv 24 hrs. Bars 11-2 am; entertainment. Ck-out noon. Coin lndry. Convention facilities. Business center. In-rm modem link. Concierge. Gift shops. Airport transportation. Exercise equipt; steam rm, sauna. Health club privileges. Microwaves avail. Luxury level. Cr cds: A, D, DS, MC, V.

🅓 🐾 ⇆ 🏃 🐕 👋 🏃

★ ★ ★ ★ **THE BROWN PALACE HOTEL.** *321 17th St (80202).* 303/297-3111; fax 303/293-9204; res 800/321-2599. www.brownpalace.com. Topped with beautiful stained glass, the breathtaking nine-story atrium lobby of this hotel has impressed distinguished visitors since 1892. The 237-room property sits in the center of the business district and offers various dining options including the antique-filled Palace Arms for Southwest-influenced Continental cuisine. Over 13,000 square feet of special event space shares the same nostalgic opulence as the lobby. 241 rms, 10 story. S, D $99-$275; each addl $15; suites $675-$1,125; under 12 free; wkend rates; package plans. Valet parking. Crib free. Pet accepted, some restrictions. TV; cable (premium), VCR avail. 5 restaurants (see PALACE ARMS). Afternoon tea noon-4:30 pm. Rm serv 24 hrs. Bar noon-midnight; entertainment. Ck-in 3 pm, ck-out noon. Meeting rms. Business center. In-rm modem link. Valet serv. Shopping arcade. Bellhops. Concierge. Barber. Exercise equipt. Massage avail. Health club privileges. Pool privileges. Some refrigerators. Golf nearby. Cr cds: A, C, D, DS, ER, JCB, MC, V.

★ **CAMBRIDGE HOTEL.** 1560 Sherman St (80203). 303/831-1252; fax 303/831-4724; toll-free 800/877-1252. 31 suites, 3 story. S, D $129-$139; under 12 free. Crib $10. Valet parking $10. TV; cable (premium). Complimentary continental bkfst. Complimentary coffee in rms. Ck-out noon. Meeting rms. Business servs avail. In-rm modem link. Luggage handling. Valet serv. Concierge. Health club privileges. Minibars, refrigerators; microwaves avail. Antique furnishings, oil paintings, original prints. Cr cds: A, D, DS, MC, V.

★★ **EXECUTIVE TOWER HOTEL.** 1405 Curtis St (80202). 303/571-0300; fax 303/825-4301; toll-free 800/525-6651. www.exectowerhotel.com. 337 rms, 16 story. S, D $69-$169; each addl $10; suites $130-$300; under 16 free; wkend rates. Garage parking $9/day. Crib free. Pet accepted, some restrictions. TV; cable (premium), VCR avail. Heated indoor pool; whirlpool. Restaurants 6:30 am-9 pm, wkends to 10 pm. Rm serv. Bar 4 pm-midnight. Ck-out noon. Coin lndry. Meeting rms. Business servs avail. In-rm modem link. Valet serv. Tennis. Rooftop running track. Racquetball. Exercise equipt. Rec rm. Refrigerators avail. Cr cds: A, C, D, DS, ER, JCB, MC, V.

★★★ **HOTEL MONACO.** 1717 Champa St (80202). 303/296-1717; fax 303/296-1818; toll-free 800/397-5380. www.monaco-denver.com. 189 rms, 7 story, 32 suites. S, D $159-$259; under 18 free. Crib avail. Pet accepted. Valet parking $21/day. TV; cable (premium), VCR avail. Complimentary coffee in rms. Restaurant 7 am-11 pm. Rm serv 24 hrs. Bar. Ck-out noon. Meetings rms. Business center. Bellhops. Concierge serv. Gift shop. Exercise equipt. Bike rental. Cr cds: A, D, DS, ER, JCB, MC, V.

★★★ **HOTEL TEATRO.** 1100 14th St (80202). 303/228-1100; fax 303/228-1101; toll-free 888/727-1200. www.hotelteatro.com. 111 rms, 9 story, 8 suites. S, D $255-$295; suites $1,450; under 18 free. Crib avail. Pet accepted. Valet parking $24/day. TV; cable (premium). Supervised children's activities. Complimentary coffe in rms, newspaper, toll-free calls. Restaurant 7 am-11 pm. Rm serv 24 hrs. Bar. Ck-out noon. ck-in 3 pm. Meeting rms. Business servs avail. In-rm modem link. Bellhops. Concierge. Valet serv. Exercise equipt. Health club privileges. Golf, tennis privileges. Refrigerators. Some balconies. Cr cds: A, C, D, DS, ER, JCB, MC, V.

★★★ **HYATT REGENCY DENVER.** 1750 Welton St (80202). 303/295-1234; fax 303/292-2472; toll-free 800/233-1234. www.denver.regency.hyatt.com. 511 rms, 26 story. S, D $85-$275; each addl $25; suites $350-$1,000; wkend rates. Crib avail. Garage, valet parking $15. TV; cable (premium). Indoor pool; poolside serv. Complimentary coffee in rms. Restaurant 6 am-11 pm. Bar 10:30-2 am. Ck-out noon. Meeting rms. Business center. In-rm modem link. Concierge. Airport transportation. Tennis. Exercise equipt. Health club privileges. Bathrm phones, minibars; refrigerators avail. Luxury level. Cr cds: A, D, DS, MC, V.

★★★ **HYATT REGENCY TECH CENTER.** 7800 E Tufts Ave (80237). 303/779-1234; fax 303/850-7164; res 800/233-1234. www.techcenter.hyatt.com. 450 rms, 11 story. S, D $200; each addl $25; suites $350-$1,500; under 18 free; wkend plans. Crib free. TV; cable (premium), VCR avail (movies). Indoor pool; whirlpool, poolside serv. Complimentary coffee in rms. Restaurants 6:30 am-11 pm. Bar 3 pm-1 am; Sun to midnight. Ck-out noon. Convention facilities.

Business center. In-rm modem link. Concierge. Gift shop. Valet parking. Airport transportation. Lighted tennis. Exercise equipt; sauna. Health club privileges. Refrigerators; some bathrm phones; microwaves avail. Luxury level. Cr cds: A, C, D, DS, ER, JCB, MC, V.

⊡ 🛏️ ➰ 🕴️ 🏊 🔥 🏃

★ ★ ★ **LOEWS GIORGIO HOTEL.** *4150 E Mississippi Ave (80246). 303/782-9300; fax 303/758-6542; toll-free 800/235-6397. www.loewshotels. com.* 183 rms, 11 story. S $199-$229; D $219-$249; each addl $20; suites $259-$900; under 18 free; wkend rates from $79. Crib free. Pet accepted, some restrictions. TV; cable (premium), VCR avail (movies). Complimentary coffee in rms, Complimentary newspaper. Restaurant (see TUSCANY). Rm serv 24 hrs. Bar noon-1 am. Ck-out 11 am. Meeting rms. Business center. Concierge. Gift shop. Valet parking. Exercise equipt. Health club privileges. Bathrm phones, minibars; some refrigerators; microwaves avail. Library. Cr cds: A, C, D, DS, MC, V.

⊡ 🐾 🕴️ ➰ 🔥 🏃

★ ★ ★ **THE MAGNOLIA DENVER.** *818 17th St (80202). 303/607-9000; fax 303/607-0101; toll-free 888/915-1110. www.themagnoliahotel.com.* 244 rms, 10 story. S, D $175-$250; suites $275; under 18 free. Crib avail. Pet accepted. TV; cable (premium). Valet parking $21/day. Complimentary continental bkfst. Ck-out 11 am. Meeting rms. Business center. In-rm modem link. Concierge. Exercise equipt. Airport transportation avail. Cr cds: A, C, D, DS, JCB, MC, V.

🔥 🐾 🏃 🏃

★ ★ ★ **MARRIOTT CITY CENTER DENVER.** *1701 California St (80202). 303/297-1300; fax 303/298-7474; toll-free 800/228-9290. www.marriott.com.* 614 rms, 19 story. S, D $169-$195; suites $225-$825; under 18 free; wkend plans. Crib free. Pet accepted, some restrictions. Valet parking; fee. TV; cable (premium), VCR avail. Indoor pool; whirlpool. Coffee in rms. Restaurant 6:30 am-10 pm. Rm serv to midnight. Bar 11-2 am. Ck-out noon. Convention facilities. Business center. In-rm modem link. Concierge. Shopping arcade. Exercise equipt; sauna. Bathrm phones; refrig-

erators avail. Luxury level. Cr cds: A, C, D, DS, MC, V.

🐾 ➰ 🕴️ 🔥 🏃

★ ★ ★ **MARRIOTT SOUTHEAST DENVER.** *6363 E Hampden Ave (80222). 303/758-7000; fax 303/691-3418; toll-free 800/228-9290. www. marriott.com.* 595 rms, 11 story. S, D $82-$154; suites $150-$350; under 18 free; wkend package plan. Crib free. Pet accepted, some restrictions. TV; cable (premium), VCR avail. 2 pools, 1 indoor; whirlpool, poolside serv. Coffee in rms. Restaurant 6 am-11 pm. Bar 11 am-midnight. Ck-out 1 pm. Coin lndry. Convention facilities. Business center. In-rm modem link. Concierge. Shopping arcade. Barber, beauty shop. Covered parking. Airport transportation. Exercise equipt. Game rm. Some bathrm phones, refrigerators. Balconies; some private patios. Luxury level. Cr cds: A, C, D, DS, ER, JCB, MC, V.

⊡ 🐾 ➰ 🕴️ ➰ 🔥 SC 🏃

★ ★ ★ **MARRIOTT TECH CENTER DENVER.** *4900 S Syracuse St (80237). 303/779-1100; fax 303/740-2523; toll-free 800/228-9290. www.marriott.com.* 626 rms, 2-10 story. S, D $179; suites $260-$500; under 18 free; wkend plans. Crib free. Pet accepted. TV; cable (premium), VCR avail. 2 pools, 1 indoor; whirlpool. Coffee in rms. Restaurant 5:30-1 am. Bar 11 am-midnight. Ck-out noon. Convention facilities. Business center. In-rm modem link. Shopping arcade. Valet parking. Exercise equipt; sauna. Health club privileges. Refrigerators. Some balconies. Cr cds: A, C, D, DS, ER, JCB, MC, V.

⊡ 🐾 ➰ 🕴️ ➰ 🔥 SC 🏃

★ ★ **OXFORD HOTEL.** *1600 17th St (80202). 303/628-5400; fax 303/628-5413; toll-free 800/228-5838. www. theoxfordhotel.com.* 80 rms, 5 story, 9 suites. S, D $149-$369; each addl $10; suites from $275; under 12 free. Crib avail. Valet parking $12. TV; cable (premium), VCR avail. Complimentary continental bkfst. Restaurant 11 am-2 pm, 5-10 pm; Fri, Sat to 11 pm; Sun 7 am-10 pm. Rm serv 24 hrs. Bar. Ck-out 1 pm. Meeting rms. Business servs avail. In-rm modem link. Concierge. Barber, beauty shop, spa. Exercise rm; steam rm. Whirlpool. Minibars. Elegant, European-style; many antiques. First luxury hotel built in Denver (1891). Cr cds: A, C, D, DS, MC, V.

★★★ **RADISSON HOTEL DENVER STAPLETON PLAZA.** *3333 Quebec St (80207). 303/321-3500; fax 303/322-7343; res 800/333-3333. www.radisson.com.* 300 rms, 11 story. S, D $85-$149; each addl $10; suites $275-$350; under 18 free; wkly, wkend package plans. Crib free. TV; cable (premium). Heated pool; whirlpool, poolside serv. Complimentary coffee. Restaurant 6 am-11 pm. Rm serv. Bars from 4 pm. Ck-out noon. Convention facilities. Business center. In-rm modem link. Coin lndry. Shopping arcade. Free garage parking. Free airport transportation. Valet serv. Exercise rm; sauna, steam rm. Balconies. Refrigerator avail. Built around 11-story atrium; glass-enclosed elvtrs. Cr cds: A, C, D, DS, ER, JCB, MC, V.

★★★ **RENAISSANCE DENVER.** *3801 Quebec St (80207). 303/399-7500; fax 303/321-1966; res 800/468-3571. www.renaissancehotels.com.* 400 rms, 12 story. S, D $105-$125; each addl $10; suites $150-$600; under 18 free. Crib free. TV; cable (premium), VCR avail. 2 heated pools; 1 indoor, whirlpool, poolside serv. Complimentary coffee in rms. Restaurant 6 am-10 pm. Rm serv. Bar 11-1 am. Ck-out 2 pm. Convention facilities. Business center. In-rm modem link. Coin lndry. Concierge. Gift shop. Covered parking. Airport transportation. Exercise equipt; steam rm. Many refrigerators. Balconies. 10-story central atrium. Luxury level. Cr cds: A, C, D, DS, MC, V.

★★★ **WARWICK HOTEL.** *1776 Grant St (80203). 303/861-2000; fax 303/839-8504; toll-free 800/525-2888.* 194 rms, 15 story. S, D $165-$175; each addl $20; suites $200-$800; under 18 free; wkend package plan. Crib free. Garage $10. Pet accepted. TV; cable (premium). Rooftop pool; poolside serv. Complimentary continental bkfst. Restaurant 6:30 am-2 pm, 5-10 pm; Fri, Sat 7-11 am, 5-10 pm. Rm serv 24 hrs. Bar 11 am-midnight. Ck-out 1 pm. Meeting rms. Business servs avail. In-rm modem link. Concierge. Airport transportation, RR station, bus depot transportation. Health club privileges. Bathrm phones, refrigerators; many wet bars; microwaves avail. Many balconies. Cr cds: A, C, D, DS, JCB, MC, V.

★★★ **WESTIN TABOR CENTER DENVER.** *1672 Lawrence St (80202). 303/572-9100; fax 303/572-7288; res 800/937-8461. www.westin.com/taborcenter.* 430 rms, 19 story. S, D $205; each addl $15; suites $425-$1,200; under 18 free. Crib free. Pet accepted, some restrictions. Garage $10-$15. TV; cable (premium), VCR avail. Indoor/outdoor pool; whirlpool, poolside serv. Restaurants 6 am-11 pm. Rm serv 24 hrs. Bar 5 pm-1:30 am; pianist Tues-Sat. Ck-out 1 pm. Convention facilities. Business center. In-rm modem link. Shopping arcade. Exercise equipt; sauna, steam rm. Health club privileges. Refrigerators, minibars; some bathrm phones. Some balconies. Luxury level. Cr cds: A, C, D, DS, ER, JCB, MC, V.

★★★ **WESTIN WESTMINSTER.** *10600 Westminster Blvd, Westminister (80020). 303/410-5000; fax 303/410-5005; toll-free 800/937-8461. www.westin.com.* 369 rms, 14 story, 6 suites. S, D $99-$269; suites $300-$900; each addl $20; under 18 free. Valet parking avail. Crib avail. Pet accepted, some restrictions. Heated indoor pool, whirlpool, poolside servs. TV; cable (premium). Complimentary coffee in rms. Restaurant 6:30 am-10:30 pm. Rm serv 24 hrs. Bar. Ck-out noon. Convention facilities. Business center. In-rm modem link. Concierge. Valet serv. Gift shop. Exercise equipt; sauna. Golf, tennis nearby. Hiking trail. Supervised children's activities. Fireplace, wet bar in suites. Cr cds: A, C, D, DS, JCB, MC, V.

Resort

★★★★ **OMNI INTERLOCKEN RESORT.** *500 Interlocken Blvd, Broomfield (80021). 303/438-6600; fax 303/438-7224; toll-free 800/843-6664. www.omnihotels.com.* Between Denver and Boulder, this resort is housed in the high-tech Interlocken Center. It offers spacious, well-furnished guest rooms to please the business traveler, plus a 27-hole golf course, full-service spa, and outdoor pool for leisure visitors. There are various dining options including The Meritage with its beautiful stone fireplace and outdoor patio. 390 rms, 11 story, 13 suites. S, D $109-$199; suites $239-$550; each addl $20. Complimentary valet parking. Crib free. Pet accepted; $50 refundable deposit. TV; cable (premium), VCR avail. Heated pool; whirlpool, poolside serv avail. Restaurant 6:30 am-10 pm. Rm serv 24 hrs. Bar. Ck-out noon. Conference center. Business center. In-rm modem link. Bellhops. Concierge. Valet serv. Gift shop. Exercise rm, sauna, steam rm. Massage. 27-hole golf; greens fee $65-$105 (incl cart), pro, driving range. Bike rentals. Supervised children's activities (summer). Hiking trail. Picnic facilities. Game rm. Minibars. Refrigerators in suites. Some balconies. Cr cds: A, C, D, DS, ER, JCB, MC, V.

⊡ 🗷 🛠 🕊 🖈 🖾 🖾 🖈

B&Bs/Small Inns

★★★ **CAPITOL HILL MANSION BED & BREAKFAST.** *1207 Pennsylvania St (80203). 303/839-5221; fax 303/839-9046; toll-free 800/839-9329. www.capitolhillmansion.com.* 8 rms, 7 with A/C, 3 story, 3 suites. S, D $85-$95; each addl $10; suites $105-$165. TV; cable (premium). Complimentary full bkfst. Complimentary coffee in rms. Restaurant nearby. Ck-out 11 am, ck-in 4:30-8 pm. Business servs avail. Concierge serv. Some in-rm whirlpools, fireplaces. Some balconies. Built in 1891; Romanesque style with turrets, chimneys and curved porch. Totally nonsmoking. Cr cds: A, C, D, DS, ER, JCB, MC, V.

⊡ 🐾 🖈 🖾 🖾

★★★ **CASTLE MARNE LUXURY URBAN INN.** *1572 Race St (80206). 303/331-0621; fax 303/331-0623; toll-free 800/926-2763. www.castlemarne.com.* 10 rms, 3 story. S $90; D $75. Complimentary full bkfst; afternoon refreshments. Restaurant nearby. Ck-out 11 am, ck-in 4 pm. Business center. In-rm modem link. Luggage handling. Valet serv. Concierge serv.

Gift shop. Game rm. Health club privileges. In-rm whirlpools. Some balconies. Antiques. Library/sitting rm. Built 1889; Romanesque mansion was residence of museum curator. Cheesman Park 3 blks. Totally nonsmoking. Cr cds: A, C, D, DS, MC, V.

🖈 🖾 🖾 🔥 🖈

★★★ **HAUS BERLIN BED & BREAKFAST.** *1651 Emerson St (80218). 303/837-9527; toll-free 800/659-0253. www.hausberlinbandb.com.* 4 rms, 3 story, 1 suite. S $95-$115; D $100; suite $140. TV (in 3 rms); cable (premium). Complimentary full bkfst. Restaurant nearby. Ck-out 11 am, ck-in 4-8 pm. Built in 1892 for Rev Thomas N Haskell, founder of Colorado College. Totally nonsmoking. Cr cds: A, C, D, MC, V.

🖾 🔥

★ **HOLIDAY CHALET.** *1820 E Colfax Ave (80218). 303/321-9975; fax 303/377-6556; res 800/626-4497.* 10 kit. suites, 3 story. S, D $94; each addl $5; under 12 free; wkly rates. Crib free. Pet accepted; $50 deposit & $5/day. TV; VCR. Garage parking $10/day. Complimentary bkfst. Complimentary coffee in rms. Restaurants nearby. Ck-out noon. Concierge. Microwaves avail. Restored brownstone built in 1896. Antique furniture; library; patio; 1880 salt water fish prints. Totally nonsmoking. Cr cds: A, C, D, DS, MC, V.

🐾 🗙 🖾 🔥 SC

★★ **THE LUMBER BARON INN.** *2555 W 37th Ave (80211). 303/477-8205; fax 303/477-0269; res 800/697-6552. www.lumberbaron.com.* 5 rms, 3 story. S, D $145-$235; wkend rates. TV; VCR avail (movies). Complimentary full bkfst. Complimentary coffee in rms. Restaurant nearby. Ck-out 11 am, ck-in 4 pm. Business servs avail. Luggage handling. Street parking. Lawn games. Ballrm. Fireplaces. Built in 1890. Totally nonsmoking. Cr cds: A, DS, MC, V.

🖾 🔥 SC

★★★ **QUEEN ANNE BED & BREAKFAST.** *2147-51 Tremont Pl (80205). 303/296-6666; fax 303/296-2151; toll-free 800/432-4667. www.queenannebnb.com.* 14 rms, 3 story. S, D $75-$145; each addl $25; suites $145-$175. Complimentary full bkfst; afternoon refreshments. Ck-out noon, ck-in 3 pm. Business servs avail. In-rm modem link. Health club privileges. Some in-rm whirlpools. Built in 1879; antiques; garden; fountain. In the Clement Historic District. Totally nonsmoking. Cr cds: A, MC, V.

★★ **VICTORIA OAKS INN.** *1575 Race St (80206). 303/355-1818; fax 303/331-1095; toll-free 800/662-6357.* 9 rms, 2 share bath, 3 story. S $60-$85; D $70-$95. TV in sitting rm. Complimentary continental bkfst; afternoon refreshments. Ck-out noon, ck-in 3 pm. In-rm modem link. Kitchen, lndry privileges. 1896 mansion, Victorian antiques. Cr cds: A, C, D, DS, MC, V.

All Suites

★★★ **THE BURNSLEY ALL-SUITE HOTEL.** *1000 Grant St (80203). 303/830-1000; fax 303/830-7676; toll-free 800/231-3915. www.burnsley.com.* 80 kit. suites, 16 story. S, D $119-$149; suites $149-$189; each addl $15. TV; cable (premium). Pool. Complimentary full bkfst. Complimentary coffee in rms. Restaurant 6:30 am-2 pm, 6-9 pm. Rm serv to 11 pm. Bar from 11 am. Ck-out noon. Meeting rms. Business center. Garage parking. Health club privileges. Microwaves. Balconies. Converted apartment building in residential area, near State Capitol. Cr cds: A, D, DS, MC, V.

★★★ **EMBASSY SUITES.** *7525 E Hampden Ave (80231). 303/696-6644; fax 303/337-6202; res 800/362-2779. www.winhotel.com.* 206 suites, 7 story. S $139-$169; each addl $10; under 18 free; wkend rates. Crib free. TV; cable (premium), VCR avail. Indoor pool; whirlpool. Complimentary full bkfst. Coffee in rms. Restaurant 11:30 am-2 pm, 5-10 pm. Bar to 2 am; Sun to midnight. Ck-out 1 pm. Coin lndry. Meeting rms. Business center. In-rm modem link. Gift shop. Exercise equipt; sauna, steam rm. Refrigerators, microwaves, minibars.

Balconies. Cr cds: A, C, D, DS, JCB, MC, V.

★★★ **EMBASSY SUITES.** *4444 Havana St (80239). 303/375-0400; fax 303/371-4634; toll-free 800/345-0087. www.placetostay.com.* 210 suites, 7 story. Suites $124-$145; each addl $12; under 12 free; ski plans, wkend package. Crib free. Pet accepted, some restrictions; $50 deposit. TV; cable (premium), VCR avail. Indoor pool; whirlpool. Complimentary full bkfst. Coffee in rms. Restaurant 11 am-11 pm. Bar to 1 am. Ck-out 1 pm. Coin lndry. Meeting rms. Business servs avail. In-rm modem link. Gift shop. Free airport transportation. Exercise equipt; steam rm, sauna. Refrigerators, microwaves, minibars. Cr cds: A, D, DS, MC, V.

Extended Stay

★★ **RESIDENCE INN BY MARRIOTT.** *2777 Zuni St (80211). 303/458-5318; fax 303/433-0182; toll-free 800/331-3131. www.residenceinn. com.* 154 kit. suites, 2 story. S $89-$149; D $109-$155. Crib free. Pet accepted; $10. TV; cable. Heated pool; whirlpool. Complimentary continental bkfst. Restaurant 6:30 am-9:30 pm. Bar. Ck-out 11 am. Meeting rms. Business servs avail. Valet serv. Free grocery shopping serv. RR station, bus depot transportation. Exercise equipt. Health club privileges. Refrigerators, microwaves; many fireplaces. Private patios, balconies. Cr cds: A, C, D, DS, JCB, MC, V.

Restaurants

★★ **AUBERGINE CAFE.** *225 E 7th Ave (80203). 303/832-4778.* Hrs: 11:30 am-10 pm; Fri to 11 pm; Sat 4-11 pm; Sun 4-9 pm. Closed Mon; major hols. Res accepted. Mediterranean menu. Serv bar. A la carte entrees: lunch $10-$12, dinner $11-$20. Child's menu. Specialties: roasted eggplant, stewed mussels, roast tuscan chicken. Outdoor dining. Cr cds: A, DS, MC, V.

★ ★ **BABY DOE'S MATCHLESS MINE.** *2520 W 23rd Ave (80211). 303/433-3386.* Hrs: 11 am-2:30 pm, 4:30-10 pm; Fri, Sat to 11 pm; Sun 4-10 pm; Sun brunch 9 am-2:30 pm. Res accepted. Lunch $6.50-$12.95, dinner $12-$32. Sun brunch $17.95. Child's menu. Specializes in seafood, steak. Parking. Replica of Matchless Mine in Leadville; memorabilia of era. Panoramic view of city. Cr cds: A, D, DS, MC, V.
D SC ➤

★ ★ **BAROLO GRILL.** *3030 E 6th Ave (80206). 303/393-1040.* Hrs: 5-10:30 pm. Closed Sun, Mon; major hols. Res accepted. Northern Italian menu. Bar. A la carte entrees: dinner $17-$27. Complete meal: dinner $38.95. Child's menu. Specialties: wine-marinated duck, tuna puttanesca, lamb chops. Free valet parking. Outdoor dining. Paintings. Cr cds: A, D, DS, MC, V.
D

★ **BENNY'S.** *301 E 7th Ave (80203). 303/894-0788.* Hrs: 8 am-11 pm; Sat, Sun from 9 am. Closed Thanksgiving, Dec 25. Res accepted. Mexican menu. Bar. Bkfst $3.50-$4.85, lunch, dinner $4.25-$8.45. Specialties: sir-loin burrito, fish tacos, grilled chicken tacos. Parking. Outdoor dining. Casual decor. Cr cds: A, D, DS, MC, V.
D ➤

★ ★ **BISTRO ADDE BREWSTER.** *250 Steele St (80206). 303/388-1900.* Hrs: 11:30 am-10 pm; Fri, Sat to 11 pm. Closed Sun; major hols. Res accepted. Continental menu. Bar. Lunch $8-$20, dinner $8-$30. Specialties: salmon salad, bistro burger, gravlax. Outdoor dining in season. Bistro atmosphere. Cr cds: A, D, MC, V.
D

★ **BRITTANY HILL.** *9350 Grant, Thornton (80229). 303/451-5151.* Hrs: 11 am-2 pm, 4-9 pm; Fri, Sat to 11 pm; Sun 4-10 pm; Sun brunch 9 am-2:30 pm. Res accepted. Bar to 11 pm. Lunch $6.95-$8.95, dinner $13.95-$25.95. Sun brunch $17.95. Specializes in prime rib, steak, fresh seafood. Patio deck. Scenic view of city, mountains. Cr cds: A, C, D, DS, ER, MC, V.
D SC ➤

★ ★ ★ **BROKER.** *821 17th St (80202). 303/292-5065. www.denver.citysearch. com.* Hrs: 11 am-2:30 pm, 5-11 pm; Sat, Sun from 5 pm. Closed Dec 25. Res accepted. Continental menu. Bar.

16th Century Mall

Lunch $6.95-$19.95, dinner $24-$39. Specialties: prime rib, filet Wellington. In vault & board rms of converted bank (1903). Cr cds: A, D, DS, MC, V.

★★ **BUKHORN EXCHANGE.** *1000 Osage St (80204). 303/534-9505. www.buckhorn.com.* Hrs: 11 am-2 pm, 5:30-9:30 pm; Fri, Sat 5-10 pm; Sun 4-9 pm. Closed major hols. Res accepted. Bar. Lunch $6.95-$14, dinner $17-$39. Specializes in steak, buffalo, elk. Entertainment Wed-Sat. Roof garden dining. Historical landmark & museum, built 1893. Cr cds: A, C, D, DS, MC, V.

★★ **COOS BAY BISTRO.** *2076 S University Blvd (80210). 303/744-3591.* Hrs: 11:15 am-2 pm, 5:30-10 pm; Fri, Sat 5-10:30 pm. Closed major hols. Res accepted. Italian, French menu. Bar. Lunch $4.50-$10, dinner $7-$16. Specialties: Thai pasta, marinated duck breast with blackberry sauce, seared ahi tuna. Outdoor dining. Totally nonsmoking. Cr cds: A, D, MC, V.
D

★★ **DENVER BUFFALO COMPANY.** *1109 Lincoln St (80203). 303/832-0880. www.denverbuffalo company.com.* Hrs: 11 am-2:30 pm, 5-9 pm; Fri, Sat to 10 pm; Sun 4-9 pm. Closed Jan 1, Memorial Day, Dec 25. Res accepted. Bar. Lunch $5-$12, dinner $15-$38. Child's menu. Specializes in buffalo, fish, game. Seasonal entertainment. Valet parking. Outdoor dining. Western decor. Cr cds: A, D, DS, MC, V.
D

★★ **DENVER CHOPHOUSE & BREWERY.** *1735 19th St (80202). 303/296-0800.* Hrs: 11 am-2:30 pm, 4:30 pm-midnight; Sun 4:30-10 pm. Res accepted. Bar. Lunch $7.25-$13.95, dinner $9-$24.95. Specializes in steaks, seafood. Jazz Thurs-Sat. Outdoor dining. Historic warehouse converted into restaurant; microbrewery. Cr cds: A, D, MC, V.
D

★ **EMPRESS SEAFOOD.** *2825 W Alameda Ave (80219). 303/922-2822.* Hrs: 11 am-9 pm; Sat, Sun from 10:30 am. Chinese menu. Bar. A la carte entrees: lunch $4.25-$13, dinner $6-

$13. Specializes in seafood. Oriental artwork. Cr cds: A, D, DS, MC, V.
D

★★ **FOURTH STORY.** *2955 E 1st Ave (80206). 303/322-1824. www. fourthstory.com.* Hrs: 11 am-4 pm, 5-10 pm; Sun brunch 11 am-3 pm. Closed some major hols. Res accepted. Contemporary Amer menu. Bar. Lunch $6-$14, dinner $11-$24. Sun brunch $7-$12. Child's menu. Specializes in fresh seafood. Entertainment Sun, Mon. Casual dining above bookstore. View of mountains. Cr cds: A, D, DS, MC, V.
D

★★ **FRESH FISH CO.** *7800 E Hampden Ave (80237). 303/740-9556. www. freshfishco.citysearch.com.* Hrs: 11:30 am-2:30 pm, 5-11 pm; Mon, Tues 5-10 pm; Sat from 4:45 pm; Sun brunch 10 am-2 pm. Closed Dec 25. Res accepted. Bar. Lunch $6.25-$12.95, dinner $13.95-$38.95. Sun brunch $16.95. Child's menu. Specializes in calamari, salmon, lobster. Parking. Many large aquariums throughout restaurant. Cr cds: A, D, DS, MC, V.
D

★★★ **HIGHLANDS GARDEN CAFE.** *3927 W 32nd Ave (80212). 303/458-5920.* Hrs: 11 am-2 pm, 5-9 pm; Sun brunch 10 am-2 pm. Closed Mon; major hols. Res accepted. Wine list. Lunch $7-$12, dinner $14-$28. Sun brunch $6.50-$12. Specialties: lamb loin chops, bouillabaisse, salmon in poblano pepper. Outdoor dining. Two victorian houses converted into restaurant. Cr cds: A, MC, V.
D

★★ **IL FORNAIO.** *1631 Wazee St (80202). 303/573-5050. www.ilfornaio. com.* Hrs: 11:30 am-11 pm; Fri, Sat to midnight. Closed July 4, Thanksgiving, Dec 25. Res accepted. Italian menu. Bar. A la carte entrees: lunch $7.95-$21.50, dinner $8.95-$21.50. Child's menu. Menu changes monthly. Valet parking. Outdoor dining. Totally nonsmoking. Cr cds: A, D, MC, V.
D

★★★ **IMPERIAL CHINESE.** *431 S Broadway (80209). 303/698-2800.*

www.imperialchinese.com. Hrs: 11 am-10 pm; Fri to 10:30 pm; Sat noon-10:30 pm; Sun 4-10 pm. Closed July 4, Thanksgiving, Dec 25. Chinese menu. Bar. Wine list. A la carte entrees: lunch $6.25-$8.95, dinner $7.95-$15.95. Specialties: sesame chicken, whole steamed bass. Parking. Contemporary Chinese decor with many artifacts. Cr cds: A, C, D, MC, V.
[D]

★ ★ **INDIA'S RESTAURANT.** *3333 S Tamarac (80231). 303/755-4284.* Hrs: 11:30 am-2:15 pm, 5:30-9:30 pm; Fri to 10 pm; Sat noon-2:15 pm, 5:30-10 pm; Sun 5:30-9 pm. Res accepted. Northern Indian menu. Bar. Lunch $6.95-$10.95, dinner $7.95-$15.95. Complete meal: dinner $16.95-$34.95. Specialties: vaishnav thali, akbar boti, ticca jehangir. Parking. Indian decor. Cr cds: A, D, DS, MC, V.
[D]

★ **JACKSON'S SPORTS GRILL.** *10001 Grant St, Thornton (80229). 303/457-2100.* Specializes in wings, hot sandwiches. Hrs: 11 am-11 pm; Fri, Sat to 1 am. Closed Easter, Thanksgiving, Dec 25. Wine list. Amer menu. Lunch, dinner $6.99-$11.99. Cr cds: A, D, DS, MC, V.
[D] [⟲]

★ **JAPON RESTAURANT.** *1028 S Gaylord St (80209). 303/744-0330.* Hrs: 11:30 am-2 pm, 5-10 pm; Fri, Sat to 11:30 pm; Sun from 5 pm. Closed July 4, Thanksgiving. Res accepted. Japanese menu. Serv bar. Lunch $5-$10, dinner $10-$25. Specializes in sushi. Industrial decor. Totally nonsmoking. Cr cds: A, D, DS, MC, V.

★ **JAX FISH HOUSE.** *1539 17th St (80202). 303/292-5767. www.jaxfish housedenver.citysearch.com.* Hrs: 4-10 pm; Fri, Sat to 11 pm; Sun to 9 pm. Closed most major hols. Seafood menu. Bar. Dinner $8.95-$24.50. Child's menu. Specialties: filet mignon of tuna, oyster bar, cioppino. Jazz Tues. Street parking. Totally nonsmoking. Cr cds: A, D, MC, V.
[D]

★ ★ ★ ★ **KEVIN TAYLOR RESTAURANT.** *1106 14th St (80202). 303/820-2600.* All the elements for a superb evening are brought together

in this stylishly elegant restaurant. Professional, attentive service and a fine wine list compliment chef Kevin Taylor's imaginative New American cuisine. Starters include a creamy lobster essence with morel mushrooms and garlic flan. Fresh seafood, wild game, and rack of lamb are just a few highlights. French influenced menu. Specializes in seared ahi tuna on jasmine rice, venison, foie gras. Hrs: 5:30-10:30 pm. Closed Sun; hols. Res accepted. Wine list. Dinner $25-$36. Cr cds: A, D, MC, V.
[D]

★ **LAS DELICIAS.** *439 E 19th Ave (80203). 303/839-5675.* Hrs: 8 am-9 pm; Fri, Sat to 10 pm; Sun from 9 am. Closed Thanksgiving, Dec 25. Res accepted. Mexican menu. Bkfst $1.99-$6, lunch, dinner $2.25-$9.25. Specialties: carnitas estilo michoacan, fajitas estilo michoacan. Street parking. Family-owned since 1976. Cr cds: A, D, DS, MC, V.
[D] [⟲]

★ ★ **LE CENTRAL.** *112 E 8th Ave (80203). 303/863-8094. www.lecentral. com.* Hrs: 11:30 am-2:30 pm, 5:30-10 pm; Sun 5-9 pm; Sat, Sun brunch 11 am-2 pm. Closed most major hols. Res accepted. French menu. Serv bar. Lunch $5.95-$7.95, dinner $8.50-$14.95. Sat, Sun brunch $5-$8. Specializes in country French dishes. Cr cds: A, MC, V.

★ ★ **MEL'S.** *235 Fillmore (80206). 303/333-3979. www.melsbarandgrill. com.* Hrs: 11:30 am-2:30 pm, 5:30-9:30 pm; Sun from 5 pm. Closed major hols. Res accepted. Contemporary continental menu. Bar. Wine list. A la carte entrees: lunch $8-$15, dinner $12-$26. Specializes in seafood, pasta, lamb. Jazz nightly. Outdoor dining. Cr cds: A, D, DS, MC, V.
[D]

★ ★ ★ **MORTON'S OF CHICAGO.** *1710 Wynkoop St (80202). 303/825-3353. www.mortons.com.* Hrs: 5:30-11 pm; Sun 5-10 pm. Closed major hols. Bar from 5 pm. Wine list. A la carte entrees: dinner $18.95-$29.95. Specializes in steak, lobster. Valet parking. Menu recited. Cr cds: A, D, MC, V.
[D] [⟲]

★ **OLD SPAGHETTI FACTORY.**
1215 18th St (80202). 303/295-1864.
www.osf.com. Hrs: 11:30 am-2 pm, 5-
9:30 pm; Fri to 10:30 pm; Sat 4:45-
10:30 pm; Sun 4-9:30 pm. Closed
Thanksgiving, Dec 24, 25. Italian
menu. Bar. Lunch $3.40-$5.65, dinner $4.70-$9. Specialties: homemade
lasagne, chicken Parmesan. Located
on ground floor of Tramway Cable
Bldg (1889). Trolley car, antique display. Cr cds: A, D, DS, MC, V.
D ⮔

★★★★ **PALACE ARMS.** *321 17th St*
(80202). 303/297-3111. www.brown
palace.com. Located downtown in
the century-old landmark hotel The
Brown Palace, this classic continental dining room has touches of the
Southwest on its menu with items
including buffalo filet with smoked
cheddar polenta. The impressive,
antique-filled room is decorated with
22 Revolutionary War battle flag
replicas and a dispatch case, bridle,
and pair of pistols believed to have
belonged to Napoleon. Continental,
regional American menu. Specializes
in rack of lamb, Chilean sea bass.
Own baking. Hrs: 11:30 am-2 pm, 6-
10 pm; Sat from 5:30 pm; Sun from
6 pm. Res accepted. Extensive wine
list. A la carte entrees: lunch $8.50-
$16, dinner $29-$42. Valet parking.
Jacket. Cr cds: A, D, DS, ER, JCB,
MC, V.
D

★★★ **PAPILLON CAFE.** *250*
Josephine Ave (80206). 303/333-7166.
www.papilloncafe.com. Hrs: 11 am-3
pm, 5-10 pm; Fri, Sat to 11 pm; Sun
5-9 pm. Closed Jan 1, Memorial Day,
July 4. Res accepted. French, Asian
menu. Bar. Wine list. A la carte
entrees: lunch $8-$12, dinner $16-
$25. Child's menu. Specialties:
Bangkok scallops, Louisiana crab
cakes, shrimp fritters. Contemporary
decor. Chef-owned. Totally nonsmoking. Cr cds: A, D, DS, MC, V.
D

★ **POTAGER.** *1109 Ogden St (80218).*
303/832-5788. www.coloradocuisine.
com. Hrs: 5-11 pm. Closed Mon, Sun;
also major hols. Wine, beer. A la
carte entrees: dinner $10-$20. Specialties: roasted chicken, grilled
salmon, twice-baked cheese souffle.

Parking. Outdoor dining. Totally
nonsmoking. Cr cds: A, MC, V.
D

★ **RACINES.** *850 Bannock St (80204).*
303/595-0418. Hrs: 7 am-midnight;
Mon to 11 pm; Sat 8 am-midnight;
Sun 8 am-11 pm. Closed Thanksgiv-
ing, Dec 24, 25. Res accepted. Bar.
Bkfst $2.50-$6.50, lunch $5.25-$8.95,
dinner $5.25-$13.50. Specializes in
big salads, fresh fish. Own pastries.
Parking. Outdoor dining. Cr cds: A,
D, DS, MC, V.
D ⮔

★★ **RADEX.** *100 E 9th Ave (80206).*
303/861-7999. French menu. Specializes in salmon paillard with cucum-
ber dill beurre blanc and jasmine
rice, pork loin with shiitake mushrooms and mashed potatoes. Hrs: 11
am-3 pm, 5 pm-midnight; Fri, Sat 5
pm-1 am. Closed major hols. Res
accepted. Wine list. Lunch $8-$12;
dinner $11-$20. Entertainment. Outstanding art collection. Cr cds: A, D,
DS, MC, V.
D ⮔

★★ **REDFISH.** *1701 Wynkoop*
(80202). 303/595-0443. www.redfish
america.com. Cajun menu. Specializes
in crawfish etouffee, jambalaya,
blackened redfish. Hrs: 11:30 am-
midnight; Fri to 1 am; Sat 4 pm-1
am; Sun to 9 pm. Res accepted. Wine
list. Lunch $4.95-$17.95; dinner
$7.95-$18.95. Entertainment: jazz. Cr
cds: A, DS, MC, V.
D ⮔

★ **ROCKY MOUNTAIN DINER.** *800*
18th St (80202). 303/293-8383. www.
rockymountaindiner.com. Hrs: 11 am-
11 pm; Sun 10 am-9 pm. Closed
most major hols. Res accepted (dinner). Bar. Lunch, dinner $4.95-
$18.95. Child's menu. Specialties:
buffalo meatloaf, duck enchiladas.
Outdoor dining. Saloon-style decor,
Western motif. Cr cds: A, D, DS,
MC, V.
D

★★★ **SACRE BLEU.** *410 E 7th St*
(80203). 303/832-6614. www.sacrebleu
denver.com. French Provencal cuisine
with a Mediterranean influence
menu. Specializes in seared ahi tuna,
oven roasted poussain, foie gras ravioli. Hrs: 5-10:30 pm. Res accepted.

Wine list. Dinner $17-$25. Entertainment: DJ Thurs-Mon. Cr cds: A, D, DS, MC, V.

[D] [⊒]

★★ **STARFISH.** *300 Fillmore St (80206). 303/333-1133. www.starfish. com.* Specializes in calamari, crab cakes, fresh fish. Own desserts. Hrs: 11:30 am-10 pm; Fri, Sat to midnight. Closed Sun; major hols. Res accepted. Bar. Lunch $5.95-$9.95; dinner $11.95-$25.95. Entertainment: pianist. Contemporary decor with ocean theme; framed posters, original artwork. Cr cds: A, D, DS, MC, V.

[D]

★★★ **STRINGS.** *1700 Humboldt St (80218). 303/831-7310. www.strings restaurant.com.* Hrs: 11 am-10 pm; Fri, Sat to 11 pm; Sun 5-10 pm. Closed some major hols. Res accepted. Bar. Wine list. Lunch $10-$17, dinner $18-$30. Child's menu. Specializes in pastas, daily menu. Valet parking. Outdoor dining. Six dining areas, each with its own decor and ambience. Cr cds: A, D, DS, MC, V.

[D]

★★★★ **TANTE LOUISE.** *4900 E Colfax Ave (80220). 303/355-4488. www.tantelouise.com.* Housed in a renovated Victorian bungalow, this romantic dining room has attracted guests for over 25 years with its contemporary French cuisine. Varied tastes can be accommodated in either the large main dining room, one of several more intimate areas, or the outdoor patio. Continental menu. Specializes in duck, roast rack of lamb, game. Own baking. Hrs: 5:30-10 pm. Closed Sun. Res accepted. Bar. Wine cellar. Dinner $19-$32.95. Valet parking. Outdoor dining. French decor. Cr cds: A, D, DS, MC, V.

[D] [⊒]

★★ **THREE SONS.** *2915 W 44th Ave (80211). 303/455-4366.* Hrs: 11 am-9:30 pm; Sun from 4 pm; early-bird dinner Tues-Thurs 4-7 pm. Closed Mon; also most major hols. Italian menu. Bar. Lunch $6.95-$10.25, dinner $10.95-$17.95. Child's menu. Specialties: roast chicken, lasagna, cappellini Madonna. Parking.

Romanesque decor. Family-owned since 1951. Cr cds: MC, V.

[D]

★★ **TOMMY TSUNAMI'S.** *1432 Market St (80202). 303/534-5050. www.larimersquare.com.* Hrs: 11 am-11 pm; Thurs to midnight; Fri to 1 am; Sat 4:30 pm-1 am; Sun 4:30-11 pm. Closed Thanksgiving, Dec 25. Res accepted. Pacific Rim menu. Bar. Lunch $6.75-$17.95, dinner $13.95-$23.95. Specializes in sushi, teriyaki, noodles. Outdoor dining. Japanese influenced modern decor; sushi bar. Totally nonsmoking. Cr cds: A, DS, MC, V.

[D]

★ **TRINITY GRILLE.** *1801 Broadway (80202). 303/293-2288. www.trinity grille.com.* Hrs: 11 am-2:30 pm, 5:30-10 pm; Sat from 5:30 pm. Closed Sun; most major hols. Res accepted. Bar. Lunch $4.50-$12.95, dinner $8.95-$29.95. Specializes in Maryland crab cakes, fresh seafood. Casual dining. Cr cds: A, D, DS, MC, V.

[D] [⊒]

★★★ **TUSCANY.** *4150 E Mississippi Ave (80246). 303/782-9300.* Hrs: 6 am-10 pm; Sat, Sun from 7 am. Res accepted; required Sun, hols. Northern Italian menu. Bar noon-midnight. Wine cellar. Bkfst $2.50-$12.50, lunch $8.25-$16, dinner $12.50-$25. Sun brunch $28.95. Child's menu. Specializes in pasta, seafood. Pianist Thurs-Sun. Harpist Sun brunch. Valet parking. Quiet, elegant dining rm; fireplace, frescoes. Outdoor dining. Braille menu. Cr cds: A, D, DS, MC, V.

[D] [⊒]

★ **WAZEE SUPPER CLUB.** *1600 15th St (80202). 303/623-9518. www. wazeesupperclub.com.* Hrs: 11-2 am; Sun noon-midnight. Closed Jan 1, Dec 25. Res accepted (Mon-Thurs). Bar. A la carte entrees: lunch, dinner $3.75-$19.45. Specializes in pizza, sandwiches. Sat night entertainment. Street parking. Cr cds: A, MC, V.

[D] [⊒]

★★★ **WELLSHIRE INN.** *3333 S Colorado Blvd (80222). 303/759-3333. www.wellshireinn.* Hrs: 7-10 am, 11:30 am-2:30 pm, 5-10 pm; Fri to 11 pm; Sat 11:30 am-2:30 pm, 5-11 pm; Sun 10 am-2 pm (brunch), 5-9 pm. Closed Jan 1, Memorial Day, Labor Day. Res accepted. Bar. Bkfst $4.75-$9.75, lunch $8.25-$12.95, dinner $14.95-$28. Sun brunch $6.95-$12.95. Specializes in salmon, rack of lamb, steak. Outdoor dining. Tudor-style inn. Totally nonsmoking. Cr cds: A, D, DS, MC, V.

D

★ **WYNKOOP BREWING COMPANY.** *1634 18th St (80202). 303/297-2700. www.wynkoop.com.* Hrs: 11-2 am; Sun 10 am-midnight. Closed Thanksgiving, Dec 25. Bar. Lunch $4.95-$7.50, dinner $5.95-$16.95. Specializes in continental pub cuisine. Outdoor dining. In J.S. Brown Mercantile Bldg (1899). Brewery kettles displayed; beer brewed on premises. Cr cds: A, D, DS, MC, V.

D

★ **ZAIDY'S DELI.** *121 Adams St (80206). 303/333-5336. www.zaidys deli.com.* Hrs: 7 am-8 pm; Mon, Tues to 3 pm; Sat, Sun 8 am-7 pm. Closed Thanksgiving, Rosh Hashanah, Yom Kippur. Res accepted. Bar. Bkfst $3.25-$8.50, lunch $4.50-$8, dinner $5.95-$9. Child's menu. Specializes in blintzes, deli sandwiches. Own baking, soups. Outdoor dining. Totally nonsmoking. Cr cds: A, MC, V.

D

★★ **ZENITH.** *815 17th St (80202). 303/293-2322. www.hotelnet.com.* Hrs: 11 am-11 pm; Sat from 5 pm; Sun 5-10 pm. Closed some major hols. Res accepted. Contemporary Amer menu. Bar. Lunch $7.25-$11.50, dinner $10.95-$20.75. Child's menu. Specialties: roasted sea bass, steak frites, vegetarian entrees. Own baking. Valet parking (dinner). Mediterranean atmosphere; palm trees, atrium ceiling, murals. Bldg was bank lobby in 1920s. Cr cds: A, D, MC, V.

D

Unrated Dining Spots

ANNIE'S CAFE. *4012 E 8th Ave (80220). 303/355-8197.* Hrs: 6:30 am-9 pm; Sat 8 am-9 pm; Sun 8 am-3 pm. Closed major hols. Bar. A la carte entrees: bkfst $3.50-$5.50, lunch $3.50-$5.95, dinner $4-$7.95. Child's menu. Specializes in chili,

hamburgers. Parking.Old fashioned drug store decor. Totally nonsmoking. Cr cds: DS, MC, V.

CHIPOTLE GRILL. *745 Colorado (80206). 303/333-2121. www.chipotle. com.* Hrs: 11 am-10 pm. Closed Thanksgiving, Dec 25. Mexican menu. Beer. A la carte entrees: $3.95-$4.75. Specializes in chicken fajitas, barbacoa, vegetable burritos. Parking. Outdoor dining. Cr cds: MC, V.

D

Denver International Airport Area

(C-5) *See also Denver*

Services and Information

Information. 800/AIR-2-DEN.

Lost and Found. 303/342-4062.

Weather. 303/337-2500.

Airlines. Air Canada, America West, American, Continental, Delta, Frontier, Lone Star, Lufthansa, Martinair Holland, Mexicana, Midwest Express, Northwest, Reno Air, TWA, United, USAir, Vanguard.

Motels/Motor Lodges

★★ **BEST WESTERN EXECUTIVE HOTEL.** *4411 Peoria St, Denver (80239). 303/373-5730; fax 303/375-1157; res 866/608-9330. www.best western.com.* 199 rms, 2-3 story. Apr-Sept: S, D $69-$74; each addl $10; suites $129; under 18 free; lower rates rest of yr. Crib avail. Pet accepted; $10. TV; cable (premium). Heated pool. Complimentary full bkfst. Complimentary coffee in rms. Restaurant 6 am-midnight. Rm serv. Bar 11-1 am. Ck-out noon. Coin lndry. Meeting rms. Business servs avail. In-rm modem link. Valet serv. Bellhops. Concierge. Free airport transportation. Exercise equipt. Balconies. Some refrigerators. Cr cds: A, C, D, DS, MC, V.

D 🐾 🌅 🏋 🐾 🔥

★★ **HAMPTON INN.** *1500 S Abilene St, Aurora (80012). 303/369-8400; fax*

303/369-0324; res 800/426-7866. www.hampton-inn.com. 132 rms, 4 story. S $69-$78; D $74-$88; under 18 free. Crib free. TV; cable (premium). Heated pool. Complimentary buffet bkfst. Restaurants nearby. Coffee in rms. Ck-out noon. Coin lndry. Meeting rms. Business servs avail. In-rm modem link. Valet serv. Health club privileges. Some refrigerators; microwaves avail. Cr cds: A, C, D, DS, MC, V.

D ⌦ ⌦ ⌦

Hotels

★★★ **DOUBLETREE DENVER.** 3203 Quebec St, Denver (80207). 303/321-3333; fax 303/329-5233; res 800/222-8733. www.doubletree.com. 571 rms, 9 story. S, D $59-$149; suites $350-$500; each addl $10; under 18 free; wkend rates. Crib avail. Pet accepted; $50 deposit. TV; cable, VCR avail. Indoor pool; whirlpool. Coffee in rms. Restaurant 6 am-11 pm. Rm serv 24 hrs. Bar 5 pm-2 am, Sun to midnight. Ck-out noon. Convention facilities. Business center. In-rm modem link. Free airport transportation. Exercise equipt; sauna. Refrigerators avail. Some balconies. Sun deck. Cr cds: A, C, D, DS, MC, V.

D ⌦ ⌦ ⌦ ⌦ ⌦ ⌦ ⌦

★★★ **DOUBLETREE DENVER SOUTHEAST.** 13696 E Iliff Pl, Aurora (80014). 303/337-2800; fax 303/752-0296; toll-free 800/528-0444. www.doubletree.com. 248 rms, 6 story. S $130; D $150; each addl $10; suites $150; under 18 free; wkend rates. Crib free. TV; cable (premium), VCR avail. Indoor pool; poolside serv. Restaurant 6:30 am-10 pm. Bar 11-2 am. Ck-out noon. Business center. In-rm modem link. Gift shop. Tennis privileges. Golf privileges. Exercise equipt. Health club privileges. Cr cds: A, D, DS, MC, V.

⌦ ⌦ ⌦ ⌦ ⌦ ⌦

Restaurant

★ **LA CUEVA.** 9742 E Colfax Ave, Aurora (80010). 303/367-1422. Hrs: 11 am-9 pm. Closed most major hols. Mexican menu. Bar. Lunch, dinner $2.95-$9.95. Specialties: chile rellenos, premium margaritas. Parking. Family-owned since 1974. Cr cds: A, MC, V.

D

Dillon

(C-4) *See also Breckenridge, Georgetown, Leadville, Vail*

Pop 802 **Elev** 8,858 ft **Area code** 970 **Zip** 80435

Information Summit County Chamber of Commerce, PO Box 214, Frisco 80443; 800/530-3099

Web www.summitnet.com

The entire town was moved in the early 1960s to make way for Dillon Lake, a reservoir for the Denver water system. The new Dillon, a modern, planned community, has become a popular resort area in the midst of wonderful mountain scenery. Ranger District offices of the Green Mountain Reservoir (see KREMMLING) and the White River National Forest, Arapaho division, (see GLENWOOD SPRINGS) are located in Dillon.

What to See and Do

Arapaho National Forest. Campgrounds, picnic grounds, and winter sports areas on more than one million acres. Of special interest are Lake Dillon, Arapaho National Recreation Area with five reservoirs, and Mt Evans Wilderness Area with the 14,264-ft-high Mt Evans, which has the highest auto road in the US. N, S, and E via US 6, CO 9. For information contact the Visitor Center, Arapaho and Roosevelt national forests, 1311 S College, Fort Collins 80526. Phone 970/498-2770. Camping ¢¢¢

Copper Mountain Resort Ski Area. Six-person, four high-speed quad, five triple, five double chairlifts; six surface lifts; patrol, school, rentals, snowmaking; cafeteria, restaurants, bar, nursery. One hundred twenty-six runs; longest run aprrox three mi; vertical drop 2,601 ft. (Nov-Apr, daily) X-country skiing. Half-day rates. Athletic club. Summer activities incl boating, sailing, rafting; hiking, bicycling, horseback riding, golf; jeep tours. Chairlift also operates to summit of mountain (late June-Sept, daily). 9 mi SW at jct I-70 and CO 91. Phone 970/968-2882 or 800/458-8386.

Keystone Resort Ski Area. Four ski mountains. Patrol, school, rentals. Snowmaking at Keystone, North Peak, and The Outback. Cafeteria, restaurant, bar, nursery, lodge. (Late Oct-early May) X-country skiing, night skiing, ice-skating, snowmobiling, sleigh rides. Shuttle bus service. Combination and ½-day ski rates; package plans. Summer activities incl boating and rafting, gondola rides; golf, tennis, horseback riding, bicycling, and jeep riding. 6 mi E on US 6. Phone 800/222-0188. ¢¢¢¢ The four ski mountains here are

Arapahoe Basin. Triple, four double chairlifts. Sixty-one runs; longest run 1½ mi; vertical drop 1,670 ft. (Mid-Nov-June) ¢¢¢¢

Keystone Mountain. Six-passenger gondola; two triple, eight double, four quad, two high-speed chairlifts; four surface lifts. Fifty-three runs; longest run three mi; vertical drop 2,340 ft. (Late Oct-early May) Night skiing on 13 runs (mid-Nov-early Apr).

North Peak. High-speed gondola; quad and triple chairlifts. Nineteen runs; longest run 2½ mi; vertical drop 1,620 ft. (Mid-Nov-late Apr) ¢¢¢¢

The Outback. High-speed quad chairlift. Seventeen runs; longest run 2½ mi, vertical drop 1,520 ft. (Mid-Nov-late Apr) ¢¢¢¢

Lake Dillon. Fishing, boating, rafting (ramps, rentals, marinas); hiking, picnicking, camping. Jeep tours (fee). (Daily) Just S of town in Arapaho National Forest on 3,300 acres. Phone 970/468-5400. **FREE**

Silverthorne Factory Stores. Mall contains over 45 outlet stores. Snack bars. (Daily) 2 mi N to I-70, exit 205, in Silverthorne. Phone 970/468-9440.

Special Event

Mountain Community Fair. Silverthorne. Second wkend July. Phone 970/513-8081.

Motels/Motor Lodges

★★ **BEST WESTERN PTARMIGAN LODGE.** 652 Lake Dillon Dr (80435). 970/468-2341; fax 970/468-6465; res 800/780-7234. www.bestwestern.com. 69 rms, 1-2 story, 4 kits. No A/C. Late Dec-early Apr: S, D $110-$130; each addl $5-$15; under 12 free; kit. units $10 addl; lower rates rest of yr. Crib free. Pet accepted; $50 deposit, $15. TV; cable (premium). Complimentary continental bkfst. Restaurant adj 7 am-2:30 pm, 5-10 pm. Bar. Ck-out 11 am. Meeting rm. Business servs avail. Coin lndry. Free ski area transportation. Downhill/x-country ski 5½ mi. Whirlpool. Sauna. Boating. Microwaves avail. Some refrigerators, balconies. On lake. Cr cds: A, D, DS, MC, V.

★★★ **FOUR POINTS BY SHERATON.** 560 Silverthorne Ln, Silverthorne (80498). 970/468-6200; fax 970/468-7829; res 800/325-3535. www.sunstonehotels.com. 160 rms, 6 story, 18 suites. Nov-Mar: S, D $79-$169; suites $209-$279; ski plans; hols (7-day min); lower rates rest of yr. Crib free. TV; cable (premium). Pool; whirlpool. Complimentary continental bkfst. Complimentary coffee in rms. Restaurant 11:30 am-11 pm; Sat, Sun to 3:30 pm. Rm serv. Bar. Ck-out 10 am. Coin lndry. Meeting rms. Business servs avail. Gift shop. Ski, bicycle rental. Downhill/x-country ski 4 mi. Game rm. Cr cds: A, C, D, DS, MC, V.

★★ **HOLIDAY INN.** 1129 N Summit Blvd, Frisco (80443). 970/668-5000; fax 970/668-0718; res 800/465-4329. www.holiday-inn.com/summitcounty. 217 rms, 3-6 story. Late Dec-Mar: S, D $62-$149; lower rates rest of yr. TV; cable (premium). Indoor pool; whirlpool. Restaurant 6:30 am-2 pm, 5-10 pm. Rm serv. Bar 5-10 pm; Fri, Sat to 11 pm. Coffee in rms. Ck-out 11 am. Coin lndry. Meeting rms. Business servs avail. In-rm modem link. Valet serv. Gift shop. Downhill/x-country ski 10 mi. Exercise equipt; sauna. Massage. Game rm. Rec rm. Some refrigerators. Balconies. Cr cds: A, C, D, DS, JCB, MC, V.

★ **SILVERTHORNE DAYS INN.** *580 Silverthorne Ln, Silverthorne (80498). 970/468-8661; fax 970/468-1421; res 800/329-7466. www.daysinn.com.* 73 rms, 4 story, 15 kits. Nov-Apr: S, D $89-$129; suites, kit. units $99-$199; under 18 free; lower rates rest of yr. Crib free. Pet accepted; $10. TV; cable (premium). Wading pool, whirlpool. Sauna. Complimentary continental bkfst. Restaurant nearby. Ck-out 11 am. Coin lndry. Business servs avail. Downhill/x-country ski 6 mi. Golf, tennis nearby. Some fireplaces, wetbars; refrigerators, microwaves avail. Cr cds: A, C, D, DS, JCB, MC, V.

★ **SNOWSHOE MOTEL.** *521 Main St, Frisco (80443). 970/668-3444; fax 970/668-3883; toll-free 800/445-8658. www.snowshoemotel.com.* 37 rms, 2 story, 9 kits. No A/C. Late Dec-Mar: S, D $90; kit. units $5-$7 addl; lower rates rest of yr. TV; cable (premium), VCR avail. Complimentary continental bkfst. Whirlpool. Sauna. Restaurant nearby. Ck-out 10 am. Business servs avail. Downhill ski 6 mi; x-country ski 1 mi. Some refrigerators, microwaves. Cr cds: A, D, DS, MC, V.

Resort

★★★ **COPPER MOUNTAIN RESORT.** *509 Copper Rd (80443). 907/968-2882; fax 970/968-6227; res 888/263-5302. www.ski-copper.com.* 560 units in 19 bldgs, 1-7 story. S, D $99-$225; each addl $15; full condo units (1-2 bedrm) $129-$545; under 14 free; higher rates late Dec (5-day min); 3-day min early Mar-early Apr; AP, MAP avail; package plans. Crib free. TV; cable (premium), VCR avail (movies $4). Indoor pool; whirlpool. Playground. Supervised child's activities; ages 3-12. Complimentary coffee in rms. Dining rm. Rm serv. Box lunches. Picnics. Bar 11-2 am. Ck-out 11 am, ck-in 4 pm. Grocery. Coin lndry. Package store. Convention facilities. Business center. In-rm modem link. Some services limited in summer. Valet serv. Concierge. Sports dir. Indoor tennis, pro. 18-hole golf, pro, putting green, driving range. Paddleboats. Downhill/x-country ski on site. Ice-skating, ski rentals; sleigh rides. Bicycle rentals.

Lawn games. Guides. Entertainment. Exercise rm; steam rm, sauna. Massage. Many refrigerators, fireplaces; microwaves avail. Many balconies. Picnic tables, grills. Extensive grounds on 250 acres. Cr cds: A, D, DS, MC, V.

★★★ **KEYSTONE LODGE.** *22101 US Hwy 6, Keystone (80435). 970/496-4202.* 152 rms, 5 story. S, D $300-$425; each addl $25; suites $500-$1,800; under 12 free; Crib free. TV; cable (premium), VCR (free movies) Heated pool; whirlpool, poolside serv. Coffee in rms. Restaurants 7 am-10 pm. Bar 4-11 pm; entertainment. Ck-out 11 am. Meeting rms. Business servs avail. In-rm modem link. Concierge. Downhill/x-country ski. Golf privileges. Fitness center. Cr cds: A, MC, V.

B&Bs/Small Inns

★★★ **CREEKSIDE INN.** *51 W Main St, Frisco (80443). 970/668-5607; fax 970/668-8635; toll-free 800/668-7320. www.creeksideinn-frisco.com.* 7 rms, 2 story. No A/C. Rm phone avail. Late Dec-early Jan: S $125-$155; D $100-$160; each addl $15; higher rates wk of Dec 25; lower rates rest of yr. Cable TV in common area. Whirlpool. Complimentary full bkfst. Restaurant nearby. Ck-out 11 am, ck-in 4-7 pm. Business servs avail. Gift shop. Downhill/x-country ski 2 mi. View of mountains; Ten Mile Creek at edge of backyard. Totally nonsmoking. Cr cds: DS, MC, V.

★★ **LARK MOUNTAIN INN B&B.** *109 Granite St, Frisco (80443). 970/668-5237; fax 970/668-1988; res 800/668-5275. www.toski.com/lark.* 7 air-cooled rms, 2 share bath, 1 with shower only, 2 story. No rm phones. Mid-Feb-Apr: S, D $130-$160; family, wkend, wkly rates; ski plans; higher rates hols (5-day min); lower rates rest of yr. Children over 8 yrs only. TV; cable; VCR avail (movies). Complimentary full bkfst. Restaurant adj 6 am-11 pm. Ck-out 10 am, ck-in 3-6 pm. Business servs avail. Luggage handling. Downhill ski 7 mi; x-country ski 2 mi. Whirlpool. Microwaves avail. Some balconies. Picnic tables. Log timber inn with over 400 hand-

stripped rails used in the porch.
Totally nonsmoking. Cr cds: A, MC, V.
🔥 ⚡ ⛷ 🏊 🔥 SC

★ ★ **SKI TIP LODGE.** *764 Montezuma Rd, Keystone (80435). 970/496-
4950; fax 970/496-4940.* 11 rms, 2
share bath, 2 story, 2 suites. No A/C.
No rm phones. Late Dec-early Jan: S,
D $70-$174; suites $144-$204; wkly
rates; ski plans; lower rates rest of yr.
Crib free. Whirlpool. Complimentary
complimentary bkfst in summer.
Restaurant (see SKI TIP LODGE). Bar.
Business servs avail. Tennis. Down-
hill/x-country ski on site. Health
club privileges. Mid-1800s stagecoach
stop. Totally nonsmoking. Cr cds: A,
C, D, DS, JCB, MC, V.
🔥 ⚡ ⛷ 🎿 🏊 🔥

Restaurants

★ ★ ★ **ALPENGLOW STUBE.** *22101
US Hwy 6, Keystone (80435). 970/468-
4386.* Hrs: 11 am-2 pm, 5-8:30 pm.
Closed Sun; also mid-Apr-late June &
early Sept-late Nov. Res required.
Continental menu. Bar. Wine list.
Complete 6-course meal $75; 7-
course menu $88. Specializes in game
dishes, rack of lamb. Separate vegetarian menu. Alpine atmosphere in
large log structure, native stone fireplace. Totally nonsmoking. Cr cds: A,
C, D, DS, MC, V.
D

★ ★ **BLUE SPRUCE INN.** *20 Main
St, Frisco (80443). 970/668-5900.
www.thebluespruce.com.* Hrs: 5-10 pm.
Res accepted. No A/C. Continental
menu. Bar. Dinner $31.95-$36.95.
Specializes in lamb, fresh fish, poul-
try. Own desserts. Parking. Cr cds: A,
C, D, DS, ER, MC, V.
D 🎿

★ ★ ★ **KEYSTONE RANCH.** *Keystone Rd, Keystone (80435). 970/468-
4161. www.snow.com.* Seatings: 5:30
& 8:15 pm. Res required. No A/C.
Bar. Wine list. Complete meals: dinner $67. Child's menu. Specializes in
wild game, elk medallion. Valet parking. Log ranch house with view of
mountains; fireplace. Cr cds: A, C, D,
DS, MC, V.

★ ★ ★ **SKI TIP LODGE.** *764 Montezuma Rd, Keystone (80435). 970/468-
4202. www.skiralston.com.* Hrs: 5:45-9

pm. Res accepted; required wkends.
Bar. Complete meal: dinner $49.
Child's menu. Specialties: pinenut-
encrusted roast rack of lamb, venison
chop, champagne-poached salmon.
Own baking. Parking. Former stagecoach stop; Western decor. View of
lake & mountains. Totally nonsmoking. Cr cds: A, C, D, DS, ER, MC, V.

Dinosaur National Monument (A-1)

*(88 mi W of Craig on US 40 to
monument headquarters)*

About ⅔ of the 325-square-mile
monument is in Colorado. Access to
this backcountry section, a land of
fantastic, deeply eroded canyons of
the Green and Yampa rivers, is via
the Harpers Corner Road, starting at
monument headquarters on US 40,
two miles east of Dinosaur, Colorado. At Harpers Corner, the end of
this 32-mile surfaced road, a one-
mile foot trail leads to a promontory
overlooking the Green and Yampa
rivers.

The entrance to the Dinosaur
Quarry section in Utah is at the junction of US 40 and UT 149 in Jensen,
Utah, 13 miles east of Vernal. Seven
miles north on UT 149 is the
Dinosaur Quarry; four to five miles
farther is the Green River campground. No lodgings are available
other than campgrounds.

Visitor centers and one quarry section campground are open all year.
The remainder are often closed by
snow approximately mid-November
to mid-April. For detailed information contact Superintendent, 4545 E
US 40, Dinosaur 81610; 970/374-
3000.

What to See and Do

Camping, picnicking. Green River
campground near Dinosaur Quarry
in Utah (Memorial Day-Labor Day;
fee); Lodore and Echo Park (fee),
Deerlodge campgrounds in Colorado;
Harpers Corner has picnic facilities.

Dinosaur Quarry. Remarkable fossil deposit; exhibit of 150-million-yr-old dinosaur remains; preparation laboratory on display. (Daily; extended hrs in summer; closed Jan 1, Thanksgiving, Dec 25) 7 mi N of Jensen, Utah, on UT 149. Per vehicle ¢¢

Fishing. Utah or Colorado license required.

Monument Headquarters and Information Center. At park entrance in Colorado. Display panels; audiovisual program, talks. (June-Labor Day, daily; rest of yr, Mon-Fri closed hols) **FREE**

Other activities. Self-guided nature trails (all yr), eve campfire programs, guided nature walks, children's programs, dinosaur talks (summer). Backpacking on marked trails; obtain permit at visitor centers.

River rafting. Permit must be obtained in advance from National Park Service. Guided trips from various concessionaires. Obtain list at visitor centers or from the superintendent.

Durango

(F-2) *See also Cortez*

Founded 1880 **Pop** 13,922 **Elev** 6,523 ft **Area code** 970 **Zip** 81301
Information Durango Area Chamber Resort Association, 111 S Camino Del Rio, PO Box 2587; 970/247-0312, 800/525-8855, or 800/GO-DURANGO
Web www.durango.org

What to See and Do

Big-game hunting in season. Vallecito Lake Resort Area. San Juan National Forest. Also on Bureau of Land Mangement.

Diamond Circle Theatre. Professional turn-of-the-century melodrama and vaudeville performances (June-Sept, nightly; closed Sun). Advance res advised. In Strater Hotel (see HOTELS). Phone 907/247-3400. ¢¢¢¢

Fishing. Lemon Dam, 12 mi NE on Florida Rd. Vallecito Lake, 18 mi NE on Florida Rd. Also Pine, Animas, Dolores rivers.

Mesa Verde National Park. (see). 37 mi W on US 160.

San Juan National Forest. This forest of nearly two million acres incl the Weminuche Wilderness, Colorado's largest designated wilderness, with several peaks topping 14,000 ft, as well as the South San Juan and Lizard Head wildernesses. The Colorado Trail begins in Durango and traverses the backcountry all the way to Denver. Recreation incl fishing in high mountain lakes and streams, boating, whitewater rafting; hiking, biking, camping, and four-wheel driving. The San Juan Skyway is a 232-mi auto loop through many of these scenic areas. (Daily) N on US 550; E and W on US 160. For information contact the Supervisor, 15 Burnette Ct. Phone 970/247-4874.

⭐ **The Silverton (Durango & Silverton Narrow Gauge Railroad).** America's last regularly scheduled narrow-gauge passenger train, in service since 1882, runs between Durango and Silverton, using original passenger coaches and steam engines. The 3½-hr trip each way passes over spectacular southwest Colorado Rocky Mtn scenery and through the Canyon of Rio de Las Animas. (Mid-May-Oct, daily) Under five free if not occupying seat. A winter holiday train excursion is also in operation (day before Thanksgiving-mid-Apr; closed Dec 24 and 25). Depot, 479 Main Ave. For details, check with the passenger agent. Durango. Phone 970/247-2733. In San Juan National Forest is Tall Timber Resort (see RESORTS), accessible only by the Silverton Railroad or by helicopter.

Durango & Silverton Narrow Gauge Railroad Museum. Museum in conjunction with Durango & Silverton Narrow Gauge Railroad that contains exhibits on steam trains, historic photos, railroad art, and restored railroad cars and a locomotive that can be entered. (Hrs correspond to the train depot hrs) 479 Main Ave. Phone 970/247-2733. ¢¢

Skiing. Purgatory Resort. Quad, three triple, five double chairlifts; patrol, school, rentals; five restaurants, five bars, nursery, lodge, specialty stores. Seventy runs; longest run two mi; vertical drop 2,029 ft. (Late Nov-early

Apr) X-country skiing. Multiday, half-day rates. Chairlift and alpine slide also operate mid-June-Labor Day (daily; fee); other summer activities. 25 mi N on US 550, in San Juan National Forest. Phone 800/982-6103. ¢¢¢¢

Southern Ute Indian Cultural Museum. Historical museum contains archival photos, turn-of-the-century Ute clothing, tools, and accessories. Multimedia presentation. Gift shop. (Mon-Sat; closed hols) 23 mi SE via US 160 and CO 172 in Ignacio. Phone 970/563-9583.

Special Events

Snowdown Winter Carnival. Last wk Jan. Phone 970/247-8163.

Iron Horse Bicycle Classic. Memorial Day wkend. Phone 970/259-4621.

Durango Cowboy Gathering. First wkend Oct.

Motels/Motor Lodges

★ **ALPINE MOTEL.** *3515 N Main Ave (81301). 970/247-4042; fax 970/385-4489; toll-free 800/818-4042.* 25 rms, 1 & 2 story. Mid-May-Aug: S, D $38-$84; lower rates rest of yr. Crib free. Pet accepted, some restrictions. TV; cable (premium). Restaurant nearby. Ck-out 11 am. In-rm modem link. Microwaves avail. Cr cds: A, C, D, DS, MC, V.

★★ **BEST WESTERN DURANGO INN.** *21382 US 160 (81301). 970/247-3251; fax 970/385-4835; res 800/780-7234. www.durangoinn.com.* 71 rms, 2 story. June-Sept: S, D $102-$155; under 12 free; ski plans; higher rates Christmas hols; lower rates rest of yr. Crib avail. TV; cable (premium), VCR avail (movies). Heated pool; whirlpool. Sauna. Playground. Complimentary continental bkfst, coffee in rms. Restaurant 5-10 pm. Bar from 4 pm. Ck-out 11 am. Meeting rm. Business servs avail. In-rm modem link. Valet serv. Game rm. Some refrigerators. Balconies. Cr cds: A, C, D, DS, MC, V.

★★ **BEST WESTERN LODGE.** *49617 Hwy 550 N (81301). 970/247-9669; fax 970/247-9681; res 800/780-*7234. *www.bestwestern.com.* 32 air-cooled rms, 25 kit. units, 2 story, 21 suites. Sept-Mar: S, D, suites $99-$279; under 12 free; higher rates Christmas hols; lower rates rest of yr. Crib free. Pet accepted; $10/day. TV; cable (premium), VCR avail (movies). Heated indoor pool; whirlpool. Complimentary continental bkfst, coffee in rms. Restaurant 4-10 pm. Bar. Ck-out 11 am. Business servs avail. In-rm modem link. Downhill/x-country ski adj. Golf nearby. Game rm. Exercise equipt. Refrigerators. Picnic tables. Cr cds: A, C, D, DS, MC, V.

★★ **DAYS INN.** *1700 County Rd 203 (81301). 970/259-1430; fax 970/259-5741; res 800/329-7466. www.daysinn durango.com.* 94 rms, 3 story. Mid-May-Sept: S, D $89-$109; each addl $9; under 18 free; lower rates rest of yr. Crib free. Pet accepted. TV; cable (premium). Heated indoor pool; whirlpools. Complimentary continental bkfst, coffee in rms. Ck-out 11 am. Meeting rm. Business servs avail. In-rm modem link. Coin lndry. Gift shop. Exercise equipt; sauna. Massage. Cr cds: A, C, D, DS, MC, V.

★★ **DURANGO LODGE.** *150 E 5th St (81301). 970/247-0955; fax 970/385-1882. www.durangolodge.com.* 39 rms, 2 story. May-Oct: S, D $45-$96; each addl $5; under 17 free; lower rates rest of yr. Crib free. TV; cable. Pool; whirlpool. Complimentary continental bkfst, coffee in rms. Restaurant nearby. Ck-out noon. Some refrigerators. Balconies. Golf nearby. Cr cds: A, C, D, DS, MC, V.

★ **ECONO LODGE.** *2002 Main Ave (81301). 970/247-4242; fax 970/385-4713; toll-free 800/424-4777. www. econolodge.com.* 43 rms, 2 story. Late-May-Sept: S, D $69-$169; each addl $4; suites $97; under 18 free; ski plans; higher rates Dec 25; lower rates rest of yr. Crib free. TV; cable (premium). Pool; whirlpool. Complimentary continental bkfst. Restaurant nearby. Ck-out 11 am. Business servs avail. In-rm modem link. Refrigerators, microwaves avail. Golf,

San Juan National Forest

x-country skiing nearby. Cr cds: A, D, DS, MC, V.

★★ **HAMPTON INN.** *3777 Main Ave (81301). 970/247-2600; fax 970/259-8012; toll-free 800/426-7866. www. hamptoninn.com.* 76 rms, 3 story. May-Sept: S, D $99-$129; suites $135; under 18 free; lower rates rest of yr. Crib free. TV; cable (premium), VCR avail (movies). Heated indoor pool. Complimentary continental bkfst, coffee in rms. Restaurant opp 11 am-10 pm. Ck-out 11 am. Coin lndry. Meeting rms. Business servs avail. In-rm modem link. Valet serv. Golf nearby. Cr cds: A, C, D, DS, MC, V.

★★ **RAMADA LIMITED DURANGO.** *3030 N Main Ave (81301). 970/259-1333; fax 970/247-3854; toll-free 800/252-8853. www. ramada.com.* 48 rms, 2 story. No elvtr. Late-May-Sept: S, D $75-$140; each addl $10; lower rates rest of yr. Crib free. TV; cable (premium). Heated pool; whirlpool. Sauna. Complimentary continental bkfst, coffee in rms. Restaurant nearby. Ck-out noon. Business servs avail. In-rm modem link. Skiing nearby. Cr cds: A, C, D, DS, MC, V.

★ **RODEWAY INN.** *2701 N Main Ave (81301). 970/259-2540; fax 970/247-9642; toll-free 800/752-6072. www.*
rodewayinndurango.com. 30 rms, 2 story. Late-May-Sept: S, D $75-$109; each addl $5; under 17 free; lower rates rest of yr. Crib free. Pet accepted, some restrictions; $7. TV; cable (premium). Heated indoor pool; whirlpool. Complimentary continental bkfst. Restaurant nearby. Ck-out 11 am. Coin lndry. Business servs avail. In-rm modem link. Some refrigerators. Microwaves, coffeemakers avail. Picnic area. Cr cds: A, C, D, DS, MC, V.

Hotels

★★★ **DOUBLETREE.** *501 Camino Del Rio (81301). 970/259-6580; fax 970/259-4398; res 800/222-8733. www.doubletree.com.* 159 rms, 3 story. Mid-May-mid-Oct: S, D $170-$210; each addl $15; suites $300; under 18 free; ski plans; higher rates late Dec; lower rates rest of yr. Crib free. Pet accepted; $10. TV; cable (premium). Heated indoor pool; whirlpool. Coffee in rms. Restaurant 6 am-10 pm. Rm serv. Bar from 11:30 am. Ck-out noon. Coin lndry. Meeting rms. Business servs avail. In-rm modem link. Bellhops. Concierge. Valet serv. Gift shop. Beauty shop. Free airport transportation. Exercise equipt; sauna. Private patios, balconies. Refrigerators avail. Cr cds: A, C, D, DS, MC, V.

★ ★ ★ **STRATER HOTEL.** *699 Main Ave (81301). 970/247-4431; fax 970/259-2208. www.strater.com.* 93 rms, 4 story. Mid-May-mid-Oct, Washington's birthday, late Dec: S, D $139-$250; lower rates rest of yr. Crib avail. TV; cable (premium). Complimentary full bkfst (winter). Restaurant 6 am-1:30 pm, 5-9:30 pm. Rm serv. Bar 11-2 am; entertainment. Ck-out 11 am. Business servs avail. In-rm modem link. Bellhops. Concierge. Valet parking. Whirlpool. Built 1887; Victorian decor, many antiques. Unique 1890 Diamond Belle Bar. Summer theater. Cr cds: A, C, D, DS, MC, V.

[D] [⚡] [☂] [✈] [⊠] [🔥] [SC]

Resorts

★ **IRON HORSE INN.** *5800 N Main Ave (81301). 970/259-1010; fax 970/385-4791; toll-free 800/748-2990. www.ironhorseinndurango.com.* 143 bi-level rms. Mid-May-mid-Sept: S, D $99-$119; each addl $5; under 12 free. Crib avail. Pet accepted; $10/day. TV; cable (premium). Heated indoor pool; whirlpool. Restaurant 6:30-10 am, 5-10 pm. Complimentary continental bkfst, coffee in rms. Ck-out 11 am. Coin lndry. Meeting rms. Business servs avail. In-rm modem link. Free airport transportation. Exercise equipt; sauna. Game rm. Lawn games. Refrigerators, fireplaces. Cr cds: A, C, D, DS, MC, V.

[D] [🐟] [⚡] [☂] [⊠] [👫] [✈] [⊠] [🔥]

★ ★ ★ ★ ★ **TALL TIMBER.** *1 Silverton Star Rte (80901). 970/259-4813. www.talltimberresort.com.* The historic Silverton train, which winds through scenic forests and canyons, is one of only two ways to access this family-friendly resort. The other is by helicopter. The accommodations are just as inspiring as the adventurous arrival; two-story condominium units with rustic wood paneling and stone fireplaces include three meals a day and round-trip transportation from Durango. 10 suites, 2 story. No A/C. No rm phones. AP, July 2-Sept and mid-Dec-early Jan, wkly: 7 days, 6 nights: S $4,300; D $4,600; 4 days, 3 nights: S $3,200; D $3,600; 3-12 yrs 50 percent less; under 3 yrs $400; transfer from Durango incl; lower rates mid-May-July 1, Oct. Closed rest of yr. Crib free. Indoor/outdoor pool; whirlpools. Sauna. Coffee in rms. Dining rm 7:30-9:30 am, 12:30-1:30 pm, 6:30-7:30 pm. Box lunches, helicopter picnics. Ck-out 10:30 am, ck-in 3:30 pm. Gift shop. Tennis. 9-hole, par-3 golf, putting green, driving range. Stocked pond for children. Downhill ski 3 min by air; x-country ski on site. Hiking trails. Lawn games. Massage. Refrigerators; wet bars. Balconies. Library. Totally nonsmoking. Cr cds: MC, V.

[⚡] [☂] [✈] [👫] [⊠] [⊠] [🔥] [🎿]

★ ★ ★ **TAMARRON RESORT.** *40292 US 550 N (81301). 970/259-2000; fax 970/382-7822; toll-free 800/678-1000. www.tamarron.com.* 102 kit. units, 4 story. May-Sept: S, D $109-$350; each addl $20; suites $350-$550; under 13 free; family rates; package plans. Valet parking avail. Crib free. Pet accepted; $15. TV; cable (premium), VCR avail. Complimentary continental bkfst, coffee in rms. Restaurants. Rm serv 24 hrs. Box lunches. Snack bar. Ck-out noon, ck-in 3 pm. Coin lndry. Package store. Meeting rms. Business servs avail. In-rm modem link. Bellhops. Valet serv. Concierge. Gift shop. Shopping arcade. Airport transportation. Lighted tennis, pro. 18-hole golf, greens fee $100, pro, putting green, driving range. Downhill ski 15 mi; x-country ski on site; rental equipt avail. Snowmobiles. Sleighing. Tobogganing. Hiking. Bicycle rentals. Social dir. Rec rm. Game rm. Exercise equipt; sauna, steam rm. Massage. Spa. Fishing/hunting guides. Heated indoor/outdoor pool; whirlpool, poolside serv. Playground. Supervised child's activities (Memorial Day-Labor Day); ages 4-15. Refrigerators. Bathrm phones; in-rm whirlpool, wet bar in suites. Balconies. Picnic tables, grills. Cr cds: A, D, DS, MC, V.

[D] [🐟] [⚡] [☂] [✈] [👫] [🚴] [⊠] [👫] [✈] [⊠] [🔥]

B&Bs/Small Inns

★ ★ **APPLE ORCHARD INN.** *7758 County Rd 203 (81301). 970/247-0751; fax 970/385-6976; toll-free 800/426-0751. www.appleorchardinn.com.* 10 rms, 1-2 story, 6 cottages. May-mid-Oct: S $120-$195; each addl $15; under 8 free; ski plans; higher rates Dec 22-Jan 2; lower rates rest of yr. TV; cable (premium), VCR avail. Whirlpool. Complimentary full bkfst; afternoon refreshments. Coffee in rms. Ck-out 11 am, ck-in 4-7 pm. Coin lndry. In-rm modem link. Luggage handling. Downhill ski 20 mi. Refrigerators. Picnic tables. Private patios. Farmhouse on 4½ acres. Totally nonsmoking. Cr cds: A, DS, MC, V.

★★ **COUNTRY SUNSHINE BED & BREAKFAST.** 35130 US 550N (81301). 970/247-2853; fax 970/247-1203; toll-free 800/383-2853. www.countrysunshine.com. 6 air-cooled rms, 2 story. No rm phones. Mid-May-Oct: S, D $95-$125; each addl $15; ski packages; lower rates rest of yr. TV; cable (premium), VCR in common rm. Complimentary full bkfst. Ck-out 10:30 am, ck-in 4-6 pm. Business servs avail. Downhill ski 12 mi; x-country ski on site. Whirlpool. Picnic tables, grills. Antiques. Art gallery. Library/sitting rm. Totally nonsmoking. Cr cds: A, C, D, DS, MC, V.

★★ **LELAND HOUSE BED & BREAKFAST SUITES.** 721 E 2nd Ave (81301). 970/385-1920; fax 970/385-1967; toll-free 800/664-1920. www.leland-house.com. 10 air-cooled rms, 2 story, 10 kits. Mid-May-mid-Oct: S, D $109-$139; each addl $20; suites $149-$320; ski plan. Crib avail. Pet accepted. TV; cable (premium), VCR avail (free movies). Complimentary full bkfst; afternoon refreshments. Complimentary coffee in rms. Restaurant adj 11 am-10 pm. Ck-out 11 am, ck-in 3-7 pm. Business servs avail. In-rm modem link. Refrigerators. Fireplaces in suites. Picnic tables. Restored apartment building (1927); many antiques. Totally nonsmoking. Cr cds: A, C, D, DS, MC, V.

★★★ **LIGHTNER CREEK INN.** 999 County Rd 207 (81301). 970/259-1226; fax 970/259-9526; toll-free 800/268-9804. www.lightnercreekinn.com. 10 rms, 2 story. No A/C. No rm phones. Mid-May-Sept: S, D $65-$205; each addl $25; lower rates rest of yr. Children over 6 only. Complimentary full bkfst; afternoon refreshments. Complimentary coffee in sun rm. Ck-out 11 am, ck-in 4-6 pm.

Business servs avail. In-rm modem link. Gift shop. Some fireplaces. Country French house built 1903; many antiques, baby grand piano. Gazebo. Totally nonsmoking. Cr cds: A, MC, V.

★★★ **NEW ROCHESTER HOTEL.** 726 E 2nd Ave (81301). 970/385-1920; fax 970/385-1967; toll-free 800/664-1920. www.rochesterhotel.com. 15 rms, 2 story, 2 suites, 1 kit. unit. Mid-May-Oct: S, D, suites $139-$209; each addl $15; ski plans; lower rates rest of yr. Pet accepted, some restrictions. TV; cable (premium), VCR avail (free movies). Complimentary continental bkfst. Restaurant opp 11 am-10 pm. Ck-out 11 am, ck-in 3 pm. Meeting rm. Business servs avail. Luggage handling. Some refrigerators. Restored hotel originally built in 1892. Each rm is named and decorated for a movie that was filmed in the area. Totally nonsmoking. Cr cds: A, C, D, DS, MC, V.

Guest Ranches

★★ **COLORADO TRAILS RANCH.** 12161 County Rd 240 (81301). 970/247-5055; fax 970/385-7372; toll-free 800/323-3833. www.coloradotrails.com. 33 air-cooled rms in 13 cabins. No rm phones. AP, wkly: $1,175-$1,600/person; family rates. Closed Oct-May. Heated pool; whirlpool. Free supervised child's activities from 5 yrs. Teen club. Dining rm (3 sittings): 7:30-9 am, 12:30 pm, 6:30 pm. Box lunches, snack bar, picnics. Ck-out 10 am, ck-in 2 pm. Lndry facilities. Meeting rms. Business servs avail. Gift shop. Free airport transportation. Sports dir. Waterskiing. Hiking. Trap shooting. Hayrides. Archery. Lawn games. Entertainment. Game rm. Fish guides. On 450 acres; adj to San Juan National Forest. Cr cds: A, D, DS, MC, V.

★★ **LAKE MANCOS RANCH.** 42688 County Rd N, Mancos (81328). 970/533-7900; fax 970/533-7858; toll-free 800/325-9462. www.lakemancosranch.com. 13 cabins, 4 rms in lodge. No A/C. No rm phones. Early June-Aug, AP, wkly (from Sun): S, D $1,150/person; family rates; lower rates Sept-early Oct. Closed rest of yr.

Crib free. Heated pool; whirlpool. Free supervised child's activities (mid-June-late Aug); from 4 yrs. Dining rm. Box lunches; snacks. Ck-out 10 am, ck-in 2 pm. Coin lndry. Business servs avail. Airport, bus depot transportation. Sports dir. Lawn games. Soc dir; entertainment. Jeep tours, hayrides. Rec rm. Refrigerators. Private patios. Secluded mountain location. Established in 1956. Cr cds: DS, MC, V.

★★★ **WILDERNESS TRAILS GUEST RANCH.** 23486 County Rd 501, Bayfield (81122). 970/247-0722; fax 970/247-1006; toll-free 800/527-2624. www.wildernesstrails.com. 20 rms in 10 cabins. No A/C. No rm phones. AP, June-late Aug, wkly: S $1,900; D $2,960; family rates; lower rates early-mid-June & Sept. Closed rest of yr. Adults only (Sept). Heated pool; whirlpool. Playground. Free supervised child's activities from age 3. Dining rm: bkfst 7:30-9 am, lunch noon, dinner from 6 pm. Setups. Box lunches, picnics, cookouts. Ck-out 10 am, ck-in 3 pm. Coin lndry. Meeting rms. Gift shop. Airport, bus depot transportation. Waterskiing, rafting, boats, motor boats. Overnight camping. Hayrides. 4-wheel driving trips. Lawn games. Entertainment; line dancing, movies. Rec rm. Game rm. Fishing guide. Picnic tables, grills. Fireplace in lounge. Porches, patios. Mountain resort. Totally nonsmoking. Cr cds: DS, MC, V.

★★★ **WIT'S END GUEST RANCH AND RESORT.** 254 County Rd 500, Bayfield (81122). 970/884-4113; fax 970/884-3261; toll-free 800/236-9483. 35 kit. cabins, 1-2 story. AP, Memorial Day-Labor Day (7-day min): D, cabins $3,500-$4,000; under 5 free; lower rates rest of yr. Crib free. TV; VCR (free movies). Heated pool; whirlpool. Free supervised child's activities (June-Labor Day); from 5 yrs. Dining rm 7 am-3 pm, 5-9 pm. Rm serv. Box lunches. Bar; entertainment. Ck-out 10 am, ck-in 4 pm. Free lndry. Meeting rms. Business servs avail. In-rm modem link. Gift shop. Airport, bus depot transportation. Tennis. X-country ski on site. Horse stables. Hay rides. Snowmobiles, sleighing. Mountain bikes.

Soc dir. Fishing/hunting guides. Microwaves avail. Picnic tables, grills. In valley on 550 acres; all cabins are adj to a river or pond. Stone fireplaces, knotty pine interiors. Totally nonsmoking. Cr cds: A, DS, MC, V.

All Suite

★★ **JARVIS SUITE.** 125 W 10th St (81301). 970/259-6190; toll-free 800/824-1024. www.durangohotel.com. 21 kit. suites, 3 story. June-Aug: S, D $99-$159; each addl $10; under 12 free; lower rates rest of yr. Crib $10. TV; cable (premium), VCR avail. Complimentary coffee in rms. Restaurant opp 7 am-11 pm. Ck-out 11 am. Coin lndry. Whirlpool. Refrigerators, microwaves. Restored historic hotel (1888). Cr cds: A, C, D, DS, MC, V.

Restaurants

★★ **ARIANO'S ITALIAN RESTAURANT.** 150 E College Dr (81301). 970/247-8146. Hrs: 5-10 pm; early-bird dinner to 6:30 pm. Closed Thanksgiving, Dec 25. Northern Italian menu. Bar. Dinner $10-$27. Child's menu. Specialties: chicken Vincent, veal Marsala, fettucine Napolitano. Own pasta. Turn-of-the-century building originally a saloon and brothel. Totally nonsmoking. Cr cds: A, C, MC, V.

★ **CARVER BREWING CO.** 1022 Main Ave (81301). 970/259-2545. Hrs: 6:30 am-10 pm; Sun to 1 pm. Closed Jan 1, Thanksgiving, Dec 25. Southwestern menu. Bar from 4 pm; brew pub. Bkfst $3.25-$5.95, lunch $4.75-$8.95, dinner $4.75-$17.95. Specializes in chicken stew bread bowl. Street parking. Cr cds: A, MC, V.

★★ **FRANCISO'S.** 619 Main Ave (81301). 970/247-4098. Hrs: 11 am-10 pm. Mexican, Amer menu. Bar. Lunch $6.25-$9.50, dinner $8.75-$23.95. Child's menu. Specializes in steak, fresh seafood, chicken. Own desserts. Mexican decor. Family-owned. Cr cds: A, C, D, DS, MC, V.

★ ★ **PALACE.** *505 Main Ave (81301). 970/247-2018. www.palacerestaurants. com.* Hrs: 11 am-10 pm. Closed Sun Nov-May; Dec 25. Res accepted. Amer menu. Bar. Lunch $5.95-$9.95, dinner $12-$28. Specialty: elk medallion. Street parking. Outdoor dining. Cr cds: A, D, DS, MC, V.
D

★ ★ **RED SNAPPER.** *144 E 9th St (81301). 970/259-3417. www.frontier. net/~theredsnapper.* Hrs: 5-10 pm. Closed Thanksgiving, Dec 25. Bar. Dinner $14.50-$38. Child's menu. Specializes in grilled fresh seafood, steaks, prime rib. Salad bar. Own desserts. Parking. Fish tanks. Turn-of-the-century building (1904). Totally nonsmoking. Cr cds: A, DS, MC, V.
D

Englewood

(C-5) *See also Denver, Lakewood*

Pop 31,727 **Elev** 5,369 ft
Area code 303
Information Greater Englewood Chamber of Commerce, 770 W Hampden Ave, #110, 80110, phone 303/789-4473; or the South Metro Denver Chamber of Commerce, 7901 S Park Plaza #110, Littleton 80120, phone 303/795-0142

What to See and Do

Castle Rock Factory Shops. More than 40 outlet stores; food court. (Daily) Approx 24 mi S on I-25, exit 184, in Castle Rock. Phone 303/688-4494.

The Museum of Outdoor Arts. Outdoor sculpture garden on 400 acres. Guided tours avail (fee). Lunchtime summer performance series (Wed). (Daily; closed hols) 1 mi S on S Broadway, then 4 mi E on E Arapahoe Rd, then N on Greenwood Plaza Blvd. Phone 303/741-3609. **FREE** The museum incl

    Fiddlers Green Amphitheatre. Host to summer concerts. Phone 303/220-7000.

Motel/Motor Lodge

★ ★ **HAMPTON INN.** *9231 E Arapahoe Rd (80112). 303/792-9999; fax 303/790-4360; res 800/426-7866. www.hamptoninn.com.* 152 rms, 5 story. S $69-$89; D $79-$99; under 18 free. Crib free. Pet accepted. TV; cable (premium), VCR avail. Pool. Complimentary continental bkfst. Complimentary coffee in rms. Restaurant nearby. Ck-out noon. Coin lndry. Meeting rms. Business servs avail. In-rm modem link. Valet serv. Exercise equipt. Health club privileges. Refrigerators, microwaves avail. Cr cds: A, C, D, DS, MC, V.
D ☐ ☐ ☐ ☐ SC ☐

Hotels

★ ★ ★ **HILTON DENVER TECH SOUTH.** *7801 E Orchard Rd, Denver (80111). 303/779-6161; fax 303/689-7080; res 800/445-8667. www.hilton. com.* 305 rms, 6 story. S, D $109-$149; suites $195-$275; under 18 free; wknd rates. Crib free. TV; cable (premium), VCR avail. Indoor/outdoor pool. Coffee in rms. Restaurant 6 am-10 pm. Rm serv 24 hrs. Bars 11 am-midnight. Ck-out noon. Convention facilities. Business servs avail. In-rm modem link. Bellhops. Valet serv. Gift shop. Exercise equipt; sauna. Balconies. Atrium. Cr cds: A, C, D, DS, JCB, MC, V.
D ☐ ☐ ☐ ☐ ☐ SC

★ ★ ★ **SHERATON DENVER TECH CENTER.** *7007 S Clinton (80112). 303/799-6200; fax 303/799-4828; res 800/325-3535. www.sheraton.com.* 263 rms, 10 story. S, D $150; each addl $10; under 12 free. Crib free. TV; cable (premium). Heated pool; whirlpool, poolside serv. Complimentary coffee in rms. Restaurant 6:30 am-10 pm. Bar 11:30-2 am. Ck-out noon. Convention facilities. Business center. In-rm modem link. Concierge. Gift shop. Airport transportation. Exercise equipt. Some bathrm phones; microwaves avail. Luxury level. Cr cds: A, C, D, DS, MC, V.
D ☐ ☐ ☐ ☐ ☐

Resort

★ ★ ★ **INVERNESS HOTEL & GOLF CLUB.** *200 Inverness Dr W (80112). 303/799-5800. www.inverness hotel.com.* 302 rms, 5 story. S, D $159-$279; each addl $10; suites $259-$379; under 18 free; golf plans. Crib free. TV; cable (premium), VCR avail. 2 pools, 1 indoor; whirlpool, poolside serv. Restaurant (see THE SWAN). Bar 11-1 am. Ck-out noon. Convention facilities. Business center. In-rm modem link. Concierge. Gift shop. Valet parking. Airport, RR station, bus depot transportation. Lighted tennis. 18-hole golf, greens fee $110, putting green, driving range. Pro shop. Exercise rm; sauna. Rec rm. Health club privileges. Minibars. Balconies. Near Centennial Airport. Luxury level. Cr cds: A, D, DS, JCB, MC, V.

All Suite

★★ **EMBASSY SUITES DENVER SOUTH.** *10250 E Costilla Ave, Centennial (80112). 303/792-0433; fax 303/790-1944; res 800/362-2779. www.embassysuitesdenver.com.* 236 suites, 9 story. Suites $159; each addl $10; under 12 free; wkend rates. Crib free. TV; cable (premium). Indoor pool; whirlpool. Complimentary full bkfst. Complimentary coffee in rms. Restaurant 11 am-10 pm. Bar. Ck-out noon. Meeting rms. Business servs avail. In-rm modem link. Gift shop. Exercise equipt. Game rm. Refrigerators, microwaves. Cr cds: A, C, D, DS, MC, V.

Extended Stay

★★ **RESIDENCE INN BY MARRIOTT DENVER SOUTH.** *6565 S Yosemite St (80517). 303/740-7177; fax 303/741-9426; res 800/331-3131. www.residenceinn.com.* 128 kit. suites, 1-2 story. S, D $129-$165; each addl free; wkend, wkly, monthly rates. Crib free. Pet accepted; $5/day. TV; cable (premium). Heated pool; whirlpool. Complimentary continental bkfst. Restaurant nearby. Ck-out noon. Coin lndry. Business servs avail. In-rm modem link. Valet serv. Health club privileges. Refrigerators, microwaves; many fireplaces. Private patios, balconies. Picnic tables, grills. Cr cds: A, C, D, DS, ER, JCB, MC, V.

Restaurants

★ **COUNTY LINE SMOKEHOUSE & GRILL.** *8351 Southpark Ln, Littleton (80120). 303/797-3727.* Hrs: 11 am-2 pm, 5-9 pm; Sat, Sun to 10 pm. Closed Thanksgiving, Dec 24 & 25. Bar. Lunch $5.95-$9.50, dinner $8.95-$15.95. Child's menu. Specializes in baby back ribs, mixed barbecue platter, grilled items. Own ice cream. Parking. Covered deck dining with view of mountains and McClellan Lake. Rustic decor; 40s and 50s memorabilia. Totally nonsmoking. Cr cds: A, C, D, DS, ER, MC, V.

★★ **FRATELLI'S.** *1200 E Hampden Ave (80110). 303/761-4773.* Hrs: 6:30 am-10 pm; Fri, Sat to 11 pm; Sun 8 am-9 pm. Closed July 4, Thanksgiving, Dec 25. Italian menu. Bar. Bkfst $3-$7, lunch $5-$12, dinner $7-$15. Child's menu. Specialties: pollo Fratelli, lasagne. Parking. Four dining areas. Antique bar built for Grand Tabor Hotel in Leadville. Family-owned for 33 yrs. Cr cds: A, C, D, DS, ER, MC, V.

★★ **P.F. CHANG'S CHINA BISTRO.** *8315 S Park Meadows Center Dr, Littleton (80124). 303/790-7744. www.pfchangs.com.* Hrs: 11 am-11 pm; Fri, Sat to midnight. Closed Thanksgiving, Dec 25. Chinese menu. Bar. A la carte entrees: lunch $5.95-$13.95, dinner $7.95-$15.95. Specializes in traditional Chinese dishes from Mongolia, Szechwan, Canton, Hunan, and Peking. Parking. Outdoor dining. Chinese decor. Cr cds: A, D, MC, V.

★ **SAFFRON.** *6600 S Quebec (80111). 303/290-9705.* Hrs: 11:30 am-2 pm, 5:30-9 pm; Fri to 10 pm; Sat 5:30-10 pm. Closed Sun; some major hols. Res accepted. Continental menu. Bar. Lunch $6.50-$9.95, dinner $12.95-$19.95. Specializes in Mediterranean dishes. Parking. Three dining rms. Contemporary decor. Cr cds: A, C, D, DS, ER, MC, V.

★★★ **THE SWAN.** *200 Inverness Dr W (80112). 303/799-5800. www.invernesshotel.com.* Hrs: 6-10 pm.

Closed Sun, Mon. Res accepted. Continental/Amer menu. Bar. Extensive wine list. Dinner $28-$45. Child's menu. Specialties: rack of lamb, smoked salmon and prawns. Classical guitarist, harpist Tues-Sat. Valet parking. Fine dining. Cr cds: A, C, D, DS, ER, MC, V.

[D]

★ ★ ★ **Z' TEJAS GRILL.** *8345 S Park Meadows Center Dr, Littleton (80124). 303/768-8191. www.ztejas.com.* Hrs: 11 am-10 pm; Fri, Sat to 11 pm; Sat, Sun brunch 11 am-3 pm. Closed Thanksgiving, Dec 25. Res accepted. Southwestern menu. Bar. Lunch $6-$12, dinner $8-$16. Sat, Sun brunch $6-$8. Child's menu. Specialties: voodoo tuna, mashed potato rellino, stuffed pork tenderloin. Parking. Southwestern atmosphere. Cr cds: A, DS, MC, V.

[D]

Estes Park

(B-5) *See also Fort Collins, Granby, Grand Lake, Loveland, Lyons*

Settled 1875 **Pop** 5,413 **Elev** 7,522 ft
Area code 970 **Zip** 80517
Information Information Center at the Chamber of Commerce, 500 Big Thompson Ave, PO Box 3050; 970/586-4431 or 800/443-7837
Web www.rockymtntrav.com/estes/

What to See and Do

⭐ **Aerial Tramway.** Two cabins, suspended from steel cables, move up or down Prospect Mtn at 1,400 ft per min. Superb view of Continental Divide during trip; picnic facilities at 8,896-ft summit; panoramic dome shelter; snack bar. (Mid-May-mid-Sept, daily) 420 Riverside Dr, 2 blks S of Elkhorn St. Phone 970/586-3675 or 970/756-6921. ¢¢¢

Big Thompson Canyon. One of the most beautiful canyon drives in the state. E on US 34.

Enos Mills Original Cabin. (1885) On this family-owned 200-acre nature preserve stands the cabin of Enos Mills, regarded as the "Father of Rocky Mountain National Park." In the shadow of Longs Peak, the cabin

contains photos, notes, and documents of the famed naturalist. Nature guide (fee) and self-guided nature trails. (May-Oct, daily; rest of yr, by appt) 8 mi S on CO 7. Phone 970/586-4706. **FREE**

Estes Park Area Historical Museum. Three facilities incl a building that served as headquarters for Rocky Mtn National Park from 1915-1923. Exhibits on history of the park, the town, and surrounding area. (Apr-Sept, daily; Oct-Mar, wkends only) 200 Fourth St, across from lake. Phone 970/586-6256. ¢¢

Estes Park Ride-a-Kart. Go-karts, bumper boats and cars, mini-golf, and mini-train in miniature Western town. Separate fees. (May-Sept, daily) 2250 Big Thompson Ave, 1 mi E on US 34. Phone 970/586-6495.

Fishing, boating, hiking, horseback riding, mountain climbing. Fishing for trout in local lakes and streams. Fishing license needed at Estes Park. Boating on Lake Estes; motors, boats for rent; permit required for private boats; docks (mid-May-early Sept, daily). More than 1,500 mountain-trained horses and ponies are used for bkfst rides, pack trips. National Park Service conducts guided hikes in Rocky Mtn National Park (see); climbers attempt Longs Peak (14,255 ft). Certified guides also avail in town.

Fun City Amusement Park. Bumper cars (fee); 15-lane giant slide and spiral slide (fee); arcade; miniature golf; two 18-hole golf courses; go-karts. (Mid-May-mid-Sept, daily) 455 Prospect. Phone 970/586-2070.

Rocky Mountain National Park. (see). 3 mi W on US 34, 36.

Roosevelt National Forest. More than 780,000 acres of icy streams, mountains, and beautiful scenery. Trout fishing; hiking trails, winter sports area, picnicking, camping. Of special interest are the Cache la Poudre River, five wilderness areas, and the Peak to Peak Scenic Byway. Surrounds town on north, east, and south. For information contact the Visitor Center, 1311 S College, Fort Collins 80526. Phone 970/498-1100. **FREE**

Special Events

Estes Park Music Festival. Rocky Ridge Music Center. Chamber, symphonic, and choral concerts. Early June-late Aug. Phone 970/586-9203.

Horse shows. Wkends June-Sept.

Rooftop Rodeo. Rodeo parade, nightly dances, kids jamboree. Five days mid-July.

Scottish-Irish Highland Festival. Athletic and dance competitions, arts and crafts shows, magic shows, folk dancing. Wkend after Labor Day. Phone 970/586-6104.

Motels/Motor Lodges

★ **ALPINE TRAIL RIDGE INN.** *927 Moraine Ave (80517). 970/586-4585; fax 970/586-6249; toll-free 800/233-5023. www.alpinetrailridgeinn.com.* 48 rms, 1 kit. suite. No A/C. June-early Sept: S $52-$102; D $58-$107; each addl $8; kit. suite $138; golf plans; lower rates May-mid-June, early Sept-mid-Oct. Closed rest of yr. Crib $8. TV; cable. Heated pool. Coffee in lobby. Restaurant 7 am-9 pm. Bar. Ck-out 10:30 am. Business servs avail. Airport transportation. Refrigerators; microwaves avail. Some balconies. Mountain views. Cr cds: A, C, D, DS, MC, V.

[D] [≈] [≥] [⟨⟩]

★★ **ASPEN WINDS.** *1051 Fall River Ct (80517). 970/586-6010; fax 970/586-3626; toll-free 800/399-6010. www.estes-park.com/aspenwinds.* 16 units, 2 story. Late May-mid-Sept: S, D $125-$169; each addl $10; wkly rates; lower rates rest of yr. Crib free. TV; cable (premium), VCR. Complimentary coffee in rms. Restaurant nearby. Ck-out 10 am. Business servs avail. In-rm whirlpools, refrigerators, microwaves, fireplaces. Balconies. Picnic tables, grills. On river. Mountain view. Cr cds: A, DS, MC, V.

[D] [⟨] [≥] [⟨⟩] [SC]

★ **BEST WESTERN SILVER SADDLE.** *1260 Big Thompson Ave (80517). 970/586-4476; fax 970/586-5530; res 800/780-7234. www.bestwestern.com.* 55 rms, 1 story. June-late Aug: S, D $109-$199; lower rates rest of yr. Crib free. TV; cable (premium), VCR avail. Heated pool; whirlpool. Playground. Complimentary continental bkfst, coffee in rms. Restaurant nearby. Ck-out 10 am. Coin lndry. Business servs avail. In-rm modem link. Refrigerators, microwaves, balconies. Some fireplaces. Picnic tables, grills. Cr cds: A, C, D, DS, MC, V.

[D] [≈] [≥] [⟨⟩] [SC]

★★★ **BOULDER BROOK ON FALL RIVER.** *1900 Fall River Rd (80517). 970/586-0910; fax 970/586-8067; toll-free 800/238-0910. www.estes-park. com/boulderbrook.* 19 air-cooled kit. suites, 1-2 story. May-Oct (3-day min): suites $99-$129; each addl $10; wkly rates; lower rates rest of yr. Crib free. TV; cable (premium), VCR (free movies). Complimentary coffee in rms. Ck-out 10 am. Business servs avail. In-rm modem link. Airport transportation. Whirlpool. Valet serv. X-country ski 7 mi. Microwaves; some in-rm whirlpools, fireplaces. Balconies. Picnic tables, grills. On banks of Fall River. Totally nonsmoking. Cr cds: A, D, MC, V.

[≈] [✈] [≥] [⟨⟩] [SC]

★★ **COMFORT INN.** *1450 Big Thompson Ave (80517). 970/586-2358; fax 970/586-4473; res 800/228-5150. www.comfortinn.com.* 75 rms, 1-2 story. June-Aug: S, D $85-$190; each addl $8; under 18 free; 2-day min stay wkends; lower rates rest of yr; closed Nov-Apr. Crib $3. TV; cable. Heated pool; whirlpool. Complimentary continental bkfst, coffee in rms. Restaurant nearby. Ck-out 10:30 am. Business servs avail. Airport transportation. X-country ski 8 mi. Some refrigerators; microwaves avail. Some balconies. Picnic tables. Cr cds: A, C, D, DS, ER, JCB, MC, V.

[D] [⟨] [≈] [≥] [⟨⟩]

★★ **DEER CREST.** *1200 Fall River Rd (80517). 970/586-2324; fax 970/586-8693; toll-free 800/331-2324. www. estes-park.com/deercrest.* 26 air-cooled rms, 1 A/C, 2 story, 8 suites, 6 kit. units. S $59-$79; D $64-$89; June-Sept: S, D, suites, kit. units $85-$120; each addl $20; lower rates rest of yr. Adults only. TV; cable (premium). Heated pool; whirlpool. Restaurant nearby. Ck-out 10 am. Airport transportation. X-country ski 7 mi. Refrigerators, microwaves. Balconies.

Picnic tables, grills. On Fall River. Totally nonsmoking. Cr cds: MC, V.
⊠ ⊠ ⊠ ⊠ **SC**

★★ **FAWN VALLEY INN.** *2760 Fall River Rd (80517). 970/586-2388; fax 970/586-0394; toll-free 800/525-2961. www.fawnvalleyinn.com.* 25 condos (1-2 bedrms), 1-2 story. No A/C. S, D $110-$180; 3-day min in season. TV; cable (premium). Heated pool; whirlpool. Restaurant. Bar. Ck-out 11 am. Meeting rms. In-rm modem link. Refrigerators, microwaves; many fireplaces. Balconies. Picnic tables, grills. Golf nearby. 8 acres on Fall River. Cr cds: A, DS, MC, V.
D ⊠ ⊠ ⊠ ⊠

★★ **HOLIDAY INN ROCKY MOUNTAIN PARK.** *101 S St. Vrain (80517). 970/586-2332; fax 970/586-2038; res 800/465-4329. www.holiday-inn.com.* 150 rms, 3-4 story, 5 suites. Mid-June-late Aug: S, D $98-$129; each addl $8; suites $229; under 18 free; lower rates rest of yr. Crib free. TV; cable (premium). Indoor pool; whirlpool. Restaurant 7 am-1:30 pm, 5-9 pm. Rm serv. Bar 3 pm-2 am; Sun to midnight. Ck-out 11 am. Coin lndry. Meeting rms. Business servs avail. Bellhops. Airport transportation. X-country ski 7 mi. Exercise equipt. Holidome. Game rm. Cr cds: A, C, D, DS, JCB, MC, V.
D ⊠ ⊠ ⊠ ⊠ ⊠

★★ **MCGREGOR MOUNTAIN LODGE.** *2815 Fall River Rd (80517). 970/586-3457; fax 970/586-4040; toll-free 800/835-8439. www.mcgregor mountainlodge.com.* 19 units, 10 cottages. No A/C. No rm phones. June-Sept: S, D $49-$99; each addl $10; kit. cottages $115-$265; wkly rates; lower rates rest of yr. Crib $5. TV; cable, VCR. Playground. Complimentary coffee in lobby. Restaurant nearby. Ck-out 11 am, ck-in 3 pm. Grocery, coin lndry ½ mi. Business servs avail. Airport transportation. Whirlpool. Lawn games. Many refrigerators, fireplaces, microwaves. Private patios. Covered barbecue area; picnic tables, grills. On 10 acres overlooking Fall River Canyon. Rocky Mtn National Park adj. Cr cds: DS, MC, V.
D ⊠ ⊠ ⊠

★ **OLYMPUS MOTOR LODGE.** *2365 Big Thompson Hwy 34 (80517).* *970/586-8141; fax 970/586-8143; toll-free 800/248-8141. www.estes-park. com/olympus.* 17 rms, 8 A/C. Memorial Day-mid-Sept: S, D $85-$175; each addl $8; wkly rates; lower rates, family rates rest of yr. Crib $5. Pet accepted, some restrictions. TV; cable. Complimentary coffee in lobby, rms. Restaurant 11 am-8 pm. Ck-out 10 am. Meeting rms. Airport transportation. Lawn games. Some refrigerators, microwaves. Picnic tables, grills. Golf nearby. Cr cds: A, C, D, DS, MC, V.
D ⊠ ⊠ ⊠ ⊠

★ **PONDEROSA LODGE.** *1820 Fall River Rd (80517). 970/586-4233; toll-free 800/628-0512. www.estes-park. com/ponderosa.* 19 rms, 2 story. No A/C. No rm phones. Mid-Jun-Sep S, D $94-$117; each addl $5; kits. $17-$250; under 6 free; package plans; summer (2-, 3-, 5-day min); lower rates rest of yr. Crib free. TV; cable (premium). Playground. Complimentary coffee in lobby. Restaurant nearby. Ck-out 10 am. X-country ski 2 mi. Fireplaces; some refrigerators, microwaves. Balconies. Picnic tables, grills. Hiking. Fishing. Cr cds: A, DS, MC, V.
D ⊠ ⊠ ⊠ ⊠

★★★ **SUNNYSIDE KNOLL RESORT.** *1675 Fall River Rd (80517). 970/586-5759; toll-free 800/586-5212. www.sunnysideknoll.com.* 15 rms, 7 kit. units. No A/C. No rm phones. June-Sept: S, D $75-$149; kit. units $92-$239 (3-day min); wkly rates; lower rates rest of yr. Children over 12 yrs only. TV; cable (premium), VCR (movies). Heated pool; whirlpools. Complimentary coffee in rms. Restaurant nearby. Ck-out 11 am. X-country ski 2 mi. Rec rm. Exercise equipt. Refrigerators, fireplaces; some in-rm whirlpools. Private patios. Picnic tables, grills. Cr cds: DS, MC, V.
⊠ ⊠ ⊠ ⊠ ⊠

★ **TRAPPERS MOTOR INN.** *553 W Elkhorn Ave (80517). 970/586-2833; toll-free 800/552-2833. www.estes-park. com/trappers.* 20 rms, 2 story. 3 A/C. Mid-June-early Sept: S, D $52-$72; under 10 free; lower rates rest of yr. TV; cable (premium). Playground. Complimentary coffee in lobby. Restaurant nearby. Ck-out 10 am. Lawn games. Whirlpool. Some refrigerators; microwaves avail. Picnic tables. Cr cds: A, MC, V.

Hotel

★★★ **THE STANLEY HOTEL.** *333 Wonderview Hotel (80517). 970/586-3371; fax 970/586-4964; toll-free 800/976-1377. www.stanleyhotel.com.* 140 rms, 4 story. Mid-May-mid-Oct: S, D $99-$149; each addl $20; suites $159 under 18 free. Crib free. TV; cable (premium). Heated pool. Playground. Complimentary coffee. Restaurant 7 am-9 pm. Rm serv. Bar; entertainment Fri-Sat. Ck-out 11 am. Meeting rm. Gift shop. Tennis. Valet serv. Exercise equipt. Health club privileges. Some fireplaces. Refrigerators avail. Built in 1909 by automaker F. O. Stanley. Cr cds: A, D, DS, MC, V.

Resorts

★ **BIG THOMPSON TIMBERLANE LODGE.** *740 Moraine Ave (80517). 970/586-3137; fax 970/586-3719; toll-free 800/898-4373. www.bigthompson timberlanelodge.com.* 54 rms, 36 kits. June-early Sept: S, D, cottages $89-$315; each addl $20; 1-3-bedrm cabins $89-$315; wkly rates; lower rates rest of yr. Crib $10. TV; cable (premium), VCR avail. Pool; wading pool; whirlpool. Playground. Complimentary coffee. Restaurant adj 7 am-10 pm. Ck-out 10 am. Coin lndry. Refrigerators; microwaves avail. Picnic tables, grills. On Big Thompson River. Cr cds: A, D, DS, MC, V.

B&B/Small Inn

★★★ **ROMANTIC RIVERSONG INN.** *1765 Lower Broadview Rd (80517). 970/586-4666; fax 970/577-0699. www.romanticriversong.com.* 9 rms, 1-2 story, 6 suites. No A/C. No rm phones. S, D $150-$275; each addl $50, suites $160-$275. Children over 12 yrs only. Complimentary full bkfst; afternoon refreshment. Dinner with advance reservation. Ck-out noon, ck-in 4-7 pm. Airport transportation. Many in-rm whirlpools; some refrigerators. Fireplaces. Balconies. Picnic tables. Located on 28 acres, adj to Rocky Mtn National Park; scenic views. Many ponds, trails. Built 1928; decorated with a blend of antique and modern country furnishings. Totally nonsmoking. Cr cds: DS, MC, V.

Guest Ranches

★★ **ASPEN LODGE RANCH.** *6120 Hwy 7 (80517). 970/586-8133; res 800/332-6867.* 59 units, 36 rms in lodge, 23 cottage units. No A/C. S, D $185-$260, weekly rates; family rates; AP June-Aug. Crib free. TV in lobby. Pool; whirlpool. Playground. Free supervised child's activities (June-Sept); ages 3-12. Dining rm (public by res) 7 am-10 pm. Box lunches, barbecue, bkfst rides. Bar. Ck-out 11 am, ck-in 4 pm. Meeting rms. Business center. Concierge. Gift shop. Airport transportation. Sports dir. Tennis. X-country ski on site. Ice-skating, snowshoeing. Hayrides, overnight cookouts. Mountain bike rentals. Lawn games. Handball. Paddle boats. Entertainment. Game rm. Rec rm. Exercise rm; sauna. Picnic tables, grills. Petting zoo (summer months). Cr cds: A, D, DS, MC, V.

★ **WIND RIVER RANCH.** *5770 S St. Vrain (80517). 970/586-4212; fax 970/586-2255; res 800/523-4212. www.windriverranch.com.* 15 units, 4 rms in lodge, 13 cottages (1-3-bedrm). S $200; D $400; No rm phones. June-Aug, AP (3-day min): $850-$1,350/wk. Closed rest of yr. Heated pool; whirlpool. Playground. Free supervised child's activities (June-Aug). Dining rm: 8-9 am, 12:30-1:30 pm, 6-7 pm. Box lunches. Ck-out 10 am, ck-in 3 pm. Grocery, coin lndry, package store 7 mi. Meeting rms. Business center. Airport, bus depot transportation. Hiking, rafting. Many fireplaces. Many private porches. Cr cds: A, DS, MC, V.

Cottage Colonies

★ **COLORADO COTTAGES.** *1241 High Dr (80517). 970/586-4637; toll-free 800/468-1236. www.estes-park.com/colocottage.* 10 cottages. Memorial Day-Sept: S, D $84-$115; each addl $5; wkly rates; lower rates rest of yr. Crib avail. TV; cable (premium). Restaurant nearby. Ck-out 10 am, ck-in 3-8 pm. Refrigerators, fireplaces. Some microwaves. Picnic tables, grills. Cr cds: A, MC, V.

★ **IDLEWILDE COTTAGES BY THE RIVER.** 2282 Hwy 66 (80517). 970/586-3864; fax 970/586-9217. www.idlewilde.net. 13 kit. cottages. No A/C. No rm phones. Mid-May-mid-Oct: 1-3-bedrm cottages $75-$230; each addl $10. Closed rest of yr. Crib free. TV; cable. Playground. Restaurant nearby. Ck-out 10 am, ck-in 3 pm. Grocery, coin lndry, package store 1 mi. Whirlpool. Lawn games. Refrigerators. Library. Screened porches. Picnic tables, grill. Knotty pine interiors. No cr cds accepted.

★★ **MACHIN'S COTTAGES IN THE PINES.** 2450 Eagle Cliff Rd (80517). 970/586-4276. 17 kit. cottages, 4 one-bedrm, 9 two-bedrm, 4 three-bedrm. Kit. cottages $80-$175; each addl $12; wkly rates. Closed Oct-late May. Crib $3. Pet accepted, some restrictions. TV; cable (premium). Playground. Ck-out 10 am, ck-in 3 pm. Grocery, coin lndry, package store 1 mi. Gift shop. Hiking trails. Microwaves. Patios. Picnic tables, grills. On 14 acres. Cr cds: A, MC, V.

★★★ **STREAMSIDE CABINS.** 1260 Fall River (80517). 970/586-6464; fax 970/586-6272; toll-free 800/321-3303. www.streamsidecabins.com. 19 kit. cabins & cabin suites. Summer: cabins $115-$240; cabin suites $120-$175; each addl $15; package plans; lower rates rest of yr. Crib free. TV; cable (premium), VCR (free movies). Whirlpool; steamrm. Playground. Complimentary coffee in rms. Restaurant adj. Ck-out 10:30 am, ck-in 3 pm. Grocery, coin lndry, package store ½ mi. Business servs avail. X-country ski 6 mi. Hiking. Lawn games. Fireplaces, refrigerators; microwaves avail. Some in-rm whirlpools. Porches, decks. Picnic tables, grills. On 17 acres on Fall River. Totally nonsmoking. Cr cds: A, DS, MC, V.

Restaurants

★★★ **BLACK CANYON INN.** 800 MacGregor Ave (80517). 970/586-9344. www.estespark.com/blackcanyon. Hrs: 11:30 am-2 pm, 5-9 pm. Closed Mon. Res accepted. Continental menu. Bar. Lunch $6.95-$9.95, dinner $14.95-$25.95. Child's menu. Specializes in seafood, wild game. Parking. Built in 1927 of rough-cut logs. Two-story moss & rock fireplace. Cr cds: A, DS, MC, V.
[D]

★★★ **FAWN BROOK INN.** CO 7 Business Loop, Allens Park (80510). 303/747-2556. Hrs: Mid-May-Aug: 5-8:30 pm; off-season hrs vary. Closed Mon. Res accepted. No A/C. Continental menu. Bar. Dinner $26.50-$44. Child's menu. Specialties: roast duckling, venison. Parking. Intimate dining areas. Rustic Austrian decor. Cr cds: A, MC, V.

★ **MAMA ROSE'S.** 338 E Elkhorn Ave (80517). 970/586-3330. Hrs: 7-11 am, 4-9 pm; winter from 4 pm. Closed major hols; Jan, Feb; also Mon-Wed (winter). Italian menu. Bar. Buffet: bkfst $5.95. Dinner $6.95-$14.95. Child's menu. Specialties: veal Parmesan, chicken Parmesan, fettucine Alfredo. Outdoor dining. Victorian decor; large fireplace. Totally nonsmoking. Cr cds: A, C, DS, ER, MC, V.
[D]

★★ **NICKY'S.** 1350 Fall River Rd (80517). 970/586-5376. www.nickys resort.com. Hrs: 7 am-10 pm. Continental menu. Bar 11 am-midnight. A la carte entrees: bkfst $3.50-$5.75, lunch $3-$16.75, dinner $6.75-$52.75. Child's menu. Specializes in Greek & Italian dishes, prime rib. Salad bar. Parking. Outdoor dining. Family-owned. Cr cds: A, C, DS, ER, MC, V.
[D]

Evergreen

(C-5) *See also Central City, Denver, Golden, Idaho Springs*

Pop 9,216 **Elev** 7,040 ft
Area code 303 **Zip** 80439

Information Evergreen Area Chamber of Commerce, 29029 Upper Bear

Creek Rd #202, PO Box 97; 303/674-3412

Web www.evergreenchamber.org

What to See and Do

Hiwan Homestead Museum. Restored 17-rm log lodge (1880); Native American artifacts, changing exhibits. Tours (Tues-Sun; closed hols). 4208 S Timbervale Dr. Phone 303/674-6262. **FREE**

International Bell Museum. More than 5,000 bells of widely varying size and age, many historic, artistic, or unusual. (Memorial Day-Labor Day, Tues-Sun) 30213 Upper Bear Creek Rd, off CO 74. Phone 303/674-3422. ¢¢

Special Events

Rodeo Weekend. Rodeo, parade. Phone 303/298-0220. Father's Day wkend.

Mountain Rendezvous. At Hiwan Homestead Museum (see). Craft and trapping demonstrations by mountain men; food, entertainment, old-fashioned games. Phone 303/674-6262. First Sat Aug.

B&B/Small Inn

★★★ **HIGHLAND HAVEN CREEK-SIDE INN.** *4395 Independence Trl (80439). 303/674-3577; fax 303/674-9088; toll-free 800/459-2406. www.highlandhaven.com.* 16 rms, 9 with shower only, 1-2 story, 6 suites, 6 kit. cottages. No A/C. S, D $95-$275; suites $150-$270; kit. cottages $130-$220; under 12 free; wkly rates. TV; cable (premium), VCR avail. Complimentary full bkfst. Restaurant nearby. Ck-out 11 am, ck-in 3 pm. Massage. Health club privileges. Some in-rm whirlpools; microwaves avail. Some fireplaces, balconies. On Bear Creek. Cr cds: A, D, DS, MC, V.
⬧ 🗷 🛇

Fairplay

(C-4) *See also Breckenridge, Buena Vista*

Settled 1859 **Pop** 610 **Elev** 9,920 ft
Area code 719 **Zip** 80440

Information Town Clerk, 400 Front St, PO Box 267; 719/836-2622

What to See and Do

Monument to Prunes, a Burro. In memory of a faithful burro named Prunes who packed supplies to every mine in Fairplay for more than 60 yrs. Front St. Phone 719/836-2622.

Pike National Forest. (see COLORADO SPRINGS) Camping. A Ranger District office is located at jct of US 285 and CO 9. (Daily) Phone 719/836-2031. **FREE**

South Park City Museum. Restoration of mining town incl 42 original buildings, 60,000 artifacts (ca 1860-1900); exhibits on trading, mining, social aspects of era. (Mid-May-mid-Oct, daily; rest of yr, by appt) 100 4th St. Phone 719/836-2387. ¢¢

Special Events

World's Championship Pack Burro Race. Commemorating the burros who packed supplies for the miners; 28-mi course uphill to Mosquito Pass and return. Last full wkend July.

South Park Historical Foundation, Inc. 100 4th St. More than 30 historic buildings are incl in this painstaking restoration of 19th-century boomtown Colorado. Phone 719/836-2387. Mid-May-mid-Oct.

Florissant Fossil Beds National Monument

(D-5) *See also Colorado Springs, Cripple Creek, Manitou Springs*

(22 mi W of Manitou Springs on US 24)

Florissant Fossil Beds National Monument consists of 6,000 acres once partially covered by a prehistoric lake. Thirty-five million years ago, ash and mud flows from volcanoes in the area buried a forest of redwoods, filling the lake and fossilizing its living organisms. Insects, seeds, and leaves of the Eocene Epoch are preserved in perfect detail as well as remarkable samples of standing petrified sequoia stumps. On the grounds are nature trails, picnic areas, and a restored 19th-century homestead. Guided tours are available. The visitor center is two miles south on Teller County Road 1 (daily; closed January 1, Thanksgiving, December 25). Contact the Superintendent, PO Box 185, Florissant 80816; phone 719/748-3253. Per family ¢¢; Per person ¢

Fort Collins

(A-5) See also Greeley, Loveland

Settled 1864 **Pop** 118,652 **Elev** 5,003 ft **Area code** 970

Information Fort Collins Convention & Visitors Bureau, 3745 E Prospect Rd, Suite 200; 970/491-3388

Web www.ftcollins.com

What to See and Do

Colorado State University. (1870) 24,500 students. Land-grant institution with an 833-acre campus. Pingree Park at 9,500 ft, adj to Rocky Mtn National Park, is the summer campus for natural resource science education and forestry. Main entrance at W Laurel and Howes Sts, W of College Ave. Phone 970/491-1101.

Discovery Center Science Museum. Hands-on science and technology museum features more than 70 educational exhibits. (Sun afternoons; closed hols) 703 E Prospect Rd. Phone 970/472-3990. ¢¢

Fort Collins Museum. Exhibits incl a model of the city's namesake, the army post Fort Collins; fine collection of Folsom points and Native American beadwork; display of historic household, farm, and business items; three historic cabins; changing exhibits. (Tues-Sun; closed hols) 200 Mathews St. Phone 970/221-6738. **FREE**

Industrial tour. Anheuser-Busch Brewery. Tour of the brewery that produces millions of barrels of Budweiser and other beers annually, incl exhibits on the history of the company, a look at the brewing facilities, early beer advertising, and the famous Clydesdale horses. (June-Sept, daily; Oct-May, Mon and Thurs-Sun) 2351 Busch Dr (I-25 exit 271). Phone 970/490-4691. **FREE**

Lincoln Center. Incl theater for the performing arts, concert hall, sculpture garden, art gallery, and display areas with changing exhibits. (Daily) 417 W Magnolia. Phone 970/221-6730. **FREE**

Lory State Park. Approx 2,500 acres. Nearby is Horsetooth Reservoir. Waterskiing, boating (ramps, rentals); nature trails, hiking, stables, picnicking. (Daily) 9 mi NW in Bellvue. Phone 970/493-1623. ¢¢

Scenic circle drives. Eleven colorful drives, from 50 to 200 mi, incl trip through beautiful Poudre Canyon and Cameron Pass (10,285 ft) in Roosevelt National Forest (see ESTES PARK). Inquire at Fort Collins Convention & Visitors Bureau.

Motels/Motor Lodges

★★ **BEST WESTERN KIVA INN.** *1638 E Mulberry St (80524). 970/484-2444; fax 970/221-0967; toll-free 888/299-5482. www.bestwestern.com.* 63 rms, 1-2 story. S, D $89-$105; each addl $5; under 17 free; higher rates special events. Crib free. TV; cable (premium). Heated pool; whirlpool. Complimentary continental bkfst. Complimentary coffee in rms. Restaurant adj 7 am-midnight. Ckout 11 am. Coin lndry. Business servs avail. In-rm modem link. Exercise equipt; sauna. Sundries. Refrigerators, microwaves. Some private patios. Cr cds: A, D, DS, MC, V.
D 🏃 ⊠ 🐾 SC ⊠

★★ **BEST WESTERN UNIVERSITY INN.** *914 S College Ave (80524). 970/484-1984; fax 970/484-1987; res 800/780-7234. www.bestwestern.com.* 74 rms, 2 story. May-Sept: S, D $65-$114; suites $95-$155; under 12 free. Crib free. Pet accepted; $10/night. TV; cable (premium). Heated pool. Complimentary continental bkfst, coffee in rms. Restaurant nearby. Ckout 11 am. Coin lndry. Business servs avail. Exercise equipt. In-rm modem link. Cr cds: A, D, DS, MC, V.
D 🐾 ⊠ ⊠ 🐾 🏃

★★ **HOLIDAY INN.** *3836 E Mulberry St (80524). 970/484-4660; fax 970/484-2326; res 800/465-4329. www.holiday-inn.com.* 197 rms, 2-4 story. Mid-May-mid-Sept: S, D $99-$109; each addl $10; under 18 free; higher rates: graduation, special events; lower rates rest of yr. Crib free. Pet accepted. TV; cable (premium), VCR avail. Indoor pool; wading pool, whirlpool. Restaurant 6 am-2 pm, 5-10 pm. Rm serv. Bar 4 pm-2 am; Sun to 10 pm. Coffee in rms. Ck-out noon. Coin lndry. Meeting rms. Business servs avail. In-rm modem link. Gift shop. Exercise equipt; sauna. Rec rm. Game rm. Sun deck. Holidome. Golf, tennis nearby. Some balconies. Cr cds: A, C, D, DS, MC, V.

Hotel

★ ★ ★ **MARRIOTT FORT COLLINS.** *350 E Horsetooth Rd (80525). 970/226-5200; fax 970/282-0561; res 800/548-2635. www.marriott.com.* 230 rms, 6 story. S, D $69-$179; suites $159; under 18 free. Pet accepted; $10/day. TV; cable (premium); VCR avail. Heated indoor/outdoor pool; whirlpool. Restaurant 6 am-2 pm, 5-9 pm. Rm serv. Bar 4:30 pm-1 am. Coffee in rms. Ck-out noon. Coin lndry. Meeting rms. Business center. In-rm modem link. Coin lndry. Concierge. Gift shop. Valet serv. X-country ski 15 mi. Exercise equipt. Refrigerators avail. Luxury level. Cr cds: A, D, DS, JCB, MC, V.

B&B/Small Inn

★ ★ **PORTER HOUSE B & B INN.** *530 Main St, Windsor (80550). 970/686-5793; fax 970/686-7046; toll-free 888/686-5793. www.bbonline.com/ co/porterhouse.* 4 rms, 2 with shower only. D $95-$155; each addl $15; golf plans. Children over 12 only. TV; cable (premium). Whirlpool. Complimentary full bkfst. Restaurant nearby. Ck-out 11 am, ck-in 4-6 pm. Meeting rm. Business servs avail. In-rm modem link. Luggage handling. Street parking. Airport transportation. Microwaves avail. Golf privileges. Picnic tables, grills. Built in 1898. Totally nonsmoking. Cr cds: A, D, DS, MC, V.

Fort Morgan

(B-6) *See also Sterling*

Pop 11,034 **Elev** 4,330 ft
Area code 970 **Zip** 80701
Information Fort Morgan Area Chamber of Commerce, 300 Main St, PO Box 971; 970/867-6702 or 800/354-8660
Web www.fortmorganchamber.com

What to See and Do

Fort Morgan Museum. Permanent and changing exhibits depicting history of northeast Colorado. Pamphlet for self-guided walking tour of historic downtown. (Mon-Sat) 414 Main St. Phone 970/867-6331. **FREE**

Jackson Lake State Park. Swimming, waterskiing, fishing, boating (rentals, ramps); picnicking (shelters), concession, groceries, camping, wildlife watching. Standard fees. (Daily) I-76 W to CO 39, 7¼ mi N to County Y5, then 2½ mi W to County 3. Phone 970/645-2551. ¢¢

Special Events

Glenn Miller Festival. Big band music. Third wkend June. Phone 970/867-6702.

Rodeo. 10 mi E in Brush. World's largest amateur rodeo. Wkend early July.

Festival in the Park. Arts, crafts, parade, pancake bkfst. Third wkend July. Phone 970/867-3808.

Motels/Motor Lodges

★ ★ **BEST WESTERN PARK TERRACE INN.** *725 Main (80701). 970/867-8256; fax 970/867-8257; res 800/780-7234. www.bestwestern.com.* 24 rms, 2 story. Mid-May-Sept: S, D $54-$75; special events (2-day min); lower rates rest of yr. Crib $3. Pet accepted; $10 deposit. TV; cable (premium). Heated pool; whirlpool, poolside serv avail. Coffee in rms. Restaurant adj 6 am-9 pm; summer hrs vary. Ck-out 11 am. In-rm modem link. Picnic table. Some refrigerators, microwaves avail. Cr cds: A, C, D, DS, MC, V.

★ **CENTRAL MOTEL.** *201 W Platte Ave (80701). 970/867-2401.* 19 rms. May-Sept: S, D $39-$74; each addl $5; suites from $59.95; under 10 free; lower rates rest of yr. Pet accepted, some restrictions. TV; cable (premium). Complimentary coffee. Restaurant nearby. Ck-out 11 am. Refrigerators, microwaves. Grill Cr cds: A, D, Discover, MC, V.

Georgetown

(C-4) *See also Central City, Dillon, Golden, Idaho Springs, Winter Park*

Founded 1859 **Pop** 1,088 **Elev** 8,512 ft **Area code** 303 **Zip** 80444
Information Town of Georgetown Visitor Information, PO Box 426; 303/569-2555

What to See and Do

Georgetown Loop Historic Mining and Railroad Park. Park features mine, crushing mill, and reconstructed mine buildings. Also here is the reconstructed Georgetown Loop Railroad that carries visitors on a scenic 6½-mi round-trip, which incl the reconstructed Devil's Gate Viaduct. This railroad was used in the late 1800s for shipping of ore and it was hailed as an engineering marvel. Crossing itself once, turning nearly 3½ circles and crossing four bridges, it connected Georgetown with Silver Plume during the boomtown era. A scheduled stop is made at the mine area for tours. The train leaves from Devil's Gate Viaduct (W on I-70 to exit 228, then ½ mi S on Old US 6) or Silver Plume (I-70, exit 226). Five or six round-trips/day. (Late May-early Oct, daily) Phone 303/670-1686 or 303/569-2403. ¢¢¢

Hamill House Museum. (1867) Early Gothic Revival house acquired by William A. Hamill, Colorado silver magnate and state senator; period furnishings. Partially restored carriage house and office. (Late May-Sept, daily; rest of yr, by appt) 305 Argentine St. Phone 303/569-2840. ¢¢

Hotel de Paris Museum. (1875) Internationally known hostelry built and operated by Louis Dupuy; elaborately decorated; original furnishings; courtyard. (Memorial Day-Labor Day, daily; rest of yr, Sat and Sun) 409 6th St. Phone 303/569-2311. ¢¢

Skiing. Loveland Ski Area. Quad, two triple, five double chairlifts, Pomalift, Mighty-mite; patrol, school, rentals, snowmaking; cafeteria, restaurants, bars, nursery. Sixty runs; longest run 1½ mi; vertical drop 1,680 ft. (Mid-Oct-mid-May, daily) 12 mi W on I-70, exit 216. ¢¢¢¢

B&B/Small Inn

★ **MAD CREEK BED & BREAKFAST.** *167 Park Ave., Empire (80438). 303/569-2003; toll-free 888/266-1498.* 3 rms, 2 share bath, 2 story. No A/C. No rm phones. S $55; D $85; each addl $10. Children over 10 yrs only. TV in main rm; VCR. Whirlpool. Complimentary full bkfst; afternoon refreshments. Ck-out 10:30 am, ck-in 4:30 pm. Downhill/x-country ski 20 mi. Victorian cottage built in 1881; stone fireplace. Totally nonsmoking. Cr cds: MC, V.

Guest Ranch

★★ **NORTH FORK.** *55395 US 285, Shawnee (80475). 303/838-9873; fax 303/838-1549; toll-free 800/843-7895.* 6 rms, 3 cottages. No A/C. No rm phones. AP, July-Aug, wkly: S $1,295; 6-12 yrs, $1,095; 2-6 yrs, $300-$895; lower rates May-June & early-mid-Sept. Closed rest of yr. Crib free. Heated pool; whirlpool. Free supervised child's activities (June-Aug); ages 1-6. Complimentary coffee in rms. Dining rm 7:30-8:30 am, 12:30 pm & 6:30 pm sittings. Box lunches. Picnics. Ck-out 10 am, ck-in 3 pm. Grocery, package store 6 mi. Meeting rms. Gift shop. Free guest lndry. Airport transportation. Horse stables. Hiking. Massage. Lawn games. Game rm. Fishing guides, clean and store. Refrigerator in cottages. Some porches. Picnic tables, grills. On South Platte River. No cr cds accepted.

Restaurant

★ **HAPPY COOKER.** *412 6th St (80444). 303/569-3166.* Hrs: 7 am-4 pm; Sat, Sun to 5 pm. Closed

Thanksgiving, Dec 25. Wine, beer. Bkfst, lunch $3.50-$7.95. Child's menu. Specializes in waffles, chili, cinnamon rolls. Outdoor dining. Homestyle atmosphere. Cr cds: A, D, DS, MC, V.

D

Glenwood Springs

(C-3) *See also Aspen, Snowmass Village*

Settled 1885 **Pop** 7,736 **Elev** 5,763 ft
Area code 970 **Zip** 81601
Information Chamber Resort Association, 1102 Grand Ave; 970/945-6589 or 888/4-GLENWOOD
Web www.glenscape.com

What to See and Do

Mineral pools and baths.

Glenwood Hot Springs Pool. Two outdoor pools, two blks long, are fed by warm mineral water and open yr-round; the recreational pool is 90°F, the thermal 104°F; also children's pool, miniature golf, water slide (summer). Lifeguards, athletic club, bathhouse, lodge, restaurant. (Daily) On US 6, 24 off I-70 exit 116. Phone 970/945-6571. ¢¢¢¢

River rafting, kayaking, hunting, fishing, camping, hiking, biking, golf, horseback riding, pack trips. For details and locations, inquire at the Chamber.

Scenic drives. Beautiful Hanging Lake and Bridal Veil Falls are a two-mi hike from the road. The marble quarries in the Crystal River Valley are the source of stones for the Lincoln Memorial in Washington, D.C., and the Tomb of the Unknown Soldier in Arlington National Cemetery. On CO 133, visit Redstone, Marble, and Maroon peaks. I-70 provides access to Lookout Mtn and Glenwood Canyon.

Skiing. Sunlight Mountain Resort. Triple, two double chairlifts; surface tow; patrol, school, rentals; cafeteria, bar, nursery. 67 runs; longest run 2½ mi; vertical drop 2,010 ft. Snowmo-

biling (Late Nov-early Apr, daily) Half-day rates. Also x-country touring center, 10 mi. 10 mi SW via County 117. Phone 970/945-7491 or 800/445-7931. ¢¢¢¢

White River National Forest. More than 2,500,000 acres in the heart of the Colorado Rocky Mtns. Recreation at 70 developed sites with boat ramps, picnicking, campgrounds (fee), and observation points; Holy Cross, Flat Tops, Eagles Nest, Maroon Bells-Snowmass, Raggeds, Collegiate Peaks, and Hunter-Frying Pan wildernesses (check with local ranger for information before entering wildernesses or any backcountry areas). Many streams and lakes with trout fishing; large deer and elk populations; Dillon, Green Mtn, and Ruedi reservoirs. Winter sports at 11 ski areas. N, W, E, and S of town. Contact the Supervisor's Office, Old Federal Building, 9th and Grand, PO Box 948. Phone 970/945-2521.

Special Events

Strawberry Days Festival. Arts and crafts fair, rodeo. Third wkend June.

Garfield County Fair & Rodeo. 27 mi W in Rifle. Late Aug. Phone 970/625-2514.

Motels/Motor Lodges

★ ★ **BEST WESTERN ANTLERS.** *171 W Sixth St (81601). 970/945-8535; fax 970/945-9388; toll-free 800/626-0609. www.bestwestern.com.* 100 units, 1-2 story, 13 suites. Mid-May-Sept: S, D $79-$229; Under 17 free; lower rates rest of yr. Crib $5. TV; cable (premium). Heated pool; whirlpool. Playground. Complimentary continental bkfst, coffee in rms. Restaurant nearby. Ck-out 11 am. Coin lndry. Business servs avail. In-rm modem link. Free RR station transportation. Downhill/x-country ski 10 mi. Balconies. Exercise equipt. Lawn games. Picnic tables. Cr cds: A, C, D, DS, ER, JCB, MC, V.

D ⊠ ≈ ⊠ 🏊 🕉

★ ★ **HAMPTON INN.** *401 W 1st St (81601). 970/947-9400; fax 970/947-9440; res 800/426-7866. www.hamptoninn.com.* 70 rms, 3 story. Late-May-Sept: S, D $84-$119; each addl $10; under 18 free; ski plan;

lower rates rest of yr. Crib free. TV; cable (premium). Complimentary continental bkfst, coffee in rms. Restaurant opp 7 am-10 pm. Meeting rms. Business servs avail. In-rm modem link. Ck-out 11 am. Coin lndry. Downhill/x-country ski 10 mi. Exercise equipt. Heated indoor pool; whirlpool. Refrigerators, microwaves. Cr cds: A, C, D, DS, JCB, MC, V.

⊠ ⊠ ⊠ ⊠ ⊠ ⊠ SC

★★ **HOT SPRINGS LODGE.** *415 E 6th St (81602). 970/945-6571; fax 970/947-2950; toll-free 800/537-7946. www.hotspringspool.com.* 107 units, 5 story. Mid-May-Sept: S, D $129-$162; each addl $7; ski plans; lower rates rest of yr. Crib avail. TV; cable (premium). Hot springs pool; whirlpool; wading pool; lifeguard; poolside serv; water slide. Complimentary continental bkfst, coffee in rms. Restaurant 7 am-8 pm; winter to 3 pm. Bar 2-10 pm. Ck-out noon. Coin lndry. Meeting rm. Business servs avail. In-rm modem link. Bellhops. Covered parking. Airport, RR station, bus depot transportation. Miniature golf. Downhill/x-country ski 10 mi. Exercise rm; steam rm, sauna. Massage. Some refrigerators. Private patios, balconies. Picnic tables. Cr cds: A, C, D, DS, MC, V.

⊠ ⊠ ⊠ ⊠ ⊠ ⊠

★ **RUSTY CANNON MOTEL.** *701 Taughenbaugh Blvd, Rifle (81650). 970/625-4004; fax 970/625-3604; res 866/625-4004. www.rustycannon motel.com.* 88 rms, 2 story. S, D $46-$54; each addl $5; package plans. Crib free. Pet accepted, some restrictions; $20 deposit. TV; cable (premium). Heated pool; sauna. Complimentary coffee in lobby, rms. Restaurant adj 6:30 am-10 pm. Ck-out 11 am. In-rm modem link. Coin lndry. Valet serv. Some refrigerators, microwaves. Golf, ski privileges. Horseback riding. Cr cds: A, C, D, DS, MC, V.

⊠ ⊠ ⊠ ⊠ ⊠ ⊠ ⊠

Resort

★★ **REDSTONE INN HISTORIC LANDMARK.** *82 Redstone Blvd, Carbondale (81623). 970/963-2526; fax 970/963-2527; toll-free 800/748-2524. www.redstoneinn.com.* 35 air-cooled rms, 3 story, 3 suites. No elvtr. June-mid-Oct: S, D $56-$128; suites $142-$188; package plans. Crib avail. Pet accepted. TV; cable (premium). Heated pool; whirlpool. Restaurant 8 am-9 pm. Bar. Ck-out 11 am. Meeting rms. Business servs avail. Massage. Tennis. X-country ski ¼ mi. Exercise equipt. Pool table. Fishing. Golf privileges. Horseback riding. Built in 1902; antiques, fireplace, clocktower. Cr cds: A, DS, MC, V.

⊠ ⊠ ⊠ ⊠ ⊠ ⊠ ⊠ ⊠ ⊠

B&B/Small Inn

★★★ **MOUNT SOPRIS INN.** *165 Mt Sopris Ranch Rd, Carbondale (81623). 970/963-2209; fax 970/963-8975; toll-free 800/437-8675. www.mtsoprisinn.com.* 13 rms, 2 story, 1 kit. unit. S, D $165; each addl $25; kit. unit $175. TV; cable (premium). VCR in lounge. Age 16 and over only. Heated pool; whirlpool. Complimentary full bkfst. Meeting rm. Business servs avail. In-rm modem link. Golf privileges, greens fee $80. Downhill/x-country ski 15 mi. Rec rm. Microwaves avail. Balconies. Western log complex of 3 bldgs on 14 acres. Totally nonsmoking. Cr cds: A, MC, V.

⊠ ⊠ ⊠ ⊠ ⊠ ⊠

Cottage Colony

★ **AVALANCHE RANCH.** *12863 Hwy 133, Redstone (81623). 970/963-2846; fax 970/963-3141; toll-free 877/963-9339. www.avalancheranch. com.* 12 kit. cabins. No A/C. No rm phones. Cabins (3-day min): D $99-$175; each addl $10; under 8 free. Crib free. Pet accepted, some restrictions; $10. TV in main rm, VCR avail. Playground. Complimentary coffee in rms. Ck-out 11 am, ck-in 3-5 pm. Business servs avail. Rec rm. Lawn games. Picnic tables, grills. Petting zoo. On Crystal River. Renovated 1913 farmhouse with antiques; rustic log cabins. Totally nonsmoking. Cr cds: DS, MC, V.

⊠ ⊠ ⊠ ⊠ ⊠

Restaurants

★ **CRYSTAL CLUB CAFE.** *467 Redstone Blvd, Redstone (81623). 970/963-9515.* Hrs: 11:30 am-10 pm. Closed Mon-Thurs, Nov-May. No A/C. Italian, Amer menu. Bar. Lunch $5.50-$8, dinner $5.50-$15.75. Child's menu. Specializes in chicken Marsala, soups, homeade bread. Parking. Outdoor dining. Country mountain decor; stone fireplace. Overlooks Crystal River. Cr cds: MC, V.

★★ **FLORINDO'S.** *721 Grand Ave (81601). 970/945-1245.* Hrs: 11:30 am-3 pm, 5-10:30 pm; Sat from 5 pm. Closed Sun; Easter, Memorial Day, Thanksgiving, Dec 25. Italian menu. Serv bar. Lunch $6.95-$7.95, dinner $10.95-$18.95. Child's menu. Specialties: salmon in parchment paper, veal chops. Art deco-style decor. Totally nonsmoking. Cr cds: MC, V.
D

★ **LOS DESPERADOS.** *0055 Mel Rey Rd (81601). 970/945-6878.* Hrs: 11:30 am-10 pm; Sun from 11 am; Mon from 5 pm. Closed some major hols. Res accepted. Mexican menu. Bar. Lunch $5.50-$9, dinner $6.50-$15.25. Child's menu. Specializes in enchiladas, fajitas. Parking. Outdoor dining. Mexican decor. Family-owned. Cr cds: A, C, DS, MC, V.
D ⬦

★★ **RIVER'S RESTAURANT.** *2525 S Grand Ave (81601). 970/928-8813. www.theriversrestaurant.com.* Hrs: 4-10 pm; Sun brunch 9 am-2 pm. Closed Dec 25. Res accepted. Bar. Dinner $15-$32.95. Sun brunch $5-$10. Child's menu. Specialties: smoked trout pate, elk medallions. Parking. Outdoor dining. View of Roaring Fork River. Cr cds: A, MC, V.
D

Golden

(C-5) *See also Central City, Denver, Evergreen, Idaho Springs*

Founded 1859 **Pop** 17,159

Information Greater Golden Chamber of Commerce, PO Box 1035, 80402; 303/279-3113 or 800/590-3113

What to See and Do

Astor House Hotel Museum. (1867) First stone hotel west of the Mississippi. Period furnishings. Self-guided and guided tours (res required) Victorian gift shop. (Tues-Sat; closed hols) 822 12th St. Phone 303/278-3557. ¢¢

Colorado Railroad Museum. An 1880-style railroad depot houses memorabilia and operating model railroad. More than 50 historic locomotives and cars from Colorado railroads displayed outside. (Daily; closed Thanksgiving, Dec 25) 17155 W 44th Ave (10th St E of Golden). Phone 303/279-4591 or 800/365-6263. ¢¢¢

Colorado School of Mines. (1874) 3,150 students. World-renowned institution devoted exclusively to education of mineral, energy, and material engineers and applied scientists. Tours of campus. Main entrance at 19th and Elm Sts. On campus are

Edgar Mine. Experimental mine operated by Colorado School of Mines, state government, and by manufacturers for equipt testing. (Mon-Fri, by appt) Located in Idaho Springs (see). Phone 303/567-2911. ¢¢¢

Geology Museum. Mineral and mining history exhibits. (Mon-Sat) 16th and Maple Sts. Phone 303/273-3815. **FREE** Off campus is

USGS National Earthquake Information Center. (Mon-Fri, by appt; closed hols) Illinois and 17th Sts. Phone 303/273-8500. **FREE**

Golden Gate Canyon State Park. On 12,000 acres. Nature and hiking trails, x-country skiing, picnicking, camping (dump station, electrical hook-ups). Visitor center. Panorama Point Overlook provides 100-mi view of the Continental Divide. Standard fees. (Daily) 2 mi N via CO 93, then left on Golden Gate Canyon Rd and continue W for 15 mi. Phone 303/582-3707. ¢¢

Golden Pioneer Museum. Houses more than 4,000 items dating from Golden's territorial capital days; incl household articles, clothing, furniture; mining, military, and ranching equipt; unique Native American doll collection. (Mon-Sat) Wheelchair accessible. 923 10th St. Phone 303/278-7151. **Donation**

Heritage Square. Old-fashioned shopping area with 1880s atmosphere. Incl more than 40 unique craft and gift shops, cafes, bumper cars, and alpine slide (rides, early

May-late Sept). (Daily; closed Jan 1, Thanksgiving, Dec 25) Jct CO 40, 93. Phone 303/279-2789.

Historic buildings.

Armory Building. Largest cobblestone building in the US. Approx 3,000 wagon loads of cobblestones were used in the construction. The rocks are from Clear Creek and the quartz from Golden Gate Canyon. 13th and Arapahoe Sts.

⭐ **Industrial tour. Coors Brewing Company.** Tours of Coors brewing and malting processes. Tours for hearing impaired and foreign guests may be arranged. Children welcome when accompanied by an adult. (Mon-Sat) 13th and Ford Sts. Phone 303/277-2337. **FREE**

Lariat Trail. Leads to Denver Mountain Parks. Lookout Mtn, 5 mi W off US 6, is the nearest peak. Phone 800/590-3113. At summit are

Buffalo Bill Memorial Museum and Grave. Comprehensive history of one of the American West's most famous characters, Buffalo Bill Cody. Picnic area. (May-Oct, daily; rest of yr, Tues-Sun; closed Dec 25) Phone 303/526-0747. ¢¢

Rocky Mountain Quilt Museum. Houses more than 250 quilts. Five exhibits each yr. (Tues-Sat) 1111 Washington Ave. Phone 303/277-0377. ¢¢

Special Event

Buffalo Bill Days. Parade, golf tournament. July.

Motels/Motor Lodges

★★ **LA QUINTA INN.** *3301 Youngfield Service Rd (80401). 303/279-5565; fax 303/279-5841; toll-free 800/687-6667. www.laquinta.com.* 129 rms, 3 story. S, D $79-$99; under 18 free. Crib free. Pet accepted. TV; cable (premium). Pool. Complimentary continental bkfst. Coffee in rms. Restaurant nearby. Ck-out noon. Coin lndry. Meeting rms. Business servs avail. In-rm modem link. Valet serv. Health club privileges. Cr cds: A, C, D, DS, MC, V.
🄳 �＂ ⛱ 🔀 🔥 SC

★★★ **TABLE MOUNTAIN INN.** *1310 Washington Ave (80401). 303/277-9898; fax 303/271-0298; res 303/277-9898. www.tablemountaininn.*

com. 32 rms, 2 story, 3 suites. S, D $87-$105; each addl $5; suites $130-$145; under 12 free; wkend rates. Crib free. TV; cable (premium), VCR avail. Complimentary coffee in rms. Restaurant (see TABLE MOUNTAIN INN). Rm serv. Bar from 11 am. Ck-out 11 am. Meeting rms. Business servs avail. In-rm modem link. Airport transportation. Health club privileges. Refrigerators; microwaves avail. Balconies. Southwestern decor. Cr cds: A, MC, V.
✈ 🌐 SC

Hotels

★★★ **MARRIOTT.** *1717 Denver W Blvd (80401). 303/279-9100; fax 303/271-0205; res 800/228-2800. www.marriott.com.* 307 rms, 6 story. June-Sept: S, D $71-$139; suites $275-$350; under 18 free; package plans; lower rates rest of yr. Crib free. TV; cable (premium). Complimentary coffee in rms. Restaurant 6 am-2 pm, 5-10 pm. Rm serv 5-2 am. Bar from 2 pm. Ck-out noon. Convention facilities. Business servs avail. In-rm modem link. Bellhops. Sundries. Gift shop. Coin lndry. Exercise equipt; sauna. Indoor/outdoor pool; whirlpool. Game rm. Bathrm phones; wet bar in suites; microwaves avail. Cr cds: A, C, D, DS, MC, V.
🄳 🌰 🔀 ⛱ 🏋 🔀 ♿ 🌐

★★★ **MARRIOTT DENVER WEST.** *1717 Denver West Blvd (80401). 303/279-9100; fax 303/271-0205. www.marriott.com.* 305 units, 6 story, 2 suites. S, D $134-$180. Crib free. Pet accepted; $10. TV; cable, VCR avail. Heated pool; whirlpool, poolside serv. Restaurant 6 am-10:30 pm. Complimentary coffee in rms, newspaper. Coin lndry. Meeting rms. Exercise equipt; sauna. Bellhops. Valet serv. Gift shop. Sundries. Cr cds: A, C, D, DS, JCB, MC, V.
🄳 🌐 SC 🌰 ⛱ 🏋

Restaurants

★★ **CHART HOUSE.** *25908 Genesee Trail Rd (80401). 303/526-9813.* Hrs: 5-10 pm; Sun 4:30-9 pm. Res accepted. Bar to 11 pm; wkends to midnight. Dinner $15-$26.95. Child's menu. Specializes in beef, seafood. Salad bar. Nautical decor.

View of mountains & city. Cr cds: A, D, DS, MC, V.

D

★ **CODY INN CONTINENTAL CUI-SINE.** *866 Lookout Mountain Rd (80401). 303/526-0232.* Hrs: 5-11 pm; Sun brunch 11 am-2 pm. Closed Mon; Dec 25. Res accepted. Continental menu. Bar. Dinner $14-$21. Sun brunch $9. Child's menu. Specializes in veal, duck, steak. Intimate atmosphere. Cr cds: MC, V.

D ➡

★★ **SIMMS LANDING.** *11911 W 6th Ave (80401). 303/237-0465. www. simmslanding.com.* Hrs: 11 am-10 pm; Fri, Sat to 11 pm; Sun brunch 9 am-2:30 pm. Closed Dec 25. Lunch $4.99-$8.99, dinner $7.99-$39.99. Buffet: lunch $7.99. Sun brunch $15.99. Child's menu. Specializes in prime rib, steak, fresh seafood. Valet parking. Outdoor dining. Panoramic view of Denver; nautical setting. Cr cds: A, DS, MC, V.

D SC ➡

★★ **TABLE MOUNTAIN INN.** *1310 Washington Ave (80401). 303/216-8020. www.tablemountaininn.com.* Hrs: 6:30 am-11 pm; Sat from 7 am; Sun from 8 am; Sun brunch to 2 pm. Res accepted. Southwestern menu. Bar to 11 pm. Bkfst $5-$7, lunch $6-$8.50, dinner $7.95-$18.95. Sun brunch $6-$9. Child's menu. Specialties: grilled Navajo flat bread, chicken tortilla soup, buffalo. Own baking. Outdoor dining. Southwestern decor. Cr cds: A, C, D, DS, ER, MC, V.

D ➡

Granby

(B-4) *See also Grand Lake, Kremmling, Winter Park*

Pop 1,525 **Elev** 7,939 ft
Area code 970 **Zip** 80446
Information Greater Granby Area Chamber of Commerce, PO Box 35; 970/887-2311 or 800/325-1661
Web www.rkymtnhi.com/granbycoc

What to See and Do

Arapaho National Recreation Area. Incl Shadow Mtn, Willow Creek, Monarch, Grand, and Granby lakes. Boating, fishing; hunting, camping (fee), picnicking, horseback riding. (Daily) 6 mi NE on US 34. Contact US Forest Service, PO Box 10. Phone 970/887-4100. ¢¢

Grand County Historical Association. Museum exhibits depict the history of skiing, ranching, and Rocky Mtn railroads; archaeological finds; reconstructed old buildings, wagons, and tools. (Memorial Day-Labor Day, Tues-Sat, Sun afternoons) 10 mi W via US 40 in Hot Sulphur Springs. Phone 970/725-3939.

Rocky Mountain National Park. (see). Entrance 15 mi N via US 34 at Grand Lake.

Skiing. SilverCreek Ski Area. Two triple, double chairlifts; Pomalift; patrol, school, rentals, snowmaking; concession, cafeteria, bar, nursery, day-lodge. Twenty-two runs; longest run 6,100 ft; vertical drop 1,000 ft. (Dec-mid-Apr) Snowboarding, sleigh rides. Health club. 3 mi SE on US 40. Phone 629/102-0800. ¢¢¢¢

Motel/Motor Lodge

★ **TRAIL RIDERS.** *215 E Agate Ave (80446). 970/887-3738.* 11 rms, 5 suites. S $35, D $45; suites $49-$65. Crib avail. Pet accepted, some restrictions. TV; cable (premium). Coffee in rms. Restaurant adj 11 am-10 pm. Ck-out 10 am. Free RR station transportation. Refrigerators, microwaves. Cr cds: A, DS, MC, V.

Resort

★★ **INN AT SILVERCREEK.** *62927 US 40, Silver Creek (80451). 970/887-2131; fax 970/887-4083; toll-free 800/927-4386. www.silvercreeklodging. com.* 342 rms, 3 story, 252 kits. No A/C. Feb-Mar: S, D $89; kit. units $119-$299; ski plan; higher rates late Dec; lower rates rest of yr. Crib free. Pet accepted; $12/day. TV; cable (premium). Pool; whirlpool. Bar 4-11 pm, Fri, Sat to 1 am. Ck-out 10 am, ck-in 4 pm. Coin lndry. Convention facilities. Shopping arcade. Lighted tennis. Downhill ski 1 mi. Ski

rentals. Fishing. Sleigh rides. Racquetball. Whitewater rafting. Mountain bikes. Hot-air balloon rides.
Exercise equipt; sauna. In-rm
whirlpools; many refrigerators, fireplaces. Private patios, balconies. Cr
cds: A, C, D, DS, MC, V.

Guest Ranches

★★★★ **C LAZY U RANCH.** *3640
CO 125 (80446). 970/887-3344; fax
970/887-3917. www.clazyu.com.* Much
of this ranch's pole-pine construction
was completed in 1946, but it began
as a 1919 dude ranch. A fantastic
place for families, the main lodge
and patio house are decorated with
Southwestern furnishings and
remain a destination for year-round
recreation: cross-country skiing,
snowshoeing, or a sleigh ride in winter; horseback riding, fly-fishing, or
square dancing in summer and fall. 3
rms in lodge, 41 one-to-five rm units
in cottages. No A/C. No rm phones.
AP (7-day min), June-Aug, wkly: S, D
$2,070-$3,680/person; ski plan;
lower rates early June, Sept, and mid-
Dec-Mar. Closed rest of yr. TV in
game rm; VCR avail (free movies).
Heated pool; whirlpool, poolside
serv. Playground. Free supervised
children's activities; ages 3-18. Complimentary coffee in rms. Dining rm
(guests only). Barbecues, outdoor
buffets. Bars 11-12:30 am. Ck-out 10
am, ck-in 3 pm. Free lndry facilities.
Meeting rms. Business servs avail.
Valet serv. Gift shop. Tennis, pro.
Paddle boats. Stocked lake. Downhill
ski 20 mi; x-country ski on site.
Sleighing, tubing, tobogganing, ice-
skating, winter horseback riding. Racquetball. Skeet, trap range. Trail
rides. Hayrides. Lawn games. Rec rm.
Entertainment. Exercise equipt;
sauna. Massage. Fishing guides;
cleaning and storage. Some fireplaces. Library. No cr cds accepted.

★★ **DROWSY WATER RANCH.**
*County Rd 219 (80446). 970/725-
3456; fax 970/725-3611; toll-free
800/845-2292. www.drowsywater.com.*
8 rms in lodge, 9 cottages. No A/C.
AP, June-mid-Sept, wkly: S $1,230; D
$1,150/person; each addl $1,000;
under 5, $520; 3-day rates Sept.
Closed rest of yr. Crib free. Heated
pool; whirlpool. Playground. Free
supervised child's activities (June-
Aug); ages 1-13. Family-style meals in
lodge; also trail bkfst, buffets, cookouts, picnicking. Ck-out 11 am, ck-in
2:30 pm. Coin lndry 7 mi. Meeting
rms. Business servs avail. Gift shop.
Free local RR station, bus depot
transportation. Soc dir. Lawn games.
Fishing, hunting guides. Riding, hiking trails. Hayrides. Rodeo events.
Staff show. Square dancing. Optional
white water rafting ($40/person),
pack ($35/person) trips. Some private
porches. No cr cds accepted.

Restaurant

★ **LONGBRANCH & SCHATZI'S
PIZZA.** *165 E Agate Ave (80446).
970/887-2209.* Hrs: 11 am-9 pm, Fri,
Sat to 9:30 pm; Sun 5-9 pm. Closed
Thanksgiving, Dec 25; also mid-Apr-
mid-May & mid-Oct-mid-Nov. Res
accepted. Eclectic menu. Bar. Lunch
$4.50-$7.50, dinner $5.50-$17.50.
Child's menu. Specializes in German
dishes. Own baking, pasta. Street
parking. Western atmosphere;
wagon-wheel lights, brick fireplace.
Totally nonsmoking. Cr cds: C, D,
DS, ER, MC, V.

Grand Junction

(C-1)

Settled 1881 **Pop** 41,986 **Elev** 4,597 ft
Area code 970

Information Visitor & Convention
Bureau, 740 Horizon Dr, 81506;
970/244-1480 or 800/962-2547

Web www.visitgrandjunction.com

What to See and Do

Colorado National Monument. (see).
12 mi SW on NY 64.

Cross Orchards Historic Farm. Operated 1896-1923 by owners of Red
Cross shoe company. Living history
farm with historically costumed
guides interprets the social and agricultural heritage of western Colorado. Restored buildings and equipt
on display; narrow gauge railroad
exhibit and country store. Demon-

strations, special events. (Tues-Sun) 3073 Patterson Rd. Phone 970/434-9814. ¢¢

Dinosaur Hill. Self-guided walking trail interprets quarry of paleontological excavations. (Daily) 5 mi W, 1½ mi S of Fruita on CO 340. **FREE**

⭐ **Grand Mesa National Forest.** This 346,221-acre alpine forest incl a flat-top, basalt-capped tableland at 10,500 ft. There are more than 300 alpine lakes and reservoirs, many with trout; boat rentals are avail. The mesa is also a big-game hunting area, with horses avail for rent. There are excellent areas for x-country skiing, snowmobiling, picnicking, and camping (fee at some campgrounds); there is also a lodge and housekeeping cabins. From the rim of Lands End, westernmost spot on Grand Mesa, there is a spectacular view of much of western Colorado. Also located within the forest is Powderhorn Ski Resort and the Crag Crest National Recreational Trail. Ranger District offices are located in Grand Junction and Collbran and for Uncompaghre Forest to the southwest as well. Approx 40 mi E via I-70 and CO 65. Contact the Forest Supervisor, 2250 US 50, Delta 81416. Phone 970/874-7691.

Museum of Western Colorado. Features exhibits on regional, social, and natural history of the Western Slope; collection of small weapons; wildlife exhibits. (Mon-Sat) Tours by appt. 248 S 4th St. Phone 970/242-0971. ¢

Rabbit Valley Trail Through Time. A 1 ½ mi self-guided walking trail through a paleontologically significant area. Fossilized flora and fauna from the Jurassic Age. No pets allowed. (Daily) 30 mi W on I-70, 2 mi from UT border. Phone 970/241-9210. **FREE**

Riggs Hill. A ¾ mi, self-guided walking trail in an area where bones of the Brachiosaurus dinosaur were discovered in 1900. (Daily) Jct of S Broadway and

Meadows Way. Phone 970/241-9210. **FREE**

River Rafting. On the Colorado, Green, and Yampa rivers. Two-day to five-day whitewater raft trips. Contact Adventure Bound, Inc., 2392 H Rd, 81505. Phone 800/423-4668. ¢¢¢¢

Skiing. Powderhorn Ski Resort. Quad, two double chairlifts; surface lift; patrol, school, rentals, snowmaking; snack bar, restaurants, bar, day-lodge. Twenty-nine runs; longest run two mi; vertical drop 1,650 ft. (Mid-Dec-mid-Apr, daily) X-country trails (7 mi), snowboarding, snowmobiling, sleigh rides. Half-day rates. Summer activities incl fishing, rafting trips, biking, horseback riding, western cookouts. 20 mi E via I-70, exit 49. E on CO 65. Phone 970/268-5700 or 800/241-6997. ¢¢¢¢

State parks.

Colorado River. Swimming, fishing; picnicking, camping. Grocery nearby. Standard fees. 15 mi E, off I-70 exit 47. Phone 970/464-0548 or 970/434-3388.

Highline Lake. Swimming, water-skiing, fishing, boat ramps, shelters; waterfowl hunting, picnicking, camping. Standard fees. 18 mi NW on I-70 to Loma, then 6 mi N on CO 139. Phone 970/858-7208.

Special Events

Colorado Stampede. Rodeo. Third wk June.

Colorado Mountain Winefest. Wine tastings, outdoor events. Late Sept. Phone 970/256-1531.

Colorado River

Motels/Motor Lodges

★★ **BEST WESTERN SANDMAN.** *708 Horizon Dr (81506). 970/243-4150; fax 970/243-1828; toll-free 800/780-7234. www.bestwestern.com.* 80 rms, 2 story. Mid-May-mid-Oct: S $48-$56; D $52-$60; each addl $4; under 12 free; lower rates rest of yr. Crib free. TV; cable. Heated pool; whirlpool. Complimentary coffee in lobby, rms. Restaurant adj open 24 hrs. Ck-out 11 am. Coin lndry. Business servs avail. In-rm modem link. Free airport transportation. Refrigerators. Cr cds: A, C, D, DS, MC, V.

⬛ 🏊 🛤 🐾 SC

★★ **BUDGET HOST INN.** *721 Horizon Dr (81506). 970/243-6050; fax 970/243-0310; res 800/283-4678. www.budgethost.com.* 55 rms, 2 story. Mid-May-mid-Oct: S, D $45-$96; each addl $5; under 12 free; lower rates rest of yr. Crib free. Pet accepted, some restrictions. TV; cable (premium). Heated pool. Playground. Complimentary coffee in lobby, rms. Restaurant adj 6 am-10 pm. Ck-out 11 am. Coin lndry. Cr cds: A, C, D, DS, MC, V.

⬛ 🐾 🏊 🛤 🐾

★★ **GRAND VISTA HOTEL.** *2790 Crossroads Blvd (81506). 970/241-8411; fax 970/241-1077; res 800/800-7796. www.grandvistahotel.com.* 158 rms, 6 story. S $75; D $85; each addl $10; suites $85-$105; under 18 free; wkend rates. Pet accepted. TV; cable (premium). Indoor pool; whirlpool. Complimentary coffee. Restaurant 6 am-2 pm, 5-10 pm. Rm serv. Bar 11-1 am, Sun to midnight. Ck-out noon. Meeting rms. Business servs avail. In-rm modem link. Gift shop. Free airport, RR station, bus depot transportation. Health club privileges. Cr cds: A, C, D, DS, MC, V.

⬛ 🐾 🏊 ✈ 🛤 🐾 SC

★★ **HOLIDAY INN.** *755 Horizon Dr (81506). 970/243-6790; toll-free 888/489-9796. www.holiday-inn.com.* 292 rms, 2 story. S, D $69-$79; each addl $6; suites $83-$89; under 20 free. Crib free. Pet accepted. TV; cable (premium), VCR avail. 2 pools, 1 indoor; whirlpool. Coffee in rms. Restaurant 6 am-10 pm. Rm serv. Bar 5 pm-1:30 am, Sun to midnight; entertainment. Ck-out 11 am. Coin lndry. Meeting rms. Business servs avail. In-rm modem link. Bellhops. Free airport, RR station, bus depot transportation. Putting green. Exercise equipt; sauna. Holidome. Game rm. Cr cds: A, C, D, DS, ER, JCB, MC, V.

⬛ 🐾 🏊 🎾 🛤 🐾 SC

★★ **RAMADA.** *752 Horizon Dr (81506). 970/243-5150; fax 970/242-3692; res 800/272-6232. www.ramadagj.com.* 100 rms, 2 story. S, D $54-$69; each addl $5; under 17 free. Crib free. TV; cable (premium), VCR avail (movies). Heated pool; whirlpool. Restaurant 6 am-10 pm. Coffee in rms. Ck-out noon. Coin lndry. Meeting rms. Business servs avail. In-rm modem link. Bellhops. Free airport, RR station, bus depot transportation. Private patios, balconies. Microwaves avail. Cr cds: A, C, D, DS, ER, JCB, MC, V.

⬛ 🐱 🏊 🛤 🐾 SC

★ **WEST GATE INN.** *2210 Hwy 6 & 50 (81505). 970/241-3020; fax 970/243-4516; toll-free 800/453-9253. www.gj.net/wgi.* 100 rms, 2 story. June-Oct: S $54; D $64; each addl $6; under 11 free; lower rates rest of yr. Crib free. Pet accepted. TV; cable (premium). Heated pool. Restaurant 6 am-10 pm. Bar 3 pm-2 am. Ck-out 11 am. Coin lndry. Meeting rms. Business servs avail. Cr cds: A, C, D, DS, MC, V.

⬛ 🐾 🏊 🛤 🐾

Hotel

★★ **ADAM'S MARK.** *743 Horizon Dr (81506). 970/241-8888; fax 970/242-7266; res 888/444-2326. www.adamsmark.com.* 264 units, 8 story. May-Oct: S $89-$139; D $99-$149; each addl $10; suites $119-$295; family, wkend rates; golf, ski plans; lower rates rest of yr. Crib free. Pet accepted; $50. TV; cable (premium). Heated pool; whirlpool, poolside serv. Playground. Restaurant 6 am-11 pm. Bar 11-2 am. Ck-out noon. Convention facilities. Business servs avail. Gift shop. Free airport, RR station, bus depot transportation. Lighted tennis. Exercise equipt. Game rm. Lawn games. Bathrm phones. Luxury level. Cr cds: A, D, DS, MC, V.

⬛ 🐾 🐱 💺 🎾 🏊 🎾 ✈ 🛤 🐾

Restaurants

★ ★ **FAR EAST RESTAURANT.** *1530 North Ave US 6 (81501).* 970/242-8131. Hrs: 11 am-9:30 pm; Fri, Sat to 10 pm. Closed major hols. Res accepted. Chinese, Amer menu. Bar. Lunch $3.95-$9.95, dinner $4.45-$9.95. Child's menu. Specializes in Szechwan, Cantonese dishes. Fountain. Family-owned. Cr cds: A, C, D, DS, ER, MC, V.

[D] ⊟

★ **STARVIN' ARVIN'S.** *752 Horizon Dr (81506).* 970/241-0430. Hrs: 6 am-10 pm. Closed Thanksgiving, Dec 25. Bkfst $1.99-$4.95, lunch $2.99-$4.99, dinner $3.99-$9.99. Child's menu. Specializes in chicken-fried steak, beef. Own pastries. Casual atmosphere; antique photographs. Cr cds: A, C, D, DS, ER, MC, V.

[D] [SC] ⊟

★ ★ **WINERY RESTAURANT.** *642 Main St (81501).* 970/242-4100. www. wineryrestaurant.com. Hrs: 5-10 pm. Closed Dec 25. Res accepted. Bar from 4:30 pm. Dinner $7.50-$26.90. Specializes in steak, seafood. Salad bar. Restored 1890s building. Totally nonsmoking. Cr cds: A, D, DS, MC, V.

[D]

Grand Lake

(B-4) *See also Estes Park, Granby*

Pop 447 **Elev** 8,380 ft **Area code** 970
Zip 80447
Information Grand Lake Area Chamber of Commerce, PO Box 57; 970/627-3402 or 800/531-1019
Web www.grandlakechamber.com

What to See and Do

Hiking, fishing, boating, horseback riding. Boat rentals avail from Gala Marina. Horseback riding can be scheduled with Winding River Resort. Other outdoor activities abound in summer at Grand Lake, Shadow Mtn Lake, and Lake Granby.

National Park Service lectures, field trips. (Summer) **FREE**

Rocky Mountain National Park. (see). Just N on US 34.

Snowmobiling and cross-country skiing. Back areas of Arapaho National Forest (see DILLON), portion of Trail Ridge Rd, and local trails around Grand Lake, Shadow Mtn, and Granby Lakes. (Nov-May) Inquire locally for details.

Special Events

Winter Carnival. Ice-skating, snowmobiling, snow sculptures, ice-fishing derby, ice-golf tournament. Last wkend Jan and first wkend Feb.

Rocky Mountain Repertory Theatre. Community Building, Town Sq. Three musicals change nightly, Mon-Sat. Res advised. For schedule contact PO Box 1682 or phone Chamber of Commerce or 970/627-3421 (during event). Late June-late Aug.

Buffalo Barbecue & Western Week Celebration. Parade, food; Spirit Lake Mountain Man rendezvous. Third wk July.

Lipton Cup Sailing Regatta. Early Aug.

Motels/Motor Lodges

★ **BIGHORN LODGE BEST VALUE INN.** *613 Grand Ave (80447).* 970/627-8101; fax 970/627-3771; toll-free 888/315-2378. www.rkymtnhi. com/bighorn. 20 rms, 2 story. Jan-May, mid-Oct-mid-Dec: S, D $55-$80; each addl $10; higher rates special events. Crib $5. TV; cable. Whirlpool. Restaurant nearby. Ck-out 10 am. Business servs avail. Downhill ski 18 mi; x-country ski 1 mi. Some refrigerators, microwaves. Cr cds: A, D, DS, MC, V.

[D] ⊱ ⊠ 🐾

★ ★ **WESTERN RIVIERA.** *419 Garfield St (80447).* 970/627-3580; fax 970/627-3320. www.westernriv.com. 25 rms, 2 story, 6 kit. cabins. Mid-June-mid-Sept: S, D $65-$95; each addl $5; family units $95; cabins (3-day min) $100; lower rates rest of yr. Crib $5. TV; cable. Whirlpool. Complimentary coffee in lobby. Restaurant adj. Ck-out 10 am. Business servs avail. Downhill ski 18 mi; x-country ski 1 mi. Some refrigerators. Fireplace in lobby. On lakefront; scenic view. Cr cds: A, C, D, DS, MC, V.

🄳 ⚹ 🛄 🐟 🖼 🔥

Resorts

★★ **DRIFTWOOD LODGE.** *12255 US 34 (80447). 970/627-3654; toll-free 800/766-1123. www.rkymtnhi. com/driftwood.* 17 units, 9 kits. No A/C. Mid-May-Sept, mid-Dec-early Jan: S $40-$65; D $60-$80; each addl $5; 2-rm units $65-$86; lower rates rest of yr. Crib free. TV; cable. Heated pool; wading pool, whirlpool, sauna. Playground. Ck-out 10 am. Business servs avail. In-rm modem link. RR station, bus depot transportation. Downhill ski 16 mi; x-country ski 4 mi. Snowmobiling. Lawn games. Some refrigerators. Picnic tables, grills. Overlooks lake. Cr cds: DS, MC, V.

⚹ 🛄 🐟 🛩 🖼 🔥

★ **GRAND LAKE LODGE.** *15500 US 34 (80447). 970/627-3967; fax 970/627-9495. www.grandlakelodge. com.* 56 units, 1-2 story, 24 kit. units, 32 cottages. No rm phones. June-mid-Sept: S, D, kit. units, cottages $70-$145. Closed rest of yr. Crib $10. Heated pool; whirlpool. Playground. Dining rm 7:30-10 am, 11:30 am-2:30 pm, 5:30-9 pm; Sun 9:30 am-1:30 pm. Bar 11 am-midnight; entertainment Wed-Sun. Ck-out 10 am. Coin lndry. Meeting rms. Gift shop. Game rm. Lawn games. Picnic tables, grills. Overlooks Grand Lake and Shadow Mtn Reservoir; surrounded by national park. Cr cds: A, DS, MC, V.

🐟 🔥

B&B/Small Inn

★★ **SPIRIT MOUNTAIN RANCH.** *3863 County Rd 41 (80447). 970/887-3551. www.fcinet.com/spirit.* 4 air-cooled rms, 2 story. No rm phones. S, D $130; each addl $30. Children over 10 yrs only. Whirlpool. Complimentary full bkfst; afternoon refreshments. Ck-out 11 am, ck-in 4 pm. Business servs avail. Luggage handling. Downhill ski 15 mi; x-country ski on site. Game rm. Lawn games. Bicycles. Picnic tables, grills. Totally nonsmoking. Cr cds: DS, MC, V.

🄳 🐟 🖼 🔥

Restaurants

★★★ **CAROLINE'S CUISINE.** *9921 US 34 #27 (80447). 970/627-9404. www.sodaspringsranch.com.* Hrs: 5-9 pm; Fri, Sat to 9:30 pm. Closed 2 wks Apr, 2 wks Nov. Res accepted. French, Amer menu. Bar. Wine list. Dinner $13.95-$21.95. Child's menu. Specialties: steak Diane, escargot Provençale. Pianist Sat. Parking. Outdoor dining. 3 dining rms; European decor. Art gallery upstairs. Cr cds: A, DS, MC, V.

🄳 🍽

★ **E. G.'S GARDEN GRILL.** *1000 Grand Ave (80447). 970/627-8404.* Hrs: 11 am-10 pm; hrs vary by season. Closed Dec 25. Res accepted. No A/C. Bar. Lunch $5.95-$11.95, dinner $6.95-$21. Child's menu. Specialties: mustard catfish, baby back ribs, shrimp enchiladas. Street parking. Outdoor dining. Totally nonsmoking. Cr cds: A, MC, V.

🄳

Great Sand Dunes National Monument

(F-4) See also Alamosa

(35 mi E and N of Alamosa via US 160, CO 150)

The Great Sand Dunes, tallest in North America, lie along the base of the Sangre de Cristo Mountains, on the floor of the San Luis Valley. The dunes, some of which reach a height of over 700 feet, are trapped here by the mountains, providing endless changes in color and mood. Warm and inviting by day, yet eerie and forbidding by moonlight, they have inspired strange legends of wild, web-footed horses and mysteriously disappearing wagon trains and herds of sheep. During the late spring and early summer a stream flows along the edge of the dunes. A self-guided nature trail and picnic areas are nearby. A campground is open all year (fee). The visitor center is open daily; closed winter hols. Interpretive programs are offered Memorial Day-

Labor Day. Contact the Superintendent, 11500 CO 150, Mosca 81146; 719/378-2312. ¢¢

What to See and Do

Great Sand Dunes Four-Wheel Drive Tour. A 12-mi, two-hr round-trip tour through Great Sand Dunes National Monument; spectacular scenery; stops for short hikes on dunes. (May-Oct, daily) Five-person minimum. For information contact Great Sand Dunes Oasis, Mosca 81146. Phone 719/378-2222. ¢¢¢¢

Greeley

(A-5) *See also Fort Collins, Loveland*

Founded 1870 **Pop** 76,930 **Elev** 4,664 ft **Area code** 970 **Zip** 80631

Information Convention & Visitors Bureau, 902 7th Ave; 970/352-3566 or 800/449-3866

Web www.greeleycvb.com

What to See and Do

Centennial Village. Restored buildings show the growth of Greeley and Weld County from 1860 to 1920; period furnishings; tours, lectures, special events. (Apr-Oct, Tues-Sun) N 14th Ave and A St. Phone 970/350-9220 or 970/350-9224. ¢¢

Fort Vasquez. Reconstructed adobe fur trading post of the 1830s contains exhibits of Colorado's fur trading and trapping industries, the Plains Indians, and archaeology of the fort. (Wed-Sat, Sun afternoons; Memorial Day-Labor Day, Sun afternoons) 18 mi S on US 85 near Platteville. Phone 970/785-2832. **FREE**

Meeker Home. (1870) The house of city founder Nathan Meeker contains many of his belongings, as well as other historical mementos. (Apr-Oct, Tues-Sat; closed hols) 1324 9th Ave. Phone 970/350-9220. ¢¢

Municipal Museum. County history archives, pioneer life exhibits; library; tours. (Tues-Sat; closed hols) 919 7th St. Phone 970/350-9220. **FREE**

University of Northern Colorado. (1889) 10,500 students. 11th Ave between 20th and 24th Sts, 16th to 20th Sts between 8th and 11th Aves. Phone 970/351-1890 or 970/351-1889. On the 236-acre campus are

James A. Michener Library. Colorado's largest university library. Collection incl materials owned by Michener while writing the book *Centennial.* Phone 970/351-1890.

Mariani Art Gallery. Features faculty, student, and special exhibitions. Multipurpose University Center. Phone 970/351-4890. **FREE**

Special Events

Independence Stampede Greeley Rodeo. Late June-July 4. Phone 970/356-7787.

Weld County Fair. First wk Aug. Phone 970/356-4000.

Motel/Motor Lodge

★★ **BEST WESTERN INN.** *701 8th St (80631). 970/353-8444; fax 970/353-4269; toll-free 800/780-7234. www.bestwestern.com.* 148 rms, 3 story. S, D $78-$138; each addl $10; suites $125-$155; under 18 free. Crib free. Pet accepted; $50. TV; cable (premium). Heated indoor pool. Complimentary continental bkfst, coffee in rms. Restaurant 6 am-10 pm. Rm serv. Bar 11 am-midnight. Ck-out 11 am. Meeting rms. Business servs avail. In-rm modem link. Valet serv. Free health club privileges. Refrigerators, microwaves. Some balconies. Cr cds: A, C, D, DS, MC, V.
D ⊷ ≍ ⊠ 🐾 SC

Gunnison

(D-3) *See also Crested Butte*

Settled 1874 **Pop** 5,409 **Elev** 7,703 ft

Information Gunnison Country Chamber of Commerce, 500 E Tomichi Ave, Box 36; 970/641-1501

Web www.gunnison-co.com

What to See and Do

Alpine Tunnel. Completed by Denver, South Park & Pacific Railroad in 1881 and abandoned in 1910, this railroad tunnel, 11,523 ft above sea level, is

1,771 ft long. (July-Oct) 36 mi NE via US 50, County 765, 3 mi E of Pitkin on dirt road.

Cumberland Pass. (12,200 ft) Gravel road linking towns of Pitkin and Tincup. (July-Oct) 36 mi NE via US 50, County 765.

Curecanti National Recreation Area. Named for the Ute Chief Curicata, who roamed and hunted in this territory. This area along the Gunnison River drainage incl Blue Mesa, Morrow Point, and Crystal reservoirs. Elk Creek Marinas, Inc., offers boat tours on Morrow Point Lake (Memorial Day-Labor Day, daily); phone 970/641-0402 for res. Blue Mesa Lake has waterskiing, windsurfing, fishing, boating (ramps, rentals); picnicking, camping (fee). The Elk Creek Visitor Center is 16 mi W (mid-Apr-Oct, daily). 5 mi W on US 50. Contact Superintendent, 102 Elk Creek. Phone 970/641-0406 or 970/641-2337. **FREE**

Gunnison National Forest. Forest contains 27 peaks more than 12,000 ft high within 1,662,839 acres of magnificent mountain scenery. Activities incl fishing; hiking, picnicking, camping. A four-wheeling and a winter sports area is nearby (see CRESTED BUTTE). Also within the forest are West Elk Wilderness and portions of the Maroon Bells-Snowmass, Collegiate Peaks, La Garita, and Raggeds wilderness areas. N, E, and S on US 50. A Ranger District office is located in Gunnison. Phone 970/641-0471.

Gunnison Pioneer Museum. County and area history; pioneer items, narrow-gauge railroad, 1905 school house. (Memorial Day-Labor Day, Sun afternoons) E edge of town on US 50. Phone 970/641-4530. ¢¢

Old mining town of Tincup. Inquire locally about other mining towns; "20-Circle Tour" ghost town maps provided free at the Visitor Center, 500 E Tomichi Ave (US 50). 40 mi NE on County Rd 765. Phone 970/641-1501.

Taylor Park Reservoir. Road runs through 20-mi canyon of Taylor River. Fishing, boating; hunting, camping (fee). (Memorial Day-Sept, daily) 10 mi N on CO 135 to Almont, then 22 mi NE on County Rd 742 (CO 59) in Gunnison

National Forest. Phone 970/641-2922. **FREE**

Western State College of Colorado. (1901) 2,500 students. In the college library is the **Jensen Western Colorado Room** containing a collection of books and materials relating to western Colorado history and culture. Escalante Dr between N Adams and N Colorado Sts. Phone 970/943-2103.

Special Event

Cattlemen's Days, Rodeo, and County Fair. Third full wkend July.

Motels/Motor Lodges

★★ **BEST WESTERN TOMICHI VILLAGE INN.** *41883 E US Hwy 50 (81230). 970/641-1131; fax 970/641-9554; res 800/780-7234. www.best western.com/tomichivillageinn.* 49 rms, 2 story. June-Sept: S, D $80-$130; each addl $5; higher rates special events; lower rates rest of yr. Crib $5. TV; cable (premium). Heated indoor pool; whirlpool. Complimentary continental bkfst, coffee in rms. Restaurant 6:30-9:30 am, 5-9 pm. Ck-out 11 am. Coin lndry. Meeting rms. In-rm modem link. Free airport transportation. Exercise equipt. Refrigerators, balconies. Corral facilities in hunting season. Cr cds: A, C, D, DS, MC, V.
🖼 🏋 ✈ ⊠ 🐾 SC

★★ **HOLIDAY INN EXPRESS.** *400 E Tomichi Ave Hwy 50 (81230). 970/641-1288; fax 970/641-1332; toll-free 800/486-6476. www.holiday-inn. com.* 54 rms, 1-2 story. June-Sept: S, D $90-$110; each addl $5; under 19 free; ski plans; lower rates rest of yr. Crib free. TV; cable (premium). Heated indoor pool; whirlpool. Complimentary continental bkfst. Restaurant nearby. Ck-out noon. Meeting rm. Business servs avail. In-rm modem link. Valet serv. Free airport, bus depot transportation. Exercise equipt. Cr cds: A, C, D, DS, MC, V.
🖼 🏋 ⊠ 🐾 SC

★★ **RAMADA.** *1011 W Rio Grande Ave (81230). 970/641-2804; fax 970/641-1420; res 800/272-6232. www.ramada.com.* 36 rms, 2 story. Late-May-Oct: S, D $59-$99; each addl $6; under 19 free; lower rates rest of yr. Crib free. Pet accepted;

$10. TV; cable. Indoor pool; whirl-pool. Complimentary continental bkfst. Coffee in rms. Refrigerators avail. Ck-out 11 am. Cr cds: A, D, DS, ER, JCB, MC, V.

⊡ 🏊 📶 🔥 SC 🐾

★ **SUPER 8 MOTEL.** *411 E Tomichi Ave (81230). 970/641-3068; fax 970/641-1332; toll-free 800/800-8000. www.super8.com.* 52 rms, 2 story. Mid-June-Sept: S, D $71.88-$78.88; each addl $5; ski plan. Crib $5. TV; cable (premium). Complimentary continental bkfst. Restaurant adj 6 am-9 pm. Ck-out 11 am. In-rm modem link. Free airport transportation. Horseback riding. Skiing nearby. Cr cds: A, C, D, DS, MC, V.

🏋 🏊 📶 🔥 SC

★★ **WATER WHEEL INN.** *37478 Hwy 50 (81230). 970/641-1650; toll-free 800/642-1650.* 52 rms, 2 story. Mid-June-Sep: S, D $55-$85; each addl $5; suites $100; lower rates rest of yr. TV; cable (premium). Whirl-pools. Complimentary continental bkfst. Restaurant nearby. Ck-out 11 am. Meeting rm. Business servs avail. In-rm modem link. Free airport, bus depot transportation. Exercise equipt. 18-hole golf adj. Balconies. Cr cds: A, D, DS, MC, V.

🏋 🏌 ✈ 📶 🔥 SC

B&B/Small Inn

★★ **MARY LAWRENCE INN.** *601 N Taylor St (81230). 970/641-3343; fax 970/641-6719; toll-free 888/331-6863. www.commerceteam.com/mary.html.* 7 rms, 2 story. No A/C. No rm phones. S, D $$85-$135; each addl $15; ski plan. TV in suites. Whirlpool. Complimentary full bkfst. Ck-out 11 am, ck-in 4-6 pm. Some fireplaces. Free airport transportation. Italianate inn built 1885 was women's boarding house. Many antiques. Totally non-smoking. Cr cds: A, MC, V.

✈ 📶 🔥

Guest Ranches

★★ **HARMEL'S RANCH RESORT.** *6748 County Rd 742, Almont (81210). 970/641-1740; fax 970/641-1944; toll-free 800/235-3402.* 8 lodge rms, 19 kit. cottages, 11 suites. No A/C. No rm phones. Mid-June-Aug, AP: S

$119-$150; D $170-$299; each addl $60; lower rates mid-May-mid-June, Sept, Oct. Closed rest of yr. Crib free. TV in rec rm. Heated pool; whirl-pool. Playground. Free supervised child's activities. Complimentary full bkfst, coffee in rms. Dining rm 7:30-9:30 am, noon-1 pm, 6-9 pm. Box lunches, cookouts. Bar 4-10 pm. Ck-out 10 am, ck-in 2 pm. Grocery. Coin lndry. Meeting rms. Tackle store. Gift shop. Sauna. Massage. Free airport, bus depot transportation. Whitewater rafting. Trap shooting. Horseback riding. Hayrides. Square dancing. Bicycles (rentals). Lawn games. Rec rm. Game rm. Refrigerators. Picnic tables. 300 acres on Taylor River. Cr cds: A, MC, V.

⊡ 🐎 🏌 🏊 📶 🔥

★★ **POWDERHORN GUEST RANCH.** *1525 County Rd 27, Powderhorn (81243). 970/641-0220; fax 970/642-1399.* 14 air-cooled cabins (1-2-bedrm). AP, June-late Sept, wkly: cabins $1,295/person under 12 $995/wk. Closed rest of yr. Crib free. Heated pool; whirlpool. Playground, children's fishing pond. Complimentary coffee in rms. Box lunches. Snack bar. Ck-out noon, ck-in 2 pm. Coin lndry. Free airport transportation. Horse trail rides. Hiking. Rafting. Lawn games. Rec rm. Refrigerators. Picnic tables, grills. Playground. Family-oriented ranch in remote area along Cebolla Creek. Cr cds: A, D, DS, MC, V.

🐎 🏌 🏊 🔥

★ **WAUNITA HOT SPRINGS RANCH.** *8007 County Rd 887 (81230). 970/641-1266; fax 970/641-0650; toll-free 888/232-9337. www. waunita.com.* 18 rms, 1-2 story. AP, wkly, June-mid-Sept: S $1,400; D $700-$1,300; lower group rates mid-Dec-Mar. Closed rest of yr. Crib free. TV in lobby; VCR avail (movies). Hot spring-fed pool; whirlpool. Supervised children's activities. Playground. Complimentary full bkfst. Dining rm 7:30-9 am; lunch (1 sitting) 12:30 pm, dinner (1 sitting) 6:30 pm. Box lunches. Ck-out noon, ck-in 2-5 pm. Coin lndry. Massage. Steam rm. Free local airport, bus depot transportation. Square dancing. Game rm. Hayrides, jeep trips, rafting. Overnight camping. Petting zoo. Fishing/hunting guides; fish cleaning and storage. Cr cds: A, DS, MC, V.

Restaurant

★★ **TROUGH.** *US 50 (81230). 970/641-3724.* Hrs: 5:30-10 pm; Fri & Sat to 10:30 pm. Closed Easter, Thanksgiving, Dec 25. No A/C. Bar 4 pm-2 am. Dinner $10.95-$31.95. Child's menu. Specializes in steak, prime rib, fresh seafood. Totally nonsmoking. Cr cds: A, C, D, DS, MC, V.
[D]

Idaho Springs

(C-4) *See also Central City, Denver, Dillon, Georgetown, Golden*

Settled 1859 **Pop** 1,889 **Elev** 7,524 ft
Area code 303 **Zip** 80452
Information Visitors Center, PO Box 97; 303/567-4382 or 800/685-7785

What to See and Do

Argo Town, USA. Reproduction of Western mining town; incl shops and **Argo Gold Mill.** This mill was first operated in 1913 to support mines intersected by the "mighty Argo" Tunnel; today it offers guided tours that unfold the history of the mill and the story of mining. **Clear Creek Mining and Milling Museum** illustrates the role of mining in the past. **Double Eagle Gold Mine** is an authentic and truly representative gold mine with direct access from the Argo Gold Mill. (Daily) 2350 Riverside Dr. Phone 303/567-2421. ¢¢¢

Colorado School of Mines-Edgar Mine. Experimental mine operated by students, also by government for training and by manufacturers for equipment testing; one-hr guided tour hrly (mid-June-mid-Aug, Tues-Sat; rest of yr, by appt). Colorado Ave and 8th St, ½ mi N on 8th St. Contact Mining Department, Colorado School of Mines, Golden 80401. Phone 303/567-2911. ¢

Jackson Monument. George J. Jackson made the first major gold discovery in Colorado here on Jan 1, 1859.

Hwy 103 in front of Clear Creek Secondary School. Phone 800/685-7785. **FREE**

Phoenix Gold Mine. The only working gold mine in the state that is open to the public. (Daily; closed Dec 25) Approx 2½ mi SW via Stanley Rd to Trail Creek Rd. Phone 303/567-0422 or 800/685-7785. ¢¢¢

St. Mary's Glacier. Park car approx one mi NW of Alice, then proceed ½ mi on foot. 12 mi NW via I-70, Fall River Rd to Alice, a ghost town.

Special Event

Gold Rush Days. Parades, picnic, foot races, mining contests, arts and crafts. Aug.

B&B/Small Inn

★★★ **ST. MARY'S GLACIER BED AND BREAKFAST.** *336 Crest Dr (80452). 303/567-4084.* 7 rms, 3 story, 1 suite. No A/C. No elvtr. S, D $89-$139; suites $159; package plan. Crib free. Pet accepted, some restrictions. TV in common rm; VCR avail (movies). Complimentary full bkfst. Ck-out 11 am, ck-in 4-7 pm. In-rm modem link. Game rm. Some in-rm whirlpools. Some balconies. Totally nonsmoking. Cr cds: A, DS, MC, V.

Keystone (C-4)

(see Dillon)

Kremmling

(B-4) *See also Granby*

Pop 1,578 **Elev** 7,360 ft
Area code 970 **Zip** 80459

What to See and Do

Green Mountain Reservoir. Waterskiing, fishing, boating (ramps); picnicking, groceries, camping (fee). (Daily) 16 mi S on CO 9. Contact Dillon Ranger District, Box 620, Silverthorne 80498. Phone 970/468-5400.

Guest Ranch

★★ **LATIGO RANCH.** *201 County Rd 1911 (80459). 970/724-9008; toll-free 800/227-9655. www.latigotrails. com.* 10 air-cooled cottages. AP, June-Aug, wkly: cottages $1,600/person; family rates; lower rates Sept-mid-Nov, mid-Dec-Mar. Closed rest of yr. Crib free. Heated pool; whirlpool. Playground. Free supervised child's activities (June-Sept); ages 3-14. Complimentary coffee in rms. Dining rm 7:30-9 am, 12:30-1:30 pm, 6:30-8 pm. Box lunches. Picnics. Entertainment nightly. Ck-out 4 pm, ck-in 2 pm. Coin lndry. Meeting rms. Business servs avail. Gift shop. Airport, RR station transportation. X-country ski on site. Tobogganing. Horse stables. Hiking. Lawn games. Soc dir. Rec rm. Game rm. Fishing/hunting guides, clean and store. Refrigerators. Porches. Picnic tables. On lake. No cr cds accepted.

La Junta (E-7)

Settled 1875 **Pop** 7,568 **Elev** 4,066 ft
Area code 719 **Zip** 81050
Information Chamber of Commerce, 110 Santa Fe Ave; 719/384-7411

What to See and Do

Bent's Old Fort National Historic Site. The fort has been reconstructed as accurately as possible to its appearance in 1845-1846; the furnishings are antique and reproductions. The original structure, located on the Mountain Branch of the Santa Fe Trail, was built as a privately owned frontier trading post (ca 1833). The old fort played a central role in the "opening of the west." For 16 yrs, until its abandonment in 1849, the fort was an important frontier hub of American trade and served as a rendezvous for trappers, Native Americans, and Hispanic traders on the Santa Fe Trail. It also served as the center of Army operations to protect the traders using the Santa Fe Trail. Self-guided tour. Summer "living history" programs. (Daily; closed Jan 1, Thanksgiving,

Dec 25) 8 mi NE on CO 109 and 194 E. Phone 719/383-5010. ¢

★ **Koshare Indian Kiva Museum.** Housed in a domed building, a copy of ceremonial kivas in the Southwest, the museum features Native American baskets, arrowheads, paintings, and carvings, as well as paintings by Southwestern artists. (Daily; closed hols) 115 W 18th St. Phone 719/384-4411. ¢

Otero Museum. History of Otero County and surrounding areas. Santa Fe Railroad history; artifacts. (June-Sept, Mon-Sat) 218 Anderson. Phone 719/384-7500. **FREE**

Special Events

Koshare Indian Dances. In Kiva Museum. Dances by nationally famous Boy Scout troop. Sat eves. Late June-early Aug. Phone 719/384-4411.

Arkansas Valley Fair and Exposition. Rocky Ford. Fairgrounds, grandstand. Colorado's oldest continuous fair. Highlight is "watermelon day," when every visitor receives free watermelon. Phone 719/254-7483. One wk late Aug.

Early Settlers Day. Fiddlers contest, crafts, parade. Sat after Labor Day.

Koshare Winter Night Ceremonial. In Kiva Museum. Nightly performances. Wk of Dec 25 and first wkend Jan. Phone 719/384-4411.

Motels/Motor Lodges

★★ **BEST WESTERN BENT FORT'S INN.** *10950 US 50, Las Animas (81054). 719/456-0011; fax 719/456-2550; res 800/780-7234. www.bestwestern.com.* 38 rms, 2 story. S $49; D $59; each addl $6; under 18 free. Pet accepted, some restrictions. TV; cable. Pool. Restaurant 6 am-8 pm. Rm serv. Bar 5-10 pm. Comlimentary full bkfst, coffee in rms. Ck-out 11 am. Meeting rms. Business servs avail. In-rm modem link. Free airport, bus depot transportation. Cr cds: A, C, D, DS, MC, V.

★★ **QUALITY INN.** *1325 E Third St (81050). 719/384-2571; fax 719/384-5655; res 800/228-5151.* 76 rms, 2 story. S $44-$58; D $52-$70; each addl $4; suites $79; under 18 free. Crib $5. Pet accepted, some restrictions. TV; cable (premium), VCR avail (movies). Heated indoor/outdoor pool; whirlpool, poolside serv. Complimentary bkfst, coffee in rms. Restaurant 6 am-9 pm. Rm serv. Bar. Meeting rms. Business servs avail. Free airport, RR station transportation. Exercise equipt. Refrigerator in suites. Cr cds: A, C, D, DS, ER, JCB, MC, V.

D ⬛ 🏊 🍴 🔖 ♿

Restaurant

★ **CHIARAMONTE'S.** *27696 Harris Rd (81050). 719/384-8909.* Hrs: 11 am-2 pm, 5-9 pm; Sat from 5 pm; Sun to 2 pm. Closed major hols. Res accepted. Continental menu. Bar. Lunch $4.35-$7.95, dinner $6.75-$14.75. Specializes in steak, seafood. Own soups. Cr cds: DS, MC, V.

Lake City (E-3)

Pop 375 **Elev** 8,671 ft **Area code** 970 **Zip** 81235

Information Chamber of Commerce, PO Box 430; 970/944-2527 or 800/569-1874

Web www.hinsdale-county.com

What to See and Do

Alpine Triangle Recreation Area. Approx 250,000 acres administered by Bureau of Land Management and the US Forest Service for primitive and motorized recreation, mining, grazing, and watershed protection. The area has five peaks that are more than 14,000 ft high; excellent backpacking and fishing; habitat for deer, elk, mountain sheep, black bear. Many historical mining tramways, stamp mills, and ghost towns are scattered throughout the area. Mill Creek Campground (14 mi SW) has a picnic area and 22 tent and trailer sites with water (Memorial Day-Oct, daily, weather permitting; fee for camping). Lake San Cristobal (three mi south of town), the second-largest natural lake in the state, was formed by the Slumgullion earthflow 700 yrs ago. Williams Creek (ten mi southwest) has picnic areas and 21 tent and trailer sites with water (Memorial Day-Oct, daily; fee for camping).

Southwest of town is the site where Alferd Packer murdered and mutilated five prospectors in the winter of 1873-1874. South and west of town; access by the Alpine Loop National Backcountry Byway (four-wheel drive necessary in some places). Phone 970/641-0471.

Hinsdale County Historical Society Tours. Weekly guided walking tours, about two hrs long, to historic homes, the local cemetery, and "ghostly" sites. (Mid-June-Labor Day; call for specific dates and times). 130 Silver St, PO Box 303. Phone 970/944-2050. ¢¢

Hinsdale County Museum. Small museum with exhibits on the trial of notorious cannibal Alferd Packer and the area's silver-mining history, plus a furnished 1870s-era Victorian home. (Daily mid-June-Labor Day; varied hrs rest of yr) 130 Silver St at 2nd St. Phone 970/944-2050. ¢

Special Events

Alferd Packer Barbeque Cookoff. Late May.

Ghost Town Narration Tours. Aug.

Motel/Motor Lodge

★ ★ **MELODY C. CRYSTAL LODGE.** *2175 US 149S (81235). 970/944-2201; fax 970/944-2503; toll-free 800/984-1234. www.crystallodge.net.* 19 rms, 1-2 story, 5 suites, 4 cottages. No A/C. No rm phones. Memorial Day-Sept (2-day min): S, D $55; each addl $10; suites, cottages $75-$120; under 2 free; ski rates; lower rates rest of yr. Crib free. Pet accepted, some restrictions; $25. TV; cable (premium) VCR avail. Whirlpool. Restaurant. Ck-out 10 am. Meeting rms. Business servs avail. X-country ski 1 mi. Many refrigerators. Surrounded by San Juan Mountains. Totally nonsmoking. Cr cds: MC, V.

⬛ 🔖 🔖 ♿

Lakewood

(C-5) *See also Denver, Englewood, Golden*

Pop 144,126 **Elev** 5,450 ft **Area code** 303

Information West Chamber Serving Jefferson County, PO Box 280748, 80228-0748; 303/233-5555

What to See and Do

Bear Creek Lake Park. Approx 2,600 acres. Waterskiing school, fishing, boating (ten hp limit, rentals, marina); hiking, bicycle trails, picnicking, camping (no electricity). Archery. View of downtown Denver from Mt Carbon. (Daily; closed Jan 1, Thanksgiving, Dec 25) ¼ mi E of CO 470 on Morrison Rd. Phone 303/697-6159. ¢

Crown Hill Park. This 168-acre nature preserve incl Crown Hill Lake and a wildlife pond. Fishing; hiking, bicycle, bridle trails. (Daily) W 26th Ave at Kipling St (CO 391). Phone 303/271-5925. **FREE**

Lakewood's Heritage Center. Nature, art, and historical exhibits in 127-acre park. Turn-of-the-century farm; one-rm schoolhouse; vintage farm machinery; Barn Gallery with permanent and changing exhibits, interpretive displays. Lectures, workshops; visitor center. (Tues-Sun) 797 S Wadsworth Blvd (CO 121), just S of Alameda Blvd (CO 26). Phone 303/987-7850. ¢¢

Motels/Motor Lodges

★★ **COMFORT INN.** 3440 S Vance St (80227). 303/989-5500; fax 303/989-2981; toll-free 800/228-5150. www.comfortdenver.com. 123 rms, 2 story, 4 suites. S $70; D $78; each addl $10; suites $110; under 18 free; wkly, wkend rates. Crib free. Pet accepted; $50 refundable. TV; cable (premium). Heated pool; whirlpool. Complimentary continental bkfst, coffee in rms. Restaurant opp open 24 hrs. Ck-out noon. Coin lndry. Meeting rm. Business servs avail. In-rm modem link. Valet serv. Airport transportation. Exercise equipt. Health club privileges. Some refrigerators. Microwaves avail. Cr cds: A, C, D, DS, ER, MC, V.

D ▧ ⬤ ◢ ➚ ➗ ❄ SC

★★★ **FOUR POINTS BY SHERATON.** 137 Union Blvd (80226). 303/969-9900; fax 303/989-9847; res 888/625-5144. www.starwood.com/fourpoints. 170 rms, 6 story. S $79-

$99; D $89-$109; each addl $10; under 18 free; wkend rates. Crib free. TV; cable (premium), VCR avail. Heated pool; whirlpool. Complimentary full bkfst. Complimentary coffee in rms. Restaurant 6 am-2 pm, 4:30-10 pm. Bar. Ck-out noon. Meeting rms. Business servs avail. In-rm modem link. Exercise equipt; sauna. Health club privileges. Some refrigerators. Cr cds: A, C, D, DS, ER, JCB, MC, V.

D ⬤ ◢ ➚ ➗ ➗ ❄ ➗ SC

★★ **HAMPTON INN.** 3605 S Wadsworth Blvd (80235). 303/989-6900; fax 303/985-4730; toll-free 800/426-7866. www.hamptoninn.com. 150 rms, 4 story. S, D $59; each addl $10-$13; under 18 free. Crib avail. TV; cable (premium). Heated pool. Complimentary continental bkfst, coffee in rms. Restaurant adj 11-1 am. Ck-out noon. Coin lndry. Meeting rms. Business servs avail. In-rm modem link. Valet serv. Exercise equipt. Some refrigerators; microwaves avail. Cr cds: A, C, D, DS, ER, JCB, MC, V.

D ➚ ➗ ➗ ➗ ➗

★★ **HOLIDAY INN.** 7390 W Hampden Ave (80227). 303/980-9200; fax 303/980-6423; toll-free 800/465-4329. www.holiday-inn.com. 190 rms, 6 story. S, D $105; each addl $10; suites $150; under 19 free. Crib free. Pet accepted; $50 deposit. TV; cable (premium). Heated pool; whirlpool. Complimentary coffee in rms. Restaurant 6-11 am, 5-10 pm. Rm serv. Bar 4 pm-midnight. Ck-out noon. Coin lndry. Meeting rms. Business servs avail. In-rm modem link. Bellhops. Valet serv. Gift shop. Exercise equipt; sauna. Health club privileges. Some refrigerators. Cr cds: A, C, D, DS, JCB, MC, V.

D ➚ ◢ ➚ ➗ ➗ SC

Hotel

★★★ **SHERATON DENVER WEST.** 360 Union Blvd (80228). 303/987-2000; fax 303/969-0263; res 800/325-3535. www.sheraton.com. 242 rms, 12 story. S, D $140-$175; each addl $15; under 18 free; package plans; wkend rates. Crib free. TV; cable (premium), VCR avail. Indoor pool; whirlpool. Coffee in rms. Restaurant 6:30 am-

9:30 pm. Bar 11-2 am; Sun to midnight. Ck-out 1 pm. Convention facilities. Business center. In-rm modem link. Concierge. Valet serv. Gift shop. Barber, beauty shop. Exercise rm; sauna, steam rm. Massage. Some refrigerators. Luxury level. Cr cds: A, C, D, DS, MC, V.

D ⇔ 🕺 ⤴ 🐾 🚶

Restaurants

★★★ **240 UNION.** *240 Union (80228). 303/989-3562. www.240 union.com.* Hrs: 11 am-10 pm; Fri to 10:30 pm; Sat 5-10:30 pm; Sun 5-9 pm. Closed major hols. Res accepted. Continental menu. Bar. Lunch $9-$12, dinner $9-$24. Child's menu. Specializes in seafood, chicken, lamb. Parking. Outdoor dining. Cr cds: A, C, D, DS, ER, MC, V.

D ⤴

★ **DARDANO'S.** *11968 W Jewell Ave (80228). 303/988-1991. www.dardanos restaurant.com.* Hrs: 5-9 pm; Fri to 10 pm; Sat 4-10 pm; Sun from 4 pm. Closed Mon; Thanksgiving, Dec 24, 25. Res accepted. Italian, Amer menu. Bar. Dinner $6-$16. Child's menu. Specialty: prime rib. Own pasta. Italian decor. Family-owned. Cr cds: D, DS, MC, V.

D SC ⤴

★★★ **THE FORT.** *19192 CO 8, Morrison (80465). 303/697-4771. www.thefort.com.* Hrs: 5:30-10 pm; Sat from 5 pm; Sun 4-9 pm. Closed Dec 24 and 25. Res accepted. Southwestern menu. Bar. Dinner $14.95-$39.95. Child's menu. Specializes in game. Outdoor dining. Multiple dining areas in adobe building patterned after Bent's Fort. Southwestern artifacts; kiva fireplaces. View of Denver. Cr cds: A, C, D, DS, ER, MC, V.

D

★★ **GRADY'S AMERICAN GRILL.** *5140 S Wadsworth Blvd (80123). 303/973-5140.* Hrs: 11 am-10 pm; Fri, Sat to 11 pm; Sun to 10 pm. Closed Thanksgiving, Dec 25. Res accepted. Bar. Lunch, dinner $5.50-$16.95. Child's menu. Specialties: prime rib, mesquite-grilled salmon. Parking. Outdoor dining. Three dining areas on two levels. Cr cds: A, C, D, DS, ER, MC, V.

D ⤴

Unrated Dining Spot

CASA BONITA OF DENVER. *6715 W Colfax Ave (80214). 303/232-5115. www.casabonitadenver.com.* Hrs: 11 am-9:30 pm; Fri, Sat to 10 pm. Closed Thanksgiving, Dec 25. Mexican, Amer menu. Lunch, dinner $6.49-$8.89. Child's menu. Entertainment: musicians, divers, gunfights, magician, puppet show, dancing monkeys in costume. Parking. Carnival atmosphere, Mexican decor; 30-ft waterfall. Cr cds: A, C, D, DS, ER, MC, V.

D ⤴

Lamar (E-8)

Pop 8,869 **Elev** 3,622 ft
Area code 719 **Zip** 81052
Information Chamber of Commerce, 109A E Beech St; 719/336-4379

What to See and Do

Big Timbers Museum. Named for the giant cottonwoods on the banks of the Arkansas River. Museum with newspapers, art, drawings, artifacts of area history. (Daily, afternoons; closed hols) 7517 US 50. Phone 719/336-2472. **FREE**

Motels/Motor Lodges

★★ **BEST WESTERN COW PALACE INN.** *1301 N Main St (81052). 719/336-7753; fax 719/336-9598; toll-free 800/678-0344. www.bestwestern.com.* 95 rms, 2 story. June-Aug: S $84-$94; D $89-$99; each addl $5; lower rates rest of yr. Crib free. Pet accepted. TV; cable (premium), VCR avail. Indoor pool; whirlpool, poolside serv. Complimentary bkfst buffet. Coffee in rms. Restaurant 5 am-10 pm. Rm serv. Bar 11-2 am; Sun to midnight. Ck-out 11 am. Meeting rms. Business servs avail. Gift shop. Barber, beauty shop. Free airport, RR station, bus depot transportation. Golf privileges, greens fee $4, driving range. Health club privileges. Refrigerators, microwaves. Enclosed courtyard; tropical gardens. Cr cds: A, C, D, DS, MC, V.

D 🐾 🕺 ⇔ ✈ ⤴ 🐾 SC

★ **BLUE SPRUCE.** *1801 S Main St (81052). 719/336-7454; fax 719/336-4729.* 30 rms. S $30; D $36-$38; each addl $4. Crib free. Pet accepted. TV; cable (premium). Pool. Complimentary continental bkfst. Restaurant nearby. Ck-out 11 am. Free airport, RR station, bus depot transportation. Cr cds: A, D, DS, MC, V.

Leadville

(C-4) *See also Buena Vista, Dillon, Vail*

Settled 1860 **Pop** 2,821 **Elev** 10,430 ft
Area code 719 **Zip** 80461

Information Greater Leadville Area Chamber of Commerce, 809 Harrison Ave, PO Box 861; 719/486-3900 or 888/264-5344

Web www.leadvilleusa.com

What to See and Do

Earth Runs Silver. Video presentation featuring Leadville's legendary mining camp with music and narration. (Daily; closed Jan 1, Thanksgiving, Dec 25) 809 Harrison Ave. Phone 719/486-3900 or 800/933-9301. ¢¢

Healy House-Dexter Cabin. The restored Healy House, built in 1878, contains many fine Victorian-era furnishings. Dexter Cabin, built by early mining millionaire James V. Dexter, appears on the outside to be an ordinary two-rm miner's cabin; built as a place to entertain wealthy gentlemen, the cabin's interior is surprisingly luxurious. (Memorial Day-Labor Day, daily) 912 Harrison Ave. Phone 719/486-0487. ¢¢

Heritage Museum and Gallery. Diorama and displays depict local history; scale-model replica of Ice Palace, Victorian costumes, memorabilia of mining days. Changing exhibits of American art. (Mid-May-Oct, daily) 9th St and Harrison Ave. Phone 719/486-1878. ¢¢

Leadville, Colorado & Southern Railroad Train Tour. Departs from old depot at 326 E 7th St for 23-mi round-trip scenic ride following the headwaters of the Arkansas River through the Rocky Mtns. (Memorial Day-Oct, daily) Phone 719/486-3936. ¢¢¢¢

Leadville National Fish Hatchery. The original hatchery building constructed in 1889 is still in use. Approx 45 tons of brook, lake, brown, and cutthroat trout are produced here annually. Hiking and ski-touring trails are nearby. (Daily) 7 mi SW via US 24, CO 300. Phone 719/486-0189. **FREE**

The Matchless Mine. When H.A.W. Tabor died in 1899, his last words to his wife, Baby Doe, were "Hold on to the Matchless," which had produced as much as $100,000 a month in its bonanza days. Faithful to his wish and ever hopeful, the once fabulously rich Baby Doe lived on in poverty in the little cabin next to the mine for 36 yrs; in it, she was found frozen to death in 1935. The cabin is now a museum. (June-Labor Day, daily) 1¼ mi E on E 7th St. Phone 719/486-1899. ¢¢

National Mining Hall of Fame and Museum. History and technology exhibits of the mining industry. Hall of Fame dedicated to those who have made significant contributions to the industry. (May-Oct, daily; rest of yr, Mon-Fri; closed winter hols) 120 W 9th St. Phone 719/486-1229. ¢¢

Skiing. Ski Cooper. Triple, double chairlift; Pomalift, T-bar; patrol, school, rentals; snowcat tours; cafeteria, nursery. Twenty-six runs; longest run 1½ mi; vertical drop 1,200 ft. (Late Nov-early Apr, daily) Groomed x-country skiing (15 mi). Summit of Tennessee Pass, 10 mi N on US 24. Phone 719/486-3684. ¢¢¢¢

⭐ **Tabor Opera House.** (1879) Now a museum, this theater was elegantly furnished at the time of construction. At the time, Leadville had a population of 30,000. The theater was host to the Metropolitan Opera, the Chicago Symphony, and most of the famous actors and actresses of the period. Their pictures line the corridors. Many of the original furnishings, much of the scenery, and the dressing areas are still in use and on display. The Tabor box, where many dignitaries were Tabor's guests, is part of the theater tour. Summer shows (inquire locally). Self-guided tours (Memorial Day-

Sept, daily) 308 Harrison Ave. Phone 719/486-8409. ¢¢

Special Events

Crystal Carnival. First wkend Mar.

Boom Days & Burro Race. First full wkend Aug.

Victorian Christmas & Home Tour. First Sat Dec.

Motel/Motor Lodge

★ **SUPER 8.** *1128 S Hwy 24 (80461). 719/486-3637; res 800/800-8000. www.super8.com.* 58 rms, 3 story. No A/C. No elvtr. Mid-June-mid-Sept: S, D $65-$109; under 12 free. Crib free. TV; cable (premium). Complimentary continental bkfst, coffee in lobby. Business servs avail. In-rm modem link. Ck-out 10 am. Sauna. Game rm. Cr cds: A, C, D, DS, MC, V.

Hotel

★ **DELAWARE HOTEL.** *700 Harrison Ave (80461). 719/486-1418; fax 719/486-2214; toll-free 800/748-2004. www.delawarehotel.com.* 36 rms, 32 with shower only, 3 story, 4 suites. No elvtr, A/C. S, D $70-$119; each addl $7; suites $119-$139; ski plan; under 12 free. Crib avail. TV; cable (premium). Complimentary continental bkfst. Restaurant 7-9:30 am. Ck-out 11 am. Meeting rm. Business servs avail. Whirlpool. Historic hotel (1886); Victorian lobby. Cr cds: A, DS, MC, V.

B&B/Small Inn

★ **ICE PALACE INN BED & BREAKFAST.** *813 Spruce St (80461). 719/486-8272; fax 719/486-0345; toll-free 800/754-2840. www.icepalaceinn.com.* 5 air-cooled rms, 2 story, 1 suite. No rm phones. June-Sept: D $89-$149; each addl $15. Crib free. TV; VCR (movies). Whirlpool. Complimentary full bkfst; afternoon refreshments. Ck-out 11 am, ck-in 4-6 pm. Fireplaces. Gift shop. Built in 1879. Totally nonsmoking. Cr cds: A, C, D, DS, MC, V.

Restaurant

★ **HIGH COUNTRY.** *115 Harrison Ave (80461). 719/486-3992.* Hrs: 11 am-10 pm; off-season 11 am-9 pm. Closed some major hols. Lunch $3.50-$6, dinner $5-$11.95. Specialty: prime rib. Three dining areas. Mounted wildlife. Cr cds: C, MC, V.

Limon (C-6)

Pop 2,071 **Elev** 5,365 ft
Area code 719 **Zip** 80828

Motels/Motor Lodges

★★ **BEST WESTERN INN.** *925 T Ave (80828). 719/775-0277; fax 719/775-2921; res 800/780-7234. www.bestwestern.com.* 47 rms, 2 story. S $50-$65; D $65-$75; each addl $5; under 12 free; family rates. Crib $6. Pet accepted; $15. TV; cable (premium). Complimentary continental bkfst, coffee in lobby. Restaurant opp 6 am-11 pm. Ck-out 11 am. Coin lndry. In-rm modem link. Indoor pool. Some in-rm whirlpools. Cr cds: A, D, DS, MC, V.

★ **PREFERRED MOTOR INN.** *158 E Main (80828). 719/775-2385; fax 719/775-2901; res 800/530-3956.* 57 rms. S $28-$38; D $46-$62; each addl $4; suites $65-$100. Crib $4. Pet accepted; $4. TV; cable (premium). Indoor pool; whirlpool. Restaurant nearby. Ck-out 10 am. Meeting rms. Free airport, bus depot transportation. Balconies. Cr cds: A, D, DS, MC, V.

★ **SAFARI MOTEL.** *637 Main St (80828). 719/775-2363; fax 719/775-2316; toll-free 800/330-7021.* 28 rms, 1-2 story. June-Sept: S, D $40-$67; each addl $4; suites $70; lower rates rest of yr. Pet accepted; $5. TV; cable (premium). Pool. Playground. Complimentary coffee in rms. Restaurant opp. Ck-out 10 am. Coin lndry. In-rm modem link. Private patios. Cr cds: A, D, DS, MC, V.

B&B/Small Inn

★★ **MIDWEST COUNTRY INN.**
*795 Main St (80828). 719/775-2373;
fax 719/775-8808; toll-free 888/610-
6683.* 32 rms, 2 story. June-Aug: S
$36; D $42-$44; each addl $4; suites
$55; lower rates rest of yr. TV; cable.
Coffee in lobby. Restaurant nearby.
Ck-out 10 am, ck-in 2 pm. Gift shop.
Garden. Cr cds: A, C, D, DS, MC, V.
⬜ 🔥

Restaurant

★ **FIRESIDE JUNCTION.** *2295 9th St
(80828). 719/775-2396.* Hrs: 6 am-10
pm. Closed Dec 24-25. Res accepted.
Mexican, Amer menu. Serv bar. Bkfst
$4-$7, lunch $5-$8, dinner $6.50-
$13.99. Child's menu. Specializes in
chicken-fried steak. Salad bar. Parking. Cr cds: A, DS, MC, V.
[D] ⬜

Longmont

(B-5) *See also Boulder, Denver, Loveland,
Lyons*

Founded 1870 **Pop** 71,093 **Elev** 4,979
ft **Area code** 303
Information Chamber of Commerce,
528 Main St, 80501; 303/776-5295
Web www.longmontchamber.org

What to See and Do

Longmont Museum. Changing and
special exhibits on art, history, space,
and science; permanent exhibits on
the history of Longmont and the St.
Vrain Valley. (Tues-Sat, Sun afternoons) 400 Quail Rd. Phone
303/651-8374. **FREE**

Special Events

Boulder County Fair and Rodeo. Fairgrounds. Phone 303/441-3927 or
303/772-7170. Nine days early Aug.

Rhythm on the River. St. Vrain
Greenway, Roger's Grove. Phone
303/776-6050. Sept.

Hotel

★★ **RAINTREE PLAZA.** *1900 Ken
Pratt Blvd (80501). 303/776-2000; fax*

*303/678-7361; toll-free 800/843-8240.
www.raintreeplaza.com.* 211 rms, 2
story. S, D $129-$145; each addl $10;
suites $225-$275; under 18 free.
Valet parking avail. Crib free. Pet
accepted; $50 (nonrefundable). TV;
cable (premium). Heated pool. Complimentary continental bkfst. Coffee
in rms. Restaurant 6 am-2 pm, 5-10
pm; Sat 6 am-1 pm, 5-10 pm. Rm
serv. Bar. Ck-out noon. Free lndry
facilities. Meeting rms. Business servs
avail. In-rm modem link. Valet serv.
Airport transportation. Exercise
equipt; steam rm, sauna. Wet bars,
refrigerators. Cr cds: A, C, D, DS, ER,
JCB, MC, V.
[D] 🐾 ⬜ 🧍 ✈ ⬜ 🔥

Loveland

(B-5) *See also Estes Park, Fort Collins,
Greeley, Longmont, Lyons*

Founded 1877 **Pop** 50,608 **Elev** 4,982
ft **Area code** 970
Information Visitor Center/Chamber
of Commerce, 5400 Stone Creek Circle, 80538; 970/667-5728 or 800/258-
1278
Web www.loveland.org

What to See and Do

Boyd Lake State Park. Swimming,
waterskiing, fishing, boating (ramps,
rentals); picnicking (shelters, showers), camping (dump station). Standard fees. (Daily) 1 mi E on US 34,
then 2 mi N. Phone 970/669-1739.
¢¢¢

Special Events

Dog racing. Cloverleaf Kennel Club.
4 mi E at jct US 34, I-25. Races
nightly. Matinees Mon, Wed, Sat, and
Sun. Pari-mutuel betting. No minors.
Phone 970/667-6211. Mar-June.

Larimer County Fair and Rodeo.
Mid-Aug.

B&B/Small Inn

★★★ **CATTAIL CREEK INN BED &
BREAKFAST.** *2665 Abarr Dr (80538).
970/667-7600; fax 970/667-8968; toll-
free 800/572-2466. www.cattailcreek
inn.com.* 8 rms, 2 story. S, D $105-

$170; each addl $10; golf plans; package plans. Children over 14 yrs only. TV; cable (premium). Complimentary full bkfst. Ck-out 11 am, ck-in 4-9 pm. 27-hole golf privileges. Balconies. Totally nonsmoking. Cr cds: A, DS, MC, V.

Guest Ranch

★★★ **SYLVAN DALE GUEST RANCH.** *2939 N County Rd 31D (80538). 970/667-3915; fax 970/635-9336; toll-free 877/667-3999. www. sylvandale.com.* 9 cabins (1-3-bedrm units); ;wagon wheel bunkhouse,; 1-2 story. No A/C in cabins. Mid-June-early Sept, 6 days: AP $838/adult, $669/ages 5-12, $48/ages 1-4; lower rates rest of yr. Crib free. Heated pool. Playground. Free supervised child's activities (mid-June-Labor Day). Complimetary full bkfst. Dining rm (public by res). Box lunches, cookouts, bkfst rides, overnight pack trips. Ck-out 11 am, ck-in 3 pm. Grocery ¼ mi. Meeting rms. Business center. Free bus depot, airport transportation. Tennis. Lawn games. Rec rm. Entertainment, square dancing. Horseback riding. Hiking. Hay rides.Grills. Trout-stocked lake. Some fireplaces, balconies. Working ranch on 3,000 acres bordered by Roosevelt National Forest. Totally nonsmoking. No cr cds accepted.

Restaurants

★★★ **CACTUS GRILL NORTH.** *281-A E 29th St (80538). 970/663-1550.* Hrs: 11 am-10 pm; Sun-Tues to 9 pm. Closed Dec 25. Res accepted. Mexican, Amer menu. Bar. Lunch, dinner $5-$17. Child's menu. Specialties: chicken enchiladas, tacos al carbon. Outdoor dining. 5 dining areas. Cr cds: A, D, DS, MC, V.

★★ **SUMMIT.** *3208 W Eisenhower (80537). 970/669-6648.* Hrs: 11:30 am-2 pm, 5-10 pm; Sat from 5 pm; Sun brunch 10 am-2 pm; Easter & Mother's Day 9 am-6 pm. Closed Dec 25. Res accepted. Bar 4 pm-midnight. Lunch, dinner $8.95-$14.95. Child's menu. Specializes in steak, seafood.

Salad bar. Outdoor dining. Mountain view. Cr cds: A, C, D, DS, ER, MC, V.

Lyons

(B-5) *See also Boulder, Estes Park, Longmont, Loveland*

Pop 1,585 **Elev** 5,360 ft
Area code 303 **Zip** 80540
Information Chamber of Commerce, PO Box 426; 303/823-5215. The Visitors Center at 4th and Broadway is staffed Memorial Day-Labor Day, daily; phone 303/823-6640

Special Event

Good Old Days Celebration. Midway, parade, flea market, craft fair, food. Phone 303/823-5215. Last wkend June.

Guest Ranch

★★ **PEACEFUL VALLEY RANCH.** *475 Peaceful Valley Rd (80540). 303/747-2881; fax 303/747-2167; toll-free 800/955-6343. www.peacefulvalley. com.* 42 rms in 3 lodges; 10 cabins. No A/C. Many rm phones. AP, Memorial Day-Labor Day: S $1,300-$1,560; D $1,210-$1,460/person/week; family rates; lower rates rest of yr. TV in lounge. Indoor pool; wading pool, whirlpool. Sauna. Playground. Supervised children's activities (Memorial Day-Labor Day); ages 3-18. Dining rm (public by res) 8-9 am, noon, 6 pm. Box lunches, picnics, barbecues. Ck-out 10 am, ck-in 2-4 pm. Coin lndry. Meeting rms. Business center. Gift shop. Denver airport, RR station, bus depot transportation. Downhill/x-country ski ½ mi. Backcountry tours; overnight pack trips. Soc dir; entertainment, square dancing (summer), campfires. Snowmobiling, snowshoeing, mountain biking. Petting zoo. Sleigh rides. Rec rm. Varied social program. Some fireplaces. Mountain setting on 300 acres. Cr cds: A, D, DS, MC, V.

Restaurants

★ **ANDREA'S GERMAN CUISINE.** *216 E Main St (80540). 303/823-5000.*

Hrs: 8 am-9 pm. Closed Wed; Dec 25. Res accepted. German menu. Bar. Bkfst $2.95-$7.95, lunch $4.95-$12.95, dinner $6.95-$18.95. Specialties: pepper steak, sauerbraten. Bavarian folk music Fri, Sat. Bavarian decor. Cr cds: A, C, D, DS, ER, MC, V.

D 🖼

★ ★ ★ **BLACK BEAR INN.** *42 E Main St (80540). 303/823-6812. www.black bearinn.com.* Hrs: 11 am-2:30 pm, 5:30-10 pm; Sat from 5:30 pm, Sun noon-9 pm. Closed Mon, Tues; also Jan-mid-Feb. Res accepted; required wkends. Continental menu. Bar. Wine list. Lunch $7.75-$15, dinner $23-$26. Specializes in veal, fresh seafood. Patio dining. Swiss, Bavarian decor; fireplace; many European antiques. Cr cds: A, C, D, DS, ER, MC, V.

D

★ ★ ★ **LA CHAUMIERE.** *CO 36 (80540). 303/823-6521.* Hrs: 5:30-10 pm; Sun 2-9 pm. Closed Mon. Res accepted. Continental menu. Serv bar. A la carte entrees: dinner $12.50-$23.50. Complete meals: Sun $17. Child's menu. Specializes in sweetbreads, wild game, seafood. Own ice cream. Fireplace. European-style atmosphere. View of mountains. Cr cds: A, C, MC, V.

D

Manitou Springs

(D-5) *See also Colorado Springs*

Founded 1872 **Pop** 4,980 **Elev** 6,320 ft **Area code** 719 **Zip** 80829

Information Chamber of Commerce, 354 Manitou Ave; 719/685-5089 or 800/642-2567

Web www.manitousprings.org

What to See and Do

Cave of the Winds. Fascinating 45-min guided tour through underground passageways filled with beautiful stalactites, stalagmites, and flowstone formations created millions of yrs ago. Tours leave every 15 min (daily). Light jacket and comfortable shoes recommended. Laser light show in canyon (May-Sept, Fri, Sat eves; rest of yr, daily) is 15 stories high and is accompanied by music. (May-Sept, daily) From Manitou Ave and US 24, go 6 mi W on US 24 to Cave of the Winds Rd; turn right and continue ½ mi to visitor center. Phone 719/685-5444. Cave tour ¢¢¢¢ Laser show ¢¢¢

Iron Springs Chateau. Melodrama dinner theater featuring a traditional "olio" show. Named for the mineral-rich water beneath the ground. (Mon-Sat) 444 Ruxton Ave. Phone 719/685-5104. ¢¢¢¢

Manitou Cliff Dwellings Museum. Outdoor southwestern Native American preserve; architecture of the cliff-dwelling natives, A.D. 1100-1300. Native American dancing (June-Aug). Museum (Mar-Nov, daily). W on US 24. Phone 719/685-5242. ¢¢¢

Miramont Castle Museum. (ca 1895) A 46-rm, four-story Victorian house featuring nine styles of architecture, miniatures and doll collection, tea rm, soda fountain, gardens. (Tues-Sun; closed Easter, Thanksgiving, Dec 25) 9 Capitol Hill Ave. Phone 719/685-1011. ¢¢

Pikes Peak Cog Railway. (See COLORADO SPRINGS) Phone 719/685-5401.

Motels/Motor Lodges

★ **BEST VALUE INN VILLA MOTEL.** *481 Manitou Ave (80829). 719/685-5492; fax 719/685-4143; res 888/315-2378. www.villamotel.com.* 47 rms, 2 story, 7 kits. Memorial Day-Labor Day: S $46-$89; D $55-$89; kits. $98-$103; lower rates rest of yr. Crib free. TV; cable (premium). Heated pool; whirlpool. Complimentary coffee in lobby. Restaurant opp 7 am-10 pm. Ck-out 11 am. Coin lndry. Business servs avail. Picnic tables. Cr cds: A, C, D, DS, MC, V.

🐾 ⚡ 🏊 ❄ 🐕 SC

★ **REDWING MOTEL.** *56 El Paso Blvd (80829). 719/685-5656; fax 719/685-9547; toll-free 800/733-9547. www.pikes-peak.com/redwing.* 27 rms, 2 story, 11 kits. S $30-$49; D $38-$64; kit. units $10 addl. Crib free. Pet accepted. TV; cable. Heated pool. Playground. Complimentary coffee in rms. Restaurant nearby. Ck-out 10 am. Some refrigerators; microwaves avail. Cr cds: A, DS, MC, V.

★ **SILVER SADDLE MOTEL.** *215 Manitou Ave (80829). 719/685-5611; toll-free 800/772-3353. www.silver-saddle.com.* 54 rms, 1-2 story. Mid-May-mid-Sept: S $69-$79; D $79-$84; under 18 free; each addl $6; suites $99.50-$129.50; lower rates rest of yr. Crib free. TV; cable (premium), VCR avail. Pool; whirl-pool. Complimentary coffee. Restaurant nearby. Ck-out 10:30 am. Some in-rm whirlpools. Cr cds: A, C, D, DS, MC, V.

B&Bs/Small Inns

★★ **BLACK BEAR INN OF PIKES PEAK.** *5250 Pikes Peak Hwy, Cascade (80809). 719/684-0151; toll-free 877/732-5232. www.blackbearinn pikespeak.com.* 9 rms (shower only), 2 story. S $70; D $85; each addl $10. Children over 10 yrs only. TV; cable. Whirlpool. Complimentary full bkfst. Restaurant opp 5:30-9 pm. Ck-out 10:30 am, ck-in 4-6 pm. Luggage handling. X-country ski 8 mi. View of mountains. Totally nonsmoking. Cr cds: DS, JCB, MC, V.

★★ **EASTHOLME IN THE ROCK-IES.** *4445 Haggerman Ave, Cascade (80809). 719/684-9901; toll-free 800/672-9901. www.eastholme.com.* 6 rms, 3 with shower only, 1 share bath, 3 story, 2 cottages. No A/C. No rm phones. S $75; D $99; each addl $15; cottage $135. Complimentary full bkfst. Restaurant nearby. Ck-out 11 am, ck-in 4 pm. Originally a hotel built in 1885; many antiques. Totally nonsmoking. Cr cds: A, DS, MC, V.

★★★ **RED CRAGS BED & BREAK-FAST INN.** *302 El Paso Blvd (80829). 719/685-1920; fax 719/685-1073; toll-free 800/721-2248. www.redcrags.com.* 7 air-cooled rms, 4 story. S, D $95; each addl $20. Children over 10 yrs only. Whirlpool. Complimentary full bkfst; afternoon refreshments. Restaurant nearby. Ck-out 11 am, ck-in 4-6 pm. Gift shop. Mansion (1870) originally built as a clinic. On bluff with view of Pikes Peak, Garden of Gods. Antiques, fireplaces. Totally nonsmoking. Cr cds: A, DS, MC, V.

Restaurants

★★★ **BRIARHURST MANOR.** *404 Manitou Ave (80829). 719/685-1864. www.briarhurst.com.* Hrs: 5:30-9 pm. Res accepted. Continental menu. Bar. Wine cellar. Dinner $10.50-$29.95; Wed night buffet $17.95. Complete meals: dinner $18-$37.95. Child's menu. Specialties: Rocky Mountain rainbow trout, châteaubriand, rack of lamb. Own baking. Outdoor dining. Homegrown fresh vegetables & herbs. Tudor manor (1876); origi-nally residence of founder of Mani-tou Springs. Cr cds: A, MC, V.

★★★ **CRAFTWOOD INN.** *404 El Paso Blvd (80829). 719/685-9000. www.craftwood.com.* Hrs: from 5 pm. Closed Jan 1, Dec 25. Res accepted. Bar. Wine cellar. Dinner $10-$25. Specializes in Colorado cuisine, wild game, seafood. Outdoor dining. Built in 1912 on 1½ acres of landscaped gardens; view of Pikes Peak. Casual country elegance. Totally nonsmok-ing. Cr cds: A, D, DS, MC, V.

★★ **MISSION BELL INN.** *178 Crys-tal Park Rd (80829). 719/685-9089. www.missionbellinn.com.* Hrs: 5-9:30 pm. Closed Jan 1, Thanksgiving, Dec 25; also Mon from Oct-May. Res accepted. Mexican menu. Serv bar. Dinner $8.50-$10.25. Specialties: stuffed pepper, stuffed sopapilla, fried ice cream. Outdoor dining. Family-owned. Cr cds: MC, V.

★★ **STAGE COACH.** *702 Manitou Ave (80829). 719/685-9400. www. stagecoachinn.com.* Hrs: 4:30-9:30 pm. Closed Jan 1, Dec 25. Res accepted. Bar. Dinner $5.50-$20.95. Child's menu. Specialties: prime rib, buffalo steak. Own pastries. Outdoor dining. Historic log stage stop built 1881. Fireplace. Cr cds: A, C, DS, ER, MC, V.

Mesa Verde National Park

(F-1) *See also Cortez, Durango*

(8 mi E of Cortez, 36 mi W of Durango, on US 160 to park entrance, then 15 mi S to Visitor Center)

Mesa Verde, Spanish for "green table," is a large plateau towering 1,500 to 2,000 feet above the surrounding valleys. The home of the farming Pueblo for more than eight centuries, it is famous for well-preserved, pre-Columbian cliff dwellings in the shallow alcoves of its many canyon walls.

Public campgrounds, including trailer sites (15 hookups), four miles from park entrance, are open in non-freezing weather (May-October; fee). Speed limit within the park is 35 miles per hour or as posted. The park is open year-round. Golden Eagle Passport accepted (see MAKING THE MOST OF YOUR TRIP). Per vehicle (weekly) ¢¢

Because of the fragile nature of the cliff dwellings, one regulation is rigidly enforced: the cliff dwellings are entered *only* while rangers are on duty (all year, weather permitting).

What to See and Do

Cliff Dwelling Tours. The cliff dwellings can be entered *only* while rangers are on duty. During the summer, five cliff dwellings may be visited at specific hrs; during the winter there are trips to Spruce Tree House only, weather permitting. Obtain daily tickets for Cliff Palace, Balcony House, and Long House tours at Far View Visitor Center. Balcony House tours are limited to 50 persons; Cliff Palace tours are limited to the first 60; and Long House tours are limited to 40 persons. Phone 970/529-4461. The cliff dwellings that are open to the public are

Balcony House. Noted for ladder and tunnel features; accessible only by 32-ft-long ladder. Ranger-guided mid-May to mid-Oct. On Cliff Palace Loop Rd, 25-min drive from visitor center. Phone 970/529-4461. ¢

Cliff Palace. First major dwelling to be discovered (1888). More than 200 living rms, 23 kivas, numerous

Cliff Palace, Mesa Verde National Park

storage rms. Guided tours in summer, fall, and spring; closed winter. On Cliff Palace Loop Rd, 20-min drive from visitor center. Phone 970/529-4461. ¢

Long and Step Houses and Badger House Community. Ranger-conducted (Long) and self-guided (Step) trips (Memorial Day-Labor Day); inquire at Visitor Center or museum for details. On Wetherill Mesa, 12 mi from visitor center. Phone 970/529-4461.

Spruce Tree House. Best preserved in Mesa Verde; contains 114 living rms and eight ceremonial rms, called kivas. Self-guided tour to site in summer; ranger-guided rest of yr. In canyon behind museum. Phone 970/529-4461.

★ **Far View Visitor Center.** All visitors are recommended to stop at center first. (May-Sept, daily) 15 mi S of park entrance. Phone 970/529-4461.

Mesa Top Loop & Cliff Palace Loop. Two six-mi, self-guided loops afford visits to ten excavated mesa-top sites illustrating 700 yrs of architectural development; views of 20 to 30 cliff dwellings from canyon rim vantage points. (Daily; closed during heavy snowfalls) Enter at crossroads near museum. Phone 970/529-4461.

Museum. Exhibits tell story of Mesa Verde people: their arts, crafts, industries. (Daily) Park headquarters, 21 mi S of park entrance. Phone 970/529-4461. **FREE**

Park Point Fire Lookout. Elevation, 8,572 ft. Spectacular views of entire Four Corners area of Colorado, Arizona, New Mexico, and Utah. Access road closed in winter. Halfway between park entrance and headquarters. Phone 970/529-4461.

Picnic areas. One at headquarters and one on each loop of Mesa Top Loop Rd. Phone 970/529-4461.

Motel/Motor Lodge

★★ **FAR VIEW LODGE IN MESA VERDE.** *1 Navajo Hill, Mile 15 (81328). 970/529-4421; fax 970/533-7831; res 800/449-2288.* 150 rms, 1-2 story. No A/C. No rm phones. Late Apr-late Oct: S, D $83-$103; each addl $8; under 12 free. Closed rest of yr. Crib $4. Pet accepted, some restrictions. Restaurant 6:30 am-9 pm; dining rm 5-9:30 pm. Rm serv

24 hrs. Bar 4-11 pm. Ck-out 11 am. Meeting rms. Coin lndry. Gift shop. Some refrigerators. Private balconies. Picnic tables. Hiking trails. Mesa Verde tours avail. Educational programs. View of canyon. Camping sites, trailer facilities. General store, take-out serv, coin showers. Totally nonsmoking. Cr cds: A, D, DS, JCB, MC, V.

D 🛥 🖾 🔥 SC

Monte Vista

(F-4) *See also Alamosa*

Pop 4,529 **Elev** 7,663 ft
Area code 719 **Zip** 81144
Information Chamber of Commerce, 1035 Park Ave; 719/852-2731 or 800/562-7085
Web www.monte-vista.org

What to See and Do

Historical Society Headquarters. In 1875 library; information about history of Monte Vista. (Apr-Dec, Mon-Fri afternoons) 110 Jefferson St. **FREE**

Monte Vista National Wildlife Refuge. Created as a nesting, migration, and wintering habitat for waterfowl and other migratory birds. Marked visitor tour road. 6 mi S via CO 15. Contact the Refuge Manager, 9383 El Rancho Lane, Alamosa 81101. Phone 719/589-4021. **FREE**

Special Events

Monte Vista Crane Festival. Ski-Hi Park. Tours of refuge to view cranes and other wildlife. Arts, crafts, workshops. Phone 719/852-3552 or 719/852-2692. Mid-Mar.

Ski-Hi Stampede. Ski-Hi Park. Rodeo, carnival, arts and crafts show, street parade, barbecue, Western dances. Phone 719/852-2055. Last wkend July.

San Luis Valley Fair. Ski-Hi Park. Phone 719/589-2271 719/852-2692. Mid-Aug.

Motels/Motor Lodges

★★ **BEST WESTERN MOVIE MANOR.** *2830 W US 160 (81144).*

719/852-5921; fax 719/852-0122; res 800/528-1234. tollfree 800/771-9468 *www.bestwestern.com.* 60 rms, 2 story. May-Labor Day: S $77-$87; D $81-$95; each addl $5; under 12 free lower rates rest of yr. Pet accepted. TV; cable (premium). Playground. Restaurant 6 am-2 pm, 5-10 pm. Bar from 5 pm. Ck-out 11 am. Meeting rm. Business servs avail. Exercise equipt. Drive-in movies visible from rms; speakers in most rms. Cr cds: A, C, D, DS, MC, V.

★★ **COMFORT INN.** *1519 Grand Ave (81144). 719/852-0612; fax 719/852-3585; res 800/228-5150. www.comfortinn.com.* 45 rms, 2 story. May-mid-Oct: S $60-$70; D $70-$90; each addl $5; under 18 free; lower rates rest of yr. Crib free. Pet accepted. TV; cable (premium). Indoor pool; whirlpool. Complimentary continental bkfst. Restaurant nearby. Ck-out 11 am. Business servs avail. In-rm modem link. Cr cds: A, C, D, DS, MC, V.

Montrose

(D-2) *See also Delta, Ouray*

Founded 1882 **Pop** 12,344 **Elev** 5,806 ft **Area code** 970 **Zip** 81401

Information Chamber of Commerce, 1519 E Main St; 970/249-5000 or 800/923-5515

Web www.montrosechamber.com

What to See and Do

Black Canyon of the Gunnison National Monument. (see).

Montrose County Historical Museum. Collections of antique farm machinery; archaeological artifacts; pioneer cabin with family items; tool collection; early electrical equipt; Montrose newspapers 1896-1940. (May-Sept, daily) Main St and Rio Grande, in Depot Building. Phone 970/249-2085. ¢

Ridgway State Park. This 2,320-acre park incl four recreational areas and a reservoir. Swimming, waterskiing, scuba diving, sailing, sailboarding, boating (marina); hiking, bicycling, x-country skiing, sledding, picnicking, playground, improved camping, lndry, concession. Standard fees. (Daily) 20 mi S on US 550. Phone 970/626-5822. Per vehicle ¢¢

Scenic Drive. Owl Creek Pass. Drive 23 mi S on US 550 to the left-hand turnoff for Owl Creek Pass, marked by a US Forest Service sign, then E 7 mi along Cow Creek to Debbie's Park. In this meadow, Debbie Reynolds was filmed in the wild west bkfst scene in *How the West Was Won*. The next eight mi climb to the crest of Owl Creek Pass at 10,114 ft. Fifteen mi from the pass is **Silver Jack Reservoir**, an area with good fishing and scenic hiking trails. About 20 mi N, the road joins US 50 at Cimarron. The road is not recommended for large trucks or RVs and may be impassable in inclement weather.

Ute Indian Museum and Ouray Memorial Park. On home grounds of Chief Ouray and his wife, Chipeta. History of the Utes in artifacts and objects of 19th- and early 20th-century Ute craftsmanship, clothing, dioramas, photographs. Self-guided tours. (Daily; Nov-May, Mon-Sat) 17253 Chipeta Dr, 3 mi S on US 550. Phone 970/249-3098. ¢¢

Motels/Motor Lodges

★★ **BEST WESTERN RED ARROW MOTOR INN.** *1702 E Main St; US 50 (81402). 970/249-9641; fax 970/249-8380; res 800/780-7234. www.bestwestern.com/redarrow.* 60 rms, 2 story. May-Oct: S, D $89-$109; suites $109-$125; children free; lower rates rest of yr. Crib free. Pet accepted; $8. TV; cable (premium), VCR avail. Heated pool; whirlpool. Playground. Complimentary coffee in rms. Restaurant adj. Ck-out 11 am. Coin lndry. Meeting rms. Business center. In-rm modem link. Concierge. Free airport, bus depot transportation. Valet serv. Exercise equipt. Lawn games. Bathrm phones, refrigerators; some in-rm whirlpools. Many private patios, balconies. Cr cds: A, C, D, DS, MC, V.

★ **BLACK CANYON.** *1605 E Main St (81401). 970/249-3495; fax 970/249-*

0990; toll-free 800/348-3495. www.toski.com/black-canyon.com. 49 rms, 1-2 story. May-Sept: S, D $59-$79; each addl $5; suites $95; under 12 free; lower rates rest of yr; ski, golf packages. Crib $5. Pet accepted, some restrictions; $5. TV; cable (premium). Heated pool; whirlpool. Complimentary continental bkfst. Complimentary coffee in rms. Restaurant nearby. Ck-out 11 am. Meeting rms. Business servs avail. Some refrigerators, balconies. Microwaves avail. Cr cds: A, C, D, DS, MC, V.

★★ **COUNTRY LODGE.** 1624 E Main St (81401). 970/249-4567; fax 970/249-3082. www.countrylodge.com. 22 rms. 1 cabin. June-Sept: S, D $62-$78; each addl $5; kit. units $10 addl; lower rates rest of yr. Crib free. TV; cable. Heated pool; whirlpool. Playground. Complimentary coffee in lobby. Restaurant nearby. Ck-out 11 am. Some refrigerators; microwaves avail. Cr cds: A, C, D, DS, MC, V.

★ **SAN JUAN INN.** 1480 S Townsend (81401). 970/249-6644; fax 970/249-9314; toll-free 888/681-4159. www.sanjuaninn.com. 51 rms, 2 story. May-Oct: S, D $40-$89; each addl $5; under 13 free; lower rates rest of yr. Crib free. Pet accepted; $6. TV; cable (premium). Heated indoor pool; whirlpool. Playground. Complimentary coffee in lobby. Restaurant adj 6 am-10 pm. Ck-out 11 am. Coin lndry. Free airport transportation. Refrigerators, microwaves avail. Cr cds: A, C, D, DS, MC, V.

★ **WESTERN MOTEL.** 1200 E Main St (81401). 970/249-3481; fax 970/249-3471; toll-free 800/445-7301. www.westernmotel.com. 28 rms, 1-2 story. June-Labor Day: S, D $40-$115; each addl $4; lower rates rest of yr. Crib $4. Pet accepted; $5. TV; cable (premium), VCR avail. Heated pool; whirlpool; sauna. Complimentary continental bkfst. Restaurant nearby. Ck-out 10 am. Some refrigerators. Microwaves avail. Sun deck. Cr cds: A, C, D, DS, MC, V.

Restaurants

★★ **GLENN EYRIE RESTAURANT.** 2351 S Townsend Ave (81401). 970/249-9263. Hrs: 5-9 pm; Closed Sun, Mon; Jan 1, July 4, Dec 25. Res accepted. Serv bar. American menu. Dinner $15-$30. Child's menu. Specializes in fresh fish. Cr cds: A, DS, MC, V.

★ **WHOLE ENCHILADA.** 44 S Grand Ave (81401). 970/249-1881. Hrs: 11 am-10 pm. Closed Sun. Res accepted. Bar to 10:30 pm. Lunch, dinner $4.50-$9.50. Specializes in Mexican dishes. Outdoor dining. Cr cds: A, DS, MC, V.

Norwood

(E-1) See also Telluride

Pop 438 **Elev** 7,006 ft **Area code** 970 **Zip** 81423

What to See and Do

Miramonte Lake. Fishing, boating, windsurfing. Fishing also in San Miguel River, Gurley Lake, Ground Hog Reservoir, and nearby streams and mountain lakes. Inquire locally for information, permits. 18 mi SW.

Uncompahgre National Forest. More than 940,000 acres of alpine forest ranging in elevation from 7,500 to 14,000 ft, with many peaks higher than 13,000 ft. Fishing; hunting, hiking, picnicking, camping (fee at some campgrounds). Four-wheel drive areas. Snowmobiling, x-country skiing. Within the forest are Big Blue and Mt Sneffles wilderness areas and portions of Lizard Head Wilderness Area. Also within the forest is a portion of the San Juan Skyway. North, east and south of town. Contact the Forest Service, 1150 Forest St, PO Box 388. Phone 970/327-4261.

Special Event

San Miguel Basin Fair and Rodeo. Fairgrounds. Fair and rodeo. Phone 970/327-4393. Last full wkend July.

Ouray

(E-2 *See also Montrose, Silverton*

Settled 1876 **Pop** 813 **Elev** 7,811 ft
Area code 970 **Zip** 81427
Information Ouray Chamber Resort
Assn, PO Box 145; 970/325-4746 or
800/228-1876
Web www.ouraycolorado.com

What to See and Do

Bachelor-Syracuse Mine Tour. Mine
in continuous operation since 1884.
Guided tour aboard a mine train,
advances 3,350 ft horizontally into
Gold Hill (mine temperature 47°F).
Within the mine, visitors see mining
equipt, visit work areas, and learn
how explosives are used. Gold panning. Outdoor cafe. (Late May-Sept,
daily; closed July 4) County 14, 1 mi
N via US 550, Dexter Creek Rd exit.
Phone 970/325-0220. ¢¢¢

Bear Creek Falls. Road crosses bridge
over 227-ft falls; an observation
point is nearby. 3 mi S on US 550.
Phone 970/325-4746.

Box Cañon Falls Park. Canyon Creek
has cut a natural canyon 20 ft wide,
400 ft deep. View of thundering falls
from floor of canyon is reached by
stairs and suspended bridge. Picnic
tables are avail in beautiful settings.
Children must be accompanied by
an adult. (Daily) ½ mi S on US 550.
Phone 970/325-4464.

Jeep trips. Guides take visitors to
ghost towns, mountain passes, and
mines, many above the timberline;
some full-day trips. (Mid-May-mid-
Oct, daily) Also jeep rentals. Phone
970/325-4746. Trips ¢¢¢¢

Ouray County Historical Museum.
Former hospital constructed in 1887
now houses artifacts; mining, ranching, and Ute relics. (Daily) 420 6th
Ave. Phone 970/325-4576. ¢¢

Recreation.

    Fishing. In lakes and streams.
Hunting, riding, biking, hiking
in surrounding mountains. **Ski**
course with rope tow at edge of
town; designed for children and
beginners (free).

    Hot Springs Pool. Outdoor, mil-
lion-gallon pool fed by natural

mineral hot springs; sulphur-free.
Bathhouse; spa. (Daily) Ouray City
Park, US 550 N. Phone 970/325-
4638. ¢¢

Special Events

Artists' Alpine Holiday & Festival.
National exhibit, competition in all
media. One wk mid-Aug. Phone
970/626-3611.

Ouray County Fair & Rodeo. 12 mi N
in Ridgway. Labor Day wkend.

Imogene Pass Mountain Marathon.
The 18-mi course starts at Ouray's
7,800-ft elevation, crosses over Imogene Pass (13,114 ft), and ends at
Main St, Telluride (8,800 ft). Race
route follows old mining trail. Phone
970/728-1299. Sat after Labor Day.
Phone 970/255-1002.

Motels/Motor Lodges

★★ **BOX CANYON LODGE & HOT
SPRING.** *45 Third Ave (81427).*
970/325-4981; fax 970/325-0223; toll-
free 800/327-5080. www.boxcanyon
ouray.com. 38 rms, 2 story. No A/C.
Mid-June-Sept: D $100; each addl
$10; suites $115-$165; higher rates
Christmas hols; lower rates rest of yr.
Crib $5. TV; cable (premium), Com-
plimentary coffee in rms. Restaurant
nearby. Ck-out 11 am. Outdoor
whirlpools fed from mineral hot
springs. Fireplace in suites. Some
refrigerators. Balconies. Sun decks. At
mouth of canyon; scenic view. Near
river. Cr cds: A, D, DS, MC, V.
⊡ ⬛ ⬛ ⬛ ⬛

★ **CASCADE FALLS LODGE.** *120
6th Ave (81427). 970/325-4394; fax
970/325-4947; toll-free 888/466-8729.*
19 rms, 1-2 story. No A/C. Apr-Oct:
S, D $40-$94; each addl $5. Closed
mid-Oct-mid-Apr. Crib free. TV; cable
(premium). Whirlpool. Complimentary continental bkfst, coffee in rms.
Restaurant nearby. Ck-out 10:30 am.
Refrigerators, microwaves. Balconies.
Picnic tables. Playground. Sun deck.
Cr cds: DS, MC, V.
⬛ ⬛ ⬛ ⬛ ⬛

★★ **COMFORT INN.** *191 5th Ave
(81427). 970/325-7203; fax 970/325-
4840; res 800/228-5150. www.ouray
comfortinn.com.* 33 rms, 2 story. June-
mid-Sept: S, D $59-$107; each addl
$6; under 18 free; lower rates rest of

yr. Crib $3. Whirlpool. TV; cable (premium). Complimentary continental bkfst, coffee in rms. Restaurant nearby. Ck-out 11 am. Coin lndry. Business servs avail. In-rm modem link. Refrigerators avail. Golf nearby. Mountain views. Cr cds: A, C, D, DS, MC, V.

[symbols]

★ ★ **MATTERHORN MOTEL.** *201 6th Ave (81427). 970/325-4938; fax 970/325-7335; toll-free 800/334-9425. www.ouraycolorado.com/matthorn.html.* 25 air-cooled rms, 2 story, 3 suites. Late June-Sept: S, D $77-$97; each addl $6; suites $99; lower rates Apr-early June, Oct. Closed rest of yr. Crib $5. TV; cable (premium). Heated pool; whirlpool. Complimentary coffee in rms. Restaurant nearby. Ck-out 11 am. Business servs avail. In-rm modem link. Cr cds: D, DS, MC, V.

[symbols]

★ ★ **OURAY CHALET INN.** *510 Main St; Hwy 550 (81427). 970/325-4331; fax 970/325-4504; res 800/924-2538. www.ouraychaletinn.com.* 30 rms, 2 story. Late June-mid-Sept: S, D $55-$97; each addl $4; under 12 free; lower rates rest of yr. Closed mid-Oct-mid May. TV; cable (premium). Complimentary coffee in rms. Restaurant adj 6 am-9 pm. In-rm modem link. Ck-out 11 am. Free bus depot transportation. Whirlpool. Cr cds: A, C, DS, MC, V.

[symbols]

★ ★ **OURAY VICTORIAN INN & TOWNHOMES.** *50 3rd Ave (81427). 970/325-7222; fax 970/325-7225; toll-free 800/846-8729. www.ouraylodging. com.* 38 rms, 2 story, 4 suites. No A/C. Late-June-Sept: S, D $65-$100; each addl $6; suites $120; under 6 free; ski plans; lower rates rest of yr. Crib free. Pet accepted. TV; cable (premium). 2 whirlpools. Complimentary continental bkfst (Oct-May). Complimentary coffee in rms. Restaurant nearby. Ck-out 11 am. Meeting rms. Business servs avail. In-rm modem link. Picnic tables. Playground. On river. Cr cds: A, C, D, DS, MC, V.

[symbols]

★ **RIDGWAY-TELLURIDE SUPER 8.** *373 Palomino Tr, Ridgway (81432). 970/626-5444; fax 970/626-5888; res 800/800-8000. www.super8.com.* 52 rms, 2 story. Mid-June-Labor Day: S, D $55-$75; each addl $7; under 13 free; ski plan; higher rates some hols; lower rates rest of yr. Crib $5. Pet accepted; $25 deposit. TV; cable (premium). Heated indoor pool; whirlpool. Sauna. Restaurant nearby. Ck-out 11 am. Coin lndry. Business servs avail. In-rm modem link. Refrigerators in suites. Mountain views. Cr cds: A, C, D, DS, MC, V.

[symbols]

B&Bs/Small Inns

★ ★ ★ **CHINA CLIPPER BED BREAKFAST INN.** *525 2nd St (81427). 970/325-0565; fax 970/325-4190; toll-free 800/315-0565. www. chinaclipperinn.com.* 12 air-cooled rms, 3 with shower only, 2 story. Memorial Day-mid-Oct: S, D $75-$175; each addl $10; package plans; hols 2-day min; lower rates rest of yr. Children over 15 yrs only. Crib free. TV in 9 rms; cable (premium), VCR avail. Whirlpool. Complimentary full bkfst; evening refreshments. Restaurants nearby. Ck-out 10:30 am, ck-in 2 pm. In-rm modem link. Coin lndry. X-country ski 5 mi. Some in-rm whirlpools, refrigerators, microwaves, fireplaces. Some balconies. Elegant decor. Totally nonsmoking. Cr cds: DS, MC, V.

[symbols]

★ ★ ★ **DAMN YANKEE COUNTRY INN.** *100 6th Ave (81427). 970/325-4219; fax 970/325-4339; toll-free 800/845-7512. www.montrose.net/ users/damnyank.* 10 air-cooled rms, 3 story, 3 suites. June-Sept: S, D $81-$190; each addl $15; suites $145-$185; special rates (winter); ski plans; lower rates rest of yr. Children over 16 yrs only. TV; cable (premium), VCR avail. Complimentary full bkfst. Restaurant nearby. Ck-out 11 am, ck-in 3 pm. Street parking. Balconies. Some in-rm whirlpools, fireplaces. Surrounded by San Juan Mtns. Whirlpool in gazebo. Totally nonsmoking. Cr cds: DS, MC, V.

[symbols]

★ ★ ★ **ST. ELMO HOTEL.** *426 Main St (81427). 970/325-4951; fax 970/325-0348. www.stelmohotel.com.* 9 rms, 2 story. No rm phones. Mid-May-mid-Oct: D $85-$135; each addl $20; package plans; lower rates rest of yr. TV in sitting rm; cable (premium). Complimentary full bkfst. Restaurant (see BON TON). Bar. Ck-out 11 am, ck-in 1 pm. Business servs avail. Whirlpool. Sauna. Restored 1898 hotel; antiques. Totally non-smoking. Cr cds: A, D, DS, MC, V.

Restaurants

★ ★ **BON TON.** *426 Main St (81427). 970/325-4951.* Hrs: 5-10 pm; winter 5:30-9 pm; Sun brunch 9:30 am-1 pm. Closed Dec 25. Res accepted. Italian menu. Bar. Dinner $12-$25. Sun brunch $8.95. Child's menu. Specializes in pasta, seafood, steak. Built 1898. Outdoor dining. Casual dining. Totally nonsmoking. Cr cds: A, D, DS, MC, V.
D

★ **BUEN TIEMPO.** *515 Main St (81427). 970/325-4544. www.stelmo hotel.com.* Hrs: 4-10 pm; winter 5:30-9 pm. Closed Dec 25. No A/C. Mexican, Southwestern menu. Bar. Dinner $5-$15. Specialties: carne adovada, carne asada. Outdoor dining. Casual dining. In 1891 bldg, originally a hotel. Totally nonsmoking. Cr cds: A, DS, MC, V.
D

★ **CECILIA'S.** *630 Main St (81427). 970/325-4223.* Hrs: 6:30 am-9 pm. Closed mid-Oct-mid-May. Amer menu. Bkfst $3.80-$6.75, lunch $4.50-$6.65, dinner $6.30-$15.75. Child's menu. Specializes in home-made soup, homemade pastries. Entertainment. In vintage movie theater. Cr cds: MC, V.
D

Pagosa Springs

(F-3)

Founded 1880 **Pop** 1,207 **Elev** 7,105 ft **Area code** 970 **Zip** 81147

Information Chamber of Commerce, 402 San Juan St, PO Box 787; 970/264-2360 or 800/252-2204

Web www.pagosa-springs.com

What to See and Do

Chimney Rock Archaeological Area. Area features twin pinnacles, held sacred by the Anasazi; Fire Tower, which offers a spectacular view of ruins; and Great House, which sits atop a mesa accessible only by a steep-walled narrow causeway. Guided tours only (four scheduled tours daily). SE via US 151. Phone 970/883-5359 or 970/264-2268. ¢¢

Fred Harman Art Museum. Displays of original paintings by Fred Harman, Western artist and comic illustrator best remembered for his famous Red Ryder and Little Beaver comic strip. Also rodeo, movie, and Western memorabilia. (Late May-early Oct, daily; rest of yr, Mon-Fri; closed July 4) 2 mi W on US 160, across from jct Piedra Rd. Phone 970/731-5785. ¢¢

Navajo State Park. Waterskiing, fishing, boating (ramps, rentals); picnicking (shelters), groceries, restaurant, camping (dump station). Visitor center. Standard fees. (Daily) 17 mi W on US 160, then 18 mi S on CO 151 near Arboles. Phone 970/883-2208. Per vehicle ¢¢

Rocky Mountain Wildlife Park. Zoo exhibits animals indigenous to the area; wildlife museum; wildlife photography displays. (May-Nov, daily; rest of yr, Mon-Tues, Thurs-Sat afternoons) 5 mi S on US 84. Phone 970/264-4515. ¢¢

Wolf Creek Pass. (10,857 ft) Scenic drive across the Continental Divide. The eastern approach is through the Rio Grande National Forest (see SOUTH FORK), the western approach through the San Juan National Forest (see DURANGO). Best time to drive through is Sept; spectacular views of aspens changing color. Drive takes approx one hr. 20 mi NE via US 160. Phone 970/264-5639. Nearby is

Treasure Mountain. Begin at top of Wolf Creek Pass, just east of summit marked where Continental Divide Trail winds southward and connects with Treasure Mtn Trail. Legend states that in 1790, 300 men mined five million dollars in gold and melted it into bars, but were forced to leave it behind. The gold has never been found.

Wolf Creek Ski Area. Two triple, two double chairlifts; Pomalift; patrol, school, rentals; cafeteria, restaurant, bar, day lodge. Fifty runs; longest run two mi; vertical drop 1,425 ft. (Early Nov-Apr, daily) Shuttle bus service. ¢¢¢¢¢

Special Event

Winter Fest. Winter carnival, individual and team events for all ages. Early Feb. Phone 970/264-2360.

Motels/Motor Lodges

★ **HIGH COUNTRY LODGE.** *3821 E Hwy 160 (81147).* 970/264-4181; *fax* 970/264-4185; *res* 800/862-3707. *www.highcountrylodge.com.* 29 units, 19 A/C, 2 story, 4 kit. cottages. S $50-$66; D $55-$81; each addl $5; kit. cottages $75-$83; under 12 free; wkly rates; ski plans. Crib free. TV; cable. Complimentary continental bkfst. Restaurant adj 5:30-9 pm. Ck-out 11 am. Coin lndry. Meeting rms. In-rm modem links. Exercise equipt. Downhill ski 20 mi; x-country ski 3 mi. Whirlpool. Cr cds: A, C, D, DS, MC, V.

🄳 ⬆️ 🅗 🏊 🏃 ⛷️ 🔥

★★ **PAGOSA SPRINGS INN.** *3565 Hwy 60 W, Pagosa Spring (81147).* 970/731-3400; *fax* 970/731-3402; *toll-free* 888/221-8088. *www.pagosasprings inn.com.* 97 rms, 3 story. May-Sept: S $70; D $75; golf, ski plans; lower rates rest of yr. Crib free. Pet accepted. TV; cable (premium). Complimentary coffee in lobby. Restaurant nearby. Ck-out 11 am. Meeting rms. Business servs avail. X-country ski 3 mi. Indoor pool; whirlpool. Game rm. Bathrm phones, refrigerators; some in-rm whirlpools. Cr cds: A, D, DS, MC, V.

🄳 🐾 🏊 ⛷️ 🔥

Resorts

★★ **PAGOSA LODGE.** *3505 W Hwy 160 (81147).* 970/731-4141; *fax* 970/731-4343; *toll-free* 800/523-7704. *www.pagosalodge.com.* 101 rms, 2-3 story. Late May-Oct: S, D $100-$110; under 13 free; ski, golf plans; some lower rates rest of yr. TV; cable. Indoor pool. Playground. Restaurants 6:30-11 am, 5-9 pm. Box lunches, snacks. Bar 4 pm-2 am. Ck-out 11 am, ck-in 4 pm. Meeting rms. Busi-

ness servs avail. Airport transportation. Exercise equipt; sauna, steam rm. Tennis, pro. 18-hole & 9-hole golf, greens fee, pro, putting green, driving range. Canoes, rowboats. Whitewater rafting. X-country ski on site. Sleigh rides. Hot-air balloon rides. Jeep tours. Bicycle rentals. Lawn games. Rec rm. 6,500-ft private airstrip. Private patios. Picnic tables. On lake. Cr cds: A, D, DS, MC, V.

🄳 ⬆️ 🅗 ⛷️ 🏃 🏊 🏃 🎣

★ **THE SPRING INN.** *165 Hot Springs Blvd (81147).* 970/264-4168; *fax* 970/264-4707; *toll-free* 800/225-0934. *www.pagosa.net/springinn.* 37 rms. S $83-$145; D $83-$180; each addl $5; ski plan. TV; cable (premium), VCR. Complimentary coffee in lobby. Restaurant opp 6 am-10 pm. Ck-out noon. Whirlpools. Game rm. Microwaves avail. Hot springs; unlimited use to guests. Cr cds: D, DS, MC, V.

🄳 ⬆️ 🅗 🏊 🔥

Restaurants

★ **ELKHORN CAFE.** *438 Pagosa St (81147).* 970/264-2146. Hrs: 6 am-9 pm. Closed some major hols. Res accepted. Mexican, Amer menu. Bkfst $1.85-$6.25, lunch $1.25-$6, dinner $2.50-$8.50. Child's menu. Specialties: bkfst burrito, stuffed sopapilla. Casual dining. Family-owned. Cr cds: A, DS, MC, V.

🄳

★★ **RIVERSIDE.** *439 San Juan St (81157).* 970/264-2175. Hrs: 7 am-10 pm. Closed Thanksgiving, Dec 25. No A/C. Southwestern, Amer menu. Wine, beer. Bkfst $3-$7, lunch $3-$8, dinner $6-$12. Child's menu. Outdoor dining. Specializes in beef, chicken. Faces river; view of hot springs. Totally nonsmoking. Cr cds: A, DS, MC, V.

🄳 🆂🅲

Pueblo

(E-5) *See also Cañon City, Colorado Springs*

Settled 1842 **Pop** 102,121 **Elev** 4,695 ft **Area code** 719

Information Chamber of Commerce, PO Box 697, 81002; 719/542-1704; or the Pueblo Visitors Information Center, 302 N Santa Fe Ave, 81003. The Visitors Information Center is open daily.

Web www.pueblochamber.org

What to See and Do

City parks. Approx 700 acres of parks within city. Two of the largest are

City Park. Swimming pool (Memorial Day-Labor Day, daily; fee), children's fishing; 9-hole, 18-hole golf and driving range (fee); tennis, picnicking, zoo (fee); herds of wildlife, children's farm, Eco Center, Rainforest. Historical carousel area (Memorial Day-Labor Day, daily; fee). Thirty-five mi river trail system. Park (daily). Goodnight Ave. Phone 719/542-1704. **FREE**

Mineral Palace Park. Swimming pool (fee), children's fishing; picnicking. Rose garden, greenhouse. Pueblo Art Guild Gallery with local artists exhibits (Sat and Sun; closed Dec-Feb). Main St. Phone 719/566-1745 or 719/542-1704. **FREE**

El Pueblo Museum. Full-sized replica of Old Fort Pueblo, which served as a base for fur traders and other settlers from 1842-1855. Exhibits on the Anasazi, steel and ore production, and narrow-gauge railroads. (Daily; closed Thanksgiving, Dec 25) 324 W First St. Phone 719/583-0453. ¢¢

Fred E. Weisbrod Aircraft Museum. Outdoor museum features static aircraft display. Adj is the **B-24 Aircraft Memorial Museum**, with indoor displays of the history of the B-24 bomber. Guided tours. (Daily; closed hols) Pueblo Memorial Airport. Phone 719/948-3355 or 719/948-9219. ¢¢

The Greenway and Nature Center of Pueblo. Small reptile exhibit and Raptor Center, special nature programs (by appt). Also 36 miles of hiking and biking trails (rentals). Cafe. (Tues-Sun; closed Jan 1, Thanksgiving, Dec 25) 5200 Nature Center Rd, 5 mi W via US 50. Phone 719/549-2414.

Lake Pueblo State Park. Swimming, waterskiing, boating; hiking, camping (dump station). Standard fees.

(Daily) 6 mi W via CO 96 or US 50 W. Phone 719/561-9320. ¢¢

Rosemount Victorian House Museum. This 37-rm mansion contains original Victorian furnishings and the McClelland Collection of world curiosities. (Tues-Sun; closed hols; also closed Jan) 419 W 14th St. Phone 719/545-5290. ¢¢¢

Sangre de Cristo Arts and Conference Center. Four art galleries incl the Francis King Collection of Western Art on permanent display; changing art exhibits; children's museum, workshops, dance studios, theater; gift shop. (Mon-Sat; closed hols) 210 N Santa Fe Ave. Phone 719/295-7200. ¢

San Isabel National Forest. On 1,109,782 acres. Three sections of forest lie adj to this highway with picnicking, camping, and two winter sports areas: Monarch and Ski Cooper. In the southern part of the forest is the Spanish Peaks National Natural Landmark. Collegiate Peaks, Mt Massive, and Holy Cross Wilderness areas are also within the forest, as well as four wilderness study areas. Colorado's highest peak, Mt Elbert (14,433 ft), is within the forest south of Leadville (see). NW and W via US 50. Contact the Supervisor, 2840 Kachina Dr. Phone 719/545-8737. Also in forest is

Lake Isabel. A 310-acre recreation area. Fishing, boating (no motors); picnicking, camping. No swimming. 43 mi SW via I-25, CO 165 or 32 mi SW on CO 76.

University of Southern Colorado. (1975) 4,000 students. Developed from Pueblo Junior College established in 1933. Chemistry Building has Geological Museum with mineral, rock, and fossil exhibits, maps (academic yr, Mon-Fri; closed hols; free). 2200 Bonforte Blvd. Campus tours (Mon-Fri, by appt), contact Admissions Office, Administration Building. Phone 719/549-2461.

Special Events

Colorado State Fair. Fairgrounds, Prairie Ave. PRCA rodeo, grandstand and amphitheater entertainment, livestock and agricultural displays, industrial and high technology displays, home arts, fine arts and crafts, carnival. Phone 719/561-8484 or 800/444-FAIR. Aug-Sept.

Pueblo Greyhound Park. 3215 Lake Ave, S on I-25. Pari-mutuel betting. Phone 719/566-0370. Satellite betting Apr-Sept. Live racing Oct-Mar.

Motels/Motor Lodges

★★ **BEST WESTERN INN AT PUEBLO WEST.** 201 S McCulloch Blvd, Pueblo West (81007). 719/547-2111; fax 719/547-0385; res 800/780-7234. www.bestwestern.com/innatpueblow. 79 rms, 2 story. June-Sept: S $50-$69; D $55-$74; each addl $5; under 12 free; lower rates rest of yr. Crib free. Pet accepted, some restrictions. TV; cable (premium). Pool. Coffee in rms. Restaurant 6 am-10 pm. Ck-out 11 am. Meeting rms. Business servs avail. Exercise equipt. Gift shop. Private patios. Cr cds: A, C, D, DS, MC, V.
🄳 ⬦ ⚮ 🕅 ⬩ 🔥 SC

★★ **COMFORT INN.** 4645 N Freeway Rd (I-25) (81008). 719/542-6868; fax 719/-542-6868 res 800/228-5150. www.comfortinn.com. 60 rms, 2 story. Memorial Day-Aug: S, D $60-$85; each addl $5; lower rates rest of yr. TV; cable (premium). Indoor pool. Complimentary continental bkfst. Restaurant nearby. Ck-out 11 am. Coin lndry. Business servs avail. In-rm modem link. Cr cds: A, DS, JCB, MC, V.
🄳 ⚮ ⬩ 🔥

★ **DAYS INN.** 4201 N Elizabeth (81008). 719/543-8031; fax 719/546-1317; res 800/329-7466. www.daysinn.com. 58 rms, 2 story. S $45-$59; D $55-$69; each addl $6; suites $75-$135; under 13 free. Crib free. TV; cable (premium). Indoor pool; whirlpool. Complimentary continental bkfst. Restaurant nearby. Ck-out 11 am. Coin lndry. Business servs avail. Exercise equipt. Refrigerator, microwave in suites. Cr cds: A, C, D, DS, MC, V.
🄳 ⚮ 🕅 ⬩ 🔥 SC

★★ **HAMPTON INN.** 4703 N Freeway (81008). 719/544-4700; fax 719/544-6526; res 800/426-7866. www.sunstonehotels.com. 111 rms, 2 story. S $59-$79; D $79-$99; under 19 free; golf plans. Crib avail. TV; cable (premium), VCR avail. Heated pool. Complimentary bkfst buffet.

Coffee in rms. Ck-out noon. Coin lndry. Meeting rm. Business servs avail. Exercise equipt. Valet serv. Some refrigerators, microwaves. Cr cds: A, C, D, DS, MC, V.
🄳 ⚮ 🕅 ⬩ 🔥

★★ **HOLIDAY INN.** 4001 N Elizabeth St (81008). 719/543-8050; fax 719/545-2271; toll-free 800/465-4329. www.holiday-inn.com. 193 rms, 2 story. S $59-$99; D $69-$109; each addl $10; suites $150-$250; under 17 free. Crib free. TV; cable. Indoor pool; whirlpool. Coffee in rms. Restaurant 6 am-2 pm, 5-10 pm. Rm serv. Bar 4 pm-2 am, Sun to midnight. Ck-out 11 am. Coin lndry. Meeting rms. Business center. In-rm modem link. Bellhops. Free airport, bus depot transportation. Exercise equipt. Game rm. Cr cds: A, C, D, DS, MC, V.
🄳 ⬥ ⚮ 🕅 ⬩ 🔥 🔥

★★ **WINGATE INN.** 4711 N Elizabeth St (81008). 719/586-9000; toll-free 800/993-7232; res 800/228-1000. www.wingateinns.com. 84 rms, 3 story. Mid-May-Labor Day: S $69-$79; D $79-$89; each addl $10; suites $119; under 18 free; lower rates rest of yr. Crib avail. TV; cable (premium). Indoor pool; whirlpool. Complimentary continental bkfst. Complimentary coffee in rms. Restaurant nearby. Ck-out 11 am. Meeting rms. Business center. In-rm modem link. Exercise equipt. Some refrigerators; microwave in suites. Cr cds: A, C, D, DS, JCB, MC, V.
⚮ 🄳 🕅 ⬩ 🔥 🔥

Hotel

★★★ **MARRIOTT PUEBLO.** 110 W First St (81003). 719/542-3200; toll-free 888/236-2427. www.marriott.com. 164 rms, 7 story. S, D $150-$225; under 17 free. Crib avail. TV; cable (premium). Indoor pool; whirlpool. Restaurant 6:30 am-10 pm. Bar to midnight. Ck-out noon. Meeting rms. Business center. In-rm modem link. Concierge. Exercise equipt. Minibars; many refrigerators in suites. Cr cds: A, C, D, DS, MC, V.
🔥 🔥 🕅 ⬩

B&B/Small Inn

★★★ **ABRIENDO INN.** *300 W Abriendo Ave (81004). 719/544-2703; fax 719/542-6544. www.bedand breakfastinns.org.* 10 rms, 3 story, 1 suite. S, D $110-$115; each addl $15; suite $84. Children over 6 yrs only. TV, cable; VCR. Complimentary full bkfst. Restaurant nearby. Ck-out 11 am, ck-in 3:30-9 pm. Business servs avail. In-rm modem link. Built in 1906; antiques. Totally nonsmoking. Cr cds: A, D, MC, V.

Restaurants

★★ **CAFE DEL RIO.** *5200 Nature Center Rd (81003). 719/549-2029.* Hrs: 11 am-9 pm; Sun brunch 10 am-2 pm. Closed Mon. Res accepted. Serv bar. Lunch $4.25-$9.95, dinner $9.95-$18.95. Sun brunch $12.95. Child's menu. Specializes in steak, seafood, chicken. Own soups. Parking. Outdoor dining. Scenic view of Arkansas river; adobe building built by volunteers. Cr cds: A, D, DS, MC, V.

★★ **GAETANO'S.** *910 US 50 W (81008). 719/546-0949.* Hrs: 11 am-10 pm; Sat from 4 pm; early-bird dinner 4-6 pm. Closed Sun; Jan 1, Dec 25. Res accepted. Italian, Amer menu. Bar. Lunch $4.95-$8.95. Complete meals: dinner $6.95-$17.95. Child's menu. Specializes in steak, seafood, lasagne. Casual dining. Outdoor dining. Family-owned. Cr cds: A, C, D, DS, ER, MC, V.

★★★ **LA RENAISSANCE.** *217 E Routt Ave (81004). 719/543-6367.* Hrs: 11 am-2 pm, 5-9 pm; Sat from 5 pm. Closed Sun; some major hols. Res accepted. Continental menu. Bar. Wine list. Complete meals: lunch $5.95-$10.95, dinner $9.95-$22.95. Specialties: baby back ribs, prime rib. Church built in 1886; garden rm. Totally nonsmoking. Cr cds: A, D, DS, MC, V.

Rocky Mountain National Park

(B-4) *See also Estes Park, Granby, Grand Lake, Loveland, Lyons*

(Park headquarters is 3 mi W of Estes Park on US 36; western entrance at Grand Lake)

More than 100 years ago, Joel Estes built a cabin on Fish Creek, one of the higher sections of north-central Colorado. Although the Estes family moved away, more settlers soon followed, and the area became known as Estes Park. Described by Albert Bierstadt, one of the great 19th-century landscape artists of the West, as America's finest composition for the painter, the land west of where Estes settled was set aside as Rocky Mountain National Park in 1915.

Straddling the Continental Divide, with valleys 8,000 feet in elevation and 114 named peaks more than 10,000 feet high, the 415-square-mile park contains a staggering profusion of peaks, upland meadows, sheer canyons, glacial streams, and lakes. Dominating the scene is Longs Peak, with its east face towering 14,255 feet above sea level. The park's forests and meadows provide sanctuary for more than 750 varieties of wildflowers, more than 260 species of birds, and such indigenous mammals as deer, wapiti (American elk), bighorn sheep, beaver, and other animals. There are five campgrounds, two of which take reservations from May to early September (fee; write Destinet, 9450 Carroll Park Dr, San Diego CA, 92121-2256; 800/365-2267). Some attractions are not accessible during winter months. $10/car/week; Golden Eagle Passport accepted (see MAKING THE MOST OF YOUR TRIP). Contact Superintendent, Rocky Mountain National Park, Estes Park 80517-8397; 970/586-1206.

What to See and Do

Bear Lake Road. Scenic drive (plowed in winter months) into high

mountain basin is rimmed with precipitous 12,000- to 14,000-ft peaks.
At end of road self-guided nature
trail circles Bear Lake. Other trails
lead to higher lakes, gorges, glaciers.
Bus service (summer).

⭐ **Headquarters Building.** Information (publications sales, maps); program on park (daily); guided walks
and illustrated eve programs (summer only; daily). Just outside east
entrance station on US 36 approach.

Moraine Park Museum. Exhibits,
information, publications sales,
maps. (May-Sept, daily) One mi
inside park from Beaver Meadows
entrance.

Never Summer Ranch. Historic pioneer homestead and preserved 1920s
dude ranch. (Weather permitting,
mid-June-Labor Day, daily) 10 mi N
of Grand Lake entrance on Trail
Ridge Rd. Phone 970/627-3471.

Trail Ridge Road. Above-the-treeline
road roughly parallels a trail once
used by Utes and Arapahos; 8 mi of
full 48-mi length is above 11,000 ft;
entire drive provides views of Rocky
Mtn grandeur and, far to the east,
the Great Plains; overlooks provide
stopping places for views of Longs
Peak and Forest Canyon. Self-guided
tour brochure can be obtained at
park headquarters and visitor centers; Alpine Visitor Center at Fall
River Pass has exhibits on alpine tun-
dra ecology (summer, daily). Road
closed to transmountain travel mid-
Oct-late May. West of Estes Park to
Grand Lake, crossing Continental
Divide.

Salida

(D-4) *See also Buena Vista*

Founded 1880 **Pop** 5,504 **Elev** 7,036
ft **Area code** 719 **Zip** 81201
Information Heart of the Rockies
Chamber of Commerce, 406 W US
50; 719/539-2068

What to See and Do

The Angel of Shavano. Every spring
the snow melts on the 14,239-ft
slopes of Mt Shavano leaving an outline called "The Angel."

**Arkansas Headwaters State Recre-
ation Area.** Area of 5,000 acres, with
an outstanding waterway that cuts
its way through rugged canyons for
148 mi, from Leadville to Pueblo.
One of the world's premier water-
ways for kayaking and whitewater
rafting; fishing, boating (ramps);
hiking, bridle trails; picnicking,
camping. Interpretive programs.
(Daily) US 24, 285, and 50. Visitor
Center, 301 W Sackett. Phone
719/539-7289. ¢

Jeep tours. To mountainous areas
inaccessible by car, over trails, old
railroad beds. Outfitters offer ½-hr,
½-day, and full-day trail rides; fishing, hunting, photography, and pack
trips. Contact Chamber of Commerce for details.

Monarch Scenic Tram. Continuous
trips to deck and observatory at
12,000 ft offer panoramic views of
Rocky Mtns. (May-Sept, daily) US 50
at Monarch Pass. Phone 719/539-
4789. ¢¢

Mountain Spirit Winery. Family-
operated boutique winery. Five acres
with apple orchard, homestead.
Tours, tastings (Memorial Day-Labor
Day, wkends). 13 mi W of Salida on
US 50. Phone 719/539-1175. **FREE**
Tastings also at

Mountain Spirit Winery. Tasting
rm, art gallery, gift shop. (Mon-Sat)
201 F St. Phone 719/539-7848.
FREE

Mount Shavano Fish Hatchery. State-
operated hatchery. (Daily) ½ mi W
on CO 291, US 50. Phone 719/539-
6877.

Salida Museum. Museum features
mineral display, Native American
artifacts, early pioneer household
display, mining and railroad display.
(Late May-early Sept, daily) Phone
719/539-7483. ¢¢

**Skiing. Monarch Ski & Snowboard
Area.** Four double chairlifts; patrol,
school, rentals; cafeteria, restaurant,
bar, nursery. Fifty-four runs; longest
run two mi; vertical drop 1,160 ft.
(Mid-Nov-mid-Apr, daily) Multiday,
half-day rates. X-country skiing. 18
mi W on US 50 at Monarch Pass
(11,312 ft). Phone 996/766-9719.
¢¢¢¢

Tenderfoot Drive. Spiral drive encir-
cling Mt Tenderfoot. Views of surrounding mountain area and upper
Arkansas Valley. W on CO 291.

Special Events

FIBArk River International Whitewater Boat Race. International experts compete in a 26-mi kayak race. Other events incl slalom, raft, foot, and bicycle races. Father's Day wkend. Phone 719/539-7997.

Artwalk. Downtown Historic District. Local artisans, craftspeople, and entertainers display artwork. Last wkend June.

Chaffee County Fair. Five days last wkend July. Phone 719/539-6151.

Christmas Mountain USA. Three-day season opener; more than 3,500 lights outline a 700-ft Christmas tree on Tenderfoot Mtn; parade. Day after Thanksgiving. Phone 719/539-2068.

Motels/Motor Lodges

★ **BEST WESTERN COLORADO LODGE.** *352 W Rainbow Blvd (81201). 719/539-2514; fax 719/539-4316; res 800/780-7234. www.best western.com.* 35 rms. May-Oct: S, D $70-$79; each addl $5; lower rates rest of yr. Crib free. TV; cable (premium). Indoor pool; whirlpool. Sauna. Complimentary continental bkfst, coffee in rms. Restaurant opp 6 am-9 pm. Ck-out 10 am. Coin lndry. Business servs avail. In-rm modem link. Free local airport, bus depot transportation. Tennis, volleyball, shuffleboard, basketball, picnic facilities adj. Downhill ski 16 mi; x-country ski 12 mi. Refrigerators. Cr cds: A, C, D, DS, MC, V.
⊠ ⊠ 🕭 ⊁ 🖈

★ **TRAVELODGE.** *7310 W US 50 (81201). 719/539-2528; fax 719/539-7235; res 800/578-7878. www.salidatravelodge.com.* 27 rms, 10 with shower only, 2 story, 3 cottages. S, D $65-$99; each addl $5; cottages $66-$77; under 10 free; package plans. Crib free. Pet accepted $3-$5. TV; cable (premium), VCR avail. Heated pool; 2 whirlpools. Complimentary continental bkfst, coffee in rms. Restaurant nearby. Ck-out 11 am. Meeting rm. Business servs avail. Downhill/x-country ski 18 mi. Fishing, rafting. Refrigerators, microwaves avail. Cr cds: A, C, D, DS, MC, V.
🐾 🕭 ⊁ ⊠ ✈ ⊠ 🕭 SC

B&B/Small Inn

★★ **TUDOR ROSE BED & BREAKFAST.** *6720 County Rd 104 (81201). 719/539-2002; fax 719/530-0345; toll-free 800/379-0889. www.thetudorrose. com.* 6 rms, 2 share bath, 3 story, 2 suites. S, D $85-$165; each addl $20; suites $120; children over 10 yrs only. TV; VCR (movies) in common rm. Whirlpool. Complimentary full bkfst; afternoon refreshments. In-rm modem link. Ck-out 11 am, ck-in 4-7 pm. Luggage handling. Hiking trail. Downhill ski 18 mi; x-country ski 7 mi. Horseback riding. Some in-rm TVs, VCRs, CD players, whirlpools, refrigerators. Country manor located on hill. Overnight horse stabling $9.50/horse/day. Totally nonsmoking. Cr cds: DS, MC, V.
⊠ ⊠ 🕭

Restaurants

★★ **COUNTRY BOUNTY.** *413 W Rainbow Blvd (81201). 719/539-3546.* Hrs: 6:30 am-9 pm. Closed Thanksgiving, Dec 24-25. Res accepted. Amer, Mexican menu. Bkfst $2.25-$5.75, lunch $2.75-$6.95, dinner $5.50-$15. Child's menu. Specialty: almond chicken Shanghai. Dining rm overlooking garden and mountains. Totally nonsmoking. Cr cds: A, C, DS, MC, V.
D SC

★ **WINDMILL.** *720 E Rainbow Blvd (81201). 719/539-3594.* Hrs: 11 am-9 pm; Fri, Sat to 10 pm. Closed Thanksgiving, Dec 25. Res accepted. Bar. Lunch $5.95-$13.50, dinner $6.95-$16.95. Child's menu. Specializes in Tex-Mex dishes. Rustic decor. Cr cds: A, C, DS, ER, MC, V.
D SC ⊣

Silverton

(E-2) *See also Durango, Ouray*

Settled 1874 **Pop** 531 **Elev** 9,318 ft
Area code 970 **Zip** 81433

Information Chamber of Commerce, 414 Greene St; 970/387-5654 or 800/752-4494

Web www.silverton.org

What to See and Do

Circle Jeep Tour. Mapped jeep route with historical information to many mines and ghost towns. Contact the Chamber of Commerce. Phone 970/387-5654 or 800/752-4494. ¢

Old Hundred Gold Mine Tour. Guided one-hr tour of underground mine offers view of mining equipt, crystal pockets, veins; learn about methods of hardrock mining. (Memorial Day-Sept, daily). 5 mi E via CO 110, on County Rd 4A. Phone 970/387-5444 or 800/872-3009. ¢¢¢¢

San Juan County Historical Society Museum. Located in old three-story jail. Mining and railroad artifacts from Silverton's early days. (Memorial Day-mid-Oct, daily) Main St. Phone 970/387-5838. ¢¢

The Silverton. Narrow-gauge train (see DURANGO). Phone 970/247-2733.

Special Events

Iron Horse Bicycle Classic. Bicycles race the Silverton narrow-gauge train. Late May. Phone 970/259-4621.

Silverton Jubilee Folk Music Festival. Late June. Phone 970/387-5737.

Brass Band Festival. Mid-Aug. Phone 800/752-4497.

Hardrockers Holiday. Mining skills competition. Mid-Aug. Phone 800/752-4497.

B&Bs/Small Inns

★★ **ALMA HOUSE BED AND BREAKFAST.** *220 E 10th St (81433). 970/387-5336; fax 970/387-5974; toll-free 800/267-5336.* 10 air-cooled rms, 2½ story, 6 with bath, 4 share bath. No rm phones. S, D $79-$99; suites $130. Crib free. Pet accepted, some restrictions; $10. TV; cable (premium). Complimentary full bkfst. Ck-out 11 am, ck-in 2 pm. Business servs avail. Luggage handling. Built 1898. Victorian furnishings. Some fireplaces. Totally nonsmoking. Cr cds: A, DS, MC, V.

★★★ **WYMAN HOTEL.** *1371 Greene St (81433). 970/387-5372; fax 970/387-5745; toll-free 800/609-7845. www.silverton.org/wymanhotel.* 18 air-cooled rms, 2 story. Apr-Oct, Jan-Mar: S, D $100-$195; package plans; each addl $20, under 14 $15. Closed Nov, Dec, Mar, Apr. Crib free. Pet accepted; $15. TV; cable (premium), VCR (free movies). Complimentary full bkfst; afternoon refreshments. Restaurant nearby. Ck-out 10:30 am, ck-in after 3-8 pm. Business servs avail. In-rm modem link. Luggage handling. Some refrigerators. Street parking. Built 1902. Victorian furnishings. Totally nonsmoking. Cr cds: A, DS, MC, V.

Restaurant

★ **HANDLEBARS.** *117 W 13th (81433). 970/387-5395. www.handlebarsco.com.* Hrs: 10:30 am-10 pm. Closed Nov-Apr. No A/C. Bar to 2 am. Lunch $3.75-$8.95, dinner $5.95-$22.95. Specialties: baby back ribs, chicken-fried steak. Own chili & soup. Built in 1881; display of antique mining and museum wildlife artifacts. Cr cds: DS, MC, V.

Snowmass Village

(C-3) *See also Aspen, Glenwood Springs*

Pop 1,822 **Elev** 8,604 ft
Area code 970 **Zip** 81615
Information Snowmass Resort Association, 38 Village Square, PO Box 5566; 970/923-2000 or 800/766-9627

What to See and Do

Bicycle trips and jeep trips. Throughout the Snowmass/Aspen area. Transportation and equipt provided. (June-Sept) Contact Blazing Adventures, Box 5929. Phone 970/923-4544. ¢¢¢¢

Krabloonik Husky Kennels. Half-day dog-sled trips by res (Dec-Apr). Kennel tours (mid-June-Sept, Mon-Sat). 5 mi SW of CO 82 on Divide Rd. Contact PO Box 5517. Phone 970/923-3953. Trips ¢¢¢

River rafting. Snowmass Whitewater. Half-day, full-day, and overnight trips on the Arkansas, Roaring Fork, Colorado, Gunnison, and Dolores rivers. Trips range from scenic floats for beginners to exciting runs for experienced rafters. (May-Oct daily, depending on snow melt) Transportation to site. 70 Snowmass Village Mall. Phone 970/923-4544 or 800/282-7238. ¢¢¢¢

Skiing. Snowmass Ski Area. Seven quad, two triple, six double chairlifts; two platter pulls; patrol, school, rentals, snowmaking; restaurants, bar, nursery. Eighty-three runs; longest run five mi, vertical drop 4,406 ft. (Late Nov-mid-Apr, daily) X-country skiing (50 mi). Shuttle bus service from Aspen. Phone 970/923-1220. ¢¢¢¢

Motels/Motor Lodges

★★★ **SILVERTREE.** *100 Elbert Ln (81615). 970/923-3520; fax 970/923-5192; toll-free 800/837-4255. www.silvertreehotel.com.* 261 rms, 2-7 story. No A/C. Late Nov-early Apr: S, D $145-$550; each addl $25; suites $295-$2,950; under 12 free; family rates in summer; higher rates midlate Dec; varied lower rates rest of yr. Crib free. Pet accepted. TV; cable (premium). 2 heated pools; whirlpool, poolside serv. Playground. Coffee in rms. Restaurant 7 am-10 pm. Rm serv. Bar 11:30-1 am; entertainment. Ck-out 10 am. Coin lndry. Meeting rms. Business center. In-rm modem link. Valet serv. Concierge. Shopping arcade. Beauty shop. Free local airport transportation. Downhill/x-country ski on site. Ski rentals. Exercise rm; steam rm. Massage. Bicycle rentals. Lawn games. Refrigerators. Private patios, balconies. Cr cds: A, C, D, DS, MC, V.

★★ **STONEBRIDGE INN.** *300 Carriage Way (81615). 970/923-2420; fax 970/923-5889; toll-free 800/213-3214. www.stonebridgeinn.com.* 95 rms, 7 story. Feb-mid Mar: S, D $175-$245; suites $235-$300; under 12 free; ski plans; higher rates hols; lower rates rest of yr. Crib free. TV; cable (premium), VCR avail (movies). Heated pool; whirlpool. Sauna. Complimentary continental bkfst. Complimentary coffee in rms. Bar 3:30-11 pm. Ck-out 10 am. Coin lndry. Meeting rms. Business servs avail. Bellhops. Valet serv. Concierge. Sundries. Mas-sage. Free airport transportation. Downhill ski on site; x-country ski ½ mi. Refrigerators. Some balconies. Picnic tables. Cr cds: A, MC, V.

Resorts

★★ **CRESTWOOD LODGE.** *400 Wood Rd (81615). 970/923-2450; fax 970/923-5018; toll-free 800/356-5949. www.thecrestwood.com.* 122 air-cooled kit. condos (1-3 bedrm), 3 story. No elvtr. Feb-Mar: S, D $310-$778; each addl $25; under 13 free in summer (2 max); ski plans; higher rates Christmas hols; lower rates rest of yr. TV; cable (premium), VCR (movies $4). Heated pool; whirlpool. Complimentary coffee. Ck-out 10 am. Guest lndry. Meeting rms. Business servs avail. In-rm modem link. Bellhops. Valet serv. Airport transportation. Downhill/x-country ski on site. Exercise equipt; sauna. Health club privileges. Refrigerators, microwaves, fireplaces. Balconies. Grills. Cr cds: A, C, D, DS, MC, V.

★★★ **SNOWMASS CLUB.** *0239 Snowmass Club Cir (81615). 970/923-5600; fax 970/923-6944; toll-free 800/525-0710. www.snowmassclub.com.* 76 hotel rms, 4 story, 62 villas. Mid-Nov-mid-Apr: S, D $130-$355; each addl $20; villas $199-$809; under 12 free; wkly, ski, golf plans; higher rates hols; lower rates rest of yr. TV; cable (premium), VCR avail. 2 heated pools; wading pool, whirlpool, poolside serv. Supervised children's activities; ages 6 months-8 yrs. Complimentary coffee in rms. Restaurant (see also SAGE). Box lunches. Rm serv. Bar 11 am-midnight. Ck-out noon, villas 10 am, ck-in 4 pm. Grocery, package store 1 mi. Coin lndry. Meeting rms. Business center. Gift shop. Free valet parking. Concierge. Free airport, ski area transportation. Sports dir. Lighted and indoor tennis, pro. 18-hole golf, pro, putting green, driving range. Downhill ski 1 mi; x-country ski on site. Ski rentals. Snowmobiling, sleighing. Exercise rm; sauna, steam rm. Massage. Refrigerators; microwaves avail. Private patios, balconies. Cr cds: A, D, DS, MC, V.

★ ★ **WILDWOOD LODGE.** *40 Elbert Ln (81615). 970/923-3550; fax 970/923-5494; toll-free 800/445-1642. www.wildwood-lodge.com.* 148 rms, 3-4 story. Nov-Mar: S, D $69-$195; each addl $25; suites $175-$600; under 12 free; ski plans; higher rates hols; lower rates rest of yr. Crib free. Pet accepted. TV; cable (premium), VCR avail. Heated pool; whirlpool, poolside serv. Complimentary continental bkfst (winter). Complimentary coffee in rms. Restaurant 5-10 pm. Rm serv. Bar. Ck-out 10 am. Coin lndry. Meeting rms. Business servs avail. In-rm modem link. Bellhops. Valet serv. Concierge. Free airport transportation. Downhill/x-country ski 1 blk. Health club privileges. Refrigerators; microwaves avail. Patios, balconies. Cr cds: A, C, D, DS, MC, V.

⬛🔧🐟🛋️🏊🏊♨️⛷️🔥

Restaurants

★ ★ ★ **KRABLOONIK.** *4250 Divide Rd (81615). 970/923-3953. www. krabloonik.com.* Hrs: summer 6-10 pm (closed Tues); winter 11 am-2 pm, 5:30-10 pm. Closed mid-Apr-May, Oct-Thanksgiving. Res accepted. No A/C. Continental menu. A la carte entrees: dinner $22.50-$49.50. Prix fixe: lunch $25. Specializes in fresh seafood, wild game. Rustic atmosphere. Dogsled rides in winter; kennel tours in summer. Totally nonsmoking. Cr cds: MC, V.

⬛

★ ★ ★ **SAGE.** *239 Snowmass Circle (81615). 970/923-0923.* Hrs: 7 am-10 pm; early-bird dinner 5-7 pm. Res accepted. Contemporary Amer menu. Bar 10 am-midnight. Bkfst $7-$9.50, lunch $7-$14, dinner $14-$23. Child's menu. Specialties: Rocky Mountain herb-crusted trout, pan-seared halibut, roasted lamb loin. Valet parking. Outdoor dining. Cr cds: A, C, D, DS, MC, V.

⬛↗️

★ ★ **TOWER.** *45 Village Sq (81615). 970/923-4650.* Hrs: 11:30 am-3 pm, 5:30-10 pm; summer from 6 pm. Res accepted (dinner). Bar. Lunch $5-$8, dinner $14-$24. Child's menu. Specialties: elk tenderloin, cedar-planked salmon, shrimp pasta. Comedy, magic. Outdoor dining. Casual

mountain-lodge decor; view of mountains. Totally nonsmoking. Cr cds: D, DS, MC, V.

⬛↗️

South Fork

(F-3) *See also Monte Vista*

Pop 604 **Elev** 8,200 ft **Area code** 719 **Zip** 81154

Information Visitors Center, PO Box 1030; 719/873-5512 or 800/571-0881

Web www.southfork.org

What to See and Do

Rio Grande National Forest. This rugged forest surrounding the San Luis Valley incl Wolf Creek Pass (10,850 ft) (see PAGOSA SPRINGS). Within the forest is the rugged Sangre de Cristo backcountry and parts of Weminuche, South San Juan, and La Garita wildernesses. Fishing, boating; hunting, hiking, downhill and x-country skiing, snowmobiling, picnicking, camping. North, south, and west of town. Contact Forest Headquarters, 1803 W US 160, Monte Vista 81144. Phone 719/852-5941. In forest are

Creede. (pop 653) Frontier mining town. 22 mi NW on CO 149.

Wolf Creek Ski Area. (see). 18 mi SW on US 160.

Special Events

Creede Repertory Theater. 21 mi NW on CO 149 in Creede. Classic and modern comedies, drama, musicals. Advance res suggested. Nightly Tues-Sun; also Wed and Fri afternoons; children's matinee Sat in Aug. Contact PO Box 269, Creede 81130. Phone 719/873-5512. Early June-Labor Day. Phone 719/658-2540.

Logger Days Festival. Logging competition, crafts, food, music. Third wkend July.

Motel/Motor Lodge

★ **WOLF CREEK LODGE.** *31042 W Hwy 160 (81154). 719/873-5547; fax 719/873-5027; toll-free 800/874-0416. www.southforkco.com/wclodge.* 49 air-cooled rms, 1-2 story, 18 kit. units. S

$45-$50; D $62-$68; kit. units $50-$68; ski plans; wkly rates. Crib free. Pet accepted. TV; cable. Playground. Ck-out 10 am. Meeting rms. Business servs avail. Downhill ski 18 mi; x-country ski 3 mi. Snowmobiling. Horseback riding. Fishing. Hiking. Whirlpool. Microwaves avail. Cr cds: A, MC, V.

D 🐾 🎿 ⚡ 🛄 🔥

Steamboat Springs (A-3)

Settled 1875 **Pop** 9,815 **Elev** 6,695 ft
Area code 970 **Zip** 80477
Information Steamboat Springs Chamber Resort Association, PO Box 774408; 970/879-0880 or 800/922-2722
Web www.steamboat-chamber.com

What to See and Do

Routt National Forest. More than one million acres incl the 139,898-acre Mt Zirkel Wilderness and 38,870 acres of the 235,230-acre Flat Tops Wilderness. Fishing; hunting, winter sports area, hiking, picnicking, camping. Contact the Supervisor, 29587 W US 40, Suite 20, 80487. A Ranger District office is also located in town. North, east, south, and southwest of town. Phone 970/879-1722.

Scenic drives. The following drives are accessible in summer and are well-maintained paved and gravel-surfaced roads. Impressive view of valley and Howelsen Ski Complex. Fish Creek Falls (283 ft) 3 mi E. Picnic area. Buffalo Pass (10,180 ft) 15 mi NE. Impressive road atop Continental Divide leading to formerly inaccessible trout-filled lakes. Rabbit Ears Pass (9,680 ft) 22 mi SE. Additional information avail at information centers.

Skiing.

   Howelsen Hill Ski Complex. International ski/jump complex incl a double chairlift, Pomalift, rope tow, five ski jumping hills; patrol; ice-skating, snowboarding. Eve skiing avail. (Dec-Mar, daily) Also summer activities. Off US 40 on

River Rd via 5th St bridge. Phone 970/879-4300. ¢¢¢¢

   Steamboat. Gondola; four high-speed quad, quad, six triple, seven double chairlifts; two surface tows; patrol, school, rentals, snowmaking; cafeterias, restaurants, bars, nursery. One hundred forty-two runs; longest run three mi; vertical drop 3,668 ft. (Late Nov-early Apr, daily) X-country skiing (14 mi). Multiday, half-day rates. Snowboarding. Gondola also operates mid-June-mid-Sept (daily; fee) 3 mi E on US 40. Phone 800/922-2722. ¢¢¢¢

Steamboat Health & Recreation Association. Three hot pools fed by 103°F mineral water; lap pool, saunas, exercise classes, massage, weight rm, tennis courts (summer). (Daily) 136 Lincoln Ave, east end of town. Phone 970/879-1828. ¢¢ Also here is

   Hot Slide Hydrotube. Tube slide with 350 ft of hot water. (Daily) Phone 970/879-1828. ¢¢

Steamboat Lake State Park. Swimming, waterskiing, fishing, boating (ramps); picnicking, camping. Standard fees. (Daily) 26 mi N on County 129. Phone 970/879-3922. ¢¢

Strawberry Park Natural Hot Springs. Mineral springs feed four pools; water cooled from 160°F to 105°F. Changing area; picnicking, camping, cabins. (Daily) 7 mi NE at 44200 County 36. Phone 970/879-0342.

Tread of Pioneers Museum. Victorian house with period rms and furnishings. Pioneer and cattle ranching artifacts, Native American displays, permanent ski exhibit tracing the evolution of skiing. (Fall/Spring, Tues-Sat; Summer/Winter, Mon-Sat) 8th and Oak Sts. Phone 970/879-2214. ¢¢

Special Events

Cowboy Roundup Days. Rodeos, parade, entertainment. July 4th wkend.

Mustang Round-Up. Mid-June.

Rainbow Weekend. Balloon rally, arts and crafts fair, concerts, rodeo. Mid-July.

Winter Carnival. Snow and ski competitions, parade. Early Feb.

Motels/Motor Lodges

★ **ALPINER LODGE.** *424 Lincoln Ave (80488). 970/879-1430; fax 970/879-6044; toll-free 800/538-7519. www. steamboat-lodging.com.* 33 rms, 2 story. Mid-Nov-Mar: S, D $69-$99; each addl $10; under 12 free; lower rates rest of yr. Crib free. Pet accepted. TV; cable (premium). Complimentary coffee in rms. Restaurant opp 6 am-10 pm. Ck-out 10 am. Business servs avail. In-rm modem link. Downhill ski 1 mi; x-country ski ½ mi. Microwaves, refrigerators avail. Cr cds: A, C, D, DS, MC, V.

🅳 🐾 🍴 🏊 🏋 🐾 🔥

★★ **BEST WESTERN PTARMIGAN INN.** *2304 Apres Ski Way (80477). 970/897-1730; fax 970/879-6044; res 800/780-7234. www.steamboat-lodging.com.* 77 rms, 47 A/C, 3-4 story. Late Nov-mid-Apr: S, D $72-$234; each addl $10; under 18 free; higher rates late Dec; package plans; varied lower rates rest of yr. Closed early Apr-late May. Crib free. Pet accepted. TV; cable, VCR. Heated pool; whirlpool. Sauna. Complimentary coffee. Restaurant. Rm serv. Bar 4-10 pm. Ck-out 10 am. Coin lndry. Business servs avail. In-rm modem link. Valet serv. Downhill/x-country ski on site. Ski rentals, storage. Refrigerators. Balconies. View of Mt Werner, valley. Cr cds: A, C, D, DS, MC, V.

🐾 🍴 🏊 🔥

★★ **HOLIDAY INN.** *3190 S Lincoln Ave (80477). 970/879-2250; fax 970/879-0251; toll-free 800/654-3944. www.holidayinnsteamboat.com.* 82 rms, 2 story. Late Jan-Mar: S, D $129-$169; each addl $10; under 19 free; higher rates late Dec-early Jan; lower rates rest of yr. Crib free. Pet accepted, some restrictions; $10/night. TV; cable (premium), VCR avail. Heated pool; wading pool, whirlpool. Restaurant 6 am-11 pm. Rm serv. Bar 4-11 pm. Coffee in rms. Ck-out 11 am. Coin lndry. Meeting rm. Business servs avail. In-rm modem link. Valet serv. Downhill/x-country ski 1 mi. Exercise equipt. Game rm. Lawn games.

Some refrigerators; microwaves avail. Cr cds: A, C, D, DS, MC, V.

🅳 🐾 🏊 🏋 🐾 🔥 SC

Hotel

★★★ **SHERATON.** *2200 Village Inn Court (80477). 970/879-2220; fax 970/879-7686; toll-free 800/848-8877. www.steamboat-sheraton.* 311 rms, 8 story. S, D $99-$259; each addl $15; suites $249-$649; kit. units $139-$580; under 17 free; ski, golf plans; varied lower rates June-mid-Sept, Thanksgiving-mid-Dec, Jan. Closed mid-Apr-mid-May, mid-Oct-mid-Nov. TV; cable (premium). Heated pool; whirlpool. Complimentary coffee in rms. Dining rm 6:30 am-2 pm, 5:30-10 pm. Rm serv. Bar 2 pm-1 am. Ck-out 11 am, ck-in 5 pm. Coin lndry. Convention facilities. Business servs avail. Bellhops. Concierge. Shopping arcade. Tennis privileges. 18-hole golf privileges, pro, greens fee $80. Downhill/x-country ski on site; rentals. Exercise rm; sauna. Health club privileges. Game rm. Refrigerators; microwaves avail. Private patios. Picnic tables. Cr cds: A, C, D, DS, MC, V.

🅳 🐾 🏋 🏊 🏋 🏃 🏊 🏋 🔥

Resort

★★ **GLEN EDEN RESORT.** *54737 US 129, Clark (80428). 970/879-3906; fax 970/870-0858; toll-free 800/882-0854. glenedenresort.com.* 28 kit. cottages, 1-2 story. Jan-Sept: cottages $115-$145; each addl $20; under 17 free; higher rates mid-Dec-early Jan; lower rates rest of yr. Crib free. TV; VCR avail (movies $2). Heated pool; whirlpools. Playground. Dining rm 11:30 am-9 pm. Bar. Ck-out 10 am, ck-in 4 pm. Coin lndry. Grocery ½ mi. Meeting rms. Business servs avail. Tennis. Downhill ski 20 mi; x-country ski on site. Bicycles avail. Lawn games. Microwaves. Balconies. Picnic tables, grills. Cr cds: A, DS, MC, V.

🅳 🐾 🏊 🏋 🏊 ✈ 🐾 🔥

B&B/Small Inn

★★ **SKY VALLEY LODGE.** *31490 US Hwy 40 (80477). 970/879-7749; fax 970/879-7752; res 800/538-7519. www.steamboat-lodging.com.* 24 rms, 3 story. No A/C. No elvtr. Late Nov-mid-Apr: S, D $69-$189; each addl $10; higher rates Christmas; lower rates rest of yr. Crib free. Pet accepted, some restrictions. TV; cable. Complimentary bkfst. Dining rm 7-10 am, noon-2 pm, 5-8 pm (in season). Bar 3-11 pm. Ck-out 11 am. Meeting rms. Business servs avail. In-rm modem link. Downhill ski 7 mi; x-country ski 5 mi. Whirlpool. Sauna. Totally nonsmoking. Cr cds: A, C, D, DS, MC, V.

🖼️ 🖼️ 🖼️ SC 🖼️

Guest Ranches

★ ★ ★ ★ **THE HOME RANCH.** *54880 County Rd 129, Clark (80428). 970/879-1780; fax 970/879-1795.* Sprawled at the northern end of Elk River Valley, this authentic ranch is family-oriented and offers summer and fall horseback riding programs (led by experienced wranglers) for all ages. Nightly activities and other back-to-nature recreations, including fly-fishing in the summer and skiing in the winter, keep guests entertained. There are eight private cabins and six lodge rooms available. 6 rms in lodge, 8 cottages. No rm phones. AP, June-early Oct and mid-Dec-Mar, wkly: D $3,500-$4,600; each addl $1,650/wk. Closed rest of yr. Heated pool; whirlpool. Sauna. Playground. Supervised child's activities; ages 6-16. Complimentary coffee in rms. Dining rm 8-9 am, noon-1 pm, dinner (1 sitting) 7 pm; children's dinner 5:30 pm. Box lunches, snacks, picnics. Ck-out 10 am, ck-in 4 pm. Business servs avail. Valet serv. Free local airport, bus depot transportation. Downhill ski 20 mi; x-country ski on site. Sleighing, tobogganing, ski instructor. Guided hiking. Horse riding instruction avail. Lawn games. Soc dir; entertainment nightly, movies. Rec rm. Fishing guides. Fly-fishing instruction avail. Petting zoo for children. Refrigerators, wood stoves. Private whirlpool in each cabin. Private porches. Ranch team roping, barbecue. Library. Cr cds: A, MC, V.

D 🖼️ 🖼️ 🖼️ 🖼️ 🖼️ 🖼️

★ ★ ★ ★ **VISTA VERDE RANCH.** *31100 Seedhouse Rd, Steamboat Springs (80428). 970/879-3858; fax 970/879-1413; toll-free 800/526-7433. www.vistaverde.com.* This dude ranch is set on a 500-acre retreat in Rocky Mountain high country and is surrounded by national forest. Although the idea is to get back in touch with nature, the accommodations don't skimp on creature comforts. Cabins have down comforters, woodstoves, and private hot tubs, and all lodge rooms have balconies with views of the ranch. 8 cabins, 1-2 story, 3 lodge rms. No A/C. Early June-late Sept, AP (7-day min): S, D $1,750-$1,850/person/wk; under 8, $1,250-$1,350/wk; lower rates June-Sept, Dec-Mar. Playground. Free supervised children's activities (late May-mid-Sept). Coffee in rms. Box lunches, snack bar, picnics. Dining rm. Meeting rms. Business servs avail. Guest lndry. Gift shop. Free airport, bus depot transportation. Lake swimming. X-country ski on site. Sleighing, tobogganing. Mountain bikes. Guided hiking trips. Float and backpack trips; gold-panning expeditions. Rock climbing with guide. Hot-air ballooning. Hayrides. Cattle drives. Dog sledding. Lawn games. Rec rm. Game rm. Entertainment; movies in lodge. Whirlpool. Exercise equipt; sauna. Massage. Fish/hunt guides. Refrigerators. Wood stoves. Private porches. Totally nonsmoking. No cr cds accepted.

🖼️ 🖼️ 🖼️ 🖼️ 🖼️ 🖼️

Villa/Condo

★ ★ **RANCH AT STEAMBOAT SPRINGS.** *1 Ranch Rd (80487). 970/879-3000; fax 970/879-5409; toll-free 800/525-2002. www.ranch-steamboat.com.* 88 1-4-bedrm kit. condos, 2 story. No A/C. Feb-Mar, Dec: S $115-$430; D $135-$495; lower rates rest of yr. TV; cable (premium), VCR avail (movies $3.50). Heated pool; whirlpool. Supervised child's activities (Nov-Apr); ages 3-13. Ck-out 10 am. Free lndry facilities. Meeting rms. Business servs avail. In-rm modem link. Concierge. Garage. Tennis. Downhill/x-country ski 1½ mi. Exercise equipt; sauna. Microwaves. Balconies. Picnic tables, grills. On 35 acres. Cr cds: A, DS, MC, V.

🖼️ 🖼️ 🖼️ 🖼️ 🖼️ 🖼️

Restaurants

★★★ **ANTARES.** *57 1/2 8th St (80477). 970/879-9939.* Hrs: 5:30-10 pm; hrs vary off-season. Closed Thanksgiving. Res accepted. Continental menu. Bar. Wine list. Dinner $10-$25. Child's menu. Specialties: tournedos of beef, sesame-crusted ahi tuna, Thai chili-sauteed prawns. Jazz Fri-Sat. Street parking. 1909 bldg has Victorian-era furnishings; Victrola, large picture windows, stone fireplace. Cr cds: A, D, MC, V.
🖼️

★★ **LA MONTANA.** *2500 Village Dr (80477). 970/879-5800.* Hrs: 5:30-10 pm; summer from 6 pm. Closed Thanksgiving. Res accepted. Southwestern, Mexican menu. Bar 5-10 pm. Dinner $9.25-$22.95. Child's menu. Specialties: elk loin with pecans, fajitas, red chili pasta. Parking. Outdoor dining. Cr cds: DS, MC, V.

★★★ **L'APOGEE.** *911 Lincoln Ave (80487). 970/879-1919. www.lapogee. com.* Hrs: 5:30-10:30 pm. Res accepted. Bar. Wine cellar. French menu. Dinner $18-$28. Child's menu. Specialties: oysters Rockefeller, wild mushrooms, filet mignon. Menu changes every 3 months. 1886 building. Patio dining. Totally nonsmoking. Cr cds: A, D, V.
D

★★ **ORE HOUSE AT THE PINE GROVE.** *1465 Pine Grove Rd (80477). 970/879-1190. www.orehouseatthe pinegrove.com.* Hrs: 5-9:30 pm. Res accepted. Bar. Dinner $11.95-$29.50. Child's menu. Specializes in steak, prime rib, fresh seafood. Salad bar. Parking. Outdoor dining. Old ranch decor. Fireplaces; ranch antiques. Cr cds: A, DS, MC, V.
D **SC**

★★ **STEAMBOAT BREWERY.** *811 Yampa Ave (80477). 970/879-4774.* Hrs: 11:30 am-10 pm. Res accepted. Bar. Lunch $5.50-$7.95, dinner $9.95-$21.95. Child's menu. Specializes in fresh seafood, steak. Outdoor dining overlooking river and ski jump. Cr cds: A, MC, V.
D

★ **WINONA'S DELI-BAKERY.** *617 Lincoln Ave (80477). 970/879-2483.* Hrs: 7 am-9 pm. Closed Thanksgiving, Dec 25. Wine, beer. Bkfst $1.95-$5.95, lunch $5-$7, dinner $7-$12. Specializes in deli sandwiches, pastries. Child's menu. Outdoor dining. Totally nonsmoking. Cr cds: MC, V.
D

Sterling (A-7)

Pop 11,360 **Elev** 3,939 ft
Area code 970 **Zip** 80751

Information Logan County Chamber of Commerce, 109 N Front St, PO Box 1683; 970/522-5070 or 800/544-8609

Web www.logancountychamber.com

What to See and Do

Outdoor sculptures. Sterling is known as the "City of Living Trees" because of the unique carved trees found throughout town. A self-guided tour map shows where to find the 16 sculpted trees created by a local sculptor. Call the Logan County Chamber of Commerce for more information.

Overland Trail Museum. Village of seven buildings. Collections of Native American artifacts, cattle brands, farm machinery; archaeological and paleontological exhibits, one-rm schoolhouse, fire engine, children's displays; local historical items; park and picnic area. (Apr-Oct, daily; rest of yr, Tues-Sat) 21053 County Rd 26½, just off I-76. Phone 970/522-3895. **FREE**

Motels/Motor Lodges

★★ **BEST WESTERN SUNDOWNER.** *Overland Tr St (80751). 970/522-6265; toll-free 800/780-7234. www.bestwestern.com.* 30 rms. S $70; D $79; each addl $7; under 12 free. Crib avail. Pet accepted; $10/night. TV; cable (premium), VCR avail. Heated pool; whirlpool. Complimentary continental bkfst, coffee in lobby. Restaurant nearby. Ck-out 11 am. Coin lndry. Business servs avail. In-rm modem link. Exercise equipt. Balconies. Picnic tables, grills. Cr cds: A, C, D, DS, MC, V.
🐾 🛏️ 🏋️ ⛱️ 🏊 SC

★ **COLONIAL MOTEL.** *915 S Division Ave (80751). 970/522-3382; toll-*

free 888/522-2901. 14 rms. S $32; D $38-$44; each addl $3; under 10 free; wkly rates in winter. Pet accepted. TV; cable (premium). Coffee in rms. In-rm modem links. Ck-out 10 am. Some refrigerators; microwaves avail. Cr cds: A, DS, MC, V.

★★ **RAMADA INN.** 22246 E Hwy 6 (80751). 970/522-2625; fax 970/522-1321; res 888/298-2054. www.ramada. com. 100 rms, 2 story. S $50-$72; D $57-$81; each addl $7; under 18 free. Crib free. Pet accepted, some restrictions. TV; cable (premium). Indoor pool; whirlpool. Complimentary coffee in rms. Restaurant 6 am-10 pm. Bar 3:30-10 pm. Ck-out noon. Meeting rms. Business servs avail. In-rm modem link. Valet serv. Exercise equipt; sauna. Game rm. Cr cds: A, C, D, DS, enroute, JCB, MC, V.

B&B/Small Inn

★★★ **ELK ECHO RANCH.** 47490 Weld County Rd 155, Stoneham (80754). 970/735-2426; fax 970/735-2427. www.wapiti.net/co/eer.htm. 4 rms, 3 story. No rm phones. S $89; D $99; each addl $10-$20. Complimentary full bkfst. Ck-out 11 am, ck-in 4 pm. Luggage handling. Rustic log cabin lodge. Totally nonsmoking. Cr cds: MC, V.

Restaurant

★ **T.J. BUMMER'S.** 203 Broadway (80751). 970/522-8397. Hrs: 5:30 am-9 pm; Oct-Apr to 8 pm. Closed most major hols. Bkfst $2.99-$5.95, lunch $3.95-$6.95, dinner $5.95-$14.95. Child's menu. Specializes in chicken-fried steak and chicken. Guitarist Fri, Sat. Rustic antiques. Totally nonsmoking. Cr cds: A, DS, MC, V.
SC

Telluride

(E-2) See also Norwood

Settled 1878 **Pop** 2,221 **Elev** 8,800 ft
Area code 970 **Zip** 81435

Information Telluride Visitor Services, 666 W Colorado Ave, Box 653; 970/728-4431 or 888/605-2578
Web www.telluride.com

What to See and Do

Bear Creek Trail. A two-mi canyon walk with view of tiered waterfall. (May-Oct) S end of Pine St.

Bridal Veil Falls. Highest waterfall in Colorado. Structure at top of falls was once a hydroelectric power plant, which served the Smuggler-Union Mine operations. It has been recently renovated and now provides auxiliary electric power to Telluride. 2½ mi E on CO 145.

Skiing. Telluride Ski Resort. Three-stage gondola; four quad, two triple, two double chairlifts; one surface lift; patrol, school, rentals; restaurants, nursery. Sixty-six runs; longest run three mi; vertical drop 3,522 ft. (Thanksgiving-early Apr, daily) X-country skiing, heliskiing, ice-skating, snowmobiling, sleigh rides. Shuttle bus service and two in-town chairlifts. Contact PO Box 653. Phone 800/801-4832. ¢¢¢¢

Telluride Gondola. Passengers are transported from downtown Telluride, over ski mountain, and to Mt Village. (Early June-early Oct and late Nov-mid-Apr, daily) Four gondola terminals: Station Telluride, Oak St; Station St. Sophia, on the ski mountain; stations Mt Village and Village Parking in Mt Village. **FREE**

Telluride Historical Museum. Built in 1893 as the community hospital, this historic building houses artifacts, historic photos, and exhibits that show what Telluride was like in its Wild West days. (Tues-Sun) 317 N Fir St. Phone 970/728-3344. **FREE**

Special Events

Balloon Rally. Early June.

Bluegrass Festival. Town Park. Late June.

Jazz Celebration. Town Park. Early Aug.

Chamber Music Festival. Mid-Aug. Phone 970/728-6769.

Mountain Film Festival. Labor Day wkend. Phone 970/728-4401.

Telluride Airmen's Rendezvous & Hang Gliding Festival. Mid-Sept.

Motel/Motor Lodge

★★★ **ICE HOUSE LODGE AND CONDOMINIUMS.** *310 S Fir St (81435). 970/728-6300; fax 970/728-6358; toll-free 800/544-3436. www. icehouselodge.com.* 42 air-cooled rms, 3 story, 16 condos. S, D, condos $145-$250; each addl $15; under 13 free; higher rates: music, film festivals, ski season, special events. Valet parking avail. Crib free. TV; cable (premium), VCR avail. Heated pool; whirlpool. Complimentary continental bkfst. Restaurant nearby. Ck-out 11 am (10 am winter). Meeting rms. Business servs avail. In-rm modem link. Gift shop. Bellhops. Valet serv. Concierge. Free covered parking. Downhill ski ½ blk; x-country ski adj. Steam rm. Minibars. Balconies. Cr cds: A, C, D, DS, JCB, MC, V.

Hotel

★★★ **HOTEL COLUMBIA.** *300 W San Juan Ave (81435). 970/728-0660; fax 970/728-9249; toll-free 800/201-9505. www.columbiatelluride.com.* 21 rms, 2 suites, 4 story. No A/C. S $230-$285. Penthouse $234-$440. Crib free. Pet accepted, some restrictions; $25. TV; cable (premium), VCR every room, movies avail. Outdoor whirlpool. Complimentary covered parking, continental bkfst. Coffee in rms. Restaurant (see COSMOPOLITAN). Rm serv. Bar 4 -9 pm. Ck-out 11 am. Lndry. Library/sitting rm. Business servs avail. In-rm modem link. Bellhops. Valet serv. Concierge. Downhill/x-country ski/snowboard on site. Exercise equipt. Health club nearby. Minibars, refrigerators, fireplaces, down comforters, balconies. Cr cds: A, MC, V.

Resort

★★★ **WYNDHAM PEAKS RESORT & GOLDEN DOOR SPA.** *136 Country Club Dr (81435). 970/728-6800; fax 970/728-6175; toll-free 800/789-2220. www.peaksresort.com.* 174 rms, 6 story, 28 suites. Jan-Mar: S, D $375-$565; suites $685-$1,300; under 18 free; golf, ski plans; higher rates Dec hols; lower rates rest of yr. Closed mid-Apr-May. Crib $10. Pet accepted, some restrictions; $50. TV; cable (premium), VCR (free movies). 2 pools, 1 indoor; whirlpools, lifeguard, poolside serv. Supervised children's activities. Complimentary coffee in lobby. Dining rm 7 am-11 pm. Box lunches. Rm serv 7 am-11 pm. Bar. Ck-out noon, ck-in 4 pm. Meeting rms. Business center. In-rm modem link. Bellhops. Valet serv. Concierge. Gift shop. Barber/beauty shop. Covered valet parking $18/day. Free airport transportation. Sports dir. Tennis, pro. 18-hole golf (May-Oct), greens fee $160 (incl cart), pro, putting green, driving range. Downhill/x-country ski on site; rentals. Snowmobiles, sleighing. Hiking. Exercise rm; sauna. Massage. Microwaves avail. Refrigerators, minibars. Some balconies. Cr cds: A, C, D, DS, MC, V.

B&Bs/Small Inns

★ **MANITOU LODGE.** *333 S Fir St (80751). 970/728-4011; fax 970/728-3716; toll-free 800/538-7754.* 12 rms, 2 story. No A/C. Mid-Feb-Mar: S, D $145-$170; higher rates: festivals, hols; lower rates rest of yr. TV; cable (premium). Complimentary continental bkfst. Restaurant nearby. Ck-out 10 am, ck-in 4 pm. Downhill ski 1 blk; x-country ski on site. Whirlpool. Refrigerators. Antiques. Cr cds: A, D, DS, MC, V.

★★★ **NEW SHERIDAN HOTEL.** *231 W Colorado Ave (81435). 970/728-4351; fax 970/728-5024; toll-free 800/200-1891. www.newsheridan. com.* 26 air-cooled rms, 8 share baths, 3 story, 8 suites. Late-Dec-Jan: S, D $150-$275; each addl $15; suites $295-$400; under 12 free; ski plans; lower rates rest of yr. Crib free. TV; cable (premium). Complimentary full bkfst; afternoon refreshments. Restaurant 5:30-10 pm. No rm serv. Bar 3 pm-2 am. Ck-out 11 am. Meeting rms. Business servs avail. In-rm modem link. Concierge. Downhill/x-country ski 2 blks. Exercise equipt; whirlpools. Valet parking avail. Luggage handling. Concierge. Built in 1895. Rooftop whirlpool and sun deck. Game rm. Some in-rm whirlpools. Totally nonsmoking. Cr cds: A, D, MC, V.

★ ★ ★ **SAN SOPHIA BED &
BREAKFAST.** *330 W Pacific Ave
(81435). 970/728-3001; fax 970/728-
6226; toll-free 800/537-4781. www.
sansophia.com.* 16 air-cooled rms, 2
story. S, D $135-$300; each addl $25;
higher rates: music & film festivals,
Dec-Mar. Closed Apr, Nov. Children
over 9 yrs only. TV; cable (premium),
VCR (free movies). Complimentary
full bkfst; afternoon refreshments.
Ck-out 11 am, ck-in 3 pm. Business
servs avail. In-rm modem link. Fishing. Horseback riding. Downhill ski 1
blk; x-country ski on site. Luggage
handling. Whirlpool. Some balconies. Modern frame structure built
in Victorian style with octagon tower
observatory; bay windows; library;
sitting rm. Interiors blend Victorian
and modern Southwest design;
stained and etched glass, period furnishings. Mountain views. Totally
nonsmoking. Cr cds: A, MC, V.
⚓ 🏷 ⤢ ⛷ 🔥

Restaurants

★ ★ ★ **COSMOPOLITAN.** *300 W
San Juan (81435). 970/728-1292.
www.cosmotelluride.com.* French/Amer
menu. Specializes in whole roast duck.
Hrs: 6-9:30 pm. Dinner $19-$32.
Patio heated dining. Res accepted. Bar.
Entertainment. Cr cds: A, MC, V.
D

★ **FLORADORA.** *103 W Colorado
Ave (81435). 970/728-3888.* Hrs: 11
am-10 pm. Southwestern, Amer
menu. Bar to midnight. Lunch $5-
$10, dinner $6.95-$18.95. Child's
menu. Specializes in steak, pasta, fajitas. Stained-glass windows, Tiffany-
style lamps. Totally nonsmoking. Cr
cds: A, DS, MC, V.
D

Trinidad

(F-6) See also Walsenburg

Settled 1859 **Pop** 9,078 **Elev** 6,025 ft
Area code 719 **Zip** 81082
Information Trinidad-Las Animas
County Chamber of Commerce, 309
Nevada Ave; 719/846-9285
Web www.trinidadco.com

What to See and Do

**A. R. Mitchell Memorial Museum of
Western Art.** Features Western paintings by Arthur Roy Mitchell, Harvey
Dunn, Harold von Schmidt, and
other famous artists; Western and
Native American artifacts; Hispanic
religious folk art. Housed in a 1906
former department store with original tin ceiling, wood floors, horse-
shoe-shaped mezzanine. (Apr-Sept,
Mon-Sat; also by appt; closed hols)
150 E Main St. Phone 719/846-4224.
FREE

Trinidad History Museum. Colorado
Historical Society administers this
museum complex. The Baca House
(1870) is a restored nine-rm, two-
story adobe house purchased by a
wealthy Hispanic sheep rancher. The
Bloom House (1882) is a restored
Victorian mansion and garden built
by cattleman and banker Frank C.
Bloom. The Santa Fe Museum is also
here. Guided tours (Memorial Day-
Sept, daily; rest of yr, by appt) 300 E
Main St, on the historic Santa Fe
Trail. Phone 719/846-7217. ¢¢

Trinidad Lake State Park. A 2,300-
acre park with a 900-acre lake. Waterskiing, fishing, boating (ramps);
nature trails, mountain biking, picnicking, playground, camping (electrical hookups, showers, dump
station). Interpretive programs
(Memorial Day-Labor Day, Fri, Sat,
hols) Standard fees. (Daily) 3 mi W
on CO 12. Phone 719/846-6951. ¢¢

Motels/Motor Lodges

★ **BUDGET HOST DERRICK
MOTEL.** *10301 Santa Fe Tr (81082).
719/846-3307; fax 719/846-3309.*
tollfree 800/283-4678 *www.trinidadco.
com/budgethost.* 26 rms. June-mid-
Sept: S $39.95-$59.95; D $49.95-
$69.95; wkly rates; lower rates rest of
yr. Crib $5. Pet accepted; $3. TV,
cable. Whirlpool. Complimentary
continental bkfst, coffee in rms.
Restaurant nearby. Ck-out 11 am.
Free airport, RR station, bus depot
transportation. Lawn games. Coin
lndry. Microwaves, refrigerators avail.
Picnic tables, grills. Features 107-ft
oil derrick. Located along the Mountain Branch of the Santa Fe Trail. Cr
cds: A, DS, MC, V.
D 🐾 SC ⚓ ⛷ 🔥

★ **BUDGET SUMMIT INN.** *9800 Santa Fe Trail Dr (81082). 719/846-2251.* 44 rms, 21 with shower only, 2 story. Memorial Day-Labor Day: S $40-$60; D $45-$70; each addl $10; lower rates rest of yr. Pet accepted; $3. TV; cable. Whirlpool. Complimentary continental bkfst. Restaurant adj open 24 hrs. Ck-out 11 am. Coin lndry. Meeting rm. Business servs avail. In-rm modem link. Gift shop. Rec rm. Lawn games. Some refrigerators; microwaves avail. Cr cds: A, MC, V.

⬛ 🐾 🏊 🔥

★★ **HOLIDAY INN.** *3125 Toupal Dr (81082). 719/846-4491; fax 719/846-2440; res 800/465-4329. www.holiday-inn.com.* 113 rms, 2 story. June-Sept: S $89-$109; D $99-$119; each addl $10; under 18 free; lower rates rest of yr. Crib free. Pet accepted, some restrictions. TV; cable (premium). Indoor pool; whirlpool, poolside serv. Coffee in rms. Restaurant 6 am-10 pm. Rm serv from 7 am. Bar 5 pm-midnight. Ck-out noon. Coin lndry. Meeting rms. Business servs avail. In-rm modem link. Gift shop. Game rm. Exercise equipt. Lawn games. Some bathrm phones, refrigerators; microwaves avail. Cr cds: A, C, D, DS, ER, JCB, MC, V.

⬛ 🐾 🏊 🏋 🔥

Restaurant

★★ **CHEF LIU'S CHINESE RESTAURANT.** *1423 Santa Fe Tr (81082). 719/846-3333.* Hrs: 11 am-9:15 pm; Fri & Sat to 9:45 pm. Closed Thanksgiving; also Mon from Thanksgiving-Mar. Res accepted. Chinese menu. Bar. Lunch $3.75-$4.50, dinner $4.95-$16.95. Specialties: sweet & sour volcano shrimp, Peking beef, pepper steak. Parking. Chinese decor. Cr cds: A, MC, V.

⬛ 🍴

Vail

(C-4) *See also Dillon, Leadville*

Pop 4,531 **Elev** 8,160 ft

Information Vail Valley Tourism & Convention Bureau, 100 E Meadow Dr; 970/476-1000 or 800/525-3875

Snowboarding in Vail

Web visitvailvalley.com

What to See and Do

Colorado Ski Museum & Ski Hall of Fame. Skiing artifacts and photographs tracing the history of skiing in Colorado for more than 120 yrs. (Memorial Day-late Sept and late Nov-mid Apr, Tues-Sun; closed hols) 231 S Frontage, in Vail Village Transportation Center. Phone 970/476-1876. ¢

Skiing.

Beaver Creek/Arrowhead Resort. Six quad, three triple, four double chairlifts; patrol, rentals, snowmaking; cafeteria, restaurants, bar, nursery. Longest run 2¾ mi; vertical drop 4,040 ft. (Late Nov-mid-Apr, daily) X-country trails and rentals (Nov-Apr), ice-skating, snowmobiling, sleigh rides. Chairlift rides (July-Aug, daily; Sept, wkends; fee). 10 mi W on I-70, exit 167, then 3 mi S. Phone 970/949-5750. Summer ¢¢¢¢ Winter ¢¢¢¢

Vail Ski Resort. Gondola; thirteen high-speed quad, two fixed-grip quad, three triple, six double chairlifts; nine surface lifts; patrol, school, rentals, snowmaking; cafeterias, restaurants, bars, nursery. Longest run 4½ mi; vertical drop

3,360 ft. (Late Nov-mid-Apr, daily) X-country trails, rentals (Nov-Apr; fee), ice-skating, snowmobiling, sleigh rides. Gondola and Vista Bahn (June-Aug, daily; May and Sept, wkends; fee). In town on I-70, exit 176. Phone 970/476-9090. Summer ¢¢¢ Winter ¢¢¢¢

Special Event

Taste of Vail. Early Apr. Phone 888/311-5665.

Motels/Motor Lodges

★ **MOUNTAIN HAUS RESORT & SPA.** *292 E Meadow Dr (81657). 970/476-2434; fax 970/476-3007; toll-free 800/237-0922. www.mountain haus.com.* 72 rms, 5 story, 64 kit. units. No A/C. Jan-Apr: S, D $120-$240; kit. units $230-$600; wkly rates; higher rates hols; lower rates rest of yr. Crib avail. Garage parking $15. TV; cable (premium), VCR (movies). Complimentary coffee in rms. Restaurant opp 7 am-10 pm. Bar from 6 pm. Ck-out 10 am. Meeting rms. Business servs avail. Bellhops. Concierge. Coin lndry. Downhill/x-country ski 1 blk. Exercise equipt; sauna. Massage. Pool; whirlpool. Fireplaces. Many balconies. Cr cds: A, C, D, DS, MC, V.

★★ **SITZMARK LODGE.** *183 Gore Creek Dr (81657). 970/476-5001; fax 970/476-8702; res 800/525-3875.* 35 rms, 3 story, 1 kit. No A/C. Mid-Apr-mid-Nov: S $61-$91; D $66-$97; each addl $10; under 12 free in summer; higher rates: hols, ski season. Crib $5. TV; cable (premium). Pool; whirlpool. Sauna. Complimentary continental bkfst (winter). Restaurant 6-10 pm. Bar. Ck-out 11 am. Coin lndry. Business servs avail. In-rm modem link. Shopping arcade. Covered parking. Downhill/x-country ski ½ blk. Refrigerators; some fireplaces. Balconies. Cr cds: DS, MC, V.

Hotels

★★ **HOTEL GASTHOF GRAMSHAMMER.** *231 E Gore Creek Dr (81657). 970/476-5626; fax 970/476-8816; toll-free 800/610-7374. www.pepis.com.* 28 units, 6 kit. units, 4 story. No A/C. Thanksgiving-Easter: S, D, kit. units $83-$225; each addl $40; under 12 free in summer; lower rates Memorial Day-mid-Nov. Closed rest of yr. TV; cable, VCR avail. Complimentary continental bkfst. Restaurant 11:30 am-3 pm, 5:45-10 pm. Bar 11:30-2 am. Ck-out 11 am. Business servs avail. Valet serv. Shopping arcade. Downhill ski 1 blk. Ski rental; ski shop. Health club privileges. Some refrigerators, fireplaces; microwaves avail. Some balconies. Austrian decor. Cr cds: A, D, DS, MC, V.

★★ **VAIL ATHLETIC CLUB HOTEL & SPA.** *352 E Meadow Dr (81657). 970/476-0700; fax 970/476-6451; toll-free 800/822-4754. www.vailmountain lodge-spa.com.* 38 air-cooled rms, 3 story, 9 suites, 7 kit. units. Feb-Mar: S, D $350-$375; suites $765-$1,300; kit. units $445; under 12 free; higher rates hols; lower rates rest of yr. Crib free. TV; cable (premium), VCR avail. Indoor pool; whirlpool. Complimentary continental bkfst. Complimentary coffee in rms. Restaurant 7-10 am, 5:30-10 pm. Rm serv. Bar 5 pm-closing. Ck-out 11 am. Coin lndry. Meeting rms. Business servs avail. In-rm modem link. Bellhops. Valet serv. Concierge. Beauty shop, spa. Free covered parking. Tennis privileges. Golf privileges, greens fee $85, pro, putting green, driving range. Downhill/x-country ski 3 blks. Exercise rm; sauna. Refrigerators; some wet bars, microwaves. Balconies. Cr cds: A, C, D, DS, MC, V.

Resorts

★★★ **BEAVER CREEK LODGE - MOUNTAIN SUITES HOTEL.** *26 Avondale Ln (81620). 970/845-9800; fax 970/845-8242; res 800/525-7280. www.beavercreeklodge.net.* 73 air-cooled suites, 6 story. Feb-Mar: S, D $250-$550; each addl $20; under 12 free; 7-day min Dec 25; lower rates rest of yr. Crib free. Valet parking $10. TV; cable (premium), VCR (movies). Indoor/outdoor pool; whirlpool. Complimentary bkfst. Complimentary coffee in rms. Restaurant 7 am-10 pm. Bar. Ck-out noon. Coin lndry. Meeting rms. Business servs avail. In-rm modem link. Concierge. Barber, beauty shop. 18-

hole golf privileges. Downhill/x-country ski ½ blk. Exercise equipt; sauna. Massage. Refrigerators, microwaves, fireplaces. Some balconies. Cr cds: A, MC, V.

★ ★ ★ **CHARTER AT BEAVER CREEK.** *120 Offerson Rd (81620). 970/949-6660; fax 970/949-6709; toll-free 800/525-6660. www.thecharter. com.* 64 lodge rms, 4-6 story, 156 condos. Late Nov-mid-Apr: S, D $140-$310; suites $210-$1,160; ski, golf plans; higher rates late Dec; lower rates rest of yr. Crib avail. TV; cable (premium). VCR (movies). 2 pools, 1 indoor; wading pool, whirlpool. Supervised children's activities (Jan-Apr); ages 4-12. Coffee in rms. Dining rm 7-10:30 am, 11:30 am-2 pm, 5:30-9:30 pm; summer 7 am-2 pm, 5-11 pm. Box lunches. Bar 4-10 pm; summer 5-11 pm. Ck-out 11 am, ck-in 4 pm. Meeting rms. Business servs avail. In-rm modem link. Bellhops. Concierge. Beauty shop. Valet parking. Ski shop. Tennis privileges, pro. 18-hole golf privileges opp, pro. Downhill/x-country ski on site. Sleighing. Snowmobiles. Exercise rm; sauna, steam rm. Massage. Refrigerators. Fireplace in condos. Balconies. Cr cds: A, MC, V.

★ ★ **THE CHATEAU AT VAIL.** *13 Vail Rd (81657). 970/476-5631; fax 970/476-2508; toll-free 800/451-9840. www.chateauvail.com.* 120 rms, 4 story. Nov-Mar, July-Sept: S $145; D $165; each addl $25; under 18 free; lower rates rest of yr. Crib avail. Pool; whirlpool. TV; cable. Complimentary coffee in rms. Restaurant 7 am-9 pm. Bar. Ck-out 11 am-3 pm. Meeting rms. Free airport transportation. Sauna, steam rm. Golf, 18 holes. Tennis, 4 courts. Downhill skiing. Hiking trail. Cr cds: A, D, DS, MC, V.

★ ★ ★ **INN AT BEAVER CREEK.** *10 Elk Track Ln, Avon (81620). 970/845-7800; fax 970/845-5279; res 800/859-8242. www.innatbeavercreek.com.* 45 air-cooled rms, 4 story. Late Jan-Mar: S, D $330-$370; each addl $25; suites $800; higher rates late Dec; lower rates rest of yr. Crib free. TV; cable (premium). VCR avail. Heated pool; whirlpool. Complimentary covered parking. Complimentary continental bkfst. Coffee in rms. Restaurant nearby. Bar 3-10 pm. Ck-out 10 am. Free lndry. Meeting rms. Business servs avail. In-rm modem link. Bellhops. Valet serv. Concierge. Downhill/x-country ski on site. True ski in and ski out. Exercise equipt; sauna, steam rm. Health club privileges. Refrigerators, microwaves. Cr cds: A, C, D, DS, MC, V.

★ ★ **LION SQUARE LODGE.** *660 W Lionshead Pl (81657). 970/476-2281; fax 970/476-7423; toll-free 800/525-5788. www.lionsquare.com.* 108 units, 3-7 story, 83 townhouses. No A/C. Nov-Apr: S $109-$400; D $189-$450; townhouses $260-$800; under 17 free; lower rates rest of yr. Crib free. Free garage parking. TV; cable (premium), VCR. Heated pool; whirlpool. Sauna. Supervised children's activities (Nov-Apr); ages 5-12. Coffee in rms. Restaurant 6-10 pm. Ck-out 10 am. Coin lndry. Meeting rms. Business servs avail. Valet serv. Concierge. Ski shop. Downhill ski adj; x-country ski on site. Health club privileges. Lawn games. Refrigerators, microwaves. Balconies. Picnic tables, grills. On creek; adj to gondola. Cr cds: A, D, DS, MC, V.

★ ★ ★ ★ **THE LODGE & SPA AT CORDILLERA.** *2205 Cordillera Way, Edwards (81632). 970/926-2200; fax 970/926-2486; toll-free 800/877-3529. www.cordillera-vail.com.* This luxurious chateau-style lodge is a member of Small Luxury Hotels of the World and is situated 20 minutes from the Vail/Beaver Creek ski areas. The secluded 6,500-acre setting features 56 rooms with earthy colors, rustic pine accents, and balconies or terraces overlooking the Rockies. 56 rms, 3 story. S $150-$495; D $150-$595; suites $275-$950; under 16 free. Crib free. TV; cable (premium), VCR avail. 2 pools, 1 indoor; indoor/outdoor whirlpool. Restaurant (see also RESTAURANT PICASSO). Box lunches. Rm serv 6 am-10 pm. Bar; entertainment wkends. Ck-out noon, ck-in 4 pm. Meeting rms. Business center. In-rm modem link. Valet serv. Concierge. Beauty shop. Tennis, pro. 3 golf courses, 2 18-hole, 1 10-hole, greens fee $180, pro. Downhill ski 8 mi; x-country ski on site; rentals. Hiking.

Bicycle rentals. Horseback riding. Extensive exercise rm; sauna, steam rm. Many fireplaces, sleeping lofts. Many balconies, private decks. Totally nonsmoking. Cr cds: A, D, DS, MC, V.

★★★★ **THE LODGE AT VAIL.** *174 E Gore Creek Dr (81657). 970/476-5011; fax 970/477-3741. www.lodgeat vail.com.* Renowned for its relaxed luxury and impeccable personal service, The Lodge offers various levels of accommodations to suit its guests. Standard guest rooms are individually decorated, and offer courtyard, poolside, or Vail Village views; studio guest rooms offer similar views and feature large balconies, full kitchens, and wood-burning fireplaces; luxury rooms feature oversized bathrooms with heated marble floors and separate soaking tub and shower. The epitome of luxury, the 3,800-square-foot Penthouse Suite, features breathtaking views of Vail Mountain and the International Ski Run, and private mountainside terraces. The Lodge's fine dining restaurant, The Wildflower, offers an eclectic array of creative American cuisine prepared with the freshest and finest in produce, seafood, and meat. 124 rms, 2 story. S, D $125-$350; under 18 free. Crib avail. TV; cable (premium). Restaurant 6:30 am-10 pm. Bar to midnight. Ck-out noon. Meeting rms. Concierge. Downhill skiing. Minibars; many refrigerators. Cr cds: A, C, D, DS, MC, V.

★★★ **MARRIOTT MOUNTAIN RESORT.** *715 W Lionshead Cir (81657). 970/476-4444; fax 970/476-1647; toll-free 888/236-2427. www.marriott.com.* 350 units, 6 story, 40 kits. Some A/C. Jan-Mar: S, D $175-$375; kit. units, suites $300-$825; under 18 free; ski, package plans; higher rates Christmas hols; lower rates rest of yr. Crib free. TV; cable (premium). 2 pools, 1 indoor; whirlpool, poolside serv (summer). Coffee in rms. Restaurants 7 am-11 pm; summer to 10 pm. Bars to midnight. Ck-out 11 am, ck-in 4 pm. Coin lndry. Convention facilities. Business center. In-rm modem link. Valet serv. Concierge. Gift shop. Beauty shop. Tennis. Golf privileges.

Downhill/x-country ski ¼ mi. Ski rentals. Exercise rm; steam rm. Spa. Refrigerators; some microwaves, fireplaces. Balconies. Cr cds: A, C, D, DS, ER, JCB, MC, V.

★★★★ **PARK HYATT BEAVER CREEK RESORT.** *50 E Thomas Pl, Avon (81620). 970/949-1234; fax 970/949-4164; res 800/233-1234. www.beavercreek.hyatt.com.* At the base of the Gore Range Mountains, this 1,700-acre resort in Beaver Creek Village affords guests a ski-in/ski-out location. There are eight whirlpools and a 20,000-square-foot spa for relaxing tired muscles after a hard day on the slopes. In the summer months a Robert Trent Jones, Jr. golf course is nearby with guaranteed tee times for guests. 275 rms, 6 story, 30 suites. Dec-Mar: S, D $400-$585; each addl $25; suites $1,050-$2,300; under 18 free; ski, golf plans; lower rates rest of yr. Crib free. Valet parking $18. TV; cable (premium), VCR avail. Heated pool; whirlpool, poolside serv. Playground. Supervised child's activities; ages 5-12. Complimentary coffee in rms. Dining rm 6 am-10 pm. Box lunches, picnics, deli. Rm serv 6 am-midnight. Bar 11:30-1:30 am; entertainment. Ck-out noon, ck-in 4 pm. Coin lndry. Convention facilities. Business center. In-rm modem link. Bellhops. Valet serv. Concierge. Shopping arcade. Barber, beauty shop. Rec dir. Tennis, pro. 18-hole golf privileges, greens fee $135, pro, putting green, driving range. Downhill/x-country ski on site. Hiking. Bicycle rentals. Lawn games. Exercise rm; sauna, steam rm. Spa. Fishing/hunting guides. Refrigerators. Balconies. Cr cds: A, C, D, DS, JCB, MC, V.

★★★ **PINES LODGE.** *141 Scott Hill Rd, Avon (81620). 970/845-7900; fax 970/845-7809.* 60 air-cooled rms, 4 story, 12 kit. units. Early-Jan-Mar: S, D $200-$425; each addl $25; suites $500-$1,800; under 12 free; ski, golf packages; higher rates Christmas hols; lower rates rest of yr. Crib free. TV; cable (premium), VCR (free movies) Heated pool; whirlpool, poolside serv. Coffee in rms. Restaurant 7 am-10 pm. Bar 4-11 pm; entertainment. Ck-out 11 am. Meeting rms. Business servs avail. In-rm modem link. Concierge. Downhill/x-country ski adj. Tennis. Golf privileges. Exercise equipt. Massage. Game rm. Refrigerators. Many balconies. Traditional Alpine structure; high-pitched roofs, dormers, towers. Modern Alpine interior; stone fireplaces, pine furnishings. Cr cds: A, C, D, DS, MC, V.

★★★ **SONNENALP RESORT OF VAIL.** *20 Vail Rd (81657). 970/476-5656; fax 970/476-1639; toll-free 800/654-8312. www.sonnenalp.com.* 149 rms, 3 villas (3-4 story). Some A/C. Early Jan-early Apr: S $172-$497; D $190-$515; each addl $25; suite $370-$1,440; under 5 free; package plans; higher rates Christmas season; lower rates rest of yr. TV; cable (premium), VCR avail (movies avail). 2 indoor/outdoor pools; whirlpool. Supervised children's activities; infant-6 yrs. Restaurant 7 am-10 pm. Rm serv. Bar. Ck-out 11 am. Meeting rms. Business center. In-rm modem link. Bellhops. Valet serv. Concierge. Free valet parking. Tennis privileges. 18-hole golf privileges, pro, putting green, driving range. Downhill/x-country ski ¼mi. Exercise equipt; sauna, steam rm. Game rm. Some balconies. Cr cds: A, D, MC, V.

★★★ **VAIL CASCADE RESORT.** *1300 Westhaven Dr (81657). 970/476-7111; fax 970/479-7020; res 800/420-2424.* 289 rms, 4 story. Late Nov-mid-Apr: S, D $309-$429; suites $500-$995; under 18 free; package plans; lower rates rest of yr. Crib free. Valet parking $12. TV; cable (premium), VCR avail (movies). Heated pool; whirlpool, poolside serv. Coffee in rms. Restaurants 6:30 am-10 pm. Rm serv 24 hrs. Bars 3:30 pm-1:30 am; entertainment. Ck-out noon. Meeting rms. Business center. In-rm modem link. Concierge. Shopping arcade. Beauty shop. Tennis. Downhill/x-country ski on site. Exercise rm; sauna, steam rm. Spa. Ski rentals. Mountain bike rentals. Refrigerators, minibars. Private patios, balconies. On river. Cr cds: A, C, D, DS, JCB, MC, V.

B&Bs/Small Inns

★★ **BEST WESTERN VAILGLO LODGE.** *701 W Lionshead Cir (81658). 970/476-5506; fax 970/476-3926; res 800/780-7234. www.best western.com.* 34 air-cooled rms, 4 story. Feb-Mar, Dec: S, D $99-$250; each addl $25; under 8 free; lower rates rest of yr. Crib free. TV; cable (premium). Heated pool; whirlpool. Complimentary continental bkfst. Restaurant adj 7-3 am. Ck-out noon. In-rm modem link. Valet serv. Downhill/x-country ski 1 blk. Refrigerators. Balconies. Cr cds: A, C, D, DS, MC, V.

★★ **BLACK BEAR INN OF VAIL.** *2405 Elliott Rd (81657). 970/476-1304; fax 970/476-0433. www.vail.net/blackbear.* 12 rms, 2 story. Mid-Nov-mid-Apr: S, D $105-$200; each addl $35; higher rates Dec 25; lower rates mid-May-mid-Nov. Closed mid-Apr-mid May. TV in sitting rm; cable (premium). Complimentary full bkfst. Restaurant opp 7 am-11 pm. Ck-out 11 am, ck-in 3-7 pm. Meeting rm. Business servs avail. In-rm modem link. Downhill/x-country ski 1½mi. Whirlpool. Game rm. Lawn games. Antiques; on banks of Gore Creek. Totally nonsmoking. Cr cds: DS, MC, V.

★★★ **CHRISTIANA AT VAIL.** *356 E Hanson Ranch Rd (81657). 970/476-5641; fax 970/476-0470; res 800/530-3999. www.christiania.com.* 22 air-cooled rms, 3 story, 6 suites. Jan-Mar: S, D $185-$350; suites $250-$500; kit. suite $375; Dec, Feb & Mar (7-day min); lower rates rest of yr. Crib $10. Parking $5. TV; cable, VCR avail. Heated pool. Sauna. Complimentary continental bkfst. Ck-out 11 am, ck-in 4 pm. Business servs avail. Luggage handling. Downhill/x-country ski adj. Minibars; microwaves avail. Bavarian-style inn. Some antiques, hand-carved furnishings. Totally nonsmoking. Cr cds: A, MC, V.

Restaurants

★ **ALPENROSE.** *100 E Meadow Dr (81657). 970/476-3194.* Hrs: 11 am-10 pm; Mon to 5 pm. Closed Tues; also mid-Apr-late-May & mid-Oct-mid-Nov. Res accepted. No A/C. German, Continental menu. Bar. Lunch $7-$9, dinner $19-$25. Specializes in veal, fresh fish, European pastries. Outdoor dining, two terraces. Cr cds: A, D, DS, MC, V.

★ ★ ★ **BEANO'S CABIN.** *42 Avondale Ln, Avon (81620). 970/845-5770.* Hrs: 5-10 pm. Closed Mon, Tues in summer; also mid-Apr-May. Summer brunch 11 am-2 pm. Res required. Bar. Complete meals: dinner $85. Summer brunch $45-$65. Child's menu. Specializes in seafood, venison filet, chicken. Guitarist. Outdoor dining. Access by horse-drawn wagon, van or on horseback; winter months by sleigh. Rustic mountain cabin. Totally nonsmoking. Cr cds: A, DS, MC, V.
D

★ **BLU'S.** *193 E Gore Creek Dr (81657). 970/476-3113.* Hrs: 9 am-11 pm. Bar. Bkfst $5.95-$9.95, lunch $4.50-$9.95, dinner $8-$20. Specializes in eclectic Amer cuisine. Child's menu. Outdoor dining. Cr cds: A, D, DS, MC, V.
D ⌐ᶾ

★ **CHILI WILLY'S.** *101 Main St, Minturn (81645). 970/827-5887. www.chiliwilly.com.* Hrs: 11 am-10 pm; Labor Day-Memorial Day 5-10 pm. Closed Thanksgiving, Dec 25. Bar. Lunch $4.95-$11.95, dinner $8.95-$16.95. Child's menu. Specializes in Tex-Mex and vegetarian dishes. Parking. Outdoor dining. Rustic decor; casual atmosphere. Cr cds: A, DS, MC, V.
D

★ ★ **GOLDEN EAGLE INN.** *118 Beaver Creek Pl (81657). 970/949-1940.* Hrs: 11:30 am-10 pm. Res accepted. Bar. Lunch $6-$10, dinner $15-$27. Child's menu. Specialties: beef tenderloin au poiue, smoked chicken fettucine, roast loin of elk. Parking. Outdoor dining. 3 dining areas. Cr cds: A, C, D, MC, V.
D

★ ★ ★ **GROUSE MOUNTAIN GRILL.** *141 Scott Hill Rd, Avon (81620). 970/949-0600.* Hrs: summer 6-10 pm; winter hrs vary. Closed mid-Apr-mid-May. American menu. Bar. Wine cellar. A la carte entrees: dinner $25.50-$34. Specialties:

grilled beef tenderloin with mushrooms, dry aged NY stilton stuffed roasted onion and port reduction, horseradish mashed potatoes. Free valet parking. Outdoor dining. Entertainment: jazz keyboards and vocals. Cr cds: A, MC, V.
D

★ ★ **LANCELOT INN.** *201 E Gore Creek Dr (81657). 970/476-5828. www.lancelotinn.com.* Hrs: 11:30 am-2:30 pm, 6-10 pm. Closed lunch exc summer; also May. Res accepted. No A/C. Bar 5 pm-closing. Lunch $5.95-$8.95, dinner $12.95-$26.95. Child's menu. Specializes in prime rib, Colorado beef, fresh seafood. Outdoor dining in summer. Overlooks landscaped creek. Totally nonsmoking. Cr cds: A, MC, V.
D

★ ★ ★ **LEFT BANK.** *183 Gore Creek Dr (81657). 970/476-3696.* Hrs: 5:30-10 pm. Closed Wed; Memorial Day, Dec 25; mid-Apr-mid-June, Oct-mid-Nov. Res accepted. No A/C. French menu. Bar. Wine list. Dinner $18.95-$29.95. Specialties: rack of lamb, sauteed elk medallions, fresh seafood. Own pastries. European decor. Cr cds: A, MC, V.
D

★ **MINTURN COUNTRY CLUB.** *131 Main St, Minturn (81645). 970/827-4114.* Specializes in seafood, steak, chicken. Hrs: 5:30-10 pm. Closed Dec 25. Res accepted. Wine, beer. Dinner $9.95-$30. Child's menu. Entertainment. Cr cds: MC, V.
D

★ ★ ★ ★ **MIRABELLE AT BEAVER CREEK.** *55 Village Rd, Beaver Creek (81657). 970/949-7728. www.mirabelleatbeavercreek.com.* Classic French food is served in this converted farm house. Every detail of the sophisticated experience is overseen by the Belgian chef/owner Daniel Joly. Excellent wines and fine service complement the food. French, Belgian menu. Specializes in loin of elk, rack of lamb, lobster with creamy polenta. Own pastries, ice cream. Hrs: 6-10 pm. Closed Sun; also May and mid-Oct-mid-Nov. Res accepted. Dinner $17-$28. Parking. Outdoor dining. Built 1898; believed to be on site of first house in Beaver Creek. Cr cds: A, DS, MC, V.

[D]

★★ **MONTAUK SEAFOOD GRILL.**
549 W Lionshead Mall (81657).
970/476-2601. www.montaukseafood
grill.com. Hrs: 3-10 pm; summer months 5-9:30 pm. Closed Thanksgiving. Res accepted. Bar. Dinner $15.95-$21.95. Specialties: Hawaiian ahi, crispy calamari, tempura shrimp. Outdoor dining. View of mountains. Totally nonsmoking. Cr cds: A, DS, MC, V.

[D]

★★★ **RESTAURANT PICASSO.**
2205 Cordillera Way, Edwards (81632).
970/926-2200. Hrs: 7-10 am, 11:30 am-2 pm, 6-9pm. Res accepted. French menu. Bar. Wine cellar. A la carte entrees: lunch $4.50-$15, dinner $13.99-$34.95. Pianist Thurs-Sat. Valet parking. Outdoor dining during lunch. Overlooks mountain range. Original Picasso paintings. Totally nonsmoking. Cr cds: A, C, D, DS, ER, MC, V.

[D]

★★★★ **SPLENDIDO AT THE CHATEAU.** *17 Chateau Ln, Beaver Creek (81620). 970/845-8808. splendidobeavercreek.com.* The lofty setting of this New-American restaurant offers a fantastic view of Beaver Creek Valley. Chef David Walford has much to be proud of with a creative menu, impressive wine list, and cozy European setting. Nonetheless, the staff manages service without pretense and the adjacent piano bar lends a relaxing, classic note. In sum, the name says it all. Hrs: 6-10 pm. Closed May, Oct. A la carte entrees: dinner $28-$38. Res required. Bar. Entertainment; pianist. Valet parking. Child's menu. Cr cds: A, C, D, DS, MC, V.

★★★ **SWEET BASIL.** *193 E Gore Creek Dr (81657). 970/476-0125. www.sweetbasil-vail.com.* Hrs: 11:30 am-2:30 pm, 5:30-10 pm. Res accepted. No A/C. Bar. Lunch $5.95-$9.50, dinner $22-$28. Specializes in fresh fish, homemade pasta. Outdoor dining. Totally nonsmoking. Cr cds: A, MC, V.

★★ **THE TYROLEAN.** *400 E Meadow Dr (81657). 970/476-2204. www.tyrolean.net.* Hrs: 6-10 pm.

Closed late Apr-May. Res accepted. Continental menu. Bar. Wine list. Dinner $16-$34. Child's menu. Specializes in wild game, steak, fresh seafood. Outdoor dining. 3-level dining area. Large logging sled chandelier. Austrian atmosphere. Cr cds: A, MC, V.

[image]

★★★★ **THE WILDFLOWER.** *174 Gore Creek Dr (81657). 970/476-5011.* This flowery dining room at the luxurious Lodge at Vail shines through local competition with chef Thomas Gay's beautiful, sophisticated cuisine. Guests will be mesmerized by the views of snowcapped mountains, Vail Village, and quaint chalets. The nationwide praise is warranted considering the creative dishes, such as applewood-roasted venison with polenta and onion jam, and the fairly priced wine list. American menu. Specialties: green peppercorn, and herb-crusted swordfish, Alaskan halibut, lamb T-bone, applewood grilled tenderloin of beef. Hrs: 6-10 pm; closed Mon during winter. Res accepted. A la carte entrees: $22-$38. Valet parking. Cr cds: A, D, DS, MC, V.

[D] [image]

Walsenburg

(F-5) *See also Trinidad*

Founded 1873 **Pop** 4,182 **Elev** 6,182 ft **Area code** 719 **Zip** 81089
Information Chamber of Commerce, 400 Main St, Railroad Depot; 719/738-1065

What to See and Do

Francisco Fort Museum. Original adobe trading fort (1862) now contains exhibits of pioneer cattle ranching and commercial mining. The site also has a saloon, blacksmith shop, one-rm schoolhouse, and collection of Native American artifacts. (Late May-early Oct, Wed-Sun) 16 mi SW on US 160 and CO 12 in La Veta. Phone 719/742-5501. ¢¢

Lathrop State Park. Swimming, waterskiing, fishing, boating (ramps); golf, picnicking (shelters), camping (dump station). Visitor Center. Standard fees. (Daily) 3 mi W on US 160. Phone 719/738-2376. ¢¢

Walsenburg Mining Museum. Exhibits on the history of coal mining in Huerfano County, the Trinidad coal fields, and Raton basin. (May-Sept, Mon-Sat; rest of yr, by appt) W 5th St, Old County Jail Building. Phone 719/738-1992. ¢

Motel/Motor Lodge

★★ **BEST WESTERN RAMBLER MOTEL.** I-25, exit 52 (81089). 719/738-1121; fax 719/738-1093; res 800/780-7234. www.bestwestern.com. 35 rms. Mid-May-early Sept: S $62-$77; D $77-$87; under 18 free; lower rates rest of yr. Crib free. Pet accepted, some restrictions. TV. Heated pool. Restaurant 6 am-9 pm. Coffee in lobby. Ck-out 11 am. In-rm modem link. Free bus depot transportation. Cr cds: A, C, D, DS, MC, V.

Restaurant

★★ **IRON HORSE.** 503 W 7th St (81089). 719/738-9966. Hrs: 11 am-2 pm, 4:30-10 pm; Sat & Sun from 4:30 pm. Winter hrs vary. Closed Thanksgiving, Dec 24 & 25; 3 wks Feb. Bar. Lunch $4.25-$7.50, dinner $7.95-$15.95. Specializes in steak, ribs, chicken. Parking. 3 dining rms in turn-of-the-century armory. Cr cds: A, DS, MC, V.

Winter Park

(B-4) See also Central City, Georgetown, Granby, Idaho Springs

Pop 662 **Elev** 9,040 ft **Area code** 970 **Zip** 80482
Information Winter Park/Fraser Valley Chamber of Commerce, PO Box 3236; 800/903-7275
Web www.winterpark-info.com

What to See and Do

Skiing. Winter Park Resort. Eight high-speed quad, five triple, seven double chairlifts; patrol, school, rentals, snowmaking; cafeterias, restaurants, bars. NASTAR and coin-operated race courses. (Mid-Nov-mid-Apr, daily) The five interconnected mountain areas incl **Winter Park, Mary Jane,** and **Vasquez Ridge.** One hundred thirty-four runs; longest run five mi; vertical drop 2,610 ft. Half-day rates. Chairlift and alpine slide also operate late June-mid-Sept (daily). Bicycle rentals, miniature golf (summer, fee). 1 mi SE off US 40. Phone 970/726-5514. ¢¢¢¢ Within resort is

The Children's Center. An all-inclusive ski center for children (inquire about ages) with children's ski slopes, rentals, school, and day care (winter); human maze, 18-hole frisbee golf, indoor/outdoor climbing wall (summer). Phone 970/726-5514. ¢¢¢¢

Motels/Motor Lodges

★ **HIGH MOUNTAIN LODGE INC.** 425 County Rd 5001 (66211). 970/726-5958; fax 970/726-9796; res 800/772-9987. www.himtnlodge.com. 12 air-cooled rms, 2 story. Mid-Dec-early Apr: $80/person; wkly rates; higher rates special events; lower rates rest of yr. Closed May. Crib avail. Pet accepted, some restrictions. TV in rec rm; VCR avail. Complimentary full bkfst. Restaurant nearby. Bar. Ck-out 10 am. Concierge. Coin lndry. RR station transportation. Downhill/x-country ski 9 mi. Exercise equipt; sauna. Indoor pool; whirlpool. Massage. Game rm. Lawn games. Refrigerators, microwaves, fireplaces. Some balconies. Picnic tables, grills. Opp stream. Cr cds: MC, V.

★ **WOODSPUR LODGE.** 111 Van Anderson Dr (80482). 970/726-8417; fax 970/726-8553; toll-free 800/626-6562. 32 air-cooled rms, 18 with shower only, 2 story. Mid-Dec-early Apr, MAP: S $95; D $156; under 3 free; lower rates rest of yr. Crib free. TV in common rm; cable. Complimentary coffee in lobby. Restaurant nearby. Bar (in season) 5-11 pm. Ck-out 10 am. Meeting rms. Business servs avail. Concierge. Free RR station transportation. Downhill ski 3 mi; x-country ski on site. Sauna.

Whirlpools. Game rm. Rec rm. Lawn games. Some balconies. Picnic tables. Cr cds: DS, MC, V.

Hotels

★★ GASTHAUS EICHLER HOTEL.
78786 US 40 (80482). 970/726-4244; fax 970/726-5175; toll-free 800/543-3899. 15 air-cooled rms. Mid-Nov-mid-Apr: S $59-$129; D $89-$169; under 5 free; lower rates rest of yr. Crib avail. TV; cable. Restaurant (see GASTHAUS EICHLER). Bar 7:30 am-11 pm. Ck-out 10 am. Business servs avail. Concierge. Free RR station, bus depot transportation. Downhill/x-country ski 2 mi. In-rm whirlpools. Cr cds: A, MC, V.

★★ VINTAGE HOTEL. *100 Winter Park Dr (80482). 970/726-8801; fax 970/726-9230; toll-free 800/472-7017. www.vintagehotel.com.* 118 air-cooled rms, 5 story, 90 kit. units. Mid-Nov-mid-Apr: S, D $60-$185; suites $385-$475; higher rates mid-Dec-early Jan; lower rates rest of yr. Crib free. Pet accepted. TV; cable (premium). Heated pool; whirlpool. Continental bkfst. Complimentary coffee in rms. Restaurant 7 am-10 pm. Rm serv (seasonal). Bar 3 pm-midnight. Ck-out 11 am. Coin lndry. Meeting rms. Business servs avail. In-rm modem link. Gift shop. Free RR station, bus depot transportation. Downhill/x-country ski. Exercise equipt; sauna. Game rm. Picnic tables. Cr cds: A, D, DS, MC, V.

Resort

★★ IRON HORSE RESORT.
257 Winter Park Dr (80482). 970/726-8851; fax 970/726-2321; toll-free 800/621-8190. www.ironhorse-resort.com. 126 kit. condos, 6 story. Nov-Apr: condos $99-$499; higher rates Dec 25-Jan 1; lower rates rest of yr. Crib $5. TV; cable (premium). Indoor/outdoor pool; whirlpool. Complimentary coffee in rms. Restaurant 7-10 am, 11:30 am-2:30 pm, 5-9:30 pm; summer hrs vary. Bar 3 pm-midnight. Ck-out 10 am, ck-in 4 pm. Grocery 4 mi. Coin lndry. Package store 2 mi. Meeting rms. Business center. Bellhops. Concierge.

Free RR station, bus depot transportation. Downhill/x-country ski on site. Hiking. Lawn games. Game rm. Exercise equipt; steam rms. Microwaves. Balconies. Picnic tables, grills. On river. Cr cds: A, D, DS, MC, V.

B&Bs/Small Inns

★★ ARAPAHOE SKI LODGE.
78594 Hwy 40 (78753). 970/726-8222; res 800/453-2525. www.winterpark-info.com/wpfv/arapahoe/index.html. 11 rms, 2 story. No A/C. No rm phones. Mid-Dec-early Apr: S $54-$132; D $65-$178; each addl $46-$51; MAP avail; hols (5-day min); lower rates rest of yr. Closed Apr, May, Oct. Crib free. TV in lounge; cable (premium). Complimentary full bkfst. Restaurant 7:30-9 am, 6-7:15 pm. Bar 3-10 pm. Ck-out 10 am. Meeting rms. Business servs avail. Concierge. Downhill ski 3 mi; x-country ski 10 mi. Sauna. Indoor pool; whirlpool. Game rm. Rec rm. Picnic tables. Totally nonsmoking. Cr cds: A, DS, JCB, MC, V.

★★★ GRAND VICTORIAN AT WINTER PARK. *78542 Fraser Valley Pkwy (80482). 970/726-5881; fax 970/726-5602; toll-free 800/204-1170.* 10 rms, 3 story. Rm phones avail. Mid-Dec-Mar: S, D $155-$235; lower rates Apr, June-mid-Dec. Closed May. Children over 12 yrs only. TV in some rms. Complimentary full bkfst; afternoon refreshments. Restaurant nearby. Ck-out 11 am, ck-in 4 pm. In-rm modem link. Downhill ski 2 mi; x-country ski 5 mi. Some in-rm whirlpools, fireplaces. Some balconies. Victorian architectural style. Totally nonsmoking. Cr cds: A, D, DS, MC, V.

Restaurants

★★★ DINNING ROOM AT SUNSPOT. *Winter Park Ski Resort (80482). 970/726-1446.* Hrs: 11 am-2 pm, 5:30-8 pm; Sun-Wed to 2 pm. Closed May-Oct. Res accepted; required dinner. No A/C. Bar. Extensive wine list. Lunch $10-$15. Complete meals: dinner $49-$59. Child's menu. Specialties: venison medallion au poivre; shiitake mushroom and

fresh herb-encrusted sea bass;
Sonoma County rabbit. Own baking.
Restaurant located at 10,700-ft altitude, reached by gondola;
panoramic views of Continental
Divide. Totally nonsmoking. Cr cds:
A, D, DS, MC, V.
D

★★ **GASTHAUS EICHLER.** *78786*
US 40 (80482). 970/726-5133. Hrs:
7:30 am-2 pm, 5-9 pm; early-bird
dinner 5-6 pm. Res accepted. No
A/C. German, Amer menu. Bar. Bkfst
$2.75-$7.25, lunch $4.25-$8.50, dinner $12.95-$39. Child's menu. Specializes in apple strudel, German
cuisine. Own pasta. Outdoor dining.
Alpine chalet features an antler chandelier and stained glass windows. Cr
cds: A, MC, V.
SC →

★★ **RANDI'S IRISH SALOON.**
78521 US 40 (80482). 970/726-1186.
Hrs: 7:30-1:30 am. Irish menu. Bar.
Prices: $6.95-$9.95. Child's menu.
Specializes in Irish food, stew, steak
and mushroom pie. Outdoor dining.
Chalet-style bldg with fireplace,
early-Amer furnishings; patio has
rock garden and fountain. Cr cds: A,
C, D, DS, MC, V.
D SC →

NEVADA

Famous for gambling and glamorous nightlife, Nevada also has a rich history and tradition, magnificent scenery, and some of the wildest desert country on the continent.

Tourism is still the lifeblood of Nevada, with some 42 million visitors a year coming for a vacation or convention. Because of its central location and lack of inventory tax on goods bound out of state, Nevada is becoming increasingly important as a warehousing center for the western states.

Gambling (Nevadans call it "gaming") was first legalized in the Depression year of 1931, the same year residency requirements for obtaining a divorce were relaxed. Gaming is strictly controlled and regulated in Nevada, and casinos offer each bettor a fair chance to win. Taxes derived from the casinos account for nearly half of the state's revenue.

Population: 1,998,257
Area: 110,567 square miles
Elevation: 470-13,143 feet
Peak: Boundary Peak
   (Esmeralda County)
Entered Union: October 31,
   1864 (36th state)
Capital: Carson City
Motto: All for our country
Nickname: Silver State
Flower: Sagebrush
Bird: Mountain Bluebird
Tree: Piñon and Bristlecone
   Pine
Fair: August, 2003 in Reno
Time Zone: Pacific
Website:
   www.travelnevada.com

Most Nevadans feel it is preferable to license, tax, and regulate gambling strictly than to tolerate the evils of bribery and corruption that inevitably accompany illegal gambling activities. While the state enforces numerous regulations, such as those barring criminals and prohibiting cheating, it does not control odds on the various games.

Although Nevada has little rainfall and few rivers, water sports are popular on a few large lakes, both natural and man-made. These include Lakes Tahoe, Mead, and Lahontan, Pyramid Lake, and Walker Lake.

Mining and ranching have always been important facets of Nevada's economy. Sheep raising became important when millions of sheep were needed to feed the hungry miners working Nevada's Comstock Lode and California's Mother Lode. Most of these sheepherders were Basque. Although today's sheepherder is more likely Peruvian or Mexican, the Basques are still an important influence in the state.

Because of Nevada's arid land, cattle have to roam over a wide area; therefore, ranches average more than 2,000 acres in size. Most Nevada beef cattle are shipped to California or the Midwest for fattening prior to marketing.

Known for its precious metals, Nevada produces more than $2.6 billion worth of gold and silver a year. Eerie ghost towns still hint at the romantic early days of fabulous gold and silver strikes that made millionaires overnight and generated some of the wildest history in the world. In the southern part of the state, the deserted mining camps of Rhyolite, Berlin, Belmont, Goodsprings, and Searchlight, to name a few, still delight explorers. Industrial metals and minerals also have an impact on the economy.

The fur traders of the 1820s and 1830s, Jedediah Smith, Peter Ogden, and Joseph Walker and the Frémont expeditions, guided by Kit Carson in 1848, were the first to report on the area that is now Nevada.

The Mormons established a trading post in 1851. Now called Genoa, this was Nevada's first non-Indian settlement. Gold was found along the Carson River in Dayton Valley in May of 1850. A decade later the fabulous Comstock Lode (silver and gold ore) was discovered. The gold rush was on and Virginia City mushroomed into a town of 20,000. Formerly a part of Utah and New Mexico Territory, ceded by Mexico in 1848, Nevada became a territory in 1861, a state in 1864. Before Europeans arrived, Nevada was the home of the Paiute, the Shoshone, and the Washoe, and even earlier, the Basketmakers.

Note: It is illegal to pick many types of wildflowers in Nevada, as well as gathering rocks. It is also illegal in this dry land to toss away lighted cigarette butts.

When to Go/Climate

Temperatures vary greatly in Nevada—from scorching desert days in Death Valley to bone-chilling night freezes in the Sierra Nevada. The entire state is arid. You may want to avoid visiting Nevada in the hot summer months of June, July, and August, when daytime temperatures can remain above 100 degrees in many parts of the state.

AVERAGE HIGH/LOW TEMPERATURES (°F)

ELKO

Jan 37/13	**May** 69/37	**Sept** 78/39
Feb 43/20	**June** 80/47	**Oct** 66/30
Mar 50/25	**July** 91/50	**Nov** 49/23
Apr 60/30	**Aug** 89/49	**Dec** 37/14

LAS VEGAS

Jan 57/34	**May** 88/60	**Sept** 95/66
Feb 63/39	**June** 100/69	**Oct** 82/54
Mar 69/44	**July** 106/76	**Nov** 67/43
Apr 78/51	**Aug** 103/74	**Dec** 58/34

Parks and Recreation Finder

Directions to and information about the parks and recreation areas below are given under their respective town/city sections. Please refer to those sections for details.

NATIONAL PARK AND RECREATION AREAS

Key to abbreviations. I.H.S. = International Historic Site; I.P.M. = International Peace Memorial; N.B. = National Battlefield; N.B.P. = National Battlefield Park; N.B.C. = National Battlefield and Cemetery; N.C.A. = National Conservation Area; N.E.M. = National Expansion Memorial; N.F. = National Forest; N.G. = National Grassland; N.H.P. = National Historical Park; N.H.C. = National Heritage Corridor; N.H.S. = National Historic Site; N.L. = National Lakeshore; N.M. = National Monument; N.M.P. = National Military Park; N.Mem. = National Memorial; N.P. = National Park; N.Pres. = National Preserve; N.R.A. = National Recreational Area; N.R.R. = National Recreational River; N.Riv. = National River; N.S. = National Seashore; N.S.R. = National Scenic Riverway; N.S.T. = National Scenic Trail; N.Sc. = National Scientific Reserve; N.V.M. = National Volcanic Monument.

Place Name	Listed Under
Great Basin N.P.	same
Lake Mead N.R.	same
Toiyabe N.F.	RENO

STATE PARK AND RECREATION AREAS

Key to abbreviations. I.P. = Interstate Park; S.A.P. = State Archaeological Park; S.B. = State Beach; S.C.A. = State Conservation Area; S.C.P. = State Conservation Park; S.Cp. = State Campground; S.F. = State Forest; S.G. = State Garden;

S.H.A. = State Historic Area; S.H.P. = State Historic Park; S.H.S. = State Historic Site; S.M.P. = State Marine Park; S.N.A. = State Natural Area; S.P. = State Park; S.P.C. = State Public Campground; S.R. = State Reserve; S.R.A. = State Recreation Area; S.Res. = State Reservoir; S.Res.P. = State Resort Park; S.R.P. = State Rustic Park.

Place Name	Listed Under
Berlin-Ichthyosaur S.P.	AUSTIN
Cave Lake S.P.	ELY
Floyd Lamb S.P.	LAS VEGAS
Fort Churchill S.H.P.	YERINGTON
Lahontan S.R.A.	FALLON
Lake Tahoe Nevada S.P.	INCLINE VILLAGE
Rye Patch S.R.A.	LOVELOCK
Spring Mountain Ranch S.P.	LAS VEGAS

CALENDAR HIGHLIGHTS

JANUARY

Cowboy Poetry Gathering (Elko). Working cowpersons participate in storytelling verse. Demonstrations; country music. Phone 773/738-7508.

MAY

Laughlin Riverdays (Laughlin). World's longest line dance, carnival, golf tournament. Contact Laughlin Chamber of Commerce. Phone 800/227-5245.

JUNE

Fallon Air Show (Fallon). Fallon Naval Air Station. Military exhibition flying, civilian aerobatics, aircraft displays; Blue Angels Demonstration Team. Phone 775/423-2544.

Helldorado Days (Las Vegas). Rodeos, parades, carnival, street dance, chili cook-off; Western theme throughout. Phone 702/870-1221.

Kit Carson Rendezvous (Carson City). Mountain man encampment, Civil War camp, Native American village with competition dancing, music, arts and crafts, and food vendors. Contact Carson City Convention & Visitors Bureau. Phone 775/687-7410 or 800/638-2321.

Winnemucca Basque Festival (Elko). Contests in weightlifting, sheep-hooking, other skills of mountaineers; dancing, feast. Phone 775/623-5071.

AUGUST

Nevada State Fair (Reno). Fairgrounds. Exhibits, entertainment, rides, games, and more. Phone 775/688-5767.

SEPTEMBER

National Championship Air Races (Reno). Stead Air Field. The world's longest-running air race, featuring four race classes—Unlimited, Formula One, AT-6, and Biplane. Skywriting, aerobatics, and displays. Phone 775/972-6663.

OCTOBER

Invensys Classic (Las Vegas). PGA tournament with more than $4.5 million in prize money.

DECEMBER

National Finals Rodeo (Las Vegas). Thomas and Mack Center. Nation's richest professional rodeo, featuring 15 finalists in seven rodeo disciplines. Phone 702/895-3900.

Valley of Fire S.P.	same
Ward Charcoal Ovens S.H.P.	ELY

Water-related activities, hiking, riding, various other sports, picnicking, and visitor centers, as well as camping, are available in many of these areas. "Roughing it" may be necessary in remote areas. Camping on a first-come, first-served basis; $3-$9/night. Boat launching $2-$6, except Lake Tahoe; (covers all fees, including boat launching). Inquire locally about road conditions for areas off paved highways. Carry drinking water in remote areas. Pets on leash only. For detailed information contact Nevada Division of State Parks, 1300 S Curry St, Carson City 89703-5202, phone 775/687-4384.

SKI AREAS

Place Name	Listed Under
Diamond Peak Ski Resort	INCLINE VILLAGE
Mount Rose Ski Area	INCLINE VILLAGE

FISHING AND HUNTING

Nevada's streams and lakes abound with trout, bass, mountain whitefish, and catfish. Most fishing areas are open year-round. There are some exceptions; inquire locally. Nonresident license: $51 for one year or $12 for one day. Special use stamp ($3) for Lake Mead, Lake Mohave, and the Colorado River; $5 annual trout stamp required to take or possess trout.

There is an abundance of wildlife—mule deer, quail, ducks, geese, and partridges. Deer hunting season lasts four to five wks from the first two weekends in October; season varies in some counties. Nonresident hunting license: $111 plus $200 for deer tag and processing. Deer hunting with bow and arrow: nonresidents $111 for license and $155 for tag and processing. Archery hunts usually held August 8 through September 4, prior to rifle season.

For digest of fishing and hunting regulations write to the Nevada Division of Wildlife, PO Box 10678, Reno 89520, phone 775/688-1500.

Driving Information

Safety belts are mandatory for all persons anywhere in vehicle. Children under five years and under 40 pounds in weight must be in an approved safety seat anywhere in vehicle. For further information phone 877/368-7828.

INTERSTATE HIGHWAY SYSTEM

Use the following list as a guide to access interstate highways in Nevada. You should always consult a map to confirm driving routes.

Highway Number	Cities/Towns within ten miles
Interstate 15	Las Vegas, Overton.
Interstate 80	Battle Mountain, Elko, Lovelock, Reno, Winnemucca.

Additional Visitor Information

Nevada Magazine, an illustrated bimonthly magazine, and *Nevada's Events Guide* (free), may be obtained by contacting the Nevada Commission on Tourism, 401 N Carson St, Carson City 89701, phone 775/687-4322 or 800/NEVADA-8.

For information about the Lake Mead area, write the Public Affairs Officer, Lake Mead National Recreation Area, Boulder City 89005.

Information on camping, fishing and hunting, water sports, gambling, ghost towns, mining, agriculture, and the state capitol and museum may also be obtained from the Commission on Tourism (see above).

Gambling

Gambling is limited to those 21 or over. Children are welcome in restaurants, and many casinos have child-care facilities.

SCENIC NEVADA

This tour from Reno, which can be accomplished over one or two days, combines the scenic beauty and recreational opportunities of Lake Tahoe with historic sites from Nevada's mining days. From Reno go south on US 395 to NV 431 (the Mount Rose Scenic Byway), which heads west and southwest as it climbs to an 8,911-foot pass and then drops down to Lake Tahoe, providing splendid panoramic views of the lake. Continue on NV 431 to NV 28 and Incline Village, a good base from which to enjoy the beach, swimming, fishing, and the spectacular views at Lake Tahoe Nevada State Park. The sandy beach at the park's Sand Harbor section is delightful but also very popular; those looking for more solitude can opt for Memorial Point and Hidden Beach, less-frequented areas of the state park. Those visiting from late July through August might want to experience the Lake Tahoe Shakespeare Festival, with shows at an outdoor theater at Sand Harbor. Also in Incline Village is the Ponderosa Ranch, a western theme park where the popular television series *Bonanza* was filmed from 1959 to 1973. Tours of the ranch house film set are given, and the ranch also includes an Old West town with a working blacksmith shop, a saloon, a church, historic wagons and automobiles, a petting farm, pony rides, and staged gunfights.

From Incline Village, continue south on NV 28 along Lake Tahoe's eastern shore, then take US 50 east to Carson City. Part of the Lake Tahoe Scenic Byway, this route offers panoramic views of the lake and nearby mountains. Carson City, Nevada's capital, is roughly the half-way point of this tour and a good spot to spend the night. Founded in 1858, Carson City features numerous historic sites, including the handsome State Capitol, built in 1871, with a dome of silver. Attractions also include the 1864 Bowers Mansion, built of granite and furnished with many original pieces; the Warren Engine Company No. 1 Fire Museum, where you'll see a variety of historic firefighting equipment; and the Nevada State Railroad Museum, with three steam locomotives and numerous freight and passenger cars.

Carson City is also an especially family-friendly city, with lots of activities and attractions for children. There are several fun exhibits for kids at the Nevada State Museum, such as a full-size replica of a ghost town and an underground mine tunnel. Preteens especially enjoy the Children's Museum of Northern Nevada, which boasts numerous interactive exhibits including Musical Hands, in which a motion detector helps children "conduct" an orchestra; a small-scale grocery store; and a Show Box that produces body prints. The Children's Museum also has a fire engine that kids can climb on and the huge walk-on piano from the 1988 Tom Hanks movie *Big*.

Now head northeast on US 50 to NV 341, which you follow north to picturesque Virginia City, an historic mining town that had its heyday in the 1870s. Beautifully restored, Virginia City today offers a glimpse into its opulent and sometimes wicked past with historic buildings, a mine, and a working steam train. To see the epitome of 19th-century extravagance stop at The Castle, an 1868 Victorian mansion known for its marble fireplaces, crystal chandeliers, and silver doorknobs. Other attractions include Piper's Opera House, which hosted the major stars of the late 1800s, and the Mackay Mansion, built in 1860 as the headquarters of mining magnate John Mackay. Western history is highlighted at The Way It Was Museum and Wild West Museum. Those interested in Virginia City's seamier side won't want to miss the Nevada Gambling Museum, with antique slot machines, cheating devices, and other gambling memorabilia; and the Bullette Red Light Museum, which features a mock bordello with Oriental art and vintage erotica, as well as a reproduction of a 19th-century doctor's office with antique medical equipment. Tours are offered at the Choller, an 1860s gold and silver mine, and steam train rides through the historic mining district are offered by the Virginia & Truckee Railroad. To return to Reno, take NV 341 north to US 395 north. **(APPROX 100 MI)**

Austin

(C-4) *See also Battle Mountain*

Settled 1862 **Pop** 350 **Elev** 6,525 ft
Area code 775 **Zip** 89310
Information Chamber of Commerce,
PO Box 212; 775/964-2200

What to See and Do

Berlin-Ichthyosaur State Park.
Approx 1,070 acres. Fossilized
remains of marine reptiles, some up
to 50 ft long, with fish-shaped bodies
and long, narrow snouts. The ghost
town of Berlin is also here. Hiking
and nature trails, picnicking, camping facilities (fee, dump station).
(Daily) Standard fees. 50 mi SW via
US 50, then 30 mi S on NV 361 to
Gabbs, then 22 mi E on NV 844, in
Toiyabe National Forest. Phone
775/964-2440. ¢¢

Hickison Petroglyph Recreation Site.
Native American drawings carved in
stone (ca 1000 B.C.-A.D. 1500); near
former Pony Express trail. Picnicking,
camping; no drinking water avail.
(Daily) 24 mi E on US 50. Phone
775/635-4000. **FREE**

The Lander County Courthouse.
Oldest county courthouse in the
state and one of the plainest. Its
sturdy construction, without frills,
suited the early residents.

Mountain biking. Many miles of biking trails through central Nevada's
varied terrain. Brochure describing
designated trails avail from Chamber
of Commerce or Tyrannosaurus Rix
Mountain Bike & Specialties. Phone
775/964-1212.

Other old buildings. Stores, churches,
hotels, and saloons. Stokes Castle is a
century-old, three-story stone building that can be seen for miles. Phone
775/964-1133.

The Reese River *Reveille.* Published
from May 16, 1863 to 1993; complete files are preserved.

Battle Mountain (B-5)

Settled 1868 **Pop** 2,871 **Elev** 4,512 ft
Area code 775 **Zip** 89820

Motels/Motor Lodges

★ **BEST INN & SUITES.** *650 W
Front St (89820). 775/635-5200; fax
775/635-5699; res 800/237-8466.
www.bestinn.com.* 72 rms, 2 story. S
$49; D $51; each addl $5; under 12
free. Pet accepted. TV; cable (premium). Coffee in lobby. Restaurant
adj open 24 hrs. Ck-out 11 am. Business servs avail. Some refrigerators.
Picnic table, grill. Western theme. Cr
cds: A, C, D, DS, MC, V.

★★ **COMFORT INN.** *521 E Front St
(89820). 775/635-5880; fax 775/635-
5788; toll-free 800/228-5150. www.
comfortinn.com.* 72 rms, 3 story. June-
Aug: S, D $56-$61; each addl $5;
under 6 free. Crib $5. Pet accepted;
$20 deposit. TV; cable (premium).
Heated pool; whirlpool. Complimentary continental bkfst. Restaurant adj
11 am-9 pm. Ck-out 11 am. Coin
lndry. Meeting rms. Business servs
avail. Refrigerators. Cr cds: A, C, D,
DS, MC, V.

Boulder City

(G-7) *See also Henderson, Lake Mead
National Recreation Area, Las Vegas*

Founded 1931 **Pop** 14,966 **Elev** 2,500
ft **Area code** 702
Information Chamber of Commerce,
1305 Arizona St; 702/293-2034
Web www.bouldercitychamber.com

Special Events

Boulder Damboree. Central Park.
July 4. Phone 702/293-9256.
Art in the Park. Wilbur Square,
Bicentennial, and Escalante parks.

First full wkend Oct. Phone 702/293-4111.

Motels/Motor Lodges

★ **EL RANCHO BOULDER.** *725 Nevada Hwy (89005). 702/293-1085; fax 702/293-3021.* 39 rms. S, D $60-$150; family, wkly rates. TV; cable (premium). Pool. Complimentary coffee in lobby. Restaurant adj 6 am-midnight. Ck-out 11 am. Meeting rms. Airport transportation. Refrigerators. Cr cds: A, D, DS, MC, V.
D ⬡ ⬡ ⬡ ⬡

★ **HACIENDA INN AND CASINO.** *US 93 (89005). 702/293-5000; fax 702/293-5608; res 800/245-6380.* 378 rms, 17 story. S, D $29-$69; each addl $3.27; under 12 free. Crib $3. TV. Heated pool. Restaurant open 24 hrs. Bar; entertainment Thurs-Sun. Ck-out 11 am. Gift shop. Casino. Some private patios, balconies. View of Lake Mead. Cr cds: A, D, DS, MC, V.
D ⬡ ⬡ ⬡

★ **SUPER 8.** *704 Nevada Hwy (89005). 702/294-8888; fax 702/293-4344; res 800/800-8000. www.super8. com.* 114 rms, 3 story. S, D $42.88-$79.88; suites $75.88-$200.88; wkly, monthly rates. Crib $5. TV; cable (premium). Indoor pool; whirlpool. Restaurant 7 am-10 pm. Bar. Ck-out noon. Meeting rms. Airport transportation. Game rm. Picnic tables. Cr cds: A, DS, MC, V.
D ⬡ ⬡ ⬡ ⬡

Caliente

(E-7) *See also Las Vegas, Overton*

Pop 1,123 **Elev** 4,395 ft
Area code 775 **Zip** 89008
Information Chamber of Commerce, PO Box 553; 775/726-3129
Web www.lincolncountynevada.com

What to See and Do

State parks and recreation areas.
  Beaver Dam. (Check conditions locally; trailers over 24 ft not recommended) More than 2,200 acres set amid pine forests and lofty cliffs. Fishing; hiking, picnicking, camping. (Apr-Oct) 6 mi N on US 93, then 28 mi E on improved gravel road. Phone 775/728-4460.
  Cathedral Gorge. This 1,633-acre park is a long, narrow valley cut into tan bentonite clay formations. Peculiar erosion has created unique patterns, fluting the gorge walls and forming isolated towers that resemble cathedral spires. Hiking, picnicking, camping facilities. 14 mi N on US 93. Phone 775/728-4460.
  Echo Canyon. A 920-acre park. Swimming, fishing on 65-acre reservoir (daily), boat launching; picnicking, camping (dump station). 25 mi N on US 93, then 4 mi E on NV 322, then 10 mi SE on NV 323. Phone 775/728-4460.
  Spring Valley. A 1,630-acre park. Boating and fishing on Eagle Valley Reservoir; picnicking, camping (dump station). (Daily) 26 mi N on US 93 to Pioche, then 18 mi E on NV 322. Phone 775/728-4460.

Special Events

Lincoln County Homecoming. Barbecue, celebrity auction, art show. Memorial Day wkend. Phone 775/726-3129.

Lincoln County Fair and Rodeo. Mid-Aug. Phone 775/962-5103.

Meadow Valley Western Days. Hayrides, rodeo, talent show. Third wkend Sept. Phone 775/726-3129.

Carson City

(D-2) *See also Incline Village, Reno, Stateline, Virginia City*

Founded 1858 **Pop** 52,457 **Elev** 4,687 ft **Area code** 775 **Zip** 89701
Information Convention & Visitors Bureau, 1900 S Carson St, Suite 200; 775/687-7410 or 800/638-2321
Web www.carson-city.org

What to See and Do

Bowers Mansion. (1864) The Bowers built this $200,000 granite house with the profits from a gold and silver mine. Their resources were soon depleted, leaving them penniless and forcing Mrs. Bower to become the

"Washoe seeress," telling fortunes for a living. Half-hr guided tours of 16 rms with many original furnishings. (Memorial Day-Labor Day, daily; May, Sept, and Oct, wkends). Swimming pool (Memorial Day-Labor Day; fee) and picnicking in adj park. 10 mi N in Washoe Valley. Phone 775/849-0201. ¢¢

State Capitol. (1871) Large stone structure with Doric columns and a silver dome. Houses portraits of past Nevada governors. (Mon-Fri) 101 N Carson St. Phone 775/684-5700. Near the capitol are

Nevada State Museum. Former US Mint. Exhibits of Nevada's natural history and anthropology; life-size displays of Nevada ghost town, Native American camp with artifacts and walk-through "Devonian sea." A 300-ft mine tunnel with displays runs beneath the building. (Daily; closed Jan 1, Thanksgiving, Dec 25) 600 N Carson St. Phone 775/687-4810. ¢¢

Nevada State Railroad Museum. Exhibits 50 freight and passenger cars, as well as three steam locomotives that once belonged to the Virginia and Truckee railroad. Houses pictorial history gallery and artifacts of the famed Bonanza Rd. Motor car rides (summer wkends; fee) and steam-engine rides (summer hols and some

MINING AND MONEY IN CARSON CITY

Home to Nevada's largest historical homes district and the State Capitol, a walking tour of Carson City offers a good viewpoint for investigating the heady days of the Old West's 19th-century mining boom. The legendary Comstock Lode, one of the era's richest silver strikes, was discovered in nearby Virginia City in 1859, creating the need for a US Mint in the area. As a result, Carson City was home to a US Mint from 1870 to 1895, pressing more than $50 million in coinage during that span. A half-century after it closed, the Mint building became the Nevada State Museum (600 North Carson Street), a good starting point for a tour of Carson City on foot. The museum mixes natural and cultural history in a collection of archaeological finds, dioramas, Indian baskets, and an antique—and operational—coin press. From the Nevada State Museum, it's only two blocks north on Carson Street to the Children's Museum of Northern Nevada (813 North Carson Street), the area's best attraction for kids. Backtracking south on Carson Street, you'll pass through Carson City's primary casino district in the vicinity of Spear and Telegraph streets. The casinos house the majority of the restaurants in downtown Carson City, so this is a good opportunity to grab a bite to eat. Continuing south on Carson Street for three blocks, the quarried sandstone Nevada State Capitol (just east of the intersection of Carson and Second streets) is the cornerstone of a beautifully landscaped plaza that is also home to the state's Supreme Court, Legislative Building, and Library and Archives Building (where Nevada Historic Marker Guides are available on the second floor). Just southeast of the Capitol plaza on Stewart Street is the Warren Engine Company No. 1 Museum (777 South Stewart Street), with exhibits, photographs, and memorabilia detailing the oldest continuously operating firefighting company in the West. From here, it is just a block north on Stewart Street to Fifth Street; take Fifth west to Nevada Street and walk three blocks north to King Street, on which you'll want to go west once again. At 449 West King Street is the Brewery Arts Center, a showcase for the work of local artists in the former Carson Brewing Company building, which was built in 1864 and is currently on the National Historic Register. The Arts Center is in the heart of Carson City's most historic neighborhood. A good way to cap the walking tour is to follow the Kit Carson Trail to get a peek at the city's "Talking Houses" by continuing west on King Street, turning right on Mountain Street, and going north to Robinson Street. At the Mountain-Robinson intersection are a pair of notable mansions: the Governor's Mansion and the Bliss Mansion. On the short walk back east on Robinson Street to the Nevada State Museum, you'll pass several more historic structures. (For information on the self-guided walking tour of the entire 2½-mile Kit Carson Trail, contact the Carson City Convention and Visitor's Bureau.)

wkends; fee). Museum (daily). 2180 Carson at Fairview Dr. Phone 775/687-6953. ¢

State Library Building. Files of Nevada newspapers and books about the state. (Mon-Fri; closed hols) 100 N Stewart. Phone 775/684-3360. **FREE**

Warren Engine Company No. I Fire Museum. Currier and Ives series "The Life of a Fireman," old photographs, antique fire-fighting equipment, state's first fire truck (restored), 1863 Hunneman hand-pumper, 1847 four-wheel cart. Children under 18 must be accompanied by adult. 777 S Stewart St. Phone 775/887-2210. **FREE**

Special Events

Kit Carson Rendezvous. Mountain man encampment, Civil War camp, Native American village with competition dancing, music, arts and crafts and food vendors. Second wkend June. Phone 775/687-7410.

Nevada Day Celebration. Commemorates admission to the Union. Grand Ball, parades, exhibits. Four days late Oct. Phone 775/687-7410.

Motels/Motor Lodges

★ **MILL HOUSE INN.** *3251 S Carson St (89701). 775/882-2715; fax 775/882-2415.* 24 rms. May-Oct: S $45-$85; each addl $5; under 12 free; higher rates: wkends, hols; lower rates rest of yr. Crib $5. TV; cable. Heated pool (seasonal). Complimentary coffee in lobby. Restaurant nearby. Ck-out 11 am. Picnic tables. Cr cds: A, D, DS, MC, V.
🐾 ⇌ ⊠ 🐾

★★ **PARK INN HARDMAN HOUSE.** *917 N Carson St (89701). 775/882-7744; fax 775/887-0321; toll-free 800/626-0793. www.parkinn.com.* 62 rms, 3 story. May-Oct: S $79; D $89; each addl $6; suites $95-$129; higher rates: wkends, hols, air races; lower rates rest of yr. Crib free. TV; cable. Complimentary coffee in lobby. Restaurant nearby. Ck-out 11 am. Business servs avail. Garage parking. Some refrigerators; some wet bars. Cr cds: A, C, D, DS, MC, V.
⊠ 🐾 **SC**

Restaurants

★★ **ADELE'S.** *1112 N Carson St (89701). 775/882-3353.* Hrs: 11 am-midnight. Closed Sun; also wk of Dec 31-mid-Jan. Res accepted. Bar. Complete meals: lunch $7.95-$18.95, dinner $17.95-$44.95. Specializes in seafood, steak, roast duck. Comstock Victorian decor in Second Empire house. Cr cds: MC, V.
D

★★ **CARSON NUGGET STEAK HOUSE.** *507 N Carson St (89701). 775/882-1626. www.ccnugget.com.* Hrs: 5-10 pm. Res accepted. Bar open 24 hrs. Dinner $9.95-$17.95. Child's menu. Specializes in seafood, prime rib, steak. Valet parking. Western decor. Also on premises are buffet dining rm and coffee shop open 24 hrs. Cr cds: A, D, DS, MC, V.
D SC ⊣

★ **SILVANA'S.** *1301 N Carson St (89701). 775/883-5100.* Hrs: 5-10 pm. Closed Sun, Mon; Dec 25. Res accepted. Italian menu. Bar. Dinner $10.95-$19.95. Specializes in pasta, seafood, steak. European decor. Cr cds: A, C, MC, V.
D

Crystal Bay

(see Incline Village)

Elko (B-5)

Settled ca 1870 **Pop** 16,708
Elev 5,067 ft **Area code** 775
Zip 89801
Information Chamber of Commerce, 1405 Idaho St; 775/738-7135 or 800/428-7143
Web www.elkonevada.com

On the Humboldt River, Elko is the center of a large ranching area. Originally a stopping point for wagon trains headed for the West Coast, its main sources of revenue today are tourism, ranching, gold mining, gaming, and a large service industry.

What to See and Do

Humboldt National Forest. Some of the features of this more than two million-acre forest are its eight wilderness areas, spectacular canyons, streams, and old mining camps. Fishing; hunting, picnicking, camping (May-Oct; fee). 20 mi SE on NV 228 (Ruby Mountain District), or 70 mi N on NV 225 (Mountain City and Jarbridge Districts). Contact Supervisor, 976 Mountain City Hwy. Phone 775/738-5171. ¢¢

Licensed casinos, nightclubs. Particularly along Idaho St. Phone 775/738-2111.

Northeastern Nevada Museum. Three galleries feature art, historical, Native American, and nature exhibits of area. Pioneer vehicles and original 1860 pony express cabin on grounds. (Daily; closed Jan 1, Thanksgiving, Dec 25) 1515 Idaho St. Phone 775/738-3418. ¢¢

Special Events

Cowboy Poetry Gathering. Working cowpersons participate in storytelling verse. Demonstrations; music. Last full wk Jan. Phone 775/738-7135.

National Basque Festival. Contests in weightlifting, sheephooking, other skills of mountaineers; dancing, feast. Wkend early July. Phone 775/738-7135.

County Fair and Livestock Show. Horse racing. Four days Labor Day wkend. Phone 775/738-7135.

Motels/Motor Lodges

★★ **BEST WESTERN ELKO INN EXPRESS.** *837 Idaho St (89801). 775/738-7261; fax 775/738-0118; res 800/780-7234. www.bestwestern.com.* 49 rms, 2 story. Mid-May-Sept: S $44-$54; D $54-$64; each addl $5; suites $79; higher rates special events; varied lower rates rest of yr. Crib $5. TV; cable (premium). Heated pool. Complimentary continental bkfst. Ck-out noon. Business servs avail. Cr cds: A, D, DS, MC, V.
🄳 ⏚ ⋈ ⊠ 🔥

★★ **RED LION INN AND CASINO.** *2065 E Idaho St (89801). 775/738-2111; fax 775/753-9859; res 800/545-0044. www.* 223 rms, 3 story. S

$69-$79; D $79-$89; each addl $10; suites $259; under 18 free. Crib free. Pet accepted. TV; cable (premium). Heated pool. Coffee in rms. Restaurant open 24 hrs. Bar; entertainment. Ck-out noon. Business servs avail. Gift shop. Barber, beauty shop. Free airport transportation. Game rm. Casino. Cr cds: A, DS, MC, V.
🄳 🐾 ⋈ ⊠ 🔥

★★ **SHILO INN.** *2401 Mountain City Hwy (89801). 775/738-5522; fax 775/738-6247; toll-free 800/222-2244. www.shiloinns.com.* 70 rms, 2 story, 16 kit. units. S, D $69.95-$129.95; kit. units $69-$119; under 12 free; wkly rates; higher rates special events. Crib free. Pet accepted; $7. TV; cable (premium), VCR avail. Indoor pool; whirlpool. Complimentary continental bkfst. Restaurant nearby. Ck-out noon. Coin lndry. Meeting rm. Business servs avail. In-rm modem link. Sundries. Free airport, RR station, bus depot transportation. Exercise equipt; sauna. Bathrm phones, refrigerators, wet bars. Cr cds: A, C, D, DS, MC, V.
🄳 🐾 📶 ⋈ 🏃 ✈ ⊠ 🔥 SC

★ **SUPER 8 MOTEL.** *1755 Idaho St (89801). 775/738-8488; fax 775/738-4637; toll-free 800/800-8000. www.super8.com.* 75 rms, 2 story. Late May-Sept: S, D $40.88-$55.88; each addl $3; under 12 free; higher rates special events; lower rates rest of yr. Crib free. TV; cable (premium). Complimentary coffee in lobby. Restaurant nearby. Ck-out 11 am. Business servs avail. Cr cds: A, C, D, DS, MC, V.
🄳 ⊠ 🔥 SC

Hotel

★★ **HIGH DESERT INN.** *3015 E Idaho St (89801). 775/738-8425; fax 775/753-7906; toll-free 888/394-8303.* 170 rms, 4 story. Apr-Oct: S $64-$84, D $74-$94; each addl $10; higher rates: Cowboy Poetry Gathering, Mining Exposition; lower rates rest of yr. Crib free. Pet accepted. TV; cable. Indoor pool; whirlpool. Coffee in rms. Restaurant 6 am-10 pm. Rm serv. Bar 4 pm-midnight. Ck-out noon. Coin lndry. Meeting rms. Valet serv. Free airport, RR station, bus

depot transportation. Exercise equipt.
Cr cds: A, D, DS, MC, V.

Ely (D-6)

Settled 1868 **Pop** 4,041 **Elev** 6,427 ft
Area code 775 **Zip** 89301
Information White Pine Chamber of
Commerce, 636 Aultman St;
775/289-8877

What to See and Do

Cave Lake State Park. A 1,240-acre
area; 32-acre reservoir provides swimming, fishing (trout), boating; picnicking, camping (dump station,
showers). (Daily; access may be
restricted in winter) Standard fees. 8
mi S on US 93, then 7 mi E on Suc-
cess Summit Rd, NV 486. Phone
775/728-4467 or 775/728-4460.

Humboldt National Forest. (see
ELKO) Phone 775/578-3521.

Nevada Northern Railway Museum.
Located in the historic Nevada
Northern Railway Depot (1906).
Phone 775/289-2085. Museum ¢¢
Train excursions ¢¢¢¢

**Ward Charcoal Ovens State Historic
Park.** Six stone beehive charcoal
ovens used during the 1870 mining
boom. Hunting in season. Picnicking. 7 mi SE on US 6/50/93, then 11
mi W on Cave Valley Rd, a gravel
road. Phone 775/728-4467.

White Pine Public Museum. 1905
stagecoach, early-day relics and
mementos, mineral display. (Daily)
2000 Aultman St. Phone 775/289-
4710. **FREE**

Special Events

Auto races. Open road auto races.
Phone 775/289-8877. Third wkend
May and Sept.

Pony Express Days. Pari-mutuel betting. Phone 775/289-8877. Last two
wkends Aug.

White Pine County Fair. Third
wkend Aug. Phone 775/289-8877.

Motels/Motor Lodges

★ **JAIL HOUSE MOTEL & CASINO.**
*211 5th St (89301). 775/289-3033; fax
775/289-8709; toll-free 800/841-5430.*
47 rms, 2 story. S $42; D $46-$51;
each addl $5. Crib free. TV; cable
(premium). Restaurant 5 am-9 pm.
Ck-out 11 am. Casino. Cr cds: A, C,
D, DS, MC, V.

★★ **RAMADA INN & COPPER
QUEEN CASINO.** *805 E 7th St
(89301). 775/289-4884; fax 775/289-
1492; toll-free 888/298-2054. www.
ramada.com.* 65 rms, 2 story. S $60-
$70; D $65-$75; each addl $5. Crib
free. Indoor pool; whirlpool. TV;
cable (premium). Complimentary
continental bkfst. Restaurant 11 am-
10 pm. Bar. Ck-out noon. Business
servs avail. Free airport transportation. Some refrigerators. Casino. Cr
cds: A, C, D, DS, MC, V.

Fallon (C-3)

Pop 7,536 **Elev** 3,963 ft
Area code 775 **Zip** 89406
Information Chamber of Commerce,
65 S Maine St, Ste C; 775/423-2544
Web www.fallonchamber.com

What to See and Do

Lahontan State Recreation Area.
Approx 30,000 acres with a 16-mi-
long reservoir. Water sports, fishing,
boating (launching, ramps); picnicking, camping (dump station). Standard fees. 18 mi W on US 50. Phone
775/867-3500.

Special Events

Fallon Air Show. Fallon Naval Air Station. Military exhibition flying, civilian aerobatics, aircraft displays; Blue
Angels Demonstration Team. Ground
events and static displays of vintage
and modern aircraft. Late spring-
early summer. Phone 775/426-2880.

All Indian Rodeo. Rodeo events,
parade, powwow, Native American
dances, arts, games. Phone 775/423-
2544. Third wkend July.

Motels/Motor Lodges

★★ **BEST INN & SUITES.** *1830 W Williams Ave (89406). 775/423-5554; fax 775/423-0663; toll-free 888/691-6388. www.bestinn.com.* 82 rms, 2 story. Apr-Oct: S, D $51-$65; suites $75-$100; under 18 free; lower rates rest of yr. Crib free. TV; cable, VCR avail. Indoor pool. Complimentary continental bkfst. Ck-out noon. Business servs avail. Sundries. Coin lndry. Some refrigerators, microwaves, in-rm whirlpools. Cr cds: A, C, D, DS, ER, JCB, MC, V.
[D] [⊠] [⊠] [♨] [SC]

★ **BONANZA INN AND CASINO.** *855 W Williams Ave (89406). 775/423-6031; fax 775/423-6282.* 75 rms, 2 story. S $40; D $46; each addl $5; suite $59-$76; under 12 free. Crib $5. Pet accepted; $20. TV; cable (premium). Restaurant open 24 hrs. Bar. Ck-out 11 am. Business servs avail. Casino. RV park. Cr cds: A, C, D, DS, MC, V.
[D] [🐾] [⊠] [♨] [SC]

★ **WESTERN MOTEL.** *125 S Carson St (89407). 775/423-5118; fax 775/423-4973.* 22 rms, 2 story. S $39; D $43; each addl $5. Crib $4. Pet accepted, some restrictions; $3. TV. Heated pool. Complimentary continental bkfst. Restaurant nearby. Ck-out 11 am. Refrigerators. Cr cds: A, MC, V.
[🐾] [⊠] [⊠] [♨] [SC]

Gardnerville

(D-2) *See also Carson City, Stateline*

Pop 3,357 **Elev** 4,746 ft
Area code 775 **Zip** 89410
Information Carson Valley Chamber of Commerce & Visitors Authority, 1513 US 395 N; 775/782-8144 or 800/727-7677
Web www.carsonvalleynv.org

What to See and Do

Mormon Station State Historic Park. Fort/stockade. Museum exhibits relics of the early pioneer days and the first white settlement in state. Also picnicking, tables, grills. (Mid-May-mid-Oct, daily) 4 mi N via US 395, then 4 mi W on NV 57 in Genoa. Phone 775/782-2590.

Special Events

Carson Valley Days. Parade, arts and crafts, rodeo, sport tournaments. Second wkend June. Phone 775/782-8144.

Carson Valley Fine Arts & Crafts Street Celebration. Street celebration with hundreds of crafters, treasures, entertainment, and food. Sept. Phone 775/782-8144.

Hotel

★★★ **CARSON VALLEY INN HOTEL CASINO.** *1627 US 395 N, Minden (89423). 775/782-9711; fax 775/782-4772; toll-free 800/321-6983. www.cvinn.com.* 153 rms, 4 story. Apr-Oct: S, D $65-$95; each addl $6; suites $129-$169; under 12 free; ski, golf pkgs; higher rates: wkends, hols; lower rates rest of yr. Crib free. TV. Supervised children's activities; ages 4-12. Restaurants. Rm serv 6 am-10 pm. Bar; entertainment. Ck-out noon. Meeting rms. Business servs avail. Bellhops. Gift shop. Valet serv. Downhill ski 15 mi; x-country ski 18 mi. Health club privileges. Whirlpool. Game rm. Some bathrm phones, refrigerators. Casino. Stained-glass wedding chapel. Cr cds: A, C, D, DS, MC, V.
[D] [⊠] [⊠] [♨] [SC]

Great Basin National Park

(5 mi W of Baker on NV 488)

Established as a national park in 1986, Great Basin includes Lehman Caves (formerly Lehman Caves National Monument), Wheeler Peak (elevation 13,063 feet), the park's only glacier, and Lexington Arch, a natural limestone arch more than six stories tall. The park consists of 77,092 acres of diverse scenic, ecologic, and geologic attractions.

Of particular interest in the park is Lehman Caves, a large limestone solution cavern. The cave contains numerous limestone formations, including shields and helictites. Temperature in the cave is 50°F; jackets are recommended.

The 12-mile Wheeler Peak Scenic Drive reaches to the 10,000-foot elevation mark of Wheeler Peak. From there, hiking is possible to the summit. Backcountry hiking and camping are permitted. The Lexington Arch is located at the south end of the park.

Camping is allowed at three campgrounds located along the Wheeler Peak Scenic Drive: the Wheeler Peak Campground, the Upper Lehman Creek Campground, and the Lower Lehman Campground. Baker Creek Campground is located approximately five miles from park headquarters. Picnic facilities are available near park headquarters.

Park headquarters and the Visitor Center are located at Lehman Caves (daily; closed Jan 1, Thanksgiving, Dec 25; extended hrs in summer). Also here is a souvenir and snack shop (early Apr-mid-Oct; daily). For further information contact the Superintendent, Great Basin National Park, Baker 89311; 775/234-7331.

Hawthorne (E-3)

Pop 3,311 **Elev** 4,320 ft
Area code 775 **Zip** 89415
Information Chamber of Commerce, 932 E St, PO Box 1635; 775/945-5896

What to See and Do

Walker Lake. Named for the trapper and scout Joseph Walker, this is a remnant of ancient Lake Lahontan. It is 15 mi long and five mi wide. Fishing is good for cutthroat trout in these alkaline and saline waters; swimming, water skiing, boating (landing). Camping sites. The US Bureau of Land Management maintains one recreational area: Sportsman's Beach (boat launching;

camping; free). 12 mi N on US 95. Phone 775/885-6000. Also here is

Walker Lake State Recreation Area. Approx 280 acres. Swimming, fishing, boating (launching ramp); picnicking, shade structures. Phone 775/885-6000. **FREE**

Motels/Motor Lodges

★ **EL CAPITAN RESORT CASINO.** *540 F St (89415). 775/945-3321; fax 775/945-2193; res 800/922-2311.* 103 rms, 1-2 story. S, D $41-$45; each addl $7; under 12 free. Crib free. Pet accepted; $10 deposit. TV; cable. Heated pool. Restaurant open 24 hrs. Bar. Ck-out 1 pm. Meeting rms. Sundries. Game rm. Refrigerators. Casino. Cr cds: A, C, D, DS, MC, V.
🐾 D 🐾 ⇌ ✕ ⇴ 🔥

★ **SAND & SAGE LODGE.** *1301 E Fifth (89415). 775/945-3352; fax 775/945-3353.* 37 rms, 2 story. S $29.95; D $34.95; each addl $5; kit. units $6 addl. Crib free. Pet accepted, some restrictions. TV; cable (premium). Pool. Complimentary coffee in lobby. Restaurant nearby. Ck-out 11 am. Refrigerators, microwaves. Cr cds: A, DS, MC, V.
🐾 ⇌ ✕ 🔥

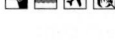

Henderson

(G-6) See also Boulder City, Lake Mead National Recreation Area, Las Vegas

Settled 1942 **Pop** 175,381 **Elev** 1,960 ft **Area code** 702 **Zip** 89015
Information Chamber of Commerce, 590 S Boulder Hwy; 702/565-8951
Web www.hendersonchamber.com

What to See and Do

Clark County Heritage Museum. Exhibit center with county "timeline." Railroad, early residence exhibits; commercial print shop, outdoor mining, farming display; gift shop. (Daily; closed Jan 1, Thanksgiving, Dec 25) 1830 S Boulder Hwy. Phone 702/455-7955. ¢

Ethel M. Chocolates Factory & Cactus Garden. Self-guided tours of famous chocolate factory and adj catcus garden. Free samples. Shops. (Daily, hrs vary) 1 Sunset Way, at jct Mt Vista. Phone 702/433-2500. **FREE**

Special Event

Heritage Days. Summer months. Phone 702/565-8951.

Motel/Motor Lodge

★★ **BEST WESTERN.** *85 W Lake Mead Dr (89015). 702/564-1712; fax 702/564-7642; toll-free 800/780-7234. www.bestwestern.com.* 59 rms, 2 story. S $51-$99; D $56-$125; under 12 free; higher rates: hols, special events. Crib free. TV; cable (premium). Complimentary continental bkfst. Restaurant nearby. Ck-out 11 am, ck-in 3 pm. Heated pool. Refrigerators. Cr cds: A, C, D, DS, MC, V.
🄳 ⚊ 🆂🅲

Hotel

★★ **SUNSET STATION CASINOS.** *1301 W Sunset Rd (89014). 702/547-7777; fax 702/547-7744; res 888/786-7389. www.sunsetstation.com.* 450 rms, 20 story, 52 suites. S, D $49-$139; each addl $10; suites $69-$179; under 12 free; wkend, hol rates; higher rates special events. Crib $10. TV; cable (premium). Complimentary coffee in rms. Restaurant open 24 hrs. Entertainment. Ck-out noon, ck-in 3 pm. Meeting rms. Business servs avail. Concierge. Shopping arcade. Barber, beauty shop. Heated pool; poolside serv. Cr cds: A, D, DS, ER, JCB, MC, V.
🄳 ⚊ ⚊ 🔥

Restaurants

★★★ **CARVER'S.** *2061 W Sunset Rd (89014). 702/433-5801.* Hrs: 5-9:30 pm; Fri, Sat to 11 pm; Sun to 9 pm. Closed Dec 25. Res accepted. Dinner $16.50-$24. Specializes in top sirloin, veal, lamb. Art Deco decor; fireplace. Cr cds: A, C, D, DS, ER, MC, V.
🄳 ⚊

★ **RAINBOW CLUB.** *122 Water St (89015). 702/565-9777. www.rainbow clubcasino.com.* Open 24 hrs. Bar. Bkfst $1.39-$4.50, lunch $3.50-$4.10,

dinner $4.95-$8.95. Specializes in filet mignon. In casino.
🄳 ⚊

Incline Village

(D-2) *See also Stateline*

Pop 9,952 **Elev** 6,360 ft
Area code 775 **Zip** 89451
Information Lake Tahoe Incline Village/Crystal Bay Visitors Bureau, 969 Tahoe Blvd; 775/832-1606 or 800/GO-TAHOE
Web www.gotahoe.com

What to See and Do

Lake Tahoe Nevada State Park. Approx 14,200 acres on the eastern shore of beautiful Lake Tahoe consisting of five management areas. Gently sloping sandy beach, swimming, fishing, boating (ramp); hiking, mountain biking, x-country skiing. Picnic tables, stoves. No camping. Standard fees. (Daily) On NV 28. Phone 775/831-0494.

Ponderosa Ranch Western Studio and Theme Park. Cartwright House seen in the *Bonanza* television series. Frontier town with 1870 country church; vintage autos; bkfst hayrides (fee); amusements May-Oct. Convention facilities. (Daily) On Tahoe Blvd (NV 28). Phone 775/831-0691. ¢¢¢¢

Skiing.

Diamond Peak Ski Resort. Three quads, three double chairlifts; patrol, school, rentals, snowmaking; cafeteria, bar, lodge. Thirty runs; longest run approx 2½ mi; vertical drop 1,840 ft. (Mid-Dec-mid-Apr, daily) Jct NV 28 and Country Club Dr. Phone 775/832-1177. ¢¢¢¢

Mount Rose Ski Area. Two quads, two triple, one six-person chairlift; patrol, rentals, school; bar, cafeteria, deli; sport shop. Longest run 2½ mi; vertical drop 1,440 ft. (Mid-Nov-mid-Apr, daily) 12 mi NE on NV 431. Phone 775/849-0704. ¢¢¢¢

Special Event

Lake Tahoe Winter Games Festival.
Diamond Peak Ski Resort (see). Early
Mar. Phone 775/832-1177.

Hotels

★★★ **CAL-NEVA RESORT HOTEL,
SPA AND CASINO.** *2 Stateline Rd,
Crystal Bay (89402). 775/832-4000;
fax 775/831-9007; toll-free 800/225-
6382. www.calnevaresort.com.* 200
rms, 9 story. S, D $79-$179; suites
$199-$269; under 10 free; higher
rates hols (2-4-day min). Crib $10.
TV; cable. Heated pool; whirlpool.
Complimentary coffee in rms.
Restaurant 7 am-11 pm; summer to 2
am. Bar. Ck-out noon. Meeting rms.
Business servs avail. Concierge. Shopping arcade. Barber, beauty shop.
Tennis. Exercise equipt; sauna. Balconies. On lake. Cr cds: A, C, D, DS,
ER, JCB, MC, V.

🄳 ⬤ ⬤ ⬤ ⬤ ⬤ ⬤ SC

★★ **TAHOE BILTMORE HOTEL
AND CASINO.** *5 NV 28, Crystal Bay
(89402). 775/831-0660; fax 775/833-
6715; res 800/245-8667. www.tahoe
biltmore.com.* 92 rms, 4 story. June-
Sept: S, D $59-$139; hols (2-day
min); lower rates rest of yr. Crib $5.
TV; cable (premium). Complimentary
full bkfst. Restaurant open 24 hrs.
Bar; entertainment. Ck-out 11 am.
Meeting rms. Business servs avail.
Downhill/x-country ski 5 mi. Pool.
Some refrigerators, microwaves.
Some balconies. Opp beach. Cr cds:
A, DS, MC, V.

⬤ ⬤ ⬤ ⬤ ⬤ ⬤

Resort

★★★ **HYATT REGENCY LAKE
TAHOE RESORT AND CASINO.**
*1111 Country Club Dr (89450).
775/832-1234; fax 775/831-7508; res
800/553-3288. www.hyatt.com.* This
property is a top pick for rustic, luxury accommodations on the North
Shore of Lake Tahoe. Although it's
not located on a ski mountain, the
resort makes every effort to help you
get to and enjoy the sites around the
lake including snow skiing, snowmobiling, hiking, tennis, golf, and water
sports. Spa services are offered
through the fitness center. The hotel
itself houses a small but charmingly
old-style casino, a private hotel

beach, and a destination restaurant
with arguably one of the best dining
views of the lake. Three additional
restaurants in the main resort building, Ciao Mein (an Italian and Asian
bistro), Sierra Grill (American), and
Cutthroat Saloon (Western saloon),
round out the dining options. 449
rms, 12 story. June-Sept, wkends,
hols: S, D $180-$350; each addl $25;
suites $610-$1565; cottages $690-
$1385; under 18 free; ski packages;
lower rates rest of yr. Crib free. TV;
cable (premium). Heated pool; whirlpool, poolside serv. Supervised children's activities (daily in season; Fri,
Sat evenings off-season); ages 3-12.
Restaurants. Rm serv. Bar. Ck-out 11
am. Convention facilities. Business
center. Concierge. Shopping arcade.
Free valet parking. Downhill ski 1½
mi; x-country ski 6 mi. Children's
arcade. Rec rm. Lawn games. Bicycles
avail. Minibars; refrigerators avail.
Wet bar in cottages. Cottages have
balconies. Casino. Private beach.
Luxury level. Cr cds: A, C, D, DS,
JCB, MC, V.

🄳 ⬤ ⬤ ⬤ ⬤ ⬤ ⬤ SC ⬤

B&B/Small Inn

★★ **INN AT INCLINE AND
CONDO.** *1003 Tahoe Blvd (NV 28)
(89451). 775/831-1052; fax 775/831-
3016; toll-free 800/824-6391. www.
innatincline.com.* 38 rms, 2 story. No
A/C. Mid-June-late Sept: S, D $99-
$139; each addl $15; under 18 free;
lower rates rest of yr. TV; cable (premium). Indoor pool; whirlpool.
Sauna. Complimentary continental
bkfst. Restaurant nearby. Ck-out 11
am. Business servs avail. Downhill
ski 1 mi; x-country ski 6 mi. Some
refrigerators. Some balconies. Cr cds:
A, DS, MC, V.

🄳 ⬤ ⬤ ⬤ ⬤

Restaurants

★ **LAS PANCHITAS.** *930 Tahoe Blvd
(NV 28) (89451). 775/831-4048.* Hrs:
11 am-10 pm; Sat, Sun from noon.
Closed Thanksgiving, Dec 25. Mexican menu. Bar. Lunch $5.25-$11.95,
dinner $7.55-$11.95. Specialties: fajitas, chile rellenos. Outdoor dining.
Rustic Mexican decor. Cr cds: A, C,
MC, V.

⬤

Lake Mead, near Las Vegas

★★★ **LONE EAGLE GRILLE ON THE LAKE.** *111 Country Club Dr (89450). 775/832-3250.* Hrs: 11:30 am-2:30 pm, 6-10 pm; Sun brunch 10:30 am-2:30 pm. Res accepted. Bar 11 am-midnight. Wine cellar. Lunch $12-$16, dinner $30-$40. Sun brunch $25. Child's menu. Specialties: prime rib, eagle-rubbed chicken. Guitarist and vocalist Fri, Sat. Valet parking. Outdoor dining. Cr cds: A, C, D, DS, ER, MC, V.
D

Lake Mead National Recreation Area

(X-0) *See also Boulder City, Overton*

(4 mi NE of Boulder City on US 93)

What to See and Do

Davis Dam. (see BULLHEAD CITY, AZ) Phone 702/293-8431.

⭐ Hoover Dam. Tour of dam and powerhouse (daily; closed Dec 25). Old exhibit building houses model of a generating unit and topographical model of Colorado River Basin. New Visitor Center exhibits audiovisual presentation, theater, and lectures from guides. Approx 8 mi E of Boulder City on US 93. Phone 702/293-8421. Tour ¢¢

Lake Mead Cruises. A 90-min sightseeing cruise to Hoover Dam on paddlewheeler *Desert Princess*. Bkfst and dinner cruises avail. (Daily exc Dec 25) Concessioner of National Park Service. Lake Mead Marina. 7 mi E of Boulder City on Lakeshore Dr, at Lake Mead Resort Area. Phone 702/293-6180. ¢¢¢¢

Swimming, fishing, boating, camping, hiking. Developed areas in Nevada: Boulder Beach on Lake Mead, 6 mi NE of Boulder City; Las Vegas Bay, 10 mi NE of Henderson; Callville Bay, 24 mi NE of Henderson; Overton Beach, 9 mi S of Overton; Echo Bay, 23 mi S of Overton; Cottonwood Cove, 14 mi E of Searchlight. Developed areas in Arizona: Willow Beach on Lake Mohave, 18 mi S of Hoover Dam (no camping); Temple Bar on Lake Mead, 50 mi E of Hoover Dam; Katherine on Lake Mohave, 3 mi N of Davis Dam (campgrounds, stores, restaurants, motels, marinas, boat ramps in these areas). (All these sites, except Willow Beach and Overton Beach, have campgrounds,

$10/site/night; stores, restaurants, marinas, and boat ramps.) Contact Superintendent, Lake Mead National Recreation Area, 601 Nevada Hwy, Boulder City 89005-2426. Phone 702/293-8906.

Lake Tahoe

(see Lake Tahoe Area in California book)

Las Vegas

(G-6) *See also Boulder City, Henderson*

Settled 1905 **Pop** 478,434 **Elev** 2,020 ft **Area code** 702
Information Las Vegas Convention/Visitors Authority, Convention Center, 3150 Paradise Rd, 89109; 702/892-7575
Web www.lasvegas24hours.com

Las Vegas, Nevada's largest city, became a major entertainment center after World War II. Near Hoover Dam and Lake Mead National Recreation Area (see), the city has public buildings and entertainment facilities designed to attract vacationers. Famous for glittering nightclubs, bars, gambling casinos, and plush hotels, Las Vegas also offers tennis, racquetball, bowling, water sports, snow skiing, golf, fishing and hunting, hiking and riding trails, and tours to nearby points of interest. The townsite covers 53 square miles on a plain encircled by distant mountains. Beyond its suburban fringe lies the desert.

Two natural springs and green meadows made the Las Vegas valley a favorite camping place in the 1840s for caravans following the Old Spanish Trail from Santa Fe to California. It was first settled by the Spanish in 1829. American settlement began in 1855, when Brigham Young sent 30 settlers to build a fort and stockade here. The Mormons tried mining in the area but found that the ore was hard to smelt and the metal made poor bullets. Later this "lead" was discovered to be a galena ore carrying silver.

The Mormons abandoned the settlement in 1857; from 1862-1899 it was operated as a ranch. Las Vegas was really born in 1905, with the advent of the railroad. A tent town sprang up; streets were laid out, and permanent buildings followed. In 1911 the city of Las Vegas was created by an act of the legislature.

A Ranger District office of the Toiyabe National Forest is located here.

Transportation

Car Rental Agencies. See IMPORTANT TOLL-FREE NUMBERS.
Public Transportation. Citizens Area Transit, 702/455-4481.
Rail Passenger Service. Amtrak 800/872-7245.

Airport Information

Las Vegas McCarran International Airport. Information 702/261-5211; weather 702/248-4800.

What to See and Do

Bonnie Springs Old Nevada. Historic Western mining town features narrow-gauge railroad, museums, shops, entertainment; 1890 melodramas. Also restaurants, motel, riding stables, and petting zoo. (Daily) 20 mi W via W Charleston Blvd. Phone 702/875-4191. ¢¢

Floyd Lamb State Park. Approx 2,000 acres. Small lakes; fishing. Picnicking. No overnight camping. 10 mi N via US 95. Phone 702/486-5413. ¢¢

Guinness World of Records Museum. Interactive computers bring the famous Guinness book to life. Displays; rare videos; special exhibit on Las Vegas. Gift shop. (Daily) 2780 Las Vegas Blvd S. Phone 702/792-3766. ¢¢¢

Imperial Palace Auto Collection. More than 300 antique and classic cars on display. Large collection of Duesenbergs. Also cars belonging to the King of Siam and Howard Hughes. (Daily) 3535 Las Vegas Blvd, on fifth-floor parking area of hotel. Phone 702/794-3174. ¢¢¢

Las Vegas Art Museum. Changing exhibits. (Tues-Sun; closed hols)

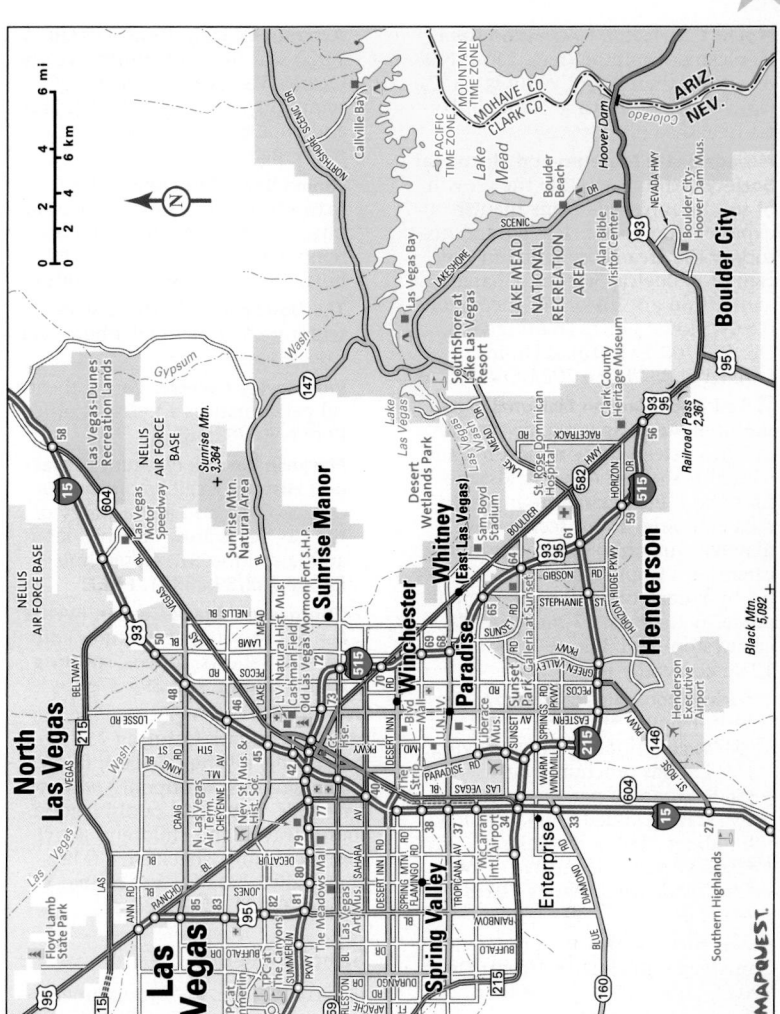

9600 W Sahara Ave. Phone 702/360-8000. ¢¢

Las Vegas Convention/Visitors Authority. The largest single-level convention center in the country; 1.3 million square ft of exhibit and meeting space. Paradise Rd, S of town. Phone 702/892-0711.

Las Vegas Motor Speedway. Motorsports complex covers 1,500 acres and features a 1½-mi superspeedway, 2½-mi road course, ½-mi dirt oval, drag strip, Go-Kart tracks, racing schools and fantasy camps, and other attractions. Home to NASCAR, IRL, and AMA racing. Tours. (Daily; event schedule varies) 7000 Las Vegas Blvd N. Phone 702/644-4444.

Las Vegas Natural History Museum. Wildlife collection featuring animated dinosaurs and shark exhibits. (Daily; closed Thanksgiving, Dec 25) 900 Las Vegas Blvd N. Phone 702/384-3466. ¢¢

Liberace Foundation and Museum. Displays memorabilia of Liberace's career, incl antique and custom cars, miniature and full-size pianos, the world's largest rhinestone, and a portion of his million-dollar wardrobe. Showcases contain awards, gifts from fans and dignitaries, and personal items. Museum store. (Daily; closed Jan 1, Dec 25) 1775 E Tropicana Ave, 2½ mi E of Strip. Phone 702/798-5595. ¢¢¢

Mount Charleston Recreation Area. Picnicking, camping (fee). 15 mi NW on US 95, then 21 mi W on NV 157, which leads to Toiyabe National Forest (see RENO).

Nevada State Museum and Historical Society. Exhibits explore the growth of southern Nevada from Spanish explorers to present. The natural history of the area is presented in the Hall of Biological Science. Changing exhibits on art, history of the region. (Daily; closed Jan 1, Thanksgiving, Dec 25) 700 Twin Lakes Dr, in Lorenzi Park. Phone 702/486-5205. ¢

⭐ **Red Rock Canyon National Conservation Area.** Spectacular view of the area's steep canyons and red and white hues of the Aztec sandstone formation. Picnicking, hiking trails, rock climbing; 13-mi scenic drive (daylight hrs only); limited primitive camping. Visitor center; nature walks led by Bureau of Land Management ranger-naturalists. 17 mi W on W Charleston Blvd. Phone 702/363-1922. ¢¢ Nearby is

> **Spring Mountain Ranch State Park.** Visitor center at main ranch house (daily; closed Jan 1, Thanksgiving, Dec 25) has brochures with self-guided tours of park and interpretive trails. Guided tours of ranch buildings (daily). Picnicking. (Daily) Approx 18 mi W on W Charleston Blvd. Phone 702/875-4141. ¢¢

Scenic Airlines. Day trips to Grand Canyon. Contact 2105 Airport Dr, 89032. Phone 702/736-8900 or 800/634-6801. ¢¢¢¢

Southern Nevada Zoological Park. Apes, monkeys, tiger, ostriches, exotic bird collection, and Southwestern desert animals. Also here is an endangered species breeding program. (Daily; closed Jan 1, Thanksgiving, Dec 25) 1775 N Rancho Dr. Phone 702/647-4685. ¢¢

⭐ **The Strip.** Las Vegas's biggest attraction, with dazzling casinos, roulette wheels, luxurious hotels, glamorous chorus lines, and top entertainers. Some shows are free; some require buying food or drink. Make res. Las Vegas Blvd, S of town. Phone 702/735-1616.

University of Nevada, Las Vegas. (1957) 19,500 students. Campus tours arranged in advance. Phone 702/895-3443. On campus are

Artemus W. Ham Concert Hall. A 1,900-seat theater featuring yearly Charles Vanda Master Series of symphony, opera, and ballet. Jazz and popular music concerts also performed here.

Donna Beam Fine Art Gallery. Exhibits by professional artists, faculty, students; emphasis on contemporary art. (Mon-Fri; closed hols) Phone 702/895-3893. **FREE**

The Flashlight. A 38-ft-tall steel sculpture by Claes Oldenburg and Coosje von Bruggen.

Judy Bayley Theatre. Varied theatrical performances all yr. Box office Phone 702/895-3801.

Marjorie Barrick Museum of Natural History. Exhibits of the biology, geology, and archaeology of the Las Vegas area, incl live desert animals. (Mon-Sat; closed hols) Phone 702/895-3381. **FREE**

Thomas and Mack Center. Events center (18,500-seat) features concerts, ice shows, rodeos, sporting events. Phone 702/895-3761.

Wet 'n Wild Las Vegas. Aquatic amusement park featuring 75-ft water slide; rafting (rentals), flumes, water cannons, whirlpools, whitewater rapids, waterfalls, pools, lagoon, four-ft waves, and children's activities. Picnicking; snack bars. (May-Sept, daily) 2601 Las Vegas Blvd S. Phone 702/737-3819. ¢¢¢¢

Special Events

Invensys Classic. PGA tournament with more than $4.5 million in prize money. Oct. Phone 702/256-0111.

National Finals Rodeo. Thomas and Mack Center. Nation's richest professional rodeo, featuring 15 finalists in seven rodeo disciplines. Dec. Phone 702/895-3761.

Motels/Motor Lodges

★ **ARIZONA CHARLIE'S HOTEL AND CASINO.** *740 S Decatur Blvd (89107). 702/258-5111; fax 702/258-5192; res 800/342-2695. www.arizonacharlies.com.* 257 rms, 7 story. S, D $38.95-$138.95; suites $125-$300. Crib free. TV; cable (premium). Heated pool; lifeguard. Restaurant open 24 hrs. Bar. Ck-out 11 am, ck-in 3 pm. Bellhops. Business servs avail. Valet serv. Gift shop. Game rm. Airport transportation. Casino. Cr cds: A, C, D, DS, ER, JCB, MC, V.

★★ **BEST WESTERN MCCARRAN INN.** *4970 Paradise Rd (89119). 702/798-5530; fax 702/798-7627; res 800/937-8376. www.bestwestern.com.* 99 rms, 3 story. S, D $49-$109; each addl $7; suites $90-$179; under 17 free; higher rates: national hols, major events. TV. Heated pool. Complimentary continental bkfst. Coffee in rms. Restaurant nearby. Coin lndry. Ck-out noon. Business servs avail. Free airport transportation. Cr cds: A, C, D, DS, ER, MC, V.

★★ **COURTYARD BY MARRIOTT.** *3275 Paradise Rd (89109). 702/791-3600; fax 702/796-7981; res 800/321-2211. www.courtyard.com.* 137 rms, 3 story, 12 suites. S, D $89-$169; higher rates: conventions, hol wkends. Crib free. TV; cable (premium). Heated pool; whirlpool. Complimentary coffee in rms. Restaurant 6:30 am-2 pm; 5-10 pm. Bar 5-11 pm. Ck-out noon. Coin lndry. Meeting rms. Business servs avail. In-rm modem link. Valet serv. Free airport transportation. Exercise equipt. Some refrigerators. Balconies. Cr cds: A, D, DS, JCB, MC, V.

★ **DAYS INN.** *707 E Fremont St (89101). 702/388-1400; fax 702/388-9622; res 800/325-2344. www.daysinn. com.* 147 units, 3 story. Feb-Nov: S, D $28-$199; each addl $10; suites $49-$249; under 18 free; lower rates rest of yr. Crib free. TV. Heated pool; lifeguard. Restaurant 7 am-7 pm. Ck-out noon. Cr cds: A, C, D, DS, JCB, MC, V.

★★ **ECONO LODGE.** *211 E Flamingo Rd (89109). 702/733-7800; fax 702/733-7353; res 800/634-6774. www.econolodge.com.* 121 rms, 2 story. S, D $55-$195; under 12 free. Crib $8. TV. Heated pool. Complimentary continental bkfst. Ck-out 11 am. Cr cds: A, D, DS, MC, V.

★★ **FAIRFIELD INN.** *3850 Paradise Rd (89109). 702/791-0899; fax 702/791-2705; res 800/228-2800.* *www.fairfieldinn.com.* 129 rms, 4 story. S, D $59-$159; under 18 free. Crib free. TV; cable (premium). Heated pool; whirlpool. Complimentary continental bkfst. Restaurants nearby. Ck-out noon. Meeting rms. In-rm modem link. Free airport transportation. Cr cds: A, C, D, DS, ER, JCB, MC, V.

★★ **LA QUINTA INN.** *3970 Paradise Rd (89109). 702/796-9000; fax 702/796-3537; toll-free 800/531-5900. www.laquinta.com.* 251 units, 3 story, 21 kits. S, D $59.99-$99.99; under 18 free; suites $109-$189. Crib free. Pet accepted, some restrictions. TV; cable (premium). Heated pool. Complimentary continental bkfst. Ck-out noon. Coin lndry. Meeting rms. Business servs avail. In-rm modem link. Bellhops. Free airport transportation. In-rm whirlpools, refrigerators. Private patios, balconies. Cr cds: A, D, DS, JCB, MC, V.

★ **LA QUINTA INN LAS VEGAS.** *3782 Las Vegas Blvd S (89109). 702/739-7457; fax 702/736-1129; res 800/531-5900. www.laquinta.com.* 38 rms, 3 story. S, D $100-$135; each addl $10; under 18 free. Crib free. Pet accepted. TV; cable. Pool. Complimentary continental bkfst. Restaurant nearby. Ck-out noon, ck-in 3 pm. Business servs avail. Free airport transportation. Cr cds: A, C, D, DS, MC, V.

★★ **TRAVELODGE.** *5075 Koval Ln (89119). 702/736-3600; fax 702/736-0726; res 800/578-7878. www. travelodge.com.* 106 rms, 2 story. S, D $39-$159; under 18 free. Crib free. TV; cable (premium). Pool. Complimentary continental bkfst. Restaurant adj open 24 hrs. Ck-out 11 am. Business servs avail. Cr cds: A, C, D, DS, ER, JCB, MC, V.

★ **TRAVELODGE.** *2028 E Fremont St (89101). 702/384-7540; fax 702/384-0408; res 888/578-7878. www. travelodge.com.* 58 rms, 2 story. S, D $30-$70; each addl $5; family rates. Crib free. TV; cable. Pool. Complimentary coffee in rms. Restaurant nearby. Ck-out 11 am. Cr cds: A, D, DS, MC, V.

★ **WESTWARD HO CASINO AND HOTEL.** *2900 Las Vegas Blvd S (89109). 702/731-2900; fax 702/731-3544; res 800/634-6803. www. westwardho.com.* 776 rms, 2-3 story. S, D $30.90-$80.90; each addl $15; 2-bedrm apt $120-$210; package plan. TV. 7 pools, 1 heated; whirlpools. Restaurant open 24 hrs. Rm serv. Bars; entertainment. Ck-out 11 am. Free airport transportation. Some refrigerators; microwaves avail. Casino. Cr cds: A, D, DS, ER, JCB, MC, V.

Hotels

★★★ **ALADDIN RESORT & CASINO.** *3667 Las Vegas Blvd (89109). 702/736-0111; fax 702/785-9600; res 877/333-9474. www.aladdin casino.com.* 2,600 rms, 30 story. S, D $150-$295; each addl $25. Crib free. TV; cable (premium). Pool; whirl-pool, poolside serv. Restaurant open 24 hrs. Bars; entertainment. Ck-out

noon. Convention facilities. Business center. In-rm modem link. Shopping arcade. Barber, beauty shop. Exercise rm; sauna. Spa. Game rm. Casino. Refrigerators in suites. Cr cds: A, D, DS, ER, JCB, MC, V.

★★★ **BALLY'S.** *3645 Las Vegas Blvd (89109). 702/967-4111; fax 702/967-4405; toll-free 888/742-9248. www. ballyslv.com.* 2,832 rms, 26 story. S, D $59-$280; each addl $15; suites $340-$2,400; under 18 free; package plans. Crib free. TV; cable (premium), VCR avail. Heated pool; whirlpool, pool-side serv. Restaurant open 24 hrs. Bars; entertainment. Ck-out 11 am. Convention facilities. Business servs avail. In-rm modem link. Shopping arcade. Barber, beauty shop. Lighted tennis, pro. Exercise equipt; sauna. Game rm. Some bathrm phones, refrigerators. Casino, wedding chapel. Cr cds: A, C, D, DS, ER, JCB, MC, V.

★★ **BARBARY COAST HOTEL.** *3595 Las Vegas Blvd S (89109). 702/737-7111; fax 702/894-9954; toll-free 888/227-2279. www.barbarycoast casino.com.* 200 rms, 8 story. S, D $39-$89; each addl $10; suites $175-$550; under 12 free. Crib free. TV; cable (premium). Restau-rant (see also DRAI'S OF LAS VEGAS). Bar. Ck-out noon. Gift shop. Free valet, covered parking. Casino. Cr cds: A, C, D, DS, JCB, MC, V.

★★★★ **BELLAGIO LAS VEGAS.** *3600 Las Vegas Blvd S (89109). 702/693-7111; fax 702/693-8546; res 888/987-6667. www.bellagiolasvegas. com.* You can almost imag-ine you've entered an Ital-ian resort upon stepping into Bellagio, complete with its own lake and a miraculous dancing water show. Gaming tables have pretty canopies in Mediter-ranean colors, the spa is a sea of pink marble, and the pool feels like it could be part of Marquis' palazzo.

Paris Hotel

For those in need of culture, there is a small art gallery with an impressive collection of post-impressionist and early modern paintings and a host of star chefs have restaurants in the hotel. 3,005 rms, 36 story. S, D $159-$799; suites $375-$6,000; each addl $40. Adults only. TV; cable (premium). Heated pool; poolside serv, whirlpool, lifeguard. Exercise rm. 12 restaurants. Entertainment. Beauty salon. Massage. Cr cds: A, C, D, DS, ER, JCB, MC, V.

★★ **BINIONS HORSESHOE HOTEL AND CASINO.** *128 E Fremont St (89125). 702/382-1600; fax 702/382-1574; toll-free 800/937-6537. www.binions.com.* 366 rms, 22 story. S, D $19-$39 (2-night min wkends). Crib free. TV; cable (premium). Heated pool. Restaurant open 24 hrs. Bar. Ck-out noon. Gift shop. Casino. Cr cds: A, C, D, DS, ER, JCB, MC, V.

★★★ **BOULDER STATION HOTEL AND CASINO.** *4111 Boulder Hwy (89112). 702/432-7777; fax 702/432-7744; toll-free 800/683-7777. www.boulderstation.com.* 300 rms, 16 story. S, D $29.99-$89.99; suites $125-$250; under 12 free. Crib free. TV; cable. Pool. Restaurant open 24 hrs. Ck-out noon. Business servs avail. In-rm modem link. Shopping arcade. Victorian-era railroad decor. Cr cds: A, C, D, DS, ER, JCB, MC, V.

★ **BOURBON STREET HOTEL AND CASINO.** *120 E Flamingo Rd (91761). 702/737-7200; fax 702/794-3490; toll-free 800/634-6956. www.bourbonstreethotel.com.* 166 rms, 9 story. S, D $29-$49; under 17 free. TV. Pool privileges. Restaurant open 24 hrs. Ck-out 11 am. Meeting rms. Concierge. Gift shop. Near airport. Cr cds: A, D, DS, ER, JCB, MC, V.

★★★ **CAESAR'S PALACE.** *3570 Las Vegas Blvd S (89109). 702/731-7110; fax 702/731-7172; res 800/634-6661. www.caesars.com.* 2,500 rms, 14-32 story. S, D $99-$500; each addl $15; suites $450-$2,800; under 13 free. TV; cable (premium), VCR avail (movies). Crib avail. 3 pools, 2 whirlpools, lifeguard. Restaurants.

(see also EMPRESS COURT). Bars. Circus Maximus, star entertainment. Ck-out noon. Convention facilities. Business center. In-rm modem link. Concierge. Shopping arcade. Barber, beauty shop. Free parking. Exercise rm; sauna, steam rm. Massage. Solarium. Racquetball. Handball. Game rm. Casino. Bathrm phones; many whirlpools. Many bilevel suites with wet bar, refrigerators, fireplaces. Cr cds: A, C, D, DS, ER, JCB, MC, V.

★★ **CALIFORNIA HOTEL AND CASINO.** *12 Ogden St (89101). 702/385-1222; fax 702/388-2670; res 800/634-6255. www.thecali.com.* 851 rms, 11 story. S, D $50-$60; each addl $10; under 12 free; package plans. Crib free. TV. Pool. Restaurant open 24 hrs. Bar. Ck-out noon. Gift shop. Refrigerators. Casino. Cr cds: A, C, D, DS, ER, JCB, MC, V.

★★ **CASTAWAYS.** *2800 E Fremont St (89104). 702/385-9123; fax 702/383-9238; toll-free 800/826-2800. www.castaways-lv.com.* 453 rms, 19 story. S, D $29-$89; suites $149-$195; under 12 free. Crib $5. TV. Heated pool; lifeguard. Restaurants open 24 hrs. Bar. Ck-out noon. Meeting rms. Business servs avail. Gift shop. Barber, beauty shop. Free airport transportation. Game rm. Casino; bingo parlor. 106-lane bowling. Cr cds: A, D, DS, MC, V.

★★ **CIRCUS CIRCUS.** *2880 Las Vegas Blvd S (89109). 702/734-0410; fax 702/734-5897; res 877/224-2287. www.circuscircus-lasvegas.com.* 3,773 rms, 35 story, 100 suites. S, D $39-$89; each addl $10; suites $79-$225; under 12 free. Crib $12. TV. 3 pools, 1 heated; poolside serv, lifeguard. Restaurants open 24 hrs (see also THE STEAK HOUSE). Bars; entertainment. Ck-out 11 am. Meeting rms. Business servs avail. In-rm modem link. Shopping arcade. Barber, beauty shop. Health club privileges. Casino, performing circus, and midway housed together in tentlike structure. Cr cds: A, D, DS, ER, JCB, MC, V.

★ **EL CORTEZ HOTEL AND CASINO.** *600 E Fremont St (89125). 702/385-5200; fax 702/385-9765; res 800/634-6703. www.elcortez.net.* 303 rms, 15 story. S, D $25-$40; each addl $3, suites $50. Crib free. TV; cable (premium). Restaurant 4:30-11 pm. Rm serv 7 am-7 pm. Bar open 24 hrs. Ck-out noon. Meeting rms. Shopping arcade. Barber, beauty shop. Free valet parking. Casino. Cr cds: A, D, MC, V.

🄳 🖾 🔥

★★ **EMERALD SPRINGS-HOLIDAY INN.** *325 E Flamingo Rd (89109). 702/732-9100; fax 702/731-9784; toll-free 800/732-7889. www.holidayinn lasvegas.com.* 150 units, 3 story, 140 suites. Mid-Sept-May: S $79-$89; D $79-$139; each addl $15; suites $129-$199; under 19 free; higher rates: hols, special events; lower rates rest of yr. TV; cable (premium), VCR avail. Heated pool; whirlpool, pool-side serv. Complimentary coffee in rms. Restaurant 6:30 am-11 pm. Bar noon-2 am. Ck-out noon, ck-in 3 pm. Meeting rms. Concierge. Free airport transportation. Exercise equipt. Refrigerators; wet bars. Cr cds: A, D, DS, ER, JCB, MC, V.

🄳 🖾 🏃 ✈ 🖾 🔥

★★ **EXCALIBUR HOTEL & CASINO.** *3850 Las Vegas Blvd S (89109). 702/597-7100; fax 702/597-7009; res 800/777-7622. www.excalibur-casino.com.* 4,000 rms, 28 story, 38 suites. S, D $49-$299; each addl $12; suites $325; higher rates: wkends, hols. Crib $10. TV; cable (premium). 2 heated pools; poolside serv, lifeguard. Restaurants open 24 hrs (see also CAMELOT and SIR GAL-LAHAD'S). Dinner theater. Bar open 24 hrs; entertainment. Ck-out. Business servs avail. In-rm modem link. Health club privileges. Shopping arcade. Barber, beauty shop. Whirlpools, refrigerators in suites. Casino. Castlelike structure with Medieval/Old English interiors based upon legend of King Arthur and Round Table. Cr cds: A, D, DS, ER, JCB, MC, V.

🄳 🖾 🖾 🔥

★ **FIESTA CASINO HOTEL.** *2400 N Rancho Dr (89130). 702/631-7000; fax 702/631-6588; res 800/731-7333. www.fiestacasinohotel.com.* 100 rms, 5 story. S, D $39-$100; under 18 free. Crib free. TV; cable. Restaurant open 24 hrs (see also GARDUNOS). No rm serv. Ck-out noon. Meeting rms. Gift shop. Heated pool. Casino. Game rm. Free airport transportation. Near North Las Vegas Airport. Cr cds: A, D, DS, ER, JCB, MC, V.

🄳 🖾 🖾 🔥

★★ **FITZGERALD'S CASINO AND HOTEL.** *301 Fremont St (89101). 702/388-2400; fax 702/388-2181; toll-free 800/274-5825. www.fitzgeralds. com.* 638 rms, 34 story, 14 suites. S, D $25-$150; suites $150-$300; under 18 free. Crib $10. TV. Restaurant open 24 hrs. Rm serv. Bar. Ck-out noon. Business servs avail. Concierge. Gift shop. Casino. Cr cds: A, C, D, DS, JCB, MC, V.

🄳 🖾 🔥

★★ **FLAMINGO LAS VEGAS.** *3555 Las Vegas Blvd S (89109). 702/733-3111; fax 702/733-3528; toll-free 800/308-8899. www.flamingolasvegas. com.* 3,642 rms, 28 story. S, D $55-$300; each addl $16; suites $500-$700; family rates; package plan. Crib free. TV; cable (premium). 5 pools; whirlpools, poolside serv, life-guard. Restaurant open 24 hrs. Bar; stage show. Ck-out noon. Convention center. Business center. In-rm modem link. Shopping arcade. Barber, beauty shop. Free valet parking. Tennis privileges. Exercise equipt; sauna, steam rm. Some bathrm phones; refrigerators avail. Casino. Cr cds: A, C, D, DS, ER, JCB, MC, V.

🄳 🖾 🏃 🖾 🔥 SC 🐾 🏌

★★ **FOUR QUEENS HOTEL AND CASINO.** *202 E Fremont St (89101). 702/385-4011; fax 702/387-5160; toll-free 800/634-6045. www.fourqueens. com.* 700 rms, 19 story. S, D $49-$199; each addl $15; suites $99-$349; under 2 free. TV. Restaurant open 24 hrs. Bar; entertainment. Ck-out noon. Meeting rms. Business servs avail. Garage parking. Wet bar in suites. Casino. Cr cds: A, C, D, DS, MC, V.

🄳 🖾 🔥

★★★★ **FOUR SEASONS HOTEL LAS VEGAS.** *3960 Las Vegas Blvd S (89119). 702/632-5000; fax 702/632-5195; toll-free 888/632-5000. www. fourseasons.com.* A dramatic private drive, lush greenery, and an ivory facade welcome guests to this rare enclave of tranquility off Las Vegas Boulevard. Although the 424 rooms are actually located on the 35th through 39th floors of the Mandalay Bay tower, this luxury hotel's quiet, nongaming atmosphere is impeccably maintained. The garden-surrounded pool and full-service spa offer the requisite indulgences. 424 rms, 5 story, 86 suites. S, D $225-$300; suites $400-$3,000; under 18 free. Crib avail. Pet accepted, some restrictions. Parking $9/day. TV; cable (premium). Heated pool. Exercise rm. Concierge. Valet serv. Rm serv 24 hrs. Restaurants. Bar 5 pm-midnight. Ck-out noon, ck-in 3 pm. Cr cds: A, D, DS, JCB, MC, V.

★ **FREMONT HOTEL & CASINO.** *200 E Fremont St (89125). 702/385-3232; fax 702/385-6270; res 800/634-6460. www.fremontcasino.com.* 423 rms, 14 story. S, D $35-$110; suites $50-$150; package plan. Crib free. TV. Restaurant open 24 hrs. Bars. Ck-out noon. Gift shop. Casino. Cr cds: A, C, D, DS, ER, JCB, MC, V.

★★ **FRONTIER HOTEL AND GAMBLING HALL.** *3120 Las Vegas Blvd S (89109). 702/794-8200; fax 702/794-8327; res 800/634-6966. www.frontierlv.com.* 984 rms, 16 story, 416 suites. S, D $39-$109; suites $59-$129; under 12 free; wkends, hols (min stay required); higher rates special events. Crib $15. TV. Restaurant open 24 hrs. Bar. Ck-out noon. Meeting rms. Business center. In-rm modem link. Concierge. Shopping arcade. Barber, beauty shop. Pool; whirlpool, poolside serv, lifeguard. Some bathrm phones. Casino. Cr cds: A, D, DS, ER, JCB, MC, V.

★★ **GOLD COAST HOTEL AND CASINO.** *4000 W Flamingo Rd (89103). 702/367-7111; fax 702/367-8575; res 888/402-6278. www.goldcoastcasino.com.* 711 rms, 10 story. S, D $30-$129; suites $175-$225; family rates; package plan. TV; cable (premium). Heated pool. Supervised children's activities. Restaurant open 24 hrs. Bars; entertainment. Ck-out noon. Convention facilities. Business servs avail. Barber, beauty shop. Free valet parking. Exercise equipt. Game rm. Bowling. Some bathrm phones. Refrigerators avail. Casino. Movie theaters. Dance hall. Cr cds: A, C, D, DS, ER, JCB, MC, V.

★★★ **GOLDEN NUGGET.** *129 E Fremont St (89101). 702/385-7111; fax 702/386-6970; toll-free 800/846-5336. www.goldennugget.com.* 1,907 rms, 18-22 story. S, D $59-$129; each addl $20; suites $275-$375. Crib free. TV; cable, VCR avail. Heated pool; whirlpool, poolside serv, lifeguard. Restaurants open 24 hrs (see also LILY LANGTRY'S and STEFANO'S). Bar; entertainment. Ck-out noon. Convention facilities. Business center. In-rm modem link. Gift shop. Barber, beauty shop. Exercise rm; sauna, steam rm. Massage. Casino. Some bathrm phones. Cr cds: A, C, D, DS, ER, JCB, MC, V.

★ **GOLD SPIKE HOTEL AND CASINO.** *400 E Ogden Ave (89101). 702/384-8444; fax 702/384-8767; res 800/634-6703.* 107 rms, 7 story. S, D $25-$30; suites $40; under 12 free. TV. Restaurant open 24 hrs. Ck-out noon. Business servs avail. Cr cds: A, C, D, DS, MC, V.

★★★ **HARD ROCK HOTEL AND CASINO.** *4455 Paradise Rd (89109). 702/693-5000; fax 702/693-5010; res 800/473-7625. www.hardrockhotel.com.* 340 rms, 11 story. S, D $59-$329; suites $209-$750. Crib free. TV; cable (premium). Heated pool; lifeguard. Restaurants (see HARD ROCK CAFE, Unrated Dining). Ck-out noon. Concierge. Sundries. Gift shop. Exercise rm. Airport transportation. Cr cds: A, C, D, DS, ER, JCB, MC, V.

★★★ **HARRAH'S CASINO HOTEL.** *3475 Las Vegas Blvd S (89109). 702/369-5000; fax 702/693-5010; toll-free 800/427-7247. www.harrahs.com.* 2,673 rms, 35 story. S, D $50-$300; each addl $15; under 12 free; higher rates special events. Crib. TV; cable. Heated pool; whirlpool, poolside serv, lifeguard. Restaurant (see also THE RANGE STEAKHOUSE). Bar; entertainment exc Sun. Ck-out noon. Coin lndry. Convention facilities.

Business servs avail. Shopping arcade. Barber, beauty shop. Valet parking; covered parking free. Exercise equipt; sauna. Massage. Barber/beauty shop. Gift shop. Game rm. Balconies. Casino. Wedding chapel. Cr cds: A, D, DS, ER, JCB, MC, V.

⬛ 🛏 🐾 SC 🍴 ⚓

★★★ **HILTON LAS VEGAS.** *3000 Paradise Rd (89109). 702/732-5111; fax 702/794-3611; res 800/732-7117. www.lvhilton.com.* 3,174 rms, 30 story, 300 suites. S, D $55-$359; each addl $25; 1-2 bedrm suites $350-$1,200; lanai suites $330-$350. Crib free. TV. Rooftop pool; whirlpool, poolside serv; poolside serv. Restaurant open 24 hrs. Bars; entertainment. Ck-out noon. Convention facilities. Business center. In-rm modem link. Shopping arcade. Barber, beauty shop. Free valet parking. Lighted tennis, pro. Exercise rm; sauna. Massage. Game rm. Some bathrm phones, refrigerators. Private patios, balconies. Casino. Cr cds: A, D, DS, ER, JCB, MC, V.

⬛ 🏊 🛏 🍴 🔥 🏃

★★ **HOTEL SAN REMO.** *115 E Tropicana Ave (89109). 702/739-9000; fax 702/736-1120; res 800/522-7366. www.sanremolasvegas.com.* 711 rms, 19 story. S, D $42-$259; each addl $15; suites $102-$220; higher rates: hols, conventions. Crib $15. TV. Heated pool; poolside serv. Restaurant open 24 hrs, dining rm 5-11 pm. Bar; entertainment. Ck-out 11 am. Meeting rms. Business servs avail. In-rm modem link. Gift shop. Free garage parking. Casino. Cr cds: A, D, DS, ER, JCB, MC, V.

⬛ 🛏 🔥

★ **IMPERIAL PALACE.** *3535 Las Vegas Blvd (89109). 702/731-3311; fax 702/735-8578; res 800/634-6441. www.imperialpalace.com.* 2,700 rms, 19 story. S, D $52-$152; each addl $15; suites $152-$452; package plan; higher rates hols. Crib $15. TV; cable (premium). Heated pool; whirlpool. Restaurant open 24 hrs. Bar; entertainment. Ck-out noon. Convention facilities. Business servs avail. In-rm modem link. Shopping arcade. Barber, beauty shop. Free valet, covered parking. Exercise equipt. Some bathrm phones, refrigerators. Private balconies. Casino. Antique auto exhibit. Cr cds: A, C, D, DS, ER, JCB, MC, V.

⬛ 🛏 🍴 🔥

★ **LADY LUCK CASINO HOTEL.** *206 N 3rd St (89101). 702/477-3000; fax 702/477-7021; res 800/523-9582. www.ladyluck.com.* 792 rms, 17 and 25 story, 118 suites. Feb-Mar, Sept-Oct: S, D $39-$99; suites $49-$100; package plans; lower rates rest of yr. TV. Heated pool; lifeguard. Restaurant open 24 hrs. Bar. Ck-out noon. Free garage parking. Airport transportation. Refrigerators. Casino. Cr cds: A, D, DS, MC, V.

⬛ 🛏 🔥

★★ **LAS VEGAS CLUB HOTEL AND CASINO.** *18 E Fremont St (89109). 702/385-1664; fax 702/380-5793; res 800/634-6532. www.vegasclubcasino.net.* 410 rms, 16 story, 5 suites. S, D $29-$85; under 12 free; suites $150-$500; higher rates: hols, special events. Crib free. TV; cable. Restaurant open 24 hrs. Ck-out noon. Business servs avail. Shopping arcade. Cr cds: A, C, D, DS, MC, V.

⬛ 🛏 🔥

★★★ **LUXOR.** *3900 Las Vegas Blvd S (89119). 702/262-4000; fax 702/262-4857; toll-free 888/288-1000. www.luxor.com.* 4,408 rms, 30 story, 400 suites. S, D $59-$299; suites $159-$359; under 12 free. Crib $10. TV; cable (premium), VCR avail. 5 pools, 1 heated; wading pool, poolside serv, lifeguard. Restaurants open 24 hrs (see also SACRED SEA). Bar; entertainment. Ck-out noon. Business center. Concierge. Shopping arcade. Barber, beauty shop. Massage. Exercise equipt; sauna. Casino. Pyramid-shaped hotel with replica of the Great Sphinx of Giza. Extensive landscaping with Egyptian theme. Cr cds: A, C, D, DS, ER, JCB, MC, V.

🛏 🔥 🍴 🛏 🏃

★★ **MAIN STREET STATION.** *200 N Main St (89101). 702/387-1896; fax 702/388-4421; res 800/465-0711.* 406 rms, 15 story. S, D $37-$100; higher rates hols. Crib free. TV; cable (premium). Restaurant open 24 hrs. Ck-out noon. Meeting rms. Business center. In-rm modem link. Concierge. Shopping arcade. Cr cds: A, C, D, DS, ER, JCB, MC, V.

⬛ 🛏 🐾

★★★ **MANDALAY BAY RESORT AND CASINO.**
3950 Las Vegas Blvd S (89119). 702/632-7777; fax 702/632-7108; toll-free 877/632-7000. www. mandalaybay.com. 3,219 rms, 36 story, 403 suites. S, D $89-$389; $35 each addl; suites $149-$12,000. Crib $20. TV; cable (premium). 15 restaurants. 4 lounges; entertainment. Ck-out 11 am. 24-hr rm serv. Exercise rm; spa, massage. 3 pools; lifeguard, whirlpool, wading pool, beach. In-rm modem and fax link. Bathrm phones. Cr cds: A, C, D, DS, MC, V.

One of the many places to wed in Las Vegas

★★★ **MGM GRAND HOTEL.** *3799 Las Vegas Blvd S (89109). 702/891-7777; fax 702/891-1030; toll-free 877/880-0880. www.mgmgrand.com.* 5,005 rms, 30 story, 740 suites. S, D $69-$399; suites $109-$750; under 12 free; higher rates hols. Crib free. TV; cable (premium). Pools; whirlpool; poolside serv, lifeguard. Supervised children's activities; ages 3-12. Restaurants open 24 hrs (see also COYOTE CAFE, EMERIL'S NEW ORLEANS, and WOLFGANG PUCK'S CAFE). Bars; entertainment. Ck-out 11 am. Convention facilities. Business center. In-rm modem link. Concierge. Shopping arcade. Barber, beauty shop. Exercise rm; steam rm. Spa. Game rm. Airport transportation. Cr cds: A, D, DS, ER, JCB, MC, V.

★★★ **THE MIRAGE HOTEL AND CASINO.** *3400 Las Vegas Blvd S (89177). 702/791-7111; fax 702/791-7446; res 800/374-9000. www.mgm-mirage.com.* 3,044 rms, 30 story. S, D $79-$499; each addl $30; suites $375-$1,625. Crib free. TV; VCR avail. Pool; whirlpool. Restaurant (see also RENOIR). Bar; entertainment. Ck-out noon. Convention facilities. Business center. In-rm modem link. Concierge. Shopping arcade. Barber, beauty shop. Valet parking. Exercise rm. Massage. Bathrm phone, refrigerator, wet bar in suites. Casino. Atrium features tropical rain forest; behind front desk is 20,000-gallon aquarium with sharks and tropical fish. On 100 acres with dolphin and white tiger habitats. Cr cds: A, D, DS, ER, JCB, MC, V.

★★★ **MONTE CARLO RESORT & CASINO.** *3770 Las Vegas Blvd S (89030). 702/730-7777; fax 702/730-7250; res 800/311-3999. www.montecarlo.com.* 3,002 rms, 32 story. S, D $59-$299; suites $99-$559; under 12 free. Crib free. TV; cable (premium), VCR avail. Pool; poolside serv, lifeguard. Restaurant open 24 hrs. Ck-out 11 am. Gift shop. Concierge. Convention facilities. Business center. In-rm modem link. Tennis. Exercise rm. Cr cds: A, D, DS, ER, JCB, MC, V.

★★★ **NEW YORK-NEW YORK HOTEL & CASINO.** *3790 Las Vegas Blvd S (89109). 702/740-6969; fax 702/740-6920; toll-free 800/693-6763. www.nynyhotelcasino.com.* 2,033 rms,

45 story. S, D $60-$200; each addl $20; under 12 free; wkends, hols (min stay required). Crib free. TV; cable (premium). Restaurant open 24 hrs (see also IL FORNAIO). Bar. Ck-out noon. Convention facilities. Business center. In-rm modem link. Concierge. Shopping arcade. Barber, beauty shop. Free garage parking. Pool; whirlpool, poolside serv, life-guard. Rec rm. Some bathrm phones. Hotel re-creates New York City's famous landmarks and attractions including the Statue of Liberty and the Manhattan Express. Cr cds: A, C, D, DS, ER, JCB, MC, V.

★★ **ORLEANS HOTEL AND CASINO.** *4500 W Tropicana Ave (89103). 702/365-7111; fax 702/365-7500; res 800/675-3267. www.orleans casino.com.* 839 rms, 21 story, 24 suites. S, D $49-$325; each addl $10; under 12 free; wkends (2-day min); higher rates hols. Crib free. TV; cable (premium). Restaurants open 24 hrs. Bar; entertainment. Ck-out noon. Meeting rms. Business center. Shopping arcade. Barber, beauty shop. Pool; poolside serv, lifeguard. Refrigerators avail. Cr cds: A, C, D, DS, ER, JCB, MC, V.

★★ **PALACE STATION HOTEL AND CASINO.** *2411 W Sahara Ave (89102). 702/367-2411; fax 702/544-2411; res 800/544-2411. www.palace station.com.* 1,028 rms, 21 story. S, D $39.99-$129; each addl $10; under 12 free. Crib free. TV. Heated pool; whirlpool. Restaurants open 24 hrs. Bars; entertainment. Ck-out noon. Business servs avail. Exercise equipt. Barber, beauty shop. Gift shop. Garage parking. Game rm. Casino, bingo. Cr cds: A, C, D, DS, ER, JCB, MC, V.

★★★ **PARIS LAS VEGAS.** *3645 Las Vegas Blvd (89109). 702/946-7000; fax 702/946-4405; res 877/796-2096. www.parislasvegas.com.* 2,916 rms, 30 story. S, D $99-$300; each addl $25. Crib free. TV. Heated pool; whirlpool, poolside serv. Restaurant open 24 hrs. Bars; entertainment. Ck-out 11 am. Convention facilities. Business center. In-rm modem link. Shopping arcade. Barber, beauty shop. Exercise

rm; sauna. Massage. Casino. Cr cds: A, D, DS, ER, JCB, MC, V.

★★ **PLAZA HOTEL AND CASINO.** *1 Main St (89125). 702/386-2110; fax 702/386-2378; res 702/386-2110. www.plazahotelcasino.com.* 1,037 rms, 25 story. S, D $35-$125; suites $70-$250; under 12 free. Crib $8. TV; VCR avail. Heated pool; wading pool. Restaurant open 24 hrs. Bar. Ck-out noon. Coin lndry. Convention facili-ties. Business servs avail. Shopping arcade. Barber. Tennis. Casino. Cr cds: A, C, D, DS, ER, JCB, MC, V.

★★ **RIVIERA HOTEL AND CASINO.** *2901 Las Vegas Blvd S (89109). 702/734-5110; fax 702/794-9483; res 800/634-6753. www.the riviera.com.* 2,072 rms, 24 story, 170 suites. S, D $59-$159; each addl $20; suites $225-$500; package plan. Crib free. TV; cable (premium). Heated pool; poolside serv, lifeguard. Restau-rant open 24 hrs. Bar; name enter-tainment. Ck-out 11 am. Convention facilities. Business center. In-rm modem link. Shopping arcade. Bar-ber, beauty shop. Exercise equipt; sauna, steam rm. Some refrigerators. Bathrm phone in some suites. Some balconies. Casino. Cr cds: A, C, D, DS, ER, JCB, MC, V.

★★ **SAHARA HOTEL AND CASINO.** *2535 Las Vegas Blvd S (89109). 702/737-2111; fax 702/791-2027; res 888/696-2121. www.sahara hotelandcasino.com.* 1,720 rms, 2-27 story, 60 suites. S, D $39-$169; each addl $12; suites $200-$369; under 12 free; package plans. Crib $10. TV; cable (premium). Heated pool; pool-side serv, lifeguard. Whirlpool. Restaurant open 24 hrs. Bar; star entertainment. Ck-out noon. Con-vention facilities. Business center. In-rm modem link. Shopping arcade. Barber, beauty shop. Free covered parking. Health club privileges. Many bathrm phones. Private patios, bal-conies. Casino. Cr cds: A, C, D, DS, ER, JCB, MC, V.

★★★ **ST. TROPEZ HOTEL.** *455 E Harmon Ave (89109). 702/369-5400; fax 702/369-1150; toll-free 800/666-5400. www.sttropezlasvegas.com.* 149

suites, 2 story. Suites $49-$249; family rates. Crib free. TV; VCR. Heated pool; poolside serv. Complimentary continental bkfst. Complimentary coffee in rms. Restaurant adj 11-3 am. Bar. Ck-out noon. Meeting rms. Business servs avail. In-rm modem link. Bellhops. Concierge. Shopping arcade. Airport transportation. Exercise equipt. Refrigerators, minibars. Cr cds: A, D, DS, ER, JCB, MC, V.

[D] [icons]

★★ **SAM'S TOWN HOTEL AND GAMBLING HALL.** *5111 Boulder Hwy (89122). 702/456-7777; fax 702/454-8107; res 800/634-6371. www.samstownlv.com.* 648 rms, 9 story. S, D $39.99-$140; suites $125-$225; under 12 free. Crib free. TV; cable. Heated pool; whirlpool, lifeguard. 10 restaurants (some open 24 hrs). Ck-out noon. Coin lndry. Convention facilities. Business servs avail. In-rm modem link. Shopping arcade. Casino, bowling center. Old West decor; atrium. Cr cds: A, D, DS, ER, JCB, MC, V.

[D] [icons]

★★ **SANTA FE STATION CASINO.** *4949 N Rancho Dr (89130). 702/658-4900; fax 702/658-4919; res 702/658-4949. www.stationcasino.com.* 200 rms, 5 story. S, D $39.99-$79.99; each addl $5; under 13 free; higher rates some hols. TV; cable. Heated pool; whirlpool. Supervised children's activities. Restaurant. Bar; entertainment. Ck-out noon. Meeting rm. Business servs avail. Gift shop. Game rm. Bowling lanes. Ice rink. Cr cds: A, D, DS, ER, JCB, MC, V.

[D] [icons]

★★ **SILVERTON HOTEL CASINO.** *3333 Blue Diamond Rd (89139). 702/263-7777; fax 702/896-5635; res 866/668-6688. www.silvertoncasino.com.* 300 rms, 4 story. S, D $29-$45; suites $59-$89; under 12 free; higher rates hols. Crib free. TV; cable (premium). 2 pools; wading pool, whirlpool, poolside serv, lifeguard. Restaurant open 24 hrs. Rm serv. Ck-out noon. Coin lndry. Meeting rms. Business servs avail. In-rm modem link. Shopping arcade. Game rm. RV park. Cr cds: A, C, D, DS, ER, JCB, MC, V.

[D] [icons]

★★ **STARDUST RESORT AND CASINO.** *3000 Las Vegas Blvd S (89109). 702/732-6111; fax 702/732-6296; res 800/634-6757. www.stardustlv.com.* 1,552 rms, 32 story, 161 suites. Jan-May, Oct-Nov: S, D $60-$125; suites $90-$250. Crib free. TV. 2 pools; lifeguard, poolside serv. Restaurants open 24 hrs. Bar; entertainment. Ck-out noon. Convention facilities. Business servs avail. In-rm modem link. Shopping arcade. Barber, beauty shop. Health club privileges. Game rm. Some bathrm phones, refrigerators. Some private patios, balconies. Casino. Cr cds: A, D, DS, ER, JCB, MC, V.

[D] [icons]

★★ **STRATOSPHERE HOTEL AND CASINO.** *2000 Las Vegas Blvd S (89104). 702/380-7777; fax 702/380-7732; res 800/998-6932. www.stratlv.com.* 2,444 rms, 24 story, 125 suites. S, D $39.95-$249; under 13 free, suites $99-$499. Ck-out 11 am. Crib free. TV; cable (premium). Heated pool; lifeguard. Whirlpool. Exercise equipt. Refrigerators in suites. Casino. Cr cds: A, D, DS, ER, JCB, MC, V.

[D] [icons]

★★ **TEXAS GAMBLING HALL AND HOTEL.** *2101 Texas Star Ln, North Las Vegas (89032). 702/631-1000; fax 702/631-1087; res 800/654-8888. www.texasstation.com.* 200 rms, 6 story. S, D $39-$169; under 12 free; suites $169-$360. Crib $5. TV; cable. Pool; poolside serv. Coffee in rms. Restaurants open 24 hrs. Ck-out noon. Gift shop. Game rm. Cr cds: A, D, DS, ER, JCB, MC, V.

[D] [icons]

★★★ **TREASURE ISLAND AT THE MIRAGE.** *3300 Las Vegas Blvd S (89109). 702/894-7111; fax 702/894-7446; toll-free 800/288-7206. www.treasureisland.com.* 2,679 rms, 36 story. S, D $59-$400; suites $120-$600. Crib $25. TV; cable, VCR avail. Heated pools; wading pool, poolside serv, lifeguard. Restaurants open 24 hrs. Bars; entertainment. Ck-out noon. Convention facilities. Business center. In-rm modem link. Shopping arcade. Barber, beauty shop. Exercise equipt. Refrigerators. Casino. Arcade entertainment complex. Buccaneer

Bay Village adventure attraction. Cr cds: A, C, D, DS, ER, JCB, MC, V.

★★ **TROPICANA RESORT AND CASINO.** *3801 Las Vegas Blvd S (89193). 702/739-2222; fax 702/739-2492; toll-free 888/826-8767. www. tropicanalv.com.* 1,878 rms, 22 story. S, D $49-$79; each addl $15. TV; cable (premium). 3 pools; whirlpool, poolside serv, lifeguard. Restaurant open 24 hrs. Bar; entertainment. Ck-out 11 am. Convention facilities. Business center. In-rm modem link. Shopping arcade. Barber, beauty shop. Gift shop. Exercise equipt; sauna. Some bathrm phones, refrigerators. Private patios, balconies. Casino. Cr cds: A, C, D, DS, ER, JCB, MC, V.

★★★★ **VENETIAN RESORT HOTEL & CASINO.** *3355 Las Vegas Blvd S (89109). 702/414-1000; fax 702/414-1100; res 877/283-6423. www.venetian.com.* This re-creation of Venice has produced an impressive hotel and casino resort. The grand lobby sparkles like the palace of the Doges. Service is excellent throughout the hotel, as is the quality of the food and other amenities. A number of top restaurants and shops make for a fine stay. The fitness center and spa, run by Canyon Ranch, is one of the most comprehensive anywhere, and includes treatments, aerobics and other classes, rock climbing, and more. Even a ride on a gondola down the Grand Canal is surprisingly entertaining. 3,036 rms, 35 story. S, D $99-$250; each addl $25. Crib free. TV; cable (premium). Pool; whirlpool, poolside serv. Restaurant open 24 hrs. Bars; entertainment. Ck-out noon. Convention facilities. Business center. In-rm modem link. Shopping arcade. Barber, beauty shop. Free valet parking. Exercise rm; sauna. Spa. Casino. Cr cds: A, D, DS, MC, V.

Resorts

★★ **CASABLANCA.** *950 W Mesquite Blvd, Mesquite (89027). 702/346-7529; fax 702/346-6888. www.casablancaresort.com.* 500 rms, 10 story. S, D $39-$89. Crib free. TV; cable (premium). Heated pool; poolside serv. Restaurant open 24 hrs. Bars; entertainment. Ck-out 11 am.

Meeting rms. Business center. In-rm modem link. Exercise rm; sauna. Spa. Massage. Tennis. 18-hole golf; greens fee $45. Casino. Cr cds: A, D, DS, ER, JCB, MC, V.

★★★★ **HYATT REGENCY LAKE LAS VEGAS RESORT.** *101 Montelago Blvd, Henderson (89011). 702/567-1234; fax 702/567-6112; res 800/633-7313. www.hyatt.com.* Situated on the shores of Lake Las Vegas and surrounded by a Jack Nicklaus designed golf course, this Mediterranean inspired resort offers a variety of recreational and dining options. The Moroccan architecture and Arabesque decor creates a soothing oasis in the desert, about 30 minutes from the Strip and a world away in terms of relaxation and calm. 496 rms, 6 story, 47 suites. S, D $119-$319; each addl $25; suites $2,400. Crib free. TV; cable (premium). Heated pool; whirlpool, poolside serv, lifeguard. Restaurant open 24 hrs. Bars; entertainment. Ck-out noon. Convention facilities. Business center. In-rm modem link. Shopping arcade. Barber, beauty shop. Golf, 36 holes, green fee $210. Exercise rm; sauna. Massage. Balconies. Refrigerators. Casino. Cr cds: A, D, DS, JCB, MC, V.

All Suites

★★★ **ALEXIS PARK RESORT HOTEL.** *375 E Harmon Ave (89109). 702/796-3300; fax 702/796-3354; res 800/582-2228. www.alexispark.com.* 500 suites, 2 story. 1-bedrm $45-$500; 2-bedrm $300-$1,150; each addl $15; under 12 free. Crib avail. TV; cable (premium), VCR avail. 3 pools, 1 heated; whirlpool; poolside serv. Restaurant 6 am-3 pm, 6-11 pm (see also PEGASUS). Bar 4 pm-midnight; entertainment. Ck-out 11 am. Convention facilities. Business center. In-rm modem link. Concierge. Gift shop. Barber, beauty shop. Exercise equipt; sauna, steam rm. Refrigerators, minibars; some bathrm phones, in-rm whirlpools. Cr cds: A, D, DS, MC, V.

★★★ **CROWNE PLAZA HOTEL.** *4255 S Paradise Rd (89109). 702/369-4400; fax 702/369-3770; toll-free 800/227-6963. www.crowneplaza.com.*

201 suites, 6 story. S, D $79-$189; each addl $20; under 18 free. Crib free. Pet accepted; fee. TV; cable (premium), VCR avail. Heated pool; poolside serv. Complimentary coffee in rms. Restaurant 6 am-2 pm, 5-10 pm. Bar 11 am-midnight. Ck-out noon. Meeting rms. Business center. In-rm modem link. Concierge. Gift shop. Free airport transportation. Exercise equipt; sauna. Minibars. Cr cds: A, C, D, DS, ER, JCB, MC, V.

★★★ **MARRIOTT SUITES.** *325 Convention Center Dr (89109). 702/650-2000; fax 702/650-9466; res 888/236-2427. www.marriott.com.* 278 rms, 17 story. S, D $129-$269; each addl $25. Crib free. TV. Heated pool; whirlpool. Restaurant 6 am-11 pm. Bars; entertainment. Ck-out noon. Meeting rms. Business center. In-rm modem link. Exercise rm; sauna. Game rm. Airport transportation. Cr cds: A, D, DS, MC, V.

★★★ **RIO SUITE HOTEL AND CASINO.** *3700 W Flamingo Rd (89103). 702/777-7777; fax 702/777-2360; res 800/752-9746. www.playrio. com.* 2,500 suites, 41 story. Suites $59-$359; each addl $25; mid-wk rates. TV; cable (premium). 4 pools; whirlpools. Complimentary coffee in rms. Restaurant open 24 hrs (see also ANTONIO'S). Bar; entertainment. Ck-out noon. Convention facilities. Business servs avail. Concierge. Shopping arcade. Barber, beauty shop. Exercise equipt. Massage. Refrigerators. Building facade of red and blue glass trimmed in neon. Casino. Cr cds: A, C, D, DS, ER, JCB, MC, V.

Extended Stay

★★ **RESIDENCE INN BY MARRIOTT.** *3225 Paradise Rd (89109). 702/796-9300; fax 702/796-9562; res 800/331-3131. www.residenceinn.com.* 192 kit. units, 1-2 story. S $99-$219; D $129-$399. Crib free. Pet accepted, some restrictions; fee. TV; cable (premium), VCR (movies $3.50). Heated pool; whirlpool. Complimentary continental bkfst. Restaurant adj 6:30 am-9 pm. Ck-out noon. Coin lndry. Meeting rms. Business servs avail.

Free airport transportation. Balconies. Picnic tables, grills. Cr cds: A, C, D, DS, ER, JCB, MC, V.

Villa/Condo

★★ **CARRIAGE HOUSE.** *105 E Harmon Ave (89109). 702/798-1020; toll-free 800/221-2301. www.carriagehouse lasvegas.com.* 155 kit. suites, 9 story. S, D $89-$300; children free; wkly rates; higher rates: special events, hols. Crib free. TV; cable (premium). Heated pool; whirlpool. Complimentary coffee in rms. Restaurant 7-10 am, 5-11 pm. Bar from 5 pm. Ck-out 11 am. Coin lndry. Business servs avail. In-rm modem link. Free airport transportation. Tennis. Microwaves. Cr cds: A, C, D, DS, ER, JCB, MC, V.

Restaurants

★★ **ANTONIO'S.** *3700 W Flamingo Rd (89103). 702/252-7737.* Hrs: 5-11 pm. Res required. Italian menu. Bar. Dinner $17-$40. Specialties: aragosta sardinia, ossobuco Milanese, scallopine piccata. Guitarist Fri, Sat. Valet parking. Elegant dining; crystal chandeliers, marble columns. Cr cds: A, D, MC, V.

★★★★ **AQUA.** *3600 Las Vegas Blvd S (89109). 702/693-7223. www. bellagiolasvegas.com.* Located amidst the over-the-top luxury of the Bellagio, this satellite of Michael Mina and Charles Condy's California restaurant serves inventive seafood. Adjacent to the hotel's Gallery of Fine Art, the restaurant itself holds two commissioned Robert Rauschenberg paintings. It looks, feels, and is expensive, but to dine like a high roller, even for just one night, makes it a worthy destination. Contemporary American menu. Specialty: whole foie gras. Hrs: 5:30-11 pm. Res required. Dinner: $28-$90. Valet parking. Jacket. Cr cds: A, C, D, MC, V.

★★★ **AUREOLE.** *3950 Las Vegas Blvd (89119). 702/632-7401. www. aureolerestaurant.com.* Progressive Amer cuisine. Hrs: 6-11 pm. Dinner:

$55-$95. Complete meals: $50-$60. Res accepted. Valet parking. Bar to 1 am. Jacket. Cr cds: A, C, D, DS, ER, JCB, MC, V.

[D]

★★ **BERTOLINI'S.** *3500 Las Vegas Blvd S (89109). 702/735-4663.* Hrs: 11 am-midnight; Fri, Sat to 1 am. Italian menu. Bar. A la carte entrees: lunch, dinner $10.95-$25.95. Specializes in pasta. Conservative Italian decor. Cr cds: A, D, MC, V.

[D] [≡]

★ **CAFE NICOLLE.** *4760 W Sahara Ave (89102). 702/870-7675. www. cafenicolle.com.* Hrs: 11 am-11 pm. Continental menu. Bar. Early-bird specials. Lunch $7.50-$11.75, dinner $14.95-$26.95. Specializes in lamb chops, steak, seafood. Entertainment 7-11 pm, Tues-Sat. Outdoor dining. Casual decor. Cr cds: A, D, MC, V.

[D] [≡]

Freemont Street

★★ **CAMELOT.** *3850 Las Vegas Blvd S (89109). 702/597-7449. www. excalibur-casino.com.* Hrs: 5-11 pm. Closed Mon, Tues. Res required. Continental menu. Bar. Wine cellar. A la carte entrees: dinner $30-$60. Specializes in fish, prime rib, veal. Valet parking. Large fireplace. Cr cds: A, D, MC, V.

[D] [≡]

★ **CATHAY HOUSE.** *5300 W Spring Mountain Rd (89102). 702/876-3838. www.cathayhouse.com.* Hrs: 11 am-11 pm. Chinese menu. Bar. Lunch $8.25-$15.95, dinner $8.25-$26. Specialties: strawberry chicken, orange-flavored beef. Chinese decor. Cr cds: A, DS, MC, V.

[D] [≡]

★ **CHAPALA.** *2101 S Decatur Blvd (89102). 702/871-7805.* Hrs: 11 am-11 pm; Fri, Sat to midnight. Closed some major hols. Res accepted. Mexican menu. Bar. Lunch, dinner $8.75-$19.50. Child's menu. Specialties: fajitas, enchilada ranchero. Cr cds: A, D, MC, V.

[D] [≡]

★★★ **CHINOIS.** *3500 Las Vegas Blvd S (89109). 702/737-9700. www. wolfgangpuck.com.* Hrs: 11:30 am-10 pm; Fri-Sun to midnight. Res required. Asian menu. Bar. Wine list. Lunch, dinner $14.95-$30. Child's menu. Specialty: Shanghai lobster. Valet parking. Oriental decor; waterfall, Oriental garden. Cr cds: A, D, DS, MC, V.

[D] [≡]

★★ **COYOTE CAFE.** *3799 Las Vegas Blvd S (89109). 702/891-7777. www. coyotecafe.com.* Hrs: 7:30 am-11 pm. Res accepted. Southwestern menu. Bar. Bkfst $3-$8, lunch $8-$18, dinner $24-$42. Specialties: chicken tacos, black beans. Valet parking. Southwestern decor; artwork, cacti. Cr cds: A, D, DS, ER, JCB, MC, V.

[D] [≡]

★★ **DRAI'S OF LAS VEGAS.** *3595 Las Vegas Blvd S (89109). 702/737-0555. www.draislasvegas.com.* American menu. Hrs: 5:30-11 pm; Sat, Sun to midnight. Res required. Bar. A la carte entrees: dinner $24-$35. Specializes in lobster, steak, seafood. Jazz Fri, Sat. Valet parking. Intimate atmosphere; unique oil paintings. Cr cds: A, D, DS, ER, JCB, MC, V.

[D] [≡]

★★★ **EMERIL'S NEW ORLEANS.**
3799 Las Vegas Blvd (89109). 702/891-7374. www.emerils.com. Hrs: 11 am-2:30 pm, 5:30-10:30 pm. Res accepted. French menu. Bar. Complete meals: lunch $15-$25, dinner $20-$31. Specializes in seafood. French Quarter decor. Pictures of New Orleans. Cr cds: A, C, D, DS, ER, MC, V.
D

★★★ **EMPRESS COURT.** *3570 Las Vegas Blvd S (89109). 702/731-7731. www.caesars.com.* Hrs: 6-11 pm. Res accepted. Cantonese menu. Bar. Complete meals: dinner $30-$80. Specializes in shark fin dishes. Valet parking. Elegant dining. Jacket. Cr cds: A, C, D, DS, ER, MC, V.
D

★★ **FASOLINI'S PIZZA CAFE.** *222 S Decatur Blvd (89107). 702/877-0071.* Hrs: noon-9 pm. Closed Sun; Jan 1, Easter, Dec 25. Italian menu. Beer, wine. Lunch, dinner $5.95-$15.95. Child's menu. Specialties: chicken cacciatore, spaghetti, pizza. Art Deco decor; posters of famous movies. Cr cds: A, D, MC, V.
D

★★ **FERRARO'S.** *5900 W Flamingo Rd (89103). 702/364-5300. www.ferraroslasvegas.com.* Hrs: 5:30-11 pm. Closed Dec 25. Res accepted. Italian menu. Bar. Dinner $12-$32.50. Specializes in pasta, seafood, steak. Pianist. Parking. Patio dining. Italian decor. Cr cds: A, C, D, DS, ER, MC, V.
D

★ **GARDUNOS.** *2400 N Rancho Dr (89130). 702/631-7000. www.gardunosrestaurants.com.* Hrs: 11 am-10 pm; Fri, Sat to 11 pm. Closed Thanksgiving, Dec 25. Mexican menu. Bar. Lunch $6.25-$12.50, dinner $10-$12.50. Specializes in pollo, carnes, fajitas. Valet parking avail. Old Mexican village decor. Cr cds: A, D, DS, ER, MC, V.
D

★ **GOLDEN STEER STEAK HOUSE.** *308 W Sahara Ave (89109). 702/384-4470.* Hrs: 5-11 pm. Closed Thanksgiving, Dec 25. Res accepted. Bar. Dinner $18.50-$55. Child's menu. Specializes in steak, seafood. Valet parking. 1890s Western decor. Family-owned. Cr cds: A, D, MC, V.
D

★★ **HAMADA OF JAPAN.** *365 E Flamingo Rd (89109). 702/733-3005. www.hamadaofjapan.com.* Hrs: 11 am-4 pm; 5 pm-4 am. Res accepted. Japanese cuisine. Bar. Lunch $7.95-$11.95. Dinner $13.50-$47.50. Valet parking. Artwork, aquarium. Cr cds: A, D, DS, JCB, MC, V.
D

★★ **IL FORNAIO.** *3790 Las Vegas Blvd S #13 (89109). 702/650-6500. www.ilfornaio.com.* Hrs: 8:30 am-midnight. Res required. Northern Italian menu. Bar. Wine list. A la carte entrees: lunch, dinner $6.50-$28.50. Specialties: antipasto, minestrone. Valet parking. Cr cds: A, D, DS, JCB, MC, V.
D

★ **LANDRY'S SEAFOOD HOUSE.** *2610 W Sahara (89102). 702/251-0101.* Hrs: 11 am-10:15 pm; Fri, Sat to 11:15 pm. Closed Dec 25. Bar. Early-bird specials. Lunch $7.99-$11.99, dinner $13.99-$26.99. Child's menu. Specializes in seafood, pasta, beef. Contemporary decor. Cr cds: A, D, MC, V.
D

★★ **LAWRY'S THE PRIME RIB.** *4043 Howard Hughes Pkwy (89109). 702/893-2223. www.lawrysonline.com.* Hrs: 5-10 pm; Fri, Sat to 11 pm. Res accepted. Bar. Wine cellar. Dinner $20-$40. Specializes in prime rib, lobster. Art Deco decor; red velvet booths, fireplace. Meats carved tableside. Cr cds: A, C, D, DS, ER, MC, V.
D

★★★★ **LE CIRQUE.** *3600 Las Vegas Blvd S (89109). 702/693-8100. www.lecirque.com.* The Maccioni family strikes again. This time in the glitzy Bellagio, miles from their original New York outpost of famed, haute-French cuisine. Visitors can still expect the signature, artfully crazy decor and playful circus theme. Although the menu makes guests smile, dining here is a momentous event, especially when paired with the world-class wine list of over 400 selections. French cuisine. Hrs: 5:30-10:30 pm. Res required. Dinner: $28-

$39. Tasting menu $75-$120. Jacket. Valet parking. Cr cds: A, C, D, MC, V. ⒟

★★ **LILY LANGTRY'S.** *129 E Fremont St (89101). 702/385-7111. www. goldennugget.com.* Hrs: 5-11 pm. Res accepted. Cantonese menu. Bar. Wine cellar. A la carte entrees: dinner $9.95-$36. Specialties: lobster Cantonese, Chinese pepper steak, moo goo gai pan. Own baking. Valet parking. Oriental decor. Cr cds: A, D, DS, ER, JCB, MC, V. ⒟ ⊒

★★★★ **LUTECE.** *3355 Las Vegas Blvd S (89109). 702/414-2220. www. lutece.com.* This Las Vegas outpost of one of New York's most famous restaurants has a distinctly urban feel. The severe decor (black and white with curved wood accents) may leave you cold, but chef Eberhard Mueller's menu will warm you up. Though not daring, the food is all very well prepared and the service is professional and attentive. Specialties: roasted monkfish, chanterelles and asparagus risotto, tournedos of beef. Own baking. Valet parking. Hrs: 5:30-11 pm. Bar. Wine cellar. A la carte entrees: dinner $41-$55. Cr cds: A, DS, MC, V.

★ **MARRAKECH.** *3900 Paradise Rd (89109). 702/737-5611. www. marrakech-lv.com.* Hrs: 5:30-11 pm. Closed Dec 25. Res accepted. Moroccan menu. Bar. Complete six-course meal: dinner $26.95. Specialties: shish kebob, chicken in light lemon sauce, shrimp scampi. Belly dancers. French Moroccan decor. Cr cds: A, D, MC, V. ⒟ ⊒

★★ **MAYFLOWER CUISINIER.** *4750 W Sahara Ave (89102). 702/870-8432. www.mayflowercuisinier.com.* Hrs: 11 am-3 pm, 5-10 pm; Sat 5-11 pm. Closed Sun; major hols. Res accepted. Chinese menu. Bar. Lunch $6.95-$9.95, dinner $12.95-$22.95. Specialties: roast duck, boneless chicken, Thai shrimp. Outdoor dining. Oil paintings. Totally nonsmoking. Cr cds: A, D, MC, V. ⒟

★★★★ **NOBU.** *4455 Paradise Rd (89109). 702/693-5090. www.hard rockhotel.com.* This Las Vegas outpost of the New York City favorite is every bit as good (maybe better) than the original. In the middle of the desert, the sushi couldn't be fresher. The black cod in sweet miso rendition is superb. The service is friendly and attentive. If it is available, don't miss the bread pudding for dessert. The atmosphere is bright and cheery with lots of exposed wood, a long, dramatic sushi bar, and interesting lighting. Easily one of the top restaurants in all of Vegas. Specializes in sushi. Hrs: 6-10 pm. Bar. Wine list. A la carte entrees: dinner $18-$30. Cr cds: A, C, D, DS, MC, V.

★★★ **OSTERIA DEL CIRCO.** *3600 Las Vegas Blvd (89109). 702/693-8150. www.osteriadelcirco.com.* Hrs 11:30 am-2 pm; 5:30-11 pm. Northern Italian cuisine. Dinner $20-$85. Jacket. Res req 60 days in advance. Cr cds: A, C, D, DS, MC, V. ⒟ ⊒

★★★ **PALM.** *3500 Las Vegas Blvd S, Suite A (89109). 702/732-7256. www. thepalm.com.* Hrs: 11:30 am-11 pm. Res accepted. Bar. Wine list. A la carte entrees: lunch $10-$14, dinner $16-$64. Specializes in prime beef, seafood, chops. Valet parking. Counterpart of famous New York restaurant. Caricatures of celebrities on walls. Cr cds: A, C, D, DS, ER, JCB, MC, V. ⒟ ⊒

★★★ **PEGASUS.** *375 E Harmon Ave (89109). 702/796-3353.* Hrs: 6 am-10 pm. Res accepted. American menu. Bar. Wine cellar. A la carte entrees: bkfst $6-$10, lunch $8.95-$15.95, dinner $12.95-$18.95. Bkfst buffet $10. Specialties: filet mignon, prime steak. Valet parking. Cr cds: A, D, MC, V. ⒟ ⒮⒞ ⊒

★★★★ **PICASSO.** *3600 Las Vegas Blvd S (89109). 702/693-7223. www. bellagiolasvegas.com.* Surrounded by more than 30 original works by Picasso, it's easy to lose sight of your food, until the first dish from chef Julian Serrano arrives, and what a piece of art it is. Contemporary French cooking is rarely more refined than in the hands of this master. An excellent wine list, literally buckets of fresh flowers, and doting service round out the whole dining experience, which is anything but abstract. Cuisine: French with Spanish flair. Hrs: 6-10 pm; Fri, Sat to 11 pm.

Closed Wed. Res required. Dinner $69-$89. Valet parking. Jacket required. Cr cds: A, D, DS, MC, V.
D

★★★ **PRIME.** 3600 Las Vegas Blvd S (89109). 702/693-7223. www.bellagio lasvegas.com. Specialities: prime meat, seafood, chops. Hrs: 5:30-10 pm. Dinner $32-$74. Cr cds: A, D, MC, V.
D ➘

★★★ **THE RANGE STEAKHOUSE.** 3475 Las Vegas Blvd S (89109). 702/369-5000. www.harrahs.com. Hrs: 5:30-11 pm, Fri-Sun to midnight. Res accepted. Bar. A la carte entrees: dinner $19.99-$53.99. Specializes in steak, lamb, veal. Valet parking. Cr cds: A, C, D, DS, ER, JCB, MC, V.
D ➘

★★★★ **RENOIR.** 3400 Las Vegas Blvd S (89109). 702/791-7223. www. mgm-mirage.com. Chef Alessandro Stratta's superb blend of contemporary French and Southwestern cuisine is exquisitely presented, and the doting service at this Mirage dining venue makes everyone feel like a high roller. Original Renoir paintings are the focal point of the jewel box of a dining room while patterned fabric wall coverings and splendid floral arrangements enhance the already impressive decor. French cuisine. Specialties: foie gras with peppered pineapple and aged balsamic vinegar, asparagus cannelloni, Maui onions in puff pastry. A la carte entrees: dinner $29-$44. Seasonal menu and vegetable tasting: $95. Res required. Valet parking. Cr cds: A, C, D, DS, ER, MC, V.
D

★★ **ROMANO'S MACARONI GRILL.** 2400 W Sahara Ave (89102). 702/248-9500. www.macaronigrill.com. Hrs: 11 am-10 pm; Fri, Sat to 11 pm. Closed Thanksgiving, Dec 25. Italian menu. Bar. Lunch $7-$9, dinner $6.50-$17.95. Child's menu. Specializes in pizza, pasta, seafood. Italian country decor. Cr cds: A, D, MC, V.
D ➘

★★★ **RUTH'S CHRIS STEAK HOUSE.** 3900 Paradise Rd (89109). 702/791-7011. www.ruthschris.com. Hrs: 11 am-11 pm; Fri, Sat to midnight. Closed Thanksgiving, Dec 25.

Res accepted. Bar. Wine list. A la carte entrees: dinner $20.95-$35.95. Specializes in steak. 3 dining rms, contemporary decor. Cr cds: A, C, D, DS, ER, MC, V.
D ➘

★★ **SACRED SEA.** 3900 Las Vegas Blvd S (89119). 702/262-4756. www. luxor.com. Hrs: 5-11 pm. Res accepted. Bar. Dinner $25-$42. Specialties: Alaskan king crab, lobster tail, black angus filet. Own pasta. Valet parking. Pianist. Egyptian decor, artwork. Cr cds: A, D, DS, MC, V.
D ➘

★★ **SFUZZI.** 3200 Las Vegas Blvd S (89109). 702/699-5777. Hrs: 11:30 am-11 pm; Sun from 11 am. Res accepted. Northern Italian menu. Bar. Lunch $4-$12, dinner $12-$20. Specialties: skillet-roasted sea bass, osso buco, grilled Atlantic salmon. Outdoor dining. Exterior features Italian village facade. Cr cds: A, C, D, ER, MC, V.
D ➘

★ **SHALIMAR.** 3900 S Paradise Rd (89109). 702/796-0302. www. shalimar.com. Hrs: 11:30 am-2 pm, 5:30-10 pm; Sat, Sun from 5:30 pm. Res accepted. Northern Indian menu. Serv bar. Buffet: lunch $6.95. A la carte entrees: dinner $10.50-$15.95. Specialties: chicken tandoori, lamb Shalimar, lamb and seafood curries. Contemporary decor. Cr cds: A, D, MC, V.
D SC ➘

★ **SIR GALAHAD'S.** 3850 Las Vegas Blvd S (89109). 702/597-7448. www. excalibur-casino.com. Hrs: 5-10 pm; Fri-Sat to 11 pm. Res required. English menu. Bar. Complete meals: dinner $15.95-$38.95. Specialty: prime rib. Valet parking. Medieval decor with suits of armor and cast-iron chandeliers. Cr cds: A, DS, MC, V.
D ➘

★★★ **SMITH & WOLLENSKY STEAKHOUSE.** 3767 Las Vegas Blvd S (89109). 702/862-4100. www.smith andwollensky.com. Specializes in crackling pork shank, grilled Atlantic salmon. Hrs: 11:30-3 am. Res accepted. Extensive wine list. Lunch $10-$24, dinner $19.50-$50. Valet parking. Cr cds: A, D, DS, ER, MC, V.
D ➘

★★★ **SPAGO.** *3500 Las Vegas Blvd S (89109). 702/399-6300. www.wolfgang puck.com.* Hrs: 11-12:30 am. Res accepted. Varied menu. Bar. Wine cellar. A la carte entrees: lunch $9.50-$18.50. Dinner $15-$30. Specialties: pizza, chicken salad. Jazz pianist Sun. Parking. Modern artwork. Art Deco, wrought iron design. Counterpart of famous restaurant in West Hollywood. Cr cds: A, DS, MC, V.
D 🅳

★ **STAGE DELI.** *3500 Las Vegas Blvd S (89109). 702/893-4045. www.ark restaurants.com.* Hrs: 8:30 am-11 pm; Fri, Sat to 11:30 pm. Res accepted. Wine, beer. Bkfst $4.95-$7.95, lunch $4.75-$12.95, dinner $9.95-$13.95. Specializes in deli fare. New York deli atmosphere; posters of Broadway shows. Cr cds: A, D, DS, ER, MC, V.
D 🅳

★★ **THE STEAK HOUSE.** *2880 Las Vegas Blvd (89114). 702/734-0410.* Hrs: 5-10 pm; Sat, Sun to 11 pm. Sun brunch 10 am-2 pm. Res accepted. Bar. Dinner $18395-$29.95. Sun brunch $19.95. Specializes in filet, crab legs, halibut. Western decor. Valet parking. Cr cds: A, D, DS, ER, JCB, MC, V.
D 🅳

★★ **STEFANO'S.** *129 E Fremont St (89101). 702/385-7111. www.golden nugget.com.* Hrs: 6-11 pm; Fri, Sat 5:30-midnight. Italian menu. Bar. Wine cellar. A la carte entrees: dinner $13.95-$34.95. Specializes in northern Italian food. Parking. Singing waiters. Murals of Italy. Cr cds: A, D, DS, MC, V.
D 🅳

★★ **TILLERMAN.** *2245 E Flamingo Rd (89109). 702/731-4036. www. tillerman.com.* Hrs: 5-11 pm. Closed major hols. Res accepted. Wine list. Dinner $20-$49. Specializes in fresh fish, steak, pasta. Valet parking. Atrium, garden, loft dining areas. Cr cds: A, D, MC, V.
D 🅳

★★★ **TOP OF THE WORLD.** *2000 S Las Vegas Blvd (89104). 702/380-7711. www.stratlv.com.* Hrs: 11 am-11 pm; Fri, Sat to midnight. Res required. Bar. Extensive wine list. Dinner $27-$48. Specializes in steak, salmon, lobster. Entertainment. Rotating restaurant from 1,000-ft elevation. Valet parking. Cr cds: A, D, MC, V.
D 🅳

★ **VIVA MERCADOS.** *6182 W Flamingo Rd (89103). 702/871-8826. www.vivamercados.com.* Hrs: 11 am-10 pm; Fri, Sat to 11 pm. Closed Sun; major hols. Res accepted (dinner). Mexican menu. Bar. Lunch $6.25-$12.75, dinner $11.95-$25.95. Specialties: orange roughy, camerones rancheros, mariscos vallarta. Mexican decor. Cr cds: A, DS, MC, V.
D 🅳

★ **WOLFGANG PUCK'S CAFE.** *3799 Las Vegas Blvd S (89109). 702/895-9653. www.mgmgrand.com.* Hrs: 8 am-11 pm; Fri, Sat to 1 am. Bar. A la carte entrees: bkfst, lunch, dinner $5.95-$30.95. Specialties: wood-burning oven pizza, rotisserie chicken. Ultramodern decor. Cr cds: A, MC, V.
D 🅳

★ **XINH-XINH.** *220 W Sahara Ave (89102). 702/471-1572.* Hrs: 10 am-10 pm. Vietnamese menu. Wine, beer. Lunch $5.95-$7.95, dinner $8.95-$12.95. Specializes in Vietnamese cuisine. Cr cds: A, D, MC, V.
🅳 D

★ **YOLIE'S BRAZILIAN STEAK-HOUSE & SEAFOOD.** *3900 Paradise Rd (89109). 702/794-0700. www. yoliesbraziliansteakhouse.com.* Hrs: 11 am-11 pm; Sat from 5 pm. Res accepted. Brazilian menu. Bar. Lunch $6.95-$12.95, dinner $14.95-$24. Specializes in steak, lamb. Cr cds: A, D, MC, V.
D 🅳

★★ **Z' TEJAS GRILL.** *3824 S Paradise Rd (89109). 702/732-1660. www. ztejas.com.* Hrs: 11 am-10 pm; Fri to 11 pm; Sat, Sun 4-11 pm. Closed Thanksgiving, Dec 25. Res accepted. Southwestern menu. Bar. Lunch $6.25-$10.95, dinner $8.95-$16.95. Specialties: crab-stuffed shrimp, pork roast Vera Cruz. Southwestern decor. Valet parking. Totally nonsmoking. Cr cds: A, D, MC, V.
D

Unrated Dining Spots

BATTISTA'S HOLE-IN-THE-WALL. *4041 Audrie St (89109). 702/732-*

1424. Hrs: 4:30-11 pm. Closed Thanksgiving, Dec 24-25. Res accepted. Italian menu. Bar. Complete meals: dinner $15.95-$29.95. Specializes in fresh pasta. Parking. Casual atmosphere. Family-owned. Cr cds: A, C, D, DS, ER, MC, V.

D ⊒

COUNTRY INN. *1401 Rainbow Blvd (89109). 702/254-0520.* Hrs: 7 am-10 pm; wkends to 11 pm. Closed Dec 25. Wine, beer. Bkfst $2.25-$6.50, lunch, dinner $6.95-$12.95. Child's menu. Specializes in turkey, fish, steak. Cr cds: A, D, DS, MC, V.

D SC ⊒

HARD ROCK CAFE. *4475 Paradise Rd (89109). 702/733-8400. www.hard rockcafe.com.* Hrs: 11 am-11:30 pm. Bar. Lunch, dinner $5.50-$13.95. Specializes in chicken, ribs. Entertainment Fri. Valet parking. Rock 'n roll memorabilia. Cr cds: A, D, DS, MC, V.

D ⊒

SAM WOO BBQ. *4215 Spring Mountain Rd (89102). 702/368-7628.* Hrs: 10-5 am. Chinese menu. Lunch $5-$10, dinner $10-$24. Specializes in barbecue, fried rice, seafood. Chinese decor.

Laughlin

(H-7) *Also see Bullhead City, AZ; Kingman, AZ*

Pop 7,076 **Elev** 520 ft **Area code** 702
Zip 89029
Information Chamber of Commerce, PO Box 77777; 800/227-5245
Web www.laughlinchamber.com

Special Event

Laughlin Riverdays. Rodeo, bull-riding, off-road racing, golf tournament. Phone 702/298-2214. Mid-May.

Motel/Motor Lodge

★★ **RAMADA INN.** *2121 S Casino Dr (89029). 702/298-4200; fax 702/298-6403; res 800/243-6846.* 1,501 rms, 24 story. S, D $39-$59; suites $65-$200; higher rates: hols, gaming tournaments. Crib $7. TV; cable. Heated pool; poolside serv. Restaurant open 24 hrs. Bar; entertainment. Ck-out 11 am. Gift shop. Valet parking. Free airport transportation. Game rm. Refrigerator, wet bar in suites. Opp river. Railroad station theme; full-size train runs around hotel. Cr cds: A, D, DS, ER, JCB, MC, V.

D ⤓ ⊠ 🔥

Hotels

★ **COLORADO BELLE HOTEL AND CASINO.** *2100 S Casino Dr (89029). 702/298-4000; fax 702/299-0669; toll-free 800/477-4837. www. coloradobelle.com.* 1,201 rms, 6 story, 53 suites. S, D $23-$125; each addl $4. Crib $7. TV. 2 heated pools; whirlpool. Restaurant open 24 hrs. Limited rm serv. Bar; entertainment. Ck-out 11 am. Business servs avail. Shopping arcade. Free airport transportation. Casino. Adj to replica of three-deck Mississippi paddlewheeler. Cr cds: A, D, DS, ER, JCB, MC, V.

D ⤓ ⊠ 🔥 SC

★★ **DON LAUGHLIN'S RIVERSIDE HOTEL.** *1650 Casino Dr (89029). 702/298-2535; fax 702/298-2695; res 800/227-3849. www.riversideresort. com.* 1,404 rms, 28 story. S, D $39-$79; suites $69-$300; higher rates wkends. Crib $8. TV; cable. 2 pools. Restaurant open 24 hrs. Bars; entertainment. Ck-out 11 am. Convention facilities. Business center. In-rm modem link. Free airport transportation. Bathrm phones. Balconies. Movie theaters. Casino. Bus depot on premises. Boat dockage on Colorado River; RV spaces. Cr cds: A, C, D, DS, ER, JCB, MC, V.

D ⤓ ♿ ⊠ 🔥 🏃

★ **EDGEWATER HOTEL AND CASINO.** *2020 S Casino Dr (89029). 702/298-2453; fax 702/298-4271. www.edgewater-casino.com.* 1,413 rms, 6-26 story, 75 suites. S, D $29-$48; each addl $4; suites $75-$100; higher rates hols; under 12 free. Crib $7. TV. Pool; whirlpool. Restaurant open 24 hrs. Bar; entertainment. Ck-out 11 am. Gift shop. Covered parking. Free airport transportation. Some balconies. On river. Cr cds: A, C, D, DS, ER, JCB, MC, V.

★★★ **FLAMINGO LAUGHLIN.** *1900 S Casino Dr (89029). 702/298-5111; fax 702/298-5116. www. laughlinflamingo.com.* 1,912 rms, 18 story, 60 suites. Mar-Oct: S, D $29-$55; each addl $9; suites $170-$270; family rates; higher rates: wknds, hols; lower rates rest of yr. Crib free. TV; cable (premium). Heated pool. Restaurant open 24 hrs. Rm serv 6 am-midnight. Bar; entertainment. Ck-out 11 am. Meeting rms. Business servs avail. Shopping arcade. Free garage parking. Free airport transportation. Lighted tennis. Game rm. Wet bar in suites. Refrigerators avail. Casino. On 18-acre site along Colorado River. Cr cds: A, C, D, DS, ER, JCB, MC, V.

★★★ **GOLDEN NUGGET.** *2300 S Casino Dr (89028). 702/298-7222; fax 702/298-7122; res 800/950-7700. www.gnlaughlin.com.* 300 rms, 4 story. S, D $29-$99; under 12 free; higher rates wknds. Crib free. TV; cable. Pool; whirlpool, poolside serv. Restaurants open 24 hrs. Bar. Ck-out noon. Business servs avail. Shopping arcade. Free airport transportation. On Colorado River. Cr cds: A, DS, ER, JCB, MC, V.

★ **RIVER PALMS.** *2700 S Casino Dr (89029). 702/298-2242; fax 702/298-2196; toll-free 800/835-7903. www. rvrpalm.com.* 1,003 rms, 3-25 story. S, D $24-$65; suites $200-$250. Crib free. TV. Heated pool; whirlpool. Restaurant open 24 hrs. Bar; entertainment. Ck-out 11 am. Convention facilities. Business servs avail. Shopping arcade. Free valet parking. Free airport transportation. Exercise equipt. Game rm. Cr cds: A, D, DS, ER, JCB, MC, V.

Lovelock (C-3)

Settled early 1840s **Pop** 2,003
Elev 3,977 ft **Area code** 775
Zip 89419

Information Pershing County Chamber of Commerce, 25 W Marzen Lane, PO Box 821; 775/273-7213

What to See and Do

Courthouse Park. The only round courthouse still in use. Shaded picnic grounds; swimming pool. (May-Aug, daily) Phone 775/273-7213. ¢

Rye Patch State Recreation Area. Approx 27,500 acres on 200,000-acre reservoir; swimming, waterskiing, fishing, boating (launching ramps); picnicking, camping (dump station). Standard fees. 23 mi N on I-80. Phone 775/538-7321.

Special Event

Frontier Days. Parade, races, rodeo. Late July or early Aug. Phone 775/273-7213.

Lunar Crater (X-0)

(Near US 6 between Tonopah and Ely)

This is a vast field of cinder cones and frozen lava. The crater is a steep-walled pit, 400 feet deep and three-quarters of a mile in diameter, created by volcanic action about 1,000 years ago. The earth exploded violently, heaving cinders, lava, and rocks the size of city blocks high into the air. Awed by the remains, pioneers named the pit Lunar Crater.

Overton

(G-7) *See also Las Vegas*

Pop 3,000 **Elev** 1,270 ft
Area code 702 **Zip** 89040

What to See and Do

Lost City Museum of Archaeology. An agency of the state of Nevada, the museum is located on a restored portion of Pueblo Grande de Nevada. The museum has an extensive collection of ancient Native American artifacts, fossils, and semiprecious gems. There is also a picnic area. The curator and staff have travel tips and information on the area; gift shop.

(Daily; closed Jan 1, Thanksgiving, Dec 25) 1 mi S on NV 169. Phone 702/397-2193. ¢

Pyramid Lake

(X-0) *See also Reno*

(36 mi N of Reno on NV 445)

Surrounded by rainbow-tinted, eroded hills, this is a remnant of prehistoric Lake Lahontan, which once covered 8,400 square miles in western Nevada and northeastern California. The largest natural lake in the state, Pyramid is about 30 miles long and from 7 to 9 miles wide, with deep-blue sparkling waters. It is fed by scant water from the diverted Truckee River and by brief floods in other streams. Since the Newlands Irrigation Project deprives it of water, its level is receding.

General John C. Frémont gave the lake its name when he visited the area in 1844, apparently taking it from the tufa (porous rock) islands that jut up from the water. One, 475 feet high, is said by Native Americans to be a basket inverted over an erring woman. Though turned to stone, her "breath" (wisps of steam from a hot spring) can still be seen. Another is called Stone Mother and Basket. At the north end there is a cluster of sharp spires known as the Needles. Anahoe Island, in the lake, is a sanctuary and breeding ground for more than 10,000 huge white pelicans.

An air of mystery surrounds the area, bred by the murmuring waves, the spires and domes with their wisps of steam, and the ever-changing tints of the folded, eroded hills. At nearby Astor Pass, railroad excavations uncovered a horse skull, fragmentary remains of an elephant, bison, and camel, all believed to have lived on the lakeshore in prehistoric times.

Pyramid Lake abounds with Lahonton cutthroat trout; it is one of the top trophy trout lakes in the United States. All rights belong to the Native Americans. For information about roads, fishing, and boat permits, contact the Sutcliffe Ranger Station or Pyramid Lake Fisheries, Star Rte, Sutcliffe 89510; 775/476-0500. Camping, boating, and fishing at Pyramid Lake are considered by many to be the best in the state. Day use ¢¢

Visitor centers, located in the hatcheries at Sutcliffe and between Nixon and Wadsworth, describe the land, lake, and people through photographs and displays (daily).

Reno

(C-2) *See also Carson City, Incline Village, Virginia City*

Founded 1868 **Pop** 180,480
Elev 4,498 ft **Area code** 775
Information Chamber of Commerce, 1 E. First St, 16th Floor, 89501 775/337-3030. For information on cultural events contact the Sierra Arts Foundation, 200 Flint St, 89501; 775/329-2787
Web www.reno-sparkschamber.org

What to See and Do

National Automobile Museum. More than 200 vehicles on display. Theater presentation; period street scenes. (Daily; closed Thanksgiving, Dec 25) 10 Lake St S. Phone 775/333-9300. ¢¢

Nevada Museum of Art. Changing art exhibits by international, national, regional, and local artists. (Tues-Sun; closed hols) 100 W Virginia St. Phone 775/329-3333. ¢¢

Pyramid Lake. (see). 55 N Main St. Phone 585/394-4975. ¢

Sierra Nevada bus tours. To Virginia City, Ponderosa Ranch, Lake Tahoe, and other nearby points. Contact 2050 Glendale Ave, Sparks 89431. Phone 775/331-1147.

Toiyabe National Forest. Approx three million acres, partly in California. Trout fishing; big-game hunting, saddle and pack trips, campsites (fees vary), picnicking, winter sports. Berlin-Ichthyosaur State Park (see AUSTIN), Lake Tahoe (see CALIFORNIA) and Mt Charleston Recreation

Area (see LAS VEGAS) are in the forest. (Daily) 10 mi W on I-80, then W on NV 27. Contact Public Affairs Officer, 1200 Franklin Way, Sparks 89431. Phone 775/331-6444. **FREE**

University of Nevada-Reno. (1874) 12,000 students. The campus covers 200 acres on a plateau overlooking the Truckee Meadows, in the shadow of the Sierra Nevada Mtns. Opened in Elko, it was moved to Reno and reopened in 1885. Tours of campus. 9th and N Virginia Sts. Phone 775/784-4865. On campus are

> **Fleischmann Planetarium.** Northern Nevada's only planetarium, this facility features star shows, movies, astronomy museum, telescope viewing (Fri eves), and more. (Daily; closed Jan 1, Thanksgiving, Dec 25) Phone 775/784-4812. ¢¢¢

> **Mackay School of Mines Museum.** Minerals, rocks, fossils, and mining memorabilia. (Mon-Fri; closed hols) Phone 775/784-6987. **FREE**

> **Nevada Historical Society Museum.** Prehistoric and modern Native American artifacts; ranching, mining, and gambling artifacts. Carson City Mint materials; museum tours; research and genealogy library (Tues-Sat). Museum (Mon-Sat; closed hols, Oct 31). 1650 N Virginia St. Phone 775/688-1190. **Donation**

Special Events

Rodeo. Reno Livestock Events Center. Downtown contests and celebrations on closed streets. Phone 775/329-3877. Late June.

Nevada State Fair. Fairgrounds, Wells St. Phone 775/688-5767. Late Aug.

National Championship Air Races. Reno/Stead Airport. Phone 775/972-6663. Four days mid-Sept.

Motels/Motor Lodges

★ ★ **BEST WESTERN AIRPORT PLAZA.** *1981 Terminal Way (89502). 775/348-6370; fax 775/348-9722; res 800/648-3525. www.bestwestern.com.* 270 rms, 3 story. S $79-$99; D $79-$119; each addl $10; suites $125-$250; kit. unit $275; under 12 free; higher rates: hols, special events. Crib free. TV; cable (premium), VCR avail. Pool; whirlpool. Restaurant 5:30 am-11 pm. Rm serv. Bar 11-1

am. Ck-out noon. Meeting rms. Business center. In-rm modem link. Bellhops. Valet serv. Airport transportation. Putting green. Exercise equipt; sauna. Health club privileges. Refrigerators avail. Some fireplaces. Mini-casino. Cr cds: A, C, D, DS, MC, V.

[D] [⇌] [🏋] [🚶] [🔥]

★ ★ **LA QUINTA INN.** *4001 Market St (89502). 775/348-6100; fax 775/348-8794; res 800/531-5900. www.laquinta.com.* 130 rms, 2 story. S $61-$69; D $61-$77; each addl $8; under 18 free. Crib free. Pet accepted. TV; cable. Pool. Complimentary continental bkfst. Coffee in rms. Ck-out noon. Business servs avail. Free airport transportation. Cr cds: A, C, D, DS, MC, V.

[D] [🐾] [⇌] [✈] [📪] [🔥]

★ **RODEWAY INN RENO.** *2050 Market St (89502). 775/786-2500; fax 775/786-3884; res 800/228-2000. www.choicehotels.com.* 211 units, 4 story, 70 kit suites (no equipt). Late May-Oct: S $39, D $189; each addl $9; kit. suites $64-$189; under 18 free; wkly rates; higher rates: wkends, hols, special events; lower rates rest of yr. Crib free. Pet accepted; $10/day. TV; cable. Pool; whirlpool. Sauna. Complimentary continental bkfst. Restaurant nearby. Ck-out noon. Coin lndry. Business servs avail. Airport, casino transportation. Microwaves in kit. units. Cr cds: A, C, D, DS, JCB, MC, V.

[D] [🐾] [⇌] [📪] [🔥]

★ **VAGABOND INN.** *3131 S Virginia St (89502). 775/825-7134; fax 775/825-3096; res 800/522-1555. www.vagabondinns.com.* 129 rms, 2 story. May-Oct: S $45-$65; D $49-$69; each addl $5; under 18 free; higher rates special events, hols; lower rates rest of yr. Crib free. Pet accepted, some restrictions; $10/day. TV; cable (premium). Pool. Complimentary continental bkfst. Restaurant adj 11-4 am. Ck-out 11 am. Business servs avail. Airport, RR station, bus depot transportation. Health club privileges. Some private patios, balconies. Cr cds: A, D, DS, MC, V.

[🐾] [⇌] [📪] [🔥]

Reno all aglow

Hotels

★★★ **ATLANTIS CASINO RESORT.** *3800 S Virginia St (89502). 775/825-4700; fax 775/826-7860; res 800/723-6500. www.atlantiscasino. com.* 973 rms, 27 story. May-Sept: S, D $69-$125; each addl $10; suites $165-$275; under 18 free; ski, golf rates; higher rates: wkends, hols, special events; lower rates rest of yr. Crib free. TV; cable. Heated pool; whirlpool. Restaurant open 24 hrs (see also ATLANTIS). Bar; entertainment. Ck-out 11 am. Convention facilities. Business servs avail. Free valet parking. Free airport transportation. Spa. Some in-rm whirlpools. Casino. Cr cds: A, C, D, DS, ER, MC, V.

★★★ **CIRCUS CIRCUS HOTEL AND CASINO.** *500 N Sierra St (89503). 775/329-0711; fax 775/328-9652; toll-free 800/648-5010. www. circusreno.com.* 1,572 rms, 23 and 28 story. S, D $39-$69; each addl $10; minisuites $69-$99; under 13 free; ski/golf packages; higher rates: wkends, hols, special events. Crib free. TV; cable. Restaurant open 24 hrs. Bar; entertainment. Ck-out noon. Business servs avail. Gift shop. Free covered valet parking. Airport transportation. Health club privileges. Rec rm. Casino. Midway, arcade games. Free circus acts. Cr cds: A, C, DS, JCB, MC, V.

★★★ **ELDORADO HOTEL & CASINO.** *345 N Virginia St (89505). 775/786-5700; fax 775/348-7513; res 800/648-5966. www.eldoradoreno.com.* 817 rms, 26 story. July-Oct: S, D $69-$89; each addl $10; suites $110-$495; under 12 free; higher rates: wkends, hols; lower rates rest of yr. Crib free. TV; cable. Heated pool; whirlpool, poolside serv. Restaurants open 24 hrs. Rm serv 24 hrs. Bar; entertainment. Ck-out noon. Convention facilities. Business servs avail. In-rm modem link. Concierge. Gift shop. Airport transportation. Garage; free valet parking. Health club privileges. Wet bar in some suites; some bathrm phones, refrigerators. Casino. Cr cds: A, D, DS, MC, V.

★★ **FITZGERALD'S CASINO HOTEL.** *255 N Virginia St (89501). 775/785-3300; fax 775/786-3686. www.fitzgeralds.com.* 351 rms, 16 story. May-Oct: S, D $36-$88; each addl $10; suites $90-$140; under 13 free; higher rates: wkends, hols; lower rates rest of yr. TV; cable. Restaurants open 24 hrs. Rm serv 6 am-9 pm. Bars; entertainment. Ck-out 11 am. Free valet parking. Casino. Cr cds: A, D, DS, MC, V.

★★★ **GOLDEN PHOENIX.** *255 N Sierra St (89501). 775/322-1111; fax 775/785-7086.* 604 rms, 20 story. May-Sept: S, D $52-$229; each addl $10; suites $145-$395; under 19 free; higher rates hols; lower rates rest of yr. Crib free. TV; cable. Restaurants open 24 hrs. Bars; entertainment. Rm serv 24 hrs. Ck-out 11 am. Convention facilities. Business center. In-rm modem link. Gift shop. Free valet parking. Airport transportation. Exercise equipt. Casino. Cr cds: A, C, D, DS, JCB, MC, V.

★★★ **HARRAH'S.** *219 N Center St (89504). 775/786-3232; fax 775/788-3274; toll-free 800/427-7247. www. harrahs.com.* 952 rms, 26 story, no rms on 1st 3 floors. May-Oct: S, D $79-$189; each addl $10; suites $210-$425; higher rates wkends; lower rates rest of yr. Crib free. Pet accepted, some restrictions. TV; cable. Heated pool; whirlpool. Restaurant open 24 hrs. Bars; entertainment. Ck-out noon. Convention facilities. Business center. In-rm modem link. Gift shop. Barber, beauty shop. Covered parking; valet. Free airport, transportation. Sauna, steam rm. Massage. Game rm. Rec rm. Casino. Some bathrm phones. Some private patios. Cr cds: A, C, D, DS, JCB, MC, V.

★★★ **HILTON RENO.** *2500 E Second St (89595). 775/789-2000; fax 775/789-1678; res 800/648-5080. www.hilton.com.* 2,000 rms, 27 story. S, D $69-$199; each addl $10; suites $149-$900; package plans. Crib free. TV; cable. Pool; whirlpool, poolside serv, lifeguard. Restaurants open 24 hrs (see also THE STEAK HOUSE). Bars; entertainment. Ck-out 11 am. Convention facilities. Meeting rms. Business center. Shopping arcade. Barber, beauty shop. Free valet parking. Free airport transportation. Driving range. Exercise rm; sauna, steam rm. Spa. Massage. Rec rm. Bowling. Some bathrm phones, refrigerators; wet bars. Casino. Cr cds: A, C, D, DS, MC, V.

★★★ **JOHN ASCUAGA'S NUGGET.** *1100 Nugget Ave, Sparks (89431). 775/356-3300; fax 775/356-4198; res 800/648-1177. www. janugget.com.* 1,407 rms, 29 story. S, D $99-$189; each addl $10; suites $145-$450; under 18 free. Crib free. TV; cable. Indoor/outdoor pool; whirlpool, poolside serv. Restaurants open 24 hrs. Bars; entertainment. Ck-out 11 am. Convention facilities. Business center. Concierge. Gift shop. Beauty shop. Free valet parking. Free airport transportation. Exercise equipt. Massage. Casino. Cr cds: A, C, D, DS, MC, V.

★★ **JOHN ASCUAGA'S NUGGET COURTYARD.** *1100 Nugget Ave, Sparks (89431). 775/356-3300; fax 775/356-4198; res 800/648-1177. www.janugget.com.* 157 rms, 5 story. S, D $79-$119; under 18 free. Crib free. TV; cable. Heated pool; poolside serv. Complimentary coffee in lobby. Ck-out 11 am. Business servs avail. Free parking. Sundries. Free airport transportation. Health club privileges. Some balconies. Wedding chapel. Cr cds: A, C, D, DS, MC, V.

★★★ **PEPPERMILL HOTEL AND CASINO.** *2707 S Virginia St (89502). 775/826-2121; fax 775/689-7178; toll-free 800/648-6992. www.peppermill casino.com.* 1,070 rms, 16 story. S, D $49-$100; suites $109-$399; under 15 free. Crib free. Valet parking. TV; cable. 2 heated pools; whirlpool. Restaurant open 24 hrs. Bars; entertainment. Ck-out noon. Meeting rms. Business servs avail. Gift shop. Barber, beauty shop. Free airport transportation. Exercise equipt; sauna. Minibars. Casino. Cr cds: A, D, DS, MC, V.

★★★ **SIENA HOTEL SPA CASINO.** *One S Lake St (89505). 775/337-6260; res 877/743-6233. www.sienareno.com.* 214 rms, 9 story. S, D $99-$189. Crib free. TV; cable. Restaurant open 24 hrs. Bars; entertainment. Ck-out noon. Business center. In-rm modem link. Exercise rm; sauna. Spa. Massage. Casino. Cr cds: A, C, D, DS, MC, V.

★★★ **SILVER LEGACY RESORT AND CASINO.** *407 N Virginia St (89501). 775/329-4777; fax 775/325-7474; res 800/687-7733. www.silver legacyresort.com.* 1,720 rms, 38 story. July-Oct: S, D $59-$119; each addl $10; suites $100-$200; under 12 free; lower rates rest of yr. TV; cable. Pool; whirlpool, poolside serv. Restaurant open 24 hrs. Bar. Ck-out 11 am. Convention facilities. Business servs avail. Barber, beauty shop. Valet serv. Free airport transportation. Cr cds: A, C, D, DS, JCB, MC, V.

D 🖘 🏖 🏊

Restaurants

★★★ **ATLANTIS.** *3800 S Virginia St (89502). 702/825-4700. www.atlantis. reno.nv.us.* Hrs: 5-10 pm; Fri, Sat to 10:30 pm. Res accepted. Continental menu. Dinner $19.95-$28.95. Specialties: flaming coconut prawns, Alaskan king crab. Valet parking. Brightly decorated interior resembles underwater terrain; large saltwater aquarium completes illusion. Cr cds: A, C, D, DS, ER, MC, V.

D 🖃

★★ **BRICKS RESTAURANT AND WINE BAR.** *1695 S Virginia St (89502). 775/786-2277.* Hrs: 11:30 am-2 pm, 5-10 pm; Sat from 5 pm. Closed Sun; major hols. Res accepted. Continental menu. Bar 4-11 pm. Lunch $6.95-$12.95, dinner $11.95-$21.95. Specialties: shrimp scampi risotto, pork tenderloin, chicken pesto. Intimate atmosphere. Cr cds: A, DS, MC, V.

D

★★ **FAMOUS MURPHY'S.** *3127 S Virginia St (89502). 775/827-4111. www.famousmurphys.com.* Hrs: 11 am-2 pm, 5-10 pm; Sat, Sun 10 am-2 pm, 5-10 pm. Res accepted. Bar to 3:30 am. Lunch $4.95-$12.95, dinner $10.95-$22.95. Child's menu. Specializes in steak, seafood, pasta. Oyster bar. Pub atmosphere. Cr cds: A, C, DS, ER, MC, V.

D 🖃

★★ **GLORY HOLE.** *4201 W 4th St (89503). 775/786-1323.* Hrs: 5-10:30 pm. Closed Thanksgiving. Bar. Dinner $10-$42.95. Specializes in steak, fresh seafood, chicken. Salad bar. Old

West saloon, mining camp decor. Cr cds: A, C, D, DS, ER, MC, V.

D 🖃

★★★ **ICHIBAN JAPANESE STEAK HOUSE.** *210 N Sierra St (89501). 775/323-5550.* Hrs: 4:30-10 pm; Fri, Sat to 11 pm. Res accepted. Japanese menu. Bar. A la carte entrees: dinner $8.95-$15.95. Complete meals: $14.95-$26.95. Child's menu. Specializes in steak, seafood, chicken. Sushi bar. Cr cds: A, C, D, DS, ER, MC, V.

D SC 🖃

★★ **PALAIS DE JADE.** *960 W Moana Ln #107 (89509). 775/827-5233.* Hrs: 11 am-10 pm. Closed most maj hols. Res accepted. Bar. Lunch $5.50-$7.50, dinner $5.50-$17.95. Specialties: Jade crispy shrimp, sesame chicken, orange-flavored beef. Chinese decor. Cr cds: A, MC, V.

D 🖃

★★ **RAPSCALLION.** *1555 S Wells Ave (89502). 775/323-1211. www. rapscallion.com.* Hrs: 11:30 am-10 pm; Fri, Sat 5-10:30 pm; Sun brunch 10 am-2 pm. Closed Thanksgiving, Dec 25. Res accepted. Bar 11-1 am; Sat to 2 am; Sun from 10 am. A la carte entrees: lunch, dinner $5.95-$18.95. Sun brunch $4.95-$7.95. Specializes in seafood. Parking. Outdoor dining. 1890s San Francisco decor. Cr cds: A, MC, V.

D 🖃

★★★ **THE STEAK HOUSE.** *2500 E 2nd St (89595). 775/789-2270. www. hilton.com.* Hrs: 5-10 pm; early-bird dinner to 6 pm. Res accepted. Setups. Wine list. A la carte entrees: $24-$70. Specialties: Winnemucca potatoes, broiled swordfish. Valet parking. Cr cds: A, DS, MC, V.

D 🖃

South Lake Tahoe (C-2)

(see South Lake Tahoe in California book)

Sparks (C-2)

(see Reno)

Stateline (X-0)

Pop 1,215 **Elev** 6,360 ft
Area code 775 **Zip** 89449

Motel/Motor Lodge

★★ **LAKESIDE INN AND CASINO.**
*Hwy 50 at Kingsbury Grade (89449).
775/588-7777; fax 775/588-4092; toll-
free 800/624-7980. www.lakesideinn.
com.* 124 rms, 2 story. Mid-June-mid-
Oct: S, D $89-$119; each addl $10;
suites $120-$235; package plans in
winter; under 16 free; lower rates rest
of yr. Crib free. TV; cable. Pool. Complimentary coffee in rms. Restaurant
open 24 hrs. Bars. Gift shop. Ck-out
noon. Sundries. Downhill ski 2 mi;
x-country. Game rm. Wet bar in
suites. Casino. Cr cds: A, C, D, DS,
MC, V.
🆔 ⊁ ⇰ ⊠ 🏂 SC

Hotels

★★★ **CAESAR'S TAHOE.** 55 US 50
(89449). *775/588-3515; fax 775/586-
2068; toll-free 888/829-7630. www.
caesars.com.* 440 rms, 15 story. S, D
$89-$225; each addl $10; suites $300-
$650; under 12 free; ski pkgs. Crib
$10. TV; cable (premium). Indoor
pool; whirlpool. Coffee in rms.
Restaurant open 24 hrs. Bar; entertainment. Ck-out noon. Convention
facilities. Business center. Concierge.
Shopping arcade. Barber, beauty
shop. Free valet parking. Lighted tennis. Exercise equipt; steam rm, sauna.
Massage. Game rm. Bathrm phones;
some refrigerators, in-rm whirlpools.
Casino. Cr cds: A, C, D, DS, MC, V.
🆔 🏌 🏋 ⊁ ⇰ 🏂 ⊠ 🏊 🏂

★★★ **HARRAH'S LAKE TAHOE
HOTEL CASINO.** *Hwy 50 (89449).
775/588-6611; fax 775/586-6607; toll-
free 800/648-3773. www.harrahstahoe.
com.* 532 rms, 18 story. S, D $79-

$209; each addl $20; suites $199-
$950; ski packages; higher rates:
wkends, hols. Crib free. Pet accepted.
TV; cable, VCR avail. Indoor pool,
whirlpool, poolside serv. 6 restaurants with one open 24 hrs (see also
FRIDAY'S STATION and SUMMIT).
Rm serv 24 hrs. Bars; theater-restau-
rant; entertainment. Ck-out noon.
Convention facilities. Business servs
avail. Concierge. Shopping arcade.
Barber, beauty shop. Free covered
valet parking. Exercise equipt; sauna,
steam rm. Massage. Game rm.
Casino. Microwaves, refrigerators
avail. Butler serv in suites. Cr cds: A,
C, D, DS, ER, JCB, MC, V.
🆔 ⊁ 🏌 🏋 ⇰ 🏂 🔥

★★★ **HARVEY'S RESORT HOTEL
AND CASINO.** *Stateline Ave (US 50)
(89449). 775/588-2411; fax 775/588-
6643; toll-free 800/427-2789. www.
harveys.com.* 740 rms, 19 story. S, D
$99-$229; each addl $20; suites $275-
$725; pkg plans; higher rates
wkends, hols. Crib free. TV; cable.
Pool; whirlpool. Poolside serv. 8
restaurants (see also LEWELLYN'S
and SAGE ROOM). Rm serv 24 hrs. 6
bars open 24 hrs; entertainment. Ck-
out noon. Convention facilities.
Business center. Concierge. Shopping
arcade. Barber, beauty shop. Covered
parking; free valet, self-park. Airport
transportation (fee). Exercise rm. Spa.
Game rm. Casino. Bathrm phones;
minibars; wet bar in suites. Tahoe's
first gaming establishment (1944). Cr
cds: A, C, D, DS, JCB, MC, V.
🆔 ⇰ 🏂 ⊠ 🔥 SC 🏂

★★ **HORIZON CASINO RESORT.**
*50 US 50 (89449). 775/588-6211; fax
775/588-1344; toll-free 800/648-3322.
www.horizoncasino.com.* 539 rms, 15
story. Mid-June-mid-Sept: S, D $119-
$169; each addl $10; suites $300-
$600; higher rates: hols, special
events; lower rates rest of yr. Crib
free. TV; cable. Heated pool (seasonal); whirlpools, poolside serv, lifeguard. Restaurants open 24 hrs. Bars;
entertainment. Ck-out noon. Convention facilities. Business servs avail.
Concierge. Gift shop. Barber, beauty
shop. Free garage parking. Downhill
ski 1 mi; x-country ski 15 mi. Exercise rm. Massage. Game rm. Wet bar
in suites. Some balconies. Casino. Cr
cds: A, C, D, DS, JCB, MC, V.
🆔 ⊁ ⇰ 🔥 ⊠ 🏊 SC

Restaurants

★★ **CHART HOUSE.** *392 Kingsbury Grade (89449).* 775/588-6276. *www. chart-house.com.* Hrs: 5:30-10 pm; Sat 5-10:30 pm. Res accepted. Bar from 5 pm; Sat from 4:30 pm. Dinner $15.50-$31.95. Child's menu. Specialties: teriyaki sirloin, prime rib. Salad bar. Outdoor dining. View of lake. Cr cds: A, C, D, DS, ER, MC, V. Ⓓ

★★★ **FRIDAY'S STATION STEAK & SEAFOOD GRILL.** *US 50 (89449).* 775/588-6611. *www.harrahs.com.* Hrs: 5:30-9:30 pm; Fri to 10 pm; Sat to 10:30 pm. Res accepted. Bar. A la carte entrees: dinner $16-$32. Specializes in hardwood-grilled seafood and steak. Overlooks Lake Tahoe. Cr cds: A, C, D, DS, ER, JCB, MC, V. ⒹⒺ

★★★ **LEWELLYN'S.** *US 50 (89449).* 775/588-2411. *www.harveys.com.* Hrs: 6-9:30 pm; Fri to 10 pm; Sat 5-10 pm. Sun 9:45-2 pm. Res accepted. International menu. Bar 5-11 pm. Wine list. Dinner $22-$36. Specialties: abalone, rack of lamb, wild boar. Pianist Wed-Sun. Valet parking. Elegant dining rm; view of Lake Tahoe. Totally nonsmoking. Cr cds: A, C, D, DS, MC, V. Ⓓ

★★★ **SAGE ROOM.** *US 50 (89449).* 775/588-2411. *www.harveys.com.* Hrs: 5:30-10 pm; Sat to 11 pm. Res accepted. Continental, Amer menu. Bar. Wine cellar. Dinner $18-$28. Specializes in steak, fresh seafood. Own baking. Valet parking. Dining rm interior is part of original Wagon Wheel Saloon and Gambling Hall; hand-hewn beams, redwood ceilings, Remington bronzes, Western decor. Cr cds: A, C, D, DS, MC, V. ⒹⒺ

★★★ **SUMMIT.** *US 50 (89449).* 775/588-6611. *www.harrahstahoe.com.* Hrs: 5:30-9:30 pm; Sat to 10 pm. Res accepted. Continental menu. Bar. Wine list. Dinner $22-$75. Specialties: rack of lamb, lobster Thermidor, abalone. Valet parking. Formal atmosphere; glass wine cases, views of lake. Totally nonsmoking. Cr cds: A, C, D, DS, ER, JCB, MC, V. Ⓓ

Tonopah (E-4)

Settled 1900 **Pop** 2,627 **Elev** 6,030 ft **Area code** 775 **Zip** 89049
Information Chamber of Commerce, 301 Brougher St, PO Box 869; 775/482-3859

What to See and Do

Central Nevada Museum. Historical, mining, and gem displays. (Daily; closed Dec 25) Logan Field Rd. Phone 775/482-9676. **Donation**

Rock collecting. Historic mining park. Rich variety of minerals. (Daily) Phone 775/482-9274.

Motels/Motor Lodges

★★ **BEST WESTERN HI-DESERT INN.** *320 Main St (89049).* 775/482-3511; fax 775/482-3300; res 800/780-7234. *www.bestwestern.com.* 62 rms, 2 story. S $49; D $69; each addl $6. Crib $8. Pet accepted, some restrictions. TV; cable (premium). Pool; whirlpool. Complimentary continental bkfst. Restaurant nearby. Ck-out 11 am. Cr cds: A, D, DS, ER, JCB, MC, V. ⒹⓀⓈⓃⓀ

★ **JIM BUTLER MOTEL.** *100 S Main St (89049).* 775/482-3577; fax 775/482-5240; toll-free 800/635-9455. 24 rms, 2 story. S, D $34-$42. Crib $5. Pet accepted, some restrictions. TV; cable (premium). Complimentary coffee in lobby. Restaurant adj 24 hrs. Ck-out 11 am. Some refrigerators. Cr cds: A, C, D, DS, MC, V. ⓀⓃⓀ**SC**

★ **SILVER QUEEN MOTEL.** *255 Erie Main (89049).* 775/482-6291; fax 775/482-3190; toll-free 800/210-9218. 85 rms, 1-2 story. No elvtr. S $33; D $45; kit. units $45. Crib $4. Pet accepted. TV; cable (premium), VCR avail (movies). Pool. Restaurant adj 6 am-10 pm. Bar 11 am-midnight. Ck-out 11 am. Some refrigerators, microwaves. Cr cds: A, C, D, DS, MC, V. ⓀⓃⓀ

★ **STATION HOUSE HOTEL AND CASINO.** *1100 Erie Main St (89049).* 775/482-9777; fax 775/482-8762. 78 rms, 3 suites, 2 story. S $36; D $39; each addl $2; suites $58-$80; under

11 free. Crib free. TV; cable (premium). Complimentary coffee in rms. Restaurant open 24 hrs. Bar; entertainment exc Mon. Ck-out 11 am. Meeting rms. Shopping arcade. Free bus depot transportation. Cr cds: A, D, DS, MC, V.

D ⊠ 🔥

Valley of Fire State Park

(X-0) *See also Las Vegas, Overton*

(37 mi NE of Las Vegas on I-15, then 18 mi SE on NV 169)

This park offers a geologically incredible 38,480-acre area that gains its name from the red, Jurassic-period sandstone formed 150 million years ago. Fine examples of Native American petroglyphs can be seen throughout the park. Picnicking, camping (dump station). Group use areas, visitor center. Standard fees. Phone 702/397-2088.

Virginia City

(D-2) *See also Carson City, Reno*

Settled 1859 **Pop** 750 **Elev** 6,220 ft **Area code** 775 **Zip** 89440

Information Chamber of Commerce, South C Street, PO Box 464; 775/847-0311

What to See and Do

The Castle. (1868) Built by Robert N. Graves, a mine superintendent of the Empire Mine, the building was patterned after a castle in Normandy, France. It was once referred to as the "house of silver doorknobs." Filled with international riches; original furnishings. (Memorial Day wkend-Oct; daily) 70 South B St. Phone 775/847-0275. ¢¢

Special Event

Camel Races. Early Sept. Phone 775/847-0311.

Wendover (X-0)

(see Wendover, UT)

Winnemucca (B-4)

Settled ca 1850 **Pop** 7,174 **Elev** 4,299 ft **Area code** 775 **Zip** 89445
Information Humboldt County Chamber of Commerce, 30 W Winnemucca Blvd; 775/623-2225

The Castle, Virginia City

What to See and Do

Humboldt Museum. Historical museum features Native American artifacts; bottles; pioneers' home items, tools, utensils; local history; antique auto display; old country store. (Mon-Fri, also Sat afternoons; closed hols) Jungo Rd and Maple Ave. Phone 775/623-2912. **Donation**

Motels/Motor Lodges

★★ **BEST WESTERN GOLD COUNTRY INN.** *921 W Winnemucca Blvd (89445). 775/623-6999; fax 775/623-9190; toll-free 800/346-5306. www.bestwestern.com.* 71 rms, 2 story. June-Labor Day: S, D $65-$75; each addl $10; under 12 free; lower rates rest of yr. Crib $5. Pet accepted, some restrictions. TV; cable (premium). Heated pool. Complimentary coffee in lobby. Restaurant adj open 24 hrs. Ck-out noon. Business servs avail. In-rm modem link. Airport transportation. Cr cds: A, D, DS, MC, V.

🄳 🐾 ➽ 🏊 🔥

★ **DAYS INN.** *511 W Winnemucca Blvd (89445). 775/623-3661; fax 775/623-4234; toll-free 800/548-0531. www.daysinn.com.* 50 rms, 2 story. June-Labor Day: S $60; D $65; each addl $5; lower rates rest of yr. Crib $5. Pet accepted. TV; cable (premium). Heated pool. Coffee in lobby. Restaurant nearby. Ck-out noon. Cr cds: A, C, D, DS, MC, V.

🐾 ➽ 🏊 🔥

★★ **RED LION INN AND CASINO.** *741 W Winnemucca Blvd (89445). 775/623-2565; fax 775/623-2527; toll-free 800/633-6435.* 105 units, 2 story. June-Oct: S, D $79-$89; each addl $10; suites $99-$150; under 12 free; lower rates rest of yr. Crib $5. Pet accepted, some restrictions; $50 deposit. TV; cable (premium), VCR avail. Heated pool. Restaurant open 24 hrs. Bar. Ck-out noon. Business servs avail. Airport transportation. Game rm. Some balconies. Casino. Cr cds: A, C, D, DS, ER, JCB, MC, V.

🄳 🐾 ➽ 🏊 🔥

★ **VAL-U-INN MOTEL.** *125 E Winnemucca Blvd (89445). 775/623-5248; fax 775/623-4722; res 800/443-7777.* 80 rms, 3 story. No elvtr. Mid-May-Sept: S $45-$50; D $48-$57; each addl $5; lower rates rest of yr. Crib $4. Pet accepted; $5. TV; cable (premium), VCR avail. Heated pool. Sauna, steam rm. Continental bkfst. Restaurant nearby. Ck-out noon. Business servs avail. Cr cds: A, D, DS, MC, V.

🄳 🐾 ➽ 🏊 🔥 **SC**

Hotel

★ **WINNERS HOTEL AND CASINO.** *185 W Winnemucca Blvd (89445). 775/623-2511; fax 775/623-3976; toll-free 800/648-4770. www.winnerscasino.com.* 37 rms, 2 story. May-Labor Day: S, D $35; each addl $5; suites $70; lower rates rest of yr. Pet accepted. TV; cable (premium). Continental bkfst in lobby. Restaurant nearby. Ck-out 11 am. Coin lndry. Cr cds: A, C, D, DS, MC, V.

🄳 🐾 ➽ 🔥

Restaurant

★ **ORMACHEA'S.** *180 Melarky St (89445). 775/623-3455.* Hrs: 4-10 pm. Closed Mon; some major hols. Basque, Amer menu. Bar. Complete meals: dinner $10.25-$17. Child's menu. Specializes in Basque dishes. Cr cds: A, C, D, DS, ER, MC, V.

Yerington (D-2)

Pop 2,883 **Elev** 4,384 ft

Information Mason Valley Chamber of Commerce, 227 S Main St; 775/463-2245

Web www.yerington.net

What to See and Do

Fort Churchill State Historic Park. This post was established when the rush to the Comstock began as protection against the Paiutes. It was garrisoned from 1860-1869. Adobe walls of the old buildings exist in a state of arrested decay. The visitor center has displays. Picnicking, trails, camping facilities on 1,232 acres. Phone 775/577-2345. ¢¢

Lyon County Museum. Complex incl a general store, natural history building, blacksmith shop, schoolhouse. (Thurs-Sun; closed Thanksgiving, Dec 25) 215 S Main. Phone 775/463-6576. **FREE**

NEW MEXICO

Fray Marcos de Niza first saw what is now New Mexico in May, 1539. From a nearby mesa he viewed the Zuni pueblo of Hawikíúh, not far from the present Gallup. He returned to Mexico with tales of cities of gold which so impressed the Viceroy that in 1540 he dispatched Francisco Coronado with an army and Fray Marcos as his guide. They found no gold and very little of anything else. Coronado returned home two years later a broken man.

While others came to New Mexico before him for a variety of purposes, Don Juan de Oñate established the first settlement in 1598. Don Pedro de Peralta founded Santa Fe as the capital in 1609. Spanish villages were settled all along the Rio Grande until 1680 when the Pueblo, with Apache help, drove the Spaniards out of New Mexico in the famous Pueblo Revolt.

Population: 1,819,046
Area: 121,593 square miles
Elevation: 2,817-13,161 feet
Peak: Wheeler Peak (Taos County)
Entered Union: January 6, 1912 (47th state)
Capital: Santa Fe
Motto: It grows as it goes
Nickname: Land of Enchantment
Flower: Yucca
Bird: Chaparral (roadrunner)
Tree: Piñon
Fair: September, 2003 in Albuquerque
Time Zone: Mountain
Website: www.newmexico.org

Twelve years later, Don Diego de Vargas reconquered the province with little resistance. The territory grew and prospered, though not entirely without conflict, since the Spanish were determined to maintain control at any cost. They forbade trade with the French of Louisiana, their nearest neighbors and rivals.

In 1810 Napoleon overran Spain; in 1821 Mexico won its independence and formed a republic. The following year William Becknell of Missouri brought the first wagons across the plains and blazed what was later called the Santa Fe Trail. After the Mexican War of 1846 New Mexico became a US territory, joining the Union in 1912.

New Mexico is a land of contrasts. Traces of prehistoric Folsom Man and Sandia Man, whose ancestors may have trekked across the Bering Strait land bridge from Asia, have been found here. Working in the midst of antiquity, scientists at Los Alamos opened up the new atomic world.

Southern New Mexico has fascinating desert country and cool, green, high forests popular with campers, anglers, and vacationers. In the north it also has desert lands, but most of this area is high mountain country with clear streams and snow which sometimes stays all year. Spanish-speaking farmers mix with Native Americans and urban Americans in the plazas of Santa Fe and Albuquerque.

Where sheep and cattle were once the only industry, extractive industries—of which oil and uranium are a part—now yield nearly five billion dollars a year.

Native Americans in New Mexico

Native Americans occupied New Mexico for centuries before the arrival of Europeans. The exploring Spaniards called them Pueblo Indians because their tightly-clustered communities were not unlike Spanish *pueblos,* or villages. The Apache and Navajo, who arrived in New Mexico after the Pueblo people, were seminomadic wanderers. The Navajo eventually adopted many of the Pueblo ways, although their society is less structured and more individualistic than the Pueblo. The main Navajo reservation straddles New Mexico and Arizona (see SHIPROCK). The Apache, living closer to the Plains Indians, remained more nomadic.

The 19 Pueblo groups have close-knit communal societies and cultures, even though they speak six different languages. Their pueblos are unique places to visit. In centuries-old dwellings craftspeople make and sell a variety of wares. The religious ceremonies, which include many dances and songs, are quite striking and not to be missed. While some pueblos are adamantly uninterested in tourists, others are trying to find a way to preserve those aspects of their ancient culture they most value while taking advantage of what is most beneficial to them in non-Native American culture and ways.

Tourists are welcome at all reservations in New Mexico on most days, though there are various restrictions. Since the religious ceremonies are sacred, photography is generally prohibited. This may also be true of certain sacred areas of the pueblo (in a few cases, the entire pueblo). Sometimes permission to photograph or draw is needed, and fees may be required. The

Santuario de Chimayo

ancient culture and traditions of these people hold great meaning; visitors should be as respectful of them as they would be of their own. Questions should be directed to the pueblo governor or representative at the tribal office.

More can be learned about New Mexico's Native Americans and their origins at the many museums and sites in Santa Fe (see), the visitor center at Bandelier National Monument (see) and the Indian Pueblo Cultural Center (see ALBUQUERQUE). For further information contact the Office of Indian Affairs, 228 E Palace Ave, Santa Fe 87501, phone 505/827-6440.

When to Go/Climate

Extreme variations in elevation and terrain make New Mexico's weather unpredictable and exciting. One minute the sun may be shining, the next could bring a cold, wind-whipping thunderstorm. Mountain temperatures can be freezing in winter; summers in the desert are hot and dry.

AVERAGE HIGH/LOW TEMPERATURES (°F)

ALBUQUERQUE

Jan 47/22	**May** 80/49	**Sept** 82/55
Feb 54/26	**June** 90/58	**Oct** 71/43
Mar 61/32	**July** 93/64	**Nov** 57/31
Apr 71/40	**Aug** 89/63	**Dec** 48/23

ROSWELL

Jan 54/25	**May** 85/55	**Sept** 86/59
Feb 60/29	**June** 94/62	**Oct** 77/47
Mar 68/36	**July** 95/67	**Nov** 66/35
Apr 77/45	**Aug** 92/65	**Dec** 56/26

CALENDAR HIGHLIGHTS

JANUARY

New Year's Celebration (Albuquerque). Taos Pueblo. Turtle dance. Albuquerque Convention Center. Phone 505/768-4575.

APRIL

Trinity Site Tour (Alamogordo). Visit to the site of the first A-bomb explosion; only time the site is open to the public. Phone 505/437-6120 or 800/826-0294.

JUNE

New Mexico Arts & Crafts Fair (Albuquerque). Fairgrounds. Exhibits and demonstrations by craftsworkers representing Spanish, Native American, and other North American cultures. Concerts in Popejoy Hall on the University of New Mexico campus. Phone 505/844-9043.

JULY

Taos Pueblo Pow-Wow (Taos). Taos Pueblo. Intertribal dancers from throughout US, Canada, and Mexico participate; competition. Phone 505/758-1028.

AUGUST

Inter-Tribal Indian Ceremonial (Gallup). Red Rock State Park. A major Native American festival; more than 50 tribes from the US, Canada, and Mexico participate in parades, rodeos, games, contests, dances, art and crafts sales. Phone 505/863-3896 or 800/233-4528.

Fiesta at Santo Domingo Pueblo (Santa Fe). Corn dance. This fiesta is probably the largest and most famous of the Rio Grande pueblo fiestas. Phone 505/465-2214.

Indian Market (Santa Fe). Santa Fe Plaza. One of largest juried displays of Native American art in the country. Dances, art. Make reservations at lodgings well in advance. Phone 505/983-5220 or 800/777-CITY.

SEPTEMBER

New Mexico State Fair (Albuquerque). Horseracing, rodeo, midway; entertainment. Phone 505/265-1791.

Enchanted Circle Century Bike Tour (Red River). Nearly 1,000 cyclists participate in a 100-mile tour around the Enchanted Circle (Red River, Angel Fire, Taos, Questa). Contact Chamber of Commerce. Phone 505/754-2366 or 800/348-6444.

Santa Fe Fiesta (Santa Fe). Sweeney Center. This ancient folk festival, dating back to 1712, features historical pageantry, religious observances, arts and crafts shows, street dancing. Celebrates the reconquest of Santa Fe by Don Diego de Vargas in 1692. Make reservations well in advance. Phone 505/955-6200 or 800/777-2489.

Southern New Mexico State Fair & Rodeo (Las Cruces). Phone 505/524-8612.

DECEMBER

Red Rock Balloon Rally (Gallup). Convention & Visitors Bureau. Phone 505/863-3841 or 800/242-4282.

Christmas Festivals (Acoma Pueblo). San Estevan del Rey Mission, Old Acoma; dances, luminarias. Tourist Visitation Center. Phone 505/740-4966 or 800/747-0181.

Parks and Recreation Finder

Directions to and information about the parks and recreation areas below are given under their respective town/city sections. Please refer to those sections for details.

NATIONAL PARK AND RECREATION AREAS

Key to abbreviations. I.H.S. = International Historic Site; I.P.M. = International Peace Memorial; N.B. = National Battlefield; N.B.P. = National Battlefield Park; N.B.C. = National Battlefield and Cemetery; N.C.A. = National Conservation Area; N.E.M. = National Expansion Memorial; N.F. = National Forest; N.G. = National Grassland; N.H.P. = National Historical Park; N.H.C. = National Heritage Corridor; N.H.S. = National Historic Site; N.L. = National Lakeshore; N.M. = National Monument; N.M.P. = National Military Park; N.Mem. = National Memorial; N.P. = National Park; N.Pres. = National Preserve; N.R.A. = National Recreational Area; N.R.R. = National Recreational River; N.Riv. = National River; N.S. = National Seashore; N.S.R. = National Scenic Riverway; N.S.T. = National Scenic Trail; N.Sc. = National Scientific Reserve; N.V.M. = National Volcanic Monument.

Place Name	Listed Under
Aztec Ruins N.M.	AZTEC
Bandelier N.M.	same
Capulin Volcano N.M.	RATON
Carlsbad Caverns N.P.	same
Carson N.F.	TAOS
Chaco Culture N.H.P.	same
Cibola N.F.	ALBUQUERQUE
El Malpais N.M. & N.C.A.	GRANTS
El Morro N.M.	same
Fort Union N.M.	LAS VEGAS
Gila Cliff Dwellings N.M.	SILVER CITY
Gila N.F.	SILVER CITY
Lincoln N.F.	ALAMOGORDO
Pecos N.H.P.	SANTA FE
Petroglyph N.M.	ALBUQUERQUE
Salinas Pueblo Missions N.M.	same
Santa Fe N.F.	SANTA FE
White Sands N.M.	same

STATE PARK AND RECREATION AREAS

Key to abbreviations. I.P. = Interstate Park; S.A.P. = State Archaeological Park; S.B. = State Beach; S.C.A. = State Conservation Area; S.C.P. = State Conservation Park; S.Cp. = State Campground; S.F. = State Forest; S.G. = State Garden; S.H.A. = State Historic Area; S.H.P. = State Historic Park; S.H.S. = State Historic Site; S.M.P. = State Marine Park; S.N.A. = State Natural Area; S.P. = State Park;

S.P.C. = State Public Campground; S.R. = State Reserve; S.R.A. = State Recreation Area; S.Res. = State Reservoir; S.Res.P. = State Resort Park; S.R.P. = State Rustic Park.

Place Name	Listed Under
Bluewater Lake S.P.	GRANTS
Bottomless Lakes S.P.	ROSWELL
Brantley Lake S.P.	CARLSBAD
Cimarron Canyon S.P.	ANGEL FIRE
City of Rocks S.P.	DEMING
El Vado Lake S.P.	CHAMA
Heron Lake S.P.	CHAMA
Hyde Memorial S.P.	SANTA FE
Living Desert Zoo and Gardens S.P.	CARLSBAD
Morphy Lake S.P.	LAS VEGAS
Navajo Lake S.P.	AZTEC
Oasis S.P.	PORTALES
Oliver Lee S.P.	ALAMOGORDO
Pancho Villa S.P.	DEMING
Red Rock S.P.	GALLUP
Rio Grande Nature Center S.P.	ALBUQUERQUE
Rockhound S.P.	DEMING
Storrie Lake S.P.	LAS VEGAS
Sugarite Canyon S.P.	RATON

Water-related activities, hiking, riding, various other sports, picnicking, camping, and visitor centers are available in many of these areas. Most parks are open all year. Day-use fee per vehicle is $4 at most parks. Camping: $8-$10/day; electrical hookups $4 (where available); sewage hookups $4. Limit 14 consecutive days during any 20-day period; pets on leash only. Annual entrance passes and camping permits available. For further information contact the New Mexico State Park and Recreation Division, PO Box 1147, Santa Fe 87504-1147, phone 888/NM-PARKS.

SKI AREAS

Place Name	Listed Under
Angel Fire Ski Resort	ANGEL FIRE
Sandia Peak Tramway Ski Area	ALBUQUERQUE
Santa Fe Ski Area	SANTA FE
Sipapu Ski Area	TAOS
Ski Apache Resort	RUIDOSO
Snow Canyon Ski Area	CLOUDCROFT
Taos Valley	TAOS

For ski reports call Snowphone from November-April for a two-minute tape on snow conditions, 505/984-0606.

FISHING AND HUNTING

Nonresident fishing license (includes trout stamp): annual $40; five-day $17; one-day $9. Nonresident hunting license: deer $190-$310; bear $160; cougar $210; elk $281-$756; antelope $192; turkey $75. (Fees include $1 vendor fee.)

New Mexico, with six of the seven life zones found on the North American continent, has a large number of wildlife species, among them four varieties of deer, as well as mountain lion, bear, elk, Rocky Mountain and Desert Bighorn sheep, oryx, antelope, javelina, Barbary sheep, ibex, wild turkey, goose, duck, quail, pheasant, and squirrel. There is good fishing for trout in mountain streams and lakes; bass, bluegill, crappie, walleye, and catfish can also be found in many of the warmer waters.

Hunting and fishing regulations are complex and vary from year to year. For detailed information contact the New Mexico Game and Fish Department, Villagra Bldg, 408 Galisteo, Santa Fe 87503, phone 800/862-9310.

Driving Information

Safety belts are mandatory for all persons in front seat of vehicle. Children under 11 yrs must be in an approved passenger restraint anywhere in vehicle: ages 5-10 may use a regulation seat belt; ages 1-4 may use a regulation seat belt in back seat, however, in front seat children must use an approved safety seat; under age one must be in an approved safety seat. Phone 505/827-0427.

INTERSTATE HIGHWAY SYSTEM

The following alphabetical listing of New Mexico towns in *Mobil Travel Guide* shows that these cities are within ten miles of the indicated Interstate highways. A highway map should, however, be checked for the nearest exit.

Highway Number	Cities/Towns within ten miles
Interstate 10	Deming, Las Cruces.
Interstate 25	Albuquerque, Las Cruces, Las Vegas, Raton, Santa Fe, Socorro, Truth or Consequences.
Interstate 40	Albuquerque, Gallup, Grants, Santa Rosa, Tucumcari.

Additional Visitor Information

For free information, contact the New Mexico Department of Tourism, Lamy Building, Room 751, 491 Old Santa Fe Trail, Santa Fe 87503, phone 505/827-7400 or 800/733-6396. *New Mexico,* a colorful, illustrated magazine, is published monthly; to order, contact *New Mexico Magazine* at the Lew Wallace Building, 495 Old Santa Fe Trail, Santa Fe 87501, phone 505/827-7447 or 800/435-0715.

There are several welcome centers in New Mexico; visitors who stop by will find information and brochures helpful when planning stops at points of interest. They are located in Anthony (24 mi S of Las Cruces on I-10); Chama (just off US 64/84); Gallup (I-40 exit 22); Glenrio (31 mi E of Tucumcari on I-40); La Bajada (11 mi S of Santa Fe on I-25); Lordsburg (on I-10); Raton (off I-25); Santa Fe (downtown); and Texico (7 mi E of Clovis on US 70/84).

THE WILD (AND NOT SO WILD) WEST

This two- to three-day tour from Las Cruces offers a combination of scenic and technological wonders, hiking and fishing opportunities, and a glimpse into the Wild West. From Las Cruces head northeast on US 70 to White Sands National Monument. This huge beach may lack an ocean but offers a seemingly endless expanse of sparkling white gypsum dunes. You'll drive among the dunes along a 16-mile scenic drive, which also provides access to the monument's four hiking trails. Or just take off on foot into the dunes, where kids will have endless hours of fun sliding down the mountains of sand on oversized plastic saucers (available at the monument's gift shop). Visiting the monument is best either early or late in the day, when the dunes display mysterious and often surreal shadows.

Continue northeast on US 70 to Alamogordo, a good spot to spend the night. Attractions here include the Space Center, where you can test your skills as a pilot in a Space Shuttle simulator, explore the International Space Hall of Fame, and see a show at the Tombaugh Omnimax Theater. Also in town is the Alameda Park Zoo and the Toy Train Depot, a museum containing a fascinating collection of toy trains, some dating from the 1800s. The Depot is lots of fun for kids, but its biggest fans are probably baby boomers who reminisce about their childhood trains as they examine the best and sometimes worst electric trains of the '40s and '50s, including Lionel's tremendous marketing flop—the pink train just for girls. About 12 miles south of Alamogordo via US 54 is Oliver Lee Memorial State Park, with a short, pleasant nature trail along a shaded stream, plus a rugged hiking trail that climbs up the side of a mountain and offers spectacular views. The park also includes the ruins of a pioneer cabin and a museum that tells the story of the site's often violent past.

From Alamogordo, go north on US 54 to Tularosa, where you can visit Tularosa Vineyards to sample the local wine and stop at the small but interesting Tularosa Basin Historical Society Museum. Then head east on US 70 into the Sacramento Mountains to the resort community of Ruidoso, whose name (Spanish for "noisy") comes from the babbling Ruidoso Creek. Surrounded by the Lincoln National Forest, this picturesque town is a good base for hiking and fishing and is another possibility for overnight lodging. Nearby is the village of Ruidoso Downs, home of Ruidoso Downs Race Track, which offers quarter horse and thoroughbred racing, and the Hubbard Museum of the American West, with displays on horses, horse racing, and related items. Head east out of Ruidoso Downs to Hondo, then turn back to the northwest on US 380, which leads to Lincoln. This genuine Wild West town, which is preserved as a state monument, was the site of a jail break by famed outlaw Billy the Kid. It's also known for the notorious Lincoln County War, in which ranchers and merchants staged a lengthy and bloody battle for beef contracts for a nearby fort.

Continue west on US 380 to the town of Capitan for a visit to Smokey Bear Historical State Park, with exhibits and the grave of the orphaned bear cub who was found in a forest fire near here and became a symbol of forest fire prevention. Leaving Capitan, drive west on US 380 to the town of Carrizozo and cross US 54. Continue four miles to the Valley of Fires National Recreation Site, where a short trail provides close-up views of numerous jet-black lava formations. Now return to Carrizozo and head south on US 54 to the turnoff to Three Rivers Petroglyph Site, one of the best places in the Southwest to see prehistoric rock art. An easy trail meanders along a hillside where there are thousands of images, ranging from geometric patterns to handprints to a variety of animals (some pierced by arrows or spears) created by the Mogollon people at least 1,000 years ago. To return to Las Cruces, take US 54 south through Tularosa and Alamogordo; turn southwest on US 70. (APPROX 349 MI)

Acoma Pueblo

See also Albuquerque, Grants

Pop 4,000 **Elev** 7,000 ft
Information Tourist Visitation Center, PO Box 309, Acoma 87034; 505/740-4966 or 800/747-0181

On a mesa rising 367 feet from the surrounding plain is perhaps the oldest continuously inhabited town in the United States. The exact date of establishment is not known, but archaeologists have dated occupation of the "Sky City" to at least 1150. Legend says it has been inhabited since the time of Christ.

Acoma is a beautiful pueblo with the mission church San Esteban del Rey. This mission probably includes part of the original built by Fray Ramirez in 1629. Beams 40 feet long and 14 inches square were carried from the mountains 30 miles away; even the dirt for the graveyard was carried up by Native Americans. They farmed on the plain below and caught water in rock basins on top. The Acoma are skilled potters and excellent stockbreeders.

The pueblo is about 12 miles south of I-40 and is accessible from exit 102. Tours leave from the base of the pueblo at the Visitor Center, where a shuttle bus takes visitors to the pueblo on top of the mesa (fee). Visitors may walk down the steep, narrow "stairway" to the Visitor Center after the tour.

There is a museum with Native American pottery and history exhibits (circa 1400 to the present). (Daily) **FREE**

Acoma-made crafts, native foods, tours, and a cultural and historical exhibit can be seen at the Visitor Center below Sky City.

Once or twice a year special religious ceremonials are held at which no outsiders are permitted, but there are several festivals (see SPECIAL EVENTS) to which the public is welcome. (Daily; closed pueblo holidays, mid-July, and first or second weekend October) Your guide will explain the rules and courtesies of taking pictures (picture-taking fee; no video or movie cameras).

Approximately one mile north on NM 23 is the **Enchanted Mesa,** 400 feet high. According to an Acoma legend, the tribe lived on top of this mesa until a sudden, violent storm washed out the only way up. Visitors are not permitted to climb to the mesa.

Special Events

Governor's Feast. Old Acoma. Dances. Early Feb.

Santa Maria Feast. McCarty's Village Mission. First Sun May. Phone 800/766-4405.

Fiesta (St. Lorenzo's) Day. In Acomita. Mid-Aug.

Feast of St. Estevan. Old Acoma. Harvest dance. Early Sept.

Christmas Festivals. San Estevan del Rey Mission, Old Acoma. Dances, luminarias. Late Dec. Phone 800/766-4405.

Alamogordo

(F-4) *See also Cloudcroft, Mescalero, Ruidoso*

Founded 1898 **Pop** 35,582 **Elev** 4,350 ft **Area code** 505 **Zip** 88310
Information Chamber of Commerce, 1301 N White Sands Blvd, PO Box 518; 505/437-6120 or 800/826-0294
Web www.alamogordo.com

What to See and Do

Alameda Park Zoo. A seven-acre zoo with more than 300 native and exotic animals. (Daily; closed Jan 1, Dec 25) 10th and White Sands Blvd (US 54/70). Phone 505/439-4290. ¢¢

Lincoln National Forest. Fishing; hunting, picnicking, camping, wild cave tours, and winter sports in the Sacramento, Capitan, and Guadalupe mountains. Backpack in the White Mtn Capitan Wildernesses. Some campsites in developed areas free, some require fee. Contact the Supervisor's Office, Federal Building, 1101 New York Ave. E of town. Phone 505/434-7200.

⭐ **New Mexico Museum of Space History.** Museum features space-related artifacts and exhibits; self-guided tour (daily; closed Dec 25). 2 mi E via US 54, Indian Wells and Scenic Dr. Phone 505/437-2840. ¢¢ Combination ticket incl Museum of Space History and

Tombaugh IMAX Theater. Planetarium with Omnimax movies (daily). Features laser light shows (Fri, Sat eves). ¢¢¢

Oliver Lee State Park. (Dog Canyon) Mecca for mountain climbers, photographers, and history buffs. Early Apache stronghold, site of at least five major battles; box canyon protected by 2,000-ft bluff; mossy bluffs, cottonwood trees; Frenchy's Place, a substantial rock house with mi of stone fence. Hiking, camping (hookups, dump station). Visitor center (daily), museum, tours of restored Lee Ranch House (Sat and Sun, mid-afternoon; also by appt). 10 mi S via US 54, E on County A16. Phone 505/437-8284. Per vehicle ¢¢ Camping ¢¢¢

Three Rivers Petroglyph Site. Twenty thousand rock carvings made between A.D. 900-1400 by the Jornada Branch of the Mogollon Indian Culture; semidesert terrain; interpretive signs; reconstructed prehistoric village; six picnic sites; tent and trailer sites (no hookups). 29 mi N on US 54 to Three Rivers, then 5 mi E on county road. Phone 505/525-4300. ¢¢

Toy Train Depot. Over 1,200 ft of model railroad track and hundreds of model and toy trains are on display in five-rm, 100-yr-old train depot. Also 2-mi outdoor miniature railroad track (rides). Gift and model shop. (Wed-Sun) 1991 N White Sands Blvd, N end of Alameda Park. Phone 888/207-3564. ¢

Special Events

New Mexico Museum of Space History Induction Ceremonies. Phone 505/437-2840 or 877/333-6589. (Call for schedule.)

Trinity Site Tour. Visit to the site of the first A-bomb explosion; only time the site is open to the public. Phone 505/437-6120 or 800/826-0294. First Sat Apr and Oct.

Motels/Motor Lodges

⭐⭐ **BEST WESTERN DESERT AIRE MOTOR INN.** *1021 S White Sands Blvd (88310). 505/437-2110; fax 505/437-1898; res 800/780-7234. www.bestwestern.com.* 100 rms, 2 story. S $47-$57; D $58; under 16 free. Crib free. Pet accepted, some restrictions. TV; cable. Heated pool; whirlpool. Sauna. Complimentary continental bkfst. Ck-out noon. Coin lndry. Valet serv. Sundries. Game rm. Microwaves avail. Cr cds: A, C, D, DS, MC, V.
🖭 🐾 ➳ ⊠ 🔥

⭐⭐ **DAYS INN.** *907 S White Sands Blvd (88310). 505/437-5090; fax 505/434-5667; res 800/329-7466. www.daysinn.com.* 120 rms, 2 story. S $38-$65; D $46-$52; each addl $8. TV; cable (premium). Pool. Complimentary continental bkfst. Restaurant adj open 24 hrs. Ck-out noon. Coin lndry. Refrigerators; microwaves avail. Cr cds: A, C, D, DS, ER, JCB, MC, V.
🖭 ➳ ⊠ 🔥

⭐ **SATELLITE INN.** *2224 N White Sands Blvd (88310). 505/437-8454; toll-free 800/221-7690. www.satelliteinn.com.* 40 rms, 1-2 story. S $32-$34; D $34-$38; each addl $2; kit. unit $38-$46; family unit $36-$42. Crib free. Pet accepted. TV; cable (premium), VCR avail (movies). Pool. Restaurant adj 6 am-9 pm. Ck-out noon. Refrigerators, microwaves avail. Cr cds: A, C, D, DS, MC, V.
🐾 ➳ ⊠ 🔥

⭐⭐ **WHITE SANDS INN.** *1020 S White Sands Blvd (88310). 505/434-4200; fax 505/437-8872. www.nmohwy.com.* 92 units, 2 story, 16 suites. S $42-$54; D $50-$65; each addl $5; suites $55; under 12 free. Crib free. TV; cable (premium). Heated pool; whirlpool. Complimentary continental bkfst. Coffee in rms. Restaurant adj open 24 hrs. Ck-out noon. Coin lndry. Meeting rms. Business servs avail. Valet serv. Refrigerators, microwaves. Cr cds: A, C, D, DS, MC, V.
🖭 ➳ ⊠ 🔥

Restaurant

⭐ **CHINA WEST.** *905 S White Sands Blvd (88310). 505/437-8644.* Chinese menu. Specializes in seafood, chicken, beef. Hrs: 11 am-9 pm. Res accepted. Bar. Lunch $3.95-$6.95, dinner $9.95-$22.95. Chinese decor. Cr cds: A, D, DS, MC, V.

Albuquerque (C-3)

Founded 1706 **Pop** 448,607
Elev 5,311 ft **Area code** 505
Information Convention & Visitors Bureau, 20 First Plaza NW, PO Box 26866, 87125; 505/842-9918 or 800/284-2282

Web www.abqcvb.org

Additional Visitor Information

For further information and a list of sightseeing tours contact the Convention & Visitors Bureau, 20 First Plaza NW, 505/842-9918 or 800/284-2282. For information on public transportation phone 505/843-9200.

What to See and Do

Albuquerque Biological Park. Biological park consists of Albuquerque Aquarium, Rio Grande Botanic Garden, and Rio Grande Zoo. Aquarium consists of shark tank, eel tunnel, shrimp boat. Botanic Gardens display formal walled gardens and a glass conservatory. Zoo exhibits incl koala creek, sea lion exhibit and shows. Gift shops; restaurants. (Daily; closed Jan 1, Thanksgiving, Dec 25) 2601 Central Ave NW. Phone 505/764-6200. ¢¢¢

Albuquerque Museum. Regional museum of art and history; traveling exhibits; solar-heated building. (Tues-Sun; closed hols) 2000 Mountain Rd NW. Phone 505/243-7255. ¢¢

Cibola National Forest. More than 1½ million acres located throughout central New Mexico. Incl Mt Taylor (11,301 ft), several mountain ranges, and four wilderness areas: Sandia Mtn, Manzano Mtn, Apache Kid, and Withington. Scenic drives; bighorn sheep in Sandia Mtns. Fishing; hunting, picnicking, camping (some fees). La Cienega Nature Trail is for the dis-

abled and visually impaired. Contact the Supervisor, 2113 Osuna Rd NE, Suite A, 87113. Phone 505/346-3900.

Coronado State Monument. Coronado is said to have camped near this excavated pueblo in 1540 on his famous but unsuccessful quest for the seven golden cities of Cibola. Reconstructed, painted kiva; visitor center devoted to Southwestern culture and the Spanish influence on the area. Picnicking. (Daily; closed hols) 15 mi N on I-25, then 1 mi W on NM 44. ¢¢

Indian Pueblo Cultural Center. Owned and operated by the 19 pueblos of New Mexico. Exhibits in museum feature the story of the Pueblo culture, Pueblo Gallery with handcrafted art, Native American dance and craft demonstrations (wkends). Restaurant. (Daily; closed Jan 1, Thanksgiving, Dec 25) 2401 12th St NW. Phone 505/843-7270. ¢¢

Isleta Pueblo. (Population: 1,703; altitude: 4,885 ft) A prosperous pueblo with church originally built by Fray Juan de Salas. The church was burned during the Pueblo Rebellion of 1680 and later rebuilt; beautiful sanctuary and altar. Recreation area 4 mi NE across river incl stocked fishing lakes (fee); picnicking, camping (electricity, water avail, two-wk limit), concession. Pueblo (daily). 1905 Mountain Rd. Phone 505/869-3111. ¢¢

National Atomic Museum. History and nuclear energy science center; films, tours, exhibits depicting history of atomic age. (Daily; closed hols) Necessary identification for admission to the base incl: valid driver's license (driver only), vehicle registration, proof of insurance, car rental paperwork. Kirtland Air Force Base (E), Building 20358; 2½ mi S of I-40 on Wyoming Blvd. Phone 505/845-6670. **FREE**

New Mexico Museum of Natural History. Exhibits on botany, geology, paleontology, and zoology; naturalist center, Dynamax theater, cafe, shop. (Daily; closed hols) 1801 Mountain Rd NW. Phone 505/841-2800. ¢¢

🟦 **Old Town.** The original settlement is 1 blk N of Central Ave, the city's main street, at Rio Grande Blvd. Old Town Plaza retains a lovely Spanish flavor with many interesting shops and restaurants. (See SPECIAL EVENTS)

Petroglyph National Monument. In the West Mesa area; contains concentrated groups of rock drawings believed to have been carved on lava formations by ancestors of the Pueblo. Three walking trails along the 17-mi escarpment. Picnicking. (Daily) 3 ½ mi N of I-40. Phone 505/899-0205. Per vehicle ¢

Rio Grande Nature Center State Park. Visitor center, glass-enclosed observation rm overlooking 3 acre pond, interpretive displays on wildlife of the *bosque* (cottonwood groves) along the river, two mi of nature trails. (Daily; closed Jan 1, Thanksgiving, Dec 25) E bank of Rio Grande, at 2901 Candelaria Rd NW. Phone 505/344-7240. ¢

Rio Grande Zoo. More than 1,200 exotic animals in exhibits among a grove of cottonwoods. Rain forest, reptile house, Ape Country, Cat Walk, white tigers. (Daily; closed Jan 1, Thanksgiving, Dec 25) 903 10th St SW. Phone 505/764-6200. ¢¢

Skiing. Sandia Peak Tramway Ski Area. Area has four double chairlifts,

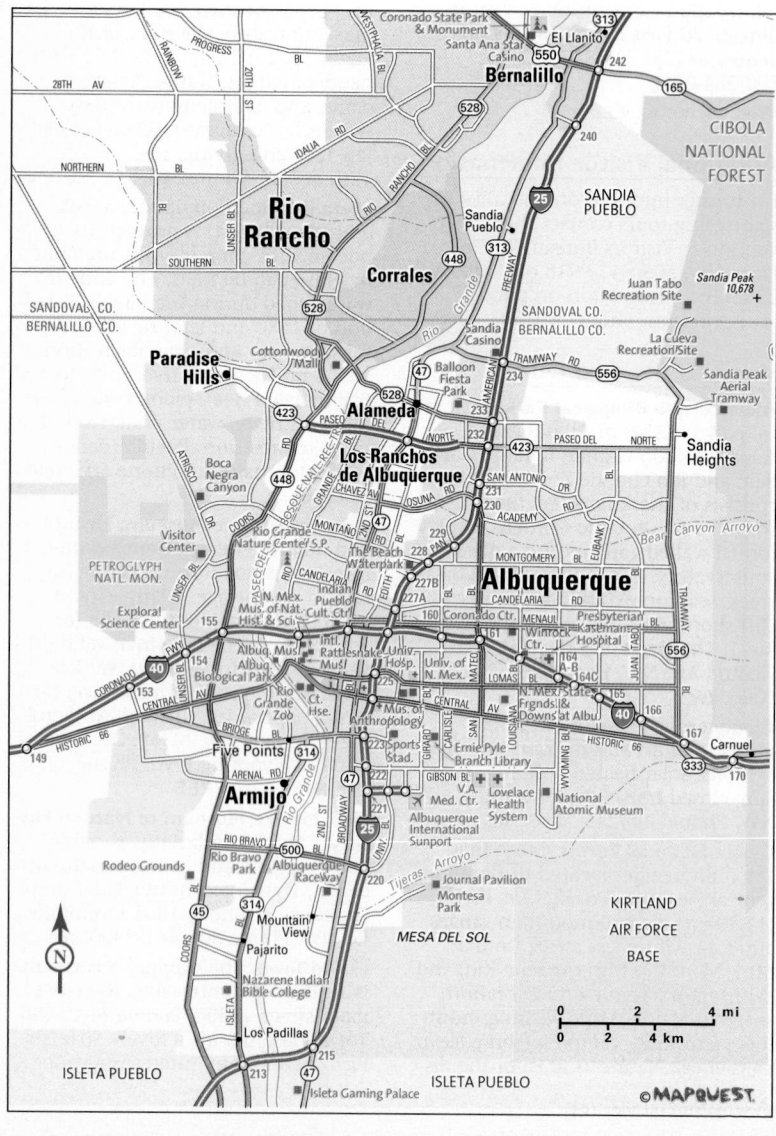

surface lift; patrol, school, rentals, snowmaking, cafe, restaurant, bar. Aerial tramway on west side of mountain meets lifts at top. Longest run over 2½ mi; vertical drop 1,700 ft. (Mid-Dec-Mar, daily) Chairlift also operates July-Labor Day (Fri-Sun; fee). 16 mi E on I-40, then 7 mi N on NM 14, then 6 mi NW on NM 536, in Cibola National Forests, Crest Scenic Byway, Sandia Mtns. Phone 505/242-9133. ¢¢¢¢

Sandia Peak Aerial Tramway. From tram base at 6,559 ft, travels almost three mi up west slope of Sandia Mtns to 10,378 ft. Hiking trail, restaurant at summit, and Mexican grill at base.(Daily; closed two wks late Apr and two wks late Oct) Parking (fee). 5 mi NE of city limits via I-25 and Tramway Rd. Phone 505/856-7325 or 505/856-6419. ¢¢¢

Telephone Pioneer Museum. Displays trace the development of the telephone from 1876-present. More than 400 types of telephones; switchboards, early equipment, old telephone directories. 110 4th St NW Phone 505/842-2937. ¢

University of New Mexico. (1889) 25,000 students. This campus shows both Spanish and Pueblo architectural influences. It is one of the largest universities in the Southwest. Special outdoor sports course for the disabled, N of Johnson Gym. E of I-25, Central Ave exit. Contact Visitor Center at the corner of Las Lomas and Redondo Sts. Phone 505/277-1989. On campus are

Fine Arts Center. Houses University Art Museum featuring more than 23,000 pieces in collection of fine arts (Tues-Fri, also Sun afternoons; phone 505/277-4001; free); Fine Arts Library, which contains the Southwest Music Archives; Rodey Theatre; 2,094-seat Popejoy Hall, home of New Mexico Symphony Orchestra and host to Best of Broadway International Theatre seasons of plays, dance, and music (phone 505/277-2111). Just NW of university's Stanford Dr and Central Ave main entrance.

Jonson Gallery. Houses archives and work of modernist painter Raymond Jonson (1891-1982) and a few works by his contemporaries.

Also exhibitions on the arts in New Mexico. (Tues-Fri; closed hols) 1909 Las Lomas NE. Phone 505/277-4967. **Donation**

Maxwell Museum of Anthropology. Permanent and changing exhibits of early man and Native American cultures with an emphasis on the Southwest. (Tues-Sat; closed hols) Redondo Dr, in Anthropology Building. Phone 505/277-4405. **FREE**

Museum of Geology and Institute of Meteoritics Meteorite Museum. Museum of Geology contains numerous samples of ancient plants, minerals, rocks, and animals. Meteorite Museum has major collection of over 200 meteorites. Both museums (Mon-Fri). Part of Earth and Planetary Science Dept, in Northrop Hall. Phone 505/277-4204. **Donation**

Special Events

Musical Theater Southwest. Highland Theater. Five musicals each season. Phone 505/262-9301. (yr-round) 4804 Central Ave SE.

Founders Day. In Old Town. Phone 505/768-3483. Late Apr.

New Mexico Arts & Crafts Fair. At Fairgrounds. Exhibits and demonstrations by craftsworkers representing Spanish, Native American, and other North American cultures. Last wkend June.

Santa Ana Feast Day. Santa Ana and Taos Pueblos. Corn dance. Late July.

Albuquerque Little Theatre. Historic community theater; Broadway productions. Phone 505/242-4750. Aug-May.

St. Augustin's Feast Day. Dances at Isleta Pueblo. Late Aug.

New Mexico State Fair. Fairgrounds, San Pedro Dr between Lomas and Central blvds. Horse racing, rodeo, midway; entertainment. Phone 505/265-1791. Sept.

New Mexico Symphony Orchestra. Concerts in Popejoy Hall on the University of New Mexico campus. Phone 505/881-9590 or 800/251-NMSO. Sept-May.

Kodak Albuquerque International Balloon Fiesta. First two wkends Oct beginning with first Sat.

Motels/Motor Lodges

★ ★ **BEST WESTERN INN AT RIO RANCHO.** *1465 Rio Rancho Blvd, Rio Rancho (87124). 505/892-1700; fax 505/892-4628; res 800/528-1902. www.innatriorancho.com.* 121 rms, 10 kits. S $55-$73; D $61-$79; each addl $6; kit. units $61-$67; under 12 free. Crib $6. Pet accepted, some restrictions; $6/day. TV; cable (premium). Pool; whirlpool, poolside serv. Coffee in rms. Restaurant 6:30 am-10 pm. Rm serv. Bar 11 am-midnight; Sun noon-midnight; entertainment. Ck-out 11 am. Coin lndry. Meeting rms. Business servs avail. In-rm modem link. Valet serv. Sundries. Gift shop. Free airport, RR station, bus depot transportation. Golf privileges, greens fee, pro, putting green, driving range. Downhill/x-country ski 20 mi. Exercise equipt. Lawn games. Microwaves avail. Some in-rm whirlpools. Picnic tables, grills. Cr cds: DS, ER, V.

★ ★ **BEST WESTERN WINROCK INN.** *18 NE Winrock Ctr (87110). 505/883-5252; fax 505/889-3206; toll-free 800/780-7234. www.bestwestern. com.* 173 rms, 2 story. S, D $69-$99; each addl $10; suites $125; under 18 free. Crib free. TV; cable. Heated pool. Complimentary bkfst buffet. Restaurant nearby. Ck-out noon. Coin lndry. Meeting rms. Business servs avail. Bellhops. Health club privileges. Some refrigerators. Cr cds: A, C, D, DS, MC, V.

★ ★ **CLUBHOUSE INN ALBU-QUERQUE.** *1315 Menaul Blvd NE (87107). 505/345-0010; fax 505/344-3911. www.clubhouseinn.com.* 137 units, 2 story, 17 kit. suites. S $74; D $84; each addl $10; kit. suites $89-$105; under 16 free; wkly, wkend rates. Crib free. TV; cable (premium). Heated pool; whirlpool. Complimentary bkfst buffet. Ck-out noon. Meeting rms. Business servs avail. Health club privileges. Private patios, balconies. Picnic tables, grills. Cr cds: A, C, D, DS, MC, V.

★ ★ **COMFORT INN EAST.** *13031 Central Ave NE (87123). 505/294-1800; fax 505/293-1088; res 800/228-5150. www.comfortinn.com.* 122 rms, 2 story. May-mid-Sept: S $49-$57; D $55-$63; each addl $6; under 18 free. Crib free. Pet accepted; $3/day. TV; cable (premium). Pool; whirlpools. Complimentary full bkfst, coffee in rms. Restaurant 6-10 am, 5-8:30 pm; Sat, Sun 6-11 am, 5-8:30 pm. Ck-out noon. Coin lndry. Meeting rms. Business servs avail. Refrigerators. Picnic area. Downhill ski 9 mi. Cr cds: A, C, D, DS, JCB, MC, V.

★ ★ **COURTYARD BY MARRIOTT.** *1920 S Yale Blvd (87106). 505/843-6600; fax 505/843-8740; res 800/321-2211. www.courtyard.com.* 150 rms, 4 story. S $61-$94; D $104; suites $115-$125; under 12 free; wkend rates. Crib free. TV; cable (premium). Indoor pool; whirlpool. Complimentary coffee in rms. Restaurant 6 am-10 am, 5-10 pm; Sat, Sun 7 am-11 am. Rm serv. Bar 4-11 pm. Ck-out noon. Meeting rms. Business servs avail. In-rm modem link. Valet serv. Free airport transportation. Downhill/x-country ski 15 mi. Exercise equipt. Refrigerator in suites. Balconies. Picnic tables. Cr cds: A, C, D, DS, JCB, MC, V.

★ **DAYS INN.** *6031 Iliff Rd NW (87121). 505/836-3297; fax 505/836-1214; toll-free 800/329-7466. www.daysinn.com.* 80 rms, 2 story. June-Oct: S $55-$75; D $60-$80; each addl $5; under 12 free. Pet accepted; $5/day. TV; cable (premium). Heated indoor pool; whirlpool. Sauna. Complimentary continental bkfst. Restaurant nearby. Ck-out 11 am. Guest lndry. Business servs avail. Downhill/x-country ski 10 mi. Cr cds: A, C, D, DS, JCB, MC, V.

★ **DAYS INN.** *13317 NE Central Ave (87123). 505/294-3297; fax 505/293-3973; res 800/329-7466. www.daysinn.com.* 72 rms, 2 story. S $52-$60; D $55-$65; each addl $5; under 12 free. Crib free. TV; cable (premium). Indoor pool; whirlpool. Sauna. Restaurant adj open 24 hrs. Ck-out 11 am. Business servs avail. Cr cds: A, C, D, DS, ER, MC, V.

★ ★ **HAMPTON INN.** *5101 Ellison NE (87109). 505/344-1555; fax 505/345-2216; toll-free 800/426-7866.*

www.hamptoninn.com. 125 rms, 3 story. S $57-$62; D $62-$67; under 18 free. Crib free. Pet accepted, some restrictions. TV; cable (premium). Heated pool. Complimentary continental bkfst. Coffee in rms. Restaurant nearby. Ck-out noon. Coin lndry. Health club privileges. Cr cds: A, C, D, DS, MC, V.

[D] [icons]

★★ **HOLIDAY INN EXPRESS.**
10330 Hotel Ave NE (87123). 505/275-8900; fax 505/275-6000; res 800/465-4329. www.holidayinnexpress.com. 104 rms, 2 story. S $75; D $84; each addl $5; suites $95-$100; under 18 free; higher rates special events. Crib free. Pet accepted; $5. TV; cable (premium), VCR avail. Complimentary continental bkfst. Complimentary coffee in rms. Restaurant 5 am-10 pm. Rm serv. Ck-out noon. Meeting rms. Business servs avail. In-rm modem link. Coin lndry. Downhill/x-country ski 15 mi. Exercise equipt; sauna. Indoor pool; whirlpool. Bathrm phones, refrigerators, microwaves. Some in-rm whirlpools, balconies. Cr cds: A, D, DS, MC, V.

[D] [icons]

★★★ **HOLIDAY INN MOUNTAINVIEW.** *2020 Menaul NE (87107). 505/884-2511; fax 505/884-5720; res 800/465-4329. www.holiday-inn.com.* 360 rms, 4-5 story. S, D $99-$109; each addl $10; under 18 free. Crib free. Pet accepted; $25. TV; cable (premium). Heated pool; whirlpool; poolside serv. Coffee in rms. Restaurant 6:30 am-2 pm, 5-10 pm. Rm serv. Bar 1 pm-1 am; Sun 11 am-midnight. Ck-out noon. Coin lndry. Meeting rms. Business servs avail. Bellhops. Valet serv. Sundries. Downhill ski 15 mi. Exercise equipt; sauna. Some private patios, balconies. Free airport transportation. Cr cds: A, D, DS, MC, V.

[D] [icons]

★ **HOWARD JOHNSON EXPRESS.**
411 Mcknight Ave NW (87102). 505/242-5228; fax 505/766-9218; res 800/446-4656. www.hojo.com. 100 rms, 4 story. S $44-$62; D $49-$79; each addl $4; suites $57.59-$63.89; under 18 free. Crib free. TV; cable (premium). Heated pool; whirlpool. Complimentary continental bkfst. Restaurant adj open 24 hrs; Sun to

11 pm. Ck-out noon. Meeting rm. Business servs avail. Some minibars. Cr cds: A, D, DS, JCB, MC, V.

[D] [icons] SC

★ **HOWARD JOHNSON HOTEL.**
15 Hotel Cir NE (87123). 505/296-4852; fax 505/293-9072; res 800/446-4656. www.hojo.com. 150 rms, 2 story. S, D $48-$88; each addl $5; under 18 free. Crib free. TV; cable (premium). Heated pool; whirlpool. Restaurant 6 am-10 pm. Rm serv. Complimentary continental bkfst, coffee in rms. Ck-out noon. Coin lndry. Business servs avail. In-rm modem link. Bellhops. Valet serv. Free airport, RR station, bus depot transportation. Exercise equipt. Some refrigerators, whirlpool suites. Cr cds: A, C, D, DS, ER, MC, V.

[D] [icons]

★★ **LA QUINTA INN.** *2116 Yale Blvd SE (87106). 505/243-5500; fax 505/247-8288; toll-free 800/531-5900. www.laquinta.com.* 105 rms, 3 story. S $69; D $75; each addl $7; suites $99; under 18 free. Crib free. Pet accepted, some restrictions. TV; cable (premium). Pool. Continental bkfst. Restaurant adj 6 am-10 pm. Ck-out noon. Coin lndry. Business servs avail. Valet serv. Free airport transportation. Downhill ski 20 mi. Microwave in suites. Cr cds: A, C, D, DS, MC, V.

[D] [icons] SC

★★ **LE BARON COURTYARD AND SUITES.** *2120 Menaul Blvd NE (87107). 505/884-0250; fax 505/883-0594. www.lebaronabq.com.* 200 units, 2 story, 33 suites. S, D $55-$64; suites $76-$135; under 12 free. Crib free. TV; cable (premium). Heated pool. Complimentary continental bkfst. Coffee in rms. Restaurant adj open 24 hrs. Ck-out noon. Coin lndry. Meeting rms. Business servs avail. Valet serv. Free airport transportation. Downhill ski 15 mi. Bathrm phones; some refrigerators. Cr cds: A, C, D, DS, MC, V.

[icons]

★★ **PLAZA INN.** *900 Medical Arts NE (87102). 505/243-5693; fax 505/843-6229; toll-free 800/237-1307. www.plazainnabq.com.* 120 rms, 5 story. S, D $85-$117; each addl $10; under 18 free. Pet accepted. TV.

Indoor pool; whirlpools. Restaurant 6 am-midnight. Bar 11-2 am; Sun noon-midnight. Ck-out noon. Coin lndry. Meeting rms. Business servs avail. Valet serv. Free airport, RR station, bus depot transportation. Downhill ski 14 mi. Exercise equipt. Health club privileges. Some refrigerators. Private patios, balconies. Cr cds: A, DS, MC, V.

★★ **RAMADA LIMITED.** *1801 Yale Blvd SE (87106). 505/242-0036; fax 505/242-0068; res 888/298-2054. www.ramada.com.* 76 rms, 3 story, 12 suites. Apr-Oct: S $55-$95; D $65-$105; each addl $10; suites $99-$105; under 18 free; wkend rates; higher rates special events; lower rates rest of yr. Crib free. TV; cable. 2 pools, 1 indoor; whirlpool. Complimentary continental bkfst. Coffee in rms. Restaurant opp 11 am-midnight. Ck-out 11 am. Meeting rms. Business servs avail. In-rm modem link. Valet serv. Coin lndry. Free airport transportation. Downhill/x-country ski 20 mi. Exercise equipt; sauna. Some refrigerators. Some balconies. Cr cds: A, C, D, JCB, MC, V.

★★ **RAMADA MOUNTAINVIEW.** *25 Hotel Cir NE (87123). 505/271-1000; fax 505/291-9028; toll-free 888/298-2054. www.ramada.com.* 205 rms, 2 story. S $49-$85; D $59-$95; each addl $10; suites $89-$150; under 18 free; wkend rates. Crib free. Pet accepted. TV; cable (premium). Coffee in rms. Heated pool. Restaurant 6 am-2 pm, 5-10 pm. Rm serv. Bar 2 pm-midnight; Sun from 1 pm. Ck-out noon. Coin lndry. Meeting rms. Business servs avail. Valet serv. Free airport transportation. Downhill ski 10 mi. Refrigerators, microwaves. Cr cds: A, C, D, DS, JCB, MC, V.

★ **TRAVELODGE-TRAMWAY.** *13139 Central Ave NE (87123). 505/292-4878; fax 505/299-1822; res 800/515-6375. www.travelodge.com.* 41 rms, 2 story. May-Dec: S, D $40-$60; each addl $5; under 17 free; lower rates rest of yr. Crib free. Pet accepted, some restrictions; $5. TV; cable (premium). Complimentary continental bkfst. Complimentary coffee in rms. Restaurant nearby. Ck-out 11 am. Business servs avail.

Downhill/x-country ski 8 mi. Cr cds: A, D, DS, MC, V.

★★ **WYNDHAM GARDEN HOTEL.** *6000 Pan American Fwy NE (87109). 505/798-4300; fax 505/798-4305; res 800/996-3426. www.wyndham.com.* 150 rms, 5 story. S $69-$135; D $69-$145; each addl $10; under 18 free. Crib free. TV; cable. Indoor/outdoor pool; whirlpool. Coffee in rms. Restaurant 6:30 am-2 pm, 5-10 pm. Rm serv. Bar 4 pm-midnight. Ck-out noon. Meeting rms. Business servs avail. Coin lndry. Exercise equipt. Some balconies. Cr cds: A, C, D, DS, MC, V.

Hotels

★★★ **CROWNE PLAZA.** *5151 San Francisco Rd NE (87109). 505/821-3333; fax 505/828-0230; toll-free 800/227-6963. www.crowneplaza.com.* 311 units, 74 suites, 10 story. S, D $132-$152; each addl $20; suites $143-$275; under 18 free. Crib free. TV; cable (premium). Indoor/outdoor pool; whirlpool, poolside serv. Coffee in rms. Restaurant 6 am-10 pm. Bar 11-2 am. Ck-out noon. Convention facilities. Business center. In-rm modem link. Concierge. Shopping arcade. Downhill ski 8 mi. Exercise equipt. Some refrigerators. Private patios. Atrium lobby; waterfall. Luxury level. Cr cds: A, D, DS, MC, V.

★★★ **DOUBLETREE HOTEL ALBUQUERQUE.** *201 Marquette NW (87102). 505/247-3344; fax 505/247-7025; res 800/222-TREE. www.doubletree.com.* 295 rms, 15 story. S, D $125-$145; each addl $10; suites $140-$475; under 18 free. Crib free. TV; cable (premium). Pool. Restaurant 6 am-10 pm. Bar 11:30-2 am; Sun from noon. Ck-out noon. Convention facilities. Business servs avail. Gift shop. Downhill ski 15 mi. Exercise equipt. Health club privileges. Cr cds: A, D, DS, MC, V.

★★★ **HILTON.** *1901 University NE (87102). 505/884-2500; fax 505/880-1196; toll-free 800/932-3322. www.hilton.com.* 264 rms, 12 story. S $89-139; D $99-$149; each addl $10; suites $395-$495; under 18 free. Crib free. Valet serv $5. TV; cable (premium). 2 pools, 1 indoor; whirlpool, poolside serv. Coffee in rms. Restaurants 6 am-11 pm. Bar 11-1 am; Sun from noon; entertainment. Ck-out noon. Coin lndry. Convention facilities. Business center. In-rm modem link. Concierge. Tennis. Downhill ski 15 mi. Exercise equipt; sauna. Health club privileges. Some bathrm phones, refrigerators. Balconies. Luxury level. Cr cds: A, C, D, DS, ER, JCB, MC, V.

[icons]

★★ **THE HOTEL BLUE.** *717 NW Central Ave (87102). 505/294-2400; fax 505/924-2465. www.thehotelblue. com.* 135 rms, 10 suites, 6 story. May-Oct: S $60-$70; D $65-$75; each addl $5; suites $75-$85; under 18 free; higher rates special events. Crib free. TV; cable (premium). Pool. Complimentary continental bkfst. Complimentary coffee in rms. Restaurant 7 am-9 pm. Rm serv. Bar. Ck-out noon. Meeting rms. Business servs avail. In-rm modem link. Bellhops. Airport, RR station transportation. Downhill ski 20 mi. Exercise equipt. Refrigerator in suites. Cr cds: A, C, D, DS, JCB, MC, V.

[icons]

★★★ **HYATT REGENCY.** *330 Tijeras NW (87102). 505/842-1234; fax 505/766-6710; toll-free 800/233-1234. www.hyatt.com.* 395 rms, 20 story. S $199; D $224; each addl $25; suites $375-$750; under 15 free. Crib free. Garage parking $8; valet $11. TV; cable (premium). Heated pool; lap pool; poolside serv. Restaurant 6:30 am-10:30 pm. Bar 11 am-midnight; entertainment. Ck-out noon. Convention facilities. Business servs avail. Concierge. Shopping arcade. Beauty shop. Downhill/x-country ski 18 mi. Exercise equipt; sauna. Health club privileges. Refrigerator, wet bar in suites. Convention center adj. Cr cds: A, C, D, DS, ER, JCB, MC, V.

[icons]

★★ **LA POSADA DE ALBU-QUERQUE.** *125 2nd St NW (87102). 505/242-9090; fax 505/242-8664; toll-free 800/777-5732. www.laposada-abq. com.* 114 rms, 10 story. S $115-$135; D $125-$145; each addl $15; suites $195-$275; under 17 free; wkend rates. Crib free. TV; cable (premium). Restaurant (see also CONRAD'S

DOWNTOWN). Bar 11 am-midnight. Ck-out noon. Meeting rms. Business servs avail. Health club privileges. Downhill ski 15 mi. Refrigerator avail. Cr cds: A, C, D, DS, MC, V.

[icons]

★★★ **MARRIOTT ALBU-QUERQUE.** *2101 Louisiana Blvd NE (87110). 505/881-6800; fax 505/888-2982; toll-free 800/228-9290. www. marriotthotels.com/abqnm/.* 411 rms, 17 story. S, D $129-$149; suites $250-$500; under 18 free; seasonal rates. Crib free. TV; cable (premium). Indoor/outdoor pool; whirlpool, poolside serv. Coffee in rms. Restaurant 6:30 am-11 pm. Bar 11 am-midnight; Sun from noon. Ck-out noon. Coin lndry. Convention facilities. In-rm modem link. Gift shop. Downhill ski 10 mi. Exercise equipt; sauna. Rec rm. Luxury level. Cr cds: A, C, D, DS, JCB, MC, V.

[icons]

★★★ **RADISSON INN.** *1901 University Blvd SE (87106). 505/247-0512; fax 505/247-1063; res 800/333-3333. www.radisson.com.* 148 rms, 2-3 story. S $75-$95; D $85-$105; each addl $10; under 18 free. Crib free. Pet accepted. TV; cable (premium). Heated pool; whirlpool, poolside serv. Restaurant 6 am-10 pm. Rm serv. Bar 2 pm-midnight. Ck-out noon. Meeting rms. In-rm modem link. Bellhops. Free airport, RR station, bus depot transportation. Downhill ski 20 mi. Health club privileges. Cr cds: A, D, DS, MC, V.

[icons]

★★★ **SHERATON ALBUQUERQUE UPTOWN.** *2600 Louisiana Blvd NE (87110). 505/881-0000; fax 505/881-3736; res 800/325-3535. www.sheraton uptown.com.* 296 rms, 8 story. S $129; D $139; each addl $10; suites $150-$300; under 18 free; wkend rates. Crib free. TV; cable (premium). Indoor pool; whirlpool. Restaurant 6 am-11 pm. Bar 11-2 am. Ck-out noon. Coin lndry. Convention facilities. Business servs avail. Gift shop. Downhill ski 7 mi. Exercise equipt. Refrigerators. Some whirlpool suites. Cr cds: A, C, D, DS, JCB, MC, V.

[icons]

★★★ **SHERATON OLD TOWN HOTEL.** *800 Rio Grande Blvd NW*

(87104). 505/843-6300; fax 505/842-9863; toll-free 800/237-2133. www.baynewmexico.com. 188 rms, 11 story. S $110-$125; D $120-$130; each addl $10; suites $150-$170; under 18 free; wkend rates. Crib free. TV; cable (premium). Heated pool; whirlpool, poolside serv. Coffee in rms. Restaurant 6 am-10:30 pm. Bar 4-11 pm. Ck-out noon. Meeting rms. Business center. In-rm modem link. Shopping arcade. Barber, beauty shop. Downhill ski 20 mi. Exercise equipt. Some refrigerators. Some balconies. In historic Old Town. Cr cds: A, D, DS, MC, V.

★★ **WYNDHAM ALBUQUERQUE HOTEL.** *2910 Yale Blvd SE (87106). 505/843-7000; fax 505/843-6307; toll-free 800/227-1117. www.wynatabq.com.* 276 rms, 14 story. S $99-$169; D $109-$179; each addl $10; suites $189-$300; under 16 free; wkend rates. Crib free. TV; cable (premium). Heated pool; poolside serv. Restaurant 6 am-11 pm. Bar 2 pm-1:30 am; Sun to midnight. Ck-out noon. Meeting rms. In-rm modem link. Gift shop. Free airport transportation. Tennis. Downhill ski 15 mi. Exercise equipt. Some refrigerators. Balconies. Cr cds: A, C, D, DS, JCB, MC, V.

B&Bs/Small Inns

★★★ **APACHE CANYON RANCH.** *4 Canyon Dr, Laguna (87026). 505/836-7220; fax 505/836-2922; toll-free 800/808-8310. www.apachecanyon.com.* 5 rms, 2 share bath, 1 guest house. Apr-Nov, MAP: S, D $90-$120; guest house $265; golf, package plans; lower rates rest of yr. Children over 12 yrs only. TV; VCR avail (movies). Complimentary coffee in rms. Ck-out 11 am, ck-in 3 pm. Business servs avail. Luggage handling. Concierge serv. Gift shop. Putting green. Exercise equipt. Massage. Many in-rm whirlpools; some fireplaces; microwaves avail. Picnic tables, grills. View of mountains. Totally nonsmoking. Cr cds: A, DS, MC, V.

★★★ **BRITTANIA & W. E. MAUGER ESTATE BED AND BREAKFAST.** *701 Roma Ave NW (87102). 505/242-8755; fax 505/842-8835; toll-free 800/719-9189. www.maugerbb.com.* 8 air-cooled rms, shower only, 3 story.

S, D $89-$199; each addl $15. Crib free. Pet accepted (fee). TV; cable (premium), VCR avail. Complimentary full bkfst; afternoon refreshments. Complimentary coffee in rms. Restaurant nearby. Ck-out 11 am, ck-in 4-6 pm. Business servs avail. In-rm modem link. Downhill/x-country ski 12 mi. Health club privileges. Sun porch. Restored Queen Anne house (1897). Cr cds: A, D, DS, MC, V.

★★★ **CASA DEL GRANJERO B&B.** *414C De Baca Ln NW (87114). 505/897-4144; fax 505/897-9788; toll-free 800/701-4144. www.innewmexico.com.* 7 rms, 2 with shower only, 5 suites, 1 kit. unit. No rm phones. S $69-$99; D, suites, kit. unit $89-$109; each addl $20; wkly, wkend, hol rates; ski plans. Children over 3 yrs only. Crib $10. TV in common rm; cable, VCR (movies). Whirlpool. Complimentary full bkfst; afternoon refreshments. Ck-out 11 am, ck-in 11 am-2 pm. Luggage handling. Concierge serv. Business center. Downhill/x-country ski 10 mi. Sauna. Lawn games. Some refrigerators; microwaves avail. Hacienda built in 1880; kiva fireplaces, carved Mexican furniture. Totally nonsmoking. Cr cds: DS, MC, V.

★★★ **CASAS DE SUENOS OLD TOWN BED AND BREAKFAST INN.** *310 Rio Grande Blvd SW (87102). 505/247-4560; fax 505/842-8493; toll-free 800/242-8987. www.casasdesuenos.com.* 20 units, 6 suites, 8 with kit. S, D $85-$250; each addl $15; suites, kit. units $110-$250; 3-day min Balloon Fiesta. Children over 12 yrs only. TV; cable (premium). Complimentary full bkfst. Restaurant nearby. Ck-out 11 am, ck-in 3 pm. Business servs avail. In-rm modem link. Separate adobe units surround courtyard; European antiques. Totally nonsmoking. Cr cds: A, C, D, DS, JCB, MC, V.

★★★ **CHOCOLATE TURTLE BED AND BREAKFAST.** *1098 W Meadowlark, Corrales (87048). 505/898-1800; fax 505/898-5328; toll-free 800/898-1842. www.collectorsguide.com/chocturtle.* 4 air-cooled rms, 3 with shower only, 1 suite. No rm phones. S, D $65-$115; each addl

$10; suite $85-$90; package plans. Children over 6 yrs only. TV in common rm; cable (premium), VCR avail (movies). Complimentary full bkfst. Restaurant nearby. Ck-out 11 am, ck-in 4-6 pm. Business servs avail. Concierge serv. Downhill ski 15 mi. Whirlpool. Totally nonsmoking. Cr cds: A, D, DS, MC, V.

★★★ **HACIENDA ANTIGUA BED AND BREAKFAST.** 6708 Tierra Dr NW (87107). 505/345-5399; fax 505/345-3855; toll-free 800/201-2986. www.haciendaantigua.com. 5 air-cooled rms. Many rm phones. S, D $119; each addl $25; 3-day min Balloon Fiesta. TV in common rm. Pool; whirlpool. Complimentary full bkfst; afternoon refreshments. Ck-out 11 am, ck-in 4-6 pm. Business servs avail. Downhill/x-country ski 12 mi. Refrigerators. Picnic tables. Spanish Colonial house built 1790 that once served as stagecoach stop; many antiques. Cr cds: MC, V.

★★★ **HACIENDA VARGAS B&B INN.** 1431 Hwy 313 Historical El Camino Real, Algodones (87001). 505/867-9115; fax 505/867-0640; toll-free 800/261-0006. www.haciendavargas.com. 3 rms, 5 suites. No rm phones. S, D $89-$109; each addl $15; suites $110-$149. Complimentary full bkfst; afternoon refreshments. Ck-out 11 am, ck-in 4 pm. Business servs avail. Site has been a stagecoach stop, train depot, and a trading post. Totally nonsmoking. Cr cds: A, MC, V.

★★★ **LA HACIENDA GRANDE.** 21 Baros Ln, Bernalillo (87004). 505/867-1887; fax 505/771-1436; res 800/353-1887. www.lahaciendagrande.com. 6 rms. S, D $99-$119; each addl $15; ski, golf plans; higher rates hols (2-day min). Children over 12 yrs only. TV; cable (premium), VCR avail (movies). Complimentary full bkfst. Complimentary coffee in rms. Ck-out 11 am, ck-in 4-6 pm. Luggage handling. Concierge serv. Business servs avail. 18-hole golf privileges, greens fee $32. Downhill/x-country ski 15 mi. Spanish hacienda built in 1750s. Rms surround courtyard with covered portico. Totally nonsmoking. Cr cds: A, MC, V.

★★★ **RIVER DANCER BED AND BREAKFAST.** 16445 Hwy 4, Jemez Springs (87025). 505/829-3262; toll-free 800/809-3262. www.riverdancer.com. 6 rms, 1 suite. Apr-Oct: S $89-$99; D $99-$129; each addl $15; suite $160; package plans; lower rates rest of yr. TV; cable (premium), VCR avail (movies). Complimentary full bkfst. Restaurant nearby. Ck-out 11 am, ck-in 2-8 pm. Concierge serv. Massage. In-rm whirlpool, refrigerator, microwave in suite. Picnic tables, grills. On river. Totally nonsmoking. Cr cds: MC, V.

All Suite

★★ **AMBERLEY SUITE HOTEL.** 7620 Pan American Fwy NE (87109). 505/823-1300; fax 505/823-2896; toll-free 800/333-9806. www.amberleysuite.com. 170 suites, 3 story. S, D $99-$138; each addl $10; under 18 free; package plans. Crib free. Pet accepted; $5. TV; cable (premium). Heated pool; whirlpool. Complimentary full bkfst; afternoon refreshments. Restaurant 6 am-10 pm. Bar 4 pm-midnight Ck-out noon. Coin lndry. Meeting rms. Business center. In-rm modem link. Gift shop. Free airport, RR station, bus depot transportation. Downhill ski 5 mi. Exercise equipt; sauna. Game rm. Refrigerators, microwaves. Courtyard; fountain. Cr cds: A, C, D, DS, ER, MC, V.

Restaurants

★★ **ANTIQUITY.** 112 Romero St NW (87104). 505/247-3545. Continental menu. Specializes in seafood, steaks, salmon. Hrs: 5-9 pm; Fri, Sat to 9:30 pm. Closed most major hols. Res accepted. Wine, beer. Dinner $14.75-$21.95. Romantic hacienda atmosphere. Antiques. Cr cds: A, DS, MC, V.

★★★ **THE ARTICHOKE CAFE.** 424 Central St (87102). 505/243-0200. Hrs: 11 am-2:30 pm, 5:30-10

pm; Sat from 5:30 pm. Closed Sun; Jan 1, Thanksgiving, Dec 25. Res accepted. Wine, beer. Lunch $4.95-$10.95, dinner $11.95-$22.95. Child's menu. Specializes in pasta, fresh seafood, lamb. Own bread. Outdoor dining. Contemporary decor. Cr cds: A, MC, V.
[D]

★★ **BARRY'S OASIS.** *445 Osua (87109).* 505/884-2324. Hrs: 11 am-2:30 pm, 5-9 pm; Fri to 10 pm; Sat noon-10 pm; Sun 5-9 pm. Closed Thanksgiving, Dec 25. Res accepted. Mediterranean, Greek menu. Bar. Lunch $4-$6, dinner $8-$19.95. Child's menu. Specialties: lamb marsala, Athenian chicken, vegetarian combination plate. Belly dancer Wed-Sat. Enclosed garden dining. Cr cds: D, DS, MC, V.
[D] [⊟]

★★ **CHEF DU JOUR.** *119 San Pasquale SW (87104).* 505/247-8998. Eclectic menu changes wkly. Specializes in fresh seasonal foods. Own baking.Hrs: 11 am-2 pm; Fri, Sat 5:30-8:30 pm. Closed Sun; major hols. Res accepted. Lunch $2.50-$7.50. Outdoor dining. Intimate atmosphere; open kitchen. Totally nonsmoking. Cr cds: MC, V.
[D]

★ **CHRISTY MAE'S.** *1400 San Pedro NE (87110).* 505/255-4740. www. christymaes.com. Specializes in grilled sandwiches, chicken. Own soup. Hrs: 11 am-8 pm. Closed Sun; hols. Lunch $4.75-$7.50, dinner $5.95-$9.50. Child's menu. Cr cds: A, C, DS, ER, MC, V.
[D] [SC] [⊟]

★★ **CONRAD'S DOWNTOWN.** *125 2nd St NW (87102).* 505/242-9090. Southwestern menu. Specializes in paella. Hrs: 6:30 am-10 pm. Res accepted (dinner). Bar. Bkfst $3.95-$7.50, lunch $3.95-$8, dinner $9.95-$22. Guitarist Fri, Sat eves. Valet parking. Cr cds: A, D, DS, MC, V.
[D] [SC] [⊟]

★ **COOPERAGE.** *7220 Lomas Blvd NE (87110).* 505/255-1657. Specializes in prime rib, lobster. Hrs: 11 am-2:30 pm, 5-10 pm; Fri to 11 pm; Sat noon-2:30 pm, 5-11 pm; Sun noon-9 pm; early-bird dinner 5-7 pm. Closed Dec 25. Res accepted. Bar to 2 am;

Sun to 9 pm. Lunch $4.50-$7.50, dinner $12.95-$27.95. Child's menu. Entertainment Thurs-Sat. Built like an enormous barrel; circular rms with many intimate corners, booths; atrium dining rm. Cr cds: A, D, DS, MC, V.
[D] [⊟]

★ **EL PINTO.** *10500 4th St NW (87114).* 505/898-1771. www.elpinto. com. Mexican menu. Specialties: chile con carne, carne adobada ribs. Hrs: 11 am-9 pm; Fri, Sat to 10 pm; Sun 10:30 am-9 pm. Closed Thanksgiving, Dec 25. Bar. Lunch $5.25-$12.95, dinner $6.50-$13.95. Child's menu. Patio dining with waterfall. Hacienda decor. Cr cds: A, DS, MC, V.
[D] [⊟]

★ **GARDUNO'S OF MEXICO.** *10551 Montgomery NE (87111).* 505/298-5000. www.gardunorestaurant.com. Contemporary Mexican menu. Specializes in enchiladas, fajitas. Hrs: 11 am-10 pm; Fri, Sat to 10:30 pm; Sun from 10:30 am; Sun brunch to 3 pm. Closed Thanksgiving, Dec 25. Bar. Lunch $4.95-$11.95, dinner $7.50-$12.95. Sun brunch $9.95. Child's menu. Entertainment Thurs-Sun. Outdoor dining. Festive atmosphere; Mexican decor. Family-owned. Cr cds: A, D, DS, MC, V.
[D] [⊟]

★★ **HIGH NOON.** *425 San Felipe St NW (87104).* 505/765-1455. Continental menu. Specializes in pepper steak, seafood. Hrs: 11 am-9 pm; Fri, Sat to 10:30 pm; Sun from noon. Closed Jan 1, Dec 25. Res accepted. Bar. Lunch $4.95-$8.95, dinner $9.50-$21.95. Guitarist Thurs-Sat. Original 2 rooms built in 1785. Colonial Mexican, Western, and Native American decor; kiva fireplaces. Cr cds: A, C, D, DS, MC, V.
[D] [SC] [⊟]

★ **LA HACIENDA DINING ROOM.** *302 San Felipe NW (87104).* 505/243-3131. Mexican, Amer menu. Specialties: enchiladas New Mexican, sopapillas. Hrs: 11 am-9 pm; summer to 10 pm. Closed Thanksgiving, Dec 25. Res accepted. Serv bar. Lunch $4.25-$9.95, dinner $7.95-$13.95. Child's menu. Entertainment Wed-Sun. Patio dining. Mexican decor in

old hacienda; antiques, Native American art. Cr cds: A, C, D, DS, MC, V.
D

★ ★ ★ **LE CAFE MICHE.** *1431 Wyoming Blvd NE (87112). 505/299-6088. www.lecafemiche.com.* French country menu. Specializes in veal, seafood. Hrs: 11 am-1:30 pm, 5:30-9 pm; Fri, Sat from 5 pm. Closed Sun, Mon (lunch only); major hols. Res accepted. A la carte entrees: lunch $7.50-$11.75, dinner $14.50-$28. Totally nonsmoking. Cr cds: A, D, DS, MC, V.
D

★ ★ **MAINE-LY LOBSTER AND STEAKHOUSE.** *3000 San Pedro Dr NE (87110). 505/878-0070.* Hrs: 5-10 pm. Closed Mon. Res accepted. Wine, beer. Dinner $10.95-$32.95. Child's menu. Specializes in fresh seafood, steak. Nautical decor. Cr cds: A, C, D, DS, MC, V.
D

★ ★ **MARIA TERESA.** *618 Rio Grande Blvd NW (87104). 505/242-3900.* Hrs: 11 am-2:30 pm, 5-9 pm; Sun brunch to 2:30 pm. Res accepted. Continental, Mexican menu. Bar 11 am-9 pm. Lunch $6.95-$10.95, dinner $12.95-$23.95. Sun brunch $10.95-$16.95. Child's menu. Fountain courtyard for lunch, cocktails. Restored adobe hacienda (1840); antique decor; art, fireplaces, walled gardens. Cr cds: A, C, D, ER, MC, V.
D

★ **M AND J.** *403 2nd St SW (87102). 505/242-4890.* Mexican menu. Specialties: tamales, carne adovada, blue corn enchilada plate. Hrs: 9 am-4 pm. Closed Sun; major hols. Lunch, dinner $5-$8.50. Child's menu. Cr cds: A, MC, V.
D SC

★ ★ **NEW CHINATOWN.** *5001 Central Ave NE (87108). 505/265-8859. www.newchinatown.org.* Hrs: 11 am-9:30 pm; Fri, Sat to 10:30 pm. Closed Thanksgiving, Dec 25. Res accepted. Chinese menu. Bar to midnight. Lunch $3.25-$5.75, dinner $6.50-$14.95. Lunch buffet $5.49. Child's menu. Specializes in Cantonese, Szechwan dishes. Piano bar. Parking. Unusual modern Chinese decor; art-

work; Chinese garden. Family-owned. Cr cds: A, D, DS, MC, V.
D

★ ★ ★ **PRAIRIE STAR.** *255 Prairie Star Rd, Bernalillo (87004). 505/867-3327.* Hrs: 5-9 pm; Fri, Sat to 10 pm. Closed Mon; Dec 25-Jan 1. Continental menu. Bar. Wine cellar. Dinner $15-$20. Specialties: chateaubriand, venison. Own baking. Adobe building; art. View of river valley, mountains. Cr cds: A, C, D, DS, ER, MC, V.
D

★ **RAGIN' SHRIMP.** *3619 Copper NE (87108). 505/254-1544. www.ragin shrimp.com.* Hrs: 11 am-9 pm; Fri to 10 pm; Sat 11:30 am-10 pm; Sun from 11:30 am. Closed most major hols. Cajun menu. Wine, beer. Lunch $5.50-$7.95, dinner $5.50-$12.95. Child's menu. Specialties: Ragin' gumbo, original shrimp, big salad. Parking. Outdoor dining. Gallery-like dining atmosphere. Totally nonsmoking. Cr cds: A, D, DS, MC, V.
D

★ **RANGE CAFE AND BAKERY.** *925 Camino del Pueblo, Bernalillo (87004). 505/867-1700. www.rangecafe.com.* Hrs: 7:30 am-9:30 pm; Fri, Sat to 10 pm. Closed Thanksgiving, Dec 25. Bar. Bkfst $3-$7.25, lunch $5-$9, dinner $8-$20. Child's menu. Specialties: chicken-fried steak, Tom's meatloaf. Parking. Totally nonsmoking. Cr cds: A, C, D, DS, ER, MC, V.
D

★ ★ ★ **SCALO.** *3500 Central Ave SE (87106). 505/255-8782.* Hrs: 11:30 am-2:30 pm, 5-11 pm; Sun 5-9 pm. Closed most major hols. Res accepted. Italian menu. Bar. Lunch $4.95-$9.95, dinner $7.95-$19.95. Specialties: salmone alla Como, filet of beef, grilled fish. Own pasta. Patio dining. Dining areas on several levels. Cr cds: A, D, DS, MC, V.
D

★ ★ **TRATTORIA TROMBINO.** *5415 Academy Blvd NE (87109). 505/821-5974.* Hrs: 11 am-2:30 pm, 5-10 pm; Fri, Sat 11 am-10:30 pm; Sun 4-9 pm. Closed Thanksgiving, Dec 25. Italian menu. Bar. Lunch $5.50-$9.95, dinner $7.95-$16.95. Child's menu. Specializes in pasta, seafood, steak. Cr cds: A, D, DS, MC, V.

D

Unrated Dining Spots

66 DINER. *1405 Central Ave NE (87106).* 505/247-1421. *www.66diner. com.* Hrs: 11 am-11 pm; Fri to midnight; Sat 8 am-midnight; Sun 8 am-10 pm. Closed major hols. Wine, beer. Bkfst $1.95-$4.25, lunch, dinner $3-$6.95. Child's menu. Specialty: green chile cheeseburger. Outdoor dining. Roadside diner; photographs, music of the '40s, '50s, and '60s. Cr cds: A, C, D, DS, ER, MC, V.

D

SOUPER SALAD. *4411 San Mateo NE (87109).* 505/883-9534. Hrs: 11 am-9:30 pm; Sun noon-8 pm. Closed Jan 1, Thanksgiving, Dec 25. Lunch, dinner $2.65-$5.95. Specializes in homemade soup, baked potatoes. Salad bar. Cr cds: A, C, D, DS, ER, MC, V.

D

Angel Fire

See also Cimarron, Red River, Taos

Pop 1,048 **Elev** 8,500 ft
Area code 505 **Zip** 87710
Information Chamber of Commerce, PO Box 547; 505/377-6661 or 800/446-8117
Web www.angelfirechamber.org

This is a family resort area high in the Sangre de Cristo Mountains of northern New Mexico.

What to See and Do

Carson National Forest. 3 mi W (see TAOS). Phone 505/587-2255.

Cimarron Canyon State Park. Region of high mountains and deep canyons has scenic 200-ft palisades; winding mountain stream has excellent trout fishing; state wildlife area. Hiking, rock climbing, wildlife viewing, winter sports, camping. Standard fees. (Daily) 15 mi NE on US 64. Phone 505/377-6271. **FREE**

Eagle Nest Lake. This 2,200-acre lake offers yr-round fishing for rainbow

trout and Kokonee salmon (fishing license required). 12 mi N on US 64. **FREE**

Skiing. Angel Fire Ski Resort. Resort has two high-speed quad, three double chairlifts; patrol, school, rentals; cafeteria, restaurants, bars. Sixty-seven runs, longest run over 3 mi; vertical drop 2,077 ft. (Thanksgiving-Mar, daily) Nordic center, snowmobiling. Summer resort incl fishing, boating, lake; 18-hole golf, tennis, mountain biking, riding stables. Conference center (all yr). 3½ mi off US 64, NM 434. Phone 505/377-6401 or 800/633-7463. ¢¢¢¢

Vietnam Veterans National Memorial. This beautiful, gracefully designed building stands on a hillside overlooking Moreno Valley and the Sangre de Cristo Mtns. It is dedicated to all who fought in Vietnam. Chapel (daily). Visitor center (Daily). 3 mi N on US 64. Phone 505/377-6900. **FREE**

Artesia

(F-6) *See also Carlsbad*

Founded 1903 **Pop** 10,692 **Elev** 3,380 ft **Area code** 505 **Zip** 88210
Information Chamber of Commerce, 107 N First St, 88210; 505/746-2744 or 800/658-6251
Web www.artesiachamber.com

What to See and Do

Historical Museum and Art Center. Pioneer and Native American artifacts; changing art exhibits. (Tues-Sat; closed hols) 503 and 505 W Richardson Ave. Phone 505/748-2390. **FREE**

Special Events

Bulldog Balloon Rally. Second wkend Nov.

Eddy County Fair. First wk Aug.

Motel/Motor Lodge

★ ★ **BEST WESTERN PECOS INN.** *2209 W Main St (88210).* 505/748-3324; fax 505/748-2868; res 800/528-1234. *www.bestwestern.com.* 81 rms, 2 story. S, D $48-$120; each addl $7; suites $100-$110. Crib free. TV; cable. Indoor pool; whirlpool. Sauna. Restaurant 6 am-9 pm; Sun 5-8 pm. Rm serv. Bar 4 am-midnight; closed Sun. Ck-out 11 am. Coin lndry. Meeting rms. Refrigerators. Some balconies. Cr cds: A, C, D, DS, MC, V.

B&B/Small Inn

★★ **HERITAGE INN.** *209 W Main St (88210). 505/748-2552; fax 505/746-4981; toll-free 800/594-7392. www. artesiaheritageinn.com.* 9 rms, 5 with shower only. No rm phones. S $50-$55; D $55-$60; each addl $10; wkly rates. Children over 15 yrs only. TV; cable (premium). Complimentary continental bkfst; afternoon refreshments. Restaurant nearby. Ck-out 11 am, ck-in 3 pm. Luggage handling. Gift shop. Individually decorated rms. Totally nonsmoking. Cr cds: A, DS, MC, V.

Restaurant

★★ **LA FONDA.** *206 W Main (88210). 505/746-9377.* Hrs: 11 am-2 pm, 5-9 pm; Sat, Sun 11 am-9 pm. Closed Jan 1, Thanksgiving, Dec 25. Mexican, Amer menu. Lunch buffet $6.75. Dinner $4.50-$9.25. Child's menu. Specialties: fajitas, burritos, enchiladas. Waterfall in lobby; arched doorways. Cr cds: A, D, DS, MC, V.

Aztec

(A-2) *See also Farmington*

Founded 1890 **Pop** 6,378 **Elev** 5,686 ft **Area code** 505 **Zip** 87410
Information Chamber of Commerce, 110 N Ash; 505/334-9551
Web www.cyberport.com/aztec

What to See and Do

Aztec Museum and Pioneer Village. Main museum houses authentic pioneer artifacts, incl mineral and fossil display, household items, farm and ranch tools, Native American artifacts. Atwood Annex has authentically furnished pioneer rms, farm equipment, sleighs, buggies, and wagons. Oil Field Museum has 1920s cable tool oil rig, oil well pumping unit, "doghouse," and tools. Pioneer Village has 12 reconstructed buildings, incl doctor's and sheriff's offices, blacksmith shop and foundry, pioneer cabin (1880), general store and post office, original Aztec jail, church. (Mon-Sat) 125 N Main. Phone 505/334-9829. ¢¢

⭐ **Aztec Ruins National Monument.** One of the largest prehistoric Native American towns, it was occupied between A.D. 1100-1300. These are ancient Pueblo ruins, misnamed Aztec by early settlers in the 1800s. The partially excavated pueblo contains nearly 450 rms, with its plaza dominated by the Great Kiva (48 ft in diameter). Instructive museum, interpretive programs in summer. Self-guided tours, trail guide avail at visitor center for the ¼-mi trail. Some portions accessible by wheelchair. (Daily; closed Jan 1, Dec 25) ½ mi N of US 550. Contact Superintendent, 84 County Rd 290. Phone 505/334-6174. ¢¢

Navajo Lake State Park. Surrounded by sandstone mesas and stands of piñon and juniper. Part of Colorado River Storage Project; reservoir extends 35 mi upstream into Colorado, totaling 15,000 surface acres of water. Standard fees. (Daily) 18 mi E via NM 173, 511. Phone 505/632-2278. ¢¢ Also in the area are

Pine River Site. Swimming, waterskiing, fishing (panfish, catfish, bass, salmon, and trout), boating (ramps, rentals, marina); picnicking (fireplaces), concession, camping (hookups). Visitor center with interpretive displays. West side.

San Juan River Recreation Area. Fishing (trout); camping. Below the dam.

Sims Mesa Site. Boat ramp; camping (dump station). East side.

Hotel

★★ **STEP BACK INN.** *103 W Aztec Blvd (87410). 505/334-1200; fax 505/334-9858; res 800/334-1255.* 39 rms, 2 story. Mid-May-mid-Oct: S, D

$78; each addl $6; under 12 free; lower rates rest of yr. Crib free. TV; cable. Restaurant nearby. Ck-out 11 am. Business servs avail. Turn-of-the-century decor. Cr cds: A, MC, V.

Bandelier National Monument

See also Los Alamos, Santa Fe

(From Los Alamos, 6 mi SW on NM 502, then 6 mi SE on NM 4 to turnoff sign)

A major portion of this 32,000-acre area is designated wilderness. The most accessible part is in Frijoles Canyon, which features cave dwellings carved out of the soft volcanic turf and houses built out from the cliffs. There is also a great circular pueblo ruin (Tyuonyi) on the floor of the canyon. These houses and caves were occupied from about 1150-1550. The depletion of resources forced the residents to abandon the area. Some of the modern pueblos along the Rio Grande are related to the prehistoric Anasazi people of the canyon and the surrounding mesa country. There is a paved one-mile self-guided trail to walk and view these sites. The monument is named after Adolph Bandelier, ethnologist and author of the novel, *The Delight Makers*, which used Frijoles Canyon as its locale. There are 70 miles of trails (free permits required for overnight trips; no pets allowed on the trails). Visitor center with exhibits depicting the culture of the pueblo region (Daily; closed January 1, December 25), ranger-guided tours (summer), campfire programs (Memorial Day-Labor Day). Campground (March-November, daily) with tent and trailer sites (fee; no showers, hookups, or reservations); grills, tables, and water. Golden Access, Golden Age, Golden Eagle Passport (see MAKING THE MOST OF YOUR TRIP). Contact the Visitor Center, HCR 1, Box 1, Suite 15, Los Alamos 87544; 505/672-3861, ext 517 or 505/672-0343 (recording). Per vehicle ¢¢¢

Capulin Volcano National Monument

29 mi E on US 64/87 to Capulin, then 3-1/2 mi N.

Dormant volcano that last erupted approximately 10,000 years ago. The strikingly symmetrical cinder cone rises more than 1,500 feet from plains, with a crater one mile in circumference and 415 feet deep. Visitors can spiral completely around the mountain on paved road to rim (daily); five states can be seen on clear days. Picnic area. Visitor center with exhibits of geology, flora, and fauna of the area (daily; closed January 1, December 25). Uniformed personnel on duty at the crater rim (summer only). Contact the Superintendent, Box 40, Capulin 88414.

Carlsbad

(G-6) *See also Artesia*

Founded 1893 **Pop** 25,625
Information Convention & Visitors Bureau, 302 S Canal, PO Box 910; 505/887-6516 or 800/221-1224 outside NM

What to See and Do

Brantley Lake State Park. This 3,000-acre park is adj to Brantley Lake on the Pecos River. Fishing, boating (ramps); picnicking (shelters), camping (hookups, dump station, showers). Visitor center. Standard fees. (Daily) 12 mi N on US 285, then 5 mi E on County Rd 30. Phone 505/457-2384. ¢¢

Carlsbad Museum & Art Center. Pueblo pottery, art, meteorite remains. Potash and mineral exhibits. Pioneer and Apache relics. McAdoo collection of paintings, bird carvings by Jack Drake, changing temporary exhibits. (Mon-Sat; closed hols) 418 W Fox St, 1 blk W of Canal St. Phone 505/887-0276. **Donation**

Lake Carlsbad Water Recreation Area. Swimming, water sports, fishing, boating; tennis, golf (fee), picnic area. Off Green St, on the Pecos River. Phone 505/887-2702.

Living Desert Zoo and Gardens State Park. This 1,100-acre park is an indoor/outdoor living museum of the Chihuahuan Desert's plants and animals. The Desert Arboretum has an extensive cactus collection. Living Desert Zoo has over 60 animal species native to the region incl mountain lions, bear, wolf, elk, bison, and an extensive aviary. (Daily; closed Dec 25) 1½ mi NW, off US 285. Phone 505/887-5516. ¢¢

Million Dollar Museum. Early Americana collection; 31 antique European doll houses, $25,000 doll collection, first car west of the Pecos, Whittlin' Cowboys Ranch. (Daily; closed Dec 25) 20 mi SW on US 62/180 to White's City, then W on NM 7. Phone 505/885-6776. ¢¢

Sitting Bull Falls. Day-use area near spectacular desert waterfall. Hiking trail to piñon and juniper forest, diverse vegetation along trail with scenic overlooks of canyons and plains. Picnicking. (Daily) 11 mi NW on US 285 to NM 137, then 30 mi SW, in Lincoln National Forest (see ALAMOGORDO). Phone 505/885-4181. **FREE**

Motels/Motor Lodges

★★ **BEST WESTERN STEVENS INN.** *1829 S Canal St (88220). 505/887-2851; fax 505/887-6338; res 800/730-2851. www.bestwestern.com.* 202 rms, 1-2 story. S, D $52; suites $62-$85; each addl $5. Crib $5. Pet accepted. TV; cable (premium), VCR (movies $4). Pool. Playground. Comlimentary bkfst buffet. Restaurant 5:30 am-10 pm; Sun 6 am-9 pm. Rm serv 7 am-9 pm. Bar 11-2 am; entertainment exc Sun. Ck-out noon. Meeting rms. Business servs avail. Sundries. Some refrigerators. Some patios. Cr cds: A, C, D, DS, JCB, MC, V.

D 🐾 ≋ 📐 🔥 🛇

★★ **CONTINENTAL INN.** *3820 National Park Hwy (88220). 505/887-0341; fax 505/885-1186; toll-free 877/887-0341.* 58 units, 2 story. S $35; D $45; each addl $5; suites

$49.95-$79.95. Crib free. Pet accepted, some restrictions; $10. TV; cable (premium). Heated pool. Restaurant nearby. Ck-out 11 am. Business servs avail. In-rm modem link. Some refrigerators. Cr cds: A, C, D, MC, V.

≋ 📐 🔥 🛇

★★★ **HOLIDAY INN.** *601 S Canal St (88220). 505/885-8500; fax 505/887-5999; res 800/465-4329. www.holiday-inn.com.* 100 rms, 2 story. Mid-June-mid-Aug: S $79-$99; D $85-$105; each addl $5; suites $77-$87; under 19 free; lower rates rest of yr. Crib free. Pet accepted; $25 deposit. TV; cable (premium), VCR avail (movies). Pool; whirlpool, poolside serv. Playground. Complimentary coffee in rms. Restaurants 6-10 am, 5:30-9:30 pm. Rm serv. Ck-out 11 am. Guest lndry. Meeting rms. Business servs avail. In-rm modem link. Bellhops. Valet serv. Tennis privileges. 36-hole golf privileges, greens fee $26, putting green, driving range. Exercise equipt; sauna. Some refrigerators. Picnic tables. Cr cds: A, C, D, DS, MC, V.

🐾 🏋 🖎 ≋ 📐 🔥 🛇 🏃 🏌

★ **SUPER 8.** *3817 National Parks Hwy (88220). 505/887-8888; fax 505/885-0126; res 800/800-8000. www.super8.com.* 60 units, 3 story. S $40.88-$48.88; D $44.88-$48.88; each addl $4; under 12 free. Crib $5. TV; cable (premium). Heated pool; whirlpool. Complimentary bkfst. Ck-out 11 am. Coin lndry. Business servs avail. Cr cds: A, D, DS, MC, V.

D ≋ 📐 🔥 🛇

Carlsbad Caverns National Park

See also Carlsbad

(27 mi SW of Carlsbad on US 62/180)

One of the largest and most remarkable in the world, this cavern extends approximately 30 miles and is as deep as 1,037 feet below the surface.

It was once known as Bat Cave because of the spectacular bat flights, still a daily occurrence at sunset during the warmer months. Cowboy and guano miner Jim White first explored and guided people through the caverns in the early 1900s, later working for the National Park Service as the Chief Park Ranger. Carlsbad Cave National Monument was established in 1923, and in 1930 the area was enlarged and designated a national park. The park contains 46,755 acres and more than 80 caves. Carlsbad Cavern was formed by the dissolving action of acidic water in the Tansill and Capitan limestones of the Permian age. When an uplift drained the cavern, mineral-laden water dripping from the ceiling formed the stalactites and stalagmites.

Hall of Giants, Carlsbad Caverns

The main cavern has two self-guided routes, a Ranger-guided Kings Palace tour, and several "off-trail" trips. The "Cavern Guide," an audio tour rented at the visitor center, enhances self-guided tours with interpretations of the caverns, interviews, and historic re-creations. Also available are tours in two backcountry caves: Slaughter Canyon Cave and Spider Cave. All guided tours require reservations.

Since the temperature in the cavern is always 56°F, be sure to carry a sweater even if it is hot outside; comfortable rubber-soled shoes are also recommended for safety. No pets; kennel available. Photography, including flash and time exposures, is permitted on self-guided trips and some guided tours. Wheelchairs can be accommodated in the elevator for a partial tour. Rangers patrol the cave. Holders of Golden Access and Golden Age passports (see MAKING THE MOST OF YOUR TRIP) receive a 50 percent discount. Picnic area at Rattlesnake Springs. Scenic 9½-mile loop drive, hiking trails, observation tower, exhibits on surface, restaurant. No camping in park, but available nearby. Bat flight programs are held each evening during the summer at the cavern entrance amphitheater.

Visitor center and museum with educational exhibits and displays. For tour reservations and fees contact the Superintendent, 3225 National Parks Hwy, Carlsbad 88220. Phone 505/785-2232 (ext 429 for reservations).

Chaco Culture National Historical Park

See also Farmington, Gallup, Grants

(From NM 44, 25 mi S on country road 7900; 3 mi S of Nageezi Trading Post; from I-40, 60 mi N of Thoreau on NM 57. Check road conditions locally; may be extremely difficult when wet)

From A.D. 900 to 1150, Chaco Canyon was a major center of Anasazi culture. A prehistoric roadway system, which included stairways carved into sandstone cliffs, extends for hundreds of miles in all directions. Ancient roads up to 30 feet wide represent the most developed and extensive road network of this period north of Central America. Researchers speculate that Chaco Canyon was the center of a vast, complex, and interdependent civilization in the American Southwest.

There are five self-guided trails with tours conducted (Memorial Day-Labor Day, times vary), as well as evening campfire programs in summer. Visitor center has museum (daily; closed January 1, December 25). Camping (fee). Contact Superintendent, PO Box 220, Nageezi, 87037-0220. Phone 505/786-7014. Per vehicle ¢¢¢

Chama

See also Dulce

Pop 1,199 **Elev** 7,800 ft
Area code 505 **Zip** 87520

What to See and Do

Cumbres & Toltec Scenic Railroad, New Mexico Express. Round-trip excursion to Osier, CO on 1880s narrow-gauge steam railroad. Route passes through backwoods country and spectacular mountain scenery; incl the four-percent-grade climb to Cumbres Pass. Warm clothing advised due to sudden weather changes. (Memorial Day-mid-Oct, daily) Also through trips to Antonito, CO with van return. Res advised; contact PO Box 789. ¢¢¢¢

El Vado Lake State Park. This park features an irrigation lake with fishing, ice fishing, boating (dock, ramps); hiking trail connects to Heron Lake, picnicking, playground, camping (hookups, dump station). Standard fees. (Daily) 15 mi S on US 84 to Tierra Amarilla, then 13 mi SW on NM 112. Phone 505/588-7247. Per vehicle ¢¢

Heron Lake State Park. Region of tall ponderosa pines. Swimming, fishing (trout, salmon), ice fishing, boating (ramp, dock); hiking, winter sports, picnicking, camping (hookups; fee). Visitor center. (Daily) 10 mi S on US 84, then 6 mi SW on NM 95. Phone 505/588-7470. Per vehicle ¢¢

Motel/Motor Lodge

★ **ELK HORN LODGE.** *HC 75 Box 45 (87520). 505/756-2105; fax 505/756-2638; toll-free 800/532-8874. www.elkhornlodge.net.* 23 motel rms, 1-2 story, 11 kit. cottages. July-Oct: S $42-$62; D $55-$72; each addl $6; kit cottages $76-$108; wkly and

lower rates rest of yr. Crib $6. Pet accepted. TV; cable. Restaurant 6 am-10 pm. Ck-out 11 am. X-country ski 5 mi. Balconies. Porches on cottages. Picnic tables, grills. On Chama River. Cr cds: A, C, D, DS, MC, V.

Cimarron

(A-5) *See also Angel Fire, Raton, Red River*

Pop 917 **Elev** 6,427 ft **Area code** 505 **Zip** 87714

Information Chamber of Commerce, PO Box 604; 505/376-2417 or 800/700-4298

What to See and Do

Cimarron Canyon State Park. 10 mi W on US 64 (see ANGEL FIRE). Phone 505/377-6271.

Old Aztec Mill Museum. (1864) Built as gristmill. Chuckwagon, mill wheels, and local historical items. (Memorial Day-Labor Day, Fri-Wed; early May and late Sept, wkends) On NM 21, S of US 64 in Old Town. Phone 505/376-2913. ¢

Philmont Scout Ranch. A 138,000-acre camp for some 20,000 Boy Scouts. Villa Philmonte, former summer home of ranch's benefactor, offers tours (mid-June-mid-Aug, daily; rest of yr, call for schedule; fee). Ernest Thompson Seton Memorial Library and Philmont Museum incl several thousand drawings, paintings, and Native American artifacts (Mon-Fri; closed hols). Kit Carson Museum (7 mi S of headquarters; mid-June-Aug, daily; fee). Camp also has buffalo, deer, elk, bear, and antelope. Headquarters is 4 mi S on NM 21. Phone 505/376-2281. **FREE**

Special Events

Maverick Club Rodeo. Rodeo for working cowboys. Parade, dance. Phone 505/376-2417. July 4.

Cimarron Days. Crafts, entertainment. Labor Day wkend. Phone 505/376-2417.

Motel/Motor Lodge

★ **CIMARRON INN & RV PARK.** *212 10th St (87714). 505/376-2268; fax 505/376-4504; toll-free 800/546-2244. www.placestostay.com.* 12 rms, 5 with shower only. S $34-$40; D $36-$46; each addl $3; under 8 free. Crib $3. Pet accepted, some restrictions; $50 deposit. TV; cable. Complimentary coffee in lobby. Restaurant nearby. Ck-out 11 am. Business servs avail. Some refrigerators, microwaves. Picnic tables, grills. Cr cds: A, D, DS, MC, V.

B&B/Small Inn

★★★ **CASA DEL GAVILAN.** *Hwy 21 S (87714). 505/376-2246; fax 505/376-2247. www.casadelgavilan. com.* 5 rms, 1 suite. No A/C. No rm phones. S, D $70-$100; suite $125; under 10 free. Crib free. Complimentary full bkfst. Restaurant nearby. Ck-out 11 am, ck-in 3 pm. Business servs avail. Southwestern adobe built in 1912. Totally nonsmoking. Cr cds: A, DS, MC, V.

Cloudcroft

(F-4) *See also Alamogordo, Mescalero, Ruidoso*

Pop 749 **Elev** 8,700 ft **Area code** 505 **Zip** 88317

Information Chamber of Commerce, PO Box 1290; 505/682-2733

Web www.cloudcroft.net

What to See and Do

Sacramento Mountains Historical Museum. Exhibits depict 1880-1910 life in the Sacramento Mtns area. (Mon, Tues, Fri-Sun) US 82, in town. Phone 505/682-2333. ¢

Ski Cloudcroft. Double chairlift, beginner tows; patrol, school, rentals, snowmaking, lodge, snack bar, cafeteria, restaurant. Vertical drop 700 ft. (Mid-Dec-mid-Mar, daily) Snowboarding. Elev 8,350-9,050 ft. 2½ mi E on US 82. Phone 505/682-2333. ¢¢¢¢

Special Event

Western Roundup. Contests, parade, street dance. Phone 505/682-2733. Mid-June.

Resort

★★★ **THE LODGE AT CLOUD-CROFT.** *1 Corona Pl (88317). 505/682-2566; fax 505/682-2715; toll-free 800/395-6343. www.thelodge-nm. com.* 60 rms, 3 story, 7 suites. No elvtr. S $102; D $120; each addl $10; suites $139-$309; package plans. Crib free. Pet accepted, $100. TV; cable (premium), VCR avail. Heated pool; whirlpool. Sauna. Restaurant (see also REBECCA'S). Bar 11-2 am. Ck-out noon, ck-in after 4 pm. Meeting rms. Business servs avail. Gift shop. 9-hole golf, greens fee, putting green, pro shop. Downhill ski 2 mi; x-country ski on site. Massage. Historic building (1899). Cr cds: A, D, DS, MC, V.

Restaurant

★★★ **REBECCA'S.** *1 Corona Pl (88317). 505/682-2566. www.thelodge-nm.com.* Hrs: 7-10:30 am, 11:30 am-2 pm, 5:30-10 pm; Sun from 10 am; Sun brunch 11 am-2 pm. Res accepted. Continental menu. Bar 11 am-midnight. Wine list. Bkfst $3.25-$9.95, lunch $5.95-$9.95, dinner $12.95-$32.95. Sun brunch $16.95. Child's menu. Specializes in beef, chicken. Own pastries. Pianist. Mountain view; early 1900s atmosphere. Cr cds: A, C, D, DS, ER, MC, V.

Clovis

(D-7) *See also Portales*

Founded 1907 **Pop** 30,954 **Elev** 4,280 ft **Area code** 505 **Zip** 88101

Information Chamber of Commerce, 215 N Main; 505/763-3435

Web www.clovis.org

What to See and Do

Clovis Depot Model Train Museum.
Built in 1907 by the Atchison,
Topeka, and Santa Fe Railway, the
Depot has been restored to its condition in the 1950s era. Features
working model train layouts, railroad memorabilia, historical displays, and an operating telegraph
station. Real train operations along
one of the busiest rail lines in the
US can be viewed from platform.
Gift shop. (Wed-Sun afternoons;
closed hols) 221 W First St. Phone
505/762-0066. ¢¢

Hillcrest Park and Zoo. Second-
largest zoo in New Mexico; more
than 500 animals, most of which are
exhibited in natural environments.
Informational programs. Park has
kiddieland with amusement rides,
outdoor and indoor swimming pool,
golf course, picnic areas, sunken garden. 10th St and Sycamore. Phone
505/769-7870. ¢¢

Special Events

Pioneer Days & PRCA Rodeo.
Parade, Little Buckaroo Rodeo. Phone
505/763-3435. First wk June.

Curry County Fair. Mid-Aug. Phone
505/763-3435.

Motels/Motor Lodges

★★ **BEST WESTERN LA VISTA
INN.** *1516 Mabry Dr (88101).
505/762-3808; fax 505/762-1422; res
800/780-7234. www.bestwestern.com.*
47 rms. S $41-$51; D $44-$54; each
addl $4; under 12 free. Crib $4. TV;
cable (premium). Pool. Ck-out 11
am. Business servs avail. Game rm.
Some refrigerators. Cr cds: A, C, D,
DS, JCB, MC, V.
🄳 ⛱ 🛏 🔥

★★ **CLOVIS INN.** *2912 Mabry Dr
(88101). 505/762-5600; fax 505/762-
6803; toll-free 800/535-3440.* 97 rms,
2 story. S $46; D $53; each addl $5;
under 12 free. Crib free. TV; cable.
Heated pool; whirlpool. Complimentary continental bkfst. Restaurant nearby. Ck-out noon. Coin
lndry. Meeting rms. Business servs
avail. Refrigerators, microwaves

avail. Picnic tables. Cr cds: A, C, D,
DS, MC, V.
🄳 ⛱ 🛏 🔥

★ **COMFORT INN.** *1616 Mabry Dr
(88101). 505/762-4591; fax 505/763-
6747; res 800/228-5150. www.
comfortinn.com.* 50 rms, 2 story. S
$33-$38; D $36-$47; each addl $5;
under 12 free. Crib free. TV; cable
(premium). Heated pool. Restaurant
adj 7 am-9 pm. Ck-out 11 am. Meeting rm. Business servs avail. Cr cds:
A, D, DS, MC, V.
⛱ 🛏 🔥

★★ **HOLIDAY INN.** *2700 E Mabry
Dr (88101). 505/762-4491; fax
505/769-0564; toll-free 800/465-4329.
www.holiday-inn.com.* 120 rms, 2
story. S $59-$95; D $64-$100; under
18 free. Crib free. TV; cable. 2 pools,
1 indoor; whirlpool, sauna. Restaurant 6 am-2 pm, 5-10 pm. Rm serv.
Bar 2-10 pm; closed Sun. Ck-out
noon. Meeting rms. Business servs
avail. In-rm modem link. Game rm.
Cr cds: A, C, D, DS, ER, JCB, MC, V.
🄳 ⛱ 🛏 **SC**

★ **NUMBER ONE VALUE INN.** *1720
Mabry Dr (88101). 505/762-2971; fax
505/762-2735.* 92 rms, 1-2 story. S
$31-$37; D $37-$44; each addl $6.
Crib free. TV; cable (premium). Pool.
Complimentary coffee. Restaurant
adj 7 am-9 pm. Ck-out 11 am. Busi-
ness servs avail. Cr cds: A, C, D, DS,
MC, V.
⛱ 🔥 **SC**

Restaurants

★ **GUADLAJARA CAFE.** *916 L
Casillas St (88101). 505/769-9965.*
Hrs: 11 am-2 pm, 5-9 pm; Sat from 5
pm. Closed Sun. Mexican menu.
Lunch, dinner $2.50-$7.55. Specialty: chile relleno con carne. Cr
cds: MC, V.
🍽

★ **LEAL'S MEXICAN FOOD.** *3100 E
Mabry Dr (88101). 505/763-4075.* Hrs:
10:30 am-9 pm; Sun to 8 pm. Closed
Thanksgiving, Dec 25. Res accepted.
Mexican, Amer menu. Lunch, dinner
$3.25-$9.99. Child's menu. Specializes in enchiladas, tacos, tamales. Cr
cds: A, DS, MC, V.
🄳 🍽

★★ **POOR BOY'S STEAKHOUSE.**
2115 N Prince (88101). 505/763-5222.
Hrs: 11 am-9 pm; Fri, Sat to 10 pm.
Res accepted. Closed Thanksgiving,
Dec 25. Lunch $3.99-$18.99, dinner
$3.99-$20.99. Child's menu. Specializes in steak, seafood. Salad bar.
Antiques. Cr cds: A, DS, MC, V.
[D] [✕]

Deming

(G-2) *See also Las Cruces*

Founded 1881 **Pop** 14,116 **Elev** 4,335
ft **Area code** 505 **Zip** 88031
Information Chamber of Commerce,
800 E Pine St, PO Box 8; 505/546-
2674 or 800/848-4955
Web www.cityofdeming.org

What to See and Do

City of Rocks State Park. This 680-
acre park features fantastic rock formations formed by a thick blanket of
volcanic ash that hardened into tuff,
and subsequently was sculpted by
wind and water; extensive cactus garden. Hiking, picnicking, camping.
Standard fees. (Daily) 28 mi NW on
US 180, then E on NM 61. Phone
505/536-2800. ¢¢

Columbus Historical Museum.
Housed in restored Southern Pacific
Depot (1902). Memorabilia of 1916
Pancho Villa raid and Camp Furlong
(Pershing expedition into Mexico);
headquarters of Columbus Historical
Society. (Daily; closed hols) 32 mi S
via NM 11 in Columbus. Phone
505/531-2620. **FREE**

Deming-Luna Mimbres Museum.
Mining, military, ranching, railroad,
Native American, and Hispanic artifacts of the Southwest. Mimbres pottery; Indian baskets; chuckwagon
with equipt; photographic display;
antique china, crystal; quilt rm;
antique dolls; bell and bottle collections; gems and minerals. Musical
center; art gallery. (Daily; closed
hols) 301 S Silver St. Phone 505/546-
2382. **FREE**

Pancho Villa State Park. Commemorates Pancho Villa's famous raid (Mar
9, 1916) into US territory. On site of

Camp Furlong, from which Brigadier
General John "Black Jack" Pershing
pursued Villa into Mexico; the first
US military action to employ motorized vehicles and airplanes. Some
original buildings still stand. Garden
of desert vegetation, hundreds of different cacti. Picnicking, playground,
camping (hookups, dump station).
Standard fees. Three mi south is Las
Palomas, Mexico. (Daily) (For Border
Crossing Regulations, see MAKING
THE MOST OF YOUR TRIP.) 32 mi S
on NM 11 near Columbus. Phone
505/531-2711. Per vehicle ¢¢

Rockhound State Park. This 1,000-
acre park is on the rugged western
slope of the Little Florida Mtns. An
abundance of agate, geodes, and
other semiprecious stones for collectors (free; limit 15 lbs). Display of
polished stones. Hiking, picnicking,
playground, camping (hookups).
Standard fees. (Daily) 5 mi S on NM
11, then 9 mi E on Access Rd 549.
Phone 505/546-6182. ¢¢

Rock hunting. "Deming Agate,"
jasper, onyx, nodules, and many
other types of semiprecious stones
abound in area. Local gem and mineral society sponsors field trips (see
SPECIAL EVENTS). Phone 505/546-
0348.

Special Events

Old West Gun Show. Fairgrounds.
Western artifacts, jewelry; military
equipment, guns, ammunition.
Phone 800/848-4955. Third wkends
Feb and Aug.

Rockhound Roundup. Fairgrounds.
More than 6,000 participants.
Guided field trips for agate, geodes,
candy rock, marble, honey onyx.
Auctions; exhibitions; demonstrations. Contact Deming Gem & Mineral Society, PO Box 1459. Phone
505/544-4158. Mid-Mar.

Great American Duck Race. Courthouse Park. Live duck racing; duck
queen, darling duckling, best-dressed
duck contests; hot-air balloon race;
tortilla toss; parade. Fourth wkend
Aug.

**Southwestern New Mexico State
Fair.** Fairgrounds. Livestock shows,
midway, parade. Phone 505/546-
8694. Early-mid-Oct.

Motels/Motor Lodges

★ **DAYS INN.** *1601 E Pine St (88030). 505/546-8813; fax 505/546-7095; res 800/329-7466. www.daysinn.com.* 57 rms, 2 story. S $36; D $44; each addl $4; suites $46-$58; under 12 free; wkly rates. Crib free. Pet accepted, some restrictions. TV; cable (premium). Pool. Complimentary continental bkfst. Ck-out 11 am. Cr cds: A, C, D, DS, MC, V.

🔲 🐾 ⛱ 🐾

★ **GRAND MOTOR INN.** *1721 E Spruce St (88031). 505/546-2632; fax 505/546-4446.* 62 rms, 2 story. S $42; D $45-$50; each addl $6; suites $65; under 12 free. Crib free. Pet accepted. TV; cable (premium). Heated pool; wading pool, poolside serv. Restaurant 6 am-10 pm. Rm serv. Bar noon-12:30 am. Ck-out noon. Meeting rms. Business servs avail. Valet serv. Free airport, RR station, bus depot transportation. Golf privileges. Cr cds: A, C, D, DS, MC, V.

🔲 🐾 ⛱ ⛳ 🐾 SC

★★ **HOLIDAY INN.** *I-10 E exit 85 (88031). 505/546-2661; fax 505/546-6308; toll-free 888/546-2661. www.holiday-inn.com.* 120 rms, 2 story. S, D $59; each addl $6; suites $79; under 19 free; higher rates last wkend Aug. Crib free. Pet accepted. TV; cable (premium). Pool. Restaurant 6 am-2 pm, 4-10 pm. Ck-out 11 am. Coin lndry. Meeting rms. Business servs avail. Sundries. Free airport, RR station, bus depot transportation. Some in-rm whirlpools. Cr cds: A, C, D, DS, JCB, MC, V.

🔲 🐾 ⛱ ⛳ 🐾 SC

Dulce

(A-3) *See also Chama*

Pop 2,623 **Elev** 6,769 ft
Area code 505 **Zip** 87528

What to See and Do

Jicarilla Apache Indian Reservation. The Jicarilla Apaches came from a group that migrated from southwestern Canada several centuries ago. The reservation is at an elevation of 6,500-8,500 ft and has excellent fishing and boating; hunting (guides avail; tribal permit required; phone 505/759-3255 for information). On US 64. Phone 505/759-3242. Primitive camping ¢¢

Special Events

Little Beaver Roundup. Jicarilla Apache Reservation (see). Parade, rodeo, dances, arts and crafts, carnival, 62-mi pony express race; baseball tournament; archery. Phone 505/759-3242. Mid-July.

Go-Jii-Ya. Stone Lake. Rodeo, powwow, foot races. Phone 505/759-3242. Mid-Sept.

Motel/Motor Lodge

★★ **BEST WESTERN JICARILLA INN.** *Jicarilla Blvd (87528). 505/759-3663; fax 505/759-3170; res 800/528-1234. www.bestwestern.com.* 42 units, 2 story. July-Jan: S $65; D $80; each addl $5; suites $90-$95; under 12 free; lower rates rest of yr. TV. Restaurant 6:30 am-9 pm. Bar 4:30 pm-1:30 am. Complimentary continental bkfst. Ck-out 11 am. Meeting rms. Gift shop. Some refrigerators. Microwave in suites. Cr cds: A, C, D, DS, ER, JCB, MC, V.

🔲 ⛳ 🐾

El Morro National Monument (Inscription Rock)

(C-1) *See also Gallup, Grants*

(From I-40, 43 mi SW of Grants off NM 53)

Here, on the ancient trail taken by the Conquistadores from Santa Fe to Zuni, is the towering cliff that served as the guest book of New Mexico. Don Juan de Oñate carved his name here in 1605; others followed him in 1629 and 1632. Don Diego de Vargas, reconqueror of New Mexico after the Pueblo Rebellion of 1680, registered his passing in 1692, and scores of other Spaniards and Americans added their names to the cliff at later dates.

The rock is pale buff Zuni sandstone. The cliff, 200 feet high, has pueblo ruins on its top; pre-Columbian petroglyphs. Visitor center and museum (daily; closed January 1, December 25; free).

Trail (fee), picnic facilities. Ranger on duty. Golden Eagle and Golden Age passports (see MAKING THE MOST OF YOUR TRIP). Primitive camping (fee). Contact the Superintendent, El Morro National Monument, Rte 2, Box 43, Ramah 87321. Phone 505/783-4226.

Española

(B-4) *See also Los Alamos, Santa Fe*

Pop 9,688 **Elev** 5,585 ft
Area code 505 **Zip** 87532
Information Española Valley Chamber of Commerce, 417 Big Rock Center; 505/753-2831
Web espanola.com/chamber

What to See and Do

Florence Hawley Ellis Museum of Anthropology. Exhibits of Native American/Spanish history. (Memorial Day-Labor Day, Tues-Sun; closed Dec; rest of yr, Tues-Sat) Phone 505/685-4333. ¢¢

Ortega's Weaving Shop. Near the Plaza del Cerro (plaza of the hill), an example of an old-style protected Spanish Colonial village. Generations of noted weavers make blankets, coats, vests, purses, rugs. (Mon-Sat) 10 mi NE via NM 76, County Rd 98 in Chimayo. Phone 505/351-4215. **FREE** Directly north of the shop is

   Galeria Ortega. Contains works by artists of northern New Mexico depicting the region's unique tricultural heritage. (May-Oct, daily; rest of yr, Mon-Sat) Phone 800/743-5921. **FREE**

Ruth Hall Museum of Paleontology. Exhibits on Triassic animals, Coelophysis, New Mexico state fossil. (Memorial Day-Labor Day, Tues-Sun;

rest of yr, Tues-Sat) Phone 505/685-4333. ¢

Whitewater rafting. Guided river excursions; ½-day, full-day, and multiday tours arranged. (Mar-Sept) Contact Santa Fe Rafting Company, PO Box 23525, Santa Fe 87502. ¢¢¢¢

Special Events

Fiesta del Valle de Española. Celebrates establishment of New Mexico's first Spanish settlement in 1598. Torch relay, vespers, candlelight procession, street dancing, arts and crafts, food, entertainment, parade (Sun). Phone Chamber of Commerce. Second wk July.

Sainte Claire Feast Day. Santa Clara Pueblo, 2 mi S via NM 30. Dancing, food, market. Mid-Aug. Phone 505/753-7326.

San Juan Feast Day. San Juan Pueblo, 5 mi N via US 84, NM 68. Dancing, food, carnival. Late June. Phone 800/793-4955 or 505/852-4400.

Tri-cultural Arts Festival. Northern New Mexico Community College. Features local artisans and their works; incl potters, weavers, woodworkers, photographers, painters, singers, and dancers. Phone Chamber of Commerce. Usually first wkend Oct.

White Water Race. Canoe, kayak, raft experts challenge 14 mi of white water below Pilar. Phone 800/222-RAFT. Mother's Day.

B&Bs/Small Inns

★★★ **INN AT DELTA.** *304 Paseo De Onate (87532). 505/753-9466; fax 505/753-9446; toll-free 800/995-8599. www.newmexico.com/delta/deltahome. htm.* 10 rms, 2 story. S, D $100-$150; each addl $10; under 12 free; hol plans. Crib avail. TV; cable. Complimentary full bkfst. Restaurant adj 5-10 pm. Ck-out noon, ck-in 3 pm. Concierge serv. Whirlpools, fireplaces. Adobe structure with Southwestern-style furnishings, hand-carved by local craftsmen. Cr cds: A, DS, MC, V.
D ⬛ 🐾 ♨ 🈁 🔥

★★★ **RANCHO DE SAN JUAN COUNTRY INN.** *US 285, MM 340 (87533). 505/753-6818; fax 505/753-6818; toll-free 800/726-7121.* 14 suites, 3 std rooms, 3 kit. units. S, D

$175-$325; suites $195-$325; kit. units $250-$325; higher rates Jan 1, Thanksgiving, Dec 25. Children over 12 yrs only. Complimentary full bkfst. Complimentary afternoon refreshments. Restaurant (see also RANCHO DE SAN JUAN COUNTRY INN). Ck-out 11 am, ck-in 2 pm. Concierge serv. Fireplaces; some in-rm whirlpools, refrigerators, microwaves. Balconies. Totally nonsmoking. Cr cds: A, DS, MC, V.

Restaurants

★★ **ANTHONY'S AT THE DELTA.** *233 Paseo de Onate (87532). 505/753-4511.* Hrs: 5-9 pm; summer to 10 pm. Closed Jan 1, Thanksgiving, Dec 25. Res accepted. Bar. Dinner $10.95-$32. Specialties: prime rib, grilled salmon. Salad bar. 4 dining areas; 2 fireplaces; hand-carved wooden furniture; art collection displayed. Many plants; courtyard with rose bushes. Cr cds: A, C, D, DS, ER, MC, V.

★★ **EL PARAGUA.** *603 Santa Cruz Rd (87532). 505/753-3211.* Hrs: 11 am-9 pm; wkends to 9:30 pm. Closed Dec 25. Res accepted. Mexican menu. Bar. A la carte entrees: lunch $5.75-$8.50, dinner $7.50-$28. Child's menu. Specialties: tacos, carne adovada. Mariachi band wkends. Stone bldg (1877); many antiques, Mexican tiles, stone fireplace. Family-owned. Cr cds: A, D, DS, MC, V.

★★ **RANCHO DE CHIMAYO.** *County Rd 98, 300, Chimayo (87522). 505/351-4444. www.ranchodechimayo. com.* Hrs: 11:30 am-9 pm. Closed Dec 25; Mon Nov-May; also 1st full wk Jan. Res accepted. Mexican, Amer menu. Bar. Lunch $4.50-$12.95, dinner $5.50-$12.95. Child's menu. Specialties: carne adovada, sopaipillas. Terrace dining. In old hacienda (1885); antiques, fireplace, original artwork. Family-owned. Cr cds: A, C, D, DS, ER, MC, V.

★★★ **RANCHO DE SAN JUAN COUNTRY INN.** *US 285 (87533). 505/753-6818; toll-free 800/726-7121. www.ranchodesanjuan.com.* French,

Amer menu. Specialties: red wine-marinated breast of duck with onion confit, risotto cake and sauteed chayote; white prawns sauteed with garlic, red pepper, and artichoke hearts with mushroom polenta and carmelized shallots; house-cured Alaskan halibut with wasabi cream. Sittings: Wed-Sat 6:30 and 8 pm; Tues sitting at 7 pm. Closed Sun, Mon; also Dec 25. Res required. Bar. Complete meals: dinner $45-$85. Parking. Outdoor dining. Totally nonsmoking. Cr cds: A, DS, MC, V.

Farmington

(A-2) *See also Aztec, Shiprock*

Founded 1876 **Pop** 37,844 **Elev** 5,395 ft **Area code** 505

Information Chamber of Commerce, 203 W Main St, 87401; 505/326-7602 or 800/448-1240

Web www.farmingtonnm.org

What to See and Do

Bisti Badlands. A federally protected wilderness area of strange geologic formations; large petrified logs and other fossils are scattered among numerous scenic landforms. No vehicles permitted beyond boundary. 37 mi S via NM 371. Phone 505/599-8900. **FREE**

Chaco Culture National Historical Park. (see). 75 mi S.

⭐ **Four Corners Monument.** Only point in the country common to four states: Arizona, Colorado, New Mexico, and Utah. 64 mi NW via US 64, NM 504, US 160. Phone 928/871-6647.

San Juan County Archaeological Research Center & Library at Salmon Ruin. Archaeological remains of a 250-rm structure built by the Pueblo (ca A.D. 1100). Museum and research center exhibit artifacts from excavation; historic structures; picnicking. (Daily; closed hols) 12 mi E on US 64 near Bloomfield. Phone 505/632-2013. ¢¢

Special Events

Farmington Invitational Balloon Rally. Hare and hound races; competitions. Memorial Day wkend. Phone 800/448-1240.

Black River Traders. Lions Wilderness Park Amphitheater. Historical drama about the Southwest's multicultural heritage, presented in outdoor amphitheater. Contact Convention and Visitors Bureau for schedule. Phone 505/325-0279. Mid-June-mid-Aug.

Connie Mack World Series Baseball Tournament. Ricketts Park. Seventeen-game series hosting teams from all over US and Puerto Rico. Aug.

San Juan County Fair. Parade; rodeo; fiddlers' contest; chili cook-off; exhibits. Mid-late Aug.

Totah Festival. Fine arts juried show. Rug auction; powwow. Labor Day wkend.

Motels/Motor Lodges

★★ **BEST WESTERN INN AND SUITES.** 700 Scott Ave (87401). 505/327-5221; fax 505/327-1565; toll-free 800/780-7234. www.bestwestern.com. 194 rms, 3 story. S, D $59-$69; each addl $10; under 12 free; wkend rates; golf plans. Crib free. Pet accepted. TV; cable (premium), VCR avail (movies $2). Indoor pool; whirlpool, poolside serv. Coffee in rms. Restaurant 6-10 am, 11 am-2 pm, 5-10 pm. Rm serv. Bar 11:30 am-midnight. Ck-out noon. Coin lndry. Meeting rms. Business servs avail. Bellhops. Valet serv. Free airport, bus depot transportation. Exercise equipt; sauna. Rec rm. Some refrigerators. Cr cds: A, C, D, DS, MC, V.

★★ **COMFORT INN.** 555 Scott Ave (87401). 505/325-2626; fax 505/325-7675; res 800/228-5150. www.comfortinn.com. 60 rms, 2 story, 18 suites. May-Oct: S $54; D $62; each addl $6; suites $59-$69; under 18 free; lower rates rest of yr. Crib $5. Pet accepted. TV; cable (premium). Pool. Complimentary continental bkfst. Complimentary coffee in rms. Ck-out 11 am. Business servs avail. In-rm modem link. Health club privileges. Refrigerator in suites. Cr cds: A, D, DS, MC, V.

★★ **HOLIDAY INN.** 600 E Broadway (87499). 505/327-9811; fax 505/325-2288; res 800/465-4329. www.holiday-inn.com. 149 rms, 2 story. S $69-$79; D $75-$85; each addl $8; under 19 free. Crib free. Pet accepted. TV; cable (premium). Pool; whirlpool. Restaurant 6 am-10 pm. Rm serv. Bar. Ck-out noon. Business servs avail. Bellhops. Free airport, bus depot transportation. Exercise equipt; sauna. Cr cds: A, D, DS, MC, V.

★★ **LA QUINTA INN.** 675 Scott Ave (87401). 505/327-4706; fax 505/325-6583; res 800/531-5900. 106 rms, 2 story. S, D $59-$74; each addl $8; under 18 free. Crib free. Pet accepted. TV; cable (premium). Heated pool. Complimentary continental bkfst. Restaurant adj open 24 hrs. Ck-out noon. Valet serv. Refrigerators avail. Picnic tables, grills. Cr cds: A, C, D, DS, MC, V.

★★ **RAMADA INN.** 601 E Broadway (87401). 505/325-1191; fax 505/325-1223; toll-free 888/325-1191. www.ramada.com. 75 rms, 3 story. Apr-Sept: S, D $67; each addl $10; suites $175; under 12 free; family rates; lower rates rest of yr. Crib free. TV; cable (premium), VCR avail. Complimentary coffee in rms. Restaurant 6:30 am-10:30 pm. Rm serv 7 am-10 pm. Ck-out noon. Meeting rms. Business servs avail. In-rm modem link. Coin lndry. Free airport transportation. Heated pool; whirlpool. In-rm whirlpool, microwave, wet bar in suites. Cr cds: A, D, DS, MC, V.

B&B/Small Inn

★★★ **CASA BLANCA INN.** 505 E La Plata St (87401). 505/327-6503; fax 505/326-5680; toll-free 800/550-6503. www.farmington-nm-lodging.com. 4 rms, 2 suites. May-Oct: S, D $65; suites $115-$125; lower rates rest of yr. TV; cable, VCR (movies). Complimentary full bkfst; afternoon refreshments. Restaurant nearby. Ck-out 11 am, ck-in 4-7 pm. Concierge serv. Business servs avail. Free airport transportation. Mission-style house built in the '50s. Totally nonsmoking. Cr cds: A, MC, V.

Restaurants

★ **CLANCY'S PUB.** *2703 E 20th St (87402). 505/325-8176. www.clancys. net.* Hrs: 11-2 am; Sun noon-midnight. Closed Easter, Thanksgiving, Dec 25. Res accepted. Mexican, Amer menu. Bar. Lunch, dinner $2.50-$11.95. Child's menu. Specializes in prime rib, hamburgers. Outdoor dining. Casual dining. Cr cds: A, D, MC, V.

★ **LA FIESTA GRANDE.** *1916 E Main St (87401). 505/397-1235.* Hrs: 11 am-9:30 pm; Fri, Sat to 10 pm; Sun to 8 pm. Closed Jan 1, Thanksgiving, Dec 25. Mexican, Amer menu. Lunch $3-$4.95, dinner $3-$8.50. Lunch buffet $4.95, Sun $5.95. Child's menu. Specializes in fajitas, sopaipillas, green chili cheeseburgers. Salad bar. Cr cds: MC, V.

Gallup (C-1)

Founded 1881 **Pop** 20,209 **Elev** 6,600 ft **Area code** 505 **Zip** 87301
Information Gallup-McKinley County Chamber of Commerce, 103 W Hwy 66, 87301; 505/722-2228
Web www.gallupchamber.com

What to See and Do

Cultural Center. Located in restored historic railroad station; ceremonial gallery, storyteller museum, Indian dances (Memorial Day-Labor Day, eves), kiva cinema, visitor center, gift shop, cafe. (Summer, Mon-Sat; winter, Mon-Fri) 201 US 66 E. Phone 505/863-4131. **FREE**

McGaffey Recreation Area. Half mi to lake. Fishing, picnicking (fireplaces, tables), tent and trailer sites. Ranger District headquarters at Grants. Fees for some activities. (May-Sept, daily) 12 mi E on I-40, then 10 mi S on NM 400 in Cibola National Forest (see ALBUQUERQUE). Phone 505/287-8833. ¢

Red Rock State Park. Desert setting with massive red sandstone buttes.

Nature trail, boarding stable. Picnicking, concession, camping (hookups; fee). Interpretive displays, auditorium/convention center, 7,000-seat arena; site of Inter-Tribal Indian Ceremonial (see SPECIAL EVENTS) and rodeos. 5 mi E via I-40 and NM 566. Phone 505/722-3839. **FREE** In the park is

Red Rock Museum. Hopi, Navajo, and Zuni artifacts; gift shop. (Summer, Mon-Sat; winter, Mon-Fri; closed winter hols) Phone 505/863-1337. **Donation**

Window Rock. This is the capital of the Navajo Reservation. The Navajo Nation Council Chambers, Navajo Tribal Museum, and Navajo Nation Zoological and Botanical Park are here. 8 mi N on US 666, then 18 mi W on NM 264, in Arizona. Phone 520/871-6436.

Zuni Pueblo. (see) 31 mi S on NM 602, then 8 mi W on NM 53.

Special Events

Inter-Tribal Indian Ceremonial. Red Rock State Park. A major Native American festival; more than 50 tribes from the US, Canada, and Mexico participate in parades, rodeos, games, contests, dances, arts and crafts sales. Second wk Aug. Phone 505/722-3839.

Navajo Nation Fair. Fairgrounds in Window Rock, AZ. Dances, ceremonials, rodeo, arts and crafts, educational and commercial exhibits, food, traditional events. Contact PO Box 2370, Window Rock, AZ 86515. Phone 928/871-6478. Five days beginning Wed after Labor Day.

Red Rock Balloon Rally. Red Rock State Park. Contact Convention and Visitors Bureau for more information. Phone 505/722-6274. First wkend Dec.

Motels/Motor Lodges

★ **BEST VALUE INN.** *2003 W US 66 (87301). 505/863-9385; fax 505/863-6532; res 800/228-2000. www.best valueinn.com.* 92 rms, 2 story. S, D $33.40-$44; each addl $4; wkly rates. Crib free. Pet accepted. TV; cable (premium). Heated pool; whirlpool. Sauna. Restaurant adj 6 am-10 pm. Ck-out noon. Meeting rm. Business servs avail. Cr cds: A, C, D, DS, ER, JCB, MC, V.

★★ **BEST WESTERN.** *1903 W US 66 (87301). 505/722-4900; fax 505/863-9952; res 800/780-7234. www.bestwestern.com.* 50 rms, 2 story. May-Oct: S $50-$65; D $55-$65; each addl $5; suites $64-$79; lower rates rest of yr. TV; cable (premium). Indoor pool; whirlpool. Complimentary continental bkfst. Complimentary coffee in rms. Restaurant nearby. Ck-out 11 am. Cr cds: A, D, DS, MC, V.

★★ **BEST WESTERN INN AND SUITES.** *3009 W 66; I-40 (87301). 505/722-2221; fax 505/722-7442; toll-free 800/780-7234. www.bestwestern. com.* 126 rms, 2 story, 25 suites. June-Sept: S $64; D $72; each addl $8; suites $70; under 12 free; higher rates special events; lower rates rest of yr. Crib free. Pet accepted, some restrictions. TV; cable (premium). Indoor pool; whirlpool. Complimentary coffee in rms. Restaurant 6-10 am, 5-9:30 pm. Rm serv. Bar 4:30-11 pm. Ck-out noon. Meeting rms. Sundries. Gift shop. Coin lndry. Exercise equipt; sauna. Game rm. Microwave in suites. Cr cds: A, C, D, DS, MC, V.

★ **DAYS INN.** *1603 W US 66 (87301). 505/863-3891; res 800/329-7466. www.daysinn.com.* 78 rms, 2 story. Apr-Oct: S, D $50-$60; each addl $5; under 18 free; lower rates rest of yr. Crib free. Pet accepted. TV; cable (premium). Heated pool. Playground. Complimentary continental bkfst. Restaurant nearby. Ck-out 11 am. Business servs avail. Coin lndry. Cr cds: A, DS, MC, V.

★ **ECONO LODGE INN.** *3101 W US 66 (87301). 505/722-3800; fax 505/722-3800; res 800/553-2666. www.econolodge.com.* 51 rms, 2 story. May-Oct: S, D $38.95-$51.95; each addl $7; suites $59.95; under 18 free; higher rates mid-Aug; lower rates rest of yr. Crib $5. Pet accepted; $5 refundable deposit. TV; cable (premium). Restaurant nearby. Ck-out 11 am. Cr cds: A, C, D, DS, JCB, MC, V.

★★ **EL RANCHO.** *1000 E US 66 (87301). 505/863-9311; fax 505/722-5917; toll-free 800/543-6351.* 75 rms, 6 kit. units. S $46-$70; D $64-$70; suites $85-$95. Crib free. Pet accepted. TV. Restaurant 6:30 am-10 pm. Bar 5 pm-1 am. Ck-out noon. Coin lndry. Meeting rms. Business servs avail. Gift shop. Cr cds: A, DS, MC, V.

★★ **HOLIDAY INN.** *2915 W US 66 (87301). 505/722-2201; fax 505/722-9616; toll-free 800/432-2211. www.holiday-inn.com.* 212 rms, 2 story. June-Aug: S, D $65-$73; each addl $5; under 19 free; lower rates rest of yr. Crib free. Pet accepted. TV; cable (premium). Indoor pool; whirlpool. Complimentary full bkfst. Restaurant 6 am-10 pm. Rm serv. Bar 4 pm-12:30am; closed Sun; entertainment. Ck-out noon. Coin lndry. Meeting rms. Business servs avail. Bellhops. Valet serv. Sundries. Free airport, RR station, bus depot transportation. Exercise equipt; sauna. Game rm. Cr cds: A, C, D, DS, JCB, V.

★ **RED ROOF INN.** *3304 W US 66 (87301). 505/722-7765; fax 505/722-4752; res 800/843-7663. www.redroof.com.* 105 rms, 2 story. May-Sept: S $35.99; D $42.99; each addl $4; suites $37.99-$65.99; under 18 free; lower rates rest of yr. Crib free. TV; cable (premium). Heated pool. Complimentary coffee in lobby. Restaurant nearby. Ck-out 11 am. Refrigerator in suites. Cr cds: A, D, DS, MC, V.

Restaurants

★ **EARL'S.** *1400 E US 66 (87301). 505/863-4201.* Hrs: 6 am-9:30 pm; Fri, Sat to 10 pm; Sun to 9 pm. Closed most major hols. Res accepted. Mexican, Amer menu. Bkfst $3.50-$5.50, lunch, dinner $4.50-$9.29. Child's menu. Salad bar. Casual family dining. Family-owned. Cr cds: A, D, MC, V.

★ **RANCH KITCHEN.** *3001 W US 66 (87301). 505/722-2537; toll-free 800/717-8818. www.ranchkitchen.com.* Hrs: 6 am-10 pm. Closed Dec 25. Res accepted. Mexican, Amer menu.

Wine, beer. Bkfst $2.95-$5.50, lunch $3.50-$7.95, dinner $5.95-$16.95. Child's menu. Specialties: beef chimichanga, Navajo taco, mesquite-smoked barbecue. Cr cds: A, D, DS, MC, V.

D SC

Grants (C-2)

Founded 1882 **Pop** 8,806 **Elev** 6,460 ft **Area code** 505 **Zip** 87020
Information Chamber of Commerce, 100 N Iron St, PO Box 297; 505/287-4802
Web www.grants.org

What to See and Do

Acoma Pueblo. Oldest continuously inhabited pueblo in North America. Provides a glimpse into well-preserved Native American culture. 32 mi SE via I-40, NM 23. Phone 800/747-0181.

Bluewater Lake State Park. Rolling hills studded with piñon and juniper trees encircle the Bluewater Reservoir. Swimming, waterskiing, fishing (trout, catfish), boating (ramps); ice-fishing, picnicking, camping (electrical hookups, dump station). Standard fees. (Daily) 19 mi W on I-40, then 7 mi S on NM 412. Phone 505/876-2391. Per vehicle ¢¢

El Malpais National Monument and National Conservation Area. These two areas total 376,000 acres of volcanic formations and sandstone canyons. Monument features splatter cones, 17-mi-long system of lava tubes. Conservation area, which surrounds the monument, incl: La Ventana Natural Arch, one of the state's largest freestanding natural arches; Cebolla and West Malpais wildernesses; and numerous Anasazi ruins. The Sandstone Bluffs Overlook, off NM 117, offers an excellent view of lava-filled valley and surrounding area. Facilities incl hiking, bicycling, scenic drives, primitive camping (acquire Backcountry Permit at Information Center or Ranger Station). Lava is rough; caution is advised. Most lava tubes accessible only by hiking trails; check with Information

Center in Grants before attempting any hikes. Monument, conservation area (daily). Information Center and visitor facility on NM 117 (daily; closed Jan 1, Thanksgiving, Dec 25). S on NM 53; or 6 mi SE on I-40, then S on NM 117. Contact Information Center, 123 E Roosevelt. Phone 505/783-4774. **FREE**

El Morro National Monument (Inscription Rock). (see). Approx 43 mi SW off NM 53.

Laguna Pueblo. (Population approx 7,000) This is one of the 19 pueblos located in the state of New Mexico. The people here speak the Keresan language. The pueblo consists of six villages: Encinal, Laguna, Mesita, Paguate, Paraje, and Seama. These villages are located along the western boundary of the pueblo. The Pueblo people sell their arts and crafts on the reservation; items such as Indian belts, pottery, jewelry, baskets, paintings, Indian kilts, and moccasins can be purchased. Visitors are welcomed to the pueblo throughout the yr and may encounter various religious observances, some of which are open to the public. However, questions concerning social and religious ceremonies should be directed to the Governor of the Pueblo. As a general rule, photographs, sketches, and tape recordings of Pueblo ceremonials are strictly forbidden. Therefore, it is most important that visitors observe these restrictions and first obtain permission from the Governor of the

Pueblo Indian buffalo dance

Pueblo before engaging in such activities. Fiestas and dances are held throughout the yr. 33 mi E off I-40. Phone 505/552-6654.

New Mexico Mining Museum. Only underground uranium mining museum in the world. Indian artifacts and relics; native mineral display. (Mon-Sat) 100 N Iron St. Phone 505/287-4802. ¢¢

Motels/Motor Lodges

★★ **BEST WESTERN INN AND SUITES.** *1501 E Santa Fe Ave (87020). 505/287-7901; fax 505/285-5751; toll-free 800/780-7234. www.bestwestern. com.* 126 rms, 2 story. S, D $60-$80; each addl $8; under 12 free; suites $65-$85. Crib free. Pet accepted, some restrictions. TV; cable (premium). Indoor pool; whirlpool. Sauna. Restaurant 6:30-9:30 am, 5-9:30 pm. Rm serv. Bar 3:30-11 pm; Fri, Sat to midnight; Sun to 11 pm. Ck-out noon. Coin lndry. Meeting rms. Business servs avail. Valet serv. Sundries, Game rm. Refrigerators avail. Cr cds: A, C, D, DS, MC, V.

Hobbs (F-7)

Founded 1927 **Pop** 28,657 **Elev** 3,650 ft **Area code** 505 **Zip** 88240

Information Chamber of Commerce, 400 N Marland; 505/397-3202

Web www.hobbschamber.org

What to See and Do

Lea County Cowboy Hall of Fame & Western Heritage Center. Local memorabilia and artifacts with emphasis on the cowboy, Native American, and oil eras. Permanent displays of Lea County history. (Mon-Sat; closed hols) New Mexico Junior College. Phone 505/392-1275. **FREE**

Special Events

Noche de Espana Music Festival. Main and Becker Sts. Incl Mexican food booths, arts and crafts booths. Phone 505/864-2830. May.

Lea County Fair. In Lovington, 20 mi NW on NM 18. Phone 505/396-5344. Aug.

Motels/Motor Lodges

★★ **BEST INN.** *501 N Marland Blvd (88240). 505/397-3251; fax 505/393-3065.* 75 rms, 2 story. S $49; D $59; each addl $7; suites $95-$119; under 18 free. Crib free. Pet accepted, some restrictions; $25. TV; cable. Heated pool. Restaurant 5 am-8 pm; dining rm 5:30-10 pm. Rm serv 6 am-10 pm. Bar 11-1:30 am; entertainment exc Sun. Ck-out 11 am. Guest lndry. Meeting rms. Business servs avail. In-rm modem link. Sundries. Cr cds: A, C, D, DS, MC, V.
⬜ 🔄 🏊 📶 🐾

★ **TRAVELODGE.** *1301 E Broadway (88240). 505/393-4101; fax 505/393-4101; res 800/578-7878. www. travelodge.com.* 72 rms. S $40-$48; D $50-$54; each addl $4. Crib $3. Pet accepted. TV; cable (premium). Pool. Complimentary full bkfst. Restaurant opp 11 am-10 pm. Ck-out noon. Business servs avail. In-rm modem link. Cr cds: A, C, D, DS, MC, V.
⬜ 🔄 🏊 📶 🐾

Restaurant

★★ **CATTLE BARON STEAK AND SEAFOOD.** *1930 N Grimes (88240). 505/393-2800.* Hrs: 11 am-9:30 pm; Fri, Sat to 10 pm; Sun to 9 pm. Closed Thanksgiving, Dec 25. Bar. Lunch $4.95-$8, dinner $7.25-$29.95. Child's menu. Specializes in steak, seafood, prime rib. Salad bar. Cr cds: A, D, DS, MC, V.
⬜ 🔄

Las Cruces

(G-3) *Also see El Paso, TX*

Founded 1849 **Pop** 74,627 **Elev** 3,896 ft **Area code** 505

Information Convention & Visitors Bureau, 211 N Water St, 88001; 505/541-2444 or 800/FIESTAS

Web www.lascrucescvb.org

What to See and Do

Aguirre Spring Recreation Site. Organ Mtn area formed by monzonite intrusions—molten rock beneath the surface. Wearing away of the crust left organ pipe rock spires. Baylor Pass and Pine Tree hiking trails. Picnicking, camping (centrally located rest rms; no drinking water). Managed by the Department of the Interior, Bureau of Land Management, Las Cruces Field Office. (Daily) 17 mi E via US 70, 5 mi S on unnumbered road. Phone 505/525-4300. Per vehicle ¢¢

Cultural Complex. Found at north end of Downtown Mall, incl the Las Cruces Museum of Fine Art & Culture, and the Braningan Cultural Center, which oversees the Bicentennial Log Cabin Museum. Developing is a Volunteers Memorial Sculpture Garden, five blks west of the complex at the Historical Sante Fe Depot in the New Mexico Railroad and Transportation Museum. (Call for schedule) 500 N Water St. Phone 505/541-2155.

Exploring by car. There are ghost mining towns, extinct volcanoes, frontier forts, mountains, and pecan orchards in the area.

Fort Selden State Monument. Frontier fort established in 1865. General Douglas MacArthur lived here as a boy (1884-1886) when his father was post commander. Famed Buffalo Soldiers were stationed here. Self-guided, bilingual trail. Visitor center has history exhibits. Picnicking. (Mon, Wed-Sun; closed winter hols) 12 mi N on I-25. Phone 505/526-8911. ¢¢

Gadsden Museum. Native American and Civil War artifacts; paintings; hand-painted china; Santo collection; history of the Gadsden Purchase. (Daily; closed hols) 2 mi SW on W Barker Rd in Mesilla. Phone 505/526-6293. ¢

Mesilla. Historic village that briefly served as the Confederate capital of the Territory of Arizona. Billy the Kid stood trial for murder here and escaped. La Mesilla consists of the original plaza and surrounding adobe buildings. There are numerous specialty shops, restaurants, art galleries, and museums. 1 mi SW. Phone 505/647-9698.

New Mexico Farm and Ranch Heritage Museum. Interactive 47-acre museum that brings to life Mexico's 3,000-yr history, farming and ranching life. Hands-on exhibits incl plowing, blacksmithing, and cow-milking. Outdoor animal and plant life. (Tues-Sun; closed hols) 1½ mi E on University Ave. Phone 505/522-4100. ¢¢

New Mexico State University. (1888) 15,500 students. On the 950-acre campus are a history museum (Tues-Sun; free), an art gallery, and an 18-hole public golf course. University Ave. Phone 505/646-3221.

White Sands Missile Range. Missiles and related equipt tested here. Actual range closed to the public; visitors welcome at the outdoor missile park and museum. (Daily; closed hols) 25 mi E on US 70. Phone 505/678-1134. **FREE**

Special Events

Whole Enchilada Fiesta. Downtown Mall. Street dancing, entertainment, crafts, food incl world's largest enchilada. Phone 505/524-6832. Last wkend Sept.

Southern New Mexico State Fair. First wkend Oct.

Renaissance Craftfaire. Young Park. Juried fair with participants in Renaissance costume. Food, entertainment. Phone 505/524-6403. Early Nov.

Our Lady of Guadalupe Fiesta. Tortugas Village, adj to town. Evening Indian dances, vespers; daytime ascent of Mt Tortugas; Mass, bonfire, and torchlight descent; fiesta. Phone 505/526-8171. Mid-Dec.

Motels/Motor Lodges

★★ **BEST WESTERN MESILA VALLEY INN.** *901 Avenida De Mesilla (88005). 505/524-8603; fax 505/526-8437; res 800/327-3314. www.best western.com.* 167 units, 2 story. S, D $59; each addl $7; under 12 free. Crib free. Pet accepted. TV; cable. Heated pool; whirlpool. Restaurant 6 am-10 pm. Rm serv. Bar 11-1:30 am; Sun noon-11 pm; entertainment. Ck-out 11 am. Coin lndry. Meeting rms. Business servs avail. Health club privileges. Some refrigerators; microwaves avail. Cr cds: A, C, D, DS, JCB, MC, V.

⊡ 🔧 ➿ ➿ 🐾

★ **DAY'S END LODGE.** *755 N Valley Dr (88005). 505/524-7753; fax 505/541-0732.* 32 rms, 2 story. S $31; D $37-$41; each addl $3; family unit $43-$50; under 18 free. Crib free. Pet accepted. TV; cable (premium). Complimentary continental bkfst. Pool. Ck-out 11 am. Business servs avail. Cr cds: A, DS, MC, V.

⊡ 🔧 ➿ 🐾 ➿

★ **DAYS INN.** *2600 S Valley Dr (88005). 505/526-4441; fax 505/526-1980; res 800/329-7466. www.daysinn. com.* 130 rms, 2 story. S $45-$50; D $49-$59; each addl $5; under 18 free. Pet accepted. TV; cable (premium). Indoor pool; poolside serv. Sauna. Restaurant 6-10 am, 5:30-9 pm. Bar 11 am-11 pm; Sat, Sun noon-10 pm. Ck-out noon. Coin lndry. Meeting rms. Business servs avail. Health club privileges. Valet serv. Some balconies. Cr cds: A, C, D, DS, MC, V.

⊡ 🔧 ➿ ➿ 🐾 SC

★ ★ **FAIRFIELD INN.** *2101 Summit Ct (88011). 505/522-6840; fax 505/522-9784; toll-free 800/228-2800. www.fairfieldinn.com.* 78 rms, 3 story. S, D $54.95-$64.95. Crib free. TV; cable (premium), VCR avail. Complimentary continental bkfst. Restaurant nearby. Ck-out noon. Business servs avail. Coin lndry. Exercise equipt. Pool. Some refrigerators, microwaves. Cr cds: A, C, D, DS, MC, V.

⊡ ➿ 🏋 ➿ 🐾 SC

★ ★ **HAMPTON INN.** *755 Avenida De Mesilla (88005). 505/526-8311; fax 505/527-2015; toll-free 888/846-6741. www.hamptoninn.com.* 117 rms, 2 story. S, D $61-$70; under 18 free. Crib free. Pet accepted. TV; cable (premium). Pool. Complimentary continental bkfst. Ck-out noon. In-rm modem link. Cr cds: A, D, DS, MC, V.

⊡ 🔧 ➿ SC

★ ★ **HOLIDAY INN.** *201 E University Ave (88005). 505/526-4411; fax 505/524-0530; res 800/465-4329. www.holiday-inn.com.* 114 rms, 2 story. S $79-$150; D $84-$175; suites $150; under 18 free. Crib free. Pet accepted, some restrictions. TV; cable (premium). Indoor pool; wading pool. Restaurant 6 am-10 pm. Rm serv. Bar 11-1 am. Ck-out noon. Coin lndry. Meeting rms. Free airport, bus depot transportation. Exercise rm. Beauty shop. Game rm. Enclosed courtyard re-creates Mexican plaza. Cr cds: A, D, DS, MC, V.

⊡ 🔧 ➿ ➿ 🐾 SC

Hotel

★ ★ ★ **HILTON.** *705 S Telshor Blvd (88011). 505/522-4300; fax 505/521-4707; toll-free 800/445-8667. www. hilton.com.* 203 units, 7 story. S $85-$110; D $90-$115; each addl $10; suites $115-$300. Crib free. Pet accepted. TV; cable; VCR avail (movies). Pool; whirlpool, poolside serv. Coffee in rms. Restaurant 6 am-2 pm, 5-10 pm. Rm serv. Bar 11-2 am; entertainment. Ck-out 1 pm. Meeting rms. Business servs avail. In-rm modem link. Gift shop. Free airport, bus depot transportation. Tennis privileges. Golf privileges. Exercise equipt. Health club privileges. Some refrigerators. Overlooks valley. Cr cds: A, C, D, DS, MC, V.

⊡ 🔧 🏋 ➿ 🏋 ➿ 🐾 SC

Resort

★ ★ **MESON DE MESILLA RESORT HOTEL.** *1803 Avenida Demesilla, Mesilla (88046). 505/525-9212; fax 505/527-4196; toll-free 800/732-6025. www.mesondemesilla.com.* 15 rms, 2 story. S $45-$50; D $65-$70. Pet accepted. TV; cable (premium). Pool. Complimentary full bkfst. Restaurant (see also MESON DE MESILLA). Bar 11:30 am-9:15 pm. Ck-out 11 am, ck-in 1 pm. Balconies. Picnic tables. Scenic views. Antique furnishings, brass beds; fireplace. Totally nonsmoking. Cr cds: A, D, DS, MC, V.

🔧 ➿ ➿ 🐾

B&B/Small Inn

★ ★ **LUNDEEN INN OF THE ARTS.** *618 S Alameda Blvd (88005). 505/526-3326; fax 505/647-1334; toll-free 888/526-3326. www.innofthearts.com.* 21 units, 2 story, 7 suites, 11 kits. S $58-$64; D $75-$85; each addl $15; suites, kit. units $85-$105; wkly rates. Crib $15. Pet accepted. TV in sitting rm; cable (premium), VCR avail. Complimentary full bkfst. Restaurant nearby. Ck-out 11 am, ck-in 4 pm. Business servs avail. Bell-hops. Lawn games. Some balconies. Microwaves avail. Picnic tables, grills. Built in 1890; antique furnishings. Library, sitting rm. Art gallery; each rm named for an artist. Cr cds: A, MC, V.

🔲 🔲

Restaurants

★ ★ **CATTLE BARON.** *790 S Telshor (88011). 505/522-7533. www.cattle baron.com.* Hrs: 11 am-9:30 pm; Fri, Sat to 10 pm. Closed Dec 25. Bar. Lunch $4.25-$6.50, dinner from $7.95. Child's menu. Specialties: blackened catfish, prime rib. Salad bar. Cr cds: A, C, D, DS, MC, V.

D 🔲

★ ★ ★ **DOUBLE EAGLE.** *308 Calle Guadalupe, Mesilla (88004). 505/523-6700. www.doubleeagledining.com.* Hrs: 11 am-10 pm; Sun brunch to 3 pm. Res accepted. Bar. Wine list. Lunch $4.95-$8.95, dinner $10.95-$24.95. Sun brunch $15.95. Specializes in steak, seafood. Outdoor dining. Fountain in patio. Restored adobe house (1848); Victorian decor, antiques. Cr cds: A, C, D, DS, ER, MC, V.

D 🔲

★ **EL COMEDOR.** *2190 Avenida de Mesilla, Mesilla (88005). 505/524-7002. www.vianet.com/elcomedor.* Hrs: 8 am-8 pm. Closed Jan 1, Thanksgiving, Dec 25. Res accepted. Southwestern menu. Wine, beer. Bkfst $2.25-$5.75, lunch, dinner $4.95-$8. Specialties: green chile con carne, taco ranchero. Cr cds: A, D, MC, V.

🔲

★ ★ ★ **MESON DE MESILLA.** *1803 Avenida de Mesilla (88005). 505/525-9212. www.mesondemesilla.com.* Hrs: 5:30-9 pm; Sun brunch 11 am-1:45 pm. Closed Mon; Jan 1, Dec 25. Res accepted. Changing menu. Bar. Complete meals: dinner $23-$26. Sun brunch $16.95. Specializes in beef, seafood. Guitarist wkends. Adobe building. Cr cds: A, C, D, DS, ER, MC, V.

Las Vegas

(B-5) *See also Santa Fe*

Founded 1835 **Pop** 14,565 **Elev** 6,470 ft **Area code** 505 **Zip** 87701

Information Las Vegas-San Miguel Chamber of Commerce, 727 Grand Ave, PO Box 128; 505/425-8631 or 800/832-5947

Web www.lasvegasnewmexico.com

What to See and Do

City of Las Vegas Museum and Rough Riders' Memorial Collection. Artifacts and memorabilia from Spanish-American War and turn-of-the-century northern New Mexico life. (May-Oct, daily; Nov-Apr, Mon-Fri). Municipal Building, 727 Grand Ave. Phone 505/425-8726. **Donation**

Fort Union National Monument. Established at this key defensive point on the Santa Fe Trail in 1851, the third and last fort built here was the largest post in the Southwest and the supply center for nearly 50 other forts in the area. It was abandoned by the military in 1891; 100 acres of adobe ruins remain. Self-guided trail with audio stations, living history programs featuring costumed demonstrations (summer). Visitor center depicts the fort's history, artifacts. (Daily; closed Jan 1, Thanksgiving, Dec 25) 20 mi NE on I-25 to Watrous/Fort Union exit 366, then 8 mi NW on NM 161. Contact Superintendent, PO Box 127, Watrous 87753. Phone 505/425-8025. ¢¢

Las Vegas National Wildlife Refuge. Nature trail, observation of wildlife, incl migratory water fowl. Hunting for dove (permit required), Canada goose (permit required, limited drawing); user's fee for hunts. (Daily; some areas Mon-Fri) 2 mi E via NM 104, then 4 mi S via NM 281. Phone 505/425-3581. **FREE**

Morphy Lake State Park. Towering ponderosa pines surround 15-acre mountain lake in Carson National Forest. Primitive use area. Fishing (trout), restricted boating (oars or electric motors only; ramp); winter sports, primitive camping. Accessible to backpackers; four-wheel-drive vehicle advisable. No drinking water avail. Standard fees. (Daily) 11 mi N on NM 518 to Sapello, then 16 mi NW off NM 94. Phone 505/387-2328. ¢¢

Storrie Lake State Park. Swimming, waterskiing, fishing, boating (ramp), windsurfing, picnicking, playground, camping (hookups). (Daily) Standard fees. 4 mi N on NM 518. Phone 505/425-7278. ¢¢

Motels/Motor Lodges

★ **BUDGET INN.** 1216 N Grand Ave (87701). 505/425-9357. 45 rms, 2 story. May-Sept: S $40-$60; D $50-$80; each addl $5; under 3 free; lower rates rest of yr. Crib $3. Pet accepted, some restrictions. TV; cable (premium). Complimentary coffee in lobby. Restaurant adj. Ck-out 11 am. Cr cds: A, C, D, DS, MC, V.
⬛ ➦ 🐾 ➖ 🔥

★★ **COMFORT INN.** 2500 N Grand Ave (87701). 505/425-1100; fax 505/454-8404; res 800/228-5150. www.comfortinn.com. 101 rms, 2 story. Mar-Oct: S $54-$65; D $59-$70; each addl $5; under 18 free; lower rates rest of yr. Crib $5. TV; cable (premium). Indoor pool; whirlpool. Complimentary continental bkfst. Ck-out 11 am. Meeting rms. Business servs avail. Patio. Picnic tables. Cr cds: A, D, DS, MC, V.
⬛ ➖ ➖ 🔥

★ **REGAL MOTEL.** 1809 N Grand Ave (87701). 505/454-1456. 50 rms. Mid-May-mid-Sept: S $30-$39; D $40-$49; under 17 free; higher rates special events; lower rates rest of yr. Crib $5. Pet accepted, some restrictions. TV; cable (premium). Complimentary coffee in lobby. Restaurant adj 6 am-9 pm. Ck-out 11 am. Cr cds: A, D, DS, MC, V.
⬛ ➦ 🐾 ➖ 🔥

★ **TOWN HOUSE MOTEL.** 1215 N Grand Ave (87701). 505/425-6717; fax 505/425-9005. 42 rms. May-Oct: S $27-$36; D $36-$44; each addl $3; under 8 free; wkly rates; higher rates: graduation, family reunions; lower rates rest of yr. Pet accepted, some restrictions; $2. TV; cable (premium). Restaurant nearby. Ck-out 11 am. Picnic tables. Cr cds: A, C, D, DS, MC, V.
⬛ ➦ ➖ 🔥

Hotel

★★ **PLAZA HOTEL.** 230 Plaza (87701). 505/425-3591; fax 505/425-9659; toll-free 800/328-1882. www.plazahotel-nm.com. 37 rms, 3 story. S $79; D $84; each addl $8; suites from $138-$146; under 17 free; some wkend rates. Crib free. Pet accepted, $10/night. TV; cable (premium). Coffee in rms. Restaurant 7 am-2 pm, 5-9 pm. Bar noon-midnight. Ck-out 11 am. Meeting rms. Business servs avail. Airport, RR station, bus depot transportation. X-country ski 5 mi. Health club privileges. Historic hotel built 1882 in the Victorian Italianate-bracketed style; interior renovated; period furnishings, antiques. Cr cds: A, D, DS, MC, V.
⬛ ➦ 🐾 🍴 ➖ ➖ 🔥 SC

Resort

★★ **INN ON THE SANTA FE TRAIL.** 1133 Grand Ave (87701). 505/425-6791; fax 505/425-0417; toll-free 888/448-8438. www.innonthe santafetrail.com. 42 rms, 12 suites. May-Sept: S $64-$69; D $74-$79; each addl $5; suites $95-$145; wkly rates; lower rates rest of yr. Crib free. Pet accepted; $5/day. Satellite TV. Heated pool; whirlpool. Complimentary continental bkfst. Restaurant opp 6:30 am-9 pm. Ck-out 11 am. Business servs avail. In-rm modem link. Lawn games. Refrigerator in suites; microwaves avail. Cr cds: A, DS, MC, V.
⬛ ➦ 🐾 🍴 ➖ 🔥 SC

Restaurants

★ **EL RIALTO.** 141 Bridge St (87701). 505/454-0037. Hrs: 10:30 am-9 pm. Closed Sun; major hols. Res accepted. Mexican, Amer menu. Bar 11 am-midnight. Complete meals: lunch, dinner $3.99-$20. Child's menu. Specializes in New Mexican dishes, seafood. Salad bar. Historic building (1890s); antiques. Cr cds: A, D, MC, V.
⬛ ➖

★ **PINOS TRUCK STOP.** 1901 N Grand Ave (87701). 505/454-1944. Hrs: 6 am-9 pm. Closed Thanksgiving, Dec 25. Mexican, Amer menu. Wine, beer. Bkfst $1.95-$7.95, lunch $3.25-$23.95, dinner $6.95-$23.95.

Child's menu. Specialties: enchilada plate, super burger. Salad bar. Casual dining. Cr cds: MC, V.

[D] [SC] [↵]

Los Alamos

(B-4) *See also Espanola, Santa Fe*

Pop 11,909 **Elev** 7,410 ft
Area code 505 **Zip** 87544
Information Los Alamos County Chamber of Commerce, 109 Central Park Sq, PO Box 460; 505/662-8105 or 800/444-0707
Web www.vla.com

What to See and Do

Bandelier National Monument. (see). 295 N Main St. Phone 585/394-1472. ¢¢

Bradbury Science Museum. Displays artifacts relating to the history of the laboratory and the atomic bomb. Exhibits on modern nuclear weapons; life sciences; materials sciences; computers; particle accelerators; geothermal, fusion, and fission energy sources. (Daily; closed hols) 15th and Central. Phone 505/667-4444. **FREE**

Jemez State Monument. Stabilized Spanish mission (1621) built by Franciscan missionaries next to a prehistoric pueblo. Self-guided bilingual trail. Visitor center has anthropology and archaeology exhibits. Picnicking. (Daily; closed hols) 18 mi N on US 4, then 9 mi S in Jemez Springs. Phone 505/829-3530. ¢¢

Los Alamos Historical Museum. Fuller Lodge Cultural Center. Artifacts, photos, other material tracing local history from prehistoric to present times; exhibit on the Manhattan Project. (Daily; closed hols) 1921 Juniper. Phone 505/662-4493. **FREE** Also here is

    Fuller Lodge Art Center and Gallery. Ground floor of Fuller Lodge's west wing. Historic log building provides setting for changing exhibits. Features arts and crafts of northern New Mexico. (Mon-Sat; closed hols) 2132

Central Ave. Phone 505/662-9331. **FREE**

Motel/Motor Lodge

★ ★ BEST WESTERN HILLTOP HOUSE HOTEL. *400 Trinity Dr at Central (87544). 505/662-2441; fax 505/662-5913; toll-free 800/462-0936. www.vla.com/hilltophouse.* 98 rms, 3 story, 33 kits. S $75; D $85; each addl $10; kit. units $76-$86; suites $98-$275; under 12 free. Crib $10. Pet accepted; $25 deposit. TV; cable (premium). Indoor pool; whirlpool. Complimentary bkfst. Restaurant 6:30-9:30 am, 11:30 am-2 pm, 5-9 pm. Rm serv. Ck-out 11 am. Coin lndry. Meeting rms. Business servs avail. In-rm modem link. Airport transportation. Sauna. Downhill/x-country ski 10 mi. Exercise equipt. Massage. Cr cds: A, C, D, DS, JCB, MC, V.

[D] [♫] [✈] [≈] [才] [N] [⚲]

Hotel

★ LOS ALAMOS INN. *2201 Trinity Dr (87544). 505/662-7211; fax 505/661-7714; toll-free 800/279-9279. www.losalamosinn.com.* 116 rms, 2-3 story. S, D $79-$99; each addl $15; under 12 free. Crib free. TV; cable. Pool; whirlpool. Complimentary bkfst. Restaurant 6:30 am-2 pm, 5-9 pm; Sun from 7 am. Bar 11 am-midnight; Sun noon-9 pm. Ck-out 12:30 pm. Meeting rms. Business servs avail. Cr cds: A, D, DS, MC, V.

[D] [≈] [N] [⚲] [SC]

B&B/Small Inn

★ RENATA'S ORANGE STREET BED AND BREAKFAST. *3496 Orange St (87544). 505/662-2651; fax 505/661-1538; res 800/662-3180. www.losalamos.com/orangestreetinn.* 8 air-cooled rms, 4 with bath, 2 story. S, D $55-$75; ski, golf plans. Children over 5 yrs only. TV in sitting rm; cable. Complimentary full bkfst. Restaurant nearby. Rm serv. Ck-out 11 am, ck-in 4-7 pm. Business servs avail. Concierge serv. Street parking. Airport transportation. Downhill/x-country ski 8 mi. Lawn games. Picnic tables, grills. Southwest and country decor; antiques, library. Totally non-smoking. Cr cds: A, D, DS, MC, V.

Restaurant

★★ **BLUE WINDOW BISTRO.** *813 Central Ave (87544). 505/662-6305.* Hrs: 11 am-2 pm, 5-9 pm; Sat 5-9 pm; Sun (brunch) 11 am-2 pm. Closed Jan 1, Thanksgiving, Dec 25. Res accepted. Continental menu. Lunch $5.75-$6.75, dinner $9.95-$15.95. Sun brunch $9.95. Child's menu. Specialty: Southwest chicken. Parking. Totally nonsmoking. Cr cds: A, C, D, DS, ER, MC, V.

Mescalero

(F-4) *See also Alamogordo, Cloudcroft, Ruidoso*

Pop 1,233 **Elev** 6,605 ft
Area code 505 **Zip** 88340

What to See and Do

Mescalero Apache Reservation. Approx 4,000 Native Americans live on this reservation. Timber, cattle, and recreation are sources of income. There is also a store, museum, and casino. Ceremonials may sometimes be observed (fee); inquire at the community center or at the Mescalero store. Most famous dances are on or around July 4 (see SPECIAL EVENT). Contact Main Tribal Office. Phone 505/671-4494. Also on reservation are

Silver Lake, Mescalero Lake, and Ruidoso Recreation Areas. Fishing; hunting for elk, deer, antelope, and bear (fall), picnicking, camping (exc at Mescalero Lake; hookups at Silver and Eagle lakes only). Some fees. Phone 505/671-4494. Per vehicle ¢¢¢

Special Event

Mescalero Apache Maidens' Ceremonial. Colorful and interesting series of dances, Mountain Spirits dance at dusk, rodeo, parade. Four days incl predawn ceremony July 4. Phone 505/671-4494.

Portales

(D-7) *See also Clovis*

Founded 1890 **Pop** 11,131 **Elev** 4,000 ft **Area code** 505 **Zip** 88130
Information Roosevelt County Chamber of Commerce, 200 E 7th; 505/356-8541 or 800/635-8036
Web www.portales.com

What to See and Do

Blackwater Draw Museum. Operated by Eastern New Mexico University. Incl 12,000-yr-old artifacts and fossils from nearby archaeological site (Mar-Oct); displays, murals tell story of early inhabitants. Films, tours (by appt). Museum (Memorial Day-Labor Day, Mon-Sat, also Sun afternoons; rest of yr, Tues-Sat, also Sun afternoons). 7 mi N on US 70. Phone 505/562-2202. ¢¢

Eastern New Mexico University. (1934) 4,000 students. On campus is the Roosevelt County Museum; exhibits depict daily lives of early Western pioneers (daily; closed hols; museum phone 505/562-2592) SW corner of town. Phone 550/562-2178.

Oasis State Park. Shifting sand dunes and towering cottonwood trees, planted in 1902 by a homesteader, form an oasis. Fishing lake; picnicking, camping (hookups, dump station). Standard fees. (Daily) 6 mi N, off NM 467. Phone 505/356-5331. Per vehicle ¢¢

Special Events

Roosevelt County Heritage Days. Rodeo, dance, barbecue, parade, contests, entertainment. Phone 505/356-8541. June.

Roosevelt County Fair. Phone 505/356-4417. Mid-Aug.

Peanut Valley Festival. Phone 505/562-2242. Late Oct.

Motel/Motor Lodge

★ **CLASSIC AMERICAN ECONOMY INN.** *1613 W 2nd St (88130). 505/356-6668; toll-free 800/901-9466.* 40 units. S $40-$50; D $45-$60; suite

$35-$50; under 18 free; wkly rates. Crib free. Pet accepted. TV; cable (premium), VCR avail. Heated pool. Playground. Complimentary continental bkfst. Complimentary coffee in rms. Ck-out noon. In-rm modem link. Coin lndry. Sundries. Airport, bus depot transportation. Refrigerators, microwaves. Picnic tables, grills. Adj to Eastern New Mexico Univ. Cr cds: A, C, D, DS, MC, V.

Raton

(A-6) *See also Cimarron; also see Trinidad, CO*

Founded 1880 **Pop** 7,282 **Elev** 6,666 ft **Area code** 505 **Zip** 87740

Information Chamber & Economic Development Council, 100 Clayton Rd, PO Box 1211; 505/445-3689 or 800/638-6161

Web www.ratonchamber.com

What to See and Do

Capulin Volcano National Monument. (see). 7 mi NW on NY 332 at jct NY 96; I-90, exit 44. Phone 585/924-3232. ¢¢

Folsom Museum. Artifacts and fossils of Folsom Man (ca 12,000 B.C.). (Memorial Day-Labor Day, daily; May and Sept, wkends; winter, by appt) 29 mi E on US 64/87, then 10 mi N on NM 325, on Main St in Folsom. Phone 505/278-2122. ¢

Raton Museum. Collections relating to the Native American, Hispanic, ranch, railroad, and mining cultures in New Mexico. (Memorial Day-Labor Day, Tues-Sat; rest of yr, Wed-Sat or by appt; closed hols) 218 S 1st St. Phone 505/445-8979. **FREE**

Sugarite Canyon State Park. This park contains 3,500 acres on the New Mexico side and offers fishing, ice fishing, boating (oars or electric motors only), tubing; seasonal bow hunting for deer and turkey, x-country skiing, ice-skating, riding trails (no rentals), picnicking, camping (fee). Visitor center. (May-Sept, daily; rest of yr by appt) 10 mi NE on NM 72 and NM 526. Phone 505/445-5607. Per vehicle ¢¢

Motels/Motor Lodges

★★ **BEST WESTERN SANDS.** *300 Clayton Rd (87740). 505/445-2737; fax 505/445-4053; res 800/780-7234. www.bestwestern.com.* 50 rms. June-Aug: S, D $49-$99; each addl $3; lower rates rest of yr. Crib free. TV; cable (premium). Heated pool; whirlpool. Playground. Coffee in rms. Restaurant 6:30 am-8 pm. Ck-out 11 am. Business servs avail. In-rm modem link. Free RR station, bus depot transportation. Some refrigerators, microwaves. Cr cds: A, C, D, DS, MC, V.

★ **BUDGET HOST MELODY LANE.** *136 Canyon Dr (87740). 505/445-3655; fax 505/445-3461; toll-free 800/283-4678. www.budgethost.com.* 27 rms. May-early Oct: S $41-$49; D $46-$54; each addl $5; wkly rates; lower rates rest of yr. Crib $5. Pet accepted. TV; cable (premium). Continental bkfst. Ck-out 11 am. Meeting rm. RR station transportation. Some in-rm steam baths; refrigerators, microwaves avail. Cr cds: A, C, D, DS, MC, V.

Restaurant

★★ **PAPPAS' SWEET SHOP.** *1201 S 2nd St (87740). 505/445-9811.* Hrs: 9 am-2 pm, 5-9 pm. Closed Sun; most major hols. Res accepted. Bar. Bkfst $3.50-$7.95, lunch $4.95-$7.95, dinner $8.95-$27.95. Child's menu. Specializes in prime rib, pasta, seafood. Pianist Sat. Decorated with many collectibles and antiques. Cr cds: A, DS, MC, V.

Red River

(A-5) *See also Angel Fire, Cimarron, Taos*

Pop 484 **Elev** 8,676 ft **Area code** 505 **Zip** 87558

Information Chamber of Commerce, Main St, PO Box 870; 505/754-2366 or 800/348-6444

Web www.redrivernewmex.com

What to See and Do

Skiing. Red River Ski Area. Two triple, three double chairlifts, surface tow; patrol, school, rentals; snow-making; snack bar, cafeteria. Fifty-seven runs, longest run over 2½ mi; vertical drop 1,600 ft. (Thanksgiving-late Mar, daily) Chairlift also operates Memorial Day-Labor Day (daily; fee). 400 Pioneer Rd. Phone 505/754-2223. ¢¢¢¢

Special Events

Mardi Gras in the Mountains. Ski slope parades, Cajun food. Feb.

Enchanted Circle Century Bike Tour. Nearly 1,000 cyclists participate in a 100-mi tour around the Enchanted Circle (Red River, Angel Fire, Taos, Questa). Sept.

Motels/Motor Lodges

★★ **ALPINE LODGE.** *417 W Main (87558). 505/754-2952; fax 505/754-6421; toll-free 800/252-2333. www. thealpinelodge.com.* 45 rms, 1-3 story, 15 kits. No A/C. No elvtr. S, D from $46; kit. units for 2-12, $35-$148. Crib $5. TV; cable (premium). Playground. Restaurant 7 am-2 pm. Bar 4 pm-close. Ck-out 10 am. Business servs avail. Downhill ski opp; x-country ski 2 mi. Some balconies. On river; at ski lift. Cr cds: A, DS, MC, V.
🅓 🛄 🏊 🛖 🔥

★ **ARROWHEAD LODGE.** *405 Pio-neer Rd (87558). 505/754-2255; fax 505/754-2588; toll-free 800/299-6547. www.redrivernm.com/arrowhead.* 19 rms, 12 kits. No A/C. S, D $45-$70; each addl $10; kit. units $50-$209. TV; cable. Complimentary coffee in lobby. Restaurant nearby. Ck-out 10 am. Airport transportation. Downhill ski on site; x-country ski 4 mi. Picnic tables, grill. Sun deck. On river. Cr cds: A, DS, MC, V.
🔥 🏊 🛄 🔥 SC

★★★ **LIFTS WEST CONDOMINI-UMS.** *201 Main St (87558). 505/754-2778; fax 505/754-6617; toll-free 800/221-1859.* 75 kit. units, 3 story. Dec-Mar: S, D $60-$115; each addl $25; suites $100-$370; studio rms $75-$155; under 12 free; higher rates Dec 25; lower rates rest of yr. Crib free. TV; cable (premium), VCR (movies). Heated pool; whirlpools.

Restaurant 8 am-2 pm. Ck-out 10 am. Lndry facilities. Meeting rms. Business servs avail. Shopping arcade. Downhill ski adj; x-country ski 7 mi. Private patios, balconies. Large atrium lobby with fireplace. Cr cds: A, C, D, JCB, MC, V.
🏊 🛄 🏊

★ **THE LODGE AT RED RIVER.** *400 E Main St (87558). 505/754-6280; fax 505/754-6304. www.redriver.com/ lodgeatrr/.* 26 rms, 2 story. No A/C. No rm phones. Mid-May-Sept, late Nov-Mar: S $46; D $78; each addl $11; ski plans; higher rates hols; lower rates rest of yr. Restaurant 7-11 am, 4:30-9 pm. Bar 5-10 pm. Ck-out 11 am. Meeting rms. Business servs avail. Downhill ski on site; x-country ski 3 mi. Rustic lodge. Cr cds: A, D, DS, MC, V.
🐾 🛌 🏊 🛄 🔥

★★ **PONDEROSA LODGE.** *200 W Main St (87558). 505/754-2988; toll-free 800/336-7787. www.redriver.com/ ponderosa.* 17 rms, 2 story, 17 kit. apts. No A/C. Dec-Mar: S, D $65-$79; each addl $10; suites $122-$245; under 12 free; higher rates Dec 25; lower rates rest of yr. Crib free. TV; cable. Ck-out 10 am. Downhill ski adj; x-country ski 4 mi. Whirlpool. Sauna. Cr cds: A, D, DS, MC, V.
🅓 🏊 🛄 🔥

★ **RED RIVER INN.** *300 W Main St (87558). 505/754-2930; fax 505/754-2943; toll-free 800/365-2930. www. redriverinn.com.* 14 rms, 3 kit. units. No A/C. June-Sept: S $37-$56; D $54-$64; kit. units $60-$66; family, hol rates; ski plans; higher rates hols; lower rates rest of yr. Crib free. TV; cable (premium). Whirlpool. Compli-mentary coffee in lobby. Restaurant nearby. Ck-out 10 am. Gift shop. Downhill ski 1 blk; x-country ski 1 mi. Exercise equipt; sauna. Picnic tables, grills. Totally nonsmoking. Cr cds: A, DS, MC, V.
🏊 🛄 🔥 SC 🏋

★ **TERRACE TOWERS LODGE.** *712 W Main St (87558). 505/754-2962; fax 505/754-2990; toll-free 800/695-6343. www.redriver.com/terracetowers. com.* 26 kit. suites, 2 story. S, D $55-$110; under 12 free; higher rates: Spring Break, Dec 25. Pet accepted. TV; cable (premium), VCR avail (movies $3). Playground. Restaurant nearby. Ck-out 10 am. Coin lndry. Downhill/x-country ski ½ mi. Whirl-pool. View of valley and mountains. Cr cds: A, D, DS, ER, MC, V.

Resort

★★ **THE RIVERSIDE.** *201 Main (87558). 505/754-2252; fax 505/754-2495; toll-free 800/432-9999. www. redriver-nm.com.* 8 rms in 2-story lodge, 30 winterized kit. cabins. No A/C. Dec-Mar: S $50-$60; D $68-$80; each addl $10; kit. units to 6, $115-$150; higher rates Dec 25, hols; lower rates rest of yr. Closed late Mar-Memorial Day. Crib $5. TV; cable. Playground. Restaurant opp 7 am-10 pm. Ck-out 10 am. Meeting rm. Business servs avail. Downhill ski adj; x-country ski 2 mi. Whirlpool. Some fireplaces. Lawn games. Patio area with picnic tables, grills. Cr cds: DS, MC, V.

Cottage Colony

★ **TALL PINE RESORT.** *1929 NM 578 (87558). 505/754-2241; fax 505/754-3134; toll-free 800/573-2241. www.tallpineresort.com.* 19 kit. cabins (1-2-bedrm). No A/C. No rm phones. May-Sept: S $75; D $120. Closed rest of yr. Crib free. Pet accepted. Playground. Ck-out 10 am, ck-in 1 pm. Maid serv wkly. Grocery, package store 1½ mi. Picnic tables, grills. 27 acres in forest; cabins along Red River. Cr cds: MC, V.

Restaurants

★★★ **BRETT'S HOMESTEAD STEAKHOUSE.** *102 High Cost Trl (87558). 505/754-6136.* Hrs: 5-9 pm. Closed Easter-mid-May, Nov. Res accepted. Wine, beer. Dinner $9.95-$30. Child's menu. Specializes in fresh trout, choice steaks, prime rib. Fireplace; many antiques. In Victorian house with duck pond. Cr cds: A, D, DS, MC, V.

★ **SUNDANCE.** *401 High St (87558). 505/754-2971. www.redrivernm.com/sundance.* Hrs: 5-9 pm. Closed Apr-mid-May. Mexican menu. Wine,

beer. Dinner $7.50-$15.50. Child's menu. Specialties: stuffed sopaipilla, fajitas, super burrito. Southwestern decor; fireplace. Gift shop. Cr cds: A, D, MC, V.

★★ **TEXAS RED'S STEAK HOUSE.** *111 E Main St (87558). 505/754-2964.* Hrs: 5-9:30 pm. Dinner $6-$28.50. Child's menu. Specialties: NY strip steak, smoked pork chops, char-broiled beef steak. Western decor. Family-owned. Cr cds: A, D, DS, MC, V.

Roswell

(E-6) *See also Artesia*

Founded 1871 **Pop** 45,293 **Elev** 3,981 ft **Area code** 505 **Zip** 88201

Information Chamber of Commerce, PO Box 70, 88202; 505/623-5695

Web www.roswellnm.org

What to See and Do

Bitter Lake National Wildlife Refuge. Wildlife observation, auto tour. Hunting in season with state license. (Daily) 13 mi NE, via US 70, 285, and US 380 exits. Phone 505/622-6755. **FREE**

Bottomless Lakes State Park. Bordered by high red bluffs, seven small lakes were formed when circulating underground water formed caverns that collapsed into sinkholes. Headquarters at Cottonwood Lake has displays and a network of trails. Beach and swimming at Lea Lake only, bathhouse, skin diving, some lakes have fishing (trout), paddleboat rentals; picnicking, camping. (Daily) 10 mi E on US 380, then 6 mi S on NM 409. Phone 505/624-6058. ¢¢

Dexter National Fish Hatchery and Technology Center. This facility is the US Fish and Wildlife Service's primary center for the study and culture of endangered fish species of the American Southwest. (Daily) Also visitor center (Apr-Oct, daily). 20 mi SE via US 285 or NM 2. Phone 505/734-5910. **FREE**

Historical Center for Southeast New Mexico. Antiques, period rms (early 1900s); turn-of-the-century furnishings, clothes; communications exhibits; research library, and archives. (Daily, afternoons; Fri, by appt) Tours by appt. 200 N Lea. Phone 505/622-8333. **FREE**

⭐ **International UFO Museum & Research Center.** Museum incl exhibits on various aspects of UFO phenomena and a video-viewing rm. Various video tapes can be viewed upon request. (Daily) 114 N Main St. Phone 505/625-9495. **FREE**

New Mexico Military Institute. (1891) 1,000 cadets. State-supported high school and junior college. Alumni Memorial Chapel, near the entrance, has beautiful windows. Also here is the General Douglas L. McBride Military Museum with an interpretation of 20th-century American military history (Tues-Fri; free). Occasional marching formations and parades. Tours. N Main St and College Blvd. Phone 505/624-8011.

Roswell Museum and Art Center. Southwest arts collection incl Georgia O'Keeffe, Peter Hurd, Henriette Wyeth; Native American, Mexican American, and western arts; Dr. Robert H. Goddard's early liquid-fueled rocketry experiments. (Mon-Sat, also Sun and hol afternoons; closed Jan 1, Thanksgiving, Dec 25) 100 W 11th St. Phone 505/624-6744. **FREE**

Spring River Park & Zoo. Zoo and children's zoo area; small lake with fishing for children 11 and under only; miniature train; antique wooden-horse carousel. Picnicking, playground. (Daily; closed Dec 25) 1306 E College Blvd. Phone 505/624-6760. **FREE**

Special Events

UFO Encounters Festival. UFO Expo trade show, alien chase, alien parade, costume contest, guest speeches. July 4 wkend. Phone 505/625-9495.

Eastern New Mexico State Fair and Rodeo. 2 mi S on US 285, at Fair Park. Phone 505/623-9411. Sept-Oct.

Motels/Motor Lodges

⭐⭐ **BEST WESTERN SALLY PORT INN & SUITES.** *2000 N Main St (88201).* 505/622-6430; fax 505/623-7631; res 800/780-7234. *www.best western.com.* 124 rms, 2 story. S, D $79; each addl $10; suites $90-$119; under 12 free. Crib free. Pet accepted. TV; cable (premium). Indoor pool; whirlpool. Complimentary full bkfst. Restaurant 6-10 am, 5-10 pm; Sun 6-11 am, 5-9 pm. Rm serv. Bar 4 pm-midnight; Fri, Sat to 1 am. Ck-out noon. Coin lndry. Meeting rms. Business servs avail. Sundries. Beauty shop. Free airport, bus depot transportation. Tennis. 18-hole golf privileges adj, putting green, driving range. Exercise equipt. Refrigerators. Cr cds: A, C, D, DS, MC, V.

⭐ **BUDGET INN.** *2200 W Second St (88201).* 505/623-3811; fax 505/623-7030; toll-free 800/806-7030. 29 rms, 2 story. S $27-$37; D $31-$45; each addl $4; kit. units $175/wk; under 16 free. Crib free. Pet accepted, some restrictions; $2. TV; cable. Pool. Coffee in lobby. Ck-out 11 am. Some refrigerators. Cr cds: A, DS, MC, V.

⭐ **FRONTIER MOTEL.** *3010 N Main St (88201).* 505/622-1400; fax 505/622-1405; toll-free 800/678-1401. *www.frontiermotelroswell.com.* 38 rms. S $28-$36; D $32-$40; each addl $4; higher rates NMMI events. Pet accepted. TV; cable (premium). Pool. Complimentary continental bkfst. Restaurant adj 5:30 am-9 pm. Ck-out 11 am. Some refrigerators. Cr cds: A, C, D, DS, MC, V.

⭐⭐ **RAMADA.** *2803 W 2nd St (88201).* 505/623-9440; fax 505/622-9708; res 800/228-2828. *www.ramada. com.* 61 rms, 2 story. S $53; D $58; each addl $5; under 18 free. Crib $5. Pet accepted; $15 deposit. TV; cable. Heated pool. Ck-out noon. Meeting rms. Business servs avail. Cr cds: A, D, DS, MC, V.

⭐⭐ **ROSWELL INN.** *1815 N Main St (88202).* 505/623-4920. *www.nmohwy. com.* 121 rms, 2 story. S $62; D $65; each addl $7; suites $95-$145; under 18 free. Crib free. TV; cable (premium). Heated pool; poolside serv. Restaurant 6 am-9 pm. Rm serv. Bar 11-1 am. Ck-out noon. Meeting rms. Free airport transportation. 18-hole golf privileges. Balconies. Cr cds: A, C, D, DS, MC, V.

Restaurant

★ **EL TORO BRAVO.** *102 S Main St (88201). 505/622-9280.* Hrs: 11 am-2:30 pm, 5-9 pm; Sat 11 am-9 pm; Sun to 2:30 pm. Res accepted. Closed most major hols. Mexican menu. Wine, beer. Lunch, dinner $1.95-$10.95. Lunch buffet (Mon-Fri) $5.55. Child's menu. Specialties: chimichangas, chile Colorado, fajitas. Bullfighting and Mexican pictures. Cr cds: A, DS, MC, V.

Ruidoso

(E-4) *See also Alamogordo, Cloudcroft, Mescalero*

Pop 7,698 **Elev** 6,911 ft
Area code 505 **Zip** 88345
Information Ruidoso Valley Chamber of Commerce, 720 Sudderth Dr, PO Box 698; 505/257-7395 or 800/253-2255
Web www.ruidoso.net

What to See and Do

Hubbard Museum of the American West. Western-themed exhibits relating to horses and pioneer life. (Daily; closed Thanksgiving, Dec 25) 841 Hwy 70W, PO Box 40, 88346. Phone 505/378-4142. ¢¢¢

Lincoln State Monument. Lincoln was the site of the infamous Lincoln County War and a hangout of Billy the Kid. Several properties have been restored, incl the Old Lincoln County Courthouse and the mercantile store of John Tunstall. Guided tours (summer, res required). (Daily; closed hols) 30 mi E on US 70, then 10 mi NW on US 380. ¢¢

Old Dowlin Mill. A 20-ft waterwheel still drives a mill more than 100 yrs old. In town. Phone 800/253-2255.

Ski Apache Resort. Resort has four-passenger gondola; quad, five triple, two double chairlifts; surface lift; patrol, school, rentals; snack bars, cafeteria, bar. Fifty-two runs, longest run over two mi; vertical drop 1,900 ft. (Thanksgiving-Easter, daily) 16 mi NW on NM 48, 532 in Lincoln National Forests. Phone 505/336-4356. ¢¢¢¢

Smokey Bear Historical State Park. Commemorates the history and development of the national symbol of forest fire prevention. The original Smokey, who was orphaned by a fire raging in the Lincoln National Forests, is buried here within sight of the mountain where he was found. Fire prevention exhibit, film. (Daily; closed Jan 1, Thanksgiving, Dec 25) 22 mi N via NM 37/48 on US 380 in Capitan. Phone 505/354-2748. ¢ Nearby is

Smokey Bear Museum. Features 1950s memorabilia of famed fire-fighting bear found in the nearby Capitan Mtns. (Daily; closed hols) Phone 505/354-2298. **FREE**

The Spencer Theater for the Performing Arts. Stunning $22 million structure offers 514 seats for professional touring musical and theater productions. Created from 450 tons of Spanish limestone, the building's design calls forth images of pyramids, mountain peaks, and sci-fi star cruisers. Inside are multiple blown glass installations by Seattle artist Dale Chihuly. (Call for schedule) Tours (Tues, Thurs). N of Ruidoso at Alto via NM 48. Phone 888/818-7872.

Special Events

Horse racing. Ruidoso Downs. Thoroughbred and quarter horse racing, pari-mutuel betting. Home of All-American Futurity, world's richest quarter horse race (Labor Day); All-American Derby and All-American Gold Cup. Phone 505/378-4431. Thurs-Sun and hols. Early May-Labor Day.

Smokey Bear Stampede. 22 mi N via NM 48 in Capitan. Fireworks, music festival, parade, dances, barbecue. Phone 505/354-2273. Early July.

Arts Festival. Phone 505/854-2261. Last full wknd July.

Aspenfest. Incl motorcycle convention, official state chili cook-off, arts and crafts. Phone 800/253-2255. Early Oct. Phone 505/257-5121.

Motels/Motor Lodges

★ ★ **BEST WESTERN SWISS CHALET.** *1451 Mechem Dr (88355). 505/258-3333; fax 505/258-5325; toll-free 800/477-9477. www.ruidoso.net/ swisschalet.* 81 rms, 2 story. June-Sept: S $69-$99; D $79-$109; each addl $10; suites $99-$150; under 12 free; lower rates rest of yr. Pet accepted, some restrictions. TV; cable (premium); VCR avail (movies). Indoor pool; whirlpool. Sauna. Restaurant 7-11 am, 5:30-9 pm; closed Mon. Rm serv. Bar 5-10 pm. Ck-out noon. Coin lndry. Meeting rms. Business servs avail. Sundries. Balconies. On hilltop. Cr cds: A, C, D, DS, ER, JCB, MC, V.

🐾 🏊 ⛷ 🔥 SC

★ **INNSBRUCK LODGE.** *601 Sudderth Dr (88345). 505/257-4071; toll-free 800/680-4447. www.ruidoso.com/ innsbruck.* 48 rms, 30 with A/C, 18 with shower only, 2 story. Mid-June-Sept: S, D $32-$60; under 10 free; wkly rates; higher rates hols; lower rates rest of yr. Crib $4-$6. TV; cable. Restaurant nearby. Ck-out 11 am. Business servs avail. Gift shop. Downhill ski 16 mi. Health club privileges. Cr cds: A, D, DS, MC, V.

⛷ ⛷ 🔥 SC

★ **SUPER 8.** *100 Cliff Dr (88345). 505/378-8180; toll-free 800/800-8000. www.super8.com.* 63 rms, 2 story. May-Sept: S $45-$58; D $53-$62; each addl $4; suites $80.88-85.88; lower rates rest of yr. Crib $3. TV; cable (premium), VCR avail (movies). Whirlpool. Sauna. Ck-out 11 am. Coin lndry. Business servs avail. Sundries. Picnic table. Cr cds: A, C, D, DS, MC, V.

D ⛷ 🔥 SC

★ ★ **VILLAGE LODGE.** *1000 Mechem Dr (88345). 505/258-5442; fax 505/258-3127; toll-free 800/722-8779. www.villagelodge.com.* 28 kit. suites, 2 story. Mid-May-mid-Sept, Nov-Easter: S, D $79-$109; each addl $10; under 13 free; higher rates hols; lower rates rest of yr. TV; cable (premium). Whirlpool. Ck-out 11 am. Business servs avail. Downhill ski 14 mi. Microwaves. Cr cds: A, DS, MC, V.

⛷ ⛷ 🔥

Hotels

★ **ENCHANTMENT INN AND SUITES.** *307 Hwy 70 W (88355). 505/378-4051; fax 505/378-5427; toll-free 800/435-0280. www.ruidoso.com/ enchantment.* 81 rms, 2 story 33 suites. S, D $65-$80; suites, kit. units $65-$185; under 18 free. TV; cable (premium). Indoor pool; whirlpool. Restaurant 7-11 am, 5-9 pm. Rm serv. Bar. Ck-out 11 am. Coin lndry. Meeting rms. Business servs avail. Downhill ski 20 mi. Picnic tables, grills. Cr cds: A, DS, MC, V.

D ⛷ ⛷ 🔥 ⛷

★ ★ **SHADOW MOUNTAIN LODGE.** *107 Main Rd (88345). 505/257-4886; fax 505/257-2000; toll-free 800/441-4331. www.smlruidoso. com.* 19 kit. units. Memorial Day-Labor Day: S, D $67-$97; each addl $10; ski plans; lower rates rest of yr. TV; cable (premium). Complimentary coffee in rms. Restaurant nearby. Ck-out 11 am. Business servs avail. Downhill ski 18 mi. Wet bars. Fireplaces. Grills. Opp river. Cr cds: A, C, D, DS, MC, V.

✈ ⛷ 🔥 ⛷

Resorts

★ **HIGH COUNTRY LODGE.** *Hwy 48, Alto (88312). 505/336-4321; fax 505/336-8205; toll-free 800/845-7265. www.ruidoso.net.* 32 kit. apts (2-bedrm). No A/C. S, D $49-$119; each addl $10; higher rates hol wkends. Pet accepted. TV; cable (premium). Indoor pool; whirlpool. Playground. Ck-out 11 am. Meeting rms. Business servs avail. Tennis. Game rm. Lawn games. Exercise rm; sauna. Fireplaces. Picnic table, grills. Lake opp. Cr cds: A, D, DS, MC, V.

🐾 ⛷ ⛷ 🎾 ⛷ 🔥

★ ★ ★ **INN OF THE MOUNTAIN GODS.** *Caprizo Canyon Rd, Mescalero (88340). 505/464-6173; res 800/545-9011. www.innofthemountaingods.com.* 253 rms, 2-5 story. June-Sep: S, D, suites $120-$150; each addl $14; under 12 free; package plans; lower rates rest of yr. Crib $14. TV; cable (premium). Heated pool; wading pool, whirlpool, poolside serv. Sauna. Dining rm 7 am-10 pm. Box lunches. Rm serv. Bars 10-1 am; entertainment. Ck-out noon, ck-in 4 pm. Convention facilities. Business servs avail. Gift shop. Airport transportation. Lighted tennis, pro. 18-hole golf, pro, putting green. Dock; rowboats, paddleboats. Game rm. Lawn games. Some refrigerators. Private patios, balconies. Casino. Cr cds: A, C, D, DS, MC, V.

B&Bs/Small Inns

★ ★ ★ **CASA DE PATRON BED AND BREAKFAST INN.** *Hwy 380 E, Lincoln (88338). 505/653-4676; fax 505/653-4671; toll-free 800/524-5202. www.casapatron.com.* 5 rms, shower only, 2 casitas, 2 suites. No A/C. No rm phones. S $69; D $79; each addl $6; casitas $97; suites $97-$107; min some hols & special events. Complimentary full bkfst. Restaurant nearby. Ck-out noon, ck-in 3-8 pm. Luggage handling. Business servs avail. Whirlpool. Sauna. Refrigerator in suites. Picnic tables. Built in 1860; antiques. This inn was the home of Juan Patron, the youngest Speaker of the House in the Territorial Legislature. Legendary figures such as Billy the Kid and Pat Garrett are said to have spent the night here. Totally nonsmoking. Cr cds: MC, V.

Villa/Condo

★ **WEST WINDS LODGE AND CONDOS.** *208 Eagle Dr (88455). 505/257-4031; toll-free 800/421-0691. www.wwlodge.com.* 21 rms, 15 condos. No A/C. No rm phones. Dec-Jan, mid-June-Sept: S, D $42-$75; each addl $5-$10; kit. units $54-$75; condominiums $75-$169; lower rates rest of yr. TV; cable. Indoor pool; whirlpool. Restaurant nearby. Ck-out 11 am. Free bus depot transportation. Downhill/x-country ski 16 mi. Grills. Cr cds: DS, MC, V.

Restaurant

★ ★ ★ **VICTORIA'S ROMANTIC HIDEAWAY.** *2117 Sudderth Dr*

(88345). 505/257-5440. www.ruidoso. net. Sitting: 6 pm. Closed Dec 25. Res required. No A/C. Sicilian menu. Wine, beer. Prix fixe: 7-course dinner $75. Specializes in traditional Sicilian entrees. Intimate dining. Cr cds: MC, V.

SC

Salinas Pueblo Missions National Monument

See also Socorro

(Approx 75 mi SE of Albuquerque via I-40, NM 337, 55)

This monument was established to explore European-Native American contact and the resultant cultural changes. The stabilized ruins of the massive 17th-century missions are basically unaltered, preserving the original design and construction. All three units are open and feature wayside exhibits, trails, and picnic areas (daily; closed January 1, December 25). Monument Headquarters, one block west of NM 55 on US 60 in Mountainair, has an audiovisual presentation and an exhibit depicting the Salinas story. (Daily; closed January 1, December 25) Contact the Superintendent, PO Box 517, Mountainair 87036; phone 505/847-2585. The three units of this monument are

Gran Quivira. Here are the massive walls of the 17th-century San Buenaventura Mission (begun in 1659 but never completed), "San Isidro" Church (circa 1639), and 21 pueblo mounds, two of which have been excavated. A self-guided trail and museum/visitor center (exhibits, seven-minute video, 40-minute video) combine to vividly portray Native American life and the cultural change that has occurred over the past 1,000 years. Various factors led to the desertion of the pueblo and the mission around 1671. Tompiro Indians occupied this and the Abó

site. Picnicking. 25 mi SE of Mountainair on NM 55. Phone 505/847-
2770.

Abó. Ruins of the mission church
of San Gregorio de Abó (circa 1622),
built by Native Americans under the
direction of Franciscan priests. This is
the only early church in New Mexico
with 40-foot buttressed curtain
walls—a style typical of medieval
European architecture. The pueblo
adjacent to the church was abandoned around 1673 because of
drought, disease, and Apache uprisings. The Abó and others from the
Salinas jurisdiction eventually moved
south with the Spanish to El Paso del
Norte, where they established the
pueblo of Ysleta del Sur and other
towns still in existence today. There
are self-guided trails throughout the
mission compound and pueblo
mounds. Picnicking (no water). 9 mi
W of Mountainair on US 60, then ¾
mi N on NM 513. Phone 505/847-
2400.

Quarai. Ruins of the Mission de la
Purísima Concepción de Cuarac,
other Spanish structures, and unexcavated Native American mounds, all
built of red sandstone. Built about
1630, it was abandoned along with
the pueblo about 1677, most likely
for the same reasons. Unlike the
other two, this site was occupied by
Tiwa-speaking people. Much of the
history is related to the Spanish-
Indian cultural conflict. The church
ruins have been excavated, and it is
the most complete church in the
monument. The visitor center has a
museum and interpretive displays.
Wayside exhibits, trail guides. Picnicking. 8 mi N of Mountainair on
NM 55, then 1 mi W on a county
road from Punta. Phone 505/847-
2290.

Santa Fe

(B-4) *See also Espanola, Las Vegas, Los
Alamos*

Founded 1607 **Pop** 62,203 **Elev** 7,000
ft **Area code** 505
Information Convention & Visitors
Bureau, PO Box 909, 87504; 505/984-
6760 or 800/777-2489
Web www.santafe.org

What to See and Do

⭐ **Canyon Road Tour.** This tour totals
about two or three mi, and there is
no better way to savor the unique
character of Santa Fe than to travel
along its narrow, picturesque old
streets. Go east on San Francisco St
to the cathedral and bear right to the
end of Cathedral Pl. Turn left on
Alameda. On the left is

Camino del Monte Sol. Famous
street on which many artists live
and work. Turn left up the hill. Off
this road are a number of interesting streets worth exploring. If traveling by car, continue down the
hill on Camino del Monte Sol
about one mi to

Canyon Road. Many artists now
live on this old thoroughfare.
Continue along Canyon Rd several
mi to

Cristo Rey Church. This is the
largest adobe structure in the US.
It contains beautiful ancient
stone reredos (altar screens).
(Mon-Fri; closed hols) Return on
Canyon Rd to

**Museum of Indian Arts and Cul-
ture.** Displays outstanding collection of the Laboratory of
Anthropology; Southwestern basketry, pottery, weaving, jewelry,
and other cultural artifacts. (Tues-
Sun; closed hols) 710 Camino Lejo.
Phone 505/476-1250. ¢¢ Across the
yard is the

Museum of International Folk Art.
Folk art collections with more than
125,000 objects from around the
world: textiles, woodcarvings, toys,
jewelry, paintings, religious articles. (Tues-Sun; closed hols) 706
Camino Lejo. Phone 505/476-
1200. ¢¢ On the same road, less
than one long blk beyond the
museum, is the

**National Park Service, Southwest
Regional Office.** (1939) Adobe
building with central patio. (Mon-
Fri; closed hols) 1100 Old Santa Fe
Tr. Phone 505/988-6011. **FREE**
From here go west a short distance
on Old Santa Fe Tr, then south on
Camino Lejo to the

St. Francis School. Turn right
across first bridge and immediately
bear left onto

St. John's College in Santa Fe.
(1964) 400 students. The first cam-

Canyon Road

Georgia O'Keeffe Museum. Houses world's largest permanent collection of O'Keeffe's work. (Sept-June, Tue, Thurs-Sat; rest of yr, daily; closed hols) 217 Johnson St. Phone 505/946-1000. ¢¢¢

Hyde Memorial State Park. Perched 8,500 ft up in the Sangre de Cristo Mtns near the Santa Fe Ski Basin; used as base camp for backpackers and skiers in the Santa Fe National Forests. X-country skiing, rentals, picnicking (shelters), playground, concession, camping (electric hookups, dump station). Standard fees. (Daily) 8 mi NE via NM 475. Phone 505/983-7175. ¢¢

pus of St. John's College is in Annapolis, MD (1696). Liberal arts. On Camino Cruz Blanca, just west of Camino del Monte Sol. Phone 505/984-6000. On Camino Cruz Blanca, just E of Camino del Monte Sol. From its intersection with Camino Cruz Blanca, walk south approx two blks on Camino del Monte Sol to Old Santa Fe Trail, then turn east. On the right is the

Wheelwright Museum. Exhibits of the arts and culture of Native Americans. Collections of Navajo textiles, silver, baskets, and Southwest pottery; traditional and contemporary artists' exhibitions; turn-of-the-century replica of Navajo Trading Post. (Mon-Sat, also Sun afternoons; closed Jan 1, Thanksgiving, Dec 25) 704 Camino Lejo. Phone 800/607-4636. **FREE** Shortest way back to town is via the Old Santa Fe Trail.

College of Santa Fe. (1947) 1,400 students. On campus are the Greer Garson Theatre Center, Communications Center, and Fogelson Library. 3 mi SW at Cerrillos Rd and St. Michael's Dr. Phone 505/473-6011.

El Rancho de las Golondrinas. Living history museum depicting Spanish Colonial life in New Mexico from 1700-1900. (June-Sept, Wed-Sun). Tours by appt (Apr-Oct). 13 mi S, off I-25. Phone 505/471-2261. ¢¢

Institute of American Indian Arts Museum. This national collection contains more than 8,000 pieces of contemporary Native American art and some historical material. Collection incl paintings, prints, drawings, sculpture, weavings, costumes, jewelry, and other artwork. (Mon-Sat) 108 Cathedral Pl. Phone 505/983-8900. ¢¢

Pecos National Historical Park. Ruins of two large Spanish mission churches and unexcavated multistory communal pueblo dwelling that once housed 2,000; it was occupied for 500 yrs. The final 17 occupants left the pueblo in 1838 and relocated to Jemez Pueblo. Once a landmark on the Santa Fe Trail. Self-guided walk through pueblo and mission, restored kivas. Visitor center with introductory film, exhibits. (Daily; closed Dec 25) 25 mi SE via US 25. Contact Superintendent, PO Box 418, Pecos 87552-0418. Phone 505/757-6414. ¢¢

San Ildefonso Pueblo. (Population: 447) This pueblo is famous for its beautiful surroundings and its black, red, and polychrome pottery, made famous by Maria Poveka Martinez. (Daily; closed winter wknds; visitors must register at the visitor center) Photography permit may be purchased at the visitor center (fee). Various festivals take place here throughout the yr (see SPECIAL EVENTS). The circular structure with the staircase leading up to its rim is a *kiva,* or ceremonial chamber. There are two shops in the pueblo plaza, and a tribal museum adjoins the governor's office. One-half mi west is a fishing lake. 16 mi N on US 84, 285, then 6 mi W on NM 502. Phone 505/455-2273. Per vehicle ¢¢

Santa Fe Children's Museum. Participatory children's exhibits of science and arts in playlike environment. Giant soap bubbles, greenhouse with pond and working microscopes, simulated rock-climbing activity involving 18-ft-high climbing wall (days vary), toddler water-play area. Also art and science programs. (June-Aug, Wed-Sun; rest of yr, Thurs-Sun; closed hols) 1050 Old Pecos Tr. Phone 505/989-8359. ¢¢

Santa Fe National Forest. This forest consists of over 1½ million acres. Fishing is excellent in the Pecos and Jemez rivers and tributary streams. Hiking trails are close to unusual geologic formations. Hot springs in the Jemez Mtns. Four wilderness areas within the forest total more than 300,000 acres. Campgrounds are provided by the Forest Service at more than 40 locations; for res call 800/280-2267. There are user fees for many areas. Forest headquarters are located here. Contact the Forest Supervisor, 1474 Rodeo Rd, 87505. Phone 505/438-7840.

Santa Fe School of Cooking. Sign up for classes offered several times wkly in traditional and contemporary Southwestern cuisine. Culinary tours involve classes with nationally renowned chefs with trips to local farms and wineries. Call for schedule. 116 W San Francisco St. Phone 505/983-4511.

Santa Fe Ski Area. Area has quad, one triple chairlift, two double chairlifts, two surface lifts; patrol, school, rentals, snowmaking; concession, cafeteria, restaurant, bar. Forty-four runs, longest run three mi; vertical drop 1,650 ft. (Thanksgiving-mid-Apr, daily) 16 mi NE via NM 475. Phone 505/982-4429. ¢¢¢¢

Santuario de Guadalupe. (ca 1785) Adobe church museum featuring Spanish Colonial art, changing exhibits, the only existing complete *lienzo* in New Mexico, the Jose de Alzibar oil on canvas of *Our Lady of Guadalupe,* garden, authentic 18th-century sacristy. (Daily; winter, Mon-Fri; closed hols) 100 Guadalupe St. Phone 505/988-2027. **Donation**

⭐ **Walking tour.** Start on Palace Ave at

The Plaza. Laid out in 1607, this famous square is where the old Santa Fe Trail ended. Incl Soldier's Monument at the center, "End of the Santa Fe Trail" marker at southeast corner, and Kearny Proclamation marker on north side. The colorful plaza is center of informal civic social life and scene of fiestas and markets. Cross Palace Ave toward the roofed portal under which Native Americans sell jewelry, pottery, and blankets, and enter

Palace of the Governors. Built in 1610, this is the oldest public building in continuous use in the US. It was the seat of government in New Mexico for more than 300 yrs. Lew Wallace, governor of the territory (1878-1881), wrote part of *Ben Hur* here in 1880. It is now a major museum of Southwestern history. The Palace, Museum of Fine Arts, Museum of Indian Arts and Culture, Museum of International Folk Art, and state monuments all make up the Museum of New Mexico. (Tues-Sun; closed hols) Phone 505/827-6483. ¢¢ Turn right (west) onto the Plaza and walk across Lincoln Ave to the

Museum of Fine Arts. (1917) Classic Southwestern Pueblo Revival architecture. More than 10,000 art objects; focus on Santa Fe and Taos artists of the early 20th century. Changing exhibits of American art and photography. Research library. (Tues-Sun; closed Jan 1, Easter, Thanksgiving, Dec 25) 107 W Palace Ave. Phone 505/476-5072. ¢¢ Turn left (north) two blks to Federal Pl. Turn right, passing the

Federal Court House. There is a monument to Kit Carson in front. Northeast of this is the monumental

Scottish Rite Temple. Modeled after part of the Alhambra. Return to the plaza along Washington Ave, turn left (east) on Palace Ave, and explore

Sena Plaza and Prince Plaza. Small shops, formerly old houses, built behind portals and around central patios. Next street east is Cathedral Pl. Turn right. On the left is the

Cathedral of St. Francis. (1869) French Romanesque cathedral built under the direction of Archbishop Lamy (prototype for Bishop Latour in Willa Cather's *Death Comes for the Archbishop*). La Conquistadora Chapel, said to be the

country's oldest Marian shrine, is here. (Daily) Tours (summer). Phone 505/982-5619. This is the eastern end of San Francisco St, Santa Fe's main street. Turn right and drop in at

La Fonda Hotel. A long-time center of Santa Fe social life. Former meeting place of trappers, pioneers, merchants, soldiers, and politicians; known as the "Inn at the End of the Trail." Just beyond, walk left (south) one blk on Old Santa Fe Tr. Here is

---

SANTA FE'S ART AND ARCHITECTURE

Every tourist's Santa Fe exploration begins at the Plaza, plotted when the town was built in 1610. A square block planted with trees and grass, it's a place to sit on park benches to study a map or just watch the parade of visitors go by. Lining the Plaza on the east, south, and west are art galleries, Native American jewelry shops, boutiques, a vintage hotel, and restaurants. Facing the Plaza on the north is the Palace of the Governors, the first stop on your walking tour. Sheltered along the portal (porch) that spans the front of the block-long, pueblo-style building—which also dates from 1610—are dozens of craft and art vendors from the region's nearby pueblos. Only pueblo Indians can sell their jewelry, blankets, beadwork, pottery, and other goods here. Inside the palace, a museum exhibits nearly 20,000 historic objects, including pottery, books, documents, and artifacts.

One block west along Palace Avenue, the Museum of Fine Arts was built in 1917 and represents the Pueblo Revival style, also called Santa Fe style, of architecture. Site of chamber music concerts, the museum exhibits work by local artists and by noted painters of the Santa Fe and Taos art colonies. Continue west on Palace another block, turning north on Grant Avenue one block, then west on Johnson Street one block. Stop inside the relatively new Georgia O'Keefe Museum to see the world's largest collection of the artist's work.

Backtrack to the Plaza, heading to the Catron Building, which forms the east "wall" of the Plaza. Inside the 1891 office building are several art galleries and stores. At the building's southern end, anchoring the southeast corner of the Plaza, is La Fonda, the oldest hotel in Santa Fe. The lobby's art and decor are worth a look, and the rooftop bar is a favorite gathering place. From the plaza, walk south two blocks on Old Santa Fe Trail to Loretto Chapel. The beautiful chapel has an irresistible story in its Miraculous Staircase. Now walk east on Water Street one block to Cathedral Place, turning left (north) on Cathedral one block to the magnificent St. Francis Cathedral, built over several years in the latter 1800s.

Directly across the street, see the Institute of American Indian Arts Museum, housing thousands of pieces of sculpture, basketry, paintings, and pottery. Cathedral ends here at Palace Avenue, which you'll follow east one long block to explore two excellent bookstores, Nicholas Potter Bookseller and Palace Avenue Books. Backtracking on Palace again to the west, Sena Plaza is on your right (on the north side of the street). Inside the lovely, flower-filled courtyard, you'll find a 19th-century hacienda that once belonged to the Sena family and is now filled with art galleries, shops and a restaurant. Wind up back at the Plaza by following Palace another long block to the west; head to the Ore House on the Plaza's west side to review the day over refreshments.

Loretto Chapel. (Chapel of Our Lady of Light) Gothic chapel built by the Sisters of Loretto, the first religious women to come to New Mexico. (Daily) Old Santa Fe Trail. Phone 505/984-7971. The problem of constructing a staircase to the choir loft here baffled workmen until an unknown carpenter appeared and built

The Miraculous Staircase. A circular stairway 22 ft high, built without central support and, according to legend, put together with wooden pegs. It makes two complete 360° turns and has 33 steps. (Daily; closed Jan 1, Thanksgiving, Dec 25) Phone 505/984-7971. ¢ Continue south along Santa Fe Tr crossing the bridge over the Santa Fe River. One blk beyond is

San Miguel Mission. Oldest church still in use in the US, originally built in the early 1600s. Santa Fe's oldest wooden *reredos* (altar screen), dated 1798. Much of the interior has been restored; audio tours. (Daily; closed hols) 401 Old Santa Fe Trail. Phone 505/983-3974. **Donation** A few yards east, on narrow De Vargas St, is the

Oldest House. Believed to be pre-Spanish; built by Native Americans more than 800 yrs ago. Walk west along De Vargas St. South is the new

State Capitol. (1966) This unique building, in modified Territorial style, is round and intended to resemble a Zia sun symbol Self-guided tours. (Memorial Day-Labor Day, daily; rest of yr, Mon-Sat; closed hols). Return to the Plaza via Old Santa Fe Tr, just east of the capitol. Phone 505/986-4589. **FREE** Return to the Plaza via Old Santa Fe Trail, just E of the capitol.

Special Events

Buffalo and Comanche dances. Fiesta at San Ildefonso Pueblo. Phone 505/867-3301. Late Jan.

Fiesta and Green Corn Dance. San Felipe Pueblo. Early May.

Spring Corn Dances. Cochiti, San Felipe, Santo Domingo, and other pueblos. Races, contests. Phone 505/843-7270. Late May-early June.

Horse racing. The Downs. 5 mi S on I-25. Thoroughbred and quarter horse racing. For res phone 505/471-3311. June-Labor Day.

St. Anthony's Feast-Comanche Dance. San Juan Pueblo. Mid-June.

Santa Fe Opera. 8 mi N on US 84/285. Presents combination of operatic classics with neglected masterpieces and an American premiere in an outdoor setting. Backstage tours (during season, Mon-Sat). Res suggested. For schedule and prices contact PO Box 2408, 87504. Phone 505/986-5955 or 505/986-5900 (box office). June-Aug.

Santa Fe Rodeo. Late June.

Santa Fe Chamber Music Festival. Contact PO Box 853, 87504; phone 505/983-2075. July-Aug.

Northern Pueblo Artist & Craftsman Show. Mid-July.

Spanish Market. Main plaza. Artisans display Spanish crafts. Phone 505/983-4038. Last full wkend July.

Fiesta at Santo Domingo Pueblo. Corn dance. This fiesta is probably the largest and most famous of the Rio Grande pueblo fiestas. Early Aug.

Indian Market. Plaza. The largest in the world with tribes from all over US. Dances, Indian art. Make res at lodgings well in advance. Phone 505/983-5220. Mid-Aug.

Invitational Antique Indian Art Show. Sweeney Center. Largest show of its kind in the country. Pre-1935 items; attracts dealers, collectors, museums. Phone 505/984-6760. Two days mid-Aug.

Santa Fe Pro Musica. Chamber orchestra and chamber ensemble perform classical and contemporary music, also performance of Messiah during Christmas season, Mozart Festival in Feb. Contact PO Box 2091, 87504; phone 505/988-4640. Sept-May.

Santa Fe Fiesta. This ancient folk festival, dating back to 1712, features historical pageantry, religious observances, arts and crafts shows, street dancing. Celebrates the reconquest of Santa Fe by Don Diego de Vargas in 1692. Make res well in advance. Phone 505/988-7575. Second wkend Sept.

Christmas Eve Celebrations. In Santa Fe and nearby villages with street fires and *farolitos* (paper bag lanterns) "to guide the Christ Child," candlelit Nacimientos (nativity scenes), and other events. Santo Domingo, Tesuque, Santa Clara, and other pueblos have Christmas dances the following three days.

Motels/Motor Lodges

★ ★ **BEST WESTERN INN OF SANTA FE.** *3650 Cerrillos Rd (87505). 505/438-3822; fax 505/438-3795; res 800/780-7234. www.bestwestern.com.* 97 rms, 3 story. Memorial Day-Labor Day: S $65-$105; D $66-$120; each addl $10; suites $95-$195; under 12 free; higher rates special events; lower rates rest of yr. Crib free. Pet accepted, some restrictions. TV; cable (premium). Indoor pool; whirlpool. Complimentary continental bkfst. Ck-out 11 am. Coin lndry. Business servs avail. Downhill/x-country ski 20 mi. Some refrigerators. Balconies. Cr cds: A, C, D, DS, MC, V.

🄳 ⌖ 🖂 ⌸ 🆖 🔥

★ ★ **BEST WESTERN LAMP-LIGHTER INN.** *2405 Cerrillos Rd (87505). 505/471-8000; fax 505/471-1397; res 800/767-5267. www.bestwestern.com.* 80 rms, 2 story. 16 kits. May-Oct: S, D $72-$85; suites $95; kit. units $95; under 18 free; lower rates rest of yr. Crib free. TV; cable (premium). Indoor pool. Sauna. Complimentary coffee in rms. Restaurant 7 am-9 pm. Bar. Ck-out 11 am. Guest lndry. Business servs avail. Refrigerators; some microwaves. Picnic tables. Cr cds: A, D, DS, MC, V.

🖂 🔥

★ ★ **COURTYARD BY MARRIOTT.** *3347 Cerrillos Rd (87505). 505/473-2800; fax 505/473-4905; toll-free 800/777-3347. www.santafecourtyard. com.* 213 rms, 3 story. May-Oct: S, D $69-$139; each addl $10; under 17 free; ski rates; higher rates: Dec 25, Indian Market; lower rates rest of yr. Crib free. TV; cable (premium). Indoor pool; whirlpools. Coffee in rms. Restaurant 7 am-1:30 pm, 5-9:30 pm. Bar. Ck-out noon. Coin lndry. Meeting rms. Business center. In-rm modem link. Gift shop. Free airport transportation. Downhill/x-country ski 17 mi. Exercise equipt. Refrigerators; microwaves avail. Some

private patios, balconies. Cr cds: A, C, D, DS, MC, V.

🄳 ⌖ 🖂 ⏀ 🆖 🔥 🆂🅲 ⚇

★ **GARRETTS DESERT INN.** *311 Old Santa Fe Tr (87501). 505/982-1851; fax 505/989-1647; toll-free 800/888-2145.* 82 rms, 2 story. July-Aug: S, D $111-$121; suites $131; lower rates rest of yr. TV; cable (premium). Heated pool. Restaurant 7 am-8 pm. Bar. Ck-out noon. Meeting rms. Business servs avail. Cr cds: A, D, DS, MC, V.

🖂 🔥

★ ★ **HOLIDAY INN.** *4048 Cerrillos Rd (87505). 505/473-4646; fax 505/473-2186; toll-free 800/465-4329. www.holiday-inn.com.* 130 rms, 4 story. Mid-June-Sept: S $89-$139; D $89-$149; each addl $10; under 18 free; lower rates rest of yr. Crib free. Pet accepted, some restrictions. TV; cable (premium). Heated indoor/outdoor pool; whirlpool, poolside serv. Complimentary coffee in rms. Restaurant 6:30 am-10 pm. Rm serv. Bar. Ck-out noon. Meeting rms. Business servs avail. In-rm modem link. Bellhops. Sundries. Airport, bus depot transportation. Downhill/x-country ski 20 mi. Exercise equipt; sauna. Refrigerator. Private patios, balconies. Cr cds: A, D, DS, MC, V.

🄳 ⌖ ⏀ 🖂 ⏀ 🆖 🔥

★ **HOWARD JOHNSON EXPRESS INN.** *4044 Cerrillos Rd (87505). 505/438-8950; fax 505/471-9129; res 800/446-4656. www.hojo.com.* 47 rms, 2 story. Mid-May-Aug: S $54-$98; D $65-$120; each addl $6; under 18 free; lower rates rest of yr. Crib avail. TV; cable (premium). Complimentary continental bkfst. Restaurant adj 6:30 am-10 pm. Ck-out 11 am. Business servs avail. Downhill/x-country ski 20 mi. Near airport. Cr cds: A, C, D, DS, MC, V.

🄳 ⌖ 🖂 🆖 🔥

★ ★ **LA QUINTA INN.** *4298 Cerrillos Road (87505). 505/471-1142; fax 505/438-7219; res 800/531-5900. www.laquinta.com.* 130 rms, 3 story. Late June-Aug: S, D $89-$100; each addl $8; suites $120-$140; under 18 free; lower rates rest of yr. Crib free. Pet accepted. TV; cable (premium). Pool. Complimentary continental bkfst. Coffee in rms. Restaurant adj open 24 hrs. Ck-out noon. Coin lndry. Downhill/x-country ski 14 mi. Refrigerators, microwaves avail. Cr cds: A, C, D, DS, MC, V.

🅳 🐾 ⛷ 🏊 ≋ 🔥

★ **LUXURY INN.** *3752 Cerrillos Rd (87505). 505/473-0567; fax 505/471-9139; toll-free 800/647-1346.* 51 rms, 2 story. May-Oct: S $35-$55; D $70-$90; under 10 free; wkly rates; ski plan; higher rates special events; lower rates rest of yr. Crib free. TV; cable (premium). Pool; whirlpool. Complimentary continental bkfst. Restaurant adj 11 am-9 pm. Ck-out 11 am. Cr cds: A, C, D, DS, MC, V.

🅳 🏊 ≋ 🔥

★ **PARK INN AND SUITES.** *2907 Cerrillos Rd (87505). 505/471-3000; fax 505/424-7561.* 101 rms, 2 story. Mid-June-Oct: S $90; D $95; each addl $5; under 17 free; ski plan; lower rates rest of yr. Crib free. Pet accepted. TV; cable (premium). Pool. Restaurant 7 am-2 pm, 6-9 pm. Bar. Meeting rms. Business servs avail. Downhill/x-country ski 20 mi. Health club privileges. Game rm. Cr cds: A, D, DS, MC, V.

🅳 🐾 🏊 ≋ 🔥 🏊

★★ **PLAZA REAL.** *125 Washington Ave (87501). 505/988-4900; fax 505/983-9322.* 56 rms, 3 story, 44 suites. June-Oct: S, D $149-$219; suites $199-$650; ski plans; lower rates rest of yr. Garage parking $10. TV; cable (premium). Restaurant 7-11 am. Bar 4-11 pm. Ck-out noon. Meeting rms. Business servs avail. In-rm modem link. Bellhops. Concierge. Health club privileges. Downhill/x-country ski 15 mi. Wet bar in suites. Refrigerators. Some balconies. Territorial-style architecture; fireplaces, handcrafted Southwestern furniture. Cr cds: A, D, DS, JCB, MC, V.

🅳 ⛷ ≋ 🔥

★★ **QUALITY INN.** *3011 Cerrillos Rd (87505). 505/471-1211; fax 505/438-9535; res 800/228-5151. www.qualityinn.com.* 99 rms, 2 story. May-Oct: S $55-$105; D $60-$105; each addl $10; under 18 free; lower rates rest of yr. Crib free. Pet accepted, some restrictions. TV; cable (premium). Heated pool. Restaurant 7 am-9 pm. Rm serv. Ck-out noon. Convention center. Meeting rm. Business servs avail. Airport trans-

portation. Downhill/x-country ski 17 mi. Some refrigerators. Balconies. Cr cds: A, C, D, DS, ER, JCB, MC, V.

🅳 🐾 ⛷ ≋ ✈ ≋ 🔥

★ **STAGE COACH INN.** *3360 Cerrillos Rd (87505). 505/471-0707.* 15 rms, 1-2 story. S, D $49-$89; each addl $10. TV; cable (premium). Restaurant nearby. Ck-out 10 am. Downhill/x-country ski 20 mi. Picnic tables, grills. Cr cds: A, MC, V.

⛷ ≋ 🔥 🆂🅲

Hotels

★★★ **ELDORADO.** *309 W San Francisco (87501). 505/988-4455; fax 505/995-4555; toll-free 800/286-6755. www.eldoradohotel.com.* 219 rms, 5 story. S, D $189-$269; suites $259-$2,000; under 18 free. Crib free. Pet accepted. Garage parking $10. TV; cable (premium), VCR avail (movies). Rooftop pool; whirlpool, poolside serv. Restaurant 7 am-9:30 pm (see also THE OLD HOUSE). Bar 11:30-2 am; entertainment. Ck-out noon. Convention facilities. Business center. In-rm modem link. Concierge. Shopping arcade. Barber, beauty shop. Downhill ski 16 mi; x-country ski 7 mi. Exercise equipt; sauna. Massage. Refrigerators, minibars. Balconies and fireplaces avail. Cr cds: A, C, D, DS, MC, V.

🅳 🐾 ⛷ ≋ 🏋 ≋ 🔥 🆂🅲 🚶

★★★ **HILTON.** *100 Sandoval St. (87501). 505/988-2811; fax 505/986-6439; toll-free 800/336-3676. www.hiltonofsantafe.com.* 157 rms, 3 story. Mid-June-Oct: S $139-$249; D $159-$269; each addl $20; suites $275-$675; family rates; ski packages; lower rates rest of yr. Crib free. TV; cable (premium), VCR avail (movies). Heated pool; whirlpool. Restaurants 6:30 am-midnight (see also PIÑON GRILL). Rm serv. Bar 11 am-11 pm. Ck-out noon. Meeting rms. Business center. In-rm modem link. Bellhops. Concierge. Exercise equipt. Gift shop. Airport transportation. Downhill ski 15 mi. Minibars. Cr cds: A, C, D, DS, JCB, MC, V.

🅳 ≋ ≋ 🏋 🔥 🆂🅲 🚶

★★★ **HOTEL LORETTO.** *211 Old Santa Fe Tr (87501). 505/988-5531; fax 505/984-7988; toll-free 800/727-5531. www.hotelloretto.com.* 140 rms, 4 story. July-Aug: S, D $279-$349;

each addl $15; under 18 free; lower rates rest of yr. Crib free. TV; cable (premium). Coffee in rms. Heated pool; poolside serv. Restaurant 7 am-9 pm; dining rm from 5:30 pm. Rm serv. Bar 11-1 am; Sun noon-midnight; entertainment. Ck-out noon. Guest lndry. Meeting rms. Business servs avail. Bellhops. Concierge. Shopping arcade. Barber, beauty shop. Massage. Downhill/x-country ski 15 mi. Refrigerators. Private patios, balconies. Adobe building. Cr cds: A, C, D, DS, MC, V.

★ ★ ★ **HOTEL SANTA FE.** *1501 Paseo De Peralta (87501). 505/982-1200; fax 505/955-7878; toll-free 800/825-9876.* 129 rms, 3 story, 89 suites. Late June-Aug: S, D $149-$209; suites $179-$219; under 17 free; ski plans; lower rates rest of yr. Crib free. TV; cable (premium). Pool; whirlpool. Restaurant (see also CORN DANCE CAFE). Bar 4 pm-midnight; entertainment Fri, Sat. Ck-out noon. Coin lndry. Meeting rms. Business servs avail. Bellhops. Valet serv. Concierge. Gift shop. Airport transportation. Downhill/x-country ski 10 mi. Health club privileges. Minibars. Balconies. Pueblo Revival architecture; original art by Native Americans. A Native American enterprise. Cr cds: A, D, DS, MC, V.

★ ★ ★ ★ **INN OF THE ANASAZI.** *113 Washington Ave (87501). 505/988-3030; fax 505/988-3277; toll-free 800/688-8100. www.innofthe anasazi.com.* The unique design of this inn is mesmerizing: timber ceilings, creamy sandstone walls, cactus in terra-cotta pots, and New Mexican art. The tranquil design, modeled after the mud and stone pueblos of the ancient Anasazi, runs through all 59 guest rooms with geometric-designed rugs, fireplaces, and four-poster beds. The restaurant showcases cuisine of the Native American, New Mexican, and American cowboy. 59 units, 3 story. Apr-Oct: S, D $249-$415; each addl $20; under 12 free; lower rates rest of yr. Crib free. Pet accepted, some restrictions; $30. Valet parking $12/day. TV; cable (premium), VCR (movies $5). Complimentary coffee in rms. Restaurant. Ck-out noon. Business

servs avail. Concierge. Tennis privileges. 18-hole golf privileges, putting green, driving range. Downhill ski 13 mi; x-country ski 7 mi. Exercise equipt. Massage. Health club privileges. Cr cds: A, D, DS, MC, V.

★ ★ ★ **INN ON THE ALAMEDA.** *303 E Alameda (87501). 505/984-2121; fax 505/986-8325; res 888/286-2122. www.inn-alameda.com.* 69 rms, 2-3 story. July-Oct: S, D $147-$197; each addl $15; suites $249-$334; lower rates rest of yr. Pet accepted. TV; cable (premium). Complimentary continental bkfst. Restaurant nearby. Bar 2:30-11 pm. Ck-out noon. Meeting rm. Business servs avail. In-rm modem link. Concierge. Valet serv. Downhill/x-country ski 15 mi. Exercise equipt. Whirlpools. Massage. Health club privileges. Private patios, balconies. Library. Kiva fireplaces. Cr cds: A, C, D, DS, MC, V.

★ ★ ★ **LA POSADA DE SANTA FE RESORT.** *330 E Palace Ave (87501). 505/986-0000; fax 505/982-6850; toll-free 800/727-5276. www.laposadade santafe.com.* 119 rms, 1-2 story. May-Oct & hols: S, D $199-$279; suites $195-$395; under 12 free; package plans; lower rates rest of yr. Crib $5. TV; cable (premium). Pool; poolside serv. Restaurant (see also STAAB HOUSE). Rm serv. Bar 11 am-midnight; Sun noon-11 pm. Ck-out noon. Meeting rms. Business servs avail. Concierge. Bellhops. Beauty shop. Downhill/x-country ski 15 mi. Many fireplaces. Adobe casitas surround Victorian/Second Empire Staab mansion (1882); guest rms either Pueblo Revival or Victorian in style. On 6 acres; gardens. Cr cds: A, D, DS, MC, V.

★ ★ ★ **RADISSON.** *750 N St Francis Dr (87501). 505/992-5800; fax 505/992-5865; toll-free 800/723-4776; res 800/333-3333. www.radisson.com.* 141 rms, 2 story. May-Dec: S, D, studio rms $139; each addl $20; suites $169-$434; ski packages; lower rates rest of yr. Pet accepted. TV; cable (premium). Heated pool; poolside serv. Restaurant 6:30 am-2 pm, 5:30-10 pm. Rm serv. Bar 4 pm-midnight; entertainment. Ck-out noon. Meet-

ing rms. Business servs avail. Bellhops. Free RR station, bus depot
transportation. Downhill/x-country
ski 18 mi. Health club privileges. Cr
cds: A, C, D, DS, JCB, MC, V.

⊡ ▨ ⩯ ▨ ▨ SC ◗

★ ★ ★ **ST. FRANCIS.** *210 Don Gaspar
Ave (87501). 505/983-5700; fax
505/989-7690; toll-free 800/529-5700.
www.hotelstfrancis.com.* 83 rms, 3
story. S, D $80-$220; each addl $15;
suites $205-$380; under 12 free;
lower rates rest of yr. Crib free. TV;
cable. Restaurant 7-10 am, 11:30 am-
2 pm, 5-10 pm; wkends 7 am-2 pm.
Rm serv. Bar noon-2 am; Sun to midnight. Ck-out 11 am. Meeting rms.
Business servs avail. In-rm modem
link. Concierge. Downhill ski 15 mi.
Refrigerators. European ambience;
antiques, original artwork. Cr cds: A,
C, D, DS, MC, V.

⊡ ▨ ⩯ ▨ SC

Resorts

★ ★ ★ **BISHOP'S LODGE.** *Bishop's
Lodge Rd (87504). 505/983-6377; fax
505/989-8739; toll-free 800/732-2240.
www.bishopslodge.com.* 111 rms in 1-
3-story lodges. No elvtr. July-Aug: S,
D $299-$729; lower rates rest of yr.
TV; cable (premium), VCR avail.
Heated pool; whirlpool, poolside
serv, lifeguard. Playground. Supervised children's activities (Memorial
Day-Sept); ages 4-12. Restaurant (see
also BISHOP'S LODGE). Child's dining rm. Rm serv. Box lunches, picnics. Bar 11:30 am-midnight; Sun
from noon. Ck-out noon, ck-in 4
pm. Business servs avail. In-rm
modem link. Concierge. Sports dir.
Tennis, pro. 18-hole golf privileges.
Stocked pond. Fishing pond for children. Downhill/x-country ski 18 mi.
Skeet, trap shooting; pro. Riding
instruction; bkfst and lunch rides;
children's rides. Lawn games. Exercise equipt; sauna. Soc dir; entertainment. Rec rm. Many refrigerators;
some fireplaces. Some private patios.
Cr cds: A, D, DS, MC, V.

⊡ ▨ ▨ ▨ ▨ ▨ ⩯ ▨ ▨ ▨

★ ★ ★ **HYATT REGENCY TAMAYA
RESORT.** *1300 Tamaya Tr, Santa Ana
Peublo (87004). 505/867-1234; res
800/633-7313. www.hyatt.com.* 350
rms, 4 story. S, D $195-$275; each
addl $20; under 17 free. Crib avail.
Pool; whirlpool, poolside serv. TV;

cable (premium), VCR avail. Complimentary coffee, newspaper in rms.
Restaurant 6 am-10 pm. Ck-out
noon. Meeting rms. Business center.
Gift shop. Exercise rm. Spa. Golf, 18
holes. Refrigerators, some minibars.
Cr cds: A, C, D, DS, JCB, MC, V.

▨ ▨ ⩯ ▨ ▨ ▨

★ ★ ★ **RANCHO ENCANTADO
RESORT.** *198 State Rd 592 (87501).
505/982-3537; fax 505/983-8269; toll-
free 800/722-9339. www.nmhotels.
com/html/sfranchencantado.html.* 39
units, 16 cottages. Late June-mid-
Oct: S, D $175-$375; each addl $10;
cottages $210-$250; ski plan; lower
rates rest of yr. Crib avail. TV. Pool;
whirlpool. Complimentary coffee in
rms. Dining rm 7-11 am, 11:30 am-2
pm, 5:30-9:30 pm. Box lunches. Picnics. Bar 11 am-11 pm. Ck-out 11
am, ck-in 3 pm. Gift shop. Grocery 3
mi. Coin lndry 8 mi. Meeting rm.
Business servs avail. Tennis; pro. X-
country ski 12 mi. Hiking trails.
Minibars. Picnic tables. Cr cds: A, C,
D, DS, MC, V.

⊡ ▨ ▨ ▨ ⩯ ▨ ▨ SC

B&Bs/Small Inns

★ ★ ★ **ADOBE ABODE.** *202 Chapelle
St (87501). 505/983-3133; fax
505/424-3027. www.adobeabode.com.*
6 rms, 3 with shower only. S, D
$120-$125; each addl $15; suite
$145-$155. TV; cable (premium).
Complimentary full bkfst. Ck-out 11
am, ck-in 2 pm. Luggage handling.
Individually decorated rms with
antiques from all over the world. Cr
cds: DS, MC, V.

▨ ▨

★ ★ ★ **ALEXANDER'S INN.** *529 E
Palace Ave (87501). 505/986-1431; fax
505/982-8572; toll-free 888/321-5123.
www.alexanders-inn.com.* 16 rms, 2
share bath, 2 with shower only; 4
suites, 2 story. Mid-Mar-mid-Nov: S,
D $100-$110; each addl $20; higher
rates: Indian Market, Dec 25; lower
rates rest of yr. Pet accepted, some
restrictions. TV; cable, VCR avail.
Whirlpool. Complimentary continental bkfst; afternoon refreshments.
Ck-out 11 am, ck-in by arrangement.
Business servs avail. Luggage handling. Concierge serv. Downhill ski
17 mi; x-country ski 10 mi. Health

club privileges. Five rms in renovated house built 1903. Totally nonsmoking. Cr cds: DS, MC, V.

★★ **DANCING GROUND OF THE SUN.** *711 Paseo De Peralta (87501). 505/986-9797; fax 505/986-8082; toll-free 800/745-9910. www.dancing ground.com.* 5 casitas, 5 kit. units, 2 story. S, D $130-$219; each addl $20. TV; cable. Complimentary continental bkfst. Complimentary coffee in rms. Restaurant nearby. Ck-out 11 am, ck-in 3-6 pm. Business servs avail. Concierge serv. Microwaves. Patios. All rms with Native American theme. Totally nonsmoking. Cr cds: MC, V.

Santa Fe pottery

★★★ **DOS CASAS VIEJAS.** *610 Agua Fria St (87501). 505/983-1636; fax 505/983-1749. www.doscasasviejas. com.* 8 rms, 1 suite. s, D $185-$215; suite $265. TV; cable (premium). Heated pool. Complimentary continental bkfst. Coffee in rms. Restaurant nearby. Ck-out noon, ck-in 3-6 pm. Business servs avail. Refrigerators. Two historical buildings in a ½-acre walled/gated compound; renovated to restore 1860s architecture. Mexican-tiled floors and wood-burning kiva fireplaces. Totally nonsmoking. Cr cds: MC, V.

★★ **EL PARADERO EN SANTA FE.** *220 W Manhattan Ave, Sante Fe (87501). 505/988-1177; fax 505/988-3577. www.elparadero.com.* 12 rms, 2 kit. suites. Apr-Oct: S $65-$135; D $70-$135; each addl $15; kit. suites $135; lower rates rest of yr. Children over 3 yrs only. Pet accepted, $100. TV in sitting rm; cable in suites. Complimentary full bkfst. Restaurant nearby. Ck-out 11 am, ck-in 2-8 pm. Downhill ski 18 mi; x-country ski 9 mi. Balconies. Renovated Spanish adobe house (ca 1820) with details from 1880 and 1912 remodelings. Library/sitting rm; skylights, fireplaces, antiques. Cr cds: A, MC, V.

★★ **EL REY INN.** *1862 Cerrillos Rd (87502). 505/982-1931; fax 505/989-9249; toll-free 800/521-1349. www. elreyinnsantafe.com.* 86 rms, 1-2 story, 9 kits. May-Oct: S $85-$95; D $99-$105; each addl $12; kit. suites $99-$185. Crib free. TV; cable (premium). Pool; whirlpool. Playground. Complimentary continental bkfst. Restaurant nearby. Ck-out noon. Coin lndry. Business servs avail. Downhill/x-country ski 17 mi. Health club privileges. Some fireplaces. Picnic tables. Cr cds: A, C, D, DS, MC, V.

★★★ **GALISTEO INN.** *9 La Vega, Galisteo (87540). 505/466-8200; fax 505/466-4008. www.galisteoinn.com.* 12 rms, 3 share bath. No A/C. No rm phones. S $70-$185; D $110-$185; each addl $25. Closed 5 wks Jan-Feb. Children over 6 yrs only. 4 TVs. Pool; whirlpool. Sauna. Complimentary full bkfst. Complimentary coffee. Restaurant Wed-Sun 6-8:30 pm. Ck-out noon, ck-in 4-6 pm. Business servs avail. Massage. Hacienda on 8 acres built in 1750s. Totally nonsmoking. Cr cds: DS, MC, V.

★★★ **GRANT CORNER INN.** *122 Grant Ave (87501). 505/983-6678; fax 505/983-1526; toll-free 800/964-9003. grantcornerinn.com.* 12 rms, 2 share bath, 3 story. June-Oct: S, D $ 145-$240; each addl $20. Children over 8 yrs only. TV; cable. Complimentary full bkfst; afternoon refreshments. Restaurant nearby. Ck-out noon, ck-in 2-6 pm. Business servs avail. Downhill/x-country ski 15 mi. Colonial manor house built 1905; antiques. Massage. Totally nonsmoking. Cr cds: A, MC, V.

★★★ GUADALUPE INN. *604 Agua Fria St (87501). 505/989-7422. www.guadalupeinn.com.* 12 rms, 2 story. Mid-Apr-mid-Jan: S, D $125-$175; each addl $15; 4-day min Indian Market; lower rates rest of yr. Crib. TV; cable (premium). Whirlpool. Complimentary full bkfst. Restaurant adj. Ck-out 11 am, ck-in 3-6 pm. Concierge serv. Business servs avail. Downhill ski 15 mi; x-country ski 10 mi. Balconies. Picnic tables. Individually decorated rms. Totally nonsmoking. Cr cds: A, DS, MC, V.

★★★ INN OF THE GOVERNORS. *101 W Alameda (87501). 505/982-4333; fax 505/989-9149; toll-free 800/234-4534. www.innofthegovernors.com.* 100 rms, 2-3 story. S, D $139-$330; each addl $15; under 18 free. Crib free. TV; cable (premium). Pool. Complimentary continental bkfst. Restaurant (see also MAÑANA). Rm serv. Bar 11:30 am-midnight; Sun from noon; entertainment. Ck-out noon. Ck-in 4 pm. Meeting rm. Business servs avail. In-rm modem link. Bellhops. Concierge. Downhill/x-country ski 14 mi. Some minibars, fireplaces. Balconies. Cr cds: A, C, D, DS, ER, JCB, MC, V.

★★★ INN ON THE PASEO. *630 Paseo De Peralta (87501). 505/984-8200; fax 505/989-3979; toll-free 800/457-9045. www.innonthepaseo.com.* 18 rms, 2-3 story. July-Oct: S, D $105-$165; suite $165; summer wkends (2-day min), Indian market. TV; cable (premium). Complimentary bkfst buffet; afternoon refreshments. Restaurant nearby. Ck-out 11 am, ck-in 3 pm. Business servs avail. Sun decks. Totally nonsmoking. Cr cds: A, D, MC, V.

★★★ LA TIENDA INN & DURAN HOUSE. *445-447 & 511 W San Francisco St (87501). 505/989-8259; fax 505/820-6931; toll-free 800/889-7611.* www.latiendabb.com. 7 rms. S, D $90-$160. Adults only. TV; cable (premium). Complimentary continental bkfst. Restaurant nearby. Ck-out 11 am, ck-in 3-6 pm. Luggage handling. Concierge serv. Downhill/x-country ski 17 mi. Territorial house built ca 1900 has 3 rms; 4 rms in Old Store adobe wing. Totally nonsmoking. Cr cds: A, MC, V.

★★★ THE MADELEINE. *106 E Faithway St (87501). 505/982-1431; fax 505/982-8572; toll-free 888/321-5123. www.madeleineinn.com.* 8 rms, 3 with shower only, 3 story, 1 suite. Apr-Oct, hols: S, D $80-$180; each addl $25; suite $135; lower rates rest of yr. Pet accepted, some restrictions. TV. Complimentary continental bkfst; afternoon refreshments. Restaurant nearby. Ck-out 11 am, ck-in 3 pm. Business servs avail. Downhill/x-country ski 17 mi. Some fireplaces. Queen Anne house (1886) with antique furnishings and sitting rm. Totally nonsmoking. Cr cds: DS, MC, V.

★★ PUEBLO BONITO BED AND BREAKFAST INN. *138 W Manhattan Ave (87501). 505/984-8001; fax 505/984-3155; toll-free 800/461-4599. www.pueblobonitoinn.com.* 18 rms, 1-2 story, 7 suites, 6 kits. No A/C. May-Oct: S, D $115-$160; each addl $15; suites, kit. units $145; lower rates rest of yr. TV; cable. Whirlpool. Complimentary buffet bkfst. Restaurant nearby. Ck-out noon, ck-in 2 pm. Downhill/x-country ski 18 mi. Fireplaces. Some balconies. Renovated adobe casitas on 1880s estate; private courtyards, gardens, mature trees. Antique furnishings, baskets. Cr cds: A, DS, MC, V.

★★★ SPENCER HOUSE BED AND BREAKFAST INN. *222 McKenzie St (87501). 505/988-3024; toll-free 800/647-0530.* 6 air-cooled rms. May-Oct: S, D $99-$165; lower rates rest of yr. Children over 12 yrs only. TV; cable (premium). Complimentary full bkfst. Restaurant nearby. Ck-out 10:30 am, ck-in 3-5 pm. Some fireplaces. Luggage handling. Downhill/x-country ski 15 mi. Country cottage atmosphere with antiques from England, Ireland and Wales. Cr cds: A, MC, V.

★★★ **TERRITORIAL INN.** *320 Artist Rd (87501). 505/982-6636; fax 505/984-8682. www.territorialinn.com.* 10 rms, 1 with shower only, 2 share bath, 2 story. S $100-$120; D $120-$140; each addl $20. Children over 10 yrs only. TV; cable (premium). Complimentary continental bkfst; eve refreshments. Restaurant nearby. Ck-out 11 am, ck-in 3 pm. Business servs avail. Downhill/x-country ski 15 mi. Health club privileges. Whirlpool. Some fireplaces. House (ca 1895) blends New Mexico's stone and adobe architecture with pitched roof, Victorian-style interior; sitting rm, antiques; garden and tree-shaded lawns more typical of buildings in the East. Cr cds: A, C, D, DS, MC, V.

★★★ **WATER STREET INN.** *427 W Water St (87501). 505/984-1193; fax 505/984-6235; toll-free 800/646-6752. www.waterstreetinn.com.* 12 rms. S, D $125-$225; each addl $15. TV; cable, VCR (movies $3). Whirlpool. Complimentary continental bkfst. Restaurant nearby. Ck-out 11 am, ck-in 2-6 pm. Business servs avail. In-rm modem link. Downhill/x-country ski 17 mi. Restored adobe building; fireplaces, antique stoves. Totally nonsmoking. Cr cds: A, DS, MC, V.

All Suite

★★ **VILLAS DE SANTA FE.** *400 Griffin St (87501). 505/988-3000; fax 505/988-4700; res 800/869-6790. www.sunterra.com.* 100 kit. suites, 4 story. May-Oct, Dec: S $155-$175, D $175-$310; lower rates rest of yr. Crib free. Pet accepted; $10/day. TV; cable (premium). Heated pool; whirlpools. Complimentary bkfst buffet. Complimentary coffee in rms. Restaurant nearby. Ck-out noon. Coin lndry. Meeting rms. Business servs avail. In-rm modem link. Bellhops. Concierge. Exercise equipt. Microwaves. Many balconies. Picnic tables. Cr cds: A, C, D, DS, MC, V.

Extended Stay

★★ **RESIDENCE INN BY MARRIOTT.** *1698 Galisteo St (87505). 505/988-7300; fax 505/988-3243; res 800/331-3131. www.residenceinn.com.* 120 kit. suites, 2 story. June-late Oct: kit. suites $169; under 12 free; wkly, ski rates; lower rates rest of yr. Crib free. Pet accepted, some restrictions; $150 deposit plus $10/day. TV; cable (premium). Heated pool; whirlpools. Complimentary buffet bkfst. Ck-out noon, ck-in 3 pm. Coin lndry. Meeting rms. Business servs avail. In-rm modem link. Valet serv. Airport transportation. Downhill ski 16 mi. Some private patios, balconies. Picnic tables, grills. Cr cds: A, C, D, DS, JCB, MC, V.

Restaurants

★★★ **THE ANASAZI.** *113 Washington Ave (87501). 505/988-3236. www.innoftheanasazi.com.* Hrs: 7-10:30 am, 11:30 am-2:30 pm, 5:30-10 pm; Sun brunch 11 am-2:30 pm. Res accepted. Contemporary Western cuisine. Bar 11 am-midnight. Wine cellar. A la carte entrees: bkfst $5.25-$9.50, lunch $8.50-$12.75, dinner $18.50-$29. Sun brunch $6-$12.75. Child's menu. Specialties: tortilla soup, fresh fish, cinnamon chile with mango salsa. Menu changes seasonally. Classical guitarist (brunch). Cr cds: A, D, DS, MC, V.

★★ **ANDIAMO.** *322 Garfield (87501). 505/995-9595.* Hrs: 5:30-9:30 pm. Closed Tues. Res accepted. Italian menu. Wine, beer. Dinner $13.50-$17.50. Child's menu. Specializes in pasta. Outdoor dining. Three dining areas. Contemporary decor. Totally nonsmoking. Cr cds: A, DS, MC, V.

★★★ **BISHOP'S LODGE.** *Bishop's Lodge Rd (87504). 505/983-6377. www.bishopslodge.com.* Hrs: 7:30-10 am, 11:30 am-2 pm, 6-9 pm; brunch 11 am-2 pm. Res required (dinner). Eclectic menu. Bar. A la carte entrees: lunch $10-$15, dinner $15-$28. Complete meals: dinner $17-$35. Buffet: bkfst $12. Child's menu. Specialties: Asian barbecued lamb with green chile, seared squash gorditas, mole grilled chicken breast. Entertainment Mon-Wed, Sat, Sun (seasonal). Parking. Outdoor dining. Adobe home was built in the early 1900s. Cr cds: A, D, DS, MC, V.

D

★ **BLUE CORN CAFE.** *133 Water St (87501). 505/438-1800.* Hrs: 11 am-11 pm. Closed Thanksgiving, Dec 25. New Mexican menu. Bar to midnight. Lunch, dinner $6.95-$9.95. Child's menu. Specialties: chile rellenos, fajitas, enchiladas. Southwestern decor; fireplace. Cr cds: A, C, D, DS, MC, V.

D [icon]

★★ **CAFE PARIS.** *31 Burro Alley (87501). 505/986-9162.* Hrs: 11:30 am-2:30 pm, 5:30-9:30 pm; Tues 11:30 am-2:30 pm. Closed Sun; also Jan 1, Dec 25. Res accepted. French cuisine. Wine, beer. A la carte entrees: lunch $5.95-$12.95, dinner $16.95-$20.95. Cafe-style dining. Totally nonsmoking. Cr cds: DS, MC, V.

★★ **CAFE PASQUAL'S.** *121 Don Gaspar (87501). 505/983-9340.* Hrs: 7 am-3 pm, 6-10:30 pm; Sun brunch 8 am-2 pm. Closed Thanksgiving, Dec 25. Res accepted. New Mexican, Amer menu. Wine, beer. Bkfst $4.75-$13.10, lunch $7.95-$10.75, dinner $14.75-$26. Sun brunch $7.95-$10.75. Specialties: grilled salmon burrito, char-grilled chicken quesadillas, char-grilled rack of lamb. Hand-painted murals; festive Old Santa Fe decor. Totally nonsmoking. Cr cds: A, DS, MC, V.

D

★★ **CELEBRATIONS.** *613 Canyon Rd (87501). 505/989-8904. www. celebrationscanyonroad.com.* Hrs: 8:30 am-2:30 pm, 5-9 pm; Sun brunch 11 am-2:30 pm. Closed Jan 1, Thanksgiving, Dec 25. Res accepted. Continental menu. Bar. Bkfst $3.95-$7.95, lunch $4.75-$7.95, dinner $7.95-$14.95. Sun brunch $5.95-$9.95. Specializes in American bistro dishes, New Orleans dishes, rack of lamb. Outdoor dining. 3 dining areas; fireplaces. Cr cds: DS, MC, V.

D

★ **CHOW'S CONTEMPORARY CHINESE.** *720 St. Michaels Dr (87505). 505/471-7120. www.chows. com.* Hrs: 11:30 am-2 pm, 5-9 pm;

Sat noon-3 pm, 5-9 pm. Closed Sun. Res accepted. Chinese menu. Wine, beer. A la carte entrees: lunch, dinner $2.95-$15.95. Specialty: green bean chicken. Outdoor dining. Contemporary Chinese decor. Cr cds: MC, V.

D

★★ **CORN DANCE CAFE.** *1501 Paseo de Peralta (87501). 505/982-1200. www.hotelsantafe.com.* Hrs: 11:30 am-2 pm, 5:30-9 pm. Res accepted. Native Amer menu. Bar to 10 pm; Fri, Sat to 11 pm. Lunch, dinner $6.25-$21.95. Specialties: little big pies, buffalo ribeye steak, Potawatomi prairie chicken. Own baking. Outdoor dining. Southwestern decor; large fireplace; Native American art and artifacts. Totally nonsmoking. Cr cds: A, MC, V.

D

★★★ **COYOTE CAFE.** *132 W Water St (87501). 505/983-1615. www. coyote-cafe.com.* Hrs: 6-9:30 pm; Sat, Sun 11 am-1:45 pm, 5:30-9:45 pm. Southwestern menu. Bar/cantina (May-Oct) 11:30 am-9:45 pm. A la carte entrees: lunch $7-$13, dinner $42.50. Specialties: cowboy rib chop, Caesar salad, griddled corn cakes with shrimp. Outdoor dining on rooftop cantina. Adobe structure; Southwestern decor; fireplace. View of mountains. Cr cds: A, C, D, DS, ER, MC, V.

D

★ **EL COMEDOR.** *727 Cerrillos Rd (87501). 505/989-7575.* Hrs: 7 am-9 pm; winter hrs vary. Closed Thanksgiving, Dec 25. Northern New Mexican menu. Wine, beer. Bkfst $3.25-$7.75, lunch $3.50-$9.50, dinner $6-$10.95. Child's menu. Patio dining. Family-owned. Cr cds: A, DS, MC, V.

D

★★ **EL MESON - LA COCINA DE ESPANA.** *213 Washington Ave (87501). 505/983-6756. www. enchantedweb.com.* Hrs: 11:30 am-2 pm, 5:30-10 pm. Closed Mon, Sun; also Jan 1, Thanksgiving, Dec 25. Res accepted. Spanish menu. Wine, beer. A la carte entrees: lunch $6-$9, dinner $15-$18. Child's menu. Specializes in tapas, paellas. Guitarist wkends. Street parking. Outdoor dining. Totally nonsmoking. Cr cds: A, C, D, DS, ER, MC, V.

D

★★ **EL NIDO.** *591 Bishops Lodge Rd, Tesuque (87574).* 505/988-4340. Hrs: Tues-Sun 6-9:30 pm. Closed Mon; Jan 1, Thanksgiving, Dec 25; also Super Bowl Sun. Res accepted. Bar. Dinner $13.95-$24.95. Specializes in fresh seafood, beef, rack of lamb. 1920 adobe building; fireplaces. Folk art of Tesuque Village. Cr cds: A, MC, V.

⌣

★★ **GABRIEL'S.** *4 Bannah Ln (87501).* 505/455-7000. Hrs: 11:30 am-9 pm; Fri, Sat to 10 pm; Sun brunch to 3 pm. Closed Thanksgiving, Dec 25. Res accepted. Southwestern, Mexican menu. Bar. Lunch $5.50-$10.75, dinner $6.95-$15.95. Sun brunch $8.50-$9.95. Child's menu. Specialties: guacamole, pato carnitas, rellenos de Santa Fe. Outdoor dining. Adobe bldg has four dining areas, two large fireplaces; Southwestern decor. Cr cds: A, D, DS, MC, V.

D SC

★ **GARDUNO'S.** *130 Lincoln Ave (87501).* 505/983-9797. www.gardunos restaurants.com. Hrs: 11 am-10 pm; Fri, Sat to 10:30 pm; Sun 10:30 am-10 pm; Sun brunch to 3 pm. Closed Thanksgiving, Dec 25. Mexican menu. Bar. Lunch $5.50-$10.95, dinner $6.50-$13.95. Sun brunch $10.95. Child's menu. Specializes in chimichangas, fajitas, seafood. Entertainment. Southwestern decor. Family-owned. Cr cds: A, D, MC, V.

D

★★★★ **GERONIMO.** *724 Canyon Rd (87501).* 505/982-1500. Built by Geronimo Lopez in 1756, this adobe home features a romantic dining room boasting crackling fireplaces, cozy banquettes, and a vaulted, beamed ceiling. The artistic, Southwestern cuisine, including mesquite-grilled salmon over roasted eggplant with olive-butter sauce, can be enjoyed inside the elegant space or out under the stars. The gracious service is a splendid finishing touch. Specializes in neoclassical, global fare. Hrs: 11:30 am-2:30 pm, 6-10 pm. Res accepted. Bar to midnight.

Lunch $18, dinner $30. Outdoor dining. Cr cds: A, MC, V.

D

★★ **IL PIATTO.** *95 W Marcy St (87501).* 505/984-1091. Hrs: 11:30 am-2 pm, 5:30-9:30 pm, Fri, Sat to 10 pm. Closed Jan 1, Thanksgiving, Dec 25. Res accepted. Italian menu. Lunch $3-$10, dinner $5-$15. Specializes in fresh pasta. Country Italian original art. Cr cds: A, MC, V.

D

★★ **INDIA PALACE.** *227 Don Gaspar (87501).* 505/986-5859. www.india palace.com. Hrs: 11:30 am-2:30 pm, 5-10 pm. Closed Super Bowl Sun. East Indian menu. Wine, beer. Lunch buffet $6.95. A la carte entrees: lunch, dinner $6.95-$24.95. Specializes in Tandoori dishes. Outdoor dining. Indian decor. Cr cds: A, D, DS, MC, V.

D ⌣

★★★ **JULIAN'S.** *221 Shelby St (87501).* 505/988-2355. Hrs: 5:30-10 pm. Closed Thanksgiving. Res accepted. Northern Italian menu. Bar. Dinner $14-$24. Specialties: pollo al agro dolci, gamberi alla marinara, piccata di vitello. Outdoor dining. Fine art; etched-glass windows; 2 fireplaces. Elegant Italian ambience. Cr cds: A, D, DS, MC, V.

D

★★ **LITTLE ANITA'S.** *2811 Cerrillos Rd (87501).* 505/473-4505. Hrs: 7 am-9 pm. Closed Thanksgiving, Dec 25. Mexican menu. Wine, beer. Bkfst $2.75-$5.95, lunch, dinner $3.95-$8. Child's menu. Specialties: chimichanga, fajitas. Southwestern decor. Cr cds: A, DS, MC, V.

D SC

★★ **MAÑANA.** *101 W Alameda (87501).* 505/982-4333. www.inn-gov. com. Hrs: 6:30 am-10 pm. Res accepted. Southwestern/Californian menu. Bar. A la carte entrees: bkfst $4-$7.50, lunch $5.50-$15.95, dinner $6.95-$16.95. Specialties: wood-fired pizza, wood-roasted salmon, blue corn pancakes. Pianist, vocalist. Patio dining. Two dining rms. Cr cds: A, D, DS, MC, V.

★★ **MARIA'S NEW MEXICAN KITCHEN.** *555 W Cordova Rd (87501).* 505/983-7929. www.marias-santafe.com. Hrs: 11 am-10 pm; Sat,

Sun from noon. Closed Thanksgiving, Dec 25. Res accepted. Bar. Lunch $4.95-$8.95, dinner $7.25-$15.75. Child's menu. Specializes in fajitas, magaritas. Extensive Mexican beer selection. Patio dining. Original art. Cr cds: A, C, D, DS, MC, V.
D

★ **MU DU NOODLES.** *1494 Cerrillos Rd (87505). 505/983-1411.* Hrs: 11:30 am-2:30 pm, 5:30-9:30 pm; Sat from 5:30 pm. Closed Sun; some major hols. Asian menu. Lunch $7-$9, dinner $13-$16. Child's menu. Specializes in rice and noodle dishes. Totally nonsmoking. Cr cds: A, C, D, DS, MC, V.
D

★★★ **THE OLD HOUSE RESTAURANT.** *309 W San Francisco St (87501). 505/988-4455. www. eldoradohotel.com.* Contemporary American menu. Hrs: 5:30-10 pm. Res accepted. Bar. Wine list. A la carte entrees: dinner $18-$27. Valet parking. Contemporary Southwestern decor. Cr cds: A, D, DS, MC, V.
D

★★ **OLD MEXICO GRILL.** *2434 Cerrillos Rd (87501). 505/473-0338.* Hrs: 11:30 am-2:30 pm, 5:30-9 pm. Closed major hols; also Super Bowl Sun. Mexican menu. Bar. A la carte entrees: lunch $6.95-$10.75, dinner $9.50-$17.95. Specializes in fajitas, tacos. Cr cds: D, DS, MC, V.
D SC

★★ **ORE HOUSE ON THE PLAZA.** *50 Lincoln Ave (87501). 505/883-8687. www.orehouseontheplaza.com.* Hrs: 11:30 am-2:30 pm, 5:30-10 pm; Sun noon-2:30 pm. Closed Thanksgiving, Dec 25. Res accepted. Bar to 1 am; entertainment Fri-Sun. Lunch $4.50-$9, dinner $14-$22. Child's menu. Specializes in steak, seafood, rack of lamb. Outdoor dining. Plaza view. Cr cds: A, MC, V.

★★ **OSTERIA D'ASSISI.** *58 S Federal Pl (87501). 505/986-5858. www. osteriadassisi.com.* Hrs: 11 am-9 pm; Fri, Sat to 10 pm. Closed Sun; Jan 1, Dec 25. Res accepted. Italian menu. Wine, beer.

Lunch $3.95-$9.75, dinner $6-$16. Specializes in pasta, pizza, panini. Outdoor dining. Country decor. Totally nonsmoking. Cr cds: A, D, MC, V.
D

★★★ **PALACE RESTAURANT AND SALOON.** *142 W Palace Ave (87501). 505/982-9891. www.palacerestaurant. com.* Hrs: 11:30 am-3 pm, 5:30-10 pm; Sun from 5:30 pm. Closed Dec 25. Res accepted. Continental, Italian menu. Bar. Lunch $4.50-$12, dinner $10.50-$24. Specializes in New Mexican lamb, seafood, pasta. Pianist. Patio dining. Turn-of-the-century Victorian decor. Cr cds: A, D, DS, MC, V.
D

★★★ **PAUL'S.** *72 W Marcy St, Pojoaque Valley (87501). 505/982-8738.* Hrs: 11:30 am-2 pm, 5:30-9 pm. Closed July 4, Dec 25. Res accepted. Wine, beer. Lunch $5.95-$8.95, dinner $14-$19. Specializes in duck, seafood, lamb. Contemporary decor. Totally nonsmoking. Cr cds: A, D, DS, MC, V.
D

★★ **THE PINK ADOBE.** *406 Old Santa Fe Trl (87501). 505/983-7712. www.thepinkadobe.com.* Hrs: 11:30 am-2:30 pm, 5:30-10 pm; Sat, Sun from 5:30 pm. Closed major hols. Res accepted. Some A/C. Bar. New Mexican, continental menu. Lunch $6.50-$8.50, dinner $10.25-$22.25. Specialties: porc Napoleone, poulet Marengo, steak Dunigan. Entertainment Tues-Thurs, Sat. Fireplace in dining rms. Historic pink adobe

Santuario de Guadalupe

building ca 1700. Family-owned. Cr cds: A, D, DS, MC, V.

D

★★ **PIÑON GRILL.** *100 Sandoval St (87501). 505/988-2811. www.hiltonof santafe.com.* Hrs: 5-10 pm. Res accepted. Bar. A la carte entrees: dinner $12-$19. Child's menu. Specializes in grilled steaks, fish, free-range poultry. High-beamed, Mission-style ceilings; Native American artifacts. Cr cds: A, D, DS, MC, V.

D

★ **PIZZERIA ESPIRITU.** *1722 St. Michaels Dr (87505). 505/424-8000.* Hrs: 11 am-9 pm. Closed Sun; also most major hols. Res accepted. Italian menu. A la carte entrees: lunch $2.50-$8.95, dinner $2.50-$12.95. Child's menu. Specializes in gourmet pizzas, pastas, salads. Parking. Outdoor dining. Cr cds: A, D, DS, MC, V.

D

★★ **PRANZO ITALIAN GRILL.** *540 Montezuma (87501). 505/984-2645.* Hrs: 11:30 am-3 pm, 5 pm-midnight; Sun from 5 pm. Closed July 4, Thanksgiving, Dec 25. Res accepted. Italian menu. Bar noon-midnight. Lunch $5.95-$9.35, dinner $5.95-$19.95. Specialties: cioppino, pizza, osso buco Milanese. Outdoor dining. Contemporary decor. Cr cds: A, C, D, DS, MC, V.

D

★★★ **RISTRA.** *548 Agua Fria (87501). 505/982-8608. www.ristra restaurant.com.* Hrs: 5:30-9:30 pm; Fri, Sat to 10 pm. Res accepted. French, Southwestern menu. Wine, beer. Dinner $15-$24. Specialties: rack of lamb, filet mignon, Alaskan halibut. Outdoor dining. Three intimate dining rms in historic home. Cr cds: A, MC, V.

D

★★★ **ROCIADA.** *304 Johnson St (87501). 505/983-3800.* French menu. Hrs: 5-10 pm. Closed Mon. Res accepted. Dinner $15-$22. Extensive wine list. Cr cds: A, MC, V.

D

★★★ **SANTACAFE.** *231 Washington Ave (87501). 505/984-1788. www. santacafe.com.* Hrs: 11:30 am-2 pm, 5:30-10:30 pm; Sat, Sun from 5:30 pm. Res accepted. Bar. A la carte entrees: lunch $6-$12, dinner $17-$24. Specializes in modern American cuisine with regional touches. Own baking. Patio dining. Historic adobe house (1850); landscaped courtyard. Cr cds: A, MC, V.

D

★ **SHED AND LA CHOZA.** *113 1/2 E Palace Ave (87501). 505/982-9030. www.sfshed.com.* Hrs: 11 am-2:30 pm, 5:30-9 pm; Mon, Tues to 2:30 pm. Closed Sun. New Mexican, Amer menu. Wine, beer. Lunch $3.75-$8, dinner $6.50-$13.95. Specializes in blue corn enchiladas, mocha cake. Patio dining. Artwork, wall hangings. Family-owned since 1953. Totally nonsmoking. Cr cds: A, D, DS, MC, V.

D

★★ **SHOHKO-CAFE.** *321 Johnson St (87501). 505/983-7288.* Hrs: 11:30 am-2 pm, 6-9:30 pm; Fri, Sat to 10 pm. Closed Sun; hols. Res accepted. Japanese menu. Wine, beer. Lunch $3.50-$6.75, dinner $8.50-$18.25. Specializes in tempura, sushi, seafood. Cr cds: A, D, MC, V.

D

★★★ **STAAB HOUSE.** *330 E Palace Ave (87501). 505/986-0000. www. laposadadesantafe.com.* Hrs: 7 am-10:30 pm. Res accepted. Continental menu. Bar 11-2 am; Sun from noon. Bkfst $5.50-$12.50, lunch $5-$10, dinner $6-$22. Child's menu. Specializes in creative Southwest cuisine. Entertainment (seasonal). Outdoor dining. In historic Staab mansion (1882); hand-crafted furniture; fireplace. On 6 acres. Cr cds: A, D, DS, MC, V.

D

★★ **STEAKSMITH AT EL GAN-CHO.** *Old Las Vegas Hwy (87505). 505/988-3333.* Hrs: 5:30-10 pm; Sun 5-9 pm. Closed most major hols. Res accepted. Continental menu. Bar from 4 pm. Complete meals: dinner $8.95-$32.95. Specializes in prime rib, fresh seafood, tapas. Southwestern decor. Cr cds: A, D, DS, MC, V.

D

★ **TECOLOTE CAFE.** *1203 Cerrillos Rd (87501). 505/988-1362.* Hrs: 7 am-2 pm. Closed Mon; Thanksgiving,

Dec 24, 25; also Fri after Thanksgiving. Southwestern, Mexican menu. Bkfst, lunch $3.25-$10. Child's menu. Specializes in bkfst dishes. Original Southwestern art. Cr cds: A, C, D, DS, MC, V.

D SC

★★ **TOMASITA'S.** *500 S Guadalupe (87501). 505/983-5721.* Hrs: 11 am-10 pm. Closed Sun; Jan 1, Thanksgiving, Dec 25. Northern New Mexican, Amer menu. Bar. Lunch $4.50-$10.50, dinner $4.95-$10.95. Child's menu. Specializes in quesadillas, burritos, enchiladas. Parking. Outdoor dining. Located in a historic train station (1904). Cr cds: MC, V.

D

★★ **VANESSIE OF SANTA FE.** *434 W San Francisco St (87501). 505/982-9966.* Hrs: 5:30-10 pm. Closed Easter, Thanksgiving, Dec 25. Bar to 2 am. A la carte entrees: dinner $12.95-$42.95. Specializes in lamb, lobster, steak. Pianist evenings. Patio dining. Cr cds: A, C, D, DS, MC, V.

D

★ **WHISTLING MOON CAFE.** *402 N Guadalupe St (87501). 505/983-3093.* Hrs: 11 am-9:30 pm. Closed July 4, Thanksgiving, Dec 25. Mediterranean menu. Wine, beer. Lunch $6-$9, dinner $7-$12. Child's menu. Specializes in lamb, salads, pasta. Outdoor dining. Mediterranean decor. Cr cds: D, DS, MC, V.

D

Unrated Dining Spots

THE BURRITO COMPANY. *111 Washington Ave (87501). 505/982-4453.* Hrs: 7:30 am-7 pm; Sun 10 am-5 pm. Closed Dec 25. Mexican menu. A la carte entrees: bkfst $2-$3.50, lunch, dinner $1.65-$4.75. Child's menu. Specializes in burritos, enchiladas. Fast-food style restaurant famous for bkfst burritos.

D

GRANT CORNER INN. *122 Grant Ave (87501). 505/983-6678. www. grantcornerinn.com.* Hrs: 8-9:30 am; Sat to 11 am; Sun to 1 pm. Res accepted. Brunch menu: $8.50-$10.50; Sun $10.50. Child's menu. Specialties: hearts of palm eggs Benedict, chile rellenos souffle, pumpkin raisin pancakes. Guitarist Sun. Out-

door dining. Colonial-style house built 1905. Cr cds: A, MC, V.

D

PLAZA. *54 Lincoln Ave (87501). 505/982-1664.* Hrs: 7 am-10 pm. Closed Thanksgiving, Dec 25. Continental menu. Wine, beer. Bkfst $2.50-$6.50, lunch $4.50-$8, dinner $6-$15. Child's menu. Specialties: blue corn enchiladas, sopaipillas, New Mexico meatloaf. Century-old building with many original fixtures; stamped-tin ceiling; photos of early Santa Fe. Art Deco lunch counter design. Family-owned since 1947. Cr cds: A, D, MC, V.

Santa Rosa (C-5)

Settled 1865 **Pop** 2,744 **Elev** 4,620 ft
Area code 505 **Zip** 88435
Information Chamber of Commerce, 486 Parker Ave; 505/472-3763 or 800/450-7084

What to See and Do

Billy the Kid Museum. Contains 60,000 items, incl relics of the Old West, Billy the Kid, and Old Fort Sumner. On display is rifle once owned by Billy the Kid. (Daily; closed first 2 wkends Jan, major hols) 1601 E Sumner Ave, 44 mi SE via US 60/84, in Fort Sumner. Phone 505/355-2380. ¢¢

City parks. Fishing in stocked lakes; picnicking. (Daily) Phone 505/472-3404. **FREE**

  Blue Hole. Clear blue lake in rock setting fed by natural artesian spring, 81 ft deep; scuba diving (permit fee). 1 mi E on Blue Hole Rd.

  Janes-Wallace Memorial Park. Also camping, small trailers allowed. 1 mi S on 3rd St.

  Park Lake. Also swimming, lifeguard (June-Aug), children's fishing only; paddleboats, canoe rentals; playground. Park Lake Dr.

  Santa Rosa Dam and Lake. Army Corps of Engineers project for flood control and irrigation. No permanent pool; irrigation pool is often avail for recreation. Fishing, boating (ramp, launch); nature trails, also trail for the disabled;

picnicking, camping (fee; electricity addl). Information center. Excellent area for photography. (Daily) 7 mi N via access road. Contact ACE, PO Box 345. Phone 505/472-3115. Per vehicle ¢¢

Tres Lagunas. Fishing; hiking, nine-hole golf (fee). ¼ mi N of US 66, E end of town.

Fort Sumner State Monument. Original site of the Bosque Redondo, where thousands of Navajo and Mescalero Apache were held captive by the US Army from 1863-1868. The military established Fort Sumner to oversee the containment. (See SPECIAL EVENTS) Visitor center has exhibits relating to the period. (Mon, Wed-Sun; closed winter hols) 3 mi E on US 54/66, then 44 mi SE on US 84, near Fort Sumner. Phone 505/355-2573. ¢¢

Puerta de Luna. Founded approx 1862, this Spanish-American town of 250 persons holds to old customs in living and working. 10 mi S on NM 91. Phone 505/472-3763. Also here is

Grzelachowski Territorial House. Store and mercantile built in 1800; this house was visited frequently by Billy the Kid. Grzelachowski had a major role in the Civil War battle at Glorieta Pass. (Daily, mid-morning-early eve; closed hols) Phone 505/472-5320. **Donation**

Rock Lake Rearing Station. State fish hatchery, rearing rainbow trout and walleyed pike. (Daily) 2 mi S off I-40. Phone 505/472-3690. **FREE**

Sumner Lake State Park. A 4,500-surface-acre reservoir created by irrigation dam. Swimming, fishing (bass, crappie, channel catfish); picnicking, camping (hookups, dump station). (Daily) Standard fees. 3 mi E on US 54/66, then 32 mi S on US 84, near Fort Sumner. Phone 505/355-2541. ¢¢

Special Events

Santa Rosa Day Celebration. Sports events, contests, exhibits. Memorial Day wkend.

Old Fort Days. Fort Sumner, downtown, and County Fairgrounds. Parade, rodeo, bank robbery, barbecue, contests, exhibits. Second wk June.

Motels/Motor Lodges

★★ **BEST WESTERN ADOBE INN.** *1501 Will Rogers Dr (88435). 505/472-3446; fax 505/472-5759; res 800/780-7234. www.bestwestern.com.* 58 rms, 2 story. S $40-$52; D $62; each addl $2. Crib $4. Pet accepted. TV; cable. Heated pool. Complimentary continental bkfst. Ck-out 11 am. Business servs avail. In-rm modem link. Sundries. Gift shop. Airport, bus depot transportation. Cr cds: A, C, D, DS, MC, V.

★★ **HOLIDAY INN EXPRESS.** *3202 Will Rogers Dr (88435). 505/472-5411; fax 505/472-3537; toll-free 800/465-4329. www.holiday-inn.com.* 67 rms, 2 story. S $55-$67; D $66-$77; each addl $10. TV; cable. Pool. Ck-out 10 am. Coin lndry. Meeting rm. Business servs avail. Cr cds: A, C, D, DS, MC, V.

Shiprock

(A-1) *See also Farmington*

Founded 1904 **Pop** 8,156 **Elev** 4,903 ft **Area code** 505 **Zip** 87420

Special Event

Shiprock Navajo Fair. Powwow, carnival, parade. Phone 505/598-8213. First wkend Oct.

Silver City

(F-1) *See also Deming*

Founded 1870 **Pop** 10,545 **Elev** 5,895 ft **Area code** 505 **Zip** 88061

Information Chamber of Commerce, 201 N Hudson; 505/538-3785

Web www.silvercity.org

What to See and Do

Gila (HEE-la) National Forest. Administers more than three million acres, incl the New Mexico part of

Apache National Forest. Also incl Gila, Blue Range, and Aldo Leopold wildernesses. Hunting, backpacking, horseback riding. Lakes Quemado, Roberts, and Snow also have fishing, boating; picnicking, camping. Fees for some activities. Surrounds town on all borders except on southeast. Contact the Information Desk, 3005 E Camino del Bosque. Phone 505/388-8201. In forest are

Catwalk of Whitewater Canyon. National recreation trail. Steel Causeway follows the course of two former pipelines that supplied water and water power in the 1890s to the historic gold and silver mining town of Graham. Causeway clings to sides of the sheer box canyon of Whitewater Creek. Access is by foot trail from Whitewater picnic ground (no water avail); access also to Gila Wilderness. (Daily) 63 mi NW of Silver City via US 180, then 5 mi NE on NM 174. Phone 505/539-2481. ¢¢

Gila Cliff Dwellings National Monument. There are 42 rms in six caves (accessible by a one-mi hiking trail), which were occupied by the Mogollon ca 1300. Well-preserved masonry dwellings in natural alcoves in the face of an overhanging cliff. Self-guided tour, camping. Forest naturalists conduct programs (Memorial Day-Labor Day). Ruins and visitor center (daily; closed Jan 1, Dec 25). 44 mi N of Silver City on NM 15. Phone 505/536-9461. ¢¢

Mogollon Ghost Town. (1878-1930s) Former gold-mining town. Weathered buildings, beautiful surroundings; nearby Whitewater Canyon was once the haunt of Butch Cassidy and his gang, as well as Vitorio and Geronimo. 75 mi NW of Silver City via US 180 on NM 159. (*Note that NM 159 is closed Nov-Apr past the ghost town*) Phone 505/539-2481. **FREE**

Phelps Dodge Copper Mine. Historic mining town is home to fort and other historic buildings. 7 mi NE on NM 15. Phone 505/538-5331.

Silver City Museum. In restored 1881 house of H. B. Ailman, owner of a rich silver mine; Victorian antiques and furnishings; Casas Grandes artifacts; memorabilia from mining town of Tyrone. (Tues-Sun; closed hols) 312 W Broadway. Phone 505/538-5921. **FREE**

Western New Mexico University. (1893) 3,000 students. West part of town. Phone 505/538-6011. On campus is

Western New Mexico University Museum. Depicts contribution of Native American, Hispanic, black, and European cultures to history of region; largest display of Membres pottery in the nation; photography, archive, and mineral collections. (Daily; closed hols) 1000 College Ave, in Fleming Hall. Phone 505/538-6386. **FREE**

Special Event

Frontier Days. Parade, dances, exhibits, food. Western dress desired. July 4.

Motels/Motor Lodges

★ **COPPER MANOR MOTEL.** *710 Silver Heights Blvd (88062).* 505/538-5392; fax 505/538-5830; toll-free 800/853-2916. 68 rms, 2 story. S $42-$45; D $48-$52; each addl $4. Crib free. TV; cable. Indoor pool. Complimentary continental bkfst. Restaurant 6 am-2 pm. Ck-out 11 am. Meeting rm. Business servs avail. Valet serv. Some refrigerators. Cr cds: A, C, D, DS, MC, V.

★ **DRIFTER MOTEL REST LOUNGE.** *711 Silver Heights Blvd (88061).* 505/538-2916; fax 505/538-5703; toll-free 800/853-2916. 69 rms, 2 story. No A/C. S $40-$45; D $44-$49; each addl $3; under 10 free. Crib free. TV; cable. Indoor/outdoor pool. Sauna. Complimentary continental bkfst. Complimentary coffee in lobby. Restaurant adj 6 am-2 pm. Bar 4 pm-2 am. Meeting rms. Business servs avail. Rec rm. Cr cds: A, C, D, DS, JCB, MC, V.

★★ **HOLIDAY MOTOR HOTEL.** *3420 Hwy 180 E (88061).* 505/538-3711; toll-free 800/828-8291. www.holidayhotel.com. 79 rms, 2 story. S $42.20-$47.59; D $47.59; each addl $4; under 12 free. Pet accepted. TV; cable (premium). Pool. Restaurant 6 am-2 pm, 5-8:30 pm; Sun 7 am-2:30 pm, 5-8:30 pm. Rm serv. Ck-out noon. Guest lndry. Meeting rms. Business servs avail. Free airport transportation. Cr cds: A, C, D, DS, MC, V.

Restaurant

★★ **BUCKHORN SALOON.** *32 Main St, Pinos Altos (88053). 505/538-9911.* Hrs: 6-10 pm. Closed Sun; Jan 1, Thanksgiving, Dec 25. Res accepted. No A/C. Bar to midnight. Dinner $7-$35. Specializes in steak, seafood. Entertainment Thurs-Sat. Four dining rms in house designed to look like Western opera house; melodrama performed some wkends. Cr cds: MC, V.

Socorro (D-3)

Pop 8,877 **Elev** 4,620 ft
Area code 505 **Zip** 87801
Information Socorro County Chamber of Commerce, 103 Francisco de Avondo, PO Box 743; 505/835-0424

What to See and Do

Bosque del Apache National Wildlife Refuge. A 12-mi self-guided auto tour loop allows visitors to view a variety of wildlife. Also walking trails. Nov-mid-Feb are best viewing months (see SPECIAL EVENTS). Visitor center has brochures and exhibits (daily). Tour loop (daily; phone for hrs and fee). 18 mi S via I-25 and NM 1. Phone 505/835-1828.

Mineral Museum. More than 12,000 mineral specimens from around the world. Free rockhounding and prospecting information. (Mon-Sat) 1 mi W of I-25 on campus of New Mexico Institute of Mining and Technology (College Ave and Leroy) at Workman Center. Phone 505/835-5154. **FREE**

National Radio Astronomy Observatory. The VLA (Very Large Array) radio telescope consists of 27 separate antennas situated along three arms of railroad track. Self-guided walking tour of grounds and visitor center. (Daily) 52 mi W on US 60,

then S on NM 52. Phone 505/835-7000. **FREE**

Old San Miguel Mission. (1615-1626) Restored; south wall was part of the original 1598 mission. Carved ceiling beams and corbels; walls are five ft thick. (Daily) Artifacts on display in church office (building south of church) (Mon-Fri). 403 El Camino Real NW, 2 blks N of the plaza. Phone 505/835-1620. **FREE**

Special Events

Conrad Hilton Open Golf Tournament. Phone 505/835-0424. Early June.

Socorro County Fair & Rodeo. Phone 505/835-0424. Labor Day wkend.

Festival of the Crane. Bosque del Apache National Wildlife Refuge. Phone 505/835-0424. Third wkend Nov.

Motels/Motor Lodges

★ **BEST INN.** *507 N California Ave (87801). 505/835-0230; fax 505/835-1993. www.bestinn.com.* 41 rms, 2 story. S $45; D $52; each addl $3. Crib $4. Pet accepted, some restrictions; $50 refundable. TV; cable (premium). Heated pool. Restaurant 6 am-9 pm. Rm serv. Ck-out 11 am. Microwaves. Cr cds: A, C, D, DS, MC, V.

★ **SAN MIGUEL INN.** *916 California Ave NE (87801). 505/835-0211; fax 505/838-1516; toll-free 800/548-7938.* 40 rms. S $45; D $49; each addl $3. TV; cable (premium). Heated pool. Complimentary continental bkfst. Coffee in rms. Restaurant opp open 24 hrs. Ck-out noon. Coin lndry. Business servs avail. Some refrigerators; microwaves avail. Cr cds: A, C, D, DS, MC, V.

★ **SUPER 8 MOTEL.** *1121 Frontage Rd NW (87801). 505/835-4626; fax 505/835-3988; toll-free 800/800-8000.* 88 rms, 2 story. S $42.88-$46.88; D $49.88-$52.88; each addl $4; under 12 free. Crib $5. TV; cable (premium). Heated pool; whirlpool. Complimentary coffee in lobby. Restaurant nearby. Ck-out 11 am. Coin lndry. Business servs avail.

Refrigerator avail. Cr cds: A, C, D, DS, MC, V.

D ⌦ ⌦ ⌦ SC

★ **THE WESTERN.** *404 First St, Magdalena (87825). 505/854-2417; fax 505/854-3217. www.thewesternmotel. com.* 6 rms, shower only. No A/C. S $33-$36; D $41-$44; each addl $4; under 10 free; wkly rates. Pet accepted, $10. TV; cable (premium). Complimentary coffee in rms. Restaurant nearby. Ck-out 11 am. Cr cds: A, D, DS, MC, V.

D ⌦ ⌦ ⌦ SC

Taos

(A-5) *See also Angel Fire, Red River*

Founded 1615 **Pop** 4,700 **Elev** 6,950 ft **Area code** 505 **Zip** 87571

Information Taos County Chamber of Commerce, 1139 Paseo Del Pueblo Sur, PO Drawer I; 505/758-3873 or 800/732-8267

Web www.taos.org

What to See and Do

Carson National Forest. On 1½ million acres. Incl Wheeler Peak, New Mexico's highest mountain at 13,161 ft, and the Valle Vidal, home to Rocky Mtn elk. Fishing (good in the 425 mi of streams and numerous small mountain lakes); hunting, hiking, winter sports, picnicking, camping (some fees). (Daily) Contact Forest Supervisor Headquarters, 208 Cruz Alta Rd. Phone 505/758-6200.

Ernest L. Blumenschein Home. Restored adobe house incl furnishings and exhibits of paintings by the Blumenschein family and other early Taos artists. Cofounder of Taos Society of Artists. (Daily) Combination tickets to other museums avail. 222 Ledoux St. Phone 505/758-0505. ¢¢

Fort Burgwin Research Center. Restored fort was occupied by First Dragoons of the US Calvary (1852-1860). Summer lecture series, music and theater performances. Operated by Southern Methodist University. (Schedule varies) 8 mi S on NM 518. Phone 505/758-8322. **FREE**

Governor Bent House Museum and Gallery. Home of New Mexico's first American territorial governor; scene of his death in 1847. Bent family possessions, Native American artifacts, western American art. (Daily; closed Jan 1, Thanksgiving, Dec 25) 117A Bent St, 1 blk N of plaza. Phone 505/758-2376. Museum ¢

Hacienda Martinez. Contains early Spanish Colonial hacienda with period furnishings; 21 rms, two large patios. Early Taos, Spanish culture exhibits. Used as fortress during raids. Living museum demonstrations. (Daily) Combination tickets to other museums avail. 708 Ranchitos Rd. 2 mi W of plaza on NM 240. Phone 505/758-1000. ¢¢

Harwood Museum of Art. Founded in 1923; features paintings, drawings, prints, sculptures, and photographs by artists of Taos from 1800-present. (Tues-Sun; closed hols) 238 Ledoux St. Phone 505/758-9826. ¢¢

Kit Carson Home and Museum. (1825) Restored house with mementos of the famous scout, mountain man and trappers rms, artifacts, gun exhibit. (Daily) Combination tickets to other museums avail. Kit Carson Rd, on US 64, ½ blk E of plaza. Phone 505/758-4741. ¢¢ Nearby is

Kit Carson Park. A 25-acre plot with bicycle/walking path. Picnic tables (grills), playground, sand volleyball pit. No camping. Graves of Kit Carson and his family. (Daily) Phone 505/758-8234. **FREE**

Millicent Rogers Museum. Native American and Hispanic arts and crafts. (Daily; closed hols) 4 mi N on NM 522. Phone 505/758-2462. ¢¢¢

Orilla Verde Recreation Area. Offers spectacular views. Park runs along banks of the Rio Grande, offering some of the finest trout fishing in the state; whitewater rafting through deep chasm north of park. Hiking, picnicking. Standard fees. (Daily) 12 mi SW via NM 68. Phone 505/751-4899. ¢¢

Ranchos de Taos. (ca 1800) This adobe-housed farming and ranching center has one of the most beautiful churches in the Southwest—the San Francisco de Asis Church. Its huge buttresses and twin bell towers only suggest the beauty of its interior. (Mon-Sat) 4 mi S on NM 68. Phone 505/758-2754. ¢¢

Rio Grande Gorge Bridge. Bridge is 650 ft above the Rio Grande; observation platforms, picnic and parking areas. 11 mi NW on US 64.

Ski areas.

Sipapu Area. Area has two triple chairlifts, two Pomalifts; patrol, school, rentals, snowmaking; accommodations, restaurant, lounge. Thirty-one runs; longest run more than one mi; vertical drop 1,065 ft. (Mid-Dec-Mar, daily) X-country skiing on forest roads and trails. Snowboarding. 25 mi SE on NM 518, 3 mi W of Tres Ritos. Phone 505/587-2240. ¢¢¢¢

Taos Ski Valley. Area has twelve chairlifts, two surface lifts; patrol, school, rentals; cafeteria, restaurants, bar; nursery, lodges. Longest run more than four mi; vertical drop 2,612 ft. (Nov-Apr, daily) 18 mi NE via NM 522, 150. ¢¢¢¢

Taos Pueblo. (Pop: 1,187) This is one of the most famous pueblos and is believed to be more than 1,000 yrs old. Within the pueblo is a double apartment house; the north and south buildings, separated by a river, are five stories tall and form a unique communal dwelling. Small buildings and corrals are scattered around these impressive architectural masterpieces. The residents here live without modern utilities such as electricity and plumbing and get their drinking water from the river. The people are independent, conservative, and devout in their own religious observances. Fees are charged for parking, photography permits. Photographs of individual Native Americans may be taken only with their consent. Do not enter any buildings that do not indicate a shop. Pueblo (daily; closed for special occasions in spring). (See SPECIAL EVENTS) 2½ mi N. Phone 505/758-1028. ¢

Van Vechten-Lineberry Taos Art Museum. Houses artwork of the Taos Founders and other local artists. (Wed-Sun) 501 N Pueblo Rd. Phone 505/758-2690. ¢¢

Special Events

Taos Talking Picture Festival. Four-day film festival showcasing independent productions. Phone 505/751-0637. Mid-Apr.

Spring Arts Festival. Three-wk festival featuring visual, performing, and literary arts. Phone 800/732-8267. May.

Chamber Music Festival. Taos Community Auditorium and Hotel St. Bernard in Taos Ski Valley. Phone 505/776-2388. Mid-June-early Aug.

Taos Rodeo. County Fairgrounds. Phone 800/732-8267. Late June or early July.

Annual Pow-Wow. Taos Pueblo. Intertribal dancers from throughout US, Canada, and Mexico participate; competition. Phone 505/758-1028. Second wkend July.

Fiestas de Santiago y Santa Ana. Traditional festival honoring the patron saints of Taos. Candlelight procession, parade, crafts, food, entertainment. Late July.

Taos Arts Festival. Arts and crafts exhibitions, music, plays, poetry readings. Phone 505/758-1028. Mid-Sept-early Oct.

San Geronimo Eve Sundown Dance. Taos Pueblo. Traditional men's dance followed next day by San Geronimo Feast Day, with intertribal dancing, trade fair, pole climb, footraces. Phone 505/758-1028. Late Sept.

Yuletide in Taos. Ski area festivities, *farolito* (paper bag lantern) tours, food and craft fairs, art events, dance performances. Phone 800/732-8267. Dec.

Taos Pueblo Dances. For a complete list of annual dances, contact the pueblo. Phone 505/758-1028.

Taos Pueblo Deer or *Matachines* Dance. Symbolic animal dance or ancient Montezuma dance. Dec 25.

Motels/Motor Lodges

★ ★ **EL PUEBLO LODGE.** *412 Paseo Del Pueblo N (87571). 505/758-8700; fax 505/758-7321; toll-free 800/433-9612.* 60 rms, 1-2 story, 16 kits. Mid-June-Oct, mid-Dec-early Apr: S $50; D $68; each addl $10; suites $105-$215; kit. units $75; wkly rates; ski plans; lower rates rest of yr. Crib free. Pet accepted. TV; cable (premium). Heated pool; whirlpool. Complimentary continental bkfst. Ck-out 11:30 am. Business servs avail. Downhill ski 17 mi; x-country ski 5 mi. Refrigerators; some microwaves. Some balconies. Cr cds: A, DS, MC, V.

★★ **HAMPTON INN.** *1515 Paseo Del Pueblo Sur (87571). 505/737-5700; fax 505/737-5701; res 800/426-7866. www.hamptoninn.com.* 71 rms, 2 story. Memorial Day-Labor Day: S, D $74-$84; under 18 free; lower rates rest of yr. Crib avail. Pet accepted. TV; cable. Complimentary continental bkfst. Complimentary coffee in rms. Restaurant opp 7 am-10 pm. Ck-out 11 am. Meeting rms. Business servs avail. In-rm modem link. X-country ski 10 mi. Indoor pool; whirlpool. Cr cds: A, C, D, DS, JCB, ER, MC, V.

★★★ **HOLIDAY INN DON FERNANDO DE TAOS.** *1005 Paseo Del Pueblo Sur (87571). 505/758-4444; fax 505/758-0055; toll-free 800/759-2736. www.holiday-inn.com.* 124 rms, 2 story. S, D $99-$115; under 19 free; wkly rates; ski plans; higher rates Christmas hols. Crib free. Pet accepted; $75 deposit. TV; cable, VCR avail. Indoor/outdoor pool; whirlpool, poolside serv. Restaurant 6:30 am-2 pm, 5-10 pm. Rm serv. Bar 3-11 pm; Fri, Sat to 1 am; Sun noon-11 pm. Ck-out 11 am. Meeting rm. Business servs avail. Tennis. 18-hole golf privileges, greens fee $27-$35, pro, putting green, driving range. Downhill ski 20 mi; x-country ski 5 mi. Fireplace in suites. Pueblo-style building; central courtyard. Cr cds: A, C, D, DS, JCB, MC, V.

★★ **QUALITY INN.** *1043 Paseo Del Pueblo Sur (87571). 505/758-2200; fax 505/758-9009; res 800/228-5151. www.qualityinn.com.* 99 rms, 2 story. Mid-June-Oct: S, D $55-$99; each addl $7; suites $95-$175; under 18 free; ski plans; higher rates Christmas hols; lower rates rest of yr. Crib free. Pet accepted. TV; cable (premium), VCR avail. Heated pool; poolside serv. Coffee in rms. Restaurant 6:30 am-2 pm, 5-9 pm. Rm serv. Bar 11 am-11 pm. Ck-out 11 am. Meeting rms. Business servs avail. In-rm modem link. Valet serv. Downhill ski 20 mi; x-country ski 5 mi. Health club privileges. Many microwaves; refrigerator, wet bar in suites. Picnic tables. Cr cds: A, C, D, DS, ER, JCB, MC, V.

★★ **RAMADA INN DE TAOS.** *615 Paseo Del Pueblo Sur (87571). 505/758-2900; fax 505/758-1662; toll-free 888/298-2054. www.ramada.com.* 124 rms, 2 story. Mid-June-Sept, mid-Dec-mid-Apr: S, D $79-$120; each addl $10; under 18 free; package plans; lower rates rest of yr. Crib free. TV; cable (premium). Indoor pool; whirlpool. Ck-out noon. Meeting rms. Business servs avail. Valet serv. Downhill ski 17 mi; x-country ski 5 mi. Some fireplaces. Cr cds: A, C, D, DS, MC, V.

Hotel

★★★ **FECHIN INN.** *227 Paseo del Pueblo Notre (87571). 505/751-1000. www.fechin-inn.com.* 85 rms, 2 story. S, D $149-$169; each addl $15. Crib avail. TV; cable (premium), VCR avail. Complimentary continental bkfst. Ck-out noon. Meeting rms. Business serv avail. Exercise rm; whirlpool. Former home of Russian artist Nicolai Fechin. Southwestern decor. Cr cds: A, C, D, DS, MC, V.

Resort

★★ **QUAIL RIDGE INN RESORT.** *88 Ski Valley Rd (87571). 505/776-2211; fax 505/776-2949; toll-free 800/624-4448. www.quailridgeinn.com.* 110 condos, 65 kits. No A/C. S, D $72-$160; each addl $10; suites $170-$300; studio rms $120-$140; under 18 free; tennis plans; higher rates ski season. TV; cable (premium), VCR. Pool; whirlpools. Supervised children's activities (June-Labor Day); ages 5-15. Dining rm 7-10 am, 6-9 pm. Bar from 4 pm. Ck-out 11 am. Meeting rms. Business servs avail. Indoor tennis, pro. Soc dir. Exercise equipt; saunas. Massage. Microwaves, fireplaces. Balconies. Cr cds: A, C, D, DS, MC, V.

B&Bs/Small Inns

★★★ **ADOBE STARS BED AND BREAKFAST INN.** *584 NM 150 (87571). 505/776-2776; fax 505/776-*

2872; toll-free 800/211-7076.
www.
taosadobe.com. 7 rms, 3 with
shower only. No A/C. Jan-Apr,
June-Oct, Dec: S $85-$170; D
$140-$180; each addl $20;
wkly rates; hols (2-day min);
higher rates Dec 25; lower
rates rest of yr. Pet accepted,
some restrictions. TV in common rm; VCR (movies). Complimentary full bkfst. Ck-out
11 am, ck-in 4 pm. Luggage
handling. Concierge serv.
Downhill/x-country ski 8 mi.
Southwestern furnishings,
regional art, kiva fireplaces.
Totally nonsmoking. Cr cds: A,
DS, MC, V.

Taos Pueblo Church

★ ★ **AMERICAN ARTISTS
GALLERY HOUSE.** *132 Frontier Ln (87571). 505/758-4446;
fax 505/758-0497; toll-free
800/532-2041. www.
taosbedandbreakfast.com.* 10
rms, 5 with shower only. No
rm phones. S, D $75-$150;
each addl $25. Children over 8
yrs only. Complimentary full bkfst.
Restaurant nearby. Ck-out 11 am, ck-
in 3-6 pm. Luggage handling.
Concierge serv. Downhill ski 18 mi;
x-country ski 8 mi. Art gallery located
in main house. Cr cds: DS, MC, V.

★ ★ **AUSTING HAUS B&B.** *1282
NM 150, Taos Ski Valley (87525).
505/776-2649; fax 505/776-8751; toll-
free 800/748-2932. www.taoswebb.
com/hotel/austinghaus.* 45 rms, 2
story. No A/C. Mid-Nov-mid-Apr: S
$108; D $120; each addl $20; under
5 free; ski plans; wkday rates; lower
rates mid-May-mid-Nov. Closed mid-
Apr-mid-May. Pet accepted. TV;
cable. Complimentary continental
bkfst. Dining rm 7:30-10 am; winter
also 6-9 pm. Ck-out 10 am, ck-in 2
pm. Lndry facilities. Business servs
avail. Downhill ski 2 mi. 2
whirlpools. Constructed of oak-
pegged heavy timbers with beams
exposed inside and out; built by
hand entirely without nails or metal
plates. Cr cds: A, DS, MC, V.

★ ★ ★ **BROOKS STREET INN.** *119
Brooks St (87571). 505/758-1489; fax*
505/758-7525; toll-free 800/758-1489.
www.brooksstreetinn.com. 6 rms. No
A/C. No rm phones. S, D $95; each
addl $20; Christmas hols (3-day
min). Adults only. Complimentary
full bkfst. Ck-out 11 am, ck-in 4-6
pm. Business servs avail. Downhill
ski 18 mi; x-country ski 5 mi. Rambling adobe house; stone fireplace in
sitting rm; artwork. Patio. Totally
nonsmoking. Cr cds: A, DS, MC, V.

★ ★ ★ **CASA DE LAS CHIMENEAS.**
*405 Cordoba Rd (87571). 505/758-
4777; fax 505/758-3976; toll-free
877/758-4777. www.visit-taos.com.* 8
rms, 1 suite. No A/C. S, D $125-$155;
each addl $15; suite $150-$170. Crib
$10. TV; cable (premium). Compli-
mentary full bkfst; afternoon refreshments. Coffee in rms. Restaurant
nearby. Ck-out 11 am, ck-in 3-6 pm.
Downhill ski 18 mi; x-country ski 15
mi. Exercise rm; sauna. Massage.
Refrigerators. Rambling adobe house
within walled garden with fountains.
Library. Kiva fireplaces; hand-carved
and antique furniture; regional art.
Totally nonsmoking. Cr cds: A, D,
MC, V.

★ ★ ★ **CASA EUROPA INN & GALLERY.** *840 Upper Ranchitos (87571). 505/758-9798; toll-free 888/758-9798. www.cacaeuropanm. com.* 7 rms, 2 story. No A/C. S $85-$105; D $95-$135; each addl $20. Crib $5. TV in sitting rm; cable (premium). Complimentary full bkfst; afternoon refreshments (seasonal). Ck-out 11 am, ck-in 3 pm. Downhill/x-county ski 16 mi. Whirlpools. Sauna. Picnic tables. Old adobe structure with courtyard. European antiques, artwork. Cr cds: A, MC, V.
🏌 🐾 ⊠ ⊠ 🔥

★ ★ ★ **COTTONWOOD INN BED AND BREAKFAST.** *#2 State Rte 230 Arroyo Seco 24609 (87529). 505/776-5826; fax 505/776-1141; toll-free 800/324-7120. www.taos-cottonwood. com.* 7 rms, 2 with shower only, 2 story. No A/C. No rm phones. S, D $85-$155. TV in common rm. Complimentary full bkfst. Restaurant nearby. Ck-out 11 am, ck-in 4-7 pm. Business servs avail. Luggage handling. Concierge serv. Downhill ski 11 mi. Sauna. Lawn games. Many fireplaces; some in-rm whirlpools, refrigerators, wet bars; microwaves avail. Some balconies. Picnic tables. Built in 1947; renovated Pueblo-style adobe. Totally nonsmoking. Cr cds: A, DS, MC, V.
🅳 🏌 🐾 ⊠ ⊠ 🔥

★ ★ **DREAMCATCHER BED AND BREAKFAST.** *416 La Lomita Rd (87571). 505/758-0613; fax 505/751-0115; toll-free 888/758-0613. dreambb. com.* 7 rms. No A/C. No rm phones. S $89; D $99; wkly rates; ski plans; higher rates Christmas hols. Complimentary full bkfst. Coffee in rms. Ck-out 11 am, ck-in 4-6 pm. Downhill ski 18 mi; x-country ski 5 mi. Whirlpool. Picnic table. Library; works by local artists; kiva fireplaces. Cr cds: A, DS, MC, V.
🅳 🏌 🐾 ⊠ ⊠ 🔥

★ ★ ★ **HACIENDA DEL SOL.** *109 Mabel Dodge Ln (87571). 505/758-0287; fax 505/758-5895. www.taos haciendadelsol.com.* 10 rms, 2 with shower only, 2 suites. No A/C. No rm phones. S $115; D $130; suites $145-$189; under 3 free; 2-day min wkends, 3-day min hols. Crib free. TV in common; cable (premium). Complimentary full bkfst; afternoon refreshments. Restaurant opp 11 am-

9 pm. Ck-out 11 am, ck-in 3 pm. Luggage handling. Concierge serv. Business servs avail. Downhill/x-country ski 18 mi. Lawn games. Refrigerators. Picnic tables. Adobe built in early 1800s. Totally nonsmoking. Cr cds: A, MC, V.
🅳 🏌 🐾 ⊠ 🔥

★ ★ ★ **THE HISTORIC TAOS INN.** *125 Paseo Del Pueblo Norte (87571). 505/758-2233; fax 505/758-5776; res 888/518-8267. www.taosinn.com.* 36 rms. Some A/C. S, D $85-$225. Crib free. TV; cable (premium). Pool; whirlpool. Restaurant (see also DOC MARTIN'S). Bar noon-10:30 pm; entertainment. Ck-out 11 am, ck-in 3 pm. Business servs avail. X-country ski 15 mi. Inn consists of number of structures, some dating from 17th century. Pueblo fireplaces; antique Taos-style furniture; Mexican tile. Meet-the-Artist Series in spring, fall. Cr cds: A, D, DS, MC, V.
🅳 🐾 ⊠ ⊠ 🔥 **SC**

★ ★ ★ **INN ON LA LOMA PLAZA.** *315 Ranchitos Rd (87571). 505/758-1717; fax 505/751-0155; toll-free 800/530-3040. vacationtaos.com.* 7 rms, 2 story, 2 kit. units. Jan-Mar, June-Oct: S $70-$240; D $80-$250; each addl $10; kit. units $170-$195; package plans; wkends (2-day min); hols (3-5 day min); lower rates rest of yr. Crib avail. TV; cable (premium). Complimentary full bkfst. Complimentary coffee in rms. Ck-out 11 am, ck-in 4-9 pm. Business servs avail. Luggage handling. Valet serv. Heated pool; whirlpool. Playground. Fireplaces. Some balconies, patio. Picnic tables. Built in 1800; Pueblo Revival architecture. Totally nonsmoking. Cr cds: A, DS, MC, V.
🅳 🐾 ⊠ ⊠ 🔥

★ ★ ★ **LA DONA LUZ INN, AN HISTORIC BED AND BREAKFAST.** *114 Kit Carson Rd (87571). 505/758-4874; fax 505/758-4541; toll-free 800/758-9187. www.ladonaluz.com.* 17 rms, 3 story. No rm phones. S, D $89; each addl $10-$15. Crib avail. Pet accepted. $10. TV; VCR (free movies). Complimentary continental bkfst. Complimentary coffee in rms. Restaurant nearby. Ck-out 11 am, ck-in 2-6 pm. Business servs avail. Downhill ski 18 mi; x-country ski 5 mi. Many fireplaces; microwaves avail. Picnic tables. Adobe building

(1800); antiques, contemporary and Native American art; fireplaces. Cr cds: A, DS, MC, V.

[icons]

★★ **LA POSADA DE TAOS.** *309 Juanita Ln (87571). 505/758-8164; fax 505/751-4696; toll-free 800/645-4803.* 6 rms, 3 with shower only. S $75-$110; D $85-$120; each addl $15. TV in common rm. Complimentary full bkfst. Restaurant nearby. Ck-out 11 am, ck-in 3-5 pm. Luggage handling. Old adobe structure with courtyard. Cr cds: A, MC, V.

[icons]

★★★ **SALSA DELI SALTO B&B INN.** *543 Hwy 150, Arroyd Selo (87529). 505/776-2422; fax 505/776-5734; toll-free 800/530-3097. www.bandbtaos.com.* 10 rms, 2 story. No A/C. No rm phones. S, D $85-$160. Children over 6 yrs only. TV in sitting rm. Heated pool; whirlpool. Complimentary full bkfst. Restaurant nearby. Ck-out 11 am, ck-in 3-7 pm. Concierge serv. Tennis. Downhill/x-country ski 8 mi. Lawn games. Some fireplaces. Balconies. Picnic tables. View of mountains or mesas. Totally nonsmoking. Cr cds: A, MC, V.

[icons]

★★ **SAN GERONIMO LODGE.** *1101 Witt Rd (87571). 505/751-3776; fax 505/751-1493; toll-free 800/894-4119. www.newmex.com/sgl.* 18 rms, 2 with shower only, 2 story. S, D $120; each addl $10; under 5 free. Crib free. TV; cable (premium). Pool; whirlpool. Complimentary full bkfst. Ck-out 11 am, ck-in 3-7 pm. Luggage handling. Downhill ski 18 mi; x-country 8 mi. Old adobe lodge with handcrafted furniture. Cr cds: A, D, DS, MC, V.

[icons]

★★★ **TOUCHSTONE LUXURY BED AND BREAKFAST.** *110 Mabel Dodge Ln (87571). 505/758-0192; fax 505/758-3498; toll-free 800/758-0192. www.taoswebb.com/touchstone.* 7 rms, 2 story. No A/C. S, D $85-$150; each addl $30. TV; cable (premium), VCR (movies). Complimentary full bkfst; afternoon refreshments. Ck-out 11 am, ck-in 4 pm. Ceiling fans; Business servs avail. Downhill ski 15 mi; x-country ski 10 mi. Adobe hacienda filled with original art; bkfst rm has view of Taos Mtn. Totally nonsmoking. Cr cds: A, MC, V.

[icons]

All Suite

★★ **COMFORT SUITES.** *1500 Paseo Del Pueblo Sur (87571). 505/751-1555; fax 505/751-1991; toll-free 888/751-1555. www.taoshotels.com//comfort suites/.* 60 suites, 2 story. S, D $60-$140; each addl $10; under 18 free; package plans. Crib free. TV; cable (premium). Complimentary continental bkfst. Complimentary coffee in rms. Restaurant adj 6:30-11 am, 5:30-10 pm. Ck-out 11 am. Meeting rms. Business servs avail. In-rm modem link. Tennis. X-country ski 15 mi. Pool; whirlpool. Refrigerators, microwaves. Cr cds: A, C, D, DS, ER, JCB, MC, V.

[icons]

Conference Center

★★★ **SAGEBRUSH INN.** *1508 S Santa Fe Rd (87571). 505/758-2254; fax 505/758-5077; toll-free 800/428-3626. www.sagebrushinn.com.* 100 rms, 2 story. S, D $65-$95; each addl $10; suites $90-$140; under 12 free. Crib $7. Pet accepted. TV; cable (premium). Pool; whirlpools. Complimentary full bkfst. Coffee in rms. Restaurant 6:30-11 am, 5:30-10 pm. Bar 3 pm-midnight; entertainment. Ck-out 11 am. Meeting rms. Business center. X-country ski 10 mi. Sundries. Many fireplaces; some refrigerators. Built in 1929 of adobe in Pueblo-Mission style; extensive art collection, antiques, Navajo rugs, pottery. Cr cds: A, C, D, DS, JCB, MC, V.

[icons]

Restaurants

★★ **APPLE TREE.** *123 Bent St (87571). 505/758-1900.* Hrs: 11:30 am-3 pm, 5:30-9 pm; Sun brunch 10 am-3 pm. Res accepted. Wine, beer. Lunch $5.95-$9.95, dinner $7.95-$19.95. Sun brunch $5.95-$9.95. Specializes in fresh seafood, New Mexican dishes. Outdoor dining. Cr cds: A, C, D, DS, MC, V.

[icon]

★★ **CASA DE VALDEZ.** *1401 Paseo del Pueblo Sur (87571).* 505/758-8777. Hrs: 11:30 am-9:30 pm; Sun from 3:30 pm. Closed Wed; Easter, Thanksgiving, Dec 25; also 3 wks after Thanksgiving. Res accepted. Southwestern menu. Serv bar. Lunch $5.95-$9.95, dinner $8.95-$25.95. Specializes in barbecue, steak. Patio. Cr cds: A, D, DS, MC, V.
🔲

★★★ **DOC MARTIN'S.** *125 Paseo Del Pueblo (87571).* 505/758-1977. *www.taoswebb.com/nmusa/hotel/ taos.inn.* Hrs: 7:30 am-2:30 pm, 5:30-9:30 pm. Res accepted. Continental, Southwestern menu. Wine list. Bkfst $4-$8, lunch $5.50-$10.50, dinner $14-$24. Specializes in fresh seafood. Own baking. In colorful, historic structure; fireplaces. Cr cds: A, D, MC, V.
🔲

★★★ **LAMBERT'S.** *309 Paseo Del Pueblo Sur (87571).* 505/758-1009. Hrs: 5:30-9 pm; Fri-Sun to 9:30 pm. Res accepted. No A/C. Wine list. Dinner $6-$20. Child's menu. Specialties: pepper-crusted loin of lamb with garlic glaze, San Francisco cheesecake. Own baking. Outdoor dining. Gardenlike setting; 3 stone fireplaces. Cr cds: A, C, DS, MC, V.
🔲 🔲 🔲

★ **MICHAEL'S KITCHEN AND BAKERY.** *304 Paseo Del Pueblo N (87571).* 505/758-4178. *www.michaelskitchen. com.* Hrs: 7 am-8:30 pm. Closed most major hols; also Nov. Mexican, Amer menu. Bkfst $2.55-$7.45, lunch $2.85-$7.55, dinner $6.05-$10.95. Child's menu. Specialties: stuffed sopapillas, Indian tacos. Cr cds: A, D, MC, V.
🔲

★★ **OGELVIE'S BAR AND GRILLE.** *103 E Plaza (87571).* 505/758-8866. Hrs: 11 am-10 pm. Bar. Lunch $5.95-$18.50, dinner $6.95-$19.50. Child's menu. Specializes in fresh seafood, steaks, New Mexican dishes. Outdoor dining. Eclectic Southwestern decor. Cr cds: A, MC, V.

★★ **STEAKOUT GRILL AND BAR.** *101 Stakeout Dr (87571).* 505/758-2042. *www.stakeoutrestaurant.com.* Hrs: 5-9:30 pm. Res accepted. Bar. Dinner $11.25-$27.50. Child's menu. Specializes in steak, seafood. Entertainment.

Outdoor dining May-Oct. Historically located adobe pueblo-style building. Cr cds: A, C, D, DS, MC, V.
🔲 🔲

★★ **TIM'S CHILE CONNECTION.** *NM 150, MM 1 (87529).* 505/776-8787. Hrs: 11 am-10 pm. Mexican, New Mexican menu. Bar. Lunch $3.50-$9.25, dinner $3.50-$16.95. Child's menu. Specializes in tamales, chile, seafood. Entertainment. Outdoor dining. Hacienda-style furnishing. Fireplaces in each rm. Cr cds: A, MC, V.
🔲

★★★ **VILLA FONTANA.** *NM 522 (87571).* 505/758-5800. *www.villa fontana.com.* Hrs: 5:30 pm-closing. Closed Sun; also Sun-Wed mid-Apr-mid-May, mid-Nov-mid-Dec. Res accepted. Bar. Northern Italian menu. A la carte entrees: dinner $19.50-$25. Specializes in wild mushrooms (seasonal), veal, fresh fish. Outdoor dining. Cr cds: A, DS, MC, V.
🔲

Truth or Consequences

(F-3)

Pop 7,289 **Elev** 4,240 ft
Area code 505 **Zip** 87901
Information Truth or Consequences/ Sierra County Chamber of Commerce, 201 S Foch St, PO Drawer 31; 505/894-3536

What to See and Do

Caballo Lake State Park. Caballo Mtns form a backdrop for this lake. Swimming, windsurfing, waterskiing, fishing (bass, crappie, pike, trout, catfish), boating (ramp); hiking, picnicking, playground, camping (hookups). Standard fees. (Daily) 18 mi S on I-25. Phone 505/743-3942. ¢¢

Canoeing, boating, and tubing. On the Rio Grande, which flows through the city.

Elephant Butte Lake State Park. This 40-mi-long lake was created in 1916 for irrigation; later adapted to hydroelectric power. Swimming, windsurfing, waterskiing, fishing (bass, crappie, pike, catfish), boating (ramp, rentals, slips, mooring, three marinas); hiking, picnicking, playground, concession, restaurant, lodge, camping (hookups), cabins. (Daily) Standard fees. 5 mi N via I-25. Phone 505/744-5421. ¢¢

Geronimo Springs Museum. Exhibits of Mimbres pottery, fossils, and photographs, and articles on local history. Ralph Edwards Room, Apache Room, Hispanic Room, and log cabin. Gift shop. (Mon-Sat; closed Jan 1, Thanksgiving, Dec 25) 211 Main St. Phone 505/894-6600. ¢

Motels/Motor Lodges

★ **ACE LODGE AND MOTEL.** *1302 N Date St (87901). 505/894-2151.* 38 rms. S $29-$32; D $34-$40; each addl $2; suites $50-$60; wkly rates. Crib $2. Pet accepted, some restrictions. TV; cable. Heated pool. Playground. Restaurant 6 am-9 pm. Bar 5 pm-2 am. Ck-out 11 am. Free airport transportation. Golf privileges. Picnic tables. Cr cds: A, C, D, DS, JCB, MC, V.

★★ **BEST WESTERN HOT SPRINGS MOTOR INN.** *2270 N Date St (87901). 505/894-6665; fax 505/894-6665; toll-free 800/780-7234. www.bestwestern.com.* 40 rms. S $55; D $60; each addl $5; under 12 free (2 max). Crib free. TV; cable (premium). Heated pool. Complimentary coffee in lobby. Restaurant adj 7 am-8 pm. Ck-out noon. Business servs avail. Cr cds: A, C, D, DS, MC, V.

★★ **QUALITY INN AT THE BUTTE.** *401 Hwy 195, Elephant Butte (87935). 505/744-5431; fax 505/744-5044; res 800/228-5150. www.qualityinn.com.* 48 rms, 2 story. Apr-Aug: S, D $69-$79; each addl $5; under 12 free; wkly rates; lower rates rest of yr. Crib $2. Pet accepted. TV; cable (premium). Complimentary coffee in rms. Restaurant 7 am-2 pm, 5-9 pm. Rm serv. Bar noon-midnight. Ck-out 11 am. Meeting rms. Business servs avail. Tennis. 18-hole golf privileges. Pool. Playground. Many balconies.

Picnic tables. On lake. Cr cds: A, C, DS, JCB, MC, V.

Restaurant

★★ **LOS ARCOS STEAK HOUSE.** *1400 N Date St (87901). 505/894-6200.* Hrs: 5-10:30 pm; Fri, Sat to 11 pm. Closed Thanksgiving, Dec 25. Res accepted. Bar to 2 am. Dinner $5.95-$38.95. Specializes in steak, lobster tail. Salad bar. Open grill. Mexican decor. Cr cds: A, D, DS, MC, V.

Tucumcari (C-6)

Settled 1901 **Pop** 5,989 **Elev** 4,096 ft **Area code** 505 **Zip** 88401

Information Tucumcari/Quay County Chamber of Commerce, 404 W Rt 66, PO Drawer E; 505/461-1694

Web www.tucumcarinm.com

What to See and Do

Conchas Lake State Park. Lake is 25 mi long. Swimming, waterskiing, fishing, boating; picnicking, camping (hookups, dump station). Standard fees. (Daily) 33 mi NW via NM 104, 433. Phone 505/868-2270. ¢¢

Tucumcari Historical Museum. Western Americana; Native American artifacts; gems, minerals, rocks, fossils; restored fire truck and caboose. (Tues-Sat) 416 S Adams St. Phone 505/461-4201. ¢

Ute Lake State Park. Created by a dam on the Canadian River. Swimming, waterskiing, fishing (bass, crappie, channel catfish), boating (marina, ramp, slips, mooring); hiking trails, picnicking, camping (hookups, dump station). Standard fees. (Daily) 22 mi NE on US 54, NM 540. Phone 505/487-2284. ¢¢

Special Event

Route 66 Festival. Rodeo, car show, parade, arts and crafts, entertainment. July.

Motels/Motor Lodges

★★ **COMFORT INN.** *2800 E Tucumcari Blvd (88401). 505/461-4094; fax 505/461-4099; res 800/228-5150. www.comfortinn.com.* 59 rms, 2 story. S $54-$60; D $61-$66; each addl $6; suites $66; under 18 free. Crib $6. Pet accepted; $6. TV. Pool. Complimentary continental bkfst. Restaurant nearby. Ck-out noon. Meeting rms. Cr cds: A, C, D, DS, MC, V.

★ **COUNTRY INN.** *1302 W Tucumcari Blvd (88401). 505/461-3140; fax 505/461-3143.* 57 rms, 2 story. S $38; D $48; each addl $10; under 18 free. Crib free. Pet accepted. TV; cable (premium). Pool. Complimentary continental bkfst. Restaurant adj 6:30 am-9 pm. Ck-out noon. Meeting rm. Cr cds: A, D, MC, V.

★ **ECONO LODGE.** *3400 Rte 66 E (88401). 505/461-4194; fax 505/461-4911; res 800/553-2666. www.econolodge.com.* 41 rms, 2 story. S $31.95; D $43.95-$48.95; each addl $7; under 17 free. Crib free. Pet accepted. TV; cable. Complimentary coffee in lobby. Restaurant nearby. Ck-out 11 am. Business servs avail. Cr cds: A, C, D, DS, MC, V.

★★ **HOLIDAY INN.** *3716 E Tucumcari Blvd (88401). 505/461-3780; fax 505/461-3931; toll-free 800/335-3780. www.holiday-inn.com.* 100 rms, 2 story. S $45-$65; D $51-$72; each addl $6; under 18 free. Crib free. Pet accepted. TV; cable. Heated pool; whirlpool. Playground. Restaurant 6 am-9 pm. Rm serv. Bar 5-10 pm. Ck-out noon. Coin lndry. Meeting rms. Business servs avail. In-rm modem link. Sundries. Exercise equipt. Cr cds: A, D, DS, MC, V.

★ **SUPER 8.** *4001 E Tucumcari Blvd (88401). 505/461-4444; fax 505/461-4320; res 800/800-8000. www.super8.com.* 63 rms, 2 story, 13 suites. S $36.88-$42.88; D $47.88-$52.88; each addl $2; suites $45.88-$47.88; under 12 free. TV; cable. Indoor pool. Restaurant nearby. Ck-out 11 am. Coin lndry. Business servs avail. Cr cds: A, DS, MC, V.

White Sands National Monument

See also Alamogordo

(15 mi SW of Alamogordo on US 70/82)

These shifting, dazzling white dunes are a challenge to plants and animals. Here, lizards and mice are white like the sand, helping them to blend in with the background. (Similarly, mice are black in the black lava area only a few miles north.)

Plants elongate their stems up to 30 feet so that they can keep their leaves and flowers above the sand. When the sands recede, the plants are sometimes left on elevated pillars of hardened gypsum bound together by their roots. Even an ancient two-

White Sands National Monument

wheeled Spanish cart was laid bare when the sands shifted.

Beach sand is usually silica, but White Sands National Monument sand is gypsum, from which plaster of paris is made. Dunes often rise to 60 feet; it is the largest gypsum dune field in the world.

White Sands National Monument encloses 143,732 acres of this remarkable area. The visitor center has an orientation video, exhibits concerning the dunes and how they were formed, and other related material (daily except December 25). Evening programs and guided nature walks in the dunes area are conducted (Memorial Day-mid-August). There is a 16-mile round-trip drive from the center; free printed guide leaflet. Picnic area with shaded tables and grills (no water); primitive backpackers' campsite (by permit only). Dunes Drive (daily except December 25).

For further information contact the Superintendent, PO Box 1086, Holloman AFB, NM 88330-1086; phone 505/672-2599.

Zuni Pueblo

(C-1) *See also Gallup*

Pop 6,367 **Elev** 6,283 ft
Area code 505 **Zip** 87327

Thirty-nine miles south of Gallup, via NM 602 and west on NM 53, is one of Coronado's "Seven Cities of Cibola." Fray Marcos de Niza reported that these cities were built of gold. When looking down on the Zuni pueblo from a distant hilltop at sunset, it does seem to have a golden glow. Marcos' story was partly responsible for Coronado's expedition of the area in 1540, which found no riches for Spain.

Zuni is linguistically unique and distinct from other Rio Grande pueblos. The people here make beautiful jewelry, beadwork, and pottery. They also have a furniture and woodworking center with colorful and uniquely painted and carved items. Zuni works are available at **Pueblo of Zuni Arts and Crafts.** Phone 505/782-5531.

A:shiwi A:wan Museum and Heritage Center displays historical photos and exhibits. (Daily) Phone 505/782-4403. The pueblo, built mainly of stone, is one story high for the most part. The old Zuni mission church has been restored and its interior painted with murals of Zuni traditional figures. A tribal permit is required for photography; certain rules must be observed.

Picnicking and camping at Eustace, Ojo Caliente, Pescado, Nutria #2, and Nutria #4 lakes. Lakes stocked by Tribal Fish & Wildlife Service; a tribal permit as well as a state fishing license is required. For further information contact the Pueblo of Zuni, PO Box 339; phone 505/782-4481.

TEXAS

The long, turbulent history of Texas as we know it goes back to 27 years after Columbus arrived in America. In 1519 Alonzo Alvarez de Piñeda explored and charted the Texas coast. Alvar Núñez Cabeza de Vaca, shipwrecked near Galveston, wandered across Texas beginning in 1528. Inspired by the tales of de Vaca, Coronado entered the state from New Mexico, bringing with him Fray Juan de Padilla, the first missionary, who was later killed by the Native Americans he tried to convert.

In 1821 Mexico won its independence from Spain, and Texas became a part of the new Mexican republic. At about this time, Moses Austin and his son, Stephen F. Austin, received permission to settle 300 American families on the Brazos. This was the beginning of Anglo-American Texas. Dissatisfaction with Mexican rule led to the Texas Revolution and the taking of San Antonio, later temporarily lost when the Alamo fell. The Revolution came to an end on the plain of San Jacinto when General Sam Houston's outnumbered troops successfully charged the Mexican Army on April 21, 1836, and Texas became an independent republic. It remained so until December 29, 1845, when Texas became the 28th state of the Union.

The character of Texas changes markedly from region to region. While the face of western Texas is largely that of the open range, eastern Texas is home to plantations where rice, sugar cane, and cotton are grown. Northern Texas is the land of the *Llanos Estacado* (staked plains), but to the southwest stand moun-

Population: 20,851,820
Area: 268,601 square miles
Elevation: 0-8,749 feet
Peak: Guadalupe Peak (Culberson County)
Entered Union: December 29, 1845 (28th state)
Capital: Austin
Motto: Friendship
Nickname: Lone Star State
Flower: Bluebonnet
Bird: Mockingbird
Tree: Pecan
Fair: September-October, 2003 in Dallas
Time Zone: Central and Mountain
Website: www.traveltex.com

Texas cowboy

tain ranges with 59 peaks at an altitude of more than 6,000 feet. South Texas is dotted with citrus groves that thrive in its semi tropical climate, as do the beach lovers that populate hundreds of miles of sand along the Gulf Coast and on the barrier islands. Central areas have an abundance of man-made lakes, making fishing and boating popular pastimes.

Industry exceeds agriculture in the Houston-Beaumont area, including a space industry that contributes millions of dollars to the state's economy. Much of the nation's oil is produced in Texas, and it also ranks at the top of the cotton and livestock industries.

When to Go/Climate

Most of Texas is relatively warm and dry. Exceptions are the Panhandle, which can get cold in winter, and East Texas and the Gulf Coast, which are often humid and wet. Tornado season runs from March-May in the North Texas Plains; hurricanes are most common in August and September along the Gulf Coast.

AVERAGE HIGH/LOW TEMPERATURES (°F)

DALLAS-FORT WORTH

Jan 54/33	**May** 83/63	**Sept** 88/67
Feb 59/37	**June** 92/70	**Oct** 79/56
Mar 68/46	**July** 97/74	**Nov** 67/45
Apr 76/55	**Aug** 96/74	**Dec** 58/36

HOUSTON

Jan 61/40	**May** 85/64	**Sept** 88/68
Feb 65/43	**June** 90/71	**Oct** 82/58
Mar 71/50	**July** 93/72	**Nov** 72/50
Apr 78/58	**Aug** 93/72	**Dec** 65/42

Parks and Recreation Finder

Directions to and information about the parks and recreation areas below are given under their respective town/city sections. Please refer to those sections for details.

NATIONAL PARK AND RECREATION AREAS

Key to abbreviations. I.H.S. = International Historic Site; I.P.M. = International Peace Memorial; N.B. = National Battlefield; N.B.P. = National Battlefield Park; N.B.C. = National Battlefield and Cemetery; N.C.A. = National Conservation Area; N.E.M. = National Expansion Memorial; N.F. = National Forest; N.G. = National Grassland; N.H.P. = National Historical Park; N.H.C. = National Heritage Corridor; N.H.S. = National Historic Site; N.L. = National Lakeshore; N.M. = National Monument; N.M.P. = National Military Park; N.Mem. = National Memorial; N.P. = National Park; N.Pres. = National Preserve; N.R.A. = National Recreational Area; N.R.R. = National Recreational River; N.Riv. = National River; N.S. = National Seashore; N.S.R. = National Scenic Riverway; N.S.T. = National Scenic Trail; N.Sc. = National Scientific Reserve; N.V.M. = National Volcanic Monument.

Place Name	Listed Under
Alibates Flint Quarries N.M.	FRITCH
Amistad N.R.A.	DEL RIO
Angelina N.F.	LUFKIN
Big Bend N.P.	same
Chamizal N.Mem.	EL PASO
Davy Crockett N.F.	LUFKIN
Fort Davis N.H.S.	ALPINE
Guadalupe Mountains N.P.	same
Lake Meredith N.R.A.	FRITCH
Lyndon B. Johnson N.H.P.	JOHNSON CITY
Padre Island	same
Palo Alto Battlefield N.H.S.	BROWNSVILLE
Sabine N.F.	JASPER

CALENDAR HIGHLIGHTS

JANUARY

Cotton Bowl Classic (Dallas). Phone 214/634-7525 (parade) or 214/638-2695 (tickets).

FEBRUARY

Houston Livestock Show & Rodeo (Houston). Astrodome. Largest event of its kind in the world. Phone 713/791-9000.

APRIL

Fiesta San Antonio (San Antonio). Celebrating Texas heroes since 1891 with three major parades (one on the San Antonio River), sports, and food. More than 150 events held throughout city. Phone 210/227-5191.

MAY

Byron Nelson Golf Classic (Dallas). Four Seasons Resort and Club. Phone 972/717-2500.

Cinco de Mayo Celebration (Del Rio). Festival of food, music, and dance to celebrate the Mexican victory over Spain. Phone 830/775-3551.

JUNE

Juneteenth Festival (Houston). Music festival celebrating the abolition of slavery in June 1865. Phone 800/365-7575.

AUGUST

Texas Folklife Festival (San Antonio). Institute of Texan Cultures, Hemis-Fair Park. Crafts, folk music, dancing, entertainment, food representing more than 30 ethnic groups in Texas. Phone 210/458-2249.

SEPTEMBER

Pioneer Days (Fort Worth). Fort Worth Stockyards. Commemorates pioneer settlement along the Trinity River and early days of the cattle industry. Phone 817/626-7921.

Tri-State Fair (Amarillo). Second-largest after State Fair. Wk-long festival, rodeo, and carnival with New Mexicans and Oklahomans. Phone 806/376-7767.

State Fair of Texas (Dallas). State Fair Park. America's largest state fair. Phone 214/565-9931.

OCTOBER

World War II Flying Air Show (Midland). Midland International Airport. Contact Chamber of Commerce. Phone 915/563-1000.

DECEMBER

Wonderland of Lights (Marshall). Christmas festival. Courthouse, entire neighborhoods decorated by 7½ million lights. Contact Chamber of Commerce. Phone 903/935-7868.

Harbor Lights Celebration (Corpus Christi). Lighting of boats in marina. Christmas trees at Art Museum of South Texas. Contact Convention & Visitors Bureau. Phone 361/881-1888 or 800/678-6232.

Las Posadas (San Antonio). River Walk. Song and candlelight procession has been a tradition for more than 250 yrs. Held in conjunction with Fiesta de las Luminarias, the fiesta of lights, when the River Walk is lined with candles. Reenactment of the Holy Family's search for an inn. Evening ends with piñata party in Plaza Juarez in La Villita. Phone 210/224-6163.

STATE PARK AND RECREATION AREAS

Key to abbreviations. I.P. = Interstate Park; S.A.P. = State Archaeological Park; S.B. = State Beach; S.C.A. = State Conservation Area; S.C.P. = State Conservation Park; S.Cp. = State Campground; S.F. = State Forest; S.G. = State Garden; S.H.A. = State Historic Area; S.H.P. = State Historic Park; S.H.S. = State Historic Site; S.M.P. = State Marine Park; S.N.A. = State Natural Area; S.P. = State Park; S.P.C. = State Public Campground; S.R. = State Reserve; S.R.A. = State Recreation Area; S.Res. = State Reservoir; S.Res.P. = State Resort Park; S.R.P. = State Rustic Park.

Place Name	Listed Under
Abilene S.P.	ABILENE
Admiral Nimitz Museum S.H.P.	FREDERICKSBURG
Bastrop S.P.	BASTROP
Bentsen-Rio Grande Valley S.P.	MISSION
Big Spring S.P.	BIG SPRING
Bonham S.P.	BONHAM
Buescher S.P.	BASTROP
Cleburne S.P.	CLEBURNE
Confederate Reunion Grounds S.H.P.	GROESBECK
Copano Bay Causeway S.P.	ROCKPORT
Copper Breaks S.P.	QUANAH
Davis Mountains S.P.	ALPINE
Dinosaur Valley S.P.	CLEBURNE
Eisenhower S.P.	DENISON
Eisenhower Birthplace S.H.P.	DENISON
Enchanted Rock S.N.A.	FREDERICKSBURG
Fort Lancaster S.H.P.	OZONA
Fort Parker S.P.	GROESBECK
Galveston Island S.P.	GALVESTON
Hueco Tanks S.H.P.	EL PASO
Huntsville S.P.	HUNTSVILLE
Jim Hogg S.H.P.	RUSK
José Antonio Navarro S.H.S.	SAN ANTONIO
Kerrville-Schreiner S.P.	KERRVILLE
Lake Arrowhead S.P.	WICHITA FALLS
Lake Brownwood S.P.	BROWNWOOD
Lake Casa Blanca International S.P.	LAREDO
Lake Colorado City S.P.	BIG SPRING
Lake Corpus Christi S.P.	ALICE
Lake Whitney S.P.	LAKE WHITNEY
Lubbock Lake Landmark S.H.P.	LUBBOCK
Lyndon B. Johnson S.H.P.	JOHNSON CITY
Magoffin Home S.H.S.	EL PASO
McKinney Falls S.P.	AUSTIN
Mission Tejas S.H.P.	CROCKETT
Monahans Sandhills S.P.	MONAHANS
Old Fort Parker S.H.P.	GROESBECK
Palo Duro Canyon S.P.	CANYON
Pedernales Falls S.P.	JOHNSON CITY
Possum Kingdom S.P.	same
Rusk-Palestine S.P.	RUSK

Sam Bell Maxey House S.H.P.	PARIS
Seminole Canyon S.H.P.	DEL RIO
Stephen F. Austin S.H.P.	BRENHAM
Texas State Railroad Historical Park	RUSK
Varner-Hogg Plantation S.H.P	ANGLETON

Water-related activities, hiking, horseback riding, various other sports, picnicking, and camping, as well as visitor centers, are available in many of these areas. The daily per vehicle entrance fee at most parks ranges from $2-$5; annual Texas Conservation Passport, $50. Camping: primitive $4-$9/night; water only $6-$12/night; water and electricity $9-$16/night; water, electricity, and sewer $10-$16/night; screened shelter $15-$32/night. Cabins $35-$75/night, depending on size. Pets on leash only; pets not allowed in buildings, cabins, or screened shelters. Most parks accept reservations up to 11 months in advance when you call the Central Reservations Center at 512/389-8900. Reservations require payment for each facility reserved in an amount equal to one day's user fee. Contact Texas Parks & Wildlife, Reservations, 4200 Smith School Rd, Austin 78744, phone 512/389-8950 or 800/792-1112.

There are also approximately 1,000 roadside parks maintained by the Texas Department of Transportation. Tables, benches, grills, and rubbish incinerators are provided. Some have water.

FISHING AND HUNTING

Nonresident fishing license: five-day $30; annual $30. Freshwater trout or saltwater stamp, $7. Annual nonresident hunting license: $100 for small game; $250 for big game. Nonresident five-day small game license, $35. Nonresident spring turkey license, $100. Banded bird area license $10. Stamps required for white-winged dove, $7; turkey, $5; and migratory waterfowl, $7 (state) and $15 (federal). All annual licenses expire August 31. Fees subject to change. For complete information, send for "Texas Parks & Wildlife Outdoor Annual" from the Parks & Wildlife Department, 4200 Smith School Rd, Austin 78744. Phone 512/389-8950 or 800/792-1112 in Texas. To report hunting and fishing violations call Operation Game Thief, phone 800/792-GAME.

Driving Information

Safety belts are mandatory for all persons in front seat of vehicle. Children under five years must be in an approved passenger restraint anywhere in vehicle: ages two-four may use a regulation safety belt or an approved safety seat; children under age two must use an approved safety seat. Phone 800/452-9292.

INTERSTATE HIGHWAY SYSTEM

The following alphabetical listing of Texas towns in *Mobil Travel Guide* shows that these cities are within ten miles of the indicated Interstate highways. A highway map should, however, be checked for the nearest exit.

Highway Number	Cities/Towns within ten miles
Interstate 10	Baytown, Beaumont, El Paso, Fort Stockton, Gonzales, Houston, Kerrville, Orange, Ozona, San Antonio, Seguin, Sonora, Van Horn.
Interstate 20	Abilene, Arlington-Grand Prairie, Big Spring, Dallas, Dallas/Fort Worth Airport Area, Eastland, Fort Worth, Kilgore, Longview, Marshall, Midland, Monahans, Odessa, Pecos, Sweetwater, Tyler, Weatherford.
Interstate 27	Amarillo, Canyon, Lubbock, Plainview.
Interstate 30	Arlington-Grand Prairie, Dallas, Dallas/Fort Worth Airport Area, Greenville, Mount Pleasant, Sulphur Springs, Texarkana.
Interstate 35	Arlington-Grand Prairie, Austin, Cleburne, Dallas, Dallas/Fort Worth Airport Area, Denton, Fort Worth, Gainesville, Georgetown, Hillsboro, Laredo, New

Braunfels, Salado, San Antonio, San Marcos, Temple, Waco.

Interstate 37   Corpus Christi, San Antonio.

Interstate 40   Amarillo, Shamrock.

Interstate 45   Corsicana, Dallas, Ennis, Fairfield, Galveston, Houston, Huntsville, Texas City.

Additional Visitor Information

The *Texas Almanac,* an excellent compendium published every two years by the Dallas *Morning News,* may be obtained from the Gulf Publishing Company, PO Box 2608, Houston 77252.

The Texas Department of Transportation operates 12 travel information centers on main highways entering the state, and also the Judge Roy Bean Visitor Center in Langtry and an information center in the state capitol complex. They also distribute free maps and travel literature by mail, including the *Texas State Travel Guide.* Write to *Texas,* Department of Transportation, PO Box 5064, Austin 78763. Phone 800/452-9292 (daily; 8 am-6 pm) or 800/888-8TEX (24-hr travel kit hotline).

WEST TEXAS: GHOST TOWNS, GHOST LIGHTS, AND DUDE RANCHES

From El Paso, drive east on I-10 and south on Highway 90 to Marfa, site of the filming of the 1956 movie *Giant* and home of the mysterious Marfa Ghost Lights and a mile-high golf course. Follow Highway 67 south through the Chinati Mountains to the ghost mining town of Shafter and to Presidio, then east on Ranch Road 170 (also called The River Road), one of the nation's most scenic drives. Follow the Rio Grande over steep hills and into dry gulleys, past the Big Bend Ranch State Park to the town of Lajitas, with lodgings, a saloon, dining, and a horseback trip outfitter. Head west again along Ranch Road 170 to Terlingua, a quicksilver (mercury) mining ghost town and host of the giant Chili Cook-off in November. This is the western entry point to Big Bend National Park, a rugged and forbidding expanse of 801,163 acres and Chisos Mountains scenery where hiking, camping, backcountry, and rafting trips can last from one day to three weeks. From this point, either follow TX 118 north from Terlingua through the Del Norte Mountains to Alpine, with its excellent natural history museum, railroad hotel, galleries, and dining; or take Highway 385 north from Big Bend to Marathon, a much smaller town with an excellent historic hotel, a few art galleries, and Glass Mountains glory. Then travel north on TX 118 to Fort Davis, home to sensational hiking at Davis Mountains State Park, dude ranch stays, frontier fort and buffalo soldier history exploration at Fort Davis National Historic Site, and unforgettable galaxy study at McDonald Observatory. Allow at least four days. (**APPROX 500 MI**)

Abilene

(C-4) *See also Sweetwater*

Founded 1881 **Pop** 115,930
Elev 1,738 ft **Area code** 915
Information Convention & Visitors
Bureau, 1101 N 1st St, 79601;
915/676-2556 or 800/727-7704
Web www.abilene.com/visitors

What to See and Do

Abilene State Park. Approx 600 acres
with Texas Longhorn herd. Swimming pool (Memorial Day-Labor
Day; fee), bathhouse; picnicking,
improved campsites (dump station).
Standard fees. Nearby Lake Abilene
has fishing. (Daily) 16 mi SW on FM
89 to Park Rd 32. Phone 915/572-
3204. ¢¢

Abilene Zoological Gardens. Approx
13 acres; incl indoor plant and animal habitat facility with live specimens in museum setting. (Daily;
closed Jan 1, Thanksgiving, Dec 25)
In Nelson Park, near jct Loop 322,
TX 36. Phone 915/676-6085. ¢¢

Buffalo Gap Historic Village. More
than 15 restored original buildings,
incl the first Taylor County Courthouse and jail; Museum of the Old
West. Tour incl a film on history of
Texas. (Mid-Mar-mid-Nov, daily; rest
of yr, Fri-Sun; closed Thanksgiving,
Dec 25) William and Elm Sts, Buffalo
Gap, 8 mi S on US 89. Phone
915/572-3365. ¢¢

Dyess Air Force Base. An Air Combat
Command base, first home of the B-
1B bomber. Also has C-130s, T-38s.
Linear Air Park incl 30 vintage display aircraft (daily). W on Business
20, then S on Spur 312. Stop at gate
for temporary pass. Phone 915/696-
5609. **FREE**

Fort Phantom Hill and Lake. Ruins of
1850s frontier fort, built to protect
gold miners traveling to California.
Lake has water sports (some fees).
(Daily) 14 mi N on FM 600. Phone
915/677-1309. **FREE**

Grace Museums. The former Grace
Hotel (1909), now restored and renovated, serves as the home of the
Museums of Abilene. Inside is the Art
Museum featuring permanent and
special exhibits. The Historical
Museum traces Abilene's history
from 1900-1945 through photos and
memorabilia. The Children's
Museum offers many hands-on activities. (Mon-Sat; closed hols) Free
admission Thurs eves. 102 Cypress
St. Phone 915/673-4587. ¢¢

Oscar Rose Park. Picnicking, playground, pool, gym, tennis center;
community and children's theater,
amphitheater; senior citizen center.
There are 25 other city parks. 7th
and Mockingbird Sts. Phone
915/676-6217. **FREE**

Special Events

Celebrate Abilene. Downtown. Art
festival, railroad festival, children's
activities, stew cook-off. Phone
915/676-2556. Mid-Apr.

West Texas Fair & Rodeo. Phone
915/677-4376. Fri after Labor Day.

Motels/Motor Lodges

★★ **BEST WESTERN MALL
SOUTH.** *3950 Ridgemont Dr (79606).
915/695-1262; fax 915/695-2593; res
800/528-1234. www.bestwestern.com.*
61 rms, 2 story. S $47-$55; D $53-
$63; under 12 free. Pet accepted,
some restrictions. TV; cable (premium). Pool. Complimentary continental bkfst. Restaurant adj open 24
hrs. Ck-out noon. Meeting rm. In-rm
modem link. Airport, bus depot
transportation. Refrigerators. Cr cds:
A, C, D, DS, MC, V.
🄳 🐾 🌊 🔜 🔥

★ **BUDGET HOST COLONIAL
INN.** *3210 Pine St (79601). 915/677-
2683; fax 915/677-8211; res 800/283-
4678. www.abilenebudgethostinn.com.*
100 rms, 2 story. S $43-$48; D $48-
$53; each addl $5; under 12 free.
Crib free. Pet accepted, some restrictions. TV; cable (premium). Pool;
wading pool. Restaurant 6 am-10
pm. Rm serv. Ck-out noon. Meeting
rms. Business servs avail. Cr cds: A,
C, D, DS, JCB, MC, V.
🄳 🐾 🌊 🔜 🔥

★★ **LA QUINTA MOTOR INN.**
*3501 W Lake Rd (79601). 915/676-
1676; fax 915/672-8323; res 800/687-
6667. www.laquinta.com.* 106 rms, 2
story. S $59-$63; D $66-$73; each
addl $7; suites $100; under 18 free.

Crib avail. Pet accepted; some restrictions. TV; cable (premium). Pool. Complimentary continental bkfst. Ck-out noon. Cr cds: A, C, D, DS, ER, JCB, MC, V.

🅳 🔌 ⛌ 🛏 🔥

★★ **QUALITY INN CIVIC CENTER.** *505 Pine St (79601). 915/676-0222; fax 915/673-6561; res 800/228-5151. www.qualityinn.com.* 118 rms, 2 story. S $51-$58; D $56-$63; each addl $5; suites $75-$200; under 18 free. Crib free. Pet accepted, some restrictions; $10. TV; cable (premium). Pool. Complimentary full bkfst. Restaurant 6 am-9 pm. Rm serv. Bar noon-11 pm. Ck-out noon. Meeting rms. Business servs avail. Sundries. Free airport transportation. Health club privileges. Cr cds: A, D, DS, MC, V.

🅳 🔌 ⛌ 🛏 🔥

★★ **RAMADA INN.** *3450 S Clack (79606). 915/695-7700; fax 915/698-0546; toll-free 800/676-7262. www.ramada.com.* 147 rms, 2 story. S $52-$64; D $55-$68; each addl $5; under 18 free. Crib avail. TV; cable (premium), VCR avail. Pool. Restaurant 6 am-1:30 pm, 6-9 pm. Rm serv. Bar 5 pm-midnight; entertainment. Ck-out noon. Meeting rms. Business servs avail. Coin lndry. Cr cds: A, C, D, DS, MC, V.

🅳 ⛌ 🛏 🔥 SC

★ **ROYAL INN.** *5695 S 1st St, Ste 161 (79605). 915/692-3022; fax 915/692-3137; toll-free 800/588-4386. www.royalinn-abilene.com.* 150 rms. S $24.95; D $30; each addl $4; suites $40. Crib $5. Pet accepted, some restrictions. TV; cable (premium). Pool. Restaurant 6 am-10 pm. Rm serv. Bar 10 am-midnight. Ck-out noon. Meeting rms. Business servs avail. Sundries. Microwaves avail. Cr cds: A, D, DS, MC, V.

🅳 🔌 ⛌ 🛏 🔥 SC

Hotel

★★ **CLARION HOTEL & CONVENTION CENTER.** *5403 S 1st St (79605). 915/695-2150; fax 915/698-6742; toll-free 800/252-7466. www.clarionhotel.com.* 178 rms, 3 story. S $58-$64; D $64-$69; each addl $5; suites $120-$159; under 16 free. Crib free. Pet accepted; some restrictions. TV; cable (premium). 2 pools,

1 indoor; wading pool, whirlpool, sauna. Restaurant 6 am-2 pm, 5-9 pm. Rm serv. Bar 5 pm-midnight; Sat to 1 am. Ck-out noon. Coin lndry. Meeting rms. Business center. Sundries. Some refrigerators. Microwaves avail. Cr cds: A, C, D, DS, JCB, MC, V.

🅳 🔌 ⛌ 🛏 🔥 SC 🚶

All Suite

★★★ **EMBASSY SUITES HOTEL.** *4250 Ridgemont Dr (79606). 915/698-1234; fax 915/698-2771; res 800/362-2779. www.embassysuites.com.* 176 suites, 3 story. S $86; D $96; each addl $10; under 12 free. Crib free. Pet accepted, some restrictions. TV; cable (premium). Indoor pool; whirlpool, sauna, steam rm. Complimentary full bkfst. Coffee in rms. Restaurant 11 am-2 pm, 5-10 pm. Bar to midnight; entertainment. Ck-out noon. Coin lndry. Meeting rms. Business servs avail. Bellhops. Sundries. Airport, RR station, bus depot transportation. Game rm. Health club privileges. Refrigerators, wet bars, microwaves. Garden atrium. Cr cds: A, C, D, DS, ER, JCB, MC, V.

🅳 🔌 🍴 ⛌ 🛏 🔥

Alice

(F-6) *See also Corpus Christi, Kingsville*

Pop 19,010 **Elev** 205 ft **Area code** 361 **Zip** 78332

Information Chamber of Commerce, 612 E Main, PO Box 1609; 361/664-3454

Web www.alicetx.org

What to See and Do

Lake Corpus Christi State Park. Approx 21,000 acres. Swimming, waterskiing, fishing, boating (ramp); picnicking (shelters), tent and trailer sites (dump station). Standard fees. (Daily) 25 mi NE on TX 359, then 2 mi NW on Park Rd 25. Phone 361/547-2635. ¢¢

Special Events

Fiesta Bandana. Plaza Park. Nightly entertainment; carnival, queen's court, talent show, folk dancers. Six days early May. Phone 361/664-3455.

Jim Wells County Fair. JWC Fairgrounds. Mid-Oct. Phone 361/664-3454.

Alpine

(D-2) *See also Fort Stockton, Marfa*

Founded 1882 **Pop** 5,768 **Elev** 4,481 ft **Area code** 915 **Zip** 79830
Information Chamber of Commerce, 106 N Third St; 915/837-2326

What to See and Do

Big Bend National Park. (see). 110 mi S on TX 118.

Driving tour. Davis Mountains and McDonald Observatory. (Approx 100 mi) Drive 26 mi NW on TX 118, a mountain road through scenic country, to

   Fort Davis. (Population 900, altitude 5,050 ft) Highest town in Texas. Just outside town are the restored ruins of

   Fort Davis National Historic Site. A famous frontier outpost garrisoned from 1854-1891. Museum, visitor center; restored and refurnished officers' quarters, barracks, commissary, and kitchen; sound reproduction of 1875 Retreat Parade; slide show; living history programs in summer. Self-guided trail; transportation for handicapped (free). (Daily; closed Dec 25) Golden Age Passport accepted (see MAKING THE MOST OF YOUR TRIP). Contact Superintendent, PO Box 1379, Fort Davis 79734. Phone 915/426-3224. ¢¢

Davis Mountains State Park. A 2,250-acre park. Picnicking, playground, hiking trails, restaurant, lodge, tent and trailer sites (dump station). Standard fees. (Daily) Phone 915/426-3337. ¢¢

McDonald Observatory. Has a 107-inch reflecting telescope; solar viewing, video presentations.

Guided tours (fee); evening star parties at Visitors Center (Tues, Fri, and Sat eves). (Daily; closed Jan 1, Thanksgiving, Dec 25) At the base of Mt Locke. Phone 915/426-3640. ¢¢

Museum of the Big Bend. Local Spanish, Native American, Mexican, and pioneer artifacts and historical displays. (Tues-Sun) Sul Ross State University, east of town via US 90, entrance #2. Phone 915/837-8143. **Donation**

Motels/Motor Lodges

★★ **INDIAN LODGE.** *N Hwy 118, Fort Davis (79734). 915/426-3254; fax 915/426-2022.* 39 rms, 2-3 story. S, D $55; each addl $10; suites $75-$85; under 12 free. Closed 2 wks Jan. TV; cable (premium). Pool. Restaurant 7 am-9 pm. Ck-out noon. Meeting rm. Picnic tables, grills. Pueblo-style lodge on hillside. Rustic decor. State-owned, operated. All park facilities avail. Cr cds: DS, MC, V.

D ⌧ ⌧ ⌧

★★ **LIMPIA HOTEL.** *Main St, Fort Davis (79734). 915/426-3237; fax 915/426-3983; toll-free 800/662-5517. www.hotellimpia.com.* 36 rms, 2 story, 8 with kit., 14 suites, 1 cottage. No rm phones. S, D $68; each addl $10; suites, kit. units $84-$125; cottage $99; under 12 free. Pet accepted; $10. TV; cable (premium). Complimentary coffee in lobby. Restaurant nearby. Ck-out noon. Business servs avail. Some refrigerators. Microwave in suites. Balconies. Picnic tables. Built in 1912 of locally mined pink limestone. Cr cds: A, MC, V.

D ⌧ ⌧ ⌧ SC

Restaurant

★★ **REATA.** *203 N 5th St (79830). 915/837-9232. www.reata.net.* Hrs: 11 am-2 pm, 5:30-10 pm. Closed Sun; Jan 1, Thanksgiving, Dec 25. Res accepted. Southwestern menu. Private club. Serv bar. A la carte entrees: lunch $5.95-$15.95, dinner $8.95-$28.95. Child's menu. Specialty: pepper-crusted tenderloin with port wine glaze. Own baking. Guitarist Thurs-Sat. Outdoor dining. Western decor; framed chaps, game heads on walls. Cr cds: A, MC, V.

D

Amarillo

(G-1) *See also Canyon, Pampa*

Settled 1887 **Pop** 173,627 **Elev** 3,676 ft **Area code** 806
Information Convention and Visitor Council, 1000 S Polk St, 79101; 806/374-1497 or 800/692-1338
Web www.amarillo-cvb.org

What to See and Do

Amarillo Museum of Art. Features broad range of paintings, photographs, sculptures, and textiles from 20th-century American art to Southeast Asian treasures. Exhibits change every seven wks. (Tues-Sun) 2200 S Van Buren. Phone 806/371-5050. **FREE**

American Quarter Horse Heritage Center & Museum. Many hands-on and interactive exhibits, video presentations, artifacts, and live demonstrations on the history and significance of "America's breed." Heritage Gallery traces chronology of development; Performance Gallery incl rodeo, ranching, and racing aspects and features the American Quarter Horse Hall of Fame. Research library; 70-seat orientation theater. (May-Aug, daily; rest of yr, Mon-Sat; closed Jan 1, Thanksgiving, Dec 25) 2601 I-40 E, at Quarter Horse Dr. Phone 806/376-5181. ¢¢

Carson County Square House Museum. Museum depicts the history and development of the Texas Panhandle region from the era of Native American hunters through ranching and railroads to the discovery of oil and the industrialization of the region. Complex incl historic house, furnished dugout dwelling, Santa Fe caboose, barn, branding diorama, pioneer bank, general store, windmill, blacksmith shop, natural history hall, and two art galleries. (Daily; closed hols) 26 mi NE via US 60 at 5th and Elsie Sts (TX 207) in Panhandle. Phone 806/537-3524. **FREE**

Don Harrington Discovery Center. Exhibits focus on science, health,

and technology; more than 75 hands-on exhibits. Planetarium shows, 360° films (summer). Helium Monument is a steel memorial to the gas found in abundance in the area; also incl a time capsule. (Tues-Sun; closed hols) 1200 Streit Dr, 5 mi W on I-40, 1 mi N of Coulter exit. Phone 806/355-9548. ¢¢

Livestock auction. More than 200,000 cattle sold each yr. (All yr, Tues) E 3rd and Manhattan Sts. Phone 806/373-7464. **FREE**

Palo Duro Canyon State Park. (See CANYON) 18 mi S on I-27, then 10 mi E on TX 217.

Thompson Park. Pool (June-Aug, daily; fee); amusement park (mid-Mar-Sept, daily; fee). Amarillo Zoo has animals indigenous to the plains (Tues-Sun). NE 24th St and US 87. Phone 806/378-3036. **FREE**

Wonderland Amusement Park. 25 rides and 30 attractions, incl a double-loop roller coaster and water rides. (June-Aug, daily; Apr-May, wkends only) N on US 87/287 N, River Rd exit. Phone 800/383-4712. ¢¢¢¢

Special Events

Cowboy Morning Breakfast. Horse-drawn wagons run to bkfst site, rim of Palo Duro Canyon; bkfst cooked on open fire. Exhibition roping and branding. Phone 800/658-2613. Apr-Oct. (Daily)

FUNFEST. Thompson Park. Phone 806/374-0802. Memorial Day wkend.

Coors Ranch Rodeo. Tri-State fairgrounds. Phone 806/376-7767. Mid-June.

Tri-State Fair. Second-largest after State Fair. Phone 806/376-7767. Mid-Sept.

Motels/Motor Lodges

★ **DAYS INN AIRPORT/DOWN-TOWN.** *1701 I-40 E (79102). 806/379-6255; fax 806/379-8204; res 800/329-7466. www.daysinn.com.* 119 rms, 5 story. S $55-$80; D $65-$80; each addl $5; under 12 free. Crib free. TV; cable (premium). Heated pool. Complimentary bkfst buffet. Restaurant opp 6 am-9 pm. Ck-out noon. Meeting rm. Business servs avail. Airport transportation. Health club privileges. Cr cds: A, C, D, DS, MC, V.

★★ **HAMPTON INN.** *1700 I-40 E (79103). 806/372-1425; fax 806/379-8807; res 800/426-7866. www. hamptoninn.com.* 116 rms, 2 story. June-Sept: S, D $61-$70; under 18 free; lower rates rest of yr. Crib free. Pet accepted. TV; cable (premium). Pool. Complimentary continental bkfst. Restaurant adj open 24 hrs. Ck-out noon. Business servs avail. Health club privileges. Cr cds: A, C, D, DS, MC, V.

★★ **HOLIDAY INN.** *1911 I-40 E (79102). 806/372-8741; fax 806/372-2913; toll-free 800/465-4329. www. holiday-inn.com.* 248 rms, 4 story. June-July: S, D $89.95; each addl $10; under 19 free; lower rates rest of yr. Crib free. Pet accepted. TV; cable (premium). Indoor pool; wading pool. Restaurants 6 am-1 pm, 5:30-10 pm. Rm serv. Bar 4 pm-1 am. Ck-out noon. Coin lndry. Meeting rms. Business servs avail. In-rm modem link. Bellhops. Sundries. Free airport transportation. Exercise equipt. Game rm. Balconies. Cr cds: A, D, DS, MC, V.

★★ **HOMEGATE STUDIOS AND SUITES.** *6800 I-40 W (79106). 806/358-7943; fax 806/358-8475; res 888/456-4283. www.homegate.com.* 126 kit. suites, 2 story. S, D $65-$75; each addl $8; under 18 free. Crib free. TV; cable. Heated pool; whirlpool. Business servs avail. In-rm modem link. Valet serv. Exercise equipt. Refrigerators. Picnic tables, grills. Cr cds: A, C, D, DS, MC, V.

★ **TRAVELODGE.** *2035 Paramount Blvd (79109). 806/353-3541; fax 806/353-0201; res 800/578-7878. www.travelodge.com.* 100 rms, 2 story. S $58; D $62; each addl $5; under 17 free. Crib free. TV; cable (premium). Heated pool. Restaurant nearby. Ck-out noon. Meeting rm. Business servs avail. In-rm modem link. Health club privileges. Cr cds: A, C, D, DS, MC, V.

Hotel

★★★ **RADISSON.** *7909 E I-40 (79118). 806/373-3303; fax 806/373-3353; toll-free 800/333-3333. www. radisson.com.* 206 rms, 2 story. June-Aug: S $82; D $92; each addl $10; suites $149-$199; under 12 free; lower rates rest of yr. Crib free. TV; cable (premium). Indoor pool; poolside serv. Coffee in rms. Restaurant 6 am-10 pm. Rm serv. Bar; entertainment Fri-Sat. Ck-out noon. Meeting rms. Business servs avail. In-rm modem link. Bellhops. Valet serv. Free airport transportation. Exercise equipt. Game rm. Minibars. Cr cds: A, C, D, DS, ER, JCB, MC, V.

Restaurant

★★ **BIG TEXAN STEAK RANCH.** *7701 I-40 E (79104). 806/372-6000. www.bigtexan.com.* Hrs: 10:30 am-10:30 pm. Res accepted. Bar. Lunch, dinner $4.50-$29.95. Child's menu. Specializes in Texas prime beef steak, rattlesnake, buffalo. Strolling musicians. Frontier Western decor. Family-owned. Cr cds: A, DS, MC, V.

Angleton

(E-7) *See also Brazosport, Galveston, Houston*

Pop 18,130 **Elev** 31 ft **Area code** 979 **Zip** 77515

Information Chamber of Commerce, 445 E Mulberry, PO Box 1356, 77516; 979/849-6443

What to See and Do

Varner-Hogg Plantation State Historical Park. Stately house (ca 1835) in 66-acre park. Period furnishings; family memorabilia. Tours (Wed-Sun, fee). Picnicking. 15 mi W via TX 35, in West Columbia. Phone 979/345-4656. **FREE**

Special Event

Brazoria County Fair. Rodeo, livestock exhibition, exhibits. Phone 979/849-6416. Ten days early Oct.

Aransas Pass

(F-6) *See also Corpus Christi, Port Aransas, Rockport*

Founded ca 1830 **Pop** 8,138 **Elev** 5 ft
Area code 361 **Zip** 78336
Information Chamber of Commerce, 130 W Goodnight, 78336; 800/633-3028
Web www.aransaspass.org

Special Event

Shrimporee. Parade, arts and crafts, entertainment. Late Sept. Phone 361/758-2750.

Motel/Motor Lodge

★ **DAYS INN SUITES.** *410 E Goodnight Ave (78336). 361/758-7375; fax 361/758-8105; toll-free 877/430-2444. www.daysinn.com.* 32 rms, 18 suites. S $55-$100; D $65-$100; each addl $10; suites $70-$150. Crib free. Pet accepted, some restrictions. TV; cable (premium). Pool. Complimentary continental bkfst. Restaurant nearby. Ck-out noon. Meeting rms. Business servs avail. In-rm modem link. Exercise equipt. Game rm. Refrigerators, microwaves. Picnic tables, grills. Cr cds: A, C, D, DS, MC, V.
🄳 🔧 🛄 ⚡ 🏊 🏃 🗯 🔥

Arlington-Grand Prairie

(C-6) *See also Dallas, Dallas/Fort Worth Airport Area, Fort Worth*

Pop 261,721 **Elev** 616 ft
Area code Arlington, 817; Grand Prairie, 972
Information Arlington Convention & Visitors Bureau,1905 E Randol Mill

Rd, 76011; 817/265-7721 or 800/433-5374. Grand Prairie Tourist Information located at I-30 and Belt Line Rd; 972/263-9588 or 800/288-8386
Web www.arlington.org

What to See and Do

The Palace of Wax. Onion-domed structure houses a collection of wax figures in exhibits with themes incl Hollywood, history, religion, fairy tales, horrors, and the Old West. Visitors can view figure-making studio to see actual pieces under construction. Gift shop, concession, arcade. (Daily; closed Thanksgiving, Dec 25) 601 E Safari Pkwy, I-30 at Belt Line Rd exit N, Grand Prairie. Phone 972/263-2391. ¢¢¢ Also here is

  Ripley's Believe It or Not!. Features galleries filled with antiques, oddities, curiosities, and illusions from the collection of Robert L. Ripley. Phone 972/263-2391.

Professional sports.

  Texas Rangers (MLB). The Ballpark at Arlington, jct TX 360 and I-30. Phone 817/273-5222.

River Legacy Living Science Center. Hands-on, interactive exhibits depicting the thriving ecosystem along the Trinity River. (Tues-Sat; closed hols). 703 NW Green Oaks Blvd, Arlington. Phone 817/860-6752. ¢

Six Flags Over Texas. This 205-acre entertainment center has more than 100 rides, shows, and other attractions. Texas history under flags of Spain, France, the Republic of Texas, the Confederacy, Mexico, and the US is presented, with a separate section of the park devoted to each flag. Skylines of Dallas and Fort Worth are visible from 300-ft-high observation deck atop oil derrick. Park is circled by narrow-gauge railway; other rides incl wooden roller coaster, Runaway Mine Train, parachute ride, double-loop roller coaster, biplane ride, Roaring Rapids river rafting; Looney Tunes Land, with special rides and play activities for small children; Southern Palace musical productions and other attractions. Restaurants. (Late May-early Sept, daily; mid-Mar-late May and early Sept-mid-Nov, wkends) Admission incl all rides. Just W of jct TX 360, I-30, Arlington.

Contact PO Box 90191, Arlington 76004. Phone 817/640-8900. ¢¢¢¢¢

Special Event

Horse racing. Lone Star Park, 1000 Lone Star Pkwy, N of jct I-30 in Grand Prairie. Pari-mutuel thoroughbred racing (mid-Apr-late July, Wed-Sun). Quarter Horse Fall Meeting of Champions (early Oct-late Nov, Thurs-Sun). Also simulcast thoroughbred racing (daily). Phone 972/263-7223.

Motels/Motor Lodges

★★ **COURTYARD BY MARRIOTT.** *1500 Nolan Ryan Expy, Arlington (76011). 817/277-2774; fax 817/277-3103; res 800/321-2211. www.courtyard.com.* 147 rms, 3 story, 14 suites. Mar-Oct: S, D $89; each addl $10; suites $109; under 18 free; wkend, hol rates; higher rates special events; lower rates rest of yr. Crib free. TV; cable (premium), VCR avail. Heated indoor/outdoor pool; whirlpool, poolside serv. Complimentary coffee in lobby. Restaurant 6:30-10:30 am; Sat, Sun 7 am-noon. Bar 4-10 pm. Ck-out noon. Meeting rms. Business servs avail. Valet serv. Coin lndry. Exercise equipt. Game rm. Some refrigerators. Many balconies. Cr cds: A, C, D, DS, JCB, MC, V.

★★ **FAIRFIELD INN BY MARRIOTT.** *2500 E Lamar Blvd, Arlington (76006). 817/649-5800; toll-free 800/228-2800; res 800/228-2800. www.fairfieldinn.com.* 109 rms, 3 story. May-Sept: S $69.95; D $79.95; under 18 free; lower rates rest of yr. Crib free. TV; cable (premium). Heated pool. Complimentary continental bkfst. Restaurant nearby. Ck-out noon. Business servs avail. In-rm modem link. Sundries. Health club privileges. Cr cds: A, D, DS, MC, V.

★★ **HAMPTON INN-DFW/ARL.** *2050 N Hwy 360, Grand Prairie (75050). 972/988-8989; fax 972/623-0004; res 800/426-7866. www.hamptoninn.com.* 140 rms, 4 story. S $69-$75; D $75; under 18 free. Crib avail. TV; cable (premium). Pool. Complimentary continental bkfst. Complimentary coffee in rms. Restaurant nearby. Ck-out noon. Coin lndry. Business servs avail. In-rm modem link. Valet serv. Free airport transportation. Exercise rm. Cr cds: A, C, D, DS, MC, V.

★★ **HAWTHORN SUITES HOTEL ARLINGTON.** *2401 Brookhollow Plaza Dr, Arlington (76006). 817/640-1188; fax 817/649-4720; res 800/527-1133. www.hawthorn.com.* 26 rms, 130 suites, 3 story, 104 kit. suites. S $85-$110; D $95-$120; suites $110-$180; wkend rates. Crib free. Pet accepted, some restrictions; $50 plus $5/day. TV; cable (premium), VCR avail (movies). Pool; whirlpool. Complimentary full bkfst. Restaurant nearby. Ck-out noon. Coin lndry. Meeting rms. Business servs avail. Valet serv. Exercise equipt. Microwaves. Balconies, picnic tables, grills. Cr cds: A, C, D, DS, MC, V.

★★ **HOLIDAY INN ARLINGTON-NEAR SIX FLAGS.** *1507 N Watson Rd, Arlington (76006). 817/640-7712; fax 817/640-3174; res 800/465-4329. www.holiday-inn.com.* 237 rms, 5 story. S $79-$99; D $84-$104; each addl $5; under 19 free. Crib free. TV; cable (premium), VCR avail. Indoor/outdoor pool; wading pool, whirlpool. Restaurant 6:30 am-2 pm, 5-10 pm. Rm serv. Bar 4:30 pm-midnight. Ck-out noon. Coin lndry. Meeting rms. Business servs avail. In-rm modem link. Bellhops. Valet serv. Free airport transportation. Exercise equipt. Some refrigerators. Some private patios, balconies. Cr cds: A, D, DS, MC, V.

Hotels

★★★ **HILTON.** *2401 E Lamar Blvd, Arlington (76006). 817/640-3322; fax 817/652-0243; res 800/445-8667. www.hilton.com.* 309 rms, 15 story. S $99-$145; D $125-$159; each addl $10; suites $179; under 18 free; wkend rates. Crib free. TV; cable (premium). Pool; whirlpool, poolside serv. Restaurant 6 am-11 pm. Bar noon-2 am. Ck-out noon. Coin lndry. Convention facilities. Business center. In-rm modem link. Concierge. Gift shop. Airport transportation. Exercise equipt; sauna.

Health club privileges. Cr cds: A, D, DS, MC, V.

★ ★ ★ **RADISSON SUITES.** *700 Ave H E, Arlington (76011). 817/640-0440; fax 817/649-2480; res 800/333-3333.* 203 rms, 7 story, 186 suites. S, D $114-$139; each addl $10; under 12 free. Crib free. TV; cable. Indoor pool. Complimentary full bkfst. Restaurant 11:30 am-2 pm, 5:30-10 pm. Bar. Ck-out noon. Meeting rms. Business servs avail. Gift shop. Sauna. Health club privileges. Game rm. Refrigerators, wet bars. Cr cds: A, C, D, DS, MC, V.

★ ★ **WYNDHAM ARLINGTON DFW AIRPORT SOUTH.** *1500 Convention Center Dr, Arlington (76011). 817/261-8200; fax 817/548-2865; res 800/996-3426. www.wyndham.com/ arlington.* 310 rms, 18 story. S $159; D $169; each addl $10; suites $145-$350; under 16 free; wkend rates. Crib free. TV; cable (premium). Pool; poolside serv. Restaurant 6:30 am-10 pm. Bar 2 pm-2 am. Ck-out noon. Coin lndry. Meeting rms. Business center. In-rm modem link. Concierge. Sundries. Gift shop. Exercise equipt. Health club privileges. Game rm. Some refrigerators. Luxury level. Cr cds: A, C, D, DS, MC, V.

All Suites

★ ★ **AMERISUITES.** *2380 East Rd, Arlington (76011). 817/649-7676; fax 817/649-7753; res 800/833-1516. www.amerisuites.com.* 128 suites, 6 story. June-Sept: S $109-$129; D $109-$139; under 17 free; lower rates rest of yr. Crib free. TV; cable (premium). Pool. Complimentary continental bkfst. Ck-out noon. Meeting rms. Business center. Coin lndry. Exercise equipt. Health club privileges. Microwaves. Cr cds: A, D, DS, MC, V.

★ ★ **COUNTRY SUITES - ARLINGTON.** *1075 Wet N Wild Way, Arlington (76011). 817/261-8900; fax 817/274-0343; toll-free 800/456-4000. www.countryinns.com.* 132 kit. suites, 3 story. May-Sept: suites $109; each addl $10; under 18 free; lower rates

rest of yr. TV; cable (premium). Heated pool; wading pool, whirlpool. Playground. Complimentary continental bkfst. Restaurant nearby. Ck-out noon. Coin lndry. Meeting rms. Business servs avail. Sundries. Valet serv. Free airport transportation. Health club privileges. Microwaves. Cr cds: A, D, MC, V.

Restaurants

★ ★ ★ **CACHAREL.** *2221 E Lamar Blvd, Arlington (76006). 817/640-9981.* Hrs: 11:30 am-2 pm, 6-10 pm; Sat from 6 pm. Closed Sun; hols. Res accepted. French, American menu. Serv bar. Complete meals: lunch $8-$30, dinner $30-$60. Child's menu. Specializes in grilled ostrich steak. Own pastries. Country French decor. Menu changes daily. View of city. Totally nonsmoking. Cr cds: A, C, D, DS, ER, JCB, MC, V.

★ ★ **PICCOLO MONDO.** *829 Lamar Blvd E, Arlington (76011). 817/265-9174. www.piccolomondo.com.* Hrs: 11:30 am-2:30 pm, 5:30-10:30 pm; Fri, Sat to 11 pm; Sun 5-10 pm. Closed Jan 1, Thanksgiving, Dec 25. Res accepted. Italian menu. Bar. Lunch $8-$16, dinner $10-$30. Pianist Tues-Sat. Cozy Italian atmosphere. Cr cds: A, C, D, DS, MC, V.

Athens

(C-7) *See also Corsicana, Palestine, Tyler*

Pop 11,297 **Elev** 492 ft **Area code** 903 **Zip** 75751

Information Chamber of Commerce, 1206 S Palestine, PO Box 2600; 903/675-5181 or 800/755-7878

Web www.athenscc.org

Special Event

Texas Fiddlers' Contest and Reunion. Last Fri May. Phone 903/675-1859.

Motels/Motor Lodges

★★ **BEST WESTERN INN ON THE HILL.** *2050 Hwy 31 E (75751). 903/675-9214; fax 903/675-5963; res 800/528-1234. www.bestwestern.com.* 110 rms, 2 story. S $49-$84; D $50-$96; each addl $5; suites $110. Crib free. TV; cable (premium). Pool. Restaurant 6-10 am, 5:30-9 pm; Sun to 10 pm. Rm serv. Bar. Ck-out noon. Meeting rms. Business servs avail. Cr cds: A, C, D, DS, MC, V.

D ⮌ ↘ 🐾 SC

★★ **SPANISH TRACE INN.** *716 E Tyler St (75751). 903/675-5173; fax 903/677-1528; toll-free 800/488-5173. www.spanishtraceinn.com.* 80 rms, 2 story. S $38-$45; D $46-$50; each addl $6; suites $76; under 12 free. Crib free. TV; cable (premium). Pool. Coffee in rms. Restaurant. Rm serv. Private club 5 pm-midnight, closed Sun. Ck-out noon. Meeting rms. Business servs avail. Health club privileges. Private patios, balconies. Cr cds: A, C, D, DS, ER, JCB, MC, V.

D ⮌ ✈ ↘ 🐾

★ **VICTORIAN INN.** *1803 E Hwy 31 (75751). 903/677-1470; fax 903/677-9293. www.welcome.to/victorian-inn.* 40 rms, 2 story. S $39-$54; D $44-$59; under 12 free. TV; cable (premium). Restaurant nearby. Ck-out 11 am. Cr cds: A, DS, MC, V.

D ↘ 🐾 SC

B&B/Small Inn

★★ **THE BIRDHOUSE.** *103 E Kaufman St, Mabank (75147). 903/887-1242; fax 903/887-7621; toll-free 888/474-2687. www.inn-guide.com/birdhouse.* 4 rms, 3 with shower only, 3 story. Mar-Oct: S, D $73.50; under 18 free; package plans; lower rates rest of yr. TV; cable (premium), VCR (movies). Complimentary full bkfst. Complimentary coffee in rms. Restaurant nearby. Ck-out noon, ck-in varies. Business servs avail. In-rm modem link. Luggage handling. Coin lndry. Street parking. Fireplace in public rm. Cr cds: A, DS, MC, V.

D 🐾 SC

Restaurant

★ **PAPATILO'S.** *716 E Tyler St (75751). 903/675-5173.* Hrs: 6 am-2 pm, 5 pm-midnight; Sun brunch 11:30 am-2 pm. Bar. Bkfst $3.25-$5.75, lunch $4.25-$5.95, dinner $7.95-$13.95. Sun brunch $8.95. Child's menu. Specializes in chicken, steak, seafood. Salad bar (lunch). Old Spanish decor. Cr cds: A, D, DS, MC, V.

D SC ⮌

Austin

(D-6) *See also Georgetown, San Antonio, San Marcos*

Founded 1839 **Pop** 656,562 **Elev** 550 ft **Area code** 512

Information Convention & Visitors Bureau, 201 E 2nd St, 78701; 512/478-0098 or 800/926-2282

Web www.austintexas.org

In 1838, a party of buffalo hunters that included Mirabeau B. Lamar, vice president of the Republic of Texas, camped at a pleasant spot on the Colorado River. In 1839, Lamar, then president of the republic, suggested this same spot as the site of a permanent capital. Situated on high ground and far away from the fever dangers of the coast country, the site was selected even though it was on the frontier. Named for Stephen F. Austin, son of Moses Austin, leader of the first American colony in Texas, the new capital was planned and planned well. Situated at the foot of the Highland Lakes chain, the site was blessed with lakes—Austin and Town—which today wind their way through the heart of the city. The Capitol building, at the head of Congress Avenue, was later built on one of the hills that rises from the Colorado River Valley.

A city of handsome buildings, modern Austin boasts a unique version of New Orleans's Bourbon Street—Old Pecan Street. This seven-block strip of renovated Victorian and native limestone buildings on East 6th Street between Congress Avenue and I-35 is a National Registered Historic District with more than 60 restaurants, clubs, and shops. On weekends, thousands gather to enjoy the street performers and nightlife.

As a state center of science, research, education, and government, Austin's economy is diversified between the state bureaucracy, the University of Texas, and the research and manufacturing of high-technology electronics.

What to See and Do

Austin Museum of Art. Changing exhibits of American art since 1900; performances, films, lectures, art classes. (Tues-Sun; closed hols) 823 Congress. Phone 512/495-9224. ¢¢

Austin Steam Train Association. Vintage steam train makes scenic journey from Cedar Park and Plaza Saltillo; some trips feature hors d'oeuvres, musical entertainment, and drinks. Prices vary. (Sat-Sun) US 183 at FM 1431. Phone 512/477-8468.

Austin Zoo. (Daily; closed Thanksgiving, Dec 25) 10807 Rawhide Trail. Phone 512/288-1490. ¢¢¢

⭐ **Elisabet Ney Museum.** Former studio of Elisabet Ney, 19th-century German-Texan portrait sculptor. Houses collection of her works, some of which are in the Texas and US capitols. (Wed-Sun; closed hols) 304 E 44th St, at Ave H. Phone 512/458-2255. **FREE**

French Legation Museum. (1841) Housed the chargé d'affaires to the Republic of Texas. Creole architecture and furnishings. Restored house and gardens, reconstructed carriage house, French Creole kitchen. (Tues-Sun, afternoons; closed hols) 802 San Marcos St. Phone 512/472-8180. ¢¢

Governor's Mansion. (1856) Greek Revival architecture, American Federal and Empire furnishings. Contains former governors' memorabilia. Tours (Mon-Thurs mornings; closed state hols and special occasions). No purses, bags, or backpacks permitted on mansion grounds. 1010 Colorado between 10th and 11th Sts, in Capitol Complex. Phone 512/463-5516. **FREE**

Highland Lakes. Seven hydroelectric dams cross the Colorado River, creating a continuous series of lakes for nearly 150 mi upstream. Lake Buchanan and Lake Travis are the largest; Town Lake and Lake Austin are located within the Austin city limits. Fishing, boating; camping (exc on Town Lake). Many varied accommodations on the shores of each.

Inner Space Cavern. (See GEORGETOWN) 27 mi N off I-35.

Lady Bird Johnson Wildflower Research Center. Native plant botanical garden of national renown begun with generous grant from former First Lady, who added to her legacy by launching a national roadside beautification program in the 1960s. Numerous courtyards, terraces, arbors, and meadows, as well as an observation tower, cafe, gift store, and nature trail. (Tues-Sun) 4801 La Crosse Ave. Phone 512/292-4200. ¢¢

McKinney Falls State Park. A 641-acre park containing two waterfalls. Fishing; nature trail, hiking, picnicking, camping (dump station). Standard fees. (Daily) 7 mi SE on US 183. 5808 McKinney Falls Pkwy. Phone 512/243-1643. ¢

Mexic-Arte Museum. Nonprofit arts organization exhibits contemporary and historical art focusing on Latino culture. Museum store. (Mon-Sat) 419 Congress Ave. Phone 512/480-9373. ¢¢

Neill-Cochran House. (ca 1855) Greek Revival house built of native Austin limestone and Bastrop pine; furnishings from 18th-20th centuries. (Wed-Sun; closed hols) 2310 San Gabriel. Phone 512/478-2335. ¢

⭐ **O. Henry Home and Museum.** Victorian cottage was the residence of writer William Sydney Porter (O. Henry); original furnishings. Special events. (Wed-Sun afternoons; closed hols) 409 E 5th St. Phone 512/472-1903. **FREE**

State Capitol. A conventionally domed state capitol, larger than that of other states; built in 1888 of southwest red granite taken from Marble Falls near Burnet. A special narrow-gauge railroad was built to bring the stone to Austin. Fine statuary surrounds the building, which also has murals by W. H. Huddle. In the south wing is a guide center (daily; closed hols). Guided tours (daily; schedule may vary). 11th and

Congress Ave. Phone 512/463-0063. **FREE** On grounds is

Capitol Complex Visitor Center. Oldest government building in state has information on tours; brochures, exhibits. Gift shop. (Daily; closed hols) 112 E 11th St. Phone 512/305-8400. **FREE**

Texas State Library. Houses historical documents incl Texas Declaration of Independence; 45-ft mural offers view of Texas history. (Mon-Fri; genealogy library Tues-Sat; closed hols) Lorenzo de Zavala State Archives and Library Building, 1201 Brazos St. Phone 512/463-5514. **FREE**

University of Texas at Austin. (1883) 48,000 students. Its 15 colleges and schools and 75 departments offer some 6,500 courses, providing 260 different degree programs. The general information desk in rotunda of the main bldg offers schedules of campus events. Red River, Guadalupe, 26th St, and Martin Luther King Jr. Blvd. Phone 512/471-3434. Attractions incl

Harry Ransom Humanities Research Center. Collections of rare books and manuscripts. Gutenberg Bible on display. (Mon-Fri; closed hols) Guadalupe and 21st Sts. Phone 512/471-8944. **FREE**

THE UNIVERSITY OF TEXAS, THE CAPITOL, AND DOWNTOWN

People can't seem to agree whether the University or the Capitol represents the heart of Austin. The two grew up together and sit side-by-side, so it's important to see both. Begin on Guadalupe Street at about 24th Street, which is universally known as The Drag. Along this stretch are bookstores, music stores, clothing stores, and exceptional people-watching. To the immediate east is the main campus of the University of Texas; turn left (east) onto 22nd Street and walk about three blocks to the University of Texas tower, the South's largest bell carillon. This 1930s Beaux-Arts tower was the horrifying site of a gunman's murderous rampage in 1966. Walk north along Speedway to 24th Street and turn right (east) on 24th; continue to Trinity. There awaits the Texas Memorial Museum, a 1936 beauty housing natural history exhibits. Hike another block east to Red River, where the Lyndon Baines Johnson Library and Museum offers an in-depth look at the life and administration of the late president.

Now double back toward the middle of campus, following San Jacinto Boulevard south to 21st Street. Take 21st Street west to its intersection with University Avenue, and drink in the sight of the Littlefield Fountain, a glorious, unforgettable sculpture erected in 1933 to honor World War I veterans.

Walk south from the fountain along University to Martin Luther King Boulevard, turning left (east) to MLK at Congress Avenue. The Bob Bullock Texas History Museum offers state-of-the-art exhibits, collections, an IMAX Theater, cafe, and museum store. Walk south on Congress five blocks to the State Capitol building, a beautiful, 1888 domed design in pink granite. Immediately southeast of the capitol is the visitor center, at the corner of 11th Street and Brazos Street. Walk west on 11th to Colorado Street to see the Governor's Mansion, a stately, Greek Revival house that's been home to every governor since 1856.

Backtrack a block to Congress and turn right (south). On the left (east) side of the street is the Austin Museum of Art's downtown location and, across Eighth Street, the Jones Center for Contemporary Art. Take a moment to examine the old Majestic Theater at Seventh and Congress, which was built in 1915 and had its name changed to Paramount Theater in 1929. Also at Seventh and Congress, note the Stephen F. Austin Hotel, a lovely 1924 creation with a comfortable, ground-floor bar. Continue south on Congress another block to Sixth Street and turn left (east) for one block to the splendid Driskill Hotel, an 1886 landmark. Roam along Sixth Street to see several blocks of late 19th-century architecture in brick and limestone and to poke around art galleries, bistros, and music venues, or continue south on Congress to the Mexic-Arte Museum at Fourth and Congress.

Lyndon Baines Johnson Library & Museum. Exhibits on "Great Society," international affairs, oval office, first lady's gallery, head-of-state gifts; presidential history presented through memorabilia of political campaigns from Washington to Reagan. Changing exhibits on US history. Archives collection of documents avail for research. (Daily; closed Dec 25) 2313 Red River. On campus, 1 blk W of I-35. Phone 512/916-5137. **FREE**

Texas Memorial Museum of Science and History. Natural history exhibits dedicated to geology, paleontology, zoology, anthropology, and history. Special events. (Daily; closed hols) 2400 Trinity St. Phone 512/471-1604. **FREE**

Zilker Park. Austin's largest and most beautiful city park. 2201 Barton Springs Rd. Phone 512/974-6700. Incl

Barton Springs Pool. Spring-fed natural swimming pool nearly as long as a football field. (Apr-Oct) Phone 512/476-9044. ¢

Zilker Botanical Gardens. Phone 512/477-8672.

Zilker Hillside Theater. (See SPECIAL EVENTS) Phone 512/397-1463.

Special Events

Congress Avenue Bridge Bat Colony. Twelve blks south of State Capitol. The largest urban bat colony in North America, this 81-ft span across Town Lake provides roosting for more than a million Mexican free-tailed bats. The bats emerge from beneath the bridge each night at dusk to forage for insects. The spectacle of the colony taking flight has become one of the most popular tourist attractions in Texas, and draws thousands of people each summer. An educational kiosk is located on the north bank of the river, just east of the bridge. Best viewing is in Aug. Phone 512/327-9721. Late Mar-early Nov.

Star Texas Fair and Rodeo. Features rodeo performances. Late Mar.

Zilker Hillside Theater. Zilker Park. Free drama, ballet, classic films, musicals, and symphony concerts under the stars. Major musical featured each summer. Phone 512/397-1463. Early Apr-Oct.

Highland Lakes Bluebonnet Trail. Highland Lakes communities feature arts, crafts, and activities during wildflower season. Two wkends early Apr.

Old Pecan Street Arts Festival. First wkend May and last wkend Sept. Phone 512/441-9015.

Laguna Gloria Arts Festival. Fine arts and crafts, children's events, music, food. Apr. Phone 512/458-6073.

Motels/Motor Lodges

★ **DRURY INN & SUITES.** 6711 I-35 N (78752). 512/467-9500; fax 512/323-6198; res 800/378-7946. www.druryinn.com. 224 rms, 4 story. S $69.99-$79.99; D $79.99-$89.99; each addl $10; under 18 free. Pet accepted, some restrictions. TV; cable (premium). Pool. Complimentary continental bkfst. Restaurant adj 6 am-midnight. Ck-out noon. Meeting rms. Business servs avail. In-rm modem link. Valet serv. Sundries. Some refrigerators; microwaves avail. 4-story atrium lobby. Cr cds: A, C, D, DS, MC, V.

★ **EXEL INN OF AUSTIN.** 2711 I-35 S (78741). 512/462-9201; fax 512/462-9371; toll-free 800/367-3935. www.exelinns.com. 89 rms, 3 story. S $48.99-$59.99; D $57.99-$59.99; each addl $5; under 18 free. Pet accepted, some restrictions. TV; cable (premium). Pool. Complimentary continental bkfst. Restaurant adj open 24 hrs. Ck-out noon. Coin lndry. Health club privileges. Microwaves avail. Cr cds: A, C, D, DS, MC, V.

★★ **HAMPTON INN AUSTIN NORTH.** 7619 N I-35 (78752). 512/452-3300; fax 512/452-3124; res 800/426-7866. www.hamptoninn.com. 121 rms, 4 story. S $74-$84, D $84-$94; under 18 free. Crib free. TV; cable (premium). Pool. Complimentary continental bkfst. Restaurant adj 11 am-midnight. Ck-out noon. Meeting rm. Business servs avail. In-rm modem link. Exercise equipt. Cr cds: A, C, D, DS, JCB, MC, V.

★★ **HAMPTON INN AUSTIN SOUTH.** *4141 Governors Row (78744). 512/442-4040; fax 512/442-7122; res 800/426-7866. www.hamptoninn.com.* 123 rms, 6 story. S, D $84-$94; under 18 free; family rates. Pet accepted, some restrictions. Crib avail. TV; cable (premium). Complimentary continental bkfst. Complimentary coffee in rms. Ck-out noon. Meeting rms. Business servs avail. In-rm modem link. Exercise equipt. Pool. Cr cds: A, D, DS, MC, V.

★★ **HOLIDAY INN AUSTIN AIR-PORT SOUTH.** *3401 S I-35 (78741). 512/448-2444; fax 512/448-4999; res 800/465-4329. www.holiday-inn.com.* 210 rms, 5 story. S $69-$89; D $79-$99; each addl $10; suites $99-$149; under 18 free; wkend rates. Crib free. Pet accepted, some restrictions; $35. TV; cable (premium). Pool; whirlpool, poolside serv. Restaurant 6:30 am-10 pm; Sat, Sun from 7 am. Rm serv. Bar 5-10 pm; Fri, Sat to midnight. Ck-out noon. Coin lndry. Meeting rms. Business servs avail. In-rm modem link. Bellhops. Gift shop. Free airport transportation. Exercise equipt. Refrigerators; many bathrm phones; microwaves avail. Private patios. Cr cds: A, C, D, DS, MC, V.

★ **HOLIDAY INN EXPRESS AIR-PORT NORTH.** *7622 I-35 N (78752). 512/467-1701; fax 512/451-0966; res 800/465-4329. www.hiexpress.com.* 125 rms, 4 story. S $81-$87; D $87-$95; each addl $6; under 19 free. Crib free. TV; cable (premium). Pool. Complimentary continental bkfst. Restaurant adj 11-2 am. Ck-out noon. Meeting rms. Business servs avail. In-rm modem link. Some refrigerators; microwaves avail. Cr cds: A, C, D, DS, JCB, MC, V.

★★ **HOLIDAY INN TOWN LAKE.** *20 N I-35 (78701). 512/472-8211; fax 512/472-4636; res 800/465-4329. www.holiday-inn.com.* 320 rms, 14 story. S $99-$139, D $99-$149; each addl $10; under 18 free; wkend rates. Crib avail. Pet accepted; $125 deposit, $25 fee. TV; cable (pre-mium). Pool; whirlpool. Restaurant 6 am-2 pm, 5:30-10 pm. Rm serv. Bar noon-midnight; Fri, Sat to 1 am. Ck-out noon. Coin lndry. In-rm modem link. Bellhops. Valet serv. Sundries. Gift shop. Free covered parking. Free airport transportation. Exercise equipt; sauna. Two towers. On lake. Cr cds: A, C, D, DS, MC, V.

★★ **LA QUINTA.** *7100 I-35 N (78752). 512/452-9401; fax 512/452-0856; res 800/531-5900. www.laquinta.com.* 115 rms, 2 story. S, D $62.99-$71.99; each addl $5; suites $109-$122; under 18 free. Crib free. Pet accepted, some restrictions. TV; cable (premium). Pool. Restaurant adj open 24 hrs. Ck-out noon. Busi-ness servs avail. In-rm modem link. Cr cds: A, C, D, DS, MC, V.

★★ **LA QUINTA INN.** *2004 I-35 N, Round Rock (78681). 512/255-6666; fax 512/388-3635; res 800/531-5900. www.laquinta.com.* 116 units. 3 story. S $75-$85; D $85-$95; each addl $10, suite $115-$125. Crib free. Pet accepted, some restrictions. TV; cable (premium). Pool; whirlpool. Compli-mentary continental bkfst. Restau-rant nearby. Ck-out noon. Meeting rm. In-rm modem link. Exercise equipt; sauna. Some refrigerators; microwaves avail. Cr cds: A, C, D, DS, MC, V.

★ **RED LION HOTEL.** *6121 I-35 N (78752). 512/323-5466; fax 512/453-1945; toll-free 800/733-5466. www.redlion.com.* 300 rms, 7 story. S, D $109-$125; each addl $10; suites $150; under 18 free; wkend rates. Crib free. Pet accepted. TV; cable (premium). Pool; whirlpool, poolside serv. Restaurant 6 am-10 pm. Rm serv. Bar 4 pm-midnight; Fri, Sat to 2 am. Ck-out noon. Coin lndry. Meet-ing rms. Business servs avail. In-rm modem link. Bellhops. Gift shop. Sundries. Exercise equipt; sauna. Some refrigerators. Private patios. Cr cds: A, D, DS, MC, V.

★ **RED ROOF INN.** *8210 N Interre-gional Hwy 35 (78753). 512/835-2200; fax 512/339-9043; res 800/733-7663. www.redroof.com.* 143 rms, 4 story. S $42-$47; D $44-$56; each addl $5; suites $65-$72; under 18 free. Crib free. Pet accepted. TV; cable (pre-mium). Pool. Complimentary coffee in lobby. Restaurant adj. Ck-out noon. In-rm modem link. Cr cds: A, D, DS, MC, V.

D ☎ ⊠ ♨

★ **SUPER 8.** *8128 I-35 N (78753). 512/339-1300; fax 512/339-0820; res 800/800-8000. www.super8.com.* 123 rms, 4 story. S, D $45-$69; each addl $4; suites $78; under 18 free; hol rates. Crib free. TV; cable (premium). Pool; whirlpool. Complimentary continental bkfst. Restaurant adj 6 am-midnight. Ck-out 11 am. Meeting rm. Business servs avail. Coin lndry. Some refrigerators. Cr cds: A, D, DS, MC, V.

D ⊠ ⊠ ♨

Hotels

★★ **COURTYARD BY MARRIOTT.** *5660 I-35 N (78751). 512/458-2340; fax 512/458-8525; toll-free 800/321-2211. www.courtyard.com.* 198 rms, 9 story. S, D $79-$119; each addl $10; suites $135-$145; under 12 free; wkend rates. Crib free. TV; cable (premium). Pool; whirlpool. Complimentary coffee in rms. Restaurant 6 am-10 am; wkends 7-11 am. Bar 5-11 pm. Ck-out noon. Meeting rms. Business servs avail. In-rm modem link. Exercise equipt. Microwaves avail. Cr cds: A, C, D, DS, JCB, MC, V.

D ⊠ 🏋 ⊠ ♨

★★ **DOUBLETREE HOTEL AUSTIN.** *6505 I-35 N (78752). 512/454-3737; fax 512/454-6915; res 800/222-8733. www.doubletreehotels. com.* 350 rms, 6 story. S, D $134-$200; each addl $20; suites $149-$369; under 18 free; wkend rates. Crib free. Valet parking $9.74. TV; cable (premium). Pool; whirlpool, poolside serv. Restaurant 6:30 am-10 pm; wkends to 11 pm. Rm serv. Bar 3 pm-2 am. Ck-out noon. Convention facilities. Business center. In-rm modem link. Concierge. Gift shop. Exercise equipt. Bathrm phones; some refrigerators; microwaves avail. Balconies. Luxury level. Cr cds: A, C, D, DS, ER, JCB, MC, V.

D ⊠ 🏋 ⊠ ♨ 🏃

★★ **DRISKILL HOTEL.** *604 Brazos St (78701). 512/474-5911; fax 512/474-2214; toll-free 800/252-9367. www.driskillhotel.com.* 189 rms, 4 story. S, D $225-$275. Crib free. Pet accepted. TV; cable (premium), VCR avail. Restaurants 6:30 am-10 pm.

Bar 11 am-midnight. Ck-out noon. Meeting rms. Business center. In-rm modem link. Concierge. Exercise equipt. Refrigerators. Cr cds: A, C, D, DS, ER, JCB, MC, V.

D ☎ 🏋 ⊠ ♨ 🏃

★★★★ **FOUR SEASONS HOTEL AUSTIN.** *98 San Jacinto Blvd (78701). 512/478-4500; fax 512/478-3117; res 800/332-3442. www.fourseasons.com.* This luxurious capital city property is conveniently located across from the Convention Center and near the Capitol and the University of Texas. The expansive oak- and wildflower-covered grounds and Town Lake-side setting create a relaxing city haven. Lounge in one of the 291 rooms or suites and read a book by a Texas author from the unique lending library. 291 units, 9 story. S, D $270; suites $675-$1,400; under 18 free; wkend rates. Crib free. Covered parking $10; valet parking $14. Pet accepted, some restrictions. TV; cable (premium), VCR avail. Heated pool; whirlpool, poolside serv. Restaurant 6:30 am-10 pm; Fri, Sat to 11 pm (see also CAFE AT THE FOUR SEASONS). Rm serv 24 hrs. Bar 11-1 am, Fri-Sun to 2 am. Ck-out noon. Convention facilities. Business center. In-rm modem link. 24 hr concierge. Gift shop. Exercise rm; sauna. Massage. Bathroom phones; some refrigerators; minibar; microwaves avail. Balconies. Cr cds: A, C, D, DS, MC, V.

D ☎ ⊠ 🏋 ⊠ ♨ 🏃

★★★ **HILTON AUSTIN NORTH.** *6000 Middle Fiskville Rd (78752). 512/451-5757; fax 512/467-7644; toll-free 800/347-0330. www.austinnorth. hilton.com.* 189 rms, 9 story. S $130-$170; D $150-$190; each addl $20; suites $195-$310; family, wkend rates. Crib avail. Pet accepted, some restrictions. TV; cable (premium). Pool. Restaurant 6:30 am-11 pm; Sat, Sun from 7 am. Bar 3 pm-midnight. Ck-out noon. Meeting rms. In-rm modem link. Gift shop. Exercise equipt. Balconies. Cr cds: A, C, D, DS, ER, JCB, MC, V.

D ☎ ⊠ 🏋 ⊠ ♨ 🏃

★★★ **HYATT REGENCY AUSTIN.** *208 Barton Springs Rd (78704). 512/477-1234; fax 512/480-2069; toll-free 800/233-1234. www.hyatt.com.* 446 rms, 17 story. S $185-$225; D

$225-$265; each addl $25; suites $345-$700; under 18 free; wkend rates. Crib free. TV; cable (premium), VCR avail. Pool; whirlpool, poolside serv. Restaurant 6:30 am-midnight. Bar 4 pm-2 am. Ck-out noon. Meeting rms. Business center. In-rm modem link. Concierge. Gift shop. Exercise equipt. Balconies. Open atrium lobby. On lake. Cr cds: A, C, D, DS, JCB, MC, V.

⊡ ☒ ⊼ ☒ ☒ ⊼

★★★ **INTER-CONTINENTAL STEPHEN F. AUSTIN.** *701 Congress Ave (78701). 512/457-8800; fax 512/457-8896; toll-free 800/327-0200.* 189 rms, 16 story. S, D $195-$250; suites $375-$2,000; under 12 free; wkend rates. Crib free. TV; cable (premium), VCR avail. Indoor pool; whirlpool. Coffee in rms. Restaurants 6:30 am-midnight. Bar 3 pm-midnight. Ck-out noon. Meeting rms. Business center. In-rm modem link. Concierge. Exercise equipt; sauna. Cr cds: A, D, DS, JCB, MC, V.

⊡ ☒ ⊼ SC ⊼

★★★ **MARRIOTT.** *701 E 11th St (78701). 512/478-1111; fax 512/478-3700; res 800/228-9290. www.marriott.com.* 365 rms, 15 story. S, D $179-$199; suites $275-$575; wkend rates. Crib free. TV; cable (premium). Indoor/outdoor pool; whirlpool, poolside serv. Restaurant 6:30 am-10 pm. Rm serv to midnight. Ck-out noon. Convention facilities. In-rm modem link. Gift shop. Exercise equipt; saunas. Game rm. Some bathrm phones, refrigerators. Scenic view of city. Luxury level. Cr cds: A, C, D, DS, MC, V.

⊡ ☒ ⊼ ☒ ☒ ⊼

★★★ **MARRIOTT NORTH AUSTIN.** *2600 LaFrontera Blvd (78681). 515/733-6767; res 800/228-9290. www.marriott.com.* 295 rms, 8 story. S, D $129-$199; suites $250-$450; under 12 free; wkend rates. Crib free. TV; cable (premium), VCR avail. Indoor pool; whirlpool. Coffee in rms. Restaurants 6:30 am-midnight. Bar 11 am-midnight. Ck-out noon. Lndry serv. Meeting rms. Business center. In-rm modem link. Concierge. Gift shop. Exercise equipt. Refrigerators avail. Cr cds: A, C, D, DS, MC, V.

☒ ☒ ⊡ ⊼ ☒

★★★ **OMNI AUSTIN HOTEL AT DOWNTOWN.** *700 San Jacinto Blvd (78701). 512/476-3700; fax 512/397-4888; toll-free 800/843-6664. www.omnihotels.com.* 375 units, 20 story. S, D $149-$179; each addl $20; suites $219-$600; under 18 free; wkend rates. Crib free. Pet accepted, $50. Parking $8, valet $12. TV; cable (premium), VCR avail. Pool; whirlpool, poolside serv. Restaurant 6:30 am-10 pm. Bar 11-1 am; Fri, Sat to 2 am. Ck-out noon. Convention facilities. Business center. In-rm modem link. Shopping arcade. Exercise equipt; sauna. Massage. Some refrigerators. Luxury level. Cr cds: A, C, D, DS, ER, JCB, MC, V.

⊡ ☒ ⊼ ☒ ☒ SC ⊼ ☒

★★★ **OMNI AUSTIN HOTEL SOUTHPARK.** *4140 Governors Row (78744). 512/448-2222; fax 512/442-8028; toll-free 800/843-6664. www.omnihotels.com.* 313 rms, 14 story. S $99-$179; D $109-$189; each addl $10; suites $250-$500; under 18 free; wkend rates. Crib free. TV; cable (premium), VCR avail. Indoor/outdoor pool; whirlpool, poolside serv. Coffee in rms. Restaurant 6:30 am-10 pm. Bar 11 am-midnight; Fri, Sat to 2 am. Ck-out noon. Business servs avail. In-rm modem link. Gift shop. Free airport transportation. Exercise equipt; sauna. Some refrigerators; microwaves avail. Balconies. Cr cds: A, C, D, DS, JCB, MC, V.

⊡ ☒ ⊼ ✕ ☒ ☒ SC

★★ **RADISSON HOTEL AND SUITES AUSTIN.** *111 E Cesar Chavez St (78701). 512/478-9611; fax 512/473-8399; res 800/333-3333. www.radisson.com.* 413 rms, 12 story. S, D $99-$199; each addl $10; suites $134-$209; under 18 free. Crib free. Parking $9/day. TV; cable (premium). Pool. Restaurant 6:30 am-11 pm. Bar 11-2 am. Ck-out noon. Meeting rms. Business center. In-rm modem link. Exercise equipt. Cr cds: A, C, D, DS, ER, JCB, MC, V.

⊡ ☒ ⊼ ☒ ☒ ⊼

★★★ **RENAISSANCE AUSTIN.** *9721 Arboretum Blvd (78759). 512/343-2626; fax 512/346-7953; toll-free 800/228-9290. www.renaissancehotels.com.* 478 units, 9 story, 16 suites. S, D $109-$219; each addl $20; suites $275-$1,500; under 18 free; package plans. Crib free. Pet accepted, some restrictions. TV; cable (premium). 2 pools, 1 indoor; whirlpool, poolside serv. Restaurant 6:30 am-11 pm (see also TRATTORIA GRANDE). Bar noon-2 am. Ck-out 1 pm. Convention facilities. Business center. In-rm modem link. Concierge. Shopping arcade. Exercise equipt; sauna. Some refrigerators. Balconies. Elegant skylit atrium lobby. Luxury level. Cr cds: A, C, D, DS, ER, JCB, MC, V.

★★ **SHERATON.** *500 I-35 N (78701). 512/480-8181; fax 512/457-7990; res 800/325-3535. www.sheraton austin.com.* 254 rms, 18 story. S $119-$189; D $139-$209; each addl $10; suites $359; under 18 free; wkend rates. Crib free. Garage parking $9. TV; cable (premium). Pool. Complimentary coffee in rms. Restaurant 6:30 am-10 pm; wkends from 7 am. Bar 4 pm-midnight. Ck-out noon. Meeting rms. Business center. Gift shop. Exercise equipt. Microwaves avail. Cr cds: A, C, D, DS, JCB, MC, V.

Resorts

★★★★ **BARTON CREEK RESORT.** *8212 Barton Club Dr (78735). 512/329-4000; fax 512/329-4597; toll-free 800/336-6158. www.bartoncreek. com.* In Texas Hill Country west of Austin, this 4,000-acre resort is known for its conference and golf facilities. Masters Tom Fazio and Arnold Palmer, among others, designed the four championship golf courses, and the extensive meeting spaces offer high-tech capabilities and trained production staff. Other activity options include playing tennis, relaxing in the spa, or hiking the nature trail. 295 rms, 5 story. S $275; D $300; suites $450-$1500; under 17 free; golf, spa plans. Crib free. TV; cable (premium), VCR avail. 2 pools, 1 indoor; whirlpool, poolside serv. Dining rm 7 am-10 pm. Snack bar. Grill rm. Rm serv to midnight. Bar 11-1 am. Ck-out noon, ck-in 4 pm. Valet serv. Gift shop. Barber, beauty shop. Meeting rms. Business center. In-rm modem link. Airport transportation. Lighted tennis, pro. 72-hole golf, greens fees $125-$175, pro, putting green, driving range. Golf

school. Exercise rm; sauna, steam rm. Massage. Soc dir. Game rm. Refrigerators, minibars. Some balconies. Cr cds: A, C, D, MC, V.

★★★ **LAKEWAY INN.** *101 Lakeway Dr, Lakeway (78734). 512/261-6600; fax 512/261-7311; toll-free 800/525-3929. www.dolce.com.* 239 rms. S, D $160-$220; under 18 free; suites $240-$850; golf plan. Crib free. TV; cable (premium), VCR avail. 2 pools; whirlpool, poolside serv. Playground. Dining rm 7 am-10 pm. Rm serv. Bar 11-2 am; Sun from noon. Ck-out noon, ck-in 4 pm. Gift shop. Meeting rms. Business center. In-rm modem link. Airport transportation. Lighted tennis, pro. 36-hole golf, greens fee $61-$175, driving ranges, putting greens. Marina; charter boats, motor boats; water sports. Lawn games. Exercise equipt; sauna. Some refrigerators, fireplaces. Wet bar; microwaves avail. Private patios, balconies. Cr cds: A, D, DS, JCB, MC, V.

All Suites

★★★ **DOUBLETREE GUEST SUITES DOWNTOWN.** *303 W 15th St (78701). 512/478-7000; fax 512/478-3562; res 800/222-8733. www.doubletreehotels.com.* 189 suites, 15 story. S, D $139-$169; each addl $10; 2-bedrm suites $195-$275; under 18 free; wkly, wkend rates. Crib free. Pet accepted, some restrictions. Valet parking $8. TV; cable (premium), VCR avail. Heated pool; whirlpool, poolside serv. Complimentary coffee in rms. Restaurant 6:30 am-10 pm. Bar 11 am-midnight. Ck-out noon. Coin lndry. Meeting rms. Business center. In-rm modem link. Exercise equipt; sauna. Refrigerators, microwaves. Balconies. Cr cds: A, D, DS, MC, V.

★★★ **EMBASSY SUITES HOTEL DOWNTOWN.** *300 S Congress Ave (78704). 512/469-9000; fax 512/480-9164; res 800/362-2779. www.embassy suites.com.* 262 suites, 9 story. S, D $145-$240; each addl $10; under 18 free; wkend rates. Crib free. TV; cable (premium). Indoor pool; whirlpool.

Complimentary full bkfst. Restaurant 11 am-10 pm. Bar to 11 pm. Ck-out noon. Coin lndry. Meeting rms. Business servs avail. In-rm modem link. Exercise equipt; sauna. Refrigerators, microwaves. Cr cds: A, C, D, JCB, MC, V.

D ⊠ ⨉ ⊠ ⨀

★★ **HAWTHORN SUITES NORTH-WEST AUSTIN.** *8888 Tallwood Dr (78759). 512/343-0008; fax 512/343-6532. www.hawthorn.com.* 105 rms, 3 story, 91 kit. units. S $129-$159, D $169-$199; wkly, wkend rates. Crib free. TV; cable (premium), VCR avail (movies). Pool; whirlpool. Complimentary buffet bkfst. Coffee in rms. Ck-out noon. Coin lndry. Business servs avail. In-rm modem link. Valet serv. Health club privileges. Refrigerators, microwaves. Private patios, balconies. Picnic tables. Cr cds: A, D, DS, MC, V.

D ⊠ ⨀ ⨀

★★ **HAWTHORN SUITES SOUTH.** *4020 I-35 S (78704). 512/440-7722; fax 512/440-4815; res 800/527-1133. www.hawthorn.com.* 120 suites, 2 story. S $99-$139; D $109-$159; wkend rates. Crib free. Pet accepted; $50. TV; cable (premium). Heated pool; whirlpool. Complimentary continental bkfst. Complimentary coffee in rms. Restaurant nearby. Ck-out noon. Coin lndry. Meeting rm. Business servs avail. Valet serv. Refrigerators; microwaves. Picnic tables, grills. Cr cds: A, C, D, DS, MC, V.

D ⨀ ⊠ ⨀ ⨀

Restaurants

★★★ **BASIL'S.** *900 W 10th St (78703). 512/477-5576.* Hrs: 6-10 pm; Fri, Sat to 10:30 pm. Closed Dec 25. Res accepted. Italian menu. Wine, beer. Dinner $9.25-$21.95. Specializes in fresh seafood, beef tenderloin. Own pasta. Dining in several rooms. Cr cds: A, D, DS, MC, V.

D

★★★ **BELGIAN RESTAURANT.** *3520 Bee Caves Rd (78746). 512/328-0580.* Hrs: 11:30 am-2 pm, 6-10 pm; Fri, Sat 6-11 pm; Sun 11 am-2 pm, 6-10 pm. Closed Jan 1, July 4, Dec 25. Res accepted. Continental menu. Wine, beer. Lunch $5.95-$7.45, dinner $9.75-$23. Complete meals: din-

ner $22.50. Child's menu. Specialties: Dover sole meuniere, beef tenderloin bearnaise. Guitarist, harpist Wed-Sat. Totally nonsmoking. Cr cds: A, D, DS, MC, V.

D

★ **THE BOILING POT.** *700 E 6th St (78701). 512/472-0985. www.the boilingpot.citysearch.com.* Specializes in Cajun shellfish. Hrs: 4-10 pm; Fri, Sat 11 am-11 pm; Sun noon-10 pm. Closed Thanksgiving, Dec 24, 25. Wine list. Lunch, dinner $3.75-$34.95 Child's menu. Entertainment. Eat off table, supplied with bib and hammer. Cr cds: A, D, DS, MC, V.

D

★★★★ **CAFE AT THE FOUR SEASONS.** *98 San Jacinto Blvd (78701). 512/478-4500. www.fourseasons.com.* Located on the hotel's ground level and offering indoor and outdoor seating with a view of Town Lake, this dining room has a creative American menu and Texas Hill country decor. The most discriminating visitors will be impressed by the friendly, professional service and the striking presentations. Specializes in game, seafood, pasta. Own baking. Hrs: 6:30 am-10 pm; Fri to 11 pm; Sat 7 am-11 pm; Sun from 7 am; Sun brunch 10:30 am-2 pm. Res accepted. Bar. Wine cellar. Bkfst $4.50-$16.50, lunch $12-$20, dinner $20-$35. Sun brunch $38. Child's menu. Valet parking. Outdoor dining. Overlooks Town Lake. Cr cds: A, D, DS, MC, V.

D ⨀

★ **CHEZ NOUS.** *510 Neches St (78701). 512/473-2413. www. cheznous.citysearch.com.* Hrs: 11:45 am-2 pm, 6-10:30 pm; Sat, Sun from 6 pm. Closed Mon; Thanksgiving. French menu. Wine, beer. Lunch $8.50-$14, dinner $14.50-$21. Complete meals: dinner $17.50. Specializes in duck, lamb, seafood. Valet parking (eves). Bistro-style cafe. Cr cds: A, MC, V.

⨀

★★ **CHEZ ZEE.** *5406 Balcones Dr (78731). 512/454-2666. www.chez-zee. com.* Hrs: 7 am-10:30 pm. Closed Dec 25. Res accepted. Southwestern menu. Bar. Bkfst, lunch, dinner $6-$15. Child's menu. Specialties: chicken Caesar salad, fried pickles, creme brulee French toast. Own

desserts. Parking. Outdoor dining. Totally nonsmoking. Cr cds: A, D, DS, MC, V.
D

★★ **CITY GRILL.** *401 Sabine St (78701). 512/479-0817. www.citygrill austin.citysearch.com.* Hrs: 5-10 pm; Fri, Sat to 10:30 pm. Closed Thanksgiving, Dec 24, 25. Res accepted. Continental menu. Bar. A la carte entrees: dinner $12-$25. Child's menu. Specialties: broiled salmon, peppered steak Marsala. Valet parking. Outdoor dining. Original lumber mill built in 1896. Cr cds: A, C, D, DS, MC, V.
D

★ **COUNTY LINE ON THE HILL.** *6500 W Bee Cave Rd (78746). 512/327-1742. www.countyline.com.* Hrs: 5-9 pm; Fri, Sat to 10 pm. Closed Jan 1, Thanksgiving, Dec 24-26. Bar. Dinner $8.95-$16.95. Child's menu. Specializes in barbecued meats. Own desserts. Outdoor dining. 1940s Texas roadhouse atmosphere. View of hill country. Cr cds: A, D, DS, MC, V.
D

★★★ **DRISKILL GRILL.** *604 Brazos St (78701). 512/474-5911. www. driskillgrill.com.* Global flair menu. Specializes in steak, seafood. Hrs: 6:30 am-10 pm. Res accepted. Wine list. Bkfst, lunch $11-$16; dinner $18-$38. Entertainment. Cr cds: A, C, D, DS, ER, JCB, MC, V.
D

★★ **EASTSIDE CAFI.** *2113 Manor Rd (78722). 512/476-5858.* Specializes in pasta, beef tenderloin, homemade soup. Hrs: 11am-10 pm; Fri, Sat 10 am-11 pm; Sun 10 am-10 pm. Res accepted. Wine list. Lunch, dinner $6.95-$19.95. Brunch $6.95-$19.95. Entertainment. Garden. Cr cds: A, D, DS, MC, V.
D

★★ **FONDA SAN MIGUEL.** *2330 W N Loop (78756). 512/459-4121. www. fondasanmiguel.com.* Hrs: 5:30-9:30 pm; Fri, Sat to 10:30 pm. Sun brunch 11 am-2 pm. Mexican menu. Bar. Dinner $11.95-$18.95. Sun brunch $24.95. Child's menu. Specialties: chiles rellenos, shrimp Veracruz,

pescado al mojo de Ajo. Classic Mexican decor. Cr cds: A, D, DS, MC, V.
D

★★ **GREEN PASTURES.** *811 W Live Oak (78704). 512/444-4747. www. citysearch.com/aus/greenpastures.* Hrs: 11 am-2 pm, 6-10 pm; Sun brunch 11 am-2 pm. Closed Jan 1, Dec 25. Res accepted. Continental menu. Bar. Lunch $6.50-$12.25, dinner $16-$27. Sun brunch $23.50. Child's menu. Specialties: duck Texana, asparagus struedel, pecan-smoked salmon. Pianist Sun. Southern mansion built 1894. Family-owned. Cr cds: A, D, DS, MC, V.
D

★★★ **HUDSON'S ON THE BEND.** *3509 Ranch Rd (78734). 512/266-1369. www.hudsonsonthebend.com.* Hrs: 6-10 pm; Sat from 5:30 pm; Sun to 9 pm. Closed Dec 25. Res accepted. Continental menu. Bar. Wine list. Dinner $20-$30. Specializes in smoked quail, smoked shrimp quesadilla, pecan wood-smoked meats. Outdoor dining. Native stone house surrounded by flower and herb gardens; patio. Cr cds: A, D, DS, MC, V.
D ⊟

★ **JAIME'S SPANISH VILLAGE.** *802 Red River St (78701). 512/476-5149.* Specializes in fajitas, quesadillas, chimichangas. Hrs: 11 am-10 pm; Fri, Sat 11 am-11 pm. Closed Sun. Res accepted. Wine, beer. Lunch, dinner $5.50-$9.25. Child's menu. Entertainment. Cr cds: A, D, DS, MC, V.
D ⊟

★★★ **JEAN-PIERRE'S UPSTAIRS.** *3500 Jefferson (78731). 512/454-4811. www.jeanpierres.citysearch.com.* Hrs: 11:30 am-2 pm, 6-10 pm; Fri, Sat to 11 pm. Closed Sun; some major hols. Res accepted. Continental, Southwestern menu. Bar. Lunch $6-$11, dinner $12-$22.50. Specialties: spinach duck salad, marinated lamb chops, Texas bobwhite quail. Covered parking. Dining on 2nd floor terrace of office building. Cr cds: A, D, DS, MC, V.
D

★★★ **JEFFREY'S.** *1204 W Lynn St (78703). 512/477-5584. www.*

citysearch.com. Hrs: 5:30-10 pm; Fri, Sat to 10:30 pm. Sun 5 -9:30 pm. Res accepted. New Texas menu. Bar. Dinner $19.75-$29.75. Specializes in elk, fish, lamb. Original paintings. Menu changes daily. Cr cds: A, C, D, DS, MC, V.
D ⌐

★★ **LOUIE'S 106.** *106 E 6th (78701). 512/476-1997. www.louies106.net.* Hrs: 11:15 am-10:30 pm; Fri to 11 pm; Sat 5-11 pm; Sun 5:30-9:30 pm. Mediterranean menu. Bar. Lunch $10-$13.75, dinner $14.50-$24.50. Child's menu. Specialties: Blue Island mussels, veal chop with caramelized onion, bouillabaisse. Guitarist Fri, Sat. Valet parking. Cr cds: A, D, DS, MC, V.
D

★★ **MATT'S EL RANCHO.** *2613 S Lamar Blvd (78704). 512/462-9333. www.mattselrancho.com.* Hrs: 11 am-10 pm; Fri, Sat to 11 pm. Closed Tues; some major hols. Mexican menu. Bar. Lunch, dinner $5.50-$12.25. Child's menu. Specializes in chile rellenos, steak, Mexican seafood entrees. Patio dining. Mexican hacienda. Family-owned. Cr cds: A, D, DS, MC, V.
D SC

★ **THE OASIS-LAKE TRAVIS.** *6550 Comanche Trl (78732). 512/266-2442. www.theoasis.citysearch.com.* Hrs: 11:30 am-10 pm; Sat 11 am-11 pm; Sun 11 am-10 pm. Closed Thanksgiving, Dec 25. Mexican, American menu. Bar. Lunch $5.95-$9.95, dinner $7.95-$22.95. Specializes in shrimp, beef, fajitas. Outdoor dining. Outstanding view of Lake Travis. 32 levels of outdoor dining. Cr cds: A, DS, MC, V.
D ⌐

★ **OLD SAN FRANCISCO STEAK HOUSE.** *8709 I-35 N (78753). 512/835-9200. www.osfsteakhouse. com.* Hrs: 5-10 pm; Sat to 11 pm. Res accepted. Bar. Dinner $9.95-$55.95. Child's menu. Specializes in steak, fresh seafood. Pianist. Valet parking. Cr cds: A, C, D, DS, MC, V.
D ⌐

★ **PAPPADEAUX.** *6319 I-35 N (78752). 512/452-9363. www. pappadeaux.com.* Hrs: 11 am-3 pm, 5-10 pm; Fri, Sat to 11 pm, Sun 11 am-2 pm. Closed Thanksgiving, Dec 25. Cajun menu. Bar. A la carte entrees: lunch, dinner $8.20-$19.95. Child's menu. Specializes in Gulf Coast seafood. Totally nonsmoking. Cr cds: A, D, MC, V.
D

★★ **RUTH'S CHRIS STEAK HOUSE.** *107 W 6th St (78701). 512/477-7884. www.ruthschrisaustin. com.* Specializes in steak, lobster. Hrs: 5:30-10:30 pm; Fri, Sat to 11 pm. Closed hols. Res accepted. Bar. Wine list. Lunch, dinner $19.95-$45. Cr cds: A, D, MC, V.
D ⌐

★★ **SHORELINE GRILL.** *98 San Jacinto Blvd (78701). 512/477-3300. www.shorelinegrill.com.* Hrs: 11 am-10 pm; Fri to 10:30 pm; Sat 5-10:30 pm; Sun 5-10 pm. Closed some major hols. Res accepted. Bar. Lunch $5.95-$12.95, dinner $10.95-$23.95. Child's menu. Specializes in prime rib, seafood. Outdoor dining. Overlooks Town Lake. Cr cds: A, D, DS, MC, V.
D ⌐

★★★ **TRATTORIA GRANDE.** *9721 Arboretum Blvd (78759). 512/795-6100.* Hrs: 5-10 pm; Fri, Sat to 11 pm. Closed Sun, Mon; Dec 25. Res accepted. Italian menu. Bar. A la carte entrees: dinner $14-$27. Specializes in pasta. Entertainment Fri, Sat. Free valet parking. Arched windows overlooking arboretum, hill country. Cr cds: A, C, D, DS, ER, JCB, MC, V.
D

★ **U. R. COOKS.** *9012 Research Blvd (78758). 512/453-8350.* Hrs: 5-11 pm; Sat, Sun from noon. Closed Thanksgiving, Dec 25. Bar. Lunch, dinner $8.95-$14.95. Child's menu. Specializes in steak, seafood. Salad bar. Patio dining. Cooking area for guests to select and grill their own food. Cr cds: A, D, DS, MC, V.
D

★★ **WEST LYNN CAFE.** *1110 W Lynn (78703). 512/482-0950. www. citysearch.com/aus/westlynn.* Specializes in fettucine algreco, Thai red pepper curry. Hrs: 11:30 am-10:30 pm; Sat 11 am-10:30 pm; Sun 11 am-9:30 pm; Sat, Sun brunch 11 am-3 pm. Res accepted. Lunch $6-$10;

dinner $6-$11. Entertainment. Cr cds: A, D, DS, MC, V.

★★ **ZOOT.** *509 Hearn St (78703). 512/477-6535. www.zoot.citysearch. com.* Hrs: 5:30-10:30 pm; Fri, Sat to 11 pm; Sun brunch 11 am-2 pm. Closed some major hols. Res accepted. Wine, beer. Dinner $13.95-$24.95. Specializes in pork loin, roast chicken, tenderloin of beef. 4 small dining rms in older house. Totally nonsmoking. Cr cds: A, C, D, DS, MC, V.

Bandera

See also Kerrville, San Antonio

Founded 1850 **Pop** 957 **Elev** 1,257 ft
Area code 830 **Zip** 78003
Information Convention & Visitors Bureau, PO Box 171; 830/796-3045 or 800/364-3833
Web www.tourtexas.com/bandera

What to See and Do

Frontier Times Museum. Early Texas and frontier items; Western art gallery; bell collection; South American items; genuine shrunken head. (Daily; closed hols) 506 13th St. Phone 830/796-3864. ¢

Special Event

Cowboy Capital PRCA Rodeo. Mansfield Park Rodeo Arena. Parade, dances. Memorial Day wkend. Phone 800/364-3833.

Motel/Motor Lodge

★ **BANDERA LODGE.** *700 Hwy 16 S (78003). 830/796-3093; fax 830/796-3191.* 44 rms. Feb-Nov: S $51.75-$69; each addl $5. TV; cable (premium). Pool. Restaurant 11 am-9 pm. Bar. Ck-out 11 am. Coin lndry. Meeting rm. Trail rides avail. Cr cds: A, D, DS, MC, V.

Resorts

★★ **FLYING L GUEST RANCH.** *566 Flying L Dr (78003). 830/460-3001; fax 830/796-8455; toll-free 800/292-5134. www.flyingl.com.* 45 units (1- and 2-bedrm). Late May-early Sept: S, D $108-$199; under 3 free; golf plans; lower rates rest of yr. Crib free. TV; cable (premium). Pool. Playground. Free supervised children's activities (May-Sept, hols); ages 3-12. Complimentary coffee in rms. Dining rm 7:30-9:30 am, 5:30-7:30 pm. Snacks. Cookouts. Bar 5 pm-midnight; entertainment. Ck-out noon, ck-in 4 pm. Grocery 1½ mi. Coin lndry. Meeting rms. Business servs avail. Gift shop. Lighted tennis. 18-hole golf, greens fee (with cart) $22-$31, pro, putting green, driving range. Refrigerators, microwaves; some in-rm whirlpools. Cr cds: A, DS, MC, V.

★★ **HILL COUNTRY EQUESTRIAN LODGE.** *1580 Hay Hollar Rd (78003). 830/796-7950; fax 830/796-7970. www.hillcountryequestlodge.com.* 5 suites, 4 cabins. S, D $75-$198; family rates. Crib avail. Ck-out noon, ck-in 2 pm. Lawn games. Soc dir; Western entertainment. Fireplaces. Private patios, porches. Horseback rides twice daily. On 6,000-acre working ranch. Cr cds: A, DS, MC, V.

Guest Ranches

★★ **DIXIE DUDE RANCH.** *Ranch Rd 1077 (78003). 830/796-4481; toll-free 800/375-9255. www.dixieduderanch. com.* 2 rms in ranch house, 15 cottages, 1-3 bedrm. AP: S $100-$115; D $190-$210; family rates. Crib avail. TV. Heated pool; wading pool. Playground. Dining rm, 3 sittings: 8:20 am, 12:30 pm, 6 pm. Family-style meals; buffets, cookouts. Setups. Ck-out 11 am, ck-in 3 pm. Coin lndry 9 mi. Business servs avail. Lawn games. Soc dir; Western entertainment. Fireplaces. Private patios, porches. Horseback rides twice daily. On 725-acre working ranch. Cr cds: A, DS, MC, V.

★★★ **MAYAN DUDE RANCH.** *350 Mayan Ranch Rd (78003). 830/796-3312; fax 830/796-8205. www.mayan*

ranch.com. 67 cottages, 1-4 bedrm, 1-2 story. AP: S, D $125-$130/person; under 13, $60; 13-17, $85; wkly rates. TV. Pool. Playground. Free supervised children's activities (June-Sept). Dining rm (public by res) 7:30-10 am, 12:30-1:30 pm, 7-8 pm. Box lunches, snack bar, picnics. Bar noon-midnight. Ck-out 1 pm, ck-in 4 pm. Coin lndry. Meeting rms. Business servs avail. Airport transportation. Tennis. Tubing on Medina River. Lawn games. Soc dir (June-Sept). Entertainment. Movies. Game rm. Rec rm. Fireplace in some rms. Private patios. Picnic tables. Authenticated dinosaur tracks on property. Family-owned over 40 yrs. Cr cds: A, D, DS, MC, V.

★★ **SILVER SPUR DUDE RANCH.**
9266 Hwy 1077 (78003). 830/796-3037; fax 830/796-7170. www.silver spur-ranch.com. 9 rms, 6 cottages. AP: S $100; D $180; each addl $65; 2-day min stay. Crib free. TV. Pool. Picnics. Gift shop. Coin lndry 10 mi. Meeting rms. Horse stables. Hiking. Rec rm. Lawn games. Cr cds: MC, V.

Bastrop

See also Austin, La Grange, San Marcos

Pop 5,340 **Elev** 374 ft **Area code** 512
Zip 78602
Information Chamber of Commerce, 927 Main St; 512/321-2419
Web www.bastropchamber.com

Bastrop, named for Felipe Enrique Neri, Baron de Bastrop, is the seat of Bastrop County, one of the 23 original counties of the Republic of Texas. First settled in 1829 to protect commerce on the Old San Antonio Road, the town was subject to many Native American raids and was virtually abandoned in 1836. In 1839 it was resettled and has since flourished. The timber from the "Lost Pines of Texas," so named because the nearest similar vegetation is 100 miles away, was used in the building of the capitol at Austin.

What to See and Do

Lake Bastrop Park. (Lower Colorado River Authority) Incl a 906-acre lake. Daily entrance permit incl swimming, waterskiing, fishing, boating (launch fee); picnicking, camping (hookups, dump station), unfurnished cabins. (Daily) North Shore Recreation Area, 3 mi N on TX 95, then E on FM 1441. Phone 512/303-7666. ¢¢

State parks.

Bastrop. These 5,000 acres incl forest of "Lost Pines of Texas." Swimming pool (Memorial Day-Labor Day, daily; fee), fishing; hiking trail, 18-hole golf, picnicking, improved campsites, RV facilities, cabins. Standard fees. (Daily) 1 mi E via TX 71, Park Rd 1. Phone 512/321-2101. ¢¢

Buescher. Approx 1,000 acres. Fishing, boating (no gas motors permitted); hiking trail, picnicking, playground, improved campsites (dump station), shelters. Standard fees. (Daily) 12 mi SE via TX 71, then NE on FM 153, Park Rd 1. Phone 512/237-2241. ¢¢

Baytown

(E-7) *See also Galveston, Houston*

Settled 1824 **Pop** 66,430 **Elev** 33 ft
Area code 281
Information Chamber of Commerce, 4721 Garth Rd, Suite C, PO Box 330, 77522; 281/422-8359
Web www.baytownchamber.com

What to See and Do

Anahuac National Wildlife Refuge. This 28,564-acre refuge, bounded by East Galveston Bay and the Intracoastal Waterway, is primarily for migrating and wintering waterfowl; more than 250 bird species incl 30 varieties of geese and duck as well as pelicans, roseate spoonbills, ibis, and egrets. Natural marshlands provide food and shelter. Animals incl American alligator, nutria, and river otter. Saltwater fishing for crab and flounder; freshwater fishing only in designated areas; seasonal waterfowl hunting east of Oyster Bayou. Rest rms but no drinking water avail. 20 mi S of I-10 on TX 61, 562 to FM 1985, connecting with gravel road for 3 mi. Phone 409/267-3337. **FREE**

Baytown Historical Museum. Contains artifacts pertaining to local and pioneer history. (Tues-Sat) 220 W Defee. Phone 281/427-8768. **FREE**

Lynchburg Ferry. Oldest operating ferry in Texas, shuttling travelers across the mouth of the San Jacinto River since 1824. Trip provides access to San Jacinto Battleground and Battleship USS *Texas* (see HOUSTON). Phone 281/424-3521.

Motel/Motor Lodge

★ ★ **HAMPTON INN.** *7211 Garth Rd (77521). 281/421-1234; fax 281/421-9825; res 800/426-7866. www. hamptoninn.com.* 69 rms, 3 story. S, D $60-$84; each addl $10; under 18 free; wkend rates. Crib avail. TV; cable (premium). Complimentary continental bkfst. Complimentary coffee in rms. Restaurant adj open 24 hrs. Ck-out noon. Meeting rms. Business servs avail. In-rm modem link. Coin lndry. Pool; whirlpool. Many refrigerators. Cr cds: A, D, DS, ER, JCB, MC, V.

Beaumont

(D-8) *See also Orange, Port Arthur*

Founded 1835 **Pop** 113,866 **Elev** 24 ft

Information Convention & Visitors Bureau, 801 Main, Suite 100, PO Box 3827, 77704; 409/880-3749 or 800/392-4401

Web www.beaumontcvb.com

On January 10, 1901, a group of men working under Anthony Lucas were glumly but determinedly drilling for oil. Suddenly the pipe catapulted into the air, and oil spouted 200 feet high. This was the Lucas well in the Spindletop field. Promoters, toughs, petty thieves, and soldiers of fortune rushed to Beaumont, but the town soon brought things under control.

Later, another oil pool deeper than the original was discovered.

Located on the Neches River deep ship channel, which connects with the Intracoastal Waterway and the Gulf of Mexico, Beaumont is an important inland port and industrial city. Chemicals, synthetic rubber, oil equipment, forest products, and ships are produced here. Rice is grown in the surrounding area and milled in Beaumont.

What to See and Do

Art Museum of Southeast Texas. A permanent collection of 19th- and 20th-century American paintings, sculpture, prints, drawings, photography; contemporary folk art, decorative arts. Hosts national and international traveling exhibitions. Gift shop. (Daily; closed hols) 500 Main St. Phone 409/832-3432. **FREE**

Babe Didrikson Zaharias Memorial Museum. Trophies, artifacts, and memorabilia of "the world's greatest woman athlete." Also houses the Beaumont Visitor Information Center. (Daily; closed Dec 25) 1701 E I-10, exit 854. Phone 409/833-4622. **FREE**

Cattail Marsh. A 900-acre constructed wetland incl more than 375,000 plants and attracts over 350 bird species annually. Recreational activities incl bird-watching, hiking, biking, on over eight mi of gravel roads. Tyrell Park is adj and offers picknicking, frisbee, 18-hole golf, and children's playgrounds. (Daily) W on I-10 to Walden Rd, S to Tyrell Park entrance. Phone 409/842-0458. **FREE**

Edison Plaza Museum. Largest collection of Thomas A. Edison artifacts west of the Mississippi and the only electric industry museum in the South. Exhibits focus on Edison's inventions concerning electric light and power, the rising costs of electricity today, the future of electricity, and alternative energy sources. Incl Edison phonographs, mimeograph, dictating machine, and personal items from Edison's estate. (Mon-Fri or by appt; closed hols) 350 Pine St. Phone 409/981-3089. **FREE**

Jefferson Theatre. Full performance arts venue. Host to vaudeville in

1927 and various live performances today. Located in the orchestra pit is the original Robert Morton Wonder Organ with 778 pipes. 345 Fannin St. Phone 409/835-LIVE. **FREE**

John Jay French Museum (Historic House). (1845) Restored Greek Revival country house, re-created tannery and blacksmith shop. (Tues-Sat; closed hols) 2995 French Rd. Phone 409/898-3267. ¢¢

McFaddin-Ward House. (1906) Historic house museum, Beaux-Arts Colonial style with original family furnishings. Silver collection, Oriental rugs, porcelain, and glass; carriage house. (Tues-Sun; closed hols) Res requested. Children over eight yrs only. 1906 Calder Ave. Phone 409/832-2134. ¢¢

Spindletop/Gladys City Boomtown Museum. Re-creation of turn-of-the-century oil town; 15 buildings incl pharmacy, surveyor's office, saloon, photography studio; all contain period furnishings, artifacts. Self-guided tour. (Tues-Sun; closed hols) 3 mi S of I-10, on US 69/96/287; Lamar University campus, at US 69 and University Dr. Phone 409/835-0823. ¢¢ On grounds is

> **Lucas Gusher Monument.** A Texas granite shaft, 58 ft high, erected to commemorate the discovery of the first major oil field on the Gulf Coastal Plain.

Texas Energy Museum. Extensive modern facility encompassing history, science, and technology of energy. Permanent educational exhibits incl a 120-ft-long "History Wall," which traces energy from the 18th century to the present; a 135-gallon saltwater aquarium; and an exhibit on the 1901 "Spindletop" oil boom, featuring two lifelike animated robots. (Tues-Sun; closed hols) 600 Main St. Phone 409/833-5100. ¢

Tyrrell Historical Library. (1903) Served as the First Baptist Church until 1926. It now houses historical documents and art collections and serves as a center for genealogical research. (Tues-Sat) 695 Pearl St. Phone 409/833-2759. **FREE**

Special Events

Neches River Festival. Phone 409/835-2443. Mid-Apr. Phone 800/392-4401.

South Texas State Fair. Phone 409/832-9991. Ten days early Oct. Phone 800/392-4401.

Motels/Motor Lodges

★ ★ **BEST WESTERN JEFFERSON INN.** *1610 I-10 S (77707).* 409/842-0037; fax 409/842-0057; res 800/528-1234. www.bestwestern.com. 120 rms, 12 kits. S $59; D $67; each addl $6; kit. units $63-$69; under 18 free. Crib free. Pet accepted, some restrictions. TV; cable (premium). Pool. Complimentary continental bkfst. Coffee in rms. Ck-out noon. Coin lndry. Meeting rms. Business servs avail. In-rm modem link. Some refrigerators. Cr cds: A, C, D, DS, MC, V.

★ ★ **HOLIDAY INN.** *2095 N 11th St (77703).* 409/892-2222; fax 409/892-2231; toll-free 800/465-4329. www.holiday-inn.com. 190 rms, 6 story. S, D $63-$89.99; each addl $7; under 18 free; wkend rates. Crib free. Pet accepted, some restrictions. TV; cable (premium). Pool; poolside serv. Restaurant 6-10 am, 5:30-10 pm. Rm serv. Bar. Ck-out noon. Coin lndry. Meeting rms. Business servs avail. In-rm modem link. Bellhops. Free airport transportation. Health club privileges. Cr cds: A, C, D, DS, ER, JCB, MC, V.

★ ★ **HOLIDAY INN PLAZA.** *3950 I-10 S (77705).* 409/842-5995; fax 409/842-0315; res 800/465-4329. www.holiday-inn.com. 253 rms, 80 suites, 8 story. S $115; D $125; each addl $10; suites $120-$275; under 18 free; wkend rates. Crib free. Pet accepted; $15 refundable. TV; cable (premium), VCR avail. Indoor pool; whirlpool, poolside serv. Restaurant 6 am-10 pm. Bar. Ck-out noon. Business center. In-rm modem link. Gift shop. Free airport transportation. Exercise equipt; sauna. Game rm. Some refrigerators. Microwaves avail. 3-story waterfall in lobby. Convention center adj. Cr cds: A, C, D, DS, MC, V.

★ ★ **LA QUINTA INN.** *220 I-10 N (77702).* 409/838-9991; fax 409/832-1266; res 800/531-5900. www.laquinta.com. 122 rms, 2 story. S $69;

D $77; under 18 free. Crib free. Pet accepted, some restrictions. TV. Pool. Complimentary continental bkfst. Ck-out noon. Meeting rms. Business servs avail. In-rm modem link. Valet serv. Sundries. Microwaves avail. Cr cds: A, C, D, DS, JCB, MC, V.

Hotel

★ ★ ★ **HILTON BEAUMONT.** 2355 I-10 S (77705). 409/842-3600; fax 409/842-1355; res 800/445-8667. www.hilton.com. 284 rms, 9 story. S, D $79-$99; each addl $10; suites $129-$299; under 18 free; wkend rates. Crib free. TV; cable (premium). Pool. Complimentary coffee. Restaurant 6 am-10:30 pm. Bar 5 pm-midnight. Ck-out noon. Business servs avail. In-rm modem link. Gift shop. Free airport transportation. Golf privileges. Exercise equipt. Health club privileges. Microwaves avail. Balconies. Cr cds: A, D, DS, MC, V.

Restaurants

★ **CHULA VISTA.** 1135 N 11th St (77702). 409/898-8855. Hrs: 11 am-10 pm; Fri, Sat to 11 pm. Closed Thanksgiving, Dec 25. Res accepted. Mexican menu. Bar. Lunch $4.50-$5.70, dinner $4.95-$14.95. Child's menu. Specializes in fajitas, beef enchiladas. Entertainment Tues. Outdoor dining. Cr cds: A, D, DS, MC, V.

★ **HOFFBRAU STEAKS.** 2310 N 11th St (77703). 409/892-6911. www. hoffbrausteaks.com. Hrs: 11 am-10 pm; Fri, Sat 4-11 pm; Sun 5-10 pm. Closed Jan 1, Dec 25. Res accepted. Bar. Lunch, dinner $5.50-$16.95. Child's menu. Specializes in chargrilled steak with lemon butter sauce. Entertainment exc Sun. Outdoor dining. Cr cds: A, D, DS, MC, V.

Belton (D-6)

(see Temple)

Big Bend National Park

See also Alpine, Fort Stockton

(108 mi S of Alpine on TX 118 or 69 mi S of Marathon on US 385 to Park Headquarters)

In this park the Rio Grande, southern boundary of the United States, flows through awe-inspiring canyons with sheer rock walls rising 1,500 feet above the water; south of Marathon, the river makes the extraordinary 90-degree bend for which the park is named. This rocky wilderness, once home to dinosaurs, boasts more than 1,200 species of plants, particularly cacti in the lowest areas and juniper, piñon, oak, and scattered stands of Arizona pine, Douglas fir, Arizona cypress, and aspen in the uplands. Deer, coyote, peccaries (javelina), and more than 400 bird species may be found amid scenery as stark and magnificent as anywhere in the United States. The Sierra del Carmen and other mountain ranges visible from the park are across the border in Mexico.

The visitor center at Panther Junction contains orientation exhibits for visitors (daily); at Persimmon Gap, the entrance from Marathon, there is also a visitor contact station. At Chisos Basin, about seven miles off the connecting road within the park (watch for sign), there is a visitor center, store, restaurant, and motel; tent and trailer campgrounds (no hookups; limit 24 feet). Rio Grande Village, 20 mi SE of Panther Junction, offers a visitor center; tent and trailer campground and RV park (vehicle must accept full hookups); a store; shower facilities; gas; laundromat. Castolon, 35 miles southwest of Panther Junction, has a tent and trailer campground (no hookups) and small store. Some fees.

Floating the Rio Grande and overnight backpacking is free by permit only; inquire at visitor centers. Several self-guided trails. Park Service naturalists frequently conduct nature walks and talks. Further information, including activity schedules, can be obtained at all visitor centers in park

Rio Grande, Big Bend National Park

or by contacting the Superintendent, PO Box 129, Big Bend National Park 79834; 915/477-2251.

It is possible to drive within this 800,000-acre park to Santa Elena Canyon and to Boquillas Canyon. Both drives offer much scenery. The trip between Alpine, the park, and Marathon totals about 190 miles. To get the most out of Big Bend, plan to spend at least one night.

Fill gas tank, check oil, and carry water before entering the park. Most people go into the park by one route and out by the other.

Big Spring

(C-3) *See also Midland*

Founded 1881 **Pop** 25,233 **Elev** 2,397 ft **Area code** 915 **Zip** 79720
Information Chamber of Commerce, 215 W 3rd St, PO Box 1391, 79721; 915/263-7641 or 800/734-7641
Web www.bigspringtx.com

What to See and Do

Big Spring State Park. A 370-acre park, with picnic grounds and playground. View from top of mountain; prairie dog colony. Hiking; interpretive trail. (Day use only) Standard fees. (Daily) 1 mi W on FM 700 to Park Rd 8. Phone 915/263-4931. ¢¢

Heritage Museum. Themed exhibits, incl Indian artifacts, ranching, and oil production; large longhorn collection; Western art; changing exhibits, demonstrations. (Tues-Sat; closed hols) 510 Scurry St. Phone 915/267-8255. ¢

Lake Colorado City State Park. A 500-acre area. Swimming, waterskiing, fishing, boating (ramp); picnicking, playground, improved camping, tent and trailer sites. Standard fees. (Daily) 36 mi E via I-20, then 6 mi S via FM 2836. Phone 915/728-3931. ¢¢

Potton House. (1901) Restored turn-of-the-century, Victorian-style house; furnishings brought from England by original owners. (Tues-Sat afternoon; closed hols) 200 Gregg St. Phone 915/263-0511. ¢

Special Events

Gem & Mineral Show. Dora Roberts Building, Fairgrounds. First wkend Mar. Contact Chamber of Commerce. Phone 800/734-7641.

Rattlesnake Roundup. Late Mar. Contact Chamber of Commerce. Phone 800/734-7641.

Square Dance Festival. Mid-May. Contact Chamber of Commerce. Phone 800/734-7641.

Howard County Fair. Third wk Aug. Phone 800/734-7641.

Motel/Motor Lodge

★ ★ **BEST WESTERN.** *700 W I-20 (79720). 915/267-1601; fax 915/267-*

*6916; res 800/528-1234. www.best
western.com.* 155 rms, 2 story. S $44-
$50; D $50-$55; each addl $6; suites
$90-$125; under 12 free. Crib free.
TV; cable. Heated pool. Complimentary continental bkfst. Restaurant
open 24 hrs. Rm serv. Ck-out noon.
Meeting rms. Exercise equipt. Cr cds:
A, C, D, DS, MC, V.

Bonham

(B-7) *See also Greenville, Paris, Sherman*

Founded 1837 **Pop** 9,990 **Elev** 605 ft
Area code 903 **Zip** 75418
Information Chamber of Commerce,
110 E First St; 903/583-4811

What to See and Do

Bonham State Park. Entrance on
Park Rd 24. On 261 acres. Swimming, fishing; picnicking, ten-mi
mountain bike trail, improved campsites (dump station). (Daily) 3½ mi
SE via TX 78, FM 271. Phone
903/583-5022. ¢¢

Fort Inglish Village. Blockhouse is
replica of first building in Bonham
(1837), built to protect settlers. Log
structures, incl blacksmith shop, residential cabin, schoolhouse/church,
and general store have been moved
from surrounding county to form a
settlement. Living history demonstrations of pioneer skills. (Apr-Aug,
Tues-Sun) ½ mi W on US 82. Phone
903/640-0506. **FREE**

Lake Bonham Recreation Area.
Swimming, waterskiing, fishing,
boating (launch); nine-hole and
miniature golf, playground, tent and
trailer sites (dump station, no
hookups). Some fees. 6 mi N. Phone
903/583-8001.

Sam Rayburn House. (1916) Guided
tour of house and grounds. (Mon-Fri,
hrs vary; closed hols) 1 mi W on US
82. Phone 903/583-5558. **FREE**

Sam Rayburn Library and Museum.
Affiliated with the University of
Texas at Austin. Honors the man
who was Speaker of the US House of
Representatives for 17½ yrs. In the
library is an exact copy of the
Speaker's Capitol office, which contains a fireplace that was in the US
House of Representatives for 92 yrs,
and a crystal chandelier, more than a
century old, that has hung in both
the White House and the Capitol.
The library also contains Rayburn's
papers; published proceedings from
the first Continental Congress; books
by and about leading political figures
and American history. (Daily; closed
hols) 800 W Sam Rayburn Dr, ½ mi
W on US 82. Phone 903/583-2455.
FREE

Special Event

Fannin County Fair. Fort Inglish Park.
Phone 903/583-7453. Third wkend
Oct.

Brackettville

See also Del Rio, Eagle Pass, Uvalde

Pop 1,876 **Elev** 1,110 ft
Information Kinney County Chamber of Commerce, PO Box 386;
830/563-2466

What to See and Do

⭐ **Alamo Village.** Built for the John
Wayne movie *The Alamo* (1959).
Buildings incl stage depot, bank, jail,
and a replica of the Alamo. Entertainment (Memorial Day-Labor Day);
walk-in museums, trading post, store,
cantina. (Daily; closed Dec 21-26) 7
mi N on Ranch Rd 674. Phone
830/563-2580. ¢¢¢

Brazosport

See also Angleton, Houston

Pop 49,541 **Elev** 0-20 ft
Area code 979
Information Visitor & Convention
Council, 420 TX 332, Clute 77531;
979/265-2505 or 888/477-2505
Web www.brazosport.org

What to See and Do

Brazosport Museum of Natural Science. Emphasizing local flora and fauna; archaeological finds. Shell exhibits with collections for public study; Children's Hall; paleontology, mineralogy, and ivory displays; marine life exhibits; aquarium, simulated underwater diorama. (Mon-Sat; closed hols) 400 College Dr. Phone 979/265-7831. **FREE**

Special Events

Joyride & Rod Run. Mar. Phone 979/233-4141.

Riverfest. Last wkend Apr. Phone 979/233-3306.

Fishin' Fiesta. July.

Great Texas Mosquito Festival. Last wkend July.

Shrimp Boil and Auction. Late Aug.

Festival of Lights. Sat before Thanksgiving. Phone 979/297-4533.

Motels/Motor Lodges

★ **LA QUINTA INN.** *1126 W Hwy 332, Clute (77531). 979/265-7461; fax 979/265-3804; toll-free 800/687-6667.* 136 rms, 2 story. S $49-$56; D $56-$63; each addl $6; suites $66-$73; under 18 free. Pet accepted, some restrictions. TV; cable (premium). Pool. Complimentary continental bkfst. Coffee in rms. Restaurant adj open 24 hrs. Ck-out noon. Meeting rm. In-rm modem link. Cr cds: A, C, D, DS, ER, JCB, MC, V.
⊡ 🐾 ≈ 🛏 🔥 SC

★★ **RAMADA INN.** *925 Hwy 332 W, Lake Jackson (77566). 979/297-1161; fax 979/297-1249; toll-free 800/544-2119. www.ramadainnlakejacksontx.com.* 144 rms, 2 story. S, D $90; each addl $10; family, wkend, wkly rates. Crib free. Pet accepted, some restrictions. TV; cable. Pool. Restaurant 6 am-1 pm, 5-10 pm. Rm serv. Bar 4 pm-midnight. Ck-out 1 pm. Meeting rms. In-rm modem link. Cr cds: A, C, D, DS, JCB, MC, V.
⊡ 🐾 ≈ 🛏 🔥

Brenham

(D-6) *See also Bryan/College Station*

Founded 1844 **Pop** 13,507 **Elev** 350 ft
Area code 979 **Zip** 77833
Information Washington County Chamber of Commerce, 314 S Austin St; 979/836-3695 or 888/BRENHAM
Web www.brenhamtx.org

What to See and Do

Antique Rose Emporium. Eight-acre garden center beautifully landscaped on early settler's homestead with old garden roses, native plants, cottage garden perennials, and wildflowers. Restored buildings incl 1855 stone kitchen, 1840s log corn crib, 1850s salt box house, and 1900s Victorian home. Tours (groups by res). (Daily; closed hols) 12 mi NW on FM 50. Phone 979/836-5548. **FREE**

Baptist Historical Center. Museum with exhibits on Sam Houston, incl wardrobe; history of Texas Baptists; history of city of Independence. Baptist Church (organized in 1839, present building 1872) was site of baptism of Sam Houston. Contains historic century-old church bell, relics. (Wed-Sat; closed Jan 1, Dec 25) Across the highway are the graves of Houston's wife and mother-in-law, who requested burial within sound of the church bell. Ruins of old Baylor College, ½ mi W on FM 390. 12 mi N at intersection of FM 50 and 390 in Independence. Phone 979/836-5117. **FREE**

Blue Bell Creamery. 45-min tours of ice cream manufacturing plant. Free samples. Country store. (Mon-Fri, phone 800/327-8135 for information) FM 577 2 mi off US 290. ¢¢

Lake Somerville. Fishing, boating (ramps); hiking, picnicking, concession, camping, cabins, tent and trailer facilities. The state of Texas operates Birch Creek (phone 979/535-7763) and Nails Creek (phone 979/289-2392) state parks on the lake. The US Army Corps of Engineers operates three additional recreation areas; contact PO Box 549, 77879. Phone 979/596-1622. 15 mi NW on TX 36.

Monastery of St. Clare Miniature Horse Ranch. Home of Franciscan Poor Clare nuns. Pastures, barn. "Art Barn" gift shop sells handmade ceramics. Self-guided tours (free). Forty-five-min guided tours (fee). (Limited hrs; closed religious hols). 9 mi NE via TX 105. Phone 979/836-9652.

Pleasant Hill Winery. Winery and vineyards tours. Tasting rm, gift shop. Tours (res required). (Wkends; closed hols) 1441 Salem Rd. **FREE**

Stephen F. Austin State Historical Park. Site of San Felipe, seat of Anglo-American colonies in Texas. Monuments; replica of Austin's house. Bathhouse, fishing; picnicking, playground, gift shop, camping (tent and trailer sites, shelters). Some fees. (Daily) Approx 30 mi S via TX 36, off I-10. Phone 979/885-3613. ¢¢

Washington-on-the-Brazos State Historical Park. A 200-acre park, site of signing of Texas Declaration of Independence (1836). Picnic area. (Daily) 14 mi NE on TX 105, then 5 mi NE on FM 912. Phone 979/878-2214. **FREE** On grounds are

Anson Jones Home. Residence of last president of the Republic of Texas; period furnishings. Guided tours (daily). ¢¢

Independence Hall. Replica of hall in which Texas Declaration of Independence was signed. (Daily) ¢¢

Star of the Republic Museum. Exhibits on history and culture of the Republic of Texas; audiovisual programs; research library. Tours. (Daily; closed Thanksgiving, Dec 24-Jan 1) Phone 979/878-2214. ¢

Special Events

Texas Independence Day Celebration. Washington-on-the-Brazos State Historical Park. Reenactments, musical performances, tours of historic park. Wkend nearest Mar 2.

Bluebonnet Trails/Wildflowers Tours. Drive through countryside combining wildflowers with early Texas history; free maps. Late Mar-Apr. Phone 888/273-6426.

Washington County Fair. Held annually since 1868. Rodeos, carnival, entertainment, food. Phone 979/836-4112. Third Wed-Sat Sept.

B&B/Small Inn

★ ★ ★ **ANT STREET INN.** *107 W Commerce St (77833). 979/836-7393; fax 979/836-7595; res 800/805-2600. www.antstreetinn.com.* 13 rms, 5 with shower only, 2 story. S, D $95. Children over 12 yrs only. TV; cable. Complimentary full bkfst. Complimentary coffee in rms. Ck-out 11 am, ck-in 3 pm. Business servs avail. In-rm modem link. Luggage handling. Balconies. Built in 1899; restored turn-of-the-century decor, antiques. Totally nonsmoking. Cr cds: A, D, DS, MC, V.

Brownsville

(G-6) *See also Harlingen, Port Isabel, South Padre Island*

Founded 1848 **Pop** 139,722 **Elev** 33 ft
Area code 956
Information Brownsville Chamber of Commerce, 1600 E Elizabeth St, 78520; 956/542-4341
Web www.brownsvillechamber.com

While breezes off the Gulf make Texas's southernmost city cooler than many other cities farther north, its tropical climate remains clear. Palms, royal poinciana, citrus trees, bougainvillea, papaya, and banana trees line the streets. Brownsville and nearby South Padre Island are year-round resort areas.

Brownsville is an air, rail, and highway port of entry between the United States and Mexico and an international seaport with a 17-mile ship channel to the Gulf. Red grapefruit, oranges, lemons, limes, sorghum, and winter vegetables are grown and shipped from here. Brownsville is also an important shrimp boat port and deep-sea fishing center. The Mexican city of Matamoros is just across the Rio Grande.

Fort Taylor (later Fort Brown) was established in 1846, after Texas entered the Union. Construction of the fort precipitated the Mexican War, which began at Palo Alto Battlefield. The final land battle of the Civil War was also fought nearby. Raids of the area by Mexican bandits continued well into the early 20th century.

What to See and Do

Fishing.

Freshwater fishing. In many lakes and canals. Bass, crappie, and catfish.

Saltwater fishing. On Laguna Madre Bay, in the ship channels, or in the Gulf by charter boats from Port Isabel or South Padre Island.

Gladys Porter Zoo. Outstanding 31-acre zoo with more than 1,900 animals in their natural setting; reptile collection, free-flight aviary, children's zoo, aquarium, Australian exhibit. (Daily) 500 Ringgold St. Phone 956/546-2177. ¢¢

Gray Line bus tours. Contact PO Box 2610, South Padre Island 78597.

Matamoros, Tamaulipas, Mexico. (population 500,000) Across the Rio Grande. This is a colorful and interesting Mexican border city, with diversified industry making it one of Mexico's wealthiest towns. Life centers around the Plaza de Hidalgo and the streets that reach out from it. The market, four blks from the plaza on Calle (street) 9 and Calle 10, is an open mall of small stands. (No fruit may be brought back to the US. For Border Crossing Regulations, see MAKING THE MOST OF YOUR TRIP.)

Palmitto Ranch Battlefield. Site of the final land engagement of the Civil War (May 12-13, 1865). Confederate troops prevailed, but were ordered to surrender upon learning of Lee's capitulation at Appomattox more than a month before. Marker is 12 mi E on TX 4.

Palo Alto Battlefield National Historic Site. Historical marker gives details of the artillery battle that began the Mexican War here on May 8, 1846. 6 mi N of town on FM 1847, near jct FM 511. Visitor center with museum is at 1623 Central Blvd on the second floor of IBC Bank Building. Phone 956/541-2785. **FREE**

Port Brownsville. Harbor for shrimp boats and ships transporting various commodities. 6 mi NE on International Blvd. Phone 800/378-5395. **FREE**

Resaca de la Palma. Site of the second Mexican War battle, May 9, 1846. General Zachary Taylor defeated Mexican General Mariano Arista. Historical markers give details. North end of town, vicinity Paredes Line Rd and Coffee Port Rd.

Special Event

Charro Days. Parades, concerts, special events. Late Feb-early Mar. Phone 956/546-3721.

Motels/Motor Lodges

★★ **BEST WESTERN ROSE GARDEN.** *845 N Expy 77/83 (78520). 956/546-5501; fax 956/546-6474; toll-free 800/528-1234. www.bestwestern. com.* 121 rms, 2 story. S $45-$95; D $55-$95; each addl $8; under 18 free. Crib free. TV; cable (premium). Pool. Complimentary bkfst buffet. Ck-out noon. Coin lndry. Some refrigerators. Some balconies. Cr cds: A, C, D, DS, MC, V.

D ⊷ ⊠ 🔥 SC

★ **DAYS INN.** *715 N Frontage Rd (78520). 956/541-2201; fax 956/541-6011; res 800/329-7466. www.days inn.com.* 124 rms, 2 story. S $34-$56; D $49-$65; suites $85; under 17 free. Crib free. TV; cable (premium). Pool. Coffee in lobby. Restaurant 6 am-10 pm. Bar 4 pm-2 am. Ck-out noon. Meeting rms. In-rm modem link. Coin lndry. Valet serv. Some refrigerators. Some balconies. Cr cds: A, C, D, DS, MC, V.

D ♿ ⊷ ⊠ 🔥

★★★ **FOUR POINTS BY SHERATON.** *3777 N Expy (78520). 956/547-1500; fax 956/547-1550; res 800/325-3535. www.fourpoints.com.* 141 rms. 2 story. S, D $79-$109; each addl $10; suites $225; under 17 free; wkend rates. Pet accepted, some restrictions. TV; cable (premium). Indoor/outdoor pool; whirlpool. Coffee in rms. Restaurant 6 am-11 pm. Rm serv. Bar 4 pm-2 am; entertainment. Ck-out noon. Meeting rms. Business servs avail. In-rm modem link. Exercise equipt. Refrigerator, whirlpool in suites. Cr cds: A, D, DS, MC, V.

D 🐾 ⊷ 🏃 🔥

★★ **HOLIDAY INN.** *1900 E Elizabeth St (78520). 956/546-2201; fax 956/546-0756; toll-free 800/465-4329. www.holiday-inn.com.* 167 rms, 2 story. S $75; D $83; each addl $8; suites $95-$200; under 19 free. Crib free. TV; cable (premium). Pool; poolside serv. Restaurant 6 am-10 pm. Rm serv. Bar noon-2 am; entertainment. Ck-out noon. Convention facilities. Business servs avail. In-rm modem link. Bellhops. Valet serv. Exercise equipt. Balconies. Intl Gateway Bridge nearby. Cr cds: A, C, D, DS, MC, V.

★ **RED ROOF INN.** *2377 N Expressway 83 (78520). 956/504-2300; fax 956/504-2303; res 800/733-7663. www.redroof.com.* 124 units, 3 story, 3 suites. S $50-$70; D $54-$74; each addl $4; under 18 free; suites $68-$75. Crib free. Pet accepted, some restrictions. TV; cable (premium). Heated pool; whirlpool. Complimentary continental bkfst. Coffee in lobby. Restaurant adj 6 am-midnight. Ck-out 11 am. Meeting rm. Valet serv. Coin lndry. Some refrigerators. Cr cds: A, D, DS, MC, V.

Resort

★★★ **RANCHO VIEJO RESORT AND COUNTRY CLUB.** *1 Rancho Viejo Dr, Rancho Viejo (78575). 956/350-4000; fax 956/350-9681; toll-free 800/531-7400. www.playrancho. com.* 65 units, 1-2 story, 31 kits. S $125; D $135; each addl $10; kit. villas (1-3 bedrm) $148-$475; under 14 free; golf plans. TV; cable. Pool; wading pool, poolside serv. Dining rm 7 am-10 pm. Bar from noon; entertainment Thurs-Sat. Ck-out noon, ck-in 4 pm. Convention facilities. Business servs avail. Bellhops. Barber, beauty shop. Tennis. 36-hole golf, greens fee $40, putting green, driving range. Exercise equipt. Rec rm. Refrigerator in suites. Private patios, balconies. Cr cds: A, C, D, DS, MC, V.

Restaurants

★★ **LOS CAMPEROS.** *1440 International Blvd (78520). 956/546-8172.* Hrs: 11 am-midnight, Fri, Sat to 2 am. Res accepted. Mexican menu. Bar. Lunch $4.75-$13, dinner $7.75-$13.25. Child's menu. Specializes in chicken, steak. Entertainment Thurs-Sat. Cr cds: A, D, DS, MC, V.

★★ **VALLEY INN.** *Ruben Torres Blvd (78523). 956/546-5331.* Hrs: 8 am-10 pm; Mon-Wed to 2:30 pm; Sun to 4 pm; Sun brunch from 11:30 am. Res accepted, required for Sun brunch. Amer, Mexican menu. Bar. Bkfst $2-$4.75, lunch $4-$6.95, dinner $8.75-$24.95. Sun brunch $10.95. Specialties: red snapper, prime rib. Salad bar. View of golf course. Cr cds: A, C, D, DS, MC, V.

Brownwood

(C-5) See also Comanche

Pop 18,813 **Elev** 1,342 ft
Area code 915
Information Brown County Chamber of Commerce, 521 E Baker, PO Box 880, 76804; 915/649-9535

What to See and Do

Douglas MacArthur Academy of Freedom. Incl Hall of Christian Civilization, with one of Texas's largest murals; Mediterranean Hall, with reproduction of the Rosetta Stone; and MacArthur Exhibit Gallery, containing memorabilia of the famous general. Tours (daily; closed school hols). Howard Payne University campus, Austin and Coggin Sts. Phone 915/649-8700. **FREE**

Lake Brownwood State Park. Approx 540 acres on a 7,300-acre lake. Swimming, fishing, boating (ramps); hiking trails, picnicking, concessions (seasonal), multiuse campsites, RV facilities, cabins, shelters. (Daily) Standard fees. 16 mi NW on TX 279, then 6 mi E on Park Rd 15. Phone 915/784-5223. ¢

Motel/Motor Lodge

★★ **DAYS INN.** *515 E Commerce St (76801). 915/646-2551; fax 915/643-*

6064; *res* 800/329-7466. 138 rms, 2 story. S, D $42-$48; under 18 free. Crib $5. Pet accepted; $15. TV; cable (premium). Pool; whirlpool; sauna. Complimentary continental bkfst. Coffee in rms. Ck-out noon. Coin lndry. Meeting rms. Business servs avail. In-rm modem link. Refrigerators, microwaves avail. Cr cds: A, C, D, DS, JCB, MC, V.

D ⊶ ⊠ ⊛ SC

Bryan/College Station

(D-7) *See also Huntsville*

Pop 65,660 **Elev** Bryan, 367 ft; College Station, 308 ft **Area code** 979

Information Bryan/College Station Convention & Visitors Bureau, 715 University Dr E, College Station 77840; 979/260-9898 or 800/777-8292

Web www.b-cs.com

What to See and Do

The Brazos Valley Museum of Natural History. Exhibits focus on archeology and natural history of the Brazos Valley; incl hands-on Discovery Room featuring live animals. (Mon-Sat; closed hols) 3232 Briarcrest Dr, Bryan. Phone 979/776-2195. ¢¢¢

Messina Hof Wine Cellars. Winery and vineyard tours, lakeside picnic area. Tasting rm, gift shop. Tours (fee). (Daily; closed hols) 5 mi NE of Bryan on TX 21, Old Reliance exit, then follow signs. **FREE**

Texas A&M University. (1876) 44,000 students. This school is the oldest public institution of higher education in the state. It ranks among the top ten institutions in research and development. Enrollments in engineering, agriculture, business, veterinary medicine, and architecture are among the largest in the country. On its attractive 5,200-acre campus, limited tours are avail of the creamery, the oceanography-meteorology building with observation deck, the Memorial Student Center art exhibits, rare gun collection, nuclear science center, cyclotron, and branding iron exhibit. Aggieland Visitor

Center has audiovisual programs (Mon-Fri; two-wk advance notice requested). Phone 979/845-5851.

Motels/Motor Lodges

★★ **BEST WESTERN AT CHIMNEY HILL.** *901 University Dr , College Station (77840). 979/260-9150; fax 979/846-0467; res 800/780-7234. www.ssrs.com/bestwest/location.htm.* 98 rms, 2 story. S $59; D $60-$64; suites $125-$150; under 16 free; higher rates special events. Crib avail. TV; cable. Pool. Complimentary continental bkfst. Coffee in rms. Restaurant adj 4-10 pm. Bar to midnight. Ck-out noon. Coin lndry. Cr cds: A, C, D, DS, MC, V.

D ⊠ ⊠ ⊛ SC

★★ **COMFORT INN.** *104 Texas Ave S, College Station (77840). 979/846-7333; fax 979/846-5479; toll-free 800/228-5150. www.comfortinn.com.* 114 rms, 3 story. S $45-$70; D $50-$75; each addl $5; under 18 free; higher rates special events. TV; cable (premium) Pool; whirlpool. Complimentary continental bkfst. Ck-out noon. Coin lndry. Meeting rm. Valet serv. Free airport, bus depot transportation. Picnic tables, grills. Cr cds: A, C, D, DS, MC, V.

D ⊠ ⊠ ⊛ SC

★★ **FAIRFIELD INN.** *4613 S Texas Ave, Bryan (77802). 979/268-1552; res 800/228-2800. www.fairfieldinn.com.* 62 rms, 3 story. S, D $63.95-$115; under 18 free; higher rates special events. Crib avail. TV; cable (premium). Indoor pool; whirlpool. Complimentary continental bkfst. Restaurant opp 10 am-11 pm. Ck-out noon. Meeting rm. Game rm. Some refrigerators; microwaves avail. Cr cds: A, D, DS, MC, V.

D ⊁ ⊠ ⊠ ⊛

★★ **HAMPTON INN.** *320 S Texas Ave, College Station (77840). 979/846-0184; fax 979/268-5807; res 800/426-7866. www.hamptoninn.com.* 134 rms, 4 story. S, D $76; under 18 free; higher rates special events. Crib free. TV; cable (premium). Pool. Complimentary continental bkfst. Restaurant nearby. Ck-out noon. Meeting rm. Business servs avail. In-rm modem link. Valet serv. Airport, bus depot transportation. Cr cds: A, D, DS, MC, V.

★★ **HOLIDAY INN.** *1503 Texas Ave S, College Station (77840). 979/693-1736; res 800/465-4329. www.holiday-inn.com.* 125 rms, 6 story. S $59-$75; D $65-$75; each addl $6; under 19 free. Crib free. Pet accepted, some restrictions; $25. TV; cable (premium). Pool; poolside serv. Restaurant 6 am-2 pm, 5-9 pm; Sun 7 am-2 pm. Rm serv. Bar. Ck-out noon. Meeting rms. In-rm modem link. Free airport transportation. Health club privileges. Some refrigerators. Cr cds: A, C, DS, MC, V.

★★ **LA QUINTA MOTOR INN.** *607 Texas Ave S, College Station (77840). 979/696-7777; fax 979/696-0531; toll-free 800/531-5900. www.laquinta.com.* 176 rms. S $79-$99; D $69-$89; each addl $10; under 18 free. Crib free. Pet accepted. TV; cable (premium). Pool. Complimentary continental bkfst. Restaurant adj open 24 hrs. Ck-out noon. In-rm modem link. Free airport transportation. Texas A & M Univ opp. Cr cds: A, C, D, DS, MC, V.

★ **MANOR HOUSE INN.** *2504 Texas Ave S, College Station (77840). 979/764-9540; fax 979/693-2430; toll-free 800/231-4100. www.manorhouse inn.com.* 117 rms, 2 story. S, D $57-$62; suites $89; under 16 free; higher rates: hols, special events. Crib $7. Pet accepted; $50. TV; cable (premium). Pool. Complimentary continental bkfst. Restaurant adj open 24 hrs. Ck-out noon. Meeting rms. In-rm modem link. Valet serv. Free airport transportation. Health club privileges. Refrigerators. Cr cds: A, C, D, DS, MC, V.

Hotel

★★★ **HILTON.** *801 University Dr E, College Station (77840). 979/693-7500; fax 979/260-1931; res 800/445-8667. www.hiltoncs.com.* 303 rms, 11 story. S $100-$125; D $110-$135; each addl $10; suites $110-$250; family rates. Crib free. Pet accepted, some restrictions; $50 refundable. TV; cable (premium). Pool; poolside serv. Restaurant 6 am-10 pm; Fri, Sat to 11 pm. Bar 11 am-midnight; Fri, Sat to 1 am; Sun noon-midnight; entertainment. Meeting rms. Business servs avail. In-rm modem link. Gift shop. Free airport transportation. Exercise equipt. Some refrigerators, in-rm whirlpools. Microwaves avail. Private patios, balconies. Cr cds: A, C, D, DS, MC, V.

Restaurant

★ **JOSE'S.** *3824 Texas Ave S, Bryan (77802). 979/268-0036.* Hrs: 11 am-9:45 pm. Closed Mon; most major hols. Mexican menu. Bar. Lunch $3.95-$16.95, dinner $4.50-$16.99. Child's menu. Specialties: tacos al carbon, chimichangas, filet de Huachinango. Cr cds: A, DS, MC, V.

Burnet

See also Austin, Georgetown, Johnson City

Founded 1849 **Pop** 4,735 **Elev** 1,300 ft **Area code** 512 **Zip** 78611

Information Chamber of Commerce, 703 Buchanan Dr; 512/756-4297

Web www.burnetchamber.com

What to See and Do

Fort Croghan Museum. One of eight frontier forts established 1848-1849 to protect settlements. Two original stone bldgs, blacksmith shop, one-rm schoolhouse relocated buildings; visitor center; museum displays 1,400 early pioneer artifacts; displays relating to Civilian Conservation Corps. (Apr-Sept, Thurs-Sat) 1 mi W on TX 29. Phone 512/756-8281. **Donation**

Inks Lake State Park. A 1,200-acre recreation area. Swimming, fishing, boating (ramps); hiking, golf, concessions, campsites (dump station). Standard fees. (Daily) 9 mi W on TX 29, then S on Park Rd 4. Phone 512/793-2223. ¢¢

Lake Buchanan. Larger than Inks Lake; water sports. 3 mi W on TX 29. Phone 512/793-2803.

Longhorn Cavern State Park. In the Highland Lakes country on the Colorado River, this 639-acre tract provides picnicking facilities in addition to a museum of the Civilian Conservation Corps (CCC) and the extremely large cavern. Guided tours. (Daily) 6 mi S on US 281, then 6 mi W on Park Rd 4. Phone 512/756-4680. ¢¢¢

Special Event

Bluebonnet Festival. On the square. Second wkend Apr.

Canyon

(G-1) *See also Amarillo, Hereford*

Pop 12,875 **Elev** 3,551 ft
Area code 806 **Zip** 79015
Information Chamber of Commerce, 1518 5th Ave, PO Box 8; 806/655-1183

What to See and Do

Palo Duro Canyon State Park. Approx 16,400 acres of colorful scenery. Hiking trail, saddle horses (fee). Picnicking, concession, improved campsites (dump station). (See SPECIAL EVENT) Standard fees. (Daily) 12 mi E on TX 217 to Park Rd 5. Phone 806/488-2227. ¢¢

Panhandle-Plains Historical Museum. Texas's largest state museum; exhibits incl Western heritage, petroleum, paleontology, transportation, and fine art. (Daily; closed hols) 2401 4th Ave, on campus of West Texas A&M University. Phone 806/651-2244. ¢¢

Special Event

Texas. Amphitheater, Palo Duro Canyon State Park. Musical drama by Paul Green depicting Texas life in the 1880s. Outdoors. Pre-performance barbecue. Thurs-Tues eves. Contact PO Box 268. Phone 806/655-2181. Mid-June-late-Aug.

B&Bs/Small Inns

★★ **COUNTRY HOME BED AND BREAKFAST.** *8th St (79015). 806/655-7636. www.countryhome weddings.com.* 4 rms, 2 share baths, 2 story. No rm phones. S, D $85-$95. Crib free. Whirlpools. Complimentary full bkfst. Ck-out 11 am, ck-in 4-7 pm. Luggage handling. Country home furnished with antiques. Cr cds: A, D, MC, V.
D ⊅ 🐾 SC

★★★ **HUDSPETH HOUSE.** *1905 4th Ave (79015). 806/655-9800; fax 806/655-7457; toll-free 800/655-9809. www.hudspethinn.com.* 8 rms, 3 story. June-Aug: S, D $60-$110; lower rates rest of yr. Crib free. TV; cable (premium). Complimentary full bkfst. Business servs avail. In-rm modem link. Ck-out 11 am, ck-in 3 pm. Free airport transportation. Fireplaces. Antiques. Restored house (1909) on Texas Historical Register. Cr cds: A, DS, MC, V.
⊅ 🐾

Childress

(G-2) *See also Quanah, Vernon*

Pop 6,778 **Elev** 1,877 ft
Area code 940 **Zip** 79201
Information Chamber of Commerce, PO Box 35; 940/937-2567

What to See and Do

Childress County Heritage Museum. Housed in historic US Post Office building; prehistoric and Native American artifacts; cattle, cotton, and railroad industry exhibits; farming, ranching, and pioneer displays; period rms, antique carriage rm. (Mon-Fri or by appt) 210 3rd St NW. Phone 940/937-2261. **FREE**

Special Event

Childress County Old Settlers' Reunion. Rodeo Old Settlers Arena. Celebrated for more than 100 yrs. Memorial, parade, barbecue, rodeo, dance. Three days third wkend July. Phone 940/597-6241.

Clarendon

See also Amarillo

Founded 1878 **Pop** 1,974 **Elev** 2,727 ft **Area code** 806 **Zip** 79226
Information Chamber of Commerce, 318 S Kearney, PO Box 730; 806/874-2421 or 800/579-4023

What to See and Do

Greenbelt Lake. Swimming, water-skiing, fishing, boating (ramps, marina); 18-hole golf (fee), picnicking, camping, tent and trailer sites (hookups, dump station). Some fees. (Daily) 4 mi N on TX 70. Phone 806/874-2746. ¢

Saints Roost Museum. (Thurs-Sun; closed hols) TX 70 S. Phone 806/874-2746. **FREE**

Motel/Motor Lodge

★ **WESTERN SKIES MOTEL.** *800 W 2nd St (79226). 806/874-3501; fax 806/874-5303.* 23 rms. S $38-$40; D $45-$50; each addl $5. Crib $5. Pet accepted, some restrictions. TV; cable. Heated pool. Playground. Complimentary coffee. Restaurant nearby. Ck-out 11 am. Business servs avail. Some refrigerators. Cr cds: A, DS, MC, V.

Cleburne

(C-6) *See also Arlington-Grand Prairie, Dallas, Fort Worth*

Pop 26,005
Information Chamber of Commerce, 1511 W Henderson St, PO Box 701; 817/645-2455
Web www.cleburnechamber.com

What to See and Do

Layland Museum. Southwest Native American collection, early pottery,

fossils; Civil War exhibit, local history, Santa Fe Railroad caboose, and artifacts; research library. (Mon-Fri; closed hols) 201 N Caddo St. Phone 817/645-0940. **FREE**

State parks.

Cleburne. Approx 500 acres. Swimming, fishing, boating (ramp, rentals); hiking, picnicking, concession, improved camping, tent and trailer sites (dump station). Standard fees. (Daily) 6 mi SW on US 67, then 6 mi SW on Park Rd 21. Phone 817/645-4215. ¢

Dinosaur Valley. Approx 1,500 acres. Swimming, fishing; hiking, picnicking, playground, camping, tent and trailer sites (hookups, dump station). Standard fees. (Daily) 24 mi SW on US 67 to Park Rd 59, near Glen Rose. Phone 254/897-4588. ¢¢

Special Events

Sheriff's Posse PRCA Rodeo. Wkend mid-June.

Christmas Candle Walk. Tour of houses. Early Dec. Phone 817/641-7433.

College Station

(see Bryan/College Station)

Comanche

See also Brownwood, Stephenville

Pop 4,482 **Elev** 1,358 ft
Information Chamber of Commerce, 100 Indian Creek Dr, PO Box 65; 915/356-3233
Web www.comanchetx.org

What to See and Do

Bicentennial Park. Features Fleming Oak (more than 200 yrs old), historical markers, and stone columns from 1890 courthouse. On town square.

Comanche County Museum. Area history; 13 rms of memorabilia. (Sat and Sun, limited hrs; also by appt) 1 mi W via TX 36 on Moorman Rd. **Donation**

Old Cora. (1856) Oldest original existing courthouse in state. Southwestern corner of town square.

Proctor Lake. Swimming, waterskiing, fishing, boating (ramps); picnicking (fee), camping, tent and trailer sites (most with electricity; fee). (Daily) 10 mi NE on US 67/377. Phone 254/879-2424. ¢

Corpus Christi

(F-6) *See also Alice, Aransas Pass, Kingsville, Port Aransas, Rockport*

Founded 1839 **Pop** 277,454 **Elev** 35 ft
Area code 361
Information Convention & Visitors Bureau, 1201 N Shoreline, 78401; 361/881-1888 or 800/678-6232
Web www.corpuschristi-tx-cvb.org

Corpus Christi was established as a trading post by Colonel Henry L. Kinney in 1839. When the US Army moved in for the Mexican War in 1846, it was described as a "small village of smugglers and lawless men with but few women and no ladies." In its early days Corpus Christi grew and prospered as ranching prospered. Natural gas and oil were discovered in the early 1900s, but the city has remained a livestock and industrial center.

Corpus Christi Bay provides a landlocked harbor with a ship channel to the Gulf through Aransas Pass and Port Aransas. The bay also makes this a resort area, with fishing, swimming, and water sports.

What to See and Do

Asian Cultures Museum & Educational Center. Exhibits on the cultures of Japan, India, China, Korea, and the Philippines. (Tues-Sat; closed hols) 1809 N Chaparral. Phone 361/882-2641. ¢¢

Corpus Christi Museum of Science & History. Permanent exhibits focus on reptiles, minerals, prehistoric and marine life, history of native cultures of Central and North America, ranching, local history. Features 1554 shipwreck artifacts, incl full-scale ship replica; Children's Exhibit. (Tues-Sun; closed Jan 1, Thanksgiving, Dec 25) 1900 N Chaparral St. Phone 361/883-2862. ¢¢¢

Fishing. Fishing boats leave downtown Corpus Christi marina for bay fishing trips and at other piers incl Deep Sea Headquarters and Fisherman's Wharf in Port Aransas for Gulf trips. Skiffs for redfish trout fishing in Laguna Madre may be rented at John F. Kennedy Causeway.

Heritage Park. Nine turn-of-the-century houses in this district give visitors a glimpse of high Victorian architecture in Corpus Christi. (Wed-Sat; closed hols) 1581 N Chaparral, Heritage Park. Phone 361/883-0639. ¢¢

Padre Island. (see). Can be reached via the John F. Kennedy Causeway or from Port Aransas.

Sightseeing tours.

  Flagship Cruises. Peoples St T-Head dock, Corpus Christi Marina. Phone 361/884-1693. ¢¢¢

  Fun Time Coach USA bus tours. Contact 5875 Agnes, 78406. Phone 361/289-7113.

South Texas Institute for the Arts. Building designed by Philip Johnson; permanent and changing exhibits. Free admission Thurs. (Tues-Sun; closed hols) 1902 N Shoreline Blvd. Phone 361/825-3500. ¢¢

⭐ **Texas State Aquarium.** Ten major indoor and outdoor exhibit areas focus on marine plant and animal life indigenous to the Gulf of Mexico; changing exhibits; approx 350,000 gallons of salt water and more than 250 species of sea life. (Daily; closed Thanksgiving, Dec 25) On Corpus Christi Beach. Phone 361/881-1200. ¢¢¢

USS *Lexington*. Recently decomissioned WWII aircraft carrier nicknamed the "Blue Ghost" by Tokyo Rose. Now serves as a naval museum. (Daily; closed Dec 25) Phone 361/888-4873. ¢¢¢

Special Events

Buccaneer Days. Beauty pageant, parades, rodeo, BBQ challenges, sports events, carnival, music festival, art jamboree, and drama. Early-Apr-May. Phone 361/882-3242.

Bay Jammin' Concerts. Cole Park Amphitheater Under the Stars. Contemporary music. Thurs eves late May-mid-Aug, also Sat near July 4.

C-101 C-Sculptures. Sand castle building and sculpting. June. Phone 361/289-0111.

Summer Bayfront Concerts. Cole Park Amphitheater Under the Stars. Classic music and show tunes. Thurs eves in summer.

Texas Jazz Festival. Concerts. Phone 361/883-4500. Late July.

Bayfest. Six blks downtown closed to private vehicles; shuttle buses and trains. International foods, arts and crafts, entertainment. Phone 361/887-0868. Late Sept.

Harbor Lights Celebration. Lighting of boats in marina. Lighting of 70-ft tree of lights. Children's parade. Gingerbread and holiday tree village. First wkend Dec. Phone 361/985-1555.

Motels/Motor Lodges

★★ **COMFORT SUITES.** 3925 S Padre Island Dr (78415). 361/225-2500; fax 361/225-3000; res 800/228-5150. www.choicehotels.com. 68 suites, 2 story. S $59-$89; D $69-$99; each addl $10; under 18 free. Crib $5. TV; cable (premium). Complimentary continental bkfst. Ck-out noon. Business servs avail. In-rm modem link. Coin lndry. Exercise equipt. Pool; whirlpool. Refrigerators, microwaves. Cr cds: A, C, D, DS, JCB, MC, V.

⊡ ⇔ 🏋 ⊒ 🔥

★ **DAYS INN.** 4302 Surfside Blvd (78402). 361/882-3297; fax 361/882-6865; toll-free 800/329-7466. www.daysinn.com. 56 rms, 3 story. Mid-May-Labor Day: S, D $59-$89; each addl $5; under 12 free; lower rates rest of yr. Crib free. TV; cable. Pool. Complimentary continental bkfst. Coffee in rms. Ck-out 11 am. Business servs avail. In-rm modem link. On beach. Cr cds: A, C, D, DS, MC, V.

⊡ 🐾 ⊒ 🔥 SC

★★ **DRURY INN.** 2021 N Padre Island Dr (78408). 361/289-8200; res 800/325-8300. www.druryinn.com. 105 units, 4 story, 10 suites. S $61-$74.99; D, suites $69-$77; under 18 free. Crib free. Pet accepted, some restrictions. TV; cable (premium), VCR avail. Pool. Complimentary continental bkfst. Ck-out noon. Meeting rms. Business servs avail. In-rm modem link. Valet serv. Free airport transportation. Health club privileges. Refrigerator in suites. Cr cds: A, C, D, DS, MC, V.

⊡ 🐾 ⇔ ⊒ 🔥 SC

★ **GULFSTREAM CONDOMINIUM APARTMENTS.** 14810 Windward Dr (78418). 361/949-8061; fax 361/949-1497; toll-free 800/542-7368. 6 kit. apts (2-bedrm), 6 story. Mar-Aug: S, D $140-$190; under 12 free; lower rates rest of yr. Crib free. TV; cable. Heated pool. Complimentary coffee. Restaurant nearby. Ck-out noon. Coin lndry. Business servs avail. In-rm modem link. Game rm. Lawn games. Balconies. Cr cds: A, DS, MC, V.

⊡ 🐾 ⇔ ⊒ 🔥 SC

★★ **HOLIDAY INN.** 15202 Windward Dr (78418). 361/949-8041; fax 361/949-9139; toll-free 888/949-8041. www.holiday-inn.com. 149 rms, 6 story. Mar-early Sept: S, D $119.95-$189.95; each addl $10; under 19 free; wkly rates; lower rates rest of yr. Crib free. TV; cable (premium). 2 pools; whirlpool, poolside serv. Playground. Restaurant 6:30 am-2 pm, 5-10 pm. Rm serv. Bar 5 pm-2 am. Ck-out 11 am. Meeting rms. In-rm modem link. Tennis privileges, pro. 18-hole golf privileges, greens fee $45, pro. Exercise equipt; sauna. Game rm. Lawn games. Refrigerators, microwaves. Some balconies. Picnic tables. Swimming beach. Cr cds: A, C, D, DS, MC, V.

⊡ 🐾 🏋 🦮 ⊒ 🔥 SC 🎣 🏋

★★ **HOLIDAY INN EMERALD BEACH.** 1102 S Shoreline Blvd (78401). 361/883-5731; fax 361/883-9079; toll-free 800/465-4329. www.holiday-inn.com. 368 rms, 2-7 story. S, D $99-$129; each addl $5; under 18 free; some wkend rates. Pet accepted. TV; cable. Heated pool; whirlpool, poolside serv (summer). Playground. Restaurant 6 am-2 pm, 5-10 pm. Rm serv. Bar 11 am-midnight. Ck-out noon. Meeting rms. Business servs avail. In-rm modem link. Bellhops.

Golf privileges. Exercise equipt; sauna. Game rm. Some private patios, balconies. On beach. Cr cds: A, C, D, DS, ER, JCB, MC, V.

⊡ ⬛ ⬛ ⬛ ⬛ ⬛ ⬛ ⬛ ⬛ SC

★ **ISLAND HOUSE CONDOS.** *15340 Leeward Dr (78418). 361/949-8166; fax 361/949-8904; toll-free 800/333-8806.* 67 kit. apts, 1-3-bedrm, 3 story. May-Sept (2-day min): S, D $125-$240; lower rates rest of yr. Crib free. TV; cable. VCR avail (movies $3.25). Heated pool; wading pool. Restaurant nearby. Ck-out noon. Coin lndry. Business servs avail. Balconies. Picnic tables, grills. On beach. Cr cds: A, DS, MC, V.

⊡ ⬛ ⬛ ⬛ ⬛ ⬛

★★ **LA QUINTA.** *5155 I-37 N (78408). 361/888-5721; fax 361/888-5401; toll-free 800/531-5900. www.laquinta.com.* 123 rms, 2 story. S $65-$72; D $75-$82; suites $91; under 18 free. Crib free. Pet accepted. TV; cable (premium). Pool. Complimentary continental bkfst. Restaurant open 24 hrs. Ck-out noon. Meeting rms. Business servs avail. In-rm modem link. Valet serv. Health club privileges. Cr cds: A, C, D, DS, MC, V.

⊡ ⬛ ⬛ ⬛ SC ⬛

★★ **RAMADA INN BAYFRONT.** *601 N Water St (78401). 361/882-8100; fax 361/888-6540; toll-free 888/298-2054. www.ramada.com.* 200 rms, 10 story. Mid-June-early Sept: S $59-$79; D $59-$89; each addl $10; suites $119-$139; under 17 free; some wkend rates; lower rates rest of yr. Crib free. TV; cable (premium). Pool. Restaurant 6 am-10 pm. Bar 11-2 am. Coffee in rms. Ck-out noon. Coin lndry. Meeting rms. Business servs avail. In-rm modem link. Sundries. Gift shop. Free garage parking. Free airport transportation. Exercise equipt. Balconies. Lobby with 10-story atrium ceiling. Cr cds: A, C, D, DS, ER, JCB, MC, V.

⊡ ⬛ ⬛ SC ⬛ ⬛

★ **RED ROOF INN.** *6301 I-37 (78409). 361/289-6925; fax 361/289-2239; toll-free 800/843-7663. www.redroof.com.* 142 rms, 3 story. S $39.99-$49.99; D $39-$64; suite $74; under 18 free. Crib free. Pet accepted. TV; cable (premium). Pool; whirlpool. Complimentary coffee in lobby. Restaurant adj open 24 hrs. Ck-out 11 am. Business servs avail. In-rm modem link. Cr cds: A, D, DS, MC, V.

⊡ ⬛ ⬛ ⬛ SC

Hotels

★★★ **OMNI CORPUS CHRISTI HOTEL BAYFRONT TOWER.** *900 N Shoreline Blvd (78401). 361/882-1700; fax 361/887-6715; res 800/843-6664. www.omnihotels.com.* 474 units, 20 story. S, D $89-$145; each addl $10; suites $160-$500; under 18 free; wkend rates. Crib free. TV; cable (premium), VCR avail. Indoor/outdoor pool; whirlpool. Restaurant 6:30 am-11 pm. Bar 11 am-midnight. Ck-out noon. Meeting rms. Business center. In-rm modem link. Gift shop. Barber, beauty shop. Free garage parking. Free airport transportation. Exercise equipt; sauna. Massage. Some refrigerators. Balconies. Rms have view of bay. Cr cds: A, D, DS, MC, V.

⊡ ⬛ ⬛ ⬛ ⬛ ⬛ ⬛

★★★ **OMNI CORPUS CHRISTI HOTEL MARINA TOWER.** *707 N Shoreline Blvd (78401). 361/887-1600; fax 361/882-3113; toll-free 800/843-6664. www.omnihotels.com.* 346 units, 20 story, 19 suites. S, D $89-$160; each addl $10; suites $160-$275; under 18 free; wkend rates. Crib free. TV; cable (premium), VCR avail. Indoor/outdoor pool, whirlpool. Restaurant 6:30 am-10 pm. Bar noon-midnight. Ck-out noon. Meeting rms. Business center. In-rm modem link. Gift shop. Free garage parking. Free airport transportation. Exercise equipt; sauna. Some refrigerators. Private balconies. Rms have view of bay. Cr cds: A, D, DS, MC, V.

⊡ ⬛ ⬛ ⬛ ⬛ SC ⬛

★★★ **RADISSON BEACH HOTEL.** *3200 Surfside Blvd (78403). 361/883-9700; fax 361/883-1437; res 800/333-3333. www.radisson.com.* 251 rms, 7 story. Mid-May-mid-Sept: S, D $69-$129; each addl $10; under 12 free; lower rates rest of yr. Crib $5. TV; cable (premium). Heated pool; wading pool, whirlpool, poolside serv. Restaurant 7 am-10 pm. Rm serv. Bar 5-10 pm; Fri, Sat to 11 pm. Ck-out noon. Coin lndry. Meeting rms. Business servs avail. In-rm modem link. Valet serv. Sundries. Lawn games. Balconies. On beach. Wedding chapel. Kite museum off lobby. Near Texas State Aquarium. Cr cds: A, C, D, DS, MC, V.

Corsicana

(C-6) *See also Dallas, Ennis*

All Suite

★★★ **EMBASSY SUITES.** *4337 S Padre Island Dr (78411). 361/853-7899; fax 361/851-1310; res 800/362-2779. www.embassysuites.com.* 150 kit. suites, 3 story. S $109-$129; D $119-$139; each addl $10; under 17 free; wkend rates. Crib free. Pet accepted, some restrictions; $100. TV; cable (premium). Indoor pool; whirlpool. Complimentary bkfst. Restaurant 11 am-11 pm. Coin lndry. Meeting rms. Business servs avail. In-rm modem link. Free airport transportation. Exercise equipt; sauna. Game rm. Refrigerators. Atrium lobby with fountain, plants. Cr cds: A, D, DS, MC, V.

Restaurants

★ **CITY DINER AND OYSTER BAR.** *622 N Water St (78401). 361/883-1643.* Hrs: 11 am-9 pm; Fri, Sat to 10 pm; Sun 11:30 am-9 pm; June-Sept hrs vary. Closed Jan 1, Thanksgiving, Dec 24. Bar. Lunch $4.50-$9.95, dinner $6.50-$14.95. Child's menu. Specializes in seafood, chicken. 1950s diner decor. Cr cds: A, D, DS, MC, V.

★★ **LANDRY'S SEAFOOD HOUSE.** *600 N Shoreline Blvd (78401). 361/882-6666. www.landrysseafood house.com.* Hrs: 11 am-10 pm; Fri, Sat to 11 pm. Bar. Lunch $5.95-$8.95, dinner $7.99-$18.99. Child's menu. Specializes in seafood, steak. Own desserts. Former army housing barge. Views of bay and yacht mooring area. Patio dining. Cr cds: A, D, DS, MC, V.

★ **WATER STREET OYSTER BAR.** *309 N Water St (78401). 361/881-9448.* Hrs: 11 am-11 pm; Fri, Sat to midnight. Closed Thanksgiving, Dec 25. Lunch, dinner $4.95-$15. Child's menu. Specializes in Gulf seafood. Patio. High ceilings, oak furniture. Oyster bar. Cr cds: A, D, DS, MC, V.

Pop 24,485 **Elev** 411 ft **Area code** 903 **Zip** 75110

Information Corsicana Area Chamber of Commerce, 120 N 12th St; 903/874-4731

Web www.corsicana.org

While drilling for fresh water in 1894, citizens of Corsicana were surprised to strike oil instead. With that discovery, one of the first commercial wells west of the Mississippi was dug. This site has now been preserved as Petroleum Park, located on 12th Street in town. Mobil Oil had its beginnings in Corsicana as Magnolia Oil with the construction of the first oil refinery in Texas in 1897. This refinery was also the first of its kind in the west. The rotary drill bit now in universal use was developed by a Corsicanan.

Industries include oil field machinery, textiles, clothing, and food products. Cotton and small grains are grown in the rich blackland of the area, and beef cattle are another important industry.

What to See and Do

The Cook Center. Houses 60-ft domed planetarium, the largest in Texas; museum; indoor and outdoor fossil fuel exhibits. Movie and laser shows (fee). (Mon-Fri; closed hols) 3100 W Collin St, adj to Navarro College. Phone 800/988-5317. ¢¢

Navarro Mills Lake. Swimming, waterskiing, fishing, boating (ramps); nature trail, picnicking, playgrounds, tent and trailer sites (hookups, dump station; fee), shower facilities. (Daily) 20 mi SW on TX 31. Phone 254/578-1431. ¢¢

Pioneer Village. Seventeen restored bldgs, incl house, store, blacksmith shop, trading post, old barn, general shed, tack shed, children's play house, gristmill, jail cell, carriage house with antique vehicles, museums; pre-Civil War documents.

(Daily; closed hols) 912 W Park Ave. Phone 903/654-4846. ¢

Robert S. Reading Indian Artifact Collection. One of the largest collections of arrow points (47,000-54,000) and artifacts in the Southwest. Tours (by appt). (Mon-Fri; closed hols) Navarro College. 3 mi W on US 31. Phone 903/874-6501. **FREE**

Crockett

(C-7) *See also Huntsville, Lufkin, Palestine*

Pop 7,141 **Elev** 366 ft **Area code** 936
Information Houston County Chamber of Commerce, 1100 Edmiston Dr, PO Box 307; 936/544-2359 or 888/269-2359
Web www.crockett.org

What to See and Do

Mission Tejas State Historical Park. Named for Mission San Francisco de los Tejas, the first Spanish mission in Texas. Mission commemorative building; log house (1828-1838). Lake fishing; hiking and nature trails, picnicking, playground, tent and trailer sites (hookups, showers). Standard fees. (Daily) 22 mi NE via TX 21 near Weches, enter on Park Rd 44. Located adj to the Davy Crockett National Forest. Phone 936/687-2394. ¢¢

Monroe-Crook House. (1854) Greek Revival house built by the great-nephew of James Monroe. (Wed, Sat, Sun) 707 E Houston. Phone 936/544-5820. ¢

Special Events

World's Champion Fiddlers' Festival. Second wkend June.

Grapeland Peanut Festival. Second wkend Oct. Phone 936/544-2359.

Crockett Heritage Festival. Military reenactments, costumed characters. Last wkend Oct. Phone 936/544-2359.

Dalhart

(F-1) *See also Amarillo*

Pop 7,237 **Elev** 3,985 ft
Area code 806 **Zip** 79022
Information Chamber of Commerce, 102 E 7th St, PO Box 967; 806/249-5646
Web www.dalhart.org

Special Event

XIT Rodeo & Reunion. DRCA rodeo. 5K "Empty Saddle" run, parade, free barbecue, pony express races, tractor pull, fiddlers contest, arts and crafts, dances, antique car show. Early Aug. Phone 806/249-5646.

Motels/Motor Lodges

★★ **BEST WESTERN.** *102 Scott St (79022). 806/244-5637; fax 806/244-5803; res 800/528-1234. www.bestwestern.com.* 55 rms, 2 story. Late May-mid-Sept: S $50-$60; D $54-$62; each addl $4; higher rates rodeos; lower rates rest of yr. Crib $5. TV; cable (premium). Heated pool. Restaurant 6 am-10 pm. Ck-out 11 am. Meeting rm. Some refrigerators. Cr cds: A, C, D, DS, JCB, MC, V.
⊷ ⊠ 🐾

★★ **COMFORT INN.** *Hwy 54 E (79022). 806/249-8585; fax 806/249-2827; res 800/228-5150. www.choicehotels.com.* 36 rms. S $36-$51; D $45-$65. Crib $5. TV; cable (premium). Heated pool. Complimentary continental bkfst. Coffee in rms. Restaurant adj 11 am-10 pm. Ck-out 11 am. Business servs avail. Some refrigerators. Cr cds: A, D, DS, MC, V.
D ⊷ ⊠ 🐾

★ **DAYS INN .** *701 Liberal St (79022). 806/244-5246; fax 806/244-0805; res 800/329-7466. www.daysinn.com.* 43 rms, 2 story. S $55-$69; D $70-$120; each addl $5. Crib free. Pet accepted, some restrictions. TV; cable (premium). Indoor pool; whirlpool. Complimentary continental bkfst. Restaurant nearby. Ck-out 11 am. Business servs avail. Exercise equipt. Cr cds: A, C, D, DS, MC, V.
D ⊷ ⳓ ⊠ 🐾 ⳓ

Dallas (B-6)

Founded 1841 **Pop** 1,188,580
Elev 468 ft **Area code** 214, 972, 469

Information Dallas Convention &
Visitors Bureau, 325 N St. Paul St,
Suite 2000, 75201; 214/571-1000

Web www.dallascvb.com

Suburbs Arlington-Grand Prairie,
Denton, Ennis, Fort Worth,
Greenville, McKinney. (See individual alphabetical listings.)

The city of Dallas, the Southwest's largest business center, is also one of the nation's leading fashion centers. A variety of businesses and industries make their homes in Dallas, primarily those involved in oil, aerospace, and insurance. Far from the typical image of a Texas city, Dallas is a well-dressed, sophisticated city that tends toward formality. A major convention city, Dallas is accustomed to showing visitors a good time and is well-equipped to do so.

The city originated with the establishment of John Neely Bryan's trading post on the Upper Trinity River in 1841. Two years later the town was named Dallas, after one of several men by that name—no one is quite sure which. By the mid-1870s, Dallas had become a thriving business town with a cosmopolitan air unique to the region.

The cultivation of Dallas's urbane cultural persona began in 1855 with the arrival of French, Swiss, and Belgian settlers looking to build a Utopian colony. Among them were scientists, artists, writers, naturalists, and musicians. The colony was a failure, but the nucleus of culture remained in the heart of this young community on the frontier. Today ballet, symphony, opera, and theater are still enjoyed in Dallas, as are numerous museums and exhibitions.

Additional Visitor Information

For additional accommodations, see DALLAS/FORT WORTH AIRPORT AREA, which follows DALLAS.

For further information contact the Dallas Convention & Visitors Bureau, 1201 Elm St, Suite 2000, 75270; phone 214/571-1000; the Visitor Information Center, North Park Center; or the Visitor Information Center at West End Market Place, 603 Munger.

Transportation

Airport. Love Field, phone 214/670-6080; also see DALLAS/FORT WORTH AIRPORT AREA.

Car Rental Agencies. See IMPORTANT TOLL-FREE NUMBERS.

Public Transportation. Buses (Dallas Area Rapid Transit), phone 214/979-1111.

Rail Passenger Service. Amtrak 800/872-7245.

What to See and Do

African American Museum. Magnificent building of ivory-hued stone houses a library, research center, and numerous permanent and visiting exhibits. 3536 Grand Ave, in Fair Park. Phone 214/565-9026. **FREE**

Biblical Arts Center. Building features early Christian-era architecture; museum/gallery areas display Biblical art. Life-size replica of Garden Tomb of Christ located in Atrium Courtyard. Light and sound presentation of 124-by-20-ft oil painting featuring more than 200 Biblical characters (fee). (Tues-Sun; closed hols) 7500 Park Ln at Boedeker; 1 blk W of Central Expy (US 75). Phone 214/691-4661. **FREE**

Coach USA bus tours. Contact 710 E Davis St, Grand Prairie, 75050. Phone 972/263-0294.

Conspiracy Museum. Museum features displays, films, and old newspaper articles surrounding the assassinations of famous politicians. (Daily) 110 S Market St. Phone 214/741-3040. ¢¢

Dallas Arboretum and Botanical Garden. Four permanent, themed gardens situated on 66 acres; featured areas incl Mimi's Garden, with two acres of perennials; Jonsson Color and Palmer Fern Dell gardens. Self-guided tours. (Daily) 8617 Garland Rd, on White Rock Lake. Phone 214/327-4901. ¢¢¢

Dallas Market Center Complex. World's largest wholesale merchandise mart, consists of the World Trade Center, Trade Mart, Market Hall, International Apparel Mart-Dallas, and International Menswear Mart-Dallas. Tours by appt (fee). 2100 Stemmons Fwy. Phone 214/655-6100.

Dallas Museum of Art. Pre-Columbian, 18th- and 19th-century, and contemporary American art; African and Asian art; European painting and sculpture; decorative arts incl Bybee Collection of American Furniture and Emery Reves Collection. Special exhibitions (fees). (Tues-Sun; closed hols) 1717 N Harwood St. Phone 214/922-1200. **FREE**

Dallas Symphony Orchestra. Classical and pops programs; also pop, jazz, and country artists. (Sept-May) Morton H. Meyerson Symphony Center, Pearl and Flora Sts. Phone 214/692-0203.

Dallas Theater Center. (1959) Professional theater, occupies two performing spaces. The building at 3636 Turtle Creek Blvd, designed by Frank Lloyd Wright, houses the Kalita Humphreys Theater (approx 500 seats); at 2401 Flora St is the Arts District Theater, with flexible seating and staging arrangements. (Sept-May, Tues-Sun) Phone 214/522-8499.

Dallas Zoo. More than 1,400 mammals, reptiles, and birds on 85 landscaped acres. The 25-acre "Wilds of Africa" exhibit features a one-mi monorail ride, nature trail, African Plaza, chimpanzee forest, and gorilla conservation research center; animals roam freely through six naturalistic habitats. Parking fee. (Daily; closed Dec 25) 650 E S.R.L. Thornton Fwy, S on I-35, Marsalis exit. Phone 214/670-5656. ¢¢¢

Fair Park Dallas. Comprised of 277 landscaped acres with Art Deco buildings and numerous entertainment and cultural facilities. Site of the annual state fair (see SPECIAL EVENTS), one of the world's largest expositions. (Daily) 1300 Robert B. McCollum Blvd. Phone 214/670-8400. Here are

    Age of Steam Railroad Museum. Collection of steam locomotives and passenger cars, incl a locomotive weighing 1.2 million pounds; electric locomotive that pulled Robert F. Kennedy's funeral train. (Wed-Sun, weather permitting; during State Fair, daily) 1105 Washington St in Fair Park. Phone 214/428-0101. ¢¢

Dallas Aquarium. More than 375 species of marine, freshwater, and tropical fish; amphibians and reptiles. (Daily; closed Thanksgiving, Dec 25) 1st Ave and M.L. King Jr. Blvd. Phone 214/670-8443. ¢¢

Dallas Museum of Natural History. Fifty habitat groups exhibit diverse plant and animal life of Texas. Fossil hall exhibits animals of prehistoric Texas, incl a reconstructed tenontosaurus. Changing exhibits. (Daily; closed Jan 1, Thanksgiving, Dec 25) 3535 Grand Ave at Robert B. Cullum Blvd. Phone 214/421-3466. ¢¢¢

Hall of State. Historic landmark; fine example of American Art Deco architecture. Murals, statuary, and changing exhibits depict the history of Texas. (Tues-Sun; closed Jan 1, Dec 25) Research Center located in East Texas Room; lower floor houses Dallas Historical Society offices. 3939 Grand Ave. Phone 214/421-0281. **FREE**

Music Hall. Performances by the Dallas Opera; Dallas Summer Musicals and concerts. (See SPECIAL EVENTS) 909 1st Ave, at Parry. Phone 214/565-1116.

The Science Place. Hands-on exhibits on energy, chemistry, physics, medical sciences, growth, and development; "Kids Place" exhibit; IMAX Theatre. (Daily) Planetarium shows (daily). 1318 2nd Ave. Phone 214/428-5555. ¢¢¢

The Southwestern Bell Cotton Bowl. Scene of the college football classic each Jan 1 and other special events throughout the yr.

Texas Discovery Gardens. Gardens; tropical conservatory; Xeriscape Garden; display with Braille markers. (Tues-Sun; closed hols) 2nd Ave and M.L. King Jr. Blvd. Phone 214/428-7476. **FREE**

Grapevine Lake. Swimming, water-skiing, fishing, boating (ramps, rentals); hiking, bicycle and bridle trails, picnicking, camping (tent and trailer sites; hookups, dump station). Fee for camping, some recreation areas. (Daily) 110 Fairway Dr via TX 26. Phone 817/481-4541.

John F. Kennedy Memorial Plaza. A 30-ft monument, designed by Philip Johnson, is situated 200 yards from the spot where the president was assassinated. Main, Houston, and Market Sts.

McKinney Avenue Transit Authority. Four restored, vintage electric trolley cars operate over a three-mi route, mainly along McKinney Ave, which connects central Dallas (beginning at Ross Ave and St. Paul St) with McKinney Ave's popular restaurants, nightclubs, and shops. Some tracks date back 100 yrs to Dallas's original trolley system. (Daily) 3153 Oak Grove. Phone 214/855-0006. ¢

Meadows School of the Arts. Houses Greer Garson Theatre, with classic thrust stage design, Bob Hope and Margo Jones theaters, with university productions; Caruth Auditorium, a 490-seat concert hall with Fisk pipe organ. (Aug-May; some fees). Also Meadows Museum, with the most encyclopedic collection of 15th-20th-century Spanish art in the US; sculpture garden. (Daily; closed school hols) Southern Methodist University campus, Bishop and Binkley Blvd. ¢¢¢

Old City Park Museum. Museum of architectural and cultural history, operated by the Dallas County Heritage Society. A 13-acre park with 38 restored north-central Texas structures (1840-1910). Self-guided tours (one to two hrs) of buildings (Tues-Sun). Sights incl Millermore Mansion, gazebo, McCall's store, Brent Place restaurant. 1717 Gano St. Jct I-30, Gano and Harwood Sts. Phone 214/421-5141. ¢¢

Professional sports.

Dallas Cowboys (NFL). Texas Stadium, 2401 E Airport Fwy, Irving, TX. Phone 972/556-9900.

Dallas Mavericks (NBA). Reunion Arena, 2500 Victory Ave. Phone 214/747-MAVS.

Dallas Stars (NHL). Dr. Pepper Star Center, 2500 Victory Ave, Irving, TX.

Texas Rangers (MLB). The Ballpark at Arlington, jct of TX 360 and I-30. Phone 817/273-5222.

Six Flags Over Texas. 16 mi W, at jct TX 360, I-30. (See ARLINGTON-GRAND PRAIRIE) Phone 817/640-8900.

⭐ **"The Sixth Floor".** On sixth floor of former Texas School Book Depository Building; films, photographs, and original documents examining the life, death, and legacy of President Kennedy within the context of American history. Audio tour avail (fee). (Daily; closed Thanksgiving, Dec 25) 411 Elm St. Phone 214/747-6660. ¢¢¢

White Rock Lake and Greenbelt Park. Fishing, boating (marina), sailboat races (summer, most Sun); jogging and hiking trails, nature areas, picnicking, cultural center. (Daily) 5 mi NE on Garland Rd. Phone 214/670-8281. **FREE**

Special Events

Southwestern Bell Cotton Bowl Classic. Fair Park. Jan 1. Phone 214/634-7525.

Boat Show. Market Hall. Late January-Feb and mid-July.

Scarborough Faire Renaissance. 30 mi S on I-35 E, exit 399A, near Waxahachie. Re-creation of a 16th-century English village at market time; entertainment, jousting, crafts, games, food and drink. Phone 972/938-1888. Eight wkends, mid-Apr-early-June. ¢¢¢¢

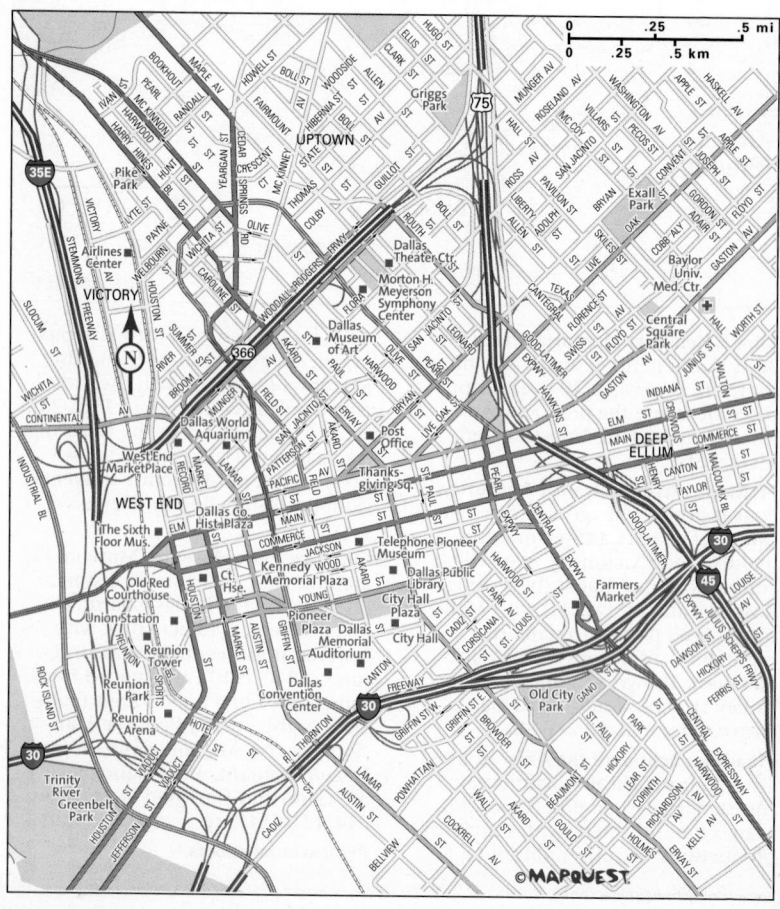

Byron Nelson Golf Classic. Four Seasons Club Resort. Phone 214/742-3896. May.

Summer musicals. Music Hall, Fair Park. Featuring Broadway musicals; Tues-Sun. Phone 214/565-1116. June-early Oct.

State Fair of Texas. State Fair Park. Phone 214/565-9931. Sept-Oct.

Dallas Opera. Music Hall, Fair Park. Internationally famed opera seasons. For schedule and tickets contact 3102 Oak Lawn Ave, Suite 450, 75219. Phone 214/443-1043. Nov-Feb.

Motels/Motor Lodges

★★ **BEST WESTERN.** *13333 N Stemmons Fwy, Farmers Branch (75234). 972/241-8521; fax 972/243-4103; res 800/528-1234. www.bestwestern.com.* 185 rms, 2 story. S, D $49-$79; each addl $6; suites $125; under 12 free; wkend rates. Pet accepted; $20 deposit. TV; cable (premium). Pool; whirlpool, sauna. Comlimentary bkfst. Coffee in rms. Restaurant 6:30 am-10 pm; hrs vary Sat, Sun. Rm serv. Bar 5 pm-2 am. Ck-out 11 am. Coin lndry. Meeting rms. Business servs avail. In-rm modem link. Valet serv. Airport transportation. Health club privileges. Microwaves avail. Cr cds: A, C, D, DS, MC, V.

⬛🔧🐾⛱✈🔼🔥🔥

★★ **BEST WESTERN .** *4154 Preferred Pl (75237). 972/298-4747; fax 972/283-1305; toll-free 800/528-1234. www.bestwestern.com.* 119 rms, 2 story. S, D $64; family, wkly, wkend, hol rates; higher rates auto races. Crib free. TV; cable (premium). Pool. Complimentary continental bkfst. Restaurant nearby. Ck-out noon. Coin lndry. Meeting rms. Business servs avail. In-rm modem link. Sundries. Microwaves avail. Adj to shopping mall. Cr cds: A, C, D, DS, MC, V.

⬛⛱🔼🔥 SC

★★ **BEST WESTERN PARK SUITES.** *640 Park Blvd E, Plano (75074). 972/578-2243; fax 972/578-0563; res 800/528-1234. www.bestwestern.com.* 83 rms, 3 story. S, D $89-$125; family rates; under 18 free. Crib free. Pet accepted, some restrictions. TV; cable (premium). Complimentary continental bkfst.

Complimentary coffee in rms. Restaurant nearby. Bar. Ck-out noon. Meeting rms. Business servs avail. In-rm modem link. Valet serv. Sundries. Coin lndry. Exercise equipt. Pool; whirlpool. Refrigerators, microwaves; some in-rm whirlpools. Cr cds: A, C, D, DS, MC, V.

⬛🔧⛱🔼🔥🔼

★★ **COMFORT INN NORTH DALLAS.** *14040 Stemmons Rd, Farmers Branch (75234). 972/406-3030; fax 972/406-2929; res 800/228-5150. www.choicehotels.com.* 50 rms, 2 story. May-Sept: S $55-$95; D $55-$110; each addl $5; family, wkend, wkly rates; higher rates special events; lower rates rest of yr. Crib free. TV; cable (premium). Complimentary continental bkfst. Coffee in rms. Restaurant adj open 24 hrs. Ck-out 11 am. Meeting rms. Business servs avail. In-rm modem link. Sundries. Coin lndry. Pool; whirlpool. Microwaves avail. Cr cds: A, C, D, DS, JCB, MC, V.

⬛🔼🔥⛱

★★ **COURTYARD BY MARRIOTT.** *2150 Market Center Blvd (75207). 214/653-1166; fax 214/653-1892; res 800/321-2211. www.courtyard.com.* 184 rms, 5 story. S, D $109-$134; each addl $10; under 12 free. Crib free. TV; cable (premium), VCR avail. Pool; whirlpool. Complimentary coffee in rms. Restaurant 6:30 am-2 pm, 4:30-10:30 pm. Bar. Ck-out 1 pm. Coin lndry. Meeting rms. Business center. In-rm modem link. Sundries. Valet serv. Exercise equipt. Health club privileges. Some refrigerators; microwaves avail. Balconies. Cr cds: A, C, D, DS, ER, JCB, MC, V.

⬛🔧🔼⛱🔼🔼🔥🔼

★★ **COURTYARD BY MARRIOTT.** *2383 Stemmons Trl (75220). 214/352-7676; fax 214/352-4914; toll-free 800/321-2211. www.courtyard.com.* 146 rms, 3 story. S $99; D $109; suites $109-$119; under 12 free; wkly rates. Crib free. TV; cable (premium). Pool; whirlpool. Complimentary coffee in rms. Bar 5-11 pm. Ck-out 1 pm. Coin lndry. Meeting rms. Business servs avail. In-rm modem link. Valet serv. Sundries. Exercise equipt.

Refrigerators, microwaves avail. Balconies. Cr cds: A, D, DS, MC, V.

★★ **DRURY INN DALLAS NORTH.**
2421 Walnut Hill Ln (75229). 972/484-3330; res 800/378-7946. www.drury inn.com. 130 rms, 4 story. S $68-$74; D $78-$84; each addl $10; under 18 free. TV; cable (premium). Pool. Complimentary continental bkfst. Coffee in rms. Restaurant adj open 24 hrs. Ck-out noon. Meeting rms. Business servs avail. In-rm modem link. Valet serv. Sundries. Some refrigerators; microwaves avail. Cr cds: A, C, D, DS, MC, V.

★★ **FAIRFIELD INN.** *2110 Market Center Blvd (75207). 214/760-8800; fax 214/760-1659; res 800/228-2800. www.fairfieldinn.com.* 117 rms, 3 story. S $69-$79; D $74-$84; each addl $5; under 12 free. Crib free. TV; cable (premium). Indoor pool; whirlpool. Complimentary continental bkfst. Restaurant adj 6:30 am-10 pm. Ck-out noon. Valet serv. Health club privileges. Cr cds: A, C, D, DS, MC, V.

★★ **HAMPTON INN DOWNTOWN.**
1015 Elm St (75202). 214/742-5678; fax 214/744-6167; res 800/426-7866. www.hamptoninn.com. 311 rms, 23 story. S, D $149; under 16 free; wkend rates; higher rates special events. Crib free. Pet accepted; $125 ($100 refundable). In/out parking $5. TV; cable (premium). Complimentary continental bkfst. Coffee in rms. Restaurant nearby. Ck-out noon. Business servs avail. In-rm modem link. Concierge. Barber. Coin lndry. Exercise equipt. Pool. Cr cds: A, C, D, DS, JCB, MC, V.

★★ **HAMPTON INN-GARLAND.**
12670 E Northwest Hwy (75228). 972/613-5000; fax 972/613-4535; toll-free 800/426-7866. www.hampton-inn.com. 125 rms, 3 story. S $45.95-$65.95; D $64.95; under 18 free. Crib free. Pet accepted. TV; cable (premium). Pool. Complimentary continental bkfst. Coffee in rms. Restaurant opp 11-2 am. Ck-out noon. Meeting rm. Business servs

avail. In-rm modem link. Valet serv. Cr cds: A, C, D, DS, ER, MC, V.

★ **HARVEY HOTEL DALLAS.** *7815 LBJ Fwy (75251). 972/960-7000; fax 972/788-4227; res 972/233-7600.* 313 rms, 3 story. S $99-$129; D $109-$139; each addl $10; suites $125-$250; under 17 free. Crib free. Pet accepted; $125 ($100 refundable). TV; cable (premium), VCR avail. Pool. Restaurant 6:30 am-11 pm. Rm serv from 6 am. Bar 11 am-midnight. Ck-out 1 pm. Meeting rms. Business servs avail. In-rm modem link. Health club privileges. Valet serv. Gift shop. Covered parking. Game rm. Microwaves avail. Cr cds: A, D, DS, MC, V.

★★ **HAWTHORN SUITES MARKET CENTER.** *7900 Brookriver Dr (75247). 214/688-1010; fax 214/638-5215; res 800/527-1133. www.hawthorn.com.* 97 kit. suites, 2 story. S $91-$118; D $169; wkend, wkly, hol rates. Crib free. Pet accepted, some restrictions; $25. TV; cable (premium). Pool. Complimentary full bkfst. Complimentary coffee in rms. Ck-out noon. Coin lndry. Meeting rms. Business servs avail. In-rm modem link. Sundries. Free airport transportation. Health club privileges. Lawn games. Microwaves avail. Balconies, patios. Cr cds: A, DS, MC, V.

★★ **HOLIDAY INN ARISTOCRAT.**
1933 Main St (75201). 214/741-7700; fax 214/939-3639; toll-free 800/231-4235. www.holiday-inn.com. 172 rms, 15 story. S $135-$179; D $145-$189; under 12 free; wkend rates. Crib $10. TV; cable (premium), VCR avail. Restaurant 6:30 am-10:30 pm. Bar 11-1 am. Ck-out noon. Meeting rms. Business servs avail. In-rm modem link. Concierge. Exercise equipt. Health club privileges. Bathrm phones, refrigerators, minibars. Historic landmark, built in 1925 by Conrad Hilton and the first to bear his name; restored to its original Sullivanesque style. Cr cds: A, C, D, DS, JCB, MC, V.

★★ **HOLIDAY INN SELECT NORTH DALLAS.** *2645 LBJ Fwy*

(75234). 972/243-3363; fax 972/243-6682; res 800/465-4329. www.holiday-inn.com. 379 rms, 6 story. S, D $129; each addl $10; suites $149-$600; under 19 free; wkend rates. Crib free. TV; cable (premium). Indoor/outdoor pool; whirlpool, poolside serv. Coffee in rms. Restaurants 6:30 am-midnight. Bar 11-1 am; Fri, Sat to 2 am. Ck-out noon. Convention facilities. In-rm modem link. Concierge. Gift shop. Exercise equipt. Some refrigerators. Some balconies. Cr cds: A, C, D, DS, MC, V.

★★ **HOLIDAY INN SELECT NORTHEAST.** 11350 LBJ Fwy (75238). 214/341-5400; fax 214/553-9349; res 800/465-4329. www.holiday-inn.com. 244 rms, 3-5 story. S, D $89-$105; under 18 free. Crib $10. TV; cable (premium). Pool. Restaurant 6 am-2 pm, 5-11 pm. Rm serv. Bar 5 pm-1 am; entertainment. Ck-out noon. Coin lndry. Meeting rms. Business servs avail. In-rm modem link. Bellhops. Valet serv. Gift shop. Exercise equipt; sauna. Microwaves avail. Luxury level. Cr cds: A, C, D, DS, MC, V.

★★ **LA QUINTA INN.** 8303 E.R.L. Thornton Fwy (75228). 214/324-3731; fax 214/324-1652; res 800/531-5900. www.laquinta.com. 102 rms, 2 story. Mar-Oct: S, D $60-$70; suites $135; each addl $10; under 18 free; higher rates wkends; lower rates rest of yr. Crib free. Pet accepted, some restrictions. TV; cable (premium). Pool. Complimentary continental bkfst. Coffee in rms. Restaurant adj 6 am-midnight. Ck-out noon. Business servs avail. In-rm modem link. Sundries. Microwaves avail. Cr cds: A, C, D, DS, MC, V.

★★ **LA QUINTA INN.** 13235 N Stemmons Fwy, Farmers Branch (75234). 972/620-7333; fax 972/484-6533; toll-free 800/687-6667. www.laquinta.com. 122 rms, 2 story. S, D $53.99-$62.99; each addl $5; under 18 free. Crib free. Pet accepted, some restrictions. TV; cable (premium). Pool. Complimentary continental bkfst. Coffee in rms. Restaurant adj 6 am-11 pm. Ck-out noon. Meeting rms. Business servs avail. In-rm

modem link. Free airport transportation. Some refrigerators; microwaves avail. Cr cds: A, C, D, DS, MC, V.

★★ **RAMADA HOTEL.** 1055 Regal Row (75247). 214/634-8550; fax 214/634-8418; res 800/272-6232. www.ramada.com. 360 units, 12 story. S, D $85; each addl $10; suites $125-$350; under 16 free. TV; cable, VCR avail. Pool; poolside serv. Restaurant 6 am-2 pm, 5-10 pm. Bar 3 pm-1 am. Ck-out noon. Coin lndry. Convention facilities. Business servs avail. Valet serv. Gift shop. Free covered parking. Free airport transportation. Game rm. Tennis. Exercise equipt. Some refrigerators. Cr cds: A, C, D, DS, ER, JCB, MC, V.

★★ **RAMADA PLAZA HOTEL.** 1011 S Akard St (75215). 214/421-1083; fax 214/428-6827; toll-free 800/527-7606. www.ramada.com. 238 rms, 12 story. S $79-$140; D $89-$150; each addl $10; suites $350-$450; under 18 free; wkend rates. Crib free. TV; cable (premium). Indoor pool; whirlpool. Restaurant 6 am-11 pm. Bar 4 pm-2 am. Ck-out noon. Meeting rms. In-rm modem link. Free garage parking. Airport transportation. Exercise equipt. Balconies. Cr cds: A, C, D, DS, ER, JCB, MC, V.

★ **SLEEP INN.** 4801 W Plano Pkwy, Plano (75093). 972/867-1111; fax 972/612-6753. www.sleepinn.com. 102 rms, 2 story. S, D $59.95-$64.95; each addl $6; under 19 free; wkend rates. Crib $10. Pet accepted; $35 first night, $10 each addl night. TV; cable. Heated pool. Complimentary continental bkfst. Restaurant nearby. Ck-out noon. Meeting rms. Business servs avail. In-rm modem link. Health club privileges. Cr cds: A, C, D, DS, ER, JCB, MC, V.

★ **SUPER 8.** 9229 Carpenter Fwy (75247). 214/631-6633; fax 214/631-6616; toll-free 800/800-8000. www.super8.com. 134 rms, 2 story. S, D $54.95-$64.95; each addl $5; suite $65; under 13 free. Crib free. TV; cable (premium), VCR avail. Pool. Complimentary continental bkfst.

Restaurant adj. Ck-out noon. Coin lndry. Meeting rms. Business servs avail. In-rm modem link. Valet serv. Free airport transportation. Exercise equipt; sauna. Bathrm phones; some refrigerators; microwaves avail. Cr cds: A, D, DS, MC, V.

⊡ ⩘ ⩔ SC ⩐ ⫐

★★ **WYNDHAM GARDEN.** *2015 Market Center Blvd (75207). 214/741-7481; fax 214/747-6191; res 800/996-3426. www.wyndham.com.* 228 rms, 11 story. S $79-$135; D $79-$145; under 18 free. Crib free. TV; cable (premium). Pool. Restaurant 6:30 am-2 pm, 5-10 pm. Coffee in rms. Ck-out noon. Coin lndry. Meeting rms. Business servs avail. In-rm modem link. Valet serv. Exercise equipt. Health club privileges. Some private patios, balconies. Cr cds: A, C, D, DS, JCB, MC, V.

⊡ ⩐ ⫐ ⩘ ⩔ SC

Hotels

★★★ **CROWNE PLAZA DALLAS MARKET CENTER.** *7050 N Stemmons Fwy (75247). 214/630-8500; fax 214/630-0037; res 800/227-6963. www.crowneplaza.com.* 354 rms, 21 story. S $129-$169; each addl $10; under 18 free; wkend rates. Crib $10. Pet accepted. TV; cable (premium). Indoor pool; whirlpool. Restaurant 6 am-2 pm, 5 pm-midnight. Bar 2 pm-midnight. Ck-out 1 pm. Coin lndry. Convention facilities. Business center. In-rm modem link. Gift shop. Exercise equipt; sauna. Cr cds: A, C, D, DS, MC, V.

⩀ ⊡ ⩐ ⫐ ⫐ ⩘ ⩔ SC ⫐

★★★ **CROWNE PLAZA-NORTH DALLAS/NEAR THE GALLERIA.** *14315 Midway Rd, Addison (75001). 972/980-8877; fax 972/788-2758; res 800/227-6963. www.crowneplaza.com.* 429 rms, 4 story. Feb-May: S, D $149-$169; each addl $10; suites $169-$189; under 12 free; wkly, wkend, hol rates. Crib free. Pet accepted, some restrictions; $125 ($100 refundable). TV; cable (premium), VCR avail. Pool; whirlpool. Restaurant 6:30 am-10 pm. Rm serv. Coin lndry. Business center. In-rm modem link. Garage parking. Airport transportation. Exercise equipt. Health club privileges. Some refriger-

ators. Microwaves. Cr cds: A, C, D, DS, JCB, MC, V.

⊡ ⩐ ⩐ ⫐ ⩘ ⩔ SC ⫐

★★★ **CROWNE PLAZA SUITES.** *7800 Alpha Rd (75240). 972/233-7600; fax 972/701-8618; toll-free 800/922-2222. www.crowneplaza.com.* 295 suites, 10 story. Suites $119-$169; each addl $10; under 17 free; some lower rates summer. Crib free. Pet accepted; $125 ($100 refundable). TV; cable. Indoor/outdoor pool; whirlpool, poolside serv. Complimentary full bkfst. Restaurant 6 am-10 pm. Bar 2 pm-midnight. Ck-out 1 pm. Coin lndry. Convention facilities. Business center. In-rm modem link. Gift shop. Exercise equipt. Refrigerators, microwaves; some bathrm phones. Cr cds: A, C, D, DS, MC, V.

⊡ ⩐ ⩐ ⫐ ⩔ ⫐

★★ **DALLAS GRAND HOTEL.** *18110 1914 Commerce St (75201). 214/747-7000; fax 214/742-1337. www.dallasgrandhotel.com.* 709 rms, 20 story. S $89-$109; D $99-$119; each addl $10; suites $149-$750; under 17 free; wkend rates. Crib free. TV; cable (premium), VCR avail. Restaurant 6:30 am-11 pm. Bar 2 pm-2 am. Ck-out noon. Coin lndry. Convention facilities. Business servs avail. In-rm modem link. Gift shop. Valet parking. Exercise equipt; whirlpools. Health club privileges. Game rm. Some refrigerators; microwaves avail. Sun deck. Cr cds: A, C, D, DS, MC, V.

⊡ ⫐ ⫐ ⩘ ⩔ SC

★★★ **DOUBLETREE HOTEL CAMPBELL CENTRE.** *8250 N Central Expy (75206). 214/691-8700; fax 214/706-0187; toll-free 800/222-8733. www.doubletreehotels.com.* 302 rms, 21 story. S, D $134; each addl $10; suites $189-$359; under 12 free; package plans; higher rates special events. Crib free. TV; cable (premium), VCR avail. Complimentary coffee in rms. Restaurant 6 am-11 pm. Bar 11 am-midnight; pianist wknds. Ck-out 11 am. Convention facilities. Business servs avail. In-rm modem link. Concierge. Gift shop. Tennis. Exercise equipt. Pool privileges. Refrigerator in suites; microwaves avail. Cr cds: A, D, DS, MC, V.

⊡ ⫐ ⫐ ⫐ ⩘ ⩔ ⫐

★★★ **THE FAIRMONT DALLAS.**
*1717 N Akard St (75201). 214/720-
5293; fax 214/720-5282; toll-free
800/527-4727. www.fairmont.com.* 550
rms, 25 story. S, D $159-$229; salon
suites $325-$500; under 17 free;
wkend rates. Crib free. Garage parking $15. TV; cable (premium), VCR
avail. Pool; wading pool, poolside
serv. Restaurant 6 am-midnight (see
also PYRAMID ROOM). Rm serv 24
hrs. Bar 11-2 am; entertainment. Ck-
out noon. Convention facilities.
Business center. In-rm modem link.
Shopping arcade. Tennis privileges.
Golf privileges. Health club privileges. Bathrm phones. Cr cds: A, C,
D, DS, MC, V.

D 🏃 ⊵ 🔥 🐾 SC 🏃 🐾

★★ **HARVEY HOTEL - PLANO.**
*1600 N Central Expy, Plano (75074).
972/578-8555; fax 972/578-9720; toll-
free 800/922-9222.* 279 rms, 3 story. S
$109-$159; D $119-$169; each addl
$10; suites $159; under 18 free. Crib
free. Pet accepted; $125 ($100
refundable). TV; cable, VCR avail.
Pool; whirlpool, poolside serv.
Restaurants 6:30 am-11 pm. Rm serv.
Bar 10 am-midnight; Sat to 1 am. Ck-
out 1 pm. Coin lndry. Meeting rms.
Business servs avail. In-rm modem
link. Bellhops. Valet serv. Sundries.
Gift shop. Game rm. Exercise equipt.
Microwaves avail; refrigerator, wet
bar in suites. Cr cds: A, C, D, DS,
MC, V.

D 🐾 ⊵ 🔥 🐾 SC

★★★ **HILTON DALLAS PARKWAY.**
*4801 LBJ Fry (75244). 972/661-3600;
res 800/445-8667. www.hilton.com.*
310 rms, 15 story. S $99-$165; D
$109-$175; each addl $10; suites
$250-$375; under 18 free; wkend,
special rates. Crib free. TV; cable (premium). Indoor/outdoor pool, whirlpool. Restaurant 6:30 am-11 pm. Bar
noon-midnight. Ck-out 1 pm. Convention facilities. Business center. In-
rm modem link. Gift shop. Exercise
equipt; sauna. Health club privileges.
Cr cds: A, C, D, DS, JCB, MC, V.

⊵ 🔥 D 🏃

★★★ **HILTON GARDEN INN.** *4090
Belt Line Rd, Addison (75001).
972/233-8000; fax 972/239-8777; res
800/445-8667. www.hilton.com.* 96
rms, 3 story, 20 suites. Feb-May, Sep-
Oct: S $119; D $129; suites $139;

each addl $10; under 18 free; lower
rates rest of yr. Crib avail. Parking
lot. Pool. TV; cable (premium), VCR
avail. Complimentary coffee in rms.
Restaurant 6 am-11 pm. Bar. Ck-out
noon, ck-in 3 pm. Meeting rms. Business center. Dry cleaning, coin lndry.
Exercise equipt. Golf. Supervised
children's activities. Cr cds: A, C, D,
DS, JCB, MC, V.

D 🏃 ⊵ 🔥 🐾 🐾 SC 🏃

★★★ **HOTEL ADOLPHUS.** *1321
Commerce St (75202). 214/742-8200;
fax 214/651-3561; res 800/223-5652.
www.hoteladolphus.com.* 426 rms, 21
story. S, D $225-$395; each addl $25;
suites $575-$2,000; under 12 free;
wkend rates. Crib free. Valet parking
$12. TV; cable (premium), VCR avail.
Restaurants 6 am-10 pm (see also
FRENCH ROOM). Rm serv 24 hrs.
Bar 11-2 am. Ck-out 1 pm. Convention facilities. Business servs avail.
In-rm modem link. Concierge. Gift
shop. Barber, beauty shop. Tennis
privileges. Golf privileges. Exercise
equipt. Health club privileges. Massage. Bathrm phones, refrigerators,
minibars; microwaves avail. Some
private patios. Cr cds: A, C, D, DS,
JCB, MC, V.

D 🏃 🔥 🔥 🐾 ⊵ 🔥

★★★★ **HOTEL CRESCENT
COURT.** *400 Crescent Ct (75201).
214/871-3200; fax 214/871-3272; res
888/767-3966. www.crescentcourt.com.*
A white, castlelike facade welcomes
visitors to this stately hotel in The
Crescent Complex, an office and
shopping development on the edge
of the business district. All 218
rooms are impeccably decorated in
gray and rose tones with marble and
brass bath fixtures. Beau Nash has
great new American cuisine and Lady
Primrose's is a magical, afternoon tea
setting. 216 rms, 7 story. S $320-
$390; D $410-$440; each addl $30;
suites $750-$1,950; under 12 free;
wkend rates. Crib free. Pet accepted,
some restrictions; $25. Garage $5.50;
valet $12. TV; cable (premium), VCR
avail. Pool; whirlpool, poolside serv.
Restaurant 6:30 am-midnight. Afternoon tea 3-5 pm. Rm serv 24 hrs. Bar
11:30-2 am. Ck-out 1 pm. Meeting
rms. Business center. In-rm modem
link. 24-hr concierge. Shopping
arcade. Free airport transportation.
Exercise rm; sauna, steam rm. Spa

$20 per day. Bathrm phones, refrigerators. Cr cds: A, C, D, MC, V.

★★★ **HOTEL INTER-CONTINENTAL DALLAS.** *15201 Dallas Pkwy, Addison (75001). 972/386-6000; fax 972/991-6937; toll-free 800/327-0200. www.intercontinental.com.* 528 rms, 16 story. S, D $195-$249; each addl $30; suites $400-$1,700; under 17 free. Crib free. Valet parking $9. TV; cable (premium), VCR avail. Indoor/outdoor pool; whirlpool, poolside serv. Restaurants 6 am-10:30 pm. Rm serv 24 hrs. Bars 11-2 am. Ck-out noon. Convention facilities. Business center. In-rm modem link. Concierge. Shopping arcade. Barber, beauty shop. Lighted tennis. Golf privileges. Exercise rm; sauna, steam rm. Bathrm phones; some refrigerators. Private patios. Luxury level. Cr cds: A, C, D, DS, JCB, MC, V.

★★★ **HYATT REGENCY DALLAS AT REUNION.** *300 Reunion Blvd (75207). 214/651-1234; fax 214/651-0018; res 800/233-1234. www.hyatt.com.* 940 rms, 28 story. S $99-$125; D $124-$150; each addl $25; suites $350-$3,000; under 18 free; wkend rates. Valet parking $12. TV; cable (premium), VCR avail (movies $5). Pool; whirlpool, poolside serv. Restaurant 6 am-midnight. Bars noon-1:30 am. Ck-out noon. Convention facilities. Business center. In-rm modem link. Gift shop. Airport transportation. Lighted tennis. Exercise equipt; sauna. Health club privileges. Minibars; some refrigerators. Luxury level. Cr cds: A, C, D, DS, JCB, MC, V.

★★★ **LE MERIDIEN DALLAS.** *650 N Pearl St (75201). 214/979-9000; fax 214/953-1931; toll-free 800/543-4300.* 407 rms, 16 story. S, D $279-$319; under 17 free; suites $400-$425; wkend rates. Crib free. TV; cable (premium), VCR avail. Coffee in rms. Restaurants 6:30 am-midnight. Bar 11 am-midnight. Ck-out noon. Meeting rms. Business center. In-rm modem link. Concierge. Gift shop. Exercise equipt. Refrigerators avail. Cr cds: A, D, DS, MC, V.

★★★ **THE MAGNOLIA.** *1401 Commerce St (75201). 214/915-6500. www.themagnoliahotel.com.* 330 rms, 18 story. S, D $225-$275; suites $250-$450; under 17 free. Crib free. TV; cable (premium), VCR avail. Coffee in rms. Restaurants 6:30 am-midnight. Bar 11 am-midnight. Ck-out noon. Meeting rms. Business center. In-rm modem link. Concierge. Gift shop. Exercise equipt. Refrigerators avail. Former headquarters for Magnolia Oil Corporation.

★★★★★ **THE MANSION ON TURTLE CREEK.** *2821 Turtle Creek Blvd (75219). 214/559-2100; fax 214/528-4187; res 888/767-3966. www.mansiononturtlecreek.com.* Originally built as a lavish home in 1925, this romantic, Italianate structure still maintains the feel of a private home. The two-to-one staff-to-guest ratio is evident in the impeccable service. Visit the restaurant, recognized as the birthplace of innovative Southwest Cuisine, for a taste of famed chef Dean Fearing's acclaimed dishes (available for room service delivery 24 hours a day). 140 rms, 9 story. S $360-$450; D $400-$490; each addl $40; suites, kit. units $645-$2,300; wkend rates. Crib free. Valet parking $15. TV; cable (premium), VCR. Heated pool; poolside serv. Restaurants 7 am-10:30 pm (see also RESTAURANT AT THE MANSION ON TURTLE CREEK). Rm serv 24 hrs. Bar 11-2 am; entertainment. Ck-out noon. Meeting rms. Business center. In-rm modem link. Concierge. Beauty shop. Airport transportation. Lighted tennis courts. Golf privileges. Exercise rm; sauna, steam rm. Health club privileges. Massage. Bathrm phones, minibars; microwaves avail; wet bar in suites. Private patios, balconies. Cr cds: A, C, D, DS, ER, JCB, MC, V.

★★★ **MARRIOTT DALLAS QUORUM BY GALLERIA.** *14901 Dallas Pkwy (75240). 972/661-2800; fax 972/934-1731; res 800/811-8664. www.marriott.com.* 548 rms, 12 story. S, D $89-$179; suites $250-$450; under 12 free; wkend rates. Crib free. TV; cable (premium), VCR avail. Heated indoor/outdoor pool; whirlpool, poolside serv. Coffee in rms. Restaurants 6:30 am-midnight. Bar

11 am-midnight. Ck-out 1 pm. Lndry serv. Convention facilities. Business center. In-rm modem link. Concierge. Gift shop. Free covered parking. Tennis. Exercise equipt; sauna. Health club privileges. Refrigerators avail. Luxury level. Cr cds: A, C, D, DS, ER, JCB, MC, V.

★ ★ ★ **MARRIOTT SOLANA DAL-LAS.** *5 Village Cir (76262). 817/430-3848; res 800/228-9290. www. marriott.com.* 198 rms, 7 story. S, D $150-$195; suites $250-$450; under 17 free; wkend rates. Crib free. TV; cable (premium), VCR avail. Outdoor pool; whirlpool. Coffee in rms. Restaurants 6:30 am-midnight. Bar 11 am-midnight. Ck-out noon. Meeting rms. Business center. In-rm modem link. Concierge. Gift shop. Exercise equipt. Refrigerators avail. Cr cds: A, D, DS, MC, V.

★ ★ ★ **MARRIOTT SUITES MAR-KET CENTER DALLAS.** *2493 N Stemmons Fwy (75207). 214/905-0050; res 800/228-9290. www. marriott.com.* 266 rms, 12 story. S, D $155-$195; under 17 free; wkend rates. Crib free. TV; cable (premium), VCR avail. Outdoor pool; whirlpool. Coffee in rms. Restaurants 6:30 am-midnight. Bar 11 am-midnight. Ck-out noon. Lndry serv. Meeting rms. Business center. In-rm modem link. Concierge. Gift shop. Exercise equipt. Refrigerators avail. Cr cds: A, D, DS, MC, V.

★ ★ ★ **THE MELROSE.** *3015 Oak Lawn Ave (75219). 214/521-5151; fax 214/521-2470; toll-free 800/635-7673. www.melrosehotel.com.* 184 rms, 8 story. S, D $175-$275; suites $250-$1,200; wkend rates. Crib free. TV; cable (premium), VCR avail. Pool privileges. Restaurant (see also THE LANDMARK). Rm serv 24 hrs. Bar 11-2 am; entertainment. Ck-out noon. Meeting rms. Business servs avail. In-rm modem link. Concierge. Gift shop. Valet parking. Free airport transportation. Health club privileges. Some refrigerators; microwaves avail. Restored 1924 hotel; library. Luxury level. Cr cds: A, C, D, DS, MC, V.

★ ★ ★ **OMNI PARK WEST.** *1590 LBJ Fwy (75234). 972/869-4300; fax 972/869-3295; res 800/843-6664. www.omnihotels.com.* 337 rms, 12 story. S, D $159-$179; suites $209-$1,200; under 17 free; wkend rates. Crib free. TV; cable (premium). Heated pool; whirlpool, poolside serv. Restaurant 6 am-10 pm. Bar 11-1 am. Ck-out noon. Convention facilities. Business center. In-rm modem link. Concierge. Gift shop. Free airport transportation. Exercise equipt; sauna. Massage. Health club privileges. Minibars. Luxury level. Cr cds: A, C, D, DS, MC, V.

★ ★ ★ **OMNI RICHARDSON HOTEL.** *701 E Campbell (75081). 972/231-9600. www.omnihotels.com.* 342 rms, 15 story. S, D $155-$195; suites $250-$450; under 17 free; wkend rates. Crib free. TV; cable (premium), VCR avail. Heated pool; whirlpool. Coffee in rms. Restaurants 6:30 am-midnight. Bar 11 am-midnight. Ck-out noon. Lndry serv. Meeting rms. Business center. In-rm modem link. Concierge. Gift shop. Exercise equipt. Refrigerators avail. Luxury level. Cr cds: A, D, DS, MC, V.

★ ★ ★ **RADISSON HOTEL AND SUITES.** *2330 W Northwest Hwy (75220). 214/353-7690; fax 214/351-2364; res 800/333-3333. www. radisson.com.* 199 rms, 8 story. S $119-$139; D $129-$159; each addl $10; suites $129-$149; under 18 free; wkly, wkend, hol rates. Crib free. Pet accepted, some restrictions; $25 deposit. TV; cable (premium). Pool; whirlpool, poolside serv. Coffee in rms. Restaurant 6:30 am-10 pm. Bar 2 pm-1 am. Ck-out noon. Coin lndry. Meeting rms. Business servs avail. In-rm modem link. Concierge. Gift shop. Free airport transportation. Exercise equipt. Health club privileges. Microwaves avail. Some balconies. Cr cds: A, C, D, DS, ER, MC, V.

★ ★ ★ **RADISSON HOTEL CEN-TRAL DALLAS.** *6060 N Central Expy (75206). 214/750-6060; fax 214/691-6581; res 800/333-3333. www. radisson.com.* 288 rms, 9 story. S, D $79-$159; each addl $10; suites $140-

$575; under 18 free; wkend rates. Crib free. Pet accepted, $100. TV; cable (premium), VCR avail. Indoor/outdoor pool; whirlpool, poolside serv. Restaurant 6:30 am-2 pm, 5-10 pm. Bar noon-1 am. Ck-out noon. Meeting rms. Business center. Gift shop. Free airport transportation. Sauna. Health club privileges. Some refrigerators; microwaves avail. Cr cds: A, C, D, DS, MC, V.

★★★ **RENAISSANCE.** *2222 N Stemmons Fwy (75207). 214/631-2222; fax 214/267-4989; toll-free 800/811-8893. www.renaissancehotels.com.* 540 rms, 30 story. S $189-$199; D $209-$219; each addl $20; suites $239-$2,000; under 18 free; wkend rates. Crib free. Pet accepted, some restrictions. TV; cable (premium), VCR avail. Heated pool; whirlpool. Complimentary coffee in rms. Restaurant 6:30 am-10 pm. Bar 3 pm-2 am; entertainment. Ck-out noon. Convention facilities. Business center. In-rm modem link. Gift shop. Exercise equipt; sauna, steam rm. Health club privileges. Three-story chandelier; art objects. Luxury level. Cr cds: A, C, D, DS, JCB, MC, V.

★★★ **RENAISSANCE DALLAS NORTH HOTEL.** *4099 Valley View Ln (75244). 972/385-9000; fax 972/458-8260; res 800/236-2427. www.renaissancehotels.com.* 300 rms, 10 story. S, D $69-$162; each addl $10; suites $175-$595; under 12 free; wkend rates (2-day min). Crib avail. TV; cable, VCR avail. Restaurant 6:30 am-10 pm. Bar noon-midnight. Ck-out noon. Convention facilities. Business center. In-rm modem link. Concierge. Tennis privileges. Golf privileges. Exercise rm. Massage. Pool; poolside serv. Luxury level. Cr cds: A, C, D, DS, MC, V.

★★★ **RENAISSANCE RICHARDSON.** *900 E Lookout Dr, Richardson (75082). 972/367-2000. www.renaissancehotels.com.* 336 rms, 12 story. S, D $175-$225; suites $250-$450; under 17 free; wkend rates. Crib free. TV; cable (premium), VCR avail. Indoor pool; whirlpool. Coffee in rms. Restaurants 6:30 am-midnight. Bar 11 am-midnight. Ck-out noon. Lndry serv. Meeting rms.

Business center. In-rm modem link. Concierge. Gift shop. Exercise equipt. Refrigerators avail.

★★★ **SHERATON.** *1241 W Mockingbird Ln (75247). 214/630-7000; fax 214/638-6943; res 800/325-3535. www.sheraton.com.* 348 rms, 13 story. S $149; D $159; each addl $10; suites $225-$550; under 18 free; wkend, hol rates. Crib free. Pet accepted, some restrictions; $50. TV; cable (premium). Pool; wading pool, poolside serv. Coffee in rms. Restaurant 6:30 am-2 pm, 5-11 pm. Bar 11-2 am. Rm serv 6 am-11 pm. Ck-out noon. Coin lndry. Convention facilities. Business servs avail. In-rm modem link. Gift shop. Free airport transportation. Exercise equipt. Health club privileges. Luxury level. Cr cds: A, C, D, DS, MC, V.

★★★ **SHERATON PARK CENTRAL HOTEL DALLAS.** *7750 LBJ Fwy (75251). 972/233-4421; res 800/325-3535.* 438 rms, 10 story. S, D $175-$225; suites $250-$450; under 17 free; wkend rates. Crib free. TV; cable (premium), VCR avail. Heated pool; whirlpool. Coffee in rms. Restaurants 6:30 am-midnight. Bar 11 am-midnight. Ck-out noon. Lndry serv. Meeting rms. Business center. In-rm modem link. Concierge. Gift shop. Exercise equipt. Refrigerators avail. Luxury level.

★★ **STONELEIGH.** *2927 Maple Ave (75201). 214/871-7111; fax 214/871-9379.* 153 units, 11 story. S, D $205-$275; each addl $15; suites $250-$350; wkend rates. Crib free. TV; cable (premium), VCR avail. Pool. Coffee in rms. Restaurants 6:30 am-11 pm (see also SUSHI). Bar 11-1 am. Ck-out noon. Business servs avail. In-rm modem link. Concierge. Valet parking. Restored 1923 hotel. Cr cds: A, C, D, DS, MC, V.

★★★ **THE WESTIN GALLERIA.** *13340 Dallas Pkwy (75240). 972/934-9494; fax 972/851-2869; toll-free 800/228-3000. www.westin.com.* 487 rms, 17 story. S, D $150-$225; suites $250-$450; under 17 free; wkend rates. Crib free. TV; cable (premium), VCR avail. Pool; whirlpool. Coffee in rms. Restaurants 6:30 am-midnight. Bar 11 am-midnight. Ck-out noon. Meeting rms. Business center. In-rm modem link. Concierge. Gift shop. Exercise equipt. Refrigerators avail. Cr cds: A, D, DS, MC, V. Cr cds: A, C, D, DS, MC, V.

★★★ WESTIN PARK CENTRAL.
12720 Merit Dr (75251). 972/385-3000; fax 972/991-4557; res 800/937-8461. www.westin.com. 545 rms, 20 story. S $185; D $195; each addl $10; suites $250-$950; under 18 free; wkend rates. Crib avail. Valet parking $12. TV; cable (premium), VCR avail. Pool; poolside serv. Restaurant (see also LAUREL'S). Rm serv 24 hrs. Ck-out 1 pm. Convention facilities. Business center. In-rm modem link. Gift shop. Concierge. Tennis. Exercise rm. Health club privileges. Bathrm phones. Luxury level. Cr cds: A, C, D, DS, ER, MC, V.

★★★ WESTIN STONEBRIAR RESORT.
1549 Legacy Dr (75034). 972/668-8000; res www.westin.com. 301 rms, 10 story. S, D $175-$225; suites $250-$450; under 17 free; wkend rates. Crib free. TV; cable (premium), VCR avail. Heated pool; whirlpool, poolside serv. Coffee in rms. Restaurants 6:30 am-midnight. Bar 11 am-midnight. Ck-out noon. Lndry serv. Meeting rms. Business center. In-rm modem link. Concierge. Gift shop. Exercise equipt. Refrigerators avail. Cr cds: A, D, DS, MC, V.

★★ WYNDHAM ANATOLE HOTEL.
2201 Stemmons Fwy (75207). 214/748-1200; fax 214/761-7520; toll-free 800/996-3426. www.wyndham.com. 1,620 rms, 27 story. S, D $195-$265; each addl $15; suites $300-$1,400; under 18 free; wkend rates. TV; cable (premium), VCR avail. 3 pools, 2 indoor; whirlpool, poolside serv. Complimentary full bkfst. Coffee in rms. Restaurants. Bar 11-2 am; entertainment. Ck-out noon. Convention facilities. Business center. In-rm modem link. Concierge. Shopping arcade. Barber, beauty shop. Garage parking; valet. Lighted tennis. Exercise rm; sauna, steam rm. Bathrm phones, refrigerators, mini-

bars. Luxury level. Cr cds: A, C, D, DS, JCB, MC, V.

B&B/Small Inn

★★★ HOTEL ST. GERMAIN.
2516 Maple Ave (75201). 214/871-2516; fax 214/871-0740. www.hotelstgermain.com. 7 suites, 3 story. S $245; D $290. TV; cable (premium). Complimentary refreshments at ck-in. Complimentary continental breakfast. Restaurant. Ck-out noon, ck-in 4 pm. Luggage handling. Valet serv. Concierge serv. 24-hr rm serv. Health club privileges. Wraparound balconies and whirlpools in 3 rms; library/sitting rm. Cr cds: A, MC, V.

All Suites

★★ CLARION SUITES.
2363 Stemmons Trail (75247). 214/350-2300; fax 214/350-5144; res 800/252-7466. www.clarionsuites.com. 96 suites, 3 story. S $104-$114; D $104-$125; under 18 free; wkend rates. Crib free. TV; cable (premium). Pool; whirlpool. Complimentary continental bkfst. Restaurant adj open 24 hrs. Ck-out noon. Coin lndry. Meeting rms. Business center. In-rm modem link. Valet serv. Gift shop. Free airport transportation. Exercise equipt. Refrigerators, microwaves. Cr cds: A, D, DS, JCB, MC, V.

★★★ COMFORT SUITES.
2287 W Northwest Hwy (75220). 214/350-4011; fax 214/350-4408; res 800/517-4000. www.comfortsuites.com. 103 suites, 3 story. S, D $94; under 18 free; wkend rates; higher rates special events. Crib free. TV; cable (premium). Complimentary continental bkfst. Complimentary coffee in rms. Restaurant opp open 24 hrs. Rm serv 11 am-10 pm. Ck-out noon. Meeting rms. Business servs avail. In-rm modem link. Valet serv. Sundries. Coin lndry. Free airport transportation. Exercise equipt. Pool; whirlpool. Refrigerators, microwaves. Cr cds: A, D, DS, JCB, MC, V.

★★★ EMBASSY SUITES.
3880 W Northwest Hwy (75220). 214/357-

4500; fax 214/357-0683; res 800/362-2779. www.embassysuites.com. 248 suites, 9 story. S $189; D $209; each addl $10; wkend rates. TV; cable (premium). Indoor pool; wading pool, whirlpool. Complimentary full bkfst. Coffee in rms. Restaurant 11 am-2 pm, 5-10 pm. Bar 4 pm-midnight; Sat, Sun to 10 pm. Ck-out noon. Guest lndry. Meeting rms. Business servs avail. In-rm modem link. Covered parking. Free airport transportation. Exercise equipt; sauna. Refrigerators, microwaves; some bathrm phones. Cr cds: A, C, D, DS, JCB, MC, V.

★ ★ ★ **SHERATON SUITES MARKET CENTER.** 2101 N Stemmons Fwy (75207). 214/747-3000; fax 214/742-5713; toll-free 800/325-3535. www.sheraton.com. 251 suites, 11 story. S, D $145-$199; each addl $15; under 18 free; wkend rates. TV; cable (premium). Indoor/outdoor pool; whirlpool. Complimentary coffee in rms. Restaurant 6 am-11 pm. Bar 11 am-midnight. Ck-out noon. Business servs avail. In-rm modem link. Sundries. Exercise equipt. Refrigerators, wet bars. Some balconies. Cr cds: A, C, D, DS, ER, JCB, MC, V.

Extended Stays

★ ★ **RESIDENCE INN BY MARRIOTT.** 6950 N Stemmons Fwy (75247). 214/631-2472; fax 214/634-9645; toll-free 800/331-3131. www.residenceinn.com. 142 kit. suites, 3 story. S $120; D $160; wkend rates. Crib free. Pet accepted; $50. TV; cable (premium). Pool; whirlpool. Complimentary continental bkfst. Complimentary coffee in rms. Ck-out noon. Coin lndry. Meeting rms. Business servs avail. Valet serv. Exercise equipt. Health club privileges. Microwaves avail. Picnic tables. Cr cds: A, D, DS, JCB, MC, V.

★ ★ **RESIDENCE INN BY MARRIOTT.** 13636 Goldmark Dr (75240). 972/669-0478; fax 972/644-2632; res 800/331-3131. www.residenceinn.com. 70 kit. suites, 1-2 story. Suites $129-$149; wkend rates. Crib free. Pet accepted, some restrictions; $60. TV; cable (premium). Pool; whirlpool. Complimentary continental bkfst.

Ck-out noon. Coin lndry. Business servs avail. In-rm modem link. Valet serv. Health club privileges. Refrigerators, microwaves, fireplaces. Private patios, balconies. Grill. Cr cds: A, D, DS, JCB, MC, V.

Restaurants

★ ★ ★ ★ **ABACUS.** 4511 McKinney Ave (75205). 214/559-3111. www.abacus-restaurant.com. Art, architecture, and chef Kent Rathbun's culinary creations come together to create this sensory-stimulating newcomer to the upper end of Dallas eateries. The professional staff is intimate with and passionate about the menu's temptations. Lobster shooters served in sake cups with a Thai broth of coconut milk, red curry and sake, are a popular appetizer; lamb, pork and a variety of fresh seafood keep guests satisfied. Contemporary American menu. Specializes in prime beef, fresh fish and seafood. Hrs: 6-10 pm. Closed Sun. Res accepted. Wine list. Dinner $26-$35. Cr cds: A, D, MC, V.

★ ★ **ADDISON CAFE.** 5290 Belt Line Rd #8, Addison (75240). 972/991-8824. Hrs: 11:30 am-2 pm, 5:30-10 pm; Sat 5:30-10 pm; Sun 5:30-9 pm. Closed hols. Res accepted. French menu. Bar. Lunch $8.95-$11.95, dinner $13-$20. Complete meals: dinner $35. Specializes in French onion soup. Elegant, romantic atmosphere. Cr cds: A, C, D, DS, MC, V.

★ ★ **ADELMO'S.** 4537 Cole Ave (75205). 214/559-0325. www.adelmos.guidelive.com. Hrs: 11:30 am-2 pm, 6-10:30 pm; Sat from 6 pm. Closed Sun; major hols. Res accepted. Mediterranean menu. Bar. Lunch $8.95-$14.50, dinner $17.95-$32.50. Specialties: 20-oz veal chop, rack of lamb, osso buco. Parking. Cr cds: A, D, DS, MC, V.

★ ★ ★ **AL BIERNAT'S.** 4217 Oak Lawn Ave (75219). 214/219-2201. www.albiernats.com. Hrs: 11:30 am-2:30 pm, 6 -10 pm Mon-Fri, 6 pm-10:30 pm Sat, 6 pm-9 pm Sun. Closed major hols. Bar 4 pm-2 am. Wine cellar. Res accepted. Free valet parking. American menu. Specialties: steak, lobster, seafood. Lunch $8-$17,

dinner $15-$32. Cigar bar. Private dining avail. Cr cds: A, D, DS, MC, V.
D

★★ **ALI-BABA.** *1905 Greenville Ave (75206). 214/823-8235.* Specializes in mazza plate, shish tawook. Hrs: 11:30 am-2 pm, 5:30-9 pm. Closed Sun, Mon. Wine list. Lunch, dinner $3.99-$9.99. Entertainment. Cr cds: A, DS, MC, V.
D

★★ **ANDIAMO.** *4151 Beltline, Addison (75001). 972/233-1515.* Specializes in stuffed pork chops. Hrs: 11 am-2:30 pm, 5-10 pm; Sat 5-10:30 pm. Closed Sun; hols. Res accepted. Wine list. Lunch $8-$15; dinner $13-$25. Cr cds: A, D, MC, V.
D

★★ **ARCODORO.** *2708 Routh St (75201). 214/871-1924. www.arcodoro. com.* Hrs: Sun-Wed 6-11 pm; Thurs-Sat to midnight. Res accepted. Sardinian cuisine. Bar. Wine list. Specializes in pizza, pasta, baked whole fish. A la carte entrees: dinner $11-$27.50. Cr crds: A, DC, MC, V
D

★★ **AUGUST MOON.** *2300 N Central Expwy, Plano (75074). 972/881-0071. www.august-moon.com.* Specializes in sesame chicken, Hunan beef. Hrs: 11 am-10 pm; Fri, Sat to 11 pm. Res accepted. Wine, beer. Lunch $6-$7, dinner $9-$25. Child's menu. Entertainment. Cr cds: D, DS, MC, V.
D

★★ **BASHA.** *2217 Greenville Ave (75206). 214/824-7794. www.basha restaurant.com.* Specializes in hummus, tabbouleh, falafel, eggplant dip. Hrs: 11 am-2:30 pm, 5:30-10 pm; Fri, Sat to 11:30 pm. Closed Sun. Res accepted. Extensive wine list. Lunch $6.25-$8.95; dinner $10.50-$16.50. Entertainment. Cr cds: A, D, DS, MC, V.
D

★★★ **BEAU NASH.** *400 Crescent Ct (75201). 214/871-3200.* Southwestern cuisine. Hrs: 6:30-11 am, 11:30 am-3 pm, 6-10:30 pm; Fri to midnight; Sat 6 pm-midnight; Sun 6-9 pm; Sat, Sun brunch 11:30 am-3 pm. Bkfst, lunch $9-$17, dinner $12-$34. Child's

menu. Valet. Bar. Cr cds: A, C, D, DS, MC, V.
D

★★★ **BISTRO A.** *6815 Snider Plaza (75205). 214/373-9911.* Middle Eastern menu. Specializes in Copper River salmon, whole snapper for two. Hrs: 11:30 am-2 pm, 5:30-10 pm; Fri, Sat 5:30-10:30 pm. Closed Sun. Res accepted. Beer. Lunch $6.50-$14.50, dinner $14.95-$23.95. Cr cds: A, D, DS, MC, V.
D

★ **BREADWINNERS.** *3301 McKinney Ave (75204). 214/754-4940. www. breadwinnerscafe.com.* Hrs: 7 am-11 pm; Mon, Tues to 4 pm; Sun 5-10 pm; Sun brunch 9 am-3 pm. Closed major hols. Res accepted. Bkfst $2.95-$6.95, lunch $4.95-$7.35, dinner $7.50-$21.95. Child's menu. Specialties: eggs Benedict, queen of hearts salad. Parking. New Orleans-style courtyard. Cr cds: A, C, D, DS, MC, V.
D

★★★ **CAFE PACIFIC.** *24 Highland Park Village (75205). 214/526-1170.* Hrs: 11:30 am-2 pm, 5:30-10 pm; Fri to 11 pm; Sat 11:30 am-2:30 pm, 5:30-11 pm. Closed Sun; some major hols. Res accepted. Bar 11 am-midnight. Wine cellar. A la carte entrees: lunch $6.90-$11.90, dinner $12.90-$26. Specializes in three-onion sea bass, smoke salmon. Valet parking. Outdoor terrace dining. View of kitchen behind glass. Cr cds: A, D, DS, MC, V.
D

★★ **CAFE PANDA.** *7979 Inwood (75209). 214/902-9500.* Specializes in Peking duck, tangerine beef. Hrs: 11 am-10:30 pm; Fri to 11:30 pm; Sat noon-11:30 pm. Closed July 4, Thanksgiving. Res accepted. Wine list. Lunch $6, dinner $10-$25. Entertainment. Cr cds: A, D, DS, MC, V.
D

★★★ **CAPITAL GRILLE.** *500 Crescent Ct, Ste 135 (75201). 214/303-0500. www.thecapitalgrille.com.* Specializes in steak, seafood. Hrs: 11:30 am-10 pm; Fri, Sat to 11 pm. Closed Thanksgiving, Dec 25, July 4. Res accepted. Wine list. Lunch $7.95-

$18.95, dinner $18.95-$32.95. Entertainment: pianist. Cr cds: A, C, D, DS, ER, JCB, MC, V.
D ⌷

★★★ **CARAVELLE.** 400 N Greenville Ave, Richardson (75081). 972/437-6388. Chinese, Vietnamese menu. Specializes in lobster with cheese, fresh clam and blackbean sauce. Hrs: 11 am-10 pm; Fri, Sat to 11 pm. Lunch $3.95-$4.50, dinner $7.50-$24.99. Cr cds: A, D, DS, ER, MC, V.
D ⌷

★ **CELEBRATION.** 4503 W Lovers Ln (75209). 214/351-2456. www.celebrationrestaurant.com. Hrs: 11 am-2:30 pm, 5:30-10 pm; Fri, Sat to 10:30 pm; Sun 11 am-10 pm. Closed Thanksgiving, Dec 24-25. Bar. American menu. Lunch $6-$7.95, dinner $6.95-$17. Child's menu. Specializes in fresh vegetables, fish, pot roast. Own breads and desserts. Parking. Rustic decor; copper tables. Cr cds: A, D, DS, MC, V.
D SC ⌷

★★ **CHAMBERLAIN'S.** 5330 Belt Line Rd, Addison (75240). 972/934-2467. www.chamberlainsrestaurant.com. Hrs: 5:30-10:30 pm; Sat to 11 pm; Sun to 9 pm. Closed hols. Res accepted. Bar from 5 pm. Dinner $18-$60. Child's menu. Specializes in aged prime beef. Valet parking. Club atmosphere with multiple dining areas; European posters. Cr cds: A, C, D, DS, MC, V.
D ⌷

★★★ **CHEZ GERARD.** 4444 McKinney Ave (75205). 214/522-6865. www.chezgerardrestaurant.com. Hrs: 11:30 am-2 pm, 6-10:30 pm; Sat from 6 pm. Closed Sun; major hols. Res accepted. French menu. Bar. A la carte entrees: lunch $7.50-$12.95, dinner $16.50-$28.50. Specializes in fish, rack of lamb. Outdoor dining. Cr cds: A, D, DS, MC, V.
⌷

★★★ **CITIZEN.** 3858 Oak Lawn Ave (75219). 214/522-7253. Pan/Asian menu. Specializes in Kobe beef, blackened cod, citrus beef. Hrs: 11:30 am-2:30 pm, 5:30-10 pm; Fri, Sat 5:30-11 pm. Res accepted. Wine list. Lunch $8-$12; dinner $18-$22. Full sushi bar. Cr cds: A, D, DS, MC, V.
D ⌷

★★ **CITY CAFE.** 5757 W Lovers Ln (75209). 214/351-2233. Hrs: 11:30 am-2:30 pm, 5:30-10 pm; Sun brunch 11 am-2:30 pm. Closed most major hols. Res accepted. Bar. Wine list. Lunch $7-$11, dinner $14-$22. Sun brunch $6-$12. Specialties: cilantro-crusted catfish, grilled venison. Valet parking. Outdoor dining. Cr cds: A, D, DS, MC, V.
D ⌷

★★★ **CIUDAD.** 3888 Oak Lawn, Ste 135 (75219). 214/219-3141. Specializes in sea bass, veal short ribs, duck. Hrs: 11:30 am-2 pm, 5-10 pm, Fri to 11 pm. Closed Sun, Mon. Res accepted. Beer, wine, liquor. Lunch $5-$10; dinner $16-$25. Cr cds: A, C, D, DS, MC, V.
D ⌷

★★ **CLAIRE DE LUNE.** 5934 Royal (75230). 214/987-2028. Menu changes seasonally. Hrs: 11:30 am-10 pm; Fri, Sat to 11 pm; Sun 11:30 am-3 pm. Closed hols. Res accepted. Wine list. Lunch $7.50-$15, dinner $12-$20. Brunch $7.50-$15. Entertainment. Cr cds: A, D, DS, MC, V.
D

★★ **DAKOTA'S.** 600 N Akard St (75201). 214/740-4001. www.dakotasrestaurant.com. Hrs: 11 am-2:30 pm, 5-10 pm; Fri to 10:30 pm; Sat 5-10:30 pm; Sun 5:30-9 pm. Closed some major hols. Res accepted. A la carte entrees: lunch $7.95-$12.95, dinner $9.95-$26.95. Specializes in fresh seafood, steaks. Own breads, pasta. Pianist Fri, Sat. Free valet parking. Patio dining with unusual 5-tiered waterfall. Cr cds: A, D, DS, MC, V.
D ⌷

★★ **DEEP ELLUM CAFE.** 2706 Elm St (75226). 214/741-9012. Specializes in salads, sandwiches, veggie dishes. Hrs: 11 am-10 pm; Sun, Mon to 2 pm. Res accepted. Wine list. Lunch $7.95-$11.95, dinner $9.95-$15.95. Brunch $7.95-$11.95. Entertainment. Cr cds: A, MC, V.
D ⌷

★★★ **DEL FRISCO'S DOUBLE EAGLE STEAK HOUSE.** 5251 Spring Valley Rd (75240). 972/490-9000. Hrs: 5-10 pm; Fri, Sat to 11 pm. Res accepted. Amer menu. Bar. Wine cellar. A la carte entrees $18-$30. Specialties: ribeye, Australian cold water

John F. Kennedy Memorial Plaza, Dallas

lobster tail. Valet parking $3. Pianist Thurs-Sun in cigar lounge. Cr cds: A, D, DS, MC, V.

D ⬛

★ ★ **DELI NEWS.** *4805 Frankford Rd; Ste 105 (75287). 972/733-3354.* NY style deli menu. Specializes in blintzes, chopped liver, Hungarian goulash, prime brisket of beef. Hrs: 7 am-9 pm; Fri, Sat to 10 pm; Sun to 4 pm. Res accepted. Lunch $4.99-$9.99, dinner $6.99-$11.99. Child's menu. Entertainment. Hand-painted wall murals. Cr cds: A, D, DS, MC, V.

D SC

★ ★ ★ **THE ENCLAVE.** *8325 Walnut Hill Ln (75231). 214/363-7487. www. theenclaverestaurant.com.* Hrs: 11 am-2 pm, 5:30-10:30 pm; Sat 5:30-11 pm. Closed Sun; major hols. Res accepted. Continental menu. Bar to 2 am. Lunch $10.25-$16.50, dinner $19.50-$24.95. Specializes in French cuisine, steak, veal. Pianist. Big band music Tues-Sat eves. Valet parking. Elegant dinner club atmosphere. Family-owned. Cr cds: A, D, DS, MC, V.

D ⬛

★ ★ ★ **FISH.** *302 S Houston (75202). 214/747-3474. www.fishdowntown. com.* Hrs: 11 am-2 pm, 5:30 pm-11 pm; Fri to 1 am; Sat 5:30 pm-1 am; Sun 5:30-11:30 pm. Closed most major hols. Res accepted. Seafood menu. Bar from 11 am. Lunch $7.95-$17.95, dinner $19.95-$39.95. Com-

plete meals: dinner $45. Specialties: green soup, Gulf crab cake, cedar-planked salmon. Piano. Valet parking. Elegant dining. Totally nonsmoking. Cr cds: A, D, DS, MC.

D ⬛

★ ★ **FISHBOWL.** *3214 Knox St (75205). 214/521-2695.* Specializes in ginger beef, soy salmon, lacquered duck. Hrs: 5-10:30 pm; Thurs to 11 pm; Fri, Sat to midnight. Bar 5 pm-2 am. Res accepted. Wine, beer. Dinner $10-$25. Entertainment. Open kitchen. Cr cds: A, MC, V.

D

★ **FOGO DE CHAO.** *4300 Belt Line Rd, Addison (75244). 972/503-7300. www.fogodechao.com.* Hrs: 11 am-2 pm, 5-10 pm; Fri to 10:30 pm; Sat 5-10:30 pm; Sun 5-10 pm. Closed Jan 1, Thanksgiving, Dec 25. Res accepted. South Brazilian menu. Bar. Wine list. Buffet: lunch $24.50, dinner $38.50. Child's menu. Specializes in picanha. Valet parking. In Southern plantation house; gaucho-style decor. Cr cds: A, D, DS, MC, V.

D

★ **FRANKI'S LI'L EUROPE.** *362 Casa Linda Plaza (75218). 214/320-0426. www.concentric.net/~frankis.* Specializes in cabbage rolls. Hrs: 11:30 am-2:30 pm, 5:30-9:30 pm; Mon to 2:30 pm; Sun brunch 11:30 am-2:30 pm. Res accepted. Extensive wine list. Lunch $6.95-$8.95; dinner $9.75-$17.95. Brunch 3-courses $15.

Child's menu. Entertainment: harpist, harmonica trio. Train goes around the ceiling. Cr cds: A, C, D, DS, ER, JCB, MC, V.
[D] [≡]

★★★★ **THE FRENCH ROOM.** *1321 Commerce St (75202). 214/742-8200.* Don't be misled by the name of this globally influenced, New American restaurant in the Adolphus Hotel. The room, designed in 1981, shows age but still feels regal. Despite the detailed menu descriptions, preparations are simple and stunning, highlighting fresh ingredients such as miso-marinated halibut with shiitakes and a light carrot-ginger sauce. Finish your meal with an exquisite souffle. Neo-classic cuisine. Specialties: Dover sole, roast rack of lamb, sautéed Norwegian salmon. Menu changes with season. Hrs: 6-9:30 pm. Closed Sun, Mon. Res accepted. Bar 6 pm-1:30 am. Wine list. Prix fixe: $52, $62, $70. Valet parking. Jacket required. Cr cds: A, D, DS, MC, V.
[D]

★★ **GERSHWIN'S.** *8442 Walnut Hill Ln (75231). 214/373-7171. www. gershwinsrestaurant.com.* Hrs: 11 am-10 pm; Fri to 11 pm; Sat 5-11 pm; Sun from 5 pm. Closed major hols. Res accepted. Bar. Lunch $5.95-$14.95, dinner $14.50-$26.95. Child's menu. Specialties: seared tuna, wild game trio, chocolate stack dessert. Own baking. Pianist. Valet parking. Outdoor dining. Contemporary decor; copper-framed windows, marble-top bar. Cr cds: A, D, DS, MC, V.
[D] [≡]

★★ **GILBERT'S NEW YORK DELICATESSEN.** *127 Preston Forrest Village (75230). 214/373-3333.* Authentic New York deli menu. Hrs: 7 am-7:45 pm; Sat from 8 am; Sun 8 am-2:45 pm. Lunch, dinner $6.95-$15. Child's menu. Entertainment. Cr cds: A, DS, MC, V.
[D]

★★ **THE GRAPE.** *2808 Greenville (75206). 214/828-1981.* Specializes in grilled beef tenderloin, seared tuna. Hrs: 11:30 am-2 pm, 5:30-10:30 pm. Res accepted. Wine list. Lunch $7-$11; dinner $12-$26.50. Entertainment. Intimate atmosphere. Cr cds: A, D, DS, MC, V.
[D]

★★ **GREEN ROOM.** *2715 Elm St (75226). 214/748-7666.* Hrs: 5:30-11 pm. Closed Jan 1, Thanksgiving, Dec 25. Res required Fri, Sat. Eclectic menu. Bar. Dinner $16-$19. Complete meal: dinner $36. Child's menu. Specializes in daily entrees and seasonal menu items. Valet parking. Outdoor dining. Casual atmosphere. Cr cds: A, C, D, DS, MC, V.
[≡]

★★ **HONG KONG ROYALE.** *221 W Polk, Richardson (75081). 972/238-8888.* Hrs: 11 am-10 pm. Res accepted. Wine, beer. Lunch $4-$8, dinner $8-$20. Entertainment. Cr cds: A, D, DS, MC, V.
[D]

★★ **INDIA PALACE.** *12817 Preston, Ste 105 (7520). 972/392-0190.* Northern Indian menu. Specializes in tandoori, leg of lamb, lamb chops. Hrs: 11:30 am-2:30 pm, 5:30-10 pm; Fri to 11 pm; Sat, Sun noon-3 pm. Res accepted. Wine, beer. Lunch $8-$12, dinner $15-$20. Child's menu. Entertainment. Cr cds: A, C, D, MC, V.
[D] [≡]

★★ **JAVIER'S.** *4912 Cole Ave (75205). 214/521-4211. www.javiers. net.* Hrs: 5:30-10:30 pm; Fri, Sat to 11 pm; Sun to 10 pm. Closed major hols. Res accepted. Continental, Mexican menu. Bar. Dinner $14.95-$20.95. Specialties: filete Cantinflas, red snapper mojo de ajo. Complimentary valet parking. Eclectic decor; antiques from Mexico. Cr cds: A, D, DS, MC, V.
[D] [≡]

★★ **KAMPAI SUSHI & GRILL.** *4995 Addison Cir, Addison (75001). 972/490-8888.* Specializes in sushi dishes. Hrs: 11:30 am-2 pm, 5-10:30 pm; Sun 5-10:30 pm. Res accepted. Wine list. Lunch $6.95-$15.95; dinner $10.95-$26.50. Entertainment. Patio dining. Cr cds: A, D, MC, V.
[D] [≡]

★★ **LA CALLE DOCE.** *1925 Skillman Ave (75206). 214/824-9900. www.lacalledoce.com.* Mexican menu. Specializes in pescado a la parrilla, paella, enchiladas de camaron. Hrs: 11 am-9:30 pm; Fri, Sat to 10:30 pm: Sun to 9 pm. Res accepted. Wine list. Lunch, dinner $4.95-$13.95. Entertainment. Porch patio. Cr cds: A, C, D, DS, MC, V.

D SC ⌐

★★★ **LA MIRABELLE.** *17610 Midway Rd (75287). 972/733-0202.* Classic French menu. Specializes in Dover sole done tableside, buffalo tenderloin. Hrs: 11:30 am-11 pm. Closed Sun, Mon. Res required Fri, Sat. Wine list. Lunch $8-$20, dinner $20-$35. Chef owned. Flaming desserts. Cr cds: MC, V.

D ⌐

★★ **L'ANCESTRAL.** *4514 Travis #124 (75205). 214/528-1081.* Hrs: 11:30 am-2 pm, 6-10 pm; Fri, Sat to 11 pm. Closed Sun; some major hols. Res accepted. Country French menu. Bar. A la carte entrees: lunch $6.25-$14.50, dinner $15.50-$21.50. Complete meals: dinner $22.50. Specializes in pepper steak, lamb tenderloin, grilled salmon. Outdoor dining. Cr cds: A, D, DS, MC, V.

D ⌐

★★★ **LANDMARK.** *3015 Oak Lawn Ave (75219). 214/522-1453.* Hrs: 6 am-2 pm, 6-10 pm; Sat 6-11 am, 6-11 pm; Sun 6 am-2 pm, brunch from 11 am. Res accepted. Bar. Wine cellar. Bkfst $7-$12, lunch $9-$14.75, dinner $19.50-$29. Sun brunch $29.50. Valet parking. Specialties: stuffed snapper, NY strip steak. Attractive decor in same 1920s style as hotel. Cr cds: A, C, D, DS, MC, V.

D

★★ **LA TRATTORIA LOMBARDI.** *2916 N Hall St (75204). 214/954-0803.* Northern menu. Specializes in fettucine den tescatore, piccata di vitello. Hrs: 11 am-2 pm. 5-10:30 pm; Sat 5-11 pm; Sun 5-10 pm. Res accepted. Wine, beer. Lunch $7.95-$16.95, dinner $11.60-$26. Entertainment. Cr cds: A, C, D, MC, V.

D ⌐

★★ **LAVENDOU.** *19009 Preston Rd; Ste 200 (75225). 972/248-1911. www.lavendou.com.* Hrs: 11:30 am-2 pm, 6-10 pm; Fri, Sat to 11 pm. Closed Sun; major hols. Res accepted. French menu. Bar. Lunch $7.95-$17.95, dinner $14.50-$28.50. Specializes in rotisserie, Southern French dishes, French pastries. Own

baking. Outdoor dining. Country French atmosphere with pottery, art. Totally nonsmoking. Cr cds: A, MC, V.

SC ⌐

★★ **LAWRY'S THE PRIME RIB.** *14655 Dallas Pkwy (75240). 972/503-6688. www.lawrysonline.com.* Hrs: 11:30 am-2 pm, 5:30-10 pm; Fri to 11 pm; Sat 5:30-11 pm; Sun 11:30 am-2 pm (brunch), 5-10 pm. Closed July 4, Dec 25. Res accepted. Bar. Wine cellar. Lunch $7.95-$12.95, dinner $15.95-$27.95. Sun brunch $8.95-$13.95. Child's menu. Specializes in prime rib, fresh fish. Free valet parking. Tableside preparation of meat chosen by patrons from silver cart; formal, Old English atmosphere. Cr cds: A, D, DS, MC, V.

D

★★★ **LOMBARDI MARE.** *5100 Beltline Rd. #410, Addison (75240). 972/503-1233.* Italian, seafood menu. Specializes in fettucine limone, fresh seafood, crème brulee. Hrs: 11 am-11 pm, Sat 5 pm-midnight; Sun 11 am-3 pm. Res accepted. Wine list. Lunch $10-$15; dinner $15-$30. Brunch $12-$20. Entertainment: jazz Sun brunch. Cr cds: A, D, MC, V.

D

★★ **LOMBARDI'S.** *311 N Market (75202). 214/747-0322.* Hrs: 11 am-11 pm; Fri to midnight; Sat 5 pm-midnight; Sun 5-10 pm. Italian menu. Bar. A la carte entrees: lunch, dinner $9-$21. Specializes in pasta, pizza. Outdoor dining. Valet parking. Cr cds: A, D, MC, V.

D

★★★ **MAGUIRE'S.** *17552 N Dallas Pkwy (75287). 972/818-0068. www. maguiresrestaurant.com.* Global menu. Specializes in filet mignon, pistachio mahi mahi, Maguire salad. Hrs: 11 am-2:30 pm, 5-10 pm; Fri to 11 pm; Sat 5-11 pm; Sun 10:30 am-2:30 pm, 5-9 pm. Res accepted. Wine list. Lunch $6-$20, dinner $10-$28. Sun brunch $10. Entertainment: jazz Sun brunch. Cr cds: A, D, DS, MC, V.

D ⌐

★★ **MARIO & ALBERTO.** *12817 Preston Valley Ctr; Ste 425 (75230).*

972/980-7296. Specializes in carne asada, shrimp Diablo. Hrs: 11 am-9 pm; Fri, Sat to 10 pm. Closed Sun. Res accepted. Wine list. Lunch $5.25-$5.75, dinner $7.85-$12. Child's menu. Entertainment. Cr cds: A, D, DS, MC, V.
D ◪

★★ **MARRAKESH.** 5027 W Lovers Ln (75209). 214/357-4104. www.dallasdinesout.com. Mediterranean menu. Specializes in lamb, sirloin and chicken kabob, pastillia, tagra. Hrs: 11 am-2 pm, 5:30-10 pm; Sat, Sun to 11 pm. Res accepted. Extensive wine list. Lunch $8-$15, dinner $8-$26.95. Entertainment: belly dancing. Cr cds: A, D, DS, MC, V.
D ◪

★★ **MARTY'S WINEBAR.** 3316 Oak Lawn Ave (75219). 214/526-4070. www.martysdfw.com. Specializes in chops, steak. Hrs: 5-10 pm. Closed Sun, Mon. Res accepted. Extensive wine list. Dinner $15-$20. Entertainment: Wed-Sat. Cr cds: A, C, D, DS, ER, JCB, MC, V.
D

★★★ **MEDITERRANEO.** 18111 Preston Rd, Ste 120 (75252). 972/447-0066. www.mediterraneo.com. French, Italian menu. Specializes in fresh seafood. Hrs: 11:30 am-2 pm, 6-10 pm; Fri to 11pm; Sat 6-11 pm; Sun 6-9 pm. Closed major hols. Res accepted. Bar. Wine list. A la carte: lunch $7.50-$13.50, dinner $15-28.50. Entertainment. Valet parking. Outdoor dining. Mediterranean villa setting. Cr cds: A, C, D, DS, MC, V.
D

★★★ **THE MERCURY GRILL.** 11909 Prescent Rd #1418 (75206). 972/960-7774. Global cuisine. Hrs: 11 am-10 pm, Fri to 11 pm; Sat 5:30-11 pm; Sun 5:30-10 pm. A la carte entrees: $16-$28. Bar. Valet. Cr cds: A, D, MC, V.
D ◪

★★ **MI COCINA.** 11661 Preston Rd (75230). 214/521-6426. Hrs: 11 am-10 pm. Mexican menu. Lunch $7.50-$9.95; dinner $10.75-$18.50. Child's menu. Specializes in enchiladas. Cr cds: A, D, DS, ER, JCB, MC, V.
D

★★ **MI PIACI.** 14854 Montfort (75240). 972/934-8424. www.mipiaci.com. Hrs: 11:30 am-10:30 pm; Fri to 11 pm; Sat 5-11 pm; Sun 5-10 pm. Closed some major hols. Res accepted. Northern Italian menu. Bar. A la carte entrees: lunch $9.95-$17.95, dinner $11.25-$32.50. Specialties: Dover sole, osso buco, linguine pirata. Own baking. Valet parking. Outdoor dining. Overlooks pond. Cr cds: A, D, DS, MC, V.
D

★★ **MODO MIO.** 18352 Dallas Pkwy (75287). 972/671-6636. Northern Italian menu. Specializes in sea bass, mahi tuna. Hrs: 5-10 pm; Fri, Sat to 11 pm. Closed Sun; hols. Res accepted. Wine list. Dinner $8-$28. Entertainment. Cr cds: A, C, D, DS, JCB, MC, V.
D ◪

★★ **MOMO'S ITALIAN.** 9191 Forest (75219). 972/234-6800. Specializes in gamberi ala momo, conchitile Quattro formatti. Hrs: 10 am-9:30 pm; Fri, Sat 4:30-10:30 pm; Sun 4:30-9 pm. Res accepted. Lunch $5.45-$6.95; dinner $11.85-$16.75. Child's menu. Entertainment. Eight salt and freshwater fish aquariums. Cr cds: A, DS, MC, V.

★★ **MONICA'S ACA Y ALLA.** 2914 Main St (75226). 214/748-7140. www.monica.com. Specializes in Mexican lasagna, green pasta, Tex-Mex. Hrs: 11 am-2 pm, 5-10 pm; Fri to midnight; Sat 11 am-3 pm, 5 pm-midnight; Sun 6-11 pm. Closed Mon; hols. Res accepted. Wine list. Lunch $4.99, dinner $6.99-$17.99. Entertainment. Cr cds: A, DS, MC, V.
D ◪

★★ **MONTE CARLO.** 15201 Dallas Pkwy, Addison (75001). 972/386-6000. www.intercontinentalhotel.com. Menu changes seasonally. Hrs: 5-10 pm. Res required. Wine, beer. Dinner $6-$28. Entertainment. Cr cds: A, C, D, DS, MC, V.
D ◪

★★★ **MORTON'S OF CHICAGO.** 501 Elm St (75202). 214/741-2277. www.mortons.com. Hrs: 5:30-11 pm; Sun 5-10 pm. Closed major hols. Res accepted. Bar. A la carte entrees: dinner $17.95-$29.95. Specializes in steak, seafood, lamb. Valet parking. Open grill; meat displayed at table for patrons to select. Cr cds: A, D, DS, MC, V.
D

★★★★ **NANA.** *2201 Stemmons Fwy (75207). 214/761-7479.* Focused mostly on grilled steaks and chops since opening in the early '80s, this restaurant's updated menu is now much more diverse. The almost overwhelming assortment of flavors makes the seven-course chef's tasting menu a safe and rewarding option. The other New American options change daily based on the market bounty, and the stunning presentations themselves are worth the visit.Specializes in fresh fish, prime beef cuts, rack of lamb. Hrs: 11:30 am-2 pm, 6-10 pm; Fri, Sat to 10:30 pm. Sun brunch 11-2 pm. Bar from noon; Sat from 5:30 pm. Res accepted. Wine list. A la carte entrees: lunch $15-$30, dinner $30-$40. Entertainment. Valet parking. Located on 27th floor; view of city. Cr cds: A, D, DS, MC, V.

★★★ **NEWPORT'S SEAFOOD.** *703 McKinney Ave (75202). 214/954-0220. www.dallasdinesout.com.* Hrs: 11:30 am-2:30 pm, 5:30-10:30 pm; Sat, Sun from 5:30 pm. Closed major hols. Bar. A la carte entrees: lunch $9-$11.50, dinner $15-$31. Specializes in mesquite-grilled seafood, steak, chicken. Extensive seafood selection. Parking. Tri-level dining in turn-of-the-century brewery; 50-ft-deep freshwater well in dining area. Cr cds: A, C, D, DS, MC, V.

★★★ **NICHOLINI'S.** *17370 Preston Rd (75252). 972/735-9868. www.dallasdinesout\n.com.* Menu changes seasonally. Hrs: 5-10 pm. Res required. Wine, beer. Dinner $6-$28. Entertainment. Cr cds: A, D, DS, MC, V.

★★★ **NICK AND SAMS.** *3008 Maple Ave (75201). 214/871-7444. www.nick-sams.com.* Steak and seafood menu. Specializes in crab cakes, filet mignon, lobster. Hrs: 5:30-10 pm, Thurs-Sat 5:30-11 pm. Res accepted. Wine list. Dinner a la carte entrees: $15-$32. Entertainment: Thurs, Fri. Two grand pianos, one in kitchen, open kitchen. Cr cds: A, D, DS, MC, V.

★★★ **OLD WARSAW.** *2610 Maple Ave (75201). 214/528-0032. www.gtesuperside.com/warsawmaner.* Hrs: 5:30-10:30 pm. Res required. French, continental menu. Bar. Wine cellar. A la carte entrees: dinner $21-$32. Specializes in lobster, steak au poivre, Dover sole. Own baking. Violinist, pianist. Valet parking. Fish tank. Family-owned. Jacket. Cr cds: A, D, DS, MC, V.

★★★ **PALM.** *701 Ross Ave (75202). 214/698-0470.* Hrs 11:30 am-10:30 pm; Sat from 5 pm; Sun 5:30-9:30 pm. Closed some major hols. Res accepted. Bar. Lunch $8.25-$13.50, dinner $14.50-$33. Specializes in prime aged beef, veal, lobster. Valet parking. Cr cds: A, C, D, MC, V.

★★ **PALOMINO.** *500 Crescent Ct #165 (75201). 214/999-1222. www.palomino.com.* Hrs: 11 am-2:30 pm, 5-11 pm; Fri to midnight; Sat 5 pm-midnight; Sun 5-9 pm. Closed Thanksgiving, Dec 25. Res accepted. Mediterranean menu. Bar to 2 am (exc Sun). Wine list. Lunch $5.95-$13.95, dinner $7.95-$24.95. Child's menu. Specializes in thin-crust pizzas, fresh seafood, lamb. Valet parking. Outdoor dining. Colorful decor; artwork. Bistro atmosphere. Cr cds: A, D, DS, MC, V.

★★★ **PAPPAS BROS. STEAKHOUSE.** *10477 Lombardy Ln (75220). 214/366-2000. www.pappasbros.com.* Specializes in prime beef, lobster tails. Hrs: 5-10; Fri, Sat to 11 pm. Closed Sun. Res accepted. Wine list. Dinner $13.97-$36.95. Pianist. Open kitchen viewing. Cr cds: A, D, MC, V. Cr cds: A, D, MC, V.

★★ **PATRIZIO.** *25 Highland Park Village (75205). 214/522-7878.* Hrs: 11 am-11 pm; Sun, Mon to 10 pm; Fri, Sat to midnight. Closed Jan 1, Thanksgiving, Dec 25. Italian menu. Bar. A la carte entrees: lunch $5.20-$7.30, dinner $6-$13.95. Specialties: angel hair pasta with artichokes, sauteed crab claws, grilled chicken portabella salad. Valet parking. Out-

door dining. Oriental rugs, original oil paintings. Cr cds: A, D, DS, MC, V.
D ⌐

★★ **PEGGY SUE BBQ.** *6600 Snider Plaza (75205).* 214/987-9188. Specializes in BBQ dishes. Hrs: 11 am-9 pm; Fri, Sat to 10 pm. Closed hols. Res accepted. Wine, beer. Lunch, dinner $4.75-$13.95. Child's menu. Entertainment. Cr cds: MC, V.

★★ **POMODORO.** *2708 Routh St (75201).* 214/871-1924. *www.arcodoro. com.* Hrs: Sun-Wed 6-11 pm; Thurs-Sat to midnight. Res accepted. Sardinian cuisine. Bar. Wine list. Specialties: grated bottarga, fresh pasta with wild boar and calamari, split veal shank. A la carte entrees: dinner $22.50-$44. Cr crds: A, DC, MC, V
D ⌐

★★★ **THE PYRAMID.** *1717 N Akard St (75201).* 214/720-5249. *www. fairmont.com.* Continental menu. Specializes in beef, veal, seafood. Own baking. Hrs: 6:30-11 am, 11:30 am-2:30 pm, 5-10:30 pm. Closed Sun. Res accepted. Bar 6 pm-1:30 am. Wine list. A la carte entrees: dinner $26-$36. Entertainment. Valet parking. Jacket required in main dining rm. Cr cds: A, C, D, DS, MC, V.
D

★★★★ **RESTAURANT AT THE MANSION ON TURTLE CREEK.** *2821 Turtle Creek Blvd (75219).* 214/559-2100. *www.rosewood-hotel. com.* Nationally recognized chef Dean Fearing, considered a founder of innovative Southwestern cuisine, presides over this hotel dining room. It is a regal space flanked by fireplaces and filled with original wood paneling, leaded glass, and antiques. Guests at the mansion can even order menu items, such as lobster taco with yellow tomato salsa and jicama salad, to their room 24 hours a day. Specialties: tortilla soup, lobster taco, crème brulée. Own baking. Hrs: noon-2:30 pm, 6-10:30 pm; Fri, Sat to 11 pm; Sun brunch 11 am-2:30 pm. Res accepted; required Fri, Sat. Bar 11-2 am. Wine cellar. A la carte entrees: lunch from $15, dinner from $26. Sun brunch $38. Valet parking. Jacket. Cr cds: A, D, DS, MC, V.
D

★★★★ **THE RIVIERA.** *7709 Inwood Rd (75209).* 214/351-0094. *www. riviera-dallas.com.* This refined, Provençal-style dining room is the perfect place to enjoy nationally recognized southern French and northern Italian cuisine. Dishes are authentic, creative, and well-presented and include a beautiful sauteed red snapper fillet with French beans, grilled portobello mushrooms, and tarragon lobster-tomato broth. A nice wine from the list or the by-the-glass offerings completes a consistently wonderful experience. Continental menu. Specializes in escargots and tortellini, rack of lamb. Hrs: 6:30-10 pm; Sat to 11 pm. Closed hols. Res accepted. Bar. Wine list. A la carte entrees: dinner $26-$39. Complete meals: dinner $45-$65. Valet parking. Country French decor. Cr cds: C, MC, V.
D

★★ **ROCK BOTTOM BREWERY.** *4050 Beltline Rd, Addison (75240).* 972/404-7456. *www.rockbottom.com.* Specializes in New York strip, Texas fire steak. Hrs: 11 am-midnight; Fri, Sat to 2 am; Sun noon-midnight. Closed July 4. Res accepted. Wine list. Lunch $5.95-$10.95, dinner $8.95-$18.95. Child's menu. Entertainment: Band Tues, Fri, Sat. Cr cds: A, C, D, ER, JCB, MC, V.
D ⌐

★★★ **ROOSTER.** *3521 Oak Grove Rd (75204).* 214/521-1234. *www.guide live.com.* Hrs: 11:30 am-2:30 pm, 5:30-10 pm; Sun 11 am-2:30 pm (brunch). Closed most major hols. Res accepted. Contemporary, regional Amer menu. Bar. Wine list. Lunch $8.50-$11, dinner $14-$26. Sun brunch $7-$15. Specialties: roasted Vidalia onion soup, molasses pecan-encrusted catfish, herb-grilled lamb loin. Own baking. Valet parking. Outdoor dining. Relaxed atmosphere has rooster theme. Cr cds: A, C, D, DS, MC, V.
D

★★ **ROUTH STREET.** *3011 Routh St (75201).* 214/526-8181. Specializes in chile relleno, chicken fried steak. Hrs: 11 am-10 pm; Fri, Sat to11 pm; Sun 10 am-10 pm. Closed Thanksgiving, Dec 25. Res accepted. Lunch $6-$8; dinner $8-$10. Child's menu.

Entertainment, garden patio. Cr cds: A, C, DS, MC, V.

⊡ ⊒

★★ **ROYAL TOKYO.** 7525 Greenville Ave (75231). 214/368-3304. www.royal tokyo.com. Hrs: 11:30 am-2 pm, 5:30-11 pm; Fri to 11:30 pm; Sat 5:30-11:30 pm; Sun 5:30-10:30 pm. Closed Thanksgiving, Dec 25. Res accepted. Japanese menu. Bar. Lunch $5-$15, dinner $14.25-$35. Child's menu. Specialties: tempura, shabu-shabu, hibachi steak. Sushi bar. Pianist. Parking. Traditional seating avail. Japanese motif; outdoor water gardens. Cr cds: A, C, D, DS, MC, V.

⊡ ⊒

★★ **RUGGERI'S.** 2911 Routh St (75201). 214/871-7377. www.dallas dinesout.com/ruggeri. Hrs: 11:30 am-2 pm, 6-11 pm; Sat, Sun from 6 pm. Closed some major hols. Res accepted. Northern Italian menu. Bar. Llunch $8.95-$13.95, dinner $10.95-$32. Specializes in fresh seafood, veal chops. Pianist. Valet parking. Cr cds: A, D, DS, MC, V.

⊡ ⊒

★★★ **RUTH'S CHRIS STEAK HOUSE.** 5922 Cedar Springs Rd (75235). 214/902-8080. www.ruth schris.com. Hrs: 5-11 pm, Sun to 10 pm. Closed Thanksgiving, Dec 25. Res accepted. Bar. Wine list. A la carte entrees: $17.95-$33.95. Specializes in steak, fresh seafood. Valet parking. Cr cds: A, C, D, DS, MC, V.

⊡ ⊒

★★★ **THE SAMBA ROOM.** 4514 Travis St, Suite #A132 (75205). 214/522-4137. www.sambaroom.com. Cuban/Latin American menu. Specializes in whole red snapper, pork tenderloin. Hrs: 5-11 pm; Fri, Sat to midnight, Sun 11 am-3 pm. Res accepted. Beer, wine. Dinner $12-$24. Brunch $12. Garage. Cr cds: A, C, D, DS, MC, V.

⊡ ⊒

★★ **SAMBUCA.** 15207 Addison Rd, Addison (75001). 972/385-8455. www. sambucajazzcafe.com. Mediterranean menu. Specializes in stuffed lobster, filet mignon. Hrs: 11:30 am-2: 30 pm, 6-11 pm; Thurs to midnight; Sat 6 pm-2 am; Sun 6-11 pm. Res

accepted. Extensive wine list. Lunch $6.95-$16.50; dinner $15-$30. Entertainment: jazz. Eclectic decor. Cr cds: DS, MC, V.

⊒

★★★ **SEVY'S GRILL.** 8201 Preston Rd, Ste 100 (75225). 214/265-7389. www.sevy.com. Hrs: 11:30 am-2:30 pm, 5-10 pm; Fri, Sat to 11 pm; Sun (brunch) 11 am-2 pm, 5-11 pm. Closed major hols. Res accepted. Bar. Lunch $6.50-$9.99, dinner $9.50-$19.79. Sun brunch $9. Specialties: smoked beef tenderloin, pan-seared salmon. Valet parking. Outdoor dining. Architectural design of dining rm inspired by Frank Lloyd Wright. Cr cds: A, C, D, DS, MC, V.

⊡ ⊒

★ **SONNY BRYAN'S.** 302 N Market St (75202). 214/744-1610. www.sonny bryansbbq.com. Hrs: 11 am-10 pm; Fri to 11 pm, Sat 6-11 pm; Sun noon-9 pm. Closed Easter, Thanksgiving, Dec 25; also Feb, Mar. Barbecue menu. Bar. Lunch $3.50-$10.99, dinner $6-$12.50. Child's menu. Guitarist exc Sun. Outdoor dining. Old West atmosphere; meats smoked on premises. Cr cds: A, D, DS, MC, V.

⊡ ⊒

★★★ **STAR CANYON.** 3102 Oak Lawn Ave, Ste 144 (75219). 214/520-7827. www.starcanyon.com. Hrs: 11:30-2pm, 6-10:30 pm; Fri, Sat to 11 pm; Sun to 9:30 pm. Closed some major hols. Res required. Wine list. A la carte entrees: dinner $16-$24. Specialties: tamale tart with roast garlic custard and Gulf crabmeat, bone-in cowboy ribeye with red chile onion rings. Valet parking. Outdoor dining. Stylish yet unpretentious dining experience among award-winning Texan decor. Cr cds: A, D, DS, MC, V.

⊡ ⊒

★★ **STONELEIGH P.** 2926 Maple Ave (75201). 214/871-2346. www. stoneleighp.com. Specializes in hamburgers, chicken sandwich. Hrs: 11 am-midnight. Closed hols. Res accepted. Wine list. Lunch, dinner $3.50-$13.95. Entertainment. Award-winning jukebox. Cr cds: A, D, DS, ER, JCB, MC, V.

⊡ ⊒

★ **SUSHI.** *2927 Maple Ave (75201). 214/871-7111.* Hrs: 11 am-2 pm, 5:30-11 pm; Fri, Sat to midnight. Closed Sun; most major hols. Res accepted. Japanese menu. Bar. Lunch, dinner $3.50-$29.50. Specialties: spider roll, granoff roll, Stoneleigh roll. Valet parking. Outdoor dining. Unique decor; kimonos and scrolls decorate walls. Totally nonsmoking. Cr cds: A, D, DS, MC, V.

★★ **TEI TEI ROBATA BAR.** *2906 N Henderson (75206). 214/828-2400. www.teiteirobata.com.* Specializes in Robata grilled seafood, Maine lobster, sushi. Hrs: 5:30-11 pm. Closed Mon. Res accepted. Wine list. Dinner $16-$100. Entertainment. Patami Room (no shoes) seats 6-12 people. Cr cds: A, MC, V.
[D] [🖥]

★★ **TEPPO.** *2014 Greenville Ave (75206). 214/826-8989. www.teppo. com.* Specializes in yakitori, sushi, chicken meatballs, beef tongue. Hrs: 5:30-11 pm; Fri, Sat to 3 am. Wine, beer. Dinner $10-$65. Entertainment. Cr cds: A, MC, V.
[🖥]

★★ **TERILLI'S.** *2815 Greenville (75206). 214/827-3993. www.terillis. com.* Specializes in capellini de angelo, chicken terreli, italchos. Hrs: 11:30-2 am; Sun, Mon to midnight. Res accepted. Wine list. Lunch $5.95-$9.25; dinner $9.75-$21.95. Sun brunch $5.95-$10.95. Jazz Tues-Sun. Patio dining. Cr cds: A, C, D, MC, V.
[D] [🖥]

★ **TIN STAR.** *2626 Howell St; Ste 100 (75204). 214/999-0059. www.tin starinc.com.* Hrs: 7 am-10 pm; Fri to 11 pm; Sat 8 am-10 pm; Sun 8 am-9 pm. Closed Thanksgiving, Dec 25. Southwestern menu. Bkfst, lunch, dinner $4.99-12.99. Child's menu. Specialty: poblano jack chicken. Cr cds: A, D, DS, MC, V.
[D]

★★ **TONY'S WINE WAREHOUSE.** *2904 Oak Lawn (75219). 214/520-9463.* Italian menu. Specializes in filet mignon, grilled salmon in lemon dill cream sauce. Hrs: 11:30 am-10 pm; Fri, Sat to 11 pm. Closed Sun. Res accepted. Wine list. Lunch $6.95-$12.95; dinner $10.95-$16.95.

Accordionist Wed. Wine tasting. Cr cds: A, D, DS, MC, V.
[D] [🖥]

★★ **TRAMONTANA.** *8220-B Westchester Ave (75225). 214/368-4188. www.mybistro.net.* New American menu. Specializes in veal osso bocco with saffron couscous, pan-roasted sea bass with lobster risotto. Hrs: 11 am-2:30 pm, 5:30-11 pm. Closed Sun, Mon; hol. Res accepted. Wine list. Lunch $6.95-$13.95; dinner $14.95-$21.95. Entertainment. Cozy bistro. Cr cds: A, MC, V.
[D]

★★ **UNCLE JULIO'S.** *4125 Lemon (75219). 214/520-6620.* Mexican menu. Specializes in broiled ribs, shrimp, quail, frog legs. Hrs: 11 am-10: 30 pm; Fri, Sat to 11:30 pm. Wine, beer. Lunch, dinner $6.95-$18.95. Child's menu. Entertainment. Cr cds: A, C, D, DS, MC, V.
[D] [🖥]

★★ **UNCLE TAI'S.** *13350 Dallas Pkwy (75240). 972/934-9998.* Hrs: 11 am-10 pm; Fri, Sat to 10:30 pm; Sun noon-9:30 pm. Closed some major hols. Res accepted. Chinese menu. Serv bar. A la carte entrees: lunch $7.50-$10.50, dinner $11-$17. Specializes in beef, chicken, seafood. Totally nonsmoking. Cr cds: A, D, MC, V.
[D]

★★ **YORK STREET.** *6047 Lewis St (75206). 214/826-0968.* Hrs: 6-10 pm; Fri, Sat to 11 pm. Closed Sun, Mon; most major hols. Res accepted. Dinner $16-$26. Specialties: sauteed soft-shelled crab, pepper steak with cognac sauce, rack of lamb Provençal. Totally nonsmoking. Cr cds: MC, V.
[D]

★★★ **YVETTE.** *14775 Midway Rd, Addison (75001). 972/503-9777. www. yvetterestaurant.com.* Hrs: 11 am-2:30 pm, 5-11 pm; Fri to midnight; Sat 5 pm-midnight. Closed Sun; Jan 1, Dec 25. Res accepted. Bar; Fri, Sat to 2 am. Wine cellar. A la carte entrees: lunch $6-$15, dinner $12-$32. Specialties: Dover sole, chateaubriand, Australian lobster tails. Musicians. Valet parking. Elegant atmosphere; ballroom, murals, wine racks. Cr cds: A, D, MC, V.
[D] [🖥]

★★ **ZIZIKI'S.** *4514 Travis St, Ste 122 (75205). 214/521-3311.* Hrs: 11 am-11 pm; Fri, Sat to midnight; Sun brunch 11 am-2 pm. Closed major hols. Mediterranean menu. Bar. Lunch $7.95-$9.95, dinner $13.95-$21.95. Sun brunch $19.95. Specialties: grilled rack of lamb, spanakopita, pasticchio. Parking. Outdoor dining. Intimate bistro setting. Cr cds: A, C, D, MC, V.

Dallas/Fort Worth Airport Area

(B-6) *See also Dallas, Fort Worth*

Services and Information

Information. 972/574-8888.
Lost and Found. 972/574-4454.
Cash Machines. Terminals 2E, 3E, 4E.
Airlines. Aeromexico, Air Canada, America West, American, British Airways, Continental, Delta, Korean Air, Lone Star, Lufthansa, Midwest Express, Northwest, Simmons, TWA, United, USAir, Vanguard, Western Pacific.

Motels/Motor Lodges

★★ **COUNTRY SUITES BY CARLSON.** *4100 W John Carpenter Fwy, Irving (75063). 972/929-4008; fax 972/929-4224; toll-free 800/456-4000. www.countryinns.com.* 72 kit. suites, 18 kit. units, 3 story. S $59-$99; D $69-$129; each addl $10; under 16 free. Crib free. Pet accepted, some restrictions; $100 deposit ($50 refundable). TV; cable (premium). Heated pool; wading pool, whirlpool. Complimentary continental bkfst. Ck-out noon. Meeting rms. Business servs avail. In-rm modem link. Coin lndry. Free airport transportation. Exercise equipt. Refrigerators, microwaves. Cr cds: A, C, D, DS, MC, V.

★★ **DRURY INN.** *4210 W Airport Fwy, Irving (75062). 972/986-1200; res 800/378-7946. www.druryinn.com.* 129 rms, 4 story. S $76-$86; D $86-$96; each addl $10; under 18 free. Crib free. Pet accepted, some restrictions. TV; cable (premium). Pool. Complimentary continental bkfst. Restaurant adj 11-2 am. Ck-out noon. Meeting rms. Business servs avail. In-rm modem link. Sundries. Free airport transportation. Health club privileges. Cr cds: A, C, D, DS, MC, V.

★★ **FAIRFIELD INN DFW AIRPORT/IRVING.** *4800 John Carpenter Frwy, Irving (75063). 972/929-7257; toll-free 800/228-2800. www.fairfield inn.com.* 109 rms, 3 story. Mar-Oct: S, D $69.95; under 18 free; lower rates rest of yr. Crib free. TV; cable (premium). Pool; whirlpool. Complimentary continental bkfst. Ck-out noon. Business servs avail. Valet serv. Cr cds: A, C, D, DS, MC, V.

★★ **HAMPTON INN.** *4340 W Airport Frwy, Irving (75062). 972/986-3606; fax 972/986-6852; toll-free 800/426-7866. www.hamptoninn.com.* 81 rms, 4 story. S $79; D $89; suites $95; under 18 free. Crib free. Pet accepted. TV; cable (premium). Pool. Complimentary continental bkfst. Restaurant adj 11-2 am. Ck-out noon. Sundries. Valet serv. Free airport transportation. Some refrigerators; microwaves avail. Health club privileges. Cr cds: A, C, D, DS, MC, V.

★★★ **HARVEY SUITES.** *4550 W John Carpenter Fwy, Irving (75063). 972/929-4499; fax 972/929-0774; res 800/922-9222.* 164 suites, 3 story. S, D $149; under 18 free; wkend rates. Crib free. Pet accepted; $25 deposit. TV; cable. Pool; whirlpool. Complimentary continental bkfst. Complimentary coffee in rms. Restaurant 6:30-9 am; Sat, Sun 7-11 am. Rm serv 5-10 pm. Bar 5 pm-midnight. Ck-out 1 pm. Coin lndry. Meeting rms. Business servs avail. In-rm modem link. Valet serv. Sundries. Gift shop. Free airport transportation. Exercise equipt. Refrigerators, wet bars; microwaves avail. Picnic tables, grills. Cr cds: A, C, D, DS, ER, JCB, MC, V.

★★ **HOLIDAY INN SELECT DFW NORTH.** *4441 Hwy 114, at Esters, Irving (75063). 972/929-8181; fax 972/929-8233; toll-free 800/339-9994. www.holiday-inn.com.* 282 rms, 8 story. S $129-$134; D $139-$149; each addl $10; suites $150-$250; under 18 free; wkend, hol rates. Crib free. TV; cable (premium). Pool; poolside serv. Coffee in rms. Restaurant 6:30 am-11 pm. Rm serv. Bar 11-1 am. Ck-out noon. Coin lndry. Meeting rms. Business center. In-rm modem link. Gift shop. Valet serv. Free airport transportation. Exercise equipt. Some refrigerators; microwaves avail. Cr cds: A, D, DS, MC, V.

⬛ 🏊 🏋 ✈ 🔅 🔥 🏃

★★ **HOLIDAY INN SELECT DFW SOUTH.** *4440 W Airport Fwy, Irving (75062). 972/399-1010; fax 972/790-8545; res 800/465-4329. www.holiday-inn.com/dfw-airports.* 409 rms, 4 story. S $69-$149; D $69-$159; each addl $10; suites $150-$350; under 18 free; wkend rates. TV; cable (premium). Indoor pool; wading pool, whirlpool. Restaurant 6 am-midnight. Rm serv. Bar 3 pm-2 am. Ck-out noon. Coin lndry. Meeting rms. Business servs avail. In-rm modem link. Bellhops. Valet serv. Sundries. Gift shop. Free airport transportation. Exercise equipt. Health club privileges. Game rm. Rec rm. Microwaves avail. Cr cds: A, C, D, DS, MC, V.

⬛ 🏊 🏋 ✈ 🔅 🔥 SC

★★ **LA QUINTA INN.** *4105 W Airport Fwy, Irving (75062). 972/252-6546; fax 972/570-4225; res 800/531-5900. www.laquinta.com.* 169 rms, 2 story. S $75-$85; D $85-$95; each addl $10; suites $100-$125; under 18 free. Crib free. Pet accepted. TV; cable (premium). Pool. Complimentary continental bkfst. Restaurant adj open 24 hrs. Ck-out noon. Meeting rm. Business servs avail. In-rm modem link. Free airport transportation. Health club privileges. Cr cds: A, C, D, DS, MC, V.

⬛ 🐾 🐕 🏊 🔅 🔥

★★ **WILSON WORLD HOTEL & SUITES.** *4600 W Airport Fwy, Irving (75062). 972/513-0800; fax 972/513-0106. www.wilsonhotels.com.* 200 rms, 5 story, 96 suites. S $69-$89; D $69-$99; suites $89-$129; under 18 free; wkend rates. Crib free. Pet accepted, some restrictions. TV; cable (pre-

mium). Indoor pool; whirlpool. Restaurant 6 am-1:30 pm, 5:30-10 pm. Bar 5 pm-midnight. Ck-out noon. Meeting rms. Business center. In-rm modem link. Gift shop. Free airport transportation. Exercise equipt. Refrigerators; microwaves avail. Cr cds: A, C, D, DS, ER, JCB, MC, V.

⬛ 🐾 🏊 🏋 ✈ 🔅 🔥 🏃

Hotels

★★★ **HILTON EXECUTIVE CONFERENCE CENTER DFW.** *1800 E Hwy 26, Grapevine (76051). 817/481-8444; fax 817/481-3160; res 800/645-1019. www.hilton.com.* 395 rms, 9 story. S, D $99-$189; each addl $15; suites $225-$950; under 18 free; wkend rates. Crib free. TV; cable (premium), VCR avail. 2 pools, 1 indoor; whirlpool, poolside serv. Coffee in rms. Restaurant 6:30 am-3 pm (see also MERITAGE GRILLE). Bars 11-2 am; entertainment. Ck-out noon. Convention facilities. Business center. In-rm modem link. Concierge. Gift shop. Free airport transportation. 8 tennis courts, 2 indoor. Golf privileges. Exercise rm; steam rm. Minibars; some bathrm phones, refrigerators. Wooded grounds with lake. Luxury level. Cr cds: A, C, D, DS, MC, V.

⬛ 🏌 🎾 🏊 🏋 ✈ 🔅 🔥 SC 🏃

★★★ **HILTON GARDEN LAS COLINAS.** *7516 Las Colinas Blvd, Irving (75063). 972/444-8434; fax 972/910-9246; toll-free 800/445-8661. www.hilton.com.* 174 rms, 5 story, 44 suites. S, D $159-$169; suites $154; under 18 free; wkend rates; wkends (2-day min); higher rates special events. Crib free. TV; cable. Complimentary continental bkfst. Complimentary coffee in rms. Restaurant nearby. Bar. Ck-out noon. Meeting rms. Business center. In-rm modem link. Valer serv. Sundries. Gift shop. Coin lndry. Exercise equipt. Pool. Refrigerators, microwaves. Grills. Cr cds: A, C, D, DS, MC, V.

⬛ 🏊 🏋 🔅 🔥 SC 🏃

★★★ **HYATT REGENCY DFW.** *International Pkwy, Dallas/Ft. Worth Airport (75261). 972/453-1234; fax 972/456-8668; res 800/233-1234. www.dfwairport.hyatt.com.* 1,369 rms, 12 story. S $79-$230; D $79-$255; each addl $25; suites $275-$1,200; under 18 free; wkend rates. TV; cable (premium), VCR avail. Heated pool; poolside serv. Restaurant open 24 hrs. Bar 11-2 am; entertainment. Ck-out noon. Convention facilities. Business center. In-rm modem link. Concierge. Shopping arcade. Free airport transportation. Indoor, outdoor tennis, pro. 36-hole golf, greens fee $75-$85, pro, putting green, driving range. Exercise equipt. Health club privileges. Many refrigerators; some bathrm phones; microwaves avail. Balconies. Luxury level. Cr cds: A, C, D, DS, ER, JCB, MC, V.

★★★ **MARRIOTT.** *8440 Freeport Pkwy, Irving (75063). 972/929-8800; fax 972/929-6501; res 800/228-9290. www.marriott.com.* 491 rms, 20 story. S, D $179-$199; suites $200-$425; under 12 free; wkend rates. Crib free. TV; cable (premium). Indoor/outdoor pool; whirlpool, poolside serv. Coffee in rms. Restaurants 6 am-11 pm. Bar 11-2 am. Ck-out 1 pm. Coin lndry. Convention facilities. Business center. In-rm modem link. Sundries. Gift shop. Free airport transportation. Tennis privileges. Golf privileges. Exercise equipt; sauna. Some refrigerators. Luxury level. Cr cds: A, C, D, DS, ER, JCB, MC, V.

★★★ **MARRIOTT DALLAS LAS COLINAS.** *223 W Las Colinas Blvd, Dallas (75039). 972/831-0000; res 800/228-9290. www.marriott.com.* 364 rms, 15 story. S, D $175-$225; suites $250-$450; under 172 free; wkend rates. Crib free. TV; cable (premium), VCR avail. Indoor pool; whirlpool. Coffee in rms. Restaurants 6:30 am-midnight. Bar 11 am-midnight. Ck-out noon. Lndry serv. Meeting rms. Business center. In-rm modem link. Concierge. Gift shop. Exercise equipt. Refrigerators avail. Cr cds: A, D, DS, MC, V.

★★★ **MARRIOTT SOUTH DALLAS FORT WORTH AIRPORT.** *4151 Centrepoint Dr, Dallas (76155). 817/358-1700; res 800/228-9290. www.marriott.com.* 295 rms, 8 story. S, D $155-$195; suites $250-$450; under 17 free; wkend rates. Crib free. TV; cable (premium), VCR avail. Indoor pool; whirlpool. Coffee in rms. Restaurants 6:30 am-midnight. Bar

11 am-midnight. Ck-out noon. Lndry serv. Meeting rms. Business center. In-rm modem link. Concierge. Gift shop. Exercise equipt. Refrigerators avail. Cr cds: A, D, DS, MC, V.

★★★ **OMNI MANDALAY HOTEL AT LAS COLINAS.** *221 E Las Colinas Blvd, Irving (75039). 972/556-0800; fax 972/556-0729; res 800/843-6664. omnihotels.com.* 410 rms, 28 story. S, D $109-$245; each addl $10; suites $225-$275; under 18 free; wkend rates. Crib free. Valet parking $8/day. TV; cable (premium), VCR avail. Heated pool; whirlpool, poolside serv (seasonal). Restaurant. Rm serv 24 hrs. Bar 11:30-1:30 am. Ck-out noon. Convention facilities. Business center. In-rm modem link. Concierge. Gift shop. Tennis privileges. Golf privileges. Exercise rm; sauna. Massage. Bathrm phones. Some private patios, balconies. Cr cds: A, C, D, DS, JCB, MC, V.

Resort

★★★★ **FOUR SEASONS RESORT AND CLUB DALLAS AT LAS COLINAS.** *4150 N MacArthur Blvd, Irving (75038). 972/717-0700; fax 972/717-2550; res 800/332-3442. www.fourseasons.com.* Located in the Las Colinas hills, this 400-acre resort offers a par-70 championship golf course, four pools, 12 tennis courts, and a spa. Corporate guests will value the 20,000-square-foot conference center and should also consider the creative, all-inclusive packages with the resort's own Byron Nelson Golf School. All 357 rooms have private balconies with fairway views. 357 rms, 9 story. S, D $305-$375; suites $600-$1,300; under 18 free; golf, spa, wkend plans. Pet accepted, some restrictions. Valet parking $5. TV; cable (premium), VCR avail. Four pools, 2 heated, wading pool, whirlpool, poolside serv. Restaurant (see also CAFE ON THE GREEN). Rm serv 24 hrs. Bar 11-2 am. Ck-out noon. Convention facilities. Business center. In-rm modem link. Concierge. Gift shop. Barber, beauty shop. 12 tennis courts, 4 indoor, pro. 18-hole golf, greens fee $150 (incl cart), pro, 2 putting greens, driving range. Exercise rm; sauna, steam rm. Massage. Lawn games. Minibars; microwaves avail. Private patios, balconies. Cr cds: A, C, D, DS, JCB, MC, V.

All Suites

★★ **AMERISUITES HOTEL.** *4235 W Airport Frwy, Irving (75062). 972/659-1272; fax 972/570-0676; res 800/833-1516. www.amerisuites.com.* 128 suites, 6 story. S $99; D $109; under 18 free; wkend rates. Crib free. TV; cable (premium). Pool. Complimentary continental bkfst. Ck-out 11 am. Meeting rms. Business servs avail. Coin lndry. Free airport transportation. Exercise equipt. Health club privileges. Refrigerators, microwaves. Cr cds: A, D, DS, MC, V.

★★ **COMFORT SUITES OF LAS COLINAS.** *1223 Greenway Cir, Irving (75038). 972/518-0606; fax 972/518-0722; res 800/517-4000. www.comfortsuites.com.* 54 suites, 3 story. S, D $99-$109; each addl $5; under 18 free. Crib free. TV; cable (premium). Complimentary continental bkfst. Ck-out 11 am. Meeting rm. Business servs avail. Valet serv. Exercise equipt. Microwaves avail. Cr cds: A, C, D, DS, MC, V.

Restaurants

★★★ **CAFE ON THE GREEN.** *4150 N MacArthur Blvd, Irving (75038). 972/717-0700. www.fshr.com.* Hrs: 6:30 am-11 pm; Sat, Sun from 7 am; Sun brunch 11 am-3 pm. Res accepted. Bar. Wine cellar. A la carte entrees: bkfst $7-$20, lunch $12-$30, dinner $35-$60. Buffet: bkfst $17, lunch $22, dinner $36. Sun brunch $47,children 6-12 $23. Serv charge 17%. Amer menu. Specialties: slow-roasted Atlantic salmon, comino-rubbed beef tenderloin,vegetable tamales. Own baking. Valet parking. Gardenlike setting; overlooks villas, pool. Cr cds: A, C, D, DS, ER, MC, V.

★★ **HANASHO.** *2938 N Belt Line Rd, Irving (75062). 972/258-0250. www.hanasho.com.* Hrs: 11:30 am-2 pm, 6-10 pm; Fri, Sat to 10:30 pm; Sun 5:30-9:30 pm. Lunch, dinner

$14-$20. Entertainment. Cr cds: A, D, MC, V.

★★ **LA BISTRO.** *722 Grapevine Hwy, Hurst (76054). 817/281-9333.* Hrs: 11 am-10 pm; Fri to 11 pm; Sat 5-11 pm. Closed most major hols. Res accepted. Italian menu. Bar. A la carte entrees: lunch $6.25-$9.95, dinner $7.95-$25.95. Child's menu. Specialties: Norwegian salmon, veal chop. Piano Tues-Sat. Parking. Intimate atmosphere. Jacket. Cr cds: A, C, D, DS, ER, MC, V.

★★★ **MERITAGE GRILLE.** *1800 TX 26 E, Grapevine (76051). 817/481-8444.* Hrs: 5-11 pm. Res accepted. Southwestern menu. Wine list. A la carte entrees: dinner $9.95-$26.95. Specializes in prime beef, steaks, chops. Valet parking. Patio dining. Dark wood paneling gives this hotel dining rm an Old World club atmosphere; view of gardens. Cr cds: A, C, D, DS, ER, MC, V.

★★ **MUSTANG CAFE.** *5205 O'Connor; Suite 105, Irving (75039). 972/869-9942. www.mustangcafe.com.* Specializes in broiled filet mignon, coconut-crusted sea bass, angel hair pasta with smoked chicken. Hrs: 11 am-10 pm; Fri to 10:30 pm; Sat 5-10:30 pm; Sun 10:30 am-2 pm, 5-9 pm. Res accepted. Wine list. Lunch $7.95-$13.95; dinner $16.95-$24.95. Brunch $18.95. Entertainment. Overlooks Mustang sculptor in Las Colinas. Cr cds: A, D, DS, MC, V.

★★★ **VIA REAL.** *4020 N MacArthur Blvd, Irving (75038). 972/650-9001. www.viareal.com.* Southwest and Mexican menu. Specializes in tentacion, flan de Mexico. Hrs: 11 am-10 pm; Fri, Sat to 11 pm. Extensive wine list. Lunch $6-$17; dinner $10-$35. Child's menu. Southwestern decor. Cr cds: A, C, D, DS, MC, V.

Unrated Dining Spot

TREVI. *221 E Las Colinas Blvd, Irving (75039). 972/556-0800.* Continental menu. Hrs: Mon-Fri 6:30 am-11 pm; Sat-Sun 7 am-11 pm. Bkfst $7-$8.50; lunch $8-$9.50; dinner $4.50-$29.

Resv accepted for large parties. Cr cds: A, C, D, DS, MC, V.

Del Rio

(E-4) *See also Brackettville, Eagle Pass, Uvalde*

Founded 1868 **Pop** 33,867 **Elev** 948 ft
Information Chamber of Commerce, 1915 Avenue F; 830/775-3551.
Web www.drchamber.com

What to See and Do

Amistad (Friendship) National Recreation Area. An international project. Six-mi-long dam forms a lake of more than 65,000 acres extending up the Rio Grande, Devil's, and Pecos rivers. Stone statue of Tlaloc, Aztec rain god, towers over Mexican end of dam; 4,000-yr-old pictographs in rock shelters in the area. Two marinas with boat ramps, gas, stores, and full facilities. Water sports, swimming; primitive camping. (Daily) 12 mi NW on US 90. Contact Amistad National Recreation Area, HCR 3 Box 5J, 78840. Phone 830/775-7491. **FREE**

Ciudad Acuña, Mexico. Across the border. Visitors often make the short trip over the river to this quaint Mexican town. Shopping, restaurants, and nightlife all serve as attractions to the tourist. (For Border Crossing Regulations, see MAKING THE MOST OF YOUR TRIP.)

Continental Ranch Tour. All-day tour of 90-yr-old ranch incl ranch headquarters, domestic livestock, native plants, rock formations, and undeveloped scenic areas of the Pecos River. Tour incl snacks and picnic lunch overlooking Pecos River. Participants should be in good physical condition and be willing to ride two hrs over rough terrain. By appt only. 50 mi NW of Del Rio in Val Verde County. Phone 830/775-6957. ¢¢¢¢

The Firehouse. The Del Rio Council for the Arts maintains an art gallery; classes and workshops in arts and special interest areas. (Mon-Sat; closed hols) 120 E Garfield. Phone 830/775-0888. **FREE**

Judge Roy Bean Visitor Center. For yrs, Bean was "the law west of the Pecos." Preserved by the state of Texas, his saloon-courtrm, the "Jersey Lily," is a historic landmark. Dioramas with sound; cactus garden. Department of Transportation visitor center. (Daily; closed hols) 60 mi NW on US 90 in Langtry. Phone 915/291-3340. **FREE**

Seminole Canyon State Historical Park. On 2,172 acres. Hiking, picnicking, camping. Prehistoric pictograph sites. Guided tours into canyon (Wed-Sun). 41 mi NW via US 90, 10 mi W of Comstock. Phone 915/292-4464. ¢¢

Val Verde Winery. Texas's oldest licensed winery, founded in 1883, is operated by the third generation of the Qualia family. Tours, tasting. (Mon-Sat; closed hols) 100 Qualia Dr. Phone 830/775-9714. **FREE**

Whitehead Memorial Museum. Memorabilia of early Southwest; Cadena folk art; grave of Judge Roy Bean; replica of Bean's Jersey Lily Saloon, hacienda and chapel, doctor's office; cabins, store, barn. (Tues-Sun; closed hols) 1308 S Main St. Phone 830/774-7568. ¢¢

Special Events

George Paul Memorial Bull Riding. Val Verde County Fairgrounds. Top riders in the world compete. Late Apr. Phone 830/775-9595.

Cinco de Mayo Celebration. Entertainment, dance, food, crafts. May 5. Phone 830/774-8541.

Diez y Seis de Septiembre. Brown Plaza. Concerts, food booths, music. Sept 16. Phone 830/774-8541.

Fiesta de Amistad. Mid-late Oct. Phone 830/775-3551.

Motels/Motor Lodges

★ ★ **BEST WESTERN.** *810 Ave F (78840).* 830/775-7511; fax 830/774-2194; res 800/528-1234. *www.bestwestern.com.* 62 rms, 2 story. S $49; D $59; each addl $10; under 18 free. Pet accepted. TV; cable (premium). Pool; whirlpool. Complimentary full bkfst. Ck-out noon. Coin lndry. Business servs avail. Cr cds: A, C, D, DS, MC, V.

★★ **LA QUINTA INN.** *2005 Ave F (78840). 830/775-7591; fax 830/774-0809; res 800/531-5900. www. laquinta.com.* 101 rms, 2 story. S $54-$70; D $62-$77; under 18 free. Crib free. Pet accepted. TV; cable (premium). Pool. Complimentary continental bkfst. Coffee in rms. Ck-out noon. Coin lndry. In-rm modem link. Cr cds: A, C, D, DS, JCB, MC, V.

★★ **RAMADA INN.** *2101 Ave F (78840). 830/775-1511; fax 830/775-1476; toll-free 800/272-6232. www. ramada.com.* 155 rms. S $55-$75; D $65-$85; each addl $10; suites $123; under 18 free; higher rates special events. Crib free. Pet accepted, some restrictions. TV; cable (premium), VCR (movies). Pool; whirlpool, poolside serv. Complimentary coffee in rms. Restaurant 6 am-2 pm, 5-10 pm; Sun 6 am-3 pm, 5-10 pm. Rm serv. Bar 4 pm-2 am. Ck-out noon. Coin lndry. Valet serv. Exercise equipt; sauna. Refrigerators. Cr cds: A, C, D, DS, JCB, MC, V.

Denison

(B-6) *See also Bonham, Gainesville, Sherman*

Founded 1872 **Pop** 22,773 **Elev** 767 ft
Area code 903

Information Chamber of Commerce, 313 W Woodard St, PO Box 325, 75021; 903/465-1551

What to See and Do

Denison Dam. Large earth-filled dam impounds Lake Texoma. Water sports; resorts. Camping (fees in some areas). Visitor center. (See LAKE TEXOMA, OK) 5 mi NW on TX 91. Phone 903/465-4990.

Eisenhower Birthplace State Historical Park. Restored house; furnishings; some of Eisenhower's personal items. Interpretive center; picnicking. (Tues-Sun; closed Jan 1, Thanksgiving, Dec 25) 208 E Day St at Lamar Ave, 4 blks E of US 69. Phone 903/465-8908. ¢

Eisenhower State Park. Approx 450 acres. Swimming, fishing (lighted pier), boating (ramps, marina); hiking trails, picnicking, playground, improved campsites, RV facilities (dump stations). Standard fees. (Daily) 5 mi NW on TX 91, then 2 mi W on FM 1310 to Park Rd 20. Phone 903/465-1956. ¢

Grayson County Frontier Village. Town replica from 1800s; 15 original structures, museum. (Daily) 2 mi SW via TX 75, Loy Lake Rd exit. Phone 903/463-2487. **FREE**

Special Event

Texoma Lakefest Regatta. Regatta, dance, lake activities. Mid-Apr. Phone 903/465-1551.

Denton

(B-6) *See also Arlington-Grand Prairie, Dallas, Fort Worth, Gainesville*

Pop 80,537 **Elev** 662 ft
Information Convention & Visitor Bureau, 414 Parkway St, PO Drawer P, 76202; 940/382-9693 or 888/381-1818
Web www.denton-chamber.org

What to See and Do

Denton County Courthouse Museum. Memorabilia and artifacts depicting Denton County history; large collections of rare antique dolls and guns; rare blue glass; Native American artifacts. (Tues-Sat afternoons; closed hols) Courthouse on the Square, 110 W Hickory, first floor. Phone 940/349-2850. **FREE**

Lewisville Lake. This 23,000-acre lake is surrounded by 11 developed park areas. Three marinas and a fishing barge provide service to boaters and anglers; swimming. Some fees. (Daily) Contact Reservoir Manager, 1801 N Mill St, Lewisville 75057. 1 mi SE via I-35E. Phone 972/219-3742.

Ray Roberts Lake State Park. Formed by the damming of the Trinity River; recreation areas around the new lake are still being developed. Isle duBois and Johnson Branch areas each offer swimming, fishing piers (cleaning stations), boating (launch, docks); nature, hiking, bridle trails; picnicking, playgrounds, primitive and improved camping, tent and trailer sites. Other areas offer limited facilities. Some fees. (Daily) Approx 12 NE via US 380 and US 377. Phone 940/686-3408. ¢¢

Texas Woman's University. (1901) 9,000 students. Graduate school and Institute of Health Sciences are coeducational. This 270-acre campus incl University Gardens; art galleries in Fine Arts Building; DAR Museum with "Gowns of First Ladies of Texas" collection in Adminstrative Conference(by appt); and the Blagg-Huey Library with "Texas Women—A Celebration of History," a self-guided tour with photos and artifacts (Daily; closed hols). University Dr and Bell Ave, NE part of town. Phone 940/898-3456. **FREE** Also on campus is

Little-Chapel-in-the-Woods. Designed by O'Neil Ford. Stained-glass windows, carved wood, mosaics made by students. A National Youth Administration (NYA) project dedicated by Eleanor Roosevelt in 1939. (Daily) **FREE**

Special Event

North Texas State Fair and Rodeo. Nine days late Aug. Phone 940/387-2632.

Motels/Motor Lodges

★★ **HOLIDAY INN.** *1500 Dallas Dr (76205).* 940/387-3511; fax 940/387-7917; res 800/465-4329. www.holiday-inn.com. 144 rms, 2 story. S, D $62-$67; each addl $5; suites $95-$150; under 18 free. Crib free. TV; cable (premium). Pool. Restaurant 6:30 am-2 pm, 5-10 pm. Rm serv. Private club 5 pm-midnight; closed Sun; entertainment. Ck-out noon. Coin lndry. Meeting rms. Business servs avail. In-rm modem link. Cr cds: A, DS, MC, V.
🄳 ⇌ 🔌 🐾 SC

★★ **RAMADA INN FANTASY SUITES.** *820 S I-35 E (76205).* 940/387-0591; fax 940/566-0792; res 800/228-2828. www.ramada.com. 84 rms, 2 story. S $58-$68; D $66-$80; each addl $10; suites $65-$199;

under 12 free; wkend rates; higher rates special events. Crib free. TV; cable (premium), VCR avail (movies). Complimentary full bkfst. Complimentary coffee in rms. Restaurant adj 6:30 am-11 pm. Ck-out noon. Meeting rms. Business servs avail. In-rm modem link. Sundries. Coin lndry. Pool. Some in-rm whirlpools, refrigerators, microwaves. Cr cds: A, C, D, DS, ER, JCB, MC, V.
🄳 ⇌ 🔌 🐾

Hotel

★★★ **RADISSON HOTEL.** *2211 I-35 E N (76205).* 940/565-8499; fax 940/384-2244; toll-free 800/333-3333. www.radisson.com. 150 rms, 8 story. S, D $89-$109; each addl $10; suites $189-$340; under 18 free; golf plans. Pet accepted, some restricions. TV; cable (premium), VCR avail. Pool. Complimentary coffee in rms. Restaurant 6 am-10 pm. Bar 11 am-midnight. Meeting rms. Business center. Tennis privileges. 18-hole golf, pro, putting green, driving range. Exercise equipt. Health club privileges. Cr cds: A, C, D, DS, ER, MC, V.
🄳 🐾 🎿 🍴 ⇌ 🏋 🔌 🐾 SC 🐾

Restaurant

★ **TRAIL DUST STEAKHOUSE.** *US 380, Aubrey (76227).* 940/440-3878. www.traildust.com. Hrs: 5-10 pm; Fri to midnight; Sat 4 pm-midnight; Sun noon-10 pm. Closed Thanksgiving, Dec 25. Western Amer menu. Bar. A la carte entrees: dinner $7.99-$22.99. Child's menu. Specialties: 14-oz or 24-oz T-bone steak, barbecued ribs, mesquite-broiled chicken. Traditional Texas atmosphere; no ties allowed. Band Thurs-Sun. Cr cds: A, D, DS, MC, V.
🄳 🍴

Dumas

(F-I) *See also Amarillo*

Pop 13,747 **Elev** 3,668 ft
Area code 806 **Zip** 79029

Information Moore County Chamber of Commerce, PO Box 735; 806/935-2123

Special Event

Dogie Days Celebration. McDade Park. Food booths, carnival rides, dances, barbecue, parade. First wkend June.

Motels/Motor Lodges

★ **BEST WESTERN WINDSOR INN.** *1701 S Dumas Ave (79029). 806/935-9644; fax 806/935-9730; res 800/780-7234. www.bestwestern.com.* 57 rms, 2 story. S $32.99-$49.99; D $40.99-$50.99; each addl $8; under 17 free. Crib free. Pet accepted. TV; cable (premium). Indoor pool; whirlpool. Restaurant nearby. Ck-out noon. Coin lndry. Exercise equipt; sauna. Some refrigerators. Cr cds: A, C, D, DS, JCB, MC, V.

D ⚓ ≈ 🏃 ⊠ 🔥 SC

★★ **COMFORT INN.** *1620 S Dumas Ave (79029). 806/935-6988; fax 806/935-6924; res 800/228-5150. www.comfortinn.com.* 50 rms, 2 story. S $49-$59; D $89-$99; each addl $5; suites $68-$88; under 12 free. Crib free. Pet accepted, some restrictions. TV; cable. Complimentary continental bkfst. Complimentary coffee in rms. Restaurant adj 11:30 am-9:30 pm. Ck-out noon. Meeting rms. Business servs avail. Exercise equipt. Indoor pool; whirlpool. Bathrm phones; many refrigerators. Cr cds: A, C, D, MC, V.

D ≈ 🏃 ⊠ 🔥

★★ **CONAKI DUMAS INN.** *1712 S Dumas Ave (79029). 806/935-6441; fax 806/935-9331; toll-free 800/396-8831.* 101 rms, 2 story. S $49-$89; D $53-$97; each addl $8; suites $125. Crib $8. Pet accepted. TV; cable (premium). Indoor pool; whirlpool. Restaurant 6 am-10 pm. Rm serv. Private club 5 pm-2 am. Ck-out noon. Meeting rms. Business servs avail. In-rm modem link. Exercise equipt. Game rm. Cr cds: A, C, D, DS, MC, V.

D ⚓ ≈ 🏃 ⊠ 🔥

★ **ECONO LODGE.** *1719 S Dumas Ave (79029). 806/935-9098; fax 806/935-7483; toll-free 800/344-2575. www.econolodge.com.* 40 rms, 2 story. Mar-July: S $38.95-$50; D $47.95-$70; each addl $3; under 18 free; wkly, wkend rates; lower rates rest of yr. Crib $5. Pet accepted. TV; cable (premium). Heated pool; whirlpool. Complimentary continental bkfst. Restaurant nearby. Ck-out 11 am. Business servs avail. Coin lndry. Some refrigerators. Cr cds: A, DS, MC, V.

⚓ ⊠ 🔥 ≈

★ **SUPER 8 MOTEL.** *119 W 17th St (79029). 806/935-6222; fax 806/935-6222; res 800/800-8000. www.super8.com.* 30 rms, 2 story. Apr-Sept, Dec: S $50.88; D $65.88; each addl $5; under 12 free; lower rates rest of yr. Pet accepted, some restrictions; $5. TV; cable. Complimentary continental bkfst. Restaurant nearby. Ck-out 11 am. Business servs avail. Refrigerators, microwaves. Cr cds: A, C, D, DS, MC, V.

D ⚓ ⊠ 🔥

Eagle Lake

See also Houston

Pop 3,664 **Elev** 170 ft **Area code** 409 **Zip** 77434

Information Chamber of Commerce, 408 E Main St, 409/234-2780

What to See and Do

Attwater Prairie Chicken National Wildlife Refuge. Approx 8,000 acres along banks of San Bernard River. Protected area for the endangered Attwater prairie chicken; large numbers of migratory and resident species. In spring, refuge is filled with wildflowers. (Daily; office Mon-Fri) 7 mi NE off FM 3013. Phone 409/234-3021. **FREE**

Prairie Edge Museum. Exhibits depicting area history, life on the prairie, flora and fauna, early rice-farming equipt. (Sat, Sun, and by appt) 408 E Main. Phone 409/234-2780. **FREE**

Special Event

Magnolia Homes Tour. 18 mi NW, in Columbus. Ten early Texas and Victorian houses are opened for tours; antique show; parade; food. Phone 409/732-8385. Four days mid-May.

Eagle Pass

(E-4) *See also Brackettville, Del Rio, Uvalde*

Founded 1849 **Pop** 22,413 **Elev** 726 ft
Area code 830
Information Chamber of Commerce, 400 Garrison St, PO Box 1188, 78853; 830/773-3224
Web www.eaglepasstexas.com

Eagle Pass is across the Rio Grande from Piedras Negras, Coahuila, Mexico (for Border Crossing Regulations see MAKING THE MOST OF YOUR TRIP). A toll bridge connects the two cities. Eagle Pass is the port of entry to Mexican Highway 57, the Constitution Highway to Mexico City via Saltillo and San Luis Potosi.

What to See and Do

Fort Duncan Park. Ten restored buildings of the fort (1849) that once housed 10,000 troops; museum (Mon-Fri). In park are ballfields, picnic area, playground, and golf course. (Daily) Enter at Adams or Monroe St. Phone 830/773-4343. **FREE**

Piedras Negras, Mexico. (Pop 280,000) Many pleasant restaurants and nightclubs. Contact the Chamber of Commerce.

Motels/Motor Lodges

★★ **BEST WESTERN EAGLE PASS.** *1923 Loop 431 (78852). 830/758-1234; fax 830/758-1235; toll-free 800/992-3245. www.bestwestern.com.* 40 rms, 2 story, 14 suites. S $72; D $78; suites $70-$80; under 12 free; family rates. Crib free. Pet accepted, some restrictions. TV; cable (premium). Restaurant opp open 24 hrs. Ck-out noon. Meeting rms. Business servs avail. In-rm modem link. Pool. Refrigerators, microwaves. Cr cds: A, C, D, DS, ER, JCB, MC, V.
🆔 🏃 🎿 ➰ 🏖 🎿

★★ **LA QUINTA INN.** *2525 E Main St (78852). 830/773-7000; fax 830/773-8852; res 800/531-5900.*

www.laquinta.com. 130 rms, 2 story. S $60-$67; D $68-$75; each addl $8; under 18 free; wkend rates. Crib free. Pet accepted. TV; cable (premium). Pool. Complimentary continental bkfst. Complimentary coffee in rms. Restaurant adj open 24 hrs. Ck-out noon. Valet serv. Meeting rms. In-rm modem link. Microwaves, refrigerators avail. Cr cds: A, D, DS, MC, V.
🆔 🏃 🎿 ➰ 🏖 🎿

Eastland

See also Abilene, Fort Worth, Weatherford

Pop 3,769 **Elev** 1,421 ft
Area code 254 **Zip** 76448
Information Chamber of Commerce, 102 S Seaman; 254/629-2332

Eastland is the home of the legend of "Old Rip," a Texas horned toad alleged to have survived for 31 years (1897-1928) sealed in the cornerstone of the county courthouse. A minor publicity sensation resulted for the town when the cornerstone was opened and the reptile discovered. Today, the remains of Old Rip are on view in the county courthouse.

Edinburg

(G-5) *See also Harlingen, McAllen, Mission*

Founded 1907 **Pop** 48,465 **Elev** 91 ft
Area code 956 **Zip** 78539
Information Chamber of Commerce, 602 W University Dr, PO Box 85; 956/383-4974
Web www.edinburg.com

What to See and Do

Hidalgo County Historical Museum. Exhibits depict regional history of Rio Grande Valley, south Texas and northern Mexico; incl Native American items, Spanish exploration, Mexican War, ranch life, steamboats, bandit era. Housed partly in 1910 County Jail Building with hanging rm (used once in 1913) and original gallows trapdoor. (Tues-Sun; closed hols) 121 E McIntyre (on Courthouse Sq). Phone 956/383-6911. ¢¢

Special Event

Fiesta Hidalgo. Five days, last wkend Feb.

El Paso

(C-1) *Also see Las Cruces, NM*

Founded 1827 **Pop** 563,662
Elev 3,762-6,700 ft **Area code** 915
Information Convention & Visitors Bureau, 1 Civic Center Plaza, 79901; 915/534-0653 or 800/351-6024
Web www.elpasocvb.com

The first authenticated expedition here was by Rodriguez Chamuscado in 1581. Juan de Oñate named the place El Paso del Norte in 1598. Several missions were founded in the area beginning in 1659. They are now considered to be among the oldest continuously active parishes in the United States. Over the years several ranches were established. The first actual settlement in what is now downtown El Paso was in 1827, adjacent to the ranch of Juan Maria Ponce de Leon.

The town remained wholly Mexican throughout the Texas Revolution. In 1846 it surrendered to US forces engaged in fighting the Mexican War. In 1848 it was divided between present-day Ciudad Juárez and what was to become El Paso proper. The border was placed in the middle of the Rio Grande, according to the terms of the treaty of Guadalupe Hidalgo. By provision of the Chamizal Treaty of 1963, the boundary has been changed, giving back to Mexico about 700 acres cut off by the shifting of the river. The disputed area was made into parkland on both sides of the border.

A military post was established in 1846 and a trading post in 1852. In 1854 the military post was named Fort Bliss. By this time the Butterfield Stage Line from St. Louis to San Francisco was carrying gold seekers to California through El Paso.

Fort Bliss was captured by Texas troops of the Confederate Army in 1861 as part of a campaign to win New Mexico. The campaign failed, and the troops gradually withdrew. El Paso returned to Union hands by the end of the Civil War.

Spanish and English are mutually spoken in both El Paso and Ciudad Juárez. International spirit runs heavy between these two cities, as does the traffic. This spirit is reflected in the Civic Center complex and in the Chamizal National Memorial.

Along with more than 400 manufacturing plants ranging from oil refineries to food processing facilities, El Paso is also home to a military training center and one of the largest air defense centers in the world.

What to See and Do

Bus tours. Trolley rides into Mexico. 1 Civic Center Plaza. Phone 915/544-0062. ¢¢¢

Chamizal National Memorial. The 55-acre area commemorates peaceful settlement of a boundary dispute between Mexico and the US. Exhibits and bilingual movie tell story of the settlement; bilingual guide service. Special events incl theater performances (see SPECIAL EVENTS). Visitor center (daily). Contact Superintendent, 800 S San Marcial, 79905. Enter from Paisano Dr; near Cordova Bridge. Phone 915/532-7273. **FREE**

Ciudad Juárez. Offers a different and fascinating experience. The markets in Ciudad Juarez have a wide variety of goods, and the stores offer better shopping than most Mexican border cities. Bullfights, fairs, and festivals abound. The best way to cross the border is to park in a lot on El Paso St, at the bridge, and walk. Take advantage of the El Paso/Juarez trolley. (For Border Crossing Regulations, see MAKING THE MOST OF YOUR TRIP.)

Concordia Cemetery. Established in 1856, this had become a primary burial site for El Paso by the 1880s.

The Boot Hill section holds the grave of gunfighter John Wesley Hardin. NW of I-10 and US 54. Phone 915/786-7733.

El Paso Holocaust Museum and Study Center. Exhibits detail tragic events that led from the rise of Nazi Germany and anti-Semitism to the death camps and, eventually, liberation. Event speakers incl liberators and survivors. (Tues-Thurs, Sun) 4401 Wallenberg Dr. Phone 915/833-5656.

El Paso Mission Trail. (Approx 20 mi) Drive E 12 mi on I-10 to Zaragosa Rd, then S 2 1/2 mi to Alameda Ave; turn left and then immediate right onto S Old Pueblo Rd, which leads to

Ysleta. (1682) Oldest mission in Texas. When founded, Ysleta was on the Mexican side of the Rio Grande, but the river shifted, leaving it in Texas. The Mission Nuestra Señora del Carmen is on US 80 and S Old Pueblo Rd. Preservation and upkeep is continuous. Some of the surrounding lands have been in cultivation every yr since its founding. This is one of the few places in the US where Egyptian long-staple cotton has been grown successfully. Also here is the

Tigua Cultural Center. The Tigua people, whose origins can be traced to 1500 B.C., maintain a cultural center, two restaurants, and a gift shop. Presentations of Tigua dances and bread-baking (Sat-Sun). (See SPECIAL EVENTS)

(Daily) 305 Ya Ya Ln. Phone 915/859-5287. **FREE**

Socorro. The Mission here (ca 1680) is the oldest parish church in continual use in the US. Continue E approx 9 mi to

San Elizario. The Presidio Chapel (1843) was built to replace the one first established in 1780. San Elizario was the site of the Salt War, a bitter struggle over rights to salt found in flats to the east.

Scenic drive. To south end of Mt Franklin gives a magnificent view of El Paso and Ciudad Juárez, particularly at night. Go north on Mesa St to Rim Rd and turn east, which will lead you to Scenic Dr.

El Paso Museum of Art. Exhibits spanning six centuries of paintings and sculpture incl American, Mexican Colonial, and pre-Columbian art, Kress Collection of Italian Renaissance works; changing exhibits. (Tues-Wed, Fri-Sun; closed hols) 1 Arts Festival Plaza. Phone 915/532-1707. **FREE**

El Paso Museum of History. Hispanic, Native American, US artifacts and El Paso history dioramas; changing exhibits. (Tues-Sun; closed hols) 12901 Gateway West, I-10 and Americas Ave. Phone 915/858-1928. **Donation**

Fort Bliss. Enter at Robert E. Lee Gate, one mi E of airport. Once the largest cavalry post in the US, Fort Bliss is now the home of the US Army Air Defense Center, one of the

Colorful El Paso

largest air defense centers in the world, where troops from all allied nations train. Phone 915/568-2121. On base are

Fort Bliss Replica Museum. Five adobe buildings replicate the original Fort Bliss army post. Period rms contain items pertaining to the history of the fort, military and civilian artifacts from 1850s-present. (Daily; closed hols) Pershing and Pleasanton rds. Phone 915/568-4518. **FREE**

US Army Air Defense Museum. Audiovisual exhibits on history of US antiaircraft gunnery and other military subjects. Changing exhibits; weapons park. (Daily; closed hols) Bldg 1735 on Marshall Rd. Phone 915/568-5412. **FREE**

Guadalupe Mountains National Park. (see). 55 mi SW via US 62/180 in Texas.

Hueco Tanks State Historic Site. More than 850 acres of cave and rock formations, ancient pictographs, vegetation, and wildlife. This is a semi-oasis in the desert where rainfall is trapped in natural basins or "huecos." Park facilities incl picnicking, improved campsites (hookups, dump station). Rock climbing. Standard fees. (Daily) 32 mi NE off US 62, Ranch Rd 2775. Phone 915/857-1135. ¢¢

Magoffin Home State Historic Site. Example of early territorial architecture (1875). Sun-dried adobe combined with Greek Revival detail created the Southwestern living style. Original family furnishings. (Daily) 1120 Magoffin Ave. Phone 915/533-5147. ¢

University of Texas at El Paso. (1914) 17,000 students. The Sun Bowl, seating 53,000, is on campus along with the Centennial Museum. Fine Arts Center with art exhibits, drama, and musical productions (fee). Off I-10, Schuster exit. Phone 915/747-5000.

Wilderness Park Museum. Archaeological and ethnological exhibits of the Southwest and man's adaptation to a desert environment; nature trail. Guided tours (by appt). (Tues-Sun; closed hols) Transmountain Rd at Gateway South. Phone 915/755-4332. **FREE**

Special Events

Southwestern International Livestock Show & PRCA Rodeo. County Coliseum. First two wks Feb.

Siglo de Oro. Chamizal National Memorial. Festival of Classical Spanish drama. Phone 915/532-7273. Two wks Mar.

Viva El Paso. McKelligon Canyon Ampitheater. Musical history of the Southwest. June-Aug. Phone 915/565-6900. Phone 800/915-8482.

St. Anthony's Day Celebration. Ysleta del Sur Reservation. Religious patron saint of the Tiguas; special food and ceremonies. Phone 915/859-7913. Mid-June.

El Paso Symphony Orchestra. Abraham Chavez Theatre. Sixteen concerts with solo artists Sept-Apr. Also summer concerts and special events. Phone 915/532-3776.

Fiesta de las Flores. El Paso County Coliseum. Carnival festivities with a Latin flavor. Phone 915/542-3464. Labor Day wkend.

Chamizal Festival. Chamizal National Memorial. Celebration of international folklife. Musicians, dancers. Phone 915/532-7273. Oct.

Horse racing. Sunland Park Race Course. 6 mi W, just off I-10 in New Mexico. Thoroughbred and quarter horse racing. Pari-mutuel betting. Water-ski shows on infield lake (Sat-Sun, weather permitting). Contact 1200 Futunity Dr, Sunland Park, NM 88063. 505/874-5200. Nov-Apr.

Sun Carnival. Festivities and sporting events; ending with the Sun Bowl. Phone 915/533-4416. Thanksgiving wkend-Dec.

Motels/Motor Lodges

★★ **COMFORT INN.** 900 N Yarbrough Dr (79915). 915/594-9111; fax 915/590-4364; res 800/228-5150. www.comfortinn.com. 200 units, 3 story. S $49; D $56; each addl $10; under 18 free. Crib free. Pet accepted. TV; cable (premium). Pool; whirlpool. Complimentary continental bkfst. Restaurant adj 10 am-8 pm. Ck-out noon. Coin lndry. Airport transportation. Balconies. Cr cds: A, D, DS, MC, V.

★★ **HOLIDAY INN SUNLAND PARK.** *900 Sunland Park Dr (79922). 915/833-2900; fax 915/833-5588; toll-free 800/658-2744. www.holidayinn sunland.com.* 178 rms, 2 story. S $79; D $84; each addl $5; suites $100-$125; under 18 free. Crib free. TV; cable (premium). Pool; wading pool, whirlpool, poolside serv. Coffee in rms. Restaurant 6 am-2 pm, 5-10 pm; wkends 7 am-10 pm. Rm serv. Bar. Ck-out noon. Meeting rms. Business servs avail. Bellhops. Valet serv. Sundries. Airport, bus depot transportation. Some microwaves. On hill overlooking Sunland Park. Cr cds: A, C, D, DS, MC, V.

🄳 ⬦ ✈ ⊠ ⊠ 🔥

★ **HOWARD JOHNSON INN.** *8887 Gateway West Blvd (79925). 915/591-9471; fax 915/591-5602; res 800/446-4656. www.hojoelpaso.com.* 140 rms, 1-2 story. S $57; D $62; each addl $5. Crib free. Pet accepted. TV; cable (premium). Pool; wading pool. Restaurant adj open 24 hrs. Ck-out 2 pm. Coin lndry. Meeting rms. Business servs avail. In-rm modem link. Bellhops. Valet serv. Free airport transportation. Exercise equipt. Some refrigerators. Private patios, balconies. Cr cds: A, C, D, DS, ER, JCB, MC, V.

🄳 ⬦ ⊠ ✕ ⊠ 🔥

★★ **LA QUINTA INN.** *6140 Gateway Blvd E (79905). 915/778-9321; fax 915/779-1505; res 800/531-5900. www.laquinta.com.* 121 rms, 2 story. S $61; D $69; each addl $8; suites $95; under 18 free. Crib free. Pet accepted. TV; cable (premium). Pool. Restaurant adj open 24 hrs. Ck-out noon. Business servs avail. In-rm modem link. Free airport transportation. Cr cds: A, C, D, DS, MC, V.

🄳 ⬦ ⊠ ⊠ 🔥

Hotels

★★★ **HILTON AT THE EL PASO AIRPORT.** *2027 Airway Blvd (79925). 915/778-4241; fax 915/772-6871; res 800/045-8667. www.hilton.com.* 272 rms, 4 story. S $112-$117; D $122-$127; each addl $10; suites $127-$137; family, wkend rates. Pet accepted. TV; cable (premium), VCR avail. Heated pool; water slide. Restaurant 6 am-11 pm. Rm serv. Bar noon-2 am. Ck-out noon. Convention facilities. Business center. In-rm modem link. Bellhops. Valet serv. Sundries. Barber, beauty shop. Free airport transportation. Exercise equipt. Microwaves avail. Cr cds: A, D, DS, MC, V.

🄳 ⬦ ⬦ ⊠ ✕ ✈ ⊠ 🔥 ✕

★★★ **HILTON CAMINO REAL HOTEL.** *101 S El Paso St (79901). 915/534-3000; fax 915/534-3024; toll-free 800/769-4300. www.hilton.com.* 359 units, 17 story. S $89-$135; D $89-$150; each addl $15; suites $155-$990; under 12 free. Crib free. Pet accepted, some restrictions; $50. TV; cable. Pool. Restaurants 6 am-11:30 pm. Rm serv 24 hrs. Bar 11-1 am; entertainment. Ck-out noon. Convention facilities. Business center. In-rm modem link. Free airport transportation. Exercise equipt; sauna. Renovated historic hotel (1912). Luxury level. Cr cds: A, C, D, DS, ER, JCB, MC, V.

🄳 ⬦ ⬦ ⊠ ✕ ✈ ⊠ 🔥 ✕

★★★ **MARRIOTT EL PASO.** *1600 Airway Blvd (79925). 915/779-3300; fax 915/772-0915; res 800/228-9290. www.marriott.com.* 296 rms, 6 story. S $124; D $139; each addl $15; suites $300-$500; wkend rates. Crib free. TV; cable (premium). Indoor/outdoor pool; whirlpool, poolside serv. Coffee in rms. Restaurant 6:30 am-2 pm; 5-10 pm. Bar noon-1 am. Ck-out 1 pm. Coin lndry. Convention facilities. Business servs avail. In-rm modem link. Valet serv. Shopping arcade. Free airport transportation. Exercise equipt; sauna. Private patios. Southwestern decor and art. Luxury level. Cr cds: A, D, DS, JCB, MC, V.

🄳 ⊠ ✕ ✈ ⊠ 🔥

B&Bs/Small Inns

★★★ **COWBOYS AND INDIANS.** *405 Mountain Vista, Santa Teresa, NM (88008). 505/589-2653; fax 505/589-4512. www.smart.net/~cowboysbb.* 4 air-cooled rms. S $70; D $77; each addl $7; package plans. Children over 12 yrs only. TV avail. Complimentary full bkfst. Complimentary coffee in rms. Restaurant nearby. Ck-out 11 am, ck-in 3 pm. In-rm modem link. Luggage handling. Concierge serv. Gift shop. Free airport, RR station transportation. Old

West atmosphere; view of Franklin Mts. Totally nonsmoking. Cr cds: A, D, MC, V.

★★★ **SUNSET HEIGHTS BED AND BREAKFAST.** *717 W Yandell Dr (79902).* 915/544-1743; fax 915/544-5119. 4 rms, 3 story. S, D $70-$165; higher rates: Sun Bowl, hols. Adults only. TV; cable, VCR avail. Pool. Spa. Complimentary full bkfst. Complimentary coffee in rms. Ck-out, ck-in noon. Business servs avail. Airport, RR station, bus depot transportation. Picnic tables, grills. Victorian-style building (1905); leaded glass, Tiffany chandeliers. Totally nonsmoking. Cr cds: A, DS, MC, V.

All Suites

★★ **CHASE SUITE HOTEL BY WOODFIN.** *6791 Montana Ave (79925).* 915/772-8000; toll-free 888/433-1936. www.woodfinsuite hotels.com. 200 rms, 2 story. S, D $99-$150; family, wkly, wkend rates. Crib free. TV; cable (premium), VCR avail. 2 heated pools; whirlpools. Complimentary buffet bkfst. Restaurant adj 11 am-midnight. Ck-out noon. Meeting rms. Business servs avail. Valet serv. Airport transportation. Refrigerators, microwaves. Private patios, balconies. Grills. Cr cds: A, C, D, DS, MC, V.

★★★ **EMBASSY SUITES.** *6100 Gateway Blvd E (79905).* 915/779-6222; fax 915/779-8846; res 800/362-2779. www.embassysuites.com. 185 suites, 8 story. S $119; D $129; under 18 free; wkend rates. Pet accepted, some restrictions; $50. TV; cable (premium), VCR avail. Indoor pool; whirlpool. Complimentary bkfst. Ck-out 1 pm. Coin lndry. Meeting rms. Business servs avail. In-rm modem link. Free airport transportation. Exercise equipt; sauna. Refrigerators, microwaves. Large atrium with fountain, pools, plants. Cr cds: A, C, D, DS, JCB, MC, V.

Restaurants

★★ **BELLA NAPOLI.** *6331 N Mesa St (79912).* 915/584-3321. Hrs: 4-10 pm; Sun from 11:30 am. Closed Mon, Tues; wk of July 4, Thanksgiving, Dec 25. Res accepted. Italian, Amer menu. Wine, beer. Lunch, dinner $6.50-$18.95. Specializes in osso buco, veal parmigiana, chicken Jerusalem. Entertainment Wed, wkends. Outdoor dining. Italian decor; twin fireplaces; gardens Cr cds: A, MC, V.

★ **CASA JURADO.** *4772 Doniphan Dr (79922).* 915/833-1151. Hrs: 11 am-9 pm; Fri, Sat to 9:30 pm; Sun noon-8 pm. Closed Mon; major hols. Mexican menu. A la carte entrees: lunch, dinner $3.85-$12.25. Specializes in chicken mole, tacos, enchiladas. Mexican decor. Cr cds: A, C, D, DS, MC, V.

★★ **CATTLEMAN'S STEAKHOUSE AT INDIAN CLIFFS RANCH.** *3045 S Fabens-Carlsbad Rd, Fabens (79838).* 915/544-3200. www.cattlemanssteak house.com. Hrs: 5-10 pm; Sat from 4 pm; Sun 12:30-9 pm. Bar. Lunch, dinner $6.95-$22.95. Child's menu. Specialties: 2-lb T-bone steak, mesquite-smoked brisket, seafood. Replica 1890s frontier fort; rustic decor. Working ranch with hay rides and BBQ dinners. Children's zoo. Gift shop. Location site for several movies. Family-owned. Cr cds: A, D, MC, V.

★★ **JAXON'S.** *4799 N Mesa St (79912).* 915/544-1188. www.jaxons. com. Hrs: 11 am-11 pm; Sun to 10 pm. Closed some major hols. Mexican, Amer menu. Bar to midnight. Lunch, dinner $4.89-$15.99. Specializes in salads, steak, Southwestern dishes. Fireplace. Cr cds: A, D, DS, MC, V.

★★ **SENOR JUAN'S GRIGGS.** *9007 Montana Ave (79925).* 915/598-3451. Hrs: 11 am-9 pm. Closed Thanksgiving, Dec 25. Res accepted. Mexican, Amer menu. Bar. A la carte entrees: lunch, dinner $3.95-$12.95. Specializes in beef and chicken enchiladas, chili. Atrium; antiques. Cr cds: MC, V.

★★ **STATE LINE.** *1222 Sunland Park Dr (79922).* 915/581-3371. Hrs: 11:30

am-2 pm, 5-9:30 pm; Fri, Sat 5-10 pm; Sun 4-9 pm. Closed some major hols. Bar. Lunch $4-$8.50, dinner $8.95-$21. Child's menu. Specializes in barbecue, steak. Own desserts, ice cream. Outdoor dining. Western decor; antique furniture, jukeboxes, cash registers. Family-owned. Cr cds: A, D, DS, MC, V.

Ennis

(C-6) *See also Arlington-Grand Prairie, Corsicana, Dallas*

Pop 16,045 **Elev** 548 ft **Area code** 972 **Zip** 75119

Information Chamber of Commerce, 108 Chamber of Commerce Dr, PO Box 1177, 75120; 972/878-2625

Web www.ennis-chamber.com

What to See and Do

Lake Bardwell. Beaches, waterskiing, fishing, boating (ramps, marina); nature trail, picnicking, tent and trailer sites (electric and water hookups, dump station). Some fees. (Daily) 4½ mi SW on TX 34. Phone 972/875-5711.

Special Events

Bluebonnet Trails. Garden Club-sponsored 40 mi of fields in profusion of blooming wildflowers. Contact the Chamber of Commerce. Mid-late Apr.

National Polka Festival. Parade, Czech costumes, arts and crafts fair. Memorial Day wkend. Phone 972/878-2625.

B&B/Small Inn

★★★ **BONNYNOOK INN.** *414 W Main, Waxanachie (75165). 972/938-7207; fax 972/937-7700; toll-free 800/486-5936.* 5 rms, 2 story. S $87; D $115; each addl $20; wkly, wkend rates. Complimentary full bkfst. Restaurant (res only) 6-8 pm; Fri, Sat seatings 7 and 9 pm. Ck-out noon, ck-in 4 pm. Meeting rms. Business servs avail. Massage. Health club privileges.

Many in-rm whirlpools, fireplaces. Picnic tables. Old World elegance with 20th-century comfort. Totally nonsmoking. Cr cds: A, C, D, DS, MC, V.

Restaurant

★ **CATFISH PLANTATION.** *814 Water St, Waxahachie (75165). 972/937-9468.* Hrs: Thurs 5-7:30 pm; Fri to 9 pm; Sat 11:30 am-9 pm; Sun 11:30 am-7:30 pm. Closed Mon-Wed; some major hols. Lunch $4.99-$10.99, dinner $6.99-$10.99. Child's menu. Specialties: fried catfish, fried shrimp, blackberry cobbler. Outdoor dining. Victorian mansion; antique furnishings and resident "ghosts." Totally nonsmoking. Cr cds: A, DS, MC, V.

SC

Fairfield

See also Palestine

Pop 3,094 **Elev** 461 ft **Area code** 903 **Zip** 75840

Information Chamber of Commerce, 900 W Commerce, PO Box 956; 903/389-5792

Web www.fairfieldtx.com

What to See and Do

Burlington-Rock Island Railroad Museum. Housed in the 1906 depot of the old Trinity & Brazos Valley Railroad; railroad artifacts, items of local history, genealogical records; also two-rm log house. Tours by appt. (Sat-Sun afternoons; closed Jan 1, Easter, Dec 25) 208 S 3rd Ave, 10 mi SW via US 84 in Teague. Phone 903/739-2408. ¢

Fairfield Lake State Park. More than 1,400 acres. Swimming, waterskiing, fishing, boating (ramps); hiking trails, picnicking, playground, improved campsites (dump station). Guided boat tours of bald eagle habitats (fee). Standard fees. (Daily) NE on US 84 to FM 2570, then E on FM 3285. Phone 903/389-4514. ¢

Freestone County Historical Museum. Old county jail (1857), two log cabins, old church, antiques exhibit, county history items, old telephone exhibit, artifacts of seven wars, Civil War letters; quilts. Tours. (Wed, Fri-Sat, also Sun afternoons; closed hols) 302 Main St. Phone 903/389-3738. ¢¢

Fort Stockton

(D-3) *See also Alpine*

Founded 1859 **Pop** 7,846 **Elev** 2,954 ft **Area code** 915 **Zip** 79735
Information Chamber of Commerce, 1000 Railroad Ave, PO Box C; 915/336-2264 or 800/336-2166
Web www.fortstockton.org

What to See and Do

Annie Riggs Hotel Museum. (1899) Turn-of-the-century hotel, later run as a boarding house; 14 of the original 15 rms feature displays on local history and the town's development. Self-guided tours. (Daily; closed hols) 301 S Main St. Phone 915/336-2167. ¢

Big Bend National Park. (see). Approx 120 mi S via US 385.

Old Fort Stockton. Some of the original 24-inch adobe-walled officers' quarters, the old guardhouse, and the fort cemetery remain; rebuilt barracks kitchen. Self-guided tours (maps avail at Chamber of Commerce Tourist Center). 4 blks off US 290 at Rooney St. Phone 915/336-2400.

Special Event

Water Carnival. Mid-July. Phone 800/336-2166.

Motels/Motor Lodges

★★ **BEST WESTERN INN.** *3201 W Dickinson (79735). 915/336-8521; fax 915/336-6513; res 800/528-1234. www.bestwestern.com.* 112 rms, 2 story. S $48-$54; D $54-$60; each addl $6; studio rms $60; under 12 free. Crib free. Pet accepted. TV; cable (premium). Pool. Restaurant 6 am-2 pm, 5-10 pm. Rm serv. Private

club 5-10 pm. Ck-out noon. Meeting rms. Business servs avail. Valet serv. Some private patios. Cr cds: A, C, D, DS, ER, JCB, MC, V.
🅳 🐾 ⇌ 🏊 🔥

★★ **LA QUINTA INN.** *2601 W I-10 (79735). 915/336-9781; fax 915/336-3634; res 800/687-6667. www. laquinta.com.* 97 rms, 2 story. S $54; D $61; each addl $7; suite $64; under 18 free. Crib free. Pet accepted, some restrictions. TV; cable (premium), VCR avail. Pool. Restaurant opp 8:30 am-11 pm. Ck-out noon. Guest lndry. Business servs avail. Cr cds: A, D, DS, MC, V.
🅳 🐾 ⇌ ✈ 🏊 🔥

Fort Worth (B-6)

Founded 1849 **Pop** 534,694 **Elev** 670 ft **Area code** 817
Information Convention & Visitors Bureau, 415 Throckmorton, 76102; 817/336-8791 or 800/433-5747
Web www.fortworth.com

Suburbs Arlington-Grand Prairie, Cleburne, Denton, Granbury, Weatherford. (See individual alphabetical listings.)

Somewhere between Dallas and Fort Worth is the dividing line between the East and the West. Dallas is sophisticated and fashionable; Fort Worth is proudly simple and open. The city's predominant industry, cattle (for a long time symbolized by the historic Fort Worth Stockyards), has been joined by the oil, grain, aircraft, and computer industries, creating a modern metropolis full of shops, restaurants, theaters, and nightspots that somehow continue to reflect a distinctly Western character.

In the mid-nineteenth century, Fort Worth was a camp (never a fort) with a garrison to protect settlers. It was later named Fort Worth in honor of General William J. Worth, a Mexican War hero. After the Civil War, great herds of longhorn cattle were driven through the area en route to the Kansas railheads. Cowboys camped with their herds outside of town and "whooped it up" at night.

By 1873 the Texas & Pacific Railroad had reached a point 26 miles east when its backers, Jay Cooke & Co, failed. The population fell from 4,000 to 1,000, and a Dallas newspaper commented that Fort Worth was a place so dead that a panther was seen sleeping on the main street. In response to this insult, Fort Worth called itself "Panther City," and the long-term feud between Fort Worth and Dallas had begun.

A group of citizens headed by K. M. Van Zandt formed the Tarrant County Construction Company and continued the building of the railroad. In 1876 the T&P had a state land grant that would expire unless the road reached Fort Worth before the legislature adjourned. While efforts were made to keep the legislature in session, practically everybody in Fort Worth went to work on the grading and laying of track.

The legislature finally decided to adjourn in two days. It seemed impossible that the line could be finished. The desperate Fort Worthians improvised cribs of ties to bridge Sycamore Creek and for two miles laid the rails on ungraded ground. The city council is said to have moved the city limits east to meet it. The first train, its whistle tied down, wheezed into town on July 19, 1876. Fort Worth had become a shipping point.

In 1882 the free school system was begun, and the first flour mill started operations. In 1883 the Greenwall Opera House was host to many famous stars. In 1870 a local banking institution, now known as Nations Bank, opened. Oil did not come in until 1917, but in the years before and since, Fort Worth has continued to grow. The headquarters for several well-known American companies are located in Fort Worth.

Transportation

Airport. See DALLAS/FORT WORTH AIRPORT AREA.

Car Rental Agencies. See IMPORTANT TOLL-FREE NUMBERS.

Public Transportation. Buses (Transportation Authority of Fort Worth). Phone 817/215-8600.

Rail Passenger Service. Amtrak 800/872-7245.

Airport Information

Dallas/Fort Worth Airport Area. For additional accommodations, see DALLAS/FORT WORTH AIRPORT AREA, which follows DALLAS.

What to See and Do

Bass Performance Hall. Opened in 1998, the $65 million masterpiece has been hailed as "the last great hall built in the 20th century." Home to the Van Cliburn International Piano Competition, the Fort Worth Symphony, the Fort Worth Opera, and the Fort Worth/Dallas Ballet. National touring productions and special concerts are offered here as well. 555 Commerce St. Phone 817/212-4280.

Benbrook Lake. Swimming, waterskiing, fishing, boating (ramps, marinas); horseback riding, golf, picnicking, concession, camping (tent and trailer sites). Fees may be charged at some recreation areas. (Daily) 4 mi S of I-20 off 77. Phone 817/292-2400. ¢¢

Botanic Garden. More than 150,000 plants of 2,000 species incl native plants and tropical plants. Conservatory (fee), fragrance garden, rose gardens, perennial garden, trial garden. Extensive Japanese garden with bridges, waterfalls, teahouses (Tues-Sun). 3220 Botanic Garden Blvd. Phone 817/871-7686. **FREE**

Cultural District.

Amon Carter Museum. Major collection of American paintings, photography, and sculpture incl works by Winslow Homer, Georgia O'Keefe, Grant Wood, Thomas Cole, Frederic Remington, and Charles Russell; changing exhibits. Building designed by Philip Johnson. 3501 Camp Bowie Blvd. Phone 817/738-1933. **FREE**

Casa Mañana Theater. Large geodesic dome houses professional performances ranging from Broadway shows to children's theater. (Tues-Sun eves, Sat and Sun matinees) 3101 W Lancaster, at University Dr.

Fort Worth Museum of Science & History. Exhibits on fossils, anthropology, geology, natural sciences and history. Hands-on, changing, and permanent exhibits. (Daily; closed Thanksgiving, Dec 24, 25) 1501 Montgomery St. Phone 817/255-9300. ¢¢¢

"Texas Gold" Statue

Fort Worth Theater. Plays, operas. (All yr) Phone 817/738-6509.

Fort Worth Zoo. More than 5,000 exotic and native specimens in a tree-shaded setting. Exhibits incl Raptor Canyon; Asian Falls, featuring Asian rhinos; also World of Primates, African Savannah, TEXAS; herpetarium and large aquarium. (Daily) 1989 Colonial Pkwy, in Forest Park; I-30 to University Dr, then 1 mi S (follow signs). Phone 817/871-7050. ¢¢ Also in Forest Park is

Kimbell Art Museum. Permanent collection dating from ancient times to early 20th century incl masterworks by El Greco, Rembrandt, Picasso, Velázquez, and many others. Asian, Mesoamerican, African, and ancient Mediterranean collections. Special exhibits. Building designed by Louis I. Kahn. (Tues-Sun; closed hols) 3333 Camp Bowie Blvd. Phone 817/332-8451. **FREE**

Log Cabin Village. Pioneer houses used by early settlers. (Tues-Sun; closed Jan 1, Thanksgiving, Dec 25) 2100 Log Cabin Village Ln at South University Dr. Phone 817/926-5881. ¢

Modern Art Museum of Fort Worth. Permanent and traveling exhibits of 20th-century paintings, sculpture, drawings, and prints, incl works by Picasso, Kelly, Pollock, and Warhol. (Tues-Sun; closed hols) 3200 Darnell St at University Dr. Phone 817/738-9215. **FREE**

Noble Planetarium. Shows change periodically. Public shows (daily). Phone 817/255-9300. ¢¢

Omni Theater. 70mm Omnimax films are screened on an 80-ft projection dome. Films change periodically. (Daily; closed Thanksgiving, Dec 24, 25) Phone 817/255-9300. ¢¢¢

⭐ **Will Rogers Memorial Center.** Will Rogers statue, Memorial Coliseum, Tower, Auditorium, Amon Carter, Jr., Exhibit Hall, Equestrian Center. Many community events are held here, incl horse shows, boxing, circuses, rodeos. 3401 W Lancaster St. Phone 817/871-8150.

Downtown.

Fort Worth Water Garden. Enormous concrete, terraced water gardens containing a wide variety of foliage, trees, and spectacular water cascades and fountains. (Daily) Just south of Fort Worth/Tarrant County Convention Center. **FREE**

Hell's Half Acre to Sundance Square. Guided walking tour of historic downtown Fort Worth. Filled with anecdotal stories of city's past and present, and tips on points of interest. Approx 2½ hrs. 100 E 8th St at Main. Phone 817/253-5909. ¢¢

150 Years of Fort Worth Museum. Museum recounts the history of the city in a series of photographs and artifacts on view in Fire Station No. 1, the city's first fire station, built in 1907. (Daily) 203 Commerce St, at 2nd St. Phone 817/255-9300. **FREE**

Sid Richardson Collection of Western Art. Permanent exhibit of 60 original paintings by renowned western artists Frederic Remington and Charles M. Russell from the private collection of oil man Sid W. Richardson. (Tues-Sun; closed hols) 309 Main St. Phone 817/332-6554. **FREE**

Sundance Square Entertainment District. Shopping, dining, art, and entertainment district of brick streets and renovated turn-of-the-century buildings. Markers along a self-guided walking tour commemorate historic locations and events; the 300 blk of Main St is especially associated with the city's colorful history and with such characters of the Old West as Butch Cassidy, the Sundance Kid, and Luke Short, an infamous western gambler who gunned down the town's marshal in front of the notorious White Elephant Saloon. Throckmorton and Calhoun Sts between 2nd and 5th Sts. Phone 817/339-7777.

Eagle Mountain Lake. A 9,200-acre impound on the West Fork of the Trininty River, the lake is home to Fort Worth Boat Club, which sponsors numerous sailing regattas. Water sports enthusiasts are served well by several marinas, which offer watercraft rentals, gas docks, restaurants, and cafes. Beaches, parks, boat ramps, bait shops. NW via TX 199 and Farm Rd 1220.

Fort Worth Nature Center & Refuge. A 3,600-acre wildlife habitat. Nature trails; picnicking. Visitor center. (Daily; closed Thanksgiving, Dec 25) 4 mi W of I-820, off TX 199. Phone 817/237-1111. **FREE**

⭐ **Fort Worth Stockyards National Historic District.** Renovated buildings now house Western-style retail shops, nightclubs, and restaurants. Site of the annual Chisholm Trail Roundup (see SPECIAL EVENTS) as well as yr-round rodeos, Wild West shows (summer), and other Western entertainment. A restored 1896 Tarantula excursion steam train travels to the stockyards from nearby Grapevine. Phone 817/625-7245. 130 E Exchange Ave. Visitor Center (daily; closed Jan 1, Dec 25). Phone 817/624-4741. ¢¢ Also here is

Billy Bob's Texas. Family fun center incl live entertainment, bull-riding, arcade, dancing, restaurant. Gift shop. (Daily) 2520 Rodeo Plaza. Phone 817/624-7117. ¢¢

Old Trail Driver's Park. East of the stockyards at 28th and Decatur Sts; adj to the stockyards to the west is Rodeo Park.

Stockyards Museum. Featuring the 1986 Texas Sesquicentennial Wagon Train Collection, the museum also contains memorabilia and hands-on artifacts of the stockyards era, the meatpacking industry, and the railroad. (Mon-Sat; closed hols) 131 E Exchange Ave, Suites 111-114. Phone 817/625-5082. **Donation**

Jubilee Theatre. A primary venue for African American theater in Texas, productions enjoy long runs and consistently good critical response. (Call for schedule) 506 Main St. Phone 817/338-4411.

Lake Worth. Boating, fishing; picnicking. 9 mi NW on TX 199.

Scenic drive. Through Trinity and Forest parks on the Clear Fork of the Trinity River. These beautiful parks have bicycle trails, a duck pond, zoo, and miniature train.

Six Flags Over Texas. (See ARLINGTON-GRAND PRAIRIE) 16 mi E on I-30, just W of jct TX 360. Phone 817/640-8900.

Thistle Hill. (1903) Restored mansion built by one of the cattle barons who made Fort Worth a major city. Guided tours (Sun-Fri). 1509 Pennsylvania Ave, at Summit Ave. Phone 817/336-1212. ¢¢

Special Events

Southwestern Exposition & Livestock Show. Will Rogers Memorial Coliseum. Late Jan-early Feb.

Texas Motor Speedway. NASCAR, Indy Racing League, and a variety of other racing classes. Phone 817/215-8500 for racing schedule and admission prices.

MAIN Street Fort Worth Arts Festival. Nine blks of historic Main St become a marketplace for arts, food, and live entertainment. One of the largest events of its kind. Phone 817/336-ARTS. Mid-Apr.

Pioneer Days. Fort Worth Stockyards. Commemorates pioneer settlement along the Trinity River and early days of the cattle industry. Mid-Sept. Phone 817/624-4741.

Motels/Motor Lodges

★★ **BEST WESTERN INN.** *2000 Beach St (76103).* 817/534-4801; fax 817/534-3761; res 800/937-8376. *www.bestwestern.com.* 192 rms, 2-3 story. S, D $69-$99; each addl $10; suites $99-$200; under 18 free. Crib free. TV; cable (premium). Pool. Coffee in rms. Restaurant 6:30 am-2 pm, 5:30-10 pm. Rm serv. Bar 4 pm-midnight. Ck-out noon. Meeting rms. Business servs avail. In-rm modem link. Tennis. Exercise equipt. Cr cds: A, DS, MC, V.

D ⚹ ⇌ ⚔ ⊠ ⚕

★★ **BEST WESTERN WEST-BRANCH INN.** *7301 W Fwy (76116).* 817/244-7444; fax 817/244-7902; toll-free 888/474-9566. 118 rms, 2 story. S $59-$69; D $59.95-$89.95; each addl $5; suites $69.95-$99; under 18 free. Crib free. Pet accepted, some restrictions. TV; cable (premium). Pool. Complimentary continental bkfst. Ck-out noon. Coin lndry. Meeting rms. Business servs avail. In-rm modem link. Some refrigerators; microwaves avail. Cr cds: A, C, D, DS, JCB, MC, V.

D ⦿ ⇌ ⊠ ⚕

★★ **COMFORT INN.** *4850 N Freeway (76137).* 817/834-8001; fax 817/834-3159; res 800/228-5150. *www.comfortinn.com.* 60 rms, 2 story. Apr-Oct: S $60; D $70-$75; each addl $5; under 18 free; lower rates rest of yr. Crib free. TV; cable (premium). Pool. Complimentary continental bkfst. Ck-out noon. Coin lndry. Business servs avail. Sundries. Microwaves avail. Cr cds: A, C, D, DS, MC, V.

D ⇌ ⊠ ⚕

★★ **COURTYARD BY MARRIOTT.** *2201 W Airport Fwy, Bedford (76021).* 817/545-2202; fax 817/545-2319; toll-free 800/321-2211. *www.courtyard.com.* 145 rms, 3 story, 14 suites. S $98; D $108; suites $118-$128; under 18 free; wkend rates. Crib free. TV; cable (premium). Pool; whirlpool. Complimentary coffee in rms. Restaurant 6:30-10:30 am; wkends 7

am-noon. Bar 4-11 pm. Ck-out noon. Coin lndry. Meeting rms. In-rm modem link. Sundries. Exercise equipt. Health club privileges. Refrigerator in suites. Patios, balconies. Cr cds: A, D, DS, MC, V.

D ⇌ ⚔ ⚶ SC

★★ **COURTYARD BY MARRIOTT.** *3150 Riverfront Dr (76107).* 817/335-1300; fax 817/336-6926; toll-free 800/321-2211. *www.courtyard.com/dfwch.* 130 rms, 2 story. S $59-$104; D $69-$114; each addl $10; suites $119-$139; under 18 free; family rates; package plans; higher rates special events. Crib free. TV; cable (premium), VCR avail (movies). Complimentary coffee in rms. Restaurant 6:30-10:30 am. Bar 5-10:30 pm. Ck-out noon. Meeting rms. Business servs avail. In-rm modem link. Valet serv. Coin lndry. Exercise equipt. Heated pool; whirlpool. Some refrigerators, microwaves. Some balconies. Cr cds: A, C, D, DS, ER, JCB, MC, V.

D ⇌ ⚔ ⊠ ⚕ SC

★★ **FAIRFIELD INN.** *1505 S University Dr (76107).* 817/335-2000; res 800/228-2800. *www.fairfieldinn.com.* 81 rms, 4 story. Feb-Dec: S $73-$80; D $78-$84; each addl $5; under 18 free; higher rates special events; lower rates rest of yr. Crib free. TV; cable (premium). Complimentary continental bkfst. Restaurant adj open 24 hrs. Ck-out noon. Meeting rms. Business servs avail. In-rm modem link. Indoor pool; whirlpool. Game rm. Some refrigerators, microwaves. Picnic tables. Cr cds: A, C, D, DS, MC, V.

D ⇌ ⊠ ⚕

★★ **HAMPTON INN.** *4681 Gemini Pl (76106).* 817/625-5327; fax 817/625-7727; res 800/426-7866. *www.hamptoninn.com.* 65 rms, 3 story. S, D $74; under 18 free; higher rates NASCAR races. TV; cable (premium). Complimentary continental bkfst. Complimentary coffee in rms. Restaurant adj 6 am-10 pm. Ck-out noon. Meeting rms. Business servs avail. In-rm modem link. Coin lndry. Pool. Refrigerators. Cr cds: A, C, D, DS, MC, V.

D ⇌ ⊠ ⚕

★★ **LA QUINTA INN & SUITES FTW-SW.** *4900 Bryant Irvin Rd*

(76132). *817/370-2700; fax 817/370-
2733; res 800/531-5900. www.
laquinta.com.* 129 rms, 4 story. S, D
$69-$175; each addl $8; suites $129;
under 18 free; higher rates special
events. Crib $10. TV; cable (pre-
mium). Complimentary continental
bkfst. Complimentary coffee in rms.
Restaurant adj 6 am-midnight. Ck-
out noon. Meeting rms. Business
servs avail. In-rm modem link. Coin
lndry. Exercise equipt. Pool; whirlpool. Refrigerators, microwaves avail.
Picnic tables. Cr cds: A.

★ **LA QUINTA INN WEST/MED-
ICAL CENTER.** *7888 W I-30 (76108).
817/246-5511; fax 817/246-8870; res
800/687-6667. www.laquinta.com.* 106
rms, 3 story. S, D $49-$59; under 18
free. Crib free. Pet accepted. TV;
cable (premium). Pool. Complimentary continental bkfst. Restaurant adj
open 24 hrs. Meeting rms. In-rm
modem link. Microwaves avail. Cr
cds: A, C, D, DS, JCB, MC, V.

★★ **RAMADA INN MIDTOWN.**
*1401 S University Dr (76107).
817/336-9311; fax 817/877-3023; res
888/298-2054. www.ramada.com.* 181
rms, 4 story. S $68; D $72; each addl
$8; suites $122-$130; under 18 free.
Crib free. Pet accepted. $10. TV;
cable (premium). Complimentary
continental bkfst. Complimentary
coffee in rms. Restaurant 6:30 am-
1:30 pm, 5-10 pm. Rm serv. Bar 5
pm-2 am. Ck-out noon. Meeting
rms. Business servs avail. In-rm
modem link. Sundries. Coin lndry.
Exercise equipt. Pool. Cr cds: A, C,
D, DS, ER, V.

★★ **RAMADA PLAZA HOTEL
CONVENTION CENTER.** *1701
Commerce St (76102). 817/335-7000;
fax 817/335-3333; res 800/228-2828.
www.ramada.com.* 434 rms, 12 story.
S $79-$129; D $89-$139; each addl
$10; suites $109-$159; under 18 free;
family rates; package plans; higher
rates NASCAR. Crib avail. Valet parking $7; garage parking $5; in/out $2.
TV; cable (premium). Complimentary coffee in rms. Restaurant open
24 hrs. Rm serv 6 am-2 pm, 5-10
pm. Bar 5 pm-2 am. Ck-out noon.
Convention facilities. Business cen-

ter. In-rm modem link. Concierge.
Gift shop. Exercise equipt. Indoor
pool; whirlpool. Refrigerator,
microwave in suites. Cr cds: A, C, D,
DS, JCB, MC, V.

Hotels

★★★ **THE ASHTON.** *610 Main St
(76102). 817/332-0100. www.the
ashtonhotel.com.* 39 rms, 6 story. S, D
$129-$179; wkend rates. Crib free.
TV; cable (premium), VCR avail.
Restaurants 7:30 am-midnight. Bar
11 am-midnight. Ck-out noon. Meeting rms. Business servs avail. In-rm
modem link. Concierge. Gift shop.
Exercise equipt. Refrigerators avail.
Cr cds: A, D, DS, MC, V.

★★★ **RADISSON PLAZA.** *815
Main St (76102). 817/870-2100; fax
817/335-3408; toll-free 800/333-3333.
www.radisson.com/ftworthtx.* 517 rms,
15 story. S $179; D $199; each addl
$10; suites $250-$1,580; under 18
free; wkend, hol rates. Crib $10.
Valet parking $8; garage parking $6.
TV; cable (premium). Pool; poolside
serv. Complimentary coffee in rms.
Restaurant 6 am-11 pm. Bar from 11
am. Ck-out noon. Convention facilities. Business center. In-rm modem
link. Concierge. Gift shop. Barber,
beauty shop. Tennis privileges. Golf
privileges. Exercise equipt; sauna.
Some refrigerators. Cr cds: A, C, D,
DS, MC, V.

★★★ **RENAISSANCE WORTHING-
TON.** *200 Main St (76102). 817/
870-1000; fax 817/338-9176; res
800/228-9290. www.renaissancehotels.
com.* 504 rms, 12 story. S $205-$225;
D $215-$245; each addl $10; suites
$450-$1,000; under 18 free; wkend
rates; packages plans. Crib free. Pet
accepted, some restrictions. Covered
parking $7; valet parking $10. TV;
cable (premium). Indoor pool; whirlpool. Restaurant 6 am-11 pm, fine
dining 6-10 pm Thurs-Sun (see also
REFLECTIONS). Rm serv 24 hrs. Bar
11-2 am; Sun from noon. Ck-out
noon. Convention facilities. Business
center. In-rm modem link.
Concierge. Club level. Shopping
arcade. Tennis. Exercise rm; sauna.

Massage. Some refrigerators. Private patios, balconies. Cr cds: A, D, DS, JCB, MC, V.

⬛🔲🔲🔲🔲🔲🔲🔲

★★★ **STOCKYARDS HOTEL.** *109 E Exchange Ave (76106). 817/625-6427; fax 817/624-2571; toll-free 800/423-8471. www.stockyardshotel.com.* 52 rms, 3 story. S $125; D $135; each addl $10; suites $160-$350; higher rates: Chisholm Trail Round-up, Pioneer Days, Dec 31. Valet parking $5. TV; cable. Coffee in rms. Restaurant 7 am-10 pm; Fri, Sat to midnight. Bar; Fri, Sat to 2 am. Ck-out noon. Business servs avail. In-rm modem link. Health club privileges. Restored turn-of-the-century hotel. Western decor. Cr cds: A, D, DS, MC, V.

⬛🔲🔲**SC**

B&B/Small Inn

★★ **BED AND BREAKFAST AT THE RANCH.** *8275 Wagley Robertson Rd (76131). 817/232-5522; fax 817/847-7420; toll-free 888/593-0352. www.bandbattheranch.com.* 4 rms, 1 with shower only, 2 story. No rm phones. S, D $95-$159; each addl $15; family rates; package plans. Crib free. TV; VCR avail (movies). Complimentary full bkfst. Ck-out 11 am, ck-in 4-6 pm. Meeting rms. Business servs avail. Concierge serv. Lighted tennis. Playground. Picnic tables, grills. Cr cds: A, MC, V.

⬛🔲🔲🔲🔲

Conference Center

★★★ **GREEN OAKS HOTEL.** *6901 West Fwy (76116). 817/738-7311; fax 817/377-1308; toll-free 800/772-2341. www.greenoakshotel.com.* 284 rms, 2-3 story. S $59-$99; D $69-$99; suites $95-$125; each addl $10; under 18 free; wkend rates; package plans. Crib free. Pet accepted. TV; cable (premium), VCR avail. 2 pools; poolside serv. Complimentary full bkfst. Restaurant 6 am-2 pm, 5-9:30 pm. Rm serv. Bars 4:30 pm-2 am; entertainment exc Sun. Ck-out noon. Convention facilities. Business servs avail. In-rm modem link. Sundries. Lighted tennis. Exercise equipt; sauna. Cr cds: A, C, D, DS, MC, V.

⬛🔲🔲🔲🔲🔲🔲

Restaurants

★ **ANGELO'S.** *2533 White Settlement Rd (76107). 817/332-0357.* Specializes in brisket, ribs. Hrs:11 am-10 pm. Wine, beer. Lunch, dinner $5-$10. Cr cds: A, MC, V.

⬛🔲

★★★ **ANGELUNA.** *215 E 4th St (76102). 817/334-0080.* Global menu. Specializes in seared red tuna, wood-grilled ribeye, Thai rice noodles. Hrs: 11:30 am-2 pm, 5-9:30 pm; Fri, Sat to 11 pm. Res accepted. Wine, beer. Lunch $8-$14; dinner $13-$29. Child's menu. Cr cds: A, MC, V.

⬛

★★★ **BALCONY OF RIDGLEA.** *6100 Camp Bowie Blvd (76116). 817/731-3719.* Hrs: 11:30 am-2 pm, 6-10 pm; Fri to 10:30 pm; Sat 6-10:30 pm. Closed Sun; major hols. Res accepted. Continental menu. Bar. Lunch $5.25-$14.95, dinner $12-$25. Specialties: chateaubriand, rack of lamb, baked red snapper. Pianist wkends. Glassed-in balcony. Cr cds: A, C, D, DS, MC, V.

⬛🔲

★★ **BELLA ITALIA WEST.** *5139 Camp Bowie Blvd (76107). 817/738-1700.* Hrs: 11:30 am-1:30 pm, 6-10 pm. Closed Sun; major hols. Res accepted. Italian menu. Bar 5-10 pm. Lunch $4.95-$9.95, dinner $10-$16. Specializes in wild game, pasta, fish. Classical guitar Fri, Sat. Parking. Outdoor dining. Italian artwork. Relaxed atmosphere. Totally nonsmoking. Cr cds: A, C, D, DS, MC, V.

⬛

★★ **BISTRO LOUISE.** *2900 S Hulen St, Ste 40 (76109). 817/922-9244. www.bistrolouise.com.* Hrs: 11 am-2 pm, 6-9 pm; Fri, Sat to 10 pm; Sat brunch 11 am-2 pm. Closed Sun; major hols. Res accepted. Mediterranean menu. Bar from 5 pm. A la carte entrees: lunch $5.95-$9.95, dinner $13.95-$24.95. Sat brunch $20. Child's menu. Specialties: Japanese macadamia shrimp, tea-smoked duck, portabella tenderloin with porcini mushroom sauce. Parking. Outdoor dining. French bistro atmosphere. Totally nonsmoking. Cr cds: A, C, D, DS, ER, MC, V.

⬛

★★★ **BLUE MESA GRILL.** *1600 S University Dr (76107). 817/332-6372. www.bluemesagrill.com.* American grill menu. Specializes in churras-caritas. Hrs: 11 am-10 pm; Fri, Sat to 11 pm; Sun from 10 am. Res accepted. Lunch $6.50-$13; dinner $7.50-$15. Child's menu. Cr cds: A, D, DS, MC, V.

★★ **CLASSIC CAFE.** *504 N Oak, Roanoke (76262). 817/430-8185.* New American menu. Specializes in Stil-ton-crusted ribeye, Asian marinated salmon. Hrs: 11 am-2:30 pm, 5-9 pm; Fri, Sat 5-10 pm. Closed Sun; hols. Res accepted. Wine list. Lunch $7.95-$14; dinner $16-$29. Child's menu. Entertainment. Old-style home decor. Cr cds: A, D, DS, MC, V.

★ **EDELWEISS.** *3801 Southwest Blvd #A (76116). 817/738-5934.* Hrs: 5-10:30 pm; Fri, Sat to 11 pm. Closed Sun, Mon; some major hols. German, Amer menu. Bar. Dinner $8.95-$19.95. Specializes in Wiener schnitzel, sauer-braten, red cabbage. Enter-tainment. Beer garden atmosphere. Family-owned. Cr cds: A, D, DS, MC, V.

★ **JOE T. GARCIA'S.** *2201 N Commerce (76106). 817/626-4356. www. joets.com.* Hrs: 11 am-11 pm. Closed Thanksgiving, Dec 25. Mexican menu. Bar. Lunch $5.25-$9, din-ner $9-$11. Child's menu. Specialties: chicken and beef fajitas, family-style dinners. Mariachi band Fri-Sun. Outdoor dining; courtyard with fountain, garden. Family-owned more than 60 yrs. Cr cds: A, DS, MC, V.

★ **MANCUSO'S.** *9500 White Settle-ment Rd (76108). 817/246-7041.* Hrs: 11 am-1:30 pm, 5-9 pm; Fri to 10 pm; Sat 5-10 pm. Closed Sun; also major hols. Res accepted. Italian menu. Wine, beer. Lunch $3.95-$6.95, dinner $5.95-$14.95. Child's menu. Specialties: Italian fish fry, lasagna, fettuccine alfredo. Parking. Outdoor dining. Building is over 100 yrs old. Cr cds: A, D, DS, MC, V.

★★★ **MICHAELS.** *3413 W 7th St (76107). 817/877-3413. www.michaels cuisine.com.* Specializes in ranch bakes crab cakes, pan-seared beef tenderloin. Hrs: 11 am-2:30 pm, 5:30-10 pm; Thurs-Sat to 11 pm. Closed Sun. Res accepted. Wine, beer. Lunch $7.50-$10.95; dinner $14.50-$28.50. Band Wed. Cr cds: A, C, D, DS, MC, V.

Sundance Square, Fort Worth

★★★ **RANDALL'S CAFI AND CHEESECAKE CO.** *907 Houston St (76102). 817/336-2253.* European menu. Menu changes seasonally. Hrs: 11 am-2 pm, to 9 pm. Fri-Sat 5:30-10 pm. Closed Sun, Mon. Res accepted. Wine, beer. Lunch $6-$12; dinner $16-$25. Cr cds: A, DS, MC, V.

★★★ **REFLECTIONS.** *200 Main St (76102). 817/882-1765. www. worthingtonhotel.com.* Specializes in wild game, seafood, veal. Own baking. Hrs: 5:30-10 pm. Sun brunch 10 am-2:30 pm. Res accepted. Bar. Wine cellar. Dinner al la carte entrees: $19.95-$35. Sun brunch $29.95. Child's menu. Pianist. Valet parking. Multi-level elegant dining. Cr cds: A, C, D, DS, MC, V.
D ⬇

★★★ **SAINT-EMILION.** *3617 W 7th St (76107). 817/737-2781.* Hrs: 6-10 pm; Sun 5:30-9 pm. Closed Mon; some major hols. Res accepted. French menu. Prix fixe: dinner $21.75-$31.75. Specializes in roast duck, imported fresh fish. Comfortable country French atmosphere. Cr cds: A, C, D, DS, MC, V.
D

★ **TOKYO STEAKHOUSE.** *8742 TX 80 W (76116). 817/560-3664.* Hrs: 11 am-2 pm, 5-10 pm; Fri to 11 pm; Sat 5-11 pm; Sun 5-10 pm. Closed some major hols. Res accepted. Japanese, Thai menu. Bar. Lunch $5.95-$12.95, dinner $10.95-$29.95. Buffet: lunch $4.50. Child's menu. Specializes in sushi, Thai dishes. Parking. Japanese decor. Tableside preparation of meals. Cr cds: A, MC, V.
D

Fredericksburg

(D-5) *See also Johnson City, Kerrville, Mason*

Founded 1846 **Pop** 8,911 **Elev** 1,742 ft **Area code** 830 **Zip** 78624
Information Chamber of Commerce/Convention & Visitors Bureau, 106 N Adams; 830/997-6523
Web www.fredericksburg-texas.com

Nearly 600 Germans came here to settle under the auspices of the Society for the Protection of German Immigrants in Texas. Surrounded by Comanches, isolated, plagued with epidemics, unfamiliar with the country, they fought a bitter battle for survival. Upright and industrious, they prospered until the Civil War when, disapproving of slavery, men hid out in the hills and fled to Mexico to avoid joining the Confederate Army. Their troubles continued during Reconstruction, but these folk persevered by being self-reliant. In 1912 they built their own railroad to connect with the nearest line; this was discontinued in 1941. In 1937, US 87 was built through the town; now US 290 and TX 16 also run through here. Today, Fredericksburg, the center of diversified farming and ranching activity, is a picturesque community with many stone houses. Fleet Admiral Chester W. Nimitz was born here.

What to See and Do

Admiral Nimitz Museum State Historical Park. Dedicated to the more than two million men and women of all services who served under Fleet Admiral Chester W. Nimitz. The restored steamboat-shaped Nimitz Hotel (1852) contains three floors of exhibits in the Museum of the Pacific War. History Walk is lined with rare guns, planes, and tanks from Pacific theater. Captured Japanese minisub. The Garden of Peace was built by the Japanese. (Daily; closed Dec 25) 340 E Main St. Phone 830/997-4379. ¢¢

Enchanted Rock State Natural Area. A 1,643-acre park with massive, 500-ft-high dome of solid granite. Native Americans believed ghost fires flickered upon its crest on moonlit nights. Geologists say creaking, groaning sounds emitted at night are result of cooling and contraction after day's heat. Nature and hiking trails, picnicking, primitive camping (no vehicular camping permitted). Standard hrs and fees. (Daily, hol schedule varies) 18 mi N off Rural Rte 965. Phone 915/247-3903. ¢¢

Pioneer Museum. Complex of several buildings, incl Weber Sunday House, log cabin. Relics of German colonists. (Daily; closed hols) 309 W Main St. Phone 830/990-8431. ¢¢

Vereins Kirche Museum. (Pioneer Memorial Building) Reproduction of the original (1847) octagonal community building; archives and local history collection. (Daily) Market Sq, opp courthouse. Phone 830/997-7832. **FREE**

Special Events

Easter Fires Pageant. Dates back more than 100 yrs. Sat eve before Easter. Phone 830/997-2359.

Educational Festival. Pioneer period crafts, dancing, entertainment. Second Sat in May. Phone 830/997-2835.

Night in Old Fredericksburg. German food, entertainment. Third wkend July. Phone 830 /997-8515.

Gillespie County Fair. Oldest county fair in Texas. Fourth wkend Aug. Phone 830/997-2359.

Food and Wine Fest. Texas wine, food, music. Late Oct. Phone 830/997-8515.

Candlelight Tour of Homes. Second Sat Dec. Phone 830/997-2835. ¢¢¢¢

Motels/Motor Lodges

★★ **COMFORT INN.** *908 S Adams St (78624). 830/997-9811; fax 830/997-2068; res 800/228-5150. www.comfortinn.com.* 46 rms, 2 story. S $59-$69; D $64-$74; each addl $6. Crib free. Pet accepted, some restrictions. TV; cable (premium). Pool. Complimentary continental bkfst. Ck-out noon. Bus depot transportation. Tennis. Picnic tables, grill. Cr cds: A, C, D, DS, JCB, MC, V.

★ **DIETZEL MOTEL.** *1141 W US Hwy 290 (78624). 830/997-3330; fax 830/997-3330.* 20 rms. S, D $42-$65; each addl $5. Crib free. Pet accepted, some restrictions; $5. TV; cable (premium). Pool. Complimentary coffee in lobby. Restaurant adj 11 am-10 pm. Ck-out 11 am. Picnic tables. Cr cds: A, DS, MC, V.

★★ **FREDERICKSBURG INN AND SUITES.** *201 S Washington St (78624). 830/997-0202; fax 830/997-5740; toll-free 800/446-0202. www.fredericksburg-inn.com.* 102 rms, 2 story, 10 suites. S, D $59-$125. TV; cable (premium). Pool. Spa. Complimentary continental bkfst. Complimentary coffee in rms. Restaurant nearby. Ck-out noon. Business servs avail. Meeting rms. Playground. Refrigerator, microwave. Cr cds: A, DS, MC, V.

★ **PEACH TREE INN.** *401 S Washington St, Fredericksbrg (78624). 830/997-2117; fax 830/990-9434; toll-free 800/843-4666. www.thepeachtreeinn.com.* 34 rms, some with shower only. S, D $40-$73.50 kit. suites $90-$110. Crib free. Pet accepted. TV; cable. Pool. Playground. Complimentary continental bkfst. Restaurant nearby. Ck-out 11 am. Lawn games. Some refrigerators, microwaves. Picnic tables. Cr cds: A, DS, MC, V.

★ **SUNDAY HOUSE INN & SUITES.** *501 E Main St (78624). 830/997-4484; fax 830/997-5607; toll-free 800/274-3762. www.sundayhouseinn.com.* 124 rms, 2-3 story. S, D $89.95; each addl $6; suites $125; under 12 free. Crib $6. Pet accepted, some restrictions. TV; cable. Pool. Restaurant 7 am-9 pm; Fri, Sat to 10 pm. Ck-out noon. Business servs avail. In-rm modem link. Cr cds: A, D, DS, MC, V.

B&B/Small Inn

★★ **MAGNOLIA HOUSE.** *101 E Hackberry St (78624). 830/997-0306; fax 830/997-0766; toll-free 800/880-4374. www.magnolia-house.com.* 5 rms, 2 story, 2 suites. S, D $95-$115; each addl $25; suite $140. Children over 12 yrs only. TV; cable (premium), VCR avail (movies). Complimentary full bkfst. Restaurant nearby. Ck-out 11 am, ck-in 2 pm. Luggage handling. Street parking. Some fireplaces; refrigerator in suite. Built in 1923. Totally nonsmoking. Cr cds: A, DS, MC, V.

Restaurants

★ **FRIEDHELM'S BAVARIAN.** *905 W Main St (78624). 830/997-6300.* Hrs: 11 am-10 pm; Sun 11:30 am-8:30 pm. Closed Mon; Thanksgiving, Dec 25. Res accepted. German menu. Bar 3-10 pm. Lunch $4.95-$14.95, dinner $6.95-$16.95. Child's menu. Specialties: jagerschnitzel, schweinerippchen. Bavarian tavern decor. Cr cds: A, DS, MC, V.

★ **MAMACITA'S.** *506 E Main St (78624). 830/997-9546.* Hrs: 11 am-

9:30 pm; Fri, Sat to 10 pm. Closed Thanksgiving, Dec 25. Res accepted. Mexican menu. Bar. Lunch $4.25-$5.25, dinner $4.95-$9.95. Child's menu. Specialties: chalupas, quesadillas, enchiladas. Mexican decor; stone fountain. Cr cds: A, D, DS, MC, V.

Freeport (E-7)

(see Brazosport)

Fritch

See also Amarillo, Pampa

Pop 2,235 **Area code** 806 **Zip** 79036
Information Chamber of Commerce, 104 N Robey, PO Box 396; 806/857-2458

What to See and Do

Hutchinson County Historical Museum. Professionally designed museum emphasizes oil boom of the 1920s and the story of Hutchinson County. Photos of Boomtown Borger; models of early houses and Fort Adobe Walls. Painting of Chief Quanah Parker, the Battle of Adobe Walls, and early Native American fighter Billy Dixon. Tools and oil field equipt, Panhandle Pueblo artifacts; dancehall, pioneer house, changing exhibits. (Mon-Sat; closed hols) 12 mi E, at 618 N Main St in Borger. Phone 806/273-0130. **FREE**

Lake Meredith Aquatic & Wildlife Museum. Life-size dioramas of small game found around lake area. Five aquariums holding 11,000 gallons of water display the variety of fish found in Lake Meredith. (Daily; closed Jan 1, Thanksgiving, Dec 25) 104 N Robey. Phone 806/857-2458. **FREE**

Lake Meredith National Recreation Area. Created by Sanford Dam on the Canadian River and stocked with walleye, bass, channel and blue catfish, crappie, and perch. Swimming, waterskiing, fishing, boating (ramps); picnicking, primitive camping (some sites rest rms, dump stations). (Daily) Phone 806/857-3151. **FREE** On S edge of lake is

Alibates Flint Quarries National Monument. Incl area of flint quarries used by Native Americans of several periods from 10,000 B.C. to A.D. 1700. Contact Lake Meredith Recreation Area, PO Box 1460. Phone 806/857-3151. **FREE**

Special Event

World's Largest Fish Fry. Borger. First Sat June. Phone 806/274-2211.

Gainesville

(B-6) *See also Denton, Sherman*

Founded 1849 **Pop** 15,538 **Elev** 738 ft
Area code 940 **Zip** 76240
Information Chamber of Commerce, 101 S Culberson, 76240; 888/585-4468.
Web www.gainesville.tx.us

What to See and Do

Lake Texoma. (See DENISON) E on US 82 then N via US 377 or US 69.

Leonard Park. Swimming pool, bathhouse (mid-May-Labor Day; fee); picnicking, playground, ballfields. Frank Buck Zoo is also here. Park (daily). 1000 W California. Phone 888/585-4468.

Morton Museum of Cooke County. Former city fire station (1884) now houses items of county history back to 1850. Tours of historic downtown area (by appt). (Tues-Sat; closed hols) 210 S Dixon St. Phone 940/668-8900. **FREE**

Moss Lake. A 1,125-acre lake with 15 mi of shoreline. Fishing, camping; picnicking. 12 mi NW. Phone 888/585-4468.

Motels/Motor Lodges

★ ★ **BEST WESTERN INN.** *2103 N I-35 (76240). 940/665-7737; fax 940/668-2651; res 800/528-1234. www.bestwestern.com.* 35 rms. S $35-$41; D $38-$44; each addl $5; under 12 free. Crib free. TV; cable (premium). Pool. Complimentary coffee in rms. Continental bkfst. Restaurant nearby. Ck-out 11 am. Cr cds: A, C, D, DS, JCB, MC, V.

★ ★ **RAMADA LIMITED.** *600 Fair Park Blvd (76241). 940/665-8800; fax 940/665-8709.* 118 rms, 2 story. S, D $57; each addl $5; under 18 free. Crib $5. TV; cable (premium). Pool. Restaurant 6:30 am-1 pm, 5-9 pm. Rm serv. Bar 5 pm-midnight, Sat to 1 am, closed Sun. Ck-out noon. Coin lndry. Meeting rms. Business servs avail. Game rm. Cr cds: A, C, D, DS, ER, JCB, MC, V.

Restaurant

★ **CLARK'S OUTPOST BBQ.** *101 N TX 377, Tioga (76271). 940/437-2414.* Hrs: 11 am-9 pm; Fri, Sat to 9:30 pm; Sun to 8:30 pm. Closed Jan 1, Thanksgiving, Dec 25. Res accepted. Bar. Lunch $3.50-$13.50, dinner $3.50-$16. Child's menu. Specializes in chicken, turkey, ribs. Western decor. Cr cds: A, D, DS, MC, V.

Galveston

(E-7) *See also Houston*

Founded 1816 **Pop** 57,247 **Elev** 20 ft
Area code 409
Information Galveston Island Convention & Visitors Bureau, 2428 Seawall Blvd, 77550; 888/425-4753
Web www.galvestontourism.com

Few American cities have histories as romantic and adventurous as Galveston's. It is generally agreed that the Spanish explorer Cabeza de Vaca, first European to see Texas, was shipwrecked on Galveston Island in 1528. From here he began his wanderings through Texas, New Mexico, and finally to Mexico, where his tales inspired later expeditions.

The pirate Jean Lafitte was lord of Galveston from 1817 until 1821. He built a house and fortress called Maison Rouge (Red House). Under Lafitte, the town was a nest of slave traders, saloon keepers, gamblers, smugglers, and pirates. One hundred Spanish ships were seized and looted during Lafitte's time, but Spain was powerless against him. Many slaves were on the pirated vessels; Lafitte's standard price for slaves was a dollar a pound.

Lafitte's occupation ended in May 1821, after the US Navy ordered him to leave. He set fire to the town, fleeing southward and into oblivion with his remaining followers.

During the Texas Revolution, the four ships of the Texas Navy were based in Galveston and managed to prevent a blockade of the Texas coast. When David Burnet, interim President of the Republic of Texas, and his cabinet came here in 1836, fleeing from Santa Ana, the town became the capital of Texas.

After the Civil War, Congress appropriated money to make Galveston a deep-water port. The town had a population of 38,000 in 1900. On September 8 of that year a hurricane with 110-mph winds struck, flooding the city, killing 6,000 and leaving 8,000 homeless. The storm drove a 4,000-ton vessel to a point 22 miles from deep water. Galveston rebuilt itself with inspired fortitude. The level of land was raised from five to 17 feet and a 17-foot-high, 16-foot-wide reinforced concrete seawall was built. The wall has withstood subsequent hurricane tides.

Galveston's wharves can berth 38 oceangoing vessels. It is the state's leading cotton port and is a sulphur and grain shipping center. It is an island city colored with blooming tropical flora. Forty blocks of the East End Historical District, protected from future development, may be seen on walking or driving tours.

With 32 miles of sandy beaches, fishing piers, deep-sea fishing, cool breezes off the Gulf and plenty of places to stay, eat, and enjoy oneself, Galveston is an ideal spot for a seaside vacation. Such vacations are its specialty, although the city is also an important medical center and international seaport.

What to See and Do

1839 Williams Home. Home of Texas pioneer, patriot, and entrepreneur Samuel May Williams, the house was saved from the wrecker's ball and meticulously restored. (Sat-Sun; closed Jan 1, Thanksgiving, Dec 25) 3601 Ave P. Phone 409/762-3933. ¢¢

Ashton Villa. (1859) This three-story brick Italianate mansion has been restored to reflect life in Galveston during the late 1800s; period furniture, many interesting details incl ornate cast-iron verandas in Gothic Revival style. Tours begin in carriage house, located on grounds, and incl the ornate Gold Room and second-floor family quarters. (Daily; closed Thanksgiving, Dec 24, 25) 2328 Broadway at 23rd St. Phone 409/762-3933. ¢¢¢

The Bishop's Palace. (1886) Four-story stone Victorian mansion, former residence of Bishop Byrne (1923-1950), is an outstanding example of this style and period; marble, mosaics, stained- and jeweled-glass windows, hand-carved stairwell and woodwork, art objects from many lands. Tours (daily; closed Dec 25). 1402 Broadway. Phone 409/762-2475. ¢¢¢

Factory Stores of America. Over 30 outlet stores can be found in this outdoor shopping area. (Mon-Sat, also Sun afternoons) Approx 15 min on I-45, exit 13, in LaMarque. Phone 409/938-3333.

Galveston Island State Park. A 2,000-acre recreational area. Swimming, fishing, boating in bay and gulf; nature trails, picnicking (shelters), improved campsites (hookups, showers, dump station). Standard fees. (Daily) 11 mi SW on FM 3005. Phone 409/737-1222. ¢¢

Galveston-Port Bolivar Ferry. Operated by Texas Department of Transportation. (Daily) Ferry Rd (Hwy 87). Phone 409/763-2386. **FREE**

Grand 1894 Opera House. Extraordinary theater with magnificent restoration hosts national touring shows and other performing arts yr-round. (Call for schedule) 2020 Postoffice St. Phone 409/765-1894.

The Great Storm. A 27-min documentary tells the story of the devastating hurricane that killed over 6,000 people and destroyed ⅓ of the city in Sept 1900. (Daily; hrly presentations) At Pier 21, 21st St at Harbor Side. Phone 409/763-8808. ¢¢

Moody Gardens. A 142-acre recreation and educational facility featuring Rain Forest Pyramid, 3-D IMAX theater, Palm Beach (Memorial Day-Labor Day, daily). 1 Hope Blvd. Phone 409/744-4673. ¢¢¢

The Strand, Galveston

Ocean Star. Step aboard an offshore rig and experience the oil and gas production work at sea through videos, interactive displays, and models from around the world. (Daily) Pier 19. Phone 409/766-7027.

Railroad Museum at the Center for Transportation and Commerce. At the foot of the historic Strand in the restored Santa Fe Union Station, the five-acre museum contains the largest collection of restored railroad equipt in the Southwest. Sound and light shows portray the history and development of Galveston Island; the miniature layout of the Port of Galveston features an HO-scale railroad. Building incl a 1930s waiting rm. (Daily; closed hols, Mardi Gras wk) 123 Rosenberg. Phone 409/765-5700. ¢¢

Recreational facilities. The 32-mi beach, with fishing piers, boats for rent, and amusements, is Galveston's prime attraction. Stewart Beach, a municipal development, is at the east end of the island. Fishing is allowed from five free county piers, by boat rental, or by charter boat for deep-sea sport. There are riding stables at Jamaica Beach on Stewart Rd and two golf courses and several tennis courts in the area. Anchorage for 300 pleasure boats and yachts at the Galveston Yacht Club, 715 Holiday Dr; also for 556 (400 covered) at the marina, 11th St at Pier 7. Phone 409/763-5668.

Seawolf Park. WWII submarine USS *Cavalla* and destroyer escort USS *Stewart* are located here; also Army tank, Navy fighter plane. Playground, picnicking, fishing pier (fee), pavilion. Parking (fee). Park (daily). Pelican Island. Phone 409/744-5738. ¢

⭐ **The Strand National Historic Landmark District.** This historic area is restored to late 1800s appearance. The Strand, once known as the "Wall Street of the Southwest," contains one of the finest concentrations of 19th-century commercial structures in the US. Many are now restored and used as apartments, restaurants, shops, and galleries. A Visitor Center is located at 2016 Strand. Various events take place here throughout the yr (see SPECIAL EVENTS). Extends between 20th and 25th Sts. Contact the Galveston Historical

Foundation, 2016 Strand, 77550. Phone 409/766-7068.

Texas Seaport Museum. Features the "tall ship Elissa," built in Scotland in 1877. The ship, crafted by Alexander Hall & Company, shipbuilders famous for their beautiful iron sailing ships, traded under five different flags and visited ports throughout the world. Rescued from the scrapyard in 1974 and restored by Galveston Historical Foundation. Audiovisual presentation on Elissa; galleries with maritime exhibits. (Daily; closed Thanksgiving, Dec 25) Pier 21. Phone 409/763-1877. ¢¢

Treasure Island Tour Train. Ninety-min, 17-mi trip around Galveston. (Daily, weather permitting) Depart from Beach Central, 2106 Seawall Blvd. Phone 409/765-9564. ¢¢¢

Special Events

Mardi Gras. On the Strand. Phone 409/766-7068. Mid-late Feb.

Historic Homes Tour. Tour of 19th-century private houses not normally open to the public. Contact Galveston Historical Foundation, 409/765-7834. First two wkends May.

Galveston Island Outdoor Musicals. Amphitheater, west of Seawall Blvd (FM 3005) on 13-mi Rd in Galveston Island State Park. Broadway, other productions. Phone 800/54-SHOWS. Mid-June-early Sept.

Dickens on the Strand. Located in the Strand National Historic Landmark District. Yuletide celebration recreates 19th-century London street scene incl live representations of Charles Dickens' characters, carolers, dancers, puppeteers, and outdoor handbell festival. Contact Galveston Historical Foundation, 2016 Strand. Phone 409/766-7068. First wkend Dec.

Motels/Motor Lodges

★★ **HARBOR HOUSE.** *Pier 21 (77550).* 409/763-3321; fax 409/765-6421; toll-free 409/763-3321. *harborhousepier21.com.* 42 rms, 3 story. S $120-$140; D $135-$155; each addl $15; suites $175; under 18 free; package plans; higher rates Mardi Gras. Crib free. TV; cable (premium). Complimentary continental bkfst. Ck-out noon. Meeting rms. Business servs avail. In-rm modem link. Shopping arcade. Marina for guests' boats. Cr cds: A, C, D, DS, MC, V.

⬛ 🛁 🖥 🐾 SC

★★ **HOLIDAY INN.** *5002 Seawall Blvd (77551). 409/740-3581; fax 409/740-4682; res 800/465-4329. www.holidayinnonthebeach.com.* 178 rms, 8 story. Mar-Aug: S, D $99-$189; each addl $5; under 18 free; suites $475; higher rates special events; lower rates rest of yr. Crib free. TV; cable (premium). Pool; wading pool, poolside serv. Restaurant 6 am-10 pm. Bar 11:30-2 am; entertainment Thurs-Sat. Ck-out noon. Coin lndry. Gift shop. Exercise equipt; sauna. Balconies. Cr cds: A, C, D, DS, MC, V.

⬛ 🖥 🧖 🐾 📶

★★ **LA QUINTA INN.** *1402 Seawall Blvd (77550). 409/763-1224; fax 409/765-8663; res 800/531-5900. www.laquinta.com.* 117 rms, 3 story. May-mid-Sept: S, D $83-$145; each addl $10; under 18 free; higher rates wkends; lower rates rest of yr. Crib free. Pet accepted, some restrictions. TV; cable (premium). Pool. Complimentary continental bkfst. Restaurant adj open 24 hrs. Ck-out noon. Business servs avail. In-rm modem link. Microwaves avail. Cr cds: A, C, D, DS, MC, V.

⬛ 🐾 🛁 🧖 🖥 📶 🐾

Hotels

★★★ **HILTON.** *5400 Seawall Blvd (77551). 409/744-5000; fax 409/740-2209; res 800/445-8667. www. galvestonhilton.com.* 150 rms, 6 story. S $89-$189; D $99-$199; each addl $10; lower rates winter. Crib free. TV; cable (premium). Heated pool; whirlpool, poolside serv. Restaurant 6 am-11 pm. Bar 11 am-11:30 pm; Fri, Sat to 1 am. Ck-out 11 am. Meeting rms. Business servs avail. In-rm modem link. Gift shop. Coin lndry. Lighted tennis. Exercise equipt; sauna. Balconies. Luxury level. Cr cds: A, D, DS, MC, V.

⬛ 🧖 🛁 🖥 📶 🐾

★★★ **SAN LUIS RESORT AND CONFERENCE CENTER.** *5222 Seawall Blvd (77551). 409/744-1500; fax 409/744-7545; toll-free 800/445-0090. www.iacconline.com.* 241 rms, 50 condos, 16 story. Memorial Day-Labor

Day: S, D $129-$229; each addl $10; condos $135-$350; suites $189-$600; under 12 free; package plans; lower rates rest of yr. Valet parking $8. TV; cable (premium). Pool; whirlpool. Restaurant 6:30 am-10:30 pm; Fri, Sat to 11 pm. Rm serv 24 hrs. Bar 11 am-midnight; Sun from noon; entertainment Thurs-Sat. Business center. In-rm modem link. Lighted tennis. Golf privileges. Exercise equipt; sauna. Massage. Microwaves, refrigerators avail. Balconies. Heliport. Cr cds: A, C, D, DS, MC, V.

⬛ 🛁 🧖 🏃 🛁 🍴 🖥 🔥 SC 🏃 🎿

★★★ **THE TREMONT HOUSE, A WYNDHAM HISTORIC HOTEL.** *2300 Ship Mechanic Row (77550). 409/763-0300; fax 409/763-1539; res 800/996-3426. www.wyndham.com.* 117 rms, 4 story. S, D $109-$250; each addl $15; suites $250-$375; under 18 free. Crib free. Valet parking $8/day. TV; cable (premium). Afternoon refreshments. Restaurant (see also MERCHANT PRINCE). Rm serv 24 hrs. Bar 11-2 am; pianist. Ck-out noon. Meeting rms. Business servs avail. Concierge. Shopping arcade. Massage. Health club privileges. 1879 bldg; 11-ft-high windows. Cr cds: A, C, D, DS, ER, JCB, MC, V.

⬛ 🖥 🐾

Resort

★★★ **THE HOTEL GALVEZ.** *2024 Seawall Blvd (77550). 409/765-7721; fax 409/765-5623. www.wyndham. com.* 231 rms, 7 story. S, D $139-$209; suites $175-$475; under 18 free. Valet parking $6. Pet accepted. TV; cable (premium). Pool; wading pool, whirlpool. Coffee in rms. Restaurant 6:30 am-2 pm, 5:30-10 pm. Bar noon-1 am; entertainment Fri, Sat. Ck-out noon. Meeting rms. Business servs avail. In-rm modem link. Gift shop. Health club privileges. Refrigerator in suites. Cr cds: A, C, D, DS, JCB, MC, V.

⬛ 🛁 🖥 🔥 🐾 🛥

Restaurants

★★ **CLARY'S.** *8509 Teichman Rd (77554). 409/740-0771.* Hrs: 11:30 am-2:30 pm, 5:30-10 pm; Fri, Sat 5-10 pm. Closed Mon. Bar. Lunch $7.50-$12, dinner $14.75-$23. Specializes in fresh seafood, steak. Own baking. Glass garden rm overlooks bayou. Family-owned. Cr cds: A, D, DS, MC, V.

⊡ ⊟

★★ **GAIDO'S.** *3828 Seawall Blvd (77550). 409/762-9625.* Hrs: 11:45 am-9 pm; Fri, Sat to 10 pm. Closed Dec 25. Bar. Lunch, dinner $12-$18. Complete meals: dinner $16.15-$23.70. Child's menu. Specializes in Gulf seafood. Nautical decor. Established 1911. Family-owned. Cr cds: A, DS, MC, V.

⊡ ⊟

★★ **THE GARDEN.** *1 Hope Blvd (77554). 409/744-4673. www.moody garden.com.* Hrs: 11 am-5 pm; Fri, Sat 11 am-4 pm, 5-8 pm; Sun buffet to 3 pm; summer hrs vary. Closed Dec 25. Continental menu. Serv bar. Lunch $5.95-$13.95, dinner $7.95-$15.95. Sun buffet $7.95. Child's menu. Specializes in Angus beef, seafood buffet. Own desserts. Entertainment Fri, Sat. Outdoor dining. View of bay, fountains. Totally nonsmoking. Cr cds: A, D, DS, MC, V.

⊡ SC

★★ **LANDRY'S SEAFOOD.** *5310 Seawall Blvd (77551). 409/744-1010.* Hrs: 11 am-11 pm; Fri, Sat to midnight; winter hrs vary. Closed Dec 25. Bar. Lunch, dinner $4.95-$18.95. Child's menu. Specialties: seafood gumbo, whole Gulf flounder, Angus steak. Outdoor dining. Casual dining. Cr cds: A, D, DS, MC, V.

⊡ ⊟

★★ **LUIGI'S RISTORANTE ITALIANO.** *2328 Strand (77550). 409/763-6500.* Hrs: 11:30 am-2:30 pm, 5:30-9 pm; Fri, Sat to 11 pm. Closed Jan 1, Thanksgiving, Dec 25. Res accepted. Italian menu. Bar. Lunch $3.95-$12.95, dinner $4.95-$22.95. Child's menu. Specializes in seafood, veal. Own desserts. Roman decor in historic Victorian building (1895). Cr cds: A, D, DS, MC, V.

⊡

★★ **MERCHANT PRINCE.** *2300 Ship Mechanic Row (77550). 409/763-0300.* Hrs: 6:30 am-10 pm; Sat to 11 pm; Sun brunch 11 am-2 pm. Res accepted. Continental, Southwestern menu. Serv bar. Bkfst $4.50-$5.25, lunch $5.95-$9.95, dinner $6.25-

$24.95. Sun brunch $11.95. Specialties: crab cakes, veal, bread pudding with bourbon sauce. Free valet parking. Atrium dining. Cr cds: A, D, DS, MC, V.

⊡

Georgetown

(D-6) *See also Austin, Burnet, Salado*

Founded 1848 **Pop** 28,339 **Elev** 758 ft
Area code 512
Information Convention and Visitor's Bureau, PO Box 409, 78627-0346; 512/930-3545 or 800/436-8696
Web www.georgetown.org

What to See and Do

Inner Space Cavern. Large stalactites, stalagmites; lighting, acoustical effects; cable car-type elevator. Cave temp constant 72°F. Guided tours (1¼ hr); 20-min max wait for tours to depart. (Daily; closed two wks before Dec 25) 1 mi S off I-35 exit 259. Phone 512/863-5545. ¢¢¢¢

Lake Georgetown. This 1,300-acre lake is surrounded by four developed park areas. Hiking trail (16½ mi), camping (fee). (Daily) 4 mi W of I-35 via FM 2338. Phone 512/930-5253. **FREE**

San Gabriel Park. Eighty acres with fishing, swimming; picnicking (shelters, barbecue facilities), ballfield, hiking; livestock show barns, rodeo arena. North edge of town, on the San Gabriel River. Phone 512/930-3595. **FREE**

Southwestern University. (1840) 1,200 students. Oldest university in Texas. Several historic buildings; chapel. Self-guided tours. (Mon-Sat) 1001 E University Ave. Phone 512/863-6511.

Special Event

Mayfair. Air show, art walk. May.

Motels/Motor Lodges

★★ **COMFORT INN.** *1005 Leander Rd (78628). 512/863-7504; fax*

512/819-9016; toll-free 800/228-5150. www.comfortinn.com. 55 rms. S $54-$72; D $59-$77; each addl $5; under 12 free. Crib free. Pet accepted, some restrictions. TV; cable, VCR avail (movies). Pool. Complimentary continental bkfst. Restaurant nearby. Ck-out noon. Microwaves avail. Cr cds: A, C, D, DS, JCB, MC, V.

★★ **LA QUINTA INN.** *333 N I-35 (78628). 512/869-2541; fax 512/863-7073; res 800/531-5900. www. laquinta.com.* 98 rms, 3 story. S $69-$89; D $79-$99; each addl $10; suites $101; under 18 free. Crib free. Pet accepted. TV; cable (premium). Pool. Complimentary continental bkfst. Restaurant 6:30 am-9 pm. Rm serv. Ck-out noon. Meeting rms. In-rm modem link. Valet serv. Cr cds: A, C, D, DS, MC, V.

Goliad

See also Victoria

Founded 1749 **Pop** 1,975 **Elev** 171 ft
Area code 361 **Zip** 77963
Information Chamber of Commerce, Market and Franklin Sts, PO Box 606; 361/645-3563

What to See and Do

Goliad State Historical Park. A 186-acre recreational area. Swimming, fishing; nature and hiking trails, picnicking, playground, improved camping, tent and trailer sites (dump station). Standard fees. (Daily) 1 mi S on US 183 to Park Rd 6. Phone 361/645-3405. ¢ Incl

Mission Espiritu Santo de Zuñiga. Reconstruction of the original established in 1749. Interpretive center in the mission contains artifacts and displays illustrating Spanish Colonial era.

Market House Museum. The Market House, restored in 1967 as a museum, was built in 1870 with stalls that were rented to sellers of meat and produce. In 1886 the building became a firehouse, home to the volunteer fire department.

Chamber of Commerce offices are here as well. (Mon-Sat; closed hols) Corner Franklin and Market Sts. Phone 361/645-3563. **FREE**

Presidio La Bahia. (1721) The only completely restored Spanish Colonial Presidio in the Western Hemisphere and the only one in North America to have participated in six wars for independence. Spanish, Mexican, and Texan soldiers once garrisoned its fortified walls. The first Declaration of Texas Independence was signed here; the first flag of Texas independence flew here. Site of the longest siege in American military history (1812-1813) and the Goliad Massacre (1836), the largest loss of life for Texas independence. Living history programs, battle reenactments, seasonal fiestas throughout the yr. (Daily; closed hols) 1 mi S on US 183. Phone 361/645-3752. ¢¢

Special Events

Goliad County Fair & Rodeo. Fairgrounds. Third wkend Mar. Phone 361/645-2492.

Stock car racing. Shady Oaks Speedway. 6 mi N off US 77A on FM 622. Phone 361/645-1963. Mar-Oct.

Tour de Goliad Bike Ride. Third Sat Oct. Phone 361/645-3563.

Gonzales

(E-6) *See also San Marcos, Seguin*

Settled 1825 **Pop** 7,202
Area code 830 **Zip** 78629
Information Chamber of Commerce, 414 St. Lawrence St, PO Box 134; 830/672-6532

What to See and Do

Gonzales County Jail Museum. Restored cells, gallows, dungeon, jailer's rm. (Daily; closed hols) 414 St. Lawrence. Phone 830/672-6532. **FREE**

Gonzales Memorial Museum. Collection of toys, guns, clothing, pictures, and letters that depict Gonzales and its history. Incl the legendary cannon. (Tues-Sun) 414 Smith St. Phone 830/672-6350. **FREE**

Gonzales Pioneer Village. Village consists of over ten reconstructed buildings from before 1900. Incl log house, blacksmith shop, printing press, grainery, working broom factory, 1890s house, and 1870s church. Special tours, programs (fees). Adj is Fort Waul, an earthen-walled Confederate fort (1864). (Sept-May, Sat-Sun; Jun-Aug, Fri-Sun) 1 mi N on US 183. Phone 830/672-2157. ¢¢

Palmetto State Park. Approx 270 acres. Swimming, fishing (pier); picnicking (shelter; fee), playground, nature and hiking trails, improved camping (hookups, dump station). Standard fees. (Daily) 12 mi NW on US 183, 2 mi W on Park Rd 11. Phone 830/672-3266. ¢

Special Events

Springfest. Tour of historic homes. Last wkend Apr. Phone 830/672-6532.

Come and Take It Celebration. Honors first shot fired for Texas independence. Parade, street dance, vintage house tours, battle reenactments. First wkend Oct. Phone 830/672-6532.

B&Bs/Small Inns

★★ **HOUSTON HOUSE BED & BREAKFAST.** *621 E St. George St (78629).* 830/672-6940; fax 830/672-6228; res 888/477-0760. *www.houston house.com.* 5 rms, 2 story. S, D $100-$150; each addl $15; higher rates special events. Children over 12 yrs only. TV; VCR (movies). Complimentary full bkfst. Complimentary coffee in rms. Ck-out 11 am, ck-in 3 pm. Fireplaces. Balconies. Built in 1895 by cattle baron. Murals, clock collection. Totally nonsmoking. Cr cds: A, MC, V.
⬜ ⬜ ⬜ SC

★ **ST. JAMES INN.** *723 St. James St (78629).* 830/672-7066. *www. stjamesinn.com.* 5 rms, 3 story, 1 suite. No elvtr. No rm phones. S $70; D $95; each addl $20; suite $95-$200; wkend, wkly rates. Children over 12 yrs only. TV; cable (premium), VCR avail (movies). Complimentary full bkfst; afternoon refreshments. Complimentary coffee in rms. Restaurant nearby. Ck-out 1

pm, ck-in 3 pm. Business servs avail. Street parking. Lawn games. Fireplaces; microwaves avail. Built in 1914. Totally nonsmoking. Cr cds: A, MC, V.
⬜ ⬜ ⬜

Graham

(B-5) *See also Mineral Wells*

Founded 1872 **Pop** 8,716 **Elev** 1,045 ft **Area code** 940 **Zip** 76450
Information Chamber of Commerce, 608 Elm St, PO Box 299; 940/549-3355 or 800/256-4844

What to See and Do

Fort Richardson State Historical Park. Approx 400 acres. Most northerly of frontier army posts in Texas, active 1867-1878. Seven restored buildings and two replicas. Interpretive center and period displays. Fishing; hiking, nature study, picnicking, improved campsites (hookups, dump station). Standard fees. (Daily) 30 mi E via US 380 in Jacksboro. Phone 940/567-3506. ¢

Possum Kingdom State Park. (see). 205 Lakeshore Dr. Phone 940/549-1803.

Motel/Motor Lodge

★★ **GATEWAY INN.** *1401 Hwy 16 S (76450).* 940/549-0222. 77 rms, 2 story. S $35; D $36-$40; each addl $4. Pet accepted; $5. TV; cable (premium). Pool; whirlpool. Complimentary coffee in rms. Restaurant 6 am-10 pm. Rm serv. Private club 11 am-midnight, Sat to 1 am. Ck-out noon. Coin lndry. Free airport transportation. Cr cds: A, C, D, DS, MC, V.
⬜ ⬜ ⬜ ⬜ ⬜ SC

Granbury

See also Arlington-Grand Prairie, Cleburne, Fort Worth

Pop 5,718 **Elev** 722 ft **Area code** 817 **Zip** 76048

Information Granbury Convention and Visitors Bureau, 100 N Crockett; 817/573-5548 or 800/950-2212

Web www.granbury.org

What to See and Do

Fossil Rim Wildlife Center. A 3,000-acre wildlife conservation center with more than 1,000 endangered, threatened, and exotic animals. Breeding programs for endangered species incl white rhinoceros, Mexican wolf, red wolf, Grevy's zebra, Arabian oryx, scimitar-horned oryx, addax, and cheetah. Ten-mi drive-through with nature trail; fossil area; petting pasture. Restaurant; gift shop. Some fees. (Daily; closed Thanksgiving, Dec 25) S on TX 144, then 3 mi SW of Glen Rose off TX 67. Phone 254/897-2960. ¢¢¢¢

Granbury Opera House. (1886) Restored opera house on historic town square. Musicals, plays, special events. (Summer, Thurs-Sun; rest of yr, Fri-Sun) 133 E Pearl St. Phone 817/573-9191.

Special Event

General Granbury Civil War Reenactment. Phone 817/573-5548. Late Sept. Phone 830/672-6532.

Motels/Motor Lodges

★ **CLASSIC INN.** *1209 N Plaza Dr (76048). 817/573-8874.* 42 rms. S $59; D $64; each addl $5; under 12 free. Crib $4. Pet accepted, some restrictions. TV; cable (premium). Pool. Complimentary continental bkfst. Restaurant adj open 24 hrs. Ck-out 11 am. Business servs avail. Refrigerators, microwaves. Lake ¼ mi; swimming beach. Cr cds: A, C, D, DS, MC, V.
🄳 🐾 🕭 🌊 📶 🔥

★★ **COMFORT INN.** *1201 N Plaza Dr (76048). 817/573-2611; fax 817/573-2695; res 800/228-5150.* www.comfortinn.com. 48 rms, 2 story. Apr-Sept: S $60-$100; D $65-$100; each addl $5; under 18 free; lower rates rest of yr. Crib $10. TV; cable (premium). Pool; whirlpool. Complimentary continental bkfst. Restaurant adj open 24 hrs. Ck-out noon. Meeting rms. Refrigerators,

microwaves. Cr cds: A, C, D, DS, JCB, MC, V.
🄳 🌊 📶 🔥

★★ **PLANTATION INN ON THE LAKE.** *1451 E Pearl St (76048). 817/573-8846; fax 817/579-0917; toll-free 800/422-2403.* 53 rms, 2 story. S $60; D $65; each addl $5; suites $75-$80; under 6 free. Pet accepted, some restrictions. TV; cable (premium). Pool; wading pool. Complimentary continental bkfst. Ck-out 11 am. Meeting rms. In-rm modem link. Health club privileges. Refrigerators; microwaves avail. Some private patios, balconies. Cr cds: A, C, D, DS, MC, V.
🄳 🐾 🕭 🌊 ✈ 📶 🔥

Resort

★ **LODGE OF GRANBURY, ON LAKE GRANBURY.** *401 E Pearl St (76048). 817/573-2606; fax 817/573-2077.* www2.itexas.net/~lodgeofgby. 58 suites, 3 story. S $65-$119; D $95-$149; May-Oct: suites $89-$165; lower rates rest of yr. Pet accepted. TV; cable (premium). Pool; whirl-pool. Complimentary coffee in rms. Private club 4 pm-midnight. Ck-out noon. Business servs avail. Lighted tennis. 18-hole golf privileges. Refrigerators, microwaves. Private patios, balconies. Picnic tables. On lake. Cr cds: A, C, D, DS, JCB, MC, V.
🄳 🐾 🕭 🎿 🏌 🌊 📶 🔥

Restaurant

★ **KELLY'S ON THE SQUARE.** *115 E Pearl (76048). 817/573-9722.* Hrs: 11:30 am-9 pm. Closed Mon; also Dec 24-Jan 1. Res accepted. Private club to midnight; Sat to 1 am. Lunch, dinner $4.95-$14.95. Child's menu. Specializes in country-fried steak, marinated rib-eye steak, dessert crêpes. Entertainment Fri, Sat. Historic building; antique furnishings. Cr cds: A, MC, V.
🄳 🍽

Grand Prairie

(see Arlington-Grand Prairie)

Greenville

(B-7) *See also Bonham, Dallas, McKinney*

Pop 23,960 **Elev** 550 ft **Area code** 903

Information Chamber of Commerce, 2713 Stonewall St, PO Box 1055, 75403; 903/455-1510

Web www.greenville-chamber.org

What to See and Do

American Cotton Museum. The story of cotton from seed to modern products. Incl history and impact of cotton in the area and special exhibits. (Tues-Sun; closed hols) 600 I-30 E at exit 95. Phone 903/450-4502. ¢¢

Lake Tawakoni. Fishing, boating (ramps), waterskiing; picnicking, cabins, tent and trailer sites. Some fees. (Daily) 16 mi S off US 69. Phone 903/662-5134. ¢¢

Mary of Puddin Hill. Fruitcake bakery, candy kitchen, and store. Tours (Oct-Dec, Mon-Sat; rest of yr varies; group tours by appt) I-30 at exit 95. Phone 903/455-6931. **FREE**

Special Events

Hunt County Fair. Fairgrounds. Second wk June. Phone 903/455-1510.

Cotton Jubilee. Multicultural and environmental entertainment; dancing, carnival, arts and crafts show. Third wkend Oct. Phone 903/455-1510.

Motels/Motor Lodges

★★ **BEST WESTERN INN AND SUITES.** *1216 I-30 W (75402). 903/454-1792; res 800/528-1234. www.bestwestern.com.* 99 rms, 2 story. S, D $49; each addl $5; suites $64; under 12 free. Crib free. TV; cable (premium). Pool. Complimentary continental bkfst. Coffee in rms. Restaurant adj open 24 hrs. Bar 2 pm-midnight; Sat to 1 am; closed Sun. Ck-out noon. Coin lndry. Meeting rm. Business servs avail. Health club privileges. Refrigerators, microwaves. Cr cds: A, C, D, DS, MC, V.
D ❋ ≋ ⩬ ⬧

★★ **RAMADA INN.** *1215 E I-30 (75402). 903/454-7000; fax 903/454-7001.* 138 rms, 2 story. S, D $58; under 18 free. Crib free. Pet accepted. TV; cable (premium). Pool; whirlpool. Complimentary full bkfst. Restaurant 6-10 am, 5-9 pm. Rm serv. Private club 3 pm-midnight. Ck-out noon. Coin lndry. Meeting rm. Business servs avail. In-rm modem link. Valet serv. Sundries. Exercise equipt; sauna. Health club privileges. Cr cds: A, C, D, DS, JCB, MC, V.
D ❋ ≋ ⫚ ⩬ ⬧ SC

Unrated Dining Spot

MARY OF PUDDIN' HILL. *201 E I-30 E (75403). 903/455-6931.* Hrs: 10 am-5 pm; Sun from 1 pm. Closed hols. A la carte entrees: lunch $3-$7.50. Child's menu. Specializes in homemade soups, gourmet sandwiches, carrot cake. Western country atmosphere; chocolate dollhouse and carousel on display. Tours of confectionery; special events. Cr cds: A, DS, MC, V.
D

Groesbeck

See also Waco

Founded 1869 **Pop** 4,291 **Elev** 478 ft **Area code** 254 **Zip** 76642

Information Chamber of Commerce, 110 N Ellis, PO Box 326; 254/729-3894

What to See and Do

Confederate Reunion Grounds State Historical Park. Approx 80 acres. Encampment formed in 1889 to perpetuate memories of fallen Confederate soldiers and to aid disabled survivors and indigent widows and orphans of the deceased. Canoeing to Fort Parker State Park on Navasota River. Swimming, fishing; hiking, bird-watching, picnicking, playground. Standard fees. (Daily) 7 mi N via TX 14, then 2½ mi W on FM 2705. Contact Park Superintendent, c/o Fort Parker State Park, 194 Pork

Rd 28, Mexia 76667. Phone 254/562-5751. ¢

Fort Parker State Park. On Lake Fort Parker, approx 1,500 acres. Swimming, fishing, boating (ramp), canoeing; hiking, picnicking, concession, improved campsites (hookups, shelters, dump station). Standard fees. (Daily) 6 mi N via TX 14, to entrance on Park Rd 28. Phone 254/562-5751. ¢

Lake Limestone. This 14,200-acre dammed lake offers two marinas with public access areas at various locations. (Daily) 18 mi SE via FM 937.

Limestone County Historical Museum. Artifacts and information relating to Limestone County; Old Fort Parker memorabilia. (Mon-Fri; closed hols) 210 W Navasota St. Phone 254/729-5064. ¢

Old Fort Parker State Historical Park. (1834) Built by the Parker family to protect a small settlement of families. In 1836, Comanches overran the fort, killing five people and capturing five more, incl Cynthia Ann Parker, nine yrs old. She grew up, married a Comanche chief, and lived with the tribe until captured 24 yrs later. She was the mother of the last great Comanche chief, Quanah Parker. Log blockhouse and stockade. Standard fees. (Daily) 4 mi N via TX 14 and Park Rd 35. Phone 254/729-5253. ¢

Special Event

Christmas at the Fort. Old Fort Parker. Live demonstration of life in 1840s. Second wkend Dec. Phone 254/562-5751.

Guadalupe Mountains National Park

See also El Paso, Van Horn, also see Carlsbad, NM

(Approx 50 mi N of Van Horn via TX 54)

Standing like an island in the desert, this spectacular expanse of the Capitan Reef is part of the world's most extensive fossil reef complex (Per-mian reef complex). The 86,416-acre park encompasses the most scenic and rugged portion of these mountains. Elevations range from 3,650 feet to 8,749 feet at Guadalupe Peak, the highest point in Texas. Besides the lofty peaks and coniferous forests there are deep canyons, a tremendous earth fault, desert lowlands, historic sites, unusual flora and fauna, outstanding scenery, and more than 80 miles of hiking trails, with possible trips ranging from five minutes to five days. Several precautions are necessary. Check with a ranger before leaving the main road; do not climb the cliffs; many desert plants have sharp spines; watch for and respect rattlesnakes; be prepared in the backcountry (stout shoes, sun protection, appropriate clothing, and water). Pets must be leashed or restrained and are not permitted on the trails or in the backcountry; firearms are not permitted in the park; wood or charcoal fires are not permitted in the park. Plan to cook on a stove using containerized fuel. Sightseeing by car is limited to the highway, but scenic. Camping, backpacking, hiking, and horseback trails (no rentals). Two drive-in campgrounds (no showers or hookups; fee): one on the southeast side at Pine Springs, and one on the north at Dog Canyon. All individual campsites are on a first-come, first-served basis. Permits (free) required for backpacking; check with the Visitor Center first. For information contact Superintendent, HC 60, Box 400, Salt Flat, TX 79847-9400; 915/828-3251.

Harlingen

(G-6) *See also Brownsville, McAllen, Port Isabel*

Pop 57,564 **Elev** 36 ft **Area code** 956

Information Chamber of Commerce, 311 E Tyler St, 78550; 956/423-5440 or 800/531-7346

Web www.harlingen.com

What to See and Do

Iwo Jima Memorial & Museum. Features the original sculpture used to cast the bronze Marine Corp Memorial in Arlington, VA, depicting the raising of the US flag over Iwo Jima during WWII. (Daily) 320 Iwo Jima Blvd. Phone 956/412-2207. **FREE**

Laguna Atascosa National Wildlife Refuge. Approx 45,000 acres with walking trails. Fishing along the Harlingen Ship Channel only. Visitor center (Oct-Apr, daily) Administrative office (all yr, Mon-Fri; closed hols). 18 mi E on FM 106, then follow signs. Phone 956/748-3607. ¢¢

Special Events

RioFest. Fair Park. Early Apr. Phone 800/531-7346.

Rio Grande Valley Birding Festival. Harlingen Municipal Auditorium Complex and Plaza de Amistad. Early-mid-Nov. Phone 800/531-7346.

Motels/Motor Lodges

★★ **COURTYARD BY MARRIOTT.** *1725 W Filmore Ave (78550). 956/412-7800; fax 956/412-7889; toll-free 888/267-8927. www.courtyardby marriottrgv.com.* 114 rms, 3 story. Aug-Apr: S, D $69; each addl $6; suites $94; under 18 free; higher rates festival wkends; lower rates rest of yr. Crib free. TV; cable (premium). Complimentary coffee in rms. Restaurant 6 am-2:30 pm, 5:30-10:30 pm. Rm serv 24 hrs. Bar 4 pm-midnight. Ck-out noon. Meeting rms. Business servs avail. In-rm modem link. Bellhops. Valet serv. Coin lndry. Free airport, RR station transportation. Exercise equipt. Pool; whirlpool. Refrigerator, microwave in suites. Some balconies. Cr cds: A, C, D, DS, MC, V.

D ⌘ 🏋 🔥

★★ **HOLIDAY INN EXPRESS.** *501 S P St (78550). 956/428-9292; fax 956/428-6152; res 800/465-4329. www.holiday-inn.com.* 129 rms, 5 story. S, D $61.50-$65.50; suites $79.95. Crib avail. TV; cable. Pool. Complimentary continental bkfst. Coffee in rms. Restaurant adj 6 am-10 pm. Ck-out noon. In-rm modem link. Coin lndry. Some refrigerators, microwaves. Cr cds: A, C, D, DS, MC, V.

D ⌘ 🔥

★★ **LA QUINTA INN.** *1002 S Expy 83 (78552). 956/428-6888; fax 956/425-5840; res 800/531-5900. www.laquinta.com.* 130 rms, 2 story. S $49-$56; D $59-$66; each addl $8; under 18 free. Crib free. Pet accepted. TV; cable (premium). Pool. Complimentary full bkfst. Restaurant adj open 24 hrs. Ck-out noon. Coin lndry. Meeting rms. Business servs avail. In-rm modem link. Valet serv. Free airport transportation. Cr cds: A, C, D, DS, MC, V.

D ⌘ ⌘ 🔥 SC

Henderson

(C-7) *See also Longview, Tyler*

Founded 1844 **Pop** 11,273 **Elev** 506 ft **Area code** 903 **Zip** 75652

Information Tourist Development Department, Chamber of Commerce, 201 N Main St; 903/657-5528

Web www.hendersontx.com

What to See and Do

Depot Museum and Children's Discovery Center. Covers Rusk County history; many activities for children ages 3-11 in renovated cotton warehouse. Several other buildings incl T. J. Walling Cabin (1841) and Arnold Outhouse (1908), the first such structure to receive a state historical marker. (Mon-Sat; closed hols) 514 N High St. Phone 903/657-4303. ¢

Howard-Dickinson House. (1805) One of the first brick houses in county. Frame wing added in 1905. Period furnishings; books, paintings, photographs, original documents. (By appt; closed hols) 501 S Main St. Phone 903/657-5256. ¢¢

Special Events

Rural Heritage Weekend. Downtown Historic District. Arts and crafts, antique tractor shows. Third wkend Apr. Phone 903/657-5528.

Syrup Festival. Syrup making, arts and crafts, entertainment. Second Sat Nov. Phone 903/657-5528.

Hereford

(G-1) *See also Amarillo, Canyon*

Pop 14,597 **Elev** 3,806 ft
Area code 806 **Zip** 79045
Information Chamber of Commerce,
701 N Main, PO Box 192; 806/364-
3333
Web www.herefordtx.com

What to See and Do

**Deaf Smith County Historical
Museum.** Furniture, clothes, farming
tools, artifacts used by pioneers of
the area; also E. B. Black Home
(1909). (Mon-Sat; closed hols) 400
Sampson St. Phone 806/363-7070.
FREE

Motel/Motor Lodge

★★ **BEST WESTERN RED CARPET
INN.** *830 W 1st St (79045). 806/364-
0540; fax 806/364-0818; res 800/528-
1234. www.bestwestern.com.* 90 rms, 2
story. S $38-$42; D $44-$50; each
addl $4; under 12 free. Pet accepted,
some restrictions. TV; cable. Pool.
Complimentary coffee in lobby.
Restaurant adj 11 am-9 pm. Ck-out
noon. Some refrigerators. Cr cds: A,
D, DS, MC, V.

Hillsboro

(C-6) *See also Arlington-Grand Prairie,
Cleburne, Corsicana, Dallas, Waco*

Founded 1853 **Pop** 8,232 **Elev** 634 ft
Area code 254 **Zip** 76645
Information Chamber of Commerce,
115 N Covington St, PO Box 358;
254/582-2481 or 800/HILLSBORO
Web www.hillsborochamber.org

What to See and Do

Confederate Research Center.
Archives and displays with emphasis
on Confederate military history. Also
here is the Audie L. Murphy Gun
Museum. (Mon-Fri; closed school
hols) Hill College, 112 Lamar Dr, in

Library Building. Phone 254/582-
2555. **FREE**

Hillsboro Outlet Center. More than
100 outlet stores can be found here.
Cafe. (Daily) 104 NE I-35. Phone
254/582-2047.

Special Event

Hill County Fair. Livestock, food, arts
and crafts exhibits. First wk Feb.
Phone 254/582-2481.

Motel/Motor Lodge

★★ **RAMADA INN.** *I-35 & US 22
(76645). 254/582-3493; fax 254/582-
2755; toll-free 877/200-3392. www.
ramada.com.* 94 rms, 2 story. S $50-
$60; D $55-$65; each addl $8; under
18 free; wkend rates. Crib free. Pet
accepted, some restrictions. TV; cable
(premium). Pool. Ck-out noon. Business servs avail. Cr cds: A, C, D, DS,
MC, V.

Houston

(E-7) *See also Galveston*

Founded 1836 **Pop** 1,953,631 **Elev** 55
ft **Area code** 713 and 281
Information Greater Houston Con-
vention & Visitors Bureau, 901
Bagby, 77002; 713/437-5200
Web www.houston-guide.com

Houston and Texas, it has been said,
grew up together. The city was
founded in the same year as the
Republic of Texas by brothers Augus-
tus and John Allen, speculators from
New York. The town became the new
nation's first capital, named after
Sam Houston, hero of the Battle of
San Jacinto and the first elected president of the Republic. When the first
steamboat chugged up the Buffalo
Bayou, its captain found stakes mark-
ing the streets of what is today the
largest city in both Texas and the
South.

Buffalo Bayou is now part of the
Houston Ship Channel, a 400-foot-
wide, 40-foot-deep, 52-mile-long
man-made waterway flowing into

the Gulf of Mexico. More than 200 industries, including petrochemical and steel plants, line its shore. Houston is a leader in both total tonnage and foreign tonnage handled by a US port.

The space industry has thrived here for years, following the establishment in 1962 of NASA's Mission Control Center (now known as the NASA Lyndon B. Johnson Space Center), 16 miles southeast, near Clear Lake City. A number of research and development and other space-related concerns are located in the greater Houston area.

In recent years, several construction and redevelopment projects have been undertaken in Houston. The city already boasts the tallest building in the US west of the Mississippi in the Texas Commerce Tower. Newer projects include a convention center, theater center, and Space Center Houston. The face of Houston promises to change continuously into the 21st century.

Conventions and tourism play an important role in the local economy. Relying on its cosmopolitan image, temperate climate, Gulf Coast location, and a myriad of shops, accommodations, and recreational and cultural activities, Houston attracts millions of visitors each year.

Transportation

Car Rental Agencies. See IMPORTANT TOLL-FREE NUMBERS.

Public Transportation. Buses (Metro Transit), phone 713/635-4000.

Rail Passenger Service. Amtrak 800/872-7245.

Airport Information

Hobby. William P. Hobby Airport. Information 713/643-4597; lost and found 713/643-4597; weather 877/792-3225; cash machines, near Southwest Airlines. **Intercontinental:** Information 281/230-3000; lost and found 281/230-3032; weather 877/792-3225; cash machines, Terminals A, B, C.

Airlines (Intercontinental). AeroMeixico, Air Canada, Air France, America West, American, Aviateca, British Airways,

Cayman Airways, Continental, Delta, KLM, Lufthansa, Northwest, Southwest, Sun Country, TACA, United, USAir, Western Pacific.

What to See and Do

Armand Bayou Nature Center. A 2,500-acre wilderness preserve and environmental education center. Interpretive building. Hiking, nature trails, bird-watching. Public demonstrations and tours (wkends). (Tues-Sun; closed hols) 8500 Bay Area Blvd, SE of town near University of Houston-Clear Lake. Phone 281/474-2551. ¢¢

Bayou Bend Collection. American decorative arts from the late 17th, 18th, and early 19th centuries; displayed in 24-rm former residence of philanthropist Miss Ima Hogg; 14-acre gardens. 1 Westcott St. Phone 713/639-7750. ¢¢¢

Children's Museum of Houston. Nine galleries cover topics ranging from science and health to history and the arts. Changing exhibits. (Memorial Day-Labor Day, daily; rest of yr, Tues-Sun; closed hols) 1500 Binz, at La Branch. Phone 713/522-1138. ¢¢

Contemporary Arts Museum. Changing exhibits by international and regional artists of contemporary painting, sculpture, photography, video. (Daily; closed hols) 5216 Montrose Blvd. Phone 713/284-8250. **FREE**

George Ranch Historical Park. A 480-acre outdoor living history museum interprets Texas history through four generations of the host family. Tour a rustic cabin, large Victorian home, and the ranch house, and attend informative lectures and exhibits. (Call for schedule) 10215 FM 762, Richmond. Phone 281/343-0218.

Gray Line bus tours. Contact 602 Sampson St, 77003. Phone 800/334-4441.

Heritage Society Tours. Museum complex of eight historic structures dating from 1820-1905; structures incl frontier cabin, Texas plantation house, Greek Revival and Victorian houses, church (ca 1890), and museum gallery. Period furnishings. One-hr tours through four structures. (Tues-Sun; no tours hols) 1100 Bagby

St, in Sam Houston Park. Phone 713/655-1912. ¢¢¢

⭐ **Hermann Park.** Approx 400 acres donated by businessman and philanthropist George Hermann. A bronze statue and fountain honoring him are located at the intersection of Fannin and N MacGregor Dr. Bounded by Fannin and Main Sts on the west, Hermann Dr on the north, Almeda Rd on the east, and N MacGregor Dr on the south. Phone 713/845-1000. Also in the park are the Garden Center, an ancient Korean pavilion, a Japanese garden, the Miller Outdoor Theatre, which stages free summer music, ballet, and theater productions and

> **Burke Baker Planetarium.** Shows (daily; closed Jan 1, Dec 25; hrs and fees vary). Phone 713/639-4600.

> **Houston Museum of Natural Science.** Archaeological, geological, petroleum, space, wildlife, and prehistoric animal exhibits. World-class gem and mineral collection. (Daily; closed Jan 1, Dec 25) Free admission on Tues after 2 pm. 1 Hermann Circle Dr. Phone 713/639-4600.

> **Houston Zoological Gardens.** Small mammals, incl vampire bat colony; reptile and primate houses, hippopotamus building, alligator display, gorilla habitat, birdhouse with tropical rain forest; aquarium with marine life; large cat facility; education center. Three-acre discovery zoo with separate contact areas. (Daily) Free admission city hols. 1513 N MacGregor Dr, N of Texas Medical Center. Phone 713/523-5888. ¢

> **Mecom Rockwell Fountain.** Considered one of the most beautiful structures in the city. Colonnade around the fountain resembles a Roman temple; the water jet in the pool rises 12 ft. Between Fannin and San Jacinto Sts.

> **Wortham IMAX Theatre.** Multimedia auditorium (seats 400) featuring films on natural science topics shown on 80-ft by six-story-high screen. (Daily; closed Jan 1, Dec 25) Phone 713/639-4600.

Historical parks.

> **Allen's Landing Park.** Site where Houston was founded (1836) by the Allen brothers. Served as first port for steamers and sailing vessels from 1837. (Daily) Downtown. At Main St and Buffalo Bayou. **FREE**

Old Market Square. Site of city's first commercial center (early 1800s). An extensive redevelopment project features a central plaza and sidewalks paved with collages of paving material taken from old Houston buildings. Photos commemorating city history are reproduced on porcelain-enameled panels decorating benches in the sq. (Daily) One blk park on Congress. Phone 713/845-1000. **FREE**

Houston Arboretum and Nature Center. A 155-acre nonprofit nature sanctuary for the protection of native trees, shrubs, and wildlife. Five mi of nature trails (daily). Guided tours (Sat-Sun afternoons). Special events and educational programs. 4501 Woodway, in Memorial Park. Phone 713/681-8433. **FREE**

Houston Ballet. Wortham Theater Center, 501 Texas Ave. Aug-June. Phone 713/227-ARTS or 800/828-2787.

Houston Grand Opera. Multiple performances of seven major productions featuring international stars (Oct-May); also special events. Wheelchair seating, infrared and live narration, headphones. Wortham Theater Center, 501 Texas Ave. Phone 713/546-0200.

Imperial Holly Corporation. Oldest continuously operated business on original site in Texas. Guided tours of all processes of sugar cane refining (Mon-Fri). Res advised. In Sugar Land, approx 20 mi SW via US 90A or US 59. Phone 281/491-9181. **FREE**

The Menil Collection. Considered one of the most outstanding private art collections in the world, endowed by Mr. and Mrs. John de Menil. Incl contemporary, surrealistic, and prehistoric art and antiquities. Housed in museum designed by renowned Italian architect Renzo Piano. (Wed-Sun) 1515 Sul Ross. Phone 713/525-9400. **FREE**

Museum of Fine Arts. Sculpture, paintings, graphics, Asian and Oceanic art, photographs, decorative arts; African, Native American, pre-Columbian artifacts and changing exhibits. Gallery lectures and tours.

(Tues-Sun; closed hols) Free admission Thurs. 1001 Bissonnet. Phone 713/639-7300. ¢¢¢

The Port of Houston. Boat tours of the port. Res required. Call for schedule. 7300 Clinton Dr at Gate 8. Phone 713/670-2416. **FREE**

Professional sports.

Houston Astros (MLB). Minutemaid Park, Crawford at Texas St.

Houston Rockets (NBA). Compaq Center, 10 Greenway Plaza. Phone 713/627-3865.

Reliant Park. Complex of entertainment and meeting/display facilities incl Reliant Center, Reliant Arena, and

Reliant Stadium. Site of sporting events, conventions, exhibitions, and concerts. Parking (fee). South Loop 610 and Kirby Dr. Phone 832/667-1400. ¢¢

Six Flags AstroWorld. A 75-acre theme park with more than 100 rides, shows, and attractions. Incl Texas Cyclone roller coaster; Dungeon Drop, a 20-story freefall; suspended coaster; children's section. Concerts at the Southern Star

Amphitheatre (adj). (Summer, daily; spring and fall, wkends) Phone 713/799-8404. ¢¢¢¢

Six Flags WaterWorld. A 15-acre family water recreation park, featuring water slides, river rapids ride, wave pool, speed slides, diving platforms, children's play area. (May, wkends; June-Aug, daily) Phone 713/799-8404. ¢¢¢¢

Rothko Chapel. Octagonal chapel houses canvases of the late Mark Rothko, Russian-born painter. On the grounds are a reflecting pool and the Broken Obelisk, a sculpture by Barnett Newman, dedicated to Dr. Martin Luther King, Jr. 3900 Yupon St. Phone 713/524-9839. **FREE**

San Jacinto Battleground. A 570-ft reinforced concrete shaft, faced with Texas fossilized buff limestone and a lone star on top, marks the site of the Battle of San Jacinto. On Apr 21, 1836, General Sam Houston suddenly attacked the superior forces of Dictator-General Santa Ana of Mexico, routed them and took Santa Ana himself prisoner. This victory ended Texas's War of Independence with

Mexico, avenged the massacre at the Alamo six wks earlier, and led to the founding of the Republic of Texas. Elevator in monument (fee). Museum with exhibits on the cultural development of Texas from Native American civilization to statehood. Multimedia presentation (fee). Monument and museum (daily; closed Dec 24, 25). Battleground (daily). 6 mi SE on Gulf Fwy (I-45) to I-610 (South Loop), then 1½ mi E to TX 225 (La Porte Fwy), then 10½ mi E to TX 134 and 3 mi W to Battleground; highway signs identify the battlefield exits beginning on the Gulf Fwy. Phone 281/479-2421. **FREE** Moored nearby is the

Battleship USS *Texas*. Presented to the state by the US Navy. The ship, a dreadnought built in 1914, saw action in WWI and WWII. Restoration in progress. (Daily; closed Dec 24, 25) Phone 281/479-2411. ¢¢

⭐ **Space Center Houston.** This hands-on facility explores the past, present, and future of America's space program. Mission Status Center has monitors showing live pictures from Mission Control, Kennedy Space Center, and space shuttle missions; briefings on current NASA projects. NASA Tour is a guided tram excursion through actual Johnson Space Center facilities, incl testing labs, design facilities, and astronaut training areas. The Feel of Space lets visitors wear a space helmet or pilot a manned maneuvering unit. Kids Space Place has Lunar Rover, Mission Kidtrol, and Lunar Jumper. Also Space Shuttle Mock-Up, Starship Gallery, five-story giant movie screen in Destiny Theater, and Space Center Plaza. (Daily; closed Dec 25) 1601 NASA Rd 1. 25 mi S on I-45, exit 25. Phone 281/244-2100. ¢¢¢¢

Theater District. Incl the Wortham Theater Center, 501 Texas Ave, phone (713/853-8000); Jesse H. Jones Hall for the Performing Arts, 615 Louisiana Ave, (713/227-3974); also Jones Plaza, 600 Louisiana Ave, which occasionally hosts outdoor performances; and Tranquility Park, 400 Rusk St, a small park opp Federal Building. Bounded by Milam, Smith, Preston, and Rusk Sts, Downtown. Also here are

Alley Theatre. Resident company presents modern and classic plays and musical theater works. (Nightly Tues-Sun; matinees Sat, Sun; also summer events) 615 Texas Ave, at Louisiana Ave. Phone 713/228-8421.

Music Hall. Presents six major indoor musical productions by Theatre Under the Stars (Oct-May, fee) and other shows. TUTS also gives free summer performances at Miller Outdoor Amphitheater, Hermann Park. 810 Bagby St, adj Sam Houston Coliseum.

University of Houston. (1927) 33,000 students. Located on 392 acres. University Center has an arboretum; the Hofheinz Pavilion is site of many sports events and concerts. The Lyndall Finley Wortham Theater complex offers mime and drama productions. Phone 713/743-9530.

Special Events

Houston Livestock Show & Rodeo. Reliant Stadium. Phone 713/791-9000. Late Feb-early Mar.

River Oaks Garden Club's Azalea Trail. Phone 713/523-2483. First two wkends Mar.

Houston International Festival. Downtown area. Dance, food, music. Apr. Phone 713/654-8808.

Summer concerts. Various parks and plazas throughout the city. May-Aug.

Juneteenth Festival. Gospel, blues, other music celebrates the abolition of slavery in Texas in June 1865. June. Phone 713/284-8352.

The Houston Symphony. Classical and Exxon Pops series (Sept-May). Sounds Like Fun children's festival (various locations; June, free). Free summer concerts at Miller Outdoor Theatre in Hermann Park. Summer concerts at Cynthia Woods Mitchell Pavilion, Jones Hall, and other locations. Jesse H. Jones Hall for the Performing Arts, 615 Louisiana. Phone 713/227-ARTS or 800/828-ARTS.

Greek Festival. Annunciation Greek Orthodox Cathedral, 3511 Yoakum Blvd. Cultural festival with Greek food, music, and dancing. Phone 713/526-5377. Early Oct.

Motels/Motor Lodges

★★ **COURTYARD BY MARRIOTT.** *3131 W Loop S (77027). 713/688-7711; fax 713/439-0989; res 800/321-*

2211. 207 rms, 6 story. S, D $69-
$109; suites $119; under 18 free;
wkend rates. Crib free. TV; cable (premium). Pool; wading pool, whirlpool. Complimentary coffee in rms.
Restaurant 6:30 am-2 pm, 5-11 pm.
Rm serv from 5 pm. Bar from 5 pm.
Ck-out noon. Meeting rms. Business
servs avail. In-rm modem link. Valet
serv. Coin lndry. Free garage parking.
Exercise equipt. Some refrigerators;
microwaves avail. Cr cds: A, C, D,
DS, MC, V.

★★ **COURTYARD BY MARRIOTT.**
2504 N Loop W (77092). 713/688-
7711; fax 713/688-3561; toll-free
800/321-2211. www.courtyard.com.
209 rms, 3 story. S, D $99; each addl
$10; suite $175; wkend rates. Crib
free. TV; cable (premium). Heated
pool; whirlpool. Coffee in rms.
Restaurant 11 am-10 pm. Bar from
11:30 am. Ck-out 1 pm. Coin lndry.
Meeting rms. Business servs avail. In-
rm modem link. Valet serv. Exercise
equipt. Some refrigerators, wet bars.
Cr cds: A, C, D, DS, MC, V.

★★ **DRURY INN & SUITES.** *1615 W*
Loop S (77027). 713/963-0700; toll-
free 800/378-7946. www.druryinn.com.
134 rms, 5 story. S $83.95-$98.95; D
$93.95-$108.95; each addl $10;
under 18 free; wkend rates. Crib
avail. Pet accepted. TV; cable (premium). Heated indoor/outdoor pool;
whirlpool. Complimentary continental bkfst. Coffee in rms. Ck-out noon.
Meeting rm. Business servs avail. In-
rm modem link. Health club privileges. Some refrigerators; microwaves
avail. Cr cds: A, C, D, DS, MC, V.

★★ **DRURY INN & SUITES WEST.**
1000 N Hwy 6 (77079). 281/558-
7007; res 800/378-7946. www.drury
inn.com. 120 rms, 5 story. S $65; D
$75; each addl $10; under 18 free;
wkend rates. Crib free. Pet accepted.
TV; cable (premium). Indoor pool;
whirlpool. Complimentary continental bkfst. Restaurant adj 11 am-10
pm. Ck-out noon. Meeting rm. In-rm
modem link. Health club privileges.
Some refrigerators; microwaves avail.
Cr cds: A, C, D, DS, MC, V.

★★ **FAIRFIELD INN.** *3131 W Loop S*
(77027). 713/961-1690; fax 713/627-
8434; res 800/228-2800. www.fairfield
inn.com. 107 rms, 2 story. S, D $44-
$79; under 18 free; wkend rates. Crib
free. TV; cable (premium). Pool.
Complimentary continental bkfst.
Restaurant adj 6 am-2 pm, 5-11 pm.
Rm serv from 5 pm. Bar from 5 pm.
Ck-out noon. Business servs avail. In-
rm modem link. Valet serv. Coin
lndry. Exercise equipt. Refrigerators,
microwaves avail. Cr cds: A, C, D,
DS, ER, JCB, MC, V.

★★ **FAIRFIELD INN.** *10155 I-10 E*
Fwy (77029). 713/675-2711; fax
713/674-6853; res 800/228-2800.
www.fairfieldinn.com. 160 rms, 2
story. S $53; D $58; each addl $5;
under 16 free. Crib free. TV; cable
(premium). Pool; wading pool. Complimentary continental bkfst. Restaurant adj 6-2 am. Ck-out noon.
Meeting rms. Business servs avail. In-
rm modem link. Coin lndry. Gazebo
Cr cds: A, C, D, DS, MC, V.

★★ **HAMPTON INN.** *502 N Sam*
Houston Pkwy (77060). 281/820-2101;
fax 281/820-9652; res 800/426-7866.
www.hamptoninn.com. 157 rms, 2
story. S $69-$79; D $75-$85; suites
$95-$150; under 18 free. Crib free.
TV; cable (premium). Indoor/outdoor
pool; whirlpool. Complimentary
continental bkfst. Coffee in rms.
Restaurant adj 6:30 am-2 pm, 5-10
pm. Rm serv. Ck-out noon. Meeting
rms. Business servs avail. Coin lndry.
Free airport transportation. Exercise
equipt. Microwaves avail. Cr cds: A,
C, D, DS, MC, V.

★★ **HAMPTON INN.** *828 Mercury*
Dr (77013). 713/673-4200; fax
713/674-6913; res 800/426-7866.
www.hamptoninn.com. 90 rms, 6
story. S, D $68-$78; under 18 free;
wkend rates. Crib free. Pet accepted;
$25 deposit. TV; cable (premium).
Pool. Complimentary continental
bkfst. Restaurant adj open 24 hrs.
Ck-out noon. Coin lndry. Business
servs avail. In-rm modem link. Valet
serv. Some refrigerators. Cr cds: A, C,
D, DS, MC, V.

★★ HAMPTON INN AND SUITES.
1715 Old Spanish Trl (77054). 713/797-0040; fax 713/797-0094; res 800/426-7866. www.hamptoninn-suites.com. 100 rms, 5 story, 28 kit. units. S, D $84; kit. units $99-$107; under 18 free. Crib avail. TV; cable (premium). Complimentary continental bkfst. Complimentary coffee in rms. Restaurant adj 10:45 am-9 pm. Ck-out noon. Meeting rms. Business servs avail. In-rm modem link. Sundries. Gift shop. Drugstore. Exercise equipt. Pool. Cr cds: A, C, D, DS, MC, V.

★★ HAMPTON INN I-10 WEST.
11333 Katy Fwy (77079). 713/935-0022; fax 713/935-0989; res 800/426-7866. www.hamptoninn.com. 120 units, 4 story. S $69-$73; D $73-$77, under 18 free; wkend rates; higher rates special events. Crib free. TV; cable (premium). Pool. Complimentary continental bkfst. Restaurant adj open 24 hrs. Ck-out noon. Meeting rm. Business center. In-rm modem link. Exercise equipt. Cr cds: A, C, D, DS, ER, JCB, MC, V.

★★ HOLIDAY INN.
8111 Kirby Dr (77054). 713/790-1900; fax 713/799-8574; res 800/465-4329. www.holiday-inn.com/hou-astrodome. 235 rms, 11 story. S, D $79-$129; each addl $10; suites $135-$395; under 19 free; wkend rates; higher rates Livestock Show and Rodeo. Crib free. TV; cable (premium). Pool; whirlpool. Restaurant 6 am-10 pm. Rm serv. Bar 11-2 am. Ck-out noon. Meeting rms. Business servs avail. In-rm modem link. Bellhops. Valet serv. Sundries. Gift shop. Exercise equipt. Some bathrm phones, refrigerators, wet bars; microwaves avail. Cr cds: A, C, D, DS, ER, JCB, MC, V.

★★★ HOLIDAY INN HOTEL & SUITES.
6800 S Main St (77030). 713/528-7744; fax 713/528-6983; res 800/465-4329. www.holiday-inn.com. 285 rms, 12 story, 212 kit. suites. S, D $72-$99; kit. suites $149-$199; under 18 free. Crib free. TV; cable. Pool. Complimentary coffee in rms. Restaurant 6:30 am-11 pm. Bar from 11 am. Ck-out noon. Coin lndry. Business servs avail. In-rm modem link. Concierge. Valet serv. Gift shop. Beauty shop. Exercise equipt. Game rm. Microwaves avail. Cr cds: A, D, DS, MC, V.

★★★ HOLIDAY INN INTERCON-TINENTAL.
15222 John F Kennedy Blvd (77032). 281/449-2311; fax 281/442-6833; res 800/465-4329. www.holiday-inn.com. 413 rms, 5 story. S, D $89-$135; each addl $10; under 18 free; wkend, wkly rates. Crib $10. Pet accepted; $125 ($100 refundable). TV; cable (premium), VCR avail. Pool; wading pool, poolside serv. Coffee in rms. Restaurant 6 am-10:30 pm. Rm serv. Bar from 11 am. Ck-out noon. Convention facilities. Business servs avail. In-rm modem link. Bellhops. Valet serv. Gift shop. Coin lndry. Free airport transportation. Lighted tennis. Exercise equipt. Lawn games. Some refrigerators; microwaves avail. Cr cds: A, C, D, DS, MC, V.

★★ HOLIDAY INN SELECT.
2712 SW Fwy (77098). 713/523-8448; fax 713/526-7948; res 800/465-4329. www.bristolhotels.com. 355 rms, 18 story, 36 suites. S $109-$129; D $129; each addl $10; suites $139-$159; under 18 free; wkend rates. Valet parking $8. TV; cable (premium), VCR avail (movies). Complimentary coffee in rms. Restaurant 6 am-11 pm. Bar noon-midnight. Ck-out noon. Convention facilities. Business center. In-rm modem link. Concierge. Gift shop. Coin lndry. Exercise equipt. Pool; whirlpool, poolside serv. Refrigerator, wet bar in suites; microwaves avail. Cr cds: A, C, D, DS, MC, V.

★★ HOLIDAY INN SELECT I-10 WEST.
14703 Park Row (77079). 281/558-5580; fax 281/496-4150; res 800/465-4329. www.holiday-inn.com. 349 rms, 20 story. S, D $99-$149; suites $250; under 18 free; wkend rates. TV; cable (premium). Indoor pool; whirlpool, poolside serv. Restaurant 6 am-10 pm. Bar 2 pm-midnight; Fri, Sat to 2 am. Ck-out noon. Convention facilities. Business center. In-rm modem link. Gift shop. Exercise equipt. Refrigerators; microwaves avail. Luxury level. Cr cds: A, C, D, DS, MC, V.

★★★ **HOMEWOOD SUITES HOTEL.** *2424 Rodgerdale Rd (77042). 713/334-2424; fax 713/787-6749. www.homewoodsuites.com.* 94 rms, 3 story, 2 suites. Jan-Mar, June-Aug, Nov: S $109; D $145; suites $119; lower rates rest of yr. Crib avail. Parking lot. Indoor pool. TV; calbe (DSS), VCR avail. Complimentary continental bkfst, newspaper, toll-free calls. Restaurant nearby. Ck-out 1 pm, ck-in 3 pm. Meeting rm. Business center. Bellhops. Dry cleaning, coin lndry. Gift shop. Exercise equipt, sauna. Golf, 18 holes. Tennis. Picnic facilities. Cr cds: A, D, DS, MC, V.

$\boxed{D}$ 🏃 🍴 🏋 🏊 🧖 ⛳ 🔥 🚶

★★ **LA QUINTA GREENWAY PLAZA.** *4015 SW Fwy (77027). 713/623-4750; fax 713/963-0599; res 800/531-5900. www.laquinta.com.* 131 rms, 2-3 story. S, D $66-$75; each addl $8; suites $82-$90; under 18 free; family units. Crib free. Pet accepted, some restrictions. TV; cable (premium). Pool. Complimentary continental bkfst. Ck-out noon. Coin lndry. Meeting rms. Microwaves avail. Cr cds: A, C, D, DS, JCB, MC, V.

$\boxed{D}$ 🐾 🏊 🧖 🔥

★★ **LA QUINTA INN.** *11113 Katy Fwy (77079). 713/932-0808; fax 713/973-2352; toll-free 800/687-6667. www.laquinta.com.* 176 rms, 2 story. S $60-$70; D $68-$78; each addl $8; under 18 free. Crib free. Pet accepted. TV; cable (premium). Pool. Complimentary continental bkfst. Coffee in rms. Restaurant adj open 24 hrs. Ck-out noon. Coin lndry. Meeting rms. In-rm modem link. Refrigerators; microwaves avail. Cr cds: A, C, D, DS, MC, V.

$\boxed{D}$ 🐾 🏊 🧖 🔥 SC

★★ **LEXINGTON HOTEL SUITES.** *16410 N Fwy 45 (77090). 281/821-1000; fax 281/821-1420; res 800/927-8483.* 247 kit. suites, 3 story. Suites $69-$129; each addl $6; under 18 free; wkly rates. Crib free. TV; cable (premium). Heated pool. Complimentary continental bkfst. Complimentary coffee in rms. Restaurant adj 6:30 am-10 pm. Ck-out noon. Coin lndry. Meeting rms. Business servs avail. In-rm modem link. Valet serv. Free airport transportation.

Health club privileges. Cr cds: A, C, D, DS, MC, V.

$\boxed{D}$ 🏊 🧖 🔥

★ **RED ROOF INN HOUSTON WEST.** *15701 Park Ten Pl (77084). 281/579-7200; fax 281/579-0732; res 800/843-7663. www.redroof.com.* 123 rms, 3 story. S $38.99-$46.99; D $41.99-$47.99; under 17 free; wkend rates. Pet accepted. TV; cable (premium). Complimentary continental bkfst. Restaurant nearby. Meeting rm. Business servs avail. In-rm modem link. Valet serv. Cr cds: A, C, D, DS, JCB, MC, V.

$\boxed{D}$ 🐾 🧖 🔥

★★★ **STAYBRIDGE SUITES.** *5190 Hidalgo St (77056). 713/355-8888; fax 713/355-4445; toll-free 800/238-8000. www.staybridge.com.* 87 rms, 4 story, 6 suites. Nov-June: S $129; D $149; suites $229; lower rates rest of yr. Crib avail. Pet accepted; fee. Parking garage. Pool; children's pool. TV; cable (premium), VCR avail. Complimentary continental bkfst. Coffee in rms. Restaurant nearby. Bar. Ck-out noon, ck-in 3 pm. Meeting rm. Business center. Dry cleaning, coin lndry. Exercise equipt. Golf, 18 holes. Tennis. Picnic facilities. Cr cds: A, C, D, DS, MC, V.

$\boxed{D}$ 🐾 🍴 🏋 🏊 ⛳ 🔥 🚶

Hotels

★★ **ADAM'S MARK.** *2900 Briarpark Dr (77042). 713/978-7400; fax 713/735-2727; res 800/444-2326. www.adamsmark.com.* 604 rms, 10 story. S, D $66-$205; each addl $10; suites $190-$730; under 18 free; wkend rates. Crib free. TV; cable (premium). Heated indoor/outdoor pool; wading pool, whirlpool, poolside serv. Restaurant 6 am-midnight. Rm serv 24 hrs. Bars 11-2 am; entertainment. Ck-out noon. Meeting rms. Business servs avail. In-rm modem link. Concierge. Gift shop. Exercise equipt; sauna. Game rm. Some refrigerators; microwaves avail. Some balconies. Artwork in lobby. Cr cds: A, C, D, DS, MC, V.

$\boxed{D}$ 🏊 🏋 🧖 🔥 SC

★★★ **CROWNE PLAZA HOUSTON BROOKHOLLOW.** *12801 Northwest Frwy (77040). 713/462-9977; fax 713/460-8725; toll-free*

800/826-1606. www.crowneplaza.com/brookhollowtx. 291 rms, 10 story. S, D $99-$109; each addl $10; suites $129-$159; under 12 free; wkend rates. Pet accepted, some restrictions. TV; cable (premium). Pool; poolside serv. Coffee in rms. Restaurant 6 am-10 pm. Rm serv. Bar 4 pm-2 am. Ck-out noon. Meeting rms. In-rm modem link. Bellhops. Valet serv. Sundries. Gift shop. Exercise equipt. Health club privileges. Some bathrm phones; refrigerator, wet bar in suites. Balconies. Cr cds: A, C, D, DS, ER, JCB, MC, V.

★★ **CROWNE PLAZA HOUSTON MEDICAL CENTER.** 6701 S Main St (77030). 713/797-1110; fax 713/797-1034; res 800/227-6963. www.crowneplaza.com. 281 rms, 10 story, 4 suites. Feb-June, Sept-Oct: S $189; suites $219; each addl $10; under 12 free; lower rates rest of yr. Crib avail. Valet parking avail. Pool; lap pool. TV; cable (DSS). Complimentary coffee in rms, newspaper, toll-free calls. Restaurant 6 am-10 pm. Bar. Ck-out noon, ck-in 3 pm. Conference center, meeting rms. Business center. Bellhops. Concierge serv. Dry cleaning, coin lndry. Gift shop. Exercise equipt, sauna. Golf. Tennis. Video games. Cr cds: A, C, D, DS, MC, V.

★★★ **DOUBLETREE AT THE ALLEN CENTER.** 400 Dallas St (77002). 713/759-0202; fax 713/759-1166; res 800/222-8733. www.doubletreehotels.com. 350 rms, 20 story. S $195-$225; D $215-$245; each addl $10; suites $329-$750; under 17 free; wkend rates. Crib free. Pet accepted, some restrictions; $75 refundable. TV; cable (premium). Restaurants 6 am-10 pm. Bar 11-2 am; entertainment Mon-Fri. Ck-out noon. Meeting rms. Business center. In-rm modem link. Concierge. Gift shop. Exercise equipt. Health club privileges. Elegant hanging tapestries. Cr cds: A, C, D, DS, MC, V.

★★★ **DOUBLETREE GUEST SUITES.** 5353 Westheimer Rd (77056). 713/961-9000; fax 713/585-2704; res 800/222-8733. www.doubletreehotels.com. 335 kit. suites, 26 story. S, D $210-$260; each addl $20; 2-bedrm suites $310; under 18 free; wkend rates. Crib free. Garage $8, valet parking $12. Pet accepted. TV; cable (premium). Pool; whirlpool, poolside serv. Restaurant 6:30 am-2 pm, 5-10 pm; Sat, Sun 6:30 am-1 pm, 5-10 pm. Rm serv 24 hrs. Bar 5 pm-midnight. Ck-out noon. Business servs avail. In-rm modem link. Coin lndry. Tennis privileges. Exercise equipt. Health club privileges. Game rm. Refrigerators. Some balconies. Cr cds: A, C, D, DS, MC, V.

★★★ **DOUBLETREE HOTEL AT POST OAK.** 2001 Post Oak Blvd (77056). 713/961-9300; fax 713/623-6685; res 800/566-5216. www.postoak.doubletreehotels.com. 449 rms, 14 story. S, D $139-$172; each addl $20; suites $210-$1,200; under 18 free; wkend rates. Crib free. Valet parking $15; garage $8. TV; cable (premium). Pool; poolside serv. Restaurant 6:30 am-11 pm. Rm serv 24 hrs. Bar 11-1 am; wkends to 2 am; Sun from noon. Ck-out noon. Convention facilities. Business center. In-rm modem link. Concierge. Shopping arcade. Barber, beauty shop. Exercise equipt; sauna. Health club privileges. Many bathrm phones; some refrigerators. Balconies. Cr cds: A, C, D, DS, JCB, MC, V.

★★★★ **FOUR SEASONS HOTEL HOUSTON.** 1300 Lamar St (77010). 713/650-1300; fax 713/652-6220; res 800/332-3442. www.fourseasons.com. This 399-room property sits in the heart of downtown's financial and business districts and offers nearly 17,000 square feet of meeting space, including 11 function rooms and The Grand Ballroom. If this chain's consistently famous service doesn't provide enough pampering, there is a full-service spa on premises. 399 rms, 30 story. S $290; D $315; each addl $30; suites $610-$3,000; under 18 free; wkend rates. Crib free. Pet accepted, some restrictions. Valet and covered parking $17/day. TV; cable (premium), VCR avail. Heated pool; whirlpool, poolside serv. Restaurant (see also DeVILLE). Rm serv 24 hrs. Bar 11-1 am; entertainment. Ck-out 1 pm. Meeting rms. Business center. In-rm modem link. Concierge. Shopping arcade. Beauty shop. Exercise equipt; sauna. Massage. Health club privileges. Bathrm phones, minibars;

some refrigerators; microwaves avail. Cr cds: A, C, D, DS, JCB, MC, V.

★★★ **HILTON AND TOWERS WESTCHASE.** *9999 Westheimer Rd (77042). 713/974-1000; fax 713/974-6866; res 800/445-8667. www. westchase.hilton.com.* 300 rms, 13 story. S, D $159-$199; each addl $15; suites $174-$204; under 18 free; wkend rates. Crib free. TV; cable (premium). Heated pool; whirlpool, poolside serv. Complimentary coffee in rms. Restaurant 6:30 am-10 pm. Rm serv 24 hrs. Bar 11:30 am-midnight. Ck-out 1 pm. Convention facilities. Business center. In-rm modem link. Concierge. Gift shop. Barber, beauty shop. Exercise equipt; sauna. Minibars. Luxury level. Cr cds: A, D, DS, MC, V.

★★★ **HILTON PLAZA.** *6633 Travis St (77030). 713/313-4000; fax 713/313-4660; res 800/441-8667. www.hilton.com.* 181 units, 19 story. S $145-$285; D $165-$290; each addl $10; wkend rates. Crib free. Garage $8 (wkends $4). TV; cable (premium). Heated pool; whirlpool, poolside serv. Coffee in rms. Restaurant 6:30 am-10 pm. Rm serv 24 hrs. Bar 4 pm-midnight; entertainment. Ck-out noon. Meeting rms. Business servs avail. In-rm modem link. Gift shop. Valet parking. Exercise equipt; sauna. Bathrm phones, refrigerators, wet bars. Adj to museums, parks, Rice Univ. Luxury level. Cr cds: A, C, D, DS, ER, JCB, MC, V.

★★★ **HOTEL DEREK.** *2525 West Loop South (77027). 713/961-3000.* 319 rms, 14 story. S $109-$144; D $119-$154; each addl $10; suites $325-$500; under 18 free; wkend rates. Crib free. Pet accepted; $25. Valet parking $11; garage. TV; cable (premium), VCR avail. Pool; whirlpool, poolside serv. Coffee in rms. Restaurant 6 am-10 pm. Bar 4 pm-midnight. Ck-out 1 pm. Convention facilities. In-rm modem link. Gift shop. Exercise equipt; sauna. Micro-

waves avail. Luxury level. Cr cds: A, C, D, DS, JCB, MC, V.

★★★ **HOTEL SOFITEL HOUSTON.** *425 N Sam Houston Pkwy E (77060). 281/445-9000; fax 281/445-9826; res 800/763-4835.* 334 rms, 8 story. S $135-$169; D $145-$179; each addl $20; suites $299-$400; under 18 free; wkend rates. Crib free. TV; cable (premium). Pool. Restaurant 6 am-11 pm. Rm serv 5:30-1 am. Bar 11 am-midnight; entertainment. Ck-out noon. Convention facilities. Business center. In-rm modem link. Concierge. Shopping arcade. Airport transportation. Exercise equipt. Massage. French bakery in lobby. Cr cds: A, C, D, DS, ER, JCB, MC, V.

★★★★ **THE HOUSTONIAN HOTEL, CLUB & SPA.** *111 N Post Oak Ln (77024). 713/680-2626; fax 713/688-6305; toll-free 800/231-2759. www.houstonian.com.* This resort is hidden on pine- and oak-wooded grounds in the center of Houston right next to the Galleria and Memorial Park. Recognized as one of the top health clubs in the country, the 125,000-square-foot Houstonian Club is complimentary for guests and neighbors a full-service spa. The splendid 18-hole, Rees Jones-designed golf course is a welcome addition. 289 rms, 4 story. S, D $269; suites $375-$1,100; under 18 free; wkend, hol rates. Crib free. TV; cable (premium). 3 heated pools; whirlpool. Supervised child's activities; ages 3-16. Restaurant (see also

Space Center Houston

OLIVETTE). Rm serv 24 hrs. Bar 3 pm-2 am; Sat, Sun from noon. Ck-out noon. Convention facilities. Business center. In-rm modem link. Concierge. Gift shop. Beauty shop. Free garage parking; valet $13. Lighted tennis, pro. Exercise rm; sauna. Spa. Game rm. Lawn games. Refrigerators, minibars. Luxury level. Cr cds: A, C, D, DS, MC, V.

🄳 🛏 🍴 ⛵ 🏊 🛀 ⓦ 🔥 🏃

★★★ **HYATT REGENCY.** *1200 Louisiana St (77002). 713/654-1234; fax 713/951-0934; toll-free 800/233-1234. www.houston.hyatt.com.* 963 rms, 30 story. S $215-$250; D $240-$275; each addl $25; suites $300-$850; under 18 free; wkend rates. Crib free. Valet parking $15; self-park $8. TV; cable (premium). Heated pool; poolside serv. Restaurant 6 am-11 pm. Bar 11-2 am. Ck-out noon. Convention facilities. Business center. In-rm modem link. Concierge. Beauty shop. Airport transportation. Exercise equipt. Health club privileges. Bathrm phones, refrigerators. Built around 30-story atrium; glass-enclosed elvtrs. Covered passage to downtown buildings. Cr cds: A, C, D, DS, JCB, MC, V.

🄳 🏊 🛀 🔥 🏃

★★★ **HYATT REGENCY HOUSTON AIRPORT.** *15747 John F Kennedy Blvd (77032). 281/987-1234; fax 281/590-8461; res 800/233-1234. www.hyatt.com.* 314 rms, 7 story. S $119-$155; D $144-$174; each addl $10; under 18 free; wkend rates; package plans. Crib free. Pet accepted; $25. TV; cable (premium). Pool; whirlpool, poolside serv. Restaurant 6 am-2 pm, 5-11 pm. Bar 11 am-midnight. Ck-out noon. Meeting rms. Business servs avail. In-rm modem link. Gift shop. Free airport transportation. Exercise equipt. Cr cds: A, C, D, DS, ER, JCB, MC, V.

🄳 🏊 ➖ 🛀

★★★ **JW MARRIOTT HOTEL ON WESTHEIMER BY THE GALLERIA.** *5150 Westheimer (77056). 713/961-1500; fax 713/961-5045; res 800/228-9290. www.marriott.com.* 508 rms, 23 story. S, D $179-$199; suites $205-$600; under 18 free; wkend rates. Crib free. Garage $8, valet parking $15, lot free. TV; cable (premium), VCR avail. Indoor/outdoor pool; whirlpool, poolside serv. Restaurant

6:30 am-2 pm, 5:30-11 pm. Bar 2 pm-midnight. Ck-out noon. Convention facilities. Business center. In-rm modem link. Concierge. Gift shop. Barber, beauty shop. Exercise equipt; sauna. Game rm. Bathrm phones; microwaves avail; refrigerator in suites. Lobby furnished with marble, rich paneling and artwork. Luxury level. Cr cds: A, C, D, DS, ER, JCB, MC, V.

🄳 🏊 🛀 🔥 🏃

★★★ **LANCASTER HOTEL.** *701 Texas Ave (77002). 713/228-9500; fax 713/223-4528; toll-free 800/231-0336.* 93 rms, 12 story. S $260; D $285; each addl $25; suites $350-$725; under 16 free; wkend rates. Crib $25. Valet parking $16. TV; cable, VCR (movies). Restaurant (see also BISTRO LANCASTER). Rm serv 24 hrs. Bars 11 am-midnight. Ck-out 1 pm. Meeting rms. In-rm modem link. Concierge. Exercise equipt. Bathrm phones, refrigerators, minibars; microwaves avail. Cr cds: A, D, DS, MC, V.

🄳 🛀 🏊

★★★ **MARRIOTT HOUSTON AIRPORT.** *18700 John F Kennedy Blvd (77032). 281/443-2310; fax 281/443-5294; res 800/228-9291. www.marriott.com.* 566 rms, 3 & 7 story. S, D $145-$155; suites $250-$350; studio rms $150-$250; under 18 free; wkend rates. Crib free. Valet parking $13. TV; cable (premium). Pool; poolside serv. Restaurant 6 am-10:30 pm. Bar 11-2 am; Sat from 4 pm; Sun noon-midnight. Ck-out 1 pm. Free lndry facilities. Convention facilities. Business center. In-rm modem link. Shopping arcade. Exercise equipt. Some refrigerators. Some private patios. Luxury level. Cr cds: A, C, D, DS, MC, V.

🄳 🏊 🛀 ✈ 🔥 🏃

★★★ **MARRIOTT MEDICAL CENTER HOUSTON.** *6580 Fannin St (77030). 713/796-0080; fax 713/770-8100; res 800/228-9290. www.marriott.com.* 386 rms, 26 story. S, D $179; suites $165-$550; under 18 free; wkend rates. Crib free. Garage $8; valet parking $14.75. TV; cable (premium), VCR avail. Indoor pool; whirlpool, poolside serv. Restaurant 6:30 am-11 pm. Ck-out noon. Coin lndry. Convention facilities. Business servs avail. In-rm modem link.

Concierge. Shopping arcade. Bus depot transportation. Exercise equipt; sauna. Refrigerators; microwaves avail. Connected to Medical Center; covered walks. Luxury level. Cr cds: A, C, D, DS, JCB, MC, V.

★★★ **MARRIOTT NORTH AT GREENSPOINT HOUSTON.** *255 N Sam Houston Pkwy E (77060). 281/875-4000; fax 281/875-6208; res 800/228-9290. www.marriotthotels. com/hougp.* 391 rms, 12 story. S, D $109-$170; suites $250-$350; under 18 free; wkend rates. Crib free. TV; cable (premium). Indoor/outdoor pool; whirlpool, poolside serv. Restaurant 6:30 am-10 pm. Bar 2 pm-2 am. Ck-out noon. Coin lndry. Convention facilities. Business center. In-rm modem link. Concierge. Gift shop. Free garage parking. Free airport transportation. Exercise equipt; sauna. Refrigerators. Luxury level. Cr cds: A, C, D, DS, MC, V.

★★★★ **OMNI HOUSTON HOTEL.** *4 Riverway (77056). 713/871-8181; fax 713/871-0719; toll-free 800/843-6664. www.omnihotels.com.* This 378-room luxury property is just a short cab drive to the Galleria. Plenty of recreation, including two pools, tennis courts and the adjacent Memorial Park golf course, along with 16,000 square feet of meeting space are all managed with graceful service. If that's not enough, fine continental dining awaits at the elegant La Reserve. 378 rms, 11 story. S, D $195-$225; each addl $25; suites $349-$1,000; under 18 free; wkend rates. Crib free. Garage: valet parking $15, self-park $7. TV; cable (premium), VCR avail. Two pools, 1 heated; whirlpool, poolside serv. Restaurant 6:30 am-11 pm (see also LA RESERVE). Rm serv 24 hrs. Bar 11:30-2 am; entertainment. Ck-out 1 pm. Meeting rms. Business center. In-rm modem link. Concierge. Tennis. Exercise rm; sauna. Massage. Mini-bars. Cr cds: A, C, D, DS, ER, JCB, MC, V.

★★★ **OMNI HOUSTON WEST-SIDE HOTEL.** *13210 Katy Fwy I-10 (77079). 281/558-8338; fax 281/558-4028; res 800/843-6664. www.omni hotels.com.* 400 rms, 5 story. S, D $159-$174; under 18 free; wkend rates. Crib free. Pet accepted; $25. TV; cable (premium). Heated pool; whirlpool, poolside serv. Complimentary coffee in rms. Restaurant 6 am-2 pm, 5-10 pm. Bar; pianist Mon-Fri. Ck-out noon. Convention facilities. Business center. In-rm modem link. Gift shop. Free garage parking. Lighted tennis. Exercise equipt. Health club privileges. Cr cds: A, C, D, DS, ER, JCB, MC, V.

★★★ **RADISSON ASTRODOME HOTEL.** *8686 Kirby Dr (77054). 713/748-3221; fax 713/950-0657; res 800/333-3333. www.radisson.com.* 631 rms, 9 story. S $69-$150; D $69-$165; each addl $10; suites $225-$375; under 18 free. Crib free. TV; cable (premium). 2 pools; whirlpool. Coffee in rms. Restaurant 6:30 am-10:30 pm. Bar 11-2 am. Ck-out noon. Meeting rms. Business center. In-rm modem link. Valet serv. Gift shop. Exercise equipt. Game rm. Beauty shop. Some refrigerators. Balconies. Cr cds: A, C, D, DS, JCB, MC, V.

★★★ **RADISSON HOTEL & CONFERENCE CENTER.** *9100 Gulf Fwy (77017). 713/943-7979; fax 713/943-1621; toll-free 800/333-3333. www. radisson.com.* 288 rms, 10 story. S $115-$140; D $125-$150; each addl $10; under 16 free; wkend rates. Crib avail. Pet accepted, some restrictions. TV; cable (premium). Indoor pool; whirlpool, poolside serv. Restaurant 6 am-midnight. Bar. Ck-out noon. Meeting rms. Business servs avail. In-rm modem link. Concierge. Gift shop. Free airport transportation. Exercise equipt; sauna. Luxury level. Cr cds: A, DS, MC, V.

★★★ **RENAISSANCE HOUSTON HOTEL.** *6 Greenway Plaza E (77046). 713/629-1200; fax 713/629-4706; res 888/236-2427. www.renaissancehotels. com.* 389 rms, 20 story. S $179; D $189; each addl $10; suites $300-$750; under 18 free; wkend rates. Crib free. Pet accepted, some restrictions. Garage parking; valet $14. TV; cable (premium). Heated pool; poolside serv. Complimentary coffee in rms. Restaurant 6 am-10 pm. Rm serv 24 hrs. Bar 11:30-2 am. Ck-out 1 pm. Convention facilities. Business servs avail. In-rm modem link. Tennis privileges. Exercise equipt; sauna. Health club privileges. Bathrm phones; some refrigerators. Cr cds: A, C, D, DS, MC, V.

★★★★ **THE ST. REGIS, HOUSTON.** *1919 Briar Oaks Ln (77027). 713/840-7600; fax 713/840-8036; res 800/325-3589. www.stregis.com.* Located in the residential River Oaks neighborhood, this luxury hotel's 180 rooms and 52 suites are near both the central business district and The Galleria. Dining highlights include the raw bar selections at the Remington Grill (the main menu includes steak, chops, and seafood), afternoon tea in the lobby lounge, and an extravagant Sunday brunch in The Astor Court. 232 rms, 12 story. S, D $295-$310; each addl $30; suites $600-$1,000; kit. units $2,500; under 18 free; wkend rates. Valet parking $17. Crib. TV; cable (premium). Heated pool; poolside serv. Restaurants. Bar; entertainment. Harpist at afternoon tea, 3-5 pm. Ck-out noon. Meeting rms. Business center. Concierge. Exercise equipt. Health club privileges. Massage. Bathrm phones, minibars; microwaves avail; whirlpool in suites. Luxury level. Cr cds: A, C, D, DS, JCB, MC, V.

★★★ **SHERATON BROOKHOLLOW.** *3000 N Loop W (77092). 713/688-0100; fax 713/688-9224; res 800/325-3535. www.sheraton.com.* 382 rms, 10 story. S, D $149-$169; family, wkend rates. Crib free. Pet accepted, some restrictions. TV; cable (premium). Heated pool; whirlpool, poolside serv. Restaurant 6 am-2 pm, 5 pm-midnight. Bar 11 am- midnight. Ck-out 1 pm. Meeting rms. In-rm modem link. Gift shop. Free garage parking. Exercise equipt; sauna. Refrigerators avail. Luxury level. Cr cds: A, D, DS, MC, V.

★★★ **SHERATON NORTH HOUSTON.** *15700 John F Kennedy Blvd (77032). 281/442-5100; 800/325-3535.* 400 rms, 15 story. S, D $175-$225; suites $250-$450; under 17 free; wkend rates. Crib free. TV; cable (premium), VCR avail. Indoor pool; whirlpool, poolside serv. Coffee in rms. Restaurants 6:30 am-midnight. Bar 11 am-midnight. Ck-out noon. Lndry serv. Meeting rms. Business center. In-rm modem link. Concierge. Gift shop. Exercise equipt. Refrigerators avail. Luxury level. Cr cds: A, D, DS, MC, V.

★★★ **THE WARWICK.** *5701 Main St (77005). 713/526-1991.* 308 rms, 10 story. S, D $125-$250; under 17 free; wkend rates. Crib free. TV; cable (premium), VCR avail. Pool; whirlpool. Coffee in rms. Restaurants 6:30 am-midnight. Bar 11 am-midnight. Ck-out noon. Meeting rms. Business center. In-rm modem link. Concierge. Gift shop. Exercise equipt. Refrigerators avail. Cr cds: A, D, DS, MC, V.

★★★ **WESTIN GALLERIA.** *5060 W Alabama (77056). 713/960-8100.* 487 rms, 17 story. S, D $150-$225; suites $250-$450; under 17 free; wkend rates. Crib free. TV; cable (premium), VCR avail. Pool; whirlpool. Coffee in rms. Restaurants 6:30 am-midnight. Bar 11 am-midnight. Ck-out noon. Meeting rms. Business center. In-rm modem link. Concierge. Gift shop. Exercise equipt. Refrigerators avail. Cr cds: A, D, DS, MC, V.

★★★ **WESTIN OAKS.** *5011 Westheimer at Post Oak (77056). 713/960-8100.* 406 rms, 15 story. S, D $150-$225; suites $250-$450; under 17 free; wkend rates. Crib free. TV; cable (premium), VCR avail. Pool; whirlpool. Coffee in rms. Restaurants 6:30 am-midnight. Bar 11 am-midnight. Ck-out noon. Meeting rms. Business center. In-rm modem link. Concierge. Gift shop. Exercise equipt. Refrigerators avail. Cr cds: A, D, DS, MC, V.

★★ **WYNDHAM GREENSPOINT HOTEL.** *12400 Greenspoint Dr (77060). 281/875-2222; fax 281/875-1652; res 800/996-3426. www.wyndham.com.* 472 rms, 16 story. S $149-$183; D $159-$193; each addl $10; suites $185-$800; under 18 free; wkend rates. TV; cable (premium). Pool. Restaurant 6 am-11 pm. Bar 4 pm-2 am; entertainment. Ck-out noon. Coin lndry. Convention facilities. Business center. In-rm modem link. Shopping arcade. Airport transportation. Exercise equipt; sauna. Health club privileges. Some refrigerators; bathrm phone in suites. Distinctive architectural design and decor. Cr cds: A, C, D, DS, ER, JCB, MC, V.

Resort

★ ★ ★ **HILTON HOUSTON NASSAU BAY AND MARINA.** *3000 Nasa Rd One (77058). 281/333-9300; fax 281/333-9748; toll-free 800/634-7230. www.nassaubayhilton.com.* 243 rms, 13 story. S $89-$134; D $99-$144; each addl $10; suites $250-$500; family, wkend rates. Crib avail. TV; cable (premium). Pool; whirlpool, poolside serv. Coffee in rms. Restaurant 7 am-10 pm; Fri to 11 pm. Bar 11 am-midnight. Ck-out 1 pm. Meeting rms. Business servs avail. In-rm modem link. Beauty shop. Exercise equipt. Sailboating, water sports. Bathrm phone in suites. Balconies with view of lake, marina. Luxury level. Cr cds: A, C, D, DS, MC, V.

B&Bs/Small Inns

★ ★ ★ **LA COLOMBE D'OR HOTEL.** *3410 Montrose Blvd (77006). 713/524-7999; fax 713/524-8923. www.cacolombedor.com.* 6 suites, 3 story. Suites $195-$575. TV; cable (premium), VCR avail. Complimentary continental bkfst. Restaurant (see also LA COLOMBE D'OR). Rm serv. Bar. Concierge serv. Ck-out noon, ck-in 3 pm. Whirlpool. Prairie-style mansion built in 1923 by Walter Fondren, founder of Humble Oil (now Exxon). Cr cds: A, MC, V.

★ ★ ★ **SARA'S BED AND BREAKFAST INN.** *941 Heights Blvd (77008). 713/868-1130; fax 713/868-3284; toll-free 800/593-1130. www.saras.com.* 14 rms, 2 share bath, 2 story. S $55-$110; D $70-$150; each addl $10; suites $150; wkly rates. TV; VCR (free movies). Complimentary bkfst. Restaurant nearby. Ck-out noon, ck-in 3 pm. Business servs avail.

Antiques, collectibles. Totally non-smoking. Cr cds: A, C, D, DS, MC, V.

All Suites

★ ★ ★ **EMBASSY SUITES.** *9090 SW Fwy (77074). 713/995-0123; fax 713/779-0703; toll-free 800/553-3417. www.winhotel.com.* 243 suites, 9 story. Suites $119-$149; each addl $10; under 18 free; wkend rates. Crib free. TV; cable (premium). Indoor pool; whirlpool. Complimentary full bkfst. Complimentary coffee in rms. Restaurant adj 11:30 am-11 pm. Ck-out noon. Meeting rms. Business servs avail. In-rm modem link. Gift shop. Exercise equipt; sauna. Game rm. Refrigerators, microwaves, wet bars; some bathrm phones. Balconies. Cr cds: A, D, DS, MC, V.

★ ★ ★ **EMBASSY SUITES NEAR THE GALLERIA.** *2911 Sage Rd (77056). 713/626-5444; fax 713/626-3883; res 800/362-2779. www.embassysuites.com.* 150 suites, 6 story. Suites $109-$229; under 18 free; family rates. Crib avail. TV; cable (premium). Complimentary full bkfst. Complimentary coffee in rms. Restaurant 6:30 am-11 pm. Rm serv from 11 am. Bar 5-11 pm. Ck-out noon. Meeting rms. Business servs avail. Bellhops. Valet serv. Sundries. Gift shop. Exercise equipt. Indoor pool; whirlpool. Refrigerators, microwaves, wet bars. Cr cds: A, D, DS, MC, V.

★ ★ ★ **RADISSON SUITES WEST.** *10655 Katy Fwy (77024). 713/461-6000; fax 713/467-2357; toll-free 800/333-3333. www.radissonhouston.com.* 173 suites, 14 story. S, D $107; each addl $10; under 10 free; package plans. Crib avail. TV; cable (premium). Complimentary full bkfst. Complimentary coffee in rms. Restaurant 6:30 am-10 pm. Bar 11 am-11 pm; wkends to midnight. Ck-out 1 pm. Meeting rms. Business servs avail. In-rm modem link. Gift shop. Pool. Refrigerators, microwaves, wet bars. Cr cds: A, C, D, DS, ER, JCB, MC, V.

★ ★ ★ **SHERATON SUITES.** *2400 W Loop S (77027). 713/586-2444; fax 713/586-2445; toll-free 888/321-4733. www.sheratonsuiteshouston.com.* 264 rms, 14 story, 22 suites. Sep-May: S $209; D $219; suites $250; each addl $10; under 18 free; lower rates rest of yr. Crib avail. Valet parking avail. Pool, whirlpool. TV; cable (DSS). Complimentary continental bkfst. Coffee in rms. Restaurant 6 am-10:30 pm. Bar. Ck-out noon, ck-in 3 pm. Conference center, meeting rms. Business servs avail. Bellhops. Concierge serv. Dry cleaning. Gift shop. Exercise equipt. Golf, 18 holes. Tennis. Video games. Cr cds: A, D, DS, JCB, MC, V.

🄳 🛐 🏋️ 🖛 🛏️ 🕭 🐾 🔥

Conference Center

★ ★ ★ **WOODLANDS RESORT.** *2301 N Millbend Dr, The Woodlands (77380). 281/367-1100; fax 281/364-6338. www.woodlandsresort.com.* 314 rms, 3 story. S $125-$160; D $140-$180; each addl $15; suites $145-$1,400; kit. units $145-$225; under 12 free; AP avail; wkend rates (seasonal), package plans. TV; cable (premium). 2 pools; wading pool, whirlpool, poolside serv. Restaurants 6 am-11 pm (see also GLASS MENAGERIE). Rm serv. 3 bars 11-2 am; Sun from noon. Ck-out noon, ck-in after 3 pm. Meeting rms. Business center. In-rm modem link. Valet serv. Gift shop. Beauty shop. Airport transportation. Indoor and outdoor lighted tennis, pro. 36-hole golf, greens fee $60-$120, 3 putting greens, 3 driving ranges, pro shop. Hiking, bicycle trails. Bicycle rentals. Game rm. Exercise rm; steam rm, sauna. Spa. Massage. Supervised children's activities (summer). Lawn games. Refrigerators; microwaves avail. Private patios, balconies. Some lake views. Outdoor sculpture garden. Cr cds: A, D, DS, MC, V.

🄳 🛐 🏋️ 🖛 🛏️ 🕭 🔥 🏃 🖛

Extended Stays

★ ★ **RESIDENCE INN BY MARRIOTT.** *7710 S Main St (77030). 713/660-7993; fax 713/660-8019; toll-free 800/331-3131. www.residenceinn. com.* 285 kit. suites. Kit. suites $79-$159; family rates. Crib free. Pet accepted; $50 and $5/day. TV; cable (premium). Heated pool; whirlpool. Complimentary continental bkfst. Bar. Ck-out noon. Meeting rms. Business servs avail. In-rm modem link. Valet serv. Lawn games. Private patios, balconies. Picnic tables, grills. Cr cds: A, C, D, DS, MC, V.

🄳 🐾 🖛 🛏️ 🔥 🆂🅲

★ ★ **RESIDENCE INN BY MARRIOTT - HOUSTON/CLEAR LAKE.** *525 Bay Area Blvd (77058). 281/486-2424; fax 281/488-8179; toll-free 800/331-3131. www.residenceinn.com/ houcl/.* 110 kit. units, 2 story. S $102; D $140; wkend rates. Crib free. Pet accepted; $50 and $6/day. TV; cable (premium). Heated pool. Complimentary continental bkfst; evening refreshments. Complimentary coffee in rms. Restaurant adj 11 am-11 pm. Ck-out noon. Coin lndry. Meeting rm. Business servs avail. In-rm modem link. Exercise equipt. Microwaves. Grills. Cr cds: A, C, D, DS, ER, JCB, MC, V.

🄳 🐾 🖛 🛏️ 🔥

Restaurants

★ ★ ★ **AMERICAS.** *1800 Post Oak Blvd (77056). 713/961-1492.* Hrs: 11:30 am-2:30 pm, 5-10 pm; Fri to 11 pm; Sat 5-11 pm. Closed Sun; most major hols. Res accepted. South American menu. Bar. Lunch $6-$12, dinner $10-$25. Child's menu. Specialties: roasted quail breast, filet of red snapper with fresh corn, plantain chips. Rain forest, Inca decor. Suspension bridge to second level. Cr cds: A, DS, MC, V.

🄳

★ ★ **A MOVEABLE FEAST.** *2202 W Alabama (77098). 713/528-3585. www.amoveablefeast.com.* Hrs: 11 am-9 pm; Sun to 6 pm. Vegetarian menu. A la carte entrees: lunch, dinner $1.50-$6.50. Child's menu. Specializes in vegetarian, vegan, natural dishes. Parking. In natural food store. Family-owned since 1971. Cr cds: A, D, DS, MC, V.

🄳

★ ★ ★ **ANTHONY'S.** *4007 Westheimer Rd (77027). 713/961-0552.* Hrs: 11:30 am-2 pm, 5:30-10 pm; Tues-Thurs to 11 pm; Fri, Sat to 11:30 pm. Closed Sun; major hols. Res accepted. Bar. Wine list. Lunch $8.95-$14.95, dinner $11.95-$26.95. Specializes in osso buco, duck, lobster and crab ravioli. Own baking. Valet parking. Open-hearth cooking. Cr cds: A, D, DS, MC, V.

★★ **ARCODORO.** *5000 Westheimer (77056). 713/621-6888. www.arcodoro. com.* Hrs: 11 am-midnight. Res accepted. Wine, beer. Specialties: handmade semolina dumplings topped with a ragu of braised baby lamb, linguini sautéed with fresh clams, gnocchetti sardi with wild boar and red wine. A la carte entrees: lunch $8-$16.50, dinner $12.50-$32.50. Entertainment. Cr cds: A, C, D, MC, V.

★★ **BACKSTREET CAFE.** *1103 S Shepherd (77019). 713/521-2239. www.backstreetcafe.net.* Hrs: 11 am-10 pm; Fri, Sat to 11 pm; Sun brunch to 3 pm. Closed some major hols. Res accepted. Bar. Lunch, dinner $8.95-$21.95. Sun brunch $8.45-$18.95. Specialties: smoked corn crab cake, fried green tomato salad, Tandoori chicken sandwich. Own baking. Valet parking. Bilevel outdoor dining. Cr cds: A, D, MC, V.

★★ **BAROQUE.** *1700 Sunset Blvd (77005). 713/523-8881.* Hrs: 11 am-2:30 pm, 5:30-10 pm; Fri to 11 pm; Sat 5:30-11 pm; Sun from 5:30 pm. Closed Dec 25. Res accepted. Eclectic menu. Bar. Lunch $10-$15, dinner $17-$26. Specialties: wild boar, gumbo, crab cakes. Own baking. 18th-century Baroque decor; ornate chandeliers, murals, antiques. Cr cds: A, C, MC, V.

★★ **BENJY'S.** *2424 Dunstan (77005). 713/522-7602. www.benjys.com.* Hrs: 11 am-2 pm, 6-10 pm; Fri to 11 pm; Sat 6-11 pm; Sun 6-9 pm; Sun brunch 11 am-2:30 pm. Closed Mon; some major hols. Res accepted. Contemporary Amer menu. Bar; Thurs-Sat to 2 am. Lunch $6-$10, dinner $8.50-$20. Specialties: polenta lasagna, sesame-crusted tuna, lobster spring roll. Jazz Thurs. Modern decor. Cr cds: A, D, MC, V.

★ **BIRRAPORETTI'S.** *500 Louisiana St (77002). 713/224-9494.* Hrs: 11 am-11 pm; Mon to 8 pm; Fri, Sat to midnight. Italian menu. Bar. Lunch, dinner $6.95-$13.95. Child's menu. Specialties: lasagne, pollo Poretti, chicken Alfredo. In Theater District. Cr cds: A, D, DS, MC, V.

★★ **BISTRO LANCASTER.** *701 Texas Ave (77002). 713/228-9502. www.lancaster.com.* Hrs: 6:30 am-11 pm; Sun from 7:30 am; Sun brunch 11 am-4 pm. Res accepted. Bar. A la carte entrees: bkfst $7.50-$11.95, lunch $5.95-$18.95, dinner $15.95-$23.95. Sun brunch $11-$23. Specialties: red pepper bisque, scrambled egg and bacon salad, crab cakes. Valet parking. Cr cds: A, DS, MC, V.

★★★ **BOULEVARD BISTRO.** *4319 Montrose Blvd (77006). 713/524-6922.* Hrs: 11 am-3 pm, 5-10 pm; Fri, Sat to 11 pm; Sat, Sun brunch 10 am-3 pm. Closed Mon; most major hols. Res accepted. Lunch $6-$8, dinner $9-$19. Sat, Sun brunch $2.50-$9. Child's menu. Specialties: Moroccan lamb shank, pistachio-crusted salmon. Outdoor dining. Parisian bistro decor. Cr cds: A, C, D, DS, ER, MC, V.

★★★★ **BRENNAN'S.** *3300 Smith St (77006). 713/522-9711. www.brennans houston.com.* Southwest adobe meets Louisiana, Cajun-Creole cuisine at this outpost of the famed New Orleans Commander's Palace. Choose the kitchen table, the shaded patio, the chef's dining room, or a variety of other private dining areas. President/managing partner Alex Brennan-Martin carries on the Texas-Creole family tradition and finishes it off with complimentary homemade pralines. Specialties: turtle soup, snapper Ponchartrain, bananas Foster. Hrs: 11:30 am-1:30 pm, 5:45-9 pm; Sat brunch 11 am-1:30 pm, dinner 5:45 -9 pm; Sun brunch 10 am-1:30 pm, dinner 5:45-9 pm. Closed Dec 24, 25. Res accepted. Bar. A la carte entrees: lunch $12-$26, dinner $17-$31. Complete meals: lunch $18.50-$24. Sat, Sun brunch $24-$34. Own baking. Sat, Sun jazz brunch. Valet parking. Outdoor dining. Elegant decor in unique building designed by John Staub as headquarters of Junior League. Family-owned. Jacket required for dinner. Cr cds: A, C, D, DS, MC, V.

D ⊒

★★★ **BROWNSTONE.** 2736 Virginia St (77098). 713/520-5666. Hrs: 11:30 am-2:30 pm, 6-10 pm; Fri, Sat to 10:30 pm. Closed Sun; Dec 25. Res accepted. Continental menu. Bar. Lunch $6.95-$15.95, dinner $19.95-$35. Prix fixe: dinner $40. Specialties: beef Wellington, potato and turnip soup, rack of lamb. Pianist; harpist Thurs-Sat. Valet parking. Outdoor poolside dining. Elegant; numerous antiques. Cr cds: A, DS, MC, V.

D

★ **BUTERA'S FINE FOODS.** 4621 Montrose Blvd (77006). 713/523-0722. Hrs: 10:30 am-10 pm; Sun to 8 pm. Closed some major hols. Wine, beer. A la carte entrees: lunch, dinner $6-$8. Specialties: chicken salad, pasta salad. Outdoor dining. Cafeteria-style serv. Cr cds: A, D, DS, MC, V.

D ⊒

★★★★ **CAFE ANNIE.** 1728 Post Oak Blvd (77056). 713/840-1111. www.cafe-express.com. Chef Robert Del Grande manages a perfect balance between strong, energetic flavors and striking simplicity with his Southwestern regional cuisine that includes dishes such as Texas farm-raised redfish with pork tamale. The dining room maintains this same balance between intricacy and simplicity with dramatic vaulted ceilings and earthy mahogany paneling. Try the prix-fixe "city lunch" for a nice sampling. Specialties: poached shrimp with Dallas mozzarella, mesquite-grilled steak, fresh red snapper. Own pastries. Hrs: 11:30 am-2 pm, 6-10 pm; Fri to 10:30 pm; Sat 6-10:30 pm. Closed Sun; hols. Res accepted. Bar. A la carte entrees: lunch $7-$17, dinner $20-$36. Prix fixe: lunch $25. Valet parking. Seasonal floral arrangements; harvest mural by local artist. Cr cds: A, DS, MC, V.

D ⊒

★ **CAFE JAPON.** 3915 Kirby Dr (77098). 713/529-1668. Hrs: 11 am-11 pm; Fri to 2 am; Sat noon-2 am; Sun noon-11 pm. Japanese menu. Wine, beer. Lunch $5.25-$9.50, dinner $9-$15. Specializes in sushi, sashimi, teriyaki. Parking. Contemporary Japanese decor. Cr cds: A, D, DS, MC, V.

D ⊒

★★ **CANYON CAFE.** 5000 Westheimer, Ste 250 (77056). 713/629-5565. Hrs: 11 am-10 pm; Fri, Sat to 11 pm; Sun brunch to 2 pm. Res accepted. Southwestern menu. Bar. Lunch $6.95-$9.95, dinner $8.95-$18.95. Sun brunch $8.95-$10.95. Child's menu. Specialties: chicken-fried tuna, desert fire pasta, barbecued cornhusk salmon. Valet parking. Outdoor dining. Southwestern decor. Cr cds: A, MC, V.

D ⊒

★★ **CAPITAL GRILLE.** 5365 Westheimer Rd (77056). 713/623-4600. www.thecapitalgrille.com. Hrs: 5-10 pm; Fri, Sat to 11 pm. Res accepted. A la carte entrees: dinner $16.95-$28.95. Specializes in dry-aged steaks. Valet parking. Elegant club atmosphere. Cr cds: A, DS, MC, V.

D ⊒

★★ **CARRABBA'S.** 3115 Kirby Dr (77098). 713/522-3131. www.carrabbas.com. Hrs: 11 am-10 pm; Fri to 11 pm; Sat noon-11 pm; Sun noon-10 pm. Closed Thanksgiving, Dec 25. Italian menu. Bar. Lunch, dinner $7.95-$20.95. Specialties: pasta Carrabba, pollo Rosa Maria, chicken Bryan Texas. Own desserts. Valet parking. Outdoor dining. Modern decor; wood-burning pizza oven. Cr cds: A, DS, MC, V.

D ⊒

★★★ **CHEZ NOUS.** 217 S Ave G, Humble (77338). 281/446-6717. Hrs: 5:30-11 pm. Closed Sun. Res accepted. French menu. Bar. Wine cellar. A la carte entrees: dinner $17.50-$29. Specialties: mesquite-grilled rib-eye steak, rack of lamb, muscovy duckling. Own desserts. Parking. French decor. Former Pentecostal church (1928). Cr cds: A, D, DS, MC, V.

D ⊒

★★ **CHIANTI CUCINA RUSTICA.** 1515 S Post Oak Ln (77056). 713/840-0303. Hrs: 11:30 am-2:30 pm, 5:30-10:30 pm; Fri to 11 pm; Sat 5:30-11 pm. Closed Sun; some major hols.

Res accepted. Italian menu. Bar. Lunch, dinner $8.75-$25. Child's menu. Specialties: antipasti misto, grilled pork chops, tortellini. Bar. Valet parking. Open-hearth cooking. View of garden from dining rm. Cr cds: A, D, MC, V.

D ⊟

★ **CHUY'S COMIDA DELUXE.** *2706 Westheimer Rd (77098). 713/524-1700. www.chuys.com.* Hrs: 11 am-11 pm; Fri, Sat to midnight. Closed Thanksgiving, Dec 25. Res accepted. Mexican menu. Bar. Lunch, dinner $4.95-$8.25. Specializes in enchiladas, fajitas. Parking. Outdoor dining. Cr cds: A, D, DS, MC, V.

D ⊟

★★ **CLIVE'S.** *517 Louisiana St (77002). 713/224-4438. www.clives. com.* Hrs: 11:30 am-2 pm, 5:30-10 pm; Thurs, Fri to 11 pm; Sat 5:30-11 pm. Closed Sun; major hols. Res accepted. Bar. Wine cellar. A la carte entrees: lunch $7.50-$16.50, dinner $17-$29.50. Specializes in steak, seafood. Own pastries. Valet parking. In Theater District. Cr cds: A, C, D, ER, MC, V.

D ⊟

★★★ **CONFEDERATE HOUSE.** *2925 Weslayan St (77027). 713/622-1936. www.confederatehouse.com.* Hrs: 11 am-2 pm, 6-10 pm; Sat from 6 pm. Closed major hols. Res accepted. Bar. Wine list. Lunch $7.50-$17, dinner $12-$26.50. Specialties: prime steak, grilled red snapper, lamb chops. Own desserts. Valet parking. Texas Colonial decor. Family-owned. Jacket (dinner). Piano bar. Cr cds: A, DS, MC, V.

D ⊟

★★ **DAILY REVIEW CAFE.** *3412 W Lamar (77019). 713/520-9217.* Hrs: 11:30 am-2 pm, 6-10 pm; Sun 10 am-2 pm. Closed Mon; most major hols. Contemporary Amer menu. Bar. Lunch $6-$10, dinner $9-$18. Sun brunch $6-$11. Specialties: lamb stew, chicken pot pie, pork chops. Valet parking. Outdoor dining. Cr cds: A, D, MC, V.

D

★★ **DAMIAN'S CUCINA ITALIA.** *3011 Smith St (77006). 713/522-0439. www.damians.com.* Hrs: 11 am-2 pm,

5:30-10 pm; Fri to 11:30 pm; Sat 5-11:30 pm. Closed Sun; some major hols. Res accepted. Italian menu. Bar. A la carte entrees: lunch, dinner $9.95-$24.95. Specialties: shrimp Damian, involtini di pollo, veal chop Milanese. Own pasta. Valet parking. Terra-cotta walls with hand-painted frescoes. Cr cds: A, C, D, MC, V.

D

★ **DONERAKI.** *7705 Westheimer Rd (77063). 713/975-9815.* Hrs: 11 am-midnight; Fri to 3 am; Sat 8-3 am; Sun 8 am-midnight. Res accepted. Mexican menu. Bar. Bkfst $5.50-$7.25, lunch, dinner $4.95-$16.95. Child's menu. Specialties: fajitas, shrimp a la Diabla, chicken enchiladas. Mariachis (dinner). Parking. Colorful Mexican decor. Cr cds: A, MC, V.

D ⊟

★★ **EMPRESS FUSION CUISINE.** *5419 FM 1960 Rd W # A (77069). 281/583-8021.* Hrs: 11 am-2:30 pm, 5-10 pm; Fri, Sat to 10:30 pm. Closed Sun; Jan 1, Thanksgiving, Dec 25. Res accepted. Pacific Rim menu. Wine, beer. Lunch $5.95-$15, dinner $8.95-$22.50. Specialties: duck a la empress, Neptune's platter. Parking. Cr cds: A, C, DS, MC, V.

D ⊟

★★ **ESCALANTE'S MEXICAN GRILLE.** *6582 Woodway (77057). 713/461-5400. www.escalantes.com.* Hrs: 11 am-10 pm; Fri, Sat to 11 pm. Closed most major hols. Mexican menu. Bar. Lunch $5.95-$10.95, dinner $8-$17. Child's menu. Specialties: fajita plate, guacamole, spinach enchiladas. Parking. Outdoor dining. Large mural; indoor colonnade. Cr cds: A, D, DS, MC, V.

D ⊟

★★ **THE FLYING DUTCHMAN.** *9 Kemah Broadwalk, Kemah (77565). 281/334-7575.* Hrs: 11 am-10 pm; wkends to 11 pm. Closed Thanksgiving, Dec 25. Res accepted. Bar. Lunch $5.95-$15.95, dinner $13.95-$18.95. Child's menu. Specializes in Gulf seafood, oyster bar, seafood gumbo. Parking. Outdoor dining with view of boat channel. Cr cds: A, C, D, DS, MC, V.

D ⊟

★ ★ **GLASS MENAGERIE.** *2301 N Millbend St (77380). 281/364-6326.* Hrs: 11:30 am-2 pm, 6-10 pm; Sun brunch 11 am-3 pm. Res accepted. Continental menu. Bar. Buffet lunch $11.95. Dinner $20-$32. Sun brunch $22.95. Specialties: steak Diane, flambe desserts. Pianist Fri-Sun. Valet parking. Views of lake. Cr cds: DS, MC, V.
D

★ **GOLDEN ROOM.** *1209 Montrose Blvd (77019). 713/524-9614.* Hrs: 11:30 am-2:30 pm, 5:30-9:30 pm; Fri to 10:30 pm; Sat 5:30-10:30 pm. Closed Sun; also Dec 25. Res accepted. Thai menu. Wine, beer. Lunch $5.95-$6.50, dinner $9.95-$14.95. Specialties: shrimp Jackson, clay pot dishes, spicy mint chicken. Parking. Oriental decor. Cr cds: A, DS, MC, V.

★ **GOODE COMPANY SEAFOOD.** *2621 Westpark (77098). 713/523-7154.* Hrs: 11 am-10 pm; Fri, Sat to 11 pm. Closed Jan 1, Thanksgiving, Dec 25. Bar. Lunch, dinner $6-$16.95. Specializes in seafood. Valet parking. Nautical decor. Cr cds: A, DS, MC, V.
D ⬛

★ ★ **GOODE COMPANY TEXAS BAR-B-Q.** *5109 Kirby Dr (77098). 713/522-2530.* Hrs: 11 am-10 pm. Closed Jan 1, Thanksgiving, Dec 25. Wine, beer. A la carte entrees: lunch, dinner $4-$9.75. Specialties: barbecued dishes, cheese bread, pecan pie. Entertainment first Fri of month. Parking. Outdoor dining. Relaxed Western atmosphere. Family-owned. Cr cds: A, D, DS, MC, V.
D

★ ★ **GREAT CARUSO.** *10001 Westheimer Rd (77042). 713/780-4900. www.houstondinnertheater.com.* Hrs: 6-10:30 pm; Fri, Sat to 11:30 pm. Closed Mon; Jan 1, Dec 25. Res accepted. Continental menu. Bar to 1 am. A la carte entrees: dinner $12.95-$21.95. Specializes in veal, steak, fish. Valet parking. Unique antique decor. Broadway and light operetta performances nightly; singing waiters and dancers. Cr cds: A, D, DS, MC, V.
D

★ ★ **GRILLE 5115.** *5115 Westheimer (77056). 713/963-8067.* Hrs: 11 am-10 pm; Fri, Sat to 11 pm. Closed Sun; Easter, Thanksgiving, Dec 25. Res accepted. Continental menu. Lunch $10-$18; dinner $13-$24. Specialties: filet mignon topped with foie gras, mixed seafood ravioli, soft shell crab with jicama cole slaw. Jazz pianist Tues-Thurs night. Valet parking. Modern decor. Cr cds: A, DS, MC, V.
D

★ ★ **GROTTO.** *3920 Westheimer Rd (77027). 713/622-3663.* Hrs: 11:30 am-11 pm; Fri, Sat to midnight; Sun to 10 pm. Closed major hols. Res accepted (6 or more). Southern Italian menu. Bar. Lunch $6.95-$9.95, dinner $6.95-$17.95. Specialties: grilled red snapper cerretto, linguine alle vongole. Own pizza, pasta. Parking. Outdoor dining. Neapolitan cafe setting; large mural on wall. Cr cds: A, C, D, DS, MC, V.
D ⬛

★ **GUADALAJARA MEXICAN GRILLE.** *12821 Kimberly Ln (77024). 713/461-5300.* Hrs: 11 am-10 pm; Fri, Sat to 11 pm. Closed Thanksgiving, Dec 25. Mexican menu. Bar. Lunch $5.50-$9.95, dinner $5.95-$13.95. Child's menu. Specializes in enchiladas, tortillas, seafood. Strolling musicians wkends. Casual dining; Mexican decor. Outdoor dining. Cr cds: A, DS, MC, V.
D ⬛

★ ★ **HUNAN.** *1800 Post Oak Blvd #184 (77056). 713/965-0808.* Hrs: 11:30 am-10:30 pm; Fri to 11:30 pm; Sat noon-11:30 pm; Sun from noon. Closed Thanksgiving. Res accepted. Chinese, Hunan menu. Bar. Lunch $6.85-$8.95, dinner $9.85-$15.50. Specialties: Hunan-style chicken and prawns, Peking duck. Parking. Chinese decor, large brass Oriental mural. Cr cds: A, DS, MC, V.
D ⬛

★ ★ **JALAPENOS.** *2702 Kirby Dr (77098). 713/524-1668.* Hrs: 11 am-10 pm; Fri, Sat to 11:30 pm; Sun brunch to 2:30 pm. Closed Thanksgiving. Res accepted. Mexican, South Amer menu. Bar. Lunch $6-$11, dinner $7-$15. Sun brunch $12.95. Child's menu. Specialties: stuffed jalapeños, spinach enchiladas, mesquite-grilled quail. Own tortillas. Central Mexican decor. Cr cds: A, C, D, DS, ER, MC, V.

★★ **KANEYAMA.** 9527 Westheimer Rd, Ste D (77063). 713/784-5168. Hrs: 11:30 am-10:30 pm; Fri, Sat to 11 pm. Closed Thanksgiving. Res accepted. Japanese menu. Bar. Lunch $5.95-$10, dinner $8.50-$20.45. Specialties: sushi, salmon teriyaki, hamachi kama. Sushi bar. Cr cds: A, C, D, DS, ER, MC, V.

★ **KHYBER.** 2510 Richmond Ave (77098). 713/942-9424. Hrs: 11 am-2 pm, 5:30-10 pm. Indian menu. Wine, beer. Lunch $7.50-$12.50, dinner $11.50-$16. Specialties: grilled lamb leg, mountain-style grilled chicken. Own baking. Outdoor dining. Indian artifacts, decorative rugs on wall; large patio. Cr cds: A, C, D, DS, MC, V.

★ **KIM SON.** 2001 Jefferson St (77003). 713/222-2461. www.kimson. com. Hrs: 11 am-11 pm; Fri, Sat to midnight. Vietnamese, Chinese menu. Bar. A la carte entrees: lunch, dinner $6.50-$13.95. Specialties: spring rolls, black pepper crab, Vietnamese fajitas. Parking. Cr cds: A, DS, MC, V.

★ **KING FISH MARKET.** 6356 Richmond (77057). 713/974-3474. Hrs: 11 am-10 pm; Fri to 11 pm; Sat noon-11 pm; Sun from noon. Res accepted. Seafood menu. Bar. Lunch $5-$10, dinner $10-$20. Child's menu. Specialties: snapper laguna, jumbo barbecue shrimp, Caribbean lobster tail. Parking. Outdoor dining. Tropical Caribbean atmosphere. Cr cds: A, C, D, DS, ER, MC, V.

★★★ **LA COLOMBE D'OR.** 3410 Montrose Blvd (77006). 713/524-7999. www.lacolombedorhouston.com. Hrs: 11:30 am-2 pm, 6-10 pm; Fri to 11 pm; Sat, Sun 6-11 pm. Res accepted. French menu. A la carte entrees: lunch $9.50-$15, dinner $22-$29. Specializes in lamb, veal, fish. Own desserts. Valet parking. 21-rm residence decorated with artwork. Cr cds: A, DS, MC, V.

★★★ **LA GRIGLIA.** 2002 W Gray St (77019). 713/526-4700. Hrs: 11:30 am-2 pm, 5:30-11 pm; Fri to midnight; Sat 5:30 pm-midnight; Sun 5:30-10 pm. Closed major hols. Res accepted. Italian menu. Bar. A la carte entrees: lunch $6.95-$14.95, dinner $8.95-$24.95. Specialties: shrimp and crab cheesecake, red snapper La Griglia, linguine pescatore. Valet parking. Outdoor dining. Colorful tilework and murals. Cr cds: A, C, D, DS, ER, MC, V.

★★ **LA MORA.** 912 Lovett (77006). 713/522-7412. www.lamora.com. Hrs: 11:30 am-2 pm, 5:30-10 pm; Fri, Sat 5:30-11 pm. Closed Sun; most major hols. Res accepted. Northern Italian menu. Bar. Lunch, dinner $10.95-$24.95. Specialties: spicy fish soup, cuscinetti, rotisserie-roasted pork loin. Valet parking. Outdoor dining, Italian villa decor. Cr cds: A, DS, MC, V.

★★★★ **LA RESERVE.** 4 Riverway (77056). 713/871-8177. A special-occasion destination where guests can experience Texas-influenced French cuisine for an expensive but justifiable price. Each item on the small menu is delicious and straightforward, like the Texas farm-raised moullard duck breast with black cherry chutney and port wine sauce. Try one of the daily changing dessert souffles or a glorious glass of reserve port to end the meal. Continental menu. Specializes in lobster, rack of Australian lamb, duck foie gras. Also vegetarian menu. Own baking. Hrs: 6:30-10 pm; Fri, Sat to 10:30 pm. Closed Sun, Mon. Bar 4 pm-midnight. Res accepted. A la carte entrees: dinner $19-$32. Table d'hôte: dinner $50-$85. Valet parking. Jacket required. Cr cds: A, C, D, DS, ER, MC, V.

★★ **LAS ALAMEDAS.** 8615 Katy Fwy (77024). 713/461-1503. Hrs: 11 am-3 pm, 6-10 pm; Fri to 11 pm; Sat 6-11 pm; Sun 11 am-3 pm (brunch),

Houston skyline

6-9 pm. Closed most major hols. Res accepted. Mexican menu. Bar. Lunch, dinner $10-$20. Sun brunch $22. Child's menu. Specialties: enchiladas verde, grilled red snapper, chile relleno. Own baking. Guitarist Tues-Sat, Sun brunch. Valet parking. Replica of 19th-century Mexican hacienda; entrance arch, stained glass. Cr cds: A, DS, MC, V.

★★ **LA STRADA.** *322 Westheimer (77006).* 713/522-7999. Hrs: 11 am-2:30 pm, 5-10 pm; Fri to 11:30 pm; Sat 11 am-3 pm, 5-11:30 pm; Sun 11 am-3:30 pm, 5:30-10 pm. Res accepted. Italian menu. Bar. Lunch, dinner $8.95-$19.95. Specialties: parmesan-crusted chicken, Joey's filet, grilled jumbo shrimp. Valet parking. Contemporary decor; Old World atmosphere. Cr cds: A, C, D, MC, V.

★★★ **LA TOUR D'ARGENT.** *2011 Ella Blvd (77008).* 713/864-9864. Hrs: 11:30 am-2 pm, 6-11 pm. Closed Sun; major hols. Res accepted; required wkends. French menu. Bar. A la carte entrees: lunch $8.50-$20, dinner $16-$31. Specializes in seafood, game, duck. Own desserts. Valet parking. Antiques. Dining in 1920s hunting lodge, Houston's oldest log cabin. Overlooks bayou. Jacket (dinner). Cr cds: A, DS, MC, V.

★★★ **MARK'S AMERICAN CUISINE.** *1658 Westheimer Rd (77006).* 713/523-3800. www.marks1658.com. Hrs: 11 am-2 pm, 6-11 pm; Fri 11 am-2 pm, 5:30 pm-midnight; Sat 5 pm-midnight; Sun 5-10 pm. Closed some major hols. Res accepted. Bar. Lunch $7-$12, dinner $15-$21. Child's menu. Specialties: hearth-roasted duck, molasses and bourbon-glazed pork, eight jewel ginger apple sauce. Valet parking. Built in 1926; former Gothic-style church. Cr cds: A, C, D, DS, ER, MC, V.

★★ **MARRAKECH.** *500 Westheimer Rd (77006).* 713/942-0800. Hrs: 6-10 pm; Fri, Sat to 11 pm. Closed Mon; most major hols. Moroccan menu. Bar. Complete meals: dinner $22-$29.50. Specialties: bastilla, couscous, lamb mrouzia. Belly dancing Fri, Sat. Parking. Outdoor dining. Moroccan decor; murals, carpets hanging on wall. Cr cds: A, C, D, DS, ER, MC, V.

★★★ **MASRAFF'S.** *1025 S Post Oak Ln (77056).* 713/355-1975. www.masraffs.com. Hrs: 11 am-10 pm; Fri to 11 pm; Sat 6-11 pm; Sun 10:30 am-11 pm. Res accepted. Wine list. Lunch $14.50-$16.50; dinner $12.50-$27. Brunch $8.50-$12.50. Cr cds: A, D, DS, MC, V.

★★★ **MAXIM'S.** *3755 Richmond Ave (77046).* 713/877-8899. www.maximshou.com. Hrs: 11:15 am-10:30 pm; Sat 5:30-11 pm. Closed Sun; major hols. Res accepted. French menu. Bar. Wine cellar. Lunch $9.75-$12, dinner

$15.75-$23.75. Specializes in Gulf seafood. Own baking. Pianist. Valet parking. Family-owned. Jacket. Cr cds: A, DS, MC, V.

D ⌐

★ ★ ★ **MCCORMICK & SCHMICK'S SEAFOOD RESTAURANT.** *1151 Uptown Park Blvd (77056). 713/840-7900. www.mccormickandschmicks. com.* Specializes in seafood. Hrs: 11 am-11 pm, Fri, Sat to midnight. Res accepted. Beer, wine. Lunch $7-$15, dinner $9-$20. Brunch $7-$15. Child's menu. Cr cds: A, D, DS, MC, V.

D ⌐

★ **MESA GRILL.** *1971 W Gray St (77019). 713/520-8900.* Hrs: 11 am-10 pm; Fri, Sat to 11 pm; Sun from 10 am; Sun brunch to 3 pm. Closed Dec 25. Res accepted. Bar; Fri, Sat to 2 am. Lunch $5.95-$9.95, dinner $7.95-$14.95. Sun brunch $14.95. Child's menu. Specialties: Adobe pie, southwestern Caesar salad, tortilla soup. Patio dining. Southwestern decor. Cr cds: A, C, D, DS, ER, MC, V.

D ⌐

★ **MINGALONE ITALIAN BAR AND GRILL.** *540 Texas Ave (77502). 713/223-0088.* Hrs: 11 am-midnight; Fri, Sat to 2 am; Sat, Sun brunch 11 am-4 pm; early-bird dinner 5-8 pm (seasonal). Res accepted. Italian menu. Bar. Lunch $5.50-$13.50, dinner $6.50-$22. Sat, Sun brunch $12.95. Child's menu. Specialties: wood-burned pizza, fried calamari, baked sardines. Own pasta. Valet parking (night). Outdoor dining. Italian decor. Cr cds: A, D, DS, MC, V.

D ⌐

★ **MO MONG.** *1201 Westheimer Rd (77006). 713/524-5664.* Hrs: 11 am-11 pm; Fri, Sat to midnight. Vietnamese menu. Bar. Lunch, dinner $3.95-$19.95. Specialties: Thai satay chicken, bu luc lac, da-nang noodles. Parking. Outdoor dining. Cr cds: A, DS, MC, V.

D ⌐

★ ★ ★ **MORTON'S OF CHICAGO.** *5000 Westheimer Rd (77056). 713/629-1946. www.mortons.com.* Hrs: 5-11 pm; Sun to 10 pm. Closed some major hols. Res accepted. Bar. A la carte entrees: dinner $17.95-$29.95.

Specializes in steak, seafood. Valet parking. Cr cds: A, D, MC, V.

D ⌐

★ ★ **NINO'S.** *2817 W Dallas St (77019). 713/522-5120.* Hrs: 11 am-2:30 pm, 5:30-10 pm; Fri to 11 pm; Sat 5:30-11 pm. Closed Sun; major hols. Res accepted. Italian menu. Bar. Lunch $8.95-$17.95, dinner $8.95-$21.95. Specializes in veal, seafood, chicken. Parking. Italian decor. Cr cds: A, C, ER, MC, V.

D ⌐

★ ★ **NIT NOI.** *2426 Bolsover (77005). 713/524-8114. www.nitnoi.com.* Hrs: 11 am-3 pm, 5-10 pm; Sat 11 am-10 pm; Sun 5-9 pm. Closed some major hols. Thai menu. Wine, beer. Lunch $5.99-$14.95, dinner $6.95-$14.95. Specialties: spring rolls, chicken basil. Totally nonsmoking. Cr cds: A, DS, MC, V.

D

★ ★ **OLIVETTE.** *111 N Post Oak Ln (77024). 713/685-6713. www. houstonian.com.* Hrs: 6:30 am-10 pm; Sat, Sun 7-10 pm. Res accepted. Wine, beer. Lunch $7-$17, dinner $7-$26. Child's menu. Entertainment. Floor-to-ceiling windows. Cr cds: A, DS, MC, V.

D

★ ★ **OTTO'S BARBECUE.** *5502 Memorial Dr (77007). 713/864-2573. www.ottosbarbecue.com.* Hrs: 11 am-9 pm. Closed Sun; some major hols. Beer. Lunch, dinner $4.75-$8.75. Child's menu. Specializes in barbecued meats. Parking. Outdoor dining. Rustic. Western decor; slogan-covered walls. Cr cds: A, D, DS, MC, V.

D ⌐

★ ★ **OUISIE'S TABLE.** *3939 San Felipe (77027). 713/528-2264. www. ouisiestable.com.* Hrs: 11 am-10 pm; Fri to 11 pm; Sat 2:30-11 pm; Sat brunch 11 am-2:30 pm. Closed Sun, Mon. Bar. Lunch $7-$14.50, dinner $11-$27. Sat brunch $7-$14.50. Specialties: Shrimp tacos, chicken curry, crab cakes. Parking. Outdoor dining. Texas Colonial style decor. Cr cds: A, C, D, DS, ER, MC, V.

D

★★ **PAPPADEAUX.** *6015 Westheimer Rd (77057). 713/782-6310. www.pappadeaux.com.* Hrs: 11 am-11 pm; Fri, Sat to midnight. Closed Thanksgiving, Dec 25. Cajun menu. Bar. Lunch $7.45-$9.95, dinner $8.95-$32.95. Specialties: fried alligator, crawfish étouffé, Angus steak. Parking. Cr cds: A, D, MC, V.
D SC

★★★ **PAPPAS BROTHERS STEAKHOUSE.** *5839 Westheimer Rd (77057). 713/780-7352.* Hrs: 5-10 pm, Fri, Sat to 11 pm. Closed Sun; most major hols. Res accepted. Bar. Wine list. A la carte entrees: dinner $18.95-$68.95. Specializes in steak, lobster. Parking. 1930s New York steakhouse atmosphere. Cr cds: A, D, MC, V.
D

★ **PAPPASITO'S CANTINA.** *6445 Richmond Ave (77082). 713/784-5253.* Hrs: 11 am-10 pm; Fri, Sat to midnight. Mexican menu. Bar. A la carte entrees: lunch $5.95-$8.95, dinner $5.95-$18.95. Specializes in seafood, enchiladas, fajitas. Own tortillas, desserts. Mexican decor. Cr cds: A, D, MC, V.
D

★ **PATRENELLAS CAFE.** *813 Jackson Hill (77007). 713/863-8223.* Hrs: 11 am-3 pm, 5-10:30 pm; Sat 5-11 pm. Closed Mon, Sun; most major hols. Res accepted. Italian menu. Lunch $6.95-$21, dinner $6.95-$25. Specialties: seafood pasta, veal marsala, involtini di melanzane. Parking. Outdoor dining. Totally nonsmoking. Cr cds: A, D, DS, MC, V.
D

★★ **P. F. CHANG'S.** *4094 Westheimer Rd (77027). 713/627-7220. www.pfchangs.com.* Hrs: 11 am-11 pm; Fri, Sat to midnight. Closed Thanksgiving, Dec 25. Chinese menu. Bar. Lunch, dinner $5.95-$12.95. Specialties: dandan noodles, Chang's spicy chicken, Szechwan seafood. Own baking, noodles. Valet parking. Outdoor dining. Upscale bistro with Oriental mural, bas-relief stone columns. Cr cds: A, C, D, ER, MC, V.
D

★ **PICO'S MEX-MEX.** *5941 Bellaire Blvd (77081). 713/662-8383.* Hrs: 9 am-10 pm; Fri, Sat to 11 pm. Closed Memorial Day, Thanksgiving, Dec 24. Mexican menu. Bar. Bkfst $3.95-$5.95, lunch $6.50-$7.95, dinner $7-$13.95. Child's menu. Specialties: huachinango, quesadillas, pollo en mole poblano. Entertainment Wed-Sun. Parking. Outdoor dining. Mexican decor; casual dining. Cr cds: A, D, DS, MC, V.
D

★★★ **POST OAK GRILL.** *1415 S Post Oak Ln (77056). 713/993-9966.* Hrs: 11 am-midnight; Mon, Tues to 11 pm; Sun 6-10 pm. Closed some major hols. Res accepted. Bar to 2 am. Wine cellar. Lunch $6.95-$14.95, dinner $8.25-$21.95. Specialties: tomatoes Manfred, fresh Gulf snapper, lemon pepper chicken. Entertainment. Valet parking. Outdoor dining. Festive ambience, colorful Toulouse-Lautrec posters. Cr cds: A, D, DS, MC, V.
D

★★ **PREGO.** *2520 Amherst St (77019). 713/529-2420.* Hrs: 11 am-10 pm; Fri to 11 pm; Sat noon-11 pm; Sun from noon. Closed some major hols. Res accepted. Italian menu. Bar. A la carte entrees: lunch, dinner $5-$20. Child's menu. Specialties: veal alla Prego, wild mushroom ravioli, Gulf Coast crab cakes. Parking. Bistro-style dining. Cr cds: A, MC, V.
D

★★★★ **QUATTRO.** *1300 Lamar St (77010).713/652-6250. www.fourseasons.com* This contemporary Italian dining room in the Four Seasons Hotel showcases inventive, worldly cuisine. Italian menu. Own baking. Hrs: 6:30 am-2:30 pm, 5-10 pm; Sun brunch 10:30 am-2 pm. Bar. Wine list. Complete meals: bkfst $15-$25. A la carte entrees: lunch $18.50-$29.50, dinner $24-$39. Sun brunch $29. Specialties: asparagus risotto scented with lemon and capers, osso bucco with saffron risotto Milanese and broccolini, pan roasted garlic shrimp with capellini pasta, tomato, shallots and white wine. Child's menu. Entertainment. Valet parking.

★★★ **RAINBOW LODGE.** *1 Birdsall St (77007). 713/861-8666. www. rainbow-lodge.com.* Hrs: 11:30 am-10:30 pm; Sat from 6 pm; Sun from 10:30 am; Sun brunch to 4 pm. Closed Mon; major hols. Res accepted. Bar. Lunch $7.25-$28, dinner $16.95-$32. Sun brunch $7.25-$15.95. Specializes in seafood, wild game. Valet parking. Outdoor dining. On Buffalo Bayou; garden, gazebo. Cr cds: A, D, DS, MC, V.
D SC ⌐

★★★ **REDWOOD GRILL.** *4611 Montrose Blvd (77006). 713/523-4611.* Hrs: 11 am-2:30 pm, 6-10:30 pm; Fri to 11 pm; Sat 6-11 pm; Sun 6-9 pm. Closed some major hols. Res accepted, required wkends. Bar. Lunch $8.95-$18.95, dinner $10.95-$21.95. Specializes in beef, chicken, fish. Valet parking. Cr cds: A, D, DS, MC, V.
D

★★ **RESA'S PRIME STEAK HOUSE.** *14641 Gladebrook (77068). 281/893-3339.* Hrs: 4:30 pm-2 am. Closed most hols. Res accepted. Bar. A la carte entrees: dinner $16.95-$22.95. Specializes in seafood, steak, beef. Entertainment. Parking. Club atmosphere. Cr cds: A, D, DS, MC, V.
D ⌐

★★ **RIVER OAKS GRILL.** *2630 Westheimer Rd (77098). 713/520-1738.* Hrs: 11 am-2 pm, 5:30-10:30 pm; Fri to 11 pm; Sat 5:30-11 pm. Closed Sun; some major hols. Res accepted; required wkends. Bar from 4 pm; Sat from 5 pm. Lunch $8.95-$16.95, dinner $13.95-$26.95. Specializes in steak, fresh seafood, chops. Pianist Tues-Sat. Valet parking. Club atmosphere; contemporary decor. Cr cds: A, D, DS, MC, V.
D ⌐

★★★ **RIVIERA GRILL.** *10655 Katy Fwy (77024). 713/365-9400. www. riveragrill.com.* French menu. Specializes in Chilean sea bass, Rivera tuna. Hrs: 11:30 am-2 pm, 6-10 pm. Closed Sun. Res accepted. Wine, beer. Lunch $9-$14; dinner $16-$31. Jazz pianist Mon-Thurs. Cr cds: A, C, D, MC, V.
D ⌐

★★★ **RIVOLI.** *5636 Richmond Ave (77057). 713/789-1900. www.the rivoli.com.* Hrs: 11:30 am-2 pm, 6-11 pm; Sat from 6 pm. Closed Sun; major hols. Res accepted. Continental menu. Bar. Wine cellar. A la carte entrees: lunch $7.95-$14.95, dinner $16.95-$31. Specialties: Dover sole stuffed with crabmeat and shrimp, rack of lamb Diablo, blackened shrimp with mustard sauce. Own pastries. Entertainment Mon-Sat. Valet parking. Jacket. Cr cds: A, D, DS, MC, V.
⌐

★★★ **ROTISSERIE FOR BEEF AND BIRD.** *2200 Wilcrest Dr (77042). 713/977-9524. www.rotisserie-beef-bird.com.* Hrs: 11:30 am-2 pm, 6-10 pm; Sat from 6 pm. Closed Sun; Jan 1, Dec 25. Res accepted. Continental menu. Bar. Wine cellar. Lunch $9.50-$12.95, dinner $18.95-$35. Specializes in roast duckling, venison, lobster. Valet parking. New England-colonial atmosphere. Jacket (dinner). Cr cds: A, D, DS, MC, V.
D

★★ **RUGGLES GRILL.** *903 Westheimer Rd (77006). 713/524-3839.* Hrs: 11:30 am-2 pm, 5:30-11 pm; Fri to midnight; Sat 5:30 pm-midnight; Sun 11 am-2:30 pm, 5:30-10 pm. Closed Mon; July 4, Thanksgiving, Dec 25. Res accepted. Bar. Lunch $5.95-$13.95, dinner $9.95-$18.95. Specialties: black pepper pasta, grilled beef filet, Texas goat cheese salad. Valet parking. Contemporary decor. Cr cds: A, D, MC, V.
D ⌐

★★★ **RUTH'S CHRIS STEAK HOUSE.** *6213 Richmond Ave (77057). 713/789-2333. www.ruthschris.com.* Hrs: 5-11 pm. Closed most major hols. Res accepted. Bar. A la carte entrees: dinner $17-$29. Specializes in steak, lamb chops, lobster. Valet parking. Cr cds: A, D, DS, MC, V.
D ⌐

★★★★ **SCOTT'S CELLAR.** *6540 San Felipe (77057). 713/785-8889. www.scottscellar.com.* This tastefully elegant restaurant combines polished, attentive service and an outstanding wine list with an imaginative menu of Pacific Rim and New American cuisine. A relatively

new venture for owner/chef Scott Chen, also owner of Empress restaurant, this destination has a loyal following. The food, service, and ambiance make it a very memorable dining experience. French menu. Specializes in crispy shrimp, foie gras. Hrs: 11 am-2:30 pm, 5:30-10:30 pm, Fri, Sat 5:30-11 pm. Closed Sun. Res accepted. Wine list. Lunch $8.95-$13; dinner $16-$30. Pianist. Cr cds: A, D, DS, MC, V.
🄳 ⊟

★★ **SHANGHAI RIVER.** *2407 West-heimer Rd (77098). 713/528-5528.* Hrs: 11 am-10 pm; Fri, Sat to 11 pm. Closed Thanksgiving. Res accepted. Chinese menu. Bar. Lunch $5.50-$6.95, dinner $5.50-$15.95. Specialties: crispy shrimp, General Tso's chicken, Peking duck. Parking. Chinese porcelains on display. Cr cds: A, D, MC, V.
🄳 ⊟

★★ **SIERRA GRILL.** *4704 Montrose Blvd (77006). 713/942-7757. www.sierragrill.com.* Hrs: 11 am-2:30 pm, 5-10:30 pm; Fri to 11:30 pm; Sat 5-11:30 pm; Sun 4-10 pm. Closed most major hols. Res accepted. Southwestern menu. Bar. Lunch $5.95-$19.95, dinner $7.50-$29.95. Specialties: filet of salmon campfire style, filet of beef tenderloin. Entertainment Wed-Sat. Valet parking. Atrium dining. Southwestern decor. Cr cds: A, D, DS, MC, V.
🄳 ⊟

★★ **SIMPOSIO.** *5591 Richmond Ave (77053). 713/532-0550. www.simposio.net.* Hrs: 11:30 am-10 pm; Fri to 11 pm; Sat 5-11 pm. Closed Sun; most major hols. Res required. Northern Italian menu. Bar. Lunch $5-$15, dinner $13-$23. Specializes in seafood, beef. Own pasta. Parking. European-style decor; elegant atmosphere. Cr cds: A, D, DS, MC, V.
🄳

★★★ **SOLERO.** *910 Prairie St (77002). 713/227-2665.* Hrs: 11 am-11 pm; Thurs, Fri to midnight; Sat 6 pm-midnight. Closed Dec 24, 25. Spanish menu. Bar to 2 am. Lunch, dinner $6.95-$9.25. A la carte entrees: lunch, dinner $2.95-$14.50. Specializes in tapas, paella. Singer Wed. Valet parking. Cr cds: A, MC, V.
🄳 ⊟

★★★ **TASCA.** *908 Congress Rd (77002). 713/225-9100.* Spanish and European influenced menu. Specializes in Chilean sea bass, pepper-crusted beef tenderloin. Hrs: 11 am-11 pm, Fri 11 am-midnight, Sat 5 pm-midnight. Closed Sun. Res accepted. Beer, wine. Lunch $5-$18; dinner $16-$29. West Coast Jazz Band Fri, Sat. Open-kitchen viewing. Cr cds: A, D, DS, MC, V.
🄳 ⊟

★★ **TASTE OF TEXAS.** *10505 Katy Frwy (77024). 713/932-6901. www.tasteoftexas.com.* Hrs: 11 am-10 pm; Fri to 11 pm; Sat 4-11 pm; Sun from 4 pm. Closed Thanksgiving, Dec 25. Bar. Lunch, dinner $4.95-$29.95. Child's menu. Specializes in steak, prime rib, lobster. Salad bar. Own baking. Historical Texan decor; many local antiques, memorabilia. Family-owned. Cr cds: A, C, D, DS, MC, V.
🄳 ⊟

★★ **TONY MANDOLA'S BLUE OYSTER.** *7947 Katy Fwy (77024). 713/680-3333.* Hrs: 11 am-2 pm, 5-10 pm; Sat from 5 pm; Sun 11 am-9 pm. Closed Thanksgiving, Dec 25. Res accepted. Italian menu. Bar. Lunch $5-$12, dinner $8-$22. Child's menu. Specialties: blackened snapper in lime butter, calamari a la Mama, baked lasagna. Own baking. Family dining; Italian decor. Cr cds: A, D, MC, V.
🄳 ⊟

★★ **TONY MANDOLA'S GULF COAST KITCHEN.** *1962 W Gray St (77019). 713/528-3474.* Hrs: 11 am-10 pm; Fri, Sat to 11 pm; Sun 5-9 pm. Closed some major hols. Res accepted. New Orleans, Cajun menu. Bar. A la carte entrees: lunch, dinner $8.95-$25.95. Child's menu. Specialties: Mama's gumbo, crawfish ravioli, blackened soft-shell crab. Parking. Outdoor dining. New Orleans bistro atmosphere. Cr cds: A, D, MC, V.
🄳 ⊟

★★★ **TONY RUPPE'S.** *3939 Montrose (77006). 713/852-0852.* Continental menu. Specializes in fish, veal. Hrs: 11 am-2 pm, 5:30-10 pm; Fri to 11 pm; Sat 5:30-11 pm. Closed Sun. Res accepted. Wine, beer. Lunch $4.25-$14.50, dinner $15.50-$29.

Child's menu. Chef table in kitchen. Cr cds: A, D, MC, V.

D

★ ★ ★ ★ **TONY'S.** *1801 Post Oak Blvd (77056). 713/622-6778.* Proprietor Tony Vallone attracts famous faces from around the globe to his landmark see-and-be-seen restaurant. The glamorous, over-the-top dining room is host to a French-Italian continental menu that changes with the seasons. Definitely order one of the amazing dessert souffles, and if you can pay the price—and most can— don't be afraid to make any special requests. Italian, continental menu. Specialties: roast duckling, osso buco, seared red snapper with crabmeat. Hrs: 6-11 pm; Fri, Sat to midnight. Closed Sun; hols. Res accepted. Bar. Wine cellar. Dinner $25-$40. Pianist, vocalist. Valet parking. Family-owned. Cr cds: A, D, DS, MC, V.

D

★ **URBANA.** *3407 Montrose (77006). 713/521-1086.* Hrs: 11 am-3 pm, 5-10:30 pm; Thurs, Fri to 11 pm; Sat 5-11 pm; Sun to 10 pm; Sun brunch 11 am-3 pm. Closed Thanksgiving, Dec 25. Res accepted. Bar. Lunch $9-$13, dinner $11-$23. Sun brunch $10. Specialties: barbecued Gulf shrimp, chicken cha-cha, yellow-fin tuna. Valet parking. Outdoor dining. Eclectic atmosphere; contemporary decor. Cr cds: A, D, DS, MC, V.

D

★ ★ **VALLONE'S.** *2811 Kirby Dr (77098). 713/526-2811.* Hrs: 5:30-11 pm; Fri, Sat to midnight. Closed Sun; major hols. Res accepted. Bar. A la carte entrees: dinner $16.95-$32.95. Specializes in prime beef, fresh seafood. Parking. Fireplace. Cr cds: A, D, DS, MC, V.

D

★ ★ **VARGO'S INTERNATIONAL CUISINE.** *2401 Fondren Rd (77063). 713/782-3888.* Hrs: 6-10 pm; Fri, Sat 5-11 pm; Sun 11 am-2 pm. Closed Dec 25. Res accepted. Continental menu. Bar. Dinner $19.95-$32.50. Sun brunch $19.95. Specializes in steaks, fresh seafood. Pianist Thurs-Sun. Valet parking. View of lake and gardens. Cr cds: A, D, DS, MC, V.

D

Huntsville

(D-7) *See also Bryan/College Station*

Pop 35,078 **Elev** 400 ft **Area code** 936 **Zip** 77340

Information Chamber of Commerce, 1327 11th St; 936/295-8113 or 800/289-0389

Web www.chamber.huntsville.tx.us

What to See and Do

Huntsville State Park. On Lake Raven, 2,083 acres. Swimming, fishing, boating (ramp, rentals); nature and hiking trails, picnicking, concession, improved campsites (hookups, dump station). Standard fees. (Daily) 6 mi S on I-45, exit 109 at Park Rd 40. Phone 936/295-5644. ¢¢

Sam Houston Memorial Museum Complex. Eight-structure complex surrounding a 15-acre park. Exhibits with artifacts pertaining to the Republic of Texas and relating to Houston and his family. Tours. (Tues-Sun; closed hols) 1836 Sam Houston Ave. Phone 936/294-1832. **FREE** Incl

> **Steamboat House.** (1858) Where Houston died. Built by Dr. Rufus W. Bailey, this house is modeled after a Mississippi steamboat, with decklike galleries running its full length. Phone 936/295-7824.

> **Woodland Home, Sam Houston's Residence.** (1848) Residence with original law office and detached replica log kitchen. Tours.

Sam Houston National Forest. Offers 161,500 acres with swimming (fee) and fishing in Double Lake and Lake Conroe for catfish, bass; hunting for deer, hogs, squirrel. Lone Star Hiking Trail (140 mi), picnicking and camping at Double Lake (fee). Primitive camping (free). Fees vary. S and E, via US 75, 190, 59, I-45. Contact San Jacinto (East) District Ranger Office. Phone 936/344-6205. **FREE**

Sam Houston's Grave. About three blks north of courthouse in Oakwood Cemetery, follow signs. Inscription is the tribute of Andrew Jackson, once his military commander: "The world will take care of Houston's fame."

Texas Prison Museum. Items on display incl a Texas electric chair ("Old Sparky"), rifles, contraband items, and examples of inmate art. (Daily; closed hols) 1113 12th St, opp courthouse. Phone 936/295-2155. ¢¢

Motels/Motor Lodges

★★ **BEST WESTERN SAM HOUSTON INN.** *613 I-45 S (77340). 936/295-9151; fax 936/295-9151; toll-free 800/491-0447.* 76 rms, 2 story. S $48; D $54; each addl $6; under 16 free. Crib free. TV; cable. Pool. Complimentary continental bkfst. Ck-out noon. Meeting rms. In-rm modem link. Cr cds: A, C, D, DS, MC, V.

★★ **LA QUINTA INN.** *124 I-45 N (77320). 936/295-6454; fax 936/295-9245; toll-free 800/687-6667. www.laquinta.com.* 120 rms, 2 story. S $54-$62; D $61-$69; each addl $7; under 18 free. Crib free. Pet accepted. TV; cable (premium). Pool; wading pool. Complimentary continental bkfst. Ck-out noon. Meeting rms. Some refrigerators. Cr cds: A, C, D, DS, MC, V.

★ **UNIVERSITY HOTEL.** *1610 Ave H at 16th St (77341). 936/291-2151; fax 936/294-1683.* 95 rms, 4 story. S $44; D $49; each addl $3; under 18 free; monthly rates. Crib free. Pet accepted, some restrictions. TV; cable. Ck-out noon. Meeting rm. Health club privileges. Refrigerators. On Sam Houston State Univ campus. Totally nonsmoking. Cr cds: A, D, MC, V.

Restaurant

★ **JUNCTION STEAK AND SEAFOOD.** *2641 11th St (77340). 936/291-2183.* Hrs: 11 am-10 pm; Fri, Sat to 10:30 pm. Closed Thanksgiving, Dec 24, 25. Res accepted. Bar. Lunch $3.95-$6.45, dinner $5.45-$15.95. Child's menu. Specializes in prime rib, catfish, shrimp. Salad bar. Restored 1840s plantation house; many antiques. Cr cds: A, D, DS, MC, V.

Irving (B-6)

(see Dallas and Dallas/Fort Worth Airport Area)

Jacksonville

(C-7) *See also Palestine, Rusk, Tyler*

Pop 13,868 **Elev** 531 ft **Area code** 903 **Zip** 75766

Information Chamber of Commerce, 526 E Commerce, PO Box 1231; 903/586-2217 or 800/376-2217

Web www.jacksonvilletexas.com

What to See and Do

Lake Jacksonville. A 1,760-acre recreation area with swimming, waterskiing, bass fishing, boating; camping and cabins (fee). (Daily) 3 mi SW via US 79, College Ave exit. Phone 903/586-5977. ¢¢

Love's Lookout State Park. Large roadside park with beautiful overlook of countryside. Woodlands, play areas, picnicking, rest rms. (All yr) 3½ mi N via US 69, Lookout exit. **FREE**

Special Events

Tomato Fest. Downtown. Children's activities. Second Sat June. Phone 903/586-2217.

Tops in Texas Rodeo. Three days. Second wk July. Phone 903/586-3285.

Jasper (D-8)

Founded 1837 **Pop** 8,247 **Elev** 228 ft **Area code** 409 **Zip** 75951

Information Chamber of Commerce, 246 E Milam; 409/384-2762

Web www.jaspercoc.org

What to See and Do

Angelina National Forest. (see LUFKIN) NW on TX 63. Phone 936/639-8620.

Beaty-Orton House. Restored Victorian gingerbread house. Museum; tours. (Mon-Fri, wkends by appt) 200 S Main. Phone 409/384-2765. ¢

Martin Dies, Jr. State Park. Approx 700 acres. Swimming, waterskiing, fishing piers, canoeing, boating (ramps); picnicking, camping (tent and trailer sites, hookups, dump station). Standard fees. (Daily) 13 mi SW on US 190 to Park Rd 48, on eastern shore of B. A. Steinhagen Lake. Phone 800/792-1112.

Reservoirs.

B. A. Steinhagen Lake. Waterskiing, fishing, boating (ramps); picnicking, concession, camping (tent and trailer sites, fee). (Daily) Headquarters located 15 mi SW on US 190, then 5 mi S on FM 92. Phone 409/429-3491. **FREE**

Sam Rayburn. Swimming, waterskiing, fishing, boating (ramps); picnicking, camping (tent and trailer sites, fee). Headquarters located 9 mi N on US 96, then 8 mi W on TX 255. Phone 409/384-5716. **FREE**

Toledo Bend Dam and Reservoir. Maintained by the Sabine River Authorities of Texas and Louisiana. Swimming, waterskiing, fishing, boating; picnicking, camping. Approx 1,200 mi of shoreline. Some fees. (Daily) Project headquarters, 9 mi N on US 96, then 26 mi E on TX 255. Phone 409/565-2273. ¢¢

Sabine National Forests. Approx 160,600 acres of rolling clay, sand hills covered with pine, hardwood forests. Toledo Bend Reservoir is on the eastern boundary of forest. Five recreation areas. Swimming, boating (launch); hiking, birding, camping (fee). (Daily) Fees vary. N and E via US 96. Contact District Ranger Office. Phone 936/639-8620.

Special Events

PRCA Lion's Club Championship Rodeo. Usually second wk May. Phone 409/384-4322.

Fall Fest. Liars Club rodeo grounds. Last Sat in Sept. Phone 409/384-2762.

Motels/Motor Lodges

★★ **HOLIDAY INN EXPRESS.** *2100 N Wheeler St (75951). 409/384-8600; res 800/465-4329. www.holiday-inn. com.* 57 rms, 2 story. S, D $57.95; under 19 free. Crib free. TV; cable (premium). Pool. Complimentary continental bkfst. Restaurant adj 11 am-10 pm. Ck-out noon. Meeting rm. Business servs avail. Coin lndry. Cr cds: A, C, D, DS, ER, JCB, MC, V.
🄳 ⛧ ⚡ ⟷ ⬚ 🔥

★★ **RAMADA INN.** *239 E Gibson St (75951). 409/384-9021; res 800/228-2828. www.ramada.com.* 100 rms. S, D $50-$55; each addl $4; under 18 free. Pet accepted. TV; cable (premium), VCR avail. Pool. Restaurant 6 am-2 pm, 5-9 pm; Sun to 2 pm. Rm serv. Bar 4 pm-midnight. Ck-out noon. Coin lndry. Meeting rms. Business servs avail. In-rm modem link. Valet serv. Some refrigerators. Picnic tables. Cr cds: A, D, DS, MC, V.
🄳 🐾 ⛧ ⟷ ⬚ 🔥

Resort

★★ **RAYBURN COUNTRY RESORT.** *1000 Wingate Blvd, Sam Rayburn (75951). 409/698-2444; fax 409/698-2372; res 800/882-1442.* 176 units, 50 rms in main bldg, 126 kit. condos. S $44.95-$49.95; D $49.95-$55.95. Crib avail. TV; cable (premium). Pool. Playground. Bar noon-midnight. Gift shop. Grocery 1 mi. Coin lndry 1 mi. Meeting rms. Business center. Lighted tennis. 27-hole golf, greens fee $28-$35, putting green, driving range. Game rm. Lawn games. Fishing guide, clean and store. Some balconies. On Lake Sam Rayburn. Cr cds: A, C, D, DS, MC, V.
🄳 ⛧ ⚡ 🎾 🏃 ⟷ ⬚ 🐾 🏃

Jefferson

See also Marshall

Founded 1836 **Pop** 2,024 **Elev** 200 ft
Area code 903 **Zip** 75657
Information Marion County Chamber of Commerce, 118 N Vale; 903/665-2672 or 888/467-3529
Web www.jefferson-texas.org

What to See and Do

Atalanta. Personal rail car of railroad magnate and financier Jay Gould. (Daily; closed Dec 25) Phone 903/665-2513. ¢

Caddo Lake State Park. (see MARSHALL) E on TX 134. Phone 903/679-3351.

Excelsior House. Built in the 1850s. President Ulysses S. Grant, President Rutherford B. Hayes, Jay Gould, and Oscar Wilde stayed here. Period furnishings. Tours (Daily; closed Dec 25). 211 W Austin St. Phone 903/665-2513. ¢¢ Opp is

> **Freeman Plantation.** Antebellum home built in 1850; restored and furnished with Victorian antiques. Tours (Mon, Tues, Thurs-Sun; closed Easter, Thanksgiving, Dec 25). 1 mi W on TX 49. Phone 903/665-2320. ¢¢

House of the Seasons. (1872) Example of the transition period between the Greek Revival and Victorian styles of architecture. The unique feature of the house is the cupola, from which the house gets its name. Each wall contains a different color stained-glass window that creates the illusion of a season of the yr. Many original furnishings and art pieces. Tours (Daily; closed Thanksgiving, Dec 25). 409 S Alley. Phone 903/665-1218. ¢¢¢

Jefferson Historical Museum. Former post office and federal court building (1888) houses Native American exhibits, gun collection, Early American items, art display. (Daily; closed hols) 223 W Austin St. Phone 903/665-2775. ¢¢

Jefferson Riverboat Landing & Depot. Narrated tour of Big Cypress Bayou. Historical sites are detailed. (Mar-Nov, daily) At Bayou St and Cypress River Bridge. Phone 903/665-2222. ¢¢¢

Lake o' the Pines. Swimming, fishing, boating; picnicking, camping (tent and trailer sites, dump station; fee). (Daily) 4 mi W on TX 49, then 4 mi W on FM 729, then 2 mi W on FM 726. Phone 903/755-2530. ¢¢

Special Events

Historical Pilgrimage. Tours of four old houses. Surrey rides. Diamond Bessie Murder Trial, Jefferson Playhouse; Henderson and Market Sts. Contact 211 W Austin. 903/665-2513. Late Apr-early May.

Christmas Candlelight Tour. Tour of four Victorian houses decorated for the season. First two wkends Dec. Phone 903/665-2672.

Motel/Motor Lodge

★ ★ **INN OF JEFFERSON.** *400 S Walcott (75657). 903/665-3983; fax 903/665-3536.* 65 rms, 2 story. S $48-$58; D $54-$64; each addl $6; suites $79-$100; under 16 free; higher rates: Mardi Gras, hol wkends, Pilgrimage, Candlelight Tour. Pet accepted, some restrictions; $20 refundable. TV; cable (premium). Complimentary continental bkfst. Pool. Restaurant adj 6 am-9 pm; Fri, Sat to 10 pm. Ck-out noon. Business servs avail. Some in-rm whirlpools. Cr cds: A, DS, MC, V.

B&Bs/Small Inns

★ ★ **1ST BED AND BREAKFAST IN TEXAS - PRIDE HOUSE.** *409 E Broadway St (75657). 903/665-2675; fax 903/665-3901; toll-free 800/894-3526. www.jeffersontexas.com.* 6 rms in house, 2 story, 4 rms in cottage. No rm phones. S, D $112; each addl $15; suite $110; mid-wk rates. TV avail. Complimentary full bkfst. Restaurant nearby. Ck-out 11:30 am, ck-in noon-3 pm. Business servs avail. Free airport transportation. Victorian residence (1889) restored with original materials. Ornate woodwork, period furnishings. Totally nonsmoking. Cr cds: A, DS, MC, V.

★ ★ **EXCELSIOR HOUSE.** *211 W Austin St (75657). 903/665-2513; fax*

903/665-9389. www.theexcelsiorhouse. com. 14 rms, 2 story. S, D $65-$95; each addl $10; suites $100. Closed Dec 24-25. TV; cable. Ck-out 11:30 am, ck-in 2:30 pm. Restored hotel (1856); elegant antique Victorian furnishings. Cr cds: A, DS, MC, V.

★★ **MCKAY HOUSE.** *306 E Delta St (75657). 903/665-7322; fax 903/665-8551. www.mckayhouse.com.* 8 rms, 4 with bath, 3 with shower only, 2 story, 3 suites. S, D $99; each addl $25; suites $135-$155; wkly, wkday rates; hols (2-day min). TV; cable (premium). Complimentary full bkfst. Restaurant nearby. Ck-out 11 am. Meeting rms. Business servs avail. In-rm modem link. Balconies. Victorian house restored with authentic antiques. Totally nonsmoking. Cr cds: MC, V.

Restaurants

★ **THE BAKERY.** *201 W Austin St (75657). 903/665-2253.* Hrs: 7 am-4 pm; Sat, Sun to 8 pm. Closed Thanksgiving, Dec 25. Res accepted. Bkfst $2.65-$4.95, lunch, dinner $1.95-$5.50. Specializes in roast beef, pastries. Own baking. In historic district. Cr cds: A, C, D, DS, ER, MC, V.

★★ **GALLEY.** *121 W Austin St (75657). 903/665-3641.* Hrs: 11 am-1:30 pm, 5-9 pm. Closed Sun, Mon; Dec 24, 25. Res accepted. Bar. Lunch $4.25-$6.50, dinner $10-$19.75. Specialty: Crab meat soup. Victorian decor, antiques. Cr cds: A, DS, MC, V.

★★★ **STILLWATER INN.** *203 E Broadway (75657). 903/665-8415. www.stillwaterinn.com.* Hrs: 6-10 pm. Closed Sun; Dec 25. Res accepted; required Sat. French, Amer menu. Private club. Wine list. Dinner $9.25-$22. Specializes in seafood, grilled meats. Own baking, ice cream. Intimate dining in restored Eastlake Victorian house (1893); antiques; herb garden. Guest rms avail. Cr cds: A, MC, V.

Johnson City
See also Austin, Burnet, Fredericksburg

Pop 1,191 **Elev** 1,193 ft
Area code 830 **Zip** 78636
Information Tourism & Visitors Bureau, PO Box 485; 830/868-7684
Web www.johnsoncity-texas.com

What to See and Do

⭐ **Lyndon B. Johnson National Historical Park.** Composed of two units: the Johnson City Unit consists of the boyhood home with visitor center and the 1860s Johnson Settlement; the LBJ Ranch Unit consists of the LBJ birthplace, family cemetery, Texas White House, and the ranch. Access to Ranch Unit by bus tour only (1¼ hrs; fee). (Daily; closed Jan 1, Dec 25) Contact Superintendent, PO Box 329. 1 blk off Main St. Phone 830/868-7128. **FREE**

Boyhood Home. (1901) Folk Victorian-style frame house, period furnishings, family heirlooms; Johnson lived here from 1913-1934. (Daily; closed Jan 1, Dec 25) **FREE** Next walk to the

Johnson Settlement. Restoration of cabin and surrounding pastures owned by the President's grandfather, a longhorn cattle driver in the mid-1800s. (Daily; closed Jan 1, Dec 25) **FREE**

Birthplace. Reconstructed two-bedrm farmhouse, typical of late 1800s structures of this region, with "dog-trot," an open hallway for ventilation. Johnson family occupied the house from 1907-1913 and 1920-1922. Adj to Birthplace is family cemetery where Johnson is buried. LBJ State Park is nearby. 13 mi W of Visitors Center via US 290, Park Rd 49 **FREE**

LBJ Ranch House ("Texas White House"). Built of limestone and wood; ranch has registered Hereford cattle. Bus tour drives by (not open to public).

Lyndon B. Johnson State Historical Park. On Pedernales River, 733 acres. Swimming and wading pools (fee), fishing; nature and hiking trails, picnicking, playground, tennis courts. Visitor center (daily; closed Dec 25) has Johnson family memorabilia and relics of previous settlers of the area. Adj is Behrens Cabin (1840), a "dogtrot" building with period furnishings. Sauer-Beckmann homestead of early 1900s is site of living history program; tours. (Daily) 14 mi W on US 290, enter on Park Rd 52. Phone 830/644-2252. **FREE**

Pedernales Falls State Park. Approx 5,000 acres. Swimming, fishing; nature, hiking, and bicycle trails; picnicking, primitive and improved camping (hookups, dump station). Standard fees. (Daily) 9 mi E on Ranch Rd 2766. Phone 830/868-7304.

Kerrville

(D-5) *See also Bandera, Fredericksburg, San Antonio*

Pop 20,425 **Elev** 1,645 ft
Area code 830 **Zip** 78028
Information Convention and Visitors Bureau, 1700 Sidney Baker, Suite 200; 830/792-3535 or 800/221-7958
Web www.kerrvilletx.com

What to See and Do

Hill Country Museum (Captain Charles Schreiner Mansion). Residence restored to house the memorabilia of more than a century of area history. (Mon-Sat) 226 Earl Garrett. Phone 830/896-8633.

Kerrville-Schreiner State Park. Approx 500 acres. Swimming, fishing, boating (ramps); hiking trail, picnicking, playground, camping (hookups, dump station). Standard fees. (Daily) 3 mi S via TX 173. Phone 830/257-5392. ¢¢

National Center for American Western Art. Rotating and permanent collections of works and memorabilia devoted to the art of the West; Western art library. (Memorial Day-Labor Day Mon-Sat, Sun afternoons; rest of yr Tues-Sat, Sun afternoons) 1550 Bandera Hwy (TX 173). Phone 830/896-2553. ¢¢

Y. O. Ranch. Acquired in 1880 by Captain Charles Schreiner, this 60-sq-mi ranch, one of the largest in Texas, has a herd of more than 1,500 longhorn cattle. The terrain resembles that of Africa. Approx 55 different species of exotic game animals, incl antelopes, zebras, giraffes, ostriches, and emus roam free. Game animals are also abundant (limited hunting); photo safaris. Tours (by res). Ranch incl general store, cabins, pool, lodge. (Daily, by res only) (See SPECIAL EVENTS) Some fees. I-10W, 18 mi W to TX 41, then 16 mi SW. Phone 830/640-3222.

Special Events

Longhorn Trail Drive. Y. O. Ranch. Heritage celebration, camping under the stars, covered wagons, and "trailblazers." Phone 830/640-3222. Wkend, spring.

Smith/Ritch Point Theatre. 6 mi W via TX 39, in Ingram. Four productions in outdoor amphitheater on the banks of the Guadalupe River. Thurs-Sat, nightly. Phone 830/367-5122. May-Aug.

Kerrville Folk Festival. Quiet Valley Ranch, 9 mi S on TX 16. Outdoor music festival. Children's concerts, crafts, camping. Phone 830/257-3600. Late May-early June.

Texas State Arts & Crafts Fair. Schreiner College campus. Concessions, entertainment, demonstrations. Phone 830/896-5711. Memorial Day wkend.

Kerrville Wine & Music Festival. Quiet Valley Ranch, 9 mi S on TX 16. Outdoor festival; concerts, wine tastings, arts and crafts, camping. Phone 830/257-3600. Labor Day wkend.

Kerr County Fair. Music, food, crafts, livestock. Phone 830/792-3535. Oct.

Motel/Motor Lodge

★★ **BEST WESTERN SUNDAY HOUSE INN.** *2124 Sidney Baker St (78028). 830/896-1313; fax 830/896-1336; res 800/528-1234. www.bestwestern.com.* 97 rms, 2 story. S, D $60-$80; each addl $6; studio, family rms $96-$115; under 12 free. Crib $6. Pet accepted; $10. TV; cable (premium). Pool. Restaurant 7 am-9 pm. Bar 5-9 pm. Ck-out noon. Meeting rms. Cr cds: A, C, D, DS, MC, V.

Resorts

★★ **INN OF THE HILLS CONFERENCE RESORT.** *1001 Junction Hwy (78028). 830/895-5000; fax 830/895-6090; toll-free 800/292-5690. www.innofthehills.com.* 200 units, 2-6 story, 10 kit. units. May-Oct: S $86-$94; D $89-$94; each addl $8; suites $130-$200; kits. $115-$165; under 18 free; wkly rates; lower rates rest of yr. Crib $10. TV; cable (premium). 5 pools, 2 indoor; wading pool; whirlpool, poolside serv (summer). Playground. Complimentary coffee in rms. Restaurant. Rm serv. Bar 3 pm-2 am; entertainment. Ck-out noon. Coin lndry. Meeting rms. In-rm modem link. Gift shop. Barber, beauty shop. Free bus depot transportation. Lighted tennis. Putting green. Health club privileges; Sauna. Microwaves. Some balconies. Cr cds: A, D, DS, MC, V.

🐕 🎿 ≈ 🎾 🔥 SC

★★ **Y.O. RANCH RESORT HOTEL & CONFERENCE CENTER.** *2033 Sidney Baker St (78028). 830/257-4440; fax 830/896-8189; toll-free 877/967-3767. www.yoresort.com.* 191 rms, 2 story. S, D $109-$119; suites $175-$259; each addl $10; package plans. Crib free. Pet accepted. TV; cable (premium). Pool; wading pool, whirlpool. Coffee in rms. Restaurant 6 am-2 pm, 5-10 pm; Fri, Sat to 10 pm. Rm serv. Bar 5 pm-2 am. Ck-out noon. Meeting rms. Business servs avail. In-rm modem link. Airport transportation. Tennis. Lawn games. Refrigerators in suites. Private patios, balconies. Western decor; Mexican tile floors. Cr cds: A, D, DS, MC, V.

🐕 🐎 🎿 ≈ 🎾 🔥 SC

Guest Ranch

★★ **LAZY HILLS GUEST RANCH.** *Henderson Branch Rd, Ingram (78025). 830/367-5600; fax 830/367-5667; toll-free 800/880-0632. www.lazyhills.com.* 25 units. S $103-$110; D $156-$170; each addl $62; under 1 yr free; 1-8 yrs $35; 9-11 yrs $40; 12-16 yrs $50; wkly rates. TV in lobby. Pool; wading pool, whirlpool. Playground. Free supervised children's activities (June-Aug); ages 3-8. Dining rm sittings: 8-9 am, noon, 6 pm. Cookouts. Ck-out noon, ck-in 4 pm. Coin lndry. Business servs avail. Gift shop. Lighted tennis. Lawn games. Rec rm. Some fireplaces. Cr cds: A, DS, MC, V.

🐕 🎿 🎿 ≈ 🎾 🔥

Restaurants

★★ **ANNEMARIE'S ALPINE LODGE.** *1001 Junction Hwy (78028). 830/257-8282.* Hrs: 6 am-10 pm; Sun to 9 pm; Sun brunch from 11 am. Res accepted. Swiss, Amer menu. Bar. Bkfst $3.75-$9.95, lunch $4.95-$12.95, dinner $5.25-$16.95. Sun brunch $13.95. Child's menu. Specialties: dessert table, birchermuesli. Salad bar. Swiss decor features Alpine horn and cow bells. Family-owned. Cr cds: A, D, DS, MC, V.

D 🍴

★ **CYPRESS GRILL.** *2124 Sidney Baker St (78028). 830/257-7171. www.bestwesternkerrville.com.* Hrs: 7 am-2 pm, 5 pm-9 pm; Sun brunch 11:30 am-2:30 pm. Res accepted. Bar. Bkfst $2.75-$6.95, lunch $5-$7.50, dinner $14.50. Sun brunch $12.95. Specializes in seafood, steak, pasta. Cr cds: A, C, D, MC, V.

D

★ **MAMACITA'S.** *215 Junction Hwy (78028). 830/895-2441.* Hrs: 11 am-9:30 pm; Fri-Sun to 10 pm. Closed Jan 1, Thanksgiving, Dec 25. Res accepted. Mexican menu. Bar. Lunch $4.95-$5.75, dinner $5.95-$9.95. Specializes in fajitas, enchiladas, steak. Mexican courtyard decor; stained-glass windows, fountain. Cr cds: A, D, DS, MC, V.

D 🍴

Kilgore

(C-7) *See also Longview, Marshall, Tyler*

Pop 11,301 **Elev** 370 ft **Area code** 903 **Zip** 75662

Information Chamber of Commerce, 813 N Kilgore St, PO Box 1582, 75663; 903/984-5022

Web www.kilgorechamber.com

What to See and Do

East Texas Oil Museum at Kilgore College. Re-creation of oil discovery and production in 1930s in largest oil field in US. Full-scale town depicting oil boom days. (Tues-Sun; special Dec hol schedule; closed Easter, Thanksgiving) Kilgore College campus, jct US 259 and Ross St. Phone 903/983-8295. ¢¢ Also on campus is

Rangerette Showcase. Museum depicts history of the famous Kilgore Rangerettes, college football's first precision drill and dance team, with photographs, scrapbooks, memorabilia, and film footage. (Mon-Sat; closed hols) 1100 Broadway. Phone 903/983-8265. **FREE**

Killeen

(D-6) *See also Burnet, Temple*

Pop 86,911 **Elev** 833 ft **Area code** 254
Information Greater Kileen Chamber of Commerce, One Santa Fe Plaza, 76541; 254/526-9551 or 800/869-8265
Web www.gkcc.com

What to See and Do

Belton Lake. (see TEMPLE) 8 mi E and N via US 190 then TX 317. Phone 254/939-1829.

Fort Hood. This 339-sq-mi army installation has the nation's largest concentration of armored power. Houses the US Army III Corps, the first Cavalry Division and the fourth Infantry. The fourth Infantry and first Cavalry museums feature military equipt and campaign exhibits (Daily, limited hrs). W of town. Phone 254/287-8506. **FREE**

Stillhouse Hollow Lake. (see SALADO) 6 mi SE via FM 2410 and US 190.

Special Event

Killeen Festival of Flags. Memorial Day wkend.

Motels/Motor Lodges

★ ★ **LA QUINTA INN.** *1112 S Fort Hood St (76541). 254/526-8331; fax 254/526-0394; res 800/531-5900. www.laquinta.com.* 105 rms, 3 story. No elvtr. S $64-$78; D $71-$78; each addl $7; suites $76-$97; under 18 free. Crib free. Pet accepted, some restrictions. TV; cable (premium). Pool. Complimentary continental bkfst. Restaurant adj open 24 hrs. Ck-out noon. In-rm modem link. Valet serv. Free airport transportation. Health club privileges. Microwaves avail. Cr cds: A, C, D, DS, MC, V.

🄳 🐾 🐈 🏋 🌊 ⛷ 🔥 🐱

★ ★ **PLAZA HOTEL.** *1721 W Central Texas Expy (76541). 254/634-1555; fax 254/519-2945; res 800/633-8756.* 148 rms, 6 story. S $76; D $81; suites $97-$115; under 12 free. Crib free. TV; cable (premium). Pool. Restaurant 6 am-1 pm, 6-9 pm; Fri, Sat to 10 pm. Rm serv. Private club noon-midnight, Fri, Sat to 2 am. Ck-out 1 pm. Meeting rms. Business servs avail. In-rm modem link. Free airport transportation. Exercise equipt. Some refrigerators. Cr cds: A, C, D, DS, MC, V.

🄳 🌊 🏋 ⛷ 🔥 **SC**

Kingsville

(F-6) *See also Alice, Corpus Christi*

Founded 1904 **Pop** 25,575 **Elev** 66 ft **Area code** 361 **Zip** 78363
Information Visitors Center, 1501 S Hwy 77, PO Box 1562; 361/592-8516 or 800/333-5032
Web www.kingsville.org

What to See and Do

King Ranch. Guided bus tours (90 min; fee) incl cattle, horses, native wildlife, drive-by of historic buildings. Museum incl 20-min film of King Ranch history, saddles, stagecoaches, automobiles. (Daily; closed hols) W of town via Santa Gertrudis Ave or TX 141. Phone 361/592-8055. ¢¢¢

Texas A&M University-Kingsville.
(1925) 6,400 students. A 1,600-acre
campus. Changing exhibits in
Gallery of Art Building featuring
famous southwestern artists. Observatory in Lon C. Hill Science Hall.
Armstrong St between Santa
Gertrudis and Corral aves. Phone
361/593-2111. Also on campus is

John E. Conner Museum. Historical
exhibits and collections of southern Texas; Kleberg Hall of Natural
History; Peeler Hall of Horns.
Regional and photo archives.
Changing exhibits. (Mon-Sat;
closed hols) 905 W Santa Gertrudis
Ave. Phone 361/593-2819. **Donation**

Special Events

**Texas A&M National Intercollegiate
Rodeo.** Northway Exposition Center.
Contestants from across Texas and
Louisiana. Late Mar. Phone 361/595-
8595.

Cactus Festival. Apr. Phone 361/592-
8516.

Fiesta de Colores. Northway Exposition Center. First wkend Oct.

Motels/Motor Lodges

★★ **HOLIDAY INN.** *3430 S Hwy 77
Bypass (78363). 361/595-5753; fax
361/595-4513; res 800/465-4329.
www.holiday-inn.com.* 75 rms, 2 story.
S $44-$49; D $49-$54; suite $125;
under 18 free. Pet accepted. TV; cable
(premium). Restaurant 6:30 am-10
pm. Rm serv avail. Bar 4 pm-midnight. Ck-out noon. Meeting rms.
Business servs avail. Coin lndry.
Pool; poolside serv. Some refrigerators. Cr cds: A, C, D, DS, MC, V.
🅳 🐕 🏊 📶 🔥

★★ **QUALITY INN.** *221 S US Hwy
77 Bypass (78363). 361/592-5251; fax
361/592-6197; toll-free 800/424-4777.
www.qualityinn.com.* 117 rms, 2 story.
S $45; D $45-$52; each addl $5;
under 18 free. Pet accepted. TV; cable
(premium). Pool; wading pool. Complimentary continental bkfst. Ck-out
noon. Meeting rms. Business servs
avail. Exercise equipt. Some refrigerators. Cr cds: A, C, D, DS, JCB, MC, V.
🅳 🐕 🏊 🏋 📶 🔥 **SC**

B&B/Small Inn

★★★ **B BAR B RANCH.** *325 E CR
2215 (78363). 361/296-3331; fax
361/296-3337. www.b-bar-b.com.* 16
rms. S, D $85-$125; each addl $25.
Children over 16 yrs only. TV; VCR
avail. Complimentary full bkfst.
Restaurant Fri, Sat 6:30-9 pm (res
only). Ck-out 11 am, ck-in 3 pm.
Business servs avail. Sauna. Pool;
whirlpool. Some in-rm whirlpools.
225 acre working ranch; part of the
King Ranch. Totally nonsmoking. Cr
cds: DS, MC, V.
🅳 🐕 🏋 🏊 📶 🔥

La Grange

See also Austin, Bastrop

Pop 4,478 **Elev** 277 ft **Area code** 979
Zip 78945
Information Chamber of Commerce,
171 S Main, "In the Old Jail";
979/968-5756 or 800/LAGRANG.
Web www.lagrangetx.org

What to See and Do

Fayette Heritage Museum. Historical
museum; changing displays; archives.
(Tues-Sun; closed hols) 855 S Jefferson. Phone 979/968-6418. **FREE**

Fayette Power Project Lake & Parks.
On 2,400-acre cooling pond for generating station. Swimming, waterskiing, fishing, boating (launch, ramps);
picnicking, tent camping (showers).
(Daily) 10 mi E via TX 159, jct TX
71. Phone 979/249-3504. ¢¢

Jersey Barnyard. Home of Belle, the
"singing and talking" cow. Tours of
dairy farm; barnyard, country store.
(Mon-Sat, also Sun afternoons; closed
hols) 3117 TX 159. Phone 979/249-
3406. ¢¢

**Monument Hill & Kreische Brewery State
Historical Park.** Memorial monument,
tomb of Texans massacred during the
Mexican uprisings (1842) and Black Bean
Episode (1843). Ruins of a German brew-
ery; guided tours (wkends). Picnic area,
nature trails. (Daily) 2 mi S off US 77 on
Spur 92, on bluff overlooking Colorado
River. Phone 979/968-5658. ¢

Old Fayette County Jail. A 114-yr-old jail; memorabilia. Information center; maps, brochures. (Mon-Sat) Phone 979/968-5756.

Winedale Historical Center. Outdoor museum maintained by the University of Texas. Six restored farm buildings; antique furniture, tools; guided tours. (Sat, Sun; Mon-Fri by appt; closed hols) 17 mi NE on TX 237 to Round Top, then 4½ mi E via FM 1457, 2714. Phone 979/278-3530. ¢¢

Special Events

Fayette County Country Fair. TX 71 and US 77. Labor Day wkend. Phone 979/968-3911.

Chilispiel. 20 mi SW on I-10 and TX 609, in Flatonia. Three-day festival is one of the largest chili cook-offs in Texas. Fourth wkend Oct.

Lake Whitney

See also Hillsboro, Waco

(17 mi SW of Hillsboro on TX 22)

What to See and Do

Whitney Lake. Swimming, waterskiing, fishing, boating (ramps); picnicking, concession, camping (tent and trailer sites, some fees). Headquarters is 7 mi SW of Whitney on TX 22. Phone 254/694-3189. On eastern shore of lake is

> **Lake Whitney State Park.** More than 900 acres offering swimming, waterskiing, fishing, boating (ramp); hiking, picnicking, playground, improved campsites (tent and trailer sites). Standard fees. (Daily) 4 mi SW of Whitney on FM 1244. Phone 254/694-3793. ¢

Laredo (F-5)

Founded 1755 **Pop** 176,576 **Elev** 420 ft **Area code** 956

Information Laredo Convention & Visitor's Bureau, 501 San Agustin, 78040; 800/361-3360 or 956/795-2200

What to See and Do

Lake Casa Blanca International State Park. Waterskiing, fishing, boating (ramp); 18-hole golf, picnicking, playground, primitive camping. (Daily) 5 mi E off US 59 on Loop 20. Phone 956/725-3826. ¢¢

Laredo Children's Museum. Two fort buildings dating from the mid-1800s house the museum. Changing hands-on exhibits and demonstrations. (Daily; closed hols) At Laredo Community College, West End Washington St. Phone 956/725-2299. ¢

LIFE Downs. Site of youth rodeos, livestock shows, other events. US 59 E, near Casa Blanca Lake. Phone 956/722-9948. ¢¢¢

Nuevo Laredo, Tamaulipas, Mexico. (Pop 575,000) Across the bridge at the end of Convent Ave. For a limited visit, it is easier to park in Laredo and walk across. (For Border Crossing Regulations, see MAKING THE MOST OF YOUR TRIP.) Nuevo Laredo is a typical border town, with stores and stands featuring Mexican goods lining the street south of the bridge. There are also many parks, fine restaurants, and popular entertainment spots.

Villa de San Agustin. Downtown area. Laredo's historical district contains many of the city's older buildings. They incl

> **Republic of the Rio Grande Museum.** (ca 1830) An example of "Laredo" architecture, this was the former capitol of the short-lived Republic; period rms, furniture. (Tues-Sun; closed hols) 1003 Zaragoza St, opp San Agustin Plaza. Phone 956/727-3480. ¢

> **San Agustin Church.** (1872) The original church was built in 1767 on the site where the city was founded. Genealogical records date back to 1789. (Daily) 214 San Agustin Ave, E of Plaza. **FREE**

Special Events

George Washington's Birthday Celebration. International fiesta with parades; jalapeño-eating festival, colonial pageant, dances, bullfights. Ten days mid-Feb. Phone 956/722-0589.

Laredo International Fair & Exposition. LIFE Downs. Stock, arts and crafts shows; horse racing, barbecue, dance. Early Mar. Phone 956/722-9948.

Expomex. Nuevo Laredo (Mexico), at Carranza Park. Fiesta, stock show, bullfight. Early Sept.

Diez Y Seis Celebration. Laredo and Nuevo Laredo. Mexican National Independence Day celebration. Mid-Sept.

Motels/Motor Lodges

★★ **COURTYARD BY MARRIOTT.** *2410 Santa Ursula Ave (78040). 956/725-5555; fax 956/724-8848; toll-free 800/321-2211. www.courtyard. com.* 110 rms, 5 story. S $69-$85; D $69-$90; each addl $10; suites $79-$95; under 18 free. Crib free. TV; cable (premium). Pool; whirlpool. Coffee in rms. Restaurant 6:30 am-10 pm; Sat, Sun 7 am-midnight. Bar 5-10 pm. Ck-out noon. Meeting rms. Business servs avail. Coin lndry. Exercise equipt. Some refrigerators. Cr cds: A, D, DS, MC, V.

🄳 ⇌ 🏋 🔀 🔥 🆂🄲

★ **FIESTA INN LAREDO.** *5240 San Bernardo (78041). 956/723-3603; fax 956/724-7697; toll-free 800/460-1176. www.fiestaone.com.* 151 rms, 2 story. S, D $69-$72; each addl $10; suites $74-$77; under 12 free. Crib free. Pet accepted; some restrictions. TV; cable (premium). Pool. Complimentary continental bkfst. Restaurant adj open 24 hrs. Ck-out noon. Meeting rms. Business center. Health club privileges. Coin lndry. Free airport transportation. Some refrigerators. Cr cds: A, D, DS, MC, V.

🄳 🐾 ⇌ 🏋 🔀 🔥 🏃

★★ **HAMPTON INN.** *7903 San Dario Ave (78041). 956/717-8888; fax 956/717-8391; res 800/426-7866. www.hamptoninn.com.* 119 rms, 5 story. S $103; D $105; under 12 free. TV; cable (premium), VCR avail. Complimentary continental bkfst. Restaurant nearby. Ck-out noon. Meeting rms. Business servs avail. In-rm modem link. Pool; whirlpool. Some refrigerators. Cr cds: A, C, D, DS, ER, JCB, MC, V.

🄳 ⇌ 🔀 🔥 🆂🄲

★★ **HOLIDAY INN CIVIC CENTER.** *800 Garden St (78040). 956/727-5800; fax 956/727-0278; res 800/465-4329.* *www.holiday-inn.com.* 203 rms, 14 story. S, D $79-$84; each addl $10; suites $149; under 12 free. TV; cable (premium), VCR avail. Complimentary coffee in rms. Restaurant 6:30-10:30 am, 11 am-3 pm, 5-10:30 pm. Rm serv. Bar 5:30 pm-2 am; entertainment. Ck-out noon. Meeting rms. Business center. In-rm modem link. Bellhops. Coin lndry. Free airport transportation. Exercise equipt. Pool; whirlpool. Microwaves avail. Cr cds: A, D, DS, MC, V.

🄳 ⇌ 🏋 🔀 🔥 🏃

★★ **LA QUINTA INN.** *3610 Santa Ursula Ave (78041). 956/722-0511; fax 956/723-6642; res 800/531-5900. www.laquinta.com.* 152 rms, 2 story. S, D $80-$87; each addl $10; suites $110; under 18 free. Pet accepted. TV; cable (premium). Pool. Complimentary continental bkfst. Restaurant adj open 24 hrs. Ck-out noon. Business servs avail. In-rm modem link. Cr cds: A, D, DS, MC, V.

🄳 🐾 ⇌ 🔀 🔥

★ **RED ROOF INN.** *1006 W Calton Rd (78041). 956/712-0733; fax 956/712-4337; res 800/843-7663. www.redroof.com.* 150 rms, 4 story. S $49.99; D $54.99-$59.99; each addl $5; under 18 free; wkly rates. Pet accepted, some restrictions. TV; cable. Complimentary coffee in lobby. Restaurant adj open 24 hrs. Ck-out noon. Business servs avail. Pool. Microwaves avail. Cr cds: A, C, D, DS, MC, V.

🄳 🐾 ⇌ 🔥

Hotel

★★ **RIO GRANDE PLAZA.** *One S Main Ave (78040). 956/722-2411; fax 956/722-4578; toll-free 877/722-2411. www.venturastreet.com.* 207 rms, 15 story. S $82-$92, D $88-$98; each addl $6; under 15 free. Crib avail. Pet accepted, some restrictions. TV; cable (premium). Complimentary coffee in rms. Restaurant 7 am-10 pm. Bar 10 am-10 pm; weekends 7 am-midnight. Ck-out noon. Coin lndry. Meeting rms. Business servs avail. In-rm modem link. Free airport transportation. Refrigerators avail. On river, overlooking Mexico. Cr cds: A, C, DS, MC, V.

🄳 🐾 ⇌ 🏋 🔀 🔥

Longview

(C-7) *See also Marshall, Tyler*

Founded 1870 **Pop** 73,344 **Elev** 289 ft
Area code 903

What to See and Do

Gregg County Historical Museum.
Artifacts, photographs; displays on
timber, cotton, corn, farming, railroads, printing, early business, and
commerce; extensive military collection. Period rm settings incl bank
president's and dentist's offices, early
1900s parlor and bedrm, log cabin,
general store. Audiovisual presentation. Tours. (Tues-Sat; closed hols)
214 N Fredonia St, in Everett Building (1910), downtown. Phone
903/753-5840. ¢

LeTourneau University. (1946) 1,700
students. Engineering, business, technology, education, aviation, arts, and
sciences. Displays on campus contain
early scale models of earthmoving
equipment invented by R. G.
LeTourneau, founder of the university; also personal mementos. 2100 S
Mobberly Ave, Memorial Student
Center, third floor. Phone 903/753-
0231.

Longview Museum of Fine Arts. Collection of Southwestern and contemporary artists; changing exhibits;
lectures, workshops and classes.
(Tues-Fri, Sat afternoons; closed hols)
215 E Tyler St. Phone 903/753-8103.
FREE

Motels/Motor Lodges

★★ **BEST WESTERN.** *3119 Estes
Pkwy (75602). 903/758-0700; fax
903/758-8705; res 800/528-1234.
www.bestwestern.com.* 193 rms, 2-4
story. S, D $69-$75; each addl $7;
suites $77-$175; under 18 free;
wkend rates. Crib free. TV; cable
(premium). Indoor/outdoor pool;
whirlpool, poolside serv. Restaurant
6 am-2 pm, 5-10 pm. Rm serv. Private club 4 pm-2 am, closed Sun.
Ck-out 1 pm. Coin lndry. Meeting
rms. Business servs avail. In-rm
modem link. Sundries. Free airport

transportation. Game rm. Cr cds: A,
C, D, DS, MC, V.

★★ **LA QUINTA INN.** *502 S Access
Rd (75602). 903/757-3663; fax
903/753-3780; res 800/531-5900.
www.laquinta.com.* 105 rms, 2 story. S
$57-$60; D $60-$71; each addl $10;
under 18 free. Crib free. Pet accepted,
some restrictions. TV; cable (premium). Pool. Complimentary continental bkfst. Coffee in rms.
Restaurant adj open 24 hrs. Ck-out
noon. Meeting rms. Business servs
avail. In-rm modem link. Valet serv.
Cr cds: A, D, DS, MC, V.

Restaurants

★★ **JOHNNY CACE'S SEAFOOD &
STEAK.** *1501 E Marshall Ave (75601).
903/753-7691. www.johnnycaces.com.*
Hrs: 11 am-10 pm; Fri, Sat to 11 pm;
Sun, Mon from 3 pm. Closed some
major hols. Creole, Cajun menu. Bar.
Lunch $3.95-$8.95, dinner $7.25-
$32.97. Child's menu. Specializes in
fresh-shucked oysters, aged beef,
broiled fresh fish. Family-owned. Cr
cds: A, C, D, DS, ER, MC, V.

★ **PAPACITA'S MEXICAN RESTAU-
RANT.** *305 W Loop 281 (75605).
903/663-1700. www.papacitas.com.*
Hrs: 11 am-10 pm; Fri, Sat to 11 pm.
Closed some major hols. Mexican
menu. Bar. Lunch $4.50-$6.75, dinner $5.95-$12.95. Child's menu. Specializes in Mexican smoked meats,
seafood. Outdoor dining. Cr cds: A,
D, DS, MC, V.

Lubbock

(B-3) *See also Plainview*

Founded 1891 **Pop** 199,564
Elev 3,241 ft **Area code** 806

Information Convention & Tourism
Bureau, 1301 Broadway, Suite 200,
79401; 806/747-5232 or 800/692-
4035

Web www.lubbockhospitality.com

What to See and Do

Buddy Holly Statue and Walk of Fame. Larger-than-life bronze statue of the rock and roll pioneer and Lubbock native. Bronze plaques honor famous country and western musicians from the area. Sixth St and Ave Q. **FREE**

Buffalo Springs Lake Recreational Area. A 1,223-acre area with 225 acres of water. Waterskiing, fishing, boating, beach, water slides (Fri-Sun); picnicking, concession, hiking, volleyball, primitive and improved camping (tent and trailer sites; fee; two-wk max). Store. (Daily) 5 mi SE on FM 835. Phone 806/747-3353. ¢

Mackenzie Park. Approx 500 acres. Incl 36-hole golf course (fee). Picnicking, grills. Amusement area (fee); prairie dog town. (Daily) Off I-27, 4 mi E on Broadway to Park Rd 18. Phone 806/763-2719. **FREE**

Science Spectrum-Omnimax. Hands-on science and technology museum with over 100 exhibits, films, and demonstrations. Kidspace; Hall of flight. Traveling exhibits. Seventy-mm projection system with domed theater screen 58 ft in diameter. (Daily) 2579 S Loop 289, between University and Indiana aves. Phone 806/745-2525. ¢¢

Texas Tech University. (1923) and **Texas Tech University Health Sciences Center.** (1969) 25,573 students. One of Texas's four major state universities; 1,800-acre campus. It offers major sports and arts attractions, incl a noted Peter Hurd mural. University and Broadway aves. Phone 806/742-1299. On campus are

　Museum of Texas Tech University. Exhibits on art, natural sciences, and history of semiarid and arid lands. Moody Planetarium. (Tues-Sun; closed hols) 4th St and Indiana Ave. Phone 806/742-2490. **FREE** An outdoor addition to the museum is

　Ranching Heritage Center. This 14-acre restoration of 36 structures represents the development of ranching in the West. (Daily; closed hols) Phone 806/742-2482. **FREE**

　Lubbock Lake Landmark State Historic Park. This major archaeological excavation has yielded

evidence of ancient peoples and extinct animals. (Tues-Sun) 2 mi N of campus at Loop 289 and Landmark Dr. Phone 806/741-0306. ¢

Wineries.

　Cap-Rock. Modern facilities with look of Southwest mission utilize classic European wine grape varieties grown in own vineyard. Tasting rm, gift shop. Tours (on the hr and ½-hr). (Daily) 5 mi S on TX 87, ½ mi E on Woodrow Rd. Phone 806/863-2704. **FREE**

　Llano Estacado Winery. Founded in 1976, this was the first modern Texas winery. Grows own award-winning grapes. Tours, tastings (Daily). 5 mi S on TX 87, 3 mi E on FM 1585. Phone 806/745-2258. **FREE**

Special Events

Lubbock Arts Festival. South Plains Fairgrounds. Phone 806/744-2787. Three days Apr.

Buddy Holly Music Festival. Historic Depot District. Phone 806/767-2686. Early Sept.

Motels/Motor Lodges

★ ★ ★ **FOUR POINTS BY SHERATON.** *505 Ave Q (79401). 806/747-0171; fax 806/747-9243; res 800/325-3535. www.fourpoints.com/lubbock.* 141 rms, 6 story. S $69-$99; D $79-$109; each addl $10; suites $150-$225; under 18 free; higher rates football wkends. Crib free. TV; cable (premium). Indoor pool. Coffee in rms. Restaurant 6 am-10 pm. Bar 4 pm-midnight; closed Sun; pianist 5-8 pm. Ck-out noon. Meeting rms. Business servs avail. In-rm modem link. Valet serv. Free airport transportation. Exercise equipt. Refrigerator, minibar in suites. Atrium. Cr cds: A, C, D, DS, MC, V.

D ⊱ ⅄ ✈ ⊠ 🖾

★ ★ **HOLIDAY INN.** *3201 S Loop 289 (79423). 806/797-3241; fax 806/793-1203; res 800/465-4329. www.holiday-inn.com.* 202 rms, 2 story. S, D $60-$90; suites $80-$150; under 18 free. Crib free. Pet accepted, some restrictions. TV; cable (premium). Indoor pool; wading pool. Restaurant 6 am-10 pm. Rm serv. Bars 4 pm-midnight; Fri, Sat to 2 am. Ck-out noon. Coin lndry. Meeting rms. Business servs avail. In-rm modem link. Bellhops. Free airport transportation. Health club privileges. Cr cds: A, C, D, DS, MC, V.

⬜ 🔄 🏊 🔼 🔥

★★ **HOLIDAY INN HOTEL & TOWERS.** *801 Ave Q (79401). 806/763-1200; fax 806/763-2656; toll-free 800/765-0330. www.holidayinn.com.* 295 rms, 6 story. S $76; D $86; each addl $10; suites $90; under 19 free. Crib free. Pet accepted. TV; cable. Indoor pool; whirlpool, poolside serv. Restaurant 6 am-10 pm. Bar 4 pm-2 am; Sun noon-midnight. Ck-out noon. Coin lndry. Convention facilities. Business servs avail. Free airport transportation. Exercise equipt, sauna. Cr cds: A, D, DS, MC, V.

⬜ 🔄 🏊 🧍 🔼 🔥

★★ **LA QUINTA INN.** *601 Ave Q (79401). 806/763-9441; fax 806/747-9325; toll-free 800/531-5900. www.laquinta.com.* 137 rms, 2 story. S $64-$76; D $69-$81; each addl $7; under 18 free. Crib free. Pet accepted. TV; cable. Pool. Complimentary continental bkfst. Restaurant adj open 24 hrs. Ck-out noon. Business servs avail. In-rm modem link. Cr cds: A, C, D, DS, MC, V.

🔄 🏊 🔼 🔥 SC

Hotels

★★ **ASHMORE INN AND SUITES.** *4019 S Loop 289 (79423). 806/785-0060; fax 806/785-6001; res 800/785-0061. www.travelweb.com.* 100 rms, 2 story, 16 suites. S $70-$80; D $75-$87; each addl $5; suites $82-$87; under 12 free; higher rates special events. Crib free. TV; cable (premium). Complimentary continental bkfst. Complimentary coffee in rms. Restaurant adj open 24 hrs. Ck-out noon. Meeting rms. Business servs avail. In-rm modem link. Bellhops. Coin lndry. Free airport transportation. Exercise equipt. Heated pool; whirlpool. Refrigerators, microwaves. Some balconies. Cr cds: A, C, D, DS, MC, V.

⬜ 🏊 🧍 ✈ 🔥 SC

★★ **LUBBOCK INN.** *3901 19th St (79410). 806/792-5181; fax 806/792-1319; toll-free 800/545-8226. www.lubbockinn.com.* 119 rms, 3 story. S, D

$45-$75; each addl $8; studio rms $90; under 12 free. Crib free. TV; cable (premium), VCR avail. Heated pool; wading pool. Restaurant 6 am-11 pm. Rm serv. Bar 10-2 am; Sun 1 pm-midnight. Ck-out noon. Meeting rms. Business servs avail. In-rm modem link. Bellhops. Sundries. Free airport, bus depot transportation. Bathrm phones; some refrigerators. Cr cds: A, DS, MC, V.

⬜ 🏊 ✈ 🔼 🔥 SC

All Suite

★★★ **BARCELONA COURT.** *5215 Loop 289 S (79424). 806/794-5353; fax 806/798-9398; toll-free 800/222-1122. www.barceloncourt.com.* 161 rms, 3 story. S, D $55-$70; each addl $5-$10; wkend rates. Crib free. TV; cable (premium). Heated pool. Complimentary full bkfst. Ck-out 11 am. Coin lndry. Meeting rms. In-rm modem link. Sundries. Free airport transportation. Balconies. Cr cds: A, MC, V.

⬜ 🏊 ✈ 🔼 🔥 SC

Extended Stay

★★ **RESIDENCE INN BY MARRIOTT.** *2551 S Loop 289 (79423). 806/745-1963; fax 806/748-1183; toll-free 800/331-3131. www.residenceinn.com.* 80 kit. suites, 2 story. S $87; D $87-$125; wkly rates. Pet accepted, $75. TV; cable (premium). Heated pool; whirlpools. Complimentary continental bkfst. Ck-out noon. Coin lndry. Meeting rms. Business servs avail. In-rm modem link. Valet serv. Free airport transportation. Refrigerators. Private patios, balconies. Picnic tables, grills. Cr cds: A, C, D, DS, JCB, MC, V.

⬜ 🏊 🔼 🔥 SC

Restaurants

★★ **CHEZ SUZETTE.** *4423 50th St (79414). 806/795-6796. www.chezsuzette.com.* Hrs: 11:30 am-2 pm, 5:30-10 pm; Fri to 10:30 pm; Sat 5:30-10:30 pm. Closed Sun; Jan 1, Thanksgiving, Dec 25. Res accepted. French, Italian menu. Bar. Lunch $4.50-$8.95, dinner $7.95-$15.95. Child's menu. Specialties: chateaubriand, snapper in puff pastry. Cr cds: A, D, DS, MC, V.

⬜ 🔼

★ **GARDSKI'S** . *2009 Broadway (79401). 806/744-2391. www.gardskis.com.* Hrs: 11 am-11 pm; Fri, Sat to midnight. Closed Thanksgiving, Dec 25. Lunch, dinner $3.95-$10.95. Specializes in gourmet hamburgers, fully aged steak, sandwiches. In 50-yr-old mansion, garden decor. Cr cds: A, C, D, DS, ER, MC, V.
⊟

★★ **HARRIGAN'S.** *3801 50th St (79413). 806/792-4648.* Specializes in prime rib. Hrs: 11 am-2 pm, 5-10 pm; Fri, Sat to 11 pm. Bar. Lunch, dinner $6-$21. Early 1920's atmosphere. Cr cds: A, C, D, DS, MC, V.
D ⊟

★ **ORLANDO'S.** *2402 Ave Q (79405). 806/747-5998. www.orlandos.com.* Hrs: 11 am-10 pm; Fri, Sat to 11 pm. Closed some major hols. Italian menu. Bar. Lunch, dinner $4.99-$15.99. Child's menu. Specialties: lasagne, fettucine, tortellini. Cr cds: A, C, D, DS, ER, MC, V.
D SC ⊟

★★ **SANTA FE.** *401 Ave Q (79401). 806/763-6114.* Hrs: 11 am-10 pm; Fri, Sat to 10:30 pm. Closed Jan 1, Thanksgiving, Dec 25. Mexican, Amer menu. Bar 4:30 pm-midnight; closed Sun. Lunch, dinner $4.75-$13.95. Child's menu. Specializes in Mexican cuisine. Cr cds: A, D, MC, V.
D SC ⊟

Lufkin

(C-7) *See also Nacogdoches*

Settled 1881 **Pop** 32,709
Area code 409 **Zip** 75901
Information Visitor & Convention Bureau, PO Box 1606; 409/634-6644

What to See and Do

Ellen Trout Park Zoo. More than 500 species of birds, reptiles, mammals; miniature train rides (summer, daily; rest of yr, wkends; fee); lake, fishing; picnicking, playground. (Daily) Loop 287 N at Martin Luther King Dr, 2 mi N. Phone 409/633-0399. ¢

Museum of East Texas. Explores visual arts and history through changing exhibits, lectures, performances, multidisciplinary programs, and films. (Tues-Sun; closed hols) 503 N Second St. Phone 409/639-4434. **FREE**

National Forests.

Angelina. Approx 153,000 acres of rolling, forested sandhills; Sam Rayburn Reservoir (see JASPER) bisects the forest. Swimming, fishing, boating (ramps); hunting, hiking, picnicking, camping (fee). Audio tape tour (free) avail at ranger station. Fees are charged at recreation sites. 21 mi E on TX 103 or 16 mi SE on US 69. Phone 409/639-8620.

Davy Crockett. Ratcliff Lake is in the forest. Approx 163,000 acres. Incl Big Slough Wilderness Area. Swimming, fishing (bass, bream, catfish), boating; hunting (deer), hiking, picnicking, concession, camping (fee) in shortleaf-loblolly pinewoods. Fees charged at recreation sites. Free audio tape tour of Ratcliff Lake and surrounding forest area avail from camp concessionaire. 17 mi W on TX 94 or TX 103. District Ranger Office. Phone 409/544-2046.

Forest Information. A visitor guide to the forests may be obtained from Forest Supervisor, 701 N First St, Lufkin. Phone 409/639-8501.

Texas Forestry Museum. Artifacts from early days of Texas logging and timber industry incl logging train, working sawmill steam engine, 100-ft fire tower, photographs, and memorabilia. (Daily; closed hols) 1905 Atkinson Dr. Phone 409/632-9535. **FREE**

Motels/Motor Lodges

★ **DAYS INN.** *2130 S 1st St (75904). 936/639-3301; fax 936/634-4266; toll-free 800/329-7466. www.daysinn.com.* 126 rms, 2 story. S $46; D $42-$47; each addl $5; suites $65-$75; under 18 free; wkend rates. Crib free. Pet accepted, some restrictions. TV; cable (premium). Pool; wading pool. Complimentary continental bkfst. Restaurant 6 am-2 pm, 5-9 pm; closed Sun. Rm serv. Bar 5 pm-midnight, Sat to 1 am, closed Sun. Ck-out noon. Coin lndry. Meeting rms. Business servs avail. Some refrigerators. Whirlpool in some suites. Cr cds: A, D, DS, MC, V.

★★ **HOLIDAY INN LUFKIN.** *4306 S First St (75901). 936/639-3333; fax 936/639-3382; toll-free 888/639-3382. www.holiday-inn.com.* 102 rms, 2 story. S $66; D $73; each addl $7; suites $65-$75; under 19 free; wkend rates (min stay required). Crib free. Pet accepted, some restrictions; $5. TV; cable (premium). Pool; poolside serv. Restaurant 6 am-2 pm, 5-10 pm. Rm serv. Bar. Ck-out noon. Coin lndry. Meeting rms. Business servs avail. In-rm modem link. Sundries. Valet serv. Free airport transportation. Health club privileges. Some refrigerators; minibar in suites. Cr cds: A, D, DS, MC, V.

★★ **LA QUINTA INN.** *2119 S 1st St (75901). 936/634-3351; fax 936/634-9475; res 800/531-5900. www. laquinta.com.* 106 rms, 2 story. S $51-$58; D $58-$65; each addl $7; suites $67; under 18 free. Crib free. Pet accepted, some restrictions. TV; cable. Pool. Complimentary continental bkfst. Restaurant adj. Ck-out noon. Meeting rms. Business servs avail. In-rm modem link. Valet serv. Cr cds: A, C, D, DS, MC, V.

Marfa

See also Alpine

Founded 1883 **Pop** 2,121 **Elev** 4,688 ft **Area code** 915 **Zip** 79843

Information Chamber of Commerce, 200 S Abbot, PO Box 635; 915/729-4942 or 800/650-9696

Web www.alpinetexas.com

Texas's highest incorporated city, Marfa is surrounded by unspoiled mountain country, rising to more than 8,000 feet in some areas. Marfa is the best starting point to travel the highway to Mexico and Chihuahua City; the Camino del Rio (River Road) to Big Bend National Park (see); and the Scenic Loop through the Davis Mountains. It offers various outdoor recreation activities and the puzzling "Marfa mystery lights," which have remained a mystery for more than 100 years. The Presidio County Courthouse (1886) and El Paisano Hotel (1930) are notable landmarks.

With mild winters and cool summers, the area offers abundant opportunities for camping, hunting, hiking, picnicking, and golfing.

What to See and Do

Chinati Foundation. Museum is spread over 15 buildings of the former army post Fort D. A. Russell. Museum houses permanent collections of Donald Judd, John Chamberlain, and others; temporary exhibits. (Thurs-Sat or by appt) 1 Calvary Row. Phone 915/729-4362. ¢¢¢

Special Event

Marfa Lights Festival. Labor Day wkend. Phone 800/650-9696.

Marshall

(C-8) *See also Longview*

Founded 1841 **Pop** 23,935 **Elev** 412 ft **Area code** 903 **Zip** 75670

Information Chamber of Commerce, 213 W Austin, PO Box 520; 903/935-7868

Web www.marshall-chamber.com

What to See and Do

Caddo Lake State Park. Approx 32,000 acres incl bayous and cypress swamp. Swimming, waterskiing, fishing, boating (ramp, rentals); nature and hiking trails, picnicking, playground, screened shelters, improved campsites, RV facilities, cabins (dump station). Standard fees. (Daily) 14 mi NE on TX 43, then ½ mi E on FM 2198. Phone 903/679-3351. ¢

Harrison County Historical Museum. Business, transportation, and communication displays; medical items; Victorian needlecraft; pressed glass, toys, Caddo Indian artifacts, pioneer relics. Memorabilia collections of

Lady Bird Johnson, journalist Bill Moyers, Olympic gold medalist George Foreman, and others. Military Room, Ethnic Group Heritage Room, Caddo Lake Room. Art gallery. (Tues-Sat; closed hols) In the old Ginocchio Hotel, a few blocks north of Hwy 80 on Washington. Phone 903/938-2680. ¢

Marshall Pottery. Twenty shops, restaurants, RV park. Tours (by appt). (Daily) US 59 to FM 31. Phone 903/938-9201. **FREE**

Michelson Museum of Art. Features paintings of Russian-born, post-impressionist Leo Michelson; special exhibits. (Tues-Sun; closed hols) Southwestern Bell Building, 216 N Bolivar. Phone 903/935-9480. ¢

T. C. Lindsey & Company. General store, in continuous operation since 1847; antiques, rural relics on display. Setting for two Walt Disney productions. (Mon-Sat; closed hols) 2 mi W of Louisiana state line via I-20, 2 mi N on FM 134 in Jonesville. Phone 903/687-3382. **FREE**

Special Events

Stagecoach Days Celebration. Stagecoach rides, gunfighters, arts and crafts. Third wkend May. Phone 903/935-7868.

Fireant Festival. Second wkend Oct. Phone 903/935-7868.

Wonderland of Lights. Christmas festival. Courthouse, entire neighborhoods decorated by 7½ million lights. Thanksgiving-Dec. Phone 903/935-7868.

Motel/Motor Lodge

★★ **GUEST INN.** *100 W I-20 (75672). 903/927-1718; fax 903/927-1747.* 46 rms, 2 story. S $45-$50; D $50-$60; each addl $4; suites $65-$75; under 16 free. Crib free. Pet accepted. TV; cable (premium). Pool. Complimentary continental bkfst. Restaurant adj 10 am-9 pm. Ck-out 11 am. Sundries. Valet serv. Some refrigerators. Cr cds: A, C, D, DS, MC, V.

Mason

See also Fredericksburg, Kerrville

Pop 2,134 **Elev** 1,550 ft
Area code 915 **Zip** 76856
Information Mason County Chamber of Commerce, PO Box 156; 915/347-5758
Web www.masontxcoc.com

What to See and Do

Eckert James River Bat Cave Preserve. One of America's largest known Mexican free-tailed bat colonies and the only bat maternity cave owned by a conservation agency. Visitors are instructed on how best to view the colony without disturbing the bats (May-Oct, Thurs-Sun eves). Preserve (all yr). Phone 915/347-5970. **FREE**

Fort Mason. Reconstructed four-rm officers' quarters on crest of Post Hill. Original foundations and stone used in reconstruction. Robert E. Lee's last command before the Civil War. Picnicking. (Daily) Post Hill St. **FREE**

Mason County Museum. Historical items housed in old schoolhouse (1870) built with stone from Fort Mason. (Mon-Fri or by appt) 300 Moody St. **FREE**

Rocks & Minerals. Collectors from all over the nation come to this area of ancient geologic outcropings for variety of rocks and minerals, especially topaz, the state gemstone.

McAllen

(G-5) See also Edinburg, Harlingen, Mission

Pop 106,414 **Elev** 124 ft
Area code 956
Information Chamber of Commerce, 10 N Broadway, PO Box 790, 78505; 956/682-2871 or 800/250-2591
Web www.mcallen.org

What to See and Do

McAllen International Museum. Art and natural science exhibits and programs. (Tues-Sun; closed hols) Free admission Thurs eves. Bicentennial Blvd at 1900 Nolana Loop. Phone 956/682-1564. ¢¢

McAllen Nature Center. Cactus gardens, nature trails, bird-watching. (Daily) 2½ mi W on TX 83 Business. Phone 956/682-1517. **FREE**

Reynosa, Mexico. (Pop 400,000) Parking area on US side of bridge. (For Border Crossing Regulations, see MAKING THE MOST OF YOUR TRIP.) Reynosa is a picturesque border town, well worth a leisurely visit. The plaza has a beautiful renovated church with high belfries and a soaring arched façade. There are nightclubs; several restaurants serve game dinners—venison and wild turkey. Dancing to Mexican music outdoors or indoors; occasional bullfights. *The Mercado* (market) tests visitors' bargaining skills. 8 mi S on TX 336.

Santa Ana National Wildlife Refuge. More than 2,000 acres of forest and lakes incl 450 plant species, 380 species of North American and Mexican birds, 12 mi of hiking trails, and 7 mi of wildlife auto tour road (avail when tram tour is not in operation). Interpretive tram tour; photo blinds; visitor center. Nature trail accessible to wheelchairs and the visually impaired. (Daily; closed Jan 1, Thanksgiving, Dec 25) 8 mi E on US 83, then 7 mi S on FM 907 and ¼ mi E on US 281. Contact Refuge Manager, Rte 2, Box 202-A, Alamo 78516. Phone 956/784-7500. Tram tour ¢¢

Virgin de San Juan del Valle Shrine. Original statue of the Virgin, rescued from flames, now stands in a new shrine. E on US 83, between McAllen and San Juan. Phone 956/787-0033.

Special Event

Candlelight Posada. Archer Park. Citywide Christmas celebration. Blends traditions of Mexico with those of America. First wkend Dec. Phone 956/682-2871.

Motels/Motor Lodges

★★ **COURTYARD BY MARRIOTT AIRPORT.** *2131 S 10th St (78503). 956/668-7800; fax 956/668-7801; toll-free 888/668-7808. www.courtyard. com.* 110 rms, 3 story. S, D $78-$84; each addl $10; suites $110-$225; under 17 free; wkend rates. Crib free. TV; cable (premium). Heated pool; whirlpool. Complimentary coffee in rms. Restaurant 6:30 am-10 pm; Sat, Sun to midnight. Bar 4-10 pm; closed Sun. Meeting rms. Coin lndry. Business servs avail. In-rm modem link. Free airport transportation. Exercise equipt. Refrigerator in suites. Balconies. Cr cds: A, D, DS, MC, V.
D ➰ ⌨ 🏌 ✈ 🏊 🔥 SC

★★ **DRURY INN.** *612 W Expy 83 (78501). 956/687-5100; res 800/378-7946. www.druryinn.com.* 89 units. S $65-$75; D $75-$80; each addl $10; under 18 free. Crib free. Pet accepted, some restrictions. TV; cable (premium), VCR avail. Pool. Complimentary continental bkfst. Restaurant adj. Ck-out noon. Meeting rm. Business servs avail. In-rm modem link. Refrigerator in suites. Cr cds: A, C, D, DS, MC, V.
D ➰ ⌨ ✈ 🏊 🔥

★★★ **FOUR POINTS BY SHERATON MCALLEN.** *2721 S 10th St (78503). 956/984-7900; fax 956/984-7997; res 800/325-3535.* 148 rms, 5 story. S $79; D $89; each addl $10; under 13 free; wkend rates. Crib free. TV; cable (premium). Pool; poolside serv, whirlpool. Coffee in rms. Restaurant 5:30 am-11 pm. Bar 11-1 am. Ck-out noon. Meeting rms. Business servs avail. In-rm modem link. Lighted tennis. Free airport transportation. Exercise equipt. Balconies. Cr cds: A, D, DS, MC, V.
D 🏌 ⌨ 🏌 ✈ 🏊 🔥

★★ **HAMPTON INN.** *300 W Expy 83 (78501). 956/682-4900; fax 956/682-6823; res 800/426-7866. www.hamptoninn.com.* 91 rms, 4 story. S $68-$74; D $78-$84; under 18 free. Crib free. Pet accepted. TV; cable. Pool. Complimentary continental bkfst. Restaurant adj. Ck-out noon. Business servs avail. In-rm modem link. Near airport. Cr cds: A, C, D, ER, MC, V.
D ➰ ⌨ ✈ 🏊 🔥

★★ **HOLIDAY INN-CIVIC CENTER.** *200 W Expy US 83 (78501). 956/686-2471; fax 956/682-7609; res 800/465-4329. www.holiday-inn.com.* 173 rms, 2 story. S $78; D $88; each addl $10; under 18 free. Crib free. Pet accepted, some restrictions. TV; cable (premium), VCR avail. 2 pools, 1 indoor; whirlpool. Coffee in rms. Restaurant 6 am-10 pm. Rm serv. Bar noon-2 am; Sun to midnight. Ck-out noon. Coin lndry. Meeting rms. Business servs avail. In-rm modem link. Bellhops. Free airport transportation. Exercise equipt; sauna. Game rm. Rec rm. Cr cds: A, C, D, DS, ER, JCB, MC, V.

★★ **HOLIDAY INN EXPRESS.** *2000 S 10th St (78503). 956/686-1741; fax 956/682-7187; toll-free 800/465-4329. www.holiday-inn.com.* 150 units. No elvtr. S $62-$79; D $65-$89; each addl $10; under 18 free. Crib free. TV; cable (premium). Pool. Complimentary continental bkfst. Complimentary coffee in rms. Ck-out noon. Meeting rm. Business servs avail. Bellhops. Coin lndry. Free airport transportation. Exercise equipt. Some refrigerators. Cr cds: A, D, DS, MC, V.

★ **LA QUINTA INN.** *1100 S 10th St (78501). 956/687-1101; fax 956/687-9265; toll-free 800/687-6667. www. laquinta.com.* 120 rms, 3 story. S $59-$65; D $61-$66; each addl $5; under 18 free. Crib free. Pet accepted. TV; cable (premium). Pool. Complimentary continental bkfst. Restaurant adj open 24 hrs. Bar 11-2 am. Ck-out noon. Meeting rm. Business servs avail. In-rm modem link. Free airport, bus depot transportation. Health club privileges. Convention Center adj. Cr cds: A, C, D, DS, MC, V.

Hotel

★★★ **RENAISSANCE CASA DE PALMAS.** *101 N Main St (78501). 956/631-1101; fax 956/631-7934; toll-free 800/537-8483. www.casadepalmas. com.* 158 rms, 3 story. S $59-$69; D $69-$79; each addl $10; suites $89-$160; under 12 free. Crib free. TV; cable (premium). Pool. Complimentary full bkfst. Restaurant. Bar 11 am-10 pm. Ck-out noon. Meeting rms. Business servs avail. In-rm modem link. Free covered parking. Free airport transportation. Tennis privileges. Golf privileges. Exercise equipt. Some

refrigerators, wet bars. Balconies. Cr cds: A, C, D, DS, JCB, MC, V.

All Suite

★★★ **EMBASSY SUITES.** *1800 S 2nd St (78503). 956/686-3000; fax 956/631-8362; toll-free 800/366-2229. www.embassy-suites.com.* 224 suites, 9 story. S $125; D $140; each addl $15; under 18 free. Crib free. TV; cable (premium). Indoor pool; whirlpool. Complimentary bkfst; evening refreshments. Coffee in rms. Restaurant 11 am-2 pm, 5-10 pm. Bar 11-1 am; entertainment. Ck-out noon. Meeting rms. Business servs avail. In-rm modem link. Gift shop. Free airport transportation. Exercise equipt; sauna. Health club privileges. Refrigerators. Balconies. Cr cds: A, C, D, DS, JCB, MC, V.

Restaurants

★ **JOHNNY'S MEXICAN FOOD.** *1010 Houston St S (78501). 956/686-9061.* Hrs: 9 am-10:30 pm; Fri, Sat to midnight. Res accepted. Mexican, Amer menu. Bar. Bkfst $2.95-$3.95, lunch $4.95-$5.95, dinner $4.95-$14.95. Child's menu. Specializes in char-broiled dishes. Strolling musicians. Family-owned. Cr cds: A, C, D, DS, MC, V.

★★ **SANTA FE STEAK.** *1918 S 10th St (78501). 956/630-2331.* Hrs: 5-10 pm; Fri, Sat to 11 pm. Closed Sun, some major hols. Southwestern menu. Dinner $9.95-$19.95. Specialties: baked orange roughy, steak Oscar. Entertainment. Outdoor dining. Cr cds: A, DS, MC, V.

★ **SPANISH ROOM.** *101 N Main St (78501). 956/631-1101.* Hrs: 11 am-2 pm, 5-10 pm. Res accepted. Mexican, Amer menu. Bar from 5 pm. Lunch, dinner $5.95-$14.95. Specialties: fajitas, tampiquena platter. Salad bar. Covered parking. Outdoor dining. Spanish Colonial-style decor. Cr cds: A, D, DS, MC, V.

McKinney

(B-6) *See also Dallas, Denton, Greenville, Sherman*

Founded 1848 **Pop** 54,369 **Elev** 632 ft
Area code 972
Information Chamber of Commerce, 1801 W Louisiana St, 75069; 972/542-0163
Web www.mckinneytx.org/chamber

What to See and Do

Heard Natural Science Museum and Wildlife Sanctuary. Natural history exhibits of north central Texas; marine life, rock, and mineral displays; historical exhibit of museum founder Bessie Heard (1886-1988); live animals; changing art shows; bird of prey rehabilitation facility; a 274-acre sanctuary along Wilson Creek incl bottomland, upland, woodland, and prairie; guided and self-guided tours of nature trails. Free museum and sanctuary admission Mon. (Daily; closed hols) Exit 38 E off US 75 to TX 5 S, follow signs (FM 1378). Phone 972/562-5566. ¢

Lavon Lake. Swimming, waterskiing, fishing, boating; hiking, horseback trail, picnicking, camping (tent and trailer sites). Some fees. (Daily) 15 mi E on US 380, then 10 mi S on TX 78. Phone 972/442-5711. **FREE**

Special Events

Wild West Fest. Downtown Sq. Antiques, crafts, entertainment. First Sat Oct. Phone 972/562-6880.

Heritage Guild's Christmas Tour of Homes. First wkend Dec. Phone 888/649-8499.

Midland

(C-3) *See also Big Spring, Odessa*

Pop 94,996 **Elev** 2,779 ft
Area code 915
Information Chamber of Commerce/Convention & Visitors Bureau, 109 N Main, PO Box 1890, 79702; 915/683-3381 or 800/624-6435
Web www.visitmidlandtx.com

What to See and Do

Commemorative Air Force and American Airpower Heritage Museum. Dedicated to the preservation of WWII combat aircraft. Planes on display change every three months. (Daily; closed Thanksgiving, Dec 25) (See SPECIAL EVENTS). 9600 Wright Dr, at Midland International Airport. Phone 915/563-1000. ¢¢

Haley Library and History Center. Rare books, archives, and Western art. Emphasis on range country and cattle industry history in Texas and the Southwest. Incl original mission bell from the Alamo, cast in 1722. Research rm. (Mon-Fri; closed hols) 1805 W Indiana. Phone 915/682-5785. **FREE**

Midland Community Theatre. Eight dramas, comedies, or musicals annually, incl special summer features. (Thurs-Sun) 2000 W Wadley Ave. Phone 915/682-2544. ¢¢¢

Museum of the Southwest. Former residence (1934) of Texas oil man Fred Turner houses permanent collection of Southwestern art and anthropology; traveling exhibits on display; children's museum with hands-on exhibits. Marian Blakemore Planetarium sky programs (Fri eves; fee). (Tues-Sun; closed hols) 1705 W Missouri Ave. Phone 915/683-2882. **FREE**

Permian Basin Petroleum Museum. Animated exhibits explain the history and development of the oil industry and the Permian Basin; walk-through diorama of ocean floor as it was 230 million yrs ago; oil well blowout action display; collection of paintings of west Texas and southeastern New Mexico. World's largest collection of antique drilling and production equipt. (Daily; closed hols) 1500 I-20 W, exit 136. Phone 915/683-4403. ¢¢

Special Events

Mex-Tex Menudo. Centennial Plaza. Chili and fajita cook-off. June. Phone 915/682-2960.

Summer Mummers. Yucca Theatre (1927), 208 N Colorado St. Topical satire staged in the manner of 1890s melodrama. Fri-Sat, June-Labor Day. Phone 915/682-4111.

Commemorative Airforce Airshow. Midland International Airport. First wkend Oct. Phone 915/563-1000.

Motels/Motor Lodges

★ ★ **BEST INN & SUITES.** *3100 W Wall St (79701). 915/699-4144; fax 915/699-7639. www.bestinn.com.* 200 rms, 3 story. S, D $59-$79; under 12 free. Crib $6. Pet accepted, some restrictions. TV; cable (premium). Indoor pool. Restaurant 6-9 am, 5-9 pm. Rm serv. Bar 4 pm-midnight. Ck-out noon. Meeting rms. Business servs avail. Free airport transportation. Exercise equipt. Cr cds: A, C, D, DS, MC, V.

⬛ 🐾 ➰ 🛏 ✈ ➰ 🐾 SC

★ **DAYS INN.** *1003 S Midkiff Ave (79701). 915/697-3155; fax 915/699-2017; toll-free 800/329-7466. www.daysinn.com.* 182 kit. units, 2 story. 1-bedrm $54-$65; 2-bedrm $80-$108. Crib free. Pet accepted, some restrictions; $75 deposit. TV; cable (premium). Heated pool; whirlpool. Complimentary continental bkfst. Restaurant nearby. Ck-out noon. Coin lndry. Business servs avail. Airport transportation. Cr cds: A, C, D, DS, MC, V.

⬛ 🐾 ➰ ➰ 🐾 SC

★ ★ ★ **HOLIDAY INN HOTEL & SUITES.** *6201 E Business Loop 20 (79762). 915/362-2311; fax 915/362-9810; res 800/465-4329. www.holiday-inn.com.* 244 rms, 3 story. S $64-$69; D $74-$79; suites $87-$150. Crib free. Pet accepted, some restrictions. TV; cable. Indoor/outdoor pool; whirlpool, poolside serv. Restaurant 6 am-9 pm. Rm serv. Bar 4-11 pm. Coin lndry. Business servs avail. In-rm modem link. Bellhops. Valet serv. Free airport, bus depot transportation. Putting green. Exercise equipt; sauna. Microwave in suites. Cr cds: A, C, D, DS, MC, V.

⬛ 🐾 ➰ 🛏 ➰ 🐾

★ ★ **LA QUINTA.** *4130 W Wall Ave (79703). 915/697-9900; fax 915/689-0617; res 800/687-6667. www.laquinta.com.* 146 rms, 2 story. S $55; D $60; under 18 free. Crib free. Pet accepted. TV; cable (premium). Pool. Complimentary continental bkfst.

Ck-out noon. Coin lndry. Business servs avail. Valet serv. Cr cds: A, D, DS, MC, V.

➰ 🐾 SC 🐾 ➰

★ ★ **MIDLAND HOLIDAY INN.** *4300 W Wall St (79703). 915/697-3181; fax 915/694-7754; res 800/465-4329. www.holiday-inn.com.* 252 rms, 2 story, 31 suites. S, D $69; each addl $10; suites $132-$159; under 18 free. Crib free. Pet accepted. TV; cable (premium). Indoor pool; whirlpool. Restaurant 6 am-9 pm. Rm serv. Bar 4-11 pm. Ck-out noon. Coin lndry. Meeting rms. Business center. Free airport transportation. Exercise equipt; sauna. Cr cds: A, C, D, DS, JCB, MC, V.

⬛ 🐾 ➰ 🛏 ✈ ➰ 🐾 SC 🛏

★ ★ **RAMADA INN AIRPORT.** *3312 S County Rd 1276 (79706). 915/561-8000; fax 915/561-5243; res 800/272-6232. www.ramada.com.* 97 rms, 3 story. S $50-$115; D $50-$125; each addl $8; under 16 free; wkend rates. Crib free. TV; cable (premium). Pool. Complimentary coffee in rms. Restaurant 6 am-9 pm. Bar 4-11 pm. Ck-out noon. Meeting rm. Business center. In-rm modem link. Bellhops. Sundries. Coin lndry. Free airport transportation. Exercise equipt. Refrigerators avail. Cr cds: A, C, D, DS, ER, JCB, MC, V.

⬛ ➰ 🛏 ✈ ➰ 🐾 SC 🛏

Hotel

★ ★ ★ **HILTON.** *117 W Wall St (79701). 915/683-6131; fax 915/683-0958; res 800/725-6131. www.hilton.com.* 249 rms, 2-11 story. S, D $125; each addl $10; suites $190-$265; wkend rates. Crib $10. Pet accepted, some restrictions; $100 refundable. TV; cable (premium), VCR avail. Pool; whirlpool, poolside serv. Restaurant 6:30 am-10 pm. Bar 4 pm-midnight; Sun from 7 pm. Ck-out noon. Meeting rms. Business servs avail. In-rm modem link. Gift shop. Free airport transportation. Exercise equipt. Health club privileges. Luxury level. Cr cds: A, C, D, DS, MC, V.

⬛ 🐾 🍴 ➰ 🛏 ➰ 🐾

Restaurants

★ **BLUE STAR INN.** *2501 W Wall (79701). 915/682-4231.* Hrs: 11 am-2 pm, 5-10 pm; Sat, Sun 11 am-10 pm. Chinese, Amer menu. A la carte entrees: lunch, dinner $3.50-$10.95. Parking. Family-owned. Cr cds: A, C, D, DS, ER, MC, V.

D ⌑

★ **LUIGI'S ITALIAN.** *111 N Big Spring St (79701). 915/683-6363.* Hrs: 11 am-10 pm; Sat 5-10 pm. Closed Sun; major hols. Res accepted. Bar. Lunch, dinner $4-$15. Child's menu. Specialties: lasagne, fettucine, spaghetti. Family-owned. Cr cds: A, C, D, DS, ER, MC, V.

D SC ⌑

★ **SHOGUN.** *4610 N Garfield (79705). 915/687-0734.* Hrs: 5-10 pm. Japanese menu. Bar. A la carte entrees: dinner $9.95-$21.25. Child's menu. Specializes in chicken teriyaki, seafood, steak. Oriental decor. Cr cds: A, D, DS, MC, V.

D ⌑

★ **TAMPICO SPANISH INN.** *2411 W Wall (79701). 915/682-5074.* Hrs: 11 am-2 pm, 5-10 pm; Sat 11 am-10 pm; Sun 11 am-4 pm. Closed Mon; July 4. Res accepted. Mexican, Amer menu. Lunch $3-$7.50, dinner $5-$9.25. Child's menu. Specialty: flautas. Own baking. Mexican decor. Family-owned. Cr cds: A, DS, MC, V.

D ⌑

★ ★ **VENEZIA.** *2101 W Wadley Ave #20 (79705). 915/687-0900.* Hrs: 11 am-1:45 pm, 5-10:15 pm; Sat from 5 pm. Closed Sun; major hols. Res accepted. Wine, beer. Lunch $5.25-$8, dinner $6-$18. Specializes in fresh seafood. Parking. Outdoor patio dining. 2 dining areas; European decor; large fireplace. Cr cds: A, C, D, DS, ER, MC, V.

D ⌑

Mineral Wells

(B-5) *See also Fort Worth, Weatherford*

Pop 16,946 **Elev** 911 ft **Area code** 940 **Zip** 76067

Information Chamber of Commerce, PO Box 1408; 940/325-2557 or 800/252-MWTX

What to See and Do

Swimming, water sports, fishing, boating. On several nearby lakes and the Brazos River. Lake Mineral Wells State Park, 4 mi E; Lake Palo Pinto, 20 mi SW; Possum Kingdom Lake, 25 mi NW.

Special Event

Palo Pinto County Livestock Association Rodeo. Second wk May. Phone 940/325-2557.

Mission

(G-5) *See also Edinburg, McAllen*

Pop 45,408 **Elev** 134 ft **Area code** 956 **Zip** 78572

Information Chamber of Commerce, 220 E 9th St; 956/585-2727 or 800/580-2700

Web www.missionchamber.com

What to See and Do

Bentsen-Rio Grande Valley State Park. Approx 600 acres. Fishing, boat ramp; nature and hiking trails, picnicking, playground, camping, tent and trailer sites (dump station). Standard fees. (Daily) 3 mi W on US 83, then 3 mi S on FM 2062 to Park Rd 43. Phone 956/585-1107. ¢¢

La Lomita Farms State Historic Site. Spanish-style structure once used as novitiate for oblate priests now houses exhibits. (Mon-Fri) 3¾ mi S on FM 1016. Phone 956/581-2725. **FREE** Nearby is

La Lomita Mission. One of several missions established. Tiny (12 by 25 ft) chapel, still used as place of worship by locals. Built by oblate priests in 1845; town of Mission is named for chapel. 3 mi S on FM 1016. Phone 956/580-8760.

Los Ebanos International Ferry. Only hand-drawn ferry across US border. (Daily, weather permitting) 17 mi W via US 83. ¢

Special Events

Texas Citrus Fiesta. Phone 956/585-9724. First wk Feb.

Texas Border Botanical & Butterfly Festival. Nature expo, seminars, butterflying field trips, park and garden tours, children's activities. Three days late Mar. Phone 956/585-2727.

Restaurant

★ **FERRELL'S PIT.** *2224 E Business Hwy 83 (78572).* 956/585-2381. Hrs: 11 am-8:30 pm. Closed Tues. Mexican, Amer menu. Lunch, dinner $3.75-$8.50. Specializes in barbecued dishes. Pit barbecue. No cr cds accepted. Cr cds: MC, V.

Monahans

(C-3) *See also Fort Stockton, Odessa, Pecos*

Pop 6,821 **Elev** 2,613 ft
Area code 915 **Zip** 79756
Information Chamber of Commerce, 401 S Dwight; 915/943-2187
Web www.monahans.org

What to See and Do

Million Barrel Museum. Texas oil boom prompted construction of an oil tank 522 ft by 426 ft to hold more than one million gallons; it was filled only once. Incl the Holman House with period furnishings; antique farming and railroad memorabilia, caboose; eclipse windmill; first Ward County jail; amphitheater; gift shop. (Tues-Sun; closed Thanksgiving, Dec 25) 2 mi E on Business Loop 20. Phone 915/943-8401. **Donation**

Monahans Sandhills State Park. Sand dunes, some 70 ft high, believed to be from the Trinity sandstone formation and collected by the Permian Sea. On 3,840 acres. Nature trail, picnicking, improved campsites (dump station). Standard fees. (Daily) 6 mi E on I-20, exit mile marker 86 to Park

Rd 41. Phone 915/943-2092. ¢ Also here is the

Sandhills Interpretive Center. Natural history, historical, archaeological, botanical, and geological displays on the area. (Daily) Incl with entrance to park.

Mount Pleasant

(B-7)

Pop 13,935 **Elev** 416 ft **Area code** 903 **Zip** 75456
Information Mount Pleasant/Titus County Chamber of Commerce, 1604 N Jefferson, PO Box 1237; 903/572-8567
Web www.mtpleasant-tx.com

Special Events

Mount Pleasant Championship Rodeo. First wkend June. Phone 903/572-3381.

Titus County Fair. Fairgrounds. Carnival, cattle show, entertainment. Last full wk Sept.

Deck the Halls. Civic Center. Arts and crafts. Sat after Thanksgiving. Phone 903/575-4190.

Motel/Motor Lodge

★ **SUPER 8.** *401 W I-30, Mount Vernon (75457).* 903/588-2882; fax 903/588-2844; res 800/800-8000. *www.super8.com.* 43 rms, 2 story. S, D $43.88-$48.88; each addl $5; under 14 free; package plans; higher rates special events. Crib free. Pet accepted, some restrictions; $5. TV; cable (premium). Complimentary continental bkfst. Restaurant nearby. Bar 11 am-9 pm. Ck-out 11 am. Business servs avail. In-rm modem link. Some refrigerators, microwaves. Picnic tables, grills. Cr cds: A, D, DS, MC, V.

Nacogdoches

(C-7) *See also Lufkin, Rusk*

Founded 1691 **Pop** 29,914 **Elev** 277 ft
Area code 936 **Zip** 75961
Information Convention & Visitors
Bureau, 513 North St, PO Drawer
631918; 936/564-7351 or 888/564-
7351
Web www.nacogdoches.org

What to See and Do

Millard's Crossing. Historic village of
restored 19th-century east Texas
homes furnished with period
antiques. Log cabin, corn crib,
chapel, Victorian parsonage, and
farmhouse reflect life of east Texas
pioneers. Guided tours. (Daily; closed
hols) 4 mi N via US 59 at 6020 North
St. Phone 936/564-6631. ¢¢

Sterne-Hoya Home. (1830) Pioneer
home of Adolphus Sterne. (Mon-Sat;
closed hols) 211 S Lanana St. Phone
936/560-5426. **FREE**

Stone Fort Museum. Rebuilt by state
in 1936 from original structure probably erected by Gil Y'Barbo in 1779.
Focus on east Texas history and
Spanish Nacogdoches. Guided tours.
(Tues-Sun; closed school hols) Vista
and Griffith blvds, Stephen F. Austin
State University campus. Phone
936/468-2408. **FREE**

Motels/Motor Lodges

★ ★ **HOLIDAY INN.** *3400 South St
(75964). 936/569-8100; fax 936/569-
0332; toll-free 800/465-4329. www.
holiday-inn.com.* 126 rms, 2 story. S
$55-$69; D $61-$74; each addl $6;
suites $69-$150; under 19 free. Crib
free. TV; cable (premium). Indoor/
outdoor pool; whirlpools. Restaurant 6-11 am, 5-10 pm. Rm serv. Private club 5-11 pm. Ck-out noon.
Coin lndry. Meeting rms. Business
servs avail. In-rm modem link. Valet
serv. Exercise equipt. Health club
privileges. Cr cds: A, C, D, DS, JCB,
MC, V.
🄳 ⇔ 🏃 ⊠ 🔥 **SC**

★ ★ **LA QUINTA INN.** *3215 South St
(75961). 936/560-5453; fax 936/560-
4372; res 800/531-5900. www.
laquinta.com.* 106 rms, 2 story. S $48-
$56; D $54-$62; each addl $6; suites
$65-$77; under 18 free. Crib free. Pet
accepted, some restrictions. TV; cable
(premium). Pool. Complimentary continental bkfst. Complimentary coffee
in lobby. Restaurant adj open 24 hrs.
Ck-out noon. Meeting rms. Business
servs avail. In-rm modem link. Valet
serv. Cr cds: A, C, D, DS, MC, V.
🄳 🐾 🦯 ⇔ 🔥

Hotel

★ **FREDONIA HOTEL & CONVEN-
TION CENTER.** *200 N Fredonia St
(75961). 936/564-1234; toll-free
800/594-5323. www.fredoniahotel.com.*
113 rms, 6 story. S $69; D $79; each
addl $10; suites $150-$175; under 18
free. Crib free. Pet accepted. TV; cable.
Pool; poolside serv. Restaurant 6:30
am-2 pm, 5:30-9 pm. Private club 5
pm-midnight; closed Sun. Ck-out 1
pm. Meeting rms. Gift shop. Some private patios. Cr cds: A, D, DS, MC, V.
🄳 🐾 ⇔ ✈ 🔥

New Braunfels

(E-5) *See also San Antonio, San Marcos*

Founded 1844 **Pop** 36,494 **Elev** 639 ft
Area code 830
Information Chamber of Commerce,
390 S Seguin Ave, PO Box 311417,
78131; 830/625-2385 or 800/572-
2626
Web www.nbcham.org

What to See and Do

Canyon Lake. A 224-ft-high earthen
dam. Swimming, waterskiing, fishing, boating (ramps), canoeing, tubing; picnicking, concession, camping
(tent and trailer sites, some hookups;
fee). Headquarters, 15 mi NW via FM
306. Phone 830/964-3341. ¢

Fishing. For bass, catfish, perch in
Lake Dunlap and Canyon Lake; for
rainbow trout in Guadalupe River.

Landa Park. A 190-acre park with spring-fed pool, swimming pool, tubing on river, glass-bottom boat rides; 18-hole golf, miniature golf, miniature train, picnicking, playground, concession. Historical markers, arboretum. Park (daily, schedule varies with season). Some fees. Landa St, 5 blks NW on TX 46. Phone 830/608-2160. **FREE**

Lindheimer Home. (ca 1852) Restored house of Ferdinand Lindheimer (1801-1879), educator, guide, botanist, and editor. (May-Aug, Mon, Tues, Thurs-Sun; rest of yr, Sat, Sun, or by appt; closed Jan 1, Dec 25) 491 Comal Ave. Phone 830/629-2943. ¢

Natural Bridge Caverns. (see SAN ANTONIO) 15 mi W via TX 46, FM 1863. Phone 210/651-6101. ¢¢¢¢

New Braunfels Museum of Art and Music. Affiliate of Smithsonian Institute. Ongoing and changing exhibits featuring Texas visual and folk artist and music history. World's largest collection of original paintings and drawings by Sister Maria Innocentia Hummel; the popular German porcelain figurines are modeled on her work. Gift shop. (Daily; closed hols) 199 Main Plaza. Phone 830/625-5636. ¢¢

Schlitterbahn Water Park. Waterslides, water rides, swimming pools. Gift shops, restaurants, hotels. (Late Apr-late Sept) 305 W Austin. Phone 830/625-2351. ¢¢¢¢

Sophienburg Museum & Archives. Memorabilia, archives of pioneer days. Changing exhibits. Museum (daily; closed hols). Archives (Mon-Fri; closed hols). 401 W Coll St. Phone 830/629-1900. ¢

Special Events

Comal County Fair. Carnival and rodeo. Late Sept. Phone 830/608-2100.

Wurstfest. German music and food, displays, dancing. Late Oct-early Nov. Phone 830/625-9167.

Motels/Motor Lodges

★ **BEST WESTERN INN & SUITES.** *1493 N I-35 (78130). 830/625-7337; res 800/528-1234. www.stonebridge hotels.com.* 60 rms, 2 story, 20 suites. S, D $49-$119; each addl $5; suites $59-$129; under 18 free. Crib free.

TV; cable (premium). Complimentary continental bkfst. Restaurant nearby. Ck-out noon. Meeting rm. Business servs avail. Coin lndry. Pool. Refrigerator, microwave in suites. Cr cds: A, C, D, DS, JCB, MC, V.

⬛ 🛁 🏊 ⛐ 🔥 **SC**

★ **HAMPTON INN.** *979 I-35 N (78130). 830/608-0123; fax 830/608-0121; res 800/426-7899. www.hampton inn.com.* 61 rms, 2 story. May-Sept: S, D $99-$139; lower rates rest of yr; each addl $10; under 18 free. TV; cable (premium). Complimentary continental bkfst. Ck-out noon. Meeting rms. Business servs avail. In-rm modem link. Coin lndry. Exercise equipt. Pool; whirlpool. Cr cds: A, C, D, DS, MC, V.

⬛ 🏊 🏋 ⛐ 🔥 **SC**

★ **HOLIDAY INN NEW BRAUN-FELS.** *1051 I-35 E (78130). 830/625-8017; fax 830/625-3130; res 800/465-4329. www.holiday-inn.com.* 140 rms, 2 story. Memorial Day-Labor Day: S, D $79-$119; each addl $5; suites $159-$179; under 18 free; lower rates rest of yr. Crib free. Pet accepted; $50. TV; cable (premium). Pool; wading pool. Complimentary coffee in rms. Restaurant 6-11 am, 5:30-10 pm. Rm serv. Bar 4 pm-midnight. Entertainment Wed, Fri-Sat. Ck-out noon. Meeting rms. Business servs avail. In-rm modem link. Coin lndry. Exercise equipt. Cr cds: A, C, D, DS, ER, JCB, MC, V.

⬛ 🐾 🏊 🏋 ⛐ 🔥 **SC**

Resort

★ **JOHN NEWCOMBE'S TENNIS RANCH.** *325 Mission Valley Rd (78131). 830/625-9105; fax 830/625-2004; toll-free 800/444-6204. www. newktennis.com.* 46 rms in lodge, motel (1-2 story); 10 cottages. S, D $65-$155; 2-bedrm kit. condos $140; tennis plans; wkly rates. Crib free. Pool; whirlpool. Supervised children's activities (June-Aug); ages 8-18. Dining rm 8-9 am, 12:30-1:30 pm, 7-8 pm. Snack bar in summer, picnics. Bar 5 pm-midnight. Ck-out 2 pm, ck-in 4 pm. Coin lndry. Business servs avail. Sports dir. 28 tennis courts (4 covered, 4 clay, 12 lighted), pro, tennis clinics. Soc dir; entertainment. Fireplace in condos.

Some private patios, balconies. Cr cds: A, D, DS, MC, V.

B&Bs/Small Inns

★ **FAUST HOTEL.** *240 S Seguin Ave (78130). 830/625-7791; fax 830/620-1530. www.fausthotel.com.* 62 rms, 4 story. May-Sept: S $89-$99; D $95-$160; each addl $5; suite $400; under 5 free; lower rates rest of yr. TV; cable. Restaurant adj. Ck-out 11 am. Health club privileges. Built 1929; many period furnishings. Cr cds: A, C, D, DS, MC, V.

★★ **THE KARBACH HAUS BED & BREAKFAST.** *487 W San Antonio St (78130). 830/625-2131; fax 830/629-1126; toll-free 800/972-5941. www.karbachhaus.com.* 6 rms, 2 with shower only, 1 kit. unit. Rm phones avail. S, D $120-$195; kit. unit $225; wkends, hols (2-day min). Children over 16 yrs only. TV; cable (premium), VCR (movies). Complimentary full bkfst. Restaurant nearby. Ck-out noon, ck-in 3-6 pm. Business servs avail. Luggage handling. Guest lndry. Pool; whirlpool. Exercise equipt. Some in-rm whirlpools; refrigerator, microwave, fireplace in kit. unit. Many balconies. Restored 1906 mansion. Totally nonsmoking. Cr cds: A, DS, MC, V.

★ **PRINCE SOLMS INN.** *295 E San Antonio St (78130). 830/625-9169; fax 830/625-2220; toll-free 800/625-9169. www.princesolmsinn.com.* 14 rms, 2 story. S, D $115-$165; suites $150-$165. Complimentary bkfst. Bar 4-11 pm. Ck-out 11 am, ck-in 2 pm. Antique furnishings, historic building. Cr cds: A, DS, MC, V.

Restaurants

★ **GRISTMILL.** *1287 Gruene Rd (78130). 830/625-0684.* Hrs: 11 am-9 pm; Fri, Sat to 10 pm; summer 11 am-10 pm. No A/C. Bar. Lunch, dinner $4.99-$14.99. Child's menu. Specializes in chicken-fried steak, grilled chicken, steaks. Entertainment Fri, Sat in summer. Outdoor dining.

Overlooks Guadalupe River. Cr cds: A, C, D, DS, MC, V.

★★ **HUISACHE GRILL.** *303 W San Antonio St (78130). 830/620-9001. www.huisache.com.* Hrs: 11 am-10 pm. Closed Thanksgiving, Dec 25. Contemporary American menu. Bar. Lunch $4.50-$10.95, dinner $6.50-$10.95. Child's menu. Specialties: herb-crusted salmon, Yucatan chicken, peppered tendertails. Own baking. Patio dining. Local art on display. Cr cds: A, D, DS, MC, V.

★ **NEW BRAUNFELS SMOKEHOUSE.** *146 TX 46E (78130). 830/625-2416. www.nbsmokehouse.com.* Hrs: 7:30 am-9 pm. Closed Easter, Thanksgiving, Dec 25. German, American menu. Wine, beer. Bkfst $4.79-$8.29, lunch, dinner $4.79-$13.49. Child's menu. Specializes in smoked meats, German potato salad, strudel. Outdoor dining. Family-owned. Cr cds: A, C, D, DS, MC, V.

Odessa

(C-3) *See also Midland, Monahans*

Founded 1881 **Pop** 90,943 **Elev** 2,890 ft **Area code** 915
Information Chamber of Commerce, 700 N Grant, Suite 200, 79760; 915/332-9111 or 800/780-4678
Web www.odessachamber.com

What to See and Do

Globe Theatre. Authentic re-creation of Shakespeare's original playhouse showcases drama ranging from Shakespeare to Broadway. Guided tours (Mon-Fri; wkends by appt). 2308 Shakespeare Rd. Phone 915/332-1586. ¢¢ Also here is

Ann Hathaway Cottage Archival & Shakespearean Library. Contains many old books, documents pertaining to Shakespeare; costumes, furnishings, and other items of the Elizabethan era.

Meteor Crater. Large crater formed more than 20,000 yrs ago. Paths through crater have interpretive signs. Picnic facilities. 8 mi W via I-20 or US 80 to Meteor Crater Rd exit. **FREE**

Presidential Museum. Changing exhibits and educational programs devoted to the people who have held or run for the office of President of the US. Collections incl images of the presidents, campaign memorabilia, signatures, political cartoons, miniature replicas of First Lady inaugural dresses. (Tues-Sat; closed hols) 622 N Lee. Phone 915/332-7123. ¢

Water Wonderland. The 18-acre park incl giant wave pools, swimming pools, water slides, inner-tube rides, bumper boats, go-carts, Kiddieland. (Late Apr-Memorial Day, wkends; Memorial Day-Labor Day, Tues-Sat) 10113 US 80 E, between Midland and Odessa; 2½ mi W of Midland International Air Terminal. Phone 915/563-1933. ¢¢¢¢

Special Events

Sandhill Hereford and Quarter Horse Show and Rodeo. Phone 915/366-3951. First wk Jan.

Jazz Festival. Wk-long jazz entertainment. May. Phone 915/362-1191.

Motels/Motor Lodges

★★ **BEST WESTERN GARDEN OASIS.** *110 W I-20 (79761). 915/337-3006; fax 915/332-1956; res 800/528-1234. www.bestwestern.com.* 118 rms, 2 story. S, D $48-$58; each addl $5; suites $85-$95; under 12 free. Crib $8. Pet accepted, some restrictions. TV; cable (premium), VCR avail (movies). Indoor pool; whirlpool, poolside serv. Restaurant 6 am-10 pm. Rm serv. Ck-out noon. Meeting rms. Business servs avail. Lndry facilities. Gift shop. Free airport, bus depot transportation. Sauna. Cr cds: A, C, D, DS, ER, JCB, MC, V.
🐾 ⌨ 🏊 📶 🔥

★★ **LA QUINTA INN.** *5001 E Business 20 (79761). 915/333-2820; fax 915/333-4208; res 800/531-5900. www.laquinta.com.* 122 rms. S $55; D $62; each addl $7; under 18 free. Crib free. Pet accepted, some restrictions. TV; cable (premium). Pool. Restaurant adj open 24 hrs. Ck-out noon. Business servs avail. Picnic tables, grills. Cr cds: A, C, D, DS, MC, V.
🐾 ⌨ 📶 🔥

Hotel

★★★ **RADISSON HOTEL & CONFERENCE CENTER.** *5200 E University Blvd (79762). 915/368-5885; fax 915/362-8958; res 800/333-3333. www.radisson.com.* 194 rms, 8 story. S $79; D $89; each addl $10; suites $100-$175; family, wkend, wkly rates. Crib $10. TV; cable (premium), VCR avail. Complimentary coffee in lobby. Restaurant 6:30 am-2 pm, 5-10 pm. Bar 4:30 pm-2 am; entertainment Fri. Ck-out noon. Meeting rms. Business servs avail. Gift shop. Free airport transportation. Health club privileges. Pool; whirlpool, poolside serv. Some balconies. Cr cds: A, C, D, DS, ER, MC, V.
🅓 ⌨ ✈ 📶 🔥

Restaurants

★★ **BARN DOOR.** *2140 N Andrew Hwy (79761). 915/337-4142.* Hrs: 11 am-9:30 pm; Fri, Sat to 10:30 pm. Closed Sun; Labor Day, Dec 24 eve & Dec 25. Res accepted. Lunch $3.95-$13.50, dinner $5.95-$19.50. Specializes in steak, seafood. Bar in old railroad depot. Victorian country decor. Cr cds: D, MC, V.
🅓 ⌨

★ **MANUEL'S CRISPY TACOS.** *1404 E 2nd St (79761). 915/333-2751.* Hrs: 11 am-9 pm; Mon to 2 pm; Fri, Sat to 10 pm. Closed most major hols. Res accepted. Mexican menu. Bar. Lunch, dinner $5.25-$14.50. Child's menu. Specializes in Mexican cooking. Family-owned. Cr cds: A, D, DS, MC, V.
🅓 ⌨

Orange

(D-8) *See also Beaumont, Port Arthur*

Founded 1836 **Pop** 18,643 **Elev** 14 ft
Area code 409 **Zip** 77630
Information Convention & Visitors
Bureau, 1012 Green Ave; 409/883-
3536 or 800/528-4906
Web www.org-tx.com/chamber

Orange is on the Sabine River, at its
junction with the Intracoastal Waterway. The deepwater port is connected with the Gulf by the
Sabine-Neches Waterway. Bayous
nearby are shaded with cypress and
pine trees. Cattle, timber, shipbuild-
ing, oil, and chemical processing
provide a diverse economy. There are
several historic structures and a
branch of Lamar University of Beaumont in town. The imposing First
Presbyterian Church with art glass
windows and a marble staircase was
among the first public buildings in
the country to be air-conditioned.

What to See and Do

Boating and fishing. On Sabine River
and Lake and in surrounding bayous.
Launching, dock facilities, marinas in
area.

Heritage House Museum. (1902) His-
toric house; changing exhibits. (Tues-
Fri; closed hols) 905 W Division St.
Phone 409/886-5385. ¢

**Lutcher Theater for the Performing
Arts.** Professional performances of
top stars in concert, Broadway musicals, and plays. Orange Civic Plaza.
Phone 409/886-5535. ¢¢¢¢

Stark Museum of Art. Built to house
the collections of the Stark family.
Fine collections of Western art, incl
originals by Russell, Remington,
Audubon, and the Taos Society of
Artists of New Mexico. The American
Indian collection incl many art
forms of the tribes of the Great
Plains and the Southwest. Displays of
Doughty and Boehm porcelain bird
sculpture and Steuben crystal. (Tues-
Sat; closed hols) 712 Green Ave.
Phone 409/883-6661. **FREE**

W. H. Stark House. (1894) Restored
Victorian house typical of wealthy
southeast Texas family; 15 rms, three
stories built of longleaf yellow pine
with gables, galleries, and windowed
turret. Original furniture, silver, woodwork, lighting, and decorative accessories; collection of cut glass in carriage
house. Stairs major part of tour. Res
required. (Tues-Sat; closed hols) Over
14 yrs only. Entrance through carriage
house, 610 Main St. 6th and Green Sts.
Phone 409/883-0871. ¢

Motels/Motor Lodges

★★ **BEST WESTERN INN.** *2630 I-
10 W (77632). 409/883-6616; fax
409/883-3427; res 800/528-1234.* 60
rms, 2 story. S $45-$53; D $51-$53;
each addl $10; under 18 free. Crib
avail. TV; cable (premium). Pool.
Complimentary coffee. Restaurant
adj 6 am-10 pm; Sun 6 am-9 pm. Ck-
out noon. In-rm modem link. Some
refrigerators. Near Orange County
Airport. Cr cds: A, C, D, DS, MC, V.

★★ **RAMADA INN.** *2610 I-10
(77632). 409/883-0231; fax 409/883-
8839; toll-free 800/272-6232. www.
ramada.com.* 125 rms, 2 story. S $58, D
$66; each addl $8; studio rms $66-
$76; suites $73-$135; under 18 free.
Crib free. Pet accepted. TV; cable (premium). Pool; wading pool. Restaurant
6 am-10 pm. Rm serv. Bar 4 pm-2 am;
Sat from 5 pm, closed Sun; entertainment Fri, Sat. Ck-out noon. Meeting
rms. Business servs avail. In-rm
modem link. Some refrigerators,
microwaves. Wet bar in some suites.
Cr cds: A, C, D, DS, MC, V.

Ozona

See also Sonora

Pop 3,436 **Elev** 2,348 ft
Area code 915 **Zip** 76943
Information Chamber of Commerce,
1110 Avenue E, PO Box 1135;
915/392-3737
Web www.ozona.com

What to See and Do

Crockett County Museum. Local historical exhibits, incl objects from early Spanish explorers; minerals, mammoth bones. Murals depicting big-game animals hunted by Paleo-Indians; simulated rock overhang shelter, artifacts dating back to 10,000 B.C. (Mon-Sat; closed hols) Courthouse Annex, 404 11th St. Phone 915/392-2837. ¢

Davy Crockett Monument. Unveiled in 1939, this statue of the famous frontiersman bears the inscription "Be sure you are right, then go ahead." South end of town sq.

Fort Lancaster State Historical Park. Ruins of Army outpost (1855-1861); 82 acres. Museum containing exhibits relating to 18th-century military life. (Daily; closed Dec 25) 33 mi W on I-10, exit 343 then 11 mi W on US 290, near Sheffield. Phone 915/836-4391. ¢

Motels/Motor Lodges

★ **TRAVELODGE.** *8 11th St (76943). 915/392-2656; fax 915/392-4152. www.travelodge.com.* 40 rms, 1-2 story. S $22-$36; D $27-$46. Crib free. TV; cable (premium). Pool. Ck-out 11 am. Cr cds: A, DS, MC, V.

Padre Island

(*North section:* see Aransas Pass, Corpus Christi, Port Aransas. *South section:* see Brownsville, Harlingen, Port Isabel, South Padre Island)

In 1962 a stretch of this long, narrow island was made a national seashore. Stretching 113 miles from Corpus Christi to a point near Port Isabel (there is a causeway from each city), the island is rarely more than three miles wide. Drivers can navigate certain parts of the island, but the majority of the seashore is open only to four-wheel drive vehicles. The Port Mansfield Ship Channel, completed in 1964, essentially divides the island in two. There are no bridges or ferries across the channel, making it neces-

sary to return to the mainland in order to reach the southern section.

Another way to explore the island is by hiking. The Grassland Trail (¾ mi) makes a loop through a grassland-and-dunes area; a guide pamphlet is available at the trailhead. Bird-watching can be an interesting diversion; more than 350 species of birds inhabit the island or are seasonal visitors. Padre Island offers swimming, excellent surf fishing, and picnicking. Camping is available at the Malaquite Beach Campground (fee) or free along the beach.

Nueces County Park, at the north end, offers picnicking, Gulf swimming, and fishing; cabañas.

For information contact Superintendent, 9405 S Padre Island Dr, Corpus Christi 78418; 512/937-2621 or 512/949-8068. The Corpus Christi Area Tourist Bureau also has details on the area; contact Box 640, Corpus Christi 78403; 800/678-OCEAN.

Palestine

(C-7) *See also Fairfield, Rusk*

Founded 1846 **Pop** 17,598 **Elev** 510 ft
Area code 903
Information Convention and Visitors Bureau, PO Box 1177, 75802; 903/723-3014 or 800/659-3484

What to See and Do

Community Forest. Fishing, piers, boat ramp; nature trails, picnicking. Fishing also on Lake Palestine, 20 mi N. 2 mi NW on US 287. **FREE**

National Scientific Balloon Facility. Research facility employs high-altitude balloons in various experiments. Interpretive video (30 min). Guided tour of facility (weather permitting; one wk advance notice requested) incl launch vehicle "Tiny Tim" and weather station. (Mon-Fri; closed hols) 5 mi N via US 287 to FM 3224. Phone 903/729-0271. **FREE**

Rusk-Palestine State Park. (See RUSK) 6 mi E on US 84. Phone 903/683-5126.

Special Events

Texas Dogwood Trail Festival. Phone 903/729-7275. Last two wkends Mar and first wkend Apr.

Hot Pepper Festival. Last Sat Oct. Phone 903/723-3014.

Motel/Motor Lodge

★ ★ **BEST WESTERN PALESTINE INN.** *1601 W Palestine Ave (75801). 903/723-4655; fax 903/723-2519; toll-free 800/523-0121. www.bestwestern. com.* 66 rms, 2 story. S $45; D $50; under 16 free. Crib $3. Pet accepted. TV; cable (premium). Pool. Playground. Restaurant 6 am-9 pm. Ck-out 1 pm. Business servs avail. In-rm modem link. Cr cds: A, D, DS, MC, V.

D ❧ ⚓ ➰ ✕ ⊠ ⚲

Pampa

(G-2) *See also Amarillo*

Pop 17,887 **Elev** 3,234 ft
Area code 806
Information Chamber of Commerce, 200 N Ballard, PO Box 1942, 79066; 806/669-3241

What to See and Do

White Deer Land Museum. Arrowhead and Native American photo collection, pioneer artifacts, historical records; rm displays with antique furnishings, machines and utensils. (Tues-Sat, limited hrs; closed hols) 116 S Cuyler St. Phone 806/669-8041. **FREE**

Special Events

Top O'Texas Junior Livestock Show & Sale. Mid-Jan. Phone 806/665-5946.

Top O'Texas Rodeo, PRCA. Second wkend July. Phone 806/669-0434.

Motel/Motor Lodge

★ ★ **BEST WESTERN NORTHGATE INN.** *2831 Perryton Pkwy (79065). 806/665-0926; fax 806/665-8027; res 800/528-1234. www.bestwestern.com/ northgateinnpampa.* 100 rms, 2 story. S, D $45-$69; lower rates rest of yr. Crib avail. TV; cable (premium). Complimentary continental bkfst. Restaurant nearby. Ck-out noon.

Business servs avail. In-rm modem link. Coin lndry. Pool. Some refrigerators, microwaves. Grills. Cr cds: A, C, D, DS, MC, V.

➰ ✕ ⊠ ⚲ SC

Restaurants

★ **DYER'S BAR-B-QUE.** *TX 60 W (79065). 806/665-4401.* Hrs: 11 am-9 pm. Closed Sun; major hols. Wine, beer. Lunch, dinner $4.50-$11. Child's menu. Specializes in barbecued ribs, chicken, steak. Western decor. Cr cds: A, DS, MC, V.

D ⊠

★ **TEXAS ROSE STEAKHOUSE.** *2537 Perryton Pkwy (79065). 806/669-1009.* Hrs: 11 am-9 pm. Closed Sun; major hols. Res accepted. Lunch, dinner $7-$20. Child's menu. Specializes in steak. Kitchen visible behind glass partition. Cr cds: A, MC, V.

D ⊠

Paris

(B-7) *See also Bonham*

Settled 1836 **Pop** 25,898 **Elev** 602 ft
Area code 903 **Zip** 75460
Information Visitor & Convention Office, 1651 Clarksville St; 903/784-2501 or 800/PARIS-TX
Web www.paristexas.com

What to See and Do

Fishing. Lake Crook, 3 mi N. Lake Pat Mayse, 12 mi N.

Sam Bell Maxey House State Historical Park. Two-story house (1867), in high Victorian Italianate style, was built by Sam Bell Maxey, Confederate major general and US Senator. Occupied by his family until 1966. Family heirlooms and furniture, some dating to 1795. (Wed-Sun; closed Jan 1, Thanksgiving, Dec 25) 812 S Church. Phone 903/785-5716. ¢

Senator A. M. and Welma Aikin, Jr. Regional Archives. Incl a gallery of memorabilia from the noted senator's career as an educational reformer; replica of his office in Austin. Local and regional archives.

(Mon-Fri; closed campus hols) On campus of Paris Junior College. Phone 903/782-0415. **FREE**

Special Events

Municipal Band Concerts. Bywaters Park. Fri nights. Second wkend June-second wkend July. Phone 903/784-2501.

CRCA Annual Rodeo. Fairgrounds. Aug.

Red River Valley Exposition. Fairgrounds. Eight days early Sept. Phone 903/785-7971.

Motel/Motor Lodge

★★ **COMFORT INN.** *3505 NE Loop 286 (75460). 903/784-7481; fax 903/784-0231; res 800/228-5150. www.comfortinn.com.* 62 rms, 2 story. S $45-$50; D $50-$60; each addl $5; under 18 free. Crib $4. TV; cable (premium). Pool. Complimentary continental bkfst. Restaurant opp 11 am-9 pm. Ck-out noon. Cr cds: A, D, DS, MC, V.
[D] [icons]

Restaurants

★ **FISH FRY.** *3500 NE Loop 286 (75460). 903/785-6144.* Hrs: 5-10 pm. Closed Sun, Mon; Jan 1, Thanksgiving, Dec 25. Res accepted. Complete meals: dinner $10-$20. Child's menu. Specializes in catfish, steak, seafood. 9 dining areas. Wildlife motif. Totally nonsmoking. Cr cds: A, MC, V.
[D]

★ **TA MOLLY'S.** *2835 NE Loop 286 (75460). 903/784-4706.* Hrs: 11 am-9 pm; Fri, Sat to 10 pm. Closed most major hols. Mexican menu. Lunch $4.85-$5.50, dinner $5.25-$7.95. Child's menu. Specialties: grilled pollo salad, pollo Monterey, quesadillas. Water fountain in center of room. Cr cds: A, D, MC, V.
[D]

Pecos

(C-2) *See also Fort Stockton, Monahans*

Pop 9,501 **Elev** 2,580 ft
Area code 915 **Zip** 79772
Information Chamber of Commerce, 111 S Cedar, PO Box 27; 915/445-2406
Web www.pecostx.com

What to See and Do

Balmorhea State Park. Spring-fed swimming pool (daily; fee); picnicking, playground, lodging, camping, tent and trailer sites (dump station). Standard fees. (Daily) 32 mi S on TX 17, near the Davis Mtns. Phone 915/375-2370. ¢¢

West of the Pecos Museum. Renovated 1904 hotel; more than 50 rms cover history of western Texas from the 1880s; incl restored Old #11 Saloon (1896), where two gunslingers were killed. (Memorial Day-Labor Day, daily; rest of yr, Tues-Sat; closed Thanksgiving; also one wk mid-Dec) 1st St and US 285. Phone 915/445-5076. ¢¢

Special Event

"West of the Pecos" Rodeo. Buck Jackson Memorial Rodeo Arena. Incl Golden Girl of the Old West contest, Old-Timer Reunion at museum, Fiesta Night in Old Pecos. Parade of floats, riding groups, and antique vehicles; barbecue. Phone 915/445-2406. Four days early July.

Motels/Motor Lodges

★★ **BEST WESTERN SWISS CLOCK INN.** *133 S Frontage Rd (79772). 915/447-2215; fax 915/447-4463; res 800/528-1234.* 104 rms. S $45-$62; D $50-$72; each addl $6. Crib free. TV; cable (premium). Pool. Complimentary bkfst. Restaurant 6 am-2 pm, 5-10 pm. Rm serv. Bar from 5 pm. Ck-out noon. Guest lndry. Meeting rm. Business servs avail. In-rm modem link. Cr cds: A, C, D, DS, MC, V.
[D] [icons] [SC]

★★ **QUALITY INN.** *4002 S Cedar St (79772). 915/445-5404; fax 915/445-2484; res 800/332-5255. www.quality inn.com.* 96 rms, 2 story. S $56; D $61; each addl $5. Crib free. TV; cable. Pool; wading pool. Restaurant 6 am-9 pm. Rm serv. Private club. Ck-out 1 pm. Meeting rm. Business servs avail. In-rm modem link. Cr cds: A, C, D, DS, ER, JCB, MC, V.

D ⊠ 🐾 SC

Plainview

(G-1) *See also Lubbock*

Founded ca 1880 **Pop** 22,336
Elev 3,300 ft **Area code** 806
Zip 79072
Information Chamber of Commerce, 710 W 5th; 806/296-7431 or 800/658-2685
Web www.texasonline.net/chamber

What to See and Do

Abraham Family Art Gallery. Dr. Malouf Abraham's donation of select artwork to the Wayland Baptist University. (Mon-Sat) Lower level of J. E. & L. E. Mabee Learning Resources Center on Wayland campus, 1900 W 7th St. Phone 806/296-5521. **FREE**

Llano Estacado Museum. Regional history and archaeology; art and science collections. Major events held yr-round. (Mar-Nov, daily; rest of yr, Mon-Fri; closed hols) 1900 W 8th St, on Wayland Baptist University campus. Phone 806/291-3660. **FREE**

Special Events

High Plains Gem & Mineral Show. Early Apr.
Bar None Rodeo. Third wkend July. Phone 806/293-2661.

Motels/Motor Lodges

★★ **BEST WESTERN CON-ESTOGA.** *600 N I-27 (79072). 806/293-9454; res 800/780-7234. www.best western.com.* 83 rms, 2 story. S, D $60-$110; each addl $7; suites $90; under 12 free. Crib free. Pet accepted, some restrictions. TV; cable (premium), VCR avail (movies). Pool. Complimentary continental bkfst.

Restaurant adj open 24 hrs. Private club 5 pm-midnight; closed Sun. Ck-out noon. Meeting rm. Business servs avail. In-rm modem link. Some bathrm phones. Some refrigerators. Cr cds: A, D, DS, MC, V.

D SC 🐾 ⊠

Plano (B-6)

(see Dallas)

Port Aransas

See also Corpus Christi, Rockport

Pop 3,370 **Elev** 7 ft **Area code** 361
Zip 78373
Information Chamber of Commerce, 421 W Cotter, PO Box 356; 361/749-5919 or 800/452-6278
Web www.portaransas.org

This resort town on Mustang Island is accessible from Aransas Pass by causeway and ferryboat or from Corpus Christi via causeway. Padre Island (see) is also nearby. Coastline of 18 miles provides good surf fishing as well as chartered-boat, deep-sea fishing for sailfish and kingfish. Swimming and surfing on the beach are popular activites. **Mustang Island State Park**, 14 miles south on TX 361, while relatively unspoiled, does have swimming with a bathhouse and showers; picnicking and camping. Beach driving is permitted. A hardtop road goes to Corpus Christi.

Special Event

Deep-Sea Roundup. Fishing contest. Early July. Phone 361/749-6339.

Motel/Motor Lodge

★★ **DUNES CONDOMINIUM.** *1000 Lantana Dr (78373). 361/749-5155; fax 361/749-5930; toll-free 800/288-DUNE.* 48 kit. units, 9 story. Mid-Mar-Labor Day (2-3 min wkends, hols): 1-3 bedrm apts $137-$275; wkly rates; lower rates rest of yr. TV; cable (premium). Heated pool; whirlpool. Complimentary coffee in lobby. Restaurant nearby. Ck-out noon. Meeting rms. Business servs avail. Tennis. Exercise equipt. Lawn games. Refrigerators. Private patios, balconies. Gulf view. On beach. Cr cds: A, C, D, MC, V.

B&B/Small Inn

★ **TARPON INN.** *200 E Cotter Ave (78373). 361/749-5555; fax 361/749-4305; toll-free 800/365-6784. www. texhillcntry.com/tarponinn.* 24 rms, 12 with shower only. No rm phones. Mar-Nov: S, D $50-$125; lower rates rest of yr. Complimentary coffee in lobby. Restaurant (see also BEULAH'S TARPON INN RESTAURANT). Ck-out noon, ck-in 2 pm. 1 blk from Gulf of Mexico. Originally built in 1886 with surplus lumber from Civil War barracks; it burned down in 1900 and was rebuilt in 1904. Cr cds: A, DS, MC, V.

Restaurant

★★ **BEULAH'S TARPON INN.** *200 E Cotter Ave (78373). 361/749-4888.* Hrs: 5-10 pm. Closed Mon, Tues; Jan 1, Labor Day, Thanksgiving; also Dec. Res accepted. Contemporary Amer menu. Wine, beer. A la carte entrees: dinner $18-$25. Specialties: filet mignon of yellow-fin tuna, crab cakes. Parking. Outdoor dining. Building was built in 1904. Cr cds: DS, MC, V.

Port Arthur

(D-8) *See also Beaumont, Orange*

Founded 1895 **Pop** 57,755 **Elev** 18 ft
Area code 409
Information Convention & Visitor Bureau, 3401 Cultural Center Dr, 77642; 409/985-7822 or 800/235-7822

What to See and Do

J. D. Murphree Wildlife Management Area. A 24,000-acre marsh. Fishing (spring, summer); waterfowl and alligator hunting (fall, winter). W on TX 73. Phone 409/736-2551. ¢¢

Museum of the Gulf Coast. Exhibits cover history and culture of area; also history of oil refining; southeast Texas musical heritage exhibit incl Janis Joplin, Tex Ritter; sports legends exhibit features Jimmy Johnson, Babe Zaharias, and others. (Daily; closed hols) 700 Procter. Phone 409/982-7000. ¢¢

Nederland Windmill Museum. Located in Tex Ritter Park is replica of Dutch windmill built to honor 1898 immigrants from Holland; artifacts from Holland; memorabilia of country-western star Tex Ritter. (Mar-Labor Day, Tues-Sun; rest of yr, Thurs-Sun; closed hols) 1500 Boston Ave, 5 mi N via TX 347 in Nederland. Phone 409/722-0279. **FREE** Adj is

> **La Maison Acadienne Museum.** Replica of French Acadian home preserves heritage of French and Cajun immigrants who settled in Nederland in early 1900s; period furniture. (Days same as Windmill Museum) Phone 409/723-1545. **FREE**

Pleasure Island. Fishing (four fishing piers, free; also charter boat fishing), crabbing (from 16½ mi of shoreline), boating (launch, marina, supplies, repair; also regattas); horseback riding (stables), picnicking, camping. Music park. Lake connects to the Intracoastal Waterway at its north end and the Port Arthur Ship Channel at its south end, 16 mi from the Gulf of Mexico. Sabine Lake, across the channel on TX 82. **FREE**

Pompeiian Villa. Built as a winter house for Isaac Ellwood of DeKalb, Illinois, in 1900, the villa, with its three-sided courtyard and decorative trim, is a copy of a Pompeiian house of A.D. 79; furnishings incl a Louis XVI parlor set; diamond-dust mirror; art nouveau Baccarat chandelier, French Savannerie rug. (Mon-Fri; closed hols) 1953 Lakeshore Dr. Phone 409/983-5977. ¢

Port of Port Arthur. Port where vessels are loaded and unloaded; 75-ton gantry crane, "Big Arthur." Tours (Mon-Fri; closed hols). 100 W Lakeshore. Phone 409/983-2011. **FREE**

Rose Hill Manor. Palatial colonial residence of Rome H. Woodworth, early Port Arthur mayor. Greek Revival style; borders the Intracoastal Waterway. Tours. (Tues-Sat, by appt; closed hols) 100 Woodworth Blvd. Phone 409/985-7292. ¢

Sabine Woods. The Audubon Society maintains two wooded bird sanctuaries near Pleasure Island. (Daily) 15 mi E on TX 87. Phone 800/235-7822. **FREE**

Sea Rim State Park. Approx 15,000 acres with a 5½-mi-long beach and some marsh areas. Swimming, fishing; nature trail, picnicking, camping (hookups, dump station); primitive beach camping. Standard fees. (Daily) 24 mi SW on TX 87. Phone 409/971-2559. ¢

Special Events

Mardi Gras of SE Texas. Downtown. Family event. Parades, carnival, entertainers, food fair. Late Feb.

Mexican Independence Day Festival. Music, children's costume parade, folk dances, food. Sept. Phone 409/724-6134.

CavOILcade. Festival honoring the oil industry; coronation of queen; carnival, parades, fireworks. Mid-Oct. Phone 409/983-1009.

Motels/Motor Lodges

★★ **HOLIDAY INN PARK CENTRAL.** 2929 Jimmy Johnson Blvd (77642). 409/724-5000; fax 409/724-7644; res 800/465-4329. www.holiday-inn.com. 163 rms, 4 story. S, D $62-$84; suites $150; under 18 free. TV; VCR avail. Pool. Restaurant 6 am-2 pm, 5-10 pm. Rm serv. Bar 5-11 pm. Ck-out noon. Meeting rms. Business servs avail. In-rm modem link. Bellhops. Free airport transportation. Health club privileges. Some refrigerators; microwaves avail. Cr cds: A, C, D, DS, JCB, MC, V.

★★ **RAMADA INN.** 3801 Hwy 73 (77642). 409/962-9858; fax 409/962-3685; res 800/228-2828. www.ramada.com. 125 rms, 2 story. S, D $58-$66; each addl $5; suites $145-$160; stu-

dio rms $65-$73; under 18 free; wkend rates. Pet accepted, some restrictions. TV; cable (premium). Pool; wading pool. Restaurant 6 am-10 pm. Rm serv. Bar 4 pm-2 am. Ck-out noon. Meeting rms. Business servs avail. Free airport transportation. Lighted tennis. Refrigerators, microwaves. Cr cds: A, C, D, DS, MC, V.

Port Isabel

See also Brownsville, Harlingen, South Padre Island

Founded 1790 **Pop** 4,865 **Elev** 15 ft
Area code 956 **Zip** 78578

Information Chamber of Commerce, 421 E Queen Isabella Blvd; 956/943-2262 or 800/527-6102

Special Events

Texas International Fishing Tournament. Marlin Marina. Marlin, tarpon, sailfish, and offshore categories; bay, tag and release, and junior divisions. Phone 956/943-8438. Late July-early Aug.

Shrimp Cook-off. Mid-Oct. Phone 956/943-2262.

Motel/Motor Lodge

★★ **YACHT CLUB HOTEL.** 700 N Yuterria St (78578). 956/943-1301; fax 956/943-2330. 22 rms, 2 story. S $42-$52; D $48-$58; each addl $10; suites $60-$70; under 12 free. TV; cable. Heated pool. Complimentary continental bkfst. Restaurant (see also YACHT CLUB RESTAURANT). On bay. Historic yacht club built 1926. Cr cds: A, C, D, DS, MC, V.

Restaurants

★ **MARCELLO'S ITALIAN RESTAURANT.** 110 N Tarnava (78578). 956/943-7611. www.marcellositalian.com. Hrs: 11:30 am-10 pm; Fri to 11 pm; Sat, Sun 5-10 pm. Closed Thanksgiving, Dec 25. Res accepted; required Fri, Sat. Italian menu. Bar.

Lunch $2.99-$7.99, dinner $7.25-$24.95. Child's menu. Specialties: fettucine, flounder primavera, pasta. Own desserts. Marble fountain at entrance. Cr cds: A, D, DS, MC, V.

D ⟶

★★ **YACHT CLUB.** *700 Yturria St (78578). 956/943-1301.* Hrs: 6-9 pm; wkends to 10 pm; early-bird dinner 5:30-6:45 pm. Closed Wed. Res accepted. Bar. Dinner $13.99-$24.95. Child's menu. Specializes in seafood, prime rib, pasta. In former yacht club built 1926. Cr cds: A, MC, V.

D ⟶

Port Lavaca

(F-6) *See also Victoria*

Founded 1815 **Pop** 12,035 **Elev** 22 ft
Area code 361 **Zip** 77979
Information Port Lavaca-Calhoun County Chamber of Commerce, 2300 TX 35 Bypass, PO Box 528; 361/552-2959 or 800/552-PORT

What to See and Do

Fishing. In Lavaca Bay (3,200-ft-long pier, lighted for night fishing) and the Gulf. Charter boats; also a number of fishing camps in area.

Special Events

Summerfest. Centers on the town's man-made beach. Beauty pageant, music, evening dances, sports tournaments, and recreational games. Third wkend June.

Calhoun County Fair. Second wk Oct. Phone 512/552-2959.

Motel/Motor Lodge

★ **DAYS INN.** *2100 N TX 35 Bypass (77979). 361/552-4511; toll-free 800/329-7466. www.daysinn.com.* 99 rms, 2 story. S $54-$64; D $57-$67; each addl $6; suites $72-$78; under 12 free. Crib free. Pet accepted. TV; cable. Pool. Complimentary continental bkfst. Restaurant 6:30 am-2 pm. Bar 5 pm-midnight Mon-Fri. Ck-out noon. Coin lndry. Meeting rms.

Business servs avail. In-rm modem link. Some refrigerators. Cr cds: A, C, D, DS, MC, V.

D ⟶ ⟶ ⟶ ⟶ SC

Possum Kingdom State Park

See also Graham, Mineral Wells

(15 mi E of Breckenridge on US 180 to Caddo, then 17 mi N on Park Rd 33)

This park, on the shores of Possum Kingdom Reservoir, is located in the Brazos River Valley. The reservoir covers 19,800 acres behind the Morris Sheppard Dam and has a 310-mile shoreline. Water sports are popular; catfish, striped bass, white bass, and crappie abound. Fishing pier. Hiking trail. Canoe, boat, pontoon, bass boat rentals available at park store.

The park covers more than 1,500 acres and offers swimming, waterskiing, boating (ramps); picnicking, playground, concessions, improved campsites, cabins. Standard fees. Phone 940/549-1803.

Quanah

See also Vernon

Pop 3,022 **Elev** 1,568 ft
Area code 940 **Zip** 79252
Information Chamber of Commerce, 220 S Main, PO Box 158; 940/663-2222

What to See and Do

Copper Breaks State Park. Approx 1,900 acres. Swimming, fishing; hiking, picnicking, playground, primitive and improved camping. Museum of local history with dioramas, artifacts; Texas Longhorn herd. Standard fees. (Daily) Contact 777 Park Rd 62. 12 mi S on TX 6. Phone 940/839-4331. ¢

Rockport

(F-6) *See also Corpus Christi*

Founded 1870 **Pop** 7,385 **Elev** 6 ft
Area code 361 **Zip** 78382
Information Chamber of Commerce,
404 Broadway; 361/729-6445 or
800/242-0071
Web www.rockport-fulton.org

Whooping cranes

What to See and Do

Aransas National Wildlife Refuge.
More than 110,000 acres, incl
Matagorda Island overlooking Gulf of
Mexico. This is the principal wintering ground for the endangered
whooping crane; it also houses deer,
alligators, and a variety of birds. Early
mornings and late afternoons are best
for viewing wildlife. Observation
tower; interpretive center; 15-mi auto
tour loop; nature trails. Wheelchair
access to observation tower (ramps).
(Daily; closed Thanksgiving, Dec 25)
Nearest gas 14 mi. 22 mi N on TX 35,
then 9 mi E on FM 774, then 7 mi SE
on FM 2040. Contact Refuge Manager, PO Box 100, Austwell 77950.
Phone 361/286-3559. ¢¢

Beaches. Rockport. Sand beach, park,
ski and yacht basins, boat launch,
bird sanctuary. **Fulton.** 3 mi N on TX
35. Yacht basin, boat launch, 1,000-ft
fishing pier, sand beach. North end
of downtown on TX 35 Business.

Boat trips. Into Aransas National
Wildlife Refuge. Bird-watching, sight-
seeing, and photography tours.
Wharf Cat leaves Rockport Harbor
(Nov-Mar), Phone 361/729-4855.
¢¢¢¢

Center for the Arts. Restored Victorian home hosts shows from sporting
art to modern expression. (Tues-Sun)
902 Navigation Cir. Phone 361/729-
5519. **FREE**

Fulton Mansion State Park. Second
Empire/Victorian mansion, built in the
mid-1870s. First and second floors
authentically fur-
nished. Spacious
lawns slope toward
the beach. (Wed-
Sun; closed Dec 25)
Between Fulton
and Rockport via
TX 35, turn E on
Henderson St.
Phone 361/729-
0386. ¢¢

State parks.

**Copano Bay
Causeway.** Fishing
piers, boating
(ramp); picnicking.
Some fees. 5 mi N
on TX 35. Phone
361/729-8633.

Goose Island. Swimming permitted, lighted fishing pier, boating
(ramp); picnicking, bird-watching,
improved campsites. Standard fees.
(Daily) 10 mi NE on TX 35, then E
on Park Rd 13, partly on mainland
and partly on nearby islands.
Phone 361/729-2858. ¢¢

Texas Maritime Museum. Explores
Texas' seafaring history, from early
Spanish discovery, through Texas
independence, emergence of river
trade, Civil War blockade-running,
and growth of fishing and offshore
drilling industries. (Tues-Sat, Sun
afternoons; closed hols) 1202 Navigation Cir, at Rockport Harbor. Phone
361/729-1271. ¢¢

Special Events

OysterFest. Food and music. First
wkend Mar. Phone 361/729-2388.

Hummer/Bird Celebration. Sept.
Phone 361/729-6445.

SeaFair Rockport. Columbus Day
wkend. Phone 361/729-6445.

Motel/Motor Lodge

★ ★ **BEST WESTERN INN BY THE BAY.** *3902 US 35 N, Fulton (78358). 361/729-8351; fax 361/729-0950; res 800/528-1234. www.bestwestern.com.* 72 rms, 2 story. S $52-$58; D $60-$64; under 12 free. Pet accepted. TV; cable (premium). Pool. Complimentary full bkfst. Restaurant nearby. Ck-out 11 am. Coin lndry. Some refrigerators. Cr cds: A, D, DS, ER, MC, V.

Restaurant

★ **DUCK INN.** *701 US 35 N (78382). 361/729-6663.* Hrs: 6 am-2:30 pm, 5-8:30 pm. Closed Mon; also Jan 1, Thanksgiving, Dec 25. Seafood menu. Bar. Bkfst $2-$5, lunch $3.65-$6.25, dinner $4.75-$16.50. Child's menu. Specialties: stuffed crab, fried shrimp, baked flounder. Family-owned since 1971. Cr cds: A, D, DS, MC, V.

Rusk

See also Jacksonville, Palestine

Pop 5,085 **Elev** 489 ft **Area code** 903 **Zip** 75785
Information Chamber of Commerce, 415 N Main St, PO Box 67; 903/683-4242

What to See and Do

Jim Hogg State Historical Park. Approx 170 acres. "Mountain Home" plantation; replica of the pioneer home of Governor Hogg and his family. Family cemetery, trails. Picnicking, playground. Flowering trees. (Fri-Sun; closed Dec 25) 2 mi NE off US 84. Phone 903/683-4850. ¢

Rusk-Palestine State Park. Incl a 15-acre lake, tennis courts, picnic area, and campsites. Standard fees. (Daily) 3 mi W on US 84. Phone 903/683-5126. ¢ Also here is

Texas State Railroad Historical Park. Four-hr round-trip excursions aboard turn-of-the-century steam-powered train to Palestine (see). Tour through locomotive cab before departure; slide show. Also runs from Palestine. (Summer, Mon and Thurs-Sun; spring and fall, Sat-Sun only) Advance res recommended. Camping adj (full hookups). Phone 903/683-2561. ¢¢¢¢

Salado

See also Georgetown, Temple

Pop 3,475 **Elev** 520 ft **Area code** 254 **Zip** 76571
Information Chamber of Commerce, PO Box 849; 254/947-5040
Web www.salado.com

What to See and Do

Stillhouse Hollow Lake. Swimming, fishing, boating (ramps, storage); picnicking, concession, primitive and improved camping (fee). Fee for some recreation areas. (Daily) Approx 5 mi NW on FM 1670. Phone 254/939-2461. **FREE**

Special Event

Art Fair. Pace Park. First full wkend Aug. Phone 254/947-5040.

Motel/Motor Lodge

★ ★ **STAGECOACH INN.** *I-35, exit 284 (76571). 254/947-5111; fax 254/947-0671; res 800/732-8994.* 82 rms, 2 story. S $71; D $78; each addl $5; suites $82; under 12 free. Crib free. TV; cable (premium). Pool; whirlpool. Playground. Restaurant (see also STAGECOACH INN DINING ROOM). Rm serv 7 am-7 pm. Private club 10 am-10 pm; winter 5-9 pm. Ck-out 1 pm. Meeting rms. Sundries. Lighted tennis. Golf privileges. Lawn games. Microwaves avail. Private patios; balconies. Landscaped grounds on Salado Creek. Cr cds: A, C, D, DS, MC, V.

Restaurants

★ ★ **SALADO MANSION.** *128 S Main St (76571).* 254/947-5157. Hrs: 11 am-9 pm; Fri, Sat to 10 pm. Closed Jan 1, Thanksgiving, Dec 25. Southwestern, Mexican menu. Bar. Lunch $4.25-$8.95, dinner $6.95-$15.95. Specializes in mesquite-grilled trout, beef tenderloin, woodgrilled vegetables. Patio dining with view of waterfall and pond. Built 1857 for a judge; antiques displayed. Totally nonsmoking. Cr cds: A, D, DS, MC, V.
[D]

★ **STAGECOACH INN DINING ROOM.** *1 Main St (76571).* 254/947-9400. Hrs: 11 am-4 pm, 5-9 pm. Res accepted. Complete meals: lunch $7.95-$11.95, dinner $12.95-$18.95. Child's menu. Specializes in prime rib, own pies. Former stagecoach stop; Early American decor. Family-owned since 1945. Cr cds: A, D, DS, MC, V.
[D]

San Angelo (C-4)

Founded 1867 **Pop** 88,439 **Elev** 1,847 ft **Area code** 915
Information Chamber of Commerce, 500 Rio Concho Dr, 76903; 915/655-4136
Web www.sanangelo-tx.com

What to See and Do

Fishing and boating. Lake Nasworthy, 6 mi SW on Knickerbocker Rd. Twin Buttes Lake, 5 mi W of city, off US 67. San Angelo State Park, 4 mi N on Arden Rd, off Mercedes St. North, Middle, and South Concho rivers.

Fort Concho National Historic Landmark. Indian Wars fort comprised of 21 restored stone buildings on 40 acres. Museum covers infantry, cavalry, artillery, and civilian life during fort's active period (1867-1889). Visitor Center on corner of Ave C and South Oakes. (Tues-Sun; closed Jan 1, Thanksgiving, Dec 25) 630 S Oakes, downtown near Concho River. Phone 915/481-2646. ¢

San Angelo State Park. Swimming, waterskiing, fishing, boating (ramps); nature, bicycle, and jogging trails; picnicking, camping (tent and trailer sites) at Dry Creek and Red Arroyo. Two off-road vehicle areas. Fee for some activities. (Daily) Just west of town off of FM 2288. Phone 915/949-4757. ¢

Special Event

Texas Wine & Food Festival. El Paseo de Santa Angela. Apr. Phone 915/653-6793.

Motels/Motor Lodges

★ **EL PATIO MOTOR INN.** *1901 W Beauregard Ave (76901).* 915/655-5711; fax 915/653-2717; res 800/677-7735. 100 rms, 2 story. S $34; D $38; under 12 free; wkly rates; higher rates rodeo. Crib avail. Pet accepted; $5/day. TV; cable (premium), VCR avail. Complimentary coffee in lobby. Ck-out noon. Business servs avail. Pool. Cr cds: A, DS, MC, V.
🐾 ➳ ≋ 🐾 SC

★ ★ ★ **HOLIDAY INN CONVENTION CENTER.** *441 Rio Concho Dr (76903).* 915/658-2828; fax 915/658-8741; toll-free 800/465-4329. www.holiday-inn.com/sanangelotx. 148 rms, 6 story. S $99; D $109; each addl $8; suites $140-$160; under 12 free. Crib free. Pet accepted, some restrictions. TV; cable (premium). Indoor pool; whirlpool, poolside serv. Restaurant 6:30 am-2 pm, 5:30-10 pm. Bar 4-11:30 pm. Ck-out noon. Meeting rms. Business servs avail. Some refrigerators. Microwaves in suites. Cr cds: A, C, D, DS, JCB, MC, V.
[D] 🐾 ⬧ ⬧ ✕ ≋ 🔥

★ ★ **INN OF THE CONCHOS.** *2021 N Bryant Blvd (76903).* 915/658-2811; fax 915/653-7560; toll-free 800/621-6091. 125 rms, 2 story. S $40-$44; D $44-$50; each addl $6; suites $85-$100; under 12 free. Crib $6. Pet accepted, some restrictions. TV; cable (premium). Pool. Restaurant adj 6 am-9 pm; Sun 7 am-2 pm. Rm serv. Bar 4 pm-2 am. Ck-out noon. Meeting rms. Sundries. Grill. Cr cds: A, D, DS, MC, V.
[D] 🐾 ≋ ≋ 🔥

★ ★ **INN OF THE WEST.** *415 W Beauregard (76903).* 915/653-2995;

fax 915/659-4393; toll-free 800/582-9668. www.bestinn.com. 75 rms, 3 story. S $43; D $55; each addl $6; under 12 free. Crib $6. Pet accepted, some restrictions. TV; cable (premium), VCR avail. Indoor pool. Restaurant 6 am-8 pm. Rm serv. Ck-out noon. Meeting rms. Business servs avail. In-rm modem link. Sun deck. Cr cds: A, C, D, DS, MC, V.

★★ **LA QUINTA INN.** *2307 Loop 306 (76904). 915/949-0515; fax 915/944-1187; toll-free 800/687-6667. www.laquinta.com. 170 rms, 2 story. S $59-$66; D $66-$81; each addl $7; suites $74; under 18 free. Crib free. Pet accepted, some restrictions. TV; cable (premium). Pool. Complimentary continental bkfst. Ck-out noon. Guest lndry. Meeting rms. Business servs avail. In-rm modem link. Health club privileges. Cr cds: A, C, D, DS, MC, V.*

Restaurants

★★ **CHINA GARDEN.** *4217 College Hill Blvd (76904). 915/949-2838.* Hrs: 11 am-10 pm; Fri, Sat to 11 pm. Closed most major hols. Chinese, Amer menu. Bar. Lunch $4.75-$12.95, dinner $5.25-$27. Child's menu. Specializes in shrimp, steak, seafood. Chinese decor. Cr cds: A, D, DS, MC, V.

★★ **ZENTNER'S DAUGHTER STEAK HOUSE.** *1901 Knickerbocker Rd (76904). 915/949-2821.* Hrs: 11 am-2 pm, 5-9:30 pm; Wed, Sun to 10 pm; Fri, Sat to 11 pm. Closed Dec 25. Bar. Lunch $4.95-$5.25, dinner $4.25-$18.95. Specializes in steak. Cr cds: A, D, DS, MC, V.

San Antonio

(E-5) See also New Braunfels, Seguin

Founded 1718 **Pop** 1,144,646
Elev 701 ft **Area code** 210

Information Convention & Visitors Bureau, 203 S St. Mary's St, PO Box 2277, 78298; 210/207-6700 or 800/447-3372
Web www.sanantoniocvb.com

In the course of its colorful history, this beautiful old city has been under six flags: France, Spain, Mexico, the Republic of Texas, Confederate States of America, and United States of America. Each has definitely left its mark.

The Mission San Antonio de Valero (the Alamo) was founded by Friar Antonio de San Buenaventura Olivares in May, 1718, near the tree-lined San Antonio River. Four more missions were built along the river during the next 13 years. All continued to operate until about 1794. In 1718, Don Martin de Alarcon, Captain General and Governor of the Province of Texas, established a military post here. San Antonio has been a military center ever since.

The Alamo is in the center of town. Here, from February 23 to March 6, 1836, Davy Crockett, Colonel James Bowie, Colonel William B. Travis, and 186 other Texans stood off General Antonio López de Santa Anna, dictator-president of Mexico, and his 5,000 troops. Every defender died in the battle. Their heroic stand was the inspiration for the famous Texas battle cry "Remember the Alamo!" Three months after the Alamo tragedy, San Antonio was almost deserted. Within a few years, however, it became a great western outpost. In the 1840s there was a heavy influx of Germans whose descendants still add to the city's cosmopolitan air. In the 1870s, new settlers, adventurers, and cowboys on long cattle drives made this a tough, hard-drinking, hard-fighting, gambling town. San Antonio has evolved into a modern, prosperous city, but it retains much of the flavor of its past.

Additional Visitor Information

The Visitor Information Center has many helpful leaflets; contact 317 Alamo Plaza, 78205; 210/270-8748. For further information contact the Convention & Visitors Bureau, PO Box 2277, 78298; 210/207-6700 or 800/447-3372. San Antonio Conservation Society, 107 King William St, 78204, 210/224-6163, provides brochures for a walking tour of the King William Historic District.

Transportation

Car Rental Agencies. See IMPORTANT TOLL-FREE NUMBERS.

Public Transportation. Buses, trolleys (Metropolitan Transit Authority), phone 210/362-2020.

Rail Passenger Service. Amtrak 800/872-7245.

Airport Information

San Antonio Intl Airport. Information 210/207-3411; lost and found 210/207-3451; cash machines, Terminals 1 and 2.

What to See and Do

Alamodome. Multipurpose dome boasts a cable-suspended roof, which is anchored from four concrete towers. This sports, concert, and convention center employs 160,000 gross sq ft of exhibit space and 30,000 sq ft of conference space with configurations for basketball, hockey, football, and major concerts (max seating 73,200). Guided tours incl executive suites, locker rms, mechanical features, and the playing field (phone for schedule). Just east of HemisFair Park, across I-37. Phone 210/207-3663. ¢¢

Auto tour. San Antonio Missions National Historical Park. Four Spanish colonial missions in San Antonio are administered by the National Park Service. Exhibits, talks, cultural demonstrations. Parishes within the missions are still active. (Daily; closed Jan 1, Thanksgiving, Dec 25) Phone 210/534-8833. **FREE**

Mission Concepcion. Established in 1731, this is one of the best preserved missions in Texas and the oldest unrestored stone mission church in the country. It is built of porous limestone found nearby. There are some fine 18th-century frescoes; the acoustics of the building are remarkable. (Daily; closed Jan 1, Thanksgiving, Dec 25) 807 Mission Rd. Phone 210/534-1540. Turn left onto Mission Rd, follow Mission Pkwy signs to

Mission San Jose. (1720) One of the largest and most successful missions in the Southwest; the church, Native American quarters, granary, and old mill have been restored. Built of tufaceous limestone, the church is famous for its carvings and masonry. The sacristy window is sometimes referred to as "Rosa's Window." Follow Napier Ave, right on Padre Dr and through underpass to Espada park. (Daily; closed Jan 1, Thanksgiving, Dec 25) 6539 San Jose Dr. Phone 210/932-1001. Here is

Espada Dam. (1740) Constructed to divert river water into irrigation ditches. Waters flow into Espada Aqueduct (see), which carries water to Mission Espada. Continue on Padre Dr (through low-water crossing) through Villamain to

Mission San Juan. (1731) A self-sufficient community was centered around this mission. Indian artisans and farmers established a trade network with their surplus. (Daily) 9101 Graf Rd. Phone 210/534-0749. Take Graf Rd back to Ashley Rd, turn right to Villamain Rd S, right on Camino Coahuilteca to

Mission Espada. (1731) Southernmost of the San Antonio chain of missions. Unusual arched doorway. Friary and chapel (exc for facade) are restored. (Daily) 10040 Espada Rd. Phone 210/627-2021. Follow Espada Rd N to

Espada Aqueduct. (1735) This 120-ft-long Spanish Colonial aqueduct carried water over Piedras Creek continuously for more than 200 yrs. Nearby farms still use water from this system. Return to Espada Rd S, turn right to Ashley and right again on Roosevelt Ave to return to San Antonio.

Brackenridge Park. This 340-acre park has picnicking, playground, athletic fields, golf, carousel, miniature train, pedal boats. Some fees. (Daily) N Broadway (US 81), 2 mi N of the Alamo. Phone 210 /207-8000. Also here are

Japanese Tea Gardens. Floral displays on walls and floor of abandoned quarry. Outdoor Grecian theater is also here. (Daily) 3800 N St. Mary's St. Phone 210/821-3120. **FREE**

Pioneer Memorial Hall. Houses collections of Texas trail drivers, pio-

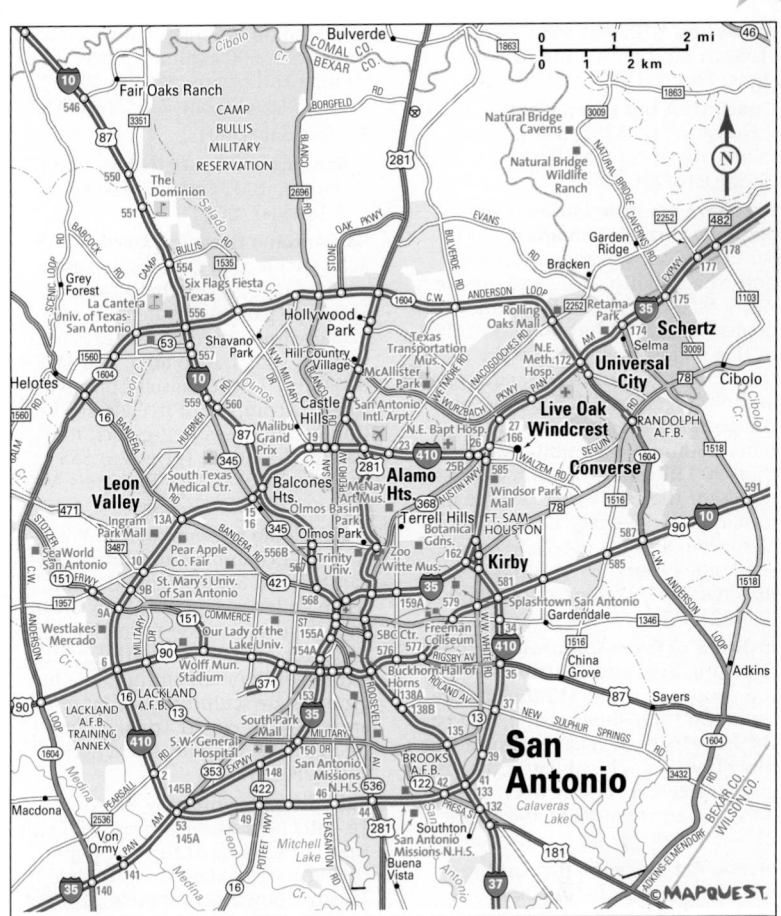

neers, and the Texas Rangers. Saddles, guns, tools, furniture, and other memorabilia illustrate lifestyle of early Texans. (Daily) 3805 Broadway. Phone 210/822-9011. ¢¢

Witte Museum. History, science, and the humanities collections and exhibits. Special attractions incl "Ancient Texans: Rock Art and Lifeways Along the Lower Pecos" and "Texas Wild: Ecology Illustrated." On museum grounds are four reconstructed early Texas houses. Changing exhibits. (Daily; closed Thanksgiving, Dec 25) 3801 Broadway at Tuleta St. Phone 210/357-1886. ¢¢

Zoological Gardens and Aquarium. Bird and antelope collections particularly notable; also children's zoo

with boat ride. (Daily) 3903 N St. Mary's St. Phone 210/734-7183. ¢¢¢

Buckhorn Saloon and Museum. Buckhorn Hall of Horns houses vast collection of horns, animal trophies, and memorabilia dating to 1881. Also Hall of Fins and Feathers, collection of birds, fish, and marine life. Buckhorn Saloon and O. Henry House. Hall of Texas History depicts memorable periods from 1534-1898. (Daily; closed Thanksgiving, Dec 25) 318 E Houston St. Phone 210/247-4000. ¢¢

Cascade Caverns Park. Located on 105-acre park is a water-formed underground cavern with spectacular rock formations. Special feature of this natural attraction is a 100-ft underground waterfall, viewed as the grand finale of a 45-min guided tour (daily). Park has picnic facilities. 14

mi NW on I-10, exit 543 Cascade Caverns Rd, then W and follow signs. Phone 830/755-8080. ¢¢¢

Coach USA bus tours. Contact 1430 E Houston St, 78202. 849 E Commerce, Rivercenter Mall, third level. Phone 210/226-1706.

Fort Sam Houston Museum and National Historic Landmark. Fort Sam Houston is headquarters for both the US Fifth Army and Brooke Army Medical Center. Museum depicts history of fort and US Army in this region from 1845 to the present. Exhibits of uniforms, equipt, and photographs detail growth of the post and events that occurred here. Audiovisual exhibits. More than 900 historic structures on base represent the era 1876-1935; the historic quadrangle once detained Geronimo and his renegade Apaches; self-guided tours. (Wed-Sun; closed hols) Off I-35, Walters St exit. Phone 210/221-1886. **FREE**

Institute of Texan Cultures. Exhibits depicting lives and contributions of the people of Texas. Multimedia presentation (four shows daily) is part of the University of Texas at San Antonio. (Tues-Sun; closed Easter, Thanksgiving, Dec 25) Parking (fee). 801 S Bowie St, in HemisFair Park. Phone 210/458-2300. ¢¢

McNay Art Museum. Incl Gothic, medieval, late 19th- and 20th-century American and European paintings; sculpture, graphic arts; rare books on theater arts, architecture, and fine arts; changing exhibits (some fees). Patio with fountains; gardens. (Tues-Sat, also Sun afternoons; closed hols) 6000 N New Braunfels, at Austin Hwy. Phone 210/824-5368. **FREE**

Natural Bridge Caverns. These caverns are still in their formative period; Sherwood Forest has totem pole formations; the Castle of the White Giants has 40-ft-high Kings Throne; 70°F. One- and 1¼-hr guided tours every 30 min. Picnicking. (Daily; closed Jan 1, Thanksgiving, Dec 25) 8 mi NE of I-35 exit 175, on FM 3009 (Natural Bridge Caverns Rd). Phone 210/651-6101. ¢¢¢

Plaza Wax Museum/Ripley's Believe It or Not!. Wax museum with more than 225 historical and entertainment figures; horror chamber. In same building, Ripley's museum with more than 500 exhibits of the strange and bizarre. (Daily) 301 Alamo Plaza. Phone 210/224-WAXX.

Professional sports.

  San Antonio Spurs (NBA). Alamodome, 100 Montana. Phone 210/554-7700.

San Antonio Botanical Gardens. 33 acres incl formal gardens, Japanese garden, rose garden, herb gardens, xeriscape gardens, garden for the visually impaired. Native Texas area features lake, native flora, and 1800s dwellings. Lucile Halsell Conservatory is a complex of five glass exhibition greenhouses. Self-guided tours. (Daily; closed Jan 1, Dec 25) 555 Funston Pl, at N New Braunfels Ave. Phone 210/207-3255. ¢¢

San Antonio Museum of Art. Works incl pre-Columbian and Latin American folk art; Spanish colonial and Asian galleries; contemporary art in the Cowden Gallery; Ewing Halsell Wing for Ancient Art, with Egyptian, Greek, and Roman antiquities. On grounds are sculpture garden, rest areas. (Daily; closed Thanksgiving, Dec 25) 200 W Jones Ave. Phone 210/978-8158. ¢¢

San Antonio Symphony. Season incl 16 pairs of classical concerts (Fri and Sat) and ten sets of three of pops concerts (Sept-May, Fri-Sun) Majestic Theatre, downtown. Phone 210/554-1010. ¢¢¢¢

Sea World of Texas. The world's largest marine life park (250 acres) offers more than 25 shows, exhibits, and attractions. Killer whale shows at 4,500-seat, multimillion-gallon "Shamu Stadium"; 300,000-gallon coral reef aquarium features many species of sharks and thousands of Indo-Pacific fishes. Sea lion, beluga whale/dolphin, and water ski shows; penguin habitat; water rides, children's play area. (Memorial Day-Mid-Aug, daily; early Mar-late May and mid-Aug-Oct, wkends) 10500 Sea World Dr, 16 mi NW via TX 151, between Loop 410 and Loop 1604. Phone 210/523-3611. ¢¢¢¢

Six Flags Fiesta Texas-9. A 200-acre amusement park dramatically set in a former limestone quarry. Four themed areas—Spassburg (German), Los Festivales (Hispanic), Crackaxle Canyon (Western), and Rockville

(1950s)—arranged around central Texas Sq, highlight live entertainment productions on seven theater stages. Features incl aeroflight thrill ride, *Dornrschen,* an early 1900s-style carousel, and *Kinderspielplatz,* a major area devoted to children's rides and amusements. Many restaurants and shops. (Mid-late Mar and Memorial Day wkend-Labor Day wkend, daily; late Mar-late May and early Sept-early Nov, Fri-Sun) 17000 I-10 W, at jct Loop 410. Phone 210/697-5050. ¢¢¢¢

Southwest School of Art & Craft. Programs incl art school, two galleries, art workshops, lectures and tours. (Mon-Sat; closed some hols) 300 Augusta, on grounds of Old Ursuline Academy and Convent (1848). Phone 210/224-1848. **FREE**

Splashtown. An 18-acre water recreation theme park with 17 rides and attractions, incl wave pool, slide complexes, and large children's play area. Changing rms, showers, lockers, rafts avail. (Memorial Day-Labor Day, daily; May and Sept, wkends) I-35 at exit 160. Phone 210/227-1400. ¢¢¢

Steves Homestead. (1876) Victorian-era mansion on banks of San Antonio River in the King William Historic District. Period furnishings; landscaped grounds have carriage house, stable, wash house. Tours (daily; closed hols) 509 King William St. Phone 210/225-5924. ¢

Sunset Station. Restored 1902 train depot serves as downtown entertainment destination with live music clubs, restaurants, and shopping. (Call for schedule) 1174 E Commerce. Phone 210/222-9481.

Texas Adventure. Multimedia show portraying the story of Texas independence with the Alamo drama as its centerpiece, this state-of-the-art presentation is impressive with surrounding special effects. (Daily) 307 Alamo Plaza. Phone 210/227-0388. ¢¢

Tower of the Americas. Stands 750 ft high; observation level at 579 ft; glass-walled elevators. Revolving restaurant at 550-ft level. (Daily) HemisFair Park. Phone 210/207-8615. ¢¢

VIA San Antonio Streetcar. Reproduction of rail streetcar that traveled the streets of San Antonio during the 1920s. Downtown route incl St. Paul's Sq, the King William District, Market Sq, and Alamo Plaza. (Daily) Phone 210/362-2020.

Vietnam War Memorial. Memorial depicts a scene from the Battle for Hill 881 South—a radioman calling for help for a wounded comrade. In front of Municipal Auditorium, corner of E Martin and Jefferson Sts.

★ **Walking tour.** Start at east side of Alamo Plaza (south of E Houston St, north of Crockett St, and east of N Alamo) and visit

The Alamo. (1718) Defended by the Texas heroes in the 1836 battle. The former church (now the shrine) and the Long Barracks Museum (formerly the Convento) are all that remain of the original mission buildings. The Long Barracks Museum contains an exhibit on Alamo history. Also on the grounds is a research library and museum-souvenir building. (Daily; closed Dec 24-25) 300 N Alamo Plaza. Phone 210/225-1391. The Coppini Cenotaph monument on Alamo Plaza shows carved figures of the heroes. It was installed to mark the Centennial of the Battle of the Alamo. Across the street and south is

Menger Hotel. A famous hostelry in which Robert E. Lee, Theodore Roosevelt, and William Jennings Bryan stayed. Bar where Roosevelt recruited the "Rough Riders" is still in use. Phone 800/345-9285.

HemisFair Park. Among HemisFair 68 buildings that remain are the Tower of the Americas and the Institute of Texan Cultures. Also here are the Henry B. Gonzalez Convention Center and Theater for the Performing Arts, urban water park, shops, restaurants. Turn left (west) on Market St to river. Phone 210/207-8572.

Arneson River Theatre. 503 Villita St. The audience sits on one side of the river; the stage is on the other. (See SPECIAL EVENTS) Climb steps through the theater and go through the arch. Phone 210/207-8610.

La Villita. South of Paseo de La Villita, west of S Alamo St, north of Nueva St, and east of S Presa St. This 250-yr-old Spanish settlement was reconstructed during 1939 to preserve its unique buildings. A haven in the midst of the city where the old arts and crafts continue to flourish, the area has three patios where various functions and festivals are held. (Daily; closed Jan 1, Thanksgiving, Dec 25) 418 Villita St. Phone 210/207-8610. Incl

Cos House. Here, on Dec 10, 1835, General Perfecto de Cos signed Articles of Capitulation after Texans had taken the town. Phone 210/207-8610. Leave La Villita and walk north on Presa St, crossing the river to the

Paseo del Rio. This 2½-mi "River Walk" along the meandering San Antonio River is lined with colorful shops, galleries, hotels, popular nightspots, and many sidewalk cafes. Water taxis provide transportation. Going west a short distance from the Tower Life Building exit is Main Plaza. Phone 210/227-4262.

San Fernando Cathedral. The original parish church of Canary Islands settlers. Phone 210/227-1297.

Military Plaza. City Hall stands in the center; on the northwest corner is a statue of Moses Austin, often called the Father of Texas. Just behind City Hall is the

Spanish Governor's Palace. (1749) Note date and Hapsburg crest in the keystone. This was the office and residence of Spanish administrators. (Daily; closed Jan 1, Thanksgiving, Dec 25; also Fiesta Fri and two wks following) 105 Plaza de Armas. Phone 210/224-0601. ¢

Casa Navarro State Historical Park. Complex of three limestone and adobe houses built circa 1850; home of a Texas patriot. Period furnishings; exhibits and documents. Tours. (Wed-Sun) 228 S Laredo St. Phone 210/226-4801. ¢

Market Square. Begins a blk west of the palace where you cross San Pedro Creek. The city market offers Mexican restaurants, shops, and entertainment. (Daily) Return to starting point east along Commerce St. Phone 210/207-8600.

Special Events

San Antonio Stock Show & Rodeo. SBC Center, 3201 E Houston St. Phone 210/225-5851. Early-mid Feb.

Dawn at The Alamo. The Alamo. Early Mar. Phone 210/225-1391.

Fiesta San Antonio. Celebrating Texas heroes since 1891 with three major parades (one on the San Antonio River), sports, and food. More than 150 events held throughout city. Phone 210/227-5191. Late Apr.

Summer Festival. Performances of Latin-flavored *Fiesta Noche del Rio*, *Fiesta Flamenca*, and *Fandango* at Arneson River Theatre. May-Aug.

Boerne Berges Fest. 30 mi NW on I-10, in Boerne. German Festival of the Hills; continuous German and country and western entertainment, arts and crafts, horse races, pig races, parade, 10K walk, special events. Father's Day wkend. Phone 830/249-4773.

Texas Folklife Festival. Institute of Texan Cultures, HemisFair Park. Crafts, folk music and dancing, entertainment, food representing more than 30 ethnic groups in Texas. Phone 210/458-2300. Early June.

Diez y Seis. Citywide. Three days of celebration mark the Sept 17 Mexican independence from Spain. Incl gala, Market Sq celebrations, parade, festivals, dance presentations, and charreadas (rodeos). Phone 210/223-3151. Mid-Sept.

Fiestas Navidenas. Market Sq. Christmas festival; bands; Mexican folk dances; Christmas foods. Phone 210/207-8600. Late Nov-Mid-Dec.

Las Posadas. River Walk. Procession assembles at La Mansion del Rio Hotel (see HOTELS). Song and candlelight procession has been a tradition for more than 250 yrs. Held in conjunction with **Fiesta de las Luminarias**, the fiesta of lights, when the River Walk is lined with candles. Reenactment of the Holy Family's search for an inn. Evening ends with piñata party in Plaza Juárez in La Villita. Phone 210/224-6163. Mid-Dec.

Motels/Motor Lodges

★★ **BEST WESTERN CONTINEN-TAL INN.** *9735 I-35 N (78233). 210/655-3510; fax 210/655-0778; res 800/528-1234. www.bestwestern.com.* 161 rms, 2 story. S $69-$79; D $79-$89. Crib free. TV; cable (premium). Pool; wading pool, whirlpools. Playground. Complimentary full bkfst. Restaurant 6 am-10 pm. Rm serv. Bar. Ck-out noon. Coin lndry. Meeting rms. Business servs avail. In-rm modem link. Sundries. Some refrigerators. Cr cds: A, C, D, DS, MC, V.

⬛ 🐾 ⬛ ⬛ ⬛ SC

★★ **CLARION HOTEL AIRPORT.** *12828 US 281 N (78216). 210/494-7600; fax 210/545-4314; res 800/362-8700. www.choicehotels.com.* 125 rms, 4 story. S $99-$170; D $109-$180; each addl $10; under 12 free. Crib free. Pet accepted, some restrictions; $50 ($25 refundable). TV; cable (premium). Indoor pool. Complimentary full bkfst; evening refreshments. Complimentary coffee in rms. Ck-out noon. Meeting rms. In-rm modem link. Valet serv. Free airport transportation. Sauna. Bathrm phones, refrigerators, microwaves; some in-rm whirlpools. Cr cds: A, C, D, DS, MC, V.

⬛ 🐾 SC ⬛ 🐾 ⬛

★★ **COURTYARD BY MARRIOTT.** *8585 Marriott Dr (78229). 210/614-7100; fax 210/614-7110; res 800/321-2211. www.courtyard.com.* 146 rms, 3 story. S, D $79-$94; wkend rates. Crib avail. TV; cable (premium). Pool; whirlpool. Complimentary coffee in rms. Restaurant 6:30-10:30 am; Sat, Sun 7 am-noon. Bar 5-10 pm. Ck-out noon. Coin lndry. Meeting rms. Business servs avail. In-rm modem link. Valet serv. Exercise equipt. Microwaves avail; refrigerator in suites. Balconies. Cr cds: A, D, DS, MC, V.

⬛ ⬛ ⬛ ⬛ ⬛

★★ **DRURY INN AND SUITES.** *95 NE Loop 410 (78216). 210/308-8100; fax 210/341-6758. www.druryinn.com.* 286 rms, 6 story. S $69.95-$79.95; D $79.95-$94.95; each addl $10; under 18 free. Crib free. Pet accepted, some restrictions. TV; cable (premium). Pool; whirlpool. Complimentary continental bkfst.

Restaurant opp 11 am-midnight. Ck-out noon. Meeting rm. Business servs avail. In-rm modem link. Free airport transportation. Refrigerators, microwaves. Picnic tables. Cr cds: A, C, D, DS, MC, V.

⬛ 🐾 ⬛ ⬛ ⬛

★ **HAMPTON INN DOWNTOWN RIVERWALK.** *414 Bowie St (78205). 210/225-8500; fax 210/225-8526; res 800/426-7688. www.hamptoninn.com.* 169 rms, 6 story. Feb-Oct: S $119; D $129; each addl $10; under 18 free; golf plans; higher rates special events; lower rates rest of yr. Crib free. TV; cable (premium). Complimentary continental bkfst. Coffee in rms. Restaurant nearby. Ck-out 11 am. Meeting rms. Business servs avail. In-rm modem link. Coin lndry. Pool. Cr cds: A, C, D, DS, MC, V.

⬛ ⬛ ⬛ ⬛ ⬛ ⬛

★★ **HAMPTON INN SIX FLAGS AREA.** *11010 I-10 W (78230). 210/561-9058; fax 210/690-5566; toll-free 877/731-4331. www.zmchotels. com.* 121 rms, 6 story. S $67-$87; D $77-$97; each addl $10; suites $119-$149; under 18 free. Crib free. TV; cable (premium). Pool. Complimentary continental bkfst. Coffee in rms. Restaurant adj open 24 hrs. Ck-out noon. Meeting rms. Business servs avail. In-rm modem link. Many refrigerators; microwaves avail. Cr cds: A, C, D, DS, MC, V.

⬛ ⬛ ⬛ ⬛ SC

★★ **HOLIDAY INN.** *217 N Saint Mary's St (78205). 210/224-2500; fax 210/223-1302; toll-free 800/445-8475. www.holiday-inn.com.* 313 rms, 23 story. S, D $139-$189; suites $225-$375; under 18 free. Crib free. Pet accepted, some restrictions. Valet parking $15. TV; cable. Heated pool; whirlpool, poolside serv. Restaurant 6:30 am-2 pm, 5:30-10 pm. Rm serv 6 am-midnight. Bar noon-12:30 am; Fri, Sat to 2 am. Ck-out noon. Convention facilities. Business servs avail. In-rm modem link. Exercise equipt. Refrigerator in suites. Balconies. View of river. Cr cds: A, C, D, DS, JCB, MC, V.

⬛ 🐾 ⬛ ⬛ ⬛ ⬛ SC

★ **HOLIDAY INN EXPRESS.** *7043 Culebra Rd (78238). 210/521-1485; fax 210/520-5924; toll-free 888/889-*

8771. *www.hiexpress.com/sat-west.* 72 rms, 2 story. S, D $59-$129; each addl $5; under 18 free. Crib free. TV; cable (premium). Pool. Complimentary continental bkfst. Restaurant adj open 24 hrs. Ck-out noon. Meeting rm. Business servs avail. In-rm modem link. Coin lndry. Refrigerators; microwaves avail. Cr cds: A, C, D, DS, JCB, MC, V.

[icons]

★★ **HOLIDAY INN EXPRESS AIRPORT.** *91 NE Loop 410 (78216). 210/308-6700; res 800/465-4329. www.holiday-inn.com.* 154 rms, 10 story. S $75-$99; D $85-$109; under 19 free. Crib free. Pet accepted, some restrictions. TV; cable (premium). Pool. Complimentary continental bkfst. Restaurant adj 11 am-midnight. Ck-out noon. Meeting rms. Business servs avail. Valet serv. In-rm modem link. Coin lndry. Free airport transportation. Microwaves, refrigerators avail. Cr cds: A, C, D, DS, MC, V.

[icons]

★★ **LA QUINTA INN.** *900 Dolorosa St (78207). 210/271-0001; fax 210/228-0663; res 800/531-5900. www. laquinta.com.* 124 rms, 2 story. S, D $79-$121; each addl $6; suites $143; under 18 free; higher rates: wkends, Fiesta wk. Crib free. Pet accepted, some restrictions. TV; cable (premium). Pool. Continental bkfst. Complimentary coffee in rms. Restaurant opp open 24 hrs. Ck-out noon. Business servs avail. In-rm modem link. Cr cds: A, C, D, DS, ER, MC, V.

[icons]

★★ **LA QUINTA INN.** *7134 NW Loop 410 (78238). 210/680-8883; fax 210/681-3877; res 800/531-5900. www.laquinta.com.* 195 rms, 3 story. S, D $59-$79; suites $89-$159; under 18 free. Crib free. Pet accepted, some restrictions. TV; cable (premium). Pool. Complimentary continental bkfst. Coffee in rms. Restaurant adj open 24 hrs. Ck-out noon. Meeting rms. In-rm modem link. Refrigerator, microwave in suites. Cr cds: A, C, D, DS, MC, V.

[icons]

★★ **PEAR TREE INN BY DRURY/SAN ANTONIO AIRPORT.** *143 NE Loop 410 (78216). 210/366-*

9300. *www.peartreeinn.com.* 125 rms, 4 story. S $58.95-$60.95; D $54.95-$69.95; each addl $10; under 18 free. Crib free. Pet accepted, some restrictions. TV; cable (premium). Pool. Complimentary bkfst. Restaurant adj 6 am-11 pm. Ck-out noon. Coin lndry. Meeting rms. Business servs avail. In-rm modem link. Free airport transportation. Some refrigerators; microwaves avail. Cr cds: A, C, D, DS, MC, V.

[icons]

★ **RED ROOF INN.** *333 Wolf Rd (78216). 210/340-4055; fax 210/340-4031; toll-free 800/843-7663. www. redroof.com.* 135 rms, 3 story. S, D $41.99-$47.99; each addl $5; under 18 free. Crib free. Pet accepted. TV; cable (premium). Complimentary coffee. Restaurant nearby. Ck-out noon. Meeting rms. Business servs avail. In-rm modem link. Free airport transportation. Cr cds: A, C, D, DS, MC, V.

[icons]

★ **TRAVELODGE SUITES.** *4934 NW Loop 410 (78229). 210/680-3351; fax 210/680-5182; res 800/578-7878. www.travelodge.com.* 201 kit. suites, 3 story. S, D $49-$89; each addl $5; under 18 free; wkly rates. Crib free. TV; cable (premium). Pool. Complimentary continental bkfst. Coffee in rms. Ck-out noon. Meeting rms. Business servs avail. Coin lndry. Free airport transportation. Health club privileges. Microwaves, refrigerators. Cr cds: A, D, DS, MC, V.

[icons]

★★★ **WOODFIELD SUITES.** *100 W Durango (78204). 210/212-5400; fax 210/212-5407; res 800/338-0008. www.woodfieldsuitessa.com.* 6 story, 151 suites. Suites $79-$149; each addl $10; under 18 free. Crib avail. Pet accepted, some restrictions, fee. Parking lot. Pool; whirlpool. TV; cable (premium). Complimentary continental bkfst, newspaper, toll-free calls. Restaurant nearby. Bar. Ck-out noon, ck-in 3 pm. Meeting rms. Coin lndry. Exercise equipt. Video games. Cr cds: A, C, D, DS, JCB, MC, V.

[icons]

Hotels

★ ★ ★ **ADAM'S MARK.** *111 Pecan St E (78205). 210/354-2800; fax 210/354-2700; res 800/444-2326. www.adamsmark.com.* 410 rms, 21 story. S, D $99-$255; suites $355-$950; under 12 free; family rates; package plans. Crib avail. Valet parking $14; garage $9. TV; cable (premium). Complimentary coffee in rms. Restaurant 6:30 am-10 pm. Rm serv 24 hrs. Bar. Ck-out noon. Convention facilities. Business servs avail. In-rm modem link. Concierge. Shopping arcade. Coin lndry. Exercise equipt. Pool; whirlpool, poolside serv. Some refrigerators. Cr cds: A, C, D, DS, JCB, MC, V.

[D] [≈] [⊀] [⊒] [⚒] [SC]

★ ★ **DOUBLETREE CLUB HOTEL SAN ANTONIO AIRPORT.** *1111 NE Loop 410 (78209). 210/828-9031; fax 210/828-3066; res 800/222-8733. www.doubletreehotels.com.* 227 rms, 10 story. S, D $69-$149; each addl $10; suites $89-$169; under 18 free. Crib avail. TV; cable (premium). Complimentary coffee in rms. Restaurant 6 am-11 pm. Bar 4-11 pm. Ck-out noon. Meeting rms. Business center. In-rm modem link. No bellhops. Free airport transportation. Exercise equipt. Pool; whirlpool. Some refrigerators, microwaves. Some balconies. Cr cds: A, C, D, DS, MC, V.

[D] [≈] [⊀] [⊒] [⚒] [SC] [⊀]

★ ★ ★ **DOUBLETREE HOTEL.** *37 NE Loop 410 (78216). 210/366-2424; fax 210/341-0410; res 800/222-8733. www.doubletreehotels.com.* 290 rms, 5 story. S $119-$169; D $129-$179; each addl $10; suites $299-$399; under 17 free; wkend rates. Crib free. TV; cable (premium). Pool; whirlpool. Coffee in rms. Restaurants (see also CASCABEL). Bar 4 pm-2 am. Ck-out noon. Convention facilities. Business servs avail. In-rm modem link. Free airport transportation. Exercise equipt; sauna. Some refrigerators. Private patios, balconies. Luxury level. Cr cds: A, D, DS, MC, V.

[D] [≈] [⊀] [⊒] [⚒]

★ ★ **FAIRMOUNT, WYNDHAM HISTORIC HOTEL.** *401 S Alamo (78205). 210/224-8800; fax 210/475-0082; toll-free 800/WYNDHAM.* *www.wyndham.com.* 37 rms, 3 story, 17 suites. S $205-$230; D $210-$230; suites $255-$550; under 12 free. Crib free. Valet parking $17. TV; cable (premium), VCR (free movies). Restaurant (see also POLO'S). Bar 11:30-1 am; entertainment Fri, Sat. Ck-out noon. Meeting rms. Business servs avail. In-rm modem link. Concierge. Exercise equipt. Bathrm phones. Balconies. Garden courtyard. Near Riverwalk. Cr cds: A, C, D, DS, MC, V.

[D] [⊀] [⊒] [⚒] [SC]

★ ★ **FOUR POINTS BY SHERATON RIVERWALK NORTH.** *110 Lexington Ave (78205). 210/223-9461; fax 210/227-4054; res 800/223-9461. www.fourpoints.com.* 324 rms, 9 story. S, D $89-$169; suites $150-$450; under 18 free. Crib free. Parking: self $6, valet $12. Pool. TV; cable (premium). Restaurant 6:30 am-2 pm, 5-10 pm. Rm serv. Bar 1 pm-midnight. Ck-out noon. Meeting rms. Business servs avail. Bellhops. Gift shop. Exercise equipt. Microwaves avail; refrigerators in suites. Balconies. On river. Cr cds: A, C, D, DS, JCB, MC, V.

[D] [≈] [⊀] [⊒]

★ ★ ★ **HILTON PALACIO DEL RIO.** *200 S Alamo St (78205). 210/222-1400; fax 210/270-0761; toll-free 800/445-8667. www.palaciodelrio. hilton.com.* 483 rms, 22 story. S $165-$215; D $185-$235; each addl $20; suites $425-$1,000; package plans. Crib free. Pet accepted, some restrictions. Garage $12, valet $25. TV; cable (premium), VCR avail. Pool; whirlpool, poolside serv. Complimentary coffee in rms. Restaurant 6:30-1 am. Bars 11:30-1:30 am; wkends to 2 am; entertainment. Ck-out 11 am. Convention facilities. Business center. In-rm modem link. Concierge. Gift shop. Tennis privileges. Golf privileges. Exercise equipt. Some bathrm phones, refrigerators; microwaves avail. Balconies. Luxury level. Cr cds: A, C, D, DS, ER, JCB, MC, V.

[D] [⬆] [⊀] [⊱] [⊀] [⊒] [⚒] [SC] [⊀] [≈]

★ ★ ★ **HYATT REGENCY SAN ANTONIO.** *123 Losoya St (78205). 210/222-1234; fax 210/227-4925; toll-free 800/233-1234. www.hyatt.com.* 632 rms, 11 story. S $149-$285; D $185-$349; each addl $25; suites

$344-$921; under 18 free; wkend rates. Garage parking $12, valet $14. TV; cable (premium), VCR avail. Pool; whirlpool, poolside serv. Restaurants 6:30 am-11 pm. Bar 11-2 am; entertainment. Meeting rms. Business center. In-rm modem link. Concierge. Shopping arcade. Exercise equipt. Minibars; some refrigerators. Balconies. River flows through lobby; waterfalls, atrium. Cr cds: A, C, D, DS, ER, JCB, MC, V.

★ ★ ★ **LA MANSION DEL RIO.** *112 College St (78205). 210/518-1000; fax 210/226-0389; res 800/292-7300. www.lamansion.com.* 337 rms, 7 story. S $199-$309; D $249-$389; each addl $25; suites $575-$1,200; under 18 free; wkend rates; package plans. Crib free. Pet accepted. Valet parking $19. TV; cable, VCR avail. Pool; poolside serv. Restaurants (see LAS CANARIAS). Rm serv 24 hrs. Bar 11-2 am; entertainment. Ck-out noon. Convention facilities. Business servs avail. In-rm modem link. Concierge. Gift shop. Airport transportation. Exercise equipt. Minibars. Private patios, balconies. Overlooks San Antonio River, courtyard. In building built in 1852. Cr cds: A, C, D, DS, ER, JCB, MC, V.

★ ★ ★ **MARRIOTT RIVERCENTER SAN ANTONIO.** *101 Bowie St (78205). 210/223-1000; fax 210/223-6239; res 800/648-4462. www.marriott hotels.com.* 1,001 units, 38 story. S, D $159-$299; each addl $20; suites $380-$1,200; under 18 free. Crib free. Pet accepted. Garage $12, valet $17. TV; cable (premium), VCR avail. Indoor/outdoor pool; whirlpool, poolside serv. Coffee in rms. Restaurant 6 am-midnight. Rm serv 24 hrs. Bar 11:30-2 am. Ck-out noon. Free lndry facilities. Convention facilities. Business center. In-rm modem link. Concierge. Shopping arcade. 18-hole golf privileges, greens fee $65-$85, pro, putting green, driving range. Exercise equipt; sauna. Some refrigerators, wet bars. Balconies. Located on the banks of the San Antonio River and adj to spectacular Rivercenter shopping complex. Luxury level. Cr cds: A, C, D, DS, ER, JCB, MC, V.

★ ★ **MARRIOTT RIVERWALK SAN ANTONIO.** *711 E Riverwalk St (78205). 210/224-4555; fax 210/224-2754; res 800/648-4462. www.marriott hotels.com.* 513 rms, 28 story. S $159-$279; D $179-$269; each addl $20; suites $380-$1,100; under 17 free; wkend rates. Crib free. Pet accepted. Garage parking $12, valet $17. TV; cable (premium), VCR avail. Indoor/outdoor pool; whirlpool. Coffee in rms. Restaurant 6:30 am-11 pm. Rm serv 24 hrs. Bar 11:30-2 am; entertainment Tues-Sat. Ck-out noon. Meeting rms. Business center. In-rm modem link. Gift shop. Golf privileges. Exercise equipt; sauna. Some bathrm phones, refrigerators. Balconies. Many rms overlook San Antonio River. Luxury level. Cr cds: A, C, D, DS, ER, JCB, MC, V.

★ ★ ★ **THE MENGER HOTEL.** *204 Alamo Plaza (78205). 210/223-4361; fax 210/228-0022; toll-free 800/345-9285. www.historicmenger.com.* 317 rms, 5 story. S $195; D $215; each addl $10; suites $275-$750; under 18 free; package plans. Crib free. Garage $13, valet $17. TV; cable (premium), VCR avail. Pool; whirlpool. Restaurant 6:30 am-10 pm; wkends to 11 pm. Rm serv 24 hrs. Bar 11 am-midnight; Sun from noon. Ck-out noon. Convention facilities. Business servs avail. In-rm modem link. Concierge. Shopping arcade. Exercise equipt; sauna. Massage. Balconies. Historic atmosphere. Alamo opp. Cr cds: A, C, D, DS, ER, MC, V.

★ ★ ★ **OMNI SAN ANTONIO HOTEL.** *9821 Colonnade Blvd (78230). 210/691-8888; fax 210/691-1128; res 800/843-6664. www.omni hotels.com.* 326 rms, 20 story. S $109-$160; D $129-$170; suites $275-$575; under 18 free; wkend rates. Crib free. Pet accepted; $50. Valet parking $7.50. TV; cable. 2 pools, 1 indoor; whirlpools, poolside serv. Complimentary coffee in rms. Restaurant 6 am-10 pm. Bar noon-1 am; entertainment. Ck-out noon. Meeting rms. Business center. In-rm modem link. Gift shop. Free airport transportation. Exercise equipt; sauna. Health club privileges. Some refrigerators. Garden with fountain.

Ck-out noon. Coin lndry. Meeting rms. Business servs avail. Free garage parking. Gift shop. Exercise equipt. Refrigerator in suites. Balconies. Cr cds: A, C, D, DS, ER, JCB, MC, V.

★ **RIVERWALK PLAZA RESORT & CONFERENCE CENTER.** *100 Villita St (78205). 210/225-1234; fax 210/226-9453; toll-free 800/554-4678. www.riverwalkplaza.com.* 133 rms, 6 story. S, D $89-$189; each addl $10; under 18 free; higher rates: Fiesta Wk, special events. Crib free. Garage parking $8 in/out. TV; cable (premium). Pool. Complimentary coffee in rms. Restaurant 6:30-10:30 am, 6-10 pm; Fri, Sat to midnight. Bar 4-10 pm. Ck-out 11 am. Meeting rms. Business center. In-rm modem link. Gift shop. Exercise equipt. Microwaves, refrigerators avail. Some balconies. Overlooks river. Cr cds: A, C, D, DS, ER, MC, V.

★★★ **ST. ANTHONY, WYNDHAM HISTORIC HOTEL.** *300 E Travis St (78205). 210/227-4392; fax 210/227-0915; toll-free 800/996-3426. www.wyndham.com.* 352 rms, 10 story, 38 suites. S, D $119-$209; each addl $15; suites $$359-$614; under 18 free; wkend rates. Crib free. Parking, $11, valet $12. TV; cable (premium). Heated pool; poolside serv. Coffee in rms. Restaurant 6 am-10 pm. Bar 11-2 am. Ck-out noon. Convention facilities. Business center. In-rm modem link. Gift shop. Exercise equipt. Refrigerators avail. This landmark property, built in 1909, is famous for its elegant lobby. Cr cds: A, C, D, DS, MC, V.

★★★ **SHERATON GUNTER HOTEL.** *205 E Houston St (78205). 210/227-3241; fax 210/227-9305; toll-free 888/999-2089. www.gunterhotel.com.* 322 rms, 12 story. S, D $129-$159; each addl $10; suites $250-$800; under 18 free. Crib free. Garage $14. TV; cable (premium). Heated pool; whirlpool. Restaurant 6 am-10 pm; Fri, Sat to 11 pm. Bar 4 pm-2 am; Sun to midnight. Ck-out noon. Convention facilities. Business servs avail. In-rm modem link. Barber. Exercise equipt. Refrigerators

The Alamo, San Antonio

Crystal chandelier, marble in lobby. Cr cds: A, D, DS, ER, JCB, MC, V.

★★★ **PLAZA SAN ANTONIO, A MARRIOTT HOTEL.** *555 S Alamo St (78205). 210/229-1000; fax 210/229-1418; res 800/648-4462. www.plazasa.com.* 252 rms, 5-7 story. S, D $109-$289; suites $350-$650; under 18 free; wkend rates. Crib free. Pet accepted, some restrictions. Valet parking $15. TV; cable (premium), VCR avail. Pool; whirlpool, poolside serv. Restaurant (see ANAQUA GRILL). Rm serv 24 hrs. Bar noon-1 am. Ck-out noon. Meeting rms. Business center. In-rm modem link. Concierge. Lighted tennis. Golf privileges. Exercise equipt; sauna. Massage. Complimentary bicycles. Microwaves avail. Private patios. Balconies. Cr cds: A, C, D, DS, JCB, MC, V.

★★ **RADISSON HOTEL SAN ANTONIO.** *502 W Durango (78207). 210/224-7155; fax 210/224-9130; res 800/333-3333. www.radisson.com/sanantoniotx.* 250 rms, 6 story. S, D $79-$169; each addl $10; suites $150-$225; under 18 free. Crib free. Pet accepted; $50 deposit. TV; cable (premium). Pool; whirlpool. Restaurant 6:30 am-10 pm. Bar noon-midnight.

avail. Built 1909. Cr cds: A, C, D, DS, JCB, MC, V.

⊡ 🏊 🏃 🛥 🔥

★★ **SIERRA ROYALE ALL SUITE HOTEL.** *6300 Rue Marielyne (78238). 210/647-0041; fax 210/647-4442; toll-free 800/289-2444. www.sierra-royale. com.* 91 kit. suites, 1-2 story. May-Sep: S $99-$130; D $139-$160; each addl $10; monthly rates; lower rates rest of yr. Crib free. TV; cable (premium). Pool; whirlpool. Complimentary continental bkfst. Coffee in rms. Restaurant nearby. Bar 5:30-7:30 pm. Ck-out noon. Lndry facilities. Meeting rm. Business servs avail. Valet serv. Health club privileges. Microwaves. Balconies. Picnic tables. Cr cds: A, C, D, DS, JCB, MC, V.

⊡ 🏊 🛥 🔥 SC

★★★ **WESTIN RIVERWALK.** *420 W Market St (78205). 210/224-6500; fax 210/444-6000; res 800/937-8461. www.westin.com.* 475 rms, 15 story. Feb-May, Oct: S $239; suites $305-$1500; lower rates rest of yr. Crib avail. Valet parking avail. Pool, poolside serv. TV; cable (premium), VCR avail. Complimentary coffee in rms, newspaper. Restaurant 6:30 am-10 pm. 24-hr rm serv. Bar. Ck-out noon, ck-in 3 pm. Conference center, meeting rms. Business center. Bellhops. Concierge serv. Dry cleaning. Gift shop. Exercise equipt, steam rm. Golf. Video games. Cr cds: A, C, D, DS, ER, JCB, MC, V.

⊡ 🏋 🏊 🏃 🛥 🔥 SC 🏃

Resorts

★★★ **HYATT REGENCY HILL COUNTRY RESORT AND SPA.** *9800 Hyatt Resort Dr (78251). 210/647-1234; fax 210/681-9681; res 800/233-1234. www.hillcountry.hyatt.com.* 500 units, 4 story. Mar-Nov: S, D $125-$315; suites $415-$2,250; under 18 free; hol, golf plans; military disc; lower rates rest of yr. Valet parking $8. TV; cable (premium). 2 heated pools; whirlpool, poolside serv. Playground. Supervised child's activities; ages 3-12. Restaurants (see ANTLERS LODGE). Rm serv 6 am-midnight. Bar 4 pm-2 am; entertainment Thurs-Sat. Ck-out noon, ck-in 4 pm. lndry. Convention facilities. Business center. In-rm modem link. Bellhops. Valet serv. Concierge. Shopping arcade. Beauty shop. Lighted tennis, pro. 18-hole

golf, greens fee $120, pro. Bicycle rentals. Hiking trail. Exercise rm; sauna. Massage. Lawn games. Rec rm. Game rm. Refrigerators; microwaves avail. Balconies. Ranch-style property on 200 landscaped acres; man-made river. Luxury level. Cr cds: A, C, D, DS, JCB, MC, V.

⊡ 🏋 🏃 🛥 🏃 🔥 🏃

★★★★ **THE WESTIN LA CANTERA RESORT.** *16641 La Cantera Pkwy (78256). 210/558-6500; fax 210/558-2400. www.westinlacantera. com.* This resort has a breathtaking winding road entrance and is spectacularly situated atop a bluff with views of the city skyline and Texas hill country. Impressive Spanish-Mediterranean architecture surrounds the lovely pools, which sit on the bluff overlooking the championship golf course. The guest rooms, suites, and casitas will exceed your expectations. 508 rms, 7 story, 24 suites. Mar-July: S, D $359; suites $1800; lower rates rest of yr. Crib avail. Valet parking avail. Pool; lap pool, children's pool, whirlpool. TV; cable (premium), VCR avail, CD avail. Complimentary coffee in rms, newspaper, toll-free calls. Restaurant 6 am-10 pm. Rm serv 24 hrs. Bar 5 pm-2 am. Ck-out noon, ck-in 3 pm. Conference center, meeting rms. Business center. Bellhops. Concierge serv. Dry cleaning. Gift shop. Exercise equipt, sauna. Golf. Tennis. Supervised children's activities. Hiking trail. Cr cds: A, C, D, DS, ER, JCB, MC, V.

⊡ 🏋 🏃 🛥 🏃 🔥 🏃

B&Bs/Small Inns

★★★ **A BECKMANN INN & CARRIAGE HOUSE BED AND BREAKFAST.** *222 E Guenther St (78204). 210/229-1449; fax 210/229-1061; toll-free 800/945-1449. www.beckmanninn. com.* 5 rms, 4 with shower only, 2 story. S, D $110-$150. Children over 12 yrs only. TV; cable. Complimentary full bkfst; afternoon refreshments. Restaurant opp 7 am-3 pm. Ck-out 11 am, ck-in 4-5 pm. Luggage handling. Refrigerators. Victorian house (1886) with wrap-around porch. Many antiques. Totally non-smoking. Cr cds: A, D, DS, MC, V.

🛥 🔥

★ **A YELLOW ROSE BED & BREAK-FAST.** *229 Madison (78204). 210/229-9903; fax 210/229-1691; toll-free 800/950-9903. www.ayellowrose.com.* 5 rms, 2 story. S, D $100-$200; wkly rates. Children over 12 yrs only. TV; cable (premium). Restaurant nearby. Ck-out 11 am, ck-in 3 pm. Luggage handling. Business servs avail. Health club privileges. Balconies. Built in 1878; antiques. Cr cds: A, DS, MC, V.
� 🔥

★★ **BEAUREGARD HOUSE.** *215 Beauregard (78204). 210/222-1198; fax 210/222-9338; toll-free 888/667-0555. www.beauregardhouse.com.* 6 rms, 2 with shower only, 3 story, 2 suites. S $114; D $124-$129; each addl $30; suite: $149; package plans. TV in sitting rm; cable. Complimentary full bkfst. Restaurant nearby. Ck-out 11 am, ck-in 3 pm. In-rm modem link. Lndry facilities. Restored Victorian house (1908) in King William District; Riverwalk 1 blk. Totally nonsmoking. Cr cds: A, DS, MC, V.
🕎 准 🔥

★★ **BRACKENRIDGE HOUSE.** *230 Madison (78204). 210/271-3442; fax 210/226-3139; toll-free 800/221-1412. www.brackenridgehouse.com.* 6 rms, 2 with shower only, 2 story. S, D $100-$200; suite $125-$250. Children over 12 yrs only. TV; cable (premium). Complimentary full bkfst. Ck-out 11 am, ck-in 3-6 pm. Individually decorated rms. Totally nonsmoking. Cr cds: A, D, DS, MC, V.
准

★ **BULLIS HOUSE INN.** *621 Pierce Ave (78208). 210/223-9426; fax 210/299-1479; toll-free 877/477-4100. www.sanantoniobb.org.* 8 rms, 4 share bath, 3 story. Some rm phones. S $55; D $89; each addl $10; under 17 free. Crib free. TV; cable (premium). Pool. Complimentary continental bkfst. Ck-out noon, ck-in 2 pm. Refrigerators. Greek Revival mansion; antiques. Cr cds: A, MC, V.
D ⇌ 🔥

★★★ **THE JACKSON HOUSE.** *107 Madison St (78204). 210/225-4045; fax 210/227-0877; toll-free 800/221-4045. www.nobleinns.com.* 6 rms, 1 with shower only, 2 story. S, D $120-$250; wkends (2-day min). Children over 12 yrs only. TV; cable (pre-mium). Complimentary full bkfst; afternoon refreshments. Restaurants nearby. Ck-out 11 am, ck-in 3 pm. Business servs avail. In-rm modem link. Luggage handling. Valet serv. Concierge serv. Indoor pool. Fireplaces; some in-rm whirlpools. Built in 1894; Victorian setting. Totally nonsmoking. Cr cds: A, D, DS, JCB, MC, V.
D ⇌ 准 🔥

★★★ **OGE HOUSE.** *209 Washington St (78204). 210/223-2353; fax 210/226-5812; toll-free 800/242-2770. www.ogeinn.com.* 10 rms, 1 with shower only, 3 story. S, D $155-$185; suite $225. Children over 16 yrs only. TV; cable. Complimentary full bkfst. Ck-out 11 am, ck-in 3 pm. Business servs avail. In-rm modem link. Luggage handling. Refrigerators; many fireplaces. Mansion built 1857 for prominent rancher; antiques. Cr cds: A, C, D, DS, MC, V.
准 🔥

★ **RIVERWALK INN.** *329 Old Guilbeau (78204). 210/212-8300; fax 210/229-9422; res 800/254-4440. www.riverwalkinn.com.* 11 rms, shower only, 2 story. S, D $130-$175; hols 2-3-day min. TV; cable. Complimentary continental bkfst. Complimentary coffee in rms. Ck-out 11 am, ck-in 3 pm. Business servs avail. In-rm modem link. Refrigerators; many fireplaces. Two authentic log cabins moved here from Tennessee. Totally nonsmoking. Cr cds: A, DS, MC, V.
准 🔥

All Suites

★★ **AMERISUITES NORTHWEST.** *4325 Amerisuites Dr (78230). 210/561-0099; fax 210/561-0513; res 800/833-1516. www.amerisuites.com.* 5 story, 128 suites. Mar-Aug: S, D $109-$199; each addl $10; under 18 free; lower rates rest of yr. Crib free. Pet accepted, some restrictions. Parking lot. Pool. TV; cable, VCR. Complimentary continental bkfst, coffee in rms, newspaper. Ck-out 11 am, ck-in 4 pm. Meeting rm. Business center. Dry cleaning, coin lndry. Exercise equipt. Golf. Cr cds: A, C, D, DS, MC, V.
D 🐾 🍴 ⇌ 🏃 准 🔥 SC 🏃

★★★ **EMBASSY SUITES.** *10110 US Hwy 281 N (78216). 210/525-9999; fax 210/525-0626; toll-free 800/362-2779. www.embassysuites.com.* 261 suites, 9 story. Suites $129-$209; each addl $20; under 18 free. Crib free. TV; cable (premium). Indoor pool; whirlpool. Complimentary full bkfst. Restaurant 11:30 am-2:30 pm, 5-10 pm; Fri, Sat to 11 pm. Bar 4 pm-midnight. Ck-out 1 pm. Coin lndry. Meeting rms. Business center. In-rm modem link. Gift shop. Free airport transportation. Exercise equipt; sauna. Game rm. Refrigerators, microwaves. Cr cds: A, C, D, DS, MC, V.

★★★ **EMBASSY SUITES NORTHWEST.** *7750 Briaridge (78230). 210/340-5421; fax 210/340-1843; res 800/362-2779. www.embassysuites.com.* 8 story, 216 suites. suites $129-$179; each addl $10; under 18 free. Crib avail. Parking lot. Indoor pool, whirlpool. TV; cable (premium). Complimentary full bkfst, coffee in rms, newspaper. Restaurant 11 am-10 pm. Bar. Ck-out noon, ck-in 3 pm. Meeting rms. Dry cleaning, coin lndry. Gift shop. Free airport transportation. Exercise privileges, sauna. Golf. Video games. Cr cds: A, D, DS, JCB, MC, V.

★★ **HOMEWOOD SUITES.** *4323 Spectrum One (78230). 210/696-5400; fax 210/696-8899. www.homewoodsuites.com.* 123 kit. units, 4 story. S $99-$119; D $119-$129; under 12 free; monthly rates. Crib free. TV; cable (premium), VCR (movies). Complimentary continental bkfst. Complimentary coffee in rms. Restaurant nearby. Ck-out noon. Meeting rms. Business center. In-rm modem link. Sundries. Grocery store. Coin lndry. Exercise equipt. Pool. Lawn games. Refrigerators, microwaves. Cr cds: A, C, D, DS, MC, V.

★★★ **HOMEWOOD SUITES RIVERWALK.** *432 W Market St. (78205). 210/222-1515; fax 210/222-1575; res 800/225-5466. www.homewood-riverwalk.com.* 10 story, 146 suites. S $139; D $249; each addl $20; under 18 free. Crib avail. Valet parking avail. Pool, whirlpool.

TV; cable (premium), VCR avail. Complimentary continental bkfst, coffee in rms, newspaper, toll-free calls. Restaurant nearby. Ck-out noon, ck-in 3 pm. Meeting rms. Business center. Bellhops. Concierge serv. Dry cleaning, coin lndry. Gift shop. Exercise equipt. Golf. Tennis. Video games. Cr cds: A, C, D, DS, MC, V.

★★ **SIERRA ROYALE ALL SUITE HOTEL.** *6300 Rue Marielyne (78238). 210/647-0041; fax 210/647-4442; toll-free 800/289-2444. www.sierra-royale.com.* 91 kit. suites, 1-2 story. May-Sept: S $99-$130; D $139-$160; each addl $10; monthly rates; lower rates rest of yr. Crib $5. TV; cable (premium). Pool; whirlpool. Complimentary continental bkfst. Complimentary coffee in rms. Restaurant nearby. Bar 5:30-7:30 pm. Ck-out noon. Lndry facilities. Meeting rm. Health club privileges. Microwaves. Balconies. Picnic tables. Cr cds: A, C, D, MC, V.

Restaurants

★★ **ALDINO CUCINA ITALIANA.** *622 NW Loop 410 (78216). 210/340-0000. www.aldinos.com.* Hrs: 11 am-11 pm. Closed Thanksgiving. Northern Italian menu. Beer, wine. Lunch $6.50-$10, dinner $7-$27. Child's menu. Pompeiian decor with broken columns. Cr cds: A, D, DS, MC, V.

★★ **ALDO'S.** *8539 Fredericksburg Rd (78229). 210/696-2536.* Hrs: 11 am-10 pm; Fri to 11 pm; Sat 5-11 pm; Sun 5 pm-10 pm. Closed most major hols. Res accepted. Italian menu. Bar. Lunch $6.50-$9.95, dinner $9.55-$23. Specialty: salmon alla Pavarotti. Outdoor dining. Intimate dining in early 1900s house. Cr cds: A, D, DS, MC, V.

★★★ **ANAQUA GRILL.** *555 S Alamo St (78205). 210/229-1000. www.plazasa.com.* Hrs: 6:30 am-2 pm, 6-10 pm; Fri, Sat to 11 pm. Res accepted. Bar. A la carte entrees: bkfst $4.25-$12.95, lunch $7.50-$12, dinner $12-$35. Child's menu. Own baking. Valet parking. Outdoor din-

ing. View of garden, courtyard, fountains. Cr cds: A, C, D, DS, MC, V.
D ⬛

★ ★ ★ **ANTLERS LODGE.** *9800 Hyatt Resort Dr (78251). 210/520-4001.* Hrs: 5:30-10 pm. Closed Mon. Res accepted. Bar. Wine list. Dinner $26-$36. Southwestern menu. Specialties: mesquite smoked prime rib. Valet parking at hotel. Southwestern decor. Cr cds: A, D, DS, MC, V.
D

★ ★ **BIGA.** *203 S St. Mary's St (78205). 210/225-0722. www.biga. com.* Hrs: 5:30-10:30 pm; Fri, Sat to 11 pm. Closed Sun; some major hols. Dinner $11-$25. Specializes in Gulf seafood, breads, wild game. Parking. In converted old mansion. Cr cds: A, D, DS, MC, V.
D ⬛

★ ★ ★ **BISTRO TIME.** *5137 Fredericksburg (78229). 210/344-6626.* Hrs: 5-9 pm; Fri, Sat to 10 pm; early-bird dinner Mon-Thurs to 6 pm. Closed Sun; July 4, Thanksgiving, Dec 25. Res accepted. Continental menu. Wine, beer. Dinner $17-$28. Specialties: lump crab cakes, steak Diane, sweetbreads. Cr cds: A, D, DS, MC, V.
D

★ ★ **BOUDRO'S A TEXAS BISTRO.** *421 E Commerce St (78205). 210/224-8484. www.boudros.com.* Hrs: 11 am-11 pm; Fri, Sat to midnight. Res accepted. Southwestern menu. A la carte entrees: lunch $5.50-$10.50, dinner $14.50-$24.50. Child's menu. Specialties: blackened prime rib, smoked ribs, quail. Outdoor dining. Dinner avail on river barges. Historic building; pictographs on walls, original artwork. Cr cds: A, D, DS, JCB, MC, V.
D ⬛

★ ★ **CAPPY'S.** *5011 Broadway St (78209). 210/828-9669.* Hrs: 11 am-3 pm, 5-10 pm; Fri, Sat to 11 pm; Sun 10:30 am- 3 pm. Closed July 4, Thanksgiving, Dec 25. Res accepted. Bar. American, Southwestern menu. Lunch $10-$15, dinner $18-$25. Specializes in mustang chicken. Parking. Outdoor dining. Local artwork on display. Totally nonsmoking. Cr cds: A, D, MC, V.
D

★ **CARRANZA MEAT MARKET.** *701 Austin St (78215). 210/223-0903.* Hrs: 11 am-2 pm, 5-10 pm; Fri to 11 pm; Sat 5-11 pm. Closed Sun; major hols. Wine, beer. Lunch, dinner $6.95-$28.50. Specializes in steak, seafood, barbecue. Parking. Originally a saloon and nightclub (1870). Family-owned. Cr cds: A.

★ **CASA RIO.** *430 E Commerce St (78205). 210/225-6718. www.casario texas.net.* Hrs: 11 am-11 pm. Closed Jan 1, Easter, Dec 25. Mexican menu. Serv bar. Lunch, dinner $4.95-$9.95. Child's menu. Specialties: green chicken enchiladas, fajitas, pollo asado. Parking. Outdoor dining. Riverboat dining by res. On San Antonio River. Family-owned. Cr cds: A, D, DS, MC, V.
D

★ ★ **CASCABEL.** *37 NE Loop 410 (78216). 210/321-4860.* Hrs: 6:30 am-10 pm; Fri, Sat to 11 pm. Res accepted. Southwestern menu. Bar. Specializes in poblano chicken. Bkfst $4.95-$7.95, lunch $8.95-$12.95, dinner $18.95-$33.95. Child's menu. Parking. Cr cds: A, D, DS, MC, V.
D

★ ★ **CRUMPET'S.** *3920 Harry Wurzbach (78209). 210/821-5454.* Hrs: 11 am-2:30 pm, 5:30-10 pm; Fri to 11 pm; Sat 11 am-3 pm, 5:30-11 pm; Sun 11 am-3 pm, 5-9 pm. Closed Jan 1, Dec 25. Res accepted. Bar. Wine list. Complete meals: lunch $6.95-$7.95, dinner $8.95-$19.50. Brunch $14.95. Specializes in beef, pasta, seafood. Own pasta, pastries. Outdoor dining. Musicians Tues-Sun. Cr cds: A, MC, V.
D SC ⬛

★ **EL JARRO DE ARTURO.** *13421 San Pedro Ave (78216). 210/494-5084.* Hrs: 11 am-10 pm; Fri, Sat to 12:30 am. Closed Thanksgiving, Dec 25. Res accepted. Mexican menu. Bar. Lunch $3.50-$6.50, dinner $6.25-$15.95. Child's menu. Specialties: green enchiladas, chili ancho chicken, black bean nachos. Own baking. Musicians Fri, Sat. Mexican decor. Family-owned. Cr cds: A, D, DS, MC, V.
D ⬛

★ ★ **EL MIRADOR.** *722 S St. Mary's St (78205).* 210/225-9444. Hrs: 6:30 am-3 pm; Wed-Sat also 5:30-10 pm; Sun 9 am-3 pm. Closed some major hols. Mexican menu. Wine, beer. Bkfst $1.50-$4, lunch $2.50-$5.50, dinner $4.50-$15. Specialties: xochitl soup, Azteca soup. Parking. Cr cds: A, DS, MC, V.
[D]

★ ★ **ERNESTO'S.** *2559 Jackson Keller (78230).* 210/344-1248. Hrs: 11:30 am-2 pm, 5:30-10 pm; Fri, Sat to 10:30 pm. Closed Sun; Jan 1, Dec 25. Mexican menu. Bar. Lunch $4.50-$13.95, dinner $7.95-$25. Specialties: green ceviche, snapper Veracruz. Storefront setting. Cr cds: A, C, D, MC, V.
[D] ⊟

★ ★ ★ **FIG TREE.** *515 Villita St (78205).* 210/224-1976. *www.figtree restaurant.com.* Hrs: 6-10 pm. Closed most major hols. Res accepted. Continental menu. Serv bar. Dinner $18.25-$29.75. Specializes in seafood, chateaubriand, rack of lamb. Outdoor dining. Elegant decor. Overlooks Riverwalk. Cr cds: A, D, DS, MC, V.

★ **FORMOSA GARDENS.** *1011 NE Loop 410 (78209).* 210/828-9988. Hrs: 11 am-2:30 pm, 5-10 pm; early-bird dinner 5-6:30 pm. Closed Thanksgiving, Dec 25. Res accepted. Chinese menu. Bar. Lunch $4.95-$5.95, dinner $6.25-$25. Specializes in Hunan, Szechuan dishes. Valet parking. Outdoor dining. Dining rm divided into small sections. Cr cds: A, DS, MC, V.
[D] ⊟

★ ★ ★ **FRANCESCA'S AT SUNSET.** *16641 La Cantera Pkwy (78256).* 210/558-6500. *www.westinlacantera. com.* Hrs: 6-10 pm; Fri, Sat to 11 pm. Closed Sun, Mon. Res accepted. Beer, wine. Eclectic/Southwestern menu. Specializes in cabrito. Dinner $23-$36. Child's menu. Cr cds: A, C, D, DS, JCB, MC, V.
[D] ⊟

★ ★ **GREY MOSS INN.** *19010 Scenic Loop Rd, Helotes (78023).* 210/695-8301. *www.grey-moss-inn.com.* Hrs: 5-10 pm. Closed Jan 1, Dec 25. Res accepted; required Fri, Sat. Serv bar. A la carte entrees: dinner $16.95-$40. Child's menu. Specializes in grilled

steaks, seafood, chicken. Own baking. Outdoor dining on patio of historic inn. Cr cds: A, D, DS, MC, V.
[D] ⊟

★ **INDIA OVEN.** *1031 Patricia Dr (78213).* 210/366-1030. *www.india oven.com.* Hrs: 11 am-2:30 pm, 5-10 pm; Sun to 10:30 pm. Res accepted. Indian menu. Bar. A la carte entrees: dinner $6.95-$11.95. Lunch buffet $5.95. Child's menu. Specialties: mixed grill tandori, rack of lamb, chicken tikka masala. Parking. Indian decor; Mughal artwork. Totally nonsmoking. Cr cds: A, D, DS, MC, V.
[D]

★ ★ **LA CANTERA GRILLE.** *16641 La Cantera Pkwy (78256).* 210/558-6500. *www.westinlacantera.com.* Hrs: 7:30 am-10 pm; Tues, Wed to 5 pm. Res accepted. Southwestern menu. Bar. Bkfst $1.55-$8.50, lunch $5.95-$11.50, dinner $17.50-$34. Specialties: chili-rubbed tenderloin of beef. Outdoor dining. Colonial Texas decor. Cr cds: A, C, D, DS, JCB, MC, V.
[D] ⊟

★ **LA FOGATA.** *2427 Vance Jackson Rd (78213).* 210/340-1337. *www. lafogata.com.* Hrs: 11 am-10 pm; Fri to 11 pm; Sat, Sun 8 am-midnight. Closed Jan 1, Dec 25. Mexican menu. Bar. Bkfst $3.25-$4.50, lunch, dinner $5.25-$14.95. Child's menu. Specialties: enchilada verdes, chile relleno, Mexican bkfst. Own tortillas. Mariachis Fri, Sat. Parking. Outdoor dining. Mexican decor. Cr cds: A, D, DS, MC, V.
[D] ⊟

★ ★ **LA FONDA.** *2415 N Main Ave (78212).* 210/733-0621. Hrs: 11 am-3 pm, 5-9 pm; Fri, Sat to 10:30 pm; Sun to 3 pm. Closed most major hols. Mexican menu. Bar. Lunch, dinner $5.95-$12. Child's menu. Specialties: shrimp a la Plancha, filet Milanesa, spinach enchiladas. Parking. Outdoor dining. Mexican decor and atmosphere. Family-owned since 1932. Cr cds: A, D, MC, V.
[D]

★ **LA MARGARITA.** *120 Produce Row (78207).* 210/227-7140. Hrs: 11 am-10 pm; Fri, Sat to midnight. Mexican menu. Bar. Lunch, dinner $5.25-$12.95. Child's menu. Specializes in

fajitas, shrimp cocktail, oyster cocktail. Entertainment. Parking. Outdoor dining. Restored farmers market building (1910). Cr cds: A, D, DS, MC, V.
D ⌐

★ ★ ★ **LAS CANARIAS.** *112 College St (78205). 210/518-1000; toll-free 800/292-7300. www.lamansion.com.* Hrs: 6:30 am-11 pm; Sun brunch 10:30 am-2:30 pm. Res accepted. Bar to midnight. Wine list. Lunch $8-$14, dinner $19-$26. Sun brunch $28.95. Child's menu. Specialties: anise-spiced barbecued duck breast, tortilla chili-dusted ahi tuna. Entertainment Fri, Sat. Overlooks Riverwalk. Totally nonsmoking. Cr cds: A, C, D, DS, ER, JCB, MC, V.
D

★ ★ ★ ★ **LE REVE.** *152 E Pecan St (79205). 210/212-2221. www.restaurantlereve.com.* Sophisticated, suave, and very French describe this small downtown eatery. Chef Andrew Weissman raises the culinary bar for the entire city with his modern renditions of classic French cooking. The charming staff is most accommodating. Contemporary French menu. Specializes in jumbo lump crab cake, crispy skin black sea bass. Hrs: 5:30-11 pm. Closed Sun, Mon. Res required. Wine list. Dinner $23-$33. Open kitchen viewing. Cr cds: A, DS, MC, V.
D

★ **LIBERTY BAR.** *328 E Josephine (78215). 210/227-1187.* Hrs: 11:30 am-10:30 pm; Fri, Sat to midnight; Sun brunch 10:30 am-2:30 pm. Res accepted. French, Mexican menu. Bar to 2 am Fri, Sat. Lunch $8-$10, dinner $10-$20. Specialties: lamb sausage, mushroom sandwiches, chicken breast with hoja santa. Parking. Oldest bar in Texas in continuous operation. Cr cds: A, MC, V.
D ⌐

★ ★ ★ **LITTLE RHEIN STEAK HOUSE.** *231 S Alamo St (78205). 210/225-2111. www.littlerheinsteak house.com.* Hrs: 5-10 pm. Closed Thanksgiving, Dec 25. Res accepted. Bar. A la carte entrees: dinner $20-$35. Child's menu. Specializes in steak, seafood, lamb chops. Terrace dining. Overlooks San Antonio River

and outdoor theater. First 2-story structure in San Antonio (1847). Cr cds: A, D, DS, MC, V.
D

★ **LONE STAR.** *237 Losoya (78205). 210/223-9374.* Hrs: 11 am-10:30 pm; Fri, Sat to midnight. Closed Thanksgiving, Dec 25. Bar. Dinner $5.95-$19.95. Child's menu. Specializes in steak. Outdoor dining. Cr cds: A, D, DS, MC, V.
D ⌐

★ **LOS BARRIOS.** *4223 Blanco Rd (78212). 210/732-6017.* Hrs: 10 am-10 pm; Fri, Sat to midnight; Sun from 9 am. Closed Easter, Thanksgiving, Dec 25. Mexican menu. Bar. Lunch, dinner $5-$14. Child's menu. Specialties: enchilada verdes, cabrito, churrasco. Entertainment Fri-Sun. Parking. Traditional Mexican dining. Family-owned. Cr cds: A, D, DS, MC, V.
D ⌐

★ ★ **MENCIUS' GOURMET HUNAN.** *7959 Fredericksburg Rd (78229). 210/615-1288.* Hrs: 11 am-2:15 pm, 5-10 pm; Sun-Tues to 9:30 pm. Closed Jan 1, Thanksgiving, Dec 25. Res accepted. Chinese menu. Bar. Lunch $4.95-$5.50, dinner $5.95-$14.95. Specialties: Mencius beef, shrimp & scallops, General Tso's chicken. Parking. Cr cds: A, DS, MC, V.
D ⌐

★ **MICHELINO'S.** *521 Riverwalk (78205). 210/223-2939. www.the sanantonioriverwalk.com.* Hrs: 11 am-10:30 pm; Fri, Sat to midnight. Northern Italian menu. Bar. Lunch $5.25-$13, dinner $7.95-$15.95. Child's menu. Specialties: fettucine verde, stuffed chicken. Outdoor dining. Cr cds: A, D, DS, MC, V.
D ⌐

★ **MI TIERRA.** *218 Produce Row (78207). 210/225-1262.* Open 24 hrs. Mexican menu. Bar noon-2 am; Sat, Sun from 10 am. Bkfst $2.50-$6.75, lunch, dinner $3.45-$9.95. Specializes in fajitas, cabrito, Mexican dinner combinations. Entertainment. Outdoor dining. Located in old farmers market building; built 1910. Family-owned. Cr cds: A, D, DS, MC, V.
D

★★★ MORTON'S OF CHICAGO.
849 E Commerce St, Ste 283 (78205). 210/228-0700. www.mortons.com. Hrs: 5-11 pm; Sun to 10 pm. Closed major hols. Res accepted. A la carte entrees: dinner $19.95-$33.95. Specializes in steak, fresh seafood. Valet parking. Elegant, contemporary decor. Cr cds: A, D, MC, V.

D ⌐

★★ OLD SAN FRANCISCO STEAK HOUSE.
10223 Sahara St (78216). 210/342-2321. www.osfsteakhouse. com. Hrs: 5-10 pm; Fri, Sat to 11 pm; Sun 4 pm-10 pm. Res accepted. Bar. Complete meals: dinner $17.95-$45.95. Child's menu. Specializes in slow-roasted prime rib. Pianist. Free valet parking. Victorian decor. Cr cds: A, D, DS, MC, V.

D SC ⌐

★★ PAESANO'S.
555 E Basse Rd; Suite 100 (78209). 210/828-5191. www.joesfood.com. Hrs: 11 am-11 pm. Closed Thanksgiving, Dec. 25. Northern Italian menu. Bar. A la carte entrees: lunch $6.95-$9.95, dinner $6.95-$26.95. Specialties: shrimp Paesano, penne al'arrabbiata, veal Christina. Parking. Outdoor dining. Cr cds: A, D, DS, MC, V.

D ⌐

★ PALOMA BLANCA.
5148 Broadway (78209). 210/822-6151. Hrs: 10:45 am-10 pm; Fri to 11 pm; Sat 8 am-11 pm; Sun to 9 pm. Closed Mon; most major hols. Res accepted. Mexican menu. Bar. Bkfst $3.99-$5.25, lunch $5.25-$8.95, dinner $6.25-$8.95. Child's menu. Specialties: pollo al cilantro, caldo tlalpeño, puntas de puerco en chile chipotle. Mariachis Fri. Eclectic, colorful Mexican decor. Cr cds: A, MC, V.

D

★ PICO DE GALLO.
111 S Leona St (78207). 210/225-6060. www.pico degallo.com. Hrs: 8 am-10 pm; Fri, Sat to 2 am. Closed Thanksgiving. Mexican menu.

Bar. Bkfst $3.95-$5.95, lunch, dinner $4.75-$8.95. Child's menu. Specializes in fajitas. Entertainment Wed-Sun. Mexican artifacts. Family-owned. Cr cds: A, D, DS, MC, V.

D

★ PIECA D'ITALIA.
502 Riverwalk (78205). 210/227-5511. www.italia riverwalk.com. Hrs: 10:30 am-10:30 pm; Fri, Sat to midnight. Closed Thanksgiving, Dec 25. Res accepted. Italian menu. Wine, beer. Lunch, dinner $5.49-$19.99. Specializes in fresh pasta, pizza, seafood. Patio dining overlooking river, many tables under Crockett St Bridge. Cr cds: A, D, DS, MC, V.

D ⌐

★★ POLO'S AT THE FAIRMOUNT.
401 S Alamo St (78205). 210/224-8800. Hrs: 6-10:30 am, 11:30 am-2 pm, 6-10 pm; Fri to 10 pm; Sun 7 am-noon. Res accepted. Continental menu. Bar 11:30-1 am. A la carte entrees: bkfst $6.95-$8.50, lunch $9-$15, dinner $22-$65. Valet parking. Jazz Thurs-Sat. Outdoor dining. Cr cds: A, D, DS, JCB, MC, V.

D

★ RIO RIO CANTINA.
421 E Commerce St (78205). 210/226-8462. www.joesfood.com. Hrs: 11 am-11 pm; Fri, Sat to midnight. Closed Thanksgiving. California, Tex-Mex menu. Bar. Lunch $6.95-$10, dinner $8.95-$24.95. Child's menu. Specialties: botano grande platter. Outdoor dining. On riverside. Cr cds: A, D, MC, V.

D ⌐

Riverwalk, San Antonio

★ ★ **ROMANO'S MACARONI GRILL.** *24116 I-10W (78257). 210/698-0003. www.macaronigrill.com.* Hrs: 11 am-10 pm; Fri, Sat to 11 pm. Closed Thanksgiving, Dec 25. Italian menu. Wine, beer. Lunch $5.25-$8.95, dinner $7.99-$16.50. Specialty: calamari fritti. Parking. Cr cds: A, D, DS, MC, V.
D ⊡

★ **ROSARIO'S.** *910 S Alamo (78210). 210/223-1806.* Hrs: 10:45 am-10 pm; Mon to 3 pm; Fri to midnight; Sat to 11 pm. Closed Sun; Thanksgiving, Dec 25. Mexican menu. Bar. Lunch $4.95-$6.95, dinner $7.95-$10.95. Specialties: enchiladas Mexicanas. Entertainment Fri, Sat. Outdoor dining. Colorful, Mexican decor. Cr cds: A, D, DS, MC, V.
D

★ ★ ★ **RUTH'S CHRIS STEAK HOUSE.** *7720 Jones Maltsberger Rd (78216). 210/821-5051. www.ruths chris-sanantonio.com.* Hrs: 11:30 am-2 pm, 5-10:30 pm; Fri to 11 pm; Sat 5-11 pm; Sun 5-10:30 pm. Closed Thanksgiving, Dec 25, Super Bowl Sunday. Res accepted. Bar. A la carte entrees: dinner $23.95-$35.95. Specializes in steak. Parking. Upscale Southwestern decor. Cr cds: A, D, DS, MC, V.
D ⊡

★ **TOWER OF THE AMERICAS.** *222 Hemisfair Plaza (78209). 210/223-3101. www.toweroftheamericas.com.* Hrs: 11 am-2 pm, 5-10 pm; Fri to 10:30 pm; Sat 11 am-2:30 pm, 5-10:30 pm; Sun 11 am-2:30 pm, 5:30-10 pm. Closed Dec 25. Res accepted. Bar 5-11 pm; Fri, Sat 11 am-midnight; Sun from 11 am. Complete meals: lunch $7-$15, dinner $12-$35. Child's menu. Specializes in lobster, steak, prime rib. Parking. Revolving tower; view of city. Cr cds: A, D, DS, MC, V.
D

★ **ZUNI GRILL.** *511 Riverwalk St (78205). 210/227-0864.* Hrs: 8 am-11 pm; Fri, Sat to midnight. Closed Dec 25. Southwestern menu. Serv bar. Bkfst, lunch $4.95-$7.95, dinner $10.95-$21.95. Child's menu. Specialties: pork loin with adobo sauce, shrimp with Chipotle chile, tortilla lasagna. Outdoor dining. Overlooks river. Cr cds: A, D, DS, MC, V.
D

Unrated Dining Spots

5050. *5050 Broadway St (78209). 210/828-4386.* Hrs: 11-2 am. Res accepted. Mexican, Amer menu. Bar. Lunch, dinner $4-$10. Child's menu. Specialties: chicken-fried steak, burgers, Tex-Mex dishes. Parking. Neighborhood bistro atmosphere; Art Deco decor. Cr cds: A, D, DS, MC, V.
⊡

BRAZIER AT LOS PATIOS. *2015 NE Loop 410 (78217). 210/655-9270.* Hrs: 11:30 am-2:30 pm; Fri, Sat 11:30 am-2:30 pm, 6-10 pm. Closed Mon; also Jan-Feb. Southwestern menu. Bar. Lunch, dinner $6.95-$17.95. Specializes in mesquite-grilled steak, fish, chicken. Parking. Outdoor dining. On Salado Creek. Cr cds: A, C, D, DS, MC, V.
⊡

DICK'S LAST RESORT. *406 Navarro St (78205). 210/224-0026. www.dicks lastresort.com.* Hrs: 11-2 am. Bar. Lunch $3.75-$16.99, dinner $10.99-$16.99. Specializes in barbecued ribs, fried catfish, honey-roasted chicken. Entertainment. Outdoor dining. Honky-tonk decor. Cr cds: A, D, DS, MC, V.
D ⊡

GAZEBO AT LOS PATIOS. *2015 NE Loop 410 (78217). 210/655-6171. www.lospatios.com.* Hrs: 11:30 am-2:30 pm; Sun 11 am-3 pm. Closed Jan 1, Thanksgiving, Dec 25. Continental, Mexican menu. Bar 11:30 am-2:30 pm. Lunch $7.95-$10.95. Dinner $12.95-$22.95. Sun brunch $13.95. Specializes in crepes, chicken, Mexican dishes. Parking. Outdoor dining. Cr cds: A, C, DS, MC, V.
⊡

GUENTHER HOUSE. *205 E Guenther St (78204). 210/227-1061. www. guentherhouse.com.* Hrs: 7 am-3 pm; Sun 8 am-2 pm. Closed Jan 1, Thanksgiving, Dec 25. Bkfst $2.95-$6.25, lunch $4.50-$6.75. Specialties: Southern sweet cream waffles, chicken salad, biscuits and gravy. Own pastries. Parking. Outdoor dining. House built by founder of Pioneer Flour Mills (1860). Museum and gift shop on grounds. Cr cds: A, D, DS, MC, V.

SCHILO'S DELICATESSEN. *424 E Commerce (78205).* 210/223-6692. Hrs: 7 am-8:30 pm. Closed Sun; most major hols. Deli menu. Bar. Bkfst $2.85-$5.35, lunch $2.85-$4.95, dinner $5.95-$8.95. Specialties: reuben sandwich, split pea soup, homemade root beer. Own desserts. German music Fri, Sat. Parking. Family-owned since 1917. Cr cds: A, DS, MC, V.

San Marcos

(E-6) *See also New Braunfels, Seguin*

Founded 1851 **Pop** 34,733 **Elev** 578 ft
Area code 512 **Zip** 78666
Information Convention & Visitors Bureau, PO Box 2310; 512/393-5900 or 800/200-5620

Fissures in the rocks of the Balcones escarpment pour out clear spring water to form the San Marcos River. A group of Franciscan monks is said to have discovered these springs on St. Mark's Day in 1709, giving the river, and hence the town, its name. This is the center of farming and ranching for this part of the black lands. To the west above the Balcones escarpment lies scenic hill country with fine deer hunting and bird-watching.

What to See and Do

Aquarena Springs. Glass-bottom boats, from which aquatic plants, fish, and spring formations can be seen; ferryboat to Hillside Gardens; Texana Village. Restaurants. Gift shop. (Daily; closed Dec 25) 1 Aquarena Springs Dr. Phone 512/245-7575. ¢¢

Fishing. From banks of the San Marcos River (license required); also scuba diving.

Lockhart State Park. Approx 260 acres. Pool (Memorial Day-Labor

Day); nine-hole golf (fee), picnicking, improved camping. Standard fees. (Daily) Approx 20 mi NE via TX 80/142. Phone 512/398-3479. ¢

San Marcos Factory Shops. Over 100 outlet stores can be found in this outdoor shopping mall. Food court. (Daily) 3939 I-35 S, at exit 200. Phone 512/396-2200.

Wonder World. Tours of cave formed by an earthquake. Cave temperature approx 70°F. Antigravity House, observation tower, train ride through wildlife park and waterfall. Picnic areas, snack bar. (Daily) 1000 Prospect St, west side of town. Phone 512/392-3760. ¢¢¢¢

Special Events

Tours of Distinction. Spring tour of historic houses and restored buildings. Departs from Charles S. Cock House Museum; docents and map/brochure. Phone 512/353-1258. First wknd May.

Texas Water Safari. Five-day, 262-mi "world's toughest boat race." Canoe race starts in San Marcos at Aquarena Center and ends in Seadrift. Contact 512/357-6113. Second Sat June.

Republic of Texas Chilympiad. Hays County Civic Center. Men's state chili championship cook-off (more than 500 entries); parade; 5K race; nightly concerts. Phone 512/396-5400. Third wknd Sept.

Motels/Motor Lodges

★ **BEST WESTERN OF SAN MARCOS.** *917 I-35 N (78666).* 512/754-7557; toll-free 800/937-8376. *www.bestwestern.com.* 50 rms, 2 story. S, D $64.95-$109; under 12 free. Crib free. Pet accepted, some restrictions. TV; cable (premium). Complimentary continental bkfst. Ck-out noon. Business servs avail. In-rm modem link. Coin lndry. Pool. Some refrigerators, microwaves. Cr cds: A, C, D, DS, JCB, MC, V.

★★ **LA QUINTA INN.** *1619 I-35 N (78666).* 512/392-8800; fax 512/392-0324; res 800/531-5900. *www.laquinta.com.* 117 rms, 2 story. S $80-$90; D $90-$97; under 18 free. Crib free. Pet accepted, some restrictions. TV; cable (premium).

Heated pool. Complimentary continental bkfst. Coffee in rms. Restaurant adj open 24 hrs. Ck-out noon. Meeting rm. In-rm modem link. Some refrigerators. Cr cds: A, C, D, DS, MC, V.

D ⌬ ⊠ ⊠ ⌬ SC

★ **WELCOME HOME INN.** *1635 Aquarena Springs Dr (78666). 512/353-8011; fax 512/396-8062.* 100 rms, 2 story. S, D $39-$89; under 18 free. TV; cable (premium). Pool. Complimentary continental bkfst. Ck-out noon. Meeting rms. Business servs avail. In-rm modem link. Cr cds: A, D, DS, MC, V.

D ⊠ ⊠ ⌬

B&Bs/Small Inns

★ ★ **BLAIR HOUSE.** *100 Spoke Hill Rd, Wimberley (78676). 512/847-1111; fax 512/847-8820; toll-free 877/549-5450. www.blairhouseinn.com.* 9 rms, 2 with shower only. No rm phones. S, D $150-$275; each addl $20; wkly rates; wkends (2-day min). Children over 11 yrs only. TV; VCR avail (movies). Complimentary full bkfst. Ck-out noon, ck-in 3 pm. Business servs avail. Many in-rm whirlpools; microwave avail. Some balconies. Art gallery. Totally nonsmoking. Cr cds: A, DS, MC, V.

D ⊠ ⌬

★ ★ **CRYSTAL RIVER INN.** *326 W Hopkins St (78666). 512/396-3739; fax 512/396-6311; toll-free 888/396-3739. www.crystalriverinn.com.* 11 rms in 3 bldgs, 2 story, 3 suites. Some rm phones. S, D $85-$150; each addl $7.50-$15; suites $110-$150. Crib $5. TV in some rms; cable. Complimentary full bkfst; afternoon refreshments. Restaurant nearby. Ck-out noon, ck-in 3 pm. Business servs avail. Converted former homes of early settlers. Picnics, themed wkends; river trips avail. Formal gardens with fountain. Cr cds: A, D, DS, MC, V.

⌬ ⊠ ⌬

★ ★ ★ **INN ABOVE ONION CREEK.** *4444 W Hwy 150 W, Kyle (78640). 512/268-1617; fax 512/268-1090; toll-free 800/579-7686. www.innabove onioncreek.com.* 9 rms, 2 story, 2 suites. S, D $140-$275. Children over 12 yrs only. TV; cable (premium), VCR (movies). Complimentary full bkfst. Ck-out 11 am, ck-in 3-6 pm. Business servs avail. In-rm modem link. Pool. Fireplaces; many in-rm whirlpools; refrigerator in suites. Some balconies. Totally nonsmoking. Cr cds: A, MC, V.

D ⊠ ⊠ ⌬

⛽ Seguin

(E-5) *See also New Braunfels, San Antonio, San Marcos*

Founded 1838 **Pop** 22,011 **Elev** 520 ft
Area code 830 **Zip** 78155
Information Chamber of Commerce, 427 N Austin St, PO Box 710; 830/379-6382 or 800/580-7322
Web www.seguintx.org

Special Events

Texas Ladies' State Chili Cook-off. Mid-Apr. Phone 830/401-2480.

Biggest Small Town Parade. July 4. Phone 830/401-2448.

Texas Youth Rodeo Association State Finals. Late July or early Aug. Phone 830/379-9997.

Guadalupe County Fair and PRCA Rodeo. Four days early Oct. Phone 830/379-1333.

Motel/Motor Lodge

★ ★ **HOLIDAY INN.** *2950 N Hwy 123 Bypass (78155). 830/372-0860; fax 830/372-3020; toll-free 800/465-4329. www.holiday-inn.com/seguintx.* 139 rms, 2 story. Late-May-Aug: S $70-$90; D $78-$98; each addl $8; lower rates rest of yr. Crib free. TV; cable (premium). Pool. Coffee in rms. Restaurant 6-10 am, 5-9 pm; Sun to 11 am. Bar 4 pm-midnight. Ck-out noon. Meeting rms. Business servs avail. Coin lndry. Exercise equipt. Cr cds: A, C, D, DS, JCB, MC, V.

D ⊠ 犬 ⊠ ⌬

Shamrock

See also Amarillo

Pop 2,029 **Elev** 2,310 ft
Area code 806 **Zip** 79079

Information Chamber of Commerce,
207 N Main; 806/256-2501

Web www.shamrocktx.net

What to See and Do

Pioneer West Museum. Renovated
hotel furnished with items depicting
pioneer days; kitchen, parlor and
bedrm, doctor and dentist offices,
Native American rm, country store,
school rm, chapel, early barbershop,
war rm, Fort Elliot rm and "Prairie-
to-the-Moon" rm honoring astronaut
Alan Bean. Located on grounds is
Justice of the Peace office and
lawyer's office building. (Call for hrs)
204 N Madden St. Phone 806/256-
3941. **Donation**

Special Event

St. Patrick's Day Celebration. Parade,
Miss Irish Rose Pageant, TRA team
roping, entertainment, dances, carnival, banquet. Wkend nearest Mar 17.

Motels/Motor Lodges

★★ **IRISH INN MOTEL.** *301 I-40 E
(79079). 806/256-2106; fax 806/256-
2106.* 157 rms, 2 story. S $40-$70; D
$44-$70; each addl $4; under 12 free.
Crib $3. Pet accepted. TV; cable, VCR
(movies). Indoor pool; whirlpool.
Restaurant open 24 hrs. Private club
5 pm-midnight. Ck-out 1 pm. Coin
lndry. Meeting rm. Business servs
avail. In-rm modem link. Some
refrigerators. Gift shop. Some refrigerators. Cr cds: A, C, D, DS, ER, JCB,
MC, V.

★ **WESTERN MOTEL.** *104 E 4th St
(79079). 806/256-3244; fax 806/256-
3244.* 24 rms, 2 story. S $35-$50; D
$40-$55; each addl $6. Crib $2. Pet
accepted. TV; cable (premium).
Restaurant 6 am-9 pm. Ck-out 11
am. Cr cds: A, C, D, DS, MC, V.

Restaurant

★ **IRISH INN.** *303 I-40 E (79079).
806/256-2332.* Open 24 hrs. Bar 5
pm-midnight. Bkfst $1.25-$7, lunch,
dinner $1.75-$15.95. Sun brunch
$5.95. Child's menu. Specializes in
steak, fish, chicken. Salad bar. Cr cds:
A, DS, MC, V.

Sherman

(B-6) *See also Bonham, Denison,
Gainesville, McKinney*

Pop 35,082 **Elev** 745 ft **Area code** 903
Zip 75090

Information Convention & Visitors
Bureau, 307 W Washington, Suite
100, PO Box 1029, 75091; 903/893-
1184 or 888/893-1188

Web www.shermantexas.com

What to See and Do

Hagerman National Wildlife Refuge.
An 11,320-acre area on Lake Texoma
provides food and rest for migratory
waterfowl of the central flyway. Fishing, boating (Apr-Sept); trail, self-
guided auto tour route, picnicking.
Visitor center. (Daily; closed hols)
NW via US 82, exit at FM 1417, go N
to Refuge Rd, follow signs to headquarters. Phone 903/786-2826. **FREE**

Lake Texoma. 13 mi N.

Red River Historical Museum. Quar-
terly exhibits; permanent exhibits
incl "Black Land, Red River," artifacts
and furniture from Glen Eden, early
plantation house whose site is now
under Lake Texoma; country store,
local history, and farm and ranch
rm. (Tues-Fri, also Sat afternoons;
closed hols) 301 S Walnut, in the historic Carnegie Library building
(1914). Phone 903/893-7623. ¢

Special Events

Lakefest Regatta. Third wkend Apr.
Phone 903/465-1551.

**Sherman Preservation League Tour
of Homes.** Third wkend Apr. Phone
903/893-4067.

National Aerobatic Championships.
Grayson County Airport. Second wk
Sept. Phone 903/786-2904.

Motel/Motor Lodge

★ ★ **EXECUTIVE INN.** *2105 Texoma
Pkwy (75090). 903/892-2161; fax
903/893-3045.* 150 rms, 2 story. S
$42-$89; D $50-$97; each addl $8;
under 17 free. Crib free. TV; cable
(premium), VCR avail. Pool; whirlpool. Restaurant 6-11:30 am. Private
club 5 pm-midnight. Coffee in rms.
Ck-out noon. Business servs avail. In-
rm modem link. Sundries. Airport
transportation. Health club privileges.
Cr cds: A, C, D, DS, ER, JCB, MC, V.

Hotel

★ ★ ★ **SHERATON INN.** *3605 S Hwy
75 (75090). 903/868-0555; fax
903/892-9396; res 800/325-3535.* 142
rms, 2 story. S, D $79-$89; each addl
$5; suites $145-$195; under 18 free.
Crib free. Pet accepted. TV; cable
(premium). Pool; wading pool, whirlpool. Restaurant 6 am-1 pm, 5-9 pm;
Sat 7:30-11 am, 5-9 pm; Sun 7:30
am-1:30 pm, 5-9 pm. Rm serv. Private club 4 pm-midnight; Sat 6 pm-1
am. Ck-out noon. Coin lndry. Meeting rms. Business servs avail. In-rm
modem link. Valet serv. Exercise
equipt. Some refrigerators. Cr cds: A,
C, D, DS, JCB, MC, V.

Snyder

See also Big Spring

Founded 1876 **Pop** 10,783 **Elev** 2,316
ft **Area code** 915 **Zip** 79549
Information Chamber of Commerce,
2302 Avenue R, PO Box 840;
915/573-3558
Web www.snydertex.com/coc/index.
htm

What to See and Do

Lake J. B. Thomas. Swimming, fishing, boating; picnicking. 17 mi SW
on TX 350.

Scurry County Museum. Local and
county historical exhibits from pre-
history to oil boom. Changing
exhibits. (Mon-Thurs) ¼ mi E off
TX 350 on Western Texas College
campus. Phone 915/573-6107. **FREE**

Special Events

Western Texas College Rodeos. First
three wkends April. Phone 915/573-
9811.

**Legends of Western Swing Music Fes-
tival.** Mid-June. Phone 903/573-3558.

Scurry County Fair. Mid-Sept. Phone
915/573-3558.

White Buffalo Festival. Early Oct.
Phone 915/573-3558.

Motels/Motor Lodges

★ **DAYS INN.** *800 E Coliseum Dr
(79549). 915/573-1166; res 800/329-
7466. www.daysinn.com.* 56 rms, 2
story. S $27; D $32; each addl $5;
suites $45; under 12 $5. Crib free.
Pet accepted. TV; cable (premium).
Pool. Restaurant 6 am-9 pm; Sat, Sun
to 2 pm. Ck-out noon. Cr cds: A, DS,
MC, V.

★ ★ **PURPLE SAGE MOTEL.** *1501 E
Coliseum Dr (79549). 915/573-5491;
fax 915/573-9027; toll-free 800/545-
5792. placestostay.com.* 45 rms. S $46-
$56; D $60-$73; each addl $3-$5;
under 12 free. Crib free. Pet accepted.
TV; cable (premium), VCR avail
(movies). Pool. Playground. Complimentary continental bkfst. Ck-out
noon. Business servs avail. Gift shop.
Health club privileges. Refrigerators;
many microwaves. Picnic tables. Cr
cds: A, C, D, DS, MC, V.

Restaurant

★ ★ **SHACK.** *1005 25th St (79549).
915/573-4921.* Hrs: 11 am-2:30 pm,
5-9:30 pm; Sun to 2:30 pm. Closed
most major hols. Lunch $4.99-
$13.99, dinner $4.99-$14.99. Special-

izes in steak, seafood. Salad bar. Old West decor. Cr cds: A, DS, MC, V.

Sonora

See also Ozona

Settled 1890 **Pop** 2,924 **Elev** 2,120 ft **Area code** 915 **Zip** 76950
Information Chamber of Commerce, 707 N Crockett Ave, PO Box 1172; 915/387-2880
Web www.sonoratx-chamber.net

What to See and Do

Caverns of Sonora. Unusually beautiful caverns with many rare and fine formations; guided tours within 30 min. Picnicking, camping and RV park avail (fee). (Daily) 8 mi W on I-10, then 7 mi S on FM 1989. Phone 915/387-3105. ¢¢¢¢

Special Event

Sutton County Days and Outlaw Pro Rodeo. Rodeo, dance, parade, children's activities. Arts and crafts, barbecue. Aug. Phone 915/387-5645.

Motel/Motor Lodge

★ **DEVIL'S RIVER DAYS INN.** *1312 N Service Rd (76950).* 915/387-3516; fax 915/387-2854; res 800/329-7466. www.daysinn.com. 99 rms, 2 story. S $40; D $60; each addl $3. Crib $4. Pet accepted, some restrictions; $2. TV; cable. Pool. Restaurant 6 am-2 pm, 5-10 pm; Sun to 2 pm. Ck-out noon. Coin lndry. Meeting rm. Business servs avail. 9-hole golf privileges. Cr cds: C, D, DS, MC, V.

South Padre Island

See also Brownsville, Harlingen, Port Isabel

Pop 2,422 **Elev** 0 ft **Area code** 956 **Zip** 78597
Information Convention & Visitors Bureau, 600 Padre Blvd; 956/761-6433 or 800/343-2368

Special Events

South Padre Island Windsurfing Blowout. May.

Independence Day Celebration & Fireworks Extravaganza. July 4. Phone 956/761-3000.

Island of Lights Festival. Late Nov-early Dec. Phone 956/761-5419.

Motel/Motor Lodge

★ **DAYS INN.** *3913 Padre Blvd (78597).* 956/761-7831; fax 956/761-2033; res 800/329-7466. www.daysinn.com. 57 rms, 2 story. Mar-Labor Day: S, D $89-$120; each addl $10; under 12 free; lower rates rest of yr. Crib free. Pet accepted; $25. TV; cable (premium). Pool; whirlpool. Ck-out noon. Coin lndry. Refrigerators. Opp ocean. Cr cds: A, C, D, DS, MC, V.

Resorts

★★ **BAHIA MAR BEACH RESORT.** *6300 Padre Blvd (78597).* 956/761-1343; fax 956/761-6287; res 800/997-2373. www.bahiamar.com. 174 rms in main 12 story bldg, 26 condos. Late May-early Sept: S, D $85-$165; each addl $10; kits. $124-$220; condos $270-$310; wkend, wkly, hol rates; higher rates spring break; lower rates rest of yr. Crib free. Pet accepted, some restrictions. TV; cable (premium). Heated pool; whirlpool, poolside serv. Restaurant 8 am-9 pm. Bar 5 pm-2 am. Ck-out noon. Lighted tennis. Exercise equipt. Balconies. Picnic tables. Swimming beach. Cr cds: A, DS, MC, V.

★★ **HOLIDAY INN SUNSPREE RESORT.** *100 Padre Blvd (78597). 956/761-5401; fax 956/761-1560; toll-free 800/531-7405. www.holiday-inn. com.* 227 rms, 6 story. Apr-Aug: S, D $99-$139; suites $159; under 19 free; lower rates rest of yr. Crib free. TV; cable. 2 pools; wading pool, whirlpool, poolside serv. Playground. Supervised children's activities. Restaurant 7 am-10 pm. Rm serv. Bar 5 pm-2 am. Ck-out noon. Coin lndry. Meeting rms. Business servs avail. In-rm modem link. Bellhops. Valet serv. Gift shop. Exercise equipt. Tennis privileges. Golf privileges. Balconies. Cr cds: A, D, DS, MC, V.

★★★ **RADISSON RESORT SOUTH PADRE.** *500 Padre Blvd (78597). 956/761-6511; fax 956/761-1602; res 800/333-3333. www.radissonspi.com.* 182 units, 2-12 story, 54 condos. Memorial Day-Labor Day: S, D $95-$200; each addl $10; condos (up to 6) $275; under 17 free; higher rates spring break; lower rates rest of yr. Crib free. TV; cable (premium). 3 pools, 1 heated; whirlpools, poolside serv. Free supervised child's activities (Memorial Day-Labor Day). Dining rm 6:30 am-10 pm; Fri, Sat to 11 pm. Box lunches, snack bar, picnics. Rm serv. Bar 11-2 am; entertainment. Ck-out 11 am, ck-in 3 pm. Meeting rms. Business servs avail. Bellhops. Gift shop. Lighted tennis, pro. Golf privileges 10 mi. Swimming beach. Boating. Lawn games. Soc dir (summer). Health club privileges. Fishing guides avail. Refrigerator in condos. Many balconies. Cr cds: A, C, D, DS, ER, MC, V.

★★★ **SHERATON SOUTH PADRE ISLAND BEACH HOTEL.** *310 Padre Blvd (78597). 956/761-6551; fax 956/761-6570; res 800/325-3535. www.sheraton.com.* 246 units, 12 story. 45 kits. June-Aug: S, D $95-$175; each addl $10; suites $250-$360; under 17 free; lower rates rest of yr. Crib free. TV; cable (premium). Pool; wading pool, whirlpool, poolside serv. Coffee in rms. Restaurants 6:30 am-10 pm. Bar 11-2 am; entertainment Tues-Sat. Ck-out 11 am. Coin lndry. Convention facilities.

Business servs avail. In-rm modem link. Gift shop. Tennis. Exercise equipt. Some refrigerators. Balconies. On beach. Cr cds: A, D, DS, MC, V.

B&B/Small Inn

★★ **BROWN PELICAN INN.** *207 W Aires Dr (78597). 956/761-2722; fax 956/761-8683. www.brownpelican.com.* 8 rms, 6 with shower only. No rm phones. Memorial Day-Labor Day, March-Easter: S, D $85-$100; each addl $15; package plans; higher rates special events; lower rates rest of yr. TV in some rms; VCR avail (movies). Complimentary continental bkfst. Restaurant adj 6-10 pm. Ck-out 11 am, ck-in 3-6 pm. Luggage handling. Gift shop. View of bay. Totally non-smoking. Cr cds: A, DS, MC, V.

Restaurants

★★ **AMBERJACKS.** *209 W Amberjack St (78597). 956/761-6500. www. dockndine.com.* Hrs: 11:30 am-10 pm; Fri, Sat to 11 pm. Closed Mon (winter). Amer, Mexican menu. Bar. Lunch $4-$8, dinner $4-$16.95. Child's menu. Specialties: rasta shrimp, sauteed amberjack, grilled snapper. Entertainment wkends. Caribbean setting. Cr cds: A, D, DS, MC, V.

★ **BLACKBEARD'S.** *103 E Saturn (78597). 956/761-2962.* Hrs: 11 am-11 pm. Closed Thanksgiving, Dec 25. Bar. Lunch, dinner $6-$16. Specializes in grilled seafood, steakburgers. Cr cds: A, D, DS, MC, V.

★ **JESSIE'S CANTINA.** *2700 Padre Blvd (78597). 956/761-4500.* Hrs: 11 am-10 pm. Closed Dec 25. Mexican menu. Bar. Lunch, dinner $4-$12. Specializes in seafood, fajitas, enchiladas. Hunting lodge atmosphere; trophies displayed. Cr cds: A, D, DS, MC, V.

★ **LA JAIBA SEAFOOD.** *2001 Padre Blvd (78597). 956/761-9878.* Hrs: 11:30 am-2:30 pm, 5-9 pm. Closed

Mon; Jan 1, Easter, Dec 25. Res accepted. Seafood menu. Bar. Lunch, dinner $4.95-$18.95. Child's menu. Specializes in Alaskan king crab, broiled baby snapper. Nautical atmosphere. Cr cds: A, D, DS, MC, V.
D ⌀

★★ **SCAMPI'S.** *206 W Aries St (78597). 956/761-1755.* Hrs: 6-10 pm. Closed Dec 12-25. Res accepted. Bar 4:30-11 pm. Dinner $13.95-$24.95. Specialties: oysters Rockefeller, flounder Georgette, scampi Italiano. Own pasta. Outdoor dining. Casual bayside dining. Cr cds: A, DS, MC, V.
⌀

★★ **SEA RANCH.** *1 Padre Blvd (78597). 956/761-1314.* Hrs: 5-10 pm; early-bird dinner 5-6:30 pm. Closed Thanksgiving, Dec 25. Seafood menu. Bar from 4:30 pm. Dinner $8.99-$24.99. Child's menu. Specialties: red snapper, shrimp, grouper. Parking. Outdoor dining. View of marina. Cr cds: A, C, DS, MC, V.
D ⌀

Stephenville

(C-5) *See also Cleburne*

Settled 1850 **Pop** 14,921 **Elev** 1,277 ft
Area code 254 **Zip** 76401
Information Chamber of Commerce, 187 W Washington; 254/965-5313 or 800/658-6490
Web www.our-town.com/~chamber

What to See and Do

Cross Timbers Country Opry. Family entertainment by country and western variety performers. (Sat eves) 1 mi E of US 281 via US 377 Bypass. Phone 254/965-4132. ¢¢¢

Dinosaur Valley State Park. (See CLEBURNE) 29 mi E on US 67.

Historical House Museum Complex. Rock English cottage (1869), two-story with bargeboards and vents with Pennsylvania hex signs. Church with fish-scaled steeple (1899); three log cabins; log corn crib (1861); late 1800s ranch house where John Tarleton (of Tarleton State University) lived; 1890s

two-rm schoolhouse; replica of carriage house containing museum of local history items. (Fri-Sun afternoons; closed hols) 525 E Washington. Phone 254/965-5880. **FREE**

Hoka Hey Fine Arts Gallery & Foundry. One of the foremost bronze foundries in the US. Here stands Robert Summers' original nine-ft sculpture of John Wayne, among various other bronzes, paintings, and prints. (Daily; closed hols) Foundry tours (by appt). 10 mi SW via US 377, in Dublin. Phone 254/445-2017. **FREE**

Tarleton State University. (1899) 6,500 students. An affiliate of Texas A&M University. Clyde Wells Fine Arts Center. Horse breeding program is one of the finest in the nation; tours of campus farm. Phone 254/968-9000.

Special Event

Dairy Fest. Family fun, games, picnic. Concert. Mid-June.

Motels/Motor Lodges

★ **DAYS INN.** *701 S Loop (76401). 254/968-3392; fax 254/968-3527; res 800/325-2525. www.daysinn.com.* 65 rms, 2 story. S $34-$65; D $40-$80; each addl $5; under 12 free. Crib free. TV; cable (premium). Pool. Ck-out 11 am. Meeting rms. Business servs avail. In-rm modem link. Cr cds: A, DS, JCB, MC, V.
D ⊠ ⌀ ⌀

★★ **HOLIDAY INN.** *2865 W Washington St (76401). 254/968-5256; fax 254/968-4255; toll-free 800/465-4329. www.holiday-inn.com.* 100 rms, 2 story. S $60-$65; D $70-$75; each addl $5; suites $125-$175; under 18 free. Crib free. Pet accepted. TV; cable (premium). Coffee in rms. Pool. Restaurant 6 am-9 pm; Sun to 3 pm. Rm serv. Private club 5 pm-midnight; closed Sun. Ck-out noon. Meeting rms. Business servs avail. In-rm modem link. Valet serv. Sundries. Cr cds: A, C, D, DS, JCB, MC, V.
D ⌀ ⊠ ⌀ ⌀ SC

★★ **HUMMINGBIRD LODGE.** *Rte 1, Box 496A, Glen Rose (76690). 254/897-2787; fax 254/897-3459. www.eaze.net/~hbird.* 6 rms, 1 with

SULPHER SPRINGS/TEXAS **569**

shower only, 2 story. S, D $92-$98; each addl $18; wkend rates. Adults only on wkends. Complimentary full bkfst. Restaurant nearby. Ck-out noon. Meeting rms. Business servs avail. Sundries. Gift shop. Whirlpool. Rec rm. Many refrigerators. Some balconies. Picnic tables, grills. 2 blks to lake. Cr cds: A, MC, V.

★ **TEXAN MOTOR INN.** *3030 W Washington (76401). 254/968-5003; fax 254/968-5060.* 30 rms. Mid-Apr-Sept: S $37.50; D $43.50; each addl $6; under 12 free. Crib avail. Pet accepted, some restrictions; $3. TV; cable (premium). Complimentary continental bkfst. Restaurant nearby. Ck-out 11 am. Business servs avail. Bus depot transportation. Microwaves avail. Cr cds: A, DS, MC, V.

Restaurant

★ **JOSE'S.** *1044 W Washington (76401). 254/965-7400.* Hrs: 11 am-9:30 pm; Fri, Sat to 10 pm. Closed Jan 1, Thanksgiving, Dec 25. Mexican, Amer menu. Lunch, dinner $2.95-$11.40. Specializes in fajitas, enchiladas, breast of chicken. Cantina atmosphere. Cr cds: A, DS, MC, V.

Sulphur Springs

(B-7) *See also Greenville*

Pop 14,551 **Elev** 530 ft **Area code** 903 **Zip** 75482

Information Tourism & Visitors Bureau, 1200 Houston St, PO Box 347; 903/885-6516 or 888/300-6623

Web www.tourtexas.com/sulphur springs

What to See and Do

City Park. Kids kingdom playground; lake, fishing, swimming pool (summer; fee). (Daily) Connally and League Sts. **FREE**

Southwest Dairy Center. Exhibits demonstrate practical application of antique processing equipt and life on an early dairy farm to modern production and transportation. Guided tours (groups by appt). (Mon-Sat; closed hols) 1210 Houston St. Phone 903/439-6455. **FREE**

Special Events

Hopkins County Dairy Festival. Civic Center. Third wk June. Phone 903/885-8071.

Fall Festival. Carnival, arts and crafts exhibits, special events. Second Sat-third Sat Sept. Phone 903/885-6515.

CRA Finals Rodeo. Civic Center. Phone 903/885-8071. Second wkend Nov.

Motels/Motor Lodges

★★ **BEST WESTERN TRAIL DUST INN.** *1521 Shannon Road E; I-30 E, exit 127 (75483). 903/885-7515; res 800/528-1234. www.bestwestern/ traildustinn.* 102 rms, 2 story. S, D $54; each addl $4; suites $65-$75; under 18 free. Crib free. TV; cable (premium); VCR avail. Pool. Playground. Complimentary continental bkfst. Coffee in rms. Restaurant adj open 24 hrs. Ck-out noon. Meeting rms. Business servs avail. Coin lndry. Health club privileges. Refrigerators. Cr cds: A, C, D, DS, ER, MC, V.

★★ **HOLIDAY INN.** *1495 Industrial Dr E (75482). 903/885-0562; res 800/465-4329. www.holiday-inn.com/ sulphursprngs.* 96 rms, 2 story. S, D $64; each addl $5; suites $75-$80; under 18 free. Crib free. Pet accepted, some restrictions. TV; cable (premium), VCR avail (movies). Pool. Complimentary coffee in rms. Restaurant 6 am-9 pm. Rm serv 6 am-10 pm. Bar 3 pm-midnight. Ck-out noon. Coin lndry. Meeting rms. Business servs avail. In-rm modem link. Valet serv. Sundries. Some refrigerators. Cr cds: A, C, D, DS, ER, JCB, MC, V.

Sweetwater

(C-4) *See also Abilene*

Founded 1881 **Pop** 11,415 **Elev** 2,164 ft **Area code** 915 **Zip** 79556
Information Chamber of Commerce, 810 E Broadway, PO Box 1148; 915/235-5488 or 800/658-6757
Web www.camalott.com/~sweetwater

What to See and Do

City-County Pioneer Museum. Historic house displays antique furniture, pioneer tools, early photographs of area; Indian artifacts; Women Air Force Service Pilots memorabilia. (Tues-Sat afternoons; closed hols) 610 E 3rd St. Phone 915/235-8547. **FREE**

Special Events

Rattlesnake Roundup. Nolan County Coliseum, north end of Elm St. Also Gun & Coin Show. Second wkend Mar. Phone 915/235-9259.

American Junior Rodeo National Finals. Nolan County Coliseum. Late July-early Aug. Phone 915/235-9259.

Motels/Motor Lodges

★★ **HOLIDAY INN.** *500 NW Georgia St (79556). 915/236-6887; fax 915/236-6887; res 800/465-4329.* 107 rms, 2 story. S, D $46-$65; each addl $5; under 19 free. Crib $5. Pet accepted. TV; cable (premium). Pool. Playground. Restaurant open 24 hrs. Rm serv. Private club 4 pm-midnight; Sat to 1 am. Ck-out noon. Coin lndry. Meeting rms. Business servs avail. Some refrigerators. Cr cds: A, C, D, DS, MC, V.
⊡ ⊡ ⊡ ⊡ ⊡ ⊡ ⊡

★ **MOTEL 6.** *510 NW Georgia St (79556). 915/235-4387; fax 915/235-8725; res 800/466-8356. www.motel6.com.* 79 rms, 2 story. S $27.99; D $31.99; each $2; under 17 free. Crib avail. Pet accepted. TV; cable (premium). Pool. Complimentary coffee in lobby. Restaurant opp open 24 hrs. Ck-out noon. Coin lndry. Cr cds: A, C, D, DS, MC, V.

Temple

(D-6) *See also Killeen, Salado, Waco*

Pop 54,514 **Elev** 736 ft **Area code** 254
Information Convention & Visitors Bureau, Municipal Building, 2 N Main, 76501; 254/298-5720

What to See and Do

Belton Lake. Swimming, waterskiing, fishing, boating (ramps); picnicking, concession, camping (tent and trailer sites, fee; hookups, dump station). (Daily) I-35 S, exit W on FM 2305. Phone 254/939-1829. ¢¢

Railroad & Heritage Museum. Exhibits in restored Santa Fe Railroad depot (1907). Baldwin locomotive 3423, Santa Fe caboose. WWII troop sleeper and other pieces of rolling stock on grounds. Picnicking, playground. (Tues-Sat; closed hols) 315 W Ave B. Phone 254/298-5172. ¢

Recreation areas. The Recreation Department maintains 26 parks, five with swimming, seven with tennis courts, three with nine-hole golf. Also 222-acre area on Belton Lake.

Special Event

Independence Day Celebration & Belton PRCA Rodeo. 8 mi SW on I-35, in Belton. Carnival, fiddlers' contest, parade, rodeo. Phone 254/939-3551. Four days early July.

Motels/Motor Lodges

★ **GUESTHOUSE INN.** *400 SW Dodgen Loop 363 (79762). 254/773-1515; fax 254/773-3622; res 800/214-8378.* 100 rms, 2 story. S $40-$45; D $46-$52; each addl $6; under 18 free; wkly, wkend rates. Crib free. Pet accepted. TV; cable (premium). Complimentary coffee in rms. Restaurant open 24 hrs. Rm serv 7 am-10 pm. Ck-out 1 pm. Meeting rms. Business servs avail. In-rm modem link. Health club privileges. Pool. Some refrigerators. Cr cds: A, C, D, DS, MC, V.
⊡ ⊡ ⊡ ⊡ ⊡ SC

★★ **LA QUINTA INN.** *1604 W Barton Ave (76501). 254/771-2980; fax 254/778-7565; res 800/531-5900. www.laquinta.com.* 106 rms, 3 story. S $59; D $66; each addl $7; suites $85-$125; under 18 free. Crib free. Pet accepted, some restrictions. TV; cable (premium). Pool. Continental bkfst. Complimentary coffee in rms. Restaurant adj open 24 hrs. Ck-out noon. Business servs avail. Microwaves avail. Sundries. Cr cds: A, C, D, DS, MC, V.

🄳 🔧 🛊 🌊 🆖 🔥

★ **TRAVELODGE.** *802 N General Bruce Dr (76504). 254/778-4411; fax 254/778-8086; res 800/578-7878. www.travelodge.com.* 132 rms, 2 story. S, D $48-$52; each addl $6; under 18 free. Crib free. Pet accepted, some restrictions. TV; cable (premium). Pool. Coffee in rms. Restaurant 6:30 am-2 pm, 5:30-10 pm; wkend hrs vary. Bar. Ck-out noon. Meeting rms. Business servs avail. In-rm modem link. Valet serv. Coin lndry. Picnic tables. Cr cds: A, MC, V.

🄳 🔧 🛊 🌊 🔥

Hotel

★★ **THE INN AT SCOTT & WHITE.** *2625 S 31st St (76504). 254/778-5511; fax 254/778-5485; toll-free 800/749-0318. www.theinnatscottandwhite.com.* 129 rms, 1-2 story. S $56-$66; D $66-$70; each addl $8; suites $135; under 18 free; wkly, wkend rates. Crib free. Pet accepted, some restrictions. TV; cable. Pool. Restaurant 6 am-10 pm. Rm serv. Private club 4-9 pm. Ck-out noon. Meeting rms. Business servs avail. Valet serv. Sundries. Barber. Gift shop. RR station, bus depot transportation. Microwaves avail. Private patios, balconies. Near Scott & White Hospital. Cr cds: A, DS, MC, V.

🄳 🔧 🌊 🆖 🔥 🆂🅲

Texarkana (B-8)

Founded 1873 **Pop** 34,782 **Elev** 336 ft
Area code 903 (TX); 870 (AR)

Information Chamber of Commerce, 819 State Line Ave, PO Box 1468, 75504; 903/792-7191
Web www.texarkanachamber.com

What to See and Do

Perot Theatre. (1924) Designed by Emil Weil to accommodate both live theater and films. This historic, 1,606-seat performing arts facility features professional and local amateur entertainment. 219 Main St. Phone 903/792-4992.

Texarkana Historical Museum. Local history displays incl Caddo artifacts, Victorian parlor, doctor's office, 1885 kitchen; changing exhibits. (Tues-Sat; closed hols) 219 State Line Ave. Phone 903/793-4831. ¢

Wright Patman Dam and Lake. Water sports (marina, ramps); hunting, picnicking, playgrounds, camping (Rocky Point, Clear Springs, Piney Point; hookups). Fee for some activities. (Daily) 12 mi SW on US 59. Phone 903/796-2419.

Special Event

Bluegrass Festival. Strange Family Bluegrass Park, George Thomas Rd. Four days May and Aug. Phone 903/791-0342.

Motels/Motor Lodges

★★ **BEST WESTERN KINGS ROW INN.** *4200 State Line Ave (71854). 870/774-3851; fax 870/772-8440; res 800/528-1234. www.bestwestern.com.* 116 rms, 2 story. S $49; D $57; each addl $5; under 12 free. Crib $2. Pet accepted, some restrictions. TV; cable (premium). Pool. Restaurant 6 am-2:30 pm. Ck-out noon. Lndry facilities. Meeting rms. Free airport transportation. Some balconies. Cr cds: A, C, D, DS, ER, JCB, MC, V.

🄳 🔧 🌊 ✈ 🆖 🔥

★★ **HOLIDAY INN EXPRESS.** *5401 N State Line Ave (75503). 903/792-3366; fax 903/792-5649; toll-free 800/342-4942. www.holiday-inn.com.* 116 rms, 3 story. S, D $79.00; suites $99; each addl $7; under 18 free. Crib free. TV; cable (premium). Pool; whirlpool. Complimentary continental bkfst. Restaurant adj. Ck-out noon. Coin lndry. Meeting rm. Business servs avail. In-rm modem link. Free airport, RR station, bus depot transportation. Health club privileges. Some refrigerators, microwaves. Cr cds: A, C, D, DS, ER, JCB, MC, V.

★★ **LA QUINTA INN.** *5201 State Line Ave (75503). 903/794-1900; fax 903/792-5506; res 800/531-5900. www.laquinta.com.* 130 rms, 2 story. May-Aug: S, D $59-$76; each addl $9; suites $82-$91; under 18 free; lower rates rest of yr. Crib free. Pet accepted. TV; cable (premium). Pool. Complimentary continental bkfst. Coffee in rms. Restaurant adj. Ck-out noon. Meeting rm. In-rm modem link. Sundries. Free airport, RR station, bus depot transportation. Cr cds: A, D, DS, MC, V.

Hotel

★★ **HOLIDAY INN TEXARKANA I-30.** *5100 N State Line Ave (71854). 870/774-3521; fax 870/772-3068; res 800/465-4329. www.holiday-inn.com.* 210 rms, 4 story. S $79; D $89; each addl $7; suite $140; under 19 free. TV; cable (premium). Heated pool; whirlpool. Complimentary coffee in rms. Restaurant 6:30 am-10 pm; Fri, Sat to 11 pm. Rm serv. Private club 11 am-10 pm; Fri, Sat to 11 pm; Sun 1-10 pm. Ck-out noon. Coin lndry. Meeting rms. Business servs avail. In-rm modem link. Bellhops. Exercise equipt; sauna. Game rm. Microwaves avail. Private patios, balconies. Cr cds: A, C, D, DS, MC, V.

B&B/Small Inn

★★ **MANSION ON MAIN BED & BREAKFAST INN.** *802 Main St (75501). 903/792-1835; fax 903/793-0878. www.bbonline.com/tx/mansion.* 4 rms, 2 with shower only, 2 story, 2 suites. S, D $60-$75; suites $99-$109. TV; cable (premium). Complimentary full bkfst. Restaurant nearby. Ck-out 11 am. Business servs avail. In-rm modem link. Built 1895; veranda columns from St. Louis World's Fair. Oak and chestnut furnishings; many antiques. Cr cds: A, MC, V.

Texas City

(E-7) *See also Galveston, Houston*

Pop 41,521 **Elev** 12 ft **Area code** 409

Information Chamber of Commerce, 8419 Emmett F. Lowry Expy, Suite 105, PO Box 1717, 77592; 409/935-1408 or 281/280-3917 (Houston)

Web www.texascitychamber.org

What to See and Do

Fishing. From three municipal fishing piers on dike extending five mi into Galveston Bay. Also at Memorial and Bay Street parks. Swimming, waterskiing, boating (ramps free); picnicking.

Texas City Museum. Two-story facility houses exhibits on history, science, technology, education, and culture. Replicas of filling station, railway depot. Discovery Center. (Tues-Sat, Sun afternoons; closed hols) 409 6th St N. Phone 409/643-5799. ¢¢

Special Events

Funfest. Competition tennis, golf, soccer; rides, dances, children's activities, fun run; barbecue cook-off. June. Phone 409/935-1408.

Shrimp Boil. Rotary Pavilion, Nessler Park. Food, dancing. Aug. Phone 888/860-1408.

Motel/Motor Lodge

★★ **LA QUINTA INN.** *1121 Hwy 146 N (77590). 409/948-3101; fax 409/945-4412; toll-free 800/687-6667. www.laquinta.com.* 120 rms, 2 story. S, D $52-$89; each addl $8; under 18 free. Crib free. Pet accepted. TV; cable (premium). Pool. Complimentary continental bkfst. Restaurant adj open 24 hrs. Ck-out noon. Meeting rms. Coin lndry. Business servs avail. Microwaves avail. Cr cds: A, C, D, DS, MC, V.

Tyler

(C-7) *See also Athens, Longview*

Founded 1846 **Pop** 83,650 **Elev** 545 ft
Area code 903
Information Convention & Visitors
Bureau, 315 N Broadway, 75702;
903/592-1661 or 800/235-5712
Web www.tylertexas.com

What to See and Do

**Brookshire's World of Wildlife
Museum & Country Store.** More
than 200 specimens of animals from
all over the world, some in natural
habitat exhibits. Replica 1920s country store stocked with authentic
items. Res advised. (Tues-Sat; closed
hols) 1600 W SW Loop 323. Phone
903/534-2169. **FREE**

Caldwell Zoo. More than 120 acres;
domestic and wild animals. (Daily;
closed Jan 1, Thanksgiving, Dec 25)
Gentry Pkwy and M. L. King Blvd,
NW part of town. Phone 903/593-
0121. **FREE**

Goodman Museum. Antebellum arti-
facts, antiques, 19th-century medical
instruments in house built ca 1860.
(Mar-Oct, Wed-Sun; rest of yr, Mon-
Fri; closed Dec 25) 624 N Broadway.
Phone 903/531-1286. **FREE**

Hudnall Planetarium. Astronomy
exhibits (Sept-mid-May, Mon-Thurs;
closed college vacations). Shows
(Sept-mid-May, Sun and Wed; closed
college vacations). On Tyler Junior
College campus, two blks from TX
64. Phone 903/510-2312. **¢**

Smith County Historical Society.
Exhibits cover history of Tyler and
Smith County. (Tues-Sun afternoons;
closed hols) Tours by appt. 201 S
College, in former Carnegie Public
Library. Phone 903/392-5993. **FREE**

⭐ **Tyler Rose Garden and Museum.**
The formal garden has 500 varieties
on 15 acres; museum, community
center. Museum and visitor center
displays photos, memorabilia, past
Rose Festival gowns. (Mon-Sat, also
Sun afternoons; closed hols) 420 Rose
Park Dr. Phone 903/531-1212. **¢¢**

Tyler State Park. Swimming, fishing,
boating (ramp, rentals); picnicking,
concession, improved campsites
(hookups, dump station). Six lakes
are within a few mi. Res advised.
Standard fees. (Daily) 2 mi N of I- 20,
exit 562. Phone 903/597-5338.

Special Events

Azalea Trail. Early Apr.

East Texas State Fair. Late Sept.
Phone 903/597-2501.

Texas Rose Festival. Parade,
pageantry; tours of rose fields. Rose
show. Late-Oct. Phone 903/597-3130.

Motels/Motor Lodges

★ **DAYS INN.** *3300 Mineola Hwy
(75702). 903/595-2451; fax 903/595-
2261; toll-free 800/329-7466. www.
daysinn.com.* 139 rms, 2 story. S $38-
$48; D $40-$50; each addl $6;
suites $65-$90; under 18 free. Crib
free. Pet accepted. TV; cable (premium), VCR avail. Pool. Complimentary continental bkfst.
Restaurant open 24 hrs. Rm serv 8
am-8 pm. Private club 4 pm-midnight. Ck-out noon. Coin lndry.
Meeting rms. Business servs avail.
Valet serv. Sundries. Barber, beauty
shop. Some refrigerators. Cr cds: A,
C, D, DS, ER, MC, V.
🐾 ➽ ⬛ 🔥 **SC**

★★ **FAIRFIELD INN.** *1945 W SW
Loop 323 (75701). 903/561-2535; res
800/228-2800. www.fairfieldinn.com.*
64 rms, 3 story, 8 suites. S $54.90-
$61; D $58.50-$65; each addl $6;
suites $72-$80; under 18 free; package plans; higher rates special events.
Crib free. TV; cable (premium). Complimentary continental bkfst. Restaurant adj 11 am-10 pm. Ck-out noon.
Meeting rms. Business servs avail.
Coin lndry. Indoor pool. Refrigerator,
microwave in suites. Cr cds: A, C, D,
DS, MC, V.
D ➽ ⬛ 🔥

★★ **HAMPTON INN.** *3130 Troup
Hwy (75701). 903/596-7752; fax
903/596-7765; res 800/426-7866.
www.hamptoninn.com.* 78 rms, 3
story. S $69-$95; D $79-$125; under
18 free; higher rates special events.
Crib free. TV; cable (premium), VCR
avail. Complimentary continental

bkfst. Complimentary coffee in rms. Restaurant nearby. Ck-out noon. Business servs avail. In-rm modem link. Valet serv. Pool; whirlpool. Refrigerators, microwaves. Cr cds: A, D, DS, MC, V.

★★ **HOLIDAY INN SOUTHEAST CROSSING.** *3310 Troup Hwy (75701). 903/593-3600; fax 903/533-9571; res 800/465-4329. www.holiday-inn.com.* 160 rms, 2 story. S, D $75-$85; suites $150; under 18 free; wkend rates. Crib free. Pet accepted. TV; cable (premium), VCR avail. Pool; poolside serv. Coffee in rms. Restaurant 6 am-1 pm, 5:30-10 pm; Sat, Sun 7 am-1 pm, 5:30-10 pm. Rm serv. Private club 5-10 pm, closed Sun. Ck-out noon. Coin lndry. Meeting rms. Business servs avail. In-rm modem link. Valet serv. Sundries. Free airport transportation. Cr cds: A, C, D, DS, MC, V.

★★ **LA QUINTA INN.** *1601 W SW Loop 323 (75701). 903/561-2223; fax 903/581-5708; res 800/531-5900. www.laquinta.com.* 130 rms, 2 story. S $72-$82; D $82-$92; each addl $10. Crib free. Pet accepted, some restrictions. TV; cable (premium). Pool. Complimentary continental bkfst. Restaurant adj open 24 hrs. Ck-out noon. Meeting rms. In-rm modem link. Valet serv. Sundries. Free airport transportation. Cr cds: A, C, D, DS, MC, V.

Hotel

★★★ **SHERATON HOTEL.** *5701 S Broadway Ave (75703). 903/561-5800; fax 903/561-9916; res 800/325-3535. www.sheraton.com.* 185 rms, 8 story. S, D $75; each addl $10; suites $105-$148; under 17 free. Crib free. TV; cable (premium). Pool; wading pool, whirlpool, poolside serv. Complimentary coffee in rms. Restaurant 6:30 am-2 pm, 5-10 pm. Private club 11 am-midnight; Sat to 1 am; Sun noon-10:30 pm; entertainment. Ck-out noon. Meeting rms. Business servs avail. In-rm modem link. Free airport transportation. Health club privileges.

Some refrigerators. Balconies. Cr cds: A, C, D, DS, MC, V.

Extended Stay

★★ **RESIDENCE INN BY MARRIOTT.** *3303 Troup Hwy (75701). 903/595-5188; fax 903/595-5719; toll-free 800/331-3131. www.residenceinn.com.* 128 kit. suites, 2 story. Kit. suites $86-$125; wkend rates. Pet accepted; $50. TV; cable (premium). Heated pool; whirlpool. Complimentary continental bkfst. Ck-out noon. Coin lndry. Meeting rms. Business servs avail. In-rm modem link. Valet serv. Sundries. Free airport transportation. Health club privileges. Sport court. Balconies. Picnic tables, grills. Cr cds: A, C, D, DS, JCB, MC, V.

Restaurants

★★ **LIANG'S CHINESE RESTAURANT.** *1828 E Southeast Loop 323 (75701). 903/593-7883.* Hrs: 11 am-10 pm; Fri, Sat to 11 pm. Closed Mon; also Thanksgiving. Res accepted. Chinese menu. Bar. Lunch $3.95-$5.50, dinner $5.25-$10.95. Child's menu. Specialties: chicken Liang-style, Suan beef. Large wood dragon sculpture. Totally nonsmoking. Cr cds: A, D, DS, MC, V.

★★ **POTPOURRI HOUSE.** *3320 Troup Hwy (75701). 903/592-4171. www.potpourrihouse.com.* Hrs: 11 am-9 pm; Fri, Sat to 9:30 pm. Closed Sun; some major hols. Res accepted. Lunch, dinner $5.95-$14.95. Specializes in steaks, seafood. Salad bar. Own baking, soups. Victorian garden decor. Totally nonsmoking. Cr cds: A, DS, MC, V.

Uvalde

(E-4) *See also Brackettville, Eagle Pass*

Founded 1855 **Pop** 14,929 **Elev** 913 ft
Area code 830 **Zip** 78801

Information Chamber of Commerce/
Convention & Visitors Bureau, 300 E
Main; 830/278-3361 or 800/588-2533

Web www.uvalde.org

What to See and Do

First State Bank. Former governor's
art and antique collections on display. (Mon-Fri) 200 E Nopal St.
Phone 830/278-6231. **FREE**

Garner Memorial Museum. Home of
Vice President John Nance Garner;
houses displays on the life and
career of Garner, and Uvalde County
history. (Mon-Sat; closed Dec 1,
hols) 333 N Park St. Phone 830/278-
5018. ¢

Garner State Park. Swimming, fishing; hiking trail, bird-watching,
miniature golf (seasonal), picnicking,
concessions, improved campsites,
screened shelters, cabins (dump station). Standard fees. (Daily) 30 mi N
on US 83, off Hwy 1050 onto Park
Rd 29. Phone 830/232-6132. ¢¢

Uvalde Grand Opera House. (1891)
Used for plays, ballets, orchestra per-
formances; also incl historical rm.
Tours (Mon-Fri; closed hols). 104 W
North St. Phone 830/278-4184.

Special Events

Sahawe Indian Dance Ceremonials.
Two wkends Feb, one wk July. Phone
830/278-2016.

Air Fiesta. Garner Field Rd. Soaring
competitions. Aug.

Motel/Motor Lodge

★★ **HOLIDAY INN.** *920 E Main St
(78801). 830/278-4511; fax 830/591-
0413; toll-free 800/465-4329. www.
holiday-inn.com.* 150 rms, 2 story. S,
D $56.95-$59.95; each addl $8; suites
$113.90-$119.90; under 18 free. Pet
accepted, some restrictions. TV; cable
(premium). Pool. Restaurant 6 am-2
pm, 5-9 pm. Rm serv. Bar 4:30-11:45
pm; closed Sun. Ck-out noon. Coin
lndry. Meeting rms. Valet serv. Cr
cds: A, C, D, DS, JCB, MC, V.

![icons]

Van Horn

Pop 2,435 **Elev** 4,010 ft
Area code 915 **Zip** 79855
Information Convention Center and
Visitors Bureau, 1801 W Broadway,
PO Box 488; 915/283-2682

Special Events

Frontier Days & Rodeo Celebration.
Held since 1899. Parade, AJRA rodeo,
Rodeo Queen contest, golf tourna-
ment, dance. Phone 915/283-2682.
Late June.

Culberson County Fair. Rodeo Arena.
Phone 915/283-2682. Late Sept.

Motels/Motor Lodges

★★ **BEST WESTERN INN OF VAN
HORN.** *1705 W Broadway (79855).
915/283-2410; fax 915/283-2143; toll-
free 800/367-7589. www.bestwestern.
com.* 60 rms. S $34-$45; D $42-$55;
each addl $4; suites $60; under 18
free. Crib $2. Pet accepted, some
restrictions. TV; cable (premium).
Pool. Complimentary continental
bkfst. Restaurant 6:15 am-10 pm. Private club 5-11 pm; closed Sun. Ck-
out noon. Business servs avail. Lndry
facilities. Gift shop. 9-hole golf privileges. Cr cds: A, C, D, DS, MC, V.

![icons]

★★ **RAMADA LIMITED.** *200 Golf
Course Dr (79855). 915/283-2780; fax
915/283-2804; res 888/298-2054.
www.ramada.com.* 98 rms, 2 story. S
$48-$58; D $52-$62; each addl $5;
under 18 free. Crib free. Pet accepted,
some restrictions. TV; cable (premium), VCR avail. Pool. Ck-out 1
pm. Bar; entertainment. Coin lndry.
Meeting rms. Business servs avail. In-
rm modem link. Sundries. Cr cds: A,
D, DS, MC, V.

![icons]

Restaurant

★ **SMOKE HOUSE.** *905 Broadway
(79855). 915/283-2453.* Hrs: 6 am-10
pm. Closed Dec 25. Res accepted.
Mexican, Amer menu. A la carte
entrees: bkfst $1.50-$5.95, lunch

$2.95-$12.95, dinner $4-$12.95. Child's menu. Specializes in smoked meats, homemade bread. Three themed dining areas. Auto museum adj. Cr cds: A, D, DS, MC, V.

Vernon

(A-5) *See also Wichita Falls*

Founded 1889 **Pop** 11,660 **Elev** 1,216 ft **Area code** 940 **Zip** 76384

Information Chamber of Commerce, 1725 Pease St, PO Box 1538, 76385; 940/552-2564 or 800/687-3137

What to See and Do

Lake Kemp. Swimming, waterskiing, fishing, boating. 25 mi S via US 183, 283.

Red River Valley Museum. Archaeological exhibits and Native American artifacts. Big-game collection incl more than 130 trophies, incl black rhino and polar bear; History of Texas Ranching Room incl a 10-by-20-ft Waggoner mural. Sculpture exhibit incl busts of famous people; traveling exhibits rm. (Tues-Sun afternoons; closed some hols) On US 70, just off US 287. Phone 940/553-1848. **FREE**

Special Event

Santa Rosa Roundup. Rodeo, parade, specialty acts, Santa Rosa Palomino Club. Third wkend May. Phone 940/552-2321.

Motels/Motor Lodges

★ **DAYS INN.** *3110 W US Hwy 287 (76384). 940/552-9982; fax 940/552-7851; toll-free 800/329-7466. www. daysinn.com.* 50 rms, 2 story. S $42; D $47. Pet accepted. TV; cable (premium), VCR avail (movies). Complimentary continental bkfst. Pool. Restaurant adj 6 am-9 pm. Ck-out 11 am. Business servs avail. Coin lndry. Some refrigerators, microwaves. Cr cds: A, C, D, DS, MC, V.

★ **GREEN TREE INN.** *3029 Morton St (76384). 940/552-5421; fax 940/552-5421; toll-free 800/600-5421.* 30 rms. S $33-$39; D $36-$42; each addl $3; under 12 free. Pet accepted. TV; cable (premium). Pool. Complimentary continental bkfst. Ck-out 11 am. In-rm modem link. Cr cds: A, C, D, DS, MC, V.

Victoria

(E-6) *See also Goliad, Port Lavaca*

Founded 1824 **Pop** 60,603 **Elev** 220 ft **Area code** 361

Information Convention & Visitors Bureau, 700 Main Center, Suite 101, PO Box 2465, 77902; 361/573-5277 or 800/926-5774

Web www.victoriachamber.org

What to See and Do

Coleto Creek Reservoir. Approx 3,100 acres of fresh water. Extensive lakefront, waterskiing, fishing (lighted pier), boating; nature trail, pavilions, picnicking, playground, improved camping (fee). (Daily) 14 mi SW via US 59S. Phone 361/575-6366. ¢¢¢

Memorial Square. Oldest public burial ground in the city. Three monuments outline history of the area. A steam locomotive and Dutch windmill are also here. Commercial and Wheeler Sts.

Riverside Park. A 562-acre site on Guadalupe River. Picnic areas, barbecue pits, playgrounds, duck pond, rose garden, hiking/biking trail; boat ramp; 27-hole golf, baseball fields, RV campsites (fee). (Daily) Red River and Memorial Sts. Phone 361/572-2767. **FREE** Within the park is

 Texas Zoo. Indoor and outdoor exhibits of animals native to Texas incl margays, ocelots, jaguarundis, and a pair of rare red wolves. (Daily; closed Jan 1, Thanksgiving, Dec 25) 110 Memorial Dr. ¢

Special Events

PRCA Rodeo. Victoria Community Center. Last wkend Feb. Phone 361/573-2651.

Victoria Jaycees Stockshow. Second wkend Mar. Phone 361/576-4300.

Bach Festival. June. Phone 361/570-5788.

Motels/Motor Lodges

★ ★ **FAIRFIELD INN.** *7502 N Navarro St (77904). 361/582-0660; toll-free 800/228-2800. www.fairfield inn.com.* 64 rms, 3 story, 8 suites. S $63.95; D $60.95; suites $66.95; under 18 free. Crib avail. TV; cable (premium). Complimentary continental bkfst. Restaurant nearby. Meeting rms. Business servs avail. In-rm modem link. Indoor pool. Refrigerator, microwave in suites. Cr cds: A, D, DS, MC, V.

🄳 ➤ ⊠ 🖟

★ ★ **HAMPTON INN.** *3112 E Houston Hwy (77901). 361/578-2030; fax 361/573-1238; res 800/426-7866. www.hamptoninn.com.* 100 rms, 2 story. S $61; D $67; under 18 free. Crib free. TV; cable (premium). Pool. Complimentary continental bkfst. Coffee in rms. Restaurant nearby. Ck-out noon. Meeting rms. Business servs avail. In-rm modem link. Free airport transportation. Health club privileges. Cr cds: A, C, D, DS, MC, V.

🄳 ➤ ✈ ⊠ 🖟 SC

★ ★ **HOLIDAY INN HOTEL AND CONVENTION CENTER.** *2705 E Houston Hwy (77901). 361/575-0251; fax 361/575-8362; res 800/465-4329. www.holidayinnvictoria.com.* 226 rms, 2 story. S $89.95; D $96.95; each addl $7-$10; suites $115; under 18 free; wkend rates. Crib free. Pet accepted. TV; cable (premium). Indoor/outdoor pool; whirlpool. Restaurant 6 am-10 pm. Rm serv. Bar 4-11 pm. Ck-out 1 pm. Coin lndry. Meeting rms. Business center. In-rm modem link. Bellhops. Valet serv. Sundries. Free airport transportation. Exercise equipt; sauna. Game rm. Some refrigerators, microwaves. Cr cds: A, C, D, DS, JCB, MC, V.

🄳 🐾 ➤ 🏋 ✈ ⊠ 🖟 🏃

★ ★ **LA QUINTA INN.** *7603 N Navarro St (77904). 361/572-3585; fax 361/576-4617; res 800/531-5900. www.laquinta.com.* 130 rms, 2 story. S $58-$72; D $67-$82; each addl $10; under 18 free. Crib free. Pet accepted, some restrictions. TV; cable (premium). Pool. Complimentary continental bkfst. Restaurant adj open 24 hrs. Ck-out noon. Meeting rm. Business servs avail. In-rm modem link. Cr cds: A, C, D, DS, MC, V.

🄳 🐾 ⊠ 🖟 🐾

★ ★ **RAMADA INN.** *3901 E Houston Hwy (77901). 361/578-2723; fax 361/272-3306; res 888/298-2054. www.ramada.com.* 126 rms, 2 story. S $55; D $59; each addl $10. Crib free. Pet accepted. TV; cable. Pool; whirlpool, poolside serv. Restaurant 6 am-10 pm, Sun to noon. Rm serv to 9 pm. Bar 5 pm-midnight; closed Sun. Ck-out noon. Meeting rms. Business servs avail. In-rm modem link. Free airport, bus depot transportation. Sauna. Cr cds: A, C, D, DS, JCB, MC, V.

🄳 ⊠ ✈ ⊠ 🖟 🐾

Restaurants

★ ★ **OLDE VICTORIA.** *207 N Navarro (77901). 361/572-8840. www. oldevictoria.com.* Hrs: 11 am-2 pm, 5-10 pm; Sat from 5 pm. Closed Sun; Thanksgiving, Dec 25. Res accepted. Continental menu. Bar. Lunch $4.95-$9.95, dinner $8.95-$18.95. Child's menu. Specialties: tournedos Capri, veal, fresh seafood. Outdoor dining. Old mansion in historic section of town. Cr cds: A, D, DS, MC, V.

🄳 ➤

★ **TEJAS CAFE.** *2902 Navarro (77901). 361/572-9433. www.tejascafe. com.* Hrs: 11 am-10:30 pm; Fri, Sat to midnight. Closed Thanksgiving, Dec 25. Bar. Lunch $4.50-$6.50, dinner $5.25-$10.25. Child's menu. Specializes in chicken, ribs, shrimp. Parking. Former grocery store. Cr cds: A, D, DS, MC, V.

🄳 ➤

★ **VERA CRUZ.** *3110 N Navarro (77901). 361/576-6015.* Hrs: 11 am-9 pm; Fri, Sat to 10 pm. Closed Sun; most major hols. Res accepted. Mexican menu. Wine, beer. Lunch $3-

$9.95, dinner $4-$9.95. Specializes in fajitas, tostadas, chile relleno. Mexican decor. Cr cds: A, MC, V.

Waco

(C-6) *See also Groesbeck, Temple*

Founded 1849 **Pop** 113,726 **Elev** 427 ft **Area code** 254

Information Tourist Information Center, PO Box 2570, 76702; 254/750-8696 or 800/922-6386 (outside Waco)

Web www.wacocvb.com

What to See and Do

Art Center Waco. Permanent and changing exhibits in renovated Mediterranean-style house. (Tues-Sat, Sun afternoon) 1300 College Dr. Phone 254/752-4371. ¢

Baylor University. (1845) 14,122 students. Chartered by the Republic of Texas in 1845, Baylor University is the oldest university in continuous existence in the state. 1311 S 5th St. Phone 254/710-1011. On the 425-acre campus are

> **Armstrong Browning Library.** World's largest collection of books, letters, manuscripts, and memorabilia of Robert Browning and Elizabeth Barrett Browning. (Mon-Sat; closed hols) 700 Speight St. Phone 254/710-3566. **FREE**

> **Governor Bill & Vara Daniel Historic Village.** A reconstructed 1890s Texas river town. (Mon-Sat) University Parks Dr, behind Alumni Center. Phone 254/710-1160. ¢¢

Strecker Museum. Biology, geology, archaeology, and anthropology exhibits; "Man's Cultural Heritage in Central Texas"; 1835 log cabin. World's largest fossil sea turtle; exhibit of local reptiles. (Mon-Sat; closed hols) Basement of Sid Richardson Science Building. Phone 254/710-1110. **FREE**

Dr. Pepper Museum. This 1906 "Home of Dr. Pepper" features exhibits, memorabilia, and a working turn-of-the-century soda fountain. (Daily, closed hols) 300 S 5th St. Phone 254/757-1024. ¢¢

Fort Fisher Park. Headquarters for Company F, Texas Rangers, Waco Tourist Information Center, and the Texas Rangers Hall of Fame and Museum. Approx 30 acres. (Daily) I-35 and University Dr, exit 335B. Phone 254/750-8630. Within the park is

> **Texas Ranger Hall of Fame & Museum.** Texas Ranger memorabilia, firearms exhibits and dioramas with wax figures depict more than 170-yr history of Texas Rangers; 20-min film, *Story of Texas Rangers;* Western art; library. (Daily; closed hols) Phone 254/750-8631. ¢¢

Lake Waco. Swimming, waterskiing, fishing, boating (ramps); nature trail, picnicking, camping (tent and trailer sites, dump station). Some fees. (Daily) Headquarters is 2 mi NW on FM 1637 (N 19th St), then approx 1½ mi W, follow signs. Phone 254/756-5359. ¢¢

Restored houses. Earle-Napier-Kinnard House. (1867) 814 S 4th St. Two-story Greek Revival home; furnished in 1860s style (summer tours Thurs-Mon). **East Terrace** (ca 1872) 100 Mill St. Two-story Italianate villa-style house built with bricks made from Brazos River clay; period furnishings. **Fort House** (1868) 503 S 4th St. Antiques and local historical exhibits in Greek Revival home. **Champe Carter McCulloch House** (1866) 407 Columbus Ave. Two-story Greek Revival home, period furnishings. (All houses: Sat and Sun; closed Easter and Thanksgiving weeks, Dec-Jan 2) Combination ticket avail. Phone 254/753-5166. ¢

Special Events

Heart o' Texas Speedway. 203 Trailwood. Stock car racing. Phone 254/829-2294. Mar-Sept.

Brazos River Festival. Art show, karaoke, the Great Texas Raft Race, food, fun, games, music. Cameron Park East. Last full wkend Apr. Cameron Park East.

Heart o' Texas Fair & Rodeo. Coliseum & Fairgrounds, 46th and Bosque Blvd. Early Oct.

Christmas on the Brazos. First full wkend Dec.

Motels/Motor Lodges

★★ **BEST WESTERN OLD MAIN LODGE.** *I-35 at 4th St (76706). 254/753-0316; fax 254/753-3811; res 800/780-7234. www.bestwestern.com/ oldmainlodge.* 84 rms. S $69; D $74; each addl $6; under 12 free; higher rates special events. Crib free. Pet accepted, some restrictions. Pool. TV; cable (premium). Complimentary continental bkfst, coffee in lobby. Restaurant adj open 24 hrs. Ck-out 1 pm. Meeting rms. Business servs avail. In-rm modem link. Valet serv. Some refrigerators; microwaves avail. Near Baylor Univ. Cr cds: A, C, D, DS, MC, V.

★★ **CLARION INN.** *801 S 4th St (76706). 254/757-2000; fax 254/757-1110; toll-free 800/252-7466. www. choicehotels.com.* 148 rms, 2 story. S $69-$85; D $74-$92; each addl $6; suites $125; under 18 free. Crib $6. TV; cable (premium). Indoor pool; whirlpool. Complimentary continental bkfst. Coffee in rms. Restaurant 11 am-2 pm, 6-9 pm. Rm serv. Bar 6 pm-midnight; closed Sun. Ck-out noon. Coin lndry. Meeting rms. Business center. In-rm modem link. Valet serv. Airport, bus depot transportation. Golf privileges. Exercise equipt. Game rm. Refrigerators, microwaves. Baylor University 1 block. Cr cds: A, C, D, DS, MC, V.

★★ **COMFORT INN.** *1430 IH 35 S (76706). 254/752-1991; fax 254/752-2084; res 800/228-5150. www.comfort inn.com.* 53 rms, 2 story. S $59-$69; D $64-$74; each addl $7; suites $89-$95; under 18 free; higher rates special events. Crib free. TV; cable (premium). Pool. Complimentary continental bkfst. Ck-out 11 am. Business servs avail. In-rm modem link. Cr cds: A, C, D, DS, MC, V.

★★ **LA QUINTA INN.** *1110 S 9th St (76706). 254/752-9741; fax 254/757-1600; toll-free 800/531-5900. www. laquinta.com.* 102 rms, 2 story. S $68-$76; D $76-$84; each addl $8; suites $88-$96; under 18 free. Crib free. Pet accepted, some restrictions. TV; cable (premium). Pool. Complimentary continental bkfst. Coffee in rms. Restaurant adj open 24 hrs. Ck-out noon. Business servs avail. In-rm modem link. Valet serv. Sundries. Microwaves avail. Baylor Univ nearby. Cr cds: A, C, D, DS, MC, V.

★★ **LEXINGTON INN.** *115 Jack Kultgen Expressway (72704). 254/754-1266; fax 254/755-8612.* 119 rms, 3 story. S $62-$74; D $69-$81; addl $7; suites $145; under 16 free. Crib free. TV; cable. Heated pool; whirlpool. Complimentary continental bkfst. Coffee in rms. Restaurant nearby. Ck-out noon. Coin lndry. Meeting rm. Business servs avail. In-rm modem link. Valet serv. Free airport transportation. Golf privileges; greens fee. Some refrigerators, microwaves. Adj Baylor Univ. Free Wed evening cookout. Cr cds: A, D, DS, MC, V.

Hotel

★★★ **HILTON WACO.** *113 S University Parks Dr (76701). 254/754-8484; fax 254/759-5506; toll-free 800/234-5244. www.hilton.com.* 199 rms, 11 story. S $79-$89; D $89-$99; each addl $10; under 12 free; higher rates special events. TV; cable (premium), VCR avail. Pool; whirlpool, poolside serv. Restaurant 6:30-1 am. Bar 11-1 am. Ck-out noon. Meeting rms. Free airport, bus depot transportation. Tennis. Refrigerators avail. On Brazos River, adj Convention Center and Indian Spring Park. Cr cds: A, C, D, DS, ER, JCB, MC, V.

Restaurant

★ **ELITE CAFE.** *2132 S Valley Mills Dr (76706). 254/754-4941.* Hrs: 11 am-10 pm; Fri, Sat to 11 pm. Closed Thanksgiving, Dec 25. Bar to midnight. Lunch, dinner $3.95-$12.95. Child's menu. Specializes in steak, fajitas, cheeseburgers. Art deco furnishings. Cr cds: A, DS, MC, V.

Weatherford

(C-6) *See also Fort Worth, Mineral Wells*

Pop 19,000 **Elev** 1,052 ft
Area code 817 **Zip** 76086
Information Chamber of Commerce, 401 Fort Worth St, PO Box 310; 817/594-3801
Web www.weatherford-chamber.com

What to See and Do

Holland Lake Park. Ten-acre municipal park; living museum of nature. An original dog-run log cabin, the first built in the county. Playground, picnicking. (Daily) Off Clear Lake Rd exit 409 from I-20.

Lake Weatherford. Water sports, fishing, boating; picnicking. (Daily) 8 mi NE on FM 1707.

Special Event

Peach Festival. Courthouse Sq. Second Sat July. Phone 817/596-3801.

Wichita Falls

(B-5) *See also Vernon*

Founded 1882 **Pop** 104,197 **Elev** 946 ft **Area code** 940
Information Convention and Visitors Bureau, 1000 Fifth St, 76301; 940/716-5500 or 800/799-6732
Web www.wichitafalls.org

What to See and Do

Kell House. (1909) Landmark with original family furnishings. High ceilings, oak floors, ornate woodwork, period pieces. Guided tour relates history of the early settlement of the area. Tours (Tues, Wed, Sun afternoons). 900 Bluff St. Phone 940/723-0623. ¢¢

Recreational facilities.

    Diversion Reservoir. Swimming, waterskiing, fishing, boating. 25 mi W via US 82, TX 258.

    Lake Arrowhead State Park. Swimming, waterskiing, fishing, boating (ramp, rentals); nature and bridle trails, picnicking, playground, improved camping (hookups, dump station). Standard fees. 15 mi SE of town via US 281 and FM 1954. Phone 940/528-2211. ¢

    Lake Kickapoo. Swimming, waterskiing, fishing, boating. 25 mi SW via US 82 to Mankins, then S off TX 25.

Trails & Tales of Boomtown, USA. Displays, photographs, and audiovisual presentations illustrate the famous 1918 Burkburnett oil boom and surrounding events. Guided bus tour (two hrs) of various sites relevant to the boom. (June-Oct, Fri and Sat; tour, Sat only) 104 W 3rd St in Burkburnett; 15 mi N on I-44 E to TX 240 W, Burkburnett exit. Phone 940/569-0460. ¢¢

Wichita Falls Museum & Art Center. Permanent and changing art and hands-on science exhibits; children's activities. Planetarium shows (Sat afternoons, fee). Museum (Tues-Sat; closed hols). 2 Eureka Cir. Phone 940/692-0923. ¢¢

Special Events

Texas Weapon Collectors Association Gun & Knife Shows. MPEC Exhibit Hall. 350 exhibitors from eight-state area; antique and modern firearms. Wkends in Jan, Mar, Aug, Nov. Phone 940/692-3766.

Home and Garden Festival. Yard and garden plants, demonstrations, seminars. Late Feb. Phone 940/696-5262.

Texas Ranch Roundup. Team competition among 11 of the largest ranches in Texas. Phone 940/322-0771. Mid Aug.

Hotter 'n Hell Bicycle Ride. Trails varying in length from 6-100 mi; race. Music; homemade ice cream contest; food and beverages. Phone 940/322-3223. Late Aug.

Texas-Oklahoma Fair. Carnival, arts and crafts, entertainment. Mid-Sept. Phone 940/720-2999.

Zephyr Days Train Show. Old-time demonstrations and dress, carriage rides, food. Early Oct. Phone 940/723-0623.

Fantasy of Lights. Midwestern State University. 3400 Taft Blvd, 2 mi SW. More than 30 magnificent Christmas displays and 18,000 lights outlining campus buildings. Begun in 1920s. Phone 940/397-4352. Dec.

Motels/Motor Lodges

★ **ECONO LODGE.** *1700 5th St (76301). 940/761-1889; fax 940/761-1505. www.econolodge.com.* 112 rms, 4 story. S, D $43; under 12 free. Crib free. TV; cable (premium). Pool. Complimentary continental bkfst. Restaurant nearby. Ck-out 11 am. Meeting rm. Business servs avail. Cr cds: A, DS, MC, V.

★ ★ ★ **HOLIDAY INN HOTEL AND SUITES.** *401 Broad St (76301). 940/766-6000; fax 940/766-5942; res 800/465-4329. www.holiday-inn.com.* 241 rms, 4 story. S $74.50; D $84.50; each addl $10; suites $99.50-$199.50; under 18 free; higher rates wkend of Hotter 'n Hell Bicycle Ride. Crib free. TV; cable. 2 pools, 1 indoor; wading pool, whirlpool, poolside serv. Restaurant 6 am-1:30 pm, 5:30-10 pm. Rm serv. Bar 4 pm-midnight; Fri, Sat 3 pm-2 am. Ck-out noon. Coin lndry. Meeting rms. Business servs avail. Bellhops. Sundries. Putting green. Exercise equipt; sauna. Game rm. Bathrm phone, refrigerator, wet bar in suites. Cr cds: A, C, D, DS, MC, V.

★ **KINGS INN.** *1211 Central Fwy (76306). 940/723-5541; fax 940/723-6342; toll-free 800/329-7466; res 800/531-5900.* 101 rms, 2 story. S $36-$48; D $39-$48; each addl $5; under 12 free. TV; cable (premium). Pool. Playground. Ck-out 11 am. Meeting rms. Business servs avail. Free airport transportation. Cr cds: A, C, D, DS, JCB, MC, V.

★ ★ **LA QUINTA INN.** *1128 Central Fwy N (76305). 940/322-6971; fax 940/723-2573; res 800/531-5900. www.laquinta.com.* 139 rms, 2 story. S $52-$69; D $59-$76; each addl $7; suites $71-$99; under 18 free. Crib free. Pet accepted. TV; cable (premium). Pool. Complimentary continental bkfst. Coffee in rms. Ck-out noon. Guest lndry. Meeting rm. Business servs avail. In-rm modem link. Valet serv. Free airport transportation. Cr cds: A, C, D, DS, V.

★ ★ **RAMADA LIMITED.** *3209 NW Fwy (76305). 940/855-0085; fax 940/855-0040; res 888/298-2054. www.ramada.com.* 83 rms, 2 story. S $59; D $65; each addl $5; suites $69-$79; under 17 free; golf plans; higher rates special events. Crib $10. Pet accepted, some restrictions. TV; cable (premium). Complimentary continental bkfst. Complimentary coffee in rms. Restaurant opp 5 am-11 pm. Ck-out noon. Business servs avail. In-rm modem link. Valet serv. Pool. Refrigerator, microwave in suites. Cr cds: A, D, DS, V.

Restaurant

★ **EL CHICO.** *1028 Central Fwy (76305). 940/322-1455. www.elchico.com.* Hrs: 11 am-10 pm; Fri, Sat to 11 pm. Closed Thanksgiving, Dec 25. Res accepted. Tex-Mex menu. Bar. A la carte entrees: lunch, dinner $2-$10.99. Child's menu. Specializes in fajitas. Mexican decor; murals, wall hangings, rugs. Cr cds: A, D, DS, MC, V.

UTAH

U tah is named for the Ute people, a nomadic tribe that populated these regions before the days of westward expansion. The state presents many natural faces, with arid desert and the deep, jagged canyons of the Colorado and Green rivers dominating the west and south and high, rugged mountains in the east and north. Utah contains examples of almost all water and land forms, many unique to the state. This natural diversity, though stimulating to the artistic eye, created an environment inhospitable to early settlers. Tribes of Ute, Piute, and Shoshone were the only people living in the region when the first white men, two Franciscan priests, passed through the area in 1776 en route to California from New Mexico. In 1819, British fur trappers began voyaging into northern Utah; by 1824 mountain men—people like Canadians Étienne Provost and Peter Skene Ogden, for whom some of Utah's towns and rivers are named—were venturing into Utah's wilds. Although these men traversed and explored much of the state, it took the determination and perseverance of a band of religious fugitives, members of the Church of Jesus Christ of Latter-day Saints, to conquer the wilderness that was Utah and permanently settle the land.

Population: 1,722,850
Area: 84,990 square miles
Elevation: 2,200-13,528 feet
Peak: Kings Peak (Duchesne County)
Entered Union: January 4, 1896 (45th state)
Capital: Salt Lake City
Motto: Industry
Nickname: Beehive State
Flower: Sego Lily
Bird: California Gull
Tree: Blue Spruce
Fair: Mid-September, 2003 in Salt Lake City
Time Zone: Mountain

Brigham Young, leader of the Mormon followers, once remarked, "If there is a place on this earth that nobody else wants, that's the place I am hunting for." On July 24, 1847, upon entering the forbidding land surrounding the Great Salt Lake, Young exclaimed, "This is the place!" Immediately the determined settlers began to plow the unfriendly soil and build dams for irrigation. Hard work and tenacity were put to the test as the Mormons struggled to convert the Utah wilderness into productive land. With little to work with—what the settlers did not have, they did without—the Mormons gradually triumphed over the land, creating the safe haven they were searching for.

The Mormon church was founded by Joseph Smith on April 6, 1830, in New York state. The religion, based on writings inscribed on golden plates said to have been delivered to Smith by an angel and translated by him into *The Book of Mormon,* drew a large following. Moving from New York to Ohio and Missouri, and then driven from Missouri and later Illinois, the church grew despite persecution and torture. When Smith was killed in Illinois, Young took over. With a zealot's determination, he headed farther west in search of a place of refuge. He found it in the Salt Lake area of Utah. Growing outward from their original settlement, Mormon pioneers and missionaries established colonies that were to become many of Utah's modern-day cities. During 1847, as many as 1,637 Mormons came to Utah, and by the time the railroad penetrated the region, more than 6,000 had settled in the state. Before his death in 1877, 30 years after entering the Salt Lake Valley, Brigham Young had directed the founding of more than 350 communities.

While the Mormon church undoubtedly had the greatest influence on the state—developing towns in an orderly fashion with wide streets, planting straight rows of poplar trees to provide wind breaks, and introducing irrigation throughout the desert regions—the church members were not the only settlers. In the latter part of the 19th century, the West's fabled pioneer era erupted. The gold rush of 1849-50 sent gold seekers pouring through Utah on their way to California. The arrival of the Pony Express in Salt Lake City in 1860 brought more immigrants, and when the mining boom hit the state in the 1870s and 1880s, Utah's mining towns appeared almost overnight. In 1900, there were 277,000 Utahns; now the population stands at more than 1,700,000, with more than 75 percent living within 50 miles of Salt Lake City. The Mormon Church continues to play an important role, with close to 60 percent of the state's population being members of the Church.

Utah's natural diversity has made it a state of magnificent beauty, with more than 3,000 lakes, miles of mountains, acres upon acres of forests, and large expanses of deserts. Its main heights, 13,000 feet or more, are reached by plateaus and mountains lifted during the Cascade disturbance of the Cenozoic period. In northern Utah, the grandeur of the Wasatch Range, one of the most rugged mountain ranges in the United States, cuts across the state north to south; the Uinta Range, capped by the white peaks of ancient glaciers, is the only major North American range that runs east to west. In the western third of the state lies the Great Basin, a land-locked drainage area that, at one time, was half covered by a large, ancient sea. At its peak, Lake Bonneville was 1,050 feet deep, 145 miles wide, and 346 miles long. The Great Salt Lake and Sevier Lake are saltwater remnants of Bonneville, and Utah Lake is a freshwater remnant. To the east, the Bonneville Salt Flats lie where the ancient lake had retreated. To the east and west extends the Colorado River Plateau, or Red Plateau. This red rock country, renowned for its brilliant coloring and fantastic rock formations, is also home to one of the largest concentrations of national parks and monuments. With its many aspects, Utah is a land designed for the traveler who loves the Western outdoors and can appreciate the awesome accomplishments of the pioneers who developed it.

When to Go/Climate

Temperatures vary across the state, but in general, summer days are hot, summer nights cool; winters are cold and snowy, except in the southwestern part of the state. The best time to visit Utah is in the spring or fall when temperatures are milder and tourist crowds have thinned out.

Snowbird and Alta ski areas

AVERAGE HIGH/LOW TEMPERATURES (°F)

ST. GEORGE

Jan 54/27	**May** 86/52	**Sept** 93/57
Feb 61/32	**June** 96/61	**Oct** 81/45
Mar 67/37	**July** 102/68	**Nov** 65/38
Apr 76/44	**Aug** 99/66	**Dec** 55/27

SALT LAKE CITY

Jan 37/19	**May** 72/46	**Sept** 79/51
Feb 44/25	**June** 83/55	**Oct** 66/40
Mar 52/31	**July** 92/64	**Nov** 51/31
Apr 61/38	**Aug** 89/62	**Dec** 38/22

Parks and Recreation Finder

Directions to and information about the parks and recreation areas below are given under their respective town/city sections. Please refer to those sections for details.

NATIONAL PARK AND RECREATION AREAS

Key to abbreviations. I.H.S. = International Historic Site; I.P.M. = International Peace Memorial; N.B. = National Battlefield; N.B.P. = National Battlefield Park; N.B.C. = National Battlefield and Cemetery; N.C.A. = National Conservation Area; N.E.M. = National Expansion Memorial; N.F. = National Forest; N.G. = National Grassland; N.H.P. = National Historical Park; N.H.C. = National Heritage Corridor; N.H.S. = National Historic Site; N.L. = National Lakeshore; N.M. = National Monument; N.M.P. = National Military Park; N.Mem. = National Memorial; N.P. = National Park; N.Pres. = National Preserve; N.R.A. = National Recreational Area; N.R.R. = National Recreational River; N.Riv. = National River; N.S. = National Seashore; N.S.R. = National Scenic Riverway; N.S.T. = National Scenic Trail; N.Sc. = National Scientific Reserve; N.V.M. = National Volcanic Monument.

Place Name	Listed Under
Arches N.P.	same
Bryce Canyon N.P.	same
Canyonlands N.P.	same
Capitol Reef N.P.	same
Cedar Breaks N.M.	same
Dinosaur N.M.	same
Dixie N.F.	CEDAR CITY
Glen Canyon N.R.A.	LAKE POWELL
Golden Spike N.H.S.	BRIGHAM CITY
Hovenweep N.M.	BLANDING
Manti-LaSal N.F.	MOAB, PRICE
Natural Bridges N.M.	same
Rainbow Bridge N.M.	same
Timpanogos Cave N.M.	same
Uinta N.F.	PROVO
Wasatch-Cache N.F.	LOGAN, SALT LAKE CITY
Zion N.P.	same

STATE PARK AND RECREATION AREAS

Key to abbreviations. I.P. = Interstate Park; S.A.P. = State Archaeological Park; S.B. = State Beach; S.C.A. = State Conservation Area; S.C.P. = State Conservation Park; S.Cp. = State Campground; S.F. = State Forest; S.G. = State Garden; S.H.A. = State Historic Area; S.H.P. = State Historic Park; S.H.S. = State Historic Site; S.M.P. = State Marine Park; S.N.A. = State Natural Area; S.P. = State Park; S.P.C. = State Public Campground; S.R. = State Reserve; S.R.A. = State Recreation Area; S.Res. = State Reservoir; S.Res.P. = State Resort Park; S.R.P. = State Rustic Park.

CALENDAR HIGHLIGHTS

JANUARY

Sundance Film Festival (Park City). Week-long festival for independent filmmakers. Workshops, screenings, and special events.

JUNE

Utah Summer Games (Cedar City). Olympic-style athletic events for amateur athletes. Phone 435/865-8421.

Utah Arts Festival (Salt Lake City). Downtown. More than 1,000 participants, 90 performing groups; Children's Art Yard, juried show with demonstrations. Ethnic food. Phone 801/322-2428.

JULY

Renaissance Fair (Cedar City). Main St City Park. Entertainment, food, and games in Renaissance style. Held in conjunction with the opening of Utah Shakespearean Festival.

JULY

Ute Stampede Rodeo (Nephi). Three-day festival featuring horse and mammoth parades, carnival, PRCA rodeo, contests, arts and crafts, concessions. Phone 435/623-7102.

Festival of the American West (Logan). Ronald V. Jensen Living Historical Farm. Historical pageant; pioneer and Native American crafts fair, art exhibition, antique quilt show, frontier town, medicine man show, log construction; Dutch-oven cook-off. Phone 435/797-1143 or 800/225-FEST.

AUGUST

Novell Showdown (Park City). PGA invitational golf tournament. Contact Park Meadows Golf Club 801/531-7029.

Railroaders Festival (Brigham City). Golden Spike National Historic Site. Relive the rush to complete transcontinental railroad. Professional railroaders pursue world record in spike driving. Contact Golden Spike National Historic Site 435/471-2209.

Bonneville National Speed Trials (Wendover). Bonneville Speedway. Held since 1914 on the Bonneville Salt Flats, which has been used as a track for racing the world's fastest cars. Car racing in competition and against the clock. Phone 805/526-1805.

SEPTEMBER

Utah State Fair (Salt Lake City). State Fair Park. Arts and crafts, live entertainment, horse show, and rodeo. Phone 801/538-FAIR.

Place Name	Listed Under
Bear Lake S.P.	GARDEN CITY
Camp Floyd S.P.	PROVO
Coral Pink Sand Dunes S.P.	KANAB
Dead Horse Point S.P.	MOAB
Deer Creek S.P.	HEBER CITY
Edge of the Cedars S.P.	BLANDING
Escalante S.P.	LOA
Fort Buenaventura S.P.	OGDEN
Goblin Valley S.P.	GREEN RIVER
Gunlock S.P.	ST. GEORGE
Hyrum S.P.	LOGAN
Iron Mission S.P.	CEDAR CITY
Red Fleet S.P.	VERNAL
Rockport S.P.	PARK CITY
Scofield S.P.	PRICE
Snow Canyon S.P.	ST. GEORGE
Stagecoach Inn S.P.	PROVO
Territorial Statehouse S.P.	FILLMORE
This is the Place S.P.	SALT LAKE CITY
Utah Lake S.P.	PROVO
Wasatch Mountain S.P.	HEBER CITY
Willard Bay S.P.	OGDEN

Water-related activities, hiking, riding, various other sports, picnicking, and visitor centers, as well as camping, are available in many of these areas. Day-use fee, including picnicking, boat launching, and museums: $5-$20 per vehicle. Camping (mid-April-October; some sites available rest of yr), $7-$16/site/night; most sites 14-day max. Advance reservations may be obtained at most developed state parks; phone 801/322-3770 (Salt Lake City) or 800/322-3770. Pets on leash only. Senior citizen and disabled permit (free; Utah residents only). For information on park facilities and permits, contact Utah State Parks & Recreation, 1594 W North Temple, Salt Lake City 84114, phone 801/538-7220.

SKI AREAS

Place Name	Listed Under
Alta Ski Area	ALTA
Beaver Mountain	GARDEN CITY
Brian Head Ski Area	CEDAR CITY
Brighton Resort	SALT LAKE CITY
Deer Valley Resort	PARK CITY
Elk Meadows	BEAVER
Mount Holly	BEAVER
Nordic Valley	OGDEN
Park City Mountain Resort	PARK CITY
Powder Mountain	OGDEN
Snowbasin	OGDEN
Snowbird Ski and Summer Resort	SNOWBIRD
Solitude	SALT LAKE CITY
Sundance	PROVO
The Canyons	PARK CITY
White Pine Touring Center	PARK CITY

A booklet and further information may be obtained from Utah Travel Council, Council Hall, Capitol Hill, 300 N State St, Salt Lake City 84114, phone 801/538-1030.

FISHING AND HUNTING

Wildlife habitat authorization $6; nonresident deer permit $198; permit for bull elk $300; once-in-a-lifetime permit for moose, bison, desert bighorn sheep, Rocky Mountain goat $1,003. For special permits, write for information and apply from early-late January (bucks, bulls, and once-in-a-lifetime draw) and early June (antlerless draw). Small game licenses $40. Deer, elk, ducks, geese, pheasants, mourning doves, and grouse are favorite quarry.

More than 3,000 lakes and hundreds of miles of mountain streams are filled with rainbow, German brown, cutthroat, Mackinaw, and brook trout; there are also catfish, walleyed pike, bass, crappie, and bluegill. Nonresident season fishing license (14 yrs and over) $45; seven-day fishing license $21; one-day fishing license $8.

Further information may be obtained from the Division of Wildlife Resources, 1594 W North Temple, Box 146301, Salt Lake City 84114-6301, phone 801/538-4700.

RIVER EXPEDITIONS

See Bluff, Green River, Moab, Salt Lake City, Vernal. For a directory of professional outfitters and river runners write Utah Travel Council, Council Hall, Capitol Hill, 300 N State St, Salt Lake City 84114, phone 801/538-1030 or 800/200-1160.

Driving Information

Safety belts are mandatory for all persons in front seat of vehicle. Children under age eight must be in an approved passenger restraint anywhere in the vehicle: ages two-seven may use a regulation safety belt; under age two must use an approved safety seat.

INTERSTATE HIGHWAY SYSTEM

Use the following list as a guide to access interstate highways in Utah. You should always consult a map to confirm driving routes.

Highway Number	Cities/Towns within ten miles
Interstate 15	Beaver, Brigham City, Cedar City, Fillmore, Nephi, Ogden, Payson, Provo, St. George, Salt Lake City.
Interstate 70	Green River, Salina.
Interstate 80	Salt Lake City, Wendover.

Additional Visitor Information

Utah Travel Council, Council Hall, Capitol Hill, 300 N State St, Salt Lake City 84114, will furnish excellent, extensive information on every section of the state and on special and annual events. Phone 801/538-1030 or 800/200-1160.

There are several visitor centers in Utah, with information and brochures about points of interest. Major centers may be found at the following locations: Utah Field House of Natural History, 235 E Main St, Vernal; St. George Information Center, Dixie Center; Echo Information Center, 2 mi E of jct I-80E, I-80N; Thompson Information Center, on I-70, 45 mi W of Utah-Colorado border; Brigham City Information Center, I-15, 5 mi N.

The Utah Fine Arts Council, 617 E South Temple, Salt Lake City 84102, phone 801/236-7555, provides information on local and statewide artists, museums, galleries, and exhibits.

WALLS OF STONE

This three- to four-day tour out of Moab includes magnificent vistas, whimsical rock formations, an early "newspaper," and the upper reaches of Lake Powell. From Moab, head south on US 191 to UT 211; follow UT 211 west to Newspaper Rock, a huge sandstone panel with petroglyphs up to 1,500 years old. Images etched into this wall of stone were left by prehistoric peoples such as the Fremonts and Ancestral Puebloans, as well as the Utes, Navajo, and European-American settlers from the 19th and early 20th centuries. From Newspaper Rock it is an easy drive west on UT 211 to the Needles District of Canyonlands National Park. You probably visited the Island in the Sky District of Canyonlands during your stay in Moab, but this section

of the park offers a different perspective. Although best explored by mountain bike or in a high-clearance four-wheel-drive vehicle, there are several roadside viewpoints from which you can see the district's namesake red-and-white-striped rock pinnacles and other formations. Several easy hikes offer additional views.

Retrace your route back to US 191, and continue south to UT 95, where you will head west to Natural Bridges National Monument. This easy-to-explore monument has a scenic drive with overlooks that offer views of three awe-inspiring natural stone bridges and some 700-year-old Ancestral Puebloan cliff dwellings. There is also prehistoric rock art and a demonstration of how solar energy is used to produce the monument's electricity. The viewpoints are short walks from parking areas, and the more ambitious can also hike to all three of the natural bridges, which were created over millions of years as water cut through solid rock.

Returning to UT 95, head northwest to the Hite Crossing section of Glen Canyon National Recreation Area. Encompassing the northern end of Lake Powell, this is one of the least developed and also least crowded areas of the recreation area. Hite has scenic views, boat rentals, and plenty of available lodging (including houseboats). This is a good opportunity for kids who have spent too much time in the car to stretch their legs and play in the water.

From Hite, continue northwest on UT 95 across rock-studded terrain to Hanksville; head north on UT 24 to the turnoff to Goblin Valley State Park. This delightful little park—sure to be a favorite of anyone with a vivid imagination—is a fantasyland where whimsical stone goblins seem to be frozen in mid-dance. From Goblin Valley, return to UT 24 and continue north to I-70. Head east to the community of Green River, which offers an ample supply of motels. Here you'll discover Green River State Park, a good spot for a picnic under the Russian olive and cottonwood trees along the river or perhaps a round of golf at the park's nine-hole championship course. Nearby, the John Wesley Powell River History Museum tells the incredible story of explorer Powell, a one-armed Civil War veteran who did what was considered impossible when he charted the Green and Colorado rivers in the late 1800s. From Green River continue east on I-70 to US 191, which leads south back to Moab.
(APPROX 448 MI)

Alta

(C-4) *See also Heber City, Park City, Salt Lake City*

Pop 370 **Elev** 8,600 ft **Area code** 435 **Zip** 84092

What to See and Do

Alta Ski Area. Three triple, five double chairlifts; four rope tows; patrol, school, rentals, snowmaking; lodges, restaurant, cafeteria. Longest run 3½ mi, vertical drop 2,020 ft. (Mid-Nov-Apr, daily) Half-day rates. On UT 210 in Little Cottonwood Canyon. Phone 435/359-1078. ¢¢¢¢

Hotel

★★ **ALTA'S RUSTLER LODGE.** *Little Cottonwood Canyon (84092).* 435/742-2200; fax 435/742-3832; res 888/532-2582. www.rustlerlodge.com. 85 rms, 5 story. No A/C. MAP: S $300-$400; D $350-$490; each addl $80; suites $520-$650/rm; under 5 free; higher rates: Dec 19, mid-Mar. Closed May-Oct. Crib free. TV in rec rm; cable. Heated pool; whirlpool. Restaurant 7:30-9:45 am, 12:30-2 pm, 6:30-9 pm. Private club 3-11 pm. Ck-out 1 pm. Coin lndry. Meeting rms. Bellhops. Downhill/x-country ski on site. Exercise equipt. Rec rm. Cr cds: A, MC, V.

[icons]

Resort

★ **ALTA LODGE.** *State Rd 210 (84092).* 435/742-3500; fax 435/742-3504; res 800/707-2582. www.alta lodge.com. 57 rms, 3 story. No elvtr. MAP, Nov-Apr: S, D $103-$467; each addl $88-$97; men's, women's dorms $98-$108; under 4 free; EP avail in summer; lower rates June-early-Oct. Closed rest of yr. TV in common area; cable, VCR avail (free movies). Supervised children's activities (Nov-Apr); ages 3-12. Restaurant 6:30-9 pm. Bar (winter). Ck-out 11 am. Meeting rms. Business servs avail. Coin lndry. Downhill/x-country ski on site. Tennis. Whirlpool. Sauna. Some fireplaces. Some balconies. Sun deck. Cr cds: D, DS, MC, V.

[icons]

Arches National Park

(E-6) *See also Moab*

(5 mi NW of Moab on US 191 to paved entrance rd)

This timeless, natural landscape of giant stone arches, pinnacles, spires, fins, and windows was once the bed of an ancient sea. Over time, erosion laid bare the skeletal structure of the earth, making this 114-square-mile area a spectacular outdoor museum. This wilderness, which contains the greatest density of natural arches in the world, was named a national monument in 1929 and a national park in 1971. More than 2,000 arches have been cataloged, ranging in size from 3 feet wide to the 105-foot-high, 306-foot-wide Landscape Arch.

The arches, other rock formations, and views of the Colorado River canyon, with the peaks of the LaSal Mountains in the distance, can be reached by car, but hiking is suggested as the best way to explore. Petroglyphs from the primitive peoples who roamed this section of Utah from A.D. 700-1200 can be seen at the Delicate Arch trailhead. This is a wildlife sanctuary; no hunting is permitted. Hiking, rock climbing, or camping in isolated sections should not be undertaken unless first reported to a park ranger at the visitor center (check locally for hours). Twenty-four miles of paved roads are open year round. Graded and dirt roads should not be attempted in wet weather. Devils Garden Campground, 18 miles north of the visitor center off US 191, provides 52 individual and 2 group camp sites (yr-round; fee; water available only March-mid-October). There is an entrance fee of $10/seven-day permit; Golden Eagle, Golden Age, and Golden Access passports accepted (see MAKING THE MOST OF YOUR TRIP). Contact the Superintendent, PO Box 907, Moab 84532; phone 435/259-8161 or 435/259-5279 (TTY).

Arches National Park

Beaver

(F-3) *See also Cedar City, Richfield*

Settled 1856 **Pop** 2,454 **Elev** 5,898 ft
Area code 435 **Zip** 84713
Information Chamber of Commerce, 1603 S Campground Rd, PO Box 760; 435/438-5081

What to See and Do

Elk Meadows and Mount Holly Ski Area. Quad, triple, three double chairlifts, one surface lift; school, rentals, shops, cafe, lodging. Longest run 2½ mi; vertical drop 1,400 ft. (Mid-Dec-Apr, daily) 18 mi E on I-15. Phone 888/881-7669.

Fishlake National Forest. (See RICH-FIELD) A Ranger District office of the forest is located in Beaver. E on UT 153. Phone 435/896-9233.

Special Event

Pioneer Days. Features parade, entertainment, horse racing; other events. Late July. Phone 435/438-5081.

Motels/Motor Lodges

★ ★ **BEST WESTERN BUTCH CASSIDY.** *161 S Main (84713). 435/438-2438; fax 435/438-1053; res 800/780-7234. www.bestwestern.com.* 35 rms, 2 story. Mid-May-Oct: S $54-$60; D $63-$70; lower rates rest of yr. Crib $3. Pet accepted, some restrictions; $5. TV; cable (premium). Heated pool; whirlpool. Coffee in rms. Restaurant 7 am-10 pm. Ck-out 11 am. Business servs avail. In-rm modem link. Downhill ski 18 mi. Sauna. Cr cds: A, C, D, DS, MC, V.

★ **DE LANO MOTEL.** *480 N Main St (84713). 435/438-2418.* 11 rms. May-Oct: S, D $34-$45; wkly rates; lower rates rest of yr. Crib free. Pet accepted. TV; cable (premium). Restaurant nearby. Ck-out 11 am. Business servs avail. Covered parking. Downhill ski 15 mi. Some refrigerators, microwaves. Cr cds: A, DS, MC, V.

★ ★ **QUALITY INN.** *781 W 1800 S (84713). 435/438-5426; fax 435/438-2493; toll-free 800/228-5151. www.qualityinn.com.* 52 rms, 2 story. June-

Oct: S $54; D $60; each addl $6; under 18 free; ski plans; lower rates rest of yr. Crib free. TV; cable. Indoor pool; whirlpool. Restaurant adj 6 am-10 pm. Ck-out 11 am. Business servs avail. Downhill/x-country ski 18 mi. Cr cds: A, C, D, DS, MC, V.

★ **SLEEPY LAGOON MOTEL.** *882 S Main St (84713). 435/438-5681; fax 435/438-9991.* 20 rms. May-Sept: S, D $40-$45; lower rates rest of yr. Crib free. Pet accepted. TV; cable. Heated pool. Complimentary continental bkfst (summer). Coffee in rms (winter). Restaurant nearby. Ck-out 11 am. Small pond. Cr cds: A, DS, MC, V.

Restaurants

★ **ARSHEL'S CAFE.** *711 N Main St (84713). 435/438-2977.* Hrs: 7 am-10 pm; Nov-Mar to 9 pm. Closed Thanksgiving, Dec 24, 25. Res accepted. Bkfst $3.10-$6.10, lunch, dinner $4.20-$10.50. Specialties: chicken-fried steak, honey pecan chicken and shrimp. Cr cds: DS, MC, V.

★★ **COTTAGE INN.** *171 S Main St (84713). 435/438-5855.* Hrs: 7 am-10 pm. Closed Dec 25. Res accepted. Bkfst $2.95-$7.95, lunch $3.95-$9.95, dinner $3.95-$14.95. Child's menu. Specializes in prime rib (Fri, Sat), chicken-fried steak. Victorian-style interior with handcrafted doll case, antiques, carvings. Cr cds: MC, V.

Blanding

(G-6) *See also Bluff, Monticello*

Settled 1905 **Pop** 3,162 **Elev** 6,105 ft **Area code** 435 **Zip** 84511

Information San Juan County Visitor Center, 117 S Main St, Box 490, Monticello 84535; 435/587-3235 or 800/574-4386

Web www.southeastutah.org

What to See and Do

Edge of the Cedars State Park. Excavated remnants of ancient dwellings and ceremonial chambers fashioned by the ancient Pueblo people. Artifacts and pictographs; museum of Native American history and culture. Visitor center. (Daily) 1 mi NW off US 191. Phone 435/678-2238. ¢

Glen Canyon National Recreation Area/Lake Powell. 4 mi S on US 191, then 85 mi W on UT 95 and UT 276. (See LAKE POWELL)

★ **Hovenweep National Monument.** Monument consists of six units of prehistoric ruins; the best preserved are the remains of pueblos (small cliff dwellings) and towers at Square Tower. Self-guided trail; park ranger on duty; visitor area (daily; closed Jan 1, Thanksgiving, Dec 25). Approx 13 mi S on US 191, then 9 mi E on UT 262 and 6 mi E on county roads to Hatch Trading Post, follow signs 16 mi to Hovenweep. Phone 970/562-4282. ¢¢¢

Natural Bridges National Monument. (see). Off Rte 21 on Charlotte St. Phone 435/692-1234. ¢¢¢

Bluff

(G-6) *See also Blanding*

Founded 1880 **Pop** 320 **Elev** 4,320 ft **Area code** 435 **Zip** 84512

Information San Juan County Visitor Center, 117 S Main St, Box 490, Monticello 84535; 435/587-3235 or 800/574-4386

Web www.southeasternutah.org

What to See and Do

★ **Tours of the Big Country.** Trips to Monument Valley, the Navajo Reservation, and into canyons of southeastern Utah explore desert plant and wildlife, history, geology, and Anasazi archaeology of this area. Naturalist-guided walking or four-wheel-drive tours. Llama rentals. Half-day, full-day, or overnight trips. (yr-round) Contact Recapture Lodge. Phone 435/672-2281. ¢¢¢¢

Wild Rivers Expeditions. Fun and educational trips on the archaeologically rich San Juan River through Glen Canyon National Recreation Area (see LAKE POWELL) and Cataract Canyon of the Colorado River. Geological formations and fossil beds. (Apr-Oct) Phone 435/672-2244. ¢¢¢¢

Special Event

Utah Navajo Fair. Third wkend Sept. Phone 800/574-4FUN.

Motel/Motor Lodge

★ **RECAPTURE LODGE.** *Hwy 191 (84512). 435/672-2281; fax 435/672-2284. www.recapturelodge.com.* 28 air-cooled rms, 1-2 story, 3 kits (equipt avail). S $38-$46; D $52-$60; each addl $2. Crib free. Pet accepted. TV; cable (premium), VCR avail. Heated pool; whirlpool. Playground. Restaurants opp 7 am-9 pm. Ck-out noon. Coin lndry. Business servs avail. Airport transportation. Lawn games. Some refrigerators. Balconies. Picnic tables, grills. Sun decks. Also units for groups, families at Pioneer House (historic building). Geologist-guided tours; slide shows. ½ mi to San Juan River. Totally nonsmoking. Cr cds: A, DS, MC, V.

Brigham City

(A-4) *See also Logan, Ogden*

Settled 1851 **Pop** 17,411 **Elev** 4,439 ft
Area code 435 **Zip** 84302
Information Chamber of Commerce, 6 N Main St, PO Box 458; 435/723-3931
Web www.bcareachamber.com

What to See and Do

Brigham City Museum-Gallery. Permanent history exhibits, rotating art exhibits; displays incl furniture, clothing, books, photographs, and documents reflecting the history of the Brigham City area since 1851. (Tues-Fri, also Sat afternoons) 24 N 300 W. Phone 435/723-6769. **FREE**

Golden Spike National Historic Site. Site where America's first transcontinental railroad was completed on May 10, 1869. Visitor cen-

ter, movies, exhibits (daily; closed Jan 1, Thanksgiving, Dec 25). Self-guided auto tour along old railroad bed. Summer interpretive program incl presentations and operating replicas of steam locomotives "Jupiter" and "119" (May-early Oct, daily). (See SPECIAL EVENTS) Golden Eagle, Golden Age, Golden Access passports accepted (see MAKING THE MOST OF YOUR TRIP). 32 mi W via UT 83 and County Rd. Contact Chief Ranger, PO Box 897. Phone 435/471-2209. ¢¢¢

Tabernacle. (1881) The tabernacle, one of the most architecturally interesting buildings in Utah, has been in continuous use since 1881. Guided tours (May-Sept, daily). 251 S Main St. Phone 435/723-5376. **FREE**

Special Events

Driving of Golden Spike. At Promontory, site where the Central Pacific and Union Pacific met. Reenactment of driving of golden spike in 1869. Locomotive replicas used. Mid-May. Phone 435/471-2209.

Railroaders Festival. Golden Spike National Historic Site. Relive the rush to complete transcontinental railroad. Professional railroaders pursue world record in spike driving. Second Sat Aug.

Box Elder County Fair. Late Aug.

Peach Days Celebration. Parade, arts and crafts, carnival; car show, entertainment. First wkend after Labor Day.

Motel/Motor Lodge

★ **HOWARD JOHNSON.** *1167 S Main St (84302). 435/723-8511; fax 435/723-0957; toll-free 800/446-4656. www.hojo.com.* 44 rms, 2 story. S $44-$54; D $51-$59; each addl $5; under 17 free. Crib free. Pet accepted, some restrictions. TV; cable (premium). Indoor pool; whirlpool. Complimentary continental bkfst. Restaurant adj. Business servs avail. Ck-out noon. Cr cds: A, C, D, DS, ER, JCB, MC, V.

Restaurant

★★ **MADDOX RANCH HOUSE.** *1900 S UT 89, Perry (84302). 435/723-8545. www.maddoxranchhouse.com.* Hrs: 11 am-9:30 pm. Closed Sun, Mon; Thanksgiving, Dec 25. Res

accepted. Lunch, dinner $6.95-
$19.95. Child's menu. Specializes in
chicken, beef, seafood. Western
decor. Family-owned. Cr cds: A, D,
DS, MC, V.

D

Bryce Canyon National Park

(G-3)

*(7 mi S of Panguitch on US 89, then 17
mi SE on UT 12 to UT 63, 3 mi to
entrance)*

Bryce Canyon is a 56-square-mile
area of colorful, fantastic cliffs created by millions of years of erosion.
Towering rocks worn to odd, sculp-
tured shapes stand grouped in striking sequences. The Paiute, who once
lived nearby, called this "the place
where red rocks stand like men in a
bowl-shaped canyon." Although
termed a canyon, Bryce is actually a
series of "breaks" in 12 large
amphitheaters—some plunging as
deep as 1,000 feet into the multicolored limestone. The formations
appear to change color as the sunlight strikes from different angles
and seem incandescent in the late
afternoon. The famous Pink Cliffs
were carved from the Claron Formation; shades of red, orange, white,
gray, purple, brown, and soft yellow
appear in the strata. Park Road follows 17 miles along the eastern edge
of the Paunsaugunt Plateau, where
the natural amphitheaters are spread
out below; plateaus covered with
evergreens and valleys filled with
sagebrush stretch away into the distance.

The visitor center at the entrance
station has complete information on
the park, including orientation
shows, geologic displays, and
detailed maps (daily; closed January
1, Thanksgiving, December 25). Park
is open year round; in winter, park
road is open to most viewpoints.
Lodging is also available April to
October. There is an entrance fee of
$10 per vehicle; Golden Eagle,
Golden Age, and Golden Access

passports are accepted (see MAKING
THE MOST OF YOUR TRIP). Shuttle
system (fee, phone for information).
Contact the Superintendent, PO Box
170001, Bryce Canyon 84717; phone
435/834-5322.

What to See and Do

Camping. North Campground (yr-
round), east of park headquarters;
Sunset Campground, two mi S of
park headquarters. Fourteen-day
limit at both sites; fireplaces, picnic
tables, rest rms, water avail. (Apr-
Oct) ¢¢

Hikes. With ranger naturalists into
canyon. (June-Aug)

Riding. Horses and mules avail,
guided trips early morning, afternoon (spring, summer, fall). Fee.

Talks. Given by rangers about history, geology, fauna, flora at campgrounds or audiotrium lodge in the
evening. (June-Aug)

Motels/Motor Lodges

★★ **BEST WESTERN RUBY'S INN.**
*UT 63, Bryce Canyon (84764).
435/834-5341; fax 435/834-5265; res
800/468-8660. www.rubysinn.com.* 368
rms, 1-3 story. June-Sept: S, D $95-
$130; each addl $5; lower rates rest
of yr. Crib free. Pet accepted, some
restrictions; $100 deposit. TV; cable,
VCR (movies). Indoor/outdoor pool;
outdoor whirlpool. Restaurant 6:30
am-9 pm; winter hrs vary. Ck-out 11
am, 4 pm. Coin lndry. Business servs
avail. Shopping arcade. Game rm. X-
country ski opp. Picnic tables. Rodeo
in summer; general store. Lake on
property. Trailer park. Cr cds: A, D,
DS, MC, V.

★★ **BRYCE CANYON LODGE.** *1
Bryce Canyon Lodge, Bryce Canyon
(84717). 435/834-5361; fax 435/834-
5330; res 888/297-2757. www.bryce
canyonlodge.com.* 114 units in cabins,
motel. Apr-Nov: motel units $110;
cabin units $121; each addl $5; suites
$135; each addl $10. Closed rest of
yr. Crib avail. Restaurant 6:30-10 am,
11 am-3:30 pm, 5:30-9:30 pm. Ck-
out 11 am, ck-in 4 pm. Coin lndry.
Bellhops. Sundries. Trail rides on
mules, horses avail. Private patios,

balconies. Original 1925 building. Cr cds: A, D, DS, MC, V.

⬜ 🔧 🏊 🔥

★★ **BRYCE CANYON PINES MOTEL.** *Hwy 12, Panguitch (84764). 435/834-5441; fax 435/834-5330; toll-free 800/892-7923. www.brycecanyon motel.com.* 50 rms, 1-2 story. May-Oct: S, D $55-$75; each addl $5; suites $85-$125; kit. cottage $95; lower rates rest of yr. Crib $5. TV; cable. Heated pool. Restaurant 6:30 am-9:30 pm. Ck-out 11 am, ck-in 2 pm. Some fireplaces, balconies. Early American decor. Cr cds: A, D, DS, MC, V.

⬜ 🏊 🔥 **SC**

Restaurant

★ **FOSTER'S STEAK HOUSE.** *UT 12 (84764). 435/834-5227.* Hrs: 7 am-10 pm; Dec-Mar from 2 pm. Beer. Bkfst $1.75-$5.99, lunch $2.99-$13.49, dinner $7.99-$22.50. Child's menu. Specializes in prime rib. Salad bar. Bakery adj. Cr cds: A, C, D, DS, ER, MC, V.

⬜

Canyonlands National Park

(F-6) *See also Moab, Monticello*

(N district: 12 mi N of Moab on US 191, then 21 mi SW on UT 313; S district: 12 mi N of Monticello on US 191, then 38 mi W on UT 211)

Spectacular rock formations, canyons, arches, spires, pictograph panels, ancestral Puebloan ruins, and desert flora are the main features of this 337,570-acre area. Set aside by Congress in 1964 as a national park, the area is largely undeveloped. Road conditions vary; primary access roads are paved and maintained, others are safe only for high clearance four-wheel-drive vehicles. For backcountry road conditions and information phone 801/259-7164.

Island in the Sky, North District, south and west of Dead Horse Point State Park (see MOAB) has Grand View Point, Upheaval Dome, and Green River Overlook. This section is accessible by passenger car via UT 313; also accessible by four-wheel-drive vehicles and mountain bikes on dirt roads.

Needles, South District, has hiking trails and four-wheel-drive roads to Angel Arch, Chesler Park, and the confluence of the Green and Colorado rivers. Also here are prehistoric ruins and rock art. This section is accessible by passenger car via UT 211, by four-wheel-drive vehicle on dirt roads, and by mountain bike.

Maze, West District, is accessible by hiking or by four-wheel-drive vehicles using unimproved roads. The most remote and least-visited section of the park, this area received its name from the many mazelike canyons. Horseshoe Canyon, a separate unit of the park nearby, is accessible via UT 24 and 30 miles of two-wheel-drive dirt road. Roads are usually passable only mid-March through mid-November.

Canyonlands is excellent for calm-water and white-water trips down the Green and Colorado rivers. Permits are required for private trips (fee; contact Reservation Office, 435/259-4351); commercial trips (see MOAB). Campgrounds, with tent sites, are located at Island in the Sky (fee) and Needles (fee); water is available only at Needles. Visitor centers are in each district (daily). There is an entrance fee of $10 per vehicle. Golden Eagle, Golden Age, Golden Access passports accepted (see MAKING THE MOST OF YOUR TRIP). Contact Canyonlands NP, 2282 S West Resource Blvd, Moab 84532; phone 435/259-7164.

Capitol Reef National Park

(F-4) *See also Loa*

(10 mi E of Richfield on UT 119, then 65 mi SE on UT 24)

Capitol Reef, at an elevation ranging from 3,900-8,800 feet, is composed of red sandstone cliffs capped with domes of white sandstone. Located in the heart of Utah's slickrock country, the park is actually a 100-mile

Canyonlands National Park

section of the Waterpocket Fold, an upthrust of sedimentary rock created during the formation of the Rocky Mountains. Pockets in the rocks collect thousands of gallons of water each time it rains. Capitol Reef was so named because the rocks formed a natural barrier to pioneer travel and the white sandstone domes resemble the dome of the US Capitol.

This 378-square-mile area was the home from A.D. 700-1350 of an ancient people who grew corn along the Fremont River. Petroglyphs can be seen on some of the sandstone walls. A schoolhouse, farmhouse, and orchards, established by early Mormon settlers, are seasonally open to the public.

The park can be approached from either east or west via UT 24, a paved road. There is a visitor center on this road about seven miles from the west boundary and eight miles from the east (daily; closed December 25). A 25-mile round-trip scenic drive starts from this point (some parts unpaved). There are evening programs and guided walks (Memorial Day-Labor Day; free). Three campgrounds are available: Fruita, approximately one mile south off UT 24, provides 70 tent and trailer sites year-round (fee); Cedar Mesa, 23 miles south off UT 24, and Cathedral, 28 miles north off

UT 24, offer five primitive sites with access depending on weather (free; no facilities). There is an entrance fee of $4 per vehicle. Golden Eagle, Golden Age, Golden Access passports accepted (see MAKING THE MOST OF YOUR TRIP). Contact the Superintendent, HC 70, Box 15, Torrey 84775; phone 435/425-3791.

Motel/Motor Lodge

★ **SUNGLOW MOTEL.** *63 E Main, Bicknell (84715).* 435/425-3821. 12 rms, 10 with A/C. Mar-mid-Nov: S, D $32-$37; each addl $2-$4. Closed rest of yr. Crib $2. Pet accepted; $5. TV; cable. Restaurant 6:30 am-10 pm. Ck-out 11 am. Cr cds: A, DS, MC, V.

Cedar Breaks National Monument

(G-2) *See also Cedar City*

(23 mi E of Cedar City via UT 14)

Cedar Breaks National Monument's major formation is a spectacular, multicolored, natural amphitheater created by the same forces that sculpted Utah's other rock formations. The amphitheater, shaped like an enormous coliseum, is 2,000 feet deep and more than three miles in diameter. It is carved out of the Markagunt Plateau and is surrounded by Dixie National Forest (see CEDAR CITY). Cedar Breaks, at an elevation of more than 10,000 feet, was established as a national monument in 1933. It derives its name from the surrounding cedar trees and the word "breaks," which means "badlands." Although similar to Bryce Canyon National Park, Cedar Breaks's formations are fewer but more vivid and varied in color. Young lava beds, resulting from small volcanic eruptions and cracks in the earth's surface, surround the Breaks area; the heavy forests include bristlecone pines, one of the oldest trees on the earth. Here, as soon as the snow melts, wildflowers bloom profusely and continue to bloom throughout the summer.

Rim Drive, a five-mile scenic road through the Cedar Breaks High Country, provides views of the monument's formations from four different overlooks. The area is open late May to mid-October, weather permitting. Point Supreme Campground, two miles north of south entrance, provides 30 tent and trailer sites (mid-June-mid-September, fee; water, rest rooms). The visitor center offers geological exhibits (June-mid-October, daily); interpretive activities (mid-June-Labor Day). There is an entrance fee of $4 per vehicle. Golden Eagle, Golden Age, Golden Access passports accepted (see MAKING THE MOST OF YOUR TRIP). Contact the Superintendent, 2390 W Hwy 56, Suite 11, Cedar City 84720; phone 435/586-9451.

Cedar City (G-2)

Settled 1851 **Pop** 20,527 **Elev** 5,834 ft
Area code 435 **Zip** 84720
Information Chamber of Commerce, 581 N Main St; 435/586-4484
Web www.chambercedarcity.org

What to See and Do

Brian Head Ski Resort. Five triple, double chairlift; patrol, school, rentals; restaurants, cafeterias, bars, nursery, ski shops, grocery, gift shops, lodging. Longest run ½ mi, vertical drop 1,700 ft. (Mid-Nov-early Apr, daily) X-country trails, rentals; snowmobiling, night skiing. Mountain biking (summer). 19 mi NE on I-15 to Parowan, then 11 mi SE on UT 143, in Dixie National Forest. Phone 435/677-2035. ¢¢¢¢

Cedar Breaks National Monument. (see). 23 mi E via UT 14.

Dixie National Forest. Camping, picnicking, hiking, mountain biking, winter sports. (Daily) 12 mi E on UT 14 to forest boundary or 17 mi SW on I-15, then W. Contact the Supervisor, PO Box 580, 84721. Phone 435/865-3200. **FREE**

Iron Mission State Park. Museum dedicated to the first pioneer iron foundry west of the Rockies; extensive collection of horse-drawn vehicles and wagons from Utah pioneer days. (Daily; closed Jan 1, Thanksgiving, Dec 25) 585 N Main. Phone 435/586-9290. ¢

Kolob Canyons Visitor Center. This section of Zion National Park (see) provides a 14-mi round-trip hike to the Kolob Arch, world's second largest, with a span of 310 ft. A five-mi scenic drive offers spectacular views of rugged peaks and sheer canyon walls 1,500 ft high. (Daily; closed Jan 1, Thanksgiving, Dec 25) 17 mi S on I-15. Phone 435/586-9548. **FREE**

Sightseeing trips. Cedar City Air Service. Trips incl Cedar Breaks National Monument and Grand Canyon, Zion, and Bryce Canyon national parks (see all); other trips avail. (Daily) Phone 435/586-3881. ¢¢¢¢

Southern Utah University. (1897) 7,000 students. Braithwaite Fine Arts Gallery (Mon-Sat; free). (See SPECIAL EVENTS) 351 W Center. Phone 435/586-7700.

Zion National Park. (see). 60 mi SE via I-15 and UT 9.

Special Events

Utah Summer Games. Olympic-style athletic events for amateur athletes. Phone 435/586-7228 or 435/586-8421. June.

Utah Shakespearean Festival. Southern Utah University campus. Shakespeare presented on outdoor stage (a replica of 16th-century Tiring House) and 750-seat indoor facility. Mon-Sat eves; preplay activities. Children over five yrs only; babysitting at festival grounds. Phone 435/586-7878 (box office). Late June-early Oct.

Renaissance Fair. Main St City Park. Entertainment, food, and games, all in the style of the Renaissance. Held in conjunction with opening of Utah Shakespearean Festival. Early July.

Motels/Motor Lodges

★★ **ABBEY INN.** *940 W 200 N (01453). 435/586-9966; fax 435/586-6522; res 800/325-5411. www.abbey inncedar.com.* 80 rms, 2 story. June-mid-Sept: S, D $78-$96; each addl $5; suites $95-$150; under 12 free; lower rates rest of yr. Crib $5. TV; cable (premium), VCR avail. Indoor pool. Complimentary continental bkfst. Coffee in rms. Restaurant adj 6 am-10 pm. Ck-out 11 am. Coin lndry. Business servs avail. In-rm modem link. Airport transportation. Refrigerators, microwaves. Near airport. Cr cds: A, C, D, DS, MC, V.

★★ **BEST WESTERN TOWN & COUNTRY.** *189 N Main (84720). 435/586-9900; fax 435/586-1664; res 800/493-4089. www.bwtowncountry. com.* 167 rms, 2 story. S $71-$86; D $79-$94; suites $94-$115. Crib free. TV. 2 pools, 1 indoor; whirlpool. Restaurant 7 am-10 pm. Complimentary continental bkfst. Ck-out 11 am, ck-in 2 pm. Coin lndry. Meeting rm. Business servs avail. Free airport transportation. Game rm. Many refrigerators, microwaves. Cr cds: A, C, D, DS, MC, V.

★★ **COMFORT INN.** *250 N 1100 W (84720). 435/586-2082; fax 435/586-3193; toll-free 800/228-5750. www. comfortinn.com.* 93 rms, 2 story. June-Sept: S, D $49-$106; each addl $5; under 12 free; lower rates rest of yr. Crib free. Pet accepted. TV; cable. Indoor pool; whirlpool. Complimentary continental bkfst. Ck-out 11 am. Business servs avail. Free airport

transportation. Cr cds: A, C, D, DS, MC, V.

Restaurant

★ **MILT'S STAGE STOP.** *Cedar Canyon Rd (84720). 435/586-9344.* Hrs: 6-10 pm. Closed Thanksgiving, Dec 25. Res accepted. Bar. Dinner $12.75-$42. Child's menu. Specializes in prime rib. Salad bar. Rustic decor. Cr cds: A, D, DS, MC, V.

Dinosaur National Monument

(C-6) *See also Vernal*

(7 mi N of Jensen on UT 149)

On August 17, 1909, paleontologist Earl Douglass discovered dinosaur bones in this area, several of them nearly complete skeletons. Since then, this location has provided more skeletons, skulls, and bones of Jurassic-period dinosaurs than any other dig in the world. The dinosaur site comprises only 80 acres of this 325-square-mile area, which lies at the border of Utah and Colorado. The back country section, most of which is in Colorado, is a land of fantastic and deeply eroded canyons of the Green and Yampa Rivers. The entire area was named a national monument in 1915.

Utah's Dinosaur Quarry section can be entered from the junction of US 40 and UT 149, north of Jensen, 13 miles east of Vernal; approximately 7 miles north on UT 149 is the fossil exhibit. Another five miles north is Green River Campground, with 90 tent and trailer sites available mid-May to mid-September. A smaller campground, Rainbow Park, provides a small number of tent sites from May to November. Lodore, Deerlodge, and Echo Park campgrounds are available in Colorado. A fee is charged at Green River, Echo Park, and Lodore (water and rest rooms available). Access to the Colorado back country section is via Harpers Corner Road, starting at monument headquarters on US 40, two miles east of Dinosaur, Colorado. This 32-mile surfaced road ends at Harpers Corner. From there a one-mile foot trail leads to a promontory overlooking the Green and Yampa rivers, more than 2,500 ft below.

Because of snow, some areas of the monument are closed from approximately mid-November to mid-April. There is an entrance fee of up to $10 per vehicle. Golden Eagle, Golden Age, Golden Access passports accepted (see MAKING THE MOST OF YOUR TRIP). Contact the Superintendent, 4545 E US 40, Dinosaur, CO 81610. Phone 970/374-3000 (headquarters).

What to See and Do

Backpacking. By permit obtainable at visitor centers; few marked trails.

⭐ **Dinosaur Quarry Information Center.** Remarkable fossil deposit exhibit of 150-million-yr-old dinosaur remains; preparation laboratory on display. (Daily; closed Jan 1, Thanksgiving, Dec 25)

Picnicking, hiking, fishing. Harpers Corner area has picnic facilities, also picnicking at campgrounds. Self-guided nature trails (all-yr), guided nature walks. State fishing license required; boating permit required (obtainable by advance lottery at the Headquarters River Office). Phone 970/374-2468.

River rafting. On Green and Yampa rivers, by advance permit from National Park Service or with concession-operated guided float trips. Information at River Office. Phone 970/374-2468.

Fillmore

(E-3) *See also Nephi, Richfield*

Settled 1856 **Pop** 2,253 **Elev** 5,135 ft
Area code 435 **Zip** 84631
Information Chamber of Commerce, City of Fillmore, 96 S Main St, PO Box 687; 435/743-6121

What to See and Do

Fishlake National Forest. E on improved gravel road (see RICH-FIELD). Phone 435/896-9233.

Territorial Statehouse State Park. Utah's first territorial capitol, built in the 1850s of red sandstone, is now a museum with extensive collection of pioneer furnishings, pictures, Native American artifacts, and early documents; also rose garden. (Mon-Sat; closed Jan 1, Thanksgiving, Dec 25) 50 W Capitol Ave. Phone 435/743-5316. ¢

Resort

★ **BEST WESTERN PARADISE INN & RESORT.** *905 N Main (84631). 435/743-6895; fax 435/743-6892; 800/780-7234. www.bestwestern.com.* 80 rms, 2 story. Mid-May-Oct: S, D $57-$63; each addl $3; lower rates rest of yr. Crib $6. Pet accepted. TV; cable (premium). Heated pool; whirlpool. Restaurant 6 am-10 pm; summer to 11 pm. Ck-out 11 am. Business servs avail. Cr cds: A, C, D, DS, ER, MC, V.

⬛⬛⬛⬛⬛

Garden City

(A-4) *See also Logan*

Settled 1875 **Pop** 357 **Elev** 5,960 ft
Area code 435 **Zip** 84028
Information Bear Lake Convention & Visitors Bureau, PO Box 26, Fish Haven, ID 83287; 208/945-2333 or 800/448-2327
Web www.bearlake.org

What to See and Do

Bear Lake. Covering 71,000 acres on the border of Utah and Idaho, this body of water is the state's second-largest freshwater lake. Approx 20 mi long and 200 ft deep, it offers good fishing for mackinaw, rainbow trout, and the rare Bonneville Cisco. Boat rentals at several resorts. On the western shore is

Bear Lake State Park. Three park areas incl state marina on west shore of lake, Rendezvous Beach on south shore, and Eastside area on east shore. Swimming, beach, waterskiing, fishing, ice fishing, boating (ramp, dock), sailing; hiking, mountain biking, x-country skiing, snowmobiling, picnicking, tent and trailer sites (rest rms, showers, hookups, dump station; fee). Visitor center. (Daily) 2 mi N on US 89. Phone 800/322-3770. ¢¢¢

Beaver Mountain Ski Area. Three double chairlifts, two surface lifts; patrol, school, rentals; day lodge, cafeteria. Twenty-two runs; vertical drop 1,600 ft. Half-day rates. (Dec-early Apr, daily) 14 mi W via US 89. Phone 435/753-0921. ¢¢¢¢

Green River (A-6)

Settled 1878 **Pop** 973 **Elev** 4,079 ft
Area code 435 **Zip** 84525
Information Green River Travel Council, 885 E Main St; 435/564-3526

Originally a mail relay station between Ouray, Colorado, and Salina, Utah, Green River now produces premium watermelons and cantaloupes on land irrigated by the Green River, one of Utah's largest rivers.

What to See and Do

Arches National Park. (see). 23 mi E on I-70 (US 50), then 54 mi S on US 191.

Goblin Valley State Park. Mi-wide basin filled with intricately eroded sandstone formations. Hiking, camping (rest rms, showers, dump station). (Daily) 50 mi W on I-70 (US 50), then 30 mi S on UT 24. Phone 435/564-3633. ¢¢

John Wesley Powell River History Museum. 20,000-sq-ft museum sits on the banks of the Green River. Contains exhibits exploring geology and geography of area; auditorium with 20-min multi-media presentation; river runner Hall of Fame. Green River Visitor Center (daily). Gift shop. Picnic area. (Daily; closed Jan 1, Thanksgiving, Dec 25) 885 E Main St. Phone 435/564-3427. ¢

River trips. On the Colorado, Green, San Juan, and Dolores rivers.

Colorado River & Trail Expeditions, Inc. PO Box 57575, Salt Lake City 84157-0575. Phone 801/261-1789. ¢¢¢¢

Holiday River and Bike Expeditions. 544 E 3900 S, Salt Lake City 84107. Phone 801/266-2087. ¢¢¢¢

Moki Mac River Expeditions. PO Box 21242, Salt Lake City 84121. Phone 801/268-6667. ¢¢¢¢

Special Event

Melon Days. Third wkend Sept.

Motels/Motor Lodges

★ ★ **BEST WESTERN RIVER TERRACE MOTEL.** *880 E Main St (84525). 435/564-3401; fax 435/564-3403; 800/528-1234. www.bestwestern.com.* 51 rms, 2-3 story. No elvtr. May-Oct: S, D $69-$79; higher rates some hols and special events; lower rates rest of yr. TV; cable (premium). Heated pool; whirlpool. Restaurant adj 6 am-10 pm. Ck-out 11 am. Private patios, balconies. On river. Cr cds: A, C, D, DS, MC, V.
🄳 🐾 ⛱ 🛏 🔥

★ **RODEWAY INN WEST WINDS.** *525 E I-70 Business Loop (84525). 435/564-3421; fax 435/564-3282; toll-free 800/228-2000. www.rodeway.com.* 42 rms, 2 story. May-Oct: S, D $49-$55; each addl $5; suites $55-$65; under 18 free; lower rates rest of yr. Crib free. TV; cable (premium). Restaurant adj open 24 hrs. Ck-out 11 am. Coin lndry. Meeting rms. Cr cds: A, C, D, DS, ER, JCB, MC, V.
🄳 🛏 🔥 🆂🅲

Restaurant

★ **TAMARISK.** *870 E Main St (84525). 435/564-8109.* Hrs: 6 am-10 pm. Closed Thanksgiving, Dec 25. Bkfst $2.20-$6.95, lunch, dinner $2.95-$13.95. Buffet: bkfst $7.95, lunch $8.95, dinner $11.95. Child's menu. Specializes in chicken, steak, fish. Salad bar. Country-style café; view of Green River. Totally non-smoking. Cr cds: A, C, D, DS, ER, MC, V.
🄳

Heber City

(C-4) *See also Alta, Park City, Provo, Salt Lake City*

Settled 1859 **Pop** 7,291 **Elev** 5,595 ft
Area code 435 **Zip** 84032
Information Heber Valley Chamber of Commerce, 475 N Main St, PO Box 427; 435/654-3666
Web www.hebervalleycc.org

What to See and Do

Deer Creek State Park. Swimming, fishing, boating (ramp); camping (fee; rest rms, showers; dump and fish cleaning stations). (Daily) 8 mi SW on US 189. Phone 435/654-0171. ¢¢¢

Heber Valley Railroad. A 90-yr-old steam-powered excursion train takes passengers through the farmlands of Heber Valley, along the shore of Deer Creek Lake and into Provo Canyon on various one-hr to four-hr trips. Restored coaches and open-air cars. Special trips some Fri, Sat eves. Res required. (May-mid-Oct, Tues-Sun; mid-Oct-Nov, schedule varies; Dec-Apr, Mon-Sat) Contact 450 S 600 W, PO Box 609. Phone 435/654-5601. ¢¢¢¢

Timpanogos Cave National Monument. (see). 16 mi SW on US 189, then 12 mi NW on UT 92.

Wasatch Mountain State Park. Approx 25,000 acres in Heber Valley. Fishing; hiking, 36-hole golf, snowmobiling, x-country skiing, picnicking, restaurant, camping (fee; hookups, dump station). Visitor center. (Daily) Standard fees. 2 mi NW off UT 224. Phone 435/654-1791.

Special Events

Wasatch County Fair. Parades, exhibits, country market, livestock shows, rodeos, dancing. First wkend Aug.

Swiss Days. 4 mi W in Midway. "Old country" games, activities, costumes. Fri and Sat before Labor Day.

Motels/Motor Lodges

★ **DANISH VIKING LODGE.** *989 S Main St (84032). 435/654-2202; fax 435/654-2770; toll-free 800/544-4066.* 34 rms, 1-2 story, 3 kits. Mid-May-mid-Sept and Christmas season: S $40-$49; D $49-$65; each addl $5; suite $99-$150; kit. units $65-$95; under 18 free; package plans; lower rates rest of yr. Crib $3. Pet accepted, some restrictions. TV; cable (premium), VCR avail. Pool; whirlpool. Sauna. Playground. Complimentary continental bkfst. Restaurant nearby. Ck-out 11 am. Coin lndry. Downhill ski 12 mi; x-country ski 7 mi. Health club privileges. Refrigerators, microwaves. Picnic tables, grills. Cr cds: A, D, DS, MC, V.

🔲🐾🏂🎣🏊🛶🔥🖋

★ **HIGH COUNTRY INN AND RV PARK.** *1000 S Main St. (84032). 435/654-0201; toll-free 800/345-9198.* 38 rms. S $45-$55; D $65-$75; each addl $5; lower rates rest of yr. Crib $5. TV; cable (premium). Heated pool; whirlpool. Playground. Complimentary continental bkfst. Restaurant adj. Ck-out 11 am. Coin lndry. Downhill ski 20 mi; x-country ski 5 mi. Refrigerators, microwaves. Picnic table. View of mountains. Cr cds: A, DS, MC, V.

🎣🏊🛶🔥🖋 SC

Resort

★★★ **THE HOMESTEAD RESORT.** *700 N Homestead Dr, Midway (84049). 435/654-1102; fax 435/654-5087; toll-free 800/327-7220. www.homestead resort.com.* 163 rms, 1-2 story, 26 suites. S, D $130; suites $180-$325; condos $250-$600; ski, golf plans. TV; cable (premium), VCR avail (movies). 2 pools, 1 indoor; whirlpool. Restaurant (see also SIMON'S FINE DINING). Bar. Ck-out noon, ck-in 4 pm. Meeting rms. Business center. Gift shop. Lighted tennis. 18-hole golf. X-country ski 10 mi. Exercise equipt; sauna. Massage. Horse stables. Wagon and buggy rides. Lawn games. Historic country inn (1886); spacious grounds, gardens, duck ponds. Cr cds: A, C, D, DS, JCB, MC, V.

🔲🐾🏂🎣🎿🏌🏊🏇🛶🔥 SC 🎿

B&B/Small Inn

★★★★ **THE BLUE BOAR INN.** *1235 Warm Springs Rd, Midway (84049). 435/654-1400; toll-free 888/650-1400. www.theblueboarinn. com.* This charming Swiss country chalet is nestled in a high valley at the foot of the Wasatch range. Each room is individually decorated with quality antiques, and the luxurious guest rooms also provide all the modern conveniences including whirlpool tubs and separate showers. 14 rms, 2 story, 3 suites. Nov-Feb, June-Aug: S $150; D $175-$295; suites $295; lower rates rest of yr. Crib avail. TV; cable (premium), VCR avail. Complimentary full bkfst. Complimentary coffee in lobby. Restaurant 8 am-9 pm, closed Mon. Ck-out noon, ck-in 3 pm. Meeting rm. Business center. Concierge serv. Dry cleaning. Gift shop. Free airport transportation. Golf. Tennis. Downhill skiing. Hiking trail. Picnic facilities. Cr cds: A, DS, MC, V.

Restaurants

★ ★ ★ ★ **THE BLUE BOAR INN RESTAURANT.** *1235 Warm Springs Rd, Midway (84049). 435/654-1400. www.theblueboarinn.com.* Well worth the 20 minute drive from Park City, this charming Tyrolean chalet offers some of the best New American cuisine in Utah. Flavors are clean and fresh as Chef Jesse Layman endeavors to accentuate the natural quality of each item. The menu changes periodically to capture the best produce and fresh seafood available. Specializes in rack of boar, duck, salmon. Hrs: 11:30 am-2:30 pm, 5:30-9:30 pm; Sun brunch 9 am-2 pm. Closed Mon. Res accepted. Wine, beer. Lunch $6-$11; dinner $17-$28. Cr cds: A, DS, MC, V.

★ ★ ★ **SIMON'S FINE DINING.** *700 N Homestead Dr, Midway (84032). 435/654-1102. www.homesteadresort. com.* Hrs: 5:30-10 pm; Sun brunch 10 am-2:30 pm; closed Mon, Tues. Res accepted. Wine list. Complete meals: dinner $23-$34. Sun brunch $17.95. Child's menu. Daily specials. Pianist. Sun brunch. Outdoor dining. Fireplaces. View of valley. Cr cds: A, D, DS, MC, V.

Kanab (G-3)

Founded 1870 **Pop** 3,564 **Elev** 4,909 ft **Area code** 435 **Zip** 84741

Information Kane County Office of Tourism, 78 E 100 S; 435/644-5033 or 800/733-5263

Web www.kaneutah.com

What to See and Do

Coral Pink Sand Dunes State Park. Six sq mi of very colorful, wind-swept sandhills. Hiking, picnicking, tent and trailer sites (fee; showers, dump station). Off-hwy vehicles allowed; exploring, photography. (Daily) 8 mi NW on US 89, then 12 mi SW on county road. Phone 435/648-2800. ¢¢

Glen Canyon National Recreation Area/Lake Powell. 68 mi E via US 89, at Wahweap Lodge and Marina (see PAGE, AZ); access in Utah at Bullfrog Marina (see LAKE POWELL). Phone 928/608-6404.

Grand Canyon Scenic Flights. Flights to Grand Canyon during daylight hrs; flight covering Bryce Canyon and Zion national parks, Lake Powell, and Coral Pink Sand Dunes. (All-yr) 2½ mi S on US 89 A. Phone 435/644-2299. ¢¢¢¢

Pipe Spring National Monument. (see ARIZONA) 20 mi W on US 389, in Arizona. Phone 435/643-7105.

Zion National Park. (see). 17 mi NW on US 89, then 25 mi W on UT 9.

Motels/Motor Lodges

★ ★ **BEST WESTERN RED HILLS.** *125 W Center St (84741). 435/644-2675; fax 435/644-5919; res 800/780-7234. www.kanabbestwestern.com.* 75 rms, 2 story. May-Oct: S, D $89; each addl $5; lower rates rest of yr. Crib free. TV; cable. Heated pool; whirlpool. Ck-out 11 am, ck-in 3 pm. Meeting rm. Business servs avail. Refrigerators. Some balconies. Cr cds: A, C, D, DS, MC.

★ **FOUR SEASONS INN.** *36 N 300 W (84741). 435/644-2635; fax*

435/644-5895. 41 rms, 2 story. Apr-Oct: S, D $68-$71; each addl $5; lower rates rest of yr. Crib $5. Pet accepted. TV; cable. Pool; wading pool. Restaurant 6:30 am-10 pm. Ck-out 11 am, ck-in 2 pm. Business servs avail. Gift shop. Cr cds: A, C, D, DS, MC, V.

★ **PARRY LODGE.** 89 E Center St (84741). 435/644-2601; fax 435/644-2605; toll-free 800/748-4104. www. infowest.com/parry. 89 rms, 1-2 story. May-Oct: S $30-$60; D $35-$75; each addl $6; family rates; lower rates rest of yr. Closed Dec-mid-Mar. Crib $6. Pet accepted; $5. TV; cable. Heated pool. Restaurant 7 am-noon, 6-10 pm. Complimentary bkfst. Ck-out 11 am, ck-in 3 pm. Coin lndry. Business servs avail. Autographed pictures of movie stars displayed in lobby. Cr cds: A, DS, MC, V.

★★ **SHILO INN.** 296 W 100 N (84741). 435/644-2562; fax 435/644-5333; toll-free 800/222-2244. www. shiloinns.com. 118 rms, 3 story. Mid-Apr-Sept: S, D $69.95-$79.95; lower rates rest of yr. Crib free. Pet accepted; $7/day. TV; cable. Heated pool; whirlpool. Complimentary continental bkfst. Ck-out noon. Coin lndry. Meeting rms. Business servs avail. Sundries. Free airport transportation. Many refrigerators. Cr cds: A, C, D, DS, MC, V.

Restaurants

★ **CHEF'S PALACE.** 176 W Center St (84741). 435/644-5052. Hrs: 6 am-11 pm; winter to 9 pm. Closed Dec 25. Res accepted. Bkfst $2.90-$8.40, lunch $3.15-$6.25, dinner $5-$38. Child's menu. Specializes in prime rib, broiled steak. Salad bar. Cr cds: A, DS, MC, V.

★ **HOUSTON'S TRAIL'S END.** 32 E Center St (84741). 435/644-2488. Hrs: 6 am-10:30 pm. Closed Thanksgiving-Mar 1. Bkfst $2.65-$5.75, lunch $3.95-$9.95, dinner $5-$15. Child's menu. Specializes in chicken fried steak, shrimp. Rustic, Western decor. Cr cds: A, C, D, DS, ER, MC, V.

Lake Powell

(G-5) Also see Page, AZ

What to See and Do

Boat trips on Lake Powell. Trips incl Canyon Explorer tour (2½ hrs) and all-day Rainbow Bridge National Monument tour; also houseboat and powerboat rentals. Res advised. (Daily) From Bullfrog or Halls Crossing marinas, both on UT 276. Phone 800/528-6154.

Glen Canyon National Recreation Area (Bullfrog Marina). This boasts more than one million acres with yr-

Glen Canyon National Recreation Area, Lake Powell

round recreation area, swimming, fishing, boating, boat tours and trips, boat rentals and repairs; picnicking, camping, tent and trailer sites (full hookups; fee), lodgings. A ranger station and visitor center is located in Bullfrog on UT 276 (Apr-Oct, daily). Phone 435/684-2243.

Lake Powell Ferry. Approx three-mi trip between Bullfrog and Hall's Crossing saves 130 mi driving around lake. (Daily; reduced hrs in winter) Contact Bullfrog Marina. Phone 435/538-1030. ¢¢¢¢¢

Motel/Motor Lodge

★ **DEFIANCE HOUSE.** *Hwy 276, Bullfrog (84533). 435/684-2233; fax 435/684-3114; toll-free 800/528-6154.* 48 units, 2 story, 8 cottages. S, D $115-$130; each addl $10; suites $59-$130; cottages $75-$175; boating tour plans; lower rates rest of yr. Crib free. Pet accepted. TV; cable. Playground. Dining rm 7 am-8 pm; summer to midnight. Bar 5-9 pm; summer to midnight. Ck-out 11 am. Coin lndry. Sundries. Gift shop. Airport transportation. Balconies. Anasazi motif; decor, artifacts. On lake; swimming. Cr cds: A, C, D, DS, MC, V.
🄳 🔧 🛅 🐾

Loa (F-4)

Pop 525 **Elev** 7,060 ft **Area code** 435 **Zip** 84747

What to See and Do

Capitol Reef National Park. (see). Approx 23 mi E via UT 24.

Escalante State Park. Petrified forest; mineralized wood and dinosaur bones. Swimming, fishing, boating (ramps) at reservoir; hiking, birdwatching, picnicking, camping (fee; rest rms, showers, dump station). (Daily) Standard fees. 65 mi S via UT 12, then 1 mi W, near Escalante. Phone 435/826-4466. ¢¢

Logan

(A-4) *See also Brigham City, Garden City*

Founded 1856 **Pop** 42,670 **Elev** 4,535 ft **Area code** 435 **Zip** 84321

Information Logan Convention & Visitors Bureau/Bridgerland Travel Region, 160 N Main; 435/752-2161 or 800/882-4433

Web www.bridgerland.com

What to See and Do

American West Heritage Center. Agricultural museum with typical Mormon family farm of WWI era; 120 acres of fields, meadows, orchards, and gardens; artifacts and machinery; costumed interpreters. (June-Sept, Tues-Sat) (See SPECIAL EVENTS) 5 mi S on US 89/91, in Wellsville. Phone 435/245-4064.

Daughters of the Utah Pioneers Museum. Exhibits depict Utah's past. 160 N Main, in Chamber of Commerce Building. (Mon-Fri) Phone 435/752-5139. **FREE**

Hyrum State Park. A 450-acre reservoir with beach swimming, waterskiing, fishing, ice fishing, boating (ramp, dock), sailing; picnicking, camping (trailer parking). (Yr-round) Standard fees. 12 mi S, off US 89/90. Phone 435/245-6866. ¢¢

Mormon Tabernacle. (1891) Gray limestone example of early Mormon building; seats 1,800. Genealogy library. (Mon-Fri) 50 N Main. Phone 435/755-5598.

Mormon Temple. (1884) The site for this massive, castellated limestone structure was chosen by Brigham Young, who also broke ground for it in 1877. Grounds are open all yr, but the temple is closed to the general public. 175 N 300 East. Phone 435/752-3611.

Utah State University. (1888) 20,100 students. On campus is the Nora Eccles Harrison Museum of Art (Mon-Fri; closed hols, also Thanksgiving wkend, Dec 22-Jan 2; free). 5th N and 7th E Sts. (Tours) Phone 435/797-1129.

Wasatch-Cache National Forest, Logan Canyon. Fishing, back country trails, hunting, winter sports, picnicking, camping. Fees charged at most recreation sites. (Daily) E on US 89 National Forest (scenic byway). A Ranger District office is located in Logan at 1500 E US 89. Phone 435/755-3620.

Willow Park Zoo. Small but attractive zoo with shady grounds and especially good bird-watching of migratory species. (Daily; closed Jan 1, Thanksgiving, Dec 25) 419 W 700 S. Phone 435/750-9893. **Donation**

Special Events

Utah Festival Opera Company. July-Aug.

American West Heritage Center. Pioneer and Native American crafts fair, art exhibition, antique quilt show; frontier town; medicine man show; log construction; Dutch-oven cooking demonstration. Hwy 8991 in Wellsville. Phone 435/245-6050. Late July-early Aug.

Cache County Fair. Rodeo, horse races, exhibits. Early Aug.

Motels/Motor Lodges

★★ **BEST WESTERN BAUGH.** *153 S Main St (84321). 435/752-5220; fax 435/752-3251; res 800/462-4154. www.bestwestern.com.* 77 rms, 1-2 story. S $59-$92; D $65-$75; each addl $6. Crib $4. TV; cable (premium), VCR avail (movies). Heated pool. Restaurant 6 am-10 pm; Sun 8 am-2 pm. Rm serv. Ck-out 11 am. Meeting rm. Business servs avail. Health club privileges. Some fireplaces; microwaves avail. Refrigerators. Sun deck. Cr cds: A, D, DS, MC, V.
D 🔄 🈂️ 🔥 SC

★★ **COMFORT INN.** *447 N Main St (84321). 435/752-9141; fax 435/752-9723; res 800/228-5150. www.comfort inn.com.* 83 rms, 2 story. S $50-$63; D $58-$60; each addl $4; suites $89; under 18 free. Crib $5. TV; cable. Indoor pool; whirlpool. Complimentary continental bkfst. Restaurant adj. Ck-out noon. Coin lndry. Meeting rms. Business servs avail. In-rm modem link. Valet serv. X-country ski 20 mi. Exercise equipt. Refrigerator in suites. Cr cds: A, C, D, DS, ER, JCB, MC, V.
D 🈂️ 🔄 🐟 ✈️ 🈂️ 🔥 SC

★ **DAYS INN LOGAN.** *364 S Main (84321). 435/753-5623; res 800/329-*

7466. www.daysinn.com. 64 rms, 2 story, 20 kit. units. S, D $36-$78; each addl $4; kit. units $48-$56; under 12 free; wkly rates Sept-May. Crib free. Pet accepted. TV; cable. Indoor pool. Complimentary continental bkfst. Restaurant nearby. Ck-out 11 am. Coin lndry. X-country ski 20 mi. Many refrigerators; some in-rm whirlpools. Cr cds: A, D, DS, MC, V.
D 🔄 🐾 🐟 🈂️ 🔥

B&Bs/Small Inns

★★★ **THE ANNIVERSARY INN.** *169 E Center St (84321). 435/752-3443; fax 435/752-8550; toll-free 800/574-7605. www.anniversaryinn. com.* 21 rms in 5 buildings, 4 suites. S, D $99-$209; suites $159-$209. Adults only. TV; cable, VCR avail (movies). Complimentary continental bkfst. Restaurant nearby. Ck-out noon, ck-in 5 pm. Downhill/x-country ski 20 mi. Microwaves avail. Lobby in historic mansion (1879); Oriental rugs, period furniture. Special theme suites, such as Swiss family, and grand bridal suite, are uniquely decorated. Totally nonsmoking. Cr cds: A, DS, MC, V.
🈂️ 🔥 🈂️

★★★ **LOGAN HOUSE INN.** *168 N 100 East (84321). 435/752-7727; fax 435/752-0092; res 800/478-7459. www.loganhouseinn.com.* 6 rms, 2 story. S, D $99-$175; each addl $15. TV; cable, VCR avail (movies). Complimentary full bkfst; afternoon refreshments. Ck-out 10:30 am, ck-in 3 pm. Business serv avail. In-rm modem link. Luggage handling. Concierge serv. Guest lndry. In-rm whirlpools, fireplaces. Built in 1898; antiques. Totally nonsmoking. Cr cds: A, D, DS, MC, V.
D 🈂️ 🔥

★★★ **PROVIDENCE INN.** *10 S Main, Providence (84332). 435/752-3432; fax 435/752-3482; toll-free 800/480-4943. www.providenceinn. com.* 17 rms, 3 story. June-Sept: S $69-$159; D $99-$229; each addl $10; suite $119-$149; under 5 free. TV; cable, VCR (movies). Complimentary full bkfst. Restaurant nearby. Ck-out 11 am, ck-in 4 pm. Business servs avail. In-rm modem link. Coin lndry. X-country ski 5 mi. Whirlpools in rms. Built in 1869;

accurately restored. Totally nonsmoking. Cr cds: A, DS, MC, V.

D ⌦ ⚒ ➤

Restaurant

★ ★ **GIA'S RESTAURANT AND DELI.** *119 S Main St (84321). 435/752-8384.* Hrs: 11 am-9:30 pm; Fri, Sat to 10 pm. Closed Dec 25. Res accepted. Italian menu. Serv bar. Lunch, dinner $6-$14.75. Child's menu. Specialties: chicken Marsala, manicotti. Italian tapestry and pictures; European decor. Family-owned. Cr cds: A, D, DS, MC, V.

D SC

Unrated Dining Spot

BLUEBIRD. *19 N Main St (84321). 435/752-3155.* Hrs: 11 am-9:30 pm; Fri, Sat to 10 pm. Closed Sun; Thanksgiving, Dec 25. Res accepted. Lunch $3-$10.45, dinner $7.50-$13. Child's menu. Limited menu. 1920s decor; ice cream, candy factory. Cr cds: A, DS, MC, V.

D

Moab (E-6)

Founded 1879 **Pop** 4,779 **Elev** 4,025 ft **Area code** 435 **Zip** 84532

Information Moab Area Travel Council, PO Box 550; 435/259-8825, 435/259-1370, or 800/635-6622

Web www.discovermoab.com

What to See and Do

Arches National Park. (see). 5 mi NW on US 191.

Canyonlands Field Institute. Educational seminars/trips featuring geology, natural and cultural history, endangered species, Southwestern literature. Many programs use Canyonlands and Arches national parks as outdoor classrms. (Mon-Fri) Contact PO Box 68, 84532. 1320 S Hwy 191. Phone 435/259-7750. ¢¢¢¢

Canyonlands National Park. (see). N district: 9 mi N on US 191, then 21 mi SW on UT 313.

Dan O'Laurie Canyon Country Museum. Exhibits on local history,

archaeology, geology, uranium, minerals of the area. Walking tour information. (Mon-Sat; closed hols) 118 E Center St. Phone 435/259-7985. ¢

Dead Horse Point State Park. Promontory rising 2,000 ft above the Colorado River, this island mesa offers views of the LaSal Mtns, Canyonlands National Park, and the Colorado River. Approx 5,200 acres in region of gorges, cliffs, buttes, and mesas. Visitor center, museum. Picnicking, limited drinking water, camping (fee; electricity, dump station). Trailer parking. (Daily) 9 mi NW on US 191, then 22 mi SW on UT 313. Phone 435/259-2614. ¢

Hole 'n the Rock. A 5,000-sq-ft dwelling carved into huge sandstone rock. Picnic area with stone tables and benches. (Daily; closed Jan 1, Thanksgiving, Dec 25) 15 mi S via US 191. Phone 435/686-2250. ¢¢

Manti-LaSal National Forest, LaSal Division. The land of the forest's LaSal Division is similar in color and beauty to some parts of the Grand Canyon, but also incl high mountains nearing 13,000 ft and pine and spruce forests. Swimming, fishing; hiking, hunting. (See MONTICELLO, PRICE) 8 mi S on US 191, then 5 mi E. Contact the Ranger District office, 125 W 200 S. Phone 435/259-7155. **FREE**

River trips. On the Green and Colorado rivers, incl Canyonlands National Park, Lake Powell (see both), and Cataract Canyon. Phone 435/259-8825.

Adrift Adventures. Oar, paddle, and motorized trips avail; one to seven days. (Early Apr-late Oct) 378 N Main St. Phone 435/259-8594. ¢¢¢¢

Canyon Voyages. Kayaking, whitewater rafting. (Early Apr-Oct) 211 N Main St. Phone 435/259-6007. ¢¢¢¢

Colorado River & Trail Expeditions, Inc. 5058 S 300 W. ¢¢¢¢

Sheri Griffith River Expeditions. Choice of rafts: oarboats, motorized rafts, paddleboats, or inflatable kayaks; one to five day trips; instruction avail. (May-Oct) PO Box 1324. Phone 435/259-8229. ¢¢¢¢

Tex's Riverways. Flatwater canoe trips, four to ten days. Confluence pick-ups avail, jet boat cruises. (Mar-Oct) PO Box 67. Phone 435/259-5101. ¢¢¢¢

Sightseeing tours.

Canyonlands By Night. Two-hr boat trip with sound-and-light presentation highlights history of area. (Apr-mid-Oct, daily, leaves at sundown, weather permitting) Res required; tickets must be purchased at office, 1861 N US 191. PO Box 328. Leaves dock at bridge, 2 mi N on US 191. Phone 435/259-5261. ¢¢¢¢

Rim Tours. Guided mountain bike tours in canyon country and the Colorado Rockies. Vehicle support for camping tours. Daily and overnight trips; combination bicycle/river trips avail. 1233 S Highway 191. Phone 435/259-5223. ¢¢¢¢

Scenic Air Tours. Flights over Canyonlands National Park and various other tours. (All-yr; closed Jan 1, Thanksgiving, Dec 25) 18 mi N on US 191, at Canyonlands Field. Contact Redtail Aviation. Phone 435/259-7421. ¢¢¢¢

Tag-A-Long Expeditions. One- to seven-day whitewater rafting trips on the Green and Colorado rivers; jetboat trips on the Colorado River; jetboat trips and four-wheel-drive tours into Canyonlands National Park; winter four-wheel-drive tours (Nov-Feb). Also Canyon Classics, one-day jetboat trips with cultural performing arts programs. (Apr-mid-Oct). 452 N Main St. Phone 435/259-8946. ¢¢¢¢¢

Trail rides. Pack Creek Ranch. Horseback rides, ranging from one to 1½ hrs, in foothills of LaSal Mtn. Guided tours for small groups; res required. (Mar-Oct; upon availability) PO Box 1270. Phone 435/259-5505. ¢¢¢¢

Special Events

Jeep Safari. Easter wk and wkend.

Butch Cassidy Days PRCA Rodeo. Second wkend June.

Moab Music Festival. First 2 wks in Sept.

Motels/Motor Lodges

★ ★ **BEST WESTERN CANYONLANDS INN.** *16 S Main St (84532). 435/259-2300; fax 435/259-2301; 800/780-7234. www.bestwestern.com.* 77 rms, 2 story, 37 suites. Mid-Mar-Oct: S, D $99.95-$109.95; each addl $8; suites $119-$249; under 12 free; higher rates special events; lower rates rest of yr. Crib free. TV; cable (premium); VCR avail. Indoor/outdoor pool. Playground. Complimentary bkfst. Coffee in rms. Restaurant adj noon-11 pm. Ck-out 11 am. Coin lndry. Meeting rms. Business servs avail. In-rm modem link. Exercise equipt. Refrigerators. Totally nonsmoking. Cr cds: A, C, D, DS, MC, V.
D 🏊 🏋 📵 🐾 SC

★ ★ **BEST WESTERN GREENWELL INN.** *105 S Main St (84532). 435/259-6151; fax 435/259-4397; 800/780-7234. www.bestwestern.com.* 72 rms, 1-2 story. Mid-Mar-Nov: S, D $69-$131; each addl $6; ; under 12 free; lower rates rest of yr. Crib free. TV; cable (premium). Heated pool whirlpool. Coffee in lobby. Restaurant 7 am-9 pm. Ck-out 11 am. Coin lndry. Exercise equipt. Refrigerators. In-rm modem links. Cr cds: A, C, D, DS, JCB, MC, V.
🏊 🏋 📵 🔥

★ **BOWEN MOTEL.** *169 N Main St (84532). 435/259-7132; fax 435/259-6641; toll-free 800/874-5439. www.bowenmotel.com.* 40 rms, 1-2 story. Mar-Oct: S, D $65-$75; each addl $6. Crib $4; under 12 free. Pet accepted $50. TV; cable (premium). Heated pool. Complimentary continental bkfst. Restaurants nearby. Ck-out 11 am. In-rm modem link. Some refrigerators. Totally nonsmoking. Cr cds: A, C, D, DS, MC, V.
🐾 🏊 📵 🔥

★ **LANDMARK INN.** *168 N Main St (84532). 435/259-6147; fax 435/259-5556; toll-free 800/441-6147. www.moab-utah.com/landmark/motel.htm.* 36 rms, 2 story. Mid-Mar-Oct: S, D $68-$86; each addl $4-$6; family rates; lower rates rest of yr. Crib $4. TV; cable (premium). Heated pool; wading pool (summer), whirlpool. Complimentary continental bkfst. Restaurant adj 7 am-midnight. Ck-out 11 am. In-rm modem link. Coin lndry. Refrigerators. Cr cds: A, C, D, DS, MC, V.

 (icons)

B&Bs/Small Inns

★★★ **CASTLE VALLEY INN.** *424 Amber Ln; HC 64 Box 2602 (84532). 435/259-6012; fax 435/259-1501; toll-free 888/466-6012. www.castlevalley inn.com.* 5 rms, 3 kit. cabins. Apr-late Nov: S, D $100-$160; cabins $155. Complimentary full bkfst. Business servs avail. Ck-out 11 am, ck-in 3-9 pm. Lawn games. Refrigerators. Cr cds: DS, MC, V.

★★ **SUNFLOWER HILL BED AND BREAKFAST.** *185 N 300 E (84532). 435/259-2974; fax 435/259-3065; res 800/662-2786. www.sunflowerhill.com.* 11 rms, 2 story, 3 suites. No rm phones. Mar-Oct: S, D $139-$199; each addl $20. Children over 10 yrs only. TV; cable (premium), VCR avail. Coin lndry. Balconies. Luggage handling. Whirlpool. Complimentary full bkfst; afternoon refreshments. Ck-out 11 am, ck-in 3-6 pm. Turn-of-the-century adobe farmhouse, cottage amid gardens. Totally nonsmoking. Cr cds: A, DS, MC, V.

Guest Ranch

★★ **PACK CREEK RANCH.** *Pack Creek Ranch Rd (84532). 435/259-5505; fax 435/259-8879. www.pack creekranch.com.* 10 kit. cottages (1-, 2- and 3-bedrm). No rm phones. S, D $180-$300; Apr-Oct, AP: $125 per person; lower rates rest of yr. Crib $10. Pet accepted. Pool; whirlpool. Sauna. Dining rm 7-10 am, 6:30-8:30 pm. Coffee in rms. Ck-out 11 am, ck-in 3 pm. Exercise equipt. Grocery, package store 16 mi. Business servs avail. Refrigerators, balconies. X-country ski nearby. Hiking. Picnic tables. A 300-acre ranch at foot of La Sal

Mtns; features trail rides. Cr cds: DS, MC, V.

Restaurant

★★ **CENTER CAFE.** *60 N 100 W (84532). 435/259-4295.* Hrs: 5:30-10 pm. Closed Thanksgiving, Dec 25; also Jan. Res accepted. Continental menu. Serv bar. A la carte entrees: dinner $16-$27. Specializes in fresh fish, grilled meats. Own pastries. Original artwork. Totally nonsmoking. Cr cds: DS, MC, V.

Monticello

(F-6) *See also Blanding*

Founded 1887 **Pop** 1,806 **Elev** 7,066 ft **Area code** 435 **Zip** 84535
Information San Juan County Visitor Center, 117 S Main St, PO Box 490; 435/587-3235 or 800/574-4386
Web www.southeastutah.org

What to See and Do

Canyonlands National Park. (see). S district: 14 mi N on US 191, then 35 mi W on UT 211 to Squaw Flats Campground Area.

Canyon Rims Recreation Area. Anticline and Needles overlooks into Canyonlands National Park are located here, as are Wind Whistle and Hatch campgrounds. 20 mi N on US 191.

Petroglyphs, near Monticello

Manti-LaSal National Forest, LaSal Division. (See MOAB, PRICE) The forest land of this division ranges from red rock canyons to high alpine terrain. Ancient ruins and rock art contrast with pine and spruce forests and aspen-dotted meadows. Fishing; hiking, snowmobiling, X-country skiing, hunting, camping (fee). 2½ mi W. Contact the Ranger District Office, 62 E 100 N. Phone 435/587-2041. **FREE**

Special Events

Monticello Pioneer Days. Parade, booths, food, games, sports. Wkend nearest July 24.

San Juan County Fair & Rodeo. Second wkend Aug.

Motels/Motor Lodges

★ ★ **BEST WESTERN WAYSIDE INN.** *197 E Central Ave (84535). 435/587-2261; fax 435/587-2920; toll-free 800/633-9700. www.bestwestern. com.* 38 rms. May-Sept: S, D $69-$74; each addl $5; suites $95; under 12 free; lower rates rest of yr. Crib $5. Pet accepted. TV; cable (premium). Heated indoor pool. Restaurant adj. Coffee in rms. Ck-out 11 am. X-country ski 6 mi. Some refrigerators. Picnic tables. Cr cds: A, C, D, DS, MC, V.
➤ ⇌ ⇘ 🐾 SC 🐾

Monument Valley (H-6)

(see Kayenta, AZ)

Natural Bridges National Monument (G-6)

(4 mi S of Blanding on US 191, then 36 mi W on UT 95, then 4 mi N on UT 275)

This 7,439-acre area of fantastically eroded and colorful terrain, made a national monument in 1908, features three natural bridges, all with Hopi names: Sipapu, a 268-foot span, and Kachina, a 204-foot span, are in White Canyon, a major tributary gorge of the Colorado River; Owachomo, a 180-foot span, is near Armstrong Canyon, which joins White Canyon. Sipapu is the second-largest natural bridge in the world. From 650 to 2,000 years ago, the ancestral Puebloan people lived in this area, leaving behind cliff dwelling ruins and pictographs that can be viewed today. Bridge View Drive, a nine-mile loop road, provides views of the three bridges from rim overlooks. There are hiking trails to each bridge within the canyon. In the park is a visitor center (daily; closed holidays in winter) and a primitive campground with 13 tent and trailer sites (all-year, fee; 26-ft combined-length limit). Car and passenger ferry service across Lake Powell is available (see LAKE POWELL). There is a $6 per vehicle entrance fee; Golden Eagle, Golden Age, Golden Access passports accepted (see MAKING THE MOST OF YOUR TRIP). Contact the Superintendent, Box 1, Lake Powell 84533; phone 435/692-1234.

Nephi

(D-4) *See also Fillmore, Payson*

Settled 1851 **Pop** 4,733 **Elev** 5,133 ft
Area code 435
Information Juab Travel Council, 4 S Main, PO Box 71, 84648; 435/623-5203 or 435/623-2411

What to See and Do

Yuba State Park. Waterskiing and walleyed pike fishing are the big attractions of this lake, as well as sandy beaches. Swimming, waterskiing, fishing, boating (ramps); picnicking, camping (fee; rest rms, showers, dump station). (Daily) 30 mi S via I-15, near Scipio. Phone 435/758-2611. ¢¢

Special Event

Ute Stampede Rodeo. Three-day festival featuring horse and mammoth parades, carnival, PRCA rodeo, contests, arts and crafts, concessions.

Phone 435/623-4407 or 435/623-5608. Second wkend July.

Motels/Motor Lodges

★★ **BEST WESTERN PARADISE INN.** *1025 S Main (84648). 435/623-0624; res 800/780-7234. www.best western.com.* 40 rms, 2 story. Mid-May-Oct: S $59; D $69; lower rates rest of yr. Crib $6. Pet accepted, some restrictions. TV; cable (premium). Heated pool; whirlpool. Complimentary continental bkfst. Restaurant nearby. Ck-out noon. Cr cds: A, C, D, DS, MC, V.
🐾 ⚁ ⚄ ⚅ ⚆

★ **ROBERTA'S COVE MOTOR INN.** *2250 S Main (84648). 435/623-2629; fax 435/623-2245; toll-free 800/456-6460.* 43 air-cooled rms, 2 story. S, D $39-$45; each addl $5; higher rates Ute Stampede. TV; cable (premium). Pool; whirlpool. Coffee in rms. Restaurant opp 6 am-9:30 pm. Ck-out 11 am. Coin lndry. Cr cds: A, C, D, DS, MC, V.
⚄ ⚅ ⚆

B&B/Small Inn

★★ **WHITMORE MANSION.** *110 S Main St (84648). 435/623-2047. www.whitmoremansion.com.* 9 rms, 5 with shower only, 3 story, 2 suites. No rm phones. S, D $78-$128; suites $118. TV in common rm, VCR avail (movies). Complimentary continental bkfst. Restaurant nearby. Ck-out 11 am, ck-in 4-8 pm. Business servs avail. Street parking. X-country ski 10 mi. Rec rm. Built in 1898; antiques. Totally nonsmoking. Cr cds: A, DS, MC, V.
⚅ ⚆ ⚇

Ogden

(B-4) *See also Brigham City, Salt Lake City*

Settled 1844 **Pop** 77,226 **Elev** 4,300 ft
Area code 801
Information Convention & Visitors Bureau, 2501 Wall Ave, 84401; 801/627-8288 or 800/255-8824
Web www.ogdencvb.org

What to See and Do

Daughters of Utah Pioneers Museum & Relic Hall. Old handicrafts, household items, pioneer clothing, furniture, and portraits of those who came to Utah prior to the railroad of 1869. Also Miles Goodyear's cabin, the first permanent house built in Utah. (Mid-May-mid-Sept, Mon-Sat) 2148 Grant Ave, in Tabernacle Sq. Phone 801/393-4460. **FREE**

Eccles Community Art Center. A 19th-century castlelike mansion that hosts changing art exhibits, plus has a dance studio and an outdoor sculpture and floral garden. (Mon-Sat; closed hols) 2580 Jefferson Ave. Phone 801/392-6935. **FREE**

Fort Buenaventura State Park. The exciting era of mountain men is brought to life on this 32-acre site, where the actual fort, Ogden's first settlement, was built in 1846 by Miles Goodyear. The fort has been reconstructed according to archaeological and historical research: no nails have been used in building the stockade; wooden pegs and mortise and tenon joints hold the structure together. (Apr-Nov) 2450 A Ave. Phone 801/621-4808. ¢¢

George S. Eccles Dinosaur Park. Outdoor display containing more than 100 life-size reproductions of dinosaurs and other prehistoric creatures, plus an educational building with a working paleontological lab and fossil and reptile displays. (Daily; closed Nov-Mar) 1544 E Park Blvd. Phone 801/393-3466. ¢¢

Hill Aerospace Museum. More than 55 aircraft on display, some indoors and suspended from ceiling. Planes incl B-29 Superfortress, SR-71 "Blackbird" reconnaissance plane, B-52 bomber, PT-71 Stearman; helicopters, jet engines, missiles; uniforms and other memorabilia. (Daily; closed Jan 1, Thanksgiving, Dec 25) 7961 Wardleigh Rd. 4 mi S on I-15 exit 341, in Roy. Phone 801/777-6868. **FREE**

Lagoon and Pioneer Village. Amusement park. Thrill rides, musical entertainment, water park, food, campground. (June-Aug, daily; late Apr-Memorial Day and Labor Day-Oct, wkends) Approx 20 mi S on I-

15, in Farmington. Phone 801/451-8000. ¢¢¢¢

Pine View Reservoir. Boating, fishing, waterskiing; camping, picnicking. Fees for activities. 9 mi E on UT 39 in Ogden Canyon in Wasatch-Cache National Forest (see SALT LAKE CITY).

Skiing.

Nordic Valley. Two chairlifts; patrol, school, rentals; snack bar, lounge. Longest run 1½ mi, vertical drop 1,000 ft. (Dec-Apr, daily) 7 mi E on UT 39, then N on UT 162. Phone 801/745-3511. ¢¢¢¢

Powder Mountain. Quad, triple, two double chairlifts, three surface tows; patrol, school, rentals; food service, lodging. (Mid-Nov-Apr, daily) Night skiing. 8 mi E on UT 39, then 11 mi N on UT 158, in Eden. Phone 801/745-3772. ¢¢¢¢

Snowbasin. Two gondolas; quad, four triple, double chairlifts; patrol, school, rentals; food service, lodges. Longest run three mi, vertical drop 2,940 ft. (Late Nov-mid-Apr, daily) 10 mi E on UT 39, then S on UT 226 in Wasatch-Cache National Forest (see SALT LAKE CITY). Phone 801/399-1135. ¢¢¢¢

Union Station—the Utah State Railroad Museum. Spencer S. Eccles Railroad Center features some of the world's largest locomotives, model railroads, films, gem and mineral displays, guided tours by "conductors." **Browning-Kimball Car Museum** has classic American cars. **Browning Firearms Museum** contains the reconstructed original Browning gun shop and inventor's models. Also here is 500-seat theater for musical and dramatic productions and an art gallery; restaurant. Visitors Bureau for northern Utah located here. (June-Sept, daily; rest of the yr, Mon-Sat; closed Jan 1, Thanksgiving, Dec 25) 2501 Wall Ave, center of Ogden. Phone 801/629-8444. ¢

Weber State University. (1889) 17,000 students. On campus are Layton P. Ott Planetarium, with natural science museum and Foucault pendulum, shows (Wed; no shows summer; fee); and Stewart Bell Tower, with 183-bell electronic carillon, performances (daily; free). Campus tours. Harrison Blvd, off US 89. Phone 801/626-6000.

Willard Bay State Park. This park features a 9,900-acre lake. Swimming, fishing, boating (ramps), sailing; picnicking, tent and trailer sites (fee; showers, dump station). (Daily) 15 mi N via I-15, exit 360, near Willard. Phone 435/734-9494. ¢¢¢

Special Events

Pioneer Days. Ogden Pioneer Stadium. Rodeo, concerts, vintage car shows, fireworks, chili cookoff. Mon-Sat eves. Mid-late July.

Utah Symphony Pops Concert. Lindquist Fountain/Plaza. Music enhanced by fireworks display. Late July.

Motel/Motor Lodge

★ **DAYS INN.** *3306 Washington Blvd (84401). 801/399-5671; fax 801/621-0321; toll-free 800/999-6841. www.daysinn.com.* 109 rms, 2 story. S $65-$70; D $80-$88; each addl $8; under 18 free. Crib free. TV; cable (premium). Indoor pool; whirlpool. Complimentary continental bkfst. Ck-out noon. Coin lndry. Business servs avail. In-rm modem link. Downhill/x-country ski 15 mi. Microwaves avail. Cr cds: A, C, D, DS, MC, V.

🄳 ⊠ ⊠ ⊠ ⊠ SC

Hotels

★★ **BEN LOMOND HISTORIC SUITES HOTEL.** *2510 Washington Blvd (84401). 801/627-1900; fax 801/394-5342; toll-free 888/627-8897. www.benlomondhotel.com.* 122 suites, 11 story. S $57-$64; D $64-$74; each addl $7; suites $129-$169; under 12 free; ski packages. Crib free. Pet accepted, some restrictions. TV; cable (premium). Complimentary full bkfst. Complimentary coffee in rms. Restaurant 11 am-10 pm. Ck-out noon. Coin lndry. Meeting rms. Business center. Free covered parking. Downhill/x-country ski 16 mi. Exercise equipt. Health club privileges. Refrigerator, microwave, wet bar in suites. Cr cds: A, DS, MC, V.

⊠ 🄳 ⊠ ⊠ ⊠ ⊠ ⊠ ⊠

★★★ **MARRIOTT OGDEN .** *247 24th St (84401). 801/627-1190; fax 801/394-6312; toll-free 888/825-3163. www.marriott.com.* 292 rms, 8 story. S, D $109; suites $150-$350; wkend rates; ski plans. TV; cable. Indoor pool; whirlpool. Coffee in rms. Restaurant 6 am-10 pm. Private club 4:30 pm-midnight. Ck-out noon. Coin lndry. Convention facilities. Business servs avail. Gift shop. Free parking. Exercise equipt. Refrigerator in suites. Cr cds: A, D, DS, JCB, MC, V.

D ≈ 🏃 ⛷ 🔥 SC

Restaurants

★★ **BAVARIAN CHALET.** *4387 Harrison Blvd (84403). 801/479-7561. www.bavarian-chalet.com.* Hrs: 5-10 pm. Closed Sun, Mon; some major hols; also July. Res accepted. German menu. Serv bar. Dinner $9.95-$20.95. Child's menu. Specialties: Wiener schnitzel, sauerbraten jaegerschnitzel. Outdoor dining. German art, wall hangings and background music create a distinctive German atmosphere. Totally nonsmoking. Cr cds: A, D, MC, V.

D

★★ **GRAY CLIFF LODGE.** *508 Ogden Canyon (84401). 801/392-6775. www.grayclifflodge.com.* Hrs: 5-10 pm; Sat to 11 pm; Sun 3-8 pm; Sun brunch 10 am-2 pm. Closed Mon; most major hols. Res accepted; required some hols. Bar. Complete meal: dinner $12.95-$30.95. Sun brunch $8.95. Child's menu. Specialties: prime rib, fresh mountain trout, lamb chops. Own baking. Converted summer home with country atmosphere. Family-owned. Totally nonsmoking. Cr cds: A, D, DS, MC, V.

D

★★ **YE LION'S DEN.** *3607 Washington Blvd (84403). 801/399-5804.* Hrs: 11 am-2 pm, 5-9 pm; Fri to 10 pm; Sat 5-10 pm; Sun noon-7 pm. Closed Jan 1, Dec 24, 25. Res accepted. Serv bar. Complete meals: lunch $5.95-$10.95, dinner $9.95-$29.95. Specializes in prime rib, steak, seafood. Open-hearth grill. Cr cds: MC, V.

D

Panguitch

(F-3) *See also Cedar City*

Settled 1864 **Pop** 1,623 **Elev** 6,624 ft
Area code 435 **Zip** 84759

Information Panguitch Chamber of Commerce, PO Box 400, 84759; 435/676-8585
Web www.infowest.com/panguitch

What to See and Do

Anasazi Indian Village State Park. Partially excavated village, believed to have been occupied from A.D. 1050-1200, is one of the largest ancient communities west of the Colorado River. Picnicking. Museum (daily; closed Jan 1, Thanksgiving, Dec 25). 75 mi E of Bryce Canyon National Park, in Boulder. Phone 435/335-7308. ¢

Cedar Breaks National Monument. (see). 35 mi SW on UT 143.

Panguitch Lake. This 8,000-ft-high lake, which fills a large volcanic basin, has fishing; resorts, public campgrounds (developed sites, fee), ice fishing, snowmobiling, x-country skiing. 17 mi SW on paved road in Dixie National Forest (see CEDAR CITY). Phone 435/676-2649.

Paunsagaunt Wildlife Museum. More than 400 animals from North America in their natural habitat can be viewed here. Also exotic game animals from Africa, India, and Europe. (May-Oct, daily) 250 E Center St. Phone 435/676-2500. ¢¢

Motel/Motor Lodge

★★ **BEST WESTERN NEW WESTERN MOTEL.** *180 E Center St (84759). 435/676-8876; toll-free 800/780-7234. www.bestwestern.com.* 55 rms. Apr-Oct: S, D $55-$85; each addl $5; suites $85-$125; lower rates rest of yr. Crib free. Pet accepted. TV; cable. Heated pool. Restaurant nearby. Ck-out 11 am. Coin lndry. Business servs avail. Some refrigerators. Some rms across street. Cr cds: A, C, DS, MC, V.

D 🐾 🐕 ⛷ ≈ 🔥

Restaurant

★ **FOY'S COUNTRY CORNER.** *80 N Main (84759). 435/676-8851.* Hrs: 6 am-9:30 pm. Closed Thanksgiving, Dec 25. Amer menu. Bkfst $2.25-$5, lunch $4-$7, dinner $5-$12. Specializes in chicken fried steak. Cr cds: A, D, DS, MC, V.

Park City

(C-4) *See also Alta, Heber City, Salt Lake City*

Founded 1868 **Pop** 7,371 **Elev** 7,080 ft **Area code** 435 **Zip** 84060
Information Park City Chamber/Visitors Bureau, 1910 Prospector Ave, PO Box 1630; or the Visitor Information Center, 750 Kearns Ave; 435/649-6100, 435/649-6104, or 800/453-1360
Web www.parkcityinfo.com

What to See and Do

Egyptian Theatre. (1926) Originally built as a silent movie and vaudeville house, now a yr-round performing arts center with a full semiprofessional theater season. (Thurs-Sat; some performances other days) 328 Main St. Phone 435/649-9371.

Factory Stores at Park City. More than 45 outlet stores. (Daily) I-80 and UT 224 at Kimball jct. Phone 435/645-7078.

Kimball Art Center. Exhibits in various media by local and regional artists. (Mon, Wed-Sun) 638 Park Ave. Phone 435/649-8882. **FREE**

Rockport State Park. Approx 1,000-acre park along east side of Rockport Lake. Opportunity for viewing wildlife, incl bald eagles (winter) and golden eagles. Swimming, waterskiing, sailboarding, fishing, boating (rentals, launch); picnicking, restaurant, concession, x-country ski trail (6 mi), camping, tent and trailer sites. (Daily) Standard fees. N on UT 248 and US 40, then 8 mi NE on I-80, Wanship exit. Phone 435/336-2241.

Skiing.

Brighton Resort. Approx 10 mi SW via UT 190 in Big Cottonwood Canyon (see SALT LAKE CITY).

The Canyons. 16 high-speed quad, triple, double chairlifts; gondola; patrol, school, rentals; restaurant, cafeteria, bar, lodge. One hundred forty trails. (Thanksgiving-Apr, daily) Phone 435/649-5400. ¢¢¢¢

Deer Valley Resort. Eight high-speed quad, eight triple, two double chairlifts; rental, patrol, school, snowmaking; restaurants, lounge, lodge, nursery. Approx 1,750 skiable acres. Vertical drop 3,000 ft. (Dec-mid-Apr, daily) Summer activities incl mountain biking, hiking, horseback riding, and scenic chairlift rides (fee). 1 mi SE on Deer Valley Dr. Phone 435/649-1000. ¢¢¢¢

Park City Mountain Resort. Gondola; quad, four double, five triple, three 6-passenger chairlifts; patrol, school, rentals, snowmaking; restaurants, cafeteria, bar. Approx 2,200 acres; 100 novice, intermediate, expert slopes and trails; 750 acres of open-bowl skiing. Lighted snowboarding. (Mid-Nov-mid-Apr, daily) Alpine slide, children's park, miniature golf in summer (fees). Summer ¢¢ Winter ¢¢¢¢

Solitude Resort. W via I-80 to I-215 S, exit 6 in Big Cottonwood Canyon (see SALT LAKE CITY).

White Pine Touring Center. Groomed x-country trails (20 km), school, rentals; guided tours. (Nov-Apr, daily) Summer mountain biking; rentals. Approx 1 mi N via UT 224 to Park City Golf Course. Phone 435/649-8710. Winter ¢¢¢

Utah Winter Sports Park. Recreational ski jumping in $25-million park built for 2002 Olympic Winter Games. Nordic, competition, freestyle, and training jumps. Lessons followed by two-hr jumping session. Also Olympic bobsled and luge track (high-speed rides avail). Day lodge, snack bar, gift shop. (Wed-Sun) 4 mi N on Bear Hollow Dr. Phone 435/658-4233. ¢¢¢¢

Special Events

Sundance Film Festival. 10-day festival for independent filmmakers. Workshops, screenings, and special events. Mid-Jan.

Uniting Fore Care Classic presented by Novell PGA Tournament. 8 mi N on UT 224, at Park Meadows. PGA Invitational Golf tournament. Aug.

Art Festival. Main St. Open-air market featuring work of more than 200 visual artists. Also street entertainment. First wkend Aug.

Motels/Motor Lodges

★★ **HAMPTON INN & SUITES.**
6609 Landmark Dr (84098). 435/645-0900; fax 435/645-9672; toll-free 800/426-7866. www.hamptoninn.com. 81 rms, 4 story, 20 suites. Dec-Mar: S $135; D $210; suites $210; each addl $8; under 13 free; lower rates rest of yr. Crib avail. Parking lot. Indoor pool; whirlpool. TV; cable (premium), VCR avail. Complimentary continental bkfst, coffee in rms, newspaper, toll-free calls. Restaurant nearby. Ck-out noon. Meeting rm. Business servs avail. Concierge serv. Dry cleaning, coin lndry. Exercise equipt. Cr cds: A, D, DS, MC, V.
🄳 ⬧ ≈ 🏂 ⬧ ♨

★★★ **HOLIDAY INN EXPRESS & SUITES.** *1501 W Ute Blvd (84098). 435/658-1600; res 800/465-4329. www.holiday-inn.com.* 76 rms, 3 story, 12 suites. Jan-Apr, July-Sept: S, D $85; suites $129; under 18 free; lower rates rest of yr. Crib avail. Pet accepted, some restrictions. Parking lot. Indoor pool. TV; cable (premium), VCR avail. Complimentary coffee in rms, newspaper, toll-free calls. Restaurant nearby. Ck-out noon. Meeting rm. Business servs avail. Dry cleaning, coin lndry. Exercise equipt, sauna, stream rm. Golf, tennis nearby. Cr cds: A, DS, MC, V.
🄳 🐾 ⬧ ⚡ 🏂 ⛷ ≈ 🏂 ✈ ⬧ ♨ 🛼

★★ **THE LODGE AT MOUNTAIN VILLAGE.** *1415 Lowell Ave (84060). 435/655-3315; fax 435/649-9162. www.davidhollands.com.* 123 rms, 3 story, 98 suites. Some A/C. Mid-Jan-Mar: S, D $55-$145; suites $145-$550; higher rates: Christmas, Presidents' Week; lower rates rest of yr. Crib free. TV; cable (premium), VCR avail (movies). Indoor/outdoor pool; whirlpool. Sauna. Bar. Ck-out 10 am. Meeting rms. Business servs avail. Downhill ski on site; x-country ski 1 mi. Refrigerators, some microwaves. Balconies. Cr cds: A, C, D, DS, MC, V.
⛷ ≈ ⬧ ♨ SC

★★★ **SHADOW RIDGE.** *50 Shadow Ridge St (84060). 435/649-4300; fax 435/649-5951; toll-free 800/754-2002. www.davidhollands.com.* 150 rms, 4 story, 50 suites. Mid-Jan-late-Mar: S, D $150-$175; condos $320-$450; ski, golf plans; higher rates mid-Dec-early Jan; lower rates rest of yr. Crib free. TV; cable, VCR avail (movies). Heated pool; whirlpool. Restaurant (seasonal). Ck-out 10 am. Lndry facilities. Meeting rms. Business servs avail. Bellhops in season. Valet serv. Downhill ski opp; x-country ski ½ mi. Golf ½ mi. Exercise equipt; sauna. Some refrigerators, fireplaces; microwaves avail. Balconies. Cr cds: A, C, D, DS, JCB, MC, V.
🏂 ⬧ 🛼 SC ≈ 🏂 ⛷

★★★ **YARROW HOTEL.** *1800 Park Ave (84060). 435/649-7000; fax 435/645-7007; res 800/927-7694. www.yarrowresort.com.* 181 rms, 2 story. S, D $79-$249; each addl $15; suites $89-$249; under 13 free; package plan; higher rates mid-Dec-Mar. Crib free. TV; cable (premium). Heated pool; whirlpools. Coffee in rms. Restaurant 6:30 am-10 pm. Rm serv. Bar. Ck-out 11 am. Coin lndry. Meeting rms. Business center. Bellhops. Concierge. Downhill ski ¼ mi; x-country ski ½ mi. Exercise equipt. Refrigerators. Microwaves avail. Balconies. Golf course adj. Cr cds: A, D, DS, JCB, MC, V.
🄳 🏂 ≈ ⬧ ♨ 🏂 ⛷ 🛼

Hotel

★★★ **MARRIOTT PARK CITY.** *1895 Sidewinder Dr (84060). 435/649-2900; fax 435/649-4852; toll-free 800/234-9003. www.parkcityutah.com.* 200 rms, 1-4 story. S, D $79-$269; each addl $15; suites $119-$400; under 18 free; ski, golf packages. Crib free. TV; cable (premium). Indoor pool; whirlpool. Restaurant 6:30 am-10 pm. Rm serv 11 am-10 pm. Bar. Ck-out noon. Meeting rms. Business center. In-rm modem link. Bellhops. Concierge. Gift shop. Garage parking. Downhill/x-country ski ½ mi. Exercise equipt; sauna. Balconies. Cr cds: A, D, DS, JCB, MC, V.
🄳 ⬧ ⚡ ⛷ ≈ 🏂 ⬧ ♨ 🛼

Resorts

★★★ **GRAND SUMMIT RESORT HOTEL & CONFERENCE CENTER.** *4000 The Canyons Resort Dr (84098). 435/649-5400; fax 435/649-7374; toll-free 888/226-9667. www.thecanyons.com.* 356 rms, 8 story, 65 suites. Jan-

Mar: S, D $119-$365; suites $300-900; lower rates rest of yr. Crib avail. Valet parking avail. Pool; whirlpool. TV; cable (premium), VCR avail. Complimentary coffee in rms, newspaper. Restaurant 7 am-10 pm. Bar. Ck-out 11 am. Conference center. Bellhops. Concierge serv. Dry cleaning, coin lndry. Gift shop. Exercise rm, sauna, steam rm. Golf nearby. Tennis. Downhill skiing. Bike rentals. Supervised children's activities. Hiking trail. Video games. Cr cds: A, D, DS, MC, V.

★★ **RADISSON RESORT.** *2121 Park Ave (84060). 435/649-5000; fax 435/649-2122; 800/333-3333. www. radisson.com.* 125 rms, 6 suites. Dec-Mar, July-Aug: S $89-$149; suites $109-$189; each addl $15; under 18 free; lower rates rest of yr. Crib avail. Pet accepted; fee. Parking garage. Indoor/outdoor pools, whirlpool. TV; cable (DSS). Complimentary full bkfst. Coffee in rms. Restaurant 6:30 am-2 pm, 5-10 pm. Bar. Ck-out noon. Meeting rms. Business servs avail. Bellhops. Concierge serv. Dry cleaning, coin lndry. Gift shop. Steam rm. Golf. Tennis. Downhill skiing. Bike rentals. Hiking trail. Video games. Cr cds: A, C, D, DS, JCB, MC, V.

★★★ **SILVER KING HOTEL.** *1485 Empire Ave (84060). 435/649-5500; fax 435/649-6647; toll-free 800/331-8652. www.silverkinghotel.com.* 64 kit. suites, 5 story. Nov-Apr: S $115-$385; D $195-$425; higher rates Sundance film festival; lower rates rest of yr. Crib free. Garage parking free. TV; cable (premium), VCR (movies). Complimentary coffee in rms. Restaurant nearby. Ck-out 11 am. Meeting rms. Business servs avail. Downhill/x-country ski 1 mi. Sauna. Health club privileges. Indoor/outdoor pool; whirlpool. Refrigerators, microwaves, fireplaces. Some in-rm whirlpools. Picnic tables, grills. Cr cds: A, DS, MC, V.

★★★★ **STEIN ERIKSEN LODGE.** *7700 Stein Way (84060). 435/649-3700; fax 435/649-5825; res 800/323-7500. www.steinlodge.com.* Perched 8,200 feet high in the Wasatch Mountains, this Deer Valley Resort lodge has a cozy, Scandinavian decor and convenient ski-in, ski-out location. For the lazy at heart, there's a year-round, outdoor pool, a hot tub, and even monthly cooking classes. Dine in The Glitretind Restaurant, or, during winter, at Valhalla for creative wild game, seafood, and traditional meat dishes. 170 rms, 13 rms in main lodge, 2 story, 59 kit. suites. Early Dec-early Apr: S, D from $350; each addl $25; kit. suites from $615; under 12 free; summer rates; ski plans; higher rates hol seasons; lower rates rest of yr. Crib free. Valet parking. TV; cable (premium), VCR, DVD avail. Heated pool, whirlpool, poolside serv. Complimentary full bkfst (winter only). Dining rms (see also GLITRETIND). Rm serv 6:30 am-11 pm. Box lunches. Bar; pianist in winter. Ck-out 11 am. Grocery 4 miles. Conference facilities. Business center. In-rm modem link. Concierge. Boutique. Underground parking. Golf privileges. Downhill ski on site; x-country ski 3 mi. Sleighing. Snowmobiles. Hot-air balloons; mountain bikes avail. Lawn games. Valet serv. Exercise equipt; sauna, steam rm. Massage. Full service spa. Refrigerators, bathrm phone, whirlpool, washer, dryer in most rms. Some fireplaces; microwaves avail. Many balconies. In-rm whirlpools. Cr cds: A, D, DS, JCB, MC, V.

B&Bs/Small Inns

★★ **1904 IMPERIAL HOTEL B&B.** *221 Main St (84060). 435/649-1904; fax 435/645-7421; toll-free 800/669-8824. www.1904imperial.com.* 10 rms, 3 story, 2 suites. No A/C. Mid-Nov-mid-Apr: S, D $140-$175; suite $190-$220; higher rates: hols, film festival; lower rates rest of yr. TV; cable. Complimentary full bkfst. Ck-out 11 am, ck-in 4 pm. Downhill ski ½ mi; x-country ski 2 mi. Restored boarding house (1904) in historic area. Cr cds: A, DS, MC, V.

★★★ **GOLDENER HIRSCH INN.** *7570 Royal St E (84060). 435/649-7770; fax 435/649-7901; toll-free 800/252-3373. www.goldenerhirschinn. com.* 20 rms, 4 story; Dec-Jan: S, D $490-$950; lower rates rest of yr; suites $950; $25 addl person. Crib free. TV; VCR. Restaurant. Bar; entertainment (winter 5 nights, summer wkend eves). Limited rm serv. Valet. Concierge. Gift shop. Exercise equipt. Business center. Fireplaces, bathrm phones. Cr cds: A, MC, V.

★ ★ ★ **OLD MINERS' LODGE.** *615 Woodside Ave (84060). 435/645-8068; fax 435/645-7420; res 800/648-8068. www.oldminerslodge.com.* 12 rms, 2 story, 3 suites. No A/C. Mid-Nov-mid-Apr: S, D $130-$275; each addl $15; higher rates mid-Dec-early Jan; lower rates rest of yr. Crib $5. Complimentary full bkfst. Restaurant nearby. Ck-out noon, ck-in 2 pm. Business servs avail. Street parking. Downhill ski 1½ blks; x-country ski 1½ mi. Whirlpool. Renovated lodging house used by miners (1889); early Western decor, fireplace, antiques. Totally nonsmoking. Cr cds: A, C, D, DS, MC, V.

★ ★ ★ **WASHINGTON SCHOOL INN.** *543 Park Ave (84060). 435/649-3800; fax 435/649-3802; res 800/824-1672. www.washingtonschoolinn.com.* 12 rms, 3 story, 3 suites. No A/C. Mid-Dec-Mar: S, D $129-$235; suites $195-$365; lower rates rest of yr. TV; cable. Complimentary full bkfst; afternoon refreshments. Restaurant nearby. Ck-out 11 am, ck-in 4 pm. Meeting rms. Business servs avail. Street parking. Downhill ski 1½ blks; x-country ski 1½ mi. Sauna. Whirlpool. Historic, stone schoolhouse (1889); antiques, sitting rm with stone and carved wood fireplace, library, bell tower, turn-of-the-century country decor. Cr cds: A, D, DS, MC, V.

Conference Center

★ ★ **PROSPECTOR SQUARE LODGE & CONFERENCE CENTER.** *2200 Sidewinder Dr (84060). 435/649-7100; fax 435/649-8377; toll-free 800/453-3812. www.prospectorlodging. com.* 230 units, 2-3 story, 125 kits. Late Nov-mid-Apr: S, D $79-$479; kit. studio rms $167-$187; 1-2-3-bedrm condos $175-$400; under 12 free; ski plan; lower rates rest of yr. TV; VCR avail. Pool. Coffee in rms.

Ck-out 11 am, ck-in 4 pm. Convention facilities. Business servs avail. In-rm modem link. Valet serv. Downhill ski ½ mi; x-country ski ¼ mi. Health club privileges. 2 whirlpools. Bicycle rentals. Refrigerators, microwaves. Some balconies. Picnic tables, grills. Cr cds: A, D, DS, MC, V.

Villa/Condo

★ **EDELWEISS HAUS HOTEL.** *1482 Empire Ave (84060). 435/649-9342; fax 435/649-4049; toll-free 800/245-6417. www.pclodge.com/edelweiss.* 45 kit units, 4 story. Nov-Mar: S, D $75-$295; each addl $10; suites, kit units $225-$290; higher rates Christmas wk; lower rates rest of yr. Crib $10. TV; cable. Heated pool; whirlpool. Restaurant nearby. Ck-out 10 am. Coin lndry. Underground parking. Downhill/x-country ski opp. Saunas. Microwaves. Balconies, patios. Cr cds: A, DS, MC, V.

Restaurants

★ ★ ★ **THE CABIN.** *4000 The Canyons Resort Dr (84098). 435/615-8060. www.thecanyons.com.* Menu changes daily. Hrs: 5:30-10 pm. Res accepted. Wine, beer. Dinner $14-$34. Child's menu. Garage. Cr cds: A, DS, MC, V.

★ ★ ★ **CHEZ BETTY.** *1637 Short Line Rd (84060). 435/649-8181. www.chez betty.com.* Menu changes seasonally. Hrs: 6-10 pm. Closed Tues, Wed. Res accepted. Wine, beer. Dinner $19-$30. Cr cds: A, DS, MC, V.

★ ★ ★ **CHIMAYO.** *368 Main St (84060). 435/649-6222. www.chimayo restaurant.com.* Specializes in ribs, Chilean sea bass. Hrs: 5:30-10 pm. Closed Mon, Tues. Res accepted. Wine list. Dinner $21-$32. Cr cds: A, DS, MC, V.

★ ★ ★ ★ **THE GLITRETIND.** *7700 Stein Way (84060). 435/649-3700. www.steinlodge.com.* This rich, European dining room is housed at the four-star Stein Eriksen Lodge perched

in the Wasatch Mountains at Deer Valley Resort. The excellent wine list is nationally recognized and the American continental menu features first-rate preparations including mustard-crusted rack of lamb with lentil and arugula strudel. The upbeat Sunday jazz brunch draws a crowd for a good reason. Specializes in fresh seafood. Own baking. Hrs: 7 am-10 pm; Sun brunch 10:30 am-2:30 pm. Res accepted. Bar from 11 am. Wine cellar. Bkfst $5-$15, lunch $6-$15, dinner $18-$34. Sun brunch $29. Child's menu. Valet parking. Outdoor dining. Cr cds: A, D, DS, MC, V.
D

★ ★ ★ **GRAPPA.** *151 Main St (84060). www.grapparestaurant.com. 435/645-0636.* Hrs: 5-10 pm (summer 5:30-9 pm. Closed Dec 24; also mid-Apr-mid-May. Res accepted. Italian menu. Serv bar. A la carte entrees: dinner $22-$36. Child's menu. Seasonal menu. Specializes in pasta. Outdoor dining. Rustic decor, stained glass windows. Totally nonsmoking. Cr cds: A, D, MC, V.

★ ★ **KAMPAI.** *586 Main St (84060). 435/649-0655.* Hrs: 6-10 pm. Closed Thanksgiving, Dec 25; also 10 days in spring. Japanese menu. Serv bar. Dinner $12.95-$24. Specializes in sushi, sashimi, tempura. Outdoor dining. Casual Japanese decor; extensive sushi bar. Totally nonsmoking. Cr cds: A, C, D, DS, ER, MC, V.
D

★ **MAIN STREET PIZZA AND NOODLE.** *530 Main St (84060). 435/645-8878.* Hrs: 11:30 am-10 pm; Fri, Sat to 11 pm. Closed Thanksgiving. Italian, Amer menu. Bar. Lunch $5-$8, dinner $8-$12. Specializes in pizza, pasta. Casual decor. Totally nonsmoking. Cr cds: A, C, D, DS, ER, MC, V.
D

★ ★ ★ ★ **RIVERHORSE CAFE** . *540 Main St (84060). 435/649-3536.* Visitors are just as likely to be drawn to this cafe by the nationally recognized musical guests as they are by the contemporary American cuisine featuring pasta, poultry, game, and seafood. Chef/manager Bill Hufferd welcomes guests—and the occasional celebrity—for dining, drinking, and dancing. Weather permitting, try to snag a second-story, balcony seat

overlooking the Main Street scene. Specialties: Macadamia-crusted halibut, seared ahi tuna, Utah rack of lamb. Own baking, pasta. Hrs: 5:30-10 pm. Closed Thanksgiving. Bar. Wine list. Res accepted. Dinner $18.50-$29.50. Child's menu. Entertainment Thurs-Sun (summer), nightly (ski season). Outdoor dining. Cr cds: A, DS, MC, V.

★ **TEXAS RED'S PIT BARBECUE AND CAFE.** *440 Main St (84060). 435/649-7337.* Hrs: 11 am-10 pm. Bar. Lunch $3.95-$5.95, dinner $5.95-$16.95. Child's menu. Specializes in pit-barbecued ribs. Restored storefront (1910); rustic Western decor. Cr cds: A, C, D, DS, MC, V.

★ ★ **ZOOM ROADHOUSE GRILL.** *660 Main St (84060). 435/649-9108. www.sundanceresort.com.* Hrs: 11:30 am-2:30 pm, 5:30-10 pm. Res accepted (dinner). Bar. Lunch $10-$23, dinner $10-$27. Child's menu. Specialties: Double R Ranch ribs, creamy wild mushroom risotto with grilled shrimp. Own baking. Outdoor dining. Former train depot with original wood floor, high ceiling, fireplace. Cr cds: A, C, D, DS, MC, V.
D

Payson

(C-4) *See also Nephi, Provo*

Settled 1850 **Pop** 12,716 **Elev** 4,648 ft **Area code** 801 **Zip** 84651

Information Chamber of Commerce, 439 West Utah Ave; 801/465-5200 or 801/465-2634

Web www.paysonchamber.com

What to See and Do

Mount Nebo Scenic Loop Drive. This 45-mi drive around the eastern shoulder of towering Mt Nebo (elevation 11,877 ft) is one of the most thrilling in Utah; Mt Nebo's three peaks are the highest in the Wasatch range. The road travels south through Payson and Santaquin canyons and then climbs 9,000 ft up Mt Nebo, offering a view of Devil's Kitchen, a brilliantly colored canyon. (This section of the drive not recommended for those who dislike heights.) The forest road continues S to UT 132; take UT 132 E to Nephi, and then drive N on I-15 back to Payson.

Payson Lake Recreation Area. Fishing, swimming; camping, hiking, backpacking. 12 mi SE on unnumbered road in Uinta National Forest (see PROVO). Phone 801/798-3571.

Special Event

Golden Onion Days. Incl community theater presentations, 5k and 10k runs, horse races, demolition derby, parade, fireworks, and picnic. Labor Day wkend.

Motel/Motor Lodge

★ ★ **COMFORT INN.** *830 N Main St (84651). 801/465-4861; fax 801/465-7686; res 800/228-5150. www.comfort inn.com.* 62 rms, 2 story, 6 kits. (no equipt). S $66-$76; D $75-$85; each addl $6; suites $130; under 18 free. Crib free. Pet accepted; $10 deposit. TV; cable (premium). Indoor pool; whirlpool. Complimentary continental bkfst. Restaurant adj open 24 hrs. Ck-out 11 am. Coin lndry. Meeting rms. Business servs avail. Exercise equipt; sauna. Cr cds: A, D, DS, MC, V.

🄳 🔧 ⌦ 🖊 🐾 🕴

Price (D-5)

Settled 1879 **Pop** 8,402 **Elev** 5,567 ft **Area code** 435 **Zip** 84501

Information Carbon County Chamber of Commerce, 90 N 100 E, #3; 435/637-2788 or 435/637-8182

Web www.carboncountychamber. com

What to See and Do

Cleveland-Lloyd Dinosaur Quarry. Since 1928, more than 12,000 dinosaur bones, representing at least 70 different animals, have been excavated on this site. Visitor center, nature trail, picnic area. (Memorial Day-Labor Day, daily; Easter-Memorial Day, wkends only) 22 mi S on UT 10, then approx 15 mi E on unnumbered road. Phone 435/637-5060. **Donation**

College of Eastern Utah Prehistoric Museum. Dinosaur displays, archaeology exhibits; geological specimens. (Memorial Day-Labor Day, daily; rest of yr, Mon-Sat) 155 E Main St. Phone 435/637-5060. **Donation**

Geology tours. Self-guided tours of Nine Mile Canyon, Native American dwellings, paintings, San Rafael Desert, Clevelan-Lloyd Dinosaur Quarry, Little Grand Canyon. Maps avail at Castle Country Travel Region or Castle Country Regional Info Center, 155 E Main. Phone 800/842-0784. Phone 435/637-3009. **FREE**

Manti-LaSal National Forest, Manti Division. (See MOAB, MONTICELLO) Originally two forests—the Manti in central Utah and the LaSal section in southeastern Utah—now under single supervision. A 1,327,631-acre area partially in Colorado, this forest has among its attractions high mountain scenic drives, deep canyons, riding trails, campsites, winter sports, fishing, and deer and elk hunting. Joe's Valley Reservoir on UT 29 and Electric Lake on UT 31 have fishing and boating. Areas of geologic interest, developed as a result of massive landslides, are near Ephraim. Some fees in developed areas. 21 mi SW on UT 10, then NW on UT 31. Contact the Ranger District office or the Forest Supervisor at 599 W Price River Dr. Phone 435/637-2817. **FREE**

Price Canyon Recreation Area. Scenic overlooks; hiking, picnicking, camping (fee). Roads have steep grades. (May-mid-Oct, daily) 15 mi N on US 6, then 3 mi W on unnumbered road. **FREE**

Scofield State Park. Utah's highest state park has a 2,800-acre lake that lies at an altitude of 7,616 ft. Fishing, boating (docks, ramps); camping (rest rms, showers), snowmobiling, ice fishing, x-country skiing in winter. (May-Oct) Standard fees. 24 mi N on US 6, then 10 mi W and S on UT 96. Phone 435/448-9449. ¢¢¢

Motels/Motor Lodges

★ ★ **BEST WESTERN CARRIAGE HOUSE.** *590 E Main St (84501). 435/637-5660; fax 435/637-5157; res 800/780-7234. bestwestern.com.* 41 rms, 2 story. S $51.95-$75.95; D $57.95-$75.95; each addl $6; suites

$61.95-$75.95. Crib free. TV; cable. Indoor pool; whirlpool. Complimentary continental bkfst. Restaurant nearby. Ck-out noon. Airport transportation. Cr cds: A, D, DS, MC, V.

⊡ ⊠ ⊠ ⊠

★ **GREENWELL INN & CONVENTION CENTER.** *655 E Main St (84501). 435/637-3520; fax 435/637-4858; toll-free 800/666-3520. www. castlenet.com/greenwell.* 125 rms, 1-2 story. May-Sept: S $34-$38; D $42-$46; each addl $5; suites $46.50-$51.50; under 18 free; lower rates rest of yr. Crib $6. Pet accepted. TV; cable. Indoor pool. Complimentary continental bkfst. Restaurant adj 6 am-9 pm. Ck-out 11 am. Meeting rm. Lndry facilities. Gift shop. Exercise equipt. Health club privileges. Refrigerators avail. Cr cds: A, C, D, DS, ER, JCB, MC, V.

⊡ ⊠ ⊠ ⊠ ⊠ ⊠ ⊠ ⊠ ⊠ ⊠

★ ★ **HOLIDAY INN.** *838 Westwood Blvd (84501). 435/637-8880; fax 435/637-7707; toll-free 800/465-4329. sunstonehotels.com.* 151 rms, 2 story. S $84-$99; D $85-$106; each addl $6; suites $99-$126; under 17 free. Crib free. TV. Indoor pool. Restaurant 6 am-10 pm. Rm serv. Bar. Ck-out noon. Meeting rms. Exercise equipt. Health club privileges. Refrigerators avail. Cr cds: A, C, D, DS, JCB, MC, V.

⊡ ⊠ ⊠ ⊠ ⊠ ⊠ SC

Restaurant

★ **CHINA CITY CAFE.** *350 E Main St (84501). 435/637-8211.* Hrs: 11 am-10 pm. Closed Thanksgiving, Dec 25. Res accepted. Chinese, Amer menu. Complete meals: lunch $5.25-$6.25, dinner $6.95-$22.45. Child's menu. Specialty: cashew chicken. Café atmosphere with Chinese decor. Cr cds: A, C, D, DS, MC, V.

⊡

Provo

(C-4) *See also Heber City, Payson, Salt Lake City*

Settled 1849 **Pop** 105,166 **Elev** 4,549 ft **Area code** 801

Information Utah County Visitors Center, 51 S University Ave, 84601; 801/370-8394 or 800/222-8824

Web www.utahvalley.org/cvb

What to See and Do

Brigham Young University. (1875) 27,000 students. Founded by Brigham Young and operated by the Church of Jesus Christ of Latter-day Saints. This is one of the world's largest church-related institutions of higher learning, with students from every state and more than 90 foreign countries. One-hr, free guided tours arranged at Hosting Center (Mon-Fri; also by appt) Phone 801/378-4678. Incl

> **Earth Science Museum.** Geological collection, extensive series of minerals and fossils. Phone 801/378-4678. **FREE**

> **Harris Fine Arts Center.** Houses B. F. Larsen Gallery and Gallery 303; periodic displays of rare instruments and music collection. Concert, theater performances. **FREE** Adj is

> **Monte L. Bean Life Science Museum.** Exhibits and collections of insects, fish, amphibians, reptiles, birds, animals, and plants. Phone 801/378-5051. **FREE**

> **Museum of Art.** Exhibits from the BYU Permanent Collection; traveling exhibits (some fees). Phone 801/378-2787. ¢¢¢

> **Museum of Peoples and Cultures.** Material from South America, the Near East, and the southwestern United States. Allen Hall, 710 N 100 E. Phone 801/378-6112. **FREE**

Camp Floyd and Stagecoach Inn State Parks. Only the cemetery and one comissary bldg remain as evidence of the pre-Civil War post that quartered the largest troop concentration in the US here between 1858-1861. Approx 400 buildings were constructed for troops deployed to the west in expectation of a Mormon rebellion. The nearby Stagecoach Inn has been restored with original period furnishings. Visitor center. Museum. (Apr-Sept daily, mid-Oct-Mar, Mon-Sat) Standard fees. 13 mi N on I-15 to Lehi, then 20 mi W on UT 73, in Cedar Valley. Phone 801/768-8932. ¢

John Hutchings Museum. Six main collections incl archaeology, ornithology and zoology, paleontology, mineralogy, and pioneer artifacts. Most of the items are from the Great Basin area. Rare sea shells, fossils, Native American artifacts. (Tues-Sat; closed hols) 17 mi NW via I-15 or UT 89/91, at 55 N Center St, in Lehi. Phone 801/768-7180. ¢¢

Pioneer Museum. Outstanding collection of Utah pioneer relics and Western art. Pioneer Village. (June-early Sept, Wed, Fri, Sat afternoons; rest of yr, by appt) 500 W 500 N, on US 89. Phone 801/377-0995. **FREE**

Springville Museum of Art. Contemporary artists. Changing exhibits. Competition in Apr, quilt show in July-Sept. Guided tours. (Hrs vary with exhibit; closed Jan 1, Easter, Dec 25) 7 mi SE via I-15 exit 263, at 126 E 400 S, in Springville. Phone 801/489-2727. **FREE**

Sundance Ski Area. Three chairlifts, rope tow; patrol, school, rentals; warming hut, restaurants. Longest run two mi, vertical drop 2,150 ft. (Late Nov-Apr, daily) X-country trails. 15 mi NE on US 189, North Fork Provo Canyon. Phone 801/225-4107. ¢¢¢¢

Timpanogos Cave National Monument. (see). 15 mi NE on UT 146 (State St), then 2 mi E on UT 29.

Uinta National Forest. Scenic drives through the 950,000-acre forest; areas incl Provo Canyon, Bridal Veil Falls, Deer Creek Dam and Reservoir, Diamond Fork Canyon, Hobble Creek Canyon, Strawberry Reservoir, and the Alpine and Mt Nebo Scenic Loop (see PAYSON); roads give an unsurpassed view of colorful landscapes, canyons, waterfalls. Stream and lake fishing; hunting for deer and elk, camping (fee), picnicking. Res accepted. South and east of town. Phone 801/377-5780.

Utah Lake State Park. Park situated on the eastern shore of Utah Lake, a 150-sq-mi, freshwater remnant of ancient Lake Bonneville, which created the Great Salt Lake. Fishing (cleaning station), boating (ramp, dock); ice-skating (winter), roller-skating (summer), picnicking, play area, camping (dump station). Visitor center. (Daily) Standard fees. 2 mi W

on Center St, off I-15. Phone 801/375-0733.

Special Event

Freedom Festival. Bazaar, carnival, parades. Early July.

Motels/Motor Lodges

★ ★ **BEST WESTERN COTTON-TREE INN.** *2230 N University Pkwy (84604). 801/373-7044; fax 801/375-5240; toll-free 800/528-1234. www.bestwestern. com.* 80 rms, 2 story. S $59-$64; D $64-$74; each addl $5; suites $150; under 18 free. Crib free. TV; cable. 2 heated pools, 1 indoor; whirlpool. Complimentary continental bkfst. Restaurant nearby. Ck-out noon. Meeting rms. Business servs avail. Valet serv. Downhill ski 15 mi. Health club privileges. Microwaves avail. Balconies. View of river. Cr cds: A, C, D, DS, MC, V.
🄳 🛉 ⚒ 🛏 🖎 🔥 SC

★ **COLONY INN NATIONAL 9.** *1380 S University Ave (84601). 801/374-6800; fax 801/374-6803; res 800/524-9999.* 80 kit. suites, 2 story. May-Oct: S $42-$52; D $58-$72; each addl $5; wkly, monthly rates; lower rates rest of yr. Crib $5. Pet accepted, some restrictions; $15 refundable and $5/day. TV; cable (premium). Heated pool. Complimentary continental bkfst. Restaurant adj. Ck-out noon. Coin lndry. Business servs avail. In-rm modem link. Downhill ski 20 mi. Cr cds: A, DS, MC, V.
🐾 ⚒ 🛏 🖎 🔥

★ **DAYS INN.** *1675 N 200 W (84604). 801/375-8600; fax 801/374-6654; res 800/329-7466. www.daysinn. com.* 49 rms, 2 story. S $44-$54; D $46-$59; each addl $5; kit. unit $65-$70; under 18 free. Crib free. Pet accepted, some restrictions. TV; cable. Heated pool. Complimentary continental bkfst. Coffee in rms. Restaurant 11 am-11 pm. Ck-out noon. Business servs avail. In-rm modem link. Downhill/x-country ski 15 mi. Some refrigerators, microwaves. Cr cds: A, C, D, DS, MC, V.
🄳 🐾 ⚒ 🖎 🔥 ⚒

★ ★ **HOLIDAY INN.** *1460 S University Ave (84601). 801/374-9750; fax*

801/377-1615; res 800/465-4329. *www.holiday-inn.com.* 78 rms, 2 story. S, D $65-$90; under 18 free. Crib $10. TV; cable (premium). Pool. Complimentary continental bkfst. Restaurant 11 am-10 pm. Rm serv. Ck-out noon. Meeting rms. Business center. Downhill ski 20 mi. Exercise equipt. Cr cds: A, C, D, DS, ER, JCB, MC, V.

★ **HOWARD JOHNSON.** *1292 S University Ave (84601). 801/374-2500; fax 801/373-1146; res 800/446-4656. www.hojo.com.* 116 rms, 2 story. Apr-mid-Sept: S $49-$79; D $54-$85; each addl $6; suites $70-$75; cabin suite $195; family rates; lower rates rest of yr. Crib free. TV; cable (premium). Heated pool; whirlpool. Restaurant. Ck-out noon. Coin lndry. Meeting rms. Business servs avail. Downhill ski 20 mi. Exercise equipt. Game rm. Microwaves avail. Cr cds: A, D, MC, V.

Hotel

★★★ **MARRIOTT PROVO.** *101 W 100 N (84601). 801/377-4700; fax 801/377-4708; res 800/228-9290. www.marriott.com.* 331 rms, 9 story. S $89-$125; D $89-$130; each addl $8; suites $99-$289; under 18 free; ski, honeymoon packages. Crib free. TV; cable (premium). Heated pool; whirlpool. Complimentary coffee in rms. Restaurant 6:30 am-10 pm. Private club 5 pm-midnight. Ck-out noon. Meeting rms. Business center. In-rm modem link. Gift shop. Covered parking. Airport transportation; free RR station, bus depot transportation. Downhill ski 14 mi. Exercise equipt; sauna. Some refrigerators, microwaves, wet bars. Cr cds: A, D, DS, MC, V.

Resort

★★★ **SUNDANCE RESORT.** *N Fork Provo Canyon (84604). 801/225-4107; fax 801/226-1937; toll-free 800/892-1600. www.sundanceresort.com.* 103 kit. units. Mid-Dec-Mar: S $185-$235; D $235-$375; suites $425; 2-3-bedrm cottages $750-$950; ski plans; lower rates rest of yr. TV; cable (premium), VCR avail (free movies). Supervised

children's activities (June-Sept); ages 6-12. Dining rms (see also FOUNDRY GRILL and THE TREE ROOM). Ck-out 11 am, ck-in 3 pm. Meeting rms. Business servs avail. Concierge. Downhill/x-country ski on site. Exercise equipt. Some fireplaces; microwaves avail. Private patios. Handmade wooden furniture; Native American art. Rustic retreat surrounded by pristine wilderness. Cr cds: A, D, DS, MC, V.

Restaurants

★ **BOMBAY HOUSE.** *463 N University Ave (84601). 801/373-6677. www. bombayhouse.com.* Hrs: 4-10:30 pm. Closed Sun; Dec 25. Res accepted. Indian menu. A la carte entrees: dinner $7.95-$15.95. Specializes in lamb, chicken, vegetables, seafood. Indian atmosphere. Cr cds: A, D, DS, MC, V.

★★ **FOUNDRY GRILL.** *RR 3 Box A-1 (84604). 801/223-4551. www.sundance resort.com.* Hrs: 7 am-10 pm; Sun 9 am-10 pm; Sun brunch to 2:30 pm. Res accepted; required Thurs-Sun dinner. Southwestern, Amer menu. Serv bar. Bkfst $1.75-$12.95, lunch, dinner $6.95-$23.95. Sun brunch $23.95. Child's menu. Specializes in pizza, pasta, steak, fish. Outdoor dining. Rustic, western decor; fireplace, bare wood floors. Totally nonsmoking. Cr cds: A, C, D, DS, ER, MC, V.

★ **MAGLEBY'S.** *1675 N 200 W (84604). 801/374-6249.* Hrs: 11 am-10 pm; Sat 4-11 pm. Closed Sun; Thanksgiving, Dec 24, 25. Res accepted. Lunch $7.95-$13.95, dinner $14.95-$26.95. Specializes in steak, seafood, deep-dish apple pie. Salad bar (lunch). Street lamps and high windows with flowerboxes; artwork for sale. Totally nonsmoking. Cr cds: A, DS, MC, V.

★★★★ **THE TREE ROOM.** *RR 3, Box A-1 (84604). 801/223-4200. www. sundanceresort.com.* Located at the base of the Sundance ski lift, this restaurant's two-story windows offer stunning views of the rugged mountains and surrounding wilderness. The upscale yet casual room is filled with beautiful displays of American Indian dolls and pottery. The sophisticated new American cuisine includes wild game, steaks, seafood, and herbs and vegetables from the resort's own organic gardens. Menu changes seasonally. Hrs: 5-10 pm. Res required. Wine, beer. Dinner $25-$38. Child's menu. Cr cds: A, C, D, DS, MC, V.

D

Rainbow Bridge National Monument (G-4)

(NW of Navajo Mountain, approachable from Arizona)

Rainbow Bridge, which rises from the eastern shore of Lake Powell, is the largest natural rock bridge in the world. It was named a national monument in 1910, one year after its sighting was documented. Carved by a meander of Bridge Creek, this natural bridge stands 290 feet tall, spans 275 feet, and stretches 33 feet at the top. One of the seven natural wonders of the world, Rainbow Bridge is higher than the nation's capitol dome and nearly as long as a football field. The monument is predominantly salmon pink in color, modified by streaks of iron oxide and manganese. In the light of the late afternoon sun, the bridge is brilliant to see. Native Americans consider the area a sacred place; legend holds that the bridge is a rainbow turned to stone.

The easiest way to reach Rainbow Bridge is a half-day round-trip boat ride across Lake Powell from Page, Arizona (see), or a full-day round-trip boat ride from Bullfrog and Halls Crossing marinas (see LAKE POWELL). The bridge also can be reached on foot or horseback via the Rainbow Trail through the Navajo Indian Reservation (see ARIZONA; permit required). Fuel and camp supplies are available at Dangling Rope Marina, accessible by boat only, ten miles downlake (south). Contact the Superintendent, Glen Canyon National

Recreation Area, PO Box 1507, Page, AZ 86040; phone 520/608-6404.

Richfield

(E-3) *See also Beaver, Fillmore, Salina*

Settled 1863 **Pop** 5,593 **Elev** 5,330 ft **Area code** 435 **Zip** 84701
Information Chamber of Commerce, PO Box 327; 435/896-4241

What to See and Do

Big Rock Candy Mountain. Multicolored mountain that Burl Ives popularized in song. 25 mi S on US 89, in Marysvale Canyon. Phone 435/896-4241.

Capitol Reef National Park. (see). 10 mi E on UT 119, then 76 mi SE on UT 24.

Fishlake National Forest. This 1,424,000-acre forest offers fishing; hunting, hiking, picnicking, camping (fee). Fish Lake, 33 mi SE via UT 119 and UT 24, then 7 mi NE on UT 25, offers high-altitude angling on six-mi-long lake covering 2,600 acres. Campgrounds (mid-May-late Oct). Contact the Supervisor's Office. Phone 435/896-9233.

Fremont Indian State Park. Museum and trails feature the Fremont people, who lived in the area from A.D. 300-1300 and then vanished. There is no explanation, only speculation, for their disappearance. Interpretive center highlights evolution of their culture; artifacts from nearby Five Fingers Ridge; nature trails lead to panels of rock art and a reconstructed pit house dwelling and granary. Fishing; camping (fee), picnicking. (Daily; closed Jan 1, Thanksgiving, Dec 25) Standard fees. 20 mi SW via I-70, at 11550 W Clear Creek Canyon Rd, in Sevier. Phone 435/527-4631.

Motels/Motor Lodges

★★ **BEST WESTERN APPLE TREE INN.** *145 S Main St (84701). 435/896-5481; fax 435/896-9465; res 800/780-7234. www.bwappletree.com.* 62 rms, 1-2 story. May-Oct: S $50-$65; D $55-$75; each addl $5; suites $58-

$102; lower rates rest of yr. Crib $4. TV; cable. Heated pool; whirlpool. Complimentary continental bkfst. Restaurant nearby. Ck-out noon. Business servs avail. Cr cds: A, C, D, DS, ER, JCB, MC, V.

[symbols]

★ **DAYS INN.** *333 N Main (84701). 435/896-6476; fax 435/996-6476; res 800/329-7466. www.daysinn.com.* 51 rms, 3 story. No elvtr. May-Oct: S $39-$75; D $59-$103; each addl $5; suites $85-$110; under 12 free; lower rates rest of yr. Crib free. Pet accepted; $50 refundable. TV; cable (premium). Heated pool; whirlpool. Sauna. Restaurant 6 am-9:30 pm. Ck-out 11 am. Meeting rms. Business servs avail. In-rm modem link. Sundries. Refrigerators. Cr cds: A, C, D, DS, ER, JCB, MC, V.

[symbols]

★★ **QUALITY INN.** *540 S Main St (84701). 435/896-5465; fax 435/896-9005; res 800/228-5151. www.quality inn.com.* 79 rms, 2 story. Mid-May-Oct: S, D $55-$80; suites $80-$110; under 18 free; lower rates rest of yr. Crib free. TV; cable. Heated pool. Complimentary continental bkfst. Restaurant adj 6 am-11 pm. Ck-out 11 am. Meeting rms. Exercise equipt. Whirlpool in suites. Cr cds: A, D, DS, MC, V.

[symbols]

★ **RICHFIELD TRAVELODGE.** *647 S Main St (84701). 435/896-9271; fax 435/896-6864; toll-free 800/549-8208. www.travelodge.com.* 40 rms, 2 story. June-Sept: S, D $65-$77; each addl $4; under 12 free; lower rates rest of yr. Crib free. Pet accepted. TV; cable. Indoor pool; whirlpool. Complimentary continental bkfst. Restaurant 5 am-10 pm. Rm servs. Ck-out noon. Meeting rms. Business servs avail. Sundries. Cr cds: A, DS, MC, V.

[symbols]

★ **ROMANICO INN.** *1170 S Main St (84701). 435/896-8471.* 29 rms, 2 story. S, D $36-$64; each addl $4; under 12 free. Crib free. Pet accepted. TV; cable. Restaurant adj 5:30-10 pm. Ck-out noon. Coin lndry. Whirlpool. Refrigerators, microwaves. Cr cds: A, C, DS, MC, V.

[symbols]

Roosevelt

(C-6) *See also Vernal*

Settled 1905 **Pop** 3,915 **Elev** 5,182 ft **Area code** 435 **Zip** 84066

Information Chamber of Commerce, 50 E 200 S 35-11, PO Box 1417; 435/722-4598

Motels/Motor Lodges

★★ **BEST WESTERN INN.** *E Hwy 40 (84066). 435/722-4644; fax 435/722-0179; res 800/780-7234. www.bestwestern.com .* 40 rms, 2 story. May-mid-Nov: S $55; D $60; lower rates rest of yr. Crib $5. TV; cable (premium). Heated pool; whirlpool. Restaurant adj 6 am-11:30 pm. Ck-out 11 am. Business servs avail. Sundries. Exercise equipt. Cr cds: A, D, DS, MC, V.

[symbols]

★ **FRONTIER MOTEL.** *75 S 200 E (98624). 435/722-2201; fax 435/722-2212.* 54 units, 2 kits. S $41-$45; D $49-$53; each addl $3; kit. units $45-$50. Crib $3. Pet accepted. TV; cable (premium). Pool. Restaurant 6 am-9:30 pm; Sun to 9 pm. Ck-out 11 am. Business servs avail. Cr cds: A, D, DS, MC, V.

[symbols]

St. George (G-2)

Founded 1861 **Pop** 49,663 **Elev** 2,761 ft **Area code** 435 **Zip** 84770

Information Washington County Travel & Convention Bureau, 425 S 700 E, Dixie Center, 84770; 435/634-5747 or 800/869-6635

What to See and Do

Brigham Young Winter Home. (1873) Two-story adobe house where the Mormon leader spent the last four winters of his life; period furnishings, garden. (Daily) 200 North and 100 West Sts. Phone 435/673-2517. **FREE**

Daughters of Utah Pioneers Collection. Regional memorabilia. (Mon-Sat; closed hols) Memorial Building, 143 N 100 E. Phone 435/628-7274. **Donation**

Jacob Hamblin Home. (1863) Native sandstone house of Hamblin, Mormon missionary to Native Americans for 32 yrs; pioneer furnishings. (Daily) 5 mi W off I-15, in Santa Clara. Phone 435/673-2161. **FREE**

Pine Valley Chapel. White frame meeting house built in 1868 as an upside-down ship by Ebenezer Bryce, a shipbuilder by trade. The walls were completed on the ground, then raised and joined with wooden pegs and rawhide. Still in use, the chapel served as both church and schoolhouse until 1919. (Memorial Day-Labor Day, daily) 30 mi N via UT 18, Central exit, in Dixie National Forest. Phone 435/634-5747. **FREE**

State parks.

Gunlock. Approx 450 undeveloped acres in scenic red rock country. A dam across the Santa Clara River has created a 240-acre lake, which offers swimming, waterskiing, fishing, boating (ramp); picnicking, primitive camping; no drinking water. (Daily) 16 mi NW on Old Hwy 91. Phone 435/628-2255. **FREE**

Snow Canyon. Flat-bottomed gorge cut into multicolored Navajo sandstone; massive erosional forms, sand dunes, Native American petroglyphs. Hiking, picnicking, improved camping areas (some hookups, dump station), trailer parking. (Daily) Standard fees. 10 mi N on UT 18. Phone 435/628-2255.

Tabernacle. Red sandstone structure built 1863-1876 with local materials; resembles colonial New England church. (Daily; closed Dec 25) Main and Tabernacle Sts. Phone 435/628-4072. **FREE**

Temple Visitor Center. On grounds of temple; guided tour of center explains local history and beliefs of the Latter-day Saints; audiovisual program. (Daily; closed Dec 25) 490 S 300 E. Phone 435/673-5181. **FREE**

Zion National Park. (see). 42 mi NE on UT 9.

Motels/Motor Lodges

★ **AMBASSADOR INN.** *1481 S Sunland Dr (84790). 435/673-7900; fax 435/673-8325; toll-free 877/373-7900. www.ambassadorinn.net.* 68 rms, shower only, 2 story. Apr-Nov: S, D $43-$74; under 18 free; higher rates Easter; lower rates rest of yr. Crib free. TV; cable. Heated pool; whirlpool. Complimentary continental bkfst. Restaurant nearby. Ck-out 11 am. Business servs avail. Cr cds: A, DS, MC, V.

★★ **BEST WESTERN CORAL HILLS.** *125 E St. George Blvd (84770). 435/673-4844; fax 435/673-5352; toll-free 800/542-7733. www.coralhills.com.* 98 rms, 2 story. Feb-Oct: S, D $51-$79; each addl $5; suites $80-$121; under 18 free; lower rates rest of yr. Crib $5. TV; cable. 2 pools, 1 indoor; wading pool, whirlpool. Complimentary continental bkfst. Restaurant opp 6 am-9:30 pm. Ck-out 11 am. Meeting rms. Business servs avail. Exercise equipt. Putting green. Rec rm. Refrigerators. Some balconies. Cr cds: A, C, D, DS, MC, V.

★ **CLARIDGE INN.** *1187 S Bluff St (84770). 435/673-7222; fax 435/634-0773; toll-free 800/367-3790.* 50 rms, 2 story. S, D $39-$49; higher rates hols. Crib $3. TV; cable. Heated pool; whirlpool. Restaurant adj open 24 hrs. Ck-out 11 am. Business servs avail. Totally nonsmoking. Cr cds: A, DS, MC, V.

★★ **COMFORT SUITES.** *1239 S Main St (84770). 435/673-7000; fax 435/628-4340; toll-free 800/517-4000. www.comfortsuites.net.* 122 units, 2 story. Feb-Aug: S, D $64-$119; under 18 free; higher rates: Easter, early Oct; lower rates rest of yr. Crib free. TV; cable. Heated pool; whirlpool. Complimentary continental bkfst. Restaurant opp open 24 hrs. Ck-out 11 am. Meeting rms. Business servs avail. Airport transportation. Refrigerators, microwaves. Cr cds: A, C, D, DS, MC, V.

★★ **HOLIDAY INN.** *850 S Bluff St (84770). 435/628-4235; fax 435/628-8157; res 800/465-4329. holidayinn stgeorge.com.* 164 rms, 2 story. S, D $89-$95; each addl $8; suites $100-$140; under 19 free. Crib free. TV; cable (premium). Indoor/outdoor pool; whirlpool. Restaurant 6 am-10 pm. Rm serv. Ck-out 11 am. Coin lndry. Meeting rms. Business servs avail. In-rm modem link. Bellhops. Shopping arcade. Airport transportation. Lighted tennis. Putting green. Game rm. Some refrigerators. Balconies. Cr cds: A, C, D, DS, MC, V.

[icons]

★★ **SINGLETREE INN.** *260 E St. George Blvd (84770). 435/673-6161; fax 435/673-7453; toll-free 800/528-8890.* 45 rms, 2 story. S, D $47-$54. Crib $5. Pet accepted. TV; cable. Heated pool; whirlpool. Continental bkfst. Restaurant 11:30 am-10 pm. Ck-out 11 am. Business servs avail. Cr cds: A, D, DS, MC, V.

[icons]

★ **SUN TIME INN.** *420 E St George Blvd (84770). 435/673-6181; toll-free 800/656-3846. www.suntimeinn.com.* 46 rms, 2 story. S, D $39-$89; each addl $4; under 16 free; wkly rates. TV; cable. Pet accepted. Crib $5. Heated pool; whirlpool. Complimentary continental bkfst. Restaurant adj 10 am-9:30 pm. Ck-out 11 am. Refrigerators, microwaves. Cr cds: A, DS, MC, V.

[icons]

B&B/Small Inn

★★★ **GREEN GATE VILLAGE.** *76 W Tabernacle St (84770). 435/628-6999; fax 435/628-6989; toll-free 800/350-6999. www.greenegate.com.* 14 rms, 1-2 story, 7 suites, 1 full house, 3 kit. units. D $85-$165; higher rates wkends; each addl $10-$25; kit. units $65-$125; wkly, monthly rates. TV; cable (premium), VCR avail (movies $2). Pool; whirlpool. Complimentary full bkfst. Dining rm Thurs-Sat 6-8 pm. Ck-out 11 am. Business servs avail. Free airport, bus depot transportation. Balconies; some fireplaces. Picnic tables, grills. Consists of 8 Victorian and pioneer houses from late 1800s; library, sitting rm, antiques, tole-painted furnishings. Totally nonsmoking. Cr cds: A, DS, MC, V.

[icons]

Salina

(E-4) *See also Richfield*

Settled 1863 **Pop** 2,393 **Elev** 5,150 ft
Area code 435 **Zip** 84654

What to See and Do

Palisade State Park. Approx 200 acres. Swimming beaches, showers, fishing, nonmotorized boating, canoe rentals, nature trail, hiking, 18-hole golf, picnicking, camping (fee; dump station). Six Mile Canyon adj. 20 mi N via US 89, then 2 mi E, near Sterling. Phone 435/835-7275. ¢¢

Special Event

Mormon Miracle Pageant. 30 mi N via US 89 in Manti, on Temple grounds. Portrays historical events of the Americas; cast of 600. Phone 435/835-3000. Early-mid-June. **FREE**

Motel/Motor Lodge

★★ **BEST WESTERN SHAHEEN'S.** *1225 S State St (84654). 435/529-7455; fax 435/529-7257; 800/528-1234. www.bestwestern.com.* 40 rms, 2 story. May-Nov: S $69.95; D $74.95; each addl $7; lower rates rest of yr. Crib $4. TV; cable (premium). Heated pool. Complimentary continental bkfst. Restaurant nearby. Ck-out 11 am. Meeting rm. Business servs avail. Sundries. Cr cds: A, C, D, DS, MC, V.

[icons]

Restaurant

★ **MOM'S CAFE.** *10 E Main St (84654). 435/529-3921.* Hrs: 7 am-10 pm. Closed Thanksgiving, Dec 25. Bkfst $2.50-$8.95, lunch $5.20-$8.50, dinner $6.25-$11.75 Child's menu. Specialties: fish and chips, liver and onions, spare ribs chicken-fried steak. Salad bar. Own pies. Homey atmosphere. Family-owned. Cr cds: DS, MC, V.

Salt Lake City

(B-4) *See also Heber City, Ogden, Park City, Provo*

Founded 1847 **Pop** 181,743
Elev 4,330 ft **Area code** 801
Information Convention & Visitors
Bureau, 90 S West Temple, 84101-
1406; 801/521-2822 or 801/534-4927
Web www.saltlake.org

Additional Visitor Information

For additional information contact
the Salt Lake Convention & Visitors
Bureau, 90 S West Temple, 84101-
1406; 801/521-2822; or the Utah
Travel Council and Visitor Information Center, Council Hall, 300 N
State St, 84114; 801/538-1030.

Transportation

Car Rental Agencies. See IMPOR-
TANT TOLL-FREE NUMBERS.

Public Transportation. Buses (Utah
Transit Authority), phone 801/287-
4636.

Rail Passenger Service. Amtrak
800/872-7245.

What to See and Do

Arrow Press Square. Once the city's
printing district, now buildings such
as Arrow Press Building (1890),
Upland Hotel (1910), and Midwest
Office Building Supply (1910) have
been reconstructed into a
retail/restaurant complex. 165 S West
Temple St. Phone 801/531-9700.

Brigham Young Monument. (1897)
Intersection of Main and South Tem-
ple Sts, at north side of intersection.
Phone 801/531-9700.

Bus tours.

   InnsBrook Tours. 3359 S Main, Ste
804, 84115. Phone 801/534-1001.

   Sightseeing USA. 553 W 100 S St,
84101. Phone 801/521-7060.

Council Hall. (1864-1866) Meeting
place of territorial legislature and city
hall for 30 yrs was dismantled and
then reconstructed in 1963 at present location; Federal/Greek-revival
style architecture. Visitor information center and office; memorabilia.
(Daily; closed Jan 1, Thanksgiving,

Dec 25) Capitol Hill, 300 N State St,
84114. Phone 801/538-1900. **FREE**

Fort Douglas Military Museum. Army
museum features history of military
in Utah from arrival of Johnston's
Army during the 1857 "Utah War"
through Vietnam. Also tours of fort
(self-guided or guided, by appt).
(Tues-Sat; closed hols) 3 mi NE,
Building 32 Potter St. Phone
801/581-1710.

Governor's Mansion. (1902) Restored
mansion of Thomas Kearns, wealthy
Utah senator of early 1900s; deco-
rated with Italian marble. Tours.
(Apr-mid-Dec, Tues and Thurs after-
noons; closed hols) 603 E South
Temple St. Phone 801/538-1005.
FREE

Hansen Planetarium. Space science
museum and library. Seasonal star
shows, stage plays (fee; schedule
varies). (Daily; closed hols) 15 S State
St. Phone 801/538-2104. **FREE**

Hogle Zoological Garden. Wildlife
exhibits; Discovery Land; bird show;
miniature train (summer). Picnicking, concession. (Daily; closed Jan 1,
Dec 25) 2600 E Sunnyside Ave.
Phone 801/582-1631. ¢¢¢

Kennecott Bingham Canyon Mine.
Open-pit copper mine 2½ mi wide
and ½ mi deep. Visitor center, observation deck, and audio presentation
explain mining operations, which
date from 1906. Gift shop.(Apr-mid-
Oct, daily) 8400 W Hwy U 111.
Phone 801/569-6248 or 801/252-
3234. ¢¢

**Lagoon Amusement Park, Pioneer
Village and Water Park.** Rides, water
slides; re-creation of 19th-century
Utah town; stagecoach and steam-
engine train rides. Camping, picnick-
ing. (Memorial Day-Aug, daily;
mid-Apr-late May and Sept, Sat and
Sun only) Parking (fee). 17 mi N on
I-15 exit 325, then N to Lagoon Dr.
Phone 800/748-5246.

Liberty Park. In 100-acre park are
Chase Mill (1852), Tracy Aviary, children's garden playground (Apr-Sept),
amusement park. Swimming; lighted
tennis, horseshoe courts, picnicking.
(Daily) 1300 South and 600 East Sts.
Phone 801/972-7800. **FREE**

Lion House. (1856) and **Beehive
House.** (1854) Family residences,
offices, and social centers for

Brigham Young and his wives and children. Guided tours of Beehive House. (Daily; closed Jan 1, Thanksgiving, Dec 25) 63 and 67 E South Temple. Phone 801/363-5466. **FREE**

Maurice Abravanel Concert Hall. The home of the Utah Symphony, this building is adorned with more than 12,000 sq ft of 24-karat gold leaf and a mile of brass railing. It has been

rated one of the acoustically best halls in the US. Free tours (by appt). The symphony has performances most wkends. 123 W South Temple. Phone 801/533-6683.

Pioneer Memorial Museum. Manuscripts, pioneer relics. Also here is **Carriage House**, with exhibits relating to transportation, incl Brigham Young's wagon, mule-drawn vehicles,

Pony Express items. One-hr guided tours (by appt). (Mon-Sat; closed hols) 300 N Main St, west side of capitol grounds. Phone 801/538-1050. **FREE**

Professional sports.

Utah Jazz (NBA). Delta Center, 301 W South Temple. Phone 801/355-3865.

Utah Starzz (WNBA). Delta Center, 301 W South Temple. Phone 801/355-DUNK.

River trips. Moki Mac River Expeditions. Offers 1-14-day whitewater trips on the Green and Colorado rivers. Contact PO Box 71242, 84171. Phone 801/268-6667. ¢¢¢¢

Salt Lake Art Center. Changing exhibits; school; lectures, seminars, films. (Tues-Sun; closed hols) 20 S West Temple. Phone 801/328-4201. **Donation**

Skiing.

Alta. 26 mi SE on UT 210 in Little Cottonwood Canyon in Alta (see). Phone 801/742-3333.

Brighton Resort. Three high-speed quad, one triple, three double chairlifts; patrol, school, rentals; lodge, restaurant, cafeteria. Sixty-four runs; longest run three mi, vertical drop 1,745 ft. (Mid-Nov-late-Apr, daily) Night skiing (Mon-Sat). Half-day rates. 25 mi SE via I-215, exit 6 in Big Cottonwood Canyon. Phone 801/532-4731. ¢¢¢¢

The Canyons. 28 mi E and S via I-80, UT 224 in Park City (see). Phone 435/649-5400.

Deer Valley Resort. 34 mi E and S via I-80, UT 224 in Park City (see). Phone 435/521-2822.

Park City Mountain Resort. 32 mi E and S via I-80, UT 224 in Park City (see).

Snowbird. 25 mi E and S via I-215, UT 210 in Little Cottonwood Canyon (see SNOWBIRD). Phone 801/521-2822.

Solitude Resort. Detachable quad, two triple, four double chairlifts; race course, patrol, school, rentals; day lodge, cafeteria, restaurants, bar. Longest run 3½ mi, vertical drop 2,047 ft. (Nov-Apr, daily) X-country center. SE via I-215, in Big

Cottonwood Canyon. Phone 801/534-1400. ¢¢¢¢

State Capitol. (1914) Constructed of Utah granite and Georgia marble, with a modern annex, capitol has a commanding view of the valley and Wasatch Mtns. Gold Room is decorated with bird's-eye marble and gold from Utah mines; ground floor has exhibits. Open daily. Guided tours every 30 min (Mon-Fri; hrs vary). 350 N Main St. Phone 801/538-1563. **FREE**

⭐ **Temple Square.** (Daily) Visitor centers provide information, exhibits and guided tours (½- to 1-hr; daily, every 15 min). N, S, and W Temple Sts and Main St. Phone 801/240-1245. **FREE** Tour incl

Assembly Hall. (1880) Tours (daily), concerts (Fri, Sat eves). Phone 801/521-2822.

Family History Library. Largest genealogy library in the world aids in compilation of family histories. (Mon-Sat) 35 N West Temple. Phone 801/240-2331. **FREE**

Museum of Church History and Art. Exhibits of Latter-day Saints church history from 1820 to present. (Daily; closed Jan 1, Easter, Thanksgiving, Dec 25) 45 N West Temple St. Phone 801/240-3310. **FREE**

Seagull Monument. (1913) Commemorates saving of the crops from crickets in 1848. Phone 801/521-2822.

Tabernacle. (1867) The self-supporting roof, an elongated dome, is 250 ft long and 150 ft wide. The tabernacle organ has 11,623 pipes, ranging from ⅝ inch to 32 ft in length. The world-famous Tabernacle Choir may be heard at rehearsal (Thurs eve) or at broadcast time (Sun morning). Organ recitals (Mon-Sat noon, Sun afternoon). Phone 801/521-2822. **FREE**

Temple. (1893) Used for sacred ordinances, such as baptisms and marriages. Closed to non-Mormons. Phone 801/521-2822.

This is the Place Heritage Park. Day-use museum park at mouth of Emigration Canyon, where Mormon pioneers first entered the valley. In park are **"This Is the Place"** Monument (1947), commemorating Brigham Young's words upon first seeing the Salt Lake City site; visitor center with audio presentation and murals of the Mormon migration; and **Old Deseret Pioneer Village**, a living museum that depicts the 1847-1869 era and pioneer life. (June-Sept, daily) 2601 Sunnyside Ave. Phone 801/582-1847. ¢¢

Timpanogos Cave National Monument. (see). 26 mi S on I-15, then 10 mi E on UT 92.

Trolley Square. Ten-acre complex of trolley barns converted into entertainment/shopping/dining center. (Daily) Bounded by 500 and 600 S Sts and 600 and 700 E Sts. Phone 801/521-9877.

University of Utah. (1850) 25,900 students. 2½ mi E, at head of 200 S St. Phone 801/581-6515. On campus are

Marriott Library. Western Americana collection, rare books, manuscripts. (Daily; closed hols, also July 24) Phone 801/581-8558. **FREE**

Pioneer Theatre Company. Two auditoriums; dramas, musicals, comedies. (Sept-May; closed hols) 300 S and 1400 E Sts. Phone 801/581-6270.

Red Butte Garden and Arboretum. More than 9,000 trees on 150 acres, representing 350 species; conservatory. Self-guided tours. Special events in summer. (Daily; closed Dec 25) On campus. Phone 801/581-4747. **FREE**

Utah Museum of Fine Arts. Representations of artistic styles from Egyptian antiquities to contemporary American paintings; 19th-century French and American paintings, furniture. (Daily; closed hols) Art & Architecture Center, south of library. Phone 801/581-7332. **FREE**

Utah Museum of Natural History. Halls of anthropology, biology, mineralology, paleontology, geology; traveling exhibits. (Daily; closed hols, also July 24) Phone 801/581-4303. ¢¢

Utah Fun Dome. Enclosed mall with entertainment, rides, bowling, roller-skating, baseball, arcades, miniature golf; cafes. Fee for activities. (Daily) S on I-15, 53rd St S exit, W to 700

West, then N to 4998 S 360 West, in Murray. Phone 801/265-3866.

Utah Opera Company. Grand opera. (Oct-May) 50 W 200 South St. Phone 801/736-6868.

Wasatch-Cache National Forest. High Uintas Wilderness Area has alpine lakes and rugged peaks; Big Cottonwood, Little Cottonwood, and Logan canyons. Forest (one million acres) has fishing, boating; deer and elk hunting, winter sports, picnicking, camping (fees). E via I-80; or N via US 89; Lone Peak Wilderness Area, 20 mi SE. Contact the Supervisor, 8230 Federal Building, 125 S State St, 84138; Phone 801/524-3900. **FREE**

Wheeler Historic Farm. Living history farm (75 acres) depicts rural life from 1890 to 1918. Farmhouse, farm buildings; animals, crops; hay rides (fee). Tour (fee). Visitors can feed animals, gather eggs, milk cows. (Daily; no rides Sun) 6351 S 900 East St, 15 mi SE on I-15, exit I-215. Phone 801/264-2241. ¢¢

ZCMI (Zion's Co-operative Mercantile Institution) Center. Department store established in 1868 by Brigham Young anchors this 85-store, enclosed, downtown shopping mall. (Mon-Sat) 36 S State St. Phone 801/321-8745. **FREE**

Special Events

Utah Arts Festival. Downtown. More than 1,000 participants, 90 performing groups; Children's Art Yard, juried show with demonstrations. Ethnic food. Last wk June. Phone 801/322-2428.

"Days of '47" Celebration. Mid-July.

Utah State Fair. State Fair Park. Phone 801/538-FAIR. Mid-Sept.

Motels/Motor Lodges

★★ **BEST WESTERN EXECUTIVE INN.** 280 W 72nd S (84047). 801/566-4141; fax 801/566-5142; res 800/327-2803. www.bestwesternexec inn.com. 92 rms, 2 story. Late Dec-Mar: S, D $59-$89; each addl $5; suites $79-$149; under 18 free; lower rates rest of yr. Crib $4. TV. Heated pool; whirlpool. Complimentary continental bkfst. Restaurant adj 6 am-midnight. Ck-out noon. Meeting rms. Business servs avail. In-rm modem link. Coin lndry. Downhill ski 15 mi; x-country ski 20 mi. Health club privileges. Many refrigerators; microwaves avail. Balconies. Cr cds: A, C, D, DS, JCB, MC, V.

D ⚡ ☷ ☷ ☷ SC

★★ **BEST WESTERN SALT LAKE PLAZA HOTEL.** *122 W South Temple St. (84101). 801/521-0130; fax 801/322-5057; res 800/780-7234. www.bestwestern.com.* 226 rms, 13 story. S, D $69-$119; each addl $10; suites $159-$269; under 18 free. Crib free. Pet accepted; $10. TV; cable. Heated pool; whirlpool. Coffee in rms. Restaurant 6 am-11 pm. Rm serv. Ck-out noon. Coin lndry. Valet serv. Bellhops. Concierge. Meeting rms. Business servs avail. In-rm modem link. Gift shop. Exercise equipt. Airport transportation. Some refrigerators. Cr cds: A, C, D, DS, JCB, MC, V.

D ☷ ☷ ☷ ☷ ☷ ☷ ☷ SC

★ **BRIGHTON SKI RESORT.** *Star Rte, Brightow (84121). 801/532-4731; fax 801/649-1787; toll-free 800/873-5512.* 22 rms, 2 story. Mid-Nov-mid-Apr: S, D $50-$120; lower rates rest of yr. TV rm. Heated pool; whirlpool. Bar. Ck-out 11:30 am. Downhill/x-country ski on site. Refrigerators. Picnic tables, grills. On creek. Cr cds: A, DS, MC, V.

D ⚡ ☷ ☷ ☷

★★ **COMFORT INN.** *200 N Admiral Byrd Rd (84116). 801/537-7444; fax 801/532-4721; res 800/228-5150. www.slccomfortinn.com.* 155 rms, 4 story. S, D $69-$139; each addl $10; under 18 free. Crib free. Pet accepted; $15. TV. Heated pool; whirlpool. Restaurant 6:30-9:30 am, 11 am-2 pm, 5-11 pm. Rm serv. Ck-out 11 am. Meeting rms. Business servs avail. Valet serv. Free airport transportation. Exercise equipt. Some refrigerators; microwaves avail. Some balconies. Cr cds: A, D, DS, MC, V.

☷ ⚡ ☷ ☷ SC ☷

★★ **COMFORT INN.** *8955 S 255 W, Sandy (84070). 801/255-4919; fax 801/255-4998; res 800/228-5150. www.comfortinn.com.* 97 rms, 2 story. S, D $64.99-$79.99; each addl $5; under 18 free. Crib $10. TV; cable (premium), VCR avail (movies $2). Indoor pool; whirlpool. Compli-

mentary continental bkfst. Ck-out noon. Meeting rm. Business servs avail. In-rm modem link. Cr cds: A, DS, MC, V.

☷ ☷ ☷ SC

★★ **COUNTRY INN AND SUITES.** *3422 S Decker Lake Dr, West Valley City (84119). 801/908-0311; fax 801/908-0315; res 800/456-4000. www.countryinns.com.* 82 rms, 3 story, 49 suites. S $79-$89; D $79-$97; each addl $8; suites $89-$97; under 18 free; wkend rates. Crib free. TV; cable. Complimentary continental bkfst. Complimentary coffee in rms. Restaurant adj 11 am-11 pm. Ck-out noon. Meeting rms. Business servs avail. In-rm modem link. Coin lndry. Free airport transportation. Indoor pool; whirlpools. Refrigerator, microwave in suites. Cr cds: A, C, D, DS, MC, V.

D ☷ ☷ ☷ ☷ SC

★★ **COURTYARD BY MARRIOTT.** *10701 S Holiday Park Dr, Sandy (93515). 801/571-3600; fax 801/572-1383; toll-free 800/321-2211. www.courtyard.com.* 124 rms, 4 story. S, D $69-$109; each addl $10; suites $150-$155; under 18 free; wkend, hol rates; ski plan. Crib free. TV; cable (premium). Indoor pool; whirlpool. Complimentary coffee in rms. Restaurant 6:30-10:30 am, 5-10 pm. Rm serv. Bar 5-10 pm. Ck-out noon. Coin lndry. Meeting rms. Business servs avail. Exercise equipt. Health club privileges. Microwaves avail. Some balconies. Cr cds: A, C, D, DS, MC, V.

D ☷ ☷ SC ☷

★ **DAYS INN AIRPORT.** *1900 W North Temple (84116). 801/539-8538; fax 801/595-1041; res 800/329-7466. www.daysinn.com.* 110 rms, 2 story. S, D $58-$105; each addl $7; suites $98-$125; under 17 free. Crib free. Pet accepted. TV; cable (premium). Indoor pool. Complimentary continental bkfst. Restaurant nearby. Ck-out 11 am. Business servs avail. In-rm modem link. Valet serv. Guest lndry. Free airport, RR station, bus depot transportation. Exercise equipt. Health club privileges. Refrigerators, microwaves. Cr cds: A, C, D, DS, JCB, MC, V.

D ⚡ ☷ ☷ ☷ ☷ ☷ SC

★★★ FOUR POINTS BY SHERA-TON AIRPORT HOTEL & CONFER-ENCE CENTER. *307 N Admiral Byrd Rd (84116). 801/530-0088; 800/325-3535. www.fourpoints.com.* 98 rms, 3 story. S, D $145-$250; each addl $20; under 17 free. Crib $15. TV; cable (premium), VCR avail. Pool. Complimentary coffee, newspaper in rms. Restaurant 6 am-10 pm. Ck-out noon. Meeting rms. Business center. Gift shop. Exercise rm. Some refrigerators. Cr cds: A, C, D, DS, MC, V.

★★ HAMPTON INN. *10690 S Holiday Park Dr, Sandy (84070). 801/571-0800; fax 801/572-0708; res 800/426-7866. www.hamptoninn.com.* 131 rms, 4 story. S, D $78-$88; under 18 free; wkly rates, ski plans. Crib free. TV; cable (premium). Indoor pool; whirlpool. Complimentary continental bkfst. Restaurant adj 6 am-11 pm. Ck-out noon. Coin lndry. Meeting rms. Business servs avail. In-rm modem link. Sundries. Free bus depot transportation. Downhill ski 14 mi. Exercise equipt. Health club privileges. Microwaves avail. Shopping center adj. Cr cds: A, D, DS, MC, V.

★★ HAMPTON INN. *2393 S 800 W, Woods Cross (84087). 801/296-1211; fax 801/296-1222; toll-free 888/834-4470. www.hamptoninn.com.* 60 rms, 3 story. S $69; D $74; suites $129; under 18 free. Crib free. Pet accepted. TV; cable (premium). Indoor pool; whirlpool. Complimentary continental bkfst. Restaurant nearby. Ck-out noon. Meeting rms. Business servs avail. In-rm modem link. Coin lndry. Free airport transportation. Health club privileges. Microwaves avail. Cr cds: A, C, D, DS, MC, V.

★★ HOLIDAY INN DOWNTOWN. *999 S Main St (84111). 801/359-8600; fax 801/359-7186; toll-free 800/933-9678. saltlakeholidayinn.com.* 292 rms, 3 story, 14 suites. S, D $89; each addl $10; under 18 free. Crib free. TV; cable, VCR avail. Indoor/outdoor pool; whirlpool. Playground. Restaurants 6 am-2 pm, 5-10 pm. Rm serv. Bar. Ck-out noon. Coin lndry. Convention facilities. Business center. Bellhops. Concierge. Gift shop. Free airport, RR station, bus depot transportation. Tennis. Exercise equipt;

sauna. Basketball court. Lawn games. Some refrigerators. Wet bar in suites. Cr cds: A, C, D, DS, JCB, MC, V.

★★ LA QUINTA INN. *7231 S Catalpa Rd, Midvale (84047). 801/566-3291; fax 801/562-5943; 800/531-5900. www.laquinta.com.* 122 rms, 2 story. S $69; D $77; each addl $8; under 18 free. Crib free. Pet accepted. TV; cable (premium). Heated pool. Continental bkfst. Complimentary coffee in rms. Restaurant adj open 24 hrs. Ck-out noon. Coin lndry. In-rm modem link. Downhill ski 15 mi; x-country ski 20 mi. Health club privileges. Microwaves avail. Cr cds: A, C, D, DS, JCB, MC, V.

★★ QUALITY INN-MIDVALLEY. *4465 Century Dr S (84123). 801/268-2533; fax 801/266-6206; res 800/228-5151. www.sunbursthospitality.com.* 131 rms, 2 story. Feb-Mar, July-Sept: S, D $65.95-$79.95; under 18 free; each addl $5; ski plan; lower rates rest of yr. Crib free. Pet accepted; $7/day. TV; cable (premium). Pool; whirlpool. Complimentary continental bkfst. Restaurant adj open 24 hrs. Ck-out noon. Coin lndry. Business servs avail. In-rm modem link. Balconies. Cr cds: A, C, D, DS, JCB, MC, V.

★★ RAMADA INN DOWNTOWN. *230 W 600 S (84101). 801/364-5200; fax 801/359-2542; res 800/272-6232. www.ramadainnslc.com.* 160 rms, 2 story. S, D $59.95-$69.95; each addl $10; under 19 free. Crib free. Pet accepted, some restrictions; $10 deposit. TV; cable. Indoor pool; whirlpool. Restaurant 6 am-10 pm; Sun 6:30 am-9 pm. Rm serv. Private club from 5 pm. Ck-out noon. Coin lndry. Meeting rms. Business servs avail. In-rm modem link. Valet serv. Free airport, RR station, bus depot transportation. Exercise equipt; sauna. Game rm. Rec rm. Microwaves avail. Cr cds: A, D, DS, MC, V.

★★ SHILO INN. *206 SW Temple St (84101). 801/521-9500; fax 801/359-6527; toll-free 800/222-2244. www.shiloinns.com.* 200 rms, 12 story. S, D $79.95-$125; each addl $12; suites $265-$425; under 12 free. Crib free.

Brigham Young Monument

TV; cable (premium), VCR (movies $3). Heated pool; whirlpool. Complimentary full bkfst. Coffee in rms. Restaurant 6 am-10 pm. Ck-out noon. Coin lndry. Meeting rms. Business servs avail. Gift shop. Free airport transportation. Exercise equipt; sauna. Wet bars, refrigerators, microwaves; some bathrm phones. Cr cds: A, D, DS, MC, V.

D ≈ 🕺 ✈ 🔌 🔥 SC

★ **SLEEP INN.** *10626 S 300 W, South Jordan (84095). 801/572-2020; fax 801/572-2459; res 800/753-3746. www.sleepinn.com.* 68 rms, shower only, 2 story. S $59-$69; D $65-$75; each addl $5; family rates. Crib free. TV; cable (premium), VCR (movies). Indoor pool. Complimentary continental bkfst. Restaurant nearby. Ck-out noon. Coin lndry. Business servs avail. In-rm modem link. Downhill ski 20 mi. Health club privileges. Cr cds: A, DS, MC, V.

D 🐾 🔌 🔥 ≈

★ **SUPER 8.** *616 S 200 W (84101). 801/534-0808; fax 801/355-7735; res 800/800-8000.* 120 rms, 4 story. S

$45.99; D $55.99; under 13 free; package plans; higher rates special events. Crib free. TV; cable (premium). Complimentary coffee in lobby. Restaurant nearby. Ck-out 11 am. Business servs avail. Sundries. Coin lndry. Some refrigerators, microwaves. Cr cds: A, C, D, DS, MC, V.

D 🕺 🔌 🔥 SC

★ **TRAVELODGE.** *524 SW Temple St (84101). 801/531-7100; fax 801/359-3814; toll-free 800/578-7878. www.travelodge.com.* 60 rms, 3 story. S $50-$72; D $58-$79; each addl $6; under 18 free. Crib free. Pet accepted. TV; cable (premium). Heated pool; whirlpool. Complimentary coffee in rms. Restaurant nearby. Ck-out noon. Business servs avail. Cr cds: A, D, DS, MC, V.

🐾 ≈ 🔌 🔥 SC

Hotels

★★ **CRYSTAL INN.** *2254 W City Center Ct, West Valley City (84119). 801/736-2000; fax 801/736-2001; toll-free 888/977-9400. www.crystalinns. com.* 122 rms, 3 story. S, D $69-$109; each addl $10; suites $129; under 18 free; wkend rates. Crib free. TV; cable (premium), VCR (movies). Complimentary full bkfst. Complimentary coffee in rms. Ck-out noon. Meeting rms. Business servs avail. In-rm modem link. Coin lndry. Free airport, RR station transportation. Indoor pool. Bathrm phones, refrigerators, microwaves. Cr cds: A, C, D, DS, MC, V.

D ≈ ✈ 🔌 🔥 SC

★★ **CRYSTAL INN - DOWNTOWN.** *230 W 500 S (84101). 801/328-4466; fax 801/328-4072; toll-free 800/366-4466. www.crystalinns. com.* 175 rms, 4 story. S, D $89-$149; each addl $10; under 18 free; ski plan. Crib free. TV; cable. Indoor pool; whirlpool. Complimentary full bkfst. Restaurant adj open 24 hrs. Ck-out noon. Coin lndry. Meeting rms. Business servs avail. In-rm modem link. Sundries. Valet serv.

Free airport transportation. Exercise equipt; sauna. Refrigerators, microwaves; some wet bars. Cr cds: A, C, D, DS, MC, V.

D ⛵ 🏋 ⛷ 🛁 SC

★★★★ **THE GRAND AMERICA.** *555 S Main St (84111). 801/258-6000; fax 801/258-6811; toll-free 800/453-9450. www.grandamerica.com.* Located in the heart of Salt Lake City, this majestic property provides breathtaking views of the Wasatch and Oquirrh Mountains and the Salt Lake Valley. The elegant guest rooms are decorated in old-world style: French cherry wood furniture, English wool carpets, and Italian marble bathrooms. 775 rms, 24 story. S, D $195-$250; each addl $20; under 17 free. Crib avail. Indoor pool. TV; cable (premium), VCR avail. Complimentary coffee, newspaper in rms. Restaurant 6 am-10 pm. Ck-out noon. Meeting rms. Business center. Gift shop. Exercise rm. Tennis. Golf. Some refrigerators, minibars. Cr cds: A, C, D, DS, MC, V.

D 🏂 🏋 ⛷ 🛁 🏊 🏋 ⛵ 🏋

★★★ **HILTON SALT LAKE AIRPORT.** *5151 Wiley Post Way (84116). 801/539-1515; fax 801/539-1113; toll-free 800/999-3736. www.hilton.com.* 287 rms, 5 story. Jan-Oct: S $79-$169; D $89-$179; each addl $10; suites $189-$299; under 18 free; family rates; pkg plans; lower rates rest of yr. Crib free. Pet accepted; $50 deposit. TV; cable (premium), VCR avail (movies). Complimentary coffee in rms. Restaurant 6 am-11 pm. Bar 4:30 pm-midnight. Ck-out 1 pm. Convention facilities. Business center. Concierge. Gift shop. Coin lndry. Free airport, RR station transportation. 9-hole golf, putting green. Exercise equipt. 2 pools, 1 indoor; whirlpool. Some in-rm whirlpools; refrigerators avail. Balconies avail. Picnic tables. Luxury level. Cr cds: A, D, DS, JCB, MC, V.

D 🏂 ⛵ 🏋 🏋 ⛵ 🏋 ✈ 🛁 🏊

★★★ **HILTON SALT LAKE CITY CENTER.** *255 S W Temple (84101). 801/328-2000; fax 801/238-4888; toll-free 800/445-8667. www.hilton. com.* 500 rms, 18 story. S, D $129-$170; each addl $20; suites $300-$450; under 18 free; wkend rates. Crib free. Pet accepted. TV; VCR avail. Indoor pool; whirlpool, poolside serv. Complimentary coffee in rms. Restaurant (see also SPENCER'S). Private club. Ck-out noon. Convention facilities. Business center. In-rm modem link. Concierge. Gift shop. Covered parking; valet. Airport, RR station, bus depot transportation avail. Exercise equipt; sauna. Some refrigerators. Luxury level. Cr cds: A, D, DS, MC, V.

D 🏂 ⛵ 🏋 ✈ 🛁 🏊 SC 🏋

★★★ **HOTEL MONACO.** *15 W 200 S (84101). 801/595-0000; fax 801/532-8500; toll-free 877/294-9710. www.monaco-saltlakecity.com.* 225 rms, 15 story, 36 suites. Jan-Apr, June, Aug-Sept: S, D $129-$325; suites $225-$260; under 18 free; lower rates rest of yr. Crib avail. Pet accepted. Valet parking. TV; cable. Complimentary coffee in rms, newspaper. Restaurant 7 am-11 pm. Bar. Ck-out noon. Meeting rms. Bellhops. Dry cleaning. Exercise equipt. Golf. Tennis. Downhill skiing. Picnic facilities. Cr cds: A, C, D, DS, JCB, MC, V.

D 🏂 ⛵ 🏋 🏋 🏋 ✈ 🛁 🏊 SC

★★★ **INN AT TEMPLE SQUARE.** *71 W S Temple (84101). 801/531-1000; fax 801/536-7272; toll-free 800/843-4668. www.theinn.com.* 90 rms, 7 story, 10 suites. S, D $115-$130; each addl $10; suites $170; under 18 free. Crib free. TV; cable, VCR avail. Pool privileges. Complimentary bkfst buffet. Dining rm 6:30-9:30 am, 11:30 am-2:30 pm, 5-10 pm. Rm serv. Ck-out noon. Business servs avail. Bellhops. Valet serv. Concierge. Free airport, RR station, bus depot transportation. Health club privileges. Bathrm phones, refrigerators. Elegant inn built in 1930; antiques from old Hotel Utah. Opp Temple Square. Totally nonsmoking. Cr cds: A, D, DS, MC, V.

D ✈ 🛁 🏊

★★★ **LA EUROPA ROYALE.** *1135 E Vine St (84121). 801/263-7999; fax 801/263-8090; toll-free 800/523-8767. www.laeuropa.com.* 9 rms, 2 story, 9 suites. Dec-Apr: S, D $130-$230; lower rates rest of yr. Crib $10. Valet parking. TV; cable (premium), VCR avail. Complimentary full bkfst, coffee in rms, newspaper, toll-free calls. Restaurant 7 am-10 pm. Bar. Ck-out noon. Meeting rms. Business center. Bellhops. Concierge serv. Dry cleaning, coin lndry. Airport transportation avail. Exercise equipt. Downhill skiing. Bike rentals. Hiking trail. Picnic facilities. Cr cds: A, C, D, DS, MC, V.

D ⛷ ✈ ⇌ 🏃 ✈ ⊠ 🏊 🚶

★ ★ ★ **LITTLE AMERICA HOTEL AND TOWERS.** *500 S Main St (84101). 801/363-6781; fax 801/596-5911; toll-free 800/453-9450. little america.com.* 850 rms, 17 story. S $75; D $85; suites $800; under 13 free. Crib free. TV; cable (premium). 2 pools, 1 indoor; wading pool, whirlpool. Restaurant 5 am-midnight; dining rm 7-10 am, 11 am-2 pm, 5-11 pm. Bar noon-midnight; entertainment. Ck-out 1 pm. Convention facilities. Business servs avail. Barber, beauty shop. Free covered parking. Free airport, RR station, bus depot transportation. Exercise equipt; sauna. Health club privileges. Many bathrm phones, refrigerators. Garden setting on 10 acres. Cr cds: A, C, D, DS, MC, V.

D ⇌ 🏃 ✈ ⊠ 🏊

★ ★ ★ **MARRIOTT CITY CENTER-SALT LAKE CITY.** *220 S State St (84111). 801/961-8700; fax 801/961-8704; 800/228-9290. www.marriott. com.* 359 rms, 12 story. S, D $150-$225; each addl $20; under 17 free. Crib free. Indoor pool. TV; cable (premium), VCR avail. Complimentary coffee, newspaper in rms. Restaurant 6 am-10 pm. Ck-out noon. Meeting rms. Business center. Gift shop. Exercise rm. Golf, tennis nearby. Some refrigerators, minibars. Cr cds: A, C, D, DS, MC, V.

D 🏃 🍴 ⇌ ⊠ 🏊 SC 🏃 ⛷ 🏃

★ ★ ★ **MARRIOTT DOWNTOWN SALT LAKE CITY.** *75 S West Temple (84101). 801/531-0800; fax 801/532-4127; res 800/228-9290. www. marriott.com/slcut/.* 515 rms, 15 story. S $109-$135; D $119-$145; suites $250-$850; family rates; package plans. Crib free. TV; cable (premium). Heated indoor/outdoor pool; whirlpool, poolside serv. Complimentary coffee in rms. Restaurant 6:30 am-11 pm; Fri, Sat to midnight. Private club. Ck-out noon. Coin lndry. Convention facilities. Business center. In-rm modem link. Concierge. Covered valet parking. Airport transportation avail. Exercise equipt; sauna. Balconies. Inside access to shopping

mall. Luxury level. Cr cds: A, C, D, DS, ER, JCB, MC, V.

D ⛷ 🏃 ⇌ 🏃 ✈ ⊠ 🏊 🚶

★ ★ ★ **MARRIOTT UNIVERSITY PARK SALT LAKE CITY.** *480 Wakara Way (84108). 801/581-1000; fax 801/584-3321; toll-free 800/637-4390. www.marriott.com.* 218 rms, 7 story, 29 suites. S, D $125-$195; suites $145-$205; under 12 free. Crib free. TV; cable (premium). Indoor pool; whirlpool. Restaurant 6:30 am-10 pm. Bar 4 pm-midnight. Ck-out noon. Meeting rms. Business center. Gift shop. Free airport, RR station, bus depot transportation. Downhill/x-country ski 15 mi. Exercise equipt. Rec rm. Refrigerators, wet bar; microwave in suites. Cr cds: A, D, DS, MC, V.

D 🏃 ⇌ 🏃 ✈ ⊠ 🏊 🚶

★ ★ **PEERY HOTEL.** *110 W 300 S (84101). 801/521-4300; fax 801/575-5014; toll-free 800/331-0073. www. peeryhotel.com.* 73 rms, 3 story. S, D $99-$149; under 16 free; wknd rates. TV; cable (premium). Restaurant. Bar. Ck-out 11 am. Meeting rms. Concierge. Airport transportation avail. Exercise equipt. Historic building (1910). Cr cds: A, C, DS, MC, V.

D ⊠ 🏊 SC 🏃

★ ★ ★ **RADISSON HOTEL SALT LAKE CITY AIRPORT.** *2177 W North Temple (84116). 801/364-5800; fax 801/364-5823; res 800/333-3333. www.radisson.com.* 126 rms, 3 story, 46 suites. S, D $89-$159; each addl $10; suites $109-$159; under 18 free; ski, golf plans. Crib free. TV; cable (premium). Heated pool. Complimentary continental bkfst. Complimentary coffee in rms. Restaurant 6:30-10 am, 11:30 am-2 pm, 5-10 pm; Sat, Sun 6:30-11 am. Rm serv. Ck-out noon. Meeting rms. Business servs avail. Bellhops. Free garage parking. Free airport, RR station, bus depot transportation. Exercise equipt. Bathrm phones, refrigerators, wet bars; some fireplaces; microwaves avail. Balconies. Cr cds: A, C, D, DS, ER, JCB, MC, V.

D ⇌ 🏃 ✈ ⊠ 🏊 SC

★ ★ ★ **SHERATON CITY CENTRE.** *150 W 500 South (84101). 801/401-2000; fax 801/531-0705; 800/325-*

3535. www.sheraton.com. 362 rms, 10 story. S, D $89-$159; each addl $10; suites $195-$399; ski plans. Crib free. Pet accepted, some restrictions; $50 deposit. TV; cable (premium), VCR avail. Pool; whirlpool, poolside serv. Restaurant 6 am-11:30 pm. Private club 11:30 am-midnight, Sun 5-10 pm. Ck-out noon. Convention facilities. Business center. In-rm modem link. Barber, beauty shop. Free airport transportation. Exercise equipt; sauna. Health club privileges. Ski rentals avail. Balconies. Luxury level. Cr cds: A, C, D, DS, JCB, MC, V.

★★ **WYNDHAM HOTEL.** 215 W S Temple (84101). 801/531-7500; fax 801/328-1289; toll-free 800/553-0075. www.wyndham.com. 381 rms, 15 story. S, D $79-$179; each addl $10; suites $179-$550; under 18 free; wkend, hol rates; ski pkgs. TV; cable (premium). Indoor pool; whirlpool. Coffee in rms. Restaurant 6 am-10 pm. Bar 3 pm-midnight. Ck-out noon. Convention facilities. Business center. In-rm modem link. Concierge. Gift shop. Airport, RR station transportation avail. Exercise equipt; sauna. Health club privileges. Microwaves avail. Adj to Delta Center. Cr cds: A, C, D, DS, ER, JCB, MC, V.

B&Bs/Small Inns

★★★ **ARMSTRONG MANSION.** 667 E 100 S (84102). 801/531-1333; fax 801/531-0282; toll-free 800/708-1333. www.armstrongmansion.com. 13 rms, 4 with shower only, 3 story. S, D $99-$229. TV; cable, VCR. Complimentary full bkfst. Restaurant nearby. Ck-out 11 am, ck-in 3 pm. Luggage handling. Downhill/x-country ski 20 mi. Built in 1893; antiques. Totally nonsmoking. Cr cds: A, MC, V.

★★★ **BRIGHAM STREET INN.** 1135 E South Temple St (84102). 801/364-4461; fax 801/521-3201. www.brightonstreetinn.citysearch.com. 9 rms, 3 story. S, D $85-$185; each addl $10. Crib free. TV; cable, VCR avail. Complimentary continental bkfst. Setups. Ck-out 11 am, ck-in 3 pm. Business servs avail. X-country

ski 15 mi. Fireplace in 5 rms. Cr cds: A, MC, V.

★★★ **SALTAIR BED AND BREAKFAST.** 164 S 900 E (84102). 801/533-8184; fax 801/595-0332; toll-free 800/733-8184. www.saltlakebandb.com. 8 rms, 3 share baths, 2 with shower only, 2 story, 3 suites. Some rm phones. S, D $55-$149; each addl $15; suites $129-$225. TV in some rms; cable (premium), VCR avail (movies). Complimentary full bkfst; afternoon refreshments. Restaurant nearby. Ck-out 11 am, ck-in 3:30 pm. X-country ski 15 mi. Health club privileges. Whirlpool. Some refrigerators, microwaves, fireplaces. Built in 1903; antiques. Totally nonsmoking. Cr cds: A, D, DS, MC, V.

★★ **WILDFLOWER BED & BREAKFAST.** 936 E 1700 South (84105). 801/466-0600; fax 801/466-4728; toll-free 800/569-0009. www.wildflowersbb.com. 5 rms, 3 story. No elvtr. S, D $85-$125; kit. unit $130-$175; under 12 free. TV; cable (premium), VCR avail. Crib free. Complimentary full bkfst. Restaurant nearby. Ck-out 11 am, ck-in 3 pm. Business servs avail. Built in 1891; antiques. Totally nonsmoking. Cr cds: A, DS, MC, V.

All Suites

★★ **CHASE SUITE HOTEL BY WOODFIN.** 765 E 400 S (84102). 801/532-5511; fax 801/531-0416; toll-free 800/237-8811. www.woodfinsuitehotels.com. 128 kit. suites (1-2-bedrm), 2 story. S, D $99-$199; Suites $159-$199; wkly, monthly rates; ski packages. Pet accepted. TV; cable (premium). Heated pool. Complimentary continental bkfst. Ck-out noon. Coin lndry. Business servs avail. In-rm modem link. Bellhops. Valet serv. Free airport, RR station, bus depot transportation. Microwaves; many fireplaces. Sport court. Cr cds: A, C, D, DS, JCB, MC, V.

★★★ **EMBASSY SUITES.** 110 W 600 S (84101). 801/359-7800; fax 801/359-3753; res 800/362-2779. www.embassy-suites.com. 241 suites, 9 story. S $89-$149; each addl $15; under 18 free; wkend, ski rates. Crib free. TV; cable (premium). Indoor pool; whirlpool. Complimentary full bkfst. Complimentary coffee in rms. Restaurant 11 am-11 pm. Private club to 1 am. Ck-out noon. Coin lndry. Meeting rms. In-rm modem link. Gift shop. Covered parking. Free airport, RR station, bus depot transportation. Exercise equipt; sauna. Refrigerators, wet bars, microwaves. Atrium lobby. Cr cds: A, D, DS, MC, V.

Restaurants

★★ **ABSOLUTE.** *52 W 200 S (84101). 801/359-0899. www. citysearch.com/slc/absolute.* Specializes in garlic-baked jumbo prawns, filet mignon cashew sea bass. Hrs: 11:30 am-10 pm, Sat 5-10 pm. Res accepted. Bar. Lunch $5-$12; dinner $13-$29. Child's menu. Entertainment. Cr cds: A, C, D, DS, MC, V. D

★★ **BABA AFGHAN.** *55 E 400 S (84111). 801/596-0786.* Hrs: 11:30 am-2:30 pm, 5-9:30 pm; Mon to 2:30 pm; Sat, Sun from 5 pm. Closed some hols. Res accepted (dinner). Afghan menu. Dinner $7.95-$14.95. Buffet: lunch $6.50. Specializes in lamb, beef, chicken. Own baking. Street parking. Afghani clothing display. Totally nonsmoking. Cr cds: A, D, DS, MC, V. D

★★ **BACI TRATTORIA.** *134 W Pierpont Ave (84101). 801/328-1500. www.gastronomy.com.* Hrs: 11:30 am-3 pm, 5-10 pm; Fri, Sat to 11 pm. Closed Sun; major hols. Italian menu. Bar. A la carte entrees: lunch $6.99-$16.99, dinner $7.99-$26.99. Specializes in fresh pasta, fresh seafood. Outdoor dining (summer). Large stained-glass partitions. Wood-burning pizza oven. Cr cds: A, C, D, DS, MC, V.

★★ **BAMBARA.** *202 S Main St (84101). 801/363-5454.* Menu changes monthly. Hrs: 7-10 am, 11:30 am-2:30 pm, 5:30-10 pm; Fri, Sat 5:30-11 pm. Res accepted. Serv bar. Bkfst $4-$6; lunch $9-$11; dinner $9-$28. Cr cds: A, D, DS, MC, V. D

★ **BENIHANA OF TOKYO.** *165 S West Temple St (84101). 801/322-2421. www.benihana.com.* Hrs: 11:30 am-2 pm, 5-9:30 pm; Fri, Sat 5-10:30 pm; Sun, hols to 9 pm. Res accepted. Japanese menu. Bar. Lunch $5.50-$14, dinner $12.50-$27.50. Child's menu. Specializes in seafood, steak, chicken. Tableside cooking. Japanese decor. Cr cds: A, C, D, DS, ER, MC, V. D

★ **COWBOY GRUB.** *2350 1/2 Foothill Blvd (84109). 801/466-8334. www.cowboygrub.net.* Hrs: 11 am-10 pm; Fri, Sat to 11 pm. Closed Sun; major hols; also July 24. Lunch, dinner $5-$15. Child's menu. Specializes in pot roast, Mexican dishes. Salad bar. Western decor. Cr cds: A, D, DS, MC, V. D

★★ **CREEKSIDE AT SOLITUDE.** *12000 Big Cottonwood Canyon, Solitude (84121). 435/649-8400. www. skisolitude.com.* Hrs: 8 am-9 pm. Res accepted (dinner). Continental menu. Lunch $7-$12, dinner $12-$20. Child's menu. Specializes in fresh seafood, pasta, wood-burning dishes. Own pasta. Jazz Fri. Outdoor dining. Mediterranean decor; windows overlook pond, ski slopes. Cr cds: A, D, DS, MC, V. D

★ **CUCINA.** *1026 E 2nd Ave (84103). 801/322-3055. www.cucinadeli.com.* Specializes in salmon, chicken, pork. Hrs: 8 am-7 pm; Sat to 6 pm; Sun 9 am-3 pm (winter); (summer) Mon-Fri 7 am-9 pm; Sat 8 am-9 pm; Sun 9 am-5 pm. Res accepted. Lunch, dinner $4.99-$9.49. Brunch $4.99-$9.49. Cr cds: A, MC, V. D

★★ **DESERT EDGE PUB.** *273 Charlie Sq (84102). 801/521-8918.* Hrs: 11 am-midnight; Thurs-Sat to 1 am; Sun noon-10 pm. Closed Dec 25. Contemporary Amer menu. Bar. Lunch, $3.95-$8.95, dinner $2.25-$10.95. Specializes in pasta, sandwiches, salads. Own pastas, beer. Outdoor dining. Informal, casual atmosphere; microbrewery. Cr cds: A, C, DS, ER, MC, V. D

★★★ **FRESCO ITALIAN CAFI.** *1513 S 1500 E (84105). 801/486-1300.* Menu changes seasonally. Hrs: 5-10 pm. Res accepted. Serv bar. Dinner $17-$23. Specialties: polenta, gnocchi with crab. Cr cds: A, C, D, DS, MC, V.

★★★ **LA CAILLE.** *9565 S Wasatch Blvd, Sandy (84092). 801/942-1751. www.lacaille.com.* Specializes in rack of lamb. Hrs: 6-10 pm; Sun brunch 10 am-1 pm. Res accepted. Wine, beer. Dinner $39-$53. Sun brunch $32. Cr cds: A, C, D, DS, ER, MC, V. D

★★★ **LOG HAVEN.** *6451 E 3800 S (84109). 801/272-8255. www.log-haven.com.* Hrs: 5:30-9 pm. Closed Jan 1, July 4, Dec 25. Res accepted.

Continental menu. Bar. Wine list. Dinner $14-$30. Child's menu. Specialties: seared rare ahi tuna, Mediterranean-style lamb top sirloin, filet mignon. Own baking. Valet parking. Outdoor dining. Renovated 1920 log mansion nestled among pine trees; views of waterfall, natural surroundings. Cr cds: A, C, D, DS, ER, MC, V. D

★★ **MANDARIN.** *348 E 900 N, Bountiful (84010). 801/298-2406. www.mandarinutah.com.* Hrs: 5-9:30 pm; Fri, Sat to 10:30 pm. Closed Sun; most major hols. Res accepted. Chinese menu. Wine, beer. Dinner $7-$13. Specialties: Szechwan shrimp, almond chicken, seasoned beef and beans. Parking. Elegant atmosphere. Unique Chinese decor; murals. Glass

---

SALT LAKE CITY'S MORMON HERITAGE

The centerpiece of downtown Salt Lake City is Temple Square, the city block bordered by three streets named Temple—West, North, and South—and Main Street on the east side. Utah's top tourist attraction, Temple Square is the hub for the Church of Jesus Christ of the Latter-Day Saints, where guests are invited to join a free guided tour that offers a glimpse of several architectural and cultural landmarks, including the Mormon Tabernacle, the Museum of Church History and Art, and the Joseph Smith Memorial Building. (Tours start at the flagpole every few minutes.) If your timing is right, you can also take in a film, choir rehearsal, or organ recital here. From Temple Square, head east on South Temple to a pair of historic homes, the Lion House (63 East South Temple) and the Beehive House (67 East South Temple). No tours are available of the Lion House, which served as Brigham Young's abode during the mid-19th century, but there is a restaurant on the lower level that is a good spot for a lunch break. Next door, the Beehive House, another former Young residence and a National Historic Landmark, offers free tours every day. Just east of these houses on South Temple is Eagle Gate (at the intersection of State Street), an impressive arch capped by a two-ton sculpture of an eagle with a 20-foot wingspan. Just south of Eagle Gate on the east side of State Street are two of Salt Lake City's standout cultural facilities, the Hansen Planetarium (15 South State Street) and the Social Hall Heritage Museum (39 South State Street). The former features daily star shows and a free space museum with hands-on exhibits; the latter includes remnants of Utah's first public building and the West's first theater. From the museum, it's best to reverse course and walk north on State Street, passing under Eagle Gate. Just beyond North Temple, hop on the paths that run through the lush City Creek Park for a break from the urban bustle and head north to the adjoining Memory Grove Park. From here, it's only a two-block walk west to the Utah State Capitol (just north of the intersection of State Street and 300 North Street), an exemplary Renaissance Revival-style structure built from Utah granite in 1915. The building is open to the public daily and guided tours are offered on weekdays. Two blocks west of the State Capitol is the Pioneer Memorial Museum (300 North Main Street), a majestic replica of the original Salt Lake Theater (demolished in 1928) with 38 rooms of relics from the area's past, including photographs, vehicles, dolls, and weapons. The museum is on the eastern edge of one of the city's oldest neighborhoods, the tree-lined Marmalade District (between 300 and 500 North streets to the north and south and Center and Quince streets to the east and west), a good place to meander and gaze at historic homes.

atrium in garden rm. Totally non-smoking. Cr cds: A, MC, V.
Ⓓ

★★ **MARKET STREET BROILER.**
260 S 1300 E (84102). 801/583-8808.
www.gastronomyinc.com. Hrs: 11 am-10 pm; Sun 4-9 pm; early-bird dinner 4-6 pm. Bar from noon. Lunch $4.99-$16.99, dinner $7.99-$29.99. Child's menu. Specializes in fresh fish, barbecued ribs. Outdoor dining. Modern decor in historic former fire station. Cr cds: A, D, MC, V.
Ⓓ

★★ **MARKET STREET GRILL.** *48 Market St (84101). 801/322-4668. www.gastronomyinc.com.* Hrs: 6:30 am-10 pm; Sat 7 am-11 pm; Fri, Sat to 11 pm; Sun 9 am-10 pm; early-bird dinner 3-7 pm; Sun brunch 9 am-3 pm. Closed Labor Day, Thanksgiving, Dec 25. Bar 11:30 am-11:30 pm. Bkfst $3.99-$9.99, lunch $5.99-$17.99, dinner $10.99-$52.99. Sun brunch $3.99-$17.99. Child's menu. Specializes in steak, seafood. In renovated 1906 hotel. Cr cds: A, C, D, DS, ER, MC, V.
Ⓓ

★★★ **METROPOLITAN.** *173 W Broadway (84110). 801/364-3472. www.themetropolitan.citysearch.com.* Hrs: 5-10 pm; Fri, Sat to 11 pm; (summer) 6-9:30 pm; Tues-Sat to 10 pm. Closed Mon, Sun; also Jan 1, Thanksgiving, Dec 25. Res accepted. Contemporary Amer menu. Bar. Wine cellar. A la carte entrees: dinner $18-$36. Complete meal: dinner $55. Specializes in fish, wild game. Own pasta. Own desserts. Street parking. Totally nonsmoking. Cr cds: A, DS, MC, V.
Ⓓ

★★ **MIKADO.** *67 W 100 South St (84101). 801/328-0929.* Hrs: 5:30-9:30 pm; Fri, Sat to 10 pm. Closed major hols. Res accepted. Japanese menu. Dinner $11-$25. Child's menu. Specialties: shrimp tempura, chicken teriyaki, beef sukiyaki. Sushi bar. Zashiki rms. Cr cds: A, D, DS, JCB, MC, V.
Ⓓ

★★★ **NEW YORKER CLUB.** *60 W Market St (84101). 801/363-0166. www.gastronomyinc.com.* Hrs: 11:30

am-10 pm; Sat 5-11 pm. Closed Sun; major hols; July 4. Res accepted. Continental menu. Bar. Wine cellar. Lunch $10-$23, dinner $20-$36. Specializes in fresh seafood, beef, veal. Own desserts. Valet parking. Cr cds: A, C, D, DS, ER, MC, V.

★★ **PIERPONT CANTINA.** *122 W Pierpont Ave (84101). 801/364-1222. www.gastronomyinc.com.* Hrs: 11:30 am-10 pm; Sat 4-11 pm, Sun 10 am-10 pm; early bird 4-7 pm. Closed Jan 1, Thanksgiving, Dec 25. Res accepted. Mexican menu. Bar. Lunch $6.99-$14.99, dinner $7.99-$19. Buffet: $4.99. Child's menu. Specializes in carnitas, seafood. Outdoor dining. Mexican decor. Totally nonsmoking. Cr cds: A, C, D, MC, V.
Ⓓ

★ **RAFAEL'S.** *889 E 9400 S, Sandy (84094). 801/561-4545.* Hrs: 11 am-9 pm; Fri, Sat to 10 pm. Closed Sun; some major hols. Mexican menu. Lunch, dinner $4.50-$10. Specializes in enchiladas, fajitas. Mexican, Indian and Aztec artwork. Cr cds: A, DS, MC, V.
Ⓓ

★★ **RINO'S.** *2302 Parleys Way (84109). 801/484-0901.* Hrs: Dinner: Mon-Sun, hrs vary. Closed major hols. Res accepted. Italian, continental menu. Serv bar. Dinner $10.99-$26.99. Patio dining. Cr cds: A, D, MC, V.
Ⓓ

★★ **RIO GRANDE CAFE.** *270 S Rio Grande St (84101). 801/364-3302. www.riograndecafe.citysearch.com.* Hrs: 11 am-2:30 pm, 5-9:30 pm; Fri to 10:30 pm; Sat 11:30 am-2:30 pm, 5-10:30 pm; Sun 4-9 pm. Closed major hols. Mexican menu. Bar. Lunch, dinner $5-$9. Child's menu. Specializes in carnitas, traditional Mexican dishes. Outdoor dining. In historic Rio Grande Depot also housing RR museum and displays. Totally nonsmoking. Cr cds: A, D, DS, MC, V.
Ⓓ

★★★ **SPENCER'S.** *255 SW Temple St (84101). 801/238-4748. www. spencersforsteaksandchops.com.* Hrs: 11:30-1:30 am; Sat, Sun from 4 pm. Res accepted. Bar. Wine cellar. A la carte entrees: lunch $6.95-$19.95, dinner $14.95-$45.95. Child's menu.

Specializes in steaks, seafood, desserts. Valet parking. Classic Chicago-style steakhouse. Cr cds: A, D, DS, MC, V.

[D]

★ **SQUATTERS PUB BREWERY.** *147 W Broadway (84101). 801/363-2739. www.squatters.com.* Hrs: 11:30-12:30 am; Sun to 11:30 pm. Closed Thanksgiving, Dec 25. Bar. Lunch, dinner $6.99-$13.99. Child's menu. Specializes in burgers, sandwiches. Own baking, pasta. Guitarist Sat, Sun. Turn-of-the-century bldg; microbrewery. Totally nonsmoking. Cr cds: A, C, D, DS, ER, MC, V.

[D]

★ **SUGARHOUSE BARBECUE.** *2207 S 700 East St (84106). 801/463-4800. www.sugarhousebbq.com.* Hrs: 11:30 am-9 pm; Fri, Sat to 10 pm; Sun noon-8 pm. Closed Jan 1, Thanksgiving, Dec 25. Barbecue menu. Beer. Lunch, dinner $4.95-$14.95. Specializes in spare ribs, pulled pork, chicken. Outdoor dining. Features architecture of Southern Utah. Separate motorcycle parking; motorcycle on display indoors. Totally nonsmoking. Cr cds: A, C, D, DS, MC, V.

[D]

★★ **TUCCI'S CUCINA ITALIA.** *4835 S Highland Dr (84117). 801/277-8338.* Hrs: 11:30 am-10 pm; Fri, Sat to 11 pm; Sun noon-9 pm. Closed Thanksgiving, Dec 25. Italian menu. Bar. Lunch $5.95-$9.95, dinner $5.95-$18.95. Child's menu. Specialties: pizza tradizionale, farfalle con sugo blanco, picatta. Outdoor dining. Colorful decor. Totally nonsmoking. Cr cds: A, DS, ER, MC, V.

[D]

★★★ **TUSCANY.** *2832 E 6200 S (84121). 801/277-9919. www.tuscanyslc.com.* Hrs: 11:30 am-2 pm, from 5:30 pm; Sat, Mon 5-10 pm. Res accepted. Italian menu. Bar. Wine list. Lunch $7-$13, dinner $11-$23. Child's menu. Specialties: linguini with clams, pesto-crusted salmon, double-cut pork chop. Own baking, pasta. Valet parking. Outdoor dining. Italian villa decor with several unique dining rms; landscaped, wooded grounds near Big Cotton-

wood Canyon. Cr cds: A, C, D, DS, ER, MC, V.

[D] [SC]

★★ **XIAO LI.** *307 W 200 S #1000 (84101). 801/328-8688.* Hrs: 11:30 am-2:30 pm, 4:30-10 pm; Fri to 11 pm; Sat 4:30-11 pm; Sun 4:30-10 pm. Closed July 4, Dec 25. Chinese menu. Serv bar. A la carte entrees: lunch, dinner $7-$12. Buffet: lunch $8. Specialties: salt and pepper shrimp, house special tofu, eggplant in garlic sauce. Parking. Asian decor. Totally nonsmoking. Cr cds: A, DS, MC, V.

Unrated Dining Spots

ARGENTINE GRILL. *6055 S 900 East (84121). 801/265-0205. www.argentine grill.citysearch.com.* Hrs: 11:30 am-3 pm, 5:30-9 pm; Fri to 10:30 pm; Sun 10 am-9 pm. Res accepted. Continental menu. Wine, beer. Lunch $7-$9, dinner $18-$23. Specialties: potato-crusted salmon, blackberry brandy chicken, Viennese breaded pork. Outdoor dining. Country home atmosphere. Totally nonsmoking. Cr cds: A, D, DS, MC, V.

[D] [SC]

LITZA'S FOR PIZZA. *716 E 400 South St (84102). 801/359-5352.* Hrs: 11 am-11 pm; Fri, Sat to midnight. Closed Sun; Thanksgiving, Dec 25. Italian menu. Lunch $5.15-$11, dinner $8-$15. Specializes in pizza. Cr cds: A, MC, V.

Snowbird

See also Alta, Park City, Salt Lake City

Pop 150 **Area code** 435 **Zip** 84092

What to See and Do

Snowbird Ski and Summer Resort. Seven double chairlifts, high-speed quad, 125-passenger aerial tram; patrol, school, rentals; restaurants, cafeteria, bar, children's center, four lodges. Elevations of 7,900-11,000 ft. (Mid-Nov-early May, daily) Summer activities (June-Oct, daily) incl rock climbing, hiking, mountain biking (rentals), tennis; tram rides; concerts (see SPECIAL EVENTS). On UT 210.

Contact PO Box 929000. Phone 435/742-2222. ¢¢¢¢

Special Event

Utah Symphony. Snowbird Ski and Summer Resort (see). Summer home of the orchestra. Several Sun afternoon concerts. July-Aug. Phone 800/385-2002.

Motel/Motor Lodge

★★★ **LODGE AT SNOWBIRD.** *Snowbird Ski & Summer Resort (84092). 801/933-2229; fax 801/933-2248; toll-free 800/453-3000. www.snowbird.com.* 123 rms, 7 story, 61 kits. No A/C. Late Nov-early May: S, D $229; suites $498; kit. studio rms $269; package plans. Crib free. TV; cable (premium), VCR avail. Heated pool; whirlpool. Saunas. Playground. Restaurant 4-10. Bar 3 pm-1 am. Ck-out 11 am. Coin lndry. Business servs avail. Bellhops. Valet serv. Downhill ski on site; x-country ski 1 mi. Fireplaces. Balconies. Cr cds: A, C, D, DS, MC, V.
🅓 ⚲ ⚲ ⚲ ⚲

Hotel

★★★ **IRON BLOSSOM LODGE.** *Hwy 210 Entry # 2 (84092). 801/742-2222; fax 801/933-2148; toll-free 800/232-9542. www.snowbird.com.* 519 rms, 11 story. Dec-Mar: S, D $229-$289; suites $389-$939; under 12 free; ski packages; lower rates rest of yr. TV; cable, VCR avail. 2 heated pools, whirlpool, poolside serv. Supervised children's activities; ages infant-13. Restaurant. Private club noon-1 am; entertainment. Ck-out 10 am. Coin lndry. Convention facilities. Business center. Concierge. Barber, beauty shop. Free garage; free valet parking. Airport transportation. Tennis. Downhill ski on site; x-country ski 1 mi. Exercise rm; sauna, steam rm. Game rm. Rec rm. Some refrigerators. Some private patios. Picnic tables. Tram allows bicycles. Cr cds: A, D, DS, MC, V.
🅓 ⚲ ⚲ ⚲ ⚲ ⚲ ⚲ ⚲

Restaurant

★★ **STEAK PIT.** *Snowbird Ctr (84092). 801/933-2260. www.snowbird.com.* Hrs: 6-10 pm. No A/C. Serv bar. Dinner $14-$42. Child's menu. Specializes in steak, seafood, chicken. Mountain view. Cr cds: A, C, D, DS, MC, V.
🅓 🆂🅲

Timpanogos Cave National Monument

(X-0) *See also Heber City, Park City, Provo*

(26 mi S of Salt Lake City on I-15, then 10 mi E on UT 92)

Timpanogos (Tim-pa-NOH-gos) Cave National Monument consists of three small, beautifully decorated underground chambers within limestone beds. The cave entrance is on the northern slope of Mount Timpanogos, monarch of the Wasatch Range. Much of the cave interior is covered by a filigree of colorful crystal formations where stalactites and stalagmites are common. However, what makes Timpanogos unique is its large number of helictites—formations that appear to defy gravity as they grow outward from the walls of the cave. Temperature in Timpanogos Cave is a constant 45°F, and the interior is electrically lighted.

The cave's headquarters are located on UT 92, eight miles east of American Fork. There is picnicking at Swinging Bridge Picnic Area, ¼ mile from the headquarters. The cave entrance is 1½ miles from headquarters via a paved trail with a vertical rise of 1,065 feet. Allow three to five hours for guided tour. No pets, no strollers, walking shoes advised, jackets and sweaters needed. Tours limited to 20 people (late May-early September, daily). Purchase tickets in advance by calling 801/756-5238 or 801/756-1679, or at the Visitor Center. Golden Age and Golden Access passports accepted (see MAKING THE MOST OF YOUR TRIP). Contact the Superintendent, Rural Route 3, Box 200, American Fork 84003; 435/756-5238. Cave tours ¢¢

Vernal

See also Roosevelt

Pop 7,714 **Elev** 5,336 ft
Area code 435 **Zip** 84078
Information Dinosaurland Travel
Board, 55 E Main St; 435/789-6932
or 800/477-5558
Web www.dinoland.com

What to See and Do

Ashley National Forest. The High
Uinta Mtns—the only major east-
west range in the US—runs through
the heart of this nearly 1½ million-
acre forest. The 1,500-ft-deep Red
Canyon, the 13,528-ft Kings Peak,
and Sheep Creek Geological Area are
also here. Swimming, fishing, boating (ramps, marinas), whitewater
rafting, canoeing; hiking and nature
trails, x-country skiing, snowmobiling, improved or back country campgrounds (fee). Visitor centers. 15 mi
N on US 191. Contact the Supervisor,
355 N Vernal Ave. Phone 435/789-
1181. **FREE**

**Daughters of Utah Pioneers
Museum.** Relics and artifacts dating
from before 1847, when pioneers
first settled in Utah; period furniture,
quilts, clothing, dolls; early doctor's,
dentist's, and undertaker's instruments; restored Little Rock tithing
office (1887). (June-wkend before
Labor Day, Mon-Sat) 500 W 200 S.
Phone 435/789-3890. **Donation**

Dinosaur National Monument. (see).
122 Canal St. Phone 315/697-3451.
Donation

**Flaming Gorge Dam and National
Recreation Area.** Area surrounds 91-
mi-long Flaming Gorge Reservoir and
502-ft-high Flaming Gorge Dam. Fishing on reservoir and river (all yr), marinas, boat ramps, waterskiing; lodges,
campgrounds (fee). River rafting below
dam. Visitor centers at dam and Red
Canyon (on secondary paved road 3
mi off UT 44). 42 mi N on US 191, in
Ashley National Forest. Contact the
Ranger District office, PO Box 279,
Manila 84046. Phone 435/784-3445.

Ouray National Wildlife Refuge.
Waterfowl nesting marshes; desert
scenery; self-guided auto tour (limited route during hunting season).

(Daily) 30 mi SW on UT 88. Phone
435/789-0351. **FREE**

Red Fleet State Park. Scenic lake
highlighted by red rock formations,
boating, swimming, fishing; camping. Several hundred well-preserved
dinosaur tracks. (Daily) 4335 N US
191. Phone 435/789-4432. **¢**

River trips. Guided whitewater trips
on the Green and Yampa rivers.

> **Adrift Adventures of Dinosaur.**
> Phone 800/824-0150. **¢¢¢¢**
>
> **Hatch River Expeditions.** 55 E
> Main St. Phone 435/789-4316.
> **¢¢¢¢**
>
> **Holiday River and Bike Expedi-
> tions.** Phone 435/266-2087. **¢¢¢¢**

Steinaker State Park. Approx 2,200
acres on west shore of Steinaker
Reservoir. Swimming, waterskiing,
fishing, boating (ramp, dock); picnicking, tent and trailer sites (fee).
(Apr-Nov; fishing all yr) 7 mi N off
US 191. Phone 435/789-4432. **¢¢**

**Utah Field House of Natural History
and Dinosaur Gardens.** Guarded outside by three life-size cement
dinosaurs, this museum has exhibits
of fossils, archaeology, life zones,
geology, and fluorescent minerals of
the region. Adj Dinosaur Gardens
contain 18 life-size model dinosaurs
in natural surroundings. (Daily;
closed Jan 1, Thanksgiving, Dec 25)
235 Main St. Phone 435/789-3799. **¢**

Western Heritage Museum. Houses
memorabilia from Uintah County's
"outlaw" past as well as other artifacts dealing with a western theme.
Incl the Thorne Collection, photographs and artifacts of the ancient
people of Utah. (Mon-Sat; closed
hols) 302 E 200 S. Phone 435/789-
7399. **FREE**

Special Events

Outlaw Trail Festival. Festivals, sporting events, entertainment, theatrical
events. Late June-mid-Aug.

Dinosaur Roundup Rodeo. Mid-July.
Phone 800/421-9635.

Uintah County Fair. Aug.

Motels/Motor Lodges

★ **WESTON PLAZA HOTEL.** *1684
W Hwy 40 (84078).* 435/789-9550;
fax 435/789-4874. 102 rms, 3 story. S,
D $52-$64; each addl $8; suites $149;
under 12 free; wkend rates. TV; cable

(premium). Indoor pool; whirlpool. Continental bkfst. Restaurant 11 am-10 pm. Bar to 1 am; entertainment exc Sun (summer). Ck-out 11 am. Meeting rms. Business servs avail. Cr cds: A, D, MC, V.

★ **WESTON'S LAMPLIGHTER INN.** *120 E Main St (84078). 435/789-0312; fax 435/781-1480.* 167 rms, 2 story. May-Aug: S $36; D $56; each addl $8; under 12 free; lower rates rest of yr. TV; cable (premium). Heated pool. Playground. Restaurant hrs vary. Ck-out 11 am. Business servs avail. Picnic tables, grills. Cr cds: A, D, MC, V.

Restaurant

★ **7-11 RANCH.** *77 E Main St (84078). 435/789-1170.* Hrs: 6 am-11 pm. Closed Sun; Jan 1, Thanksgiving, Dec 25. Res accepted. Bkfst $2-$6.45, lunch $4-$7, dinner $7.50-$12.50. Child's menu. Specializes in prime rib, roasted chicken, barbecue ribs. Western motif; gift shop. Family-owned. Totally nonsmoking. Cr cds: A, DS, MC, V.

Wendover (B-1)

Founded 1907 **Pop** 1,537 **Elev** 4,232 ft **Area code** 435 **Zip** 84083

What to See and Do

Bonneville Salt Flats. This approx 100-sq-mi area of perfectly flat salt, packed as solid as cement, is what remained after ancient Lake Bonneville, which once covered the entire area, retreated to the present-day Great Salt Lake. The area is part of the Great Salt Lake Desert. East of town.

Special Event

Bonneville National Speed Trials. Bonneville Speedway, approx 15 mi E, then N. Held since 1914 on the Bonneville Salt Flats (see), which has been used as a track for racing the world's fastest cars. Car racing in competition and against the clock. Phone 801/526-1805. Aug or Sept.

Zion National Park

(G-2) *See also Cedar City, Kanab, St. George*

(42 mi NE of St. George on UT 9)

The spectacular canyons and enormous rock formations in this 147,551-acre national park are the result of powerful upheavals of the earth and erosion by flowing water and frost. Considered the "grandfather" of Utah's national parks, Zion is one of the nation's oldest national parks and one of the state's wildest, with large sections virtually inaccessible. The Virgin River runs through the interior of the park, and Zion Canyon, with its deep, narrow chasm and multicolored, vertical walls, cuts through the middle, with smaller canyons branching from it like fingers. A paved roadway following the bottom of Zion Canyon is surrounded by massive rock formations in awe-inspiring colors that change with the light. The formations, described as temples, cathedrals, and thrones, rise to great heights—the loftiest reaching 8,726 feet. The canyon road runs seven miles to the Temple of Sinawava, a natural amphitheater surrounded by cliffs. Another route, an extension of UT 9, cuts through the park in an east-west direction, taking visitors through the mile-long Zion-Mount Carmel Tunnel, then descends through a series of switchbacks with viewpoints above Pine Creek Canyon. **Note:** An escort fee is charged for large vehicles to pass through tunnel.

Zion's main visitor center is near the south entrance (daily). Check here for maps, information on the park, and schedules of naturalist activities and evening programs. Each evening, spring through fall, park naturalists give illustrated talks on the natural and human history of the area. Pets must be kept on leash and are not permitted on trails. Vehicle lights should be checked; they must be in proper condition for driving through highway tunnel. The park is open year-round. There is an admission fee of $10/seven-day stay per vehicle; Golden Eagle Passport is accepted (see MAKING THE MOST OF YOUR TRIP). Contact Superintendent, Springdale 84767-1099; 435/772-3256.

What to See and Do

Bicycling. Permitted on roads in park, except through Zion-Mt Carmel Tunnel. Roads are narrow and no designated bicycle routes exist.

Camping. At south entrance to park: South Campground provides 140 tent or trailer sites (mid-Apr-mid-Sept); Watchman Campground provides 229 tent sites and 185 trailer sites (all yr). Lava Point Campground, 26 mi N of Virgin off UT 9, provides a minimal number of tent sites (free; no facilities). South and Watchman campgrounds ¢¢¢

Escorted horseback trips. (Mar-Oct, daily) Special guide service may be obtained for other trips not regularly scheduled. Contact Bryce/Zion Trail Rides at Zion Lodge. Phone 435/772-3967.

"Grand Circle: A National Park Odyssey". Multimedia presentation encompassing four states, 14 national parks and monuments, and numerous state parks and historic sites, plus Glen Canyon National Recreation Area (see PAGE, AZ, and LAKE POWELL, UT) and Monument Valley Navajo Tribal Park (see KAYENTA, AZ). One-hr show (Memorial Day-Labor Day). O. C. Tanner Amphitheatre in Springdale. Phone 435/673-4811. ¢¢

Guided trips, hiking tours. Conducted by ranger naturalists, who explain geology, plant life, and history. Phone 435/772-3256.

Kolob Canyons Visitor Center. (see CEDAR CITY) Phone 435/772-3256.

Mountain climbing. Should be undertaken with great care due to unstable sandstone. Climbers should consult with a ranger at the park Visitor Center. Phone 435/772-3256.

Park trails. Trails lead to otherwise inaccessible areas: the Narrows (walls of this canyon are 2,000 ft high and as little as 50 ft apart at the stream), the Hanging Gardens of Zion, Weeping Rock, the Emerald Pools. Trails range from ½-mi trips to day-long treks, some requiring tested stamina. Trails in less-traveled areas should not be undertaken without first obtaining information from a park ranger. Back country permits required for travel through the Virgin River Narrows and other canyons, and on all overnight trips (fee/person/night). Phone 435/772-3256.

Zion National Park

Zion Nature Center. Junior Ranger program for children ages 6-12. (Memorial Day-Labor Day, Mon-Fri) Adj to South Campground. Phone 435/772-2356. ¢

Motels/Motor Lodges

★★ **DRIFTWOOD LODGE.** *1515 Zion Park Blvd, Springdale (84767). 435/772-3262; fax 435/772-3702; toll-free 888/801-8811. www.driftwood lodge.net.* 42 rms, 1-2 story. S $82; D $90; each addl $4. Crib $2. Pet accepted; $10. TV. Heated pool; whirlpool. Complimentary continental bkfst. Ck-out 11 am. Business servs avail. Gift shop. Private patios, balconies. Shaded grounds; good views of park. Cr cds: A, D, DS, MC, V.

★★ **FLANIGAN'S INN.** *428 Zion Park Blvd, Springdale (84767). 435/772-3244; fax 435/772-3396; toll-free 800/765-7787. www.flanigans. com.* 34 rms, 2 story. Mid-Mar-mid-Nov: S, D $79-$119; each addl $5; lower rates rest of yr. Crib free. TV; cable (premium). Heated pool; whirlpool. Restaurant 5-10 pm. Ck-out 11 am. Small local artists' gallery. Totally nonsmoking. Cr cds: A, DS, MC, V.

★ **TERRACE BROOK LODGE.** *990 Zion Park Blvd, Springdale (84767). 435/772-3932; fax 435/772-3596; toll-free 800/342-6779.* 26 rms, 2 story. Apr-Oct: S $55; D $75; each addl $4; lower rates rest of yr. Crib $4. TV; cable (premium). Heated pool. Restaurant nearby. Ck-out 11 am, ck-in 1 pm. Refrigerators avail. Picnic tables, grills. Cr cds: DS, MC, V.

★★ **ZION LODGE.** *Zion National Park, Springdale (84767). 435/772-3213; fax 435/772-2001. www.zion lodge.com.* 75 rms in motel, 1-2 story, 40 cabins. S, D $108-$136; each addl $5; suites $136; cabins $93. Crib $5. Restaurant 6:30-10 am, 11:30 am-3 pm, 6-10 pm. Ck-out 11 am. Business servs avail. Bellhops. Sundries. Gift shop. Private porches. Cr cds: A, C, D, DS, JCB, MC, V.

Resort

★★ **CLIFFROSE LODGE AND GARDENS.** *281 Zion Park Blvd, Springdale (84767). 435/772-3234; fax 435/772-3900; toll-free 800/243-8824. www.cliffroselodge.com.* 36 rms, 2 story. May-mid-Oct: S, D $119-$145; suites $145; each addl $10; under 18 free; lower rates rest of yr. Crib $6. Pet accepted. TV; cable (premium), VCR avail. Heated pool; whirlpool. Playground. Complimentary coffee in lobby. Restaurant nearby. Ck-out 11 am, ck-in 2 pm. Picnic tables. Cr cds: A, DS, MC, V.

B&Bs/Small Inns

★★★ **NOVEL HOUSE INN.** *73 Paradise Rd, Springdale (84767). 435/772-3650; fax 435/772-3651; toll-free 800/711-8400. www.novelhouse.com.* 10 rms, 2 story. S $81; D $110. Children over 12 yrs only. Closed mid-Dec-late Jan. TV; cable. Complimentary full bkfst. Ck-out 11 am, ck-in 4-7 pm. Totally nonsmoking. Cr cds: A, DS, MC, V.

★★ **RED ROCK INN.** *998 Zion Park Blvd, Springdale (84767). 435/772-3139. www.redrockinn.com.* 5 cottages, 1 story. No rm phones. Apr-Oct: S, D $89-$140; each addl $10; suites $115-$140; under 14 free; hols 2-day min; lower rates rest of yr. TV; cable (premium), VCR avail (movies). Restaurant nearby. Ck-out 11 am, ck-in 4 pm. Business servs avail. Concierge serv. Gift shop. Massage. Some in-rm whirlpools; microwaves avail. View of canyon. Totally nonsmoking. Cr cds: A, DS, MC, V.

ATTRACTION LIST

Attraction names are listed in alphabetical order followed by a symbol identifying their classification and then city. The symbols for classification are: [S] for Special Events and [W] for What to See and Do

150 Years of Fort Worth Museum [W] *Fort Worth, TX*
16th Street Mall [W] *Denver, CO*
1839 Williams Home [W] *Galveston, TX*
Abilene State Park [W] *Abilene, TX*
Abilene Zoological Gardens [W] *Abilene, TX*
Abraham Family Art Gallery [W] *Plainview, TX*
Acoma Pueblo [W] *Grants, NM*
Admiral Nimitz Museum State Historical Park [W] *Fredericksburg, TX*
Adrift Adventures [W] *Moab, UT*
Adrift Adventures of Dinosaur [W] *Vernal, UT*
Aerial Tramway [W] *Estes Park, CO*
African American Museum [W] *Dallas, TX*
Age of Steam Railroad Museum [W] *Dallas, TX*
Agua Prieta, Sonora, Mexico [W] *Douglas, AZ*
Aguirre Spring Recreation Site [W] *Las Cruces, NM*
Air Fiesta [S] *Uvalde, TX*
Alameda Park Zoo [W] *Alamogordo, NM*
Alamo, The [W] *San Antonio, TX*
Alamodome [W] *San Antonio, TX*
Alamo Village [W] *Brackettville, TX*
Albuquerque Biological Park [W] *Albuquerque, NM*
Albuquerque Little Theatre [S] *Albuquerque, NM*
Albuquerque Museum [W] *Albuquerque, NM*
Alferd Packer Barbeque Cookoff [S] *Lake City, CO*
Alibates Flint Quarries National Monument [W] *Fritch, TX*
Allen's Landing Park [W] *Houston, TX*
Alley Theatre [W] *Houston, TX*
All Indian Rodeo [S] *Fallon, NV*
Alpine Triangle Recreation Area [W] *Lake City, CO*
Alpine Tunnel [W] *Gunnison, CO*
Alta [W] *Salt Lake City, UT*
Alta Ski Area [W] *Alta, UT*
Amarillo Museum of Art [W] *Amarillo, TX*

American Cotton Museum [W] *Greenville, TX*
American Junior Rodeo National Finals [S] *Sweetwater, TX*
American Quarter Horse Heritage Center & Museum [W] *Amarillo, TX*
American West Heritage Center [W] *Logan, UT*
American West Heritage Center [S] *Logan, UT*
Amerind Foundation [W] *Willcox, AZ*
Amistad (Friendship) National Recreation Area [W] *Del Rio, TX*
Amon Carter Museum [W] *Fort Worth, TX*
Anahuac National Wildlife Refuge [W] *Baytown, TX*
Anasazi Heritage Center and Escalante [W] *Cortez, CO*
Anasazi Indian Village State Park [W] *Panguitch, UT*
Andy Devine Days & PRCA Rodeo [S] *Kingman, AZ*
Angelina [W] *Lufkin, TX*
Angelina National Forest [W] *Jasper, TX*
Angel of Shavano, The [W] *Salida, CO*
Ann Hathaway Cottage Archival & Shakespearean Library [W] *Odessa, TX*
Annie Riggs Hotel Museum [W] *Fort Stockton, TX*
Annual Pow-Wow [S] *Taos, NM*
Anson Jones Home [W] *Brenham, TX*
Antique Rose Emporium [W] *Brenham, TX*
Apache Days [S] *Globe, AZ*
Apache-Sitgreaves National Forests [W] *Holbrook, AZ*
Apache-Sitgreaves National Forests [W] *Show Low, AZ*
Apache-Sitgreaves National Forests [W] *Springerville, AZ*
Aquarena Springs [W] *San Marcos, TX*
Arabian Horse Show [S] *Scottsdale, AZ*
Aransas National Wildlife Refuge [W] *Rockport, TX*
Arapahoe Basin [W] *Dillon, CO*
Arapaho National Forest [W] *Dillon, CO*

Arapaho National Recreation Area [W] *Granby, CO*

Arches National Park [W] *Green River, UT*

Arches National Park [W] *Moab, UT*

Arcosanti [W] *Prescott, AZ*

Argo Town, USA [W] *Idaho Springs, CO*

Arizona Cardinals (NFL) [W] *Tempe, AZ*

Arizona Diamondbacks (MLB) [W] *Phoenix, AZ*

Arizona Historical Society Pioneer Museum [W] *Flagstaff, AZ*

Arizona Historical Society Fort Lowell Museum [W] *Tucson, AZ*

Arizona Historical Society Frémont House Museum [W] *Tucson, AZ*

Arizona Historical Society Museum, Library, and Archives [W] *Tucson, AZ*

Arizona Historical Society Sanguinetti House [W] *Yuma, AZ*

Arizona Mining & Mineral Museum [W] *Phoenix, AZ*

Arizona Museum for Youth [W] *Mesa, AZ*

Arizona Opera [S] *Tucson, AZ*

Arizona Opera Company [S] *Phoenix, AZ*

Arizona Renaissance Festival [S] *Mesa, AZ*

Arizona's Antique Capital [W] *Glendale, AZ*

Arizona Science Center [W] *Phoenix, AZ*

Arizona Snowbowl Ski & Summer Resort [W] *Flagstaff, AZ*

Arizona-Sonora Desert Museum [W] *Tucson, AZ*

Arizona State Capitol Museum [W] *Phoenix, AZ*

Arizona State Fair [S] *Phoenix, AZ*

Arizona State Museum [W] *Tucson, AZ*

Arizona State University [W] *Tempe, AZ*

Arizona Temple Visitor Center [W] *Mesa, AZ*

Arizona Theatre Company [S] *Phoenix, AZ*

Arizona Theatre Company [S] *Tucson, AZ*

Arkansas Headwaters State Recreation Area [W] *Salida, CO*

Arkansas River Tours [W] *Buena Vista, CO*

Arkansas Valley Fair and Exposition [S] *La Junta, CO*

Armand Bayou Nature Center [W] *Houston, TX*

A. R. Mitchell Memorial Museum of Western Art [W] *Trinidad, CO*

Armory Building [W] *Golden, CO*

Armstrong Browning Library [W] *Waco, TX*

Arneson River Theatre [W] *San Antonio, TX*

Arrow Press Square [W] *Salt Lake City, UT*

Art Center Waco [W] *Waco, TX*

Artemus W. Ham Concert Hall [W] *Las Vegas, NV*

Art Fair [S] *Salado, TX*

Art Festival [S] *Park City, UT*

Art in the Park [S] *Boulder City, NV*

Artists' Alpine Holiday & Festival [S] *Ouray, CO*

Art Museum of Southeast Texas [W] *Beaumont, TX*

Arts Festival [S] *Ruidoso, NM*

Artwalk [S] *Salida, CO*

Arvada Center for the Arts & Humanities [W] *Denver, CO*

ASA Amateur Softball National Tournament [S] *Chandler, AZ*

Ashcroft Ghost Town [W] *Aspen, CO*

Ashley National Forest [W] *Vernal, UT*

Ashton Villa [W] *Galveston, TX*

Asian Cultures Museum & Educational Center [W] *Corpus Christi, TX*

Aspenfest [S] *Ruidoso, NM*

Aspen Highlands [W] *Aspen, CO*

Aspen Mountain [W] *Aspen, CO*

Aspen Music Festival [S] *Aspen, CO*

Aspen Theater in the Park [S] *Aspen, CO*

Assembly Hall [W] *Salt Lake City, UT*

Astor House Hotel Museum [W] *Golden, CO*

Atalanta [W] *Jefferson, TX*

Attwater Prairie Chicken National Wildlife Refuge [W] *Eagle Lake, TX*

Auditorium Theatre [W] *Denver, CO*

Austin Museum of Art [W] *Austin, TX*

Austin Steam Train Association [W] *Austin, TX*

Austin Zoo [W] *Austin, TX*

Auto races [S] *Ely, NV*

Auto tour [W] *San Antonio, TX*

Azalea Trail [S] *Tyler, TX*

Aztec Museum and Pioneer Village [W] *Aztec, NM*

Aztec Ruins National Monument [W] *Aztec, NM*

Babe Didrikson Zaharias Memorial Museum [W] *Beaumont, TX*

Bachelor-Syracuse Mine Tour [W] *Ouray, CO*

Bach Festival [S] *Victoria, TX*
Backpacking [W] *Dinosaur National Monument, UT*
Backstage Theatre [S] *Breckenridge, CO*
Balcony House [W] *Mesa Verde National Park, CO*
Balloon Rally [S] *Telluride, CO*
Balmorhea State Park [W] *Pecos, TX*
Bandelier National Monument [W] *Los Alamos, NM*
Baptist Historical Center [W] *Brenham, TX*
Bar None Rodeo [S] *Plainview, TX*
Barton Springs Pool [W] *Austin, TX*
Baseball [S] *Tucson, AZ*
Baseball Spring Training [S] *Mesa, AZ*
Baseball Spring Training [S] *Scottsdale, AZ*
Baseball Spring Training [S] *Tempe, AZ*
Bass Performance Hall [W] *Fort Worth, TX*
B. A. Steinhagen Lake [W] *Jasper, TX*
Bastrop [W] *Bastrop, TX*
Battleship USS *Texas* [W] *Houston, TX*
Bayfest [S] *Corpus Christi, TX*
Bay Jammin' Concerts [S] *Corpus Christi, TX*
Baylor University [W] *Waco, TX*
Bayou Bend Collection [W] *Houston, TX*
Baytown Historical Museum [W] *Baytown, TX*
Beaches. Rockport [W] *Rockport, TX*
Bear Creek Falls [W] *Ouray, CO*
Bear Creek Lake Park [W] *Lakewood, CO*
Bear Creek Trail [W] *Telluride, CO*
Bear Lake [W] *Garden City, UT*
Bear Lake Road [W] *Rocky Mountain National Park, CO*
Bear Lake State Park [W] *Garden City, UT*
Beaty-Orton House [W] *Jasper, TX*
Beaver Creek/Arrowhead Resort [W] *Vail, CO*
Beaver Dam [W] *Caliente, NV*
Beaver Mountain Ski Area [W] *Garden City, UT*
Belton Lake [W] *Killeen, TX*
Belton Lake [W] *Temple, TX*
Benbrook Lake [W] *Fort Worth, TX*
Bentsen-Rio Grande Valley State Park [W] *Mission, TX*
Bent's Old Fort National Historic Site [W] *La Junta, CO*
Berlin-Ichthyosaur State Park [W] *Austin, NV*
Besh-Ba-Gowah Indian Ruins [W] *Globe, AZ*
Biblical Arts Center [W] *Dallas, TX*
Bicentennial Park [W] *Comanche, TX*

Bicycle trips and jeep trips [W] *Snowmass Village, CO*
Bicycling [W] *Zion National Park, UT*
Big Bend National Park [W] *Alpine, TX*
Big Bend National Park [W] *Fort Stockton, TX*
Big-game hunting in season [W] *Durango, CO*
Biggest Small Town Parade [S] *Seguin, TX*
Big Rock Candy Mountain [W] *Richfield, UT*
Big Spring State Park [W] *Big Spring, TX*
Big Thompson Canyon [W] *Estes Park, CO*
Big Timbers Museum [W] *Lamar, CO*
Bill Dvorak's Kayak & Rafting Expeditions [W] *Buena Vista, CO*
Bill Williams Rendezvous Days [S] *Williams, AZ*
Billy Bob's Texas [W] *Fort Worth, TX*
Billy Moore Days [S] *Litchfield Park, AZ*
Billy the Kid Museum [W] *Santa Rosa, NM*
Bird Cage Theatre [W] *Tombstone, AZ*
Birthplace [W] *Johnson City, TX*
Bisbee Mining and Historical Museum [W] *Bisbee, AZ*
Bisbee Restoration Association & Historical Museum [W] *Bisbee, AZ*
Bishop's Palace, The [W] *Galveston, TX*
Bisti Badlands [W] *Farmington, NM*
Bitter Lake National Wildlife Refuge [W] *Roswell, NM*
Black Canyon of the Gunnison National Monument [W] *Delta, CO*
Black Canyon of the Gunnison National Monument [W] *Montrose, CO*
Black River Traders [S] *Farmington, NM*
Blackwater Draw Museum [W] *Portales, NM*
Blazing Adventures [W] *Aspen, CO*
Blossom & Music Festival [S] *CaÒon City, CO*
Blue Bell Creamery [W] *Brenham, TX*
Bluebonnet Festival [S] *Burnet, TX*
Bluebonnet Trails [S] *Ennis, TX*
Bluebonnet Trails/Wildflowers Tours [S] *Brenham, TX*
Bluegrass Festival [S] *Prescott, AZ*
Bluegrass Festival [S] *Telluride, CO*
Bluegrass Festival [S] *Texarkana, TX*
Bluegrass Music Festival [S] *Wickenburg, AZ*
Blue Hole [W] *Santa Rosa, NM*

Bluewater Lake State Park [W] *Grants, NM*

Boating and fishing [W] *Orange, TX*

Boat Show [S] *Dallas, TX*

Boat trips [W] *Rockport, TX*

Boat trips on Lake Powell [W] *Lake Powell, UT*

Boat trips on Lake Powell [W] *Page, AZ*

Boerne Berges Fest [S] *San Antonio, TX*

Boettcher Concert Hall [W] *Denver, CO*

Bolder Boulder [S] *Boulder, CO*

Bonelli House [W] *Kingman, AZ*

Bonham State Park [W] *Bonham, TX*

Bonneville National Speed Trials [S] *Wendover, UT*

Bonneville Salt Flats [W] *Wendover, UT*

Bonnie Springs Old Nevada [W] *Las Vegas, NV*

Bonny Lake State Park [W] *Burlington, CO*

Boom Days & Burro Race [S] *Leadville, CO*

Boothill Graveyard [W] *Tombstone, AZ*

Bosque del Apache National Wildlife Refuge [W] *Socorro, NM*

Botanic Garden [W] *Fort Worth, TX*

Bottomless Lakes State Park [W] *Roswell, NM*

Boulder Bach Festival [S] *Boulder, CO*

Boulder County Fair and Rodeo [S] *Longmont, CO*

Boulder Creek Path [W] *Boulder, CO*

Boulder Damboree [S] *Boulder City, NV*

Boulder History Museum [W] *Boulder, CO*

Boulder Museum of Contemporary Art [W] *Boulder, CO*

Boulder Reservoir [W] *Boulder, CO*

Bowers Mansion [W] *Carson City, NV*

Box CaÒon Falls Park [W] *Ouray, CO*

Box Elder County Fair [S] *Brigham City, UT*

Boyce Thompson Southwestern Arboretum [W] *Globe, AZ*

Boyce Thompson Southwestern Arboretum [W] *Mesa, AZ*

Boyd Lake State Park [W] *Loveland, CO*

Boyhood Home [W] *Johnson City, TX*

Brackenridge Park [W] *San Antonio, TX*

Bradbury Science Museum [W] *Los Alamos, NM*

Brantley Lake State Park [W] *Carlsbad, NM*

Brass Band Festival [S] *Silverton, CO*

Brazoria County Fair [S] *Angleton, TX*

Brazosport Museum of Natural Science [W] *Brazosport, TX*

Brazos River Festival [S] *Waco, TX*

Brazos Valley Museum of Natural History, The [W] *Bryan/College Station, TX*

Breckenridge Music Festival [S] *Breckenridge, CO*

Brian Head Ski Resort [W] *Cedar City, UT*

Bridal Veil Falls [W] *Telluride, CO*

Brigham City Museum-Gallery [W] *Brigham City, UT*

Brigham Young Monument [W] *Salt Lake City, UT*

Brigham Young University [W] *Provo, UT*

Brigham Young Winter Home [W] *St. George, UT*

Brighton Resort [W] *Park City, UT*

Brighton Resort [W] *Salt Lake City, UT*

Broadmoor-Cheyenne Mountain Highway [W] *Colorado Springs, CO*

Broadmoor-Cheyenne Mountain Area [W] *Colorado Springs, CO*

Brookshire's World of Wildlife Museum & Country Store [W] *Tyler, TX*

Buccaneer Days [S] *Corpus Christi, TX*

Buckhorn Saloon and Museum [W] *San Antonio, TX*

Buckskin Mountain State Park [W] *Parker, AZ*

Buddy Holly Music Festival [S] *Lubbock, TX*

Buddy Holly Statue and Walk of Fame [W] *Lubbock, TX*

Buescher [W] *Bastrop, TX*

Buffalo and Comanche dances [S] *Santa Fe, NM*

Buffalo Barbecue & Western Week Celebration [S] *Grand Lake, CO*

Buffalo Bill Days [S] *Golden, CO*

Buffalo Bill Memorial Museum and Grave [W] *Golden, CO*

Buffalo Gap Historic Village [W] *Abilene, TX*

Buffalo Springs Lake Recreational Area [W] *Lubbock, TX*

Bulldog Balloon Rally [S] *Artesia, NM*

Burke Baker Planetarium [W] *Houston, TX*

Burlington-Rock Island Railroad Museum [W] *Fairfield, TX*

Bus tours [W] *El Paso, TX*

Bus tours [W] *Salt Lake City, UT*

Butch Cassidy Days PRCA Rodeo [S] *Moab, UT*

Buttermilk [W] *Aspen, CO*

Byers-Evans House Museum [W] *Denver, CO*

Byron Nelson Golf Classic [S] *Dallas, TX*

C-101 C-Sculptures [S] *Corpus Christi, TX*

Caballo Lake State Park [W] *Truth or Consequences, NM*

Cache County Fair [S] *Logan, UT*

Cactus Festival [S] *Kingsville, TX*

Caddo Lake State Park [W] *Jefferson, TX*

Caddo Lake State Park [W] *Marshall, TX*

Caldwell Zoo [W] *Tyler, TX*

Calhoun County Fair [S] *Port Lavaca, TX*

Camel Races [S] *Virginia City, NV*

Camino del Monte Sol [W] *Santa Fe, NM*

Camp Floyd and Stagecoach Inn State Parks [W] *Provo, UT*

Camping [W] *Bryce Canyon National Park, UT*

Camping [W] *North Rim (Grand Canyon National Park), AZ*

Camping [W] *South Rim (Grand Canyon National Park), AZ*

Camping [W] *Zion National Park, UT*

Camping, picnicking [W] *Dinosaur National Monument, CO*

Candlelight Posada [S] *McAllen, TX*

Candlelight Tour of Homes [S] *Fredericksburg, TX*

Canoeing, boating, and tubing [W] *Truth or Consequences, NM*

Canyon de Chelly National Monument [W] *Window Rock, AZ*

Canyon Lake [W] *New Braunfels, TX*

Canyonlands By Night [W] *Moab, UT*

Canyonlands Field Institute [W] *Moab, UT*

Canyonlands National Park [W] *Moab, UT*

Canyonlands National Park [W] *Monticello, UT*

Canyon Rims Recreation Area [W] *Monticello, UT*

Canyon Road [W] *Santa Fe, NM*

Canyon Road Tour [W] *Santa Fe, NM*

Canyons, The [W] *Park City, UT*

Canyons, The [W] *Salt Lake City, UT*

Canyon Tours [W] *Canyon de Chelly National Monument, AZ*

Canyon Voyages [W] *Moab, UT*

CaÒon City Municipal Museum [W] *CaÒon City, CO*

Capitol Complex Visitor Center [W] *Austin, TX*

Capitol Reef National Park [W] *Loa, UT*

Capitol Reef National Park [W] *Richfield, UT*

Cap-Rock [W] *Lubbock, TX*

Capulin Volcano National Monument [W] *Raton, NM*

Carlsbad Museum & Art Center [W] *Carlsbad, NM*

Carson County Square House Museum [W] *Amarillo, TX*

Carson National Forest [W] *Angel Fire, NM*

Carson National Forest [W] *Taos, NM*

Carson Valley Days [S] *Gardnerville, NV*

Carson Valley Fine Arts & Crafts Street Celebration [S] *Gardnerville, NV*

Casa Grande Ruins National Monument [W] *Casa Grande, AZ*

Casa Grande Ruins National Monument [W] *Chandler, AZ*

Casa Grande Ruins National Monument [W] *Florence, AZ*

Casa Grande Valley Historical Society & Museum [W] *Casa Grande, AZ*

Casa MaÒana Theater [W] *Fort Worth, TX*

Casa Navarro State Historical Park [W] *San Antonio, TX*

Cascade Caverns Park [W] *San Antonio, TX*

Castle, The [W] *Virginia City, NV*

Castle Rock Factory Shops [W] *Englewood, CO*

Catalina State Park [W] *Tucson, AZ*

Cathedral Gorge [W] *Caliente, NV*

Cathedral of St. Francis [W] *Santa Fe, NM*

Cattail Marsh [W] *Beaumont, TX*

Cattlemen's Days, Rodeo, and County Fair [S] *Gunnison, CO*

Catwalk of Whitewater Canyon [W] *Silver City, NM*

Cave Lake State Park [W] *Ely, NV*

Cave of the Winds [W] *Manitou Springs, CO*

Caverns of Sonora [W] *Sonora, TX*

CavOILcade [S] *Port Arthur, TX*

Cedar Breaks National Monument [W] *Cedar City, UT*

Cedar Breaks National Monument [W] *Panguitch, UT*

Celebrate Abilene [S] *Abilene, TX*

Centennial Village [W] *Greeley, CO*

Center for Creative Photography [W] *Tucson, AZ*

Center for the Arts [W] *Rockport, TX*

Central City Music Festival [S] *Central City, CO*

Central Nevada Museum [W] *Tonopah, NV*

Chaco Culture National Historical Park [W] *Farmington, NM*

Chaffee County Fair [S] *Salida, CO*

Chamberlin Observatory [W] *Denver, CO*

Chamber Music Festival [S] *Taos, NM*

Chamber Music Festival [S] *Telluride, CO*

Chamizal Festival [S] *El Paso, TX*

Chamizal National Memorial [W] *El Paso, TX*

Champlin Fighter Museum [W] *Mesa, AZ*

Chandler Ostrich Festival [S] *Chandler, AZ*

Chapel of the Holy Cross [W] *Sedona, AZ*

Charles C. Gates Planetarium [W] *Denver, CO*

Charro Days [S] *Brownsville, TX*

Chatfield State Park [W] *Denver, CO*

Cheesman Park [W] *Denver, CO*

Cherry Creek Arts Festival [S] *Denver, CO*

Cherry Creek State Park [W] *Denver, CO*

Cheyenne Mountain Zoological Park [W] *Colorado Springs, CO*

Children's Center, The [W] *Winter Park, CO*

Children's Museum of Denver, The [W] *Denver, CO*

Children's Museum of Houston [W] *Houston, TX*

Childress County Heritage Museum [W] *Childress, TX*

Childress County Old Settlers' Reunion [S] *Childress, TX*

Chilispiel [S] *La Grange, TX*

Chimney Rock Archaeological Area [W] *Pagosa Springs, CO*

Chinati Foundation [W] *Marfa, TX*

Christmas at the Fort [S] *Groesbeck, TX*

Christmas Candlelight Tour [S] *Jefferson, TX*

Christmas Candle Walk [S] *Cleburne, TX*

Christmas Eve Celebrations [S] *Santa Fe, NM*

Christmas Festivals [S] *Acoma Pueblo, NM*

Christmas Mountain USA [S] *Salida, CO*

Christmas on the Brazos [S] *Waco, TX*

Chrysler Classic of Tucson [S] *Tucson, AZ*

Cibola National Forest [W] *Albuquerque, NM*

Cimarron Canyon State Park [W] *Angel Fire, NM*

Cimarron Canyon State Park [W] *Cimarron, NM*

Cimarron Days [S] *Cimarron, NM*

Cinco de Mayo [S] *Douglas, AZ*

Cinco de Mayo Celebration [S] *Del Rio, TX*

Circle Jeep Tour [W] *Silverton, CO*

City-County Pioneer Museum [W] *Sweetwater, TX*

City of Las Vegas Museum and Rough Riders' Memorial Collection [W] *Las Vegas, NM*

City of Rocks State Park [W] *Deming, NM*

City Park [W] *Denver, CO*

City Park [W] *Pueblo, CO*

City Park [W] *Sulphur Springs, TX*

City parks [W] *Pueblo, CO*

City parks [W] *Santa Rosa, NM*

Ciudad AcuÒa, Mexico [W] *Del Rio, TX*

Ciudad Ju·rez [W] *El Paso, TX*

Civic Center [W] *Denver, CO*

Clark County Heritage Museum [W] *Henderson, NV*

Cleburne [W] *Cleburne, TX*

Cleveland-Lloyd Dinosaur Quarry [W] *Price, UT*

Cliff Dwelling Tours [W] *Mesa Verde National Park, CO*

Cliff Palace [W] *Mesa Verde National Park, CO*

Clovis Depot Model Train Museum [W] *Clovis, NM*

Coach USA bus tours [W] *Dallas, TX*

Coach USA bus tours [W] *San Antonio, TX*

Cochise County Fair & College Rodeo [S] *Douglas, AZ*

Cochise Information Center [W] *Willcox, AZ*

Cochise Stronghold [W] *Willcox, AZ*

Coconino County Fair [S] *Flagstaff, AZ*

Coconino National Forest [W] *Flagstaff, AZ*

Cog railway [W] *Colorado Springs, CO*

Cole Park [W] *Alamosa, CO*

Coleto Creek Reservoir [W] *Victoria, TX*

College of Eastern Utah Prehistoric Museum [W] *Price, UT*

College of Santa Fe [W] *Santa Fe, NM*

Colorado Avalanche (NHL) [W] *Denver, CO*

Colorado Bug Tours [W] *Denver, CO*

Colorado History Museum [W] *Denver, CO*

Colorado History Tours [W] *Denver, CO*

Colorado Mountain Winefest [S] *Grand Junction, CO*

Colorado Music Festival [S] *Boulder, CO*

Colorado National Monument [W] *Grand Junction, CO*

Colorado Railroad Museum [W] *Golden, CO*

Colorado Rapids (MLS) [W] *Denver, CO*

Colorado River [W] *Grand Junction, CO*

Colorado River & Trail Expeditions, Inc [W] *Green River, UT*

Colorado River & Trail Expeditions, Inc [W] *Moab, UT*

Colorado River Indian Tribes Reservation [W] *Parker, AZ*

Colorado River Indian Tribes Museum, Library and Gaming Casino [W] *Parker, AZ*

Colorado Rockies (MLB) [W] *Denver, CO*

Colorado School of Mines [W] *Golden, CO*

Colorado School of Mines—Edgar Mine [W] *Idaho Springs, CO*

Colorado Shakespeare Festival [S] *Boulder, CO*

Colorado Ski Museum & Ski Hall of Fame [W] *Vail, CO*

Colorado Springs Balloon Classic [S] *Colorado Springs, CO*

Colorado Springs Fine Arts Center [W] *Colorado Springs, CO*

Colorado Springs Pioneer Museum [W] *Colorado Springs, CO*

Colorado Stampede [S] *Grand Junction, CO*

Colorado State Fair [S] *Pueblo, CO*

Colorado State University [W] *Fort Collins, CO*

Colorado Territorial Prison Museum and Park [W] *CaÒon City, CO*

Colossal Cave [W] *Tucson, AZ*

Columbia University's Biosphere 2 Center [W] *Tucson, AZ*

Columbus Historical Museum [W] *Deming, NM*

Comal County Fair [S] *New Braunfels, TX*

Comanche County Museum [W] *Comanche, TX*

Comanche Crossing Museum [W] *Denver, CO*

Come and Take It Celebration [S] *Gonzales, TX*

Commemorative Air Force and American Airpower Heritage Museum [W] *Midland, TX*

Commemorative Airforce Airshow [S] *Midland, TX*

Community Forest [W] *Palestine, TX*

Conchas Lake State Park [W] *Tucumcari, NM*

Concordia Cemetery [W] *El Paso, TX*

Confederate Research Center [W] *Hillsboro, TX*

Confederate Reunion Grounds State Historical Park [W] *Groesbeck, TX*

Congress Avenue Bridge Bat Colony [S] *Austin, TX*

Connie Mack World Series Baseball Tournament [S] *Farmington, NM*

Conrad Hilton Open Golf Tournament [S] *Socorro, NM*

Conspiracy Museum [W] *Dallas, TX*

Contemporary Arts Museum [W] *Houston, TX*

Continental Ranch Tour [W] *Del Rio, TX*

Cook Center, The [W] *Corsicana, TX*

Coors Ranch Rodeo [S] *Amarillo, TX*

Copano Bay Causeway [W] *Rockport, TX*

Copper Breaks State Park [W] *Quanah, TX*

Copper Mountain Resort Ski Area [W] *Dillon, CO*

Coral Pink Sand Dunes State Park [W] *Kanab, UT*

Coronado National Forest [W] *Sierra Vista, AZ*

Coronado National Forest [W] *Tucson, AZ*

Coronado National Memorial [W] *Sierra Vista, AZ*

Coronado State Monument [W] *Albuquerque, NM*

Corpus Christi Museum of Science & History [W] *Corpus Christi, TX*

Cosanti Foundation [W] *Scottsdale, AZ*

Cos House [W] *San Antonio, TX*

Cotton Jubilee [S] *Greenville, TX*

Council Hall [W] *Salt Lake City, UT*

County Fair and Livestock Show [S] *Elko, NV*

Courthouse Park [W] *Lovelock, NV*

Cowboy Artists of America [S] *Phoenix, AZ*

Cowboy Capital PRCA Rodeo [S] *Bandera, TX*

Cowboy Morning Breakfast [S] *Amarillo, TX*

Cowboy Poetry Gathering [S] *Elko, NV*

Cowboy Roundup Days [S] *Steamboat Springs, CO*

CRA Finals Rodeo [S] *Sulphur Springs, TX*

Crawford State Park [W] *Delta, CO*

Crawley's Monument Valley Tours, Inc [W] *Kayenta, AZ*

CRCA Annual Rodeo [S] *Paris, TX*

Creede [W] *South Fork, CO*

Creede Repertory Theater [S] *South Fork, CO*
Cripple Creek District Museum [W] *Cripple Creek, CO*
Cripple Creek-Victor Narrow Gauge Railroad [W] *Cripple Creek, CO*
Cristo Rey Church [W] *Santa Fe, NM*
Crockett County Museum [W] *Ozona, TX*
Crockett Heritage Festival [S] *Crockett, TX*
Cross Orchards Historic Farm [W] *Grand Junction, CO*
Cross Timbers Country Opry [W] *Stephenville, TX*
Crown Hill Park [W] *Lakewood, CO*
Crystal Carnival [S] *Leadville, CO*
Crystal Palace Saloon [W] *Tombstone, AZ*
Culberson County Fair [S] *Van Horn, TX*
Cultural Center [W] *Gallup, NM*
Cultural Complex [W] *Las Cruces, NM*
Cultural District [W] *Fort Worth, TX*
Cumberland Pass [W] *Gunnison, CO*
Cumbres & Toltec Scenic Railroad, Colorado Limited [W] *Alamosa, CO*
Cumbres & Toltec Scenic Railroad, New Mexico Express [W] *Chama, NM*
Curecanti National Recreation Area [W] *Gunnison, CO*
Curry County Fair [S] *Clovis, NM*
Dairy Fest [S] *Stephenville, TX*
Dallas Aquarium [W] *Dallas, TX*
Dallas Arboretum and Botanical Garden [W] *Dallas, TX*
Dallas Cowboys (NFL) [W] *Dallas, TX*
Dallas Market Center Complex [W] *Dallas, TX*
Dallas Mavericks (NBA) [W] *Dallas, TX*
Dallas Museum of Art [W] *Dallas, TX*
Dallas Museum of Natural History [W] *Dallas, TX*
Dallas Opera [S] *Dallas, TX*
Dallas Stars (NHL) [W] *Dallas, TX*
Dallas Symphony Orchestra [W] *Dallas, TX*
Dallas Theater Center [W] *Dallas, TX*
Dallas Zoo [W] *Dallas, TX*
Dan O'Laurie Canyon Country Museum [W] *Moab, UT*
Daughters of the Utah Pioneers Museum [W] *Logan, UT*
Daughters of Utah Pioneers Museum & Relic Hall [W] *Ogden, UT*
Daughters of Utah Pioneers Collection [W] *St. George, UT*

Daughters of Utah Pioneers Museum [W] *Vernal, UT*
Davis Dam [W] *Lake Mead National Recreation Area, NV*
Davis Dam and Power Plant [W] *Bullhead City, AZ*
Davis Mountains State Park [W] *Alpine, TX*
Davy Crockett [W] *Lufkin, TX*
Davy Crockett Monument [W] *Ozona, TX*
Dawn at The Alamo [S] *San Antonio, TX*
"Days of '47" Celebration [S] *Salt Lake City, UT*
Dead Horse Point State Park [W] *Moab, UT*
Dead Horse Ranch State Park [W] *Cottonwood, AZ*
Deaf Smith County Historical Museum [W] *Hereford, TX*
Deck the Halls [S] *Mount Pleasant, TX*
Deep-Sea Roundup [S] *Port Aransas, TX*
Deer Creek State Park [W] *Heber City, UT*
Deer Valley Resort [W] *Park City, UT*
Deer Valley Resort [W] *Salt Lake City, UT*
Deltarado Days [S] *Delta, CO*
Deming-Luna Mimbres Museum [W] *Deming, NM*
Denison Dam [W] *Denison, TX*
Denton County Courthouse Museum [W] *Denton, TX*
Denver Art Museum [W] *Denver, CO*
Denver Botanic Gardens [W] *Denver, CO*
Denver Broncos (NFL) [W] *Denver, CO*
Denver City and County Buildings [W] *Denver, CO*
Denver Firefighters Museum [W] *Denver, CO*
Denver Museum of Nature and Science [W] *Denver, CO*
Denver Nuggets (NBA) [W] *Denver, CO*
Denver Performing Arts Complex [W] *Denver, CO*
Denver Public Library [W] *Denver, CO*
Depot Museum and Children's Discovery Center [W] *Henderson, TX*
Desert Botanical Garden [W] *Phoenix, AZ*
Desert Caballeros Western Museum [W] *Wickenburg, AZ*
Dexter National Fish Hatchery and Technology Center [W] *Roswell, NM*

Diamond Circle Theatre [W] *Durango, CO*

Diamond Peak Ski Resort [W] *Incline Village, NV*

Dickens on the Strand [S] *Galveston, TX*

Diez y Seis [S] *San Antonio, TX*

Diez Y Seis Celebration [S] *Laredo, TX*

Diez y Seis de Septiembre [S] *Del Rio, TX*

Dinosaur Hill [W] *Grand Junction, CO*

Dinosaur National Monument [W] *Craig, CO*

Dinosaur National Monument [W] *Vernal, UT*

Dinosaur Quarry [W] *Dinosaur National Monument, CO*

Dinosaur Quarry Information Center [W] *Dinosaur National Monument, UT*

Dinosaur Roundup Rodeo [S] *Vernal, UT*

Dinosaur Valley [W] *Cleburne, TX*

Dinosaur Valley State Park [W] *Stephenville, TX*

Discovery Center Science Museum [W] *Fort Collins, CO*

Diversion Reservoir [W] *Wichita Falls, TX*

Dixie National Forest [W] *Cedar City, UT*

Dogie Days Celebration [S] *Dumas, TX*

Dog racing [S] *Loveland, CO*

Dog racing [W] *Phoenix, AZ*

Dolly Steamboat Cruises [W] *Mesa, AZ*

Don Harrington Discovery Center [W] *Amarillo, TX*

Donkey Derby Days [S] *Cripple Creek, CO*

Donna Beam Fine Art Gallery [W] *Las Vegas, NV*

Douglas Fiestas [S] *Douglas, AZ*

Douglas MacArthur Academy of Freedom [W] *Brownwood, TX*

Downtown [W] *Fort Worth, TX*

Downtown Mall [W] *Boulder, CO*

Drives to viewpoints [W] *South Rim (Grand Canyon National Park), AZ*

Drive to Cape Royal [W] *North Rim (Grand Canyon National Park), AZ*

Driving of Golden Spike [S] *Brigham City, UT*

Driving tour. Davis Mountains and McDonald Observatory [W] *Alpine, TX*

Dr. Pepper Museum [W] *Waco, TX*

Duncan Family Farms [W] *Litchfield Park, AZ*

Durango & Silverton Narrow Gauge Railroad Museum [W] *Durango, CO*

Durango Cowboy Gathering [S] *Durango, CO*

Dyess Air Force Base [W] *Abilene, TX*

Eagle Mountain Lake [W] *Fort Worth, TX*

Eagle Nest Lake [W] *Angel Fire, NM*

Early Iron Festival [S] *Alamosa, CO*

Early Settlers Day [S] *La Junta, CO*

Earth Runs Silver [W] *Leadville, CO*

Earth Science Museum [W] *Provo, UT*

Easter Fires Pageant [S] *Fredericksburg, TX*

Eastern New Mexico State Fair and Rodeo [S] *Roswell, NM*

Eastern New Mexico University [W] *Portales, NM*

East Texas Oil Museum at Kilgore College [W] *Kilgore, TX*

East Texas State Fair [S] *Tyler, TX*

Eccles Community Art Center [W] *Ogden, UT*

Echo Canyon [W] *Caliente, NV*

Echo Canyon [W] *Phoenix, AZ*

Eckert James River Bat Cave Preserve [W] *Mason, TX*

Eddy County Fair [S] *Artesia, NM*

Edgar Mine [W] *Golden, CO*

Edge of the Cedars State Park [W] *Blanding, UT*

Edison Plaza Museum [W] *Beaumont, TX*

Educational Festival [S] *Fredericksburg, TX*

Egyptian Theatre [W] *Park City, UT*

Eisenhower Birthplace State Historical Park [W] *Denison, TX*

Eisenhower State Park [W] *Denison, TX*

Elephant Butte Lake State Park [W] *Truth or Consequences, NM*

Elisabet Ney Museum [W] *Austin, TX*

Elitch Gardens [W] *Denver, CO*

Elk Meadows and Mount Holly Ski Area [W] *Beaver, UT*

Ellen Trout Park Zoo [W] *Lufkin, TX*

El Malpais National Monument and National Conservation Area [W] *Grants, NM*

El Morro National Monument (Inscription Rock) [W] *Grants, NM*

El Paso Holocaust Museum and Study Center [W] *El Paso, TX*

El Paso Mission Trail [W] *El Paso, TX*

El Paso Museum of Art [W] *El Paso, TX*

El Paso Museum of History [W] *El Paso, TX*

El Paso Symphony Orchestra [S] *El Paso, TX*

El Pomar Carriage Museum [W] *Colorado Springs, CO*

El Pueblo Museum [W] *Pueblo, CO*

El Rancho de las Golondrinas [W] *Santa Fe, NM*

El Vado Lake State Park [W] *Chama, NM*

Enchanted Circle Century Bike Tour [S] *Red River, NM*

Enchanted Rock State Natural Area [W] *Fredericksburg, TX*

Enos Mills Original Cabin [W] *Estes Park, CO*

Ernest L. Blumenschein Home [W] *Taos, NM*

Escalante State Park [W] *Loa, UT*

Escorted horseback trips [W] *Zion National Park, UT*

Espada Aqueduct [W] *San Antonio, TX*

Espada Dam [W] *San Antonio, TX*

Estes Park Area Historical Museum [W] *Estes Park, CO*

Estes Park Music Festival [S] *Estes Park, CO*

Estes Park Ride-a-Kart [W] *Estes Park, CO*

Ethel M. Chocolates Factory & Cactus Garden [W] *Henderson, NV*

Evening programs [W] *South Rim (Grand Canyon National Park), AZ*

Excelsior House [W] *Jefferson, TX*

Exploring by car [W] *Las Cruces, NM*

Expomex [S] *Laredo, TX*

Factory outlet stores [W] *Casa Grande, AZ*

Factory Stores at Park City [W] *Park City, UT*

Factory Stores of America [W] *Galveston, TX*

Fairfield Lake State Park [W] *Fairfield, TX*

Fair Park Dallas [W] *Dallas, TX*

Fall Fest [S] *Jasper, TX*

Fall Festival [S] *Sulphur Springs, TX*

Fall Festival of the Arts [S] *Tempe, AZ*

Fallon Air Show [S] *Fallon, NV*

Family History Library [W] *Salt Lake City, UT*

Fannin County Fair [S] *Bonham, TX*

Fantasy of Lights [S] *Wichita Falls, TX*

Farmington Invitational Balloon Rally [S] *Farmington, NM*

Far View Visitor Center [W] *Mesa Verde National Park, CO*

Fayette County Country Fair [S] *La Grange, TX*

Fayette Heritage Museum [W] *La Grange, TX*

Fayette Power Project Lake & Parks [W] *La Grange, TX*

Feast of St. Estevan [S] *Acoma Pueblo, NM*

Federal Court House [W] *Santa Fe, NM*

Festival in the Park [S] *Fort Morgan, CO*

Festival of Lights [S] *Brazosport, TX*

Festival of the Crane [S] *Socorro, NM*

FIBArk River International Whitewater Boat Race [S] *Salida, CO*

Fiddlers Green Amphitheatre [W] *Englewood, CO*

Fiesta and Green Corn Dance [S] *Santa Fe, NM*

Fiesta at Santo Domingo Pueblo [S] *Santa Fe, NM*

Fiesta Bandana [S] *Alice, TX*

Fiesta Bowl [S] *Phoenix, AZ*

Fiesta Days [S] *Carefree, AZ*

Fiesta de Amistad [S] *Del Rio, TX*

Fiesta de Colores [S] *Kingsville, TX*

Fiesta de las Flores [S] *El Paso, TX*

Fiesta del Presidio [W] , *AZ*

Fiesta del Valle de EspaÒola [S] *Espanola, NM*

Fiesta de Mayo [S] *Safford, AZ*

Fiesta Hidalgo [S] *Edinburg, TX*

Fiesta San Antonio [S] *San Antonio, TX*

Fiestas de Santiago y Santa Ana [S] *Taos, NM*

Fiestas Navidenas [S] *San Antonio, TX*

Fiesta (St. Lorenzo's) Day [S] *Acoma Pueblo, NM*

Fine Arts Center [W] *Albuquerque, NM*

Fireant Festival [S] *Marshall, TX*

Firehouse, The [W] *Del Rio, TX*

First State Bank [W] *Uvalde, TX*

Fishin' Fiesta [S] *Brazosport, TX*

Fishing [W] *Brownsville, TX*

Fishing [W] *Corpus Christi, TX*

Fishing [W] *Dinosaur National Monument, CO*

Fishing [W] *Durango, CO*

Fishing [W] *New Braunfels, TX*

Fishing [W] *Ouray, CO*

Fishing [W] *Paris, TX*

Fishing [W] *Port Lavaca, TX*

Fishing [W] *San Marcos, TX*

Fishing [W] *Texas City, TX*

Fishing and boating [W] *San Angelo, TX*

Fishing, boating, hiking, horseback riding, mountain climbing [W] *Estes Park, CO*

Fishing, camping [W] *Bullhead City, AZ*

Fishing. Rainbow Lake [W] *Show Low, AZ*

Fishlake National Forest [W] *Beaver, UT*

Fishlake National Forest [W] *Fillmore, UT*

Fishlake National Forest [W] *Richfield, UT*

Fiske Planetarium and Science Center [W] *Boulder, CO*

Flagship Cruises [W] *Corpus Christi, TX*

Flagstaff Festival of the Arts [S] *Flagstaff, AZ*

Flaming Gorge Dam and National Recreation Area [W] *Vernal, UT*

Flandrau Science Center & Planetarium [W] *Tucson, AZ*

The Flashlight [W] *Las Vegas, NV*

Fleischmann Planetarium [W] *Reno, NV*

Florence Hawley Ellis Museum of Anthropology [W] *Espanola, NM*

Floyd Lamb State Park [W] *Las Vegas, NV*

Flying W Ranch [W] *Colorado Springs, CO*

Focus on the Family [W] *Colorado Springs, CO*

Folsom Museum [W] *Raton, NM*

Food and Wine Fest [S] *Fredericksburg, TX*

Forest Information [W] *Lufkin, TX*

Forney Transportation Museum [W] *Denver, CO*

Fort Bliss [W] *El Paso, TX*

Fort Bliss Replica Museum [W] *El Paso, TX*

Fort Bowie National Historic Site [W] *Willcox, AZ*

Fort Buenaventura State Park [W] *Ogden, UT*

Fort Burgwin Research Center [W] *Taos, NM*

Fort Churchill State Historic Park [W] *Yerington, NV*

Fort Collins Museum [W] *Fort Collins, CO*

Fort Concho National Historic Landmark [W] *San Angelo, TX*

Fort Croghan Museum [W] *Burnet, TX*

Fort Davis [W] *Alpine, TX*

Fort Davis National Historic Site [W] *Alpine, TX*

Fort Douglas Military Museum [W] *Salt Lake City, UT*

Fort Duncan Park [W] *Eagle Pass, TX*

Fort Fisher Park [W] *Waco, TX*

Fort Garland Museum [W] *Alamosa, CO*

Fort Hood [W] *Killeen, TX*

Fort Huachuca [W] *Sierra Vista, AZ*

Fort Inglish Village [W] *Bonham, TX*

Fort Lancaster State Historical Park [W] *Ozona, TX*

Fort Mason [W] *Mason, TX*

Fort Morgan Museum [W] *Fort Morgan, CO*

Fort Parker State Park [W] *Groesbeck, TX*

Fort Phantom Hill and Lake [W] *Abilene, TX*

Fort Richardson State Historical Park [W] *Graham, TX*

Fort Sam Houston Museum and National Historic Landmark [W] *San Antonio, TX*

Fort Selden State Monument [W] *Las Cruces, NM*

Fort Sumner State Monument [W] *Santa Rosa, NM*

Fort Union National Monument [W] *Las Vegas, NM*

Fort Vasquez [W] *Greeley, CO*

Fort Verde Days [S] *Cottonwood, AZ*

Fort Verde State Historic Park [W] *Cottonwood, AZ*

Fort Worth Museum of Science & History [W] *Fort Worth, TX*

Fort Worth Nature Center & Refuge [W] *Fort Worth, TX*

Fort Worth Stockyards National Historic District [W] *Fort Worth, TX*

Fort Worth Theater [W] *Fort Worth, TX*

Fort Worth Water Garden [W] *Fort Worth, TX*

Fort Worth Zoo [W] *Fort Worth, TX*

Fort Yuma-Quechan Museum [W] *Yuma, AZ*

Fossil Rim Wildlife Center [W] *Granbury, TX*

Founders Day [S] *Albuquerque, NM*

Four Corners Monument [W] *Farmington, NM*

Francisco Fort Museum [W] *Walsenburg, CO*

Fred E. Weisbrod Aircraft Museum [W] *Pueblo, CO*

Fred Harman Art Museum [W] *Pagosa Springs, CO*

Freedom Festival [S] *Provo, UT*

Freeman Plantation [W] *Jefferson, TX*

Freestone County Historical Museum [W] *Fairfield, TX*

Fremont Center for the Arts [W] *CaÒon City, CO*

Fremont Indian State Park [W] *Richfield, UT*

French Legation Museum [W] *Austin, TX*

Freshwater fishing [W] *Brownsville, TX*

Frontier Days [S] *Lovelock, NV*

Frontier Days [S] *Silver City, NM*

Frontier Days & Rodeo Celebration [S] *Van Horn, TX*

Frontier Street [W] *Wickenburg, AZ*
Frontier Times Museum [W] *Bandera, TX*
Fuller Lodge Art Center and Gallery [W] *Los Alamos, NM*
Fulton Mansion State Park [W] *Rockport, TX*
Fun City Amusement Park [W] *Estes Park, CO*
FUNFEST [S] *Amarillo, TX*
Funfest [S] *Texas City, TX*
Fun Time Coach USA bus tours [W] *Corpus Christi, TX*
Gadsden Museum [W] *Las Cruces, NM*
Galeria Ortega [W] *Espanola, NM*
Galleria, The [W] *Denver, CO*
Galveston Island Outdoor Musicals [S] *Galveston, TX*
Galveston Island State Park [W] *Galveston, TX*
Galveston-Port Bolivar Ferry [W] *Galveston, TX*
Garden of the Gods [W] *Colorado Springs, CO*
Garden of the Gods Trading Post [W] *Colorado Springs, CO*
Garfield County Fair & Rodeo [S] *Glenwood Springs, CO*
Garner Memorial Museum [W] *Uvalde, TX*
Garner State Park [W] *Uvalde, TX*
Gem & Mineral Show [S] *Big Spring, TX*
Gem & Mineral Show [S] *Tucson, AZ*
General Granbury Civil War Reenactment [S] *Granbury, TX*
Geology Museum [W] *Golden, CO*
Geology tours [W] *Price, UT*
George Paul Memorial Bull Riding [S] *Del Rio, TX*
George Ranch Historical Park [W] *Houston, TX*
George S. Eccles Dinosaur Park [W] *Ogden, UT*
Georgetown Loop Historic Mining and Railroad Park [W] *Georgetown, CO*
George Washington's Birthday Celebration [S] *Laredo, TX*
Georgia O'Keeffe Museum [W] *Santa Fe, NM*
Geronimo Springs Museum [W] *Truth or Consequences, NM*
Ghost Town Narration Tours [S] *Lake City, CO*
Ghost towns [W] *Breckenridge, CO*
Gila Cliff Dwellings National Monument [W] *Silver City, NM*
Gila County Fair [S] *Globe, AZ*
Gila County Historical Museum [W] *Globe, AZ*

Gila (HEE-la) National Forest [W] *Silver City, NM*
Gila River Arts & Crafts Center [W] *Chandler, AZ*
Gillespie County Fair [S] *Fredericksburg, TX*
Gilpin County Historical Society Museum [W] *Central City, CO*
Gladys Porter Zoo [W] *Brownsville, TX*
Glen Canyon National Recreation Area/Lake Powell [W] *Blanding, UT*
Glen Canyon National Recreation Area/Lake Powell [W] *Kanab, UT*
Glen Canyon National Recreation Area (Bullfrog Marina) [W] *Lake Powell, UT*
Glen Canyon National Recreation Area [W] *Page, AZ*
Glenn Miller Festival [S] *Fort Morgan, CO*
Glenwood Hot Springs Pool [W] *Glenwood Springs, CO*
Globe Theatre [W] *Odessa, TX*
Goblin Valley State Park [W] *Green River, UT*
Go-Jii-Ya [S] *Dulce, NM*
Golden Gate Canyon State Park [W] *Golden, CO*
Golden Onion Days [S] *Payson, UT*
Golden Pioneer Museum [W] *Golden, CO*
Golden Spike National Historic Site [W] *Brigham City, UT*
Gold Rush Days [S] *Idaho Springs, CO*
Gold Rush Days [S] *Wickenburg, AZ*
Goliad County Fair & Rodeo [S] *Goliad, TX*
Goliad State Historical Park [W] *Goliad, TX*
Gonzales County Jail Museum [W] *Gonzales, TX*
Gonzales Memorial Museum [W] *Gonzales, TX*
Gonzales Pioneer Village [W] *Gonzales, TX*
Goodman Museum [W] *Tyler, TX*
Good Old Days Celebration [S] *Lyons, CO*
Goodyear Rodeo Days [S] *Litchfield Park, AZ*
Goose Island [W] *Rockport, TX*
Governor Bent House Museum and Gallery [W] *Taos, NM*
Governor Bill & Vara Daniel Historic Village [W] *Waco, TX*
Governor's Feast [S] *Acoma Pueblo, NM*
Governor's Mansion [W] *Austin, TX*

Governor's Mansion [W] *Salt Lake City, UT*

Grace Museums [W] *Abilene, TX*

Grady Gammage Memorial Auditorium [W] *Tempe, AZ*

Graham County Fair [S] *Safford, AZ*

Granbury Opera House [W] *Granbury, TX*

Grand 1894 Opera House [W] *Galveston, TX*

Grand Canyon Caverns [W] *Seligman, AZ*

Grand Canyon IMAX Theatre [W] *South Rim (Grand Canyon National Park), AZ*

Grand Canyon National Park [W] *Williams, AZ*

Grand Canyon Railway [W] *Williams, AZ*

Grand Canyon Scenic Flights [W] *Kanab, UT*

"Grand Circle: A National Park Odyssey" [W] *Zion National Park, UT*

Grand County Historical Association [W] *Granby, CO*

Grand Mesa National Forest [W] *Grand Junction, CO*

Grapeland Peanut Festival [S] *Crockett, TX*

Grapevine Lake [W] *Dallas, TX*

Gray Line bus tours [W] *Brownsville, TX*

Gray Line bus tours [W] *Colorado Springs, CO*

Gray Line bus tours [W] *Denver, CO*

Gray Line bus tours [W] *Houston, TX*

Gray Line bus tours [W] *Tucson, AZ*

Gray Line sightseeing tours [W] *Scottsdale, AZ*

Grayson County Frontier Village [W] *Denison, TX*

Great American Duck Race [S] *Deming, NM*

Great Sand Dunes Four-Wheel Drive Tour [W] *Great Sand Dunes National Monument, CO*

Great Sand Dunes National Monument [W] *Alamosa, CO*

The Great Storm [W] *Galveston, TX*

Great Texas Mosquito Festival [S] *Brazosport, TX*

Greek Festival [S] *Houston, TX*

Greek Theater [W] *Denver, CO*

Greenbelt Lake [W] *Clarendon, TX*

Green Mountain Reservoir [W] *Kremmling, CO*

Greenway and Nature Center of Pueblo, The [W] *Pueblo, CO*

Gregg County Historical Museum [W] *Longview, TX*

Greyhound racing [S] *Colorado Springs, CO*

Greyhound racing [S] *Denver, CO*

Greyhound racing [W] *Tucson, AZ*

Grzelachowski Territorial House [W] *Santa Rosa, NM*

Guadalupe County Fair and PRCA Rodeo [S] *Seguin, TX*

Guadalupe Mountains National Park [W] *El Paso, TX*

Guided river trips [W] *South Rim (Grand Canyon National Park), AZ*

Guided tours [W] *Kayenta, AZ*

Guided tours of Navajoland [W] *Window Rock, AZ*

Guided trips, hiking tours [W] *Zion National Park, UT*

Guinness World of Records Museum [W] *Las Vegas, NV*

Gunlock [W] *St. George, UT*

Gunnison National Forest [W] *Gunnison, CO*

Gunnison Pioneer Museum [W] *Gunnison, CO*

Hacienda Martinez [W] *Taos, NM*

Hagerman National Wildlife Refuge [W] *Sherman, TX*

Haley Library and History Center [W] *Midland, TX*

Hall of Flame Firefighting Museum [W] *Phoenix, AZ*

Hall of Life [W] *Denver, CO*

Hall of State [W] *Dallas, TX*

Hamill House Museum [W] *Georgetown, CO*

Hansen Planetarium [W] *Salt Lake City, UT*

Harbor Lights Celebration [S] *Corpus Christi, TX*

Hardrockers Holiday [S] *Silverton, CO*

Harris Fine Arts Center [W] *Provo, UT*

Harrison County Historical Museum [W] *Marshall, TX*

Harry Ransom Humanities Research Center [W] *Austin, TX*

Harwood Museum of Art [W] *Taos, NM*

Hatch River Expeditions [W] *Vernal, UT*

Hawley Lake [W] *McNary, AZ*

Headquarters Building [W] *Rocky Mountain National Park, CO*

Healy House-Dexter Cabin [W] *Leadville, CO*

Heard Museum, The [W] *Phoenix, AZ*

Heard Natural Science Museum and Wildlife Sanctuary [W] *McKinney, TX*

Heart o' Texas Fair & Rodeo [S] *Waco, TX*

Heart o' Texas Speedway [S] *Waco, TX*

Heber Valley Railroad [W] *Heber City, UT*

Helen Bonfils Theatre Complex, The [W] *Denver, CO*

Helldorado [S] *Tombstone, AZ*

Hell's Half Acre to Sundance Square [W] *Fort Worth, TX*

HemisFair Park [W] *San Antonio, TX*

HeritageAspen: Aspen's Historical Society [W] *Aspen, CO*

Heritage Days [S] *Henderson, NV*

Heritage Guild's Christmas Tour of Homes [S] *McKinney, TX*

Heritage House Museum [W] *Orange, TX*

Heritage Museum [W] *Big Spring, TX*

Heritage Museum and Gallery [W] *Leadville, CO*

Heritage Park [W] *Corpus Christi, TX*

Heritage Society Tours [W] *Houston, TX*

Heritage Square [W] *Golden, CO*

Heritage Square [W] *Phoenix, AZ*

Hermann Park [W] *Houston, TX*

Heron Lake State Park [W] *Chama, NM*

Hickison Petroglyph Recreation Site [W] *Austin, NV*

Hidalgo County Historical Museum [W] *Edinburg, TX*

Highland Lakes [W] *Austin, TX*

Highland Lakes Bluebonnet Trail [S] *Austin, TX*

Highline Lake [W] *Grand Junction, CO*

High Plains Gem & Mineral Show [S] *Plainview, TX*

Hikes [W] *Bryce Canyon National Park, UT*

Hiking [W] *North Rim (Grand Canyon National Park), AZ*

Hiking, camping, mountain biking, snowmobiling, and cross-country skiing [W] *Buena Vista, CO*

Hiking down into canyon [W] *South Rim (Grand Canyon National Park), AZ*

Hiking, fishing, boating, horseback riding [W] *Grand Lake, CO*

Hill Aerospace Museum [W] *Ogden, UT*

Hill Country Museum (Captain Charles Schreiner Mansion) [W] *Kerrville, TX*

Hill County Fair [S] *Hillsboro, TX*

Hillcrest Park and Zoo [W] *Clovis, NM*

Hillsboro Outlet Center [W] *Hillsboro, TX*

Hinsdale County Historical Society Tours [W] *Lake City, CO*

Hinsdale County Museum [W] *Lake City, CO*

Historical Center for Southeast New Mexico [W] *Roswell, NM*

Historical House Museum Complex [W] *Stephenville, TX*

Historical Museum and Art Center [W] *Artesia, NM*

Historical parks [W] *Houston, TX*

Historical Pilgrimage [S] *Jefferson, TX*

Historical Society Headquarters [W] *Monte Vista, CO*

Historic buildings [W] *Golden, CO*

Historic Homes Tour [S] *Galveston, TX*

Hiwan Homestead Museum [W] *Evergreen, CO*

Hogle Zoological Garden [W] *Salt Lake City, UT*

Hoka Hey Fine Arts Gallery & Foundry [W] *Stephenville, TX*

Hole 'n the Rock [W] *Moab, UT*

Holiday Lighted Boat Parade [S] *Parker, AZ*

Holiday River and Bike Expeditions [W] *Green River, UT*

Holiday River and Bike Expeditions [W] *Vernal, UT*

Holland Lake Park [W] *Weatherford, TX*

Home and Garden Festival [S] *Wichita Falls, TX*

Homolovi Ruins State Park [W] *Winslow, AZ*

Hoover Dam [W] *Lake Mead National Recreation Area, NV*

Hopi Artists' Exhibition [S] *Flagstaff, AZ*

Hopkins County Dairy Festival [S] *Sulphur Springs, TX*

Horse races [S] *Douglas, AZ*

Horse racing [S] *Arlington-Grand Prairie, TX*

Horse racing [S] *El Paso, TX*

Horse racing [S] *Ruidoso, NM*

Horse racing [S] *Santa Fe, NM*

Horse shows [S] *Estes Park, CO*

Hot Air Expeditions [W] *Scottsdale, AZ*

Hotel de Paris Museum [W] *Georgetown, CO*

Hot Pepper Festival [S] *Palestine, TX*

Hot Slide Hydrotube [W] *Steamboat Springs, CO*

Hot Springs Pool [W] *Ouray, CO*

Hotter 'n Hell Bicycle Ride [S] *Wichita Falls, TX*

House of the Seasons [W] *Jefferson, TX*

Houston Arboretum and Nature Center [W] *Houston, TX*

Houston Astros (MLB) [W] *Houston, TX*

Houston Ballet [W] *Houston, TX*

Houston Grand Opera [W] *Houston, TX*

Houston International Festival [S] *Houston, TX*

Houston Livestock Show & Rodeo [S] *Houston, TX*

Houston Museum of Natural Science [W] *Houston, TX*

Houston Rockets (NBA) [W] *Houston, TX*

Houston Symphony, The [S] *Houston, TX*

Houston Zoological Gardens [W] *Houston, TX*

Hovenweep National Monument [W] *Blanding, UT*

Hovenweep National Monument [W] *Cortez, CO*

Howard County Fair [S] *Big Spring, TX*

Howard-Dickinson House [W] *Henderson, TX*

Howelsen Hill Ski Complex [W] *Steamboat Springs, CO*

Hozhoni Tours [W] *Window Rock, AZ*

Hubbard Museum of the American West [W] *Ruidoso, NM*

Hubbell Trading Post National Historic Site [W] *Ganado, AZ*

Hudnall Planetarium [W] *Tyler, TX*

Hueco Tanks State Historic Site [W] *El Paso, TX*

Humboldt Museum [W] *Winnemucca, NV*

Humboldt National Forest [W] *Elko, NV*

Humboldt National Forest [W] *Ely, NV*

Hummer/Bird Celebration [S] *Rockport, TX*

Hunt County Fair [S] *Greenville, TX*

Hunting [W] *Show Low, AZ*

Huntsville State Park [W] *Huntsville, TX*

Hutchinson County Historical Museum [W] *Fritch, TX*

Hyde Memorial State Park [W] *Santa Fe, NM*

Hyrum State Park [W] *Logan, UT*

Imogene Pass Mountain Marathon [S] *Ouray, CO*

Imperial Casino Hotel [W] *Cripple Creek, CO*

Imperial Holly Corporation [W] *Houston, TX*

Imperial National Wildlife Refuge [W] *Yuma, AZ*

Imperial Palace Auto Collection [W] *Las Vegas, NV*

Independence Day Celebration & Fireworks Extravaganza [S] *South Padre Island, TX*

Independence Day Celebration & Belton PRCA Rodeo [S] *Temple, TX*

Independence Hall [W] *Brenham, TX*

Independence Stampede Greeley Rodeo [S] *Greeley, CO*

Indian Fair and Market [S] *Phoenix, AZ*

Indian Market [S] *Santa Fe, NM*

Indian Pueblo Cultural Center [W] *Albuquerque, NM*

Industrial Tour [W] *Boulder, CO*

Industrial tour. Anheuser-Busch Brewery [W] *Fort Collins, CO*

Industrial tour. Coors Brewing Company [W] *Golden, CO*

Industrial Tour. Van Briggle Art Pottery Company [W] *Colorado Springs, CO*

Inks Lake State Park [W] *Burnet, TX*

Inner Space Cavern [W] *Austin, TX*

Inner Space Cavern [W] *Georgetown, TX*

InnsBrook Tours [W] *Salt Lake City, UT*

Institute of American Indian Arts Museum [W] *Santa Fe, NM*

Institute of Texan Cultures [W] *San Antonio, TX*

International Bell Museum [W] *Evergreen, CO*

International Snow Sculpture Championships [S] *Breckenridge, CO*

International UFO Museum & Research Center [W] *Roswell, NM*

International Wildlife Museum [W] *Tucson, AZ*

Inter-Tribal Indian Ceremonial [S] *Gallup, NM*

Invensys Classic [S] *Las Vegas, NV*

Invitational Antique Indian Art Show [S] *Santa Fe, NM*

Iron Horse Bicycle Classic [S] *Durango, CO*

Iron Horse Bicycle Classic [S] *Silverton, CO*

Iron Mission State Park [W] *Cedar City, UT*

Iron Springs Chateau [W] *Manitou Springs, CO*

Island of Lights Festival [S] *South Padre Island, TX*

Isleta Pueblo [W] *Albuquerque, NM*

Iwo Jima Memorial & Museum [W] *Harlingen, TX*

Jackson Lake State Park [W] *Fort Morgan, CO*

Jackson Monument [W] *Idaho Springs, CO*

Jacob Hamblin Home [W] *St. George, UT*

Jail Tree, The [W] *Wickenburg, AZ*

James A. Michener Library [W] *Greeley, CO*

Janes-Wallace Memorial Park [W] *Santa Rosa, NM*

Japanese Tea Gardens [W] *San Antonio, TX*

Jazz Celebration [S] *Telluride, CO*

Jazz Festival [S] *Odessa, TX*

J. D. Murphree Wildlife Management Area [W] *Port Arthur, TX*

Jeep Safari [S] *Moab, UT*

Jeep tours [W] *Salida, CO*

Jeep tours [W] *Sedona, AZ*

Jeep trips [W] *Ouray, CO*

Jefferson Historical Museum [W] *Jefferson, TX*

Jefferson Riverboat Landing & Depot [W] *Jefferson, TX*

Jefferson Theatre [W] *Beaumont, TX*

Jemez State Monument [W] *Los Alamos, NM*

Jerome [W] *Cottonwood, AZ*

Jerome State Historic Park [W] *Cottonwood, AZ*

Jersey Barnyard [W] *La Grange, TX*

Jicarilla Apache Indian Reservation [W] *Dulce, NM*

Jim Hogg State Historical Park [W] *Rusk, TX*

Jim Wells County Fair [S] *Alice, TX*

John E. Conner Museum [W] *Kingsville, TX*

John F. Kennedy Memorial Plaza [W] *Dallas, TX*

John Hutchings Museum [W] *Provo, UT*

John Jay French Museum (Historic House) [W] *Beaumont, TX*

Johnson Settlement [W] *Johnson City, TX*

John Wesley Powell Memorial Museum [W] *Page, AZ*

John Wesley Powell River History Museum [W] *Green River, UT*

Jonson Gallery [W] *Albuquerque, NM*

Joyride & Rod Run [S] *Brazosport, TX*

Jubilee Theatre [W] *Fort Worth, TX*

Judge Roy Bean Visitor Center [W] *Del Rio, TX*

Judy Bayley Theatre [W] *Las Vegas, NV*

Juneteenth Festival [S] *Houston, TX*

Junior Parada [S] *Florence, AZ*

Kaibab National Forest [W] *South Rim (Grand Canyon National Park), AZ*

Kaibab National Forest [W] *Williams, AZ*

Kell House [W] *Wichita Falls, TX*

Kennecott Bingham Canyon Mine [W] *Salt Lake City, UT*

Kerr County Fair [S] *Kerrville, TX*

Kerrville Folk Festival [S] *Kerrville, TX*

Kerrville-Schreiner State Park [W] *Kerrville, TX*

Kerrville Wine & Music Festival [S] *Kerrville, TX*

Keystone Mountain [W] *Dillon, CO*

Keystone Resort Ski Area [W] *Dillon, CO*

Killeen Festival of Flags [S] *Killeen, TX*

Kimball Art Center [W] *Park City, UT*

Kimbell Art Museum [W] *Fort Worth, TX*

Kinetic Conveyance Sculpture Challenge [S] *Boulder, CO*

King Ranch [W] *Kingsville, TX*

Kit Carson County Carousel [W] *Burlington, CO*

Kit Carson County Fair & Rodeo [S] *Burlington, CO*

Kit Carson Home and Museum [W] *Taos, NM*

Kit Carson Park [W] *Taos, NM*

Kit Carson Rendezvous [S] *Carson City, NV*

Kitt Peak National Observatory [W] *Sells, AZ*

Kitt Peak National Observatory [W] *Tucson, AZ*

Kodak Albuquerque International Balloon Fiesta [S] *Albuquerque, NM*

Kolob Canyons Visitor Center [W] *Cedar City, UT*

Kolob Canyons Visitor Center [W] *Zion National Park, UT*

Koshare Indian Dances [S] *La Junta, CO*

Koshare Indian Kiva Museum [W] *La Junta, CO*

Koshare Winter Night Ceremonial [S] *La Junta, CO*

Krabloonik Husky Kennels [W] *Snowmass Village, CO*

Labor Day Rodeo [S] *Williams, AZ*

Lady Bird Johnson Wildflower Research Center [W] *Austin, TX*

La Fonda Hotel [W] *Santa Fe, NM*

Lagoon Amusement Park, Pioneer Village and Water Park [W] *Salt Lake City, UT*

Lagoon and Pioneer Village [W] *Ogden, UT*

Laguna Atascosa National Wildlife Refuge [W] *Harlingen, TX*

Laguna Gloria Arts Festival [S] *Austin, TX*

Laguna Pueblo [W] *Grants, NM*

Lahontan State Recreation Area [W] *Fallon, NV*

Lake Arrowhead State Park [W] *Wichita Falls, TX*

Lake Bardwell [W] *Ennis, TX*

Lake Bastrop Park [W] *Bastrop, TX*

Lake Bonham Recreation Area [W] *Bonham, TX*

Lake Brownwood State Park [W] *Brownwood, TX*

Lake Buchanan [W] *Burnet, TX*

Lake Carlsbad Water Recreation Area [W] *Carlsbad, NM*

Lake Casa Blanca International State Park [W] *Laredo, TX*

Lake Colorado City State Park [W] *Big Spring, TX*

Lake Corpus Christi State Park [W] *Alice, TX*

Lake Dillon [W] *Dillon, CO*

Lakefest Regatta [S] *Sherman, TX*

Lake Georgetown [W] *Georgetown, TX*

Lake Havasu State Park [W] *Lake Havasu City, AZ*

Lake Isabel [W] *Pueblo, CO*

Lake Jacksonville [W] *Jacksonville, TX*

Lake J. B. Thomas [W] *Snyder, TX*

Lake Kemp [W] *Vernon, TX*

Lake Kickapoo [W] *Wichita Falls, TX*

Lake Limestone [W] *Groesbeck, TX*

Lake Mead Cruises [W] *Lake Mead National Recreation Area, NV*

Lake Meredith Aquatic & Wildlife Museum [W] *Fritch, TX*

Lake Meredith National Recreation Area [W] *Fritch, TX*

Lake o' the Pines [W] *Jefferson, TX*

Lake Powell Ferry [W] *Lake Powell, UT*

Lake Pueblo State Park [W] *Pueblo, CO*

Lake Somerville [W] *Brenham, TX*

Lake Tahoe Nevada State Park [W] *Incline Village, NV*

Lake Tahoe Winter Games Festival [S] *Incline Village, NV*

Lake Tawakoni [W] *Greenville, TX*

Lake Texoma [W] *Gainesville, TX*

Lake Texoma [W] *Sherman, TX*

Lake Waco [W] *Waco, TX*

Lake Weatherford [W] *Weatherford, TX*

Lake Whitney State Park [W] *Lake Whitney, TX*

Lakewood's Heritage Center [W] *Lakewood, CO*

Lake Worth [W] *Fort Worth, TX*

La Lomita Farms State Historic Site [W] *Mission, TX*

La Lomita Mission [W] *Mission, TX*

La Maison Acadienne Museum [W] *Port Arthur, TX*

Landa Park [W] *New Braunfels, TX*

Lander County Courthouse, The [W] *Austin, NV*

La Paz County Fair [S] *Parker, AZ*

La Paz County Park [W] *Parker, AZ*

Laredo Children's Museum [W] *Laredo, TX*

Laredo International Fair & Exposition [S] *Laredo, TX*

Lariat Trail [W] *Golden, CO*

Larimer County Fair and Rodeo [S] *Loveland, CO*

Larimer Square [W] *Denver, CO*

Las Posadas [S] *San Antonio, TX*

Las Vegas Art Museum [W] *Las Vegas, NV*

Las Vegas Convention/Visitors Authority [W] *Las Vegas, NV*

Las Vegas Motor Speedway [W] *Las Vegas, NV*

Las Vegas National Wildlife Refuge [W] *Las Vegas, NM*

Las Vegas Natural History Museum [W] *Las Vegas, NV*

Lathrop State Park [W] *Walsenburg, CO*

Laughlin Riverdays [S] *Laughlin, NV*

Lavender Pit [W] *Bisbee, AZ*

La Villita [W] *San Antonio, TX*

Lavon Lake [W] *McKinney, TX*

Layland Museum [W] *Cleburne, TX*

LBJ Ranch House ("Texas White House") [W] *Johnson City, TX*

Lea County Cowboy Hall of Fame & Western Heritage Center [W] *Hobbs, NM*

Lea County Fair [S] *Hobbs, NM*

Leadville, Colorado & Southern Railroad Train Tour [W] *Leadville, CO*

Leadville National Fish Hatchery [W] *Leadville, CO*

Leanin' Tree Museum of Western Art [W] *Boulder, CO*

Legends of Western Swing Music Festival [S] *Snyder, TX*

Leonard Park [W] *Gainesville, TX*

LeTourneau University [W] *Longview, TX*

Lewisville Lake [W] *Denton, TX*

Liberace Foundation and Museum [W] *Las Vegas, NV*

Liberty Park [W] *Salt Lake City, UT*

Licensed casinos, nightclubs [W] *Elko, NV*

LIFE Downs [W] *Laredo, TX*

Limestone County Historical Museum [W] *Groesbeck, TX*

Lincoln Center [W] *Fort Collins, CO*

Lincoln County Fair and Rodeo [S] *Caliente, NV*

Lincoln County Homecoming [S] *Caliente, NV*

Lincoln National Forest [W] *Alamogordo, NM*

Lincoln State Monument [W] *Ruidoso, NM*

Lindheimer Home [W] *New Braunfels, TX*

Lion House [W] *Salt Lake City, UT*

Lipton Cup Sailing Regatta [S] *Grand Lake, CO*

Little Beaver Roundup [S] *Dulce, NM*

Little Britches Rodeo [S] *Burlington, CO*

Little-Chapel-in-the-Woods [W] *Denton, TX*

Little Red Schoolhouse [W] *Wickenburg, AZ*

Livestock auction [W] *Amarillo, TX*

Living Desert Zoo and Gardens State Park [W] *Carlsbad, NM*

Llano Estacado Museum [W] *Plainview, TX*

Llano Estacado Winery [W] *Lubbock, TX*

Lockhart State Park [W] *San Marcos, TX*

Log Cabin Village [W] *Fort Worth, TX*

Logger Days Festival [S] *South Fork, CO*

London Bridge Resort & English Village [W] *Lake Havasu City, AZ*

Long and Step Houses and Badger House Community [W] *Mesa Verde National Park, CO*

Longhorn Cavern State Park [W] *Burnet, TX*

Longhorn Trail Drive [S] *Kerrville, TX*

Longmont Museum [W] *Longmont, CO*

Longview Museum of Fine Arts [W] *Longview, TX*

Loretto Chapel [W] *Santa Fe, NM*

Lory State Park [W] *Fort Collins, CO*

Los Alamos Historical Museum [W] *Los Alamos, NM*

Los Ebanos International Ferry [W] *Mission, TX*

Lost City Museum of Archaeology [W] *Overton, NV*

Lost Dutchman State Park [W] *Mesa, AZ*

Love's Lookout State Park [W] *Jacksonville, TX*

Lowell Observatory [W] *Flagstaff, AZ*

Lowry Pueblo [W] *Cortez, CO*

Lubbock Arts Festival [S] *Lubbock, TX*

Lubbock Lake Landmark State Historic Park [W] *Lubbock, TX*

Lucas Gusher Monument [W] *Beaumont, TX*

Lutcher Theater for the Performing Arts [W] *Orange, TX*

Lyman Lake State Park [W] *Springerville, AZ*

Lynchburg Ferry [W] *Baytown, TX*

Lyndon Baines Johnson Library & Museum [W] *Austin, TX*

Lyndon B. Johnson National Historical Park [W] *Johnson City, TX*

Lyndon B. Johnson State Historical Park [W] *Johnson City, TX*

Lyon County Museum [W] *Yerington, NV*

Mackay School of Mines Museum [W] *Reno, NV*

Mackenzie Park [W] *Lubbock, TX*

Macky Auditorium Concert Hall [W] *Boulder, CO*

Madonna of the Trail [W] *Springerville, AZ*

Magic Town [W] *Colorado Springs, CO*

Magnolia Homes Tour [S] *Eagle Lake, TX*

Magoffin Home State Historic Site [W] *El Paso, TX*

MAIN Street Fort Worth Arts Festival [S] *Fort Worth, TX*

Manitou Cliff Dwellings Museum [W] *Manitou Springs, CO*

Manti-LaSal National Forest, LaSal Division [W] *Moab, UT*

Manti-LaSal National Forest, LaSal Division [W] *Monticello, UT*

Manti-LaSal National Forest, Manti Division [W] *Price, UT*

Marble Canyon [W] *Marble Canyon, AZ*

Marcia [W] *Craig, CO*

Mardi Gras [S] *Galveston, TX*

Mardi Gras in the Mountains [S] *Red River, NM*

Mardi Gras of SE Texas [S] *Port Arthur, TX*

Marfa Lights Festival [S] *Marfa, TX*

Mariani Art Gallery [W] *Greeley, CO*

Marjorie Barrick Museum of Natural History [W] *Las Vegas, NV*

Market House Museum [W] *Goliad, TX*

Market Square [W] *San Antonio, TX*

Marriott Library [W] *Salt Lake City, UT*

Marshall Pottery [W] *Marshall, TX*

Martin Dies, Jr. State Park [W] *Jasper, TX*

Mary of Puddin Hill [W] *Greenville, TX*

Mason County Museum [W] *Mason, TX*

Matamoros, Tamaulipas, Mexico [W] *Brownsville, TX*

Matchless Mine, The [W] *Leadville, CO*

Maurice Abravanel Concert Hall [W] *Salt Lake City, UT*

Maverick Club Rodeo [S] *Cimarron, NM*

Maxwell Museum of Anthropology [W] *Albuquerque, NM*

Mayfair [S] *Georgetown, TX*

May Natural History Museum [W] *Colorado Springs, CO*

McAllen International Museum [W] *McAllen, TX*

McAllen Nature Center [W] *McAllen, TX*

McAllister House Museum [W] *Colorado Springs, CO*

McCormick Steelman Railroad Park [W] *Scottsdale, AZ*

McDonald Observatory [W] *Alpine, TX*

McFaddin-Ward House [W] *Beaumont, TX*

McFarland State Historic Park [W] *Florence, AZ*

McGaffey Recreation Area [W] *Gallup, NM*

McKinney Avenue Transit Authority [W] *Dallas, TX*

McKinney Falls State Park [W] *Austin, TX*

McNay Art Museum [W] *San Antonio, TX*

Meadows School of the Arts [W] *Dallas, TX*

Meadow Valley Western Days [S] *Caliente, NV*

Mecom Rockwell Fountain [W] *Houston, TX*

Meeker Home [W] *Greeley, CO*

Melon Days [S] *Green River, UT*

Memorial Square [W] *Victoria, TX*

Menger Hotel [W] *San Antonio, TX*

Menil Collection, The [W] *Houston, TX*

Mesa Southwest Museum [W] *Mesa, AZ*

Mesa Territorial Day Festival [S] *Mesa, AZ*

Mesa Top Loop & Cliff Palace Loop [W] *Mesa Verde National Park, CO*

Mesa Verde National Park [W] *Cortez, CO*

Mesa Verde National Park [W] *Durango, CO*

Mescalero Apache Maidens' Ceremonial [S] *Mescalero, NM*

Mescalero Apache Reservation [W] *Mescalero, NM*

Mesilla [W] *Las Cruces, NM*

Messina Hof Wine Cellars [W] *Bryan/College Station, TX*

Meteor Crater [W] *Odessa, TX*

Meteor Crater [W] *Winslow, AZ*

Mexican Independence Day Festival [S] *Port Arthur, TX*

Mexic-Arte Museum [W] *Austin, TX*

Mex-Tex Menudo [S] *Midland, TX*

Michelson Museum of Art [W] *Marshall, TX*

Midland Community Theatre [W] *Midland, TX*

Midnight at the Oasis Festival [S] *Yuma, AZ*

Military Plaza [W] *San Antonio, TX*

Millard's Crossing [W] *Nacogdoches, TX*

Millicent Rogers Museum [W] *Taos, NM*

Million Barrel Museum [W] *Monahans, TX*

Million Dollar Museum [W] *Carlsbad, NM*

Mineral Museum [W] *Socorro, NM*

Mineral Museum [W] *Tucson, AZ*

Mineral Palace Park [W] *Pueblo, CO*

Mineral pools and baths [W] *Glenwood Springs, CO*

Mine tours [W] *Bisbee, AZ*

Miraculous Staircase, The [W] *Santa Fe, NM*

Miramont Castle Museum [W] *Manitou Springs, CO*

Miramonte Lake [W] *Norwood, CO*

Mission Concepcion [W] *San Antonio, TX*

Mission Espada [W] *San Antonio, TX*

Mission Espiritu Santo de ZuÒiga [W] *Goliad, TX*

Mission San Jose [W] *San Antonio, TX*

Mission San Juan [W] *San Antonio, TX*

Mission Tejas State Historical Park [W] *Crockett, TX*

Moab Music Festival [S] *Moab, UT*

Modern Art Museum of Fort Worth [W] *Fort Worth, TX*

Mogollon Ghost Town [W] *Silver City, NM*

Mohave County Fair [S] *Kingman, AZ*

Mohave Museum of History & Art [W] *Kingman, AZ*

Moki Mac River Expeditions [W] *Green River, UT*

Mollie Kathleen Gold Mine [W] *Cripple Creek, CO*

Molly Brown House Museum [W] *Denver, CO*

Monahans Sandhills State Park [W] *Monahans, TX*

Monarch Scenic Tram [W] *Salida, CO*

Monastery of St. Clare Miniature Horse Ranch [W] *Brenham, TX*

Monroe-Crook House [W] *Crockett, TX*

Monte L. Bean Life Science Museum [W] *Provo, UT*

Monte Vista Crane Festival [S] *Monte Vista, CO*

Monte Vista National Wildlife Refuge [W] *Monte Vista, CO*

Montezuma Castle National Monument [W] *Cottonwood, AZ*

Montezuma County Fair [S] *Cortez, CO*

Monticello Pioneer Days [S] *Monticello, UT*

Montrose County Historical Museum [W] *Montrose, CO*

Monument Headquarters and Information Center [W] *Dinosaur National Monument, CO*

Monument Hill & Kreische Brewery State Historical Park [W] *La Grange, TX*

Monument to Prunes, a Burro [W] *Fairplay, CO*

Monument Valley Navajo Tribal Park [W] *Kayenta, AZ*

Moody Gardens [W] *Galveston, TX*

Moraine Park Museum [W] *Rocky Mountain National Park, CO*

Mormon Lake Ski Center [W] *Flagstaff, AZ*

Mormon Miracle Pageant [S] *Salina, UT*

Mormon Station State Historic Park [W] *Gardnerville, NV*

Mormon Tabernacle [W] *Logan, UT*

Mormon Temple [W] *Logan, UT*

Morphy Lake State Park [W] *Las Vegas, NM*

Morton Museum of Cooke County [W] *Gainesville, TX*

Moss Lake [W] *Gainesville, TX*

Motor sports [S] *Colorado Springs, CO*

Mountain biking [W] *Austin, NV*

Mountain climbing [W] *Zion National Park, UT*

Mountain Community Fair [S] *Dillon, CO*

Mountain Film Festival [S] *Telluride, CO*

Mountain Rendezvous [S] *Evergreen, CO*

Mountain Spirit Winery [W] *Salida, CO*

Mountain Spirit Winery [W] *Salida, CO*

Mount Charleston Recreation Area [W] *Las Vegas, NV*

Mount Nebo Scenic Loop Drive [W] *Payson, UT*

Mount Pleasant Championship Rodeo [S] *Mount Pleasant, TX*

Mount Rose Ski Area [W] *Incline Village, NV*

Mount Shavano Fish Hatchery [W] *Salida, CO*

Muleback trips [W] *North Rim (Grand Canyon National Park), AZ*

Mule trip into canyon [W] *South Rim (Grand Canyon National Park), AZ*

Multiday trips [W] *South Rim (Grand Canyon National Park), AZ*

Municipal Band Concerts [S] *Paris, TX*

Municipal Museum [W] *Greeley, CO*

Museum [W] *Mesa Verde National Park, CO*

Museum of Art [W] *Provo, UT*

Museum of Art [W] *Tucson, AZ*

Museum of Church History and Art [W] *Salt Lake City, UT*

Museum of East Texas [W] *Lufkin, TX*

Museum of Fine Arts [W] *Houston, TX*

Museum of Fine Arts [W] *Santa Fe, NM*

Museum of Geology and Institute of Meteoritics Meteorite Museum [W] *Albuquerque, NM*

Museum of Indian Arts and Culture [W] *Santa Fe, NM*

Museum of International Folk Art [W] *Santa Fe, NM*

Museum of Northern Arizona [W] *Flagstaff, AZ*

Museum of Northwest Colorado [W] *Craig, CO*

Museum of Outdoor Arts, The [W] *Englewood, CO*

Museum of Peoples and Cultures [W] *Provo, UT*

Museum of Texas Tech University [W] *Lubbock, TX*

Museum of the American Numismatic Association [W] *Colorado Springs, CO*

Museum of the Big Bend [W] *Alpine, TX*

Museum of the Gulf Coast [W] *Port Arthur, TX*

Museum of the Southwest [W] *Midland, TX*

Museum of Western Colorado [W] *Grand Junction, CO*

Musical Theater Southwest [S] *Albuquerque, NM*

Music Hall [W] *Dallas, TX*

Music Hall [W] *Houston, TX*

Mustang Round-Up [S] *Steamboat Springs, CO*

Mystery Castle [W] *Phoenix, AZ*

National Aerobatic Championships [S] *Sherman, TX*

National Atomic Museum [W] *Albuquerque, NM*

National Automobile Museum [W] *Reno, NV*

National Basque Festival [S] *Elko, NV*

National Center for American Western Art [W] *Kerrville, TX*

National Center for Atmospheric Research [W] *Boulder, CO*

National Championship Air Races [S] *Reno, NV*

National Finals Rodeo [S] *Las Vegas, NV*

National Forests [W] *Lufkin, TX*

National Mining Hall of Fame and Museum [W] *Leadville, CO*

National Park Service lectures, field trips [W] *Grand Lake, CO*

National Park Service, Southwest Regional Office [W] *Santa Fe, NM*

National Polka Festival [S] *Ennis, TX*

National Radio Astronomy Observatory [W] *Socorro, NM*

National Scientific Balloon Facility [W] *Palestine, TX*

National Western Livestock Show, Horse Show, and Rodeo [S] *Denver, CO*

Native American Festival [S] *Litchfield Park, AZ*

Natural Bridge Caverns [W] *New Braunfels, TX*

Natural Bridge Caverns [W] *San Antonio, TX*

Natural Bridges National Monument [W] *Blanding, UT*

Navajo Artists' Exhibition [S] *Flagstaff, AZ*

Navajo County Fair [S] *Holbrook, AZ*

Navajo County Historical Museum [W] *Holbrook, AZ*

Navajo Lake State Park [W] *Aztec, NM*

Navajo Nation Fair [S] *Gallup, NM*

Navajo Nation Fair [S] *Window Rock, AZ*

Navajo Nation Museum [W] *Window Rock, AZ*

Navajo Nation Zoological and Botanical Park [W] *Window Rock, AZ*

Navajo State Park [W] *Pagosa Springs, CO*

Navarro Mills Lake [W] *Corsicana, TX*

Neches River Festival [S] *Beaumont, TX*

Nederland Windmill Museum [W] *Port Arthur, TX*

Neill-Cochran House [W] *Austin, TX*

Nelson Fine Arts Center and Ceramics Reserach Center [W] *Tempe, AZ*

Nevada Day Celebration [S] *Carson City, NV*

Nevada Historical Society Museum [W] *Reno, NV*

Nevada Museum of Art [W] *Reno, NV*

Nevada Northern Railway Museum [W] *Ely, NV*

Nevada State Fair [S] *Reno, NV*

Nevada State Museum [W] *Carson City, NV*

Nevada State Museum and Historical Society [W] *Las Vegas, NV*

Nevada State Railroad Museum [W] *Carson City, NV*

Never Summer Ranch [W] *Rocky Mountain National Park, CO*

New Braunfels Museum of Art and Music [W] *New Braunfels, TX*

New Mexico Arts & Crafts Fair [S] *Albuquerque, NM*

New Mexico Farm and Ranch Heritage Museum [W] *Las Cruces, NM*

New Mexico Military Institute [W] *Roswell, NM*

New Mexico Mining Museum [W] *Grants, NM*

New Mexico Museum of Natural History [W] *Albuquerque, NM*

New Mexico Museum of Space History [W] *Alamogordo, NM*

New Mexico Museum of Space History Induction Ceremonies [S] *Alamogordo, NM*

New Mexico State Fair [S] *Albuquerque, NM*

New Mexico State University [W] *Las Cruces, NM*

New Mexico Symphony Orchestra [S] *Albuquerque, NM*

Niels Petersen House Museum [W] *Tempe, AZ*

Night in Old Fredericksburg [S] *Fredericksburg, TX*

Noah's Ark Whitewater Rafting Company [W] *Buena Vista, CO*

Noble Planetarium [W] *Fort Worth, TX*

Noche de Espana Music Festival [S] *Hobbs, NM*

No Man's Land Day Celebration [S] *Breckenridge, CO*

Nordic Valley [W] *Ogden, UT*

Northeastern Nevada Museum [W] *Elko, NV*

Northern Pueblo Artist & Craftsman Show [S] *Santa Fe, NM*

North Mountain Recreation Area [W] *Phoenix, AZ*

North Peak [W] *Dillon, CO*

North Texas State Fair and Rodeo [S] *Denton, TX*

Nuevo Laredo, Tamaulipas, Mexico [W] *Laredo, TX*

Oak Creek Canyon [W] *Flagstaff, AZ*

Oak Creek Canyon [W] *Sedona, AZ*

Oasis State Park [W] *Portales, NM*

Oatman [W] *Kingman, AZ*

Ocean Star [W] *Galveston, TX*

Office of the Tombstone Epitaph [W] *Tombstone, AZ*

O. Henry Home and Museum [W] *Austin, TX*

O.K. Corral [W] *Tombstone, AZ*

Old 761 Santa Fe Steam Locomotive [W] *Wickenburg, AZ*

Old Aztec Mill Museum [W] *Cimarron, NM*

Old City Park Museum [W] *Dallas, TX*

Old Colorado City [W] *Colorado Springs, CO*

Old Cora [W] *Comanche, TX*

Old Dowlin Mill [W] *Ruidoso, NM*

Oldest House [W] *Santa Fe, NM*

Old Fayette County Jail [W] *La Grange, TX*

Old Fort Days [S] *Santa Rosa, NM*

Old Fort Parker State Historical Park [W] *Groesbeck, TX*

Old Fort Stockton [W] *Fort Stockton, TX*

Old Hundred Gold Mine Tour [W] *Silverton, CO*

Old Jail & Locomotive [W] *Clifton, AZ*

Old Market Square [W] *Houston, TX*

Old mining town of Tincup [W] *Gunnison, CO*

Old Pecan Street Arts Festival [S] *Austin, TX*

Old San Miguel Mission [W] *Socorro, NM*

Old-Time Fiddler's Contest & Festival [S] *Payson, AZ*

Old Town [W] *Albuquerque, NM*

Old Town [W] *Burlington, CO*

Old Town Artisans [W] *Tucson, AZ*

Old Trail Driver's Park [W] *Fort Worth, TX*

Old Trails Museum [W] *Winslow, AZ*

Old West Celebration [S] *Holbrook, AZ*

Old West Gun Show [S] *Deming, NM*

Oliver Lee State Park [W] *Alamogordo, NM*

Omni Theater [W] *Fort Worth, TX*

One-day trips [W] *South Rim (Grand Canyon National Park), AZ*

O'Odham Tash-Casa Grande's Indian Days [S] *Casa Grande, AZ*

Orilla Verde Recreation Area [W] *Taos, NM*

Ortega's Weaving Shop [W] *Espanola, NM*

Oscar Rose Park [W] *Abilene, TX*

Otero Museum [W] *La Junta, CO*

Other activities [W] *Dinosaur National Monument, CO*

Other old buildings [W] *Austin, NV*

Ouray County Fair & Rodeo [S] *Ouray, CO*

Ouray County Historical Museum [W] *Ouray, CO*

Ouray National Wildlife Refuge [W] *Vernal, UT*

Our Lady of Guadalupe Fiesta [S] *Las Cruces, NM*

Outback, The [W] *Dillon, CO*

Outdoor sculptures [W] *Sterling, CO*

Outlaw Trail Festival [S] *Vernal, UT*

Overland Trail Museum [W] *Sterling, CO*

OysterFest [S] *Rockport, TX*

Padre Island [W] *Corpus Christi, TX*

Palace of the Governors [W] *Santa Fe, NM*

Palace of Wax, The [W] *Arlington-Grand Prairie, TX*

Palisade State Park [W] *Salina, UT*

Palmer Park [W] *Colorado Springs, CO*

Palmetto State Park [W] *Gonzales, TX*

Palmitto Ranch Battlefield [W] *Brownsville, TX*

Palo Alto Battlefield National Historic Site [W] *Brownsville, TX*

Palo Duro Canyon State Park [W] *Amarillo, TX*

Palo Duro Canyon State Park [W] *Canyon, TX*

Palo Pinto County Livestock Association Rodeo [S] *Mineral Wells, TX*

Pancho Villa State Park [W] *Deming, NM*

Panguitch Lake [W] *Panguitch, UT*

Panhandle-Plains Historical Museum [W] *Canyon, TX*

Parada del Sol & Rodeo [S] *Scottsdale, AZ*

Park City Mountain Resort [W] *Park City, UT*

Park City Mountain Resort [W] *Salt Lake City, UT*

Parker 400 Off Road Race [S] *Parker, AZ*

Parker Dam & Power Plant [W] *Parker, AZ*

Parker Enduro-Aquasports Weekend [S] *Parker, AZ*

Park Lake [W] *Santa Rosa, NM*

Park Point Fire Lookout [W] *Mesa Verde National Park, CO*

Park system [W] *Denver, CO*

Park trails [W] *Zion National Park, UT*

Paseo de Casas [S] *Cottonwood, AZ*

Paseo del Rio [W] *San Antonio, TX*

Patagonia Lake State Park [W] *Patagonia, AZ*

Patagonia-Sonoita Creek Preserve [W] *Patagonia, AZ*

Paunsagaunt Wildlife Museum [W] *Panguitch, UT*

Payson Lake Recreation Area [W] *Payson, UT*

Peach Days Celebration [S] *Brigham City, UT*

Peach Festival [S] *Weatherford, TX*
Peanut Valley Festival [S] *Portales, NM*
Pearce-McAllister Cottage [W] *Denver, CO*
Pecos National Historical Park [W] *Santa Fe, NM*
Pedernales Falls State Park [W] *Johnson City, TX*
Permian Basin Petroleum Museum [W] *Midland, TX*
Perot Theatre [W] *Texarkana, TX*
Peterson Air & Space Museum [W] *Colorado Springs, CO*
Petrified Forest National Park [W] *Holbrook, AZ*
Petroglyph National Monument [W] *Albuquerque, NM*
Phelps Dodge Copper Mine [W] *Silver City, NM*
Philmont Scout Ranch [W] *Cimarron, NM*
Phippen Museum Fine Art Show & Sale [S] *Prescott, AZ*
Phoenix Art Museum [W] *Phoenix, AZ*
Phoenix Coyotes (NHL) [W] *Phoenix, AZ*
Phoenix Gold Mine [W] *Idaho Springs, CO*
Phoenix Mercury (WNBA) [W] *Phoenix, AZ*
Phoenix Mountains Preserve [W] *Phoenix, AZ*
Phoenix Museum of History [W] *Phoenix, AZ*
Phoenix Suns (NBA) [W] *Phoenix, AZ*
Phoenix Symphony, The [S] *Phoenix, AZ*
Phoenix Zoo [W] *Phoenix, AZ*
Picacho Peak State Park [W] *Casa Grande, AZ*
Picacho Peak State Park [W] *Tucson, AZ*
Picnic areas [W] *Mesa Verde National Park, CO*
Picnicking, hiking, fishing [W] *Dinosaur National Monument, UT*
Piedras Negras, Mexico [W] *Eagle Pass, TX*
Pike National Forest [W] *Colorado Springs, CO*
Pike National Forest [W] *Fairplay, CO*
Pikes Peak [W] *Colorado Springs, CO*
Pikes Peak Auto Hill Climb Educational Museum [W] *Colorado Springs, CO*
Pikes Peak Auto Hill Climb [S] *Colorado Springs, CO*
Pikes Peak Cog Railway [W] *Manitou Springs, CO*
Pikes Peak Ghost Town [W] *Colorado Springs, CO*

Pikes Peak Marathon [S] *Colorado Springs, CO*
Pikes Peak or Bust Rodeo [S] *Colorado Springs, CO*
Pima Air & Space Museum [W] *Tucson, AZ*
Pimeria Alta Historical Society Museum [W] *Nogales, AZ*
Pinal County Historical Society Museum [W] *Florence, AZ*
Pine River Site [W] *Aztec, NM*
Pine Valley Chapel [W] *St. George, UT*
Pine View Reservoir [W] *Ogden, UT*
Pioneer Days [S] *Beaver, UT*
Pioneer Days [S] *Fort Worth, TX*
Pioneer Days [S] *Ogden, UT*
Pioneer Days [S] *Safford, AZ*
Pioneer Days & PRCA Rodeo [S] *Clovis, NM*
Pioneer Memorial Hall [W] *San Antonio, TX*
Pioneer Memorial Museum [W] *Salt Lake City, UT*
Pioneer Museum [W] *Fredericksburg, TX*
Pioneer Museum [W] *Provo, UT*
Pioneer Theatre Company [W] *Salt Lake City, UT*
Pioneer Village [W] *Corsicana, TX*
Pioneer West Museum [W] *Shamrock, TX*
Pipe Spring National Monument [W] *Kanab, UT*
Plaza, The [W] *Santa Fe, NM*
Plaza Wax Museum/Ripley's Believe It or Not! [W] *San Antonio, TX*
Pleasant Hill Winery [W] *Brenham, TX*
Pleasure Island [W] *Port Arthur, TX*
Pompeiian Villa [W] *Port Arthur, TX*
Ponderosa Ranch Western Studio and Theme Park [W] *Incline Village, NV*
Pony Express Days [S] *Ely, NV*
Port Brownsville [W] *Brownsville, TX*
Port of Houston, The [W] *Houston, TX*
Port of Port Arthur [W] *Port Arthur, TX*
Possum Kingdom State Park [W] *Graham, TX*
Potton House [W] *Big Spring, TX*
Powder Mountain [W] *Ogden, UT*
Powerhouse Visitor Center [W] *Kingman, AZ*
Powwow and PRCA Rodeo [S] *Window Rock, AZ*
Prairie Edge Museum [W] *Eagle Lake, TX*
PRCA Lion's Club Championship Rodeo [S] *Jasper, TX*
PRCA Rodeo [S] *Victoria, TX*

Prescott Frontier Days Rodeo [S]
    Prescott, AZ
Prescott National Forest [W] *Prescott,
    AZ*
Presidential Museum [W] *Odessa, TX*
Presidio La Bahia [W] *Goliad, TX*
Price Canyon Recreation Area [W]
    Price, UT
Proctor Lake [W] *Comanche, TX*
Professional sports [W] *Arlington-
    Grand Prairie, TX*
Professional sports [W] *Dallas, TX*
Professional sports [W] *Denver, CO*
Professional sports [W] *Houston, TX*
Professional sports [W] *Phoenix, AZ*
Professional sports [W] *Salt Lake City,
    UT*
Professional sports [W] *San Antonio,
    TX*
Professional sports [W] *Tempe, AZ*
Programs [W] *North Rim (Grand
    Canyon National Park), AZ*
Pro Rodeo Hall of Fame and Ameri-
    can Cowboy Museum [W] *Col-
    orado Springs, CO*
Pueblo Grande Museum and Cultural
    Park [W] *Phoenix, AZ*
Pueblo Greyhound Park [S] *Pueblo,
    CO*
Puerta de Luna [W] *Santa Rosa, NM*
Pyramid Lake [W] *Reno, NV*
Queen Mine [W] *Bisbee, AZ*
Rabbit Valley Trail Through Time [W]
    Grand Junction, CO
Rafting [W] *CaÒon City, CO*
Railroad & Heritage Museum [W]
    Temple, TX
Railroaders Festival [S] *Brigham City,
    UT*
Railroad Museum at the Center for
    Transportation and Commerce
    [W] *Galveston, TX*
Rainbow Bridge National Monument
    [W] *Page, AZ*
Rainbow Weekend [S] *Steamboat
    Springs, CO*
Ranching Heritage Center [W] *Lub-
    bock, TX*
Ranchos de Taos [W] *Taos, NM*
Rangerette Showcase [W] *Kilgore, TX*
Raton Museum [W] *Raton, NM*
Rattlesnake Roundup [S] *Big Spring,
    TX*
Rattlesnake Roundup [S] *Sweetwater,
    TX*
Rawhide 1880s Western Town [W]
    Scottsdale, AZ
Ray Roberts Lake State Park [W] *Den-
    ton, TX*
Recreation [W] *Aspen, CO*
Recreation [W] *Ouray, CO*

Recreational facilities [W] *Galveston,
    TX*
Recreational facilities [W] *Wichita
    Falls, TX*
Recreation areas [W] *Temple, TX*
Red Butte Garden and Arboretum [W]
    Salt Lake City, UT
Red Fleet State Park [W] *Vernal, UT*
Red River Historical Museum [W]
    Sherman, TX
Red River Valley Exposition [S] *Paris,
    TX*
Red River Valley Museum [W] *Vernon,
    TX*
Red Rock Balloon Rally [S] *Gallup,
    NM*
Red Rock Canyon National Conserva-
    tion Area [W] *Las Vegas, NV*
Red Rock Fantasy of Lights [S] *Sedona,
    AZ*
Red Rock Museum [W] *Gallup, NM*
Red Rocks Park [W] *Denver, CO*
Red Rock State Park [W] *Gallup, NM*
Reese River *Reveille*, The [W] *Austin,
    NV*
Reid Park [W] *Tucson, AZ*
Reliant Park [W] *Houston, TX*
Reliant Stadium [W] *Houston, TX*
Renaissance Craftfaire [S] *Las Cruces,
    NM*
Renaissance Fair [S] *Cedar City, UT*
Republic of Texas Chilympiad [S] *San
    Marcos, TX*
Republic of the Rio Grande Museum
    [W] *Laredo, TX*
Resaca de la Palma [W] *Brownsville, TX*
Reservoirs [W] *Jasper, TX*
Restored houses. Earle-Napier-Kin-
    nard House [W] *Waco, TX*
Rex Allen Arizona Cowboy Museum
    & Cowboy Hall of Fame, The
    [W] *Willcox, AZ*
Rex Allen Days [S] *Willcox, AZ*
Reynosa, Mexico [W] *McAllen, TX*
Rhythm on the River [S] *Longmont,
    CO*
Ridgway State Park [W] *Montrose, CO*
Riding [W] *Bryce Canyon National
    Park, UT*
Riggs Hill [W] *Grand Junction, CO*
Rim Tours [W] *Moab, UT*
RioFest [S] *Harlingen, TX*
Rio Grande Gorge Bridge [W] *Taos,
    NM*
Rio Grande National Forest [W] *South
    Fork, CO*
Rio Grande Nature Center State Park
    [W] *Albuquerque, NM*
Rio Grande Valley Birding Festival [S]
    Harlingen, TX
Rio Grande Zoo [W] *Albuquerque, NM*

Riordan State Historic Park [W] *Flagstaff, AZ*

Ripley's Believe It or Not! [W] *Arlington-Grand Prairie, TX*

Riverfest [S] *Brazosport, TX*

River Legacy Living Science Center [W] *Arlington-Grand Prairie, TX*

River Oaks Garden Club's Azalea Trail [S] *Houston, TX*

River rafting [W] *Aspen, CO*

River rafting [W] *Buena Vista, CO*

River rafting [W] *Dinosaur National Monument, CO*

River rafting [W] *Dinosaur National Monument, UT*

River Rafting [W] *Grand Junction, CO*

River rafting, kayaking, hunting, fishing, camping, hiking, biking, golf, horseback riding, pack trips [W] *Glenwood Springs, CO*

River rafting. Snowmass Whitewater [W] *Snowmass Village, CO*

River-running trips [W] *Marble Canyon, AZ*

Riverside Park [W] *Victoria, TX*

River trips [W] *Green River, UT*

River trips [W] *Moab, UT*

River trips [W] *Vernal, UT*

River trips. Moki Mac River Expeditions [W] *Salt Lake City, UT*

River tubing. Salt River Recreation Inc [W] *Mesa, AZ*

Robert S. Reading Indian Artifact Collection [W] *Corsicana, TX*

Rock collecting [W] *Tonopah, NV*

Rockhound Roundup [S] *Deming, NM*

Rockhound State Park [W] *Deming, NM*

Rock hunting [W] *Deming, NM*

Rock Lake Rearing Station [W] *Santa Rosa, NM*

Rock Ledge Ranch Historic Site [W] *Colorado Springs, CO*

Rockport State Park [W] *Park City, UT*

Rocks & Minerals [W] *Mason, TX*

Rocky Mountain National Park [W] *Estes Park, CO*

Rocky Mountain National Park [W] *Granby, CO*

Rocky Mountain National Park [W] *Grand Lake, CO*

Rocky Mountain Quilt Museum [W] *Golden, CO*

Rocky Mountain Repertory Theatre [S] *Grand Lake, CO*

Rocky Mountain Wildlife Park [W] *Pagosa Springs, CO*

Rodeo [S] *Fort Morgan, CO*

Rodeo [S] *Reno, NV*

Rodeo Weekend [S] *Evergreen, CO*

Roland's Navajo Land Tours [W] *Window Rock, AZ*

Rooftop Rodeo [S] *Estes Park, CO*

Roosevelt County Fair [S] *Portales, NM*

Roosevelt County Heritage Days [S] *Portales, NM*

Roosevelt National Forest [W] *Estes Park, CO*

Roper Lake State Park [W] *Safford, AZ*

Rose Hill Manor [W] *Port Arthur, TX*

Rosemount Victorian House Museum [W] *Pueblo, CO*

Rose Tree Inn Museum [W] *Tombstone, AZ*

Roswell Museum and Art Center [W] *Roswell, NM*

Rothko Chapel [W] *Houston, TX*

Route 66 Festival [S] *Tucumcari, NM*

Routt National Forest [W] *Steamboat Springs, CO*

Royal Gorge [W] *CaÒon City, CO*

Royal Gorge Frontier Town and Railway [W] *CaÒon City, CO*

Royal Gorge Rodeo [S] *CaÒon City, CO*

Royal Gorge Route [W] *CaÒon City, CO*

Rural Heritage Weekend [S] *Henderson, TX*

Rusk-Palestine State Park [W] *Palestine, TX*

Rusk-Palestine State Park [W] *Rusk, TX*

Ruth Hall Museum of Paleontology [W] *Espanola, NM*

Rye Patch State Recreation Area [W] *Lovelock, NV*

Sabine National Forests [W] *Jasper, TX*

Sabine Woods [W] *Port Arthur, TX*

Sacramento Mountains Historical Museum [W] *Cloudcroft, NM*

Sahawe Indian Dance Ceremonials [S] *Uvalde, TX*

St. Anthony's Day Celebration [S] *El Paso, TX*

St. Anthony's Feast-Comanche Dance [S] *Santa Fe, NM*

St. Augustin's Feast Day [S] *Albuquerque, NM*

Sainte Claire Feast Day [S] *Espanola, NM*

St. Francis School [W] *Santa Fe, NM*

St. John's College in Santa Fe [W] *Santa Fe, NM*

St. Mary's Glacier [W] *Idaho Springs, CO*

St. Michaels [W] *Window Rock, AZ*

St. Patrick's Day Celebration [S] *Shamrock, TX*

St. Paul's Episcopal Church [W] *Tombstone, AZ*

Saints Roost Museum [W] *Clarendon, TX*

Sakura Square [W] *Denver, CO*

Salida Museum [W] *Salida, CO*

Salt Lake Art Center [W] *Salt Lake City, UT*
Saltwater fishing [W] *Brownsville, TX*
Sam Bell Maxey House State Historical Park [W] *Paris, TX*
Sam Houston Memorial Museum Complex [W] *Huntsville, TX*
Sam Houston National Forest [W] *Huntsville, TX*
Sam Houston's Grave [W] *Huntsville, TX*
Sam Rayburn [W] *Jasper, TX*
Sam Rayburn House [W] *Bonham, TX*
Sam Rayburn Library and Museum [W] *Bonham, TX*
San Agustin Church [W] *Laredo, TX*
San Angelo State Park [W] *San Angelo, TX*
San Antonio Botanical Gardens [W] *San Antonio, TX*
San Antonio Museum of Art [W] *San Antonio, TX*
San Antonio Spurs (NBA) [W] *San Antonio, TX*
San Antonio Stock Show & Rodeo [S] *San Antonio, TX*
San Antonio Symphony [W] *San Antonio, TX*
Sandhill Hereford and Quarter Horse Show and Rodeo [S] *Odessa, TX*
Sandhills Interpretive Center [W] *Monahans, TX*
Sandia Peak Aerial Tramway [W] *Albuquerque, NM*
San Elizario [W] *El Paso, TX*
San Fernando Cathedral [W] *San Antonio, TX*
San Gabriel Park [W] *Georgetown, TX*
San Geronimo Eve Sundown Dance [S] *Taos, NM*
Sangre de Cristo Arts and Conference Center [W] *Pueblo, CO*
San Ildefonso Pueblo [W] *Santa Fe, NM*
San Isabel National Forest [W] *Pueblo, CO*
San Jacinto Battleground [W] *Houston, TX*
San Juan County Archaeological Research Center & Library at Salmon Ruin [W] *Farmington, NM*
San Juan County Fair [S] *Farmington, NM*
San Juan County Fair & Rodeo [S] *Monticello, UT*
San Juan County Historical Society Museum [W] *Silverton, CO*
San Juan Feast Day [S] *Espanola, NM*
San Juan National Forest [W] *Durango, CO*

San Juan River Recreation Area [W] *Aztec, NM*
San Luis Valley Fair [S] *Monte Vista, CO*
San Marcos Factory Shops [W] *San Marcos, TX*
San Miguel Basin Fair and Rodeo [S] *Norwood, CO*
San Miguel Mission [W] *Santa Fe, NM*
Santa Ana Feast Day [S] *Albuquerque, NM*
Santa Ana National Wildlife Refuge [W] *McAllen, TX*
Santa Fe Chamber Music Festival [S] *Santa Fe, NM*
Santa Fe Children's Museum [W] *Santa Fe, NM*
Santa Fe Fiesta [S] *Santa Fe, NM*
Santa Fe National Forest [W] *Santa Fe, NM*
Santa Fe Opera [S] *Santa Fe, NM*
Santa Fe Pro Musica [S] *Santa Fe, NM*
Santa Fe Rodeo [S] *Santa Fe, NM*
Santa Fe School of Cooking [W] *Santa Fe, NM*
Santa Maria Feast [S] *Acoma Pueblo, NM*
Santa Rosa Dam and Lake [W] *Santa Rosa, NM*
Santa Rosa Day Celebration [S] *Santa Rosa, NM*
Santa Rosa Roundup [S] *Vernon, TX*
Santuario de Guadalupe [W] *Santa Fe, NM*
Save Our Sandrocks Nature Trail [W] *Craig, CO*
Scarborough Faire Renaissance [S] *Dallas, TX*
Scenic Airlines [W] *Las Vegas, NV*
Scenic Air Tours [W] *Moab, UT*
Scenic circle drives [W] *Fort Collins, CO*
Scenic drive [W] *El Paso, TX*
Scenic drive [W] *Fort Worth, TX*
Scenic Drive. Owl Creek Pass [W] *Montrose, CO*
Scenic drives [W] *Glenwood Springs, CO*
Scenic drives [W] *Steamboat Springs, CO*
Scenic drive to Independence Pass [W] *Aspen, CO*
Scenic flights over area [W] *Page, AZ*
Scenic flights over Grand Canyon [W] *South Rim (Grand Canyon National Park), AZ*
Schlitterbahn Water Park [W] *New Braunfels, TX*
Science Place, The [W] *Dallas, TX*
Science Spectrum-Omnimax [W] *Lubbock, TX*

Scofield State Park [W] *Price, UT*

Scottish-Irish Highland Festival [S] *Estes Park, CO*

Scottish Rite Temple [W] *Santa Fe, NM*

Scottsdale Center for the Arts [W] *Scottsdale, AZ*

Scurry County Fair [S] *Snyder, TX*

Scurry County Museum [W] *Snyder, TX*

SeaFair Rockport [S] *Rockport, TX*

Seagull Monument [W] *Salt Lake City, UT*

Sea Rim State Park [W] *Port Arthur, TX*

Seawolf Park [W] *Galveston, TX*

Sea World of Texas [W] *San Antonio, TX*

Sedona Cultural Park [W] *Sedona, AZ*

Sedona Film Festival [S] *Sedona, AZ*

Sedona Jazz on the Rocks [S] *Sedona, AZ*

Seminole Canyon State Historical Park [W] *Del Rio, TX*

Sena Plaza and Prince Plaza [W] *Santa Fe, NM*

Senator A. M. and Welma Aikin, Jr. Regional Archives [W] *Paris, TX*

Septiembre Fiesta [S] *Wickenburg, AZ*

Seven Falls [W] *Colorado Springs, CO*

Sharlot Hall Museum [W] *Prescott, AZ*

Sheriff's Posse PRCA Rodeo [S] *Cleburne, TX*

Sheri Griffith River Expeditions [W] *Moab, UT*

Sherman Preservation League Tour of Homes [S] *Sherman, TX*

Shiprock Navajo Fair [S] *Shiprock, NM*

Shrimp Boil [S] *Texas City, TX*

Shrimp Boil and Auction [S] *Brazosport, TX*

Shrimp Cook-off [S] *Port Isabel, TX*

Shrimporee [S] *Aransas Pass, TX*

Shrine of the Sun [W] *Colorado Springs, CO*

Sid Richardson Collection of Western Art [W] *Fort Worth, TX*

Sierra Nevada bus tours [W] *Reno, NV*

Sightseeing [W] *Lake Havasu City, AZ*

Sightseeing tours [W] *Corpus Christi, TX*

Sightseeing tours [W] *Denver, CO*

Sightseeing tours [W] *Moab, UT*

Sightseeing tours [W] *Santa Fe, NM*

Sightseeing trips. Cedar City Air Service [W] *Cedar City, UT*

Sightseeing USA [W] *Salt Lake City, UT*

Siglo de Oro [S] *El Paso, TX*

Silver City Museum [W] *Silver City, NM*

Silver Lake, Mescalero Lake, and Ruidoso Recreation Areas [W] *Mescalero, NM*

Silverthorne Factory Stores [W] *Dillon, CO*

Silverton, The [W] *Silverton, CO*

Silverton (Durango & Silverton Narrow Gauge Railroad), The [W] *Durango, CO*

Silverton Jubilee Folk Music Festival [S] *Silverton, CO*

Sims Mesa Site [W] *Aztec, NM*

Sipapu Area [W] *Taos, NM*

Site of First Gold Lode Discovery in Colorado [W] *Central City, CO*

Sitting Bull Falls [W] *Carlsbad, NM*

Six Flags AstroWorld [W] *Houston, TX*

Six Flags Fiesta Texas [W] *San Antonio, TX*

Six Flags Over Texas [W] *Arlington-Grand Prairie, TX*

Six Flags Over Texas [W] *Dallas, TX*

Six Flags Over Texas [W] *Fort Worth, TX*

Six Flags WaterWorld [W] *Houston, TX*

"The Sixth Floor" [W] *Dallas, TX*

Ski Apache Resort [W] *Ruidoso, NM*

Ski areas [W] *Taos, NM*

Ski Cloudcroft [W] *Cloudcroft, NM*

Ski-Hi Stampede [S] *Monte Vista, CO*

Skiing [W] *Aspen, CO*

Skiing [W] *Incline Village, NV*

Skiing [W] *Ogden, UT*

Skiing [W] *Park City, UT*

Skiing [W] *Salt Lake City, UT*

Skiing [W] *Steamboat Springs, CO*

Skiing [W] *Vail, CO*

Skiing. Angel Fire Ski Resort [W] *Angel Fire, NM*

Skiing. Breckenridge Ski Area [W] *Breckenridge, CO*

Skiing. Crested Butte Mountain Resort Ski Area [W] *Crested Butte, CO*

Skiing. Eldora Mountain Resort [W] *Boulder, CO*

Skiing. Loveland Ski Area [W] *Georgetown, CO*

Skiing. Monarch Ski & Snowboard Area [W] *Salida, CO*

Skiing. Mount Lemmon Ski Valley [W] *Tucson, AZ*

Skiing. Powderhorn Ski Resort [W] *Grand Junction, CO*

Skiing. Purgatory Resort [W] *Durango, CO*

Skiing. Red River Ski Area [W] *Red River, NM*

Skiing. Sandia Peak Tramway Ski Area [W] *Albuquerque, NM*

Skiing. Santa Fe Ski Area [W] *Santa Fe, NM*

Skiing. SilverCreek Ski Area [W] *Granby, CO*

Skiing. Ski Cooper [W] *Leadville, CO*

Skiing. Snowmass Ski Area [W] *Snowmass Village, CO*

Skiing. Sunlight Mountain Resort [W] *Glenwood Springs, CO*

Skiing. Telluride Ski Resort [W] *Telluride, CO*

Skiing. Winter Park Resort [W] *Winter Park, CO*

Slide Rock State Park [W] *Sedona, AZ*

Smith County Historical Society [W] *Tyler, TX*

Smith/Ritch Point Theatre [S] *Kerrville, TX*

Smokey Bear Historical State Park [W] *Ruidoso, NM*

Smokey Bear Museum [W] *Ruidoso, NM*

Smokey Bear Stampede [S] *Ruidoso, NM*

Smoki Museum [W] *Prescott, AZ*

Snowbasin [W] *Ogden, UT*

Snowbird [W] *Salt Lake City, UT*

Snowbird Ski and Summer Resort [W] *Snowbird, UT*

Snow Canyon [W] *St. George, UT*

Snowdown Winter Carnival [S] *Durango, CO*

Snowmass [W] *Aspen, CO*

Snowmobiling and cross-country skiing [W] *Grand Lake, CO*

Socorro [W] *El Paso, TX*

Socorro County Fair & Rodeo [S] *Socorro, NM*

Solitude Resort [W] *Park City, UT*

Solitude Resort [W] *Salt Lake City, UT*

Sommers-Bausch Observatory [W] *Boulder, CO*

Sophienburg Museum & Archives [W] *New Braunfels, TX*

Southern Nevada Zoological Park [W] *Las Vegas, NV*

Southern New Mexico State Fair [S] *Las Cruces, NM*

Southern Utah University [W] *Cedar City, UT*

Southern Ute Indian Cultural Museum [W] *Durango, CO*

South Mountain [W] *Phoenix, AZ*

South Padre Island Windsurfing Blowout [S] *South Padre Island, TX*

South Park City Museum [W] *Fairplay, CO*

South Park Historical Foundation, Inc [S] *Fairplay, CO*

South Texas Institute for the Arts [W] *Corpus Christi, TX*

South Texas State Fair [S] *Beaumont, TX*

Southwest Dairy Center [W] *Sulphur Springs, TX*

Southwestern Bell Cotton Bowl, The [W] *Dallas, TX*

Southwestern Bell Cotton Bowl Classic [S] *Dallas, TX*

Southwestern Exposition & Livestock Show [S] *Fort Worth, TX*

Southwestern International Livestock Show & PRCA Rodeo [S] *El Paso, TX*

Southwestern New Mexico State Fair [S] *Deming, NM*

Southwestern University [W] *Georgetown, TX*

Southwest School of Art & Craft [W] *San Antonio, TX*

Space Center Houston [W] *Houston, TX*

Spanish Governor's Palace [W] *San Antonio, TX*

Spanish Market [S] *Santa Fe, NM*

Spencer Theater for the Performing Arts, The [W] *Ruidoso, NM*

Spindletop/Gladys City Boomtown Museum [W] *Beaumont, TX*

Splashtown [W] *San Antonio, TX*

Spring Arts Festival [S] *Taos, NM*

Spring Corn Dances [S] *Santa Fe, NM*

Springfest [S] *Gonzales, TX*

Spring Festival of the Arts [S] *Tempe, AZ*

Spring Mountain Ranch State Park [W] *Las Vegas, NV*

Spring River Park & Zoo [W] *Roswell, NM*

Spring Valley [W] *Caliente, NV*

Springville Museum of Art [W] *Provo, UT*

Spruce Tree House [W] *Mesa Verde National Park, CO*

Square Dance Festival [S] *Big Spring, TX*

Squaw Peak Park [W] *Phoenix, AZ*

Stagecoach Days Celebration [S] *Marshall, TX*

Stanley Perry, Step-On Tours [W] *Window Rock, AZ*

Stark Museum of Art [W] *Orange, TX*

Star of the Republic Museum [W] *Brenham, TX*

Star Texas Fair and Rodeo [S] *Austin, TX*

State Capitol [W] *Austin, TX*

State Capitol [W] *Carson City, NV*

State Capitol [W] *Denver, CO*

State Capitol [W] *Salt Lake City, UT*

State Capitol [W] *Santa Fe, NM*

State Capitol Complex [W] *Denver, CO*

State Fair of Texas [S] *Dallas, TX*

State Library Building [W] *Carson City, NV*

State parks [W] *Bastrop, TX*

State parks [W] *Cleburne, TX*

State parks [W] *Grand Junction, CO*

State parks [W] *Rockport, TX*

State parks [W] *St. George, UT*

State parks and recreation areas [W] *Caliente, NV*

Steamboat [W] *Steamboat Springs, CO*

Steamboat Health & Recreation Association [W] *Steamboat Springs, CO*

Steamboat House [W] *Huntsville, TX*

Steamboat Lake State Park [W] *Steamboat Springs, CO*

Steinaker State Park [W] *Vernal, UT*

Stephen F. Austin State Historical Park [W] *Brenham, TX*

Sterne-Hoya Home [W] *Nacogdoches, TX*

Steves Homestead [W] *San Antonio, TX*

Stillhouse Hollow Lake [W] *Killeen, TX*

Stillhouse Hollow Lake [W] *Salado, TX*

Stock car racing [S] *Goliad, TX*

Stockyards Museum [W] *Fort Worth, TX*

Stone Fort Museum [W] *Nacogdoches, TX*

Storrie Lake State Park [W] *Las Vegas, NM*

Strand National Historic Landmark District, The [W] *Galveston, TX*

Strawberry Days Festival [S] *Glenwood Springs, CO*

Strawberry Park Natural Hot Springs [W] *Steamboat Springs, CO*

Strecker Museum [W] *Waco, TX*

Strip, The [W] *Las Vegas, NV*

Sugarite Canyon State Park [W] *Raton, NM*

Summer Bayfront Concerts [S] *Corpus Christi, TX*

Summer concerts [S] *Houston, TX*

Summerfest [S] *Port Lavaca, TX*

Summer Festival [S] *San Antonio, TX*

Summer Mummers [S] *Midland, TX*

Summer musicals [S] *Dallas, TX*

Sumner Lake State Park [W] *Santa Rosa, NM*

Sun Carnival [S] *El Paso, TX*

Sundance Film Festival [S] *Park City, UT*

Sundance Ski Area [W] *Provo, UT*

Sundance Square Entertainment District [W] *Fort Worth, TX*

Sunrise Park Resort [W] *McNary, AZ*

Sunset Station [W] *San Antonio, TX*

Sunshine Festival [S] *Alamosa, CO*

Sutton County Days and Outlaw Pro Rodeo [S] *Sonora, TX*

Sweitzer State Park [W] *Delta, CO*

Swift Trail, The [W] *Safford, AZ*

Swimming, fishing, boating, camping, hiking [W] *Lake Mead National Recreation Area, NV*

Swimming, water sports, fishing, boating [W] *Mineral Wells, TX*

Swiss Days [S] *Heber City, UT*

Syrup Festival [S] *Henderson, TX*

Tabernacle [W] *Brigham City, UT*

Tabernacle [W] *Salt Lake City, UT*

Tabernacle [W] *St. George, UT*

Tabor Center [W] *Denver, CO*

Tabor Opera House [W] *Leadville, CO*

Tag-A-Long Expeditions [W] *Moab, UT*

Taliesin West [W] *Scottsdale, AZ*

Talks [W] *Bryce Canyon National Park, UT*

Taos Arts Festival [S] *Taos, NM*

Taos Pueblo [W] *Taos, NM*

Taos Pueblo Dances [S] *Taos, NM*

Taos Pueblo Deer or *Matachines* Dance [S] *Taos, NM*

Taos Rodeo [S] *Taos, NM*

Taos Ski Valley [W] *Taos, NM*

Taos Talking Picture Festival [S] *Taos, NM*

Tarleton State University [W] *Stephenville, TX*

Taste of Vail [S] *Vail, CO*

Taylor Park Reservoir [W] *Gunnison, CO*

T. C. Lindsey & Company [W] *Marshall, TX*

Telephone Pioneer Museum [W] *Albuquerque, NM*

Telluride Airmen's Rendezvous & Hang Gliding Festival [S] *Telluride, CO*

Telluride Gondola [W] *Telluride, CO*

Telluride Historical Museum [W] *Telluride, CO*

Tempe Historical Museum [W] *Tempe, AZ*

Temple [W] *Salt Lake City, UT*

Temple Hoyne Buell Theatre [W] *Denver, CO*

Temple Square [W] *Salt Lake City, UT*

Temple Visitor Center [W] *St. George, UT*

Tenderfoot Drive [W] *Salida, CO*

Territorial Days [S] *Tombstone, AZ*

Territorial Prescott Days [S] *Prescott, AZ*

Territorial Statehouse State Park [W] *Fillmore, UT*

Texarkana Historical Museum [W] *Texarkana, TX*

Texas [S] *Canyon, TX*
Texas A&M National Intercollegiate Rodeo [S] *Kingsville, TX*
Texas A&M University [W] *Bryan/College Station, TX*
Texas A&M University-Kingsville [W] *Kingsville, TX*
Texas Adventure [W] *San Antonio, TX*
Texas Border Botanical & Butterfly Festival [S] *Mission, TX*
Texas Citrus Fiesta [S] *Mission, TX*
Texas City Museum [W] *Texas City, TX*
Texas Discovery Gardens [W] *Dallas, TX*
Texas Dogwood Trail Festival [S] *Palestine, TX*
Texas Energy Museum [W] *Beaumont, TX*
Texas Fiddlers' Contest and Reunion [S] *Athens, TX*
Texas Folklife Festival [S] *San Antonio, TX*
Texas Forestry Museum [W] *Lufkin, TX*
Texas Independence Day Celebration [S] *Brenham, TX*
Texas International Fishing Tournament [S] *Port Isabel, TX*
Texas Jazz Festival [S] *Corpus Christi, TX*
Texas Ladies' State Chili Cookoff [S] *Seguin, TX*
Texas Maritime Museum [W] *Rockport, TX*
Texas Memorial Museum of Science and History [W] *Austin, TX*
Texas Motor Speedway [S] *Fort Worth, TX*
Texas-Oklahoma Fair [S] *Wichita Falls, TX*
Texas Prison Museum [W] *Huntsville, TX*
Texas Ranch Roundup [S] *Wichita Falls, TX*
Texas Ranger Hall of Fame & Museum [W] *Waco, TX*
Texas Rangers (MLB) [W] *Arlington-Grand Prairie, TX*
Texas Rangers (MLB) [W] *Dallas, TX*
Texas Rose Festival [S] *Tyler, TX*
Texas Seaport Museum [W] *Galveston, TX*
Texas State Aquarium [W] *Corpus Christi, TX*
Texas State Arts & Crafts Fair [S] *Kerrville, TX*
Texas State Library [W] *Austin, TX*
Texas State Railroad Historical Park [W] *Rusk, TX*

Texas Tech University [W] *Lubbock, TX*
Texas Water Safari [S] *San Marcos, TX*
Texas Weapon Collectors Association Gun & Knife Shows [S] *Wichita Falls, TX*
Texas Wine & Food Festival [S] *San Angelo, TX*
Texas Woman's University [W] *Denton, TX*
Texas Youth Rodeo Association State Finals [S] *Seguin, TX*
Texas Zoo [W] *Victoria, TX*
Texoma Lakefest Regatta [S] *Denison, TX*
Tex's Riverways [W] *Moab, UT*
Theater District [W] *Houston, TX*
This is the Place Heritage Park [W] *Salt Lake City, UT*
Thistle Hill [W] *Fort Worth, TX*
Thomas and Mack Center [W] *Las Vegas, NV*
Thomas House Museum, The [W] *Central City, CO*
Thompson Park [W] *Amarillo, TX*
Thoroughbred Horse Racing [W] *Phoenix, AZ*
Three Rivers Petroglyph Site [W] *Alamogordo, NM*
Tigua Cultural Center [W] *El Paso, TX*
Timpanogos Cave National Monument [W] *Heber City, UT*
Timpanogos Cave National Monument [W] *Provo, UT*
Timpanogos Cave National Monument [W] *Salt Lake City, UT*
Titan Missile Museum [W] *Tucson, AZ*
Titus County Fair [S] *Mount Pleasant, TX*
Tlaquepaque [W] *Sedona, AZ*
Tohono Chul Park [W] *Tucson, AZ*
Toiyabe National Forest [W] *Reno, NV*
Toledo Bend Dam and Reservoir [W] *Jasper, TX*
Tomato Fest [S] *Jacksonville, TX*
Tombaugh IMAX Theater [W] *Alamogordo, NM*
Tombstone Courthouse State Historic Park [W] *Tombstone, AZ*
Tombstone Historama [W] *Tombstone, AZ*
Tonto National Forest [W] *Payson, AZ*
Tonto National Forest [W] *Phoenix, AZ*
Topock Gorge [W] *Lake Havasu City, AZ*
Top O'Texas Junior Livestock Show & Sale [S] *Pampa, TX*
Top O'Texas Rodeo, PRCA [S] *Pampa, TX*

Tops in Texas Rodeo [S] *Jacksonville, TX*

Tostitos Fiesta Bowl [S] *Tempe, AZ*

Tostitos Fiesta Bowl Block Party [S] *Tempe, AZ*

Totah Festival [S] *Farmington, NM*

Tour de Goliad Bike Ride [S] *Goliad, TX*

Tours of Distinction [S] *San Marcos, TX*

Tours of the Big Country [W] *Bluff, UT*

Tower of the Americas [W] *San Antonio, TX*

Toy Train Depot [W] *Alamogordo, NM*

Tradition at Superstition Mountain, The [S] *Scottsdale, AZ*

Trail rides. Pack Creek Ranch [W] *Moab, UT*

Trail Ridge Road [W] *Rocky Mountain National Park, CO*

Trails & Tales of Boomtown, USA [W] *Wichita Falls, TX*

Tread of Pioneers Museum [W] *Steamboat Springs, CO*

Treasure Island Tour Train [W] *Galveston, TX*

Treasure Mountain [W] *Pagosa Springs, CO*

Tres Lagunas [W] *Santa Rosa, NM*

Tri-cultural Arts Festival [S] *Espanola, NM*

Trinidad History Museum [W] *Trinidad, CO*

Trinidad Lake State Park [W] *Trinidad, CO*

Trinity Site Tour [S] *Alamogordo, NM*

Tri-State Fair [S] *Amarillo, TX*

Trolley Square [W] *Salt Lake City, UT*

Tubac Presidio State Historic Park [W] *Nogales, AZ*

Tucson Botanical Gardens [W] *Tucson, AZ*

Tucson: Meet Yourself [S] *Tucson, AZ*

Tucson Mountain Park [W] *Tucson, AZ*

Tucson Museum of Art [W] *Tucson, AZ*

Tucson Symphony Orchestra [S] *Tucson, AZ*

Tucumcari Historical Museum [W] *Tucumcari, NM*

Tumacacori National Historical Park [W] *Nogales, AZ*

Tusayan Museum [W] *South Rim (Grand Canyon National Park), AZ*

Tuzigoot National Monument [W] *Cottonwood, AZ*

Tyler Rose Garden and Museum [W] *Tyler, TX*

Tyler State Park [W] *Tyler, TX*

Tyrrell Historical Library [W] *Beaumont, TX*

UFO Encounters Festival [S] *Roswell, NM*

Uintah County Fair [S] *Vernal, UT*

Uinta National Forest [W] *Provo, UT*

Ullr Fest & World Cup Freestyle [S] *Breckenridge, CO*

Uncompahgre National Forest [W] *Norwood, CO*

Union Station—the Utah State Railroad Museum [W] *Ogden, UT*

United States Mint [W] *Denver, CO*

Uniting Fore Care Classic presented by Novell PGA Tournament [S] *Park City, UT*

University of Arizona [W] *Tucson, AZ*

University of Colorado Museum [W] *Boulder, CO*

University of Colorado [W] *Boulder, CO*

University of Denver [W] *Denver, CO*

University of Houston [W] *Houston, TX*

University of Nevada, Las Vegas [W] *Las Vegas, NV*

University of Nevada-Reno [W] *Reno, NV*

University of New Mexico [W] *Albuquerque, NM*

University of Northern Colorado [W] *Greeley, CO*

University of Southern Colorado [W] *Pueblo, CO*

University of Texas at Austin [W] *Austin, TX*

University of Texas at El Paso [W] *El Paso, TX*

University of Utah [W] *Salt Lake City, UT*

US Air Force Academy [W] *Colorado Springs, CO*

US Army Air Defense Museum [W] *El Paso, TX*

USGS National Earthquake Information Center [W] *Golden, CO*

US Olympic Complex and Visitor Center [W] *Colorado Springs, CO*

USS *Lexington* [W] *Corpus Christi, TX*

Utah Arts Festival [S] *Salt Lake City, UT*

Utah Festival Opera Company [S] *Logan, UT*

Utah Field House of Natural History and Dinosaur Gardens [W] *Vernal, UT*

Utah Fun Dome [W] *Salt Lake City, UT*

Utah Jazz (NBA) [W] *Salt Lake City, UT*

Utah Lake State Park [W] *Provo, UT*

Utah Museum of Fine Arts [W] *Salt Lake City, UT*

Utah Museum of Natural History [W] *Salt Lake City, UT*

Utah Navajo Fair [S] *Bluff, UT*

Utah Opera Company [W] *Salt Lake City, UT*

Utah Shakespearean Festival [S] *Cedar City, UT*

Utah Starzz (WNBA) [W] *Salt Lake City, UT*

Utah State Fair [S] *Salt Lake City, UT*

Utah State University [W] *Logan, UT*

Utah Summer Games [S] *Cedar City, UT*

Utah Symphony [S] *Snowbird, UT*

Utah Symphony Pops Concert [S] *Ogden, UT*

Utah Winter Sports Park [W] *Park City, UT*

Ute Indian Museum and Ouray Memorial Park [W] *Montrose, CO*

Ute Lake State Park [W] *Tucumcari, NM*

Ute Mountain Rodeo [S] *Cortez, CO*

Ute Mountain Tribal Park [W] *Cortez, CO*

Ute Stampede Rodeo [S] *Nephi, UT*

Uvalde Grand Opera House [W] *Uvalde, TX*

Vail Ski Resort [W] *Vail, CO*

Val Verde Winery [W] *Del Rio, TX*

Van Vechten-Lineberry Taos Art Museum [W] *Taos, NM*

Varner-Hogg Plantation State Historical Park [W] *Angleton, TX*

Verde Canyon Railroad [W] *Cottonwood, AZ*

Verde Canyon Railroad [W] *Sedona, AZ*

Verde Valley Fair [S] *Cottonwood, AZ*

Vereins Kirche Museum [W] *Fredericksburg, TX*

Veteran's Memorial Rally [S] *Cripple Creek, CO*

VIA San Antonio Streetcar [W] *San Antonio, TX*

Victor [W] *Cripple Creek, CO*

Victoria Jaycees Stockshow [S] *Victoria, TX*

Victorian Christmas & Home Tour [S] *Leadville, CO*

Vietnam Veterans National Memorial [W] *Angel Fire, NM*

Vietnam War Memorial [W] *San Antonio, TX*

Villa de San Agustin [W] *Laredo, TX*

Virgin de San Juan del Valle Shrine [W] *McAllen, TX*

Visitor Center [W] *South Rim (Grand Canyon National Park), AZ*

Viva El Paso [S] *El Paso, TX*

Walker Lake [W] *Hawthorne, NV*

Walker Lake State Recreation Area [W] *Hawthorne, NV*

Walking tour [W] *San Antonio, TX*

Walking tour [W] *Santa Fe, NM*

Walking tours [W] *Breckenridge, CO*

Walsenburg Mining Museum [W] *Walsenburg, CO*

Ward Charcoal Ovens State Historic Park [W] *Ely, NV*

Warren Engine Company No. 1 Fire Museum [W] *Carson City, NV*

Wasatch-Cache National Forest, Logan Canyon [W] *Logan, UT*

Wasatch-Cache National Forest [W] *Salt Lake City, UT*

Wasatch County Fair [S] *Heber City, UT*

Wasatch Mountain State Park [W] *Heber City, UT*

Washington County Fair [S] *Brenham, TX*

Washington-on-the-Brazos State Historical Park [W] *Brenham, TX*

Washington Park [W] *Denver, CO*

Water Carnival [S] *Fort Stockton, TX*

Water Wonderland [W] *Odessa, TX*

Weber State University [W] *Ogden, UT*

Weld County Fair [S] *Greeley, CO*

Western Heritage Museum [W] *Vernal, UT*

Western New Mexico University Museum [W] *Silver City, NM*

Western New Mexico University [W] *Silver City, NM*

Western Roundup [S] *Cloudcroft, NM*

Western State College of Colorado [W] *Gunnison, CO*

Western Texas College Rodeos [S] *Snyder, TX*

West of the Pecos Museum [W] *Pecos, TX*

"West of the Pecos" Rodeo [S] *Pecos, TX*

West Texas Fair & Rodeo [S] *Abilene, TX*

WestWorld of Scottsdale [W] *Scottsdale, AZ*

Wet 'n Wild Las Vegas [W] *Las Vegas, NV*

Wheeler Historic Farm [W] *Salt Lake City, UT*

Wheelwright Museum [W] *Santa Fe, NM*

White Buffalo Festival [S] *Snyder, TX*

White Deer Land Museum [W] *Pampa, TX*

Whitehead Memorial Museum [W] *Del Rio, TX*

White Pine County Fair [S] *Ely, NV*

White Pine Public Museum [W] *Ely, NV*

White Pine Touring Center [W] *Park City, UT*

White River National Forest [W] *Glenwood Springs, CO*

White Rock Lake and Greenbelt Park [W] *Dallas, TX*

White Sands Missile Range [W] *Las Cruces, NM*

White Water Race [S] *Espanola, NM*

Whitewater rafting [W] *Espanola, NM*

Whitney Lake [W] *Lake Whitney, TX*

Whole Enchilada Fiesta [S] *Las Cruces, NM*

W. H. Stark House [W] *Orange, TX*

Wichita Falls Museum & Art Center [W] *Wichita Falls, TX*

Wilderness Aware [W] *Buena Vista, CO*

Wilderness Park Museum [W] *El Paso, TX*

Wilderness River Adventures [W] *Page, AZ*

Wildlife World Zoo [W] *Litchfield Park, AZ*

Wild Rivers Expeditions [W] *Bluff, UT*

Wild West Days and Rendezvous of Gunfighters [S] *Tombstone, AZ*

Wild West Fest [S] *McKinney, TX*

Wild West Jeep Tours [W] *Scottsdale, AZ*

Willard Bay State Park [W] *Ogden, UT*

Williams Ski Area [W] *Williams, AZ*

Willow Park Zoo [W] *Logan, UT*

Will Rogers Memorial Center [W] *Fort Worth, TX*

Window Rock [W] *Gallup, NM*

Winedale Historical Center [W] *La Grange, TX*

Wineries [W] *Lubbock, TX*

Wings Over Willcox/Sandhill Crane Celebration [S] *Willcox, AZ*

Winter Carnival [S] *Grand Lake, CO*

Winter Carnival [S] *Steamboat Springs, CO*

Winter Fest [S] *Pagosa Springs, CO*

Winter Festival [S] *Flagstaff, AZ*

Winterskol Carnival [S] *Aspen, CO*

Witte Museum [W] *San Antonio, TX*

Wolf Creek Pass [W] *Pagosa Springs, CO*

Wolf Creek Ski Area [W] *Pagosa Springs, CO*

Wolf Creek Ski Area [W] *South Fork, CO*

Wonderland Amusement Park [W] *Amarillo, TX*

Wonderland of Lights [S] *Marshall, TX*

Wonder World [W] *San Marcos, TX*

Woodland Home, Sam Houston's Residence [W] *Huntsville, TX*

World Figure Skating Hall of Fame and Museum [W] *Colorado Springs, CO*

World's Champion Fiddlers' Festival [S] *Crockett, TX*

World's Championship Pack Burro Race [S] *Fairplay, CO*

World's Largest Fish Fry [S] *Fritch, TX*

World's Oldest Continuous PRCA Rodeo [S] *Payson, AZ*

Wortham IMAX Theatre [W] *Houston, TX*

Wright Patman Dam and Lake [W] *Texarkana, TX*

Wurstfest [S] *New Braunfels, TX*

Wyatt Earp Days [S] *Tombstone, AZ*

XIT Rodeo & Reunion [S] *Dalhart, TX*

Yaqui Indian Holy Week Ceremonials [S] *Phoenix, AZ*

Yavapai Observation Station [W] *South Rim (Grand Canyon National Park), AZ*

Y. O. Ranch [W] *Kerrville, TX*

Ysleta [W] *El Paso, TX*

Yuba State Park [W] *Nephi, UT*

Yuletide in Taos [S] *Taos, NM*

Yuma County Fair [S] *Yuma, AZ*

Yuma River Tours [W] *Yuma, AZ*

Yuma Territorial Prison State Historic Park [W] *Yuma, AZ*

Yuma Valley Railway [W] *Yuma, AZ*

ZCMI (Zion's Co-operative Mercantile Institution) Center [W] *Salt Lake City, UT*

Zephyr Days Train Show [S] *Wichita Falls, TX*

Zilker Botanical Gardens [W] *Austin, TX*

Zilker Hillside Theater [W] *Austin, TX*

Zilker Hillside Theater [S] *Austin, TX*

Zilker Park [W] *Austin, TX*

Zion National Park [W] *Cedar City, UT*

Zion National Park [W] *Kanab, UT*

Zion National Park [W] *St. George, UT*

Zion Nature Center [W] *Zion National Park, UT*

Zoological Gardens and Aquarium [W] *San Antonio, TX*

Zuni Artists' Exhibition [S] *Flagstaff, AZ*

Zuni Pueblo [W] *Gallup, NM*

LODGING LIST

Establishment names are listed in alphabetical order followed by a symbol identifying their classification and then city and state. The symbols for classification are: [AS] for All Suites, [BB] for B&Bs/Small Inns, [CAS] for Casinos, [CC] for Cottage Colonies, [CON] for Villas/Condos, [CONF] for Conference Centers, [EX] for Extended Stays, [HOT] for Hotels, [MOT] for Motels/Motor Lodges, [RAN] for Guest Ranches, and [RST] for Resorts

1904 IMPERIAL HOTEL B&B [BB]
    Park City, UT
1ST BED AND BREAKFAST IN TEXAS
    - PRIDE HOUSE [BB] Jefferson,
    TX
ABBEY INN [MOT] Cedar City, UT
A BECKMANN INN & CARRIAGE
    HOUSE BED AND BREAKFAST
    [BB] San Antonio, TX
ABRIENDO INN [BB] Pueblo, CO
ACE LODGE AND MOTEL [MOT]
    Truth or Consequences, NM
ADAM'S MARK [HOT] Denver, CO
ADAM'S MARK [HOT] Grand Junction,
    CO
ADAM'S MARK [HOT] Houston, TX
ADAM'S MARK [HOT] San Antonio,
    TX
ADOBE ABODE [BB] Santa Fe, NM
ADOBE ROSE INN BED AND
    BREAKFAST [BB] Tucson, AZ
ADOBE STARS BED AND BREAKFAST
    INN [BB] Taos, NM
ADOBE VILLAGE GRAHAM INN [BB]
    Sedona, AZ
AIRPORT TRAVELODGE [MOT]
    Yuma, AZ
ALADDIN RESORT & CASINO [HOT]
    Las Vegas, NV
ALAMO TRAVELODGE [MOT] San
    Antonio, TX
ALEXANDER'S INN [BB] Santa Fe, NM
ALEXIS PARK RESORT HOTEL [AS]
    Las Vegas, NV
ALLAIRE TIMBERS INN [BB]
    Breckenridge, CO
ALLEN PARK INN [MOT] Houston, TX
ALMA HOUSE BED AND BREAKFAST
    [BB] Silverton, CO
ALPINE INN HOLLYHOCK GIFTS
    [MOT] Ouray, CO
ALPINE LODGE [MOT] Red River, NM
ALPINE MOTEL [MOT] Durango, CO
ALPINER LODGE [MOT] Steamboat
    Springs, CO

ALPINE TRAIL RIDGE INN [MOT]
    Estes Park, CO
ALPS BORDER CANYON INN [BB]
    Boulder, CO
ALTA LODGE [RST] Alta, UT
ALTA'S RUSTLER LODGE [HOT] Alta,
    UT
AMBASSADOR INN [MOT] St. George,
    UT
AMBERLEY SUITE HOTEL [AS]
    Albuquerque, NM
AMERICAN ARTISTS GALLERY
    HOUSE [BB] Taos, NM
AMERICINN MOTEL [MOT]
    Wickenburg, AZ
AMERISUITES [AS] Arlington-Grand
    Prairie, TX
AMERISUITES [AS] Colorado Springs,
    CO
AMERISUITES [AS] Scottsdale, AZ
AMERISUITES FLAGSTAFF [AS]
    Flagstaff, AZ
AMERISUITES HOTEL [AS] Dallas/Fort
    Worth Airport Area, TX
AMERISUITES NORTHWEST [AS] San
    Antonio, TX
ANASAZI MOTOR INN [MOT] Cortez,
    CO
ANNIVERSARY INN, THE [BB] Logan,
    UT
ANTLERS ADAM'S MARK HOTEL,
    THE [HOT] Colorado Springs,
    CO
ANT STREET INN [BB] Brenham, TX
APACHE CANYON RANCH [BB]
    Albuquerque, NM
APPLE ORCHARD INN [BB] Durango,
    CO
APPLE ORCHARD INN [BB] Sedona,
    AZ
ARAPAHOE SKI LODGE [BB] Winter
    Park, CO
ARIZONA BILTMORE RESORT AND
    SPA [RST] Phoenix, AZ
ARIZONA CHARLIE'S HOTEL AND
    CASINO [MOT] Las Vegas, NV

ARIZONA GOLF RESORT AND CONFERENCE CENTER [RST] *Mesa, AZ*

ARIZONA INN [RST] *Tucson, AZ*

ARMSTRONG MANSION [BB] *Salt Lake City, UT*

ARROWHEAD LODGE [MOT] *Red River, NM*

ASHMORE INN AND SUITES [HOT] *Lubbock, TX*

ASHTON, THE [HOT] *Fort Worth, TX*

ASPEN LODGE RANCH [RAN] *Estes Park, CO*

ASPEN MEADOWS [CONF] *Aspen, CO*

ASPEN MOUNTAIN LODGE [BB] *Aspen, CO*

ASPEN SQUARE CONDOMINIUM HOTEL [HOT] *Aspen, CO*

ASPEN WINDS [MOT] *Estes Park, CO*

ATLANTIS CASINO RESORT [HOT] *Reno, NV*

A TOUCH OF SEDONA BED AND BREAKFAST [BB] *Sedona, AZ*

AUSTING HAUS B&B [BB] *Taos, NM*

AVALANCHE RANCH [CC] *Glenwood Springs, CO*

A YELLOW ROSE BED & BREAKFAST [BB] *San Antonio, TX*

BAHIA MAR BEACH RESORT [RST] *South Padre Island, TX*

BALLY'S [HOT] *Las Vegas, NV*

B & B AT SADDLEROCK RANCH [BB] *Sedona, AZ*

BANDERA LODGE [MOT] *Bandera, TX*

BARBARY COAST HOTEL [HOT] *Las Vegas, NV*

BARCELONA COURT [AS] *Lubbock, TX*

BARTON CREEK RESORT [RST] *Austin, TX*

B BAR B RANCH [BB] *Kingsville, TX*

BEAUREGARD HOUSE [BB] *San Antonio, TX*

BEAVER CREEK LODGE - MOUNTAIN SUITES HOTEL [RST] *Beaver Creek, CO*

BEAVER RUN RESORT [RST] *Breckenridge, CO*

BED AND BREAKFAST AT THE RANCH [BB] *Fort Worth, TX*

BED & BREAKFAST ON NORTH MAIN ST [BB] *Breckenridge, CO*

BELLAGIO LAS VEGAS [HOT] *Las Vegas, NV*

BEN LOMOND HISTORIC SUITES HOTEL [HOT] *Ogden, UT*

BEST INN [MOT] *Hobbs, NM*

BEST INN [MOT] *Socorro, NM*

BEST INN & SUITES [MOT] *Battle Mountain, NV*

BEST INN & SUITES [MOT] *Fallon, NV*

BEST INN & SUITES [MOT] *Midland, TX*

BEST VALUE INN [MOT] *Gallup, NM*

BEST VALUE INN - NORRIS MOTEL [MOT] *Williams, AZ*

BEST VALUE INN VILLA MOTEL [MOT] *Manitou Springs, CO*

BEST WESTERN [MOT] *Big Spring, TX*

BEST WESTERN [MOT] *Bullhead City, AZ*

BEST WESTERN [MOT] *Dalhart, TX*

BEST WESTERN [MOT] *Dallas, TX*

BEST WESTERN [MOT] *Del Rio, TX*

BEST WESTERN [MOT] *Gallup, NM*

BEST WESTERN [MOT] *Henderson, NV*

BEST WESTERN [MOT] *Lamar, CO*

BEST WESTERN [MOT] *Longview, TX*

BEST WESTERN [MOT] *Scottsdale, AZ*

BEST WESTERN ADOBE INN [MOT] *Santa Rosa, NM*

BEST WESTERN ADOBE INN [MOT] *Winslow, AZ*

BEST WESTERN AIRPORT PLAZA [MOT] *Reno, NV*

BEST WESTERN ANTLERS [MOT] *Glenwood Springs, CO*

BEST WESTERN APPLE TREE INN [MOT] *Richfield, UT*

BEST WESTERN ARIZONA INN [MOT] *Page, AZ*

BEST WESTERN ARIZONIAN INN [MOT] *Holbrook, AZ*

BEST WESTERN ARROYO ROBLE [MOT] *Sedona, AZ*

BEST WESTERN AT CHIMNEY HILL [MOT] *Bryan/College Station, TX*

BEST WESTERN BAUGH [MOT] *Logan, UT*

BEST WESTERN BENT FORT'S INN [MOT] *La Junta, CO*

BEST WESTERN BUTCH CASSIDY [MOT] *Beaver, UT*

BEST WESTERN CANYON DE CHELLY [MOT] *Canyon de Chelly National Monument, AZ*

BEST WESTERN CANYONLANDS INN [MOT] *Moab, UT*

BEST WESTERN CARRIAGE HOUSE [MOT] *Price, UT*

BEST WESTERN COLORADO LODGE [MOT] *Salida, CO*

BEST WESTERN CONESTOGA [MOT] *Plainview, TX*

BEST WESTERN CONTINENTAL INN [MOT] *San Antonio, TX*

BEST WESTERN CORAL HILLS [MOT] *St. George, UT*

BEST WESTERN COTTONTREE INN [MOT] *Provo, UT*

BEST WESTERN COTTONWOOD INN [MOT] *Cottonwood, AZ*

BEST WESTERN DENVER STAPLETON [MOT] *Denver, CO*

BEST WESTERN DESERT AIRE MOTOR INN [MOT] *Alamogordo, NM*

BEST WESTERN DESERT INN [MOT] *Safford, AZ*

BEST WESTERN DOBSON RANCH INN AND RESORT [MOT] *Mesa, AZ*

BEST WESTERN DURANGO INN [MOT] *Durango, CO*

BEST WESTERN EAGLE PASS [MOT] *Eagle Pass, TX*

BEST WESTERN ELKO INN EXPRESS [MOT] *Elko, NV*

BEST WESTERN EXECUTIVE HOTEL [MOT] *Denver International Airport Area, CO*

BEST WESTERN EXECUTIVE PARK [MOT] *Phoenix, AZ*

BEST WESTERN EXECUTIVE INN [MOT] *Salt Lake City, UT*

BEST WESTERN GARDEN OASIS [MOT] *Odessa, TX*

BEST WESTERN GOLD COUNTRY INN [MOT] *Winnemucca, NV*

BEST WESTERN GRACE INN AHWATUKEE [MOT] *Phoenix, AZ*

BEST WESTERN GRAND CANYON SQ [MOT] *South Rim (Grand Canyon National Park), AZ*

BEST WESTERN GREENWELL INN [MOT] *Moab, UT*

BEST WESTERN HI-DESERT INN [MOT] *Tonopah, NV*

BEST WESTERN HILLTOP HOUSE HOTEL [MOT] *Los Alamos, NM*

BEST WESTERN HOTEL [MOT] *Pinetop, AZ*

BEST WESTERN HOT SPRINGS MOTOR INN [MOT] *Truth or Consequences, NM*

BEST WESTERN INN [MOT] *Alamosa, CO*

BEST WESTERN INN [MOT] *Fort Stockton, TX*

BEST WESTERN INN [MOT] *Fort Worth, TX*

BEST WESTERN INN [MOT] *Gainesville, TX*

BEST WESTERN INN [MOT] *Glendale, AZ*

BEST WESTERN INN [MOT] *Greeley, CO*

BEST WESTERN INN [MOT] *Limon, CO*

BEST WESTERN INN [MOT] *Orange, TX*

BEST WESTERN INN [MOT] *Roosevelt, UT*

BEST WESTERN INN AND SUITES [MOT] *Farmington, NM*

BEST WESTERN INN AND SUITES [MOT] *Gallup, NM*

BEST WESTERN INN AND SUITES [MOT] *Grants, NM*

BEST WESTERN INN AND SUITES [MOT] *Greenville, TX*

BEST WESTERN INN & SUITES [MOT] *New Braunfels, TX*

BEST WESTERN INN AT PUEBLO WEST [MOT] *Pueblo, CO*

BEST WESTERN INN AT RIO RANCHO [MOT] *Albuquerque, NM*

BEST WESTERN INN AT THE AIRPORT [MOT] *Tucson, AZ*

BEST WESTERN INN BY THE BAY [MOT] *Rockport, TX*

BEST WESTERN INN OF SANTA FE [MOT] *Santa Fe, NM*

BEST WESTERN INN OF SEDONA [MOT] *Sedona, AZ*

BEST WESTERN INN OF VAN HORN [MOT] *Van Horn, TX*

BEST WESTERN INN ON THE HILL [MOT] *Athens, TX*

BEST WESTERN INN SUITES [MOT] *Phoenix, AZ*

BEST WESTERN INN SUITES [MOT] *Tucson, AZ*

BEST WESTERN INN SUITES [AS] *Yuma, AZ*

BEST WESTERN JEFFERSON INN [MOT] *Beaumont, TX*

BEST WESTERN JICARILLA INN [MOT] *Dulce, NM*

BEST WESTERN KINGS ROW INN [MOT] *Texarkana, TX*

BEST WESTERN KIVA INN [MOT] *Fort Collins, CO*

BEST WESTERN LAMPLIGHTER INN [MOT] *Santa Fe, NM*

BEST WESTERN LA VISTA INN [MOT] *Clovis, NM*

BEST WESTERN LE BARON HOTEL [MOT] *Colorado Springs, CO*

BEST WESTERN LODGE [MOT] *Durango, CO*

BEST WESTERN LOOKOUT LODGE [MOT] *Tombstone, AZ*

BEST WESTERN MALL SOUTH [MOT] *Abilene, TX*

BEST WESTERN MCCARRAN INN [MOT] *Las Vegas, NV*

BEST WESTERN MESILA VALLEY INN [MOT] *Las Cruces, NM*

BEST WESTERN MOVIE MANOR [MOT] *Monte Vista, CO*

BEST WESTERN NEW WESTERN MOTEL [MOT] *Panguitch, UT*

BEST WESTERN NORTHGATE INN [MOT] *Pampa, TX*

BEST WESTERN OF SAN MARCOS [MOT] *San Marcos, TX*

BEST WESTERN OLD MAIN LODGE [MOT] *Waco, TX*

BEST WESTERN PAINT PONY LODGE [MOT] *Show Low, AZ*

BEST WESTERN PALESTINE INN [MOT] *Palestine, TX*

BEST WESTERN PAPAGO INN AND RESORT HOTEL [MOT] *Scottsdale, AZ*

BEST WESTERN PARADISE INN & RESORT [RST] *Fillmore, UT*

BEST WESTERN PARADISE INN [MOT] *Nephi, UT*

BEST WESTERN PARK SUITES [MOT] *Dallas, TX*

BEST WESTERN PARK TERRACE INN [MOT] *Fort Morgan, CO*

BEST WESTERN PECOS INN [MOT] *Artesia, NM*

BEST WESTERN PLAZA INN [MOT] *Willcox, AZ*

BEST WESTERN PONY SOLDIER MOTEL [MOT] *Flagstaff, AZ*

BEST WESTERN PRESCOTTONIAN [MOT] *Prescott, AZ*

BEST WESTERN PTARMIGAN LODGE [MOT] *Dillon, CO*

BEST WESTERN PTARMIGAN INN [MOT] *Steamboat Springs, CO*

BEST WESTERN RAMBLER MOTEL [MOT] *Walsenburg, CO*

BEST WESTERN RANCHO GRANDE MOTEL [MOT] *Wickenburg, AZ*

BEST WESTERN RED ARROW MOTOR INN [MOT] *Montrose, CO*

BEST WESTERN RED CARPET INN [MOT] *Hereford, TX*

BEST WESTERN RED HILLS [MOT] *Kanab, UT*

BEST WESTERN RIVER TERRACE MOTEL [MOT] *Green River, UT*

BEST WESTERN ROSE GARDEN [MOT] *Brownsville, TX*

BEST WESTERN ROYAL GORGE [MOT] *CaÒon City, CO*

BEST WESTERN ROYAL SUN INN [MOT] *Tucson, AZ*

BEST WESTERN RUBY'S INN [MOT] *Bryce Canyon National Park, UT*

BEST WESTERN SALLY PORT INN & SUITES [MOT] *Roswell, NM*

BEST WESTERN SALT LAKE PLAZA HOTEL [MOT] *Salt Lake City, UT*

BEST WESTERN SAM HOUSTON INN [MOT] *Huntsville, TX*

BEST WESTERN SANDMAN [MOT] *Grand Junction, CO*

BEST WESTERN SANDS [MOT] *Raton, NM*

BEST WESTERN SHAHEEN'S [MOT] *Salina, UT*

BEST WESTERN SILVER SADDLE [MOT] *Estes Park, CO*

BEST WESTERN SPACE AGE LODGE [MOT] *Gila Bend, AZ*

BEST WESTERN STEVENS INN [MOT] *Carlsbad, NM*

BEST WESTERN SUNDANCE [MOT] *Delta, CO*

BEST WESTERN SUNDAY HOUSE INN [MOT] *Kerrville, TX*

BEST WESTERN SUNDOWNER [MOT] *Sterling, CO*

BEST WESTERN SUPERSTITION SPRINGS INN [MOT] *Mesa, AZ*

BEST WESTERN SWISS CHALET [MOT] *Ruidoso, NM*

BEST WESTERN SWISS CLOCK INN [MOT] *Pecos, TX*

BEST WESTERN TOMICHI VILLAGE INN [MOT] *Gunnison, CO*

BEST WESTERN TOWN & COUNTRY [MOT] *Cedar City, UT*

BEST WESTERN TRAIL DUST INN [MOT] *Sulphur Springs, TX*

BEST WESTERN TURQUOISE INN AND SUITES [MOT] *Cortez, CO*

BEST WESTERN UNIVERSITY INN [MOT] *Fort Collins, CO*

BEST WESTERN VAILGLO LODGE [BB] *Vail, CO*

BEST WESTERN VISTA INN [MOT] *Buena Vista, CO*

BEST WESTERN WAYFARERS INN [MOT] *Kingman, AZ*

BEST WESTERN WAYSIDE INN [MOT] *Monticello, UT*

BEST WESTERN WESTBRANCH INN [MOT] *Fort Worth, TX*

BEST WESTERN WESTON INN AND SUITES [MOT] *Page, AZ*

BEST WESTERN WILLIAMS [MOT] *Williams, AZ*

BEST WESTERN WINDSOR INN [MOT] *Dumas, TX*

BEST WESTERN WINROCK INN [MOT] *Albuquerque, NM*

BIGHORN LODGE BEST VALUE INN [MOT] *Grand Lake, CO*

BIG THOMPSON TIMBERLANE LODGE [RST] *Estes Park, CO*

BINIONS HORSESHOE HOTEL AND CASINO [HOT] *Las Vegas, NV*

BIRDHOUSE, THE [BB] *Athens, TX*

BISHOPS INN [MOT] *Clovis, NM*

BISHOP'S LODGE [RST] *Santa Fe, NM*

BLACK BEAR INN OF PIKES PEAK [BB] *Manitou Springs, CO*

BLACK BEAR INN OF VAIL [BB] *Vail,
CO*
BLACK CANYON [MOT] *Montrose,
CO*
BLAIR HOUSE [BB] *San Marcos, TX*
BLUE BOAR INN, THE [BB] *Heber
City, UT*
BLUE SPRUCE [MOT] *Lamar, CO*
BONANZA INN AND CASINO [MOT]
Fallon, NV
BONNYNOOK INN [BB] *Ennis, TX*
BOOMERANG LODGE [BB] *Aspen, CO*
BOULDER BROKER INN, THE [HOT]
Boulder, CO
BOULDER BROOK ON FALL RIVER
[MOT] *Estes Park, CO*
BOULDERS, THE [RST] *Carefree, AZ*
BOULDER STATION HOTEL AND
CASINO [HOT] *Las Vegas, NV*
BOURBON STREET HOTEL AND
CASINO [HOT] *Las Vegas, NV*
BOWEN MOTEL [MOT] *Moab, UT*
BOX CANYON LODGE & HOT
SPRING [MOT] *Ouray, CO*
BRACKENRIDGE HOUSE [BB] *San
Antonio, TX*
BRIAR PATCH INN [CC] *Sedona, AZ*
BRIAR ROSE BED & BREAKFAST [BB]
Boulder, CO
BRIGHAM STREET INN [BB] *Salt Lake
City, UT*
BRIGHT ANGEL LODGE [MOT] *South
Rim (Grand Canyon National
Park), AZ*
BRIGHTON SKI RESORT [MOT] *Salt
Lake City, UT*
BRITTANIA & W. E. MAUGER ESTATE
BED AND BREAKFAST [BB]
Albuquerque, NM
BROADMOOR RESORT, THE [RST]
Colorado Springs, CO
BROOKS STREET INN [BB] *Taos, NM*
BROWN PALACE HOTEL, THE [HOT]
Denver, CO
BROWN PELICAN INN [BB] *South
Padre Island, TX*
BRYCE CANYON LODGE [MOT]
Bryce Canyon National Park, UT
BRYCE CANYON PINES MOTEL
[MOT] *Bryce Canyon National
Park, UT*
BUDGET HOST COLONIAL INN
[MOT] *Abilene, TX*
BUDGET HOST INN [MOT] *Grand
Junction, CO*
BUDGET HOST INN [MOT] *Trinidad,
CO*
BUDGET HOST MELODY LANE
[MOT] *Raton, NM*
BUDGET INN [MOT] *Las Vegas, NM*
BUDGET INN [MOT] *Roswell, NM*

BUDGET SUMMIT INN [MOT]
Trinidad, CO
BULLIS HOUSE INN [BB] *San Antonio,
TX*
BURNSLEY ALL-SUITE HOTEL, THE
[AS] *Denver, CO*
CAESAR'S PALACE [HOT] *Las Vegas,
NV*
CAESAR'S TAHOE [HOT] *Stateline, NV*
CALIFORNIA HOTEL AND CASINO
[HOT] *Las Vegas, NV*
CAL-NEVA RESORT HOTEL, SPA AND
CASINO [HOT] *Incline Village,
NV*
CALUMET AND ARIZONA GUEST
HOUSE [BB] *Bisbee, AZ*
CAMBRIDGE HOTEL [HOT] *Denver,
CO*
CANON INN [MOT] *CaÒon City, CO*
CANYON TRAILS INN [MOT]
Montrose, CO
CANYON VILLA INN [BB] *Sedona, AZ*
CAPITOL HILL MANSION BED &
BREAKFAST [BB] *Denver, CO*
CAR-MAR'S SOUTHWEST BED AND
BREAKFAST [BB] *Tucson, AZ*
CARRIAGE HOUSE [CON] *Las Vegas,
NV*
CARSON VALLEY INN HOTEL
CASINO [HOT] *Gardnerville,
NV*
CASA ALEGRE BED AND BREAKFAST
INN [BB] *Tucson, AZ*
CASABLANCA [RST] *Las Vegas, NV*
CASA BLANCA INN [BB] *Farmington,
NM*
CASA DE LAS CHIMENEAS [BB] *Taos,
NM*
CASA DEL GAVILAN [BB] *Cimarron,
NM*
CASA DEL GRANJERO B&B [BB]
Albuquerque, NM
CASA DE PATRON BED AND
BREAKFAST INN [BB] *Ruidoso,
NM*
CASA EUROPA INN & GALLERY [BB]
Taos, NM
CASAS DE SUENOS OLD TOWN BED
AND BREAKFAST INN [BB]
Albuquerque, NM
CASA SEDONA BED AND BREAKFAST
[BB] *Sedona, AZ*
CASCADE FALLS LODGE [MOT]
Ouray, CO
CASCADE HILLS MOTEL [MOT]
Colorado Springs, CO
CASTAWAYS [HOT] *Las Vegas, NV*
CASTLE MARNE LUXURY
URBANINN [BB] *Denver, CO*
CASTLE VALLEY INN [BB] *Moab, UT*
CATALINA PARK INN [BB] *Tucson, AZ*

CATHEDRAL ROCK LODGE & RETREAT CENTER [CC] *Sedona, AZ*

CATTAIL CREEK INN BED & BREAKFAST [BB] *Loveland, CO*

CENTRAL MOTEL [MOT] *Fort Morgan, CO*

CHAPARRAL MOTOR INN [MOT] *Burlington, CO*

CHAPARRAL SUITES [AS] *Scottsdale, AZ*

CHARTER AT BEAVER CREEK [RST] *Beaver Creek, CO*

CHASE SUITE HOTEL BY WOODFIN [AS] *El Paso, TX*

CHASE SUITE HOTEL BY WOODFIN [AS] *Salt Lake City, UT*

CHATEAU AT VAIL, THE [RST] *Vail, CO*

CHEYENNE CANON INN [BB] *Colorado Springs, CO*

CHINA CLIPPER BED BREAKFAST INN [BB] *Ouray, CO*

CHIRICAHUA FOOTHILLS [BB] *Willcox, AZ*

CHOCOLATE TURTLE BED AND BREAKFAST [BB] *Albuquerque, NM*

CHRISTIANA AT VAIL [BB] *Vail, CO*

CIMARRON INN & RV PARK [MOT] *Cimarron, NM*

CIRCLE BAR MOTEL [MOT] *Ozona, TX*

CIRCUS CIRCUS [HOT] *Las Vegas, NV*

CIRCUS CIRCUS HOTEL AND CASINO [HOT] *Reno, NV*

CLARIDGE INN [MOT] *St. George, UT*

CLARION HOTEL AIRPORT [MOT] *San Antonio, TX*

CLARION HOTEL & CONVENTION CENTER [HOT] *Abilene, TX*

CLARION HOTEL RANDOLPH PARK [MOT] *Tucson, AZ*

CLARION HOTEL TUCSON AIRPORT [MOT] *Tucson, AZ*

CLARION INN [MOT] *Waco, TX*

CLARION SANTA RITA HOTEL & SUITES [MOT] *Tucson, AZ*

CLARION SUITES [AS] *Dallas, TX*

CLASSIC AMERICAN ECONOMY INN [MOT] *Portales, NM*

CLASSIC INN [MOT] *Granbury, TX*

CLAYDESTA INN [MOT] *Midland, TX*

C LAZY U RANCH [RAN] *Granby, CO*

CLIFF DWELLERS LODGE [MOT] *Marble Canyon, AZ*

CLIFFROSE LODGE AND GARDENS [RST] *Zion National Park, UT*

CLOVIS INN [MOT] *Clovis, NM*

CLUBHOUSE INN ALBUQUERQUE [MOT] *Albuquerque, NM*

COLONIAL MOTEL [MOT] *Sterling, CO*

COLONY INN NATIONAL 9 [MOT] *Provo, UT*

COLORADO BELLE HOTEL AND CASINO [HOT] *Laughlin, NV*

COLORADO COTTAGES [CC] *Estes Park, CO*

COLORADO TRAILS RANCH [RAN] *Durango, CO*

COMFORT INN [MOT] *Battle Mountain, NV*

COMFORT INN [MOT] *Bryan/College Station, TX*

COMFORT INN [MOT] *Cedar City, UT*

COMFORT INN [MOT] *Clovis, NM*

COMFORT INN [MOT] *Colorado Springs, CO*

COMFORT INN [MOT] *Cortez, CO*

COMFORT INN [MOT] *Dalhart, TX*

COMFORT INN [MOT] *Delta, CO*

COMFORT INN [MOT] *Denver, CO*

COMFORT INN [MOT] *Dumas, TX*

COMFORT INN [MOT] *El Paso, TX*

COMFORT INN [MOT] *Estes Park, CO*

COMFORT INN [MOT] *Farmington, NM*

COMFORT INN [MOT] *Fort Worth, TX*

COMFORT INN [MOT] *Fredericksburg, TX*

COMFORT INN [MOT] *Georgetown, TX*

COMFORT INN [MOT] *Granbury, TX*

COMFORT INN [MOT] *Holbrook, AZ*

COMFORT INN [MOT] *Lakewood, CO*

COMFORT INN [MOT] *Las Vegas, NM*

COMFORT INN [MOT] *Logan, UT*

COMFORT INN [MOT] *Monte Vista, CO*

COMFORT INN [MOT] *Ouray, CO*

COMFORT INN [MOT] *Paris, TX*

COMFORT INN [MOT] *Payson, UT*

COMFORT INN [MOT] *Prescott, AZ*

COMFORT INN [MOT] *Pueblo, CO*

COMFORT INN [MOT] *Safford, AZ*

COMFORT INN [MOT] *Salt Lake City, UT*

COMFORT INN [MOT] *Salt Lake City, UT*

COMFORT INN [MOT] *Scottsdale, AZ*

COMFORT INN [MOT] *Tucumcari, NM*

COMFORT INN [MOT] *Victoria, TX*

COMFORT INN [MOT] *Waco, TX*

COMFORT INN AIRPORT [MOT] *San Antonio, TX*

COMFORT INN EAST [MOT] *Albuquerque, NM*

COMFORT INN NORTH [MOT] *Colorado Springs, CO*

COMFORT INN NORTH DALLAS [MOT] *Dallas, TX*

COMFORT SUITES [MOT] *Corpus Christi, TX*

COMFORT SUITES [AS] *Dallas, TX*
COMFORT SUITES [MOT] *St. George, UT*
COMFORT SUITES [AS] *Taos, NM*
COMFORT SUITES OF LAS COLINAS [AS] *Dallas/Fort Worth Airport Area, TX*
CONAKI DUMAS INN [MOT] *Dumas, TX*
CONTINENTAL INN [MOT] *Carlsbad, NM*
COPPER MANOR MOTEL [MOT] *Silver City, NM*
COPPER MOUNTAIN RESORT [RST] *Copper Mountain, CO*
COPPER QUEEN HOTEL [HOT] *Bisbee, AZ*
COTTAGES AT PRESCOTT COUNTRY INN, THE [BB] *Prescott, AZ*
COTTONWOOD INN [BB] *Alamosa, CO*
COTTONWOOD INN BED AND BREAKFAST [BB] *Taos, NM*
COUNTRY HOME BED AND BREAKFAST [BB] *Canyon, TX*
COUNTRY INN [MOT] *Tucumcari, NM*
COUNTRY INN AND SUITES [MOT] *Salt Lake City, UT*
COUNTRY INN AND SUITES [MOT] *Scottsdale, AZ*
COUNTRY INN & SUITES [MOT] *Tempe, AZ*
COUNTRY INN AND SUITES - TUCSON [HOT] *Tucson, AZ*
COUNTRY LODGE [MOT] *Montrose, CO*
COUNTRY SUITES- ARLINGTON [AS] *Arlington-Grand Prairie, TX*
COUNTRY SUITES BY CARLSON [MOT] *Dallas/Fort Worth Airport Area, TX*
COUNTRY SUNSHINE BED & BREAKFAST [BB] *Durango, CO*
COURTYARD BY MARRIOTT [MOT] *Albuquerque, NM*
COURTYARD BY MARRIOTT [MOT] *Arlington-Grand Prairie, TX*
COURTYARD BY MARRIOTT [HOT] *Austin, TX*
COURTYARD BY MARRIOTT [MOT] *Dallas, TX*
COURTYARD BY MARRIOTT [MOT] *Dallas, TX*
COURTYARD BY MARRIOTT [MOT] *Fort Worth, TX*
COURTYARD BY MARRIOTT [MOT] *Fort Worth, TX*
COURTYARD BY MARRIOTT [MOT] *Harlingen, TX*

COURTYARD BY MARRIOTT [MOT] *Houston, TX*
COURTYARD BY MARRIOTT [MOT] *Houston, TX*
COURTYARD BY MARRIOTT [MOT] *Laredo, TX*
COURTYARD BY MARRIOTT [MOT] *Las Vegas, NV*
COURTYARD BY MARRIOTT [MOT] *Mesa, AZ*
COURTYARD BY MARRIOTT [MOT] *Phoenix, AZ*
COURTYARD BY MARRIOTT [MOT] *Salt Lake City, UT*
COURTYARD BY MARRIOTT [MOT] *San Antonio, TX*
COURTYARD BY MARRIOTT [MOT] *Santa Fe, NM*
COURTYARD BY MARRIOTT [MOT] *Tempe, AZ*
COURTYARD BY MARRIOTT [MOT] *Tucson, AZ*
COURTYARD BY MARRIOTT AIRPORT [MOT] *McAllen, TX*
COURTYARD BY MARRIOTT AIRPORT [MOT] *Tucson, AZ*
COURTYARD BY MARRIOTT BOULDER [MOT] *Boulder, CO*
COURTYARD BY MARRIOTT CAMELBACK [MOT] *Phoenix, AZ*
COURTYARD BY MARRIOTT DENVER STAPLETON [MOT] *Denver, CO*
COURTYARD BY MARRIOTT MAYO CLINIC [HOT] *Scottsdale, AZ*
COURTYARD BY MARRIOTT NORTH SCOTTSDALE [HOT] *Scottsdale, AZ*
COURTYARD BY MARRIOTT - PHOENIX NORTH [MOT] *Phoenix, AZ*
COWBOYS AND INDIANS [BB] *El Paso, TX*
CREEKSIDE INN [BB] *Dillon, CO*
CRESTED BUTTE ATHLETIC CLUB [BB] *Crested Butte, CO*
CRESTWOOD LODGE [RST] *Snowmass Village, CO*
CROWNE PLAZA [HOT] *Albuquerque, NM*
CROWNE PLAZA DALLAS MARKET CENTER [HOT] *Dallas, TX*
CROWNE PLAZA HOTEL [AS] *Las Vegas, NV*
CROWNE PLAZA HOUSTON BROOKHOLLOW [HOT] *Houston, TX*
CROWNE PLAZA HOUSTON MEDICAL CENTER [HOT] *Houston, TX*

CROWNE PLAZA-NORTH DALLAS/NEAR THE GALLERIA [HOT] *Dallas, TX*
CROWNE PLAZA SUITES [HOT] *Dallas, TX*
CRYSTAL INN [HOT] *Salt Lake City, UT*
CRYSTAL INN - DOWNTOWN [HOT] *Salt Lake City, UT*
CRYSTAL RIVER INN [BB] *San Marcos, TX*
DALLAS GRAND HOTEL [HOT] *Dallas, TX*
DAMN YANKEE COUNTRY INN [BB] *Ouray, CO*
DANCING GROUND OF THE SUN [BB] *Santa Fe, NM*
DANISH VIKING LODGE [MOT] *Heber City, UT*
DAY'S END LODGE [MOT] *Las Cruces, NM*
DAYS INN [MOT] *Alamogordo, NM*
DAYS INN [MOT] *Albuquerque, NM*
DAYS INN [MOT] *Albuquerque, NM*
DAYS INN [MOT] *Brownsville, TX*
DAYS INN [MOT] *Brownwood, TX*
DAYS INN [MOT] *Corpus Christi, TX*
DAYS INN [MOT] *Dalhart, TX*
DAYS INN [MOT] *Deming, NM*
DAYS INN [MOT] *Durango, CO*
DAYS INN [MOT] *Flagstaff, AZ*
DAYS INN [MOT] *Gallup, NM*
DAYS INN [MOT] *Greenville, TX*
DAYS INN [MOT] *Kingman, AZ*
DAYS INN [MOT] *Las Cruces, NM*
DAYS INN [MOT] *Las Vegas, NV*
DAYS INN [MOT] *Lufkin, TX*
DAYS INN [MOT] *Mesa, AZ*
DAYS INN [MOT] *Mesa, AZ*
DAYS INN [MOT] *Midland, TX*
DAYS INN [MOT] *Ogden, UT*
DAYS INN [MOT] *Port Lavaca, TX*
DAYS INN [MOT] *Provo, UT*
DAYS INN [MOT] *Pueblo, CO*
DAYS INN [MOT] *Richfield, UT*
DAYS INN [MOT] *Show Low, AZ*
DAYS INN [MOT] *Snyder, TX*
DAYS INN [MOT] *South Padre Island, TX*
DAYS INN [MOT] *Stephenville, TX*
DAYS INN [MOT] *Tyler, TX*
DAYS INN [MOT] *Vernon, TX*
DAYS INN [MOT] *Wichita Falls, TX*
DAYS INN [MOT] *Willcox, AZ*
DAYS INN [MOT] *Winnemucca, NV*
DAYS INN AIRPORT [MOT] *Salt Lake City, UT*
DAYS INN AIRPORT/DOWNTOWN [MOT] *Amarillo, TX*
DAYS INN—EAST [MOT] *Flagstaff, AZ*
DAYS INN LOGAN [MOT] *Logan, UT*
DAYS INN OF PRESCOTT VALLEY [MOT] *Prescott, AZ*

DAYS INN SUITES [MOT] *Aransas Pass, TX*
DEER CREST [MOT] *Estes Park, CO*
DEFIANCE HOUSE [MOT] *Lake Powell, UT*
DE LANO MOTEL [MOT] *Beaver, UT*
DELAWARE HOTEL [HOT] *Leadville, CO*
DESERT QUAIL INN [MOT] *Sedona, AZ*
DEVIL'S RIVER DAYS INN [MOT] *Sonora, TX*
DIETZEL MOTEL [MOT] *Fredericksburg, TX*
DIXIE DUDE RANCH [RAN] *Bandera, TX*
DON LAUGHLIN'S RIVERSIDE HOTEL [HOT] *Laughlin, NV*
DOS CASAS VIEJAS [BB] *Santa Fe, NM*
DOUBLE HOTEL & CASINO [HOT] *Cripple Creek, CO*
DOUBLETREE [HOT] *Durango, CO*
DOUBLETREE AT THE ALLEN CENTER [HOT] *Houston, TX*
DOUBLETREE CLUB HOTEL SAN ANTONION AIRPORT [HOT] *San Antonio, TX*
DOUBLETREE DENVER [HOT] *Denver International Airport Area, CO*
DOUBLETREE DENVER SOUTHEAST [HOT] *Denver International Airport Area, CO*
DOUBLETREE GUEST SUITES DOWNTOWN [AS] *Austin, TX*
DOUBLETREE GUEST SUITES [HOT] *Houston, TX*
DOUBLETREE GUEST SUITES— PHOENIX GATEWAY CENTER [AS] *Phoenix, AZ*
DOUBLETREE GUEST SUITES [AS] *Tucson, AZ*
DOUBLETREE HOTEL [HOT] *Colorado Springs, CO*
DOUBLETREE HOTEL [HOT] *San Antonio, TX*
DOUBLETREE HOTEL ALBUQUERQUE [HOT] *Albuquerque, NM*
DOUBLETREE HOTEL AT POST OAK [HOT] *Houston, TX*
DOUBLETREE HOTEL AUSTIN [HOT] *Austin, TX*
DOUBLETREE HOTEL CAMPBELL CENTRE [HOT] *Dallas, TX*
DOUBLETREE HOTEL REID PARK [HOT] *Tucson, AZ*
DOUBLETREE LA POSADA RESORT [RST] *Scottsdale, AZ*
DOUBLETREE PARADISE VALLEY RESORT [RST] *Scottsdale, AZ*
DREAMCATCHER BED AND BREAKFAST [BB] *Taos, NM*

DRIFTER MOTEL REST LOUNGE [MOT] *Silver City, NM*
DRIFTWOOD LODGE [RST] *Grand Lake, CO*
DRIFTWOOD LODGE [MOT] *Zion National Park, UT*
DRISKILL HOTEL [HOT] *Austin, TX*
DROWSY WATER RANCH [RAN] *Granby, CO*
DRURY INN [MOT] *Colorado Springs, CO*
DRURY INN [MOT] *Corpus Christi, TX*
DRURY INN [MOT] *Dallas/Fort Worth Airport Area, TX*
DRURY INN & SUITES [MOT] *Austin, TX*
DRURY INN & SUITES [MOT] *Houston, TX*
DRURY INN & SUITES [MOT] *McAllen, TX*
DRURY INN AND SUITES [MOT] *San Antonio, TX*
DRURY INN & SUITES WEST [MOT] *Houston, TX*
DRURY INN DALLAS NORTH [MOT] *Dallas, TX*
DUNES CONDOMINIUM [MOT] *Port Aransas, TX*
DURANGO LODGE [MOT] *Durango, CO*
EASTHOLME IN THE ROCKIES [BB] *Manitou Springs, CO*
ECONO LODGE [MOT] *Dumas, TX*
ECONO LODGE [MOT] *Durango, CO*
ECONO LODGE [MOT] *Kerrville, TX*
ECONO LODGE [MOT] *Las Vegas, NV*
ECONO LODGE [MOT] *Tucumcari, NM*
ECONO LODGE [MOT] *Wichita Falls, TX*
ECONO LODGE [MOT] *Winslow, AZ*
ECONO LODGE INN [MOT] *Gallup, NM*
ECONO LODGE INN [MOT] *Holbrook, AZ*
EDELWEISS HAUS HOTEL [CON] *Park City, UT*
EDGEWATER HOTEL AND CASINO [HOT] *Laughlin, NV*
EL CAPITAN RESORT CASINO [MOT] *Hawthorne, NV*
EL CORTEZ HOTEL AND CASINO [HOT] *Las Vegas, NV*
ELDORADO [HOT] *Santa Fe, NM*
ELDORADO HOTEL & CASINO [HOT] *Reno, NV*
ELK ECHO RANCH [BB] *Sterling, CO*
ELK HORN LODGE [MOT] *Chama, NM*
EL PARADERO EN SANTA FE [BB] *Santa Fe, NM*

EL PATIO MOTOR INN [MOT] *San Angelo, TX*
EL PRESIDIO BED & BREAKFAST [BB] *Tucson, AZ*
EL PUEBLO LODGE [MOT] *Taos, NM*
EL RANCHO [MOT] *Gallup, NM*
EL RANCHO BOULDER [MOT] *Boulder City, NV*
EL RANCHO MOTEL [MOT] *Williams, AZ*
EL REY INN [BB] *Santa Fe, NM*
EL TOVAR [HOT] *South Rim (Grand Canyon National Park), AZ*
EMBASSY SUITES [AS] *Colorado Springs, CO*
EMBASSY SUITES [AS] *Corpus Christi, TX*
EMBASSY SUITES [AS] *Dallas, TX*
EMBASSY SUITES [AS] *Denver, CO*
EMBASSY SUITES [AS] *Denver, CO*
EMBASSY SUITES [AS] *El Paso, TX*
EMBASSY SUITES [AS] *Flagstaff, AZ*
EMBASSY SUITES [AS] *Houston, TX*
EMBASSY SUITES [AS] *McAllen, TX*
EMBASSY SUITES [AS] *Phoenix, AZ*
EMBASSY SUITES [AS] *Salt Lake City, UT*
EMBASSY SUITES [AS] *San Antonio, TX*
EMBASSY SUITES [AS] *Tucson, AZ*
EMBASSY SUITES DENVER SOUTH [AS] *Englewood, CO*
EMBASSY SUITES HOTEL [AS] *Abilene, TX*
EMBASSY SUITES HOTEL DOWNTOWN [AS] *Austin, TX*
EMBASSY SUITES HOTEL TUCSON-BROADWAY [AS] *Tucson, AZ*
EMBASSY SUITES NEAR THE GALLERIA [AS] *Houston, TX*
EMBASSY SUITES NORTHWEST [AS] *San Antonio, TX*
EMBASSY SUITES PHOENIX AIRPO [AS] *Phoenix, AZ*
EMBASSY SUITES PHOENIX-NORTH [AS] *Phoenix, AZ*
EMBASSY SUITES PHOENIX/TEMPE [AS] *Tempe, AZ*
EMERALD SPRINGS-HOLIDAY INN [HOT] *Las Vegas, NV*
EMPIRE MOTEL [MOT] *Page, AZ*
ENCHANTMENT INN AND SUITES [HOT] *Ruidoso, NM*
ENCHANTMENT RESORT [RST] *Sedona, AZ*
EVANS HOUSE BED & BREAKFAST [BB] *Breckenridge, CO*
EXCALIBUR HOTEL & CASINO [HOT] *Las Vegas, NV*
EXCELSIOR HOUSE [BB] *Jefferson, TX*
EXECUTIVE INN [MOT] *Sherman, TX*

EXECUTIVE TOWER HOTEL [HOT] *Denver, CO*

EXEL INN OF AUSTIN [MOT] *Austin, TX*

FAIRFIELD INN [MOT] *Bryan/College Station, TX*

FAIRFIELD INN [MOT] *Chandler, AZ*

FAIRFIELD INN [MOT] *Dallas, TX*

FAIRFIELD INN [MOT] *Flagstaff, AZ*

FAIRFIELD INN [MOT] *Fort Worth, TX*

FAIRFIELD INN [MOT] *Houston, TX*

FAIRFIELD INN [MOT] *Houston, TX*

FAIRFIELD INN [MOT] *Las Cruces, NM*

FAIRFIELD INN [MOT] *Las Vegas, NV*

FAIRFIELD INN [MOT] *Mesa, AZ*

FAIRFIELD INN [MOT] *Tyler, TX*

FAIRFIELD INN [MOT] *Victoria, TX*

FAIRFIELD INN BY MARRIOTT [MOT] *Arlington-Grand Prairie, TX*

FAIRFIELD INN DFW AIRPORT/IRVING [MOT] *Dallas/Fort Worth Airport Area, TX*

FAIRFIELD INN NORTH [MOT] *Colorado Springs, CO*

FAIRFIELD INN PHOENIX/AIRPORT [MOT] *Phoenix, AZ*

FAIRFIELD INN SCOTTSDALE NORTH [MOT] *Scottsdale, AZ*

FAIRFIELD INN SOUTH [MOT] *Colorado Springs, CO*

FAIRMONT DALLAS, THE [HOT] *Dallas, TX*

FAIRMONT SCOTTSDALE PRINCESS, THE [RST] *Scottsdale, AZ*

FAIRMOUNT, WYNDHAM HISTORIC HOTEL [HOT] *San Antonio, TX*

FAR VIEW LODGE IN MESA VERDE [MOT] *Mesa Verde National Park, CO*

FAUST HOTEL [BB] *New Braunfels, TX*

FAWN VALLEY INN [MOT] *Estes Park, CO*

FECHIN INN [HOT] *Taos, NM*

FIESTA CASINO HOTEL [HOT] *Las Vegas, NV*

FIESTA INN LAREDO [MOT] *Laredo, TX*

FIESTA INN RESORT [RST] *Tempe, AZ*

FITZGERALD'S CASINO AND HOTEL [HOT] *Las Vegas, NV*

FITZGERALD'S CASINO HOTEL [HOT] *Reno, NV*

FLAMINGO HOTEL [MOT] *Tucson, AZ*

FLAMINGO LAS VEGAS [HOT] *Las Vegas, NV*

FLAMINGO LAUGHLIN [HOT] *Laughlin, NV*

FLAMINGO RENO [HOT] *Reno, NV*

FLANIGAN'S INN [MOT] *Zion National Park, UT*

FLYING E RANCH [RAN] *Wickenburg, AZ*

FLYING L GUEST RANCH [RST] *Bandera, TX*

FOREST VILLAS HOTEL [HOT] *Prescott, AZ*

FOUR POINTS BY SHERATON [MOT] *Brownsville, TX*

FOUR POINTS BY SHERATON [MOT] *Dillon, CO*

FOUR POINTS BY SHERATON [MOT] *Lakewood, CO*

FOUR POINTS BY SHERATON [MOT] *Lubbock, TX*

FOUR POINTS BY SHERATON MCALLEN [MOT] *McAllen, TX*

FOUR POINTS BY SHERATON RIVERWALK NORTH [HOT] *San Antonio, TX*

FOUR POINTS BY SHERATON [HOT] *Tucson, AZ*

FOUR QUEENS HOTEL AND CASINO [HOT] *Las Vegas, NV*

FOUR SEASONS HOTEL AUSTIN [HOT] *Austin, TX*

FOUR SEASONS HOTEL HOUSTON [HOT] *Houston, TX*

FOUR SEASONS HOTEL LAS VEGAS [HOT] *Las Vegas, NV*

FOUR SEASONS INN [MOT] *Kanab, UT*

FOUR SEASONS RESORT AND CLUB DALLAS AT LAS COLINAS [RST] *Dallas/Fort Worth Airport Area, TX*

FOUR SEASONS RESORT SCOTTSDALE AT TROON NORTH [RST] *Scottsdale, AZ*

FRANCISCO GRANDE RESORT AND GOLF CLUB [RST] *Casa Grande, AZ*

FRAY MARCOS HOTEL [RST] *Williams, AZ*

FREDERICKSBURG INN AND SUITES [MOT] *Fredericksburg, TX*

FREDERICKSBURG LODGE [MOT] *Fredericksburg, TX*

FREDONIA HOTEL & CONVENTION CENTER [HOT] *Nacogdoches, TX*

FREMONT HOTEL & CASINO [HOT] *Las Vegas, NV*

FRONTIER HOTEL AND GAMBLING HALL [HOT] *Las Vegas, NV*

FRONTIER MOTEL [MOT] *Roosevelt, UT*

FRONTIER MOTEL [MOT] *Roswell, NM*

GAINEY SUITES HOTEL [AS] *Scottsdale, AZ*

GALISTEO INN [BB] *Santa Fe, NM*

GARDEN OF THE GODS MOTEL [MOT] *Colorado Springs, CO*

GARRETTS DESERT INN [MOT] *Santa Fe, NM*

GASTHAUS EICHLER HOTEL [HOT] *Winter Park, CO*

GATEWAY INN [MOT] *Graham, TX*

GLEN EDEN RESORT [RST] *Steamboat Springs, CO*

GLENWOOD MOTOR INN [MOT] *Glenwood Springs, CO*

GOLD CANYON GOLF RESORT [RST] *Mesa, AZ*

GOLD COAST HOTEL AND CASINO [HOT] *Las Vegas, NV*

GOLDENER HIRSCH INN [BB] *Park City, UT*

GOLDEN NUGGET [HOT] *Las Vegas, NV*

GOLDEN NUGGET [HOT] *Laughlin, NV*

GOLD SPIKE HOTEL AND CASINO [HOT] *Las Vegas, NV*

GOLF VILLAS AT ORO VALLEY, THE [RST] *Tucson, AZ*

GOVERNOR'S HOUSE MOTEL [MOT] *Houston, TX*

GRAND AMERICA [HOT] *Salt Lake City, UT*

GRAND CANYON LODGE [MOT] *North Rim (Grand Canyon National Park), AZ*

GRAND CANYON PARK NATIONAL LODGES [MOT] *South Rim (Grand Canyon National Park), AZ*

GRAND LAKE LODGE [RST] *Grand Lake, CO*

GRAND MOTOR INN [MOT] *Deming, NM*

GRAND SUMMIT RESORT HOTEL & CONFERENCE CENTER [RST] *Park City, UT*

GRAND VICTORIAN AT WINTER PARK [BB] *Winter Park, CO*

GRAND VISTA HOTEL [MOT] *Grand Junction, CO*

GRANT CORNER INN [BB] *Santa Fe, NM*

GREAT DIVIDE LODGE BRECKENRIDGE [RST] *Breckenridge, CO*

GREAT WESTERN SUMAC LODGE [MOT] *Buena Vista, CO*

GREEN GATE VILLAGE [BB] *St. George, UT*

GREEN OAKS HOTEL [CONF] *Fort Worth, TX*

GREEN TREE INN [MOT] *Vernon, TX*

GREENWELL INN & CONVENTION CENTER [MOT] *Price, UT*

GREER LODGE [MOT] *Greer, AZ*

GUADALUPE INN [BB] *Santa Fe, NM*

GUEST HOUSE INN [BB] *Organ Pipe Cactus National Monument, AZ*

GUESTHOUSE INN [MOT] *Temple, TX*

GUEST INN [MOT] *Marshall, TX*

GUEST VILLAGE INN [MOT] *Jefferson, TX*

GULFSTREAM CONDOMINIUM APARTMENTS [MOT] *Corpus Christi, TX*

HACIENDA ANTIGUA BED AND BREAKFAST [BB] *Albuquerque, NM*

HACIENDA DEL SOL [BB] *Taos, NM*

HACIENDA INN AND CASINO [MOT] *Boulder City, NV*

HACIENDA VARGAS B&B INN [BB] *Albuquerque, NM*

HAMPTON INN [MOT] *Albuquerque, NM*

HAMPTON INN [MOT] *Amarillo, TX*

HAMPTON INN [MOT] *Baytown, TX*

HAMPTON INN [MOT] *Boulder, CO*

HAMPTON INN [MOT] *Bryan/College Station, TX*

HAMPTON INN [MOT] *Chandler, AZ*

HAMPTON INN [MOT] *Dallas, TX*

HAMPTON INN [MOT] *Dallas/Fort Worth Airport Area, TX*

HAMPTON INN [MOT] *Denver International Airport Area, CO*

HAMPTON INN [MOT] *Durango, CO*

HAMPTON INN [MOT] *Englewood, CO*

HAMPTON INN [MOT] *Flagstaff, AZ*

HAMPTON INN [MOT] *Fort Worth, TX*

HAMPTON INN [MOT] *Glendale, AZ*

HAMPTON INN [MOT] *Glenwood Springs, CO*

HAMPTON INN [MOT] *Houston, TX*

HAMPTON INN [MOT] *Houston, TX*

HAMPTON INN [MOT] *Lakewood, CO*

HAMPTON INN [MOT] *Laredo, TX*

HAMPTON INN [MOT] *Las Cruces, NM*

HAMPTON INN [MOT] *McAllen, TX*

HAMPTON INN [MOT] *New Braunfels, TX*

HAMPTON INN [MOT] *Pueblo, CO*

HAMPTON INN [MOT] *Salt Lake City, UT*

HAMPTON INN [MOT] *Salt Lake City, UT*

HAMPTON INN [MOT] *Scottsdale, AZ*

HAMPTON INN [MOT] *Scottsdale, AZ*

HAMPTON INN [MOT] *Sedona, AZ*

HAMPTON INN [MOT] *Taos, NM*

HAMPTON INN [MOT] *Tyler, TX*

HAMPTON INN [MOT] *Victoria, TX*
HAMPTON INN AND SUITES [MOT] *Flagstaff, AZ*
HAMPTON INN AND SUITES [MOT] *Houston, TX*
HAMPTON INN & SUITES [MOT] *Park City, UT*
HAMPTON INN AUSTIN NORTH [MOT] *Austin, TX*
HAMPTON INN AUSTIN SOUTH [MOT] *Austin, TX*
HAMPTON INN-DFW/ARL [MOT] *Arlington-Grand Prairie, TX*
HAMPTON INN DOWNTOWN [MOT] *Dallas, TX*
HAMPTON INN DOWNTOWN RIVERWALK [MOT] *San Antonio, TX*
HAMPTON INN-GARLAND [MOT] *Dallas, TX*
HAMPTON INN I-10 WEST [MOT] *Houston, TX*
HAMPTON INN I-17 PHOENIX/METROCENTER [MOT] *Phoenix, AZ*
HAMPTON INN PHOENIX/MESA [MOT] *Mesa, AZ*
HAMPTON INN SIX FLAGS AREA [MOT] *San Antonio, TX*
HAMPTON INN TUCSON AIRPORT [MOT] *Tucson, AZ*
HARBOR HOUSE [MOT] *Galveston, TX*
HARD ROCK HOTEL AND CASINO [HOT] *Las Vegas, NV*
HARMEL'S RANCH RESORT [RAN] *Gunnison, CO*
HARRAH'S [HOT] *Reno, NV*
HARRAH'S CASINO HOTEL [HOT] *Las Vegas, NV*
HARRAH'S LAKE TAHOE HOTEL CASINO [HOT] *Stateline, NV*
HARVEY HOTEL DALLAS [MOT] *Dallas, TX*
HARVEY HOTEL- PLANO [HOT] *Dallas, TX*
HARVEY'S RESORT HOTEL AND CASINO [HOT] *Stateline, NV*
HARVEY SUITES [MOT] *Dallas/Fort Worth Airport Area, TX*
HASSAYAMPA INN [HOT] *Prescott, AZ*
HAUS BERLIN BED & BREAKFAST [BB] *Denver, CO*
HAWTHORN SUITES [AS] *Tucson, AZ*
HAWTHORN SUITES HOTEL ARLINGTON [MOT] *Arlington-Grand Prairie, TX*
HAWTHORN SUITES HOTEL SIX FLAGS [AS] *San Antonio, TX*
HAWTHORN SUITES MARKET CENTER [MOT] *Dallas, TX*
HAWTHORN SUITES NORTHWEST AUSTIN [AS] *Austin, TX*

HAWTHORN SUITES SOUTH [AS] *Austin, TX*
HEARTHSTONE INN [BB] *Colorado Springs, CO*
HERITAGE INN [BB] *Artesia, NM*
HERMOSA INN [BB] *Scottsdale, AZ*
HIGH COUNTRY INN AND RV PARK [MOT] *Heber City, UT*
HIGH COUNTRY LODGE [MOT] *Pagosa Springs, CO*
HIGH COUNTRY LODGE [RST] *Ruidoso, NM*
HIGH DESERT INN [HOT] *Elko, NV*
HIGHLAND HAVEN CREEKSIDE INN [BB] *Evergreen, CO*
HIGH MOUNTAIN LODGE INC [MOT] *Winter Park, CO*
HILL COUNTRY EQUESTRIAN LODGE [RST] *Bandera, TX*
HILTON [HOT] *Albuquerque, NM*
HILTON [HOT] *Arlington-Grand Prairie, TX*
HILTON [HOT] *Bryan/College Station, TX*
HILTON [HOT] *Galveston, TX*
HILTON [HOT] *Las Cruces, NM*
HILTON [HOT] *Midland, TX*
HILTON [HOT] *Santa Fe, NM*
HILTON AND TOWERS WESTCHASE [HOT] *Houston, TX*
HILTON AT THE EL PASO AIRPORT [HOT] *El Paso, TX*
HILTON AUSTIN NORTH [HOT] *Austin, TX*
HILTON BEAUMONT [HOT] *Beaumont, TX*
HILTON CAMINO REAL HOTEL [HOT] *El Paso, TX*
HILTON DALLAS PARKWAY [HOT] *Dallas, TX*
HILTON DENVER TECH SOUTH [HOT] *Englewood, CO*
HILTON EXECUTIVE CONFERENCE CENTER DFW [HOT] *Dallas/Fort Worth Airport Area, TX*
HILTON GARDEN INN [HOT] *Dallas, TX*
HILTON GARDEN INN [MOT] *Flagstaff, AZ*
HILTON GARDEN INN [MOT] *Scottsdale, AZ*
HILTON GARDEN LAS COLINAS [HOT] *Dallas/Fort Worth Airport Area, TX*
HILTON HOUSTON NASSAU BAY AND MARINA [RST] *Houston, TX*
HILTON LAS VEGAS [HOT] *Las Vegas, NV*
HILTON PALACIO DEL RIO [HOT] *San Antonio, TX*

HILTON PHOENIX AIRPORT HOTEL [HOT] *Phoenix, AZ*
HILTON PHOENIX EAST/MESA [HOT] *Mesa, AZ*
HILTON PLAZA [HOT] *Houston, TX*
HILTON POINTE SQUAW PEAK [RST] *Phoenix, AZ*
HILTON POINTE TAPATIO CLIFFS [RST] *Phoenix, AZ*
HILTON RENO [HOT] *Reno, NV*
HILTON SALT LAKE AIRPORT [HOT] *Salt Lake City, UT*
HILTON SALT LAKE CITY CENTER [HOT] *Salt Lake City, UT*
HILTON SCOTTSDALE RESORT & VILLAS [HOT] *Scottsdale, AZ*
HILTON SEDONA RESORT & SPA [AS] *Sedona, AZ*
HILTON SUITES [AS] *Phoenix, AZ*
HILTON TUCSON EAST [HOT] *Tucson, AZ*
HILTON WACO [HOT] *Waco, TX*
HISTORIC TAOS INN, THE [BB] *Taos, NM*
HOLDEN HOUSE 1902 BED & BREAKFAST [BB] *Colorado Springs, CO*
HOLIDAY CHALET [BB] *Denver, CO*
HOLIDAY INN [MOT] *Alamosa, CO*
HOLIDAY INN [MOT] *Amarillo, TX*
HOLIDAY INN [MOT] *Beaumont, TX*
HOLIDAY INN [MOT] *Brownsville, TX*
HOLIDAY INN [MOT] *Bryan/College Station, TX*
HOLIDAY INN [MOT] *Carlsbad, NM*
HOLIDAY INN [MOT] *Clovis, NM*
HOLIDAY INN [MOT] *Corpus Christi, TX*
HOLIDAY INN [MOT] *Craig, CO*
HOLIDAY INN [MOT] *Deming, NM*
HOLIDAY INN [MOT] *Denton, TX*
HOLIDAY INN [MOT] *Dillon, CO*
HOLIDAY INN [MOT] *Farmington, NM*
HOLIDAY INN [MOT] *Fort Collins, CO*
HOLIDAY INN [MOT] *Gallup, NM*
HOLIDAY INN [MOT] *Galveston, TX*
HOLIDAY INN [MOT] *Grand Junction, CO*
HOLIDAY INN [MOT] *Houston, TX*
HOLIDAY INN [MOT] *Kayenta, AZ*
HOLIDAY INN [MOT] *Kingsville, TX*
HOLIDAY INN [MOT] *Lake Havasu City, AZ*
HOLIDAY INN [MOT] *Lakewood, CO*
HOLIDAY INN [MOT] *Las Cruces, NM*
HOLIDAY INN [MOT] *Lubbock, TX*
HOLIDAY INN [MOT] *Nacogdoches, TX*
HOLIDAY INN [MOT] *Price, UT*
HOLIDAY INN [MOT] *Provo, UT*

HOLIDAY INN [MOT] *Pueblo, CO*
HOLIDAY INN [MOT] *San Antonio, TX*
HOLIDAY INN [MOT] *Santa Fe, NM*
HOLIDAY INN [MOT] *Seguin, TX*
HOLIDAY INN [MOT] *St. George, UT*
HOLIDAY INN [MOT] *Steamboat Springs, CO*
HOLIDAY INN [MOT] *Stephenville, TX*
HOLIDAY INN [MOT] *Sulphur Springs, TX*
HOLIDAY INN [MOT] *Sweetwater, TX*
HOLIDAY INN [MOT] *Trinidad, CO*
HOLIDAY INN [MOT] *Tucumcari, NM*
HOLIDAY INN [MOT] *Uvalde, TX*
HOLIDAY INN ARISTOCRAT [MOT] *Dallas, TX*
HOLIDAY INN ARLINGTON-NEAR SIX FLAGS [MOT] *Arlington-Grand Prairie, TX*
HOLIDAY INN AUSTIN AIRPORT SOUTH [MOT] *Austin, TX*
HOLIDAY INN CIVIC CENTER [MOT] *Laredo, TX*
HOLIDAY INN-CIVIC CENTER [MOT] *McAllen, TX*
HOLIDAY INN CONVENTION CENTER [MOT] *San Angelo, TX*
HOLIDAY INN DON FERNANDO DE TAOS [MOT] *Taos, NM*
HOLIDAY INN DOWNTOWN [MOT] *Salt Lake City, UT*
HOLIDAY INN EMERALD BEACH [MOT] *Corpus Christi, TX*
HOLIDAY INN EXPRESS [MOT] *Abilene, TX*
HOLIDAY INN EXPRESS [MOT] *Albuquerque, NM*
HOLIDAY INN EXPRESS [MOT] *Colorado Springs, CO*
HOLIDAY INN EXPRESS [MOT] *Cortez, CO*
HOLIDAY INN EXPRESS [MOT] *Glendale, AZ*
HOLIDAY INN EXPRESS [MOT] *Gunnison, CO*
HOLIDAY INN EXPRESS [MOT] *Harlingen, TX*
HOLIDAY INN EXPRESS [MOT] *Holbrook, AZ*
HOLIDAY INN EXPRESS [MOT] *Jasper, TX*
HOLIDAY INN EXPRESS [MOT] *Litchfield Park, AZ*
HOLIDAY INN EXPRESS [MOT] *McAllen, TX*
HOLIDAY INN EXPRESS [MOT] *Payson, AZ*
HOLIDAY INN EXPRESS [MOT] *San Antonio, TX*

HOLIDAY INN EXPRESS [MOT] *Santa Rosa, NM*
HOLIDAY INN EXPRESS [MOT] *Tempe, AZ*
HOLIDAY INN EXPRESS [MOT] *Texarkana, TX*
HOLIDAY INN EXPRESS AIRPORT NORTH [MOT] *Austin, TX*
HOLIDAY INN EXPRESS AIRPORT [MOT] *San Antonio, TX*
HOLIDAY INN EXPRESS & SUITES [MOT] *Park City, UT*
HOLIDAY INN EXPRESS CRIPPLER [MOT] *Cripple Creek, CO*
HOLIDAY INN EXPRESS GLOBE [MOT] *Globe, AZ*
HOLIDAY INN EXPRESS - PRESCOTT [MOT] *Prescott, AZ*
HOLIDAY INN FLAGSTAFF [MOT] *Flagstaff, AZ*
HOLIDAY INN GARCIA TRADING POST [MOT] *Canyon de Chelly National Monument, AZ*
HOLIDAY INN HOTEL AND CONVENTION CENTER [MOT] *Victoria, TX*
HOLIDAY INN HOTEL & SUITES [MOT] *Houston, TX*
HOLIDAY INN HOTEL & SUITES [MOT] *Midland, TX*
HOLIDAY INN HOTEL AND SUITES [MOT] *Wichita Falls, TX*
HOLIDAY INN HOTEL & TOWERS [MOT] *Lubbock, TX*
HOLIDAY INN INTERCONTINENTAL [MOT] *Houston, TX*
HOLIDAY INN LUFKIN [MOT] *Lufkin, TX*
HOLIDAY INN MOUNTAINVIEW [MOT] *Albuquerque, NM*
HOLIDAY INN NEW BRAUNFELS [MOT] *New Braunfels, TX*
HOLIDAY INN NORTH GLENN [MOT] *Denver, CO*
HOLIDAY INN PALO VERDE [MOT] *Tucson, AZ*
HOLIDAY INN PARK CENTRAL [MOT] *Port Arthur, TX*
HOLIDAY INN PHOENIX-TEMPE/ASU [MOT] *Tempe, AZ*
HOLIDAY INN PHOENIX WEST [MOT] *Phoenix, AZ*
HOLIDAY INN PLAZA [MOT] *Beaumont, TX*
HOLIDAY INN ROCKY MOUNTAIN PARK [MOT] *Estes Park, CO*
HOLIDAY INN SELECT [MOT] *Houston, TX*
HOLIDAY INN SELECT DFW NORTH [MOT] *Dallas/Fort Worth Airport Area, TX*

HOLIDAY INN SELECT DFW SOUTH [MOT] *Dallas/Fort Worth Airport Area, TX*
HOLIDAY INN SELECT I-10 WEST [MOT] *Houston, TX*
HOLIDAY INN SELECT NORTH DALLAS [MOT] *Dallas, TX*
HOLIDAY INN SELECT NORTHEAST [MOT] *Dallas, TX*
HOLIDAY INN SELECT - PHOENIX AIRPORT [MOT] *Phoenix, AZ*
HOLIDAY INN SOUTHEAST CROSSING [MOT] *Tyler, TX*
HOLIDAY INN SUNLAND PARK [MOT] *El Paso, TX*
HOLIDAY INN SUNSPREE [MOT] *Scottsdale, AZ*
HOLIDAY INN SUNSPREE RESORT [RST] *South Padre Island, TX*
HOLIDAY INN TEXARKANA I-30 [HOT] *Texarkana, TX*
HOLIDAY INN TOWN LAKE [MOT] *Austin, TX*
HOLIDAY INN WILLIAMS [MOT] *Williams, AZ*
HOLIDAY MOTOR HOTEL [MOT] *Silver City, NM*
HOMEGATE STUDIOS AND SUITES [MOT] *Amarillo, TX*
HOME RANCH, THE [RAN] *Steamboat Springs, CO*
HOMESTEAD RESORT, THE [RST] *Heber City, UT*
HOMEWOOD SUITES [AS] *San Antonio, TX*
HOMEWOOD SUITES [MOT] *Scottsdale, AZ*
HOMEWOOD SUITES BY HILTON [MOT] *Phoenix, AZ*
HOMEWOOD SUITES HOTEL [MOT] *Houston, TX*
HOMEWOOD SUITES RIVERWALK [AS] *San Antonio, TX*
HORIZON CASINO RESORT [HOT] *Stateline, NV*
HOSPITALITY SUITE RESORT [MOT] *Scottsdale, AZ*
HOTEL ADOLPHUS [HOT] *Dallas, TX*
HOTEL ASPEN [HOT] *Aspen, CO*
HOTEL BLUE, THE [HOT] *Albuquerque, NM*
HOTEL BOULDERADO [HOT] *Boulder, CO*
HOTEL COLUMBIA [HOT] *Telluride, CO*
HOTEL CRESCENT COURT [HOT] *Dallas, TX*
HOTEL DEREK [HOT] *Houston, TX*
HOTEL EMILY MORGAN [HOT] *San Antonio, TX*
HOTEL GALVEZ, THE [RST] *Galveston, TX*

HOTEL GASTHOF GRAMSHAMMER [HOT] *Vail, CO*

HOTEL INTER-CONTINENTAL DALLAS [HOT] *Dallas, TX*

HOTEL JEROME [MOT] *Aspen, CO*

HOTEL LA MORE/THE BISBEE INN [BB] *Bisbee, AZ*

HOTEL LENADO [BB] *Aspen, CO*

HOTEL LORETTO [HOT] *Santa Fe, NM*

HOTEL MONACO [HOT] *Denver, CO*

HOTEL MONACO [HOT] *Salt Lake City, UT*

HOTEL SAN CARLOS [HOT] *Phoenix, AZ*

HOTEL SAN REMO [HOT] *Las Vegas, NV*

HOTEL SANTA FE [HOT] *Santa Fe, NM*

HOTEL SOFITEL HOUSTON [HOT] *Houston, TX*

HOTEL ST. GERMAIN [BB] *Dallas, TX*

HOTEL TEATRO [HOT] *Denver, CO*

HOTEL VENDOME [BB] *Prescott, AZ*

HOTEL WATERFRONT IVY [MOT] *Scottsdale, AZ*

HOT SPRINGS LODGE [MOT] *Glenwood Springs, CO*

HOUSTON HOUSE BED & BREAKFAST [BB] *Gonzales, TX*

HOUSTONIAN HOTEL, CLUB & SPA, THE [HOT] *Houston, TX*

HOWARD JOHNSON [MOT] *Brigham City, UT*

HOWARD JOHNSON [MOT] *Provo, UT*

HOWARD JOHNSON EXPRESS [MOT] *Albuquerque, NM*

HOWARD JOHNSON EXPRESS INN [MOT] *Santa Fe, NM*

HOWARD JOHNSON HOTEL [MOT] *Albuquerque, NM*

HOWARD JOHNSON INN [MOT] *El Paso, TX*

HUDSPETH HOUSE [BB] *Canyon, TX*

HUMMINGBIRD LODGE [MOT] *Stephenville, TX*

HUNT PLACER INN [BB] *Breckenridge, CO*

HYATT REGENCY [HOT] *Albuquerque, NM*

HYATT REGENCY [HOT] *Houston, TX*

HYATT REGENCY [HOT] *Phoenix, AZ*

HYATT REGENCY AUSTIN [HOT] *Austin, TX*

HYATT REGENCY BEAVER CREEK RESORT AND SPA [RST] *Vail, CO*

HYATT REGENCY DALLAS AT REUNION [HOT] *Dallas, TX*

HYATT REGENCY DENVER [HOT] *Denver, CO*

HYATT REGENCY DFW [HOT] *Dallas/Fort Worth Airport Area, TX*

HYATT REGENCY HILL COUNTRY RESORT AND SPA [RST] *San Antonio, TX*

HYATT REGENCY HOUSTON AIRPORT [HOT] *Houston, TX*

HYATT REGENCY LAKE LAS VEGAS RESORT [RST] *Las Vegas, NV*

HYATT REGENCY LAKE TAHOE RESORT AND CASINO [RST] *Incline Village, NV*

HYATT REGENCY SAN ANTONIO [HOT] *San Antonio, TX*

HYATT REGENCY SCOTTSDALE RESORT AT GAINEY RANCH [RST] *Scottsdale, AZ*

HYATT REGENCY TAMAYA RESORT [RST] *Santa Fe, NM*

HYATT REGENCY TECH CENTER [HOT] *Denver, CO*

ICE HOUSE LODGE AND CONDOMINIUMS [MOT] *Telluride, CO*

ICE PALACE INN BED & BREAKFAST [BB] *Leadville, CO*

IDLEWILDE COTTAGES BY THE RIVER [CC] *Estes Park, CO*

IMPERIAL CASINO HOTEL [HOT] *Cripple Creek, CO*

IMPERIAL PALACE [HOT] *Las Vegas, NV*

INDIAN LODGE [MOT] *Alpine, TX*

INN ABOVE ONION CREEK [BB] *San Marcos, TX*

INN AT 410 BED & BREAKFAST [BB] *Flagstaff, AZ*

INN AT BEAVER CREEK [RST] *Vail, CO*

INN AT CITADEL [BB] *Scottsdale, AZ*

INN AT DELTA [BB] *Espanola, NM*

INN AT INCLINE AND CONDO [BB] *Incline Village, NV*

INN AT SCOTT & WHITE, THE [HOT] *Temple, TX*

INN AT SILVERCREEK [RST] *Granby, CO*

INN AT TEMPLE SQUARE [HOT] *Salt Lake City, UT*

INN OF PAYSON [HOT] *Payson, AZ*

INN OF THE ANASAZI [HOT] *Santa Fe, NM*

INN OF THE CONCHOS [MOT] *San Angelo, TX*

INN OF THE GOVERNORS [BB] *Santa Fe, NM*

INN OF THE HILLS CONFERENCE RESORT [RST] *Kerrville, TX*

INN OF THE MOUNTAIN GODS [RST] *Ruidoso, NM*

INN OF THE WEST [MOT] *San Angelo, TX*

INN ON LA LOMA PLAZA [BB] *Taos, NM*

INN ON OAK CREEK, THE [BB] *Sedona, AZ*

INN ON THE ALAMEDA [HOT] *Santa Fe, NM*

INN ON THE PASEO [BB] *Santa Fe, NM*

INN ON THE RIVER [BB] *San Antonio, TX*

INN ON THE SANTA FE TRAIL [RST] *Las Vegas, NM*

INNSBRUCK INN [MOT] *Aspen, CO*

INNSBRUCK LODGE [MOT] *Ruidoso, NM*

INN SUITES HOTEL SCOTTSDALE RESORT [MOT] *Scottsdale, AZ*

INN SUITES HOTELS TEMPE/PHOENIX AIRPORT [AS] *Tempe, AZ*

INTER-CONTINENTAL STEPHEN F. AUSTIN [HOT] *Austin, TX*

INTERSTATE 8 INN [MOT] *Yuma, AZ*

INVERNESS HOTEL & GOLF CLUB [RST] *Englewood, CO*

IRISH INN MOTEL [MOT] *Shamrock, TX*

IRON BLOSSOM LODGE [HOT] *Snowbird, UT*

IRON HORSE INN [RST] *Durango, CO*

IRON HORSE RESORT [RST] *Winter Park, CO*

ISLAND HOUSE CONDOS [MOT] *Corpus Christi, TX*

JACKSON HOUSE, THE [BB] *San Antonio, TX*

JAIL HOUSE MOTEL & CASINO [MOT] *Ely, NV*

JARVIS SUITE [AS] *Durango, CO*

JIM BUTLER MOTEL [MOT] *Tonopah, NV*

JOHN ASCUAGA'S NUGGET [HOT] *Reno, NV*

JOHN ASCUAGA'S NUGGET COURTYARD [HOT] *Reno, NV*

JOHN NEWCOMBE'S TENNIS RANCH [RST] *New Braunfels, TX*

JW MARRIOTT HOTEL ON WESTHEIMER BY THE GALLERIA [HOT] *Houston, TX*

KACHINA LODGE [MOT] *South Rim (Grand Canyon National Park), AZ*

KARBACH HAUS BED & BREAKFAST, THE [BB] *New Braunfels, TX*

KEYSTONE LODGE [RST] *Dillon, CO*

KOFA INN [MOT] *Parker, AZ*

KOKOPELLI SUITES [HOT] *Sedona, AZ*

LA COLOMBE D'OR HOTEL [BB] *Houston, TX*

LA DONA LUZ INN, AN HISTORIC BED AND BREAKFAST [BB] *Taos, NM*

LADY LUCK CASINO HOTEL [HOT] *Las Vegas, NV*

LA EUROPA ROYALE [HOT] *Salt Lake City, UT*

LA FUENTE INN [MOT] *Yuma, AZ*

LA HACIENDA GRANDE [BB] *Albuquerque, NM*

LAKE MANCOS RANCH [RAN] *Durango, CO*

LAKE MOHAVE RESORT [MOT] *Bullhead City, AZ*

LAKESIDE INN AND CASINO [MOT] *Stateline, NV*

LAKEWAY INN [RST] *Austin, TX*

LA MANSION DEL RIO [HOT] *San Antonio, TX*

LANCASTER HOTEL [HOT] *Houston, TX*

LANDMARK MOTEL [MOT] *Moab, UT*

LA POSADA DE ALBUQUERQUE [HOT] *Albuquerque, NM*

LA POSADA DEL VALLE BED AND BREAKFAST [BB] *Tucson, AZ*

LA POSADA DE SANTA FE RESORT [HOT] *Santa Fe, NM*

LA POSADA DE TAOS [BB] *Taos, NM*

LA POSADA HOTEL SUITES [HOT] *Laredo, TX*

LA QUINTA [MOT] *Austin, TX*

LA QUINTA [MOT] *Corpus Christi, TX*

LA QUINTA [MOT] *Midland, TX*

LA QUINTA GREENWAY PLAZA [MOT] *Houston, TX*

LA QUINTA INN [MOT] *Albuquerque, NM*

LA QUINTA INN [MOT] *Austin, TX*

LA QUINTA INN [MOT] *Beaumont, TX*

LA QUINTA INN [MOT] *Brazosport, TX*

LA QUINTA INN [MOT] *Dallas, TX*

LA QUINTA INN [MOT] *Dallas, TX*

LA QUINTA INN [MOT] *Dallas/Fort Worth Airport Area, TX*

LA QUINTA INN [MOT] *Del Rio, TX*

LA QUINTA INN [MOT] *Denver, CO*

LA QUINTA INN [MOT] *Denver, CO*

LA QUINTA INN [MOT] *Eagle Pass, TX*

LA QUINTA INN [MOT] *El Paso, TX*

LA QUINTA INN [MOT] *Farmington, NM*

LA QUINTA INN [MOT] *Fort Stockton, TX*

LA QUINTA INN [MOT] *Galveston, TX*

LA QUINTA INN [MOT] *Georgetown, TX*
LA QUINTA INN [MOT] *Golden, CO*
LA QUINTA INN [MOT] *Harlingen, TX*
LA QUINTA INN [MOT] *Houston, TX*
LA QUINTA INN [MOT] *Huntsville, TX*
LA QUINTA INN [MOT] *Killeen, TX*
LA QUINTA INN [MOT] *Laredo, TX*
LA QUINTA INN [MOT] *Las Vegas, NV*
LA QUINTA INN [MOT] *Longview, TX*
LA QUINTA INN [MOT] *Lubbock, TX*
LA QUINTA INN [MOT] *Lufkin, TX*
LA QUINTA INN [MOT] *McAllen, TX*
LA QUINTA INN [MOT] *Nacogdoches, TX*
LA QUINTA INN [MOT] *Odessa, TX*
LA QUINTA INN [MOT] *Phoenix, AZ*
LA QUINTA INN [MOT] *Reno, NV*
LA QUINTA INN [MOT] *Salt Lake City, UT*
LA QUINTA INN [MOT] *San Angelo, TX*
LA QUINTA INN [MOT] *San Antonio, TX*
LA QUINTA INN [MOT] *San Antonio, TX*
LA QUINTA INN [MOT] *San Marcos, TX*
LA QUINTA INN [MOT] *Santa Fe, NM*
LA QUINTA INN [MOT] *Tempe, AZ*
LA QUINTA INN [MOT] *Temple, TX*
LA QUINTA INN [MOT] *Texarkana, TX*
LA QUINTA INN [MOT] *Texas City, TX*
LA QUINTA INN [MOT] *Tucson, AZ*
LA QUINTA INN [MOT] *Tyler, TX*
LA QUINTA INN [MOT] *Victoria, TX*
LA QUINTA INN [MOT] *Waco, TX*
LA QUINTA INN [MOT] *Wichita Falls, TX*
LA QUINTA INN & SUITES [MOT] *Denver International Airport Area, CO*
LA QUINTA INN & SUITES FTW-SW [MOT] *Fort Worth, TX*
LA QUINTA INN AND SUITES [MOT] *Glendale, AZ*
LA QUINTA INN AND SUITES [MOT] *Mesa, AZ*
LA QUINTA INN AND SUITES [MOT] *Scottsdale, AZ*
LA QUINTA INN LAS VEGAS [MOT] *Las Vegas, NV*
LA QUINTA INN WEST/MEDICAL CENTER [MOT] *Fort Worth, TX*
LA QUINTA MOTOR INN [MOT] *Abilene, TX*
LA QUINTA MOTOR INN [MOT] *Bryan/College Station, TX*
LARK MOUNTAIN INN B&B [BB] *Dillon, CO*
LAS VEGAS CLUB HOTEL AND CASINO [HOT] *Las Vegas, NV*
LA TIENDA INN & DURAN HOUSE [BB] *Santa Fe, NM*
LATIGO RANCH [RAN] *Kremmling, CO*
L'AUBERGE DE SEDONA [RST] *Sedona, AZ*
LAZY HILLS GUEST RANCH [RAN] *Kerrville, TX*
LAZY K BAR GUEST RANCH [RAN] *Tucson, AZ*
LE BARON COURTYARD AND SUITES [MOT] *Albuquerque, NM*
LEGACY GOLF RESORT, THE [RST] *Phoenix, AZ*
LEISURE LODGE [MOT] *Grants, NM*
LELAND HOUSE BED & BREAKFAST SUITES [BB] *Durango, CO*
LE MERIDIEN DALLAS [HOT] *Dallas, TX*
LES JARDINS HOTEL AND SUITES [HOT] *Phoenix, AZ*
LEXINGTON HOTEL SUITES [MOT] *Houston, TX*
LEXINGTON INN [MOT] *Waco, TX*
LIFTS WEST CONDOMINIUMS [MOT] *Red River, NM*
LIGHTNER CREEK INN [BB] *Durango, CO*
LIMELITE LODGE [RST] *Aspen, CO*
LIMPIA HOTEL [MOT] *Alpine, TX*
LION SQUARE LODGE [RST] *Vail, CO*
LITTLE AMERICA HOTEL [HOT] *Flagstaff, AZ*
LITTLE AMERICA HOTEL AND TOWERS [HOT] *Salt Lake City, UT*
LITTLE NELL, THE [RST] *Aspen, CO*
LODGE & SPA AT BRECKENRIDGE [RST] *Breckenridge, CO*
LODGE & SPA AT CORDILLERA, THE [RST] *Vail, CO*
LODGE AT CLOUDCROFT, THE [RST] *Cloudcroft, NM*
LODGE AT MOUNTAIN VILLAGE, THE [MOT] *Park City, UT*
LODGE AT RED RIVER, THE [MOT] *Red River, NM*
LODGE AT SEDONA, THE [BB] *Sedona, AZ*
LODGE AT SNOWBIRD [MOT] *Snowbird, UT*
LODGE AT VAIL, THE [RST] *Vail, CO*
LODGE AT VENTANA CANYON, THE [RST] *Tucson, AZ*

LODGE OF GRANBURY, ON LAKE GRANBURY [RST] *Granbury, TX*

LODGE ON THE RIVER [MOT] *Bullhead City, AZ*

LOEWS GIORGIO HOTEL [HOT] *Denver, CO*

LOEWS VENTANA CANYON RESORT [RST] *Tucson, AZ*

LOGAN HOUSE INN [BB] *Logan, UT*

LONGSTAR INN [MOT] *Gainesville, TX*

LOS ABRIGADOS LODGE [MOT] *Sedona, AZ*

LOS ABRIGADOS LODGE [MOT] *Sedona, AZ*

LOS ABRIGADOS RESORT [RST] *Sedona, AZ*

LOS ALAMOS INN [HOT] *Los Alamos, NM*

LOS OLIVOS HOTEL & SUITES [MOT] *Phoenix, AZ*

LOST VALLEY RANCH [RAN] *Colorado Springs, CO*

LUBBOCK INN [HOT] *Lubbock, TX*

LUMBER BARON INN, THE [BB] *Denver, CO*

LUNDEEN INN OF THE ARTS [BB] *Las Cruces, NM*

LUXOR [HOT] *Las Vegas, NV*

LUXURY INN [MOT] *Santa Fe, NM*

MACHIN'S COTTAGES IN THE PINES [CC] *Estes Park, CO*

MAD CREEK BED & BREAKFAST [BB] *Georgetown, CO*

MADELEINE, THE [BB] *Santa Fe, NM*

MAGNOLIA, THE [HOT] *Dallas, TX*

MAGNOLIA DENVER, THE [HOT] *Denver, CO*

MAGNOLIA HOUSE [BB] *Fredericksburg, TX*

MAIN STREET STATION [HOT] *Las Vegas, NV*

MAJESTIC MOUNTAIN INN [HOT] *Payson, AZ*

MANDALAY BAY RESORT AND CASINO [HOT] *Las Vegas, NV*

MANITOU HOTEL [BB] *Telluride, CO*

MANOR HOUSE INN [MOT] *Bryan/College Station, TX*

MANSION ON MAIN BED & BREAKFAST INN [BB] *Texarkana, TX*

MANSION ON TURTLE CREEK, THE [HOT] *Dallas, TX*

MARBLE CANYON LODGE [MOT] *Marble Canyon, AZ*

MARICOPA MANOR B&B INN [BB] *Phoenix, AZ*

MARKS HOUSE VICTORIAN BED AND BREAKFAST, THE [BB] *Prescott, AZ*

MARRIOTT [HOT] *Austin, TX*

MARRIOTT [HOT] *Dallas/Fort Worth Airport Area, TX*

MARRIOTT [HOT] *Golden, CO*

MARRIOTT ALBUQUERQUE [HOT] *Albuquerque, NM*

MARRIOTT AT MCDOWELL MOUNTAINS SCOTTSDALE [AS] *Scottsdale, AZ*

MARRIOTT BOULDER [HOT] *Boulder, CO*

MARRIOTT CITY CENTER DENVER [HOT] *Denver, CO*

MARRIOTT CITY CENTER-SALT LAKE CITY [HOT] *Salt Lake City, UT*

MARRIOTT DALLAS LAS COLINAS [HOT] *Dallas/Fort Worth Airport Area, TX*

MARRIOTT DALLAS QUORUM BY GALLERIA [HOT] *Dallas, TX*

MARRIOTT DENVER WEST [HOT] *Golden, CO*

MARRIOTT DOWNTOWN SALT LAKE CITY [HOT] *Salt Lake City, UT*

MARRIOTT EL PASO [HOT] *El Paso, TX*

MARRIOTT FORT COLLINS [HOT] *Fort Collins, CO*

MARRIOTT HOUSTON AIRPORT [HOT] *Houston, TX*

MARRIOTT MEDICAL CENTER HOUSTON [HOT] *Houston, TX*

MARRIOTT MOUNTAIN RESORT [RST] *Vail, CO*

MARRIOTT NORTH AT GREENSPOINT HOUSTON [HOT] *Houston, TX*

MARRIOTT NORTH AUSTIN [HOT] *Austin, TX*

MARRIOTT OGDEN [HOT] *Ogden, UT*

MARRIOTT PARK CITY [HOT] *Park City, UT*

MARRIOTT PHOENIX AIRPORT [HOT] *Phoenix, AZ*

MARRIOTT PLAZA SAN ANTONIO [HOT] *San Antonio, TX*

MARRIOTT PROVO [HOT] *Provo, UT*

MARRIOTT PUEBLO [HOT] *Pueblo, CO*

MARRIOTT RIVERCENTER SAN ANTONIO [HOT] *San Antonio, TX*

MARRIOTT RIVERWALK SAN ANTONIO [HOT] *San Antonio, TX*

MARRIOTT'S CAMELBACK INN [RST] *Scottsdale, AZ*

MARRIOTT'S MOUNTAIN SHADOWS RESORT & GOLF CLUB [RST] *Scottsdale, AZ*

MARRIOTT SOLANA DALLAS [HOT] *Dallas, TX*

MARRIOTT SOUTH DALLAS FORT WORTH AIRPORT [HOT] *Dallas/Fort Worth Airport Area, TX*

MARRIOTT SOUTHEAST DENVER [HOT] *Denver, CO*

MARRIOTT SUITES [AS] *Las Vegas, NV*

MARRIOTT SUITES MARKET CENTER DALLAS [HOT] *Dallas, TX*

MARRIOTT SUITES SCOTTSDALE [AS] *Scottsdale, AZ*

MARRIOTT TECH CENTER DENVER [HOT] *Denver, CO*

MARRIOTT UNIVERSITY PARK SALT LAKE CITY [HOT] *Salt Lake City, UT*

MARRIOTT UNIVERSITY PARK [HOT] *Tucson, AZ*

MARRIOTT WEST LOOP BY THE GALLERIA HOUSTON [HOT] *Houston, TX*

MARY LAWRENCE INN [BB] *Gunnison, CO*

MATTERHORN MOTEL [MOT] *Ouray, CO*

MAYAN DUDE RANCH [RAN] *Bandera, TX*

MCGREGOR MOUNTAIN LODGE [MOT] *Estes Park, CO*

MCKAY HOUSE [BB] *Jefferson, TX*

MEL-HAVEN LODGE [MOT] *Colorado Springs, CO*

MELODY C. CRYSTAL LODGE [MOT] *Lake City, CO*

MELROSE, THE [HOT] *Dallas, TX*

MENGER HOTEL, THE [HOT] *San Antonio, TX*

MESON DE MESILLA RESORT HOTEL [RST] *Las Cruces, NM*

MGM GRAND HOTEL [HOT] *Las Vegas, NV*

MICROTEL INN & SUITES [MOT] *Colorado Springs, CO*

MIDLAND HOLIDAY INN [MOT] *Midland, TX*

MIDWEST COUNTRY INN [BB] *Limon, CO*

MILLENIUM RESORT SCOTTSDALE MCCORMICK RANCH [RST] *Scottsdale, AZ*

MILL HOUSE INN [MOT] *Carson City, NV*

MIRAGE HOTEL AND CASINO, THE [HOT] *Las Vegas, NV*

MIRAVAL-LIFE IN BALANCE [RST] *Tucson, AZ*

MOLLY GIBSON LODGE [HOT] *Aspen, CO*

MONTE CARLO RESORT & CASINO [HOT] *Las Vegas, NV*

MOTEL 6 [MOT] *Sweetwater, TX*

MOTEL 6 [MOT] *Williams, AZ*

MOUNTAIN HAUS RESORT & SPA [MOT] *Vail, CO*

MOUNTAINSIDE INN [MOT] *Williams, AZ*

MOUNT SOPRIS INN [BB] *Glenwood Springs, CO*

NEW ROCHESTER HOTEL [BB] *Durango, CO*

NEW SHERIDAN HOTEL [BB] *Telluride, CO*

NEW YORK-NEW YORK HOTEL & CASINO [HOT] *Las Vegas, NV*

NORDIC INN, THE [BB] *Crested Butte, CO*

NORTH FORK [RAN] *Georgetown, CO*

NOVEL HOUSE INN [BB] *Zion National Park, UT*

NUGGET MOTEL & INN [MOT] *Carson City, NV*

NUMBER ONE VALUE INN [MOT] *Clovis, NM*

OGE HOUSE [BB] *San Antonio, TX*

OLD MINERS' LODGE [BB] *Park City, UT*

OLD TOWN GUEST HOUSE [BB] *Colorado Springs, CO*

OLYMPUS MOTOR LODGE [MOT] *Estes Park, CO*

OMNI AUSTIN HOTEL AT DOWNTOWN [HOT] *Austin, TX*

OMNI AUSTIN HOTEL SOUTHPARK [HOT] *Austin, TX*

OMNI CORPUS CHRISTI HOTEL BAYFRONT TOWER [HOT] *Corpus Christi, TX*

OMNI CORPUS CHRISTI HOTEL MARINA TOWER [HOT] *Corpus Christi, TX*

OMNI HOUSTON HOTEL [HOT] *Houston, TX*

OMNI HOUSTON WESTSIDE HOTEL [HOT] *Houston, TX*

OMNI INTERLOCKEN RESORT [RST] *Denver, CO*

OMNI MANDALAY HOTEL AT LAS COLINAS [HOT] *Dallas/Fort Worth Airport Area, TX*

OMNI PARK WEST [HOT] *Dallas, TX*

OMNI RICHARDSON HOTEL [HOT] *Dallas, TX*

OMNI SAN ANTONIO HOTEL [HOT] *San Antonio, TX*

OMNI TUCSON NATIONAL GOLF RESORT & SPA [RST] *Tucson, AZ*

ORANGE TREE GOLF RESORT [RST] *Scottsdale, AZ*

ORLEANS HOTEL AND CASINO [HOT] *Las Vegas, NV*

OURAY CHALET INN [MOT] *Ouray, CO*

OURAY VICTORIAN INN & TOWNHOMES [MOT] *Ouray, CO*

OXFORD HOTEL [HOT] *Denver, CO*

PACK CREEK RANCH [RAN] *Moab, UT*

PAGOSA LODGE [RST] *Pagosa Springs, CO*

PAGOSA SPRINGS INN [MOT] *Pagosa Springs, CO*

PALACE STATION HOTEL AND CASINO [HOT] *Las Vegas, NV*

PARIS LAS VEGAS [HOT] *Las Vegas, NV*

PARK INN HARDMAN HOUSE [MOT] *Carson City, NV*

PARRY LODGE [MOT] *Kanab, UT*

PEACEFUL VALLEY RANCH [RAN] *Lyons, CO*

PEACH TREE INN [MOT] *Fredericksburg, TX*

PEAR TREE INN BY DRURY/SAN ANTONIO AIRPORT [MOT] *San Antonio, TX*

PEERY HOTEL [HOT] *Salt Lake City, UT*

PEPPERMILL HOTEL AND CASINO [HOT] *Reno, NV*

PEPPERTREE'S BED AND BREAKFAST INN [BB] *Tucson, AZ*

PHOENICIAN, THE [RST] *Scottsdale, AZ*

PHOENIX INN [MOT] *Phoenix, AZ*

PINES LODGE [RST] *Vail, CO*

PINETOP COMFORT INN [MOT] *Pinetop, AZ*

PIONEER HOTEL AND GAMBLING HALL [HOT] *Laughlin, NV*

PLAINVIEW HOTEL & CONFERENCE [MOT] *Plainview, TX*

PLANTATION INN ON THE LAKE [MOT] *Granbury, TX*

PLAZA HOTEL [MOT] *Killeen, TX*

PLAZA HOTEL [HOT] *Las Vegas, NM*

PLAZA HOTEL AND CASINO [HOT] *Las Vegas, NV*

PLAZA INN [MOT] *Albuquerque, NM*

PLAZA REAL [MOT] *Santa Fe, NM*

PLEASANT STREET INN [BB] *Prescott, AZ*

POINTE SOUTH MOUNTAIN RESORT [RST] *Phoenix, AZ*

PONDEROSA LODGE [RST] *Estes Park, CO*

PONDEROSA LODGE [MOT] *Red River, NM*

PORTER HOUSE B & B INN [BB] *Fort Collins, CO*

POWDERHORN GUEST RANCH [RAN] *Gunnison, CO*

PREFERRED MOTOR INN [MOT] *Limon, CO*

PREMIER INNS METROCENTER [MOT] *Phoenix, AZ*

PRESCOTT RESORT CONFERENCE CENTER & CASINO [RST] *Prescott, AZ*

PRINCE SOLMS INN [BB] *New Braunfels, TX*

PROSPECTOR SQUARE CONFERENCE CENTER [CONF] *Park City, UT*

PROVIDENCE INN [BB] *Logan, UT*

PUEBLO BONITO BED AND BREAKFAST INN [BB] *Santa Fe, NM*

PURPLE SAGE MOTEL [MOT] *Snyder, TX*

QUAIL RIDGE INN RESORT [RST] *Taos, NM*

QUAIL RIDGE RESORT [RST] *Sedona, AZ*

QUALITY INN [MOT] *Beaver, UT*

QUALITY INN [MOT] *Colorado Springs, CO*

QUALITY INN [MOT] *Cottonwood, AZ*

QUALITY INN [MOT] *Denver, CO*

QUALITY INN [MOT] *Denver, CO*

QUALITY INN [MOT] *Flagstaff, AZ*

QUALITY INN [MOT] *Kingman, AZ*

QUALITY INN [MOT] *Kingsville, TX*

QUALITY INN [MOT] *La Junta, CO*

QUALITY INN [MOT] *Pecos, TX*

QUALITY INN [MOT] *Richfield, UT*

QUALITY INN [MOT] *Santa Fe, NM*

QUALITY INN [MOT] *South Rim (Grand Canyon National Park), AZ*

QUALITY INN [MOT] *Taos, NM*

QUALITY INN AND SUITES [MOT] *Denver, CO*

QUALITY INN AT THE BUTTE [MOT] *Truth or Consequences, NM*

QUALITY INN CENTRAL [MOT] *Austin, TX*

QUALITY INN CIVIC CENTER [MOT] *Abilene, TX*

QUALITY INN-MIDVALLEY [MOT] *Salt Lake City, UT*

QUALITY INN ROYAL [MOT] *Mesa, AZ*

QUALITY INN SOUTH MOUNTAIN [MOT] *Phoenix, AZ*

QUEEN ANNE BED & BREAKFAST [BB] *Denver, CO*

RADISSON [HOT] *Amarillo, TX*

RADISSON [HOT] *Santa Fe, NM*

RADISSON ASTRODOME HOTEL [HOT] *Houston, TX*

RADISSON BEACH HOTEL [HOT] *Corpus Christi, TX*

RADISSON HOTEL [HOT] *Denton, TX*
RADISSON HOTEL & CONFERENCE CENTER [HOT] *Houston, TX*
RADISSON HOTEL & CONFERENCE CENTER [HOT] *Odessa, TX*
RADISSON HOTEL AND SUITES AUSTIN [HOT] *Austin, TX*
RADISSON HOTEL AND SUITES [HOT] *Dallas, TX*
RADISSON HOTEL CENTRAL DALLAS [HOT] *Dallas, TX*
RADISSON HOTEL CITY CENTER [HOT] *Tucson, AZ*
RADISSON HOTEL DENVER STAPLETON PLAZA [HOT] *Denver, CO*
RADISSON HOTEL SALT LAKE CITY AIRPORT [HOT] *Salt Lake City, UT*
RADISSON HOTEL SAN ANTONIO [HOT] *San Antonio, TX*
RADISSON INN [HOT] *Albuquerque, NM*
RADISSON INN & SUITES [HOT] *Colorado Springs, CO*
RADISSON INN NORTH [HOT] *Colorado Springs, CO*
RADISSON PHOENIX AIRPORT HOTEL [HOT] *Phoenix, AZ*
RADISSON PLAZA [HOT] *Fort Worth, TX*
RADISSON POCO DIABLO [RST] *Sedona, AZ*
RADISSON RESORT [RST] *Park City, UT*
RADISSON RESORT & SPA [RST] *Scottsdale, AZ*
RADISSON RESORT SOUTH PADRE [RST] *South Padre Island, TX*
RADISSON SUITES [HOT] *Arlington-Grand Prairie, TX*
RADISSON SUITES INN [AS] *Yuma, AZ*
RADISSON SUITES WEST [AS] *Houston, TX*
RADISSON WOODLANDS HOTEL [HOT] *Flagstaff, AZ*
RAINTREE PLAZA [HOT] *Longmont, CO*
RAMADA [MOT] *Grand Junction, CO*
RAMADA [MOT] *Gunnison, CO*
RAMADA [MOT] *Roswell, NM*
RAMADA FOOTHILLS RESORT [MOT] *Tucson, AZ*
RAMADA HOTEL [MOT] *Dallas, TX*
RAMADA INN [MOT] *Abilene, TX*
RAMADA INN [MOT] *Brazosport, TX*
RAMADA INN [MOT] *Colorado Springs, CO*
RAMADA INN [MOT] *Del Rio, TX*
RAMADA INN [MOT] *Farmington, NM*

RAMADA INN [MOT] *Flagstaff, AZ*
RAMADA INN [MOT] *Hillsboro, TX*
RAMADA INN [MOT] *Jasper, TX*
RAMADA INN [MOT] *Laughlin, NV*
RAMADA INN [MOT] *Orange, TX*
RAMADA INN [MOT] *Port Arthur, TX*
RAMADA INN [MOT] *Sterling, CO*
RAMADA INN [MOT] *Victoria, TX*
RAMADA INN AIRPORT [MOT] *Midland, TX*
RAMADA INN & COPPER QUEEN CASINO [MOT] *Ely, NV*
RAMADA INN BAYFRONT [MOT] *Corpus Christi, TX*
RAMADA INN DE TAOS [MOT] *Taos, NM*
RAMADA INN DOWNTOWN [MOT] *Salt Lake City, UT*
RAMADA INN FANTASY SUITES [MOT] *Denton, TX*
RAMADA INN MIDTOWN [MOT] *Fort Worth, TX*
RAMADA LIMITED [MOT] *Albuquerque, NM*
RAMADA LIMITED [MOT] *Santa Rosa, NM*
RAMADA LIMITED [MOT] *Van Horn, TX*
RAMADA LIMITED [MOT] *Wichita Falls, TX*
RAMADA LIMITED DURANGO [MOT] *Durango, CO*
RAMADA MOUNTAINVIEW [MOT] *Albuquerque, NM*
RAMADA PLAZA HOTEL [MOT] *Dallas, TX*
RAMADA PLAZA HOTEL CONVENTION CENTER [MOT] *Fort Worth, TX*
RAMSEY CANYON INN [BB] *Sierra Vista, AZ*
RANCH AT STEAMBOAT SPRINGS [CON] *Steamboat Springs, CO*
RANCHO DE LOS CABALLEROS [RAN] *Wickenburg, AZ*
RANCHO DE SAN JUAN COUNTRY INN [BB] *Espanola, NM*
RANCHO ENCANTADO RESORT [RST] *Santa Fe, NM*
RANCHO SONORA INN & RV PARK [BB] *Florence, AZ*
RANCHO VIEJO RESORT AND COUNTRY CLUB [RST] *Brownsville, TX*
RAYBURN COUNTRY RESORT [RST] *Jasper, TX*
RECAPTURE LODGE [MOT] *Bluff, UT*
RED CRAGS BED & BREAKFAST INN [BB] *Manitou Springs, CO*
RED LION [MOT] *Phoenix, AZ*
RED LION HOTEL [MOT] *Austin, TX*

RED LION HOTEL HOUSTON [MOT]
Houston, TX
RED LION INN AND CASINO [MOT]
Elko, NV
RED LION INN AND CASINO [MOT]
Winnemucca, NV
RED RIVER INN [MOT] *Red River, NM*
RED ROCK INN [BB] *Zion National
Park, UT*
RED ROOF INN [MOT] *Austin, TX*
RED ROOF INN [MOT] *Brownsville,
TX*
RED ROOF INN [MOT] *Corpus Christi,
TX*
RED ROOF INN [MOT] *Gallup, NM*
RED ROOF INN [MOT] *Laredo, TX*
RED ROOF INN [MOT] *San Antonio,
TX*
RED ROOF INN HOUSTON WEST
[MOT] *Houston, TX*
RED SETTER INN [BB] *Greer, AZ*
REDSTONE INN HISTORIC
LANDMARK [RST] *Glenwood
Springs, CO*
REDWING MOTEL [MOT] *Manitou
Springs, CO*
REGAL HARVEST HOUSE [HOT]
Boulder, CO
REGAL MOTEL [MOT] *Las Vegas, NM*
RENAISSANCE [HOT] *Dallas, TX*
RENAISSANCE AUSTIN [HOT]
Austin, TX
RENAISSANCE CASA DE PALMAS
[HOT] *McAllen, TX*
RENAISSANCE DALLAS NORTH
HOTEL [HOT] *Dallas, TX*
RENAISSANCE DENVER [HOT]
Denver, CO
RENAISSANCE HOUSTON HOTEL
[HOT] *Houston, TX*
RENAISSANCE RICHARDSON [HOT]
Dallas, TX
RENAISSANCE SCOTTSDALE RESORT
[RST] *Scottsdale, AZ*
RENAISSANCE WORTHINGTON
[HOT] *Fort Worth, TX*
RENATA'S ORANGE STREET BED
AND BREAKFAST [BB] *Los
Alamos, NM*
RESIDENCE INN BY MARRIOTT [EX]
Boulder, CO
RESIDENCE INN BY MARRIOTT [EX]
Colorado Springs, CO
RESIDENCE INN BY MARRIOTT
SOUTH [EX] *Colorado Springs,
CO*
RESIDENCE INN BY MARRIOTT [EX]
Dallas, TX
RESIDENCE INN BY MARRIOTT [EX]
Dallas, TX
RESIDENCE INN BY MARRIOTT [EX]
Denver, CO

RESIDENCE INN BY MARRIOTT
DENVER SOUTH [EX]
Englewood, CO
RESIDENCE INN BY MARRIOTT [EX]
Houston, TX
RESIDENCE INN BY MARRIOTT -
HOUSTON/CLEAR LAKE [EX]
Houston, TX
RESIDENCE INN BY MARRIOTT [EX]
Las Vegas, NV
RESIDENCE INN BY MARRIOTT [EX]
Lubbock, TX
RESIDENCE INN BY MARRIOTT [EX]
San Antonio, TX
RESIDENCE INN BY MARRIOTT [EX]
Santa Fe, NM
RESIDENCE INN BY MARRIOTT [EX]
Scottsdale, AZ
RESIDENCE INN BY MARRIOTT [EX]
Tyler, TX
RESORT SUITES OF SCOTTSDALE
[RST] *Scottsdale, AZ*
RICHFIELD TRAVELODGE [MOT]
Richfield, UT
RIDGE STREET INN [BB] *Breckenridge,
CO*
RIDGWAY-TELLURIDE SUPER 8
[MOT] *Ouray, CO*
RIO GRANDE PLAZA [HOT] *Laredo,
TX*
RIO RICO RESORT AND COUNTRY
CLUB [RST] *Nogales, AZ*
RIO SUITE HOTEL AND CASINO [AS]
Las Vegas, NV
RITZ-CARLTON, PHOENIX, THE
[HOT] *Phoenix, AZ*
RIVER DANCER BED AND
BREAKFAST [BB] *Albuquerque,
NM*
RIVER MOUNTAIN LODGE [RST]
Breckenridge, CO
RIVER PALMS [HOT] *Laughlin, NV*
RIVERSIDE, THE [RST] *Red River, NM*
RIVERWALK INN [BB] *San Antonio,
TX*
RIVERWALK PLAZA RESORT &
CONFERENCE CENTER [HOT]
San Antonio, TX
RIVIERA HOTEL AND CASINO [HOT]
Las Vegas, NV
ROBERTA'S COVE MOTOR INN
[MOT] *Nephi, UT*
RODEWAY INN [MOT] *Colorado
Springs, CO*
RODEWAY INN [MOT] *Durango, CO*
RODEWAY INN [MOT] *Scottsdale, AZ*
RODEWAY INN [MOT] *Tempe, AZ*
RODEWAY INN NORTH [MOT]
Tucson, AZ
RODEWAY INN RED FEATHER
LODGE [MOT] *South Rim
(Grand Canyon National Park),
AZ*

RODEWAY INN RENO [MOT] *Reno, NV*
RODEWAY INN WEST WINDS [MOT] *Green River, UT*
ROMANICO INN [MOT] *Richfield, UT*
ROMANTIC RIVERSONG INN [BB] *Estes Park, CO*
ROOM AT THE INN [BB] *Colorado Springs, CO*
ROSWELL INN [MOT] *Roswell, NM*
ROYAL INN [MOT] *Abilene, TX*
ROYAL PALMS HOTEL AND CASITA [RST] *Phoenix, AZ*
RUSTY CANNON MOTEL [MOT] *Glenwood Springs, CO*
SAFARI MOTEL [MOT] *Limon, CO*
SAGEBRUSH INN [CONF] *Taos, NM*
SAHARA HOTEL AND CASINO [HOT] *Las Vegas, NV*
ST. ANTHONY, WYNDHAM HISTORIC HOTEL [HOT] *San Antonio, TX*
ST. ELMO HOTEL [BB] *Ouray, CO*
ST. FRANCIS [HOT] *Santa Fe, NM*
ST. JAMES INN [BB] *Gonzales, TX*
ST. MARY'S GLACIER BED AND BREAKFAST [BB] *Idaho Springs, CO*
ST. REGIS ASPEN, THE [RST] *Aspen, CO*
ST. REGIS, HOUSTON, THE [HOT] *Houston, TX*
ST. TROPEZ HOTEL [HOT] *Las Vegas, NV*
SALSA DELI SALTO B&B INN [BB] *Taos, NM*
SALTAIR BED AND BREAKFAST [BB] *Salt Lake City, UT*
SAM'S TOWN HOTEL AND GAMBLING HALL [HOT] *Las Vegas, NV*
SANCTUARY AT CAMELBACK MOUNTAIN [RST] *Scottsdale, AZ*
SAND & SAGE LODGE [MOT] *Hawthorne, NV*
SANDY POINT INN [BB] *Boulder, CO*
SAN GERONIMO LODGE [BB] *Taos, NM*
SAN JUAN INN [MOT] *Montrose, CO*
SAN LUIS RESORT AND CONFERENCE CENTER [HOT] *Galveston, TX*
SAN MIGUEL INN [MOT] *Socorro, NM*
SAN SOPHIA BED & BREAKFAST [BB] *Telluride, CO*
SANTA FE INN [MOT] *Santa Fe, NM*
SANTA FE STATION CASINO [HOT] *Las Vegas, NV*
SARA'S BED AND BREAKFAST INN [BB] *Houston, TX*

SARDY HOUSE HOTEL [BB] *Aspen, CO*
SATELLITE INN [MOT] *Alamogordo, NM*
SAVE INN [MOT] *Johnson City, TX*
SCHOOL HOUSE INN [BB] *Bisbee, AZ*
SCOTTSDALE PLAZA [RST] *Scottsdale, AZ*
SEDONA REAL INN [AS] *Sedona, AZ*
SHADOW MOUNTAIN LODGE [HOT] *Ruidoso, NM*
SHADOW RIDGE [MOT] *Park City, UT*
SHENANDOAH INN [BB] *Aspen, CO*
SHERATON [HOT] *Austin, TX*
SHERATON [HOT] *Dallas, TX*
SHERATON [HOT] *Steamboat Springs, CO*
SHERATON ALBUQUERQUE UPTOWN [HOT] *Albuquerque, NM*
SHERATON BROOKHOLLOW [HOT] *Houston, TX*
SHERATON CITY CENTRE [HOT] *Salt Lake City, UT*
SHERATON CRESCENT HOTEL [HOT] *Phoenix, AZ*
SHERATON DENVER TECH CENTER [HOT] *Englewood, CO*
SHERATON DENVER WEST [HOT] *Lakewood, CO*
SHERATON EL CONQUISTADOR [RST] *Tucson, AZ*
SHERATON GUNTER HOTEL [HOT] *San Antonio, TX*
SHERATON HOTEL [HOT] *Colorado Springs, CO*
SHERATON HOTEL [HOT] *Tyler, TX*
SHERATON INN [HOT] *Sherman, TX*
SHERATON NORTH HOUSTON [HOT] *Houston, TX*
SHERATON OLD TOWN HOTEL [HOT] *Albuquerque, NM*
SHERATON PARK CENTRAL HOTEL DALLAS [HOT] *Dallas, TX*
SHERATON PHOENIX AIRPORT HOTEL [HOT] *Tempe, AZ*
SHERATON PHOENIX EAST HOTEL & CONVENTION CENTER [HOT] *Mesa, AZ*
SHERATON SALT LAKE AIRPORT HOTEL [HOT] *Salt Lake City, UT*
SHERATON SAN MARCOS GOLF RESORT [RST] *Chandler, AZ*
SHERATON SOUTH PADRE ISLAND BEACH HOTEL [RST] *South Padre Island, TX*
SHERATON SUITES [AS] *Houston, TX*
SHERATON SUITES MARKET CENTER [AS] *Dallas, TX*

SHERATON TUCSON HOTEL &SUITE [HOT] *Tucson, AZ*
SHILO INN [MOT] *Elko, NV*
SHILO INN [MOT] *Kanab, UT*
SHILO INN [MOT] *Salt Lake City, UT*
SHILO INN [MOT] *Yuma, AZ*
SIENA HOTEL SPA CASINO [HOT] *Reno, NV*
SIERRA MESA LODGE [BB] *Ruidoso, NM*
SIERRA ROYALE ALL SUITE HOTEL [HOT] *San Antonio, TX*
SIERRA ROYALE ALL SUITE HOTEL [AS] *San Antonio, TX*
SILVER KING HOTEL [RST] *Park City, UT*
SILVER LEGACY RESORT AND CASINO [HOT] *Reno, NV*
SILVER QUEEN MOTEL [MOT] *Tonopah, NV*
SILVER SADDLE MOTEL [MOT] *Manitou Springs, CO*
SILVER SPUR DUDE RANCH [RAN] *Bandera, TX*
SILVERTHORNE DAYS INN [MOT] *Dillon, CO*
SILVERTON HOTEL CASINO [HOT] *Las Vegas, NV*
SILVERTREE [MOT] *Snowmass Village, CO*
SINGLETREE INN [MOT] *St. George, UT*
SITZMARK LODGE [MOT] *Vail, CO*
SKI TIP LODGE [BB] *Dillon, CO*
SKY RANCH LODGE [MOT] *Sedona, AZ*
SKY VALLEY LODGE [BB] *Steamboat Springs, CO*
SLEEP INN [MOT] *Dallas, TX*
SLEEP INN [MOT] *Salt Lake City, UT*
SLEEPY LAGOON MOTEL [MOT] *Beaver, UT*
SLOANS MOTEL [MOT] *Burlington, CO*
SMUGGLERS INN [MOT] *Tucson, AZ*
SNOWMASS CLUB [RST] *Snowmass Village, CO*
SNOWSHOE MOTEL [MOT] *Dillon, CO*
SONNENALP RESORT OF VAIL [RST] *Vail, CO*
SOUTHWEST INN AT EAGLE MOUNTAIN [BB] *Scottsdale, AZ*
SOUTHWEST INN AT SEDONA [BB] *Sedona, AZ*
SPANISH TRACE INN [MOT] *Athens, TX*
SPENCER HOUSE BED AND BREAKFAST INN [BB] *Santa Fe, NM*
SPIRIT MOUNTAIN RANCH [BB] *Grand Lake, CO*

SPRINGHILL SUITES [MOT] *Glendale, AZ*
SPRINGHILL SUITES [MOT] *Scottsdale, AZ*
SPRING INN, THE [RST] *Pagosa Springs, CO*
STAGECOACH INN [MOT] *Salado, TX*
STAGE COACH INN [MOT] *Santa Fe, NM*
STAGE STOP INN [MOT] *Patagonia, AZ*
STANLEY HOTEL, THE [HOT] *Estes Park, CO*
STARDUST RESORT AND CASINO [HOT] *Las Vegas, NV*
STATION HOUSE HOTEL AND CASINO [MOT] *Tonopah, NV*
STAYBRIDGE SUITES [MOT] *Houston, TX*
STEIN ERIKSEN LODGE [RST] *Park City, UT*
STEP BACK INN [HOT] *Aztec, NM*
STOCKYARDS HOTEL [HOT] *Fort Worth, TX*
STONEBRIDGE INN [MOT] *Snowmass Village, CO*
STONELEIGH [HOT] *Dallas, TX*
STRATER HOTEL [HOT] *Durango, CO*
STRATOSPHERE HOTEL AND CASINO [HOT] *Las Vegas, NV*
STREAMSIDE CABINS [CC] *Estes Park, CO*
SUMMERFIELD SUITES [AS] *Scottsdale, AZ*
SUNBURST RESORT [RST] *Scottsdale, AZ*
SUNCATCHER BED AND BREAKFAST TUCSON DESERT RETREAT [BB] *Tucson, AZ*
SUNDANCE RESORT [RST] *Provo, UT*
SUNDAY HOUSE INN & SUITES [MOT] *Fredericksburg, TX*
SUNFLOWER HILL BED AND BREAKFAST [BB] *Moab, UT*
SUNGLOW MOTEL [MOT] *Capitol Reef National Park, UT*
SUNNYSIDE KNOLL RESORT [RST] *Estes Park, CO*
SUNSET HEIGHTS BED AND BREAKFAST [BB] *El Paso, TX*
SUNSET STATION CASINOS [HOT] *Henderson, NV*
SUN TIME INN [MOT] *St. George, UT*
SUPER 8 [MOT] *Austin, TX*
SUPER 8 [MOT] *Boulder City, NV*
SUPER 8 [MOT] *Carlsbad, NM*
SUPER 8 [MOT] *Dallas, TX*
SUPER 8 [MOT] *Leadville, CO*
SUPER 8 [MOT] *Mount Pleasant, TX*
SUPER 8 [MOT] *Ruidoso, NM*
SUPER 8 [MOT] *Salt Lake City, UT*
SUPER 8 [MOT] *Tucumcari, NM*
SUPER 8 MOTEL [MOT] *Dumas, TX*

SUPER 8 MOTEL [MOT] *Elko, NV*
SUPER 8 MOTEL [MOT] *Gunnison, CO*
SUPER 8 MOTEL [MOT] *Nogales, AZ*
SUPER 8 MOTEL [MOT] *Sierra Vista, AZ*
SUPER 8 MOTEL [MOT] *Socorro, NM*
SWAN MOUNTAIN INN [BB] *Breckenridge, CO*
SYLVAN DALE GUEST RANCH [RAN] *Loveland, CO*
TABLE MOUNTAIN INN [MOT] *Golden, CO*
TAHOE BILTMORE HOTEL AND CASINO [HOT] *Incline Village, NV*
TALL PINE RESORT [CC] *Red River, NM*
TALL TIMBER [RST] *Durango, CO*
TAMARRON RESORT [RST] *Durango, CO*
TANQUE VERDE GUEST RANCH [RAN] *Tucson, AZ*
TARPON INN [BB] *Port Aransas, TX*
TEMPE MISSION PALMS [RST] *Tempe, AZ*
TERRACE BROOK LODGE [MOT] *Zion National Park, UT*
TERRACE TOWERS LODGE [MOT] *Red River, NM*
TERRITORIAL HOUSE BED AND BREAKFAST [BB] *Sedona, AZ*
TERRITORIAL INN [BB] *Santa Fe, NM*
TERRY RANCH BED AND BREAKFAST [BB] *Williams, AZ*
TEXAN MOTOR INN [MOT] *Stephenville, TX*
TEXAS GAMBLING HALL AND HOTEL [HOT] *Las Vegas, NV*
THUNDERBIRD LODGE [HOT] *Canyon de Chelly National Monument, AZ*
THUNDERBIRD LODGE [MOT] *South Rim (Grand Canyon National Park), AZ*
TOUCHSTONE LUXURY BED AND BREAKFAST [BB] *Taos, NM*
TOWN HOUSE MOTEL [MOT] *Las Vegas, NM*
TRAIL RIDERS [MOT] *Granby, CO*
TRAPPERS MOTOR INN [MOT] *Estes Park, CO*
TRAVELODGE [MOT] *Amarillo, TX*
TRAVELODGE [MOT] *Hobbs, NM*
TRAVELODGE [MOT] *Las Vegas, NV*
TRAVELODGE [MOT] *Las Vegas, NV*
TRAVELODGE [MOT] *Ozona, TX*
TRAVELODGE [MOT] *Salida, CO*
TRAVELODGE [MOT] *Salt Lake City, UT*
TRAVELODGE [MOT] *Tempe, AZ*
TRAVELODGE [MOT] *Temple, TX*

TRAVELODGE SUITES [MOT] *Mesa, AZ*
TRAVELODGE SUITES [MOT] *San Antonio, TX*
TRAVELODGE-TRAMWAY [MOT] *Albuquerque, NM*
TREASURE ISLAND AT THE MIRAGE [HOT] *Las Vegas, NV*
TREMONT HOUSE, A WYNDHAM HISTORIC HOTEL, THE [HOT] *Galveston, TX*
TRIANGLE H [MOT] *Monticello, UT*
TROPICANA RESORT AND CASINO [HOT] *Las Vegas, NV*
TUBAC GOLF RESORT [RST] *Tumacacori National Historical Park, AZ*
TUDOR ROSE BED & BREAKFAST [BB] *Salida, CO*
TWIN PALMS [HOT] *Tempe, AZ*
UNIVERSITY HOTEL [MOT] *Huntsville, TX*
VAGABOND INN [MOT] *Reno, NV*
VAIL ATHLETIC CLUB HOTEL & SPA [HOT] *Vail, CO*
VAIL CASCADE RESORT [RST] *Vail, CO*
VAL-U-INN MOTEL [MOT] *Winnemucca, NV*
VENETIAN RESORT HOTEL & CASINO [HOT] *Las Vegas, NV*
VICTOR HOTEL [BB] *Cripple Creek, CO*
VICTORIAN INN [MOT] *Athens, TX*
VICTORIAN INN & SUITES [MOT] *Midland, TX*
VICTORIA OAKS INN [BB] *Denver, CO*
VILLAGE LODGE [MOT] *Ruidoso, NM*
VILLAGER PREMIER [MOT] *Colorado Springs, CO*
VILLAS DE SANTA FE [AS] *Santa Fe, NM*
VINTAGE HOTEL [HOT] *Winter Park, CO*
VISTA VERDE RANCH [RAN] *Steamboat Springs, CO*
WAHWEAP LODGE AND MARINA [MOT] *Page, AZ*
WARWICK, THE [HOT] *Houston, TX*
WARWICK HOTEL [HOT] *Denver, CO*
WASHINGTON SCHOOL INN [BB] *Park City, UT*
WATER STREET INN [BB] *Santa Fe, NM*
WATER WHEEL INN [MOT] *Gunnison, CO*
WAUNITA HOT SPRINGS RANCH [RAN] *Gunnison, CO*
WELCOME HOME INN [MOT] *San Marcos, TX*
WESTERN, THE [MOT] *Socorro, NM*

WESTERN MOTEL [MOT] *Fallon, NV*
WESTERN MOTEL [MOT] *Montrose, CO*
WESTERN MOTEL [MOT] *Shamrock, TX*
WESTERN RIVIERA [MOT] *Grand Lake, CO*
WESTERN SKIES MOTEL [MOT] *Clarendon, TX*
WEST GATE INN [MOT] *Grand Junction, CO*
WESTIN GALLERIA, THE [HOT] *Dallas, TX*
WESTIN GALLERIA [HOT] *Houston, TX*
WESTIN LA CANTERA RESORT, THE [RST] *San Antonio, TX*
WESTIN LA PALOMA, THE [RST] *Tucson, AZ*
WESTIN OAKS [HOT] *Houston, TX*
WESTIN PARK CENTRAL [HOT] *Dallas, TX*
WESTIN RIVERWALK [HOT] *San Antonio, TX*
WESTIN STONEBRIAR RESORT [HOT] *Dallas, TX*
WESTIN TABOR CENTER DENVER [HOT] *Denver, CO*
WESTIN WESTMINSTER [HOT] *Denver, CO*
WESTON PLAZA HOTEL [MOT] *Vernal, UT*
WESTON'S LAMPLIGHTER INN [MOT] *Vernal, UT*
WESTWARD HO CASINO AND HOTEL [MOT] *Las Vegas, NV*
WESTWARD LOOK RESORT [RST] *Tucson, AZ*
WEST WINDS LODGE AND CONDOS [CON] *Ruidoso, NM*
WHITE SANDS INN [MOT] *Alamogordo, NM*
WHITE STALLION RANCH [RAN] *Tucson, AZ*
WHITMORE MANSION [BB] *Nephi, UT*
WIGWAM, THE [RST] *Litchfield Park, AZ*
WILDERNESS TRAILS GUEST RANCH [RAN] *Durango, CO*
WILDFLOWER BED & BREAKFAST [BB] *Salt Lake City, UT*
WILDWOOD LODGE [RST] *Snowmass Village, CO*
WILSON WORLD HOTEL & SUITES [MOT] *Dallas/Fort Worth Airport Area, TX*
WINDEMERE HOTEL & CONFERENCE CENTER [CONF] *Sierra Vista, AZ*
WINDMILL INN AT ST. PHILIP'S PLAZA [AS] *Tucson, AZ*

WINDMILL INN AT SUN CITY WEST [MOT] *Glendale, AZ*
WIND RIVER RANCH [RAN] *Estes Park, CO*
WINGATE INN [MOT] *Pueblo, CO*
WINNERS HOTEL AND CASINO [HOT] *Winnemucca, NV*
WIT'S END GUEST RANCH AND RESORT [RAN] *Durango, CO*
WOLF CREEK LODGE [MOT] *South Fork, CO*
WOODFIELD SUITES [MOT] *San Antonio, TX*
WOODLANDS RESORT [CONF] *Houston, TX*
WOODSPUR LODGE [MOT] *Winter Park, CO*
WYMAN HOTEL [BB] *Silverton, CO*
WYNDHAM ALBUQUERQUE HOTEL [HOT] *Albuquerque, NM*
WYNDHAM ANATOLE HOTEL [HOT] *Dallas, TX*
WYNDHAM ARLINGTON DFW AIRPORT SOUTH [HOT] *Arlington-Grand Prairie, TX*
WYNDHAM BUTTES RESORT [HOT] *Tempe, AZ*
WYNDHAM COLORADO SPRINGS [HOT] *Colorado Springs, CO*
WYNDHAM GARDEN [MOT] *Dallas, TX*
WYNDHAM GARDEN HOTEL [MOT] *Albuquerque, NM*
WYNDHAM GARDEN HOTEL [MOT] *Chandler, AZ*
WYNDHAM GARDEN HOTEL NORTH [MOT] *Phoenix, AZ*
WYNDHAM GREENSPOINT HOTEL [HOT] *Houston, TX*
WYNDHAM HOTEL [HOT] *Salt Lake City, UT*
WYNDHAM PEAKS RESORT & GOLDEN DOOR SPA [RST] *Telluride, CO*
WYNDHAM PHOENIX AIRPORT [HOT] *Phoenix, AZ*
YACHT CLUB HOTEL [MOT] *Port Isabel, TX*
YARROW HOTEL [MOT] *Park City, UT*
YAVAPAI LODGE [MOT] *South Rim (Grand Canyon National Park), AZ*
Y.O. RANCH RESORT HOTEL & CONFERENCE CENTER [RST] *Kerrville, TX*
ZAPATA RANCH [BB] *Alamosa, CO*
ZION LODGE [MOT] *Zion National Park, UT*
ZION PARK MOTEL [MOT] *Zion National Park, UT*

RESTAURANT LIST

Establishment names are listed in alphabetical order followed by a symbol identifying their classification and then city and state. The symbols for classification are: [RES] for Restaurants and [URD] for Unrated Dining Spots.

240 UNION [RES] *Lakewood, CO*
5050 [URD] *San Antonio, TX*
66 DINER [URD] *Albuquerque, NM*
7-11 RANCH [RES] *Vernal, UT*
ABACUS [RES] *Dallas, TX*
ABSOLUTE [RES] *Salt Lake City, UT*
ACACIA [RES] *Scottsdale, AZ*
ADDISON CAFE [RES] *Dallas, TX*
ADELE'S [RES] *Carson City, NV*
ADELMO'S [RES] *Dallas, TX*
AJAX TAVERN [RES] *Aspen, CO*
AL BIERNAT'S [RES] *Dallas, TX*
ALDINO CUCINA ITALIANA [RES] *San Antonio, TX*
ALDO'S [RES] *San Antonio, TX*
ALI-BABA [RES] *Dallas, TX*
ALPENGLOW STUBE [RES] *Dillon, CO*
ALPENROSE [RES] *Vail, CO*
AMBERJACKS [RES] *South Padre Island, TX*
AMERICAS [RES] *Houston, TX*
A MOVEABLE FEAST [RES] *Houston, TX*
ANAQUA GRILL [RES] *San Antonio, TX*
ANASAZI, THE [RES] *Santa Fe, NM*
ANDIAMO [RES] *Dallas, TX*
ANDIAMO [RES] *Santa Fe, NM*
ANDREA'S GERMAN CUISINE [RES] *Lyons, CO*
ANGELO'S [RES] *Fort Worth, TX*
ANGELUNA [RES] *Fort Worth, TX*
ANNEMARIE'S ALPINE LODGE [RES] *Kerrville, TX*
ANNIE'S CAFE [URD] *Denver, CO*
ANTARES [RES] *Steamboat Springs, CO*
ANTHONY'S [RES] *Houston, TX*
ANTHONY'S AT THE DELTA [RES] *Espanola, NM*
ANTICA ROMA CAFFE [RES] *Boulder, CO*
ANTIQUITY [RES] *Albuquerque, NM*
ANTLERS LODGE [RES] *San Antonio, TX*
ANTONIO'S [RES] *Las Vegas, NV*
APPLE TREE [RES] *Taos, NM*
AQUA [RES] *Las Vegas, NV*
ARCODORO [RES] *Houston, TX*

ARGENTINE GRILL [URD] *Salt Lake City, UT*
ARIANO'S ITALIAN RESTAURANT [RES] *Durango, CO*
ARIZONA KITCHEN [RES] *Litchfield Park, AZ*
ARSHEL'S CAFE [RES] *Beaver, UT*
ARTICHOKE CAFE, THE [RES] *Albuquerque, NM*
ATLANTIS [RES] *Reno, NV*
AUBERGINE CAFE [RES] *Denver, CO*
AUGUST MOON [RES] *Dallas, TX*
AUREOLE [RES] *Las Vegas, NV*
AVANTI OF PHOENIX [RES] *Phoenix, AZ*
AVANTI'S [RES] *Scottsdale, AZ*
BABA AFGHAN [RES] *Salt Lake City, UT*
BABY DOE'S MATCHLESS MINE [RES] *Denver, CO*
BABY KAY'S CAJUN KITCHEN [RES] *Phoenix, AZ*
BACI TRATTORIA [RES] *Salt Lake City, UT*
BACKSTREET CAFE [RES] *Houston, TX*
BAKERY, THE [RES] *Jefferson, TX*
BALCONY OF RIDGLEA [RES] *Fort Worth, TX*
BAMBARA [RES] *Salt Lake City, UT*
BANDERA [RES] *Scottsdale, AZ*
BARN DOOR [RES] *Odessa, TX*
BAROLO GRILL [RES] *Denver, CO*
BAROQUE [RES] *Houston, TX*
BARRY'S OASIS [RES] *Albuquerque, NM*
BASHA [RES] *Dallas, TX*
BASIL'S [RES] *Austin, TX*
BATTISTA'S HOLE-IN-THE-WALL [URD] *Las Vegas, NV*
BAVARIAN CHALET [RES] *Ogden, UT*
BEANO'S CABIN [RES] *Vail, CO*
BEAU NASH [RES] *Dallas, TX*
BELGIAN RESTAURANT [RES] *Austin, TX*
BELLA ITALIA WEST [RES] *Fort Worth, TX*
BELLA NAPOLI [RES] *El Paso, TX*
BELLA NAPOLI [RES] *Page, AZ*
BENIHANA OF TOKYO [RES] *Salt Lake City, UT*

BENJY'S [RES] *Houston, TX*
BENNY'S [RES] *Denver, CO*
BERTOLINI'S [RES] *Las Vegas, NV*
BEULAH'S TARPON INN [RES] *Port Aransas, TX*
BIGA [RES] *San Antonio, TX*
BIG NOSE KATE'S SALOON [RES] *Tombstone, AZ*
BIG TEXAN STEAK RANCH [RES] *Amarillo, TX*
BIRRAPORETTI'S [RES] *Houston, TX*
BISHOP'S LODGE [RES] *Santa Fe, NM*
BISTRO 24 [RES] *Phoenix, AZ*
BISTRO A [RES] *Dallas, TX*
BISTRO ADDE BREWSTER [RES] *Denver, CO*
BISTRO LANCASTER [RES] *Houston, TX*
BISTRO LOUISE [RES] *Fort Worth, TX*
BISTRO TIME [RES] *San Antonio, TX*
BLACKBEARD'S [RES] *South Padre Island, TX*
BLACK BEAR INN [RES] *Lyons, CO*
BLACK CANYON INN [RES] *Estes Park, CO*
BLACK FOREST RESTAURANT [RES] *Central City, CO*
BLUEBIRD [URD] *Logan, UT*
BLUE BOAR INN RESTAURANT, THE [RES] *Heber City, UT*
BLUE CORN CAFE [RES] *Santa Fe, NM*
BLUE MESA GRILL [RES] *Fort Worth, TX*
BLUE SPRUCE INN [RES] *Dillon, CO*
BLUE STAR INN [RES] *Midland, TX*
BLUE WILLOW [URD] *Tucson, AZ*
BLUE WINDOW [RES] *Los Alamos, NM*
BLU'S [RES] *Vail, CO*
BOILING POT, THE [RES] *Austin, TX*
BOMBAY HOUSE [RES] *Provo, UT*
BON TON [RES] *Ouray, CO*
BOOGIES ON THE ROCKS [URD] *Aspen, CO*
BOUDRO'S A TEXAS BISTRO [RES] *San Antonio, TX*
BOULEVARD BISTRO [RES] *Houston, TX*
BRANDING IRON STEAK HOUSE [RES] *Show Low, AZ*
BRAZIER AT LOS PATIOS [URD] *San Antonio, TX*
BREADWINNERS [RES] *Dallas, TX*
BRECKENRIDGE BREWERY [RES] *Breckenridge, CO*
BRENNAN'S [RES] *Houston, TX*
BRETT'S HOMESTEAD STEAKHOUSE [RES] *Red River, NM*
BRIARHURST MANOR [RES] *Manitou Springs, CO*
BRIAR ROSE [RES] *Breckenridge, CO*
BRICKS RESTAURANT AND WINE BAR [RES] *Reno, NV*

BRITTANY HILL [RES] *Denver, CO*
BROKER [RES] *Denver, CO*
BROWNSTONE [RES] *Houston, TX*
BUCKHORN SALOON [RES] *Silver City, NM*
BUDDY'S GRILL [RES] *Tucson, AZ*
BUEN TIEMPO [RES] *Ouray, CO*
BUFFALO BAR & GRILL [RES] *Buena Vista, CO*
BUFFALO JOE'S SMOKEHOUSE [RES] *Salt Lake City, UT*
BUKHORN EXCHANGE [RES] *Denver, CO*
BURRITO COMPANY, THE [URD] *Santa Fe, NM*
BUSTER'S [RES] *Flagstaff, AZ*
BUSTER'S [RES] *Scottsdale, AZ*
BUTERA'S FINE FOODS [RES] *Houston, TX*
BYBLOS [RES] *Tempe, AZ*
CABIN, THE [RES] *Park City, UT*
CACHAREL [RES] *Arlington-Grand Prairie, TX*
CACHE CACHE [RES] *Aspen, CO*
CACTUS GRILL NORTH [RES] *Loveland, CO*
CAFE ALPINE [RES] *Breckenridge, CO*
CAFE ANNIE [RES] *Houston, TX*
CAFE AT THE FOUR SEASONS [RES] *Austin, TX*
CAFE DE LAS PLACITA [RES] *Albuquerque, NM*
CAFE DEL RIO [RES] *Pueblo, CO*
CAFE D'OR [URD] *Dallas/Fort Worth Airport Area, TX*
CAFE JAPON [RES] *Houston, TX*
CAFE NICOLLE [RES] *Las Vegas, NV*
CAFE ON THE GREEN [RES] *Dallas/Fort Worth Airport Area, TX*
CAFE PACIFIC [RES] *Dallas, TX*
CAFE PANDA [RES] *Dallas, TX*
CAFE PARIS [RES] *Santa Fe, NM*
CAFE PASQUAL'S [RES] *Santa Fe, NM*
CAFE POCA COSA [RES] *Tucson, AZ*
CAFE SPOLETO [RES] *Albuquerque, NM*
CAFE TERRA COTTA [RES] *Tucson, AZ*
CAMELOT [RES] *Las Vegas, NV*
CANTINA [RES] *Aspen, CO*
CANTINA DEL PEDREGAL [RES] *Carefree, AZ*
CANYON CAFE [RES] *Houston, TX*
CAPITAL GRILLE [RES] *Dallas, TX*
CAPITAL GRILLE [RES] *Houston, TX*
CAPPY'S [RES] *San Antonio, TX*
CAPRICCIO [RES] *Tucson, AZ*
CARAVELLE [RES] *Dallas, TX*
CAROLINE'S CUISINE [RES] *Grand Lake, CO*
CARRABBA'S [RES] *Houston, TX*
CARRANZA MEAT MARKET [RES] *San Antonio, TX*

CARSON NUGGET STEAK HOUSE [RES] *Carson City, NV*
CARVER BREWING CO [URD] *Durango, CO*
CARVER'S [RES] *Henderson, NV*
CASA BONITA OF DENVER [URD] *Lakewood, CO*
CASA DEL SOL [RES] *Buena Vista, CO*
CASA DE VALDEZ [RES] *Taos, NM*
CASA JURADO [RES] *El Paso, TX*
CASA MANANA [RES] *Safford, AZ*
CASA RIO [RES] *San Antonio, TX*
CASCABEL [RES] *San Antonio, TX*
CATALINA GRILLE [RES] *Tucson, AZ*
CATFISH PLANTATION [RES] *Ennis, TX*
CATHAY HOUSE [RES] *Las Vegas, NV*
CATTLE BARON [RES] *Las Cruces, NM*
CATTLE BARON STEAK AND SEAFOOD [RES] *Hobbs, NM*
CATTLEMAN'S STEAKHOUSE AT INDIAN CLIFFS RANCH [RES] *El Paso, TX*
CECILIA'S [RES] *Ouray, CO*
CELEBRATION [RES] *Dallas, TX*
CELEBRATIONS [RES] *Santa Fe, NM*
CENTER CAFE [RES] *Moab, UT*
CENTURY ROOM [RES] *Aspen, CO*
C-FU GOURMET [RES] *Chandler, AZ*
CHAD'S STEAKHOUSE [RES] *Tucson, AZ*
CHAMBERLAIN'S [RES] *Dallas, TX*
CHAPALA [RES] *Las Vegas, NV*
CHAPARRAL DINING ROOM [RES] *Scottsdale, AZ*
CHARLES COURT [RES] *Colorado Springs, CO*
CHARLIE CLARK'S STEAK HOUSE [RES] *Pinetop, AZ*
CHART HOUSE, THE [RES] *Aspen, CO*
CHART HOUSE [RES] *Golden, CO*
CHART HOUSE [RES] *Scottsdale, AZ*
CHART HOUSE [RES] *Stateline, NV*
CHEF DU JOUR [RES] *Albuquerque, NM*
CHEF LIU'S CHINESE RESTAURANT [RES] *Trinidad, CO*
CHEF'S PALACE [RES] *Kanab, UT*
CHEZ BETTY [RES] *Park City, UT*
CHEZ GERARD [RES] *Dallas, TX*
CHEZ NOUS [RES] *Austin, TX*
CHEZ NOUS [RES] *Houston, TX*
CHEZ SUZETTE [RES] *Lubbock, TX*
CHEZ ZEE [RES] *Austin, TX*
CHIANTI CUCINA RUSTICA [RES] *Houston, TX*
CHIARAMONTE'S [RES] *La Junta, CO*
CHILI WILLY'S [RES] *Vail, CO*
CHIMAYO [RES] *Park City, UT*
CHINA CITY CAFE [RES] *Price, UT*
CHINA GARDEN [RES] *San Angelo, TX*

CHINA WEST [RES] *Alamogordo, NM*
CHINOIS [RES] *Las Vegas, NV*
CHIN'S [RES] *Las Vegas, NV*
CHIPOTLE GRILL [URD] *Denver, CO*
CHOMPIE'S [URD] *Phoenix, AZ*
CHOMPIE'S [RES] *Scottsdale, AZ*
CHOW'S CONTEMPORARY CHINESE [RES] *Santa Fe, NM*
CHOW THAI [RES] *Dallas, TX*
CHRISTOPHER'S FERMIER BRASSERIE [RES] *Phoenix, AZ*
CHRISTY MAE'S [RES] *Albuquerque, NM*
CHULA VISTA [RES] *Beaumont, TX*
CHUY'S COMIDA DELUXE [RES] *Houston, TX*
CITIZEN [RES] *Dallas, TX*
CITY CAFE [RES] *Dallas, TX*
CITY DINER AND OYSTER BAR [RES] *Corpus Christi, TX*
CITY GRILL [RES] *Austin, TX*
CITY GRILL [RES] *Tucson, AZ*
CIUDAD [RES] *Dallas, TX*
CLAIRE DE LUNE [RES] *Dallas, TX*
CLANCY'S PUB [RES] *Farmington, NM*
CLARK'S OUTPOST BBQ [RES] *Gainesville, TX*
CLARY'S [RES] *Galveston, TX*
CLASSIC CAFE [RES] *Fort Worth, TX*
CLIVE'S [RES] *Houston, TX*
CODY INN CONTINENTAL CUISINE [RES] *Golden, CO*
COMPASS [RES] *Phoenix, AZ*
CONFEDERATE HOUSE [RES] *Houston, TX*
CONRAD'S DOWNTOWN [RES] *Albuquerque, NM*
COOPERAGE [RES] *Albuquerque, NM*
COOS BAY BISTRO [RES] *Denver, CO*
CORN DANCE CAFE [RES] *Santa Fe, NM*
COSMOPOLITAN [RES] *Telluride, CO*
COTTAGE INN [RES] *Beaver, UT*
COTTAGE PLACE [RES] *Flagstaff, AZ*
COUNTRY BOUNTY [RES] *Salida, CO*
COUNTRY INN [URD] *Las Vegas, NV*
COUNTY LINE ON THE HILL [RES] *Austin, TX*
COUNTY LINE SMOKEHOUSE & GRILL [RES] *Englewood, CO*
COWBOY CLUB [RES] *Sedona, AZ*
COWBOY GRUB [RES] *Salt Lake City, UT*
COYOTE CAFE [RES] *Las Vegas, NV*
COYOTE CAFE [RES] *Santa Fe, NM*
CRAFTWOOD INN [RES] *Manitou Springs, CO*
CREEKSIDE AT SOLITUDE [RES] *Salt Lake City, UT*
CREW [RES] *Scottsdale, AZ*
CROSSING, THE [RES] *Yuma, AZ*

CRUMPET'S [RES] San Antonio, TX
CRYSTAL CLUB CAFE [RES] Glenwood Springs, CO
CRYSTAL PALACE DINNER THEATER [URD] Aspen, CO
CUCINA [RES] Salt Lake City, UT
CYPRESS GRILL [RES] Kerrville, TX
DAILY REVIEW CAFE [RES] Houston, TX
DAISY MAE'S STEAK HOUSE [RES] Tucson, AZ
DAKOTA'S [RES] Dallas, TX
DAMIAN'S CUCINA ITALIA [RES] Houston, TX
DANDELION [RES] Boulder, CO
DANIEL'S TRATTORIA [RES] Tucson, AZ
DARDANO'S [RES] Lakewood, CO
DEEP ELLUM CAFE [RES] Dallas, TX
DELECTABLES [RES] Tucson, AZ
DEL FRISCO'S DOUBLE EAGLE STEAK HOUSE [RES] Dallas, TX
DELI NEWS [RES] Dallas, TX
DENVER BUFFALO COMPANY [RES] Denver, CO
DENVER CHOPHOUSE & BREWERY [RES] Denver, CO
DESERT EDGE PUB [RES] Salt Lake City, UT
DEVILLE [RES] Houston, TX
DICK'S LAST RESORT [URD] San Antonio, TX
DIFFERENT POINTE OF VIEW [RES] Phoenix, AZ
DINNING ROOM AT SUNSPOT [RES] Winter Park, CO
DOC MARTIN'S [RES] Taos, NM
DON AND CHARLIE'S AMERICAN RIB AND CHOP HOUSE [RES] Scottsdale, AZ
DONERAKI [RES] Houston, TX
DONG TING [RES] Houston, TX
DONITA'S CANTINA [RES] Crested Butte, CO
DOUBLE EAGLE [RES] Las Cruces, NM
DRAI'S OF LAS VEGAS [RES] Las Vegas, NV
DRISKILL GRILL [RES] Austin, TX
DUCK AND DECANTER [URD] Phoenix, AZ
DUCK INN [RES] Rockport, TX
DYER'S BAR-B-QUE [RES] Pampa, TX
EARL'S [RES] Gallup, NM
EASTSIDE CAFI [RES] Austin, TX
ED DEBEVIC'S [URD] Phoenix, AZ
EDELWEISS [RES] Colorado Springs, CO
EDELWEISS [RES] Fort Worth, TX
E. G.'S GARDEN GRILL [RES] Grand Lake, CO
EL CAFE [RES] Laredo, TX
EL CHARRO [RES] Tucson, AZ
EL CHICO [RES] Wichita Falls, TX

EL CHORRO LODGE [RES] Scottsdale, AZ
EL COMEDOR [RES] Las Cruces, NM
EL COMEDOR [RES] Santa Fe, NM
EL ENCANTO [RES] Bullhead City, AZ
ELITE CAFE [RES] Waco, TX
EL JARRO DE ARTURO [RES] San Antonio, TX
ELKHORN CAFE [RES] Pagosa Springs, CO
EL MESAON - LA COCINA DE ESPANA [RES] Santa Fe, NM
EL MIRADOR [RES] San Antonio, TX
EL NIDO [RES] Santa Fe, NM
EL NORTENO [RES] Albuquerque, NM
EL PARAGUA [RES] Espanola, NM
EL PINTO [RES] Albuquerque, NM
EL RIALTO [RES] Las Vegas, NM
EL RINCON RESTAURANTE MEXICANO [RES] Sedona, AZ
EL TORO BRAVO [RES] Roswell, NM
EL TOVAR DINING ROOM [RES] South Rim (Grand Canyon National Park), AZ
EMERIL'S NEW ORLEANS [RES] Las Vegas, NV
EMPRESS COURT [RES] Las Vegas, NV
EMPRESS FUSION CUISINE [RES] Houston, TX
EMPRESS SEAFOOD [RES] Denver, CO
ENCLAVE, THE [RES] Dallas, TX
ERNESTO'S [RES] San Antonio, TX
ESCALANTE'S MEXICAN GRILLE [RES] Houston, TX
EUROPEAN CAFE [RES] Boulder, CO
EVANGELOS SCORDATO'S [RES] Tucson, AZ
FALCON [RES] Winslow, AZ
FAMOUS MURPHY'S [RES] Reno, NV
FAR EAST RESTAURANT [RES] Grand Junction, CO
FASOLINI'S PIZZA CAFE [RES] Las Vegas, NV
FAWN BROOK INN [RES] Estes Park, CO
FERRARO'S [RES] Las Vegas, NV
FERRELL'S PIT [RES] Mission, TX
FIG TREE [RES] San Antonio, TX
FIRESIDE JUNCTION [RES] Limon, CO
FISH [RES] Dallas, TX
FISHBOWL [RES] Dallas, TX
FISH FRY [RES] Paris, TX
FISH MARKET [RES] Phoenix, AZ
FLAGSTAFF HOUSE RESTAURANT [RES] Boulder, CO
FLORADORA [RES] Telluride, CO
FLORINDO'S [RES] Glenwood Springs, CO
FLYING DUTCHMAN, THE [RES] Houston, TX
FOGO DE CHAO [RES] Dallas, TX
FONDA SAN MIGUEL [RES] Austin, TX

FORMOSA GARDENS [RES] *San Antonio, TX*
FORT, THE [RES] *Lakewood, CO*
FOSTER'S STEAK HOUSE [RES] *Bryce Canyon National Park, UT*
FOUNDRY GRILL [RES] *Provo, UT*
FOURTH STORY [RES] *Denver, CO*
FOY'S COUNTRY CORNER [RES] *Panguitch, UT*
FRANCESCA'S AT SUNSET [RES] *San Antonio, TX*
FRANCISO'S [RES] *Durango, CO*
FRANKI'S LI'L EUROPE [RES] *Dallas, TX*
FRATELLI'S [RES] *Englewood, CO*
FRENCH ROOM, THE [RES] *Dallas, TX*
FRESCO ITALIAN CAFI [RES] *Salt Lake City, UT*
FRESH FISH CO [RES] *Denver, CO*
FRIDAY'S STATION STEAK & SEAFOOD GRILL [RES] *Stateline, NV*
FRIEDHELM'S BAVARIAN [RES] *Fredericksburg, TX*
FUEGO [RES] *Tucson, AZ*
FULL MOON GRILL [RES] *Boulder, CO*
GABRIEL'S [RES] *Santa Fe, NM*
GAETANO'S [RES] *Pueblo, CO*
GAIDO'S [RES] *Galveston, TX*
GALLEY [RES] *Jefferson, TX*
GAMEKEEPER'S GRILLE [RES] *Park City, UT*
GARDEN, THE [RES] *Galveston, TX*
GARDSKI'S [RES] *Lubbock, TX*
GARDUNOS [RES] *Las Vegas, NV*
GARDUNO'S [RES] *Santa Fe, NM*
GARDUNO'S OF MEXICO [RES] *Albuquerque, NM*
GASTHAUS EICHLER [RES] *Winter Park, CO*
GAZEBO AT LOS PATIOS [URD] *San Antonio, TX*
GERONIMO [RES] *Santa Fe, NM*
GERSHWIN'S [RES] *Dallas, TX*
GIA'S RESTAURANT AND DELI [RES] *Logan, UT*
GILBERT'S NEW YORK DELICATESSEN [RES] *Dallas, TX*
GIUSEPPE'S OLD DEPOT [RES] *Colorado Springs, CO*
GLASS MENAGERIE [RES] *Houston, TX*
GLENN EYRIE RESTAURANT [RES] *Montrose, CO*
GLITRETIND, THE [RES] *Park City, UT*
GLORY HOLE [RES] *Reno, NV*
GOLDEN EAGLE INN [RES] *Vail, CO*
GOLDEN ROOM [RES] *Houston, TX*

GOLDEN STEER STEAK HOUSE [RES] *Las Vegas, NV*
GOLDEN SWAN [RES] *Scottsdale, AZ*
GOLD ROOM, THE [RES] *Tucson, AZ*
GOODE COMPANY SEAFOOD [RES] *Houston, TX*
GOODE COMPANY TEXAS BAR-B-Q [RES] *Houston, TX*
GRADY'S AMERICAN GRILL [RES] *Lakewood, CO*
GRANT CORNER INN [URD] *Santa Fe, NM*
GRAPE, THE [RES] *Dallas, TX*
GRAPPA [RES] *Park City, UT*
GRAY CLIFF LODGE [RES] *Ogden, UT*
GREAT CARUSO [RES] *Houston, TX*
GREAT WALL OF CHINA [RES] *Tucson, AZ*
GREEKFEST [RES] *Phoenix, AZ*
GREENBRIAR INN, THE [RES] *Boulder, CO*
GREEN PASTURES [RES] *Austin, TX*
GREEN ROOM [RES] *Dallas, TX*
GREY MOSS INN [RES] *San Antonio, TX*
GRILL AT HACIENDA DEL SOL, THE [RES] *Tucson, AZ*
GRILLE 5115 [RES] *Houston, TX*
GRISTMILL [RES] *New Braunfels, TX*
GROTTO [RES] *Houston, TX*
GROUSE MOUNTAIN GRILL [RES] *Vail, CO*
GUADALAJARA MEXICAN GRILLE [RES] *Houston, TX*
GUADLAJARA CAFE [RES] *Clovis, NM*
GUENTHER HOUSE [URD] *San Antonio, TX*
GUIDO'S SWISS INN [RES] *Aspen, CO*
GURLEY STREET GRILL [RES] *Prescott, AZ*
HAMADA OF JAPAN [RES] *Las Vegas, NV*
HANASHO [RES] *Dallas/Fort Worth Airport Area, TX*
HANDLEBARS [RES] *Silverton, CO*
HAPA [RES] *Scottsdale, AZ*
HAPPY COOKER [RES] *Georgetown, CO*
HARD ROCK CAFE [URD] *Las Vegas, NV*
HARD ROCK CAFE [URD] *Phoenix, AZ*
HARRIGAN'S [RES] *Lubbock, TX*
HARRIS' [RES] *Phoenix, AZ*
HATCH COVER [RES] *Colorado Springs, CO*
HAVANA CAFE [RES] *Phoenix, AZ*
HEARTHSTONE [RES] *Breckenridge, CO*
HEARTLINE CAFE [RES] *Sedona, AZ*
HIDEAWAY [RES] *Sedona, AZ*
HIGH COUNTRY [RES] *Leadville, CO*

HIGHLANDS GARDEN CAFE [RES] *Denver, CO*
HIGH NOON [RES] *Albuquerque, NM*
HOFFBRAU STEAKS [RES] *Beaumont, TX*
HOMESTEADERS [RES] *Cortez, CO*
HONG KONG ROYALE [RES] *Dallas, TX*
HORSESHOE 2 [RES] *Breckenridge, CO*
HOUSE OF TRICKS [RES] *Tempe, AZ*
HOUSTON'S [RES] *Phoenix, AZ*
HOUSTON'S [RES] *Scottsdale, AZ*
HOUSTON'S TRAIL'S END [RES] *Kanab, UT*
HUDSON'S ON THE BEND [RES] *Austin, TX*
HUISACHE GRILL [RES] *New Braunfels, TX*
HUNAN [RES] *Houston, TX*
HUNTER STEAKHOUSE [RES] *Tempe, AZ*
HUNTER STEAKHOUSE [RES] *Yuma, AZ*
ICHIBAN JAPANESE STEAK HOUSE [RES] *Reno, NV*
IL FORNAIO [RES] *Denver, CO*
IL FORNAIO [RES] *Las Vegas, NV*
IL PIATTO [RES] *Santa Fe, NM*
IMPERIAL CHINESE [RES] *Denver, CO*
INDIA OVEN [RES] *San Antonio, TX*
INDIA PALACE [RES] *Dallas, TX*
INDIA PALACE [RES] *Santa Fe, NM*
INDIA'S RESTAURANT [RES] *Denver, CO*
IRISH INN [RES] *Shamrock, TX*
IRON HORSE [RES] *Walsenburg, CO*
JACKSON'S SPORTS GRILL [RES] *Denver, CO*
JAGS [URD] *Houston, TX*
JAIME'S SPANISH VILLAGE [RES] *Austin, TX*
JALAPENOS [RES] *Houston, TX*
JANOS RESTAURANT [RES] *Tucson, AZ*
JAPON RESTAURANT [RES] *Denver, CO*
JAVIER'S [RES] *Dallas, TX*
JAX FISH HOUSE [RES] *Denver, CO*
JAXON'S [RES] *El Paso, TX*
JEAN-PIERRE'S UPSTAIRS [RES] *Austin, TX*
JEFFREY'S [RES] *Austin, TX*
JESSIE'S CANTINA [RES] *South Padre Island, TX*
JIMMY'S AN AMERICAN RESTAURANT [RES] *Aspen, CO*
JOE T. GARCIA'S [RES] *Fort Worth, TX*
JOEY BISTRO [RES] *Sedona, AZ*
JOHNNY CACE'S SEAFOOD & STEAK [RES] *Longview, TX*
JOHNNY'S MEXICAN FOOD [RES] *McAllen, TX*
JOHN'S RESTAURANT [RES] *Boulder, CO*

JOSE'S [RES] *Bryan/College Station, TX*
JOSE'S [RES] *Stephenville, TX*
JULIAN'S [RES] *Santa Fe, NM*
JUNCTION STEAK AND SEAFOOD [RES] *Huntsville, TX*
KACHINA DOWNTOWN [RES] *Flagstaff, AZ*
KAMPAI [RES] *Park City, UT*
KAMPAI SUSHI & GRILL [RES] *Dallas, TX*
KANEYAMA [RES] *Houston, TX*
KELLY'S ON THE SQUARE [RES] *Granbury, TX*
KEN'S OLD WEST [RES] *Page, AZ*
KEVIN TAYLOR RESTAURANT [RES] *Denver, CO*
KEYSTONE RANCH [RES] *Dillon, CO*
KHYBER [RES] *Houston, TX*
KIM SON [RES] *Houston, TX*
KINGFISHER [RES] *Tucson, AZ*
KING FISH MARKET [RES] *Houston, TX*
KRABLOONIK [RES] *Snowmass Village, CO*
LA BISTRO [RES] *Dallas/Fort Worth Airport Area, TX*
LA CAILLE [RES] *Salt Lake City, UT*
LA CALLE DOCE [RES] *Dallas, TX*
LA CANTERA GRILLE [RES] *San Antonio, TX*
LA CASA PEQUENA [RES] *Payson, AZ*
LA CHAUMIERE [RES] *Lyons, CO*
LA COCINA [RES] *Aspen, CO*
LA COLOMBE D'OR [RES] *Houston, TX*
LA CREPERIE [URD] *Colorado Springs, CO*
LA CUEVA [RES] *Denver International Airport Area, CO*
LA FIESTA GRANDE [RES] *Farmington, NM*
LA FOGATA [RES] *San Antonio, TX*
LA FONDA [RES] *Artesia, NM*
LA FONDA [RES] *San Antonio, TX*
LA FONTANELLA [RES] *Phoenix, AZ*
LA FUENTE [RES] *Tucson, AZ*
LA GRIGLIA [RES] *Houston, TX*
LA HACIENDA [RES] *Scottsdale, AZ*
LA HACIENDA DINING ROOM [RES] *Albuquerque, NM*
LA JAIBA SEAFOOD [RES] *South Padre Island, TX*
LA MARGARITA [RES] *San Antonio, TX*
LAMBERT'S [RES] *Taos, NM*
LA MIRABELLE [RES] *Dallas, TX*
LA MONTANA [RES] *Steamboat Springs, CO*
LA MORA [RES] *Houston, TX*
LANCELOT INN [RES] *Vail, CO*
L'ANCESTRAL [RES] *Dallas, TX*
LANDMARK [RES] *Dallas, TX*
LANDMARK [RES] *Mesa, AZ*

LANDRY'S PACIFIC FISH COMPANY [RES] *Scottsdale, AZ*

LANDRY'S SEAFOOD [RES] *Galveston, TX*

LANDRY'S SEAFOOD HOUSE [RES] *Corpus Christi, TX*

LANDRY'S SEAFOOD HOUSE [RES] *Las Vegas, NV*

LA PETITE MAISON [RES] *Colorado Springs, CO*

LA PLACITA CAFE [RES] *Tucson, AZ*

L'APOGEE [RES] *Steamboat Springs, CO*

LA RENAISSANCE [RES] *Pueblo, CO*

LA RESERVE [RES] *Houston, TX*

LAS ALAMEDAS [RES] *Houston, TX*

LAS CANARIAS [RES] *San Antonio, TX*

LAS DELICIAS [RES] *Denver, CO*

LAS PANCHITAS [RES] *Incline Village, NV*

LA STRADA [RES] *Houston, TX*

LAST TERRITORY [RES] *Tucson, AZ*

LATILLA ROOM [RES] *Carefree, AZ*

LA TOUR D'ARGENT [RES] *Houston, TX*

LA TRATTORIA LOMBARDI [RES] *Dallas, TX*

L'AUBERGE [RES] *Sedona, AZ*

LAUDISIO [RES] *Boulder, CO*

LAURELS [RES] *Dallas, TX*

LAVENDOU [RES] *Dallas, TX*

LAWRY'S THE PRIME RIB [RES] *Dallas, TX*

LAWRY'S THE PRIME RIB [RES] *Las Vegas, NV*

LEAL'S MEXICAN FOOD [RES] *Clovis, NM*

LE BISTRO [RES] *Tucson, AZ*

LE BOSQUET [RES] *Crested Butte, CO*

LE CAFE MICHE [RES] *Albuquerque, NM*

LE CENTRAL [RES] *Denver, CO*

LE CIRQUE [RES] *Las Vegas, NV*

L'ECOLE [RES] *Scottsdale, AZ*

LEFT BANK [RES] *Vail, CO*

LE RENDEZ-VOUS [RES] *Tucson, AZ*

LE REVE [RES] *San Antonio, TX*

LE RHONE [RES] *Phoenix, AZ*

LEWELLYN'S [RES] *Stateline, NV*

L'HOSTARIA [RES] *Aspen, CO*

LIANG'S CHINESE RESTAURANT [RES] *Tyler, TX*

LIBERTY BAR [RES] *San Antonio, TX*

LILY LANGTRY'S [RES] *Las Vegas, NV*

LITTLE ANITA'S [RES] *Santa Fe, NM*

LITTLE RHEIN STEAK HOUSE [RES] *San Antonio, TX*

LITZA'S FOR PIZZA [URD] *Salt Lake City, UT*

LO CASCIO [RES] *Tempe, AZ*

LOG HAVEN [RES] *Salt Lake City, UT*

LOMBARDI MARE [RES] *Dallas, TX*

LOMBARDI'S [RES] *Dallas, TX*

LOMBARDI'S [RES] *Phoenix, AZ*

LONE EAGLE GRILLE ON THE LAKE [RES] *Incline Village, NV*

LONE STAR [RES] *San Antonio, TX*

LONGBRANCH & SCHATZI'S PIZZA [RES] *Granby, CO*

LONGHORN [RES] *Tombstone, AZ*

LON'S [RES] *Scottsdale, AZ*

LOS ARCOS STEAK HOUSE [RES] *Truth or Consequences, NM*

LOS BARRIOS [RES] *San Antonio, TX*

LOS CAMPEROS [RES] *Brownsville, TX*

LOS DESPERADOS [RES] *Glenwood Springs, CO*

LOTUS GARDEN [RES] *Tucson, AZ*

LOUIE'S 106 [RES] *Austin, TX*

LUIGI'S ITALIAN [RES] *Midland, TX*

LUIGI'S RISTORANTE ITALIANO [RES] *Galveston, TX*

LUTECE [RES] *Las Vegas, NV*

MA?ANA [RES] *Santa Fe, NM*

MACAYO [RES] *Tempe, AZ*

MACKENZIE'S CHOP HOUSE [RES] *Colorado Springs, CO*

MADDOX RANCH HOUSE [RES] *Brigham City, UT*

MAGGIE MAE'S [RES] *Colorado Springs, CO*

MAGLEBY'S [RES] *Provo, UT*

MAGUIRE'S [RES] *Dallas, TX*

MAINE-LY LOBSTER AND STEAKHOUSE [RES] *Albuquerque, NM*

MAIN STREET BAKERY & CAFE [RES] *Aspen, CO*

MAIN STREET PIZZA AND NOODLE [RES] *Park City, UT*

MAMACITA'S [RES] *Fredericksburg, TX*

MAMACITA'S [RES] *Kerrville, TX*

MAMA ROSE'S [RES] *Estes Park, CO*

MAMMA LUISA [RES] *Flagstaff, AZ*

MANCUSO'S [RES] *Fort Worth, TX*

MANCUSO'S [RES] *Scottsdale, AZ*

MANDARIN [RES] *Salt Lake City, UT*

MANDARIN PALACE [RES] *Yuma, AZ*

MANHATTAN OF LAS VEGAS [RES] *Las Vegas, NV*

MANUEL'S CRISPY TACOS [RES] *Odessa, TX*

MARCELLO'S ITALIAN RESTAURANT [RES] *Port Isabel, TX*

MARCELLO'S PASTA GRILL [RES] *Tempe, AZ*

MARCO POLO SUPPER CLUB [RES] *Scottsdale, AZ*

MARIA'S NEW MEXICAN KITCHEN [RES] *Santa Fe, NM*

MARIA'S WHEN IN NAPLES [RES] *Scottsdale, AZ*

MARIA TERESA [RES] *Albuquerque, NM*

MARILYN'S [RES] *Phoenix, AZ*
MARIO & ALBERTO [RES] *Dallas, TX*
MARIO'S [RES] *Payson, AZ*
MARKET STREET BROILER [RES] *Salt Lake City, UT*
MARKET STREET GRILL [RES] *Salt Lake City, UT*
MARK'S AMERICAN CUISINE [RES] *Houston, TX*
MARQUESA [RES] *Scottsdale, AZ*
MARRAKECH [RES] *Houston, TX*
MARRAKECH [RES] *Las Vegas, NV*
MARRAKESH [RES] *Dallas, TX*
MARTY'S WINEBAR [RES] *Dallas, TX*
MARY ELAINE'S [RES] *Scottsdale, AZ*
MARY OF PUDDIN' HILL [URD] *Greenville, TX*
MASRAFF'S [RES] *Houston, TX*
MATSUHISA [RES] *Aspen, CO*
MATTA'S [RES] *Mesa, AZ*
MATT'S EL RANCHO [RES] *Austin, TX*
MAXIM'S [RES] *Houston, TX*
MAYFLOWER CUISINIER [RES] *Las Vegas, NV*
MCCORMICK [RES] *Denver, CO*
MCCORMICK & SCHMICK'S SEAFOOD RESTAURANT [RES] *Houston, TX*
MEDITERRANEAN, THE [RES] *Boulder, CO*
MEDITERRANEO [RES] *Dallas, TX*
MEL'S [RES] *Denver, CO*
MENCIUS' GOURMET HUNAN [RES] *San Antonio, TX*
MERCHANT PRINCE [RES] *Galveston, TX*
MERCURY GRILL, THE [RES] *Dallas, TX*
MERITAGE GRILLE [RES] *Dallas/Fort Worth Airport Area, TX*
MERLINO'S BELVEDERE [RES] *CaÒon City, CO*
MESA GRILL [RES] *Houston, TX*
MESA ITALIANA [RES] *Holbrook, AZ*
MESON DE MESILLA [RES] *Las Cruces, NM*
MESQUITE TREE [RES] *Sierra Vista, AZ*
METROPOLITAN [RES] *Salt Lake City, UT*
METROPOLITAN GRILL [RES] *Tucson, AZ*
MEZZALUNA [RES] *Aspen, CO*
MI CASA MEXICAN CANTINA [RES] *Breckenridge, CO*
MICHAEL MONTI'S MESA GRILL [RES] *Mesa, AZ*
MICHAELS [RES] *Fort Worth, TX*
MICHAEL'S [RES] *Scottsdale, AZ*
MICHAEL'S KITCHEN AND BAKERY [RES] *Taos, NM*
MICHELINO'S [RES] *San Antonio, TX*
MI COCINA [RES] *Dallas, TX*
MIKADO [RES] *Salt Lake City, UT*

MILLIE'S WEST PANCAKE HAUS [URD] *Tucson, AZ*
MILT'S STAGE STOP [RES] *Cedar City, UT*
MINGALONE ITALIAN BAR AND GRILL [RES] *Houston, TX*
MINTURN COUNTRY CLUB [RES] *Vail, CO*
MI PIACI [RES] *Dallas, TX*
MIRABELLE AT BEAVER CREEK [RES] *Vail, CO*
MISSION BELL INN [RES] *Manitou Springs, CO*
MI TIERRA [RES] *San Antonio, TX*
MODO MIO [RES] *Dallas, TX*
MOLLY BUTLER [RES] *Greer, AZ*
MO MONG [RES] *Houston, TX*
MOMO'S ITALIAN [RES] *Dallas, TX*
MOM'S CAFE [RES] *Salina, UT*
MONICA'S ACA Y ALLA [RES] *Dallas, TX*
MONTAGNA [RES] *Aspen, CO*
MONTAUK SEAFOOD GRILL [RES] *Vail, CO*
MONTE CARLO [RES] *Dallas, TX*
MONTI'S [RES] *Phoenix, AZ*
MORTONI'S [RES] *Las Vegas, NV*
MORTON'S OF CHICAGO [RES] *Dallas, TX*
MORTON'S OF CHICAGO [RES] *Denver, CO*
MORTON'S OF CHICAGO [RES] *Houston, TX*
MORTON'S OF CHICAGO [RES] *San Antonio, TX*
MOTHERLODE [RES] *Aspen, CO*
MOTOWN CAFE [RES] *Las Vegas, NV*
M AND J [RES] *Albuquerque, NM*
MR C'S [RES] *Nogales, AZ*
MU DU NOODLES [RES] *Santa Fe, NM*
MURPHY'S [RES] *Prescott, AZ*
MUSTANG CAFE [RES] *Dallas/Fort Worth Airport Area, TX*
NAPA [RES] *Las Vegas, NV*
NELLIE CASHMAN'S [RES] *Tombstone, AZ*
NEW BRAUFELS SMOKEHOUSE [RES] *New Braunfels, TX*
NEW CHINATOWN [RES] *Albuquerque, NM*
NEWPORT'S SEAFOOD [RES] *Dallas, TX*
NEW YORKER CLUB [RES] *Salt Lake City, UT*
NICHOLINI'S [RES] *Dallas, TX*
NICK AND SAMS [RES] *Dallas, TX*
NICKY'S [RES] *Estes Park, CO*
NINO'S [RES] *Houston, TX*
NIT NOI [RES] *Houston, TX*
NOBU [RES] *Las Vegas, NV*
OASIS-LAKE TRAVIS, THE [RES] *Austin, TX*
OCEANA [RES] *Scottsdale, AZ*

OGELVIE'S BAR AND GRILLE [RES]
Taos, NM
OLD CHICAGO [URD] Colorado
Springs, CO
OLD CHICAGO PASTA & PIZZA
[URD] Colorado Springs, CO
OLDE VICTORIA [RES] Victoria, TX
OLD HOUSE RESTAURANT, THE
[RES] Santa Fe, NM
OLD MEXICO GRILL [RES] Santa Fe,
NM
OLD SAN FRANCISCO STEAK HOUSE
[RES] Austin, TX
OLD SAN FRANCISCO STEAK HOUSE
[RES] San Antonio, TX
OLD SPAGHETTI FACTORY [RES]
Denver, CO
OLD WARSAW [RES] Dallas, TX
OLIVES [RES] Aspen, CO
OLIVE TREE [RES] Tucson, AZ
OLIVETTE [RES] Houston, TX
ORE HOUSE AT THE PINE GROVE
[RES] Steamboat Springs, CO
ORE HOUSE ON THE PLAZA [RES]
Santa Fe, NM
ORLANDO'S [RES] Lubbock, TX
ORMACHEA'S [RES] Winnemucca, NV
OSTERIA D'ASSISI [RES] Santa Fe, NM
OSTERIA DEL CIRCO [RES] Las Vegas,
NV
OTTO'S BARBECUE [RES] Houston, TX
OUISIE'S TABLE [RES] Houston, TX
PACIFICA [RES] Aspen, CO
PAESANO'S [RES] San Antonio, TX
PALACE [RES] Durango, CO
PALACE ARMS [RES] Denver, CO
PALACE RESTAURANT AND SALOON
[RES] Santa Fe, NM
PALAIS DE JADE [RES] Reno, NV
PALM [RES] Dallas, TX
PALM [RES] Las Vegas, NV
PALM COURT [RES] Scottsdale, AZ
PALOMA BLANCA [RES] San Antonio,
TX
PALOMINO [RES] Dallas, TX
PAPACITA'S MEXICAN RESTAURANT
[RES] Longview, TX
PAPATILO'S [RES] Athens, TX
PAPILLON CAFE [RES] Denver, CO
PAPPADEAUX [RES] Austin, TX
PAPPADEAUX [RES] Houston, TX
PAPPAS BROS. STEAKHOUSE [RES]
Dallas, TX
PAPPAS BROTHERS STEAKHOUSE
[RES] Houston, TX
PAPPASITO'S CANTINA [RES]
Houston, TX
PAPPAS' SWEET SHOP [RES] Raton,
NM
PATRENELLAS CAFE [RES] Houston,
TX

PATRIZIO [RES] Dallas, TX
PAUL'S [RES] Santa Fe, NM
PEGASUS [RES] Las Vegas, NV
PEGGY SUE BBQ [RES] Dallas, TX
PENROSE ROOM [RES] Colorado
Springs, CO
P. F. CHANG'S [RES] Houston, TX
P.F. CHANG'S CHINA BISTRO [RES]
Englewood, CO
P.F. CHANG'S CHINA BISTRO [RES]
Scottsdale, AZ
PHILIPS SUPPER HOUSE [RES] Las
Vegas, NV
PICASSO [RES] Las Vegas, NV
PICCOLO MONDO [RES] Arlington-
Grand Prairie, TX
PICO DE GALLO [RES] San Antonio,
TX
PICO'S MEX-MEX [RES] Houston, TX
PIECA D'ITALIA [RES] San Antonio, TX
PIERPONT CANTINA [RES] Salt Lake
City, UT
PIERRE'S RIVERWALK CAFE [RES]
Breckenridge, CO
PIETRO'S [RES] Sedona, AZ
PINE CONE INN [RES] Prescott, AZ
PINE CREEK COOKHOUSE [RES]
Aspen, CO
PINK ADOBE, THE [RES] Santa Fe, NM
PINNACLE PEAK [RES] Tucson, AZ
PINOS TRUCK STOP [RES] Las Vegas,
NM
PI?ON GRILL [RES] Santa Fe, NM
PIÒON'S [RES] Aspen, CO
PISCHKE'S PARADISE [RES] Scottsdale,
AZ
PIZZERIA BIANCO [RES] Phoenix, AZ
PIZZERIA ESPIRITU [RES] Santa Fe,
NM
PLAZA [URD] Santa Fe, NM
POIRRIER [RES] Breckenridge, CO
POLO'S AT THE FAIRMOUNT [RES]
San Antonio, TX
POOR BOY'S STEAKHOUSE [RES]
Clovis, NM
POPPIES BISTRO CAFE [RES] Aspen,
CO
PORTERHOUSE, THE [RES] Prescott,
AZ
PORTOBELLO [RES] Albuquerque, NM
POST OAK GRILL [RES] Houston, TX
POTAGER [RES] Denver, CO
POTPOURRI HOUSE [RES] Tyler, TX
PRAIRIE STAR [RES] Albuquerque, NM
PRANZO ITALIAN GRILL [RES] Santa
Fe, NM
PREGO [RES] Houston, TX
PRESIDIO GRILL [RES] Tucson, AZ
PRIME [RES] Las Vegas, NV
PRONTO RISTORANTE [RES] Phoenix,
AZ

PYRAMID, THE [RES] *Dallas, TX*

Q'S [RES] *Boulder, CO*

QUILTED BEAR [RES] *Scottsdale, AZ*

RACINES [RES] *Denver, CO*

RADEX [RES] *Denver, CO*

RAFAEL'S [RES] *Salt Lake City, UT*

RAGIN' SHRIMP [RES] *Albuquerque, NM*

RAINBOW CLUB [RES] *Henderson, NV*

RAINBOW LODGE [RES] *Houston, TX*

RANCH KITCHEN [RES] *Gallup, NM*

RANCHO DE CHIMAYO [RES] *Espanola, NM*

RANCHO DE SAN JUAN COUNTRY INN [RES] *Espanola, NM*

RANDALL'S CAFI AND CHEESECAKE CO. [RES] *Fort Worth, TX*

RANDI'S IRISH SALOON [RES] *Winter Park, CO*

RANGE CAFE AND BAKERY [RES] *Albuquerque, NM*

RANGE STEAKHOUSE, THE [RES] *Las Vegas, NV*

RAPSCALLION [RES] *Reno, NV*

RAZZ'S [RES] *Scottsdale, AZ*

REATA [RES] *Alpine, TX*

REBECCA'S [RES] *Cloudcroft, NM*

REDFISH [RES] *Denver, CO*

RED SNAPPER [RES] *Durango, CO*

REDWOOD GRILL [RES] *Houston, TX*

REFLECTIONS [RES] *Fort Worth, TX*

REMINGTON [RES] *Scottsdale, AZ*

RENAISSANCE [RES] *Aspen, CO*

RENE AT TLAQUEPAQUE [RES] *Sedona, AZ*

RENOIR [RES] *Las Vegas, NV*

RESA'S PRIME STEAK HOUSE [RES] *Houston, TX*

RESTAURANT AT HOTEL ST. GERMAIN [URD] *Dallas, TX*

RESTAURANT AT THE MANSION ON TURTLE CREEK [RES] *Dallas, TX*

RESTAURANT CONUNDRUM [RES] *Aspen, CO*

RESTAURANT PICASSO [RES] *Vail, CO*

RHUMBA [RES] *Boulder, CO*

RICARDO'S [RES] *Las Vegas, NV*

RINO'S [RES] *Salt Lake City, UT*

RIO GRANDE CAFE [RES] *Salt Lake City, UT*

RIO RIO CANTINA [RES] *San Antonio, TX*

RISTRA [RES] *Santa Fe, NM*

RIVERHORSE CAFE [RES] *Park City, UT*

RIVER OAKS GRILL [RES] *Houston, TX*

RIVERSIDE [RES] *Pagosa Springs, CO*

RIVER'S RESTAURANT [RES] *Glenwood Springs, CO*

RIVIERA, THE [RES] *Dallas, TX*

RIVIERA GRILL [RES] *Houston, TX*

RIVOLI [RES] *Houston, TX*

ROARING FORK [RES] *Scottsdale, AZ*

ROCIADA [RES] *Santa Fe, NM*

ROCK BOTTOM BREWERY [RES] *Dallas, TX*

ROCKY MOUNTAIN DINER [RES] *Denver, CO*

ROD'S STEAK HOUSE [RES] *Williams, AZ*

ROMANO'S MACARONI GRILL [RES] *Las Vegas, NV*

ROMANO'S MACARONI GRILL [RES] *San Antonio, TX*

ROOSTER [RES] *Dallas, TX*

ROSARIO'S [RES] *San Antonio, TX*

ROSEBUDS [RES] *Sedona, AZ*

ROTISSERIE FOR BEEF AND BIRD [RES] *Houston, TX*

ROUTH STREET [RES] *Dallas, TX*

ROXSAND [RES] *Phoenix, AZ*

ROYAL PEACOCK [RES] *Boulder, CO*

ROYAL TOKYO [RES] *Dallas, TX*

RUGGERI'S [RES] *Dallas, TX*

RUGGLES GRILL [RES] *Houston, TX*

RUSTLER'S ROOSTE [RES] *Phoenix, AZ*

RUTH'S CHRIS STEAK HOUSE [RES] *Austin, TX*

RUTH'S CHRIS STEAK HOUSE [RES] *Dallas, TX*

RUTH'S CHRIS STEAK HOUSE [RES] *Houston, TX*

RUTH'S CHRIS STEAK HOUSE [RES] *Las Vegas, NV*

RUTH'S CHRIS STEAK HOUSE [RES] *Phoenix, AZ*

RUTH'S CHRIS STEAK HOUSE [RES] *San Antonio, TX*

RUTH'S CHRIS STEAK HOUSE [RES] *Scottsdale, AZ*

SACRE BLEU [RES] *Denver, CO*

SACRED SEA [RES] *Las Vegas, NV*

SAFFRON [RES] *Englewood, CO*

SAGE [RES] *Snowmass Village, CO*

SAGE ROOM [RES] *Stateline, NV*

SAGUARO CORNERS [RES] *Tucson, AZ*

ST. BERNARD INN [RES] *Breckenridge, CO*

SAINT-EMILION [RES] *Fort Worth, TX*

SAKURA [RES] *Flagstaff, AZ*

SALADO MANSION [RES] *Salado, TX*

SALSA BRAVA [RES] *Flagstaff, AZ*

SALT CELLAR [RES] *Scottsdale, AZ*

SALT CREEK [RES] *Breckenridge, CO*

SAMBA ROOM, THE [RES] *Dallas, TX*

SAMBUCA [RES] *Dallas, TX*

SAM WOO BBQ [URD] *Las Vegas, NV*

SANTACAFE [RES] *Santa Fe, NM*

SANTA FE [RES] *Lubbock, TX*

SANTA FE STEAK [RES] *McAllen, TX*

SCALO [RES] *Albuquerque, NM*

SCAMPI'S [RES] *South Padre Island, TX*

SCHILO'S DELICATESSEN [URD] *San Antonio, TX*

SCOTT'S CELLAR [RES] *Houston, TX*

SEA RANCH [RES] *South Padre Island, TX*
SENOR JUAN'S GRIGGS [RES] *El Paso, TX*
SERI MELAKA [RES] *Tucson, AZ*
SEVY'S GRILL [RES] *Dallas, TX*
SFUZZI [RES] *Las Vegas, NV*
SHACK [RES] *Snyder, TX*
SHALIMAR [RES] *Las Vegas, NV*
SHANGHAI RIVER [RES] *Houston, TX*
SHED AND LA CHOZA [RES] *Santa Fe, NM*
SHOGUN [RES] *Midland, TX*
SHOHKO-CAFE [RES] *Santa Fe, NM*
SHORELINE GRILL [RES] *Austin, TX*
SHUGRUE'S [RES] *Lake Havasu City, AZ*
SHUGRUE'S HILLSIDE GRILL [RES] *Sedona, AZ*
SIAMESE CAT [RES] *Tempe, AZ*
SIERRA GRILL [RES] *Houston, TX*
SILVANA'S [RES] *Carson City, NV*
SIMMS LANDING [RES] *Golden, CO*
SIMON'S FINE DINING [RES] *Heber City, UT*
SIMPOSIO [RES] *Houston, TX*
SIR GALAHAD'S [RES] *Las Vegas, NV*
SKI TIP LODGE [RES] *Dillon, CO*
SMITH & WOLLENSKY STEAKHOUSE [RES] *Las Vegas, NV*
SMOKE HOUSE [RES] *Van Horn, TX*
SOLEIL [RES] *Tucson, AZ*
SOLERO [RES] *Houston, TX*
SONNY BRYAN'S [RES] *Dallas, TX*
SOUPER SALAD [URD] *Albuquerque, NM*
SPAGO [RES] *Las Vegas, NV*
SPANISH ROOM [RES] *McAllen, TX*
SPENCER'S [RES] *Salt Lake City, UT*
SPLENDIDO AT THE CHATEAU [RES] *Vail, CO*
SQUATTERS PUB BREWERY [RES] *Salt Lake City, UT*
STAAB HOUSE [RES] *Santa Fe, NM*
STAGE COACH [RES] *Manitou Springs, CO*
STAGECOACH INN DINING ROOM [RES] *Salado, TX*
STAGE DELI [RES] *Las Vegas, NV*
STAR CANYON [RES] *Dallas, TX*
STARFISH [RES] *Denver, CO*
STARVIN' ARVIN'S [RES] *Grand Junction, CO*
STATE LINE [RES] *El Paso, TX*
STEAK HOUSE, THE [RES] *Las Vegas, NV*
STEAK HOUSE, THE [RES] *Reno, NV*
STEAKHOUSE AT THE GRAND CANYON [RES] *South Rim (Grand Canyon National Park), AZ*

STEAKOUT GRILL AND BAR [RES] *Taos, NM*
STEAK PIT [RES] *Snowbird, UT*
STEAKSMITH AT EL GANCHO [RES] *Santa Fe, NM*
STEAMBOAT BREWERY [RES] *Steamboat Springs, CO*
STEAMERS SEAFOOD AND RAW BAR [RES] *Phoenix, AZ*
STEFANO'S [RES] *Las Vegas, NV*
STILLWATER INN [RES] *Jefferson, TX*
STONELEIGH P [RES] *Dallas, TX*
STRATTON DINING ROOM [RES] *Cripple Creek, CO*
STRINGS [RES] *Denver, CO*
SUGARHOUSE BARBECUE [RES] *Salt Lake City, UT*
SUMMIT [RES] *Loveland, CO*
SUMMIT [RES] *Stateline, NV*
SUNDANCE [RES] *Red River, NM*
SUSHI [RES] *Dallas, TX*
SUSHI ON SHEA [RES] *Scottsdale, AZ*
SWAN, THE [RES] *Englewood, CO*
SWAN MOUNTAIN INN [RES] *Breckenridge, CO*
SWEET BASIL [RES] *Vail, CO*
SYZYGY [RES] *Aspen, CO*
TABLE MOUNTAIN INN [RES] *Golden, CO*
TACK ROOM [RES] *Laredo, TX*
TACK ROOM, THE [RES] *Tucson, AZ*
TAKAH SUSHI [RES] *Aspen, CO*
TAMARISK [RES] *Green River, UT*
TA MOLLY'S [RES] *Paris, TX*
TAMPICO SPANISH INN [RES] *Midland, TX*
TANTE LOUISE [RES] *Denver, CO*
TARBELL'S [RES] *Phoenix, AZ*
TASCA [RES] *Houston, TX*
TASTE OF TEXAS [RES] *Houston, TX*
T. COOK'S [RES] *Phoenix, AZ*
TECOLOTE CAFE [RES] *Santa Fe, NM*
TEI TEI ROBATA BAR [RES] *Dallas, TX*
TEJAS CAFE [RES] *Victoria, TX*
TEPPO [RES] *Dallas, TX*
TERILLI'S [RES] *Dallas, TX*
TERRACE DINING ROOM, THE [RES] *Scottsdale, AZ*
TEXAS RED'S PIT BARBECUE AND CAFE [RES] *Park City, UT*
TEXAS RED'S STEAK HOUSE [RES] *Red River, NM*
TEXAS ROSE STEAKHOUSE [RES] *Pampa, TX*
THAI TASTE [RES] *Dallas, TX*
THREE SONS [RES] *Denver, CO*
TILLERMAN [RES] *Las Vegas, NV*
TIM'S CHILE CONNECTION [RES] *Taos, NM*
TIN STAR [RES] *Dallas, TX*
T.J. BUMMER'S [RES] *Sterling, CO*

TOHONO CHUL TEA ROOM [URD] *Tucson, AZ*

TOKYO STEAKHOUSE [RES] *Fort Worth, TX*

TOMASITA'S [RES] *Santa Fe, NM*

TOMASO'S [RES] *Phoenix, AZ*

TOMMY TSUNAMI'S [RES] *Denver, CO*

TONY MANDOLA'S BLUE OYSTER [RES] *Houston, TX*

TONY MANDOLA'S GULF COAST KITCHEN [RES] *Houston, TX*

TONY RUPPE'S [RES] *Houston, TX*

TONY'S [RES] *Houston, TX*

TONY'S WINE WAREHOUSE [RES] *Dallas, TX*

TOP OF THE MARKET [RES] *Phoenix, AZ*

TOP OF THE ROCK [RES] *Tempe, AZ*

TOP OF THE WORLD [RES] *Breckenridge, CO*

TOP OF THE WORLD [RES] *Las Vegas, NV*

TOWER [RES] *Snowmass Village, CO*

TOWER OF THE AMERICAS [RES] *San Antonio, TX*

TRAIL DUST STEAKHOUSE [RES] *Denton, TX*

TRAMONTANA [RES] *Dallas, TX*

TRATTORIA GRANDE [RES] *Austin, TX*

TRATTORIA TROMBINO [RES] *Albuquerque, NM*

TREE ROOM, THE [RES] *Provo, UT*

TRINITY GRILLE [RES] *Denver, CO*

TRIO'S [RES] *Boulder, CO*

TROUGH [RES] *Gunnison, CO*

TRUE GRITS STEAKHOUSE [RES] *Alamosa, CO*

TUCCHETTI [RES] *Phoenix, AZ*

TUCCI'S CUCINA ITALIA [RES] *Salt Lake City, UT*

TUSCANY [RES] *Denver, CO*

TUSCANY [RES] *Salt Lake City, UT*

TYROLEAN, THE [RES] *Vail, CO*

UNCLE JULIO'S [RES] *Dallas, TX*

UNCLE TAI'S [RES] *Dallas, TX*

URBANA [RES] *Houston, TX*

U. R. COOKS [RES] *Austin, TX*

UTE CITY [RES] *Aspen, CO*

VALLEY INN [RES] *Brownsville, TX*

VALLONE'S [RES] *Houston, TX*

VANESSIE OF SANTA FE [RES] *Santa Fe, NM*

VARGO'S INTERNATIONAL CUISINE [RES] *Houston, TX*

VENEZIA [RES] *Midland, TX*

VENTANA ROOM, THE [RES] *Tucson, AZ*

VERA CRUZ [RES] *Victoria, TX*

VIA REAL [RES] *Dallas/Fort Worth Airport Area, TX*

VIC'S AT PINNACLE PEAK [RES] *Scottsdale, AZ*

VICTORIA'S ROMANTIC HIDEAWAY [RES] *Ruidoso, NM*

VILLA FONTANA [RES] *Taos, NM*

VINCENT GUERITHAULT ON CAMELBACK [RES] *Phoenix, AZ*

VIVA MERCADOS [RES] *Las Vegas, NV*

VOLTAIRE [RES] *Dallas, TX*

WATER STREET OYSTER BAR [RES] *Corpus Christi, TX*

WAZEE SUPPER CLUB [RES] *Denver, CO*

WELLSHIRE INN [RES] *Denver, CO*

WEST LYNN CAFE [RES] *Austin, TX*

WHISTLING MOON CAFE [RES] *Santa Fe, NM*

WHOLE ENCHILADA [RES] *Montrose, CO*

WIENERSTUBE [RES] *Aspen, CO*

WILDFLOWER, THE [RES] *Vail, CO*

WILD TOUCAN [RES] *Sedona, AZ*

WINDMILL [RES] *Salida, CO*

WINDOWS ON THE GREEN [RES] *Scottsdale, AZ*

WINERY RESTAURANT [RES] *Grand Junction, CO*

WINONA'S DELI-BAKERY [RES] *Steamboat Springs, CO*

WOLFGANG PUCK'S CAFE [RES] *Las Vegas, NV*

WRIGHT'S [RES] *Phoenix, AZ*

WYNKOOP BREWING COMPANY [RES] *Denver, CO*

XIAO LI [RES] *Salt Lake City, UT*

XINH-XINH [RES] *Las Vegas, NV*

YACHT CLUB [RES] *Port Isabel, TX*

YAVAPAI [RES] *Sedona, AZ*

YE LION'S DEN [RES] *Ogden, UT*

YESTER-DAVE'S GRILL, BAR AND BAKERY [RES] *Albuquerque, NM*

YOLIE'S BRAZILIAN STEAKHOUSE [RES] *Las Vegas, NV*

YORK STREET [RES] *Dallas, TX*

YVETTE [RES] *Dallas, TX*

ZAIDY'S DELI [RES] *Denver, CO*

ZEN 32 [RES] *Phoenix, AZ*

ZENITH [RES] *Denver, CO*

ZENTNER'S DAUGHTER STEAK HOUSE [RES] *San Angelo, TX*

ZIZIKI'S [RES] *Dallas, TX*

ZOOM ROADHOUSE GRILL [RES] *Park City, UT*

ZOOT [RES] *Austin, TX*

Z' TEJAS GRILL [RES] *Englewood, CO*

Z' TEJAS GRILL [RES] *Las Vegas, NV*

ZUNI GRILL [RES] *San Antonio, TX*

CITY INDEX

Looking for the Mobil Guides ...?
Call toll-free 800/653-0220 8:00 am to 5:00 pm CST

Mobil Travel Guides

Please check the guides you would like to order:

☐ 0-7627-2619-9
California
$18.95

☐ 0-7627-2618-0
Florida
$18.95

☐ 0-7627-2612-1
Great Lakes
Illinois, Indiana, Michigan,
Ohio, Wisconsin
$18.95

☐ 0-7627-2610-5
Great Plains
Iowa, Kansas, Minnesota,
Missouri, Nebraska, North
Dakota, Oklahoma, South
Dakota
$18.95

☐ 0-7627-2613-X
Mid-Atlantic
Delaware, Maryland,
Pennsylvania, Virginia,
Washington D.C., West
Virginia
$18.95

☐ 0-7627-2614-8
**New England and Eastern
Canada**
Connecticut, Maine, Massachu-
setts, New Hampshire, Rhode
Island, Vermont, Canada
$18.95

☐ 0-7627-2616-4
New York/New Jersey
$18.95

☐ 0-7627-2611-3
Northwest
Idaho, Montana, Oregon, Wash-
ington, Wyoming, Canada
$18.95

☐ 0-7627-2615-6
Southeast
Alabama, Arkansas, Georgia, Ken-
tucky, Louisiana, Mississippi,
North Carolina, South Carolina,
Tennessee
$18.95

☐ 0-7627-2617-2
Southwest
Arizona, Colorado, Nevada, New
Mexico, Texas, Utah
$18.95

Please ship the books above to:

Name: _____

Address: _____

City: _____ State _____ Zip _____

Total Cost of Book(s) $_____   ☐ Please charge my credit card.

Shipping & Handling $_____   ☐ Discover   ☐ Visa
(Please add $3.00 for
first book $1.50 for each   ☐ MasterCard   ☐ American Express
additional book)

Add 8.75% sales tax $_____   Card #_____

Total Amount $_____   Expiration _____

☐ My Check is enclosed.   Signature _____

Please mail this form to: **Mobil Travel Guides**
1460 Renaissance Dr, Suite 401
Park Ridge, IL 60068

Mobil
Travel Guide®

New England
Eastern Canada
Connecticut
Maine
Massachusetts
New Hampshire
Rhode Island
Vermont
New Brunswick
Nova Scotia
Ontario
Prince Edward
  Island
Quebec

Northwest
Idaho
Montana
Oregon
Washington
Wyoming
Alberta
British Columbia
Manitoba

Great Plains
Iowa
Kansas
Minnesota
Missouri
Nebraska
North Dakota
Oklahoma
South Dakota

Great Lakes
Illinois
Indiana
Michigan
Ohio
Wisconsin

California

New York
New Jersey

Southwest
Arizona
Colorado
Nevada
New Mexico
Texas
Utah

Southeast
Alabama
Arkansas
Georgia
Kentucky
Louisiana
Mississippi
North Carolina
South Carolina
Tennessee

Florida

Mid-Atlantic
Delaware
Maryland
Pennsylvania
Virginia
Washington, D.C.
West Virginia

Add your opinion!

Help make the Guides even more useful. Tell us about your experiences with the hotels and restaurants listed in the Guides (or ones that should be added).

Find us on the Internet at **www.mobiltravelguide.com/feedback**

Or copy the form below and mail to Mobil Travel Guides, 1460 Renaissance Dr, Park Ridge, IL 60068. All information will be kept confidential.

Your name _____   Were children with you on trip? ☐ Yes ☐ No

Street _____   Number of people in your party _____

City/State/Zip _____   Your occupation _____

Establishment name_____   ☐ Hotel ☐ Resort ☐ Restaurant
                                                ☐ Motel ☐ Inn ☐ Other

Street_____   City_____ State _____

Do you agree with our description? ☐ Yes ☐ No   If not, give reason_____

Please give us your opinion of the following: 2003 Guide rating _____ ★

Decor	Cleanliness	Service	Food
☐ Excellent	☐ Spotless	☐ Excellent	☐ Excellent
☐ Good	☐ Clean	☐ Good	☐ Good
☐ Fair	☐ Unclean	☐ Fair	☐ Fair
☐ Poor	☐ Dirty	☐ Poor	☐ Poor

Check your suggested rating
☐ ★
☐ ★★
☐ ★★★
☐ ★★★★
☐ ★★★★★

Date of visit _____   First visit? ☐ Yes ☐ No   ✓unusually good value

Comments _____

Establishment name_____   ☐ Hotel ☐ Resort ☐ Restaurant
                                                ☐ Motel ☐ Inn ☐ Other

Street_____   City_____ State _____

Do you agree with our description? ☐ Yes ☐ No   If not, give reason_____

Please give us your opinion of the following: 2003 Guide rating _____ ★

Decor	Cleanliness	Service	Food
☐ Excellent	☐ Spotless	☐ Excellent	☐ Excellent
☐ Good	☐ Clean	☐ Good	☐ Good
☐ Fair	☐ Unclean	☐ Fair	☐ Fair
☐ Poor	☐ Dirty	☐ Poor	☐ Poor

Check your suggested rating
☐ ★
☐ ★★
☐ ★★★
☐ ★★★★
☐ ★★★★★

Date of visit _____   First visit? ☐ Yes ☐ No   ☐ ✓unusually good value

Comments _____

Notes